P9-AQR-495

AN AMERICAN PROFILE— OPINIONS AND BEHAVIOR, 1972-1989

AN AMERICAN PROFILE— OPINIONS AND BEHAVIOR, 1972-1989

Floris W. Wood, Editor

Opinion Results on 300 High-Interest Issues
Derived from the General Social Survey
Conducted by the National Opinion Research Center

Chronology of World Events, 1972-1989
By Edward Weilant

• • •

With a Foreword by Tom W. Smith,
Director of the General Social Survey

Editor: Floris W. Wood
Author, Chronology of World Events, 1972–1989: Edward Weilant

Gale Research Inc. Staff

Senior Editor: Linda Metzger
Coordinating Editor: Susan L. Stetler
Coordinating Associate Editor: Wendy S. Van de Sande

Production Manager: Mary Beth Trimper
External Production Assistant: Marilyn Jackman

Art Director: Arthur Chartow
Graphic Designer: Kathleen A. Mouzakis
Keyliner: C.J. Jonik

Production Supervisor: Laura Bryant
Internal Production Associate: Louise Gagné

The paper used in this publication meets the minimum requirements of American National Standard for Information Sciences—Permanence Paper for Printed Library Materials, ANSI Z39.48-1984. ∞™

ISBN 0-8103-7723-3

Printed in the United States of America

Published in the United States by Gale Research Inc.
Published simultaneously in the United Kingdom
by Gale Research International Limited
(An affiliated company of Gale Research Inc.)

Contents

Foreword

The NORC (National Opinion Research Center) is a social science research center founded in 1941. It is a separately incorporated, nonprofit, research organization affiliated with the University of Chicago. Included among its employees are 1,000 interviewers and 100 research associates.

NORC's research activities cover sociology, political science, social psychology, economics, demography, child studies, and policy studies, including studies of political behavior, religious attitudes, economic behavior, career development, family behavior, and survey research methodology.

Since 1972, the General Social Survey (GSS)—conducted by the National Opinion Research Center—has tracked the attitudes and behaviors of the American people. Nearly 25,000 respondents have been interviewed across the 16 national surveys, and trends on hundreds of questions have been monitored. Practically every topic of contemporary concern is touched upon by the GSS. These include abortion, civil liberties, confidence in institutions, crime and punishment, governmental spending priorities, public morality, race relations, religious beliefs and behaviors, and satisfactions with jobs, family, friendships, and other domains of life.

While social scientists and other data analysts have been able to work with the data on their computers, this enormous richness has not been readily available to the non-specialist. With the publication of *An American Profile-Opinions and Behavior, 1972-1989*, Floris Wood has remedied that situation. In the 23 sections that follow, he presents hundreds of trends. Not only are the general trends given, but also they are broken out separately by gender, race, and age groups. The data are logically organized, clearly presented, and well documented.

An American Profile—Opinions and Behavior, 1972-1989 is like a giant map of social change in America over the last two decades. With it, the user can relate trends in opinion to such recent events as the Second Cold War, the Reagan Revolution, the aging of the Baby Boomers, and the myth of the Sexual Revolution. *An American Profile* is an indispensable resource for anyone interested in social change and the state of contemporary America.

Tom W. Smith
Director, General Social Survey
Chicago, Illinios
1990

Introduction

The General Social Survey (GSS) and the National Opinion Research Center (NORC), the institution at the University of Chicago that conducts the survey, were unknown to me five years ago. Then I was asked to take over the Data Archive at Bowling Green State University as part of my librarian duties. NORC, and its GSS, were household words in the Data Archive. In fact, many questions routinely asked of reference librarians could be answered with GSS data. The problem was that the data that could answer the question was on computer tape. As most reference librarians know, very few library users have time to wait for data to be run off a computer tape. The idea for *An American Profile—Opinions and Behavior, 1972-1989* was born out of the frustration of knowing where the answer to a question was, but not having it readily accessible in print form.

Scholarly articles by the score, along with numerous books using GSS data have reached the academic market. Not until recently has the general public seen GSS data in newspapers, magazines, and on network news programs. Reporters almost always cite the author of the journal article or book as the source, instead of NORC. Although some GSS data has trickled down to the public, *An American Profile—Opinions and Behavior, 1972-1989* is the first publishing effort to display massive amounts of the data in readable charts. This book is an attempt to bring the library researcher extremely valuable data that has hitherto been available only to social scientists who were adept at computer assisted analysis.

Inclusion Criteria

Since 1972, the General Social Survey has been conducted annually in early spring (March-April), providing funds are available. In 1979 and 1981, funds were lacking and the survey was not conducted.

An American Profile—Opinions and Behavior, 1972-1989 does not include all questions ever asked in the GSS. To include all questions would render the book far less readable. Many questions have been discontinued after being asked only a few years, while others have been added as topics become socially significant. Still other questions, such as those involved with analyzing friendship networks, are useless in print form because they are designed with specific computer data analysis procedures in mind. Some questions in the GSS are test questions designed to measure how different wordings influence responses.

The chief criteria for inclusion in *An American Profile—Opinions and Behavior, 1972-1989* are:

- The question should have general social significance.
- The question should have been asked at least once since 1986.
- The question should have been asked at least six of the sixteen survey years.

Obviously, even these general guidelines have not been followed with every question included in *An American Profile—Opinions and Behavior, 1972-1989*. Timeliness tended to override the six-year minimum; the questions on AIDS fall into this category. Likewise, social significance overrode both the timeliness and six-year minimum on one or two occasions.

HOW TO USE THE TABLES

Responses for Each Question Broken Down Four Ways

Each question appearing in *An American Profile—Opinions and Behavior, 1972-1989* has four tables. The question—as it is actually printed in the survey questionnaire or a close paraphrase—is repeated before each table. Notations about years in which the question was not asked appear immediately after the question. Responses explain the one or two character response codes that are used in the tables.

Table I: By Total Population. Displays the responses of the whole sample for each year the question was asked. Table I is a two-way distribution, with the years the question was asked appearing across the top of the table and the possible responses going down the left side of the table. Each cell of data is the percent of the total sample that gave the response indicated. The bottom row of each table (labeled # Surveyed) indicates the number of people who were interviewed that year and answered the question. In any interview, there are people who prefer not to answer all questions or who give evasive responses. These people were not included in the total number surveyed.

Table II: By Sex. Splits the responses by sex, so that male and female responses can be compared. Tables II, III, and IV are three-way distributions. In addition to the percentage of subjects who gave a certain response in a given year, the information is further broken down in Table II by sex, with separate tables for male and female responses. As with Table I, the years the question was asked appear across the top of the table. The far left vertical column identifies which sex is included in the table; the second vertical column indicates the response code for that question. The number surveyed, at the bottom of each table, is the total number of people surveyed in the sub-sample of sex for the years the question was asked.

Table III: By Race. Splits the responses by race, so that white, black, and other responses can be compared. Users should be aware that the group called "Other" is a very small sample. (Statistically speaking, even a sample as large as 100 can have a fairly low confidence level.) Table III breaks down the Table I responses by race and there are separate tables for white, black, and other. The far left vertical column identifies which race is included in the table; the second vertical column indicates the response code for that question. The number surveyed, at the bottom of each table, is the total number of people surveyed in the sub-sample of race for the years the question was asked.

Table IV: By Age. Breaks out the responses by nine age groups. Each age group contains a six-year span except for the last group—66+—which is open-ended. Responses in Table IV are contained in nine separate tables. The far left vertical column identifies which age group is included in the table; the second vertical column indicates the response code for that question. The number surveyed, at the bottom of each table, is the total number of people surveyed in the sub-sample of age group for the years the question was asked.

Responses to Three Types of Questions

An American Profile—Opinions and Behavior, 1972-1989 is divided into three sections based on the three types of questions asked in the GSS.

Section 1: Demography. These are questions about and relating to the respondent. Questions concern personal data (respondent's age, marital status, years of education); family demography (number of siblings, number of children); employment (current employment status, industry working in, prestige of occupation); religion (current religious preference); household (household size, dwelling type); and community (community population, region of country living in, integration of neighborhood). The Demography section contains 52 questions.

Section 2: Opinions. These are questions that deal with the opinions of the respondents on a variety of topics. Questions solicit opinions on personal conditions (satisfaction with family life, satisfaction with job); family matters (ideal family size, spanking as good discipline); human conditions (most people are trustworthy, world too bad for new children); religion (feelings toward various religious affiliations); employment (importance of good pay, importance of promotion); politics (feelings toward various countries, communism as a form of government, political leanings); race issues (whites' right to segregation, interracial marriages, black presidential candidate); women's issues (working mother relationship, female presidential candidate, woman should enhance husband's career); abortion (allow abortion on demand, for poverty, for single women); social issues (is homosexuality wrong, teenage sexual relations, feelings about pornography laws, suicide for terminally ill, pre-nuptial AIDS testing); national issues (confidence in U.S. president, government aid for poor, amount of taxes, U.S. active in world affairs); and crime (fear in neighborhood, death penalty, police use of force on murderer). The Opinions section contains 174 questions.

Section 3: Behavior. These questions deal with the behavior of the respondents in a variety of situations. Questions solicit responses on personal habits (alcohol consumption, smoking history, newspaper reading); social habits (membership in specific groups, socializing with specific groups, television viewing, x-rated movie viewing, relationships with AIDS victims, frequency of sex); religion (church attendance, tithing amount); politics (voted in election years, presidential choice); and crime (victim of violence). There are 79 questions in the Behavior section.

Interpreting the Data

The following should be considered when interpreting the data in *An American Profile—Opinions and Behavior, 1972-1989:*

Rounding. The percentages in the tables are rounded to the nearest whole number. This was done for space purposes, but some accuracy was lost. Usually the difference is not very significant but, depending on how the reader is using the data, could be an important factor.

Missing years. For various reasons—the size of the GSS questionnaire being one factor—not all questions were asked each year. As stated above, no survey was conducted in 1979 and 1981. When years other than 1979 and 1981 are missing, that fact is noted following the question.

Split questions. Occasionally the reader may find that the total number of people surveyed in a particular year is about half the number as in previous or later years. This is because NORC experimented with the question, asking half of the respondents the question worded one way and the other half with a different wording. No attempt was made to combine the two groups. The reader must decide whether this presents a problem in that too few respondents are represented in some cells of data in the years where split questionnaires were used.

Too few respondents. Some categories, especially in the race and age tables, contain so few respondents that the data is unreliable. Again, the reader must determine the level of confidence acceptable to his/her needs.

Questions about blacks. Prior to 1978, many of the questions about blacks were asked only of non-black respondents. Therefore, the data is all zeroes on the black race tables for those years. Although the race data will not be affected by this policy change, the total population, sex, and age tables could change drastically after blacks were included in 1978. However, keep in mind that prior to 1978, the respondents for these questions are not representative of the total population since blacks are excluded.

Region of country living in. The responses to this question from the demography section divide the country into several ambiguous regions. Appendix A fully defines the regions.

Restatement of questions. The survey questions as stated in *An American Profile—Opinions and Behavior, 1972-1989* are sometimes not verbatim from the GSS questionnaire. Some are restated here because they were originally part of a series of questions that were linked together with a single statement preceding the series. Others—especially in the demography section—were not directly asked but were the observation of the interviewer. For the benefit of researchers interested in using the GSS tapes, the variable name used in the GSS codebook for each question is identified in Appendix B.

Race. Race is not a very scientific concept. For most people, it has to do with genetically transmitted physical features. That concept is sometimes overridden by the ethnic history of a people or even their religion. No doubt there is some confusion among some respondents about what to report as their race. Appendix C is a list of how people responded to the question about their race, along with a count of how many people gave that response.

Helpful Features

In addition to the data from the 305 questions included in *An American Profile—Opinions and Behavior, 1972-1989*, there are other features that complement the data.

Chronology of World Events, 1972-1989. While a user may view a table and trace the trends provided therein, the data has more meaning when placed within the context of world events—world events being one major factor that affects opinion and behavior. The Chronology of World Events included in *An American Profile—Opinions and Behavior, 1972-1989* tracks the events that occurred within the survey span that may have affected question responses.

Outline of Contents. The Outline of Contents restates a brief form of each question that appears in *An American Profile—Opinions and Behavior, 1972-1989* along with the page number upon which the first table is found.

Keyword Index. The Index provides access to questions on key words and alternate words. Page number is reference to the page upon which the first table is found.

Availability of GSS Data

Data analysts may wish to access the data found in *An American Profile—Opinions and Behavior, 1972-1989* by computer. The data is distributed by the Roper Center.

The Roper Center for Public Opinion Research
P.O. Box 440
Storrs, CT 06268
(203) 486-4440

Researchers affiliated with an institution who is a member of the Interuniversity Consortium for Political and Social Research (ICPSR) may have access to the GSS tapes through their membership.

ICPSR
P.O. Box 1248
Ann Arbor, MI 48106
(313) 763-5010

Acknowledgements

The past and present administrations of the Bowling Green State University Libraries and Learning Resources have been generous with support and release time. The University's Computer Services has given freely of their expertise, especially consultants Harold Stonerock, Bob Fyfe, and the Director of Academic Computing, Dale Schroeder. The Bowling Green Data Archive Graduate and Undergraduate Assistant, Sandeep Nijhawan, Bob Kelbley, and John Samenuk kept the "ship afloat." The Science Library staff has good-naturedly endured explanations of what went wrong (and occasionally right) with the project. Tom Smith, of the National Opinion Research Center, has given exemplary scholarly cooperation in answering questions about his worthy creation, the General Social Survey. My family—Bess, Becca, and Katey—have helped make this endeavor, and all others, most gratifying.

To all of these people, I give my sincerest thanks.

Suggestions Are Welcome

The editor welcomes any comments regarding this publication. Please address correspondence to: Editor, *An American Profile—Opinions and Behavior, 1972-1989*, Gale Research Inc., 835 Penobscot Bldg., Detroit, Michigan 48226-4094; or call toll-free 1-800-347-4253.

Floris W. Wood
Bowling Green, Ohio
1990

CHRONOLOGY OF WORLD EVENTS, 1972 - 1989

1972

January 13: President Nixon announces more troops pullouts from Vietnam.
January 25: President Nixon describes a previously secret eight-point peace proposal for Vietnam.

February 21: President Nixon begins an eight-day visit to the People's Republic of China. He becomes the first U.S. President to visit the P.R.C. On February 27 both the U.S. and the P.R.C. issue the Shanghai Communique. In it the two nations agree to work toward reducing the risk of war, normalizing relations, and increasing scientific and cultural ties.
The trial of Rev. Philip Berrigan, antiwar priest, begins.

March 3: The U.S. unmanned spacecraft Pioneer 10 is launched.
March 17: President Nixon proposes congressional legislation to deny the courts the power to order busing of elementary school children to achieve racial integration.
March 22: The U.S. Senate approves the Equal Rights Amendment and sends the proposed amendment to the states for ratification.
The National Commission on Marijuana and Drug Abuse recommends an end to criminal penalties for the private possession and use of marijuana.
March 27: "Soledad Brothers" Fleeta Drumgo and John Cluchette are found innocent of the 1970 slaying of a prison guard.

April 5: The "Harrisburg 7" trial ends with a mistrial as the jury declares itself hopelessly deadlocked.
April 15: President Nixon and Canada's Prime Minister Trudeau sign a treaty to clean up the Great Lakes.
April 16: Apollo 16 is launched.

May 8: President Nixon orders the mining of North Vietnamese ports.
May 15: Alabama Governor George C. Wallace is shot and paralyzed from the waist down, while campaigning in Maryland's Democratic presidential primary.
May 22: President Nixon begins the first presidential visit to Moscow. The Moscow Summit produces a number of agreements, including the Strategic Arms Limitation Treaty (SALT) signed on May 26.
May 30: U.S. Supreme Court lets stand a California State Supreme Court ruling abolishing the death penalty in that state.

June 4: Angela Davis, black militant, is acquitted of murder, kidnapping, and criminal conspiracy charges.
June 14: U.S. District Judge Stephen J. Roth orders the integration of students in Detroit and 53 suburban school districts. The desegregation plan will require the busing of about 300,000 students.
The EPA announces an almost complete ban on the pesticide DDT.
June 17: Police arrest five men, Bernard Barker, James W. McCord, Frank Sturgis, Eugenio R. Martinez, and Virgilio R. Gonzales, for breaking into the offices of the Democratic National Committee in the Watergate apartment complex in Washington, D.C.

June 19: Airline pilots from 64 nations go on strike for one day to bring attention to their demands for action against hijackers and extortionists.

June 29: U.S. Supreme Court rules that capital punishment sentences as handed out in most courts are unconstitutional, being either cruel and unusual punishment, or being imposed in a cruel, unusual, erratic way.

July 25: Senator Thomas Eagleton, Democratic Vice Presidential candidate, confirms rumors of having a history of psychiatric treatment.

August 3: U.S. Senate ratifies the Strategic Arms Limitation Treaty (SALT 1) between the U.S. and the Soviet Union.

September 5: Arab terrorists suspend the Summer Olympics in Munich, West Germany. The terrorists enter the Olympic Village, killing two Israeli coaches and taking nine Israeli athletes hostage, all of whom were later killed in a shootout.

September 15: The five men originally accused of burglary, and former White House aides G. Gordon Liddy and E. Howard Hunt; are indicted by a federal grand jury on charges of breaking into the Democratic National Committees's headquarters located in the Watergate complex.

October 3: President Nixon and Soviet Foreign Minister Gromyko sign the documents implementing the SALT agreement at a White House ceremony.

October 12: Fighting between black and white sailors starts aboard the aircraft carrier *Kitty Hawk* and leaves 46 men injured.

November 7: President Nixon is re-elected.

November 9: The Navy reassigns over 100 crewmen of the aircraft carrier *Constellation* after the seamen, most of them black, refuse to reboard the ship before their grievances over discrimination are resolved.

November 21: The 7th Circuit Court of Appeals reverses the convictions of five of the "Chicago 7" defendants: David Dellinger, Rennard Davis, Thomas Hayden, Abbie Hoffman, and Jerry Rubin.

December 7: Apollo 17 is launched.

1973

January 11: President Nixon ends mandatory wage and price controls, except for food, health care, and construction, that were established under the Economic Stabilization Act.

January 20: President Nixon and Vice President Agnew are sworn in for their second term.

January 22: U.S. Supreme Court rules that states may not prevent a woman from having an abortion during the first six months of pregnancy.

January 27: Melvin R. Laird, Defense Secretary, announces the end of the military draft.

January 28: The Vietnam War ends for the U.S.

February 12: A 10% devaluation of the U.S. dollar against nearly all the major world currencies is announced by U.S. Secretary of the Treasury, George P. Shultz.

February 27: Members of AIM (American Indian Movement) seize the trading post and church at historic Wounded Knee on the Oglala Sioux Reservation in South Dakota.

April 30: Three of the president's top aides resign: Chief of Staff - H. R. Haldeman; Domestic Policy Assistant - John D. Ehrlichman, and Presidential Counsel - John W. Dean III. The Attorney

General, Richard G. Kleindienst, also resigns. President Nixon, in a nationwide radio and television address, denies any personal involvement in the Watergate affair, but accepts full responsibility as "top man in the organization."

May 11: Charges of espionage, theft, and conspiracy in the Pentagon Papers trial of Daniel Ellsberg and Anthony J. Russo, Jr. are dropped by presiding judge William M. Byrne.

May 17: The Senate Select Committee on Presidential Campaign Activities begins hearings on the Watergate scandal. The committee's chair is Senator Sam J. Ervin.

May 22: President Nixon releases a statement saying that there was activity in the White House to conceal some aspects of the Watergate affair, but for national security reasons.

May 25: Skylab 2 is launched.

May 29: Thomas Bradley defeats the incumbent, Sam Yorty, to become the first black mayor of Los Angeles.

June 13: President Nixon freezes retail prices for 60 days.

June 21: U.S. Supreme Court, in a series of decisions on obscenity, establishes guidelines which allow materials to be banned if they are found offensive to local standards.

July 28: Skylab 3 is launched.

October 6: The Arab-Israeli War begins.

October 10: Vice President Spiro T. Agnew resigns and pleads no contest to one charge of income tax evasion.

October 20: President Nixon fires special Watergate prosecutor Archibald Cox and Deputy Attorney General William D. Ruckelshaus; Attorney General Elliot Richardson resigns.

November 7: President Nixon speaks on national television about the energy crisis.
U.S. and Egypt agree to resume diplomatic relations.

November 10-11: U.S. Secretary of State Henry Kissinger confers with Chinese leaders.

November 16: President Nixon signs into law the Alaska Pipeline Bill which authorizes the construction of a 789-mile pipeline from Prudhoe Bay to the port of Valdez.
Skylab 4 is launched.

November 17: President Nixon: "People have got to know whether or not their president is a crook -- well, I'm not a crook."

November 25: President Nixon speaks on national television about the energy crisis.

December 6: Congressman Gerald R. Ford sworn in as Vice President.

December 17: Palestinian guerillas kill 29 people in Rome's International Airport.

1974

January: Oil companies post profit increases of over 50% for the fourth quarter of 1973 as compared to the fourth quarter of 1972.

January 2: The 55-mile-per-hour speed limit bill is signed into law by President Nixon.

January 18: Israel and Egypt agree to separate their military forces along the Suez Canal.

January 30: President Nixon's state of the union message on national television. Nixon pledges not to resign, saying "one year of Watergate is enough."

February: Americans across the U.S. complain about gasoline shortages.

February 5: Patricia Hearst is kidnapped in Berkeley, California by the Symbionese Liberation Army.

February 6: U.S. House votes to grant broad constitutional power to the Judiciary Committee to pursue its impeachment inquiry.

February 8: After 84 days in space, the Skylab astronauts splash down in the Pacific.

February 13: Alexander Solzhenitsyn is stripped of Soviet citizenship and deported to West Germany.

February 19: Federal Energy Office administrator William Simon orders emergency allocation of 84 million gallons of gasoline to 20 states.

February 22: Hijacker at Baltimore-Washington Airport kills two people, then himself.

February 25: President Nixon states at a news conference that the House cannot impeach him unless it presents evidence that he has violated criminal law.

March 1: Seven former White House and presidential campaign aides are indicted in the coverup of the Watergate scandal (H.R. Haldeman, John D. Ehrlichman, John N. Mitchell, Robert Mardian, Kenneth Parkinson, Charles W. Colson, and Gordon Strachan).

March 10: Lt. Hiroo Onoda, a Japanese soldier from WWII emerges from the Philippines and surrenders. He said he had not emerged before because his last order had been to continue guerrilla warfare.

The Pennsylvania Crime Commission reports that police corruption in Philadelphia was "ongoing, widespread, systematic, and occurring at all levels of the police department."

March 18: The Arab oil embargo against the U.S. is lifted.

April 29: President Nixon assures a national television audience that he has "nothing to hide."

May: U.S. oil companies report large increases in profits for the first quarter of 1974.

May 7: The Federal Energy Administration is established.

May 9: Impeachment hearings by the Judiciary Committee of the House of Representatives, under the chairmanship of Peter Rodino of New Jersey, open.

May 16: Richard Kleindienst becomes the first former Attorney General to be convicted of a crime.

June 30: The mother of Dr. Martin Luther King, Jr. is shot and killed while in church.

July 12: Four defendants are found guilty of conspiring to break into the office of Daniel Ellsberg's psychiatrist: John Ehrlichman, G. Gordon Liddy, Bernard L. Barker, and Eugenio R. Martinez.

July 13: The Senate Select Committee on Presidential Campaign Activities, also known as the Watergate Committee, issues its final report.

July 24: U.S. Supreme Court rules that President Nixon must give up the tapes and documents sought by Watergate Special Prosecutor Leon Jaworski, rejecting Nixon's claim of executive privilege.

July 25: U.S. Supreme Court decides against school integration by means of cross-district busing, rejecting a plan to desegregate the predominantly black Detroit schools with predominantly white suburban districts.

August 9: President Nixon resigns ... Gerald R. Ford sworn in as President.

September 8: President Ford grants an unconditional pardon to former President Nixon.

September 12: School busing protest in Boston.

September 16: President Ford offers conditional amnesty to Vietnam draft evaders and military deserters.

October 8: A program to control inflation, called WIN (Whip Inflation Now), is proposed by President Ford.

December 18: Congress passes legislation appropriating $1 billion for new jobs in 1975.

December 19: Nelson A. Rockefeller sworn in as Vice President.

December 26: CIA (Central Intelligence Agency) Director William Colby, in a report to President Ford, confirms allegations that the CIA had engaged in illegal domestic operations against antiwar and other dissidents.

1975

January: Chrysler, Ford, and General Motors Corporation offer rebates on car purchases, as the recession continues.

January 2: U.S. Secretary of State Henry Kissinger hints that the U.S. might use military force in the Middle East "to prevent the economic strangulation of the industrialized world" by Arab oil producers.

January 13: President Ford, in his State of the Union address, said to Congress, "The state of the union is not good."

February 4: President Ford and his Council of Economic Advisers warned, in their annual reports to Congress, that the economy was "in a severe recession."

February 15: Dr. Kenneth C. Edelin is found guilty of manslaughter by a Boston, Massachusetts jury after performing a legal abortion.

March 22: U.S. Secretary of State Henry Kissinger announces that his efforts to bring about a peace agreement between Egypt and Israel are suspended.

April 30: Vietnam War ends. Vietcong accept South Vietnamese President Duong Van Minh's unconditional surrender.

May 10: U.S. District Court Judge W. Arthur Garrity, Jr. releases his new busing plan to achieve desegregation in Boston's racially-troubled schools.

May 14: U.S. forces engagc Cambodian forces to free the U.S. merchant vessel *Mayaguez*.

May 27: An Alaska Supreme Court ruling has the effect of legalizing the use of marijuana in the privacy of one's own home.

President Ford, in a national television address, imposes a $1 per barrel increase in fees on imported crude oil effective June 1st.

June 5: Suez Canal reopens to all international shipping, except Israeli ships, eight years after its closing.

June 10: New York City is saved from defaulting on $729 million due June 11.

July 17: American and Soviet astronauts meet in space during the joint Apollo-Soyuz space mission.

September: Protests in several cities against court-ordered busing.

September 5: Assassination attempt on President Ford by Manson cultist Lynette "Squeaky" Fromm.

September 6: The Kentucky National Guard is called in to assist with court-ordered busing in Louisville.

September 19: U.S. Air Force officers rule that T. Sgt. Leonard P. Matlovich, a homosexual, is unfit for military service. Panel recommends he be given a general discharge.

September 22: Assassination attempt on President Ford by Sara Jane Moore.

President Ford announces new energy plan.

September 27: OPEC agrees to increase the price of oil 10%.

October 26: President Anwar el-Sadat, the first Egyptian President to make an official visit to the U.S., arrives for a 10-day visit.

November 21: U.S. Senate issues a report stating that officials of the U.S. government had instigated assassination plots against two foreign leaders and had become involved in plots that led to the deaths of three other leaders.

November 26: President Ford agrees to give federal aid in the billions to New York City to help meet its seasonal cash flow needs and to avert default.

December 1-5: President Ford travels to China, meets with Mao.
December 2: South Moluccan terrorists attack the Netherlands.
December 4: South Moluccan terrorists strike the Netherlands again.
December 21: Pro-Palestinian terrorists attack the Vienna OPEC meeting.

1976

January 8: Premier Chou En-lai of China dies.
January 26: Court-ordered busing to achieve desegregation begins peacefully in Detroit, Michigan.

February 3: President Ford states his abortion position, declares that the Supreme Court had gone "too far" in striking down anti-abortion laws.
February 5: A 35-day slowdown by physicians in California ends. They had been protesting steep increases in their medical malpractice insurance premiums.

March 15: Egypt ends its Treaty of Friendship and Cooperation with the Soviet Union, which had been established in 1971.
March 24: To prevent a possible epidemic by the swine-flu virus, President Ford requests that a national anti-flu campaign be conducted.
March 29: U.S. Supreme Court upholds a Virginia state law prohibiting homosexual acts, even if performed in private and between consenting adults.
March 31: New Jersey Supreme Court rules that comatose Karen Anne Quinlan, being kept alive by a mechanical respirator, could be disconnected from it if hospital officials agree there is no reasonable possibility she will recover.

April 22: Cheating scandal at the U.S. Military Academy; 50 third-year cadets are convicted of cheating on a take-home exam.

May 23: Cheating at the U.S. Military Academy is acknowledged by the superintendent of the Academy to be more widespread than previously reported.
May 24: Supersonic transport (SST) service to Washington, D.C. begins with flights from London and Paris by British-French Concorde jets.

July 2: U.S. Supreme Court rules that the death penalty for murder convictions is not necessarily cruel or unusual punishment, and is therefore acceptable in certain cases.
July 3: Israeli commandos free 103 hostages on a hijacked plane held at Entebbe Airport in Uganda.
July 4: Americans across the United States participate in the Bicentennial Celebration.
July 17: The Summer Olympics open in Montreal, Canada. Many nations boycott the games because of political protests.
July 20: Viking I lands on Mars.

August 19: U.S. military forces in Korea are on alert after two U.S. officers are killed in the demilitarized zone.
August 31: By this time, 28 people have died from a mysterious, unidentifed flu-like disease, following an American Legion Convention in Philadelphia, Pennsylvania.

September 3: Viking II lands on Mars.
September 6: Viktor I. Belenko, a Soviet pilot, flies his MIG-25 to Japan, and defects to the U.S.
September 8: Chinese Communist Party Chairman Mao Tse-tung dies.

October 22: Federal District Court Judge John F. Dooling rules that a federal ban against medicaid reimbursement for abortions, except when the life of the mother is endangered, is unconstitutional.

November 2: Jimmy Carter is elected President of the United States.

December 15: The *Argo Merchant*, a Liberian oil tanker, runs aground off Nantucket. In the following days, the tanker spills over seven million gallons of oil into commercial fishing grounds.
December 16: Swine-flu vaccinations are suspended after several deaths follow vaccination.
December 17: The Massachusetts Supreme Judicial Court overturns the manslaughter conviction of Dr. Kenneth C. Edelin, who was convicted in 1975 after performing an abortion.

1977

January 17: Gary Gilmore is executed in Utah, the first U.S. execution to take place in 10 years.
January 20: Jimmy Carter is sworn in as President.
January 21: President Carter grants most Vietnam draft evaders an unconditional pardon.
January 23-30: The dramatization of Alex Haley's *Roots* is watched by millions in the U.S. on television.
January 27: President Carter sends Congress an economic stimulation plan.

February 8: Cincinnati jury finds Larry Flynt, editor of the men's magazine, *Hustler*, guilty on obscenity charges.
February 14: Gunman Frederick W. Cowan, kills five, wounds five, in New Rochelle, New York.

March 5: President Carter holds his first nationwide radio call-in program.
March 16: President Carter starts his "meet the people" program in Clinton, Massachusetts.
March 17: President Carter speaks on human rights before the General Assembly at the United Nations.

April 18: President Carter, in a nationwide speech, offers his energy plan and asks the country to make "the moral equivalent of war" on energy waste.
April 19: U.S. Supreme Court rules that spanking of schoolchildren by teachers is constitutional.

June 7: Dade County voters repeal a county ordinance prohibiting discrimination because of sexual preference, after an anti-homosexual campaign in Miami, Florida; singer Anita Bryant actively involved.
June 9: U.S. Supreme Court rules that the State of New York may not prohibit the distribution of contraceptives to minors.
June 20: U.S. Supreme Court rules that states do not have to use Medicaid funds for elective abortions.
June 26: Homosexuals and their supporters respond to anti-homosexual activity with marches and rallies in cities throughout the U.S.
June 30: President Carter opposes production and deployment of the B-1 bomber as too costly and not necessary for national defense.

August 4: President Carter creates the Department of Energy with James Schlesinger as Secretary.
August 10: The "Son of Sam" killer, David R. Berkowitz, is arrested in New York City.

November 19: Egyptian President Anwar Sadat travels to Israel, meets Israeli Prime Minister Menachem Begin, discusses peace between Egypt and Israel.

December 25: President Sadat and Prime Minister Begin begin a summit meeting in Egypt, continuing their peace talks.

1978

January 17: Egyptian President Sadat recalls the Egyptian representatives from negotiations in Israel.
January 24: Nuclear powered Soviet satellite, Cosmos 954, disintegrates over Canada.

February 3: President Sadat visits President Carter at the White House.
February 14: U.S. announces the sale of $4.8 billion dollars worth of military aircraft to Egypt, Israel, and Saudi Arabia.
February 19: Egyptian commandos attempt to retake a hijacked plane in Cyprus.

March: The U.S. dollar decreases in value against foreign currencies, reaching a postwar low against the Japanese yen.
March 14: Israel invades and occupies southern Lebanon.
March 16: The U.S. Senate ratifies the first of two Panama Canal treaties that were negotiated in 1977.
March 17: Super tanker, *Amoco Cadiz*, destroys fishing off the coast of France with an oil spill.
March 24: Members of the United Mine Workers Union go back to work after 110-day strike.
March 27: President Carter proposes an urban aid program.

April 7: President Carter defers production of the neutron bomb.
April 18: U.S. Senate ratifies the second of the Panama Canal treaties.

May 20: Pioneer Venus I is launched toward Venus.

June 6: Proposition 13 is approved in California, reducing state property tax by 57%.
June 13: Israel withdraws from Lebanon.
June 28: U.S. Supreme Court supports Alan Bakke's claim of reverse discrimination, and orders him admitted to medical school.

July 25: "Test-tube baby" Louise Brown is born in England.

August 2: Pollution creates health emergency in the Love Canal area of Niagara Falls, New York.
August 8: Pioneer Venus II is launched.

September 17: President Carter helps negotiate a "framework for peace" agreement between Egypt and Israel, as the Camp David Summit comes to an end.

October 6: U.S. Senate votes to extend by 39 months the time available to the states for ratification of the Equal Rights Amendment (deadline becomes June 30, 1982).
October 15: The National Energy Act of 1978 is passed by Congress.
October 27: Israeli Prime Minister Begin and Egyptian President Sadat receive the Nobel Peace Prize.

November 19: Over 900 bodies, followers of Rev. Jim Jones, are found in Jonestown, Guyana. In a massive ritual of the Peoples' Temple religious group, members committed suicide or were executed.

December 15: President Carter announces that the U.S. and China will establish diplomatic relations on January 1, 1979.

1979

January 1: U.S. and China formally establish diplomatic relations.
January 16: The Shah of Iran, Muhammad Rezi Pahlavi, goes into exile.
January 28: Chinese leader Deng Xiaoping begins visit to the U.S.

February 1: Ayatollah Ruhollah Khomeini returns to Iran from exile in Paris, France.
February 5: Approximately 3,000 farmers demonstrate in Washington, D.C., with tractors, trucks, and campers.
February 7: The U.S. Energy Secretary warns that the loss of Iran's oil supply is "prospectively more serious" than the Middle East oil embargo of 1973-1974.
February 17: Chinese troops invade Vietnam.
February 21: U.S. District Judge upholds the right of the National Organization for Women to continue a convention boycott against states which have not ratified the Equal Rights Amendment.
February 26: President Carter asks Congress to grant him the power to order gasoline rationing, weekend gas station closings, and other conservation measures as necessary.

March 26: President Sadat and Prime Minister Begin sign a formal peace treaty between Egypt and Israel.
March 28: Major nuclear accident occurs at the Three Mile Island reactor near Harrisburg, Pennsylvania.

April 27: Texas sniper, Ira Attebury, wounds 51, kills two in San Antonio.

May 3: Margaret Thatcher is the first woman elected Prime Minister of Great Britain.
May 6: Anti-nuclear protest is held in Washington, D.C., with a crowd estimated at over 65,000.
May 8: California starts an odd-even distribution plan to solve its gasoline shortage.

June 18: U.S. President Carter and Soviet President Brezhnev sign the SALT II treaty.
June 27: U.S. Supreme Court rules that private employers can legally set up voluntary programs to help blacks in employment.

July 10: President Carter signs a proclamation on the maximum and minimum temperatures that will be allowed in commercial, government and other public buildings in order to save energy (65 degree maximum for heating, 78 degree minimum for cooling).
July 15: President Carter, in a nationwide speech on energy, connects the energy crisis with a "crisis of confidence" the country is going through.

September 27: Congress approves the formation of the Dept. of Education. (Dept. of Health, Education and Welfare renamed Dept. of Health and Human Services.)

October 3: U.S. Dept. of Agriculture announces that the Soviet Union will be allowed to buy a record amount of wheat and corn during the next year.

November 1: The Carter Administration proposes a $1.5 billion loan to Chrysler Corporation.
November 4: Iranian revolutionaries seize the U.S. Embassy in Teheran, taking about 90 hostages including 65 Americans.

December 25: Soviet Union invades Afganistan.

1980

January 4: In response to the Soviet invasion of Afghanistan, President Carter announces an end to high technology sales to the Soviets, limits Soviet fishing privileges, begins a grain embargo, and defers any new cultural or economic exchanges betweeen the U.S and the Soviet Union.

January 7: President Carter signs a bill giving Chrysler Corporation a $1.5 billion federal loan.

January 20: President Carter says that if the Soviets do not withdraw from Afghanistan by February 20, the U.S. will boycott the Summer Olympics to be held in Moscow.

January 22: Soviet dissident, Andrei Sakharov, is arrested and sent into internal exile.

January 23: President Carter, in his State of the Union speech, states that the U.S. is prepared to go to war if necessary to protect the oil-supply routes of the Persian Gulf region.

January 25: The Labor Department reports that consumer prices rose 13.3% in 1979, the largest increase in inflation in 33 years.

January 29: Canada helps six U.S. Embassy employees escape from Iran.

February 2: Operation Abscam is reported; 31 public officials including U.S. Senator Harrison A. Williams, Jr. and seven representatives were the subject of a two-year undercover investigation by the FBI.

February 7: Chrysler reports a 1979 loss of $1.1 billion.

February 24: U.N. fact finding commission begins its visit to Iran over the U.S. hostages.

February 25: President Carter says that inflation has "reached a crisis stage" and points to the inability of Congress to adopt a comprehensive energy policy.

February 26: Energy Department officials say they forsee $1.50-a-gallon gasoline by the end of the year.

March 12: John Gacy is found guilty of committing 33 murders in Illinois.

April 2: The Crude Oil Windfall Profits Tax bill signed by President Carter.

April 22: U.S. Olympic Committee backs the boycott of the Summer Games in Moscow.

April 24: U.S. attempts to rescue the Americans held hostage in Iran, mission aborted due to equipment failures.

May 17-19: Racial rioting in Miami, Florida.

May 18: Mt. St. Helens volcano erupts violently in the State of Washington.

May 29: Black civil rights leader and president of the National Urban League, Vernon Jordan Jr., is shot in Fort Wayne, Indiana.

June 27: The bill providing funds for draft registration is signed by President Carter.

June 30: The Supreme Court limits the use of medicaid funds for abortion except in cases of rape or incest or where the life of the woman is threatened.

July 2: President Carter signs a proclamation requiring registration for a possible military conscription.

September 19: A fuel explosion occurs at a nuclear missile silo in Arkansas.

September 22: War between Iran and Iraq begins.

November 4: Ronald W. Reagan is elected President by a landslide.

November 12: Voyager I passes by Saturn.

December 8: John Lennon is assassinated by Mark David Chapman.

1981

January 20: Ronald Reagan sworn in as President.
52 American hostages in Iran released after 444 days of captivity.

February 10: Justice Department announces new proposals to fight violent crime.
February 15: Federal Drug Enforcement Administration announces that, despite government efforts, only 2-5% of the illegal drug trade is being kept out of distribution.
Remains of missing children continue to be discovered in Atlanta, 17 victims thus far.
February 26: British Prime Minister Margaret Thatcher visits President Reagan in the White House.
February 27: Chrysler reports a loss of $1.71 billion in 1980.

March 5: President Reagan announces nearly $1 million in grants to finance mental health and social programs relating to the case of missing and murdered children in Atlanta.
March 19: A study sponsored by the National Institute on Alcohol Use and the National Institute on Drug Abuse reports that one-third of the nation's high school students are problem drinkers.
March 22: Postal rates increase. First class mail increases from 15 cents to 18 cents.
March 30: President Reagan is wounded in an assassination attempt by John Hinckley, Jr.

April 12: Space shuttle Columbia is launched.
April 24: President Reagan announces the lifting of the grain embargo to the U.S.S.R.

May 13: Pope John Paul II is wounded in an assassination attempt.

June 7: Israel bombs Iraqi atomic reactor near Baghdad.
June 21: Wayne B. Williams is arrested as a suspect in the Atlanta child murders.
June 25: U.S. Supreme Court decides that the Constitution allows women to be excluded from registering for the draft.

July 29: Prince Charles marries Lady Diana Spencer.
July 31: Congress approves of President Reagan's package of budget cuts; consequently, support for many domestic social programs is reduced.

August 3: Federal air traffic controllers (PATCO) begin an illegal nationwide strike and all those who fail to return to work are fired.
August 4: President Reagan's tax-cut legislation, having cleared Congress, is sent to the President for his signature.
August 19: After being fired on, U.S. Navy jets shoot down two Libyan fighters near the coast of Libya.

September 25: Sandra Day O'Connor becomes the first woman on the U.S. Supreme Court.

October 6: President Anwar el-Sadat is assassinated in Egypt.

November 12: Space shuttle Columbia is launched for a second mission.

December 10: In response to suspected terrorist plotting by Libya, President Reagan requests all Americans in Libya to leave immediately.

1982

January 8: The American Telephone and Telegraph Company agrees to divest itself of its 22 Bell telephone operating systems.

January 22: Labor Department announces the total increase for consumer prices was only 8.9% in 1981, the lowest annual increase since 1977. However, medical care costs rose 12.5% in 1981, the largest increase since the government began reporting medical costs in 1935.

January 26: President Reagan, in his State of the Union speech, announces a major plan for a "new federalism" by which states and cities would be given control over federal social programs, while the federal government would take over total responsibility for medicaid.

February 6: President Reagan's budget message calls on Congress to decrease government's social responsibilities and increase the nation's military strength.

February 22: U.S. Surgeon General C. Everett Koop announces that smoking is the most important health issue of our time.

March 2: U.S. Senate passes a bill which seeks to eliminate school busing for the purpose of racial integration.

March 8: U.S. accuses Soviets of using poison gas in Afghanistan.

March 11: Sen. Harrison A. Williams, Jr. resigns following his conviction in the Abscam scandal.

March 22: Space shuttle Columbia is launched in the first of three 1982 flights.

April 2: Argentina invades the Falkland Islands.

April 25: After an occupation of 15 years, Israel returns the Sinai Peninsula to Egypt.

June 6: Israel invades Lebanon.

June 12: Half a million people demonstrate against nuclear arms in New York City's Central Park.

June 14: Following the arrival of a task force to retake the Falkland Islands, British Prime Minister Thatcher announces that Argentine forces in Stanley have surrendered.

June 15: Soviet Union pledges no first use of nuclear arms.

June 24: Leaders of the drive to obtain ratification of the Equal Rights Amendment admit defeat.

June 25: U.S. Supreme Court rules that the First Amendment limits the right of public school administrators to remove books which they find objectionable from school libraries.

September 15: A Senate vote kills a proposal which would have banned the use of federal funds for abortions.

November 5: Unemployment in October was reported to be at its highest level since 1940.

November 10: Soviet Leader Leonid Brezhnev dies.

November 12: Yuri V. Andropov is elected to succeed Brezhnev as General Secretary of the Communist Party of the Soviet Union.

November 13: President Reagan lifts sanctions against companies selling U.S. technology for use in the Soviet natural gas pipeline to Western Europe.
Vietnam Veterans Memorial is dedicated in Washington, D.C.

1983

January 3: President Reagan declares Times Beach, Missouri, a federal disaster area because of the threat of dioxin.

January 15: The National Commission on Social Security presents its reform plan to save the Social Security system from bankruptcy.

March 2: Economy shows signs of improvement, U.S. auto production increases 53% in January and February compared with the same months in 1982.

March 8: President Reagan opposes a freeze on nuclear arms. He characterizes the Soviet Union as an "evil empire" and as the "focus of evil in the modern world."

March 9: As criticism of the Environmental Protection Agency grows, EPA Chief Anne McGill Buford resigns.

March 24: Hoping to keep the Social Security system solvent for another 75 years, the House of Representatives passes the Social Security Reform Bill.
As some states are running out of funds for unemployment benefits, President Reagan signs a bill providing $4.65 billion for jobs and emergency relief.

April 4: The space shuttle Challenger is launched, in the first of three 1983 missions.

April 12: Chicago elects its first black mayor, Harold Washington.

April 18: Explosion at the U.S. Embassy in Beirut.

April 26: The National Commission on Excellence in Education issues its report, "A Nation at Risk."

May 24: Congress approves funding for the research and development of the MX missile.
Edward N. Brandt Jr., assistant secretary of Health and Human Services, states that finding the cause of Acquired Immune Deficiency Syndrome (AIDS) has been given "No. 1 priority" by the U.S. government.

June 15: The U.S. Supreme Court limits the power of state and local governments to restrict access to legal abortions.

June 18: The space shuttle Challenger carries Dr. Sally K. Ride, who becomes the first American woman astronaut in space.

June 28: A proposed anti-abortion constitutional amendment is rejected by the U.S. Senate.

August 30: The space shuttle Challenger carries Lt. Col. Guion Bluford, who becomes the first U.S. black astronaut in space.

September 1: The Soviet Union shoots down a South Korean airliner killing all 269 passengers.

October 23: 241 U.S. servicemen die in Beirut after a terrorist truck crashes into the headquarters of the U.S. Marine compound.

October 25: President Reagan sends U.S. military forces to the island of Grenada to rescue U.S. citizens.

November 2: U.S. Justice Department sues in federal court to obtain the medical records of a severely handicapped infant known as Baby Jane Doe.

November 20: *The Day After,* a TV drama about the effects of a nuclear attack on the U.S., is shown.

November 28: Space shuttle Columbia is launched.

December 1: Former EPA official, Rita Lavelle is found guilty of perjury and of obstructing a Congressional investigation.

1984

January 3: The Federal Deposit Insurance Corporation reports that 48 federally insured banks failed in

1983, the highest number since 1939.

January 17: U.S. Supreme Court ruled that home taping with VCRs does not infringe on copyright law, unless the material is used for commercial or profit-making purpose.

February 3: Space shuttle Challenger is launched in the first of three 1984 missions.
February 9: Yuri Andropov dies and is succeeded by Konstantin U. Chernenko.
February 26: Withdrawal of U.S. Marines from Beirut is completed.

March 21: Soviet nuclear powered submarine collides in the dark with the U.S. aircraft carrier *Kittyhawk*.

April 19: French researchers announce the identification of a virus that is believed to be the cause of AIDS.
April 26: President Reagan visits China.

May 8: U.S.S.R. announces it will not compete in the Summer Olympic games in Los Angeles.

June 6: The 40th anniversary of D-Day is observed.

July 12: Democratic Presidential candidate Walter Mondale chooses a woman, Geraldine Ferraro, as his vice presidential running mate.
July 17: President Reagan signs a bill that will force states to raise the drinking age to 21, or face losing federal highway construction funds.
July 18: Gunman John Humberty kills 21 people in and near a McDonald's restaurant in San Ysidro, California.
July 28: President Reagan opens the Summer Olympic games in Los Angeles.

August 2: The Census Bureau says that the Nation's poverty rate in 1983 was at its highest level since 1965.
August 11: While testing a radio microphone, President Reagan jokes about outlawing Russia and says, "We begin bombing in five minutes."
August 16: President Reagan signs a bill which requires states to pass laws requiring employers to withhold wages from parents who fall one-month behind in making court-ordered child support payments.
August 29: A prototype of the B-1 bomber crashes during a test flight, killing the pilot.
August 30: Space shuttle Discovery is launched.

October 24: Reagan administration announces $45 million worth of aid will be sent to starving Ethiopians.

November 2: A new federal holiday is established, Martin Luther King Day, to be observed on the third Monday in January.
November 6: Reagan and Bush are reelected to the Presidency and Vice Presidency.
November 11: President Reagan dedicates the sculpture *Three Servicemen* at the Vietnam Veteran's Memorial.

December: Sales of home videocassette recorders (VCRs), introduced in 1975, are estimated to be over seven million units in 1984 by the Electronic Industries Association. Thousands of video stores including grocery, drug, and other retail stores now rent tapes.
December 22: Four teen-age boys are shot by Bernard Goetz in the New York City subway.

1985

January 15: After over 20 years of military rule, Brazil's electoral college elects a civilian president.
January 24: Space shuttle Discovery is launched in the first of four 1985 missions.

February: The "Big 3" automakers -- General Motors, Ford, and Chrysler -- report total profits in 1984 of over $9 billion.
February: The dollar ends the month with new highs against foreign currencies.
February 19: Prime Minister Margaret Thatcher visits the U.S.

March 10: Soviet leader Konstantin Chernenko dies.
March 11: Mikhail Gorbachev succeeds Chernenko.
March 12: Disarmament talks begin between the U.S. and the Soviet Union in Geneva, Switzerland.
March 15: Governor Richard Celeste orders all state-chartered savings and loan institutions in Ohio ot close for three days to prevent a run on the banks.
March 19: U.S. Senate votes to authorize the production of the MX missiles.

April 29: Space shuttle Challenger is launched in the first of three 1985 missions.
April 30: Tenth anniversary of the fall of Saigon is remembered.

May 7: 25,000 Vietnam Veterans parade past a million spectators in New York City.
May 28: President Reagan campaigns for a major revision of the U.S. tax law.

June 5: U.S. House approves economic sanctions against South Africa.
June 11: Karen Ann Quinlan dies -- more than 10 years after sinking into a coma.

September 6: The Labor Department reports that unemployment in August was at its lowest point since 1980.

October 2: Actor Rock Hudson dies of AIDS.
October 4: Space shuttle Atlantis is launched in the first of two 1985 missions.
October 11: President Reagan has Navy F-14 fighters intercept a plane carrying the four Palestinian hijackers of the cruise ship *Achille Lauro.*

December: "Crack" cocaine has become a major problem in New York, Los Angeles, and Miami. "Crack" usage spreading throughout the U.S.
December 11: The Gramm-Rudman bill to eliminate the federal budget deficit by 1991 is passed by Congress.
December 12: President Reagan signs the Gramm-Rudman bill.

1986

January 12: Space shuttle Columbia is launched.
January 20: U.S. officially observes Martin Luther King Day as a national holiday for the first time.
January 28: U.S. space shuttle Challenger explodes after liftoff killing all seven crew members.

February: Oil prices fall, stocks rally, and unemployment in January is reported at a 6-year low.
February 25: President Reagan asks Congress for $100 million in military and humanitarian aid for the Contras in Nicaragua.

March 3: The President's Commission on Organized Crime reports that the government estimates that 20 million Americans use marijuana at least once a month.

March 5: President Reagan says that if Soviet leader Gorbachev does not come to the U.S. in 1986, Reagan will not go to the U.S.S.R. in 1987.

March 20: A $100,000,000 Contra aid bill for Nicaraguan rebel forces is voted down by the House of Representatives.

March 24-25: U.S. conducts naval exercises in the Mediterranean Sea off of Libya and sinks at least two Libyan missile patrol boats.

March 25: Military aid to Honduras amounting to $20,000,000 is approved by Congress following reports of a Nicaraguan military incursion to destroy rebel Contra bases just inside the Honduran border.

April 5: A terrorist bombing in a West Berlin discotheque kills a U.S. soldier and a Turkish woman, and wounds 155 other persons, including about 60 Americans. Libya is suspected of being involved with the bombing.

April 14: The U.S. launches an air strike against Libya in retaliation for Libya's involvement in the West Berlin discotheque bombing on April 5th and for other terrorist acts.

April 25: Major nuclear accident at Chernobyl begins.

May 25: "Hands across America" raises money for the hungry and homeless.

June 9: U.S. Supreme Court rules against the Reagan Administration's "Baby Doe" ruling.

June 12: U.S. Public Health Service warns that AIDS cases will increase ten-fold by 1991.

June 19: Len Bias dies from a cocaine overdose. Two days earlier he had been chosen in the NBA draft by the Boston Celtics.

June 27: Don Rodgers of the Cleveland Browns dies from cocaine.

June 30: U.S. Supreme Court rules that the Georgia law prohibiting sodomy does not violate the constitutional right to privacy.

July 3: The Statue of Liberty's 100th birthday celebration begins.

July 9: The Attorney General's Commission on Pornography issues its report on pornography, which claims that exposure to violent pornography probably leads to acts of sexual violence.

July 17: LTV Steel files for bankruptcy.

July 23: Prince Andrew marries Sarah Ferguson.

August 21: Soviets blame Chernobyl on human error.

September 14: Terrorist bombings in Paris, France lead to the announcement of antiterrorist measures by the Premier of France.

September 29: The Soviet Union frees Nicholas Daniloff, accused spy.

September 30: The U.S. frees Gennadi Zakharov, accused spy.

October 3: Fire aboard a Soviet nuclear submarine in the Atlantic.

October 9: The U.S. Senate impeaches Federal Judge Harry Claiborne.

October 11: Reagan and Gorbachev meet in Iceland.

October 19: U.S.S.R. orders five U.S. diplomats to leave the U.S.S.R.

October 21: U.S. orders 55 Soviet diplomats to leave the U.S.

November 6: General Motors announces the closing of 11 plants employing 29,000 people.

November 14: Ivan Boesky is sentenced to pay $100 million fine for insider trading on the stock market.

November 20: The World Health Organization launches a worldwide fight against AIDS.

November 26: President Reagan, in a surprise announcement, says that money earned by arms sales to Iran was diverted to the Contras through a secret Swiss account.

December 23: Pilots Richard Rutan and Jeana Yeager land after circling the earth nonstop without refueling.

1987

January 16: Television station KRON in San Francisco accepts commercials for condoms.

January 24: About 10,000 people march in Cummings, Georgia in support of civil rights. Leaders include Coretta Scott King, Jesse Jackson, and Andrew Young.

February 2: The Children's Defense Fund reports that the U.S. has one of the highest infant mortality rates among industrialized nations.

February 10: Surgeon General C. Everett Koop supports the advertising of condoms on television.

February 12: President Reagan signs a bill to allocate emergency aid to the homeless.

February 20: Brazilian President Sarney announces that Brazil will suspend payment of interest on debts to foreign commercial banks.

March 10: The Vatican states its opposition to artificial birth technology such as artificial fertilization or insemination.

March 20: AZT, azidothymidine, is approved as a drug capable of fighting AIDS.

April 1: President Reagan declares AIDS as "public health enemy No. 1."

May-August: U.S. House and Senate committees hold public hearings on the Iran-Contra affair.

May 8: Gary Hart withdraws his bid for the Democratic presidential nomination after newspaper reports connect him with a woman other than his wife.

May 17: 37 sailors aboard the *U.S.S. Stark* in the Persian Gulf are killed by an Iraqi missile.

May 31: President Reagan supports mandatory testing of prisoners and immigrants for AIDS, along with routine AIDS testing of marriage license applicants.

June 16: The New York State Supreme Court finds Bernhard Goetz, the "subway vigilante," not guilty of attempted murder and assault.

July 22: A bill providing more than $1 billion in emergency aid to the homeless is signed by President Reagan.

July 23: President Reagan announces the members of his commission on AIDS.

August 4: President Reagan announces his peace plan for the Contras and Nicaragua's Sandinista government.

September 10-19: Pope John Paul II tours the U.S.

September 16: In Montreal, Canada, representatives of 24 countries agree to a treaty designed to protect the ozone layer in the atmosphere.

September 17: The bicentennial of the signing of the U.S. Constitution is observed.

October 19: The Dow stock market average plunges 508 points, or more than 20% in one day, in what becomes known as Black Monday.

December 8: President Reagan and Gorbachev of the Soviet Union sign an agreement to eliminate intermediate range nuclear weapons from Europe.

1988

January 5: The National Academy of Sciences releases a report on the dangers of radon gas.

February 5: Federal grand juries in Miami and Tampa indict General Manuel Antonio Noriega of Panama for aiding international drug traffickers.
The Arizona House of Representatives impeaches Governor Evan Mecham.

February 11: Lyn Nofziger, former aide to President Reagan, is found guilty of violating the 1978 Ethics in Government Act.

February 21: Evangelist Jimmy Swaggart asks for forgiveness for his sin before his congregation.

March 11: Robert McFarlane, former national security adviser, pleads guilty to having withheld information from Congress on aid to the Contras.

March 16: Iran-Contra scandal. Col. Oliver North of the National Security Council, the president's adviser for national security affairs John Poindexter, USAF General Richard Secord (Ret.), and Albert Hakim are indicted by a federal grand jury.

May-August: Drought occurs throughout many parts of the U.S.

May 16: Surgeon General C. Everett Koop declares that cigarettes and other tobacco products are addictive.

May 27: U.S. Senate ratifies the treaty on intermediate-range nuclear forces.

May 29: President Reagan visits Mikhail Gorbachev in Moscow.

June 6: The Federal Home Loan Bank Board liquidates two insolvent savings and loan associations in Costa Mesa, California. The cost is $1.35 billion.

July 3: U.S. Navy warship, the *Vincennes*, while in the Persian Gulf, fires a missile which destroys an Iranian airliner, killing all 290 persons aboard the flight.

July 5: Attorney General Edwin Meese resigns.

July 27: The Surgeon General's Report on Fitness and Health is released. The report warns that fat in the diet is a major cause of death from heart disease, cancer, and strokes. The report states that Americans need to increase their consumption of fiber and complex carbohydrates.

August 3: The U.S. House of Representatives votes to impeach U.S. District Judge Alcee Hastings of Florida.

August 20: Cease-fire in effect between Iran and Iraq.

September 5: The Federal Home Loan Bank Board agrees to provide $2 billion in aid to the insolvent American Savings & Loan Association of Stockton, California.

September 13: The Reagan administration states that it will make an overdue payment of $44 million in dues to the United Nations.

September 26: Canadian sprinter Ben Johnson tests positive for steroids and is stripped of his gold medal for the 100-meter race at the Summer Olympics in Seoul, South Korea.

September 29: The U.S. space shuttle Discovery is launched, the first shuttle launched since the Challenger disaster in 1986.

November 8: George Bush is elected President.

December 3: Space shuttle Atlantis is launched.

December 29: The Commission on Base Realignment and Closure recommends the closing of 54 military bases.

1989

January 4: U.S. Navy fighters destroy two Libyan fighters over international waters off Libya.
January 7: Emperor Hirohito of Japan dies.
January 17: Gunman Patrick Purdy kills five students, wounds 29 with a semiautomatic rifle in Stockton, California.
January 20: George Bush sworn in as President.
January 30: Joel Steinberg is found guilty of first degree manslaughter in New York City, in a case that brings national attention to child abuse.

February 6: President Bush proposes to close or sell savings and loan institutions that are failing in the savings and loan industry crisis.
February 7: After public opposition, the U.S. House of Representatives defeats a proposed federal pay raise for members of Congress.
President Bush states that he will not support a ban on the import or sale of semiautomatic weapons.
February 15: The Soviet withdrawal from Afghanistan is completed.
A price of $1 million is offered for the killing of Salman Rushdie (author of *The Satanic Verses*) by one of the aides to Ayatollah Ruhollah Khomeini of Iran.
February 21: The Iran-Contra trial of Oliver North begins in federal district court, Washington, D.C.

March 13: Space shuttle Discovery is launched.
March 14: The Bush administration bans the import of semiautomatic assault rifles after public opposition to assault rifles grows.
March 24: An environmentally disastrous oil spill begins in Alaska's Prince William Sound after the *Exxon Valdez* oil tanker runs aground.
March 26: Citizens of the Soviet Union participate in nationwide multicandidate parliamentary elections for the Congress of People's Deputies.

April 9: Approximately 300,000 people rally in Washington, D.C. in support of a woman's right to choose to have an abortion.
April 19: 47 sailors are killed in an explosion aboard the *U.S.S. Iowa*.

May 2: Hungary begins to remove the barbed-wire border fence between itself and Austria.
May 4: Lt. Col. Oliver North is acquitted of nine charges but found guilty of three other charges connected with the Iran-Contra scandal.
Space shuttle Atlantis is launched.
May 13: President Bush calls on the people of Panama to overthrow General Manuel Noriega.
May 31: Speaker of the U.S. House of Representatives, Jim Wright, resigns from office after charges of ethics violations.
Surgeon General C. Everett Koop speaks against alcohol abuse and drunk driving.

June 3: Ayatollah Ruhollah Khomeini of Iran dies.
June 4: Chinese troops crush the pro-democracy movement in Beijing and other cities throughout China.
June 16: Marilyn Harrell admits to having stolen over $5 million of the Department of Housing and Urban Development's money, while the U.S. House of Representives investigates corruption within the department.
June 21: U.S. Supreme Court rules that the burning of the American flag as a form of political protest is permitted by the U.S. Constitution.

July 3: U.S. Supreme Court rules in support of a Missouri law which puts restrictions on a woman's right to an abortion.

July 11: Secretary of Housing and Urban Development, Jack Kemp, estimates that $2 billion of the department's funds have been lost because of fraud and mismanagement.

August 8: Space shuttle Columbia is launched.

August 9: President Bush signs into law the legislation designed to rescue the savings and loan industry -- a 10-year plan to close or merge more than 500 insolvent savings and loans.

August 24: Voters choose Tadeusz Mazowiecki as Prime Minister of Poland. He becomes the first non-Communist Prime Minister in 45 years.

September 10: Thousands of East German refugees pour into Austria through Hungary, as they flee to West Germany.

October 5: Jim Baker, television evangelist, is convicted of fraud and conspiracy.

November 9: East Germany ends travel restrictions across borders, permitting citizens to travel to the West freely for the first time since the erection of the Berlin Wall.

November 21: Street vendors in New York City sell alleged chunks of the Berlin Wall.

December 5: East Germany places former leader Erich Honecker under house arrest.

December 20: The U.S. invades Panama.

December 25: Romanian dictator Nicolae Ceausescu and his wife Elena are tried and executed as a new government takes over.

I would like to give special acknowledgement to those reference books that enabled me to develop this chronology: *The World Almanac* (Newspaper Enterprise Association); *Information Please Almanac* (Houghton Mifflin); *The Encyclopedia of American Facts and Dates* by Gorton Carruth (Harper & Row); *Day By Day: The Seventies* by Thomas Leonard, Cynthia Crippen, and Marc Aronson (Facts On File); *The Annals of America* (Encyclopaedia Britannica).

Edward Weilant
Bowling Green, Ohio

Outline of Contents

SECTION 1: DEMOGRAPHY

PERSONAL DATA

FAMILY DEMOGRAPHY

EMPLOYMENT

RELIGION

HOUSEHOLD

NATIONAL ISSUES

CRIME

SECTION 3: BEHAVIOR

PERSONAL HABITS

SOCIAL HABITS

AN AMERICAN PROFILE— OPINIONS AND BEHAVIOR, 1972-1989

SECTION 1 : DEMOGRAPHY

RESPONDENT'S AGE

TABLE I: RESPONDENT'S AGE -- BY TOTAL POPULATION

Question: Respondent's age.

Responses: 18-23; 24-29; 30-35; 36-41; 42-47; 48-53; 54-59; 60-65; 66+

	YEAR															
RESPONSE	'72	'73	'74	'75	'76	'77	'78	'80	'82	'83	'84	'85	'86	'87	'88	'89
18-23	11%	11%	11%	12%	11%	11%	11%	11%	10%	8%	11%	9%	7%	9%	10%	9%
24-29	14	14	14	16	15	13	16	14	16	18	16	14	15	13	15	13
30-35	12	11	12	12	12	12	15	15	14	15	14	14	15	15	13	14
36-41	8	12	10	10	11	11	10	10	10	11	13	12	13	13	13	13
42-47	12	10	10	10	8	10	8	8	8	9	9	8	10	11	11	11
48-53	12	10	10	9	9	10	9	8	7	7	7	9	7	9	6	9
54-59	10	10	9	8	9	11	9	9	10	8	8	9	7	7	6	6
60-65	9	8	7	8	9	8	7	8	8	8	8	9	8	7	8	7
66+	14	13	15	16	17	14	15	17	17	15	16	17	18	17	19	18
# SURVEYED	1608	1500	1478	1485	1493	1523	1525	1459	1494	1592	1467	1527	1463	1461	1477	1533

TABLE II: RESPONDENT'S AGE -- BY SEX

Question: Respondent's age.

Responses: 18-23; 24-29; 30-35; 36-41; 42-47; 48-53; 54-59; 60-65; 66+

		YEAR															
SEX	RESP	'72	'73	'74	'75	'76	'77	'78	'80	'82	'83	'84	'85	'86	'87	'88	'89
	18-23	2%	12%	12%	12%	12%	11%	9%	8%	11%	8%	13%	9%	7%	9%	11%	11%
M	24-29	16	14	13	15	16	14	17	14	18	18	15	14	18	13	15	13
A	30-35	11	11	10	11	11	12	16	17	13	15	12	14	15	16	13	14
L	36-41	8	12	9	11	11	11	10	12	11	12	14	12	13	13	16	15
E	42-47	11	9	10	10	7	10	9	8	8	9	9	9	10	11	12	11
	48-53	12	9	10	9	8	11	11	9	8	7	7	10	8	10	5	9
	54-59	11	10	10	9	9	10	8	10	9	8	9	9	7	7	6	6
	60-65	8	9	8	7	8	7	6	8	7	9	8	9	8	6	8	6
	66+	2	14	17	16	17	13	14	14	16	13	12	14	14	15	15	16
# SURVEYED		805	701	689	670	667	688	642	641	635	687	597	686	619	638	638	660
SEX	RESP	'72	'73	'74	'75	'76	'77	'78	'80	'82	'83	'84	'85	'86	'87	'88	'89
	18-23	9%	11%	11%	12%	10%	11%	12%	12%	9%	8%	9%	8%	8%	9%	9%	8%
F	24-29	13	14	15	16	15	13	16	14	15	18	16	15	12	13	14	13
E	30-35	13	11	13	12	13	13	14	13	14	15	15	14	15	14	13	14
M	36-41	8	12	12	10	11	11	11	9	9	10	12	12	13	13	11	11
A	42-47	12	10	11	10	8	9	7	8	8	9	9	8	9	10	10	10
L	48-53	11	11	10	10	9	9	7	8	7	7	7	8	7	8	7	9
E	54-59	9	11	9	8	8	11	10	8	10	8	7	8	7	6	6	7
	60-65	9	7	7	8	9	8	8	8	9	8	8	8	8	8	8	8
	66+	15	13	14	15	17	15	16	19	18	16	18	20	21	19	22	20
# SURVEYED		803	799	789	815	826	835	883	818	859	905	870	841	844	823	839	873

TABLE III: RESPONDENT'S AGE -- BY RACE

Question: Respondent's age.

Responses: 18-23; 24-29; 30-35; 36-41; 42-47; 48-53; 54-59; 60-65; 66+

		YEAR															
RACE	RESP	'72	'73	'74	'75	'76	'77	'78	'80	'82	'83	'84	'85	'86	'87	'88	'89
W	18-23	10%	11%	11%	12%	11%	10%	10%	10%	9%	8%	11%	9%	7%	8%	9%	8%
H	24-29	15	14	15	15	15	13	16	14	16	18	15	14	15	12	14	13
I	30-35	12	11	11	11	13	12	15	15	13	15	13	14	14	15	13	14
T	36-41	8	11	10	10	11	11	10	11	10	11	13	12	13	13	14	13
E	42-47	12	10	10	9	8	10	8	8	7	9	9	8	10	11	11	10
	48-53	12	10	10	10	9	10	9	8	8	7	7	9	7	9	6	9
	54-59	10	10	10	9	9	11	9	9	10	8	8	8	7	7	5	6
	60-65	9	8	7	8	9	8	7	8	8	8	8	9	8	7	9	7
	66+	13	13	16	16	17	14	16	17	18	16	17	18	19	18	20	20
# SURVEYED		1345	1305	1299	1318	1356	1334	1351	1312	1313	1410	1247	1333	1243	1219	1232	1315
RACE	RESP	'72	'73	'74	'75	'76	'77	'78	'80	'82	'83	'84	'85	'86	'87	'88	'89
B	18-23	12%	11%	15%	12%	11%	13%	17%	13%	12%	10%	13%	10%	11%	12%	10%	11%
L	24-29	13	12	9	17	19	17	19	15	17	20	17	11	15	18	18	15
A	30-35	10	10	17	12	12	13	18	15	19	17	17	15	19	15	20	12
C	36-41	7	14	13	13	9	14	11	8	10	9	8	9	10	11	9	13
K	42-47	12	8	8	10	5	6	6	6	12	8	9	8	9	9	10	10
	48-53	12	12	8	9	9	7	7	10	5	7	10	9	7	8	9	10
	54-59	10	12	8	7	10	11	6	12	5	9	9	11	7	6	9	11
	60-65	9	7	9	6	12	5	4	7	6	8	4	10	8	5	2	8
	66+	15	15	13	13	14	12	11	14	12	12	13	16	14	14	12	10
# SURVEYED		259	182	172	163	128	174	158	137	154	165	168	150	183	189	184	15
RACE	RESP	'72	'73	'74	'75	'76	'77	'78	'80	'82	'83	'84	'85	'86	'87	'88	'89
O	18-23	25%	8%	14%	25%	0%	7%	13%	10%	19%	6%	13%	7%	3%	13%	18%	20%
T	24-29	25	54	29	0	33	20	6	20	26	12	19	18	22	13	23	21
H	30-35	25	0	0	25	11	20	25	30	7	12	17	18	19	19	7	8
E	36-41	0	8	14	25	22	13	31	0	15	18	17	18	19	17	10	10
R	42-47	0	0	14	25	11	20	6	10	7	6	10	9	8	11	13	15
	48-53	0	8	14	0	22	7	0	20	7	6	2	7	16	8	7	8
	54-59	0	8	0	0	0	7	6	0	11	18	10	14	0	2	7	8
	60-65	25	0	0	0	0	7	0	10	7	12	4	5	3	6	3	5
	66+	0	15	14	0	0	0	13	0	0	12	8	5	11	11	13	5
# SURVEYED		4	13	7	4	9	15	16	10	27	17	52	44	37	53	61	61

****

RESPONDENT'S MONTH OF BIRTH

TABLE I: RESPONDENT'S MONTH OF BIRTH -- BY TOTAL POPULATION

Question: What is your date of birth? NOTE: Question not asked in 1972-1975.

Responses: January; February; March; etc.

	YEAR											
RESPONSE	'76	'77	'78	'80	'82	'83	'84	'85	'86	'87	'88	'89
JAN	8%	8%	8%	9%	9%	8%	9%	9%	7%	8%	8%	9%
FEB	8	7	8	7	9	7	7	8	9	7	7	8
MAR	8	10	7	10	7	10	8	8	9	9	9	9
APR	8	8	8	8	8	7	7	9	8	9	9	8
MAY	8	7	8	8	7	6	9	7	9	7	8	9
JUN	8	8	8	8	8	9	9	9	7	8	9	8
JUL	9	8	8	8	9	8	8	9	8	8	9	8
AUG	9	9	8	9	8	9	8	9	10	9	10	9
SEP	9	9	10	9	9	9	10	9	9	9	8	9
OCT	10	10	9	9	8	9	9	7	7	8	9	7
NOV	8	8	8	8	8	9	8	8	8	9	8	8
DEC	8	8	9	8	9	9	8	8	8	8	8	8
# SURVEYED	1489	1521	1512	1462	1492	1585	1462	1529	1462	1455	1467	1500

TABLE II: RESPONDENT'S MONTH OF BIRTH -- BY SEX

Question: What is your date of birth? NOTE: Question not asked in 1972-1975.

Responses: January; February; March; etc.

		YEAR											
SEX	RESP	'76	'77	'78	'80	'82	'83	'84	'85	'86	'87	'88	'89
M	JAN	8%	9%	7%	7%	9%	7%	10%	9%	9%	8%	8%	8%
A	FEB	7	7	8	8	8	7	7	8	9	9	6	8
L	MAR	9	10	7	12	8	9	7	8	9	10	9	7
E	APR	9	8	8	9	9	8	6	10	7	9	10	9
	MAY	8	7	9	8	7	7	9	6	10	8	7	9
	JUN	7	8	7	7	8	8	8	9	7	7	8	9
	JUL	9	8	7	7	9	8	7	10	7	8	8	8
	AUG	8	8	8	7	8	9	8	10	11	8	8	8
	SEP	8	9	13	9	9	9	11	8	7	9	8	9
	OCT	9	9	8	10	6	9	8	8	7	7	10	8
	NOV	8	9	9	7	9	8	8	7	8	10	8	8
	DEC	8	7	9	8	10	9	9	7	8	7	9	9
# SURVEYED		664	687	637	641	634	685	596	687	619	637	632	643
SEX	RESP	'76	'77	'78	'80	'82	'83	'84	'85	'86	'87	'88	'89
F	JAN	8%	8%	8%	10%	9%	8%	8%	9%	6%	8%	8%	9%
E	FEB	9	7	8	7	10	7	7	7	9	6	8	8
M	MAR	7	10	8	9	6	10	8	8	9	8	9	10
A	APR	7	7	8	8	7	6	8	7	9	9	7	8
L	MAY	9	7	8	7	7	6	9	8	9	7	9	9
E	JUN	8	8	9	8	8	9	9	8	7	9	9	7
	JUL	9	8	9	8	8	8	8	9	8	8	9	8
	AUG	9	9	8	11	8	9	8	9	10	9	11	9
	SEP	9	9	8	9	9	9	9	10	10	9	8	9
	OCT	10	10	10	8	10	10	9	7	7	9	8	6
	NOV	8	8	7	9	8	9	8	9	8	8	8	8
	DEC	8	8	8	7	9	8	8	9	9	9	7	8
# SURVEYED		825	834	875	821	858	900	866	842	843	818	835	857

TABLE III: RESPONDENT'S MONTH OF BIRTH -- BY RACE

Question: What is your date of birth? NOTE: Question not asked in 1972-1975.

Responses: January; February; March; etc.

		YEAR											
RACE	RESP	'76	'77	'78	'80	'82	'83	'84	'85	'86	'87	'88	'89
W	JAN	8%	9%	8%	8%	9%	8%	9%	9%	7%	8%	8%	9%
H	FEB	8	7	8	8	9	7	7	8	9	7	8	9
I	MAR	8	10	8	10	7	10	8	8	9	9	9	9
T	APR	8	8	8	8	8	7	7	9	8	9	9	8
E	MAY	8	7	9	7	7	6	10	7	9	7	8	9
	JUN	8	8	8	8	8	9	9	9	7	8	8	8
	JUL	9	8	9	8	9	8	8	9	8	8	8	8
	AUG	9	8	8	9	8	9	8	10	10	8	9	8
	SEP	8	9	9	9	9	9	10	9	8	9	8	9
	OCT	9	10	9	9	8	10	9	7	7	8	9	7
	NOV	8	8	8	8	8	8	8	8	9	9	8	8
	DEC	8	7	8	8	9	9	8	9	8	8	8	8
# SURVEYED		1352	1334	1342	1314	1311	1406	1242	1335	1242	1214	1225	1289
RACE	RESP	'76	'77	'78	'80	'82	'83	'84	'85	'86	'87	'88	'89
B	JAN	9%	8%	8%	13%	8%	7%	11%	7%	6%	6%	7%	9%
L	FEB	9	6	8	5	11	8	7	6	9	8	5	7
A	MAR	13	10	5	9	7	7	6	7	4	6	8	7
C	APR	9	6	7	11	5	5	8	7	5	9	7	8
K	MAY	9	4	7	10	7	7	5	9	10	7	9	8
	JUN	7	9	9	8	8	9	11	11	7	10	13	10
	JUL	8	8	6	7	6	12	7	9	8	6	12	7
	AUG	4	12	6	9	8	8	10	8	10	12	10	14
	SEP	11	10	14	8	6	11	9	13	14	11	7	10
	OCT	10	8	8	7	12	7	10	7	10	6	9	5
	NOV	5	8	9	7	12	11	7	12	7	10	6	7
	DEC	6	10	12	7	10	8	10	5	10	11	8	9
# SURVEYED		128	172	154	138	154	163	168	150	183	188	182	152
RACE	RESP	'76	'77	'78	'80	'82	'83	'84	'85	'86	'87	'88	'89
O	JAN	0%	7%	13%	0%	7%	6%	2%	7%	11%	11%	12%	8%
T	FEB	22	20	0	0	11	13	6	7	3	11	2	2
H	MAR	11	7	0	10	4	13	8	5	16	8	13	8
E	APR	0	0	6	10	7	6	4	9	11	8	5	8
R	MAY	0	13	6	30	15	13	12	2	14	9	12	12
	JUN	22	13	13	10	11	6	6	0	5	6	8	8
	JUL	11	0	13	10	7	0	4	16	5	2	7	10
	AUG	0	20	6	20	7	6	13	14	5	11	8	8
	SEP	11	0	13	0	7	0	15	7	8	11	5	5
	OCT	11	7	13	0	7	6	8	16	5	13	7	12
	NOV	11	13	6	10	0	6	8	9	5	8	13	8
	DEC	0	0	13	0	15	25	15	9	11	2	8	8
# SURVEYED		9	15	16	10	27	16	52	44	37	53	60	59

TABLE IV: RESPONDENT'S MONTH OF BIRTH -- BY AGE

Question: What is your month of birth? NOTE: Question not asked in 1972-1975.

Responses: January; February; March; etc.

		YEAR											
AGE	RESP	'76	'77	'78	'80	'82	'83	'84	'85	'86	'87	'88	'89
18-23	JAN	7%	7%	8%	13%	13%	9%	5%	12%	11%	8%	4%	8%
	FEB	10	6	15	10	9	7	9	12	5	7	5	10
	MAR	9	15	4	7	7	9	8	7	6	7	11	7
	APR	6	9	4	5	7	9	14	7	11	6	9	14
	MAY	5	4	9	8	8	9	7	8	6	9	10	7
	JUN	6	7	7	6	8	7	8	5	9	13	7	10
	JUL	7	9	6	8	10	5	8	8	12	8	11	4
	AUG	9	10	9	11	5	12	9	8	11	10	13	7
	SEP	8	12	10	14	7	11	8	11	4	10	8	7
	OCT	10	8	9	7	6	5	11	4	12	6	8	7
	NOV	13	7	10	6	11	9	8	10	5	9	9	11
	DEC	10	8	10	7	7	9	8	11	7	7	6	7
# SURVEYED		162	164	163	155	148	128	160	133	108	125	141	134
AGE	RESP	'76	'77	'78	'80	'82	'83	'84	'85	'86	'87	'88	'89
24-29	JAN	7%	12%	5%	7%	8%	8%	7%	9%	6%	9%	8%	11%
	FEB	7	6	7	6	14	8	7	7	7	9	7	7
	MAR	9	6	9	7	7	7	8	8	11	7	11	10
	APR	7	6	7	8	6	6	4	7	6	13	7	7
	MAY	6	8	8	8	4	7	11	7	10	10	10	8
	JUN	7	8	8	10	10	8	9	9	6	5	9	8
	JUL	12	8	8	8	9	8	7	8	5	7	8	9
	AUG	10	10	7	11	6	9	9	7	16	11	10	9
	SEP	8	8	13	6	8	12	12	12	11	10	7	10
	OCT	10	10	10	8	8	9	8	7	9	7	7	9
	NOV	7	8	8	11	8	8	8	7	7	8	7	6
	DEC	9	9	10	9	11	9	9	11	7	4	11	8
# SURVEYED		224	204	240	202	246	285	232	217	218	193	213	197
AGE	RESP	'76	'77	'78	'80	'82	'83	'84	'85	'86	'87	'88	'89
30-35	JAN	11%	11%	8%	12%	9%	9%	12%	6%	8%	6%	7%	10%
	FEB	8	9	7	10	9	8	9	5	6	10	8	8
	MAR	7	12	7	10	6	11	7	9	8	9	8	11
	APR	5	5	7	9	11	5	9	9	7	7	5	9
	MAY	9	6	10	7	5	6	9	6	9	5	10	7
	JUN	8	9	8	8	8	8	6	11	8	11	10	5
	JUL	10	8	11	8	9	9	8	8	9	8	11	10
	AUG	9	12	6	7	9	10	9	10	8	7	6	7
	SEP	9	7	13	8	5	9	8	9	8	8	7	9
	OCT	13	9	9	9	8	10	11	8	10	11	10	7
	NOV	5	7	9	6	8	9	8	10	13	11	9	9
	DEC	8	6	6	6	11	7	8	8	7	7	7	10
# SURVEYED		186	188	227	215	202	235	200	212	221	221	192	208

TABLE IV: RESPONDENT'S MONTH OF BIRTH -- BY AGE (Continued)

Question: What is your month of birth? NOTE: Question not asked in 1972-1975.

Responses: January; February; March; etc.

		YEAR											
AGE	RESP	'76	'77	'78	'80	'82	'83	'84	'85	'86	'87	'88	'89
36-41	JAN	8%	5%	9%	8%	7%	6%	8%	11%	6%	9%	6%	6%
	FEB	9	7	4	8	6	5	5	7	13	4	5	9
	MAR	9	10	6	9	8	10	9	7	12	11	10	9
	APR	8	7	11	5	8	8	6	8	9	6	11	6
	MAY	8	10	13	4	12	7	5	8	7	11	6	8
	JUN	10	8	6	9	6	9	12	5	6	4	10	8
	JUL	8	10	9	8	8	8	11	10	10	8	8	10
	AUG	8	7	9	10	7	7	6	10	9	8	12	10
	SEP	8	10	10	11	12	8	11	5	5	8	8	7
	OCT	9	7	8	9	9	8	10	9	4	10	13	6
	NOV	8	11	7	6	9	12	7	11	10	8	6	11
	DEC	7	8	8	13	8	12	10	8	9	13	6	9
# SURVEYED		158	168	160	150	145	172	187	184	188	185	192	192
AGE	RESP	'76	'77	'78	'80	'82	'83	'84	'85	'86	'87	'88	'89
42-47	JAN	5%	7%	10%	8%	13%	5%	9%	9%	5%	9%	9%	8%
	FEB	12	7	8	4	8	8	6	9	15	4	8	12
	MAR	5	12	8	11	7	8	6	10	6	7	8	7
	APR	7	10	14	9	12	8	10	7	7	10	10	11
	MAY	11	7	5	9	10	8	12	5	10	5	6	10
	JUN	5	12	13	6	3	7	7	10	6	7	6	6
	JUL	12	3	8	6	7	8	6	11	6	11	7	8
	AUG	4	7	7	15	6	10	6	15	11	8	8	10
	SEP	11	8	5	6	6	14	16	2	11	11	10	11
	OCT	10	11	7	10	10	8	11	9	9	8	9	7
	NOV	7	8	6	8	6	8	9	8	7	12	10	6
	DEC	11	8	9	9	13	10	4	4	8	8	9	4
# SURVEYED		113	147	119	117	118	145	126	124	141	157	157	157
AGE	RESP	'76	'77	'78	'80	'82	'83	'84	'85	'86	'87	'88	'89
48-53	JAN	5%	12%	10%	11%	13%	5%	11%	8%	10%	7%	13%	9%
	FEB	8	4	6	10	10	9	6	10	9	10	8	7
	MAR	10	10	8	10	5	13	4	7	7	6	7	8
	APR	12	10	8	5	5	5	9	9	7	8	8	5
	MAY	9	8	7	9	10	6	9	10	6	5	7	8
	JUN	11	7	11	5	13	11	8	5	11	11	9	13
	JUL	8	9	8	10	10	11	9	11	6	6	8	10
	AUG	10	10	8	12	4	9	7	7	12	13	13	8
	SEP	8	7	6	6	4	4	9	7	10	6	8	8
	OCT	5	8	7	8	8	10	9	10	6	10	8	7
	NOV	11	8	8	7	11	6	9	8	6	10	3	7
	DEC	4	6	14	7	7	10	12	8	8	9	9	8
# SURVEYED		133	154	132	122	112	116	102	131	108	125	90	134

TABLE IV: RESPONDENT'S MONTH OF BIRTH -- BY AGE (Continued)

Question: What is your month of birth? NOTE: Question not asked in 1972-1975.

Responses: January; February; March; etc.

		YEAR											
AGE	RESP	'76	'77	'78	'80	'82	'83	'84	'85	'86	'87	'88	'89
54-59	JAN	11%	10%	4%	7%	6%	8%	11%	9%	8%	4%	7%	9%
	FEB	6	8	7	6	8	7	9	8	11	10	4	6
	MAR	11	6	11	13	9	11	11	4	13	8	8	9
	APR	13	9	9	10	9	11	5	10	8	10	13	8
	MAY	11	5	4	8	5	8	9	6	6	9	12	8
	JUN	5	10	11	7	9	8	10	13	4	10	12	11
	JUL	6	10	8	8	6	5	7	9	5	8	7	3
	AUG	6	8	7	3	12	8	7	8	7	6	7	7
	SEP	7	6	7	11	10	8	11	10	9	7	11	13
	OCT	10	8	12	9	9	10	9	6	8	10	4	6
	NOV	7	9	9	13	6	8	4	7	10	6	9	8
	DEC	7	11	13	4	10	8	8	10	9	10	7	9
# SURVEYED		128	167	136	136	144	133	114	134	98	98	85	95
AGE	RESP	'76	'77	'78	'80	'82	'83	'84	'85	'86	'87	'88	'89
60-65	JAN	8%	3%	10%	5%	6%	9%	9%	11%	10%	9%	14%	10%
	FEB	5	6	7	4	11	5	5	6	9	5	11	13
	MAR	7	15	7	14	9	7	7	9	5	9	8	9
	APR	8	6	8	12	6	5	5	9	11	8	5	4
	MAY	10	10	9	9	9	5	16	9	11	4	8	6
	JUN	11	8	4	9	6	10	8	12	10	11	4	6
	JUL	12	9	7	8	4	7	7	7	9	8	14	8
	AUG	8	4	12	8	16	14	8	9	8	15	3	11
	SEP	12	10	14	9	7	9	13	12	8	12	7	7
	OCT	8	18	12	7	9	10	4	4	7	4	11	8
	NOV	6	8	7	8	8	12	8	5	7	11	7	5
	DEC	7	4	2	7	9	6	10	6	6	4	8	12
# SURVEYED		133	117	107	119	116	130	111	130	114	100	118	110
AGE	RESP	'76	'77	'78	'80	'82	'83	'84	'85	'86	'87	'88	'89
66+	JAN	8%	7%	7%	7%	7%	8%	7%	8%	7%	9%	8%	7%
	FEB	10	9	11	6	8	6	9	7	8	7	8	6
	MAR	7	10	8	12	7	11	9	8	8	11	10	9
	APR	6	7	8	11	7	10	6	10	9	11	10	8
	MAY	10	8	8	8	7	5	8	6	12	7	7	12
	JUN	7	6	8	7	7	9	11	7	7	7	9	8
	JUL	8	7	8	6	10	10	7	11	9	7	7	8
	AUG	12	9	8	9	9	7	10	10	8	8	12	8
	SEP	9	11	8	9	13	8	6	10	10	10	8	11
	OCT	9	10	11	10	8	13	7	8	3	8	8	7
	NOV	6	9	7	9	8	6	11	7	8	6	7	6
	DEC	9	8	7	7	7	8	8	8	11	9	7	8
# SURVEYED		251	210	227	241	259	240	229	260	265	251	277	271

****

RESPONDENT'S RACE

TABLE I: RESPONDENT'S RACE -- BY TOTAL POPULATION

Question: What race do you consider yourself?

Responses: White; Black; Other (Note: See Appendix C for explanation of "Other")

	YEAR															
RESPONSE	'72	'73	'74	'75	'76	'77	'78	'80	'82	'83	'84	'85	'86	'87	'88	'89
BLACK	84%	87%	88%	89%	91%	88%	89%	90%	88%	89%	85%	87%	85%	83%	83%	86%
WHITE	16	12	12	11	9	12	10	10	10	10	12	10	13	13	13	10
OTHER	0	1	0	0	1	1	1	1	2	1	4	3	3	4	4	4
# SURVEYED	1613	1504	1484	1490	1499	1530	1532	1468	1506	1599	1473	1534	1470	1466	1481	1537

TABLE II: RESPONDENT'S RACE -- BY SEX

Question: What race do you consider yourself?

Responses: W = White; B = Black; O = Other (Note: See Appendix C for explanation of "Other")

		YEAR															
SEX	RESP	'72	' 73	'74	'75	'76	'77	'78	'80	'82	'83	'84	'85	'86	'87	'88	'89
M	W	83%	87%	90%	89%	90%	89%	88%	92%	89%	91%	87%	88%	87%	85%	85%	89%
	B	16	12	10	11	9	10	10	7	9	8	9	10	10	11	11	7
	O	0	1	0	0	1	1	1	1	2	1	4	3	3	4	4	4
# SURVEYED		807	701	691	670	669	693	643	641	639	690	598	688	621	641	638	660
SEX	RESP	'72	'73	'74	'75	'76	'77	'78	'80	'82	'83	'84	'85	'86	'87	'88	'89
F	W	84%	87%	86%	88%	92%	87%	89%	88%	87%	87%	84%	87%	84%	82%	82%	83%
	B	16	12	13	11	8	13	10	11	11	12	13	10	14	14	13	13
	O	0	1	1	0	0	1	1	1	1	1	3	3	2	3	4	4
# SURVEYED		806	803	793	820	830	837	889	827	867	909	875	846	849	825	843	877

TABLE IV: RESPONDENT'S RACE -- BY AGE

Question: What race do you consider yourself?

Responses: W = White B = Black O = Other (Note: See Appendix C for explanation of "Other")

		YEAR															
AGE	RESP	'72	'73	'74	'75	'76	'77	'78	'80	'82	'83	'84	'85	'86	'87	'88	'89
18-23	W	80%	88%	85%	88%	91%	85%	82%	88%	84%	86%	82%	86%	81%	76%	79%	78%
	B	19	12	15	11	9	14	17	12	13	13	14	11	19	18	13	13
	O	1	1	1	1	0	1	1	1	3	1	4	2	1	6	8	9
# SURVEYED		169	171	168	173	162	164	163	155	148	128	161	133	108	126	141	137
AGE	RESP	'72	'73	'74	'75	'76	'77	'78	'80	'82	'83	'84	'85	'86	'87	'88	'89
24-29	W	85%	87%	92%	88%	88%	84%	87%	89%	87%	88%	83%	89%	83%	79%	78%	82%
	B	15	10	7	12	11	14	12	10	11	11	13	7	13	18	16	11
	O	0	3	1	0	1	1	0	1	3	1	4	4	4	4	7	6
# SURVEYED		231	212	212	232	226	204	244	202	246	287	232	217	218	193	215	201
AGE	RESP	'72	'73	'74	'75	'76	'77	'78	'80	'82	'83	'84	'85	'86	'87	'88	'89
30-35	W	86%	89%	83%	88%	91%	86%	86%	89%	85%	87%	82%	85%	81%	82%	79%	89%
	B	14	11	17	11	8	12	13	10	14	12	14	11	15	13	18	9
	O	1	0	0	1	1	2	2	1	1	1	5	4	3	5	2	2
# SURVEYED		187	167	175	171	186	188	230	215	204	236	200	212	221	221	195	212
AGE	RESP	'72	'73	'74	'75	'76	'77	'78	'80	'82	'83	'84	'85	'86	'87	'88	'89
36-41	W	86%	85%	84%	86%	92%	84%	86%	93%	86%	90%	88%	88%	86%	84%	88%	86%
	B	14	14	15	14	7	15	11	7	11	9	7	8	10	11	9	11
	O	0	1	1	1	1	1	3	0	3	2	5	4	4	5	3	3
# SURVEYED		128	175	152	154	158	168	160	150	146	173	187	184	188	186	193	198
AGE	RESP	'72	'73	'74	'75	'76	'77	'78	'80	'82	'83	'84	'85	'86	'87	'88	'89
42-47	W	84%	90%	90%	87%	93%	90%	91%	92%	82%	90%	84%	87%	86%	85%	83%	84%
	B	16	10	9	12	6	7	8	7	16	9	12	10	12	11	12	10
	O	0	0	1	1	1	2	1	1	2	1	4	3	2	4	5	6
# SURVEYED		186	146	151	143	114	147	119	117	119	145	126	124	141	157	157	161
AGE	RESP	'72	'73	'74	'75	'76	'77	'78	'80	'82	'83	'84	'85	'86	'87	'88	'89
48-53	W	84%	85%	90%	89%	90%	91%	92%	87%	91%	90%	83%	87%	82%	84%	77%	86%
	B	16	15	10	11	8	8	8	11	7	9	16	11	12	13	18	11
	O	0	1	1	0	2	1	0	2	2	1	1	2	6	3	4	4
# SURVEYED		189	151	146	141	133	154	133	123	112	116	102	131	108	126	92	138

TABLE IV: RESPONDENT'S RACE -- BY AGE (Continued)

Question: What race do you consider yourself?

Responses: W = White B = Black O = Other (Note: See Appendix C for explanation of "Other")

		YEAR															
AGE	RESP	'72	'73	'74	'75	'76	'77	'78	'80	'82	'83	'84	'85	'86	'87	'88	'89
54-59	W	83%	86%	90%	90%	90%	88%	93%	88%	92%	87%	82%	83%	88%	87%	76%	77%
	B	17	13	10	10	10	12	7	13	6	11	13	13	12	12	19	18
	O	0	1	0	0	0	1	1	0	2	2	4	4	0	1	5	5
# SURVEYED		156	157	139	126	129	168	137	136	144	134	114	134	99	98	85	99
AGE	RESP	'72	'73	'74	'75	'76	'77	'78	'80	'82	'83	'84	'85	'86	'87	'88	'89
60-65	W	83%	90%	86%	91%	89%	91%	94%	92%	90%	88%	92%	87%	86%	87%	95%	86%
	B	17	10	14	9	11	8	6	8	9	11	6	11	13	10	3	11
	O	1	0	0	0	0	1	0	1	2	2	2	2	1	3	2	3
# SURVEYED		144	121	108	113	134	117	107	119	116	132	113	131	115	101	119	111
AGE	RESP	'72	'73	'74	'75	'76	'77	'78	'80	'82	'83	'84	'85	'86	'87	'88	'89
66+	W	82%	86%	90%	91%	93%	90%	91%	92%	93%	91%	89%	90%	89%	87%	89%	93%
	B	18	14	10	9	7	10	8	8	7	8	9	9	9	11	8	5
	O	0	1	0	0	0	0	1	0	0	1	2	1	2	2	3	1
# SURVEYED		218	200	227	232	251	213	232	242	259	241	232	261	265	253	280	275

****

RESPONDENT'S SEX

TABLE I: RESPONDENT'S SEX - BY TOTAL POPULATION

Question: Respondent's sex.

Responses: Male; Female

	YEAR															
RESPONSE	'72	'73	'74	'75	'76	'77	'78	'80	'82	'83	'84	'85	'86	'87	'88	'89
MALE	50%	47%	47%	45%	45%	45%	42%	44%	42%	43%	41%	45%	42%	44%	43%	43%
FEMALE	50	53	53	55	55	55	58	56	58	57	59	55	58	56	57	57
# SURVEYED	1613	1504	1484	1490	1499	1530	1532	1468	1506	1599	1473	1534	1470	1466	1481	1537

TABLE III: RESPONDENT'S SEX -- BY RACE

Question: Respondent's sex.

Responses: M = Male F = Female

		YEAR															
RACE	RESP	'72	'73	'74	'75	'76	'77	'78	'80	'82	'83	'84	'85	'86	'87	'88	'89
W	M	50%	47%	47%	45%	44%	46%	42%	45%	43%	44%	42%	45%	43%	44%	44%	45%
H	F	50	53	53	55	56	54	58	55	57	56	58	55	57	56	56	55
T																	
# SURVEYED		1348	1308	1304	1323	1361	1339	1358	1318	1323	1416	1251	1338	1249	1222	1234	1319
RACE	RESP	'72	'73	'74	'75	'76	'77	'78	'80	'82	'83	'84	'85	'86	'87	'88	'89
B	M	50%	46%	42%	44%	49%	39%	42%	32%	38%	33%	32%	43%	35%	38%	39%	29%
L	F	50	54	58	56	51	61	58	68	62	67	68	57	65	62	61	71
K																	
# SURVEYED		261	183	173	163	129	176	158	140	156	165	170	152	184	191	186	157
RACE	RESP	'72	'73	'74	'75	'76	'77	'78	'80	'82	'83	'84	'85	'86	'87	'88	'89
O	M	75%	54%	0%	25%	56%	67%	50%	40%	52%	50%	46%	41%	49%	47%	39%	44%
T	F	25	46	100	75	44	33	50	60	48	50	54	59	51	53	61	56
H																	
# SURVEYED		4	13	7	4	9	15	16	10	27	18	52	44	37	53	61	61

TABLE IV: RESPONDENT'S SEX -- BY AGE

Question: Respondent's sex.

Responses: M = Male F = Female

		YEAR															
AGE	RESP	'72	'73	'74	'75	'76	'77	'78	'80	'82	'83	'84	'85	'86	'87	'88	'89
18-23	M	55%	48%	51%	45%	50%	46%	37%	35%	47%	45%	50%	48%	40%	44%	48%	51%
	F	45	52	49	55	50	54	63	65	53	55	50	52	60	56	52	49
# SURVEYED		169	171	168	173	162	164	163	155	148	128	161	133	108	126	141	137
AGE	RESP	'72	'73	'74	'75	'76	'77	'78	'80	'82	'83	'84	'85	'86	'87	'88	'89
24-29	M	56%	46%	43%	44%	47%	49%	44%	44%	47%	44%	40%	44%	52%	45%	45%	42%
	F	44	54	57	56	53	51	56	56	53	56	60	56	48	55	55	58
# SURVEYED		231	212	212	232	226	204	244	202	246	287	232	217	218	193	215	202
AGE	RESP	'72	'73	'74	'75	'76	'77	'78	'80	'82	'83	'84	'85	'86	'87	'88	'89
30-35	M	46%	46%	40%	44%	41%	43%	46%	50%	40%	44%	36%	46%	42%	46%	42%	44%
	F	54	54	60	56	59	57	54	50	60	56	65	54	58	54	58	56
# SURVEYED		187	167	175	171	186	188	230	215	204	236	200	212	221	221	195	212

TABLE IV: RESPONDENT'S SEX -- BY AGE (Continued)

Question: Respondent's sex.

Responses: M = Male F = Female

		YEAR															
AGE	RESP	'72	'73	'74	'75	'76	'77	'78	'80	'82	'83	'84	'85	'86	'87	'88	'89
36-41	M	48%	47%	39%	49%	45%	45%	39%	51%	46%	49%	46%	45%	43%	44%	52%	50%
	F	52	53	61	51	55	55	61	49	54	51	54	55	57	56	48	50
# SURVEYED		128	175	152	154	158	168	160	150	146	173	187	184	188	186	193	198
AGE	RESP	'72	'73	'74	'75	'76	'77	'78	'80	'82	'83	'84	'85	'86	'87	'88	'89
42-47	M	49%	44%	45%	45%	42%	48%	50%	44%	40%	41%	41%	48%	44%	46%	48%	44%
	F	51	56	55	55	58	52	50	56	60	59	59	52	56	54	52	56
# SURVEYED		186	146	151	143	114	147	119	117	119	145	126	124	141	157	157	161
AGE	RESP	'72	'73	'74	'75	'76	'77	'78	'80	'82	'83	'84	'85	'86	'87	'88	'89
48-53	M	51%	42%	49%	42%	42%	50%	52%	47%	46%	42%	41%	50%	46%	48%	38%	44%
	F	49	58	51	58	58	50	48	53	54	58	59	50	54	52	62	56
# SURVEYED		189	151	146	141	133	154	133	123	112	116	102	131	108	126	92	138
AGE	RESP	'72	'73	'74	'75	'76	'77	'78	'80	'82	'83	'84	'85	'86	'87	'88	'89
54-59	M	54%	45%	50%	47%	48%	43%	36%	49%	40%	43%	46%	49%	42%	46%	42%	40%
	F	46	55	50	53	52	57	64	51	60	57	54	51	58	54	58	60
# SURVEYED		156	157	139	126	129	168	137	136	144	134	114	134	99	98	85	99
AGE	RESP	'72	'73	'74	'75	'76	'77	'78	'80	'82	'83	'84	'85	'86	'87	'88	'89
60-65	M	47%	53%	50%	43%	42%	44%	37%	42%	36%	45%	42%	47%	43%	39%	41%	34%
	F	53	47	50	57	58	56	63	58	64	55	58	53	57	61	59	66
# SURVEYED		144	121	108	113	134	117	107	119	116	132	113	131	115	101	119	111
AGE	RESP	'72	'73	'74	'75	'76	'77	'78	'80	'82	'83	'84	'85	'86	'87	'88	'89
66+	M	43%	50%	53%	46%	44%	41%	38%	37%	39%	38%	32%	37%	33%	38%	34%	37%
	F	57	51	47	54	56	59	62	63	61	62	68	63	67	62	66	63
# SURVEYED		218	200	227	232	251	213	232	242	259	241	232	261	265	253	280	275

****

CURRENT MARITAL STATUS

TABLE I: CURRENT MARITAL STATUS -- BY TOTAL POPULATION

Question: Are you currently married, widowed, divorced, separated or have you never been married?

Responses: MR = Married WD = Widowed DV = Divorced SP = Separated NM = Never married

	YEAR															
RESPONSE	'72	'73	'74	'75	'76	'77	'78	'80	'82	'83	'84	'85	'86	'87	'88	'89
MR	72%	72%	72%	67%	65%	64%	63%	61%	57%	60%	56%	57%	56%	55%	53%	55%
WD	9	8	8	10	11	11	10	11	11	10	10	10	12	11	11	10
DV	4	4	5	6	7	7	9	9	10	10	11	11	10	12	13	12
SP	2	3	3	3	3	4	3	3	4	3	3	4	4	4	3	4
NM	13	13	12	14	14	15	15	16	18	17	19	17	18	19	20	20
# SURVEYED	1613	1504	1484	1490	1499	1530	1531	1468	1506	1599	1473	1534	1470	1466	1481	1537

TABLE II: CURRENT MARITAL STATUS -- BY SEX

Question: Are you currently married, widowed, divorced, separated or have you never been married?

Responses: MR = Married WD = Widowed DV = Divorced SP = Separated NM = Never married

		YEAR															
SEX	RESP	'72	'73	'74	'75	'76	'77	'78	'80	'82	'83	'84	'85	'86	'87	'88	'89
MALE	MR	77%	73%	74%	72%	68%	67%	70%	66%	64%	67%	60%	63%	62%	59%	59%	62%
	WD	3	4	4	3	5	6	4	5	4	4	3	4	4	4	3	3
	DV	3	3	5	5	6	5	7	7	8	7	9	8	9	9	10	9
	SP	1	3	2	2	3	4	3	2	3	2	3	3	3	3	2	2
	NM	15	17	15	18	19	18	17	20	21	19	25	22	22	25	25	24
# SURVEYED		807	701	691	670	669	693	643	641	639	690	598	688	621	641	638	660
SEX	RESP	'72	'73	'74	'75	'76	'77	'78	'80	'82	'83	'84	'85	'86	'87	'88	'89
FEMALE	MR	67%	70%	70%	63%	63%	61%	58%	56%	51%	55%	54%	52%	52%	51%	49%	50%
	WD	14	12	12	15	16	15	15	16	17	15	15	15	17	17	17	15
	DV	5	5	6	6	7	8	10	10	12	12	13	13	11	13	14	14
	SP	3	4	3	4	4	4	3	4	4	4	3	5	5	4	4	5
	NM	11	9	10	11	10	12	14	14	16	15	15	14	15	14	16	17
# SURVEYED		806	803	793	820	830	837	888	827	867	909	875	846	849	825	843	877

TABLE III: CURRENT MARITAL STATUS -- BY RACE

Question: Are you currently married, widowed, divorced, separated or have you never been married?

Responses: MR = Married WD = Widowed DV = Divorced SP = Separated NM = Never married

		YEAR															
RACE	RESP	'72	'73	'74	'75	'76	'77	'78	'80	'82	'83	'84	'85	'86	'87	'88	'89
W	MR	74%	73%	74%	70%	67%	66%	65%	62%	59%	63%	58%	59%	59%	58%	56%	58%
H	WD	8	8	8	9	11	11	10	11	12	10	10	11	12	11	11	10
I	DV	4	4	5	6	6	7	9	9	10	10	11	11	10	11	12	11
T	SP	1	2	2	2	2	3	2	2	2	2	2	3	3	2	3	3
E	NM	12	13	12	14	13	14	14	16	16	16	19	17	16	17	18	18
# SURVEYED		348	1308	1304	1323	1361	1339	1358	1318	1323	1416	1251	1338	1249	1222	1234	1319
RACE	RESP	'72	'73	'74	'75	'76	'77	'78	'80	'82	'83	'84	'85	'86	'87	'88	'89
B	MR	60%	59%	55%	48%	40%	46%	46%	43%	37%	40%	41%	39%	40%	30%	37%	29%
L	WD	10	9	11	12	16	14	10	14	6	12	16	11	11	16	10	11
A	DV	6	4	9	7	8	7	8	9	12	12	11	14	10	14	15	17
C	SP	8	16	9	15	16	13	10	14	13	12	9	13	11	12	5	14
K	NM	16	11	16	18	21	20	27	21	31	24	23	23	27	28	33	29
# SURVEYED		261	183	173	163	129	176	157	140	156	165	170	152	184	191	186	157
RACE	RESP	'72	'73	'74	'75	'76	'77	'78	'80	'82	'83	'84	'85	'86	'87	'88	'89
O	MR	50%	69%	71%	75%	89%	60%	56%	80%	63%	67%	63%	61%	49%	57%	48%	54%
T	WD	0	0	14	0	0	0	13	0	0	0	4	7	8	9	15	7
H	DV	25	0	0	0	11	7	6	0	15	17	10	9	8	11	11	5
E	SP	0	0	14	0	0	0	13	0	4	6	2	5	5	2	5	3
R	NM	25	31	0	25	0	33	13	20	19	11	21	18	30	21	21	31
SURVEYED		4	13	7	4	9	15	16	10	27	18	52	44	37	53	61	61

TABLE IV: CURRENT MARITAL STATUS -- BY AGE

Question: Are you currently married, widowed, divorced, separated or have you never been married?

Responses: MR = Married WD = Widowed DV = Divorced SP = Separated NM = Never married

		YEAR															
AGE	RESP	'72	'73	'74	'75	'76	'77	'78	'80	'82	'83	'84	'85	'86	'87	'88	'89
18-23	MR	34%	36%	40%	36%	34%	37%	35%	35%	31%	24%	25%	24%	18%	17%	26%	15%
	WD	0	0	0	1	1	0	0	0	0	0	0	0	0	0	0	1
	DV	1	2	2	1	2	1	2	3	3	0	2	3	1	5	0	1
	SP	2	2	2	3	2	1	1	3	2	0	1	1	2	2	0	3
	NM	62	60	55	60	61	61	61	59	64	76	72	72	80	75	74	80
# SURVEYED		169	171	168	173	162	164	163	155	148	128	161	133	108	126	141	137

TABLE IV: CURRENT MARITAL STATUS -- BY AGE (Continued)

Question: Are you currently married, widowed, divorced, separated or have you never been married?

Responses: MR = Married WD = Widowed DV = Divorced SP = Separated NM = Never married

		YEAR															
AGE	RESP	'72	'73	'74	'75	'76	'77	'78	'80	'82	'83	'84	'85	'86	'87	'88	'89
24-29	MR	71%	75%	71%	65%	66%	59%	64%	61%	54%	57%	53%	54%	50%	49%	45%	43%
	WD	1	1	0	1	0	0	0	0	1	1	1	0	0	1	0	0
	DV	5	3	4	6	8	5	7	7	9	9	6	8	6	9	7	10
	SP	2	3	2	3	3	7	3	4	4	3	4	6	4	6	4	6
	NM	21	19	22	26	23	28	25	27	33	30	35	31	40	36	44	40
# SURVEYED		231	212	212	232	22	204	244	202	246	297	232	217	218	193	215	202
AGE	RESP	'72	'73	'74	'75	'76	'77	'78	'80	'82	'83	'84	'85	'86	'87	'88	'89
30-35	MR	87%	86%	82%	78%	78%	75%	73%	64%	67%	69%	62%	67%	64%	60%	57%	59%
	WD	0	2	1	2	0	2	0	1	1	0	2	0	1	0	1	1
	DV	5	4	9	5	10	10	12	13	10	12	17	14	13	13	14	9
	SP	3	2	3	6	6	5	5	6	6	5	3	2	5	4	6	7
	NM	6	6	5	9	6	9	10	16	15	14	17	17	17	24	22	24
# SURVEYED		187	167	175	171	186	188	230	215	204	236	200	212	221	221	195	212
AGE	RESP	'72	'73	'74	'75	'76	'77	'78	'80	'82	'83	'84	'85	'86	'87	'88	'89
36-41	MR	86%	84%	87%	86%	79%	74%	75%	71%	58%	66%	70%	65%	72%	67%	65%	66%
	WD	2	1	1	1	2	2	1	3	2	1	2	1	1	1	1	1
	DV	7	6	3	7	9	11	13	11	24	20	20	15	15	17	23	17
	SP	5	5	6	4	4	5	3	3	3	6	4	7	3	5	4	4
	NM	1	3	3	3	6	8	8	12	13	8	5	12	9	10	8	13
# SURVEYED		128	175	152	154	158	168	159	150	146	173	187	184	188	186	193	198
AGE	RESP	'72	'73	'74	'75	'76	'77	'78	'80	'82	'83	'84	'85	'86	'87	'88	'89
42-47	MR	84%	78%	84%	77%	82%	80%	77%	73%	67%	71%	69%	65%	64%	69%	63%	71%
	WD	4	2	3	4	3	4	3	4	3	2	4	1	1	1	3	1
	DV	5	5	8	12	8	8	12	17	18	18	18	23	20	20	23	18
	SP	4	7	2	4	4	3	1	4	7	4	3	3	8	4	4	4
	NM	3	8	3	3	4	5	7	2	5	5	6	8	7	7	7	6
# SURVEYED		186	146	151	143	114	147	119	117	119	145	126	124	141	157	157	161
AGE	RESP	'72	'73	'74	'75	'76	'77	'78	'80	'82	'83	'84	'85	'86	'87	'88	'89
48-53	MR	84%	86%	82%	82%	76%	75%	81%	69%	78%	74%	75%	73%	69%	69%	61%	64%
	WD	4	5	6	7	8	6	6	8	3	4	6	3	7	6	7	7
	DV	5	5	6	4	7	10	11	11	14	15	14	15	14	16	22	21
	SP	3	1	1	4	3	4	2	3	2	3	3	8	6	2	5	4
	NM	4	3	5	3	7	5	1	8	4	4	3	2	3	7	5	4
# SURVEYED		189	151	146	141	133	154	133	123	112	116	102	131	108	126	92	138

TABLE IV: CURRENT MARITAL STATUS -- BY AGE (Continued)

Question: Are you currently married, widowed, divorced, separated or have you never been married?

Responses: MR = Married WD = Widowed DV = Divorced SP = Separated NM = Never married

AGE	RESP	'72	'73	'74	'75	'76	'77	'78	'80	'82	'83	'84	'85	'86	'87	'88	'89
54-59	MR	86%	79%	76%	73%	76%	71%	64%	76%	74%	70%	66%	69%	64%	69%	64%	71%
	WD	6	10	14	10	11	13	15	10	8	15	8	7	17	12	14	7
	DV	2	3	8	12	5	8	10	7	10	7	18	15	8	10	15	15
	SP	3	4	1	1	4	2	5	1	3	3	4	4	5	6	5	4
	NM	3	4	1	5	4	6	6	5	6	4	4	6	6	2	2	3
# SURVEYED		156	157	139	126	129	168	137	136	144	134	114	134	99	98	85	99
AGE	RESP	'72	'73	'74	'75	'76	'77	'78	'80	'82	'83	'84	'85	'86	'87	'88	'89
60-65	MR	71%	79%	74%	74%	68%	66%	62%	65%	59%	73%	65%	63%	67%	64%	67%	67%
	WD	19	10	10	12	16	21	19	18	22	17	12	18	16	21	16	17
	DV	3	4	4	5	10	6	9	6	9	3	12	8	10	10	13	10
	SP	0	3	6	4	4	4	5	3	3	3	1	6	3	0	1	4
	NM	7	4	6	4	2	3	6	8	6	4	10	5	4	5	3	3
# SURVEYED		144	121	108	113	134	117	107	119	116	132	113	131	115	101	119	111
AGE	RESP	'72	'73	'74	'75	'76	'77	'78	'80	'82	'83	'84	'85	'86	'87	'88	'89
66+	MR	51%	52%	60%	52%	46%	46%	44%	47%	42%	45%	41%	41%	43%	38%	45%	49%
	WD	37	38	31	40	45	44	41	42	45	45	47	44	46	48	41	40
	DV	3	4	4	2	3	3	5	5	5	5	3	5	5	6	5	5
	SP	1	3	1	2	1	3	3	1	2	0	2	2	2	2	1	0
	NM	8	4	4	4	5	3	8	5	6	5	6	7	5	6	7	5
# SURVEYED		218	200	227	232	251	213	232	242	259	241	232	261	265	253	280	275

****

EVER DIVORCED

TABLE I: EVER DIVORCED -- BY TOTAL POPULATION

Question: Have you ever been divorced or legally separated? NOTE: Asked only if respondents were currently married or widowed.

Responses: Yes; No

	YEAR															
RESPONSE	'72	'73	'74	'75	'76	'77	'78	'80	'82	'83	'84	'85	'86	'87	'88	'89
MALE	15%	13%	14%	15%	14%	16%	16%	16%	18%	16%	17%	18%	19%	18%	19%	19%
FEMALE	85	87	86	85	86	84	84	84	82	84	83	82	81	82	81	81
# SURVEYED	1261	1193	1181	1143	1133	1126	1108	1041	1023	1123	976	1026	992	962	943	995

TABLE II: EVER DIVORCED -- BY SEX

Question: Have you ever been divorced or legally separated? NOTE: Asked only if respondents were currently married or widowed.

Responses: Yes; No

		YEAR															
SEX	RESP	'72	'73	'74	'75	'76	'77	'78	'80	'82	'83	'84	'85	'86	'87	'88	'89
M	YES	14%	14%	14%	17%	14%	17%	16%	16%	18%	18%	16%	17%	20%	18%	20%	20%
	NO	86	86	86	83	86	83	84	84	82	82	84	83	80	82	80	80
# SURVEYED		627	534	537	501	483	496	469	449	431	493	378	460	408	402	397	430
SEX	RESP	'72	'73	'74	'75	'76	'77	'78	'80	'82	'83	'84	'85	'86	'87	'88	'89
F	YES	15%	13%	14%	14%	13%	15%	16%	17%	18%	15%	18%	20%	18%	19%	19%	17%
	NO	85	87	86	86	87	85	84	83	82	85	82	80	82	81	81	83
# SURVEYED		634	659	644	642	650	630	639	592	592	630	598	566	584	560	546	565

TABLE III: EVER DIVORCED -- BY RACE

Question: Have you ever been divorced or legally separated? NOTE: Asked only if respondents were currently married or widowed.

Responses: Yes; No

		YEAR															
RACE	RESP	'72	'73	'74	'75	'76	'77	'78	'80	'82	'83	'84	'85	'86	'87	'88	'89
WHT	YES	13%	12%	13%	14%	13%	16%	16%	16%	18%	16%	17%	18%	18%	18%	18%	19%
	NO	87	88	87	86	87	84	84	84	82	84	83	82	82	82	82	81
# SURVEYED		1081	1062	1062	1041	1055	1014	1011	954	938	1027	845	922	876	841	820	897
RACE	RESP	'72	'73	'74	'75	'76	'77	'78	'80	'82	'83	'84	'85	'86	'87	'88	'89
BLK	YES	24%	20%	21%	26%	20%	18%	19%	14%	26%	19%	22%	19%	27%	21%	34%	18%
	NO	76	80	79	74	80	82	81	86	74	81	78	81	73	79	66	82
# SURVEYED		178	122	113	99	71	103	86	79	68	84	97	74	95	86	85	61
RACE	RESP	'72	'73	'74	'75	'76	'77	'78	'80	'82	'83	'84	'85	'86	'87	'88	'89
OTH	YES	50%	11%	33%	0%	0%	11%	18%	13%	12%	8%	15%	23%	10%	23%	16%	16%
	NO	50	89	67	100	100	89	82	88	88	92	85	77	90	77	84	84
# SURVEYED		2	9	6	3	7	9	11	8	17	12	34	30	21	35	38	37

TABLE IV: EVER DIVORCED --- BY AGE

Question: Have you ever been divorced or legally separated? NOTE: Asked only if respondents were currently married or widowed.

Responses: Yes; No

		YEAR															
AGE	RESP	'72	'73	'74	'75	'76	'77	'78	'80	'82	'83	'84	'85	'86	'87	'88	'89
18-23	YES	4%	5%	1%	6%	2%	2%	7%	6%	4%	6%	3%	3%	16%	5%	0%	0%
	NO	96	95	99	94	98	98	93	94	96	94	97	97	84	95	100	100
# SURVEYED		55	61	68	62	55	59	57	54	46	31	39	32	19	21	37	21
AGE	RESP	'72	'73	'74	'75	'76	'77	'78	'80	'82	'83	'84	'85	'86	'87	'88	'89
24-29	YES	7%	8%	4%	12%	11%	17%	14%	12%	15%	9%	13%	9%	8%	12%	9%	14%
	NO	93	92	96	88	89	83	86	88	85	91	87	91	92	88	91	86
# SURVEYED		160	160	152	153	149	121	155	122	135	167	126	118	109	95	97	88

TABLE IV: EVER DIVORCED - BY AGE (Continued)

Question: Have you ever been divorced or legally separated? NOTE: Asked only if respondents were currently married or widowed.

Responses: Yes; No

AGE	RESP	'72	'73	'74	'75	'76	'77	'78	'80	'82	'83	'84	'85	'86	'87	'88	'89
30-35	YES	11%	17%	13%	13%	11%	15%	18%	16%	20%	23%	19%	17%	18%	16%	23%	17%
	NO	89	83	87	88	89	85	82	84	80	77	81	83	82	84	77	83
# SURVEYED		157	145	145	136	141	142	168	138	139	161	126	143	142	132	114	127
AGE	RESP	'72	'73	'74	'75	'76	'77	'78	'80	'82	'83	'84	'85	'86	'87	'88	'89
36-41	YES	13%	15%	15%	24%	20%	21%	20%	23%	28%	18%	27%	27%	29%	24%	29%	22%
	NO	87	85	85	76	80	79	80	77	72	82	73	73	71	76	71	78
# SURVEYED		108	149	132	132	127	128	122	111	88	115	133	122	136	127	127	132
AGE	RESP	'72	'73	'74	'75	'76	'77	'78	'80	'82	'83	'84	'85	'86	'87	'88	'89
42-47	YES	17%	16%	20%	22%	21%	18%	19%	28%	22%	20%	23%	23%	21%	23%	25%	27%
	NO	83	84	80	78	79	82	81	72	78	80	77	77	79	77	75	73
# SURVEYED		158	117	132	116	95	121	95	90	83	104	91	82	92	109	102	115
AGE	RESP	'72	'73	'74	'75	'76	'77	'78	'80	'82	'83	'84	'85	'86	'87	'88	'89
48-53	YES	16%	15%	17%	14%	14%	20%	20%	14%	19%	18%	20%	23%	25%	22%	25%	21%
	NO	84	85	83	86	86	80	80	86	81	82	80	77	75	78	75	79
# SURVEYED		158	137	126	126	111	124	116	94	90	91	82	98	83	94	61	98
AGE	RESP	'72	'73	'74	'75	'76	'77	'78	'80	'82	'83	'84	'85	'86	'87	'88	'89
54-59	YES	19%	13%	13%	17%	14%	12%	18%	22%	17%	21%	14%	25%	22%	19%	24%	26%
	NO	81	87	87	83	86	88	82	78	83	79	86	75	78	81	76	74
# SURVEYED		142	140	123	104	111	138	107	118	117	114	84	100	79	80	66	76
AGE	RESP	'72	'73	'74	'75	'76	'77	'78	'80	'82	'83	'84	'85	'86	'87	'88	'89
60-65	YES	15%	14%	21%	10%	13%	15%	15%	16%	20%	15%	11%	14%	15%	20%	19%	16%
	NO	85	86	79	90	87	85	85	84	80	85	89	86	85	80	81	84
# SURVEYED		129	105	91	98	113	99	85	98	93	119	87	106	94	86	98	93
AGE	RESP	'72	'73	'74	'75	'76	'77	'78	'80	'82	'83	'84	'85	'86	'87	'88	'89
66+	YES	20%	12%	17%	15%	13%	16%	12%	11%	16%	14%	15%	17%	15%	16%	14%	15%
	NO	80	88	83	85	87	84	88	89	84	86	85	83	85	84	86	85
# SURVEYED		190	176	207	211	228	190	196	209	223	216	204	220	235	216	238	244

****

YEARS OF EDUCATION

TABLE I: YEARS OF EDUCATION -- BY TOTAL POPULATION

Question: Level of education respondent has attained.

Responses:
1 = No formal schooling
2 = 1st - 5th grades
3 = 6th - 10th grades
4 = 11th grade
5 = 12th grade
6 = 1st - 2nd college year
7 = 3rd - 4th college year
8 = 5th - 6th college year
9 = 7th - 8th college year

	YEAR															
RESPONSE	'72	'73	'74	'75	'76	'77	'78	'80	'82	'83	'84	'85	'86	'87	'88	'89
1	1%	0%	0%	0%	0%	0%	0%	0%	0%	0%	0%	0%	0%	0%	0%	0%
2	8	6	5	5	5	6	4	5	5	4	4	3	4	3	4	2
3	24	23	23	22	24	23	21	21	19	16	18	17	17	17	16	15
4	7	7	6	8	6	8	6	6	7	8	6	7	8	5	7	6
5	32	32	33	34	34	33	35	34	35	34	33	33	33	33	31	32
6	13	15	14	15	13	13	15	14	16	16	16	17	16	18	19	20
7	11	12	12	11	11	11	11	12	12	15	15	14	14	14	16	15
8	3	3	5	3	4	4	4	5	4	5	5	6	5	7	5	7
9	1	2	2	1	2	2	2	2	2	2	3	3	3	3	3	3
# SURVEYED	1608	1499	1481	1487	1493	1520	1526	1463	1501	1597	1470	1534	1469	1460	1478	1530

TABLE II: YEARS OF EDUCATION -- BY SEX

Question: Level of education respondent has attained.

Responses:

1 = No formal schooling
2 = 1st - 5th grades
3 = 6th - 10th grades
4 = 11th grade
5 = 12th grade
6 = 1st - 2nd college year
7 = 3rd - 4th college year
8 = 5th - 6th college year
9 = 7th - 8th college year

		YEAR															
SEX	RESP	'72	'73	'74	'75	'76	'77	'78	'80	'82	'83	'84	'85	'86	'87	'88	'89
M	1	1%	1%	1%	0%	0%	1%	1%	0%	1%	0%	0%	0%	0%	0%	0%	0%
A	2	9	8	6	6	6	6	5	5	5	4	4	4	5	5	4	4
L	3	22	22	26	20	21	23	20	20	17	17	18	16	15	15	14	11
E	4	7	7	6	8	6	7	4	5	6	7	7	7	7	5	7	5
	5	27	26	26	30	28	29	33	31	33	31	31	31	29	30	28	29
	6	15	17	16	16	17	13	15	14	17	17	13	15	16	16	19	21
	7	13	12	11	13	13	14	13	13	14	16	16	15	18	19	17	16
	8	4	4	6	3	5	5	6	8	3	6	6	8	6	8	5	9
	9	2	4	3	2	3	3	4	4	3	3	5	5	5	4	5	5
# SURVEYED		803	699	689	669	668	690	641	640	637	688	596	688	620	640	637	657
SEX	RESP	'72	'73	'74	'75	'76	'77	'78	'80	'82	'83	'84	'85	'86	'87	'88	'89
F	1	1%	0%	0%	0%	0%	0%	0%	0%	0%	0%	0%	0%	0%	0%	0%	0%
E	2	6	5	4	4	5	6	4	5	4	3	4	3	3	3	3	1
M	3	26	23	21	24	26	23	22	22	20	16	18	18	18	18	17	17
A	4	8	8	6	9	6	8	7	6	7	9	6	6	8	5	7	7
L	5	36	38	40	36	40	37	37	37	36	37	35	36	36	35	33	34
E	6	12	13	13	14	10	13	15	14	15	15	18	18	16	20	19	19
	7	9	11	12	9	10	9	10	12	11	14	15	13	12	11	14	14
	8	2	2	3	3	2	4	3	3	4	4	4	4	5	6	5	5
	9	0	1	0	1	1	0	1	1	2	1	2	1	1	2	2	2
# SURVEYED		805	800	792	818	825	830	885	823	864	909	874	846	849	820	841	873

TABLE III: YEARS OF EDUCATION -- BY RACE

Question: Level of education respondent has attained.

Responses: 1 = No formal schooling; 2 = 1st - 5th grades; 3 = 6th - 10th grades; 4 = 11th grade; 5 = 12th grade; 6 = 1st - 2nd college year; 7 = 3rd - 4th college year; 8 = 5th - 6th college year; 9 = 7th - 8th college year

		YEAR															
RACE	RESP	'72	'73	'74	'75	'76	'77	'78	'80	'82	'83	'84	'85	'86	'87	'88	'89
W	1	1%	0%	0%	0%	0%	0%	0%	0%	0%	0%	0%	0%	0%	0%	0%	0%
H	2	5	5	4	4	4	5	3	4	4	3	3	2	3	3	3	2
I	3	24	22	23	22	23	23	21	21	19	16	17	16	16	16	15	14
T	4	7	7	6	7	6	7	6	5	7	7	5	6	7	5	6	6
E	5	32	34	34	35	35	34	36	35	35	35	34	35	34	34	32	34
	6	14	15	14	15	13	12	15	15	16	15	16	17	16	17	18	20
	7	12	12	12	12	12	12	12	13	13	16	16	15	16	15	16	16
	8	4	3	5	4	4	5	5	5	4	5	5	6	6	8	5	7
	9	2	2	2	2	2	2	2	2	2	2	3	3	3	3	3	3
# SURVEYED		1347	1303	1301	1320	1356	1333	1352	1313	1318	1415	1248	1338	1248	1218	1232	1312
RACE	RESP	'72	'73	'74	'75	'76	'77	'78	'80	'82	'83	'84	'85	'86	'87	'88	'89
B	1	3%	1%	1%	2%	0%	1%	3%	0%	1%	1%	0%	1%	1%	1%	0%	1%
L	2	20	17	13	13	20	16	10	11	8	10	9	14	10	6	6	6
A	3	24	25	28	24	28	22	21	27	22	15	21	24	20	15	18	19
C	4	7	11	9	19	9	10	8	8	8	13	11	7	11	7	10	11
K	5	28	24	26	26	20	26	32	31	31	32	32	22	32	28	26	22
	6	13	12	13	10	15	15	16	9	13	21	13	18	17	24	24	24
	7	4	7	7	5	7	8	8	8	9	6	11	7	5	15	12	12
	8	0	1	2	0	2	1	2	6	4	1	3	3	3	3	3	4
	9	1	1	0	1	0	1	0	1	3	0	1	3	1	1	1	1
# SURVEYED		257	183	173	163	128	172	158	140	156	164	170	152	184	189	185	157
RACE	RESP	'72	'73	'74	'75	'76	'77	'78	'80	'82	'83	'84	'85	'86	'87	'88	'89
O	1	0%	0%	0%	0%	0%	0%	0%	0%	4%	0%	0%	0%	3%	0%	0%	2%
T	2	0	15	0	0	0	7	19	0	7	6	12	7	14	11	8	10
H	3	25	23	29	25	0	7	13	0	11	17	27	16	19	32	20	25
E	4	0	8	0	25	11	7	0	0	11	0	10	14	5	4	8	7
R	5	75	8	29	0	44	20	6	40	30	28	21	32	27	23	18	15
	6	0	15	43	25	11	13	19	20	22	11	8	11	11	15	18	23
	7	0	23	0	25	22	33	31	20	11	11	12	14	14	8	16	8
	8	0	0	0	0	11	7	6	0	4	17	6	5	3	4	7	7
	9	0	8	0	0	0	7	6	20	0	11	6	2	5	4	5	5
# SURVEYED		4	13	7	4	9	15	16	10	27	18	52	44	37	53	61	61

TABLE IV: YEARS OF EDUCATION -- BY AGE

Question: Level of education respondent has attained.

Responses:
1 = No formal schooling
2 = 1st - 5th grades
3 = 6th - 10th grades
4 = 11th grade
5 = 12th grade
6 = 1st - 2nd college year
7 = 3rd - 4th college year
8 = 5th - 6th college year
9 = 7th - 8th college year

		YEAR															
AGE	RESP	'72	'73	'74	'75	'76	'77	'78	'80	'82	'83	'84	'85	'86	'87	'88	'89
18-23	1	0%	0%	0%	0%	0%	0%	0%	0%	0%	0%	0%	0%	0%	0%	0%	0%
	2	1	1	0	0	1	0	0	0	0	2	1	1	0	1	1	1
	3	13	13	8	8	12	14	11	13	12	13	12	6	10	5	11	7
	4	13	12	15	18	12	14	15	10	17	19	14	16	15	17	19	18
	5	38	39	45	45	46	44	48	52	52	38	33	38	39	39	31	40
	6	24	24	23	24	22	21	19	16	13	20	19	23	21	25	28	20
	7	10	12	8	6	7	7	7	10	6	9	19	13	14	13	10	12
	8	1	0	0	0	0	0	0	0	0	0	2	3	1	0	0	1
	9	0	0	0	0	0	0	0	0	0	0	0	0	0	0	0	0
# SURVEYED		169	170	168	173	162	161	163	155	148	128	161	133	108	126	140	137
AGE	RESP	'72	'73	'74	'75	'76	'77	'78	'80	'82	'83	'84	'85	'86	'87	'88	'89
24-29	1	0%	0%	0%	0%	0%	0%	0%	0%	0%	0%	0%	0%	0%	0%	0%	0%
	2	2	1	0	0	0	0	2	0	1	0	1	1	0	1	0	0
	3	7	9	11	10	9	12	11	9	9	11	9	11	6	7	9	11
	4	6	5	2	5	4	5	4	3	4	6	6	6	12	4	6	6
	5	39	35	35	34	35	36	39	43	41	40	38	35	30	37	32	32
	6	17	19	18	19	22	25	16	20	20	16	22	21	18	21	23	22
	7	19	22	25	23	21	14	19	17	20	21	18	17	25	18	24	20
	8	6	5	7	7	7	6	7	6	4	4	5	7	7	11	7	8
	9	2	3	1	1	2	2	2	1	1	1	2	2	2	3	0	2
# SURVEYED		231	211	212	232	225	204	244	202	245	287	232	217	218	193	215	200
AGE	RESP	'72	'73	'74	'75	'76	'77	'78	'80	'82	'83	'84	'85	'86	'87	'88	'89
30-35	1	0%	0%	0%	0%	0%	0%	0%	0%	0%	0%	0%	0%	0%	0%	0%	0%
	2	1	4	2	2	2	4	3	1	0	2	1	0	0	1	1	2
	3	18	16	13	14	17	10	10	12	8	6	7	7	8	10	8	7
	4	7	5	5	9	6	11	4	3	5	6	4	5	6	3	4	2
	5	38	46	44	40	42	36	37	34	32	38	35	35	39	28	32	26
	6	16	15	18	13	10	12	19	17	22	20	17	22	22	23	21	29
	7	14	9	13	12	16	17	16	21	22	20	24	20	15	21	22	21
	8	4	4	3	5	5	8	9	7	6	6	8	9	5	11	8	8
	9	2	2	3	4	2	2	3	4	4	3	7	2	4	3	5	4
# SURVEYED		187	167	175	171	185	187	229	215	204	235	200	212	221	221	195	212
AGE	RESP	'72	'73	'74	'75	'76	'77	'78	'80	'82	'83	'84	'85	'86	'87	'88	'89
36-41	1	1%	0%	0%	0%	0%	0%	0%	0%	0%	0%	0%	0%	0%	0%	0%	0%
	2	4	3	1	4	1	1	3	3	2	2	2	1	2	2	1	2
	3	20	21	19	17	18	13	16	14	14	13	11	9	6	8	5	7
	4	6	7	4	8	5	6	4	4	2	3	4	4	6	2	2	2
	5	41	33	45	37	37	40	43	36	42	32	28	30	34	25	31	31
	6	11	13	13	19	13	14	17	17	17	16	24	21	18	23	27	21
	7	9	15	11	12	13	13	10	13	10	17	18	20	22	25	21	20
	8	5	5	5	1	8	10	4	8	7	13	9	8	7	11	8	11
	9	2	3	1	2	4	3	1	5	6	3	4	8	6	5	6	7
# SURVEYED		128	175	151	154	157	167	159	150	146	173	187	184	188	185	193	198

TABLE IV: YEARS OF EDUCATION -- BY AGE (Continued)

Question: Level of education respondent has attained.

Responses: 1 = No formal schooling; 2 = 1st - 5th grades; 3 = 6th - 10th grades; 4 = 11th grade; 5 = 12th grade; 6 = 1st - 2nd college year; 7 = 3rd - 4th college year; 8 = 5th - 6th college year; 9 = 7th - 8th college year

AGE	RESP	'72	'73	'74	'75	'76	'77	'78	'80	'82	'83	'84	'85	'86	'87	'88	'89
42-47	1	0%	0%	1%	0%	1%	0%	0%	0%	0%	0%	0%	0%	0%	0%	0%	0%
	2	5	3	5	5	4	7	2	2	1	2	2	2	2	3	3	2
	3	28	18	23	21	24	27	20	20	15	10	17	5	12	13	11	10
	4	9	14	6	5	6	6	2	2	7	8	5	4	4	4	10	5
	5	35	29	33	31	42	35	34	43	36	41	38	35	33	39	29	29
	6	10	13	11	14	10	8	19	15	16	18	10	27	21	18	21	25
	7	6	11	10	17	9	14	12	15	16	14	20	11	13	13	16	19
	8	3	6	9	6	2	1	6	4	3	6	3	10	11	4	5	5
	9	2	5	3	1	4	1	5	0	5	1	5	6	4	6	5	6
# SURVEYED		186	146	151	143	113	146	119	116	118	145	126	124	141	157	157	161
AGE	RESP	'72	'73	'74	'75	'76	'77	'78	'80	'82	'83	'84	'85	'86	'87	'88	'89
48-53	1	1%	1%	0%	0%	0%	0%	0%	0%	0%	0%	0%	0%	0%	0%	0%	0%
	2	6	9	5	5	5	6	2	7	7	3	8	4	6	5	2	0
	3	26	25	24	23	25	29	32	18	18	15	19	21	16	22	20	15
	4	8	9	7	11	10	6	7	9	5	10	8	5	9	7	7	7
	5	29	32	38	36	36	37	34	30	35	31	38	35	39	34	32	38
	6	16	14	10	11	9	6	10	14	14	15	9	12	11	12	10	17
	7	10	10	10	11	8	11	8	10	11	16	12	14	10	9	16	13
	8	2	1	3	1	3	2	3	8	5	7	4	6	6	7	9	9
	9	1	1	3	2	5	3	4	5	5	4	3	3	2	4	5	1
# SURVEYED		189	151	146	141	133	154	132	122	111	116	102	131	108	126	92	137
AGE	RESP	'72	'73	'74	'75	'76	'77	'78	'80	'82	'83	'84	'85	'86	'87	'88	'89
54-59	1	1%	0%	0%	0%	0%	1%	0%	0%	1%	0%	1%	0%	0%	1%	0%	1%
	2	10	8	8	5	5	6	7	5	6	4	2	8	4	3	5	4
	3	31	32	33	29	29	26	18	29	21	19	31	20	30	19	18	17
	4	8	5	5	10	5	7	7	11	8	10	8	6	8	2	7	4
	5	28	34	26	40	32	32	35	30	36	35	32	39	33	35	34	37
	6	12	10	13	9	12	11	17	11	13	13	11	10	9	19	22	15
	7	6	8	7	4	12	10	11	7	8	8	7	11	8	12	8	9
	8	3	1	7	3	3	5	2	5	3	6	5	3	3	8	4	8
	9	1	1	1	2	2	2	2	1	3	4	4	3	4	1	2	4
# SURVEYED		156	156	138	126	129	168	137	136	143	134	114	134	99	97	85	98
AGE	RESP	'72	'73	'74	'75	'76	'77	'78	'80	'82	'83	'84	'85	'86	'87	'88	'89
60-65	1	1%	2%	0%	1%	0%	0%	0%	0%	0%	1%	1%	0%	2%	0%	1%	2%
	2	13	11	6	6	13	7	7	12	6	5	8	5	10	5	6	6
	3	32	31	38	42	34	36	38	29	34	20	23	22	21	27	20	23
	4	8	8	7	7	3	8	5	3	6	9	8	13	6	1	5	7
	5	27	28	28	27	28	32	29	35	28	37	34	30	33	43	38	29
	6	8	12	8	10	15	4	7	7	15	12	13	9	10	12	11	16
	7	6	8	6	4	4	9	7	7	9	11	9	12	10	8	11	7
	8	1	1	5	2	2	3	4	4	2	2	3	4	4	4	5	7
	9	4	2	2	1	1	2	3	3	0	2	2	5	3	0	3	2
# SURVEYED		142	120	108	113	134	117	107	119	116	131	112	131	115	100	119	111

TABLE IV: YEARS OF EDUCATION -- BY AGE (Continued)

Question: Level of education respondent has attained.

Responses:
1 = No formal schooling; 2 = 1st - 5th grades; 3 = 6th - 10th grades
4 = 11th grade; 5 = 12th grade; 6 = 1st - 2nd college year
7 = 3rd - 4th college year; 8 = 5th - 6th college year; 9 = 7th - 8th college year

		YEAR															
AGE	RESP	'72	'73	'74	'75	'76	'77	'78	'80	'82	'83	'84	'85	'86	'87	'88	'89
66+	1	3%	2%	2%	3%	1%	0%	3%	0%	2%	2%	0%	1%	2%	0%	0%	0%
	2	25	16	15	15	16	22	11	14	14	11	12	8	10	10	12	5
	3	40	42	45	42	45	43	43	44	36	37	35	42	39	37	35	32
	4	3	3	5	5	5	6	6	7	8	8	4	5	6	5	7	7
	5	12	17	11	17	18	13	20	15	19	19	27	27	26	29	26	32
	6	5	10	10	9	5	7	7	8	11	11	9	7	8	9	10	14
	7	10	7	8	7	8	7	7	8	6	10	7	8	6	6	7	7
	8	1	2	3	2	1	1	2	3	3	2	4	2	2	2	1	3
	9	0	1	2	0	1	0	1	1	0	1	1	0	1	2	2	1
# SURVEYED		216	199	226	230	249	209	230	240	258	241	231	261	265	252	278	273

****

HIGHEST DEGREE EARNED

TABLE I: HIGHEST DEGREE EARNED -- BY TOTAL POPULATION

Question: Respondent's highest educational degree.

Responses:
SS = Less than High School; HS = High School
AS = Associate/Junior College; BA = Bachelor's; GR = Graduate

	YEAR															
RESPONSE	'72	'73	'74	'75	'76	'77	'78	'80	'82	'83	'84	'85	'86	'87	'88	'89
SS	40%	37%	35%	36%	35%	35%	31%	30%	30%	26%	27%	27%	27%	24%	24%	22%
HS	48	48	49	49	49	49	53	51	52	52	52	52	51	52	53	53
AS	1	1	2	2	2	2	3	3	4	4	4	4	3	4	4	6
BA	8	9	9	9	10	9	10	11	10	13	12	11	13	14	12	12
GR	3	4	5	3	4	5	4	5	5	5	5	6	5	5	6	6
# SURVEYED	1590	1489	1483	1489	1493	1524	1529	1464	1501	1597	1470	1534	1469	1457	1480	1530

TABLE II: HIGHEST DEGREE EARNED -- BY SEX

Question: Respondent's highest educational degree.

Responses: SS = Less than High School; HS = High School; AS = Associate/Junior College; BA = Bachelor's; GR = Graduate

		YEAR															
SEX	RESP	'72	'73	'74	'75	'76	'77	'78	'80	'82	'83	'84	'85	'86	'87	'88	'89
M	SS	39%	38%	38%	34%	33%	35%	28%	28%	29%	27%	27%	27%	25%	24%	24%	18%
A	HS	46	44	43	48	46	44	52	49	51	49	49	49	48	48	50	52
L	AS	1	1	1	3	2	3	2	3	4	5	3	3	4	4	5	6
E	BA	9	10	10	11	13	11	12	12	11	13	13	13	16	17	13	14
	GR	5	6	8	4	6	7	6	7	5	7	8	9	8	7	8	9
# SURVEYED		791	695	690	670	667	691	642	639	637	689	596	688	620	640	638	656
SEX	RESP	'72	'73	'74	'75	'76	'77	'78	'80	'82	'83	'84	'85	'86	'87	'88	'89
F	SS	41%	36%	33%	37%	37%	35%	33%	32%	30%	26%	27%	27%	29%	24%	25%	25%
E	HS	50	52	54	50	51	53	53	52	53	55	54	54	54	55	55	54
M	AS	1	2	2	2	1	2	3	3	4	3	4	5	3	5	4	6
A	BA	7	8	9	8	8	8	8	10	8	12	11	10	11	12	11	11
L	GR	1	3	3	3	3	3	2	3	5	4	3	3	4	4	5	4
E																	
# SURVEYED		799	794	793	819	826	833	887	825	864	908	874	846	849	817	842	874

TABLE III: HIGHEST DEGREE EARNED -- BY RACE

Question: Respondent's highest educational degree.

Responses: SS = Less than High School HS = High School
AS = Associate/Junior College BA = Bachelor's GR = Graduate

		YEAR															
RACE	RESP	'72	'73	'74	'75	'76	'77	'78	'80	'82	'83	'84	'85	'86	'87	'88	'89
W	SS	37%	34%	33%	33%	33%	33%	29%	29%	28%	25%	25%	24%	25%	23%	23%	20%
H	HS	49	51	50	51	50	50	54	52	52	52	53	54	52	52	54	55
I	AS	1	1	2	2	1	2	3	3	5	4	3	4	3	4	4	6
T	BA	9	9	10	10	10	10	10	11	10	14	13	12	14	15	13	13
E	GR	4	5	5	4	4	5	4	5	5	5	5	6	6	6	6	7
# SURVEYED		1337	1300	1303	1322	1356	1336	1355	1314	1318	1415	1248	1338	1248	1216	1233	1312
RACE	RESP	'72	'73	'74	'75	'76	'77	'78	'80	'82	'83	'84	'85	'86	'87	'88	'89
B	SS	55%	59%	53%	59%	56%	50%	42%	44%	39%	39%	39%	47%	41%	30%	32%	34%
L	HS	41	32	39	36	34	42	46	43	47	52	46	39	49	54	52	46
A	AS	0	1	1	2	4	2	4	2	1	4	5	5	3	7	7	8
C	BA	2	6	5	4	6	5	6	7	6	3	8	5	5	7	6	10
K	GR	1	3	1	0	0	1	1	4	6	2	2	4	3	2	3	2
# SURVEYED		249	177	173	163	128	173	158	140	156	164	170	152	184	188	186	157
RACE	RESP	'72	'73	'74	'75	'76	'77	'78	'80	'82	'83	'84	'85	'86	'87	'88	'89
O	SS	25%	50%	29%	50%	22%	27%	31%	0%	33%	17%	44%	34%	43%	45%	34%	43%
T	HS	75	17	71	25	44	33	31	60	52	44	35	45	38	38	36	36
H	AS	0	0	0	0	0	7	6	0	4	0	6	2	0	4	7	5
E	BA	0	25	0	25	22	20	19	20	11	17	4	11	11	9	13	8
R	GR	0	8	0	0	11	13	13	20	0	22	12	7	8	4	10	8
# SURVEYED		4	12	7	4	9	15	16	10	27	18	52	44	37	53	61	61

TABLE IV: HIGHEST DEGREE EARNED -- BY AGE

Question: Respondent's highest educational degree.

Responses: SS = Less than High School HS = High School
AS = Associate/Junior College BA = Bachelor's GR = Graduate

		YEAR															
AGE	RESP	'72	'73	'74	'75	'76	'77	'78	'80	'82	'83	'84	'85	'86	'87	'88	'89
18-23	SS	28%	26%	27%	27%	23%	27%	26%	23%	24%	28%	24%	23%	23%	19%	30%	24%
	HS	68	70	63	66	72	67	70	70	72	59	65	70	72	72	65	72
	AS	2	1	4	3	2	3	1	3	2	7	2	2	2	5	3	1
	BA	3	2	5	3	3	3	3	4	1	5	8	5	3	4	2	1
	GR	0	1	1	0	0	0	0	0	0	0	1	0	0	0	0	1
# SURVEYED		167	166	168	173	162	162	163	155	147	128	161	133	108	125	141	137
AGE	RESP	'72	'73	'74	'75	'76	'77	'78	'80	'82	'83	'84	'85	'86	'87	'88	'89
24-29	SS	16%	16%	13%	15%	12%	18%	15%	11%	16%	15%	16%	14%	14%	10%	11%	13%
	HS	59	52	57	56	60	60	59	63	58	60	60	59	55	61	60	56
	AS	2	4	2	4	5	3	5	5	8	6	6	10	5	5	7	10
	BA	19	20	25	20	20	13	19	18	16	16	16	13	23	21	19	18
	GR	4	8	3	6	4	5	3	2	2	3	3	3	4	3	3	4
# SURVEYED		227	209	212	232	225	204	244	202	246	287	232	217	218	193	251	200
AGE	RESP	'72	'73	'74	'75	'76	'77	'78	'80	'82	'83	'84	'85	'86	'87	'88	'89
30-35	SS	26%	27%	21%	27%	26%	25%	15%	13%	12%	14%	9%	11%	14%	15%	11%	11%
	HS	58	60	62	53	53	50	60	57	55	58	57	55	60	48	54	50
	AS	2	0	1	3	2	4	3	5	7	7	6	6	6	8	5	11
	BA	9	8	11	10	15	13	15	18	18	18	18	21	15	20	19	22
	GR	5	5	5	7	5	8	8	7	8	4	11	7	5	8	10	5
# SURVEYED		184	166	175	171	185	187	230	241	204	236	200	212	221	221	195	211
AGE	RESP	'72	'73	'74	'75	'76	'77	'78	'80	'82	'83	'84	'85	'86	'87	'88	'89
36-41	SS	31%	32%	25%	29%	26%	18%	24%	18%	17%	16%	16%	14%	11%	10%	7%	9%
	HS	55	47	59	57	51	56	61	55	60	52	55	54	54	46	60	51
	AS	2	2	3	1	2	2	4	3	1	1	4	6	4	8	8	10
	BA	9	11	9	10	11	14	8	15	10	18	17	17	22	26	16	16
	GR	4	8	5	2	10	9	3	9	11	12	8	10	10	9	9	14
# SURVEYED		126	173	152	154	157	168	160	150	146	173	187	184	188	185	193	198
AGE	RESP	'72	'73	'74	'75	'76	'77	'78	'80	'82	'83	'84	'85	'86	'87	'88	'89
42-47	SS	43%	35%	34%	29%	33%	39%	22%	24%	19%	19%	27%	11%	16%	17%	19%	16%
	HS	47	46	47	45	53	45	55	59	59	60	48	60	54	56	56	53
	AS	1	0	2	3	0	3	4	2	3	3	4	3	6	6	4	7
	BA	5	11	7	17	8	10	8	10	10	12	13	10	15	12	13	16
	GR	4	8	9	6	6	4	10	4	8	6	7	15	9	8	8	7
# SURVEYED		184	145	151	143	112	147	119	116	118	145	126	124	141	156	157	161

TABLE IV: HIGHEST DEGREE EARNED -- BY AGE (Continued)

Question: Respondent's highest educational degree.

Responses: SS = Less than High School HS = High School
AS = Associate/Junior College BA = Bachelor's GR = Graduate

		YEAR															
AGE		'72	'73	'74	'75	'76	'77	'78	'80	'82	'83	'84	'85	'86	'87	'88	'89
48-53	SS	39%	40%	38%	36%	41%	36%	40%	32%	31%	24%	31%	29%	31%	34%	27%	18%
	HS	50	48	49	51	44	52	45	46	50	52	49	50	51	45	42	58
	AS	1	1	1	1	0	1	2	2	4	3	3	2	3	3	2	5
	BA	6	8	6	9	9	6	8	8	9	14	12	10	8	10	18	11
	GR	4	3	5	3	6	5	5	12	7	7	5	9	6	7	10	9
# SURVEYED		188	151	146	141	133	154	132	123	111	116	102	131	108	126	92	137
AGE	RESP	'72	'73	'74	'75	'76	'77	'78	'80	'82	'83	'84	'85	'86	'87	'88	'89
54-59	SS	49%	46%	44%	42%	36%	36%	32%	41%	35%	31%	39%	38%	41%	26%	25%	28%
	HS	41	46	44	50	48	48	54	46	48	52	45	46	44	54	59	52
	AS	1	1	1	1	1	1	4	3	5	1	1	2	0	0	5	5
	BA	7	6	5	5	12	10	7	7	7	6	9	10	8	15	6	9
	GR	2	2	6	2	4	4	2	3	5	10	6	4	6	5	6	6
# SURVEYED		155	156	139	126	129	168	137	136	144	134	114	134	99	97	85	99
AGE	RESP	'72	'73	'74	'75	'76	'77	'78	'80	'82	'83	'84	'85	'86	'87	'88	'89
60-65	SS	55%	50%	52%	57%	50%	49%	50%	41%	45%	34%	40%	38%	37%	32%	31%	35%
	HS	38	41	38	38	43	37	42	45	48	51	49	46	47	59	50	49
	AS	0	0	1	1	1	1	1	1	0	2	2	1	1	3	2	1
	BA	2	6	3	2	4	7	5	8	4	10	4	8	7	3	10	7
	GR	4	3	6	3	2	6	3	5	3	3	4	8	8	3	8	8
# SURVEYED		139	120	108	113	134	116	107	119	115	131	112	131	115	100	119	111
AGE	RESP	'72	'73	'74	'75	'76	'77	'78	'80	'82	'83	'84	'85	'86	'87	'88	'89
66+	SS	73%	64%	66%	65%	67%	70%	61%	65%	61%	57%	52%	57%	57%	51%	53%	44%
	HS	19	27	23	27	24	23	28	24	28	31	36	36	33	39	38	46
	AS	0	1	1	1	0	1	1	2	3	1	3	0	1	0	2	2
	BA	6	6	5	5	6	4	6	6	5	8	6	5	6	6	4	5
	GR	2	3	5	2	2	2	3	3	2	3	3	2	3	3	3	3
# SURVEYED		216	199	226	232	250	211	231	240	258	240	231	261	265	251	279	273

****

RESPONDENT'S BIRTHPLACE

TABLE I: RESPONDENT'S BIRTHPLACE - BY TOTAL POPULATION

Question: Were you born in this country? NOTE: Question not asked in 1972-1976.

Responses: Yes; No

	YEAR										
RESPONSE	'77	'78	'80	'82	'83	'84	'85	'86	'87	'88	'89
YES	93%	94%	93%	94%	93%	94%	94%	93%	94%	94%	93%
NO	7	6	7	6	7	6	6	7	6	6	7
# SURVEYED	1528	1530	1466	1504	1598	1465	1531	1462	1458	1481	1531

TABLE II: RESPONDENT'S BIRTHPLACE - BY SEX

Question: Were you born in this country? NOTE: Question not asked in 1972-1976.

Responses: Yes; No

		YEAR										
SEX	RESP	'77	'78	'80	'82	'83	'84	'85	'86	'87	'88	'89
M	YES	93%	94%	93%	93%	94%	94%	94%	93%	94%	93%	93%
	NO	7	6	7	7	6	6	6	7	6	7	7
# SURVEYED		692	643	640	637	689	596	687	620	640	638	657
SEX	RESP	'77	'78	'80	'82	'83	'84	'85	'86	'87	'88	'89
F	YES	93%	94%	93%	95%	92%	94%	93%	92%	94%	94%	94%
	NO	7	6	7	5	8	6	7	8	6	6	6
# SURVEYED		836	887	826	867	909	869	844	842	818	843	874

TABLE III: RESPONDENT'S BIRTHPLACE - BY RACE

Question: Were you born in this country? NOTE: Question not asked in 1972-1976.

Responses: Yes; No

		YEAR										
RACE	RESP	'77	'78	'80	'82	'83	'84	'85	'86	'87	'88	'89
WHT	YES	93%	94%	93%	95%	94%	95%	95%	93%	95%	95%	95%
	NO	7	6	7	5	6	5	5	7	5	5	5
# SURVEYED		1338	1356	1316	1322	1416	1243	1337	1243	1217	1234	1314
RACE	RESP	'77	'78	'80	'82	'83	'84	'85	'86	'87	'88	'89
BLK	YES	97%	97%	96%	92%	94%	93%	95%	93%	94%	95%	96%
	NO	3	3	4	8	6	7	5	7	6	5	4
# SURVEYED		175	158	140	155	165	170	150	182	188	186	156
RACE	RESP	'77	'78	'80	'82	'83	'84	'85	'86	'87	'88	'89
OTH	YES	33%	31%	50%	63%	35%	69%	52%	62%	68%	64%	52%
	NO	67	69	50	37	65	31	48	38	32	36	48
# SURVEYED		15	16	10	27	17	52	44	37	53	61	61

TABLE IV: RESPONDENT'S BIRTHPLACE - BY AGE

Question: Were you born in this country? NOTE: Question not asked in 1972-1976.

Responses: Yes; No

		YEAR										
AGE	RESP	'77	'78	'80	'82	'83	'84	'85	'86	'87	'88	'89
18-23	YES	95%	96%	95%	97%	92%	93%	95%	93%	97%	94%	90%
	NO	5	4	5	3	8	7	5	7	3	6	10
# SURVEYED		164	163	155	147	128	161	133	107	126	141	136
AGE	RESP	'77	'78	'80	'82	'83	'84	'85	'86	'87	'88	'89
24-29	YES	96%	95%	95%	95%	95%	95%	92%	94%	94%	92%	95%
	NO	4	5	5	5	5	5	8	6	6	8	5
# SURVEYED		204	244	202	246	287	232	217	218	193	215	201
AGE	RESP	'77	'78	'80	'82	'83	'84	'85	'86	'87	'88	'89
30-35	YES	90%	93%	90%	97%	94%	92%	95%	92%	94%	95%	92%
	NO	10	7	10	3	6	8	5	8	6	5	8
# SURVEYED		188	230	215	204	236	197	212	217	221	195	212

TABLE IV: RESPONDENT'S BIRTHPLACE - BY AGE (Continued)

Question: Were you born in this country? NOTE: Question not asked in 1972-1976.

Responses: Yes; No

		YEAR										
AGE	RESP	'77	'78	'80	'82	'83	'84	'85	'86	'87	'88	'89
36-41	YES	92%	92%	95%	94%	94%	95%	90%	91%	92%	93%	94%
	NO	8	8	5	6	6	5	10	9	8	7	6
# SURVEYED		167	159	150	146	173	187	184	186	185	193	198
AGE	RESP	'77	'78	'80	'82	'83	'84	'85	'86	'87	'88	'89
42-47	YES	95%	93%	90%	93%	95%	94%	94%	91%	96%	92%	93%
	NO	5	7	10	7	5	6	6	9	4	8	7
# SURVEYED		147	119	117	119	145	126	124	141	156	157	161
AGE	RESP	'77	'78	'80	'82	'83	'84	'85	'86	'87	'88	'89
48-53	YES	93%	95%	97%	95%	91%	93%	95%	92%	93%	91%	93%
	NO	7	5	3	5	9	7	5	8	7	9	7
# SURVEYED		154	132	123	111	116	102	130	108	126	92	137
AGE	RESP	'77	'78	'80	'82	'83	'84	'85	'86	'87	'88	'89
54-59	YES	96%	96%	95%	91%	93%	94%	94%	97%	99%	92%	94%
	NO	4	4	5	9	7	6	6	3	1	8	6
# SURVEYED		168	137	135	144	134	114	133	98	98	85	98
AGE	RESP	'77	'78	'80	'82	'83	'84	'85	'86	'87	'88	'89
60-65	YES	96%	98%	92%	97%	91%	98%	97%	94%	93%	97%	94%
	NO	4	2	8	3	9	2	3	6	7	3	6
# SURVEYED		117	107	119	116	132	110	130	115	100	119	111
AGE	RESP	'77	'78	'80	'82	'83	'84	'85	'86	'87	'88	'89
66+	YES	88%	91%	90%	90%	89%	93%	93%	92%	93%	95%	94%
	NO	12	9	10	10	11	7	7	8	7	5	6
# SURVEYED		212	232	242	259	241	231	261	265	250	280	274

****

PARENT'S BIRTHPLACE

TABLE I: PARENT'S BIRTHPLACE - BY TOTAL POPULATION

Question: Were both your parents born in this country? NOTE: DK = Don't Know. Question not asked in 1972-1976.

Responses:

1 = Both born in U.S.A.
2 = Mother yes, father no
3 = Mother no, father yes
4 = Mother yes, father DK
5 = Mother no, father DK
6 = Mother DK , father yes
7 = Mother DK, father no
8 = Mother DK, father DK
9= Neither born in U.S.A.

	YEAR										
RESPONSE	'77	'78	'80	'82	'83	'84	'85	'86	'87	'88	'89
1	78%	82%	80%	80%	79%	84%	83%	82%	84%	84%	83%
2	4	4	4	4	4	4	4	3	3	3	3
3	2	2	2	3	3	1	2	2	2	2	3
4	0	0	0	0	0	0	0	0	0	0	0
5	0	0	0	0	0	0	0	0	0	0	0
6	0	0	0	0	0	0	0	0	0	0	0
7	0	0	0	0	0	0	0	0	0	0	0
8	0	0	0	0	0	0	0	0	0	0	0
9	15	11	13	13	14	10	11	12	10	11	11
# SURVEYED	1529	1529	1466	1503	1598	1464	1530	1461	1458	1477	1529

TABLE II: PARENT'S BIRTHPLACE - BY SEX

Question: Were both your parents born in this country? NOTE: DK = Don't Know. Question not asked in 1972-1976.

Responses: 1 = Both born in U.S.A. 2 = Mother yes, father no 3 = Mother no, father yes
4 = Mother yes, father DK 5 = Mother no, father DK 6 = Mother DK , father yes
7 = Mother DK, father no 8 = Mother DK, father DK 9= Neither born in U.S.A.

		YEAR										
SEX	RESP	'77	'78	'80	'82	'83	'84	'85	'86	'87	'88	'89
M	1	77%	81%	80%	79%	80%	83%	83%	82%	82%	82%	82%
A	2	4	4	6	3	3	5	3	4	3	3	4
L	3	3	2	2	3	3	1	2	3	3	2	2
E	4	0	0	0	0	0	0	0	0	0	0	0
	5	0	0	0	0	0	0	0	0	0	0	0
	6	0	0	0	0	0	0	0	0	0	0	0
	7	0	0	0	0	0	0	0	0	0	0	0
	8	0	0	0	0	0	0	0	0	0	0	0
	9	16	13	12	15	13	11	11	11	12	12	11
# SURVEYED		692	642	640	636	689	596	687	619	640	635	656
SEX	RESP	'77	'78	'80	'82	'83	'84	'85	'86	'87	'88	'89
F	1	79%	83%	81%	81%	78%	85%	83%	83%	86%	85%	83%
E	2	4	4	3	4	4	4	4	2	3	3	3
M	3	2	2	2	3	2	2	2	2	2	1	3
A	4	0	0	0	0	0	0	0	0	0	0	0
L	5	0	0	0	0	0	0	0	0	0	0	0
E	6	0	0	0	0	0	0	0	0	0	0	0
	7	0	0	0	0	0	0	0	0	0	0	0
	8	0	0	0	0	0	0	0	0	0	0	0
	9	14	10	14	12	15	9	11	13	9	10	11
# SURVEYED		837	887	826	867	909	868	843	842	818	842	873

TABLE III: PARENTS BIRTHPLACE - BY RACE

Question: Were both your parents born in this country? NOTE: DK = Don't Know. Question not asked in 1972-1976.

Responses:
1 = Both born in U.S.A. 2 = Mother yes, father no 3 = Mother no, father yes
4 = Mother yes, father DK 5 = Mother no, father DK 6 = Mother DK , father yes
7 = Mother DK, father no 8 = Mother DK, father DK 9= Neither born in U.S.A.

		YEAR										
RACE	RESP	'77	'78	'80	'82	'83	'84	'85	'86	'87	'88	'89
W	1	77%	81%	79%	80%	78%	85%	83%	82%	84%	84%	84%
H	2	5	4	4	4	4	5	4	3	3	3	4
I	3	3	3	2	3	3	2	2	3	3	2	3
T	4	0	0	0	0	0	0	0	0	0	0	0
E	5	0	0	0	0	0	0	0	0	0	0	0
	6	0	0	0	0	0	0	0	0	0	0	0
	7	0	0	0	0	0	0	0	0	0	0	0
	8	0	0	0	0	0	0	0	0	0	0	0
	9	16	12	14	13	14	9	10	12	9	10	10
# SURVEYED		1338	1355	1316	1320	1416	1242	1336	1242	1216	1230	1311
RACE	RESP	'77	'78	'80	'82	'83	'84	'85	'86	'87	'88	'89
B	1	94%	96%	94%	90%	91%	92%	91%	92%	93%	91%	92%
L	2	2	0	1	1	1	1	1	1	1	2	1
A	3	0	1	0	1	1	0	0	0	0	0	1
C	4	0	0	1	0	0	0	1	1	1	1	1
K	5	0	0	0	0	0	0	0	0	0	0	0
	6	0	0	0	0	0	0	0	0	0	0	0
	7	0	0	0	0	0	0	0	0	0	0	0
	8	1	0	1	0	0	1	1	0	0	1	1
	9	3	3	4	8	7	7	6	7	6	6	4
# SURVEYED		176	158	140	156	165	170	150	182	189	186	157
RACE	RESP	'77	'78	'80	'82	'83	'84	'85	'86	'87	'88	'89
O	1	13%	25%	30%	44%	18%	48%	41%	59%	53%	54%	34%
T	2	0	13	20	0	0	12	5	0	4	5	3
H	3	7	0	10	4	12	0	5	0	4	0	8
E	4	0	6	0	0	0	0	2	0	0	0	0
R	5	0	0	0	0	0	0	0	0	0	0	0
	6	0	0	0	0	0	0	0	0	0	0	0
	7	0	0	0	0	0	0	0	0	0	0	0
	8	0	0	0	0	0	0	0	0	0	0	0
	9	80	56	40	52	71	40	48	41	40	41	54
# SURVEYED		15	16	10	27	17	52	44	37	53	61	61

TABLE IV: PARENT'S BIRTHPLACE - BY AGE

Question: Were both your parents born in this country? NOTE: DK = Don't Know. Question not asked in 1972-1976.

Responses: 1 = Both born in U.S.A. 2 = Mother yes, father no 3 = Mother no, father yes 4 = Mother yes, father DK 5 = Mother no, father DK 6 = Mother DK , father yes 7 = Mother DK, father no 8 = Mother DK, father DK 9= Neither born in U.S.A.

		YEAR										
AGE	RESP	'77	'78	'80	'82	'83	'84	'85	'86	'87	'88	'89
18-23	1	91%	90%	88%	90%	85%	90%	90%	94%	88%	91%	77%
	2	3	3	2	1	3	1	2	1	4	0	5
	3	1	2	1	1	5	1	5	1	4	2	5
	4	0	1	0	0	1	0	0	0	0	0	0
	5	0	0	0	0	0	0	0	0	0	0	0
	6	0	0	0	0	0	0	0	0	0	0	0
	7	0	0	0	0	0	0	0	0	0	0	0
	8	0	0	1	0	0	1	0	0	0	0	0
	9	5	5	8	7	5	7	3	4	4	7	12
# SURVEYED		164	163	155	147	128	161	133	107	126	141	137
AGE	RESP	'77	'78	'80	'82	'83	'84	'85	'86	'87	'88	'89
24-29	1	89%	92%	90%	89%	90%	91%	86%	88%	90%	86%	89%
	2	1	2	2	1	2	3	3	1	1	1	1
	3	3	1	2	2	1	1	3	3	1	1	2
	4	0	0	0	0	0	0	0	0	0	0	0
	5	0	0	0	0	0	0	0	0	0	0	0
	6	0	0	0	0	0	0	0	0	0	0	0
	7	0	0	0	0	0	0	0	0	0	0	0
	8	0	0	0	0	0	0	0	0	1	0	0
	9	6	5	6	8	6	5	8	7	8	11	7
# SURVEYED		204	244	202	246	287	232	217	218	193	214	201
AGE	RESP	'77	'78	'80	'82	'83	'84	'85	'86	'87	'88	'89
30-35	1	85%	85%	85%	90%	86%	89%	92%	87%	87%	88%	90%
	2	4	3	4	3	2	4	2	1	2	4	1
	3	2	3	3	3	3	1	1	1	3	2	2
	4	0	0	0	0	0	0	0	0	0	0	0
	5	0	0	0	0	0	0	0	0	0	0	0
	6	0	0	0	0	0	0	0	0	0	0	0
	7	0	0	0	0	0	0	0	0	0	0	0
	8	0	0	0	0	0	0	0	0	0	0	0
	9	10	8	8	3	9	7	4	11	8	7	7
# SURVEYED		188	230	215	204	6	196	212	217	221	195	212

TABLE IV: PARENT'S BIRTHPLACE - BY AGE (Continued)

Question: Were both your parents born in this country? NOTE: DK = Don't Know. Question not asked in 1972-1976.

Responses:
1 = Both born in U.S.A. 2 = Mother yes, father no 3 = Mother no, father yes
4 = Mother yes, father DK 5 = Mother no, father DK 6 = Mother DK , father yes
7 = Mother DK, father no 8 = Mother DK, father DK 9= Neither born in U.S.A.

		YEAR										
AGE	RESP	'77	'78	'80	'82	'83	'84	'85	'86	'87	'88	'89
36-41	1	83%	83%	85%	84%	86%	90%	86%	84%	86%	90%	87%
	2	5	4	6	3	2	2	3	2	3	2	3
	3	2	3	2	4	6	2	1	3	1	1	3
	4	0	1	1	0	0	0	1	0	1	0	1
	5	0	0	0	0	0	0	0	0	0	0	0
	6	0	0	0	0	0	0	0	0	0	0	0
	7	0	0	0	0	0	0	0	0	0	0	0
	8	0	1	0	0	0	1	0	0	0	0	0
	9	9	8	7	8	6	6	10	11	9	7	6
# SURVEYED		168	159	150	146	173	187	184	186	185	191	198
AGE	RESP	'77	'78	'80	'82	'83	'84	'85	'86	'87	'88	'89
42-47	1	81%	81%	81%	88%	88%	89%	88%	86%	85%	79%	84%
	2	5	4	4	2	3	3	5	3	2	6	4
	3	3	2	0	3	1	1	0	0	6	4	4
	4	0	0	0	0	0	0	0	1	0	0	1
	5	0	0	0	0	0	0	0	0	1	0	0
	6	0	0	0	0	0	0	0	0	0	0	0
	7	0	0	0	0	0	0	0	0	0	0	0
	8	0	1	1	0	0	0	0	0	0	0	0
	9	10	13	14	8	8	7	7	11	6	11	8
# SURVEYED		147	119	117	118	145	126	124	141	157	157	161
AGE	RESP	'77	'78	'80	'82	'83	'84	'85	'86	'87	'88	'89
48-53	1	77%	80%	81%	72%	80%	78%	82%	82%	88%	86%	89%
	2	2	5	6	8	3	8	5	7	2	2	1
	3	2	4	2	4	1	1	2	2	2	0	1
	4	0	0	0	0	0	0	0	1	0	1	0
	5	0	0	0	0	0	0	0	0	0	0	0
	6	0	0	0	0	0	0	0	0	0	0	0
	7	0	0	0	0	0	0	0	0	0	0	0
	8	0	0	0	1	0	0	0	0	0	1	0
	9	19	11	11	15	16	13	11	7	8	10	9
# SURVEYED		154	132	123	112	116	102	130	108	126	91	138
AGE	RESP	'77	'78	'80	'82	'83	'84	'85	'86	'87	'88	'89
54-59	1	64%	80%	80%	69%	69%	76%	75%	80%	90%	82%	85%
	2	8	6	4	6	6	5	5	5	2	4	2
	3	4	1	1	2	4	3	2	3	1	1	2
	4	1	0	0	0	0	0	1	0	0	0	0
	5	0	0	0	0	0	0	0	0	0	0	0
	6	0	0	0	0	0	0	0	0	0	0	0
	7	0	0	0	0	0	0	0	0	0	0	0
	8	1	0	0	0	0	0	1	0	0	0	1
	9	24	13	15	23	21	16	17	12	7	13	10
# SURVEYED		168	137	135	144	134	114	133	98	97	85	98

TABLE IV: PARENT'S BIRTHPLACE - BY AGE (continued)

Question: Were both your parents born in this country? NOTE DK = Don't know. Question not asked in 1972-1976.

Responses:

1 = Both born in U.S.A.	2 = Mother yes, father no	3 = Mother no, father yes
4 = Mother yes, father DK	5 = Mother no, father DK	6 = Mother DK , father yes
7 = Mother DK, father no	8 = Mother DK, father DK	9= Neither born in U.S.A.

		YEAR										
AGE	RESP	'77	'78	'80	'82	'83	'84	'85	'86	'87	'88	'89
60-65	1	70%	77%	68%	77%	61%	78%	73%	76%	79%	83%	75%
	2	3	3	5	5	7	8	5	6	3	6	6
	3	2	4	3	1	3	2	4	1	2	3	0
	4	0	0	0	0	0	0	1	0	0	1	0
	5	0	0	0	0	0	0	0	0	0	0	0
	6	0	0	0	0	0	0	0	0	0	0	0
	7	0	0	0	0	1	0	0	1	0	0	0
	8	0	0	0	0	0	0	0	0	0	0	0
	9	25	17	24	17	29	12	17	17	16	8	18
# SURVEYED		117	107	119	116	132	110	130	115	100	119	110
AGE	RESP	'77	'78	'80	'82	'83	'84	'85	'86	'87	'88	'89
66+	1	64%	68%	67%	64%	61%	73%	73%	70%	70%	73%	71%
	2	6	5	4	5	6	8	3	3	7	4	5
	3	2	2	3	3	2	2	3	4	2	3	3
	4	0	1	0	0	0	0	0	0	0	0	0
	5	0	0	0	0	0	0	0	0	0	0	0
	6	0	0	0	0	0	0	0	0	0	0	0
	7	0	0	0	0	0	0	0	0	0	0	0
	8	1	0	0	0	0	0	0	0	0	0	0
	9	27	25	25	27	31	17	20	23	20	19	20
# SURVEYED		212	232	241	259	241	231	260	265	250	280	271

SIBLINGS

TABLE I: SIBLINGS - BY TOTAL POPULATION

Question: How many brothers and sisters did you have? Please count those born alive, but no longer living, as well as those alive now. Also include stepbrothers and stepsisters, and children adopted by your parents.

Responses: 0 = 0; 1 = 1; 2 = 2; 3 = 3; 4 = 4; 5 = 5; 6 = 6; 7 = 7 - 12; 8 = 13+

	YEAR															
RESPONSE	'72	'73	'74	'75	'76	'77	'78	'80	'82	'83	'84	'85	'86	'87	'88	'89
0	6%	6%	5%	6%	6%	5%	6%	5%	5%	6%	4%	6%	4%	5%	4%	5%
1	16	15	15	14	13	13	14	14	14	15	15	15	16	16	15	15
2	16	15	14	16	15	16	17	16	16	17	18	16	18	17	20	20
3	14	13	15	14	15	12	14	13	16	16	16	14	16	17	15	17
4	11	11	12	10	12	12	11	13	12	12	11	12	11	12	12	11
5	8	9	9	8	10	9	9	10	9	10	8	10	10	9	9	8
6	7	7	6	7	7	8	9	7	8	7	6	8	7	7	6	7
7	24	22	21	21	21	22	18	19	18	16	19	18	16	16	17	14
8	0	2	2	2	2	2	2	3	2	2	2	2	2	2	2	2
# SURVEYED	1606	1501	1483	1485	1498	1527	1532	1467	1502	1598	1465	1525	1467	1462	1472	1533

TABLE II: SIBLINGS - BY SEX

Question: How many brothers and sisters did you have? Please count those born alive, but no longer living, as well as those alive now. Also include stepbrothers and stepsisters, and children adopted by your parents.

Responses: 0 = 0; 1 = 1; 2 = 2; 3 = 3; 4 = 4; 5 = 5; 6 = 6; 7 = 7 - 12; 8 = 13+

		YEAR															
SEX	RESP	'72	'73	'74	'75	'76	'77	'78	'80	'82	'83	'84	'85	'86	'87	'88	'89
M	0	7%	5%	5%	6%	6%	6%	7%	4%	5%	6%	5%	6%	5%	5%	5%	6%
A	1	16	15	16	16	11	13	15	17	14	16	16	16	17	15	16	17
L	2	17	16	15	17	17	16	20	17	15	17	20	16	21	18	22	22
E	3	13	13	15	14	16	12	15	14	18	16	16	15	17	18	16	19
	4	11	12	13	9	10	11	9	13	14	11	9	11	10	12	10	10
	5	8	9	9	8	11	9	8	10	10	9	9	10	8	8	8	7
	6	6	7	7	6	7	9	6	8	7	7	7	6	6	6	6	7
	7	22	21	19	21	19	22	17	15	16	16	16	18	14	15	17	12
	8	0	3	2	2	2	2	3	3	3	1	2	2	1	1	1	1
# SURVEYED		805	700	690	668	668	692	643	640	636	689	595	684	620	640	634	660
SEX	RESP	'72	'73	'74	'75	'76	'77	'78	'80	'82	'83	'84	'85	'86	'87	'88	'89
F	0	6%	6%	5%	7%	6%	5%	6%	6%	5%	6%	4%	5%	3%	4%	4%	5%
E	1	15	15	14	12	15	13	14	12	15	14	14	15	16	16	15	14
M	2	14	15	14	16	13	16	16	15	17	17	17	16	16	15	18	19
A	3	14	13	15	14	14	13	13	13	14	16	16	14	15	17	13	16
L	4	10	9	11	10	13	13	12	13	10	12	12	12	12	12	13	11
E	5	8	8	9	9	9	9	9	10	9	10	8	10	11	9	10	10
	6	7	8	6	8	7	7	10	7	8	7	6	9	7	7	6	7
	7	26	23	23	21	23	22	18	21	20	16	21	18	18	17	18	16
	8	0	2	3	2	2	2	2	3	2	2	2	2	2	2	2	2
# SURVEYED		801	801	793	817	830	835	889	827	866	909	870	841	847	822	838	873

TABLE III: SIBLINGS - BY RACE

Question: How many brothers and sisters did you have? Please count those born alive, but no longer living, as well as those alive now. Also include stepbrothers and stepsisters, and children adopted by your parents.

Responses: 0 = 0; 1 = 1; 2 = 2; 3 = 3; 4 = 4; 5 = 5; 6 = 6; 7 = 7 - 12; 8 = 13+

		YEAR															
RACE	RESP	'72	'73	'74	'75	'76	'77	'78	'80	'82	'83	'84	'85	'86	'87	'88	'89
W	0	7%	6%	5%	6%	6%	5%	7%	4%	5%	6%	4%	5%	4%	5%	4%	5%
H	1	17	16	16	14	14	14	15	15	15	16	17	16	18	17	17	17
I	2	16	17	16	18	15	17	18	16	17	18	19	17	20	18	21	21
T	3	14	13	16	15	15	13	14	14	16	16	17	15	16	19	15	18
E	4	11	11	12	10	12	12	11	13	12	11	12	12	11	13	12	11
	5	8	8	9	8	10	9	9	10	9	9	8	10	10	8	8	8
	6	6	7	6	7	7	7	8	7	7	7	6	8	7	6	5	7
	7	21	19	19	20	20	21	17	18	16	15	16	16	13	13	15	13
	8	0	2	2	2	2	2	2	2	2	2	1	1	1	1	1	1
# SURVEYED		1342	1306	1304	1319	1360	1338	1358	1317	1322	1415	1243	1331	1247	1220	1229	1316
RACE	RESP	'72	'73	'74	'75	'76	'77	'78	'80	'82	'83	'84	'85	'86	'87	'88	'89
B	0	5%	5%	7%	6%	7%	6%	5%	11%	3%	6%	5%	8%	5%	6%	6%	5%
L	1	8	4	6	9	5	3	8	8	8	6	6	9	7	8	7	6
A	2	13	5	6	6	11	12	10	10	10	10	12	5	11	10	11	13
C	3	9	12	10	8	9	9	13	6	11	15	8	9	12	11	11	15
K	4	10	9	13	10	11	12	9	9	10	16	5	8	14	9	12	11
	5	8	10	9	11	12	7	7	8	8	10	11	10	8	14	14	11
	6	8	8	6	8	6	14	13	10	10	10	6	10	5	10	6	7
	7	38	41	37	34	35	33	27	30	35	24	38	35	31	28	29	28
	8	0	6	6	7	5	4	8	9	5	2	8	5	7	5	5	4
# SURVEYED		260	182	172	162	129	174	158	140	153	165	170	150	183	189	184	156
RACE	RESP	'72	'73	'74	'75	'76	'77	'78	'80	'82	'83	'84	'85	'86	'87	'88	'89
O	0	0%	0%	0%	0%	0%	7%	6%	0%	0%	0%	0%	0%	0%	0%	0%	3%
T	1	0	8	0	25	0	0	6	0	4	11	10	9	11	8	2	13
H	2	25	15	0	25	22	7	13	20	7	11	10	11	3	13	15	15
E	3	25	8	29	25	22	20	19	20	11	17	17	7	11	2	15	10
R	4	0	15	0	0	11	7	19	20	15	6	10	11	8	11	10	18
	5	0	15	14	0	22	20	19	20	15	17	13	14	11	13	10	7
	6	0	8	0	0	0	13	6	0	11	11	4	5	11	8	15	5
	7	50	15	43	25	22	20	13	20	30	28	33	36	43	43	24	21
	8	0	15	14	0	0	7	0	0	7	0	4	7	3	2	8	8
# SURVEYED		4	13	7	4	9	15	16	10	27	18	52	44	37	53	59	61

TABLE IV: SIBLINGS - BY AGE

Question: How many brothers and sisters did you have? Please count those born alive, but no longer living, as well as those alive now. Also include stepbrothers and stepsisters, and children adopted by your parents.

Responses: 0 = 0; 1 = 1; 2 = 2; 3 = 3; 4 = 4; 5 = 5; 6 = 6; 7 = 7 - 12; 8 = 13+

		YEAR															
AGE	RESP	'72	'73	'74	'75	'76	'77	'78	'80	'82	'83	'84	'85	'86	'87	'88	'89
18-23	0	5%	4%	4%	3%	4%	2%	3%	2%	3%	3%	2%	6%	4%	3%	4%	7%
	1	14	20	15	16	7	12	14	12	12	21	17	16	18	25	19	23
	2	16	13	15	22	16	20	16	13	26	20	23	18	21	23	28	31
	3	17	20	20	17	24	12	16	15	18	16	25	17	21	17	13	13
	4	13	9	15	16	15	13	21	23	14	16	11	14	7	10	12	8
	5	8	11	9	7	12	11	6	11	11	9	8	11	8	9	9	6
	6	8	9	7	6	4	14	6	6	3	4	2	5	7	4	6	6
	7	20	12	14	11	17	12	16	15	12	10	10	8	13	8	9	5
	8	0	3	2	2	1	3	1	1	1	1	1	5	1	1	1	1
# SURVEYED		169	156	160	159	148	151	150	147	142	119	151	124	98	116	134	13
AGE	RESP	'72	'73	'74	'75	'76	'77	'78	'80	'82	'83	'84	'85	'86	'87	'88	'89
24-29	0	7%	6%	5%	7%	6%	2%	5%	2%	3%	3%	3%	4%	2%	3%	4%	3%
	1	21	23	20	15	16	19	14	15	13	13	16	11	18	12	15	16
	2	19	20	19	25	19	15	23	22	19	21	19	20	21	18	20	27
	3	15	11	17	15	18	20	18	17	20	18	15	17	18	23	19	18
	4	10	8	12	12	15	13	11	14	15	10	11	15	13	13	13	11
	5	7	11	8	8	10	7	9	9	7	10	9	10	8	8	9	6
	6	3	5	6	4	4	6	6	8	7	8	6	7	8	8	7	5
	7	17	13	11	13	13	16	9	12	16	14	19	14	11	14	11	11
	8	0	3	1	1	0	1	3	1	2	2	2	2	1	1	2	2
# SURVEYED		229	191	200	209	210	186	226	188	220	267	214	203	204	180	201	188
AGE	RESP	'72	'73	'74	'75	'76	'77	'78	'80	'82	'83	'84	'85	'86	'87	'88	'89
30-35	0	6%	10%	5%	8%	5%	5%	5%	6%	5%	3%	6%	4%	3%	4%	2%	4%
	1	21	13	22	15	20	15	18	18	17	13	17	17	14	17	17	18
	2	22	17	17	19	16	22	23	13	20	20	23	17	19	18	23	15
	3	14	14	18	21	14	11	13	17	17	19	19	12	15	22	18	19
	4	11	13	10	4	15	14	10	11	12	17	9	10	15	16	11	12
	5	5	6	4	9	8	6	7	13	8	8	10	14	13	5	12	13
	6	6	4	4	8	8	10	7	8	8	5	3	8	3	6	5	5
	7	15	25	17	15	14	15	15	13	11	14	13	17	15	12	12	12
	8	0	0	2	2	1	1	2	1	1	2	2	1	3	1	1	2
# SURVEYED		185	147	154	161	171	170	209	203	192	221	183	197	203	204	181	199
AGE	RESP	'72	'73	'74	'75	'76	'77	'78	'80	'82	'83	'84	'85	'86	'87	'88	'89
36-41	0	9%	7%	7%	6%	9%	8%	11%	7%	6%	10%	5%	6%	3%	3%	6%	4%
	1	18	12	17	18	17	15	18	17	14	23	19	20	24	16	16	16
	2	16	17	11	19	14	23	16	22	23	18	23	19	22	19	24	23
	3	19	14	15	14	12	14	9	14	14	17	14	18	17	19	15	18
	4	9	13	11	12	12	13	7	8	12	6	9	10	10	13	12	11
	5	6	5	10	5	11	6	11	10	6	8	6	6	6	10	8	7
	6	9	9	5	8	4	6	10	6	7	5	6	7	5	9	5	6
	7	15	18	20	15	17	15	16	13	15	12	14	12	10	9	12	14
	8	0	4	5	2	3	1	3	3	2	1	2	2	3	2	2	2
# SURVEYED		128	152	129	143	139	153	146	136	132	163	171	168	176	173	181	183

TABLE IV: SIBLINGS - BY AGE (Continued)

Question: How many brothers and sisters did you have? Please count those born alive, but no longer living, as well as those alive now. Also include stepbrothers and stepsisters, and children adopted by your parents.

Responses: 0 = 0; 1 = 1; 2 = 2; 3 = 3; 4 = 4; 5 = 5; 6 = 6; 7 = 7 - 12; 8 = 13+

		YEAR															
AGE	RESP	'72	'73	'74	'75	'76	'77	'78	'80	'82	'83	'84	'85	'86	'87	'88	'89
42-47	0	10%	7%	7%	7%	11%	10%	13%	7%	7%	10%	6%	7%	6%	4%	4%	8%
	1	15	13	15	17	16	16	17	20	18	22	21	19	19	24	16	18
	2	12	20	15	13	15	15	13	17	15	17	14	21	19	15	19	20
	3	15	12	18	15	11	12	15	11	11	17	15	15	13	16	19	17
	4	14	9	16	4	9	9	9	15	6	10	9	10	14	15	7	10
	5	9	6	8	8	8	9	6	5	10	5	6	7	6	8	8	11
	6	4	12	6	5	9	5	9	6	8	6	6	6	6	3	3	5
	7	20	21	14	27	20	22	16	13	24	13	19	15	17	13	21	11
	8	0	1	1	3	3	3	2	6	2	1	4	1	1	3	3	1
# SURVEYED		184	125	139	123	101	126	111	103	101	135	107	114	131	145	136	150
AGE	RESP	'72	'73	'74	'75	'76	'77	'78	'80	'82	'83	'84	'85	'86	'87	'88	'89
48-53	0	7%	5%	8%	9%	4%	6%	5%	8%	11%	8%	5%	2%	6%	4%	5%	4%
	1	14	23	18	10	8	8	20	19	18	17	15	24	15	15	15	17
	2	11	11	15	16	18	18	18	11	12	15	18	12	19	17	20	20
	3	8	13	8	14	12	12	13	7	12	18	14	9	19	13	13	22
	4	13	13	10	9	8	15	11	11	13	9	13	12	13	13	13	9
	5	11	7	5	9	11	8	9	15	8	9	6	9	8	10	11	9
	6	11	4	5	11	10	8	6	8	7	5	6	9	6	6	4	5
	7	24	22	29	20	24	21	17	18	17	16	24	19	13	21	15	14
	8	0	2	1	1	5	3	2	3	4	3	1	4	2	2	2	0
# SURVEYED		189	125	128	122	110	133	121	108	96	102	92	114	98	109	84	131
AGE	RESP	'72	'73	'74	'75	'76	'77	'78	'80	'82	'83	'84	'85	'86	'87	'88	'89
54-59	0	3%	4%	3%	5%	5%	7%	9%	8%	8%	10%	3%	5%	7%	11%	6%	6%
	1	15	10	11	13	16	9	15	10	17	12	10	18	13	16	14	12
	2	17	18	14	10	17	14	17	15	11	10	21	18	17	11	15	15
	3	11	10	14	12	9	14	17	10	13	14	13	12	16	18	14	14
	4	10	11	13	11	7	4	9	8	8	12	9	8	8	7	13	15
	5	9	11	12	7	9	11	6	7	11	8	9	11	11	8	6	6
	6	8	13	5	10	7	11	9	10	7	11	7	5	6	10	8	8
	7	27	20	25	29	25	27	15	30	23	22	25	21	20	14	22	18
	8	0	4	4	3	4	2	4	2	2	1	4	2	1	3	1	4
# SURVEYED		156	134	125	104	106	148	124	117	127	121	98	116	87	86	73	87
AGE	RESP	'72	'73	'74	'75	'76	'77	'78	'80	'82	'83	'84	'85	'86	'87	'88	'89
60-65	0	4%	2%	6%	3%	9%	6%	4%	6%	4%	4%	4%	8%	4%	6%	7%	9%
	1	13	8	6	7	6	14	9	9	12	12	14	12	14	10	18	12
	2	15	11	16	10	16	11	12	18	8	13	13	8	17	19	13	12
	3	14	16	12	11	16	7	16	12	19	10	13	12	17	14	14	19
	4	7	7	8	10	7	13	8	18	9	11	12	12	6	9	8	7
	5	8	11	14	13	9	11	7	8	14	14	9	10	10	18	12	6
	6	4	5	9	8	7	6	13	6	11	10	9	9	10	4	4	9
	7	34	37	28	34	28	30	26	21	21	24	26	27	20	20	24	24
	8	0	2	1	4	1	3	5	3	2	2	2	2	2	1	2	2
# SURVEYED		144	96	91	91	111	96	89	103	105	118	97	114	102	90	103	93

TABLE IV: SIBLINGS - BY AGE (Continued)

Question: How many brothers and sisters did you have? Please count those born alive, but no longer living, as well as those alive now. Also include stepbrothers and stepsisters, and children adopted by your parents.

Responses: 0 = 0; 1 = 1; 2 = 2; 3 = 3; 4 = 4; 5 = 5; 6 = 6; 7 = 7 - 12; 8 = 13+

		YEAR															
AGE	RESP	'72	'73	'74	'75	'76	'77	'78	'80	'82	'83	'84	'85	'86	'87	'88	'89
66+	0	6%	6%	3%	7%	4%	3%	4%	3%	2%	7%	4%	7%	5%	6%	3%	4%
	1	10	8	7	12	9	7	5	12	11	8	9	8	11	11	11	9
	2	11	10	8	7	7	8	13	12	12	15	10	9	11	11	16	18
	3	10	11	13	10	14	7	8	11	14	12	13	14	11	13	8	14
	4	7	13	14	9	12	14	10	11	12	11	15	12	11	11	13	13
	5	9	9	10	10	12	11	14	11	9	14	10	9	15	8	8	9
	6	7	7	9	9	8	8	12	7	10	8	10	11	9	8	8	11
	7	41	35	33	34	32	38	32	30	25	23	27	28	26	30	29	22
	8	0	3	4	2	2	3	2	3	4	3	2	1	2	3	3	1
# SURVEYED		218	152	175	187	214	169	190	196	216	208	193	226	231	211	237	242

****

MOTHER EMPLOYED PRE-SCHOOL AGE

TABLE I: MOTHER EMPLOYED PRE-SCHOOL AGE - BY TOTAL POPULATION

Question: Did your mother work for as long as a year after you were born and before you started the first grade? NOTE: Asked only of respondents who lived with own mother. Question was not asked 1972-1986.

Responses: Yes; No

	YEAR		
RESPONSE	'87	'88	'89
YES	43%	47%	41%
NO	57	53	59
# SURVEYED	791	804	817

TABLE II: MOTHER EMPLOYED PRE-SCHOOL AGE - BY SEX

Question: Did your mother work for as long as a year after you were born and before you started the first grade? NOTE: Asked only of respondents who lived with own mother. Question was not asked 1972-1986.

Responses: Yes; No

		YEAR		
SEX	RESP	'87	'88	'89
M	YES	40%	45%	38%
	NO	60	55	62
# SURVEYED		435	468	465

		YEAR		
SEX	RESP	'87	'88	'89
F	YES	47%	48%	45%
	NO	53	52	55
# SURVEYED		356	336	352

TABLE III: MOTHER EMPLOYED PRE-SCHOOL AGE - BY RACE

Question: Did your mother work for as long as a year after you were born and before you started the first grade? NOTE: Asked only of respondents who lived with own mother. Question was not asked 1972-1986.

Responses: Yes; No

		YEAR		
RACE	RESP	'87	'88	'89
WHT	YES	37%	41%	37%
	NO	63	59	63
# SURVEYED		667	674	709

		YEAR		
RACE	RESP	'87	'88	'89
BLK	YES	76%	77%	73%
	NO	24	23	27
# SURVEYED		107	103	83

		YEAR		
RACE	RESP	'87	'88	'89
OTH	YES	59%	67%	60%
	NO	41	33	40
# SURVEYED		17	27	25

TABLE IV: MOTHER EMPLOYED PRE-SCHOOL AGE - BY AGE

Question: Did your mother work for as long as a year after you were born and before you started the first grade? NOTE: Asked only of respondents who lived with own mother. Question was not asked 1972-1986.

Responses: Yes; No

		YEAR		
AGE	RESP	'87	'88	'89
18-23	YES	56%	57%	55%
	NO	44	43	45
# SURVEYED		87	94	92
AGE	RESP	'87	'88	'89
24-29	YES	43%	47%	42%
	NO	57	53	58
# SURVEYED		134	148	135
AGE	RESP	'87	'88	'89
30-35	YES	45%	47%	36%
	NO	55	53	64
# SURVEYED		150	136	147

		YEAR		
AGE	RESP	'87	'88	'89
36-41	YES	39%	38%	45%
	NO	61	63	55
# SURVEYED		123	120	121
AGE	RESP	'87	'88	'89
42-47	YES	39%	43%	40%
	NO	61	57	60
# SURVEYED		94	91	95
AGE	RESP	'87	'88	'89
48-53	YES	44%	53%	41%
	NO	56	47	59
# SURVEYED		56	47	59

		YEAR		
AGE	RESP	'87	'88	'89
54-59	YES	29%	42%	43%
	NO	71	58	57
# SURVEYED		71	58	57
AGE	RESP	'87	'88	'89
60-65	YES	43%	40%	14%
	NO	57	60	86
# SURVEYED		57	60	86
AGE	RESP	'87	'88	'89
66+	YES	44%	51%	47%
	NO	56	49	53
# SURVEYED		54	70	68

****

AGE WHEN FIRST MARRIED

TABLE I: AGE WHEN FIRST MARRIED - BY TOTAL POPULATION

Question: How old were you when you first married?

Responses: -15; 15-17; 18-20; 21-23; 24-26; 27-29; 30-32; 33-35; 36+

	YEAR															
RESPONSE	'72	'73	'74	'75	'76	'77	'78	'80	'82	'83	'84	'85	'86	'87	'88	'89
-15	1%	1%	1%	1%	1%	1%	1%	1%	0%	1%	0%	0%	0%	1%	0%	0%
15-17	10	11	10	11	9	11	11	11	10	10	11	10	10	9	10	9
18-20	31	30	32	31	30	30	34	34	33	31	33	34	32	31	35	32
21-23	30	30	30	29	30	29	28	27	28	30	28	29	29	30	27	30
24-26	14	15	15	14	16	14	15	16	15	16	15	15	16	16	15	14
27-29	8	7	5	6	7	8	6	5	7	6	6	7	7	7	7	8
30-32	3	4	4	4	3	3	3	2	3	3	3	3	3	3	3	4
33-35	2	1	2	1	2	2	1	1	1	1	2	1	1	1	1	1
36+	2	2	2	2	2	2	2	2	2	2	2	1	2	2	2	2
# SURVEYED	1395	1310	1298	1270	1289	1299	1288	1215	1232	1324	1176	1260	1197	1175	1171	1222

TABLE II: AGE WHEN FIRST MARRIED - BY SEX

Question: How old were you when you first married?

Responses: -15; 15-17; 18-20; 21-23; 24-26; 27-29; 30-32; 33-35; 36+

		YEAR															
SEX	RESP	'72	'73	'74	'75	'76	'77	'78	'80	'82	'83	'84	'85	'86	'87	'88	'89
M	-15	0%	0%	0%	0%	0%	0%	0%	0%	0%	0%	0%	0%	0%	0%	0%	0%
A	15-17	3	3	3	3	2	2	3	2	2	3	3	2	4	2	4	2
L	18-20	21	19	22	21	17	22	23	22	23	24	19	22	25	22	27	23
E	21-23	37	35	33	34	35	32	34	35	33	33	35	33	34	35	29	36
	24-26	19	21	20	20	24	22	21	25	21	22	24	21	21	22	20	17
	27-29	11	10	9	10	12	12	9	8	10	10	9	12	10	10	12	12
	30-32	4	6	7	5	5	4	6	3	6	5	5	5	4	6	5	6
	33-35	3	2	3	2	3	3	2	2	2	2	2	2	1	1	1	1
	36+	4	3	3	3	2	4	2	2	3	2	4	2	2	2	2	2
# SURVEYED		677	580	585	543	544	562	533	506	502	554	447	535	482	473	474	499
SEX	RESP	'72	'73	'74	'75	'76	'77	'78	'80	'82	'83	'84	'85	'86	'87	'88	'89
F	-15	2%	1%	1%	1%	2%	1%	1%	1%	1%	1%	0%	0%	1%	1%	1%	1%
E	15-17	17	17	15	17	15	17	16	18	15	16	16	15	14	14	13	14
M	18-20	40	39	40	39	39	36	41	42	40	36	42	42	37	38	40	38
A	21-23	22	26	27	25	27	27	24	22	25	27	24	25	26	27	26	25
L	24-26	10	10	10	10	10	9	10	10	11	12	9	10	13	12	11	11
E	27-29	5	4	2	4	4	5	3	3	5	4	5	4	4	5	4	5
	30-32	2	1	1	2	2	3	1	2	1	2	1	2	2	1	2	3
	33-35	1	1	1	1	1	1	1	1	1	1	2	1	1	1	1	0
	36+	1	1	1	2	1	1	1	1	1	1	1	1	1	2	1	1
# SURVEYED		718	730	713	727	745	737	755	709	730	770	729	725	715	702	697	723

TABLE III: AGE WHEN FIRST MARRIED - BY RACE

Question: How old were you when you first married?

Responses: -15; 15-17; 18-20; 21-23; 24-26; 27-29; 30-32; 33-35; 36+

		YEAR															
RACE	RESP	'72	'73	'74	'75	'76	'77	'78	'80	'82	'83	'84	'85	'86	'87	'88	'89
W	-15	0%	0%	1%	1%	1%	0%	1%	0%	0%	0%	0%	0%	0%	1%	0%	0%
H	15-17	9	10	8	10	9	10	10	11	10	10	10	9	9	9	10	8
I	18-20	30	29	32	31	31	29	33	34	34	30	33	34	32	31	35	32
T	21-23	30	31	30	30	30	30	29	28	28	31	29	29	30	31	28	30
E	24-26	15	16	16	14	16	15	15	16	15	17	15	15	16	16	15	14
	27-29	8	7	5	7	7	8	6	5	7	6	7	7	7	7	7	8
	30-32	3	3	4	4	3	4	3	3	3	3	3	3	3	3	3	4
	33-35	2	1	2	2	2	1	2	1	1	1	2	1	1	1	1	1
	36+	2	2	2	2	2	2	2	2	2	2	2	1	1	2	1	2
# SURVEYED		1175	1140	1147	1134	1178	1152	1161	1097	1104	1189	1007	1108	1040	999	1001	1071
RACE	RESP	'72	'73	'74	'75	'76	'77	'78	'80	'82	'83	'84	'85	'86	'87	'88	'89
B	-15	3%	2%	0%	2%	4%	1%	1%	2%	2%	3%	0%	1%	0%	4%	1%	1%
L	15-17	16	16	20	19	12	15	15	19	12	19	18	14	15	9	10	17
A	18-20	34	36	33	29	19	36	46	27	25	39	32	31	31	32	33	30
C	21-23	25	25	28	20	35	21	19	26	25	14	26	22	26	28	26	27
K	24-26	9	6	8	17	13	13	11	16	14	13	15	14	16	11	14	13
	27-29	6	6	6	6	10	5	4	5	10	5	4	12	3	6	6	6
	30-32	2	4	3	3	4	1	4	1	6	3	2	2	3	6	5	5
	33-35	0	3	0	1	2	3	0	1	2	2	2	2	3	1	2	0
	36+	5	2	2	5	2	3	0	3	4	2	2	3	2	4	4	1
# SURVEYED		217	161	144	133	102	137	113	110	106	120	130	116	131	134	123	109
RACE	RESP	'72	'73	'74	'75	'76	'77	'78	'80	'82	'83	'84	'85	'86	'87	'88	'89
O	-15	0%	0%	0%	0%	0%	0%	0%	0%	0%	0%	0%	0%	0%	0%	2%	2%
T	15-17	0	22	29	0	0	10	7	0	9	0	15	3	12	10	11	17
H	18-20	33	11	43	33	11	0	14	38	32	13	28	25	31	24	36	29
E	21-23	33	33	14	0	33	20	7	13	32	47	23	33	23	24	13	33
R	24-26	33	22	14	33	22	20	50	38	9	27	13	17	19	21	19	7
	27-29	0	0	0	0	33	40	7	13	5	7	5	8	12	5	11	7
	30-32	0	0	0	0	0	0	7	0	5	7	3	11	4	2	2	5
	33-35	0	11	0	0	0	0	0	0	9	0	0	3	0	5	0	0
	36+	0	0	0	33	0	10	7	0	0	0	13	0	0	10	6	0
# SURVEYED		3	9	7	3	9	10	14	8	22	15	39	36	26	42	47	42

TABLE IV: AGE WHEN FIRST MARRIED - BY AGE

Question: How old were you when you first married?

Responses: -15; 15-17; 18-20; 21-23; 24-26; 27-29; 30-32; 33-35; 36+

		YEAR															
AGE	RESP	'72	'73	'74	'75	'76	'77	'78	'80	'82	'83	'84	'85	'86	'87	'88	'89
18-23	-15	2%	0%	0%	1%	3%	0%	2%	0%	2%	0%	0%	0%	0%	0%	0%	4%
	15-17	32	33	17	25	27	17	25	30	15	16	16	11	18	13	17	8
	18-20	59	65	61	65	54	68	57	59	67	61	65	54	64	57	67	77
	21-23	8	1	21	9	16	14	16	11	15	23	19	35	18	30	17	12
	24-26	0	0	0	0	0	0	0	0	0	0	0	0	0	0	0	0
	27-29	0	0	0	0	0	0	0	0	0	0	0	0	0	0	0	0
	30-32	0	0	0	0	0	0	0	0	0	0	0	0	0	0	0	0
	33-35	0	0	0	0	0	0	0	0	0	0	0	0	0	0	0	0
	36+	0	0	0	0	0	0	0	0	0	0	0	0	0	0	0	0
# SURVEYED		63	69	75	68	63	63	63	63	52	31	43	37	22	30	36	26
AGE	RESP	'72	'73	'74	'75	'76	'77	'78	'80	'82	'83	'84	'85	'86	'87	'88	'89
24-29	-15	1%	1%	0%	0%	1%	0%	1%	1%	0%	1%	1%	1%	0%	0%	1%	1%
	15-17	10	8	7	12	10	12	13	10	11	14	14	11	11	8	5	13
	18-20	39	37	40	36	33	42	40	42	43	39	38	33	39	35	40	28
	21-23	42	42	44	47	39	38	33	32	32	35	30	33	36	36	29	45
	24-26	8	10	10	5	16	8	12	14	13	12	16	21	12	19	25	12
	27-29	1	1	0	0	1	1	1	1	1	2	1	2	2	2	1	2
	30-32	0	0	0	0	0	0	0	0	0	0	0	0	0	0	0	0
	33-35	0	0	0	0	0	0	0	0	0	0	0	0	0	0	0	0
	36+	0	0	0	0	0	0	0	0	0	0	0	0	0	0	0	0
# SURVEYED		182	172	166	172	174	146	180	145	166	200	148	150	130	124	118	118
AGE	RESP	'72	'73	'74	'75	'76	'77	'78	'80	'82	'83	'84	'85	'86	'87	'88	'89
30-35	-15	1%	1%	1%	1%	1%	0%	0%	0%	1%	0%	0%	0%	1%	1%	0%	0%
	15-17	10	11	12	13	13	10	8	14	9	11	8	6	8	11	12	8
	18-20	35	31	39	35	35	38	37	31	33	36	36	38	35	28	34	31
	21-23	32	39	33	31	31	29	31	33	26	25	31	33	28	27	28	27
	24-26	16	12	10	12	10	11	17	18	15	18	14	11	17	21	14	16
	27-29	5	4	4	4	9	11	4	2	12	5	7	9	9	7	9	13
	30-32	1	1	1	3	1	2	2	2	5	4	4	3	2	5	3	6
	33-35	0	0	0	0	0	0	0	0	0	0	1	0	0	1	0	1
	36+	0	0	0	0	0	0	0	0	0	0	0	0	0	0	0	0
# SURVEYED		176	157	166	156	175	170	208	180	173	202	163	177	184	169	149	160

TABLE IV: AGE WHEN FIRST MARRIED - BY AGE (Continued)

Question: How old were you when you first married?

Responses: -15; 15-17; 18-20; 21-23; 24-26; 27-29; 30-32; 33-35; 36+

		YEAR															
AGE	RESP	'72	'73	'74	'75	'76	'77	'78	'80	'82	'83	'84	'85	'86	'87	'88	'89
36-41	-15	1%	0%	1%	1%	0%	1%	1%	1%	0%	1%	0%	0%	1%	0%	0%	0%
	15-17	13	11	6	9	9	10	10	11	12	9	9	7	9	7	6	8
	18-20	33	28	37	32	31	32	33	30	31	30	31	37	36	33	37	34
	21-23	31	28	35	27	33	28	27	34	33	31	32	32	28	30	30	29
	24-26	11	21	14	20	15	16	16	17	16	16	13	13	15	17	13	9
	27-29	5	5	2	4	7	11	5	3	3	6	6	4	5	8	9	11
	30-32	3	5	3	4	3	2	5	2	3	4	3	3	4	1	4	7
	33-35	1	2	2	1	1	0	3	2	2	3	3	3	3	2	1	2
	36+	2	1	0	1	0	0	0	0	0	0	3	0	0	1	1	0
# SURVEYED		126	169	147	148	148	154	147	132	126	159	175	161	170	167	176	171
AGE	RESP	'72	'73	'74	'75	'76	'77	'78	'80	'82	'83	'84	'85	'86	'87	'88	'89
42-47	-15	1%	0%	1%	1%	2%	1%	1%	0%	0%	0%	0%	0%	1%	1%	0%	1%
	15-17	10	8	8	9	9	14	9	12	12	17	11	10	7	11	8	7
	18-20	35	36	34	39	29	33	35	40	29	33	35	39	28	35	32	36
	21-23	27	26	27	24	29	31	26	25	27	24	33	23	31	30	28	34
	24-26	16	13	14	17	18	11	15	11	17	18	13	14	18	11	16	11
	27-29	7	9	6	6	6	4	6	7	10	7	2	8	10	6	9	8
	30-32	2	5	7	1	2	1	6	2	3	1	3	4	2	3	3	3
	33-35	1	1	2	1	4	1	1	1	2	0	1	3	3	2	1	0
	36+	1	2	1	1	1	3	1	3	2	1	2	0	1	2	3	0
# SURVEYED		180	135	147	139	110	140	110	114	113	136	119	114	131	142	146	151
AGE	RESP	'72	'73	'74	'75	'76	'77	'78	'80	'82	'83	'84	'85	'86	'87	'88	'89
48-53	-15	0%	1%	0%	1%	2%	1%	0%	1%	0%	0%	0%	0%	0%	1%	2%	1%
	15-17	6	10	7	9	7	10	11	4	5	13	12	13	14	9	13	11
	18-20	25	31	36	25	30	21	33	37	44	35	35	33	35	34	33	33
	21-23	35	27	29	34	35	29	28	31	30	26	25	19	25	26	37	29
	24-26	16	19	15	18	12	20	17	18	7	15	15	20	16	19	7	13
	27-29	13	7	7	6	10	10	8	2	7	6	4	9	4	4	6	5
	30-32	2	4	1	5	2	5	3	4	3	2	3	3	3	5	2	4
	33-35	2	0	2	1	1	1	0	1	1	2	1	2	1	0	0	0
	36+	1	2	2	1	1	3	0	2	4	1	4	2	2	3	0	5
# SURVEYED		178	147	138	137	124	146	132	113	107	110	99	128	104	116	86	130
AGE	RESP	'72	'73	'74	'75	'76	'77	'78	'80	'82	'83	'84	'85	'86	'87	'88	'89
54-59	-15	1%	1%	1%	0%	2%	1%	1%	0%	0%	1%	0%	1%	0%	2%	0%	0%
	15-17	8	7	8	11	6	6	8	10	10	6	6	8	11	11	12	12
	18-20	25	24	20	25	23	22	23	26	31	28	29	33	33	26	36	34
	21-23	27	30	25	25	25	32	41	29	30	30	31	32	28	25	18	29
	24-26	19	15	20	13	21	22	13	18	16	18	19	12	17	17	20	14
	27-29	7	14	8	17	11	10	9	7	6	6	8	10	4	13	5	7
	30-32	5	3	9	3	4	3	1	5	3	5	4	3	2	4	6	2
	33-35	3	4	3	3	4	1	2	2	1	2	0	1	1	0	0	1
	36+	4	3	5	4	3	5	3	3	4	5	4	2	3	2	2	1
# SURVEYED		151	151	137	118	123	158	128	129	135	126	108	126	92	96	83	94

TABLE IV: AGE WHEN FIRST MARRIED - BY AGE (Continued)

Question: How old were you when you first married?

Responses: -15; 15-17; 18-20; 21-23; 24-26; 27-29; 30-32; 33-35; 36+

		YEAR															
AGE	RESP	'72	'73	'74	'75	'76	'77	'78	'80	'82	'83	'84	'85	'86	'87	'88	'89
60-65	-15	1%	1%	0%	0%	3%	0%	1%	2%	0%	1%	0%	0%	0%	0%	0%	0%
	15-17	7	12	15	11	5	9	10	7	8	9	13	9	11	6	15	9
	18-20	20	13	20	15	27	18	32	24	24	19	22	31	25	32	32	36
	21-23	26	30	22	27	26	19	22	25	27	33	32	26	36	42	27	32
	24-26	14	20	20	26	21	22	20	21	30	20	20	19	15	8	18	10
	27-29	15	14	12	9	8	16	7	12	6	10	7	10	7	6	7	5
	30-32	4	3	5	7	6	11	7	3	4	6	1	2	2	3	0	5
	33-35	6	2	2	3	4	5	1	4	1	1	2	1	2	0	1	0
	36+	6	5	5	2	1	1	1	3	1	2	3	2	3	2	0	4
# SURVEYED		134	116	101	107	131	113	101	109	108	125	100	124	110	96	115	107
AGE	RESP	'72	'73	'74	'75	'76	'77	'78	'80	'82	'83	'84	'85	'86	'87	'88	'89
66+	-15	1%	1%	1%	2%	0%	1%	0%	1%	1%	0%	0%	0%	0%	1%	1%	0%
	15-17	9	8	10	9	7	12	8	10	9	6	13	12	10	8	10	8
	18-20	22	23	17	23	22	20	28	29	22	22	26	26	24	25	29	25
	21-23	24	27	27	23	27	31	23	22	28	32	21	26	27	29	25	25
	24-26	19	16	22	16	19	14	15	20	16	19	16	15	20	15	14	21
	27-29	12	8	9	10	11	7	9	9	10	9	13	10	8	10	10	11
	30-32	6	7	6	7	7	7	5	4	5	5	4	5	5	4	5	4
	33-35	3	3	5	4	2	4	4	3	4	2	5	1	2	2	3	2
	36+	5	6	4	6	5	4	7	4	5	4	2	4	4	6	5	3
# SURVEYED		200	192	217	220	238	204	214	223	243	229	215	238	250	234	259	262

****

NUMBER OF CHILDREN YOU HAVE HAD

TABLE I: NUMBER OF CHILDREN YOU HAVE HAD - BY TOTAL POPULATION

Question: How many children have you ever had? Please count all that were born alive at any time.

Responses: 0 = 0; 1 = 1; 2 = 2; 3 = 3; 4 = 4; 5 = 5; 6 = 6; 7 = 7; 8 = 8+

	YEAR															
RESPONSE	'72	'73	'74	'75	'76	'77	'78	'80	'82	'83	'84	'85	'86	'87	'88	'89
0	23%	25%	22%	26%	26%	25%	27%	27%	28%	27%	30%	28%	27%	29%	27%	28%
1	15	13	15	16	16	17	16	16	17	16	16	15	15	16	16	15
2	21	24	22	22	22	23	24	25	24	23	23	23	24	23	24	26
3	17	16	17	16	15	15	15	15	14	16	15	16	15	17	14	15
4	11	10	10	9	10	9	9	8	7	7	9	9	9	8	9	7
5	5	4	7	4	4	5	4	4	4	4	4	5	4	3	5	5
6	3	3	4	2	2	3	3	2	2	3	1	2	3	2	3	2
7	2	1	2	1	2	1	2	1	1	2	1	1	1	1	1	1
8	2	3	3	3	2	2	1	2	2	2	2	2	2	2	2	1
# SURVEYED	1605	1500	1477	1485	1497	1516	1526	1465	1504	1596	1456	1530	1468	1461	1480	1535

TABLE II: NUMBER OF CHILDREN YOU HAVE HAD - BY SEX

Question: How many children have you ever had? Please count all that were born alive at any time.

Responses: 0 = 0; 1 = 1; 2 = 2; 3 = 3; 4 = 4; 5 = 5; 6 = 6 7 = 7 8 = 8+

		YEAR															
SEX	RESP	'72	'73	'74	'75	'76	'77	'78	'80	'82	'83	'84	'85	'86	'87	'88	'89
M	0	26%	29%	27%	30%	32%	30%	32%	31%	31%	30%	36%	33%	31%	34%	33%	33%
A	1	14	13	16	15	15	16	15	15	16	16	13	12	15	14	14	15
L	2	20	24	21	21	20	21	23	25	24	22	23	22	22	22	24	25
E	3	17	15	15	15	15	14	13	13	15	17	13	15	15	16	11	14
	4	11	9	8	8	9	9	8	7	6	7	11	8	9	7	9	6
	5	4	4	6	4	4	4	4	4	3	3	3	6	4	2	5	4
	6	2	2	2	2	1	3	2	2	2	2	1	1	2	2	2	1
	7	2	1	1	2	2	1	2	0	1	1	1	1	1	1	1	1
	8	2	2	2	2	2	1	1	2	1	2	1	2	2	2	1	1
# SURVEYED		801	698	687	665	667	686	640	640	637	690	591	686	619	639	638	659
SEX	RESP	'72	'73	'74	'75	'76	'77	'78	'80	'82	'83	'84	'85	'86	'87	'88	'89
F	0	21%	22%	18%	23%	21%	21%	24%	23%	25%	25%	26%	24%	24%	25%	22%	24%
E	1	15	13	15	17	18	18	16	17	18	16	18	17	14	17	18	15
M	2	22	24	22	23	24	26	24	24	24	25	23	24	26	24	24	26
A	3	17	16	18	16	15	16	16	15	14	16	16	16	15	18	16	17
L	4	10	11	11	9	10	8	9	9	8	7	8	9	9	8	9	7
E	5	6	5	7	5	5	5	4	4	4	4	4	5	4	4	5	5
	6	4	4	5	3	2	2	3	3	2	3	1	2	4	2	3	3
	7	2	2	2	1	2	1	1	2	1	2	2	1	1	1	1	2
	8	2	4	3	3	3	3	2	2	3	1	3	2	2	2	2	2
# SURVEYED		804	802	790	820	830	830	886	825	867	906	865	844	849	822	842	876

TABLE III: NUMBER OF CHILDREN YOU HAVE HAD - BY RACE

Question: How many children have you ever had? Please count all that were born alive at any time.

Responses: 0 = 0; 1 = 1; 2 = 2; 3 = 3; 4 = 4; 5 = 5; 6 = 6; 7 = 7; 8 = 8+

		YEAR															
RACE	RESP	'72	'73	'74	'75	'76	'77	'78	'80	'82	'83	'84	'85	'86	'87	'88	'89
W	0	23%	25%	23%	26%	26%	25%	27%	27%	28%	28%	30%	28%	28%	29%	27%	28
H	1	15	13	16	16	16	16	15	16	17	16	15	15	14	14	15	15
I	2	22	24	22	23	22	24	24	25	24	25	24	24	25	24	25	27
T	3	19	17	17	16	16	16	15	15	15	16	15	16	15	17	15	16
E	4	10	11	10	9	10	9	9	8	8	7	9	9	9	8	9	6
	5	5	4	6	4	4	5	4	4	4	3	3	5	4	3	5	4
	6	3	3	3	2	2	2	2	2	2	2	1	2	3	2	2	2
	7	1	1	1	1	2	1	2	1	1	1	1	1	1	1	1	1
	8	2	2	2	3	2	2	1	2	2	1	2	2	2	2	1	1
# SURVEYED		1342	1304	1301	1319	1359	1328	1352	1315	1321	1414	1235	1337	1248	1219	1233	1317
RACE	RESP	'72	'73	'74	'75	'76	'77	'78	'80	'82	'83	'84	'85	'86	'87	'88	'89
B	0	27%	23%	22%	27%	26%	23%	27%	24%	24%	23%	22%	28%	22%	29%	22%	27%
L	1	15	16	14	20	17	24	22	16	21	20	22	17	17	20	23	17
A	2	18	19	17	16	18	17	20	20	22	13	16	17	24	16	20	16
C	3	10	9	14	10	12	10	12	11	14	19	13	11	14	15	12	15
K	4	12	10	8	9	9	8	7	11	4	8	11	8	7	5	9	8
	5	7	8	7	4	3	5	5	5	4	7	7	5	6	6	4	5
	6	4	3	6	6	5	5	4	4	3	4	2	5	6	3	4	1
	7	4	3	6	2	3	2	1	4	2	2	2	3	2	2	2	5
	8	4	9	8	6	6	7	3	6	6	3	5	6	3	3	4	6
# SURVEYED		259	183	169	162	129	173	158	140	156	164	169	149	183	189	186	157
RACE	RESP	'72	'73	'74	'75	'76	'77	'78	'80	'82	'83	'84	'85	'86	'87	'88	'89
O	0	50%	38%	14%	25%	22%	47%	25%	40%	41%	17%	33%	32%	24%	26%	26%	30%
T	1	25	8	14	50	22	7	13	0	15	17	17	16	16	28	20	11
H	2	0	31	14	0	33	20	38	40	26	33	15	18	19	17	20	25
E	3	0	8	14	25	0	0	6	20	7	6	15	18	11	8	11	7
R	4	0	0	0	0	11	7	6	0	0	11	12	9	14	11	10	10
	5	25	8	29	0	0	13	6	0	7	0	2	2	5	0	3	8
	6	0	8	0	0	0	0	6	0	0	11	2	0	8	2	3	5
	7	0	0	14	0	0	7	0	0	0	0	2	2	0	2	2	2
	8	0	0	0	0	11	0	0	0	4	6	2	2	3	6	5	3
# SURVEYED		4	13	7	4	9	15	16	10	27	18	52	44	37	53	61	61

TABLE IV: NUMBER OF CHILDREN YOU HAVE HAD - BY AGE

Question: How many children have you ever had? Please count all that were born alive at any time.

Responses: 0 = 0; 1 = 1; 2 = 2; 3 = 3; 4 = 4; 5 = 5; 6 = 6; 7 = 7; 8 = 8+

		YEAR															
AGE	RESP	'72	'73	'74	'75	'76	'77	'78	'80	'82	'83	'84	'85	'86	'87	'88	'89
18-23	0	70%	71%	69%	72%	77%	73%	73%	69%	80%	84%	77%	77%	84%	83%	73%	82%
	1	17	17	23	22	19	21	18	21	18	10	16	20	12	15	17	13
	2	9	10	5	6	4	6	7	8	2	4	8	2	3	1	8	2
	3	2	2	2	1	0	1	1	2	1	1	0	0	1	1	1	1
	4	1	1	0	0	0	0	0	0	0	1	0	0	0	0	1	1
	5	0	0	0	0	0	0	1	0	0	0	0	0	0	1	0	0
	6	0	0	0	0	0	0	0	0	0	0	0	0	0	0	0	0
	7	0	0	0	0	0	0	0	0	0	0	0	0	0	0	0	0
	8	0	0	0	0	0	0	0	0	0	0	0	0	0	0	0	0
# SURVEYED		169	167	166	172	161	157	161	154	148	128	159	133	108	126	141	137
AGE	RESP	'72	'73	'74	'75	'76	'77	'78	'80	'82	'83	'84	'85	'86	'87	'88	'89
24-29	0	35%	39%	38%	42%	47%	41%	44%	45%	48%	44%	51%	53%	48%	55%	52%	52%
	1	24	20	25	26	21	28	24	24	22	23	17	19	23	18	25	19
	2	23	29	24	20	19	20	22	22	22	22	20	19	18	16	18	21
	3	14	7	9	9	10	8	8	6	5	7	9	7	7	9	4	6
	4	4	4	1	3	2	2	2	1	2	2	2	2	3	2	2	0
	5	1	0	2	0	0	0	1	0	1	1	0	0	0	0	0	2
	6	0	1	0	0	0	0	0	1	0	0	0	0	0	0	0	0
	7	0	0	0	0	0	0	0	0	0	0	1	0	0	0	0	0
	8	0	0	0	0	0	0	0	0	0	0	0	0	0	0	0	0
# SURVEYED		229	212	211	231	226	202	244	202	246	286	230	217	218	193	215	202
AGE	RESP	'72	'73	'74	'75	'76	'77	'78	'80	'82	'83	'84	'85	'86	'87	'88	'89
30-35	0	12%	19%	14%	12%	9%	19%	21%	29%	27%	26%	29%	29%	25%	33%	28%	29%
	1	14	9	11	17	17	19	20	21	25	22	19	18	21	22	18	20
	2	28	32	30	35	33	32	37	29	29	28	33	33	28	25	31	28
	3	22	17	25	21	22	14	13	15	13	16	14	15	16	14	13	13
	4	14	15	9	10	10	11	4	5	5	4	5	3	6	3	6	5
	5	5	4	6	2	6	3	3	1	1	4	1	0	1	1	2	2
	6	2	2	1	1	2	1	1	0	0	1	0	1	1	0	1	1
	7	1	1	2	1	1	0	1	1	0	0	0	0	0	1	1	0
	8	2	1	2	2	1	1	0	0	0	0	0	0	0	0	0	0
# SURVEYED		187	167	175	170	186	187	230	214	204	234	196	211	221	220	194	211
AGE	RESP	'72	'73	'74	'75	'76	'77	'78	'80	'82	'83	'84	'85	'86	'87	'88	'89
36-41	0	9%	7%	7%	10%	13%	11%	11%	13%	17%	18%	17%	21%	15%	21%	15%	23%
	1	12	10	7	12	11	13	8	15	16	16	18	11	12	14	18	16
	2	17	22	24	25	28	28	28	30	31	31	29	29	39	34	31	32
	3	27	26	26	25	23	26	23	21	25	23	21	20	20	23	18	16
	4	13	14	17	13	13	14	17	8	5	6	11	11	8	5	12	7
	5	10	9	9	8	5	5	4	4	3	3	3	4	3	2	5	3
	6	9	6	3	6	1	2	4	5	1	1	1	1	1	2	0	2
	7	2	3	3	0	3	1	2	2	1	2	1	1	1	0	1	1
	8	3	3	3	1	2	1	2	1	1	1	0	1	2	0	0	1
# SURVEYED		128	175	151	154	158	167	160	149	146	173	187	184	188	186	193	197

TABLE IV: NUMBER OF CHILDREN YOU HAVE HAD - BY AGE (Continued)

Question: How many children have you ever had? Please count all that were born alive at any time.

Responses: 0 = 0; 1 = 1; 2 = 2; 3 = 3; 4 = 4; 5 = 5; 6 = 6; 7 = 7; 8 = 8+

		YEAR															
AGE	RESP	'72	'73	'74	'75	'76	'77	'78	'80	'82	'83	'84	'85	'86	'87	'88	'89
42-47	0	9%	13%	7%	10%	10%	9%	14%	4%	10%	11%	10%	10%	11%	11%	15%	11%
	1	10	8	7	10	7	10	7	11	11	12	14	15	15	16	11	14
	2	17	29	22	17	19	25	26	25	31	26	30	27	29	30	31	34
	3	24	17	24	26	22	23	21	24	25	22	21	27	21	19	21	22
	4	15	18	17	13	19	15	17	19	10	15	14	9	11	11	14	9
	5	10	5	10	10	7	10	7	9	3	3	7	6	9	6	3	6
	6	5	6	9	6	4	2	5	3	5	8	3	2	1	4	4	1
	7	5	2	3	4	6	2	3	1	2	1	0	1	2	1	1	2
	8	4	3	3	4	5	5	1	3	2	1	2	2	1	2	1	1
# SURVEYED		185	146	151	143	113	147	118	117	118	145	125	124	140	157	157	161
AGE	RESP	'72	'73	'74	'75	'76	'77	'78	'80	'82	'83	'84	'85	'86	'87	'88	'89
48-53	0	11%	10%	11%	10%	14%	16%	7%	11%	9%	9%	13%	8%	9%	14%	8%	10%
	1	12	11	5	9	13	8	11	7	12	8	11	6	11	8	5	12
	2	26	20	23	28	22	26	30	27	25	25	25	19	27	29	25	32
	3	19	23	14	18	20	20	21	21	18	22	18	24	17	17	17	20
	4	15	13	13	11	14	10	9	14	12	18	17	21	19	17	16	14
	5	7	12	18	10	7	8	8	11	8	8	8	8	5	6	15	5
	6	5	4	6	4	6	6	6	5	6	4	1	4	8	3	9	3
	7	2	2	2	4	2	3	5	1	4	3	4	5	2	2	2	3
	8	4	5	8	6	2	4	4	2	7	3	4	5	3	2	2	1
# SURVEYED		188	151	146	141	133	154	132	123	112	116	101	131	108	126	92	138
AGE	RESP	'72	'73	'74	'75	'76	'77	'78	'80	'82	'83	'84	'85	'86	'87	'88	'89
54-59	0	15%	13%	12%	20%	15%	13%	17%	15%	15%	16%	7%	19%	14%	7%	8%	9%
	1	13	17	13	9	12	16	11	10	10	15	11	8	5	19	11	13
	2	25	26	20	25	29	25	21	22	26	22	18	21	14	18	27	22
	3	20	20	24	18	19	17	20	24	17	19	25	20	23	27	19	22
	4	10	13	16	15	9	10	15	9	14	10	19	11	11	18	9	13
	5	5	3	6	6	10	6	9	7	9	7	9	14	15	5	13	7
	6	5	4	5	4	4	6	2	5	2	5	4	2	11	1	7	3
	7	3	2	1	0	1	2	2	2	2	3	4	2	0	2	4	5
	8	3	3	1	2	2	4	1	6	6	4	4	3	6	4	2	5
# SURVEYED		155	157	139	126	129	167	137	136	144	134	113	133	99	97	85	99
AGE	RESP	'72	'73	'74	'75	'76	'77	'78	'80	'82	'83	'84	'85	'86	'87	'88	'89
60-65	0	22%	23%	17%	23%	19%	22%	19%	17%	14%	12%	18%	12%	12%	12%	9%	9%
	1	15	14	18	20	18	20	15	13	10	11	12	11	6	6	9	13
	2	25	27	21	22	22	21	21	33	29	27	30	27	25	26	30	25
	3	17	16	17	13	16	15	19	16	19	22	11	14	23	27	19	20
	4	10	8	11	10	10	10	17	8	12	11	15	16	12	11	14	8
	5	5	4	7	4	5	3	6	3	8	8	8	11	7	7	11	10
	6	4	1	4	2	1	3	1	3	2	5	3	2	8	2	3	5
	7	0	1	2	1	1	2	1	2	3	2	1	2	3	3	1	4
	8	3	6	4	5	6	4	3	6	3	2	3	5	4	7	3	7
# SURVEYED		144	121	106	113	134	117	107	119	115	132	110	130	115	101	119	111

TABLE IV: NUMBER OF CHILDREN YOU HAVE HAD - BY AGE (Continued)

Question: How many children have you ever had? Please count all that were born alive at any time.

Responses: 0 = 0; 1 = 1; 2 = 2; 3 = 3; 4 = 4; 5 = 5; 6 = 6; 7 = 7; 8 = 8+

		YEAR															
AGE	RESP	'72	'73	'74	'75	'76	'77	'78	'80	'82	'83	'84	'85	'86	'87	'88	'89
66+	0	21%	25%	17%	21%	19%	21%	25%	20%	16%	17%	22%	18%	23%	18%	18%	18%
	1	16	13	21	14	19	15	17	14	21	16	18	17	14	15	18	13
	2	20	21	25	23	22	27	21	26	23	23	15	22	25	22	20	28
	3	13	17	12	17	12	15	13	12	17	21	17	17	12	19	18	21
	4	13	11	7	11	14	8	9	14	10	7	12	10	12	10	11	7
	5	7	4	5	4	4	6	4	7	4	5	5	6	4	4	5	8
	6	3	4	5	1	2	3	5	2	5	3	2	4	5	4	4	3
	7	3	2	3	2	5	2	3	2	2	4	2	1	2	2	1	1
	8	4	6	4	7	4	3	3	2	3	4	7	4	3	6	5	1
# SURVEYED		215	200	226	230	251	211	231	242	259	241	230	260	264	252	280	275

****

CURRENT EMPLOYMENT STATUS

TABLE I: CURRENT EMPLOYMENT STATUS - BY TOTAL POPULATION

Question: Last week were you working full time, part-time, going to school, keeping house, or what?

Responses:

FT = Working full time
TM = With a job, but not at work because of temporary illness, vacation, strike
SC = In school
PT = Working part time
UN = Unemployed, laid off, looking for work
RT = Retired
HK = Keeping house

	YEAR															
RESPONSE	'72	'73	'74	'75	'76	'77	'78	'80	'82	'83	'84	'85	'86	'87	'88	'89
FT	47%	44%	43%	42%	42%	51%	48%	48%	47%	47%	49%	49%	48%	53%	50%	50%
PT	8	9	7	10	9	7	9	9	10	11	11	11	10	11	11	10
TM	2	2	3	2	2	3	3	2	3	2	2	3	2	1	2	3
UN	3	2	4	4	4	2	3	3	5	5	3	3	2	2	2	2
RT	9	10	11	11	12	10	10	10	12	10	11	13	14	14	15	14
SC	4	4	3	3	3	3	2	3	2	2	3	3	3	2	4	3
HK	27	28	28	27	29	24	25	25	21	22	21	18	21	16	16	18
# SURVEYED	1589	1485	1474	1470	1490	1507	1502	1443	1475	1572	1459	1519	1447	1442	1466	1515

TABLE II: CURRENT EMPLOYMENT STATUS - BY SEX

Question: Last week were you working full time, part-time, going to school, keeping house, or what?

Responses:

FT = Working full time
TM = With a job, but not at work because of temporary illness, vacation, strike
SC = In school
PT = Working part time
UN = Unemployed, laid off, looking for work
RT = Retired
HK = Keeping house

		YEAR															
SEX	RESP	'72	'73	'74	'75	'76	'77	'78	'80	'82	'83	'84	'85	'86	'87	'88	'89
M	FT	69%	65%	61%	59%	60%	67%	70%	66%	60%	62%	64%	63%	67%	68%	63%	67%
A	PT	5	5	4	7	7	5	4	7	6	9	8	9	8	9	8	7
L	TM	3	3	4	3	3	3	4	3	4	3	3	2	1	1	2	3
E	UN	5	4	5	8	8	5	5	4	8	9	6	5	3	3	3	3
	RT	12	18	20	18	18	16	15	16	18	14	14	16	17	17	17	16
	SC	5	5	4	4	4	3	2	3	2	1	3	3	2	1	5	3
	HK	1	0	1	1	0	1	0	1	1	2	2	1	1	1	1	1
# SURVEYED		796	687	685	655	662	679	632	628	627	681	588	681	608	629	634	651
SEX	RESP	'72	'73	'74	'75	'76	'77	'78	'80	'82	'83	'84	'85	'86	'87	'88	'89
F	FT	25%	26%	27%	29%	27%	39%	31%	34%	37%	36%	39%	37%	34%	42%	39%	38%
E	PT	10	13	10	12	10	9	13	11	13	12	13	13	12	13	14	12
M	TM	2	1	2	1	1	2	2	2	2	2	2	3	3	1	2	3
A	UN	1	1	2	1	2	1	1	2	2	3	1	1	1	1	1	0
L	RT	6	4	3	5	7	5	7	6	7	7	8	11	11	11	12	13
E	SC	2	3	2	3	2	2	3	3	2	2	3	3	3	4	4	3
	HK	54	53	52	48	51	43	43	43	37	38	34	32	36	28	27	30
# SURVEYED		793	798	789	815	828	828	870	815	848	891	871	838	839	813	832	864

TABLE III: CURRENT EMPLOYMENT STATUS - BY RACE

Question: Last week were you working full time, part-time, going to school, keeping house, or what?

Responses:

FT = Working full time
TM = With a job, but not at work because of temporary illness, vacation, strike
SC = In school
PT = Working part time
UN = Unemployed, laid off, looking for work
RT= Retired
HK = Keeping house

		YEAR															
RACE	RESP	'72	'73	'74	'75	'76	'77	'78	'80	'82	'83	'84	'85	'86	'87	'88	'89
WHITE	FT	47%	44%	43%	43%	42%	52%	48%	48%	47%	48%	50%	49%	48%	53%	49%	51%
	PT	7	9	8	10	9	7	9	10	11	11	12	11	10	11	12	10
	TM	2	2	3	2	2	3	3	3	3	2	2	2	2	1	2	3
	UN	3	2	3	4	4	2	2	3	4	5	3	2	2	2	2	1
	RT	9	11	11	12	12	10	10	10	12	11	11	14	14	14	16	15
	SC	4	4	3	3	3	2	2	2	2	2	3	3	2	3	4	3
	HK	29	29	28	27	29	24	25	24	22	22	20	19	21	16	16	17
# SURVEYED		1331	1291	1295	1307	1354	1320	1331	1298	1295	1394	1241	1327	1234	1211	1221	1303
RACE	RESP	'72	'73	'74	'75	'76	'77	'78	'80	'82	'83	'84	'85	'86	'87	'88	'89
BLACK	FT	49%	42%	42%	36%	38%	49%	49%	42%	42%	41%	47%	47%	46%	53%	51%	46%
	PT	9	7	4	12	7	7	7	7	10	11	8	12	12	8	10	9
	TM	3	6	5	1	4	3	2	1	3	1	2	2	3	1	2	3
	UN	4	6	6	7	9	3	6	4	8	8	5	5	4	3	5	2
	RT	11	8	13	9	14	12	10	10	10	9	10	13	12	14	10	9
	SC	4	4	3	6	6	3	3	5	6	3	2	4	5	2	6	4
	HK	19	27	27	29	22	23	23	30	20	28	25	16	18	20	16	28
# SURVEYED		254	181	172	159	127	172	155	135	153	160	166	148	177	178	185	152
RACE	RESP	'72	'73	'74	'75	'76	'77	'78	'80	'82	'83	'84	'85	'86	'87	'88	'89
OTHER	FT	0%	54%	14%	75%	67%	67%	38%	70%	63%	50%	46%	55%	58%	45%	50%	45%
	PT	0	8	14	0	0	7	19	0	0	0	10	11	8	17	12	8
	TM	25	0	0	0	0	0	0	0	4	6	4	7	0	0	5	2
	UN	0	0	0	0	0	0	6	0	4	11	6	9	3	6	3	5
	RT	25	8	0	0	0	0	13	0	0	11	2	5	3	11	7	5
	SC	0	8	14	0	0	13	6	10	7	6	6	2	3	4	7	13
	HK	0	23	57	25	33	13	19	20	22	17	27	11	25	17	17	22
# SURVEYED		4	13	7	4	9	15	16	10	27	18	52	44	36	53	60	60

TABLE IV: CURRENT EMPLOYMENT STATUS - BY AGE

Question: Last week were you working full time, part-time, going to school, keeping house, or what?

Responses:

FT = Working full time
TM = With a job, but not at work because of temporary illness, vacation, strike
SC = In school
PT = Working part time
UN = Unemployed, laid off, looking for work
RT = Retired
HK = Keeping house

		YEAR															
AGE	RESP	'72	'73	'74	'75	'76	'77	'78	'80	'82	'83	'84	'85	'86	'87	'88	'89
18-23	FT	39%	36%	46%	38%	37%	49%	48%	49%	42%	43%	43%	42%	38%	42%	33%	36%
	PT	12	10	8	14	17	10	16	10	20	18	18	23	27	22	21	17
	TM	1	1	1	1	2	2	1	1	1	1	1	1	2	1	1	2
	UN	7	7	10	10	8	5	4	6	10	11	8	5	3	6	7	5
	RT	0	0	0	0	0	0	0	0	0	0	0	0	0	1	0	0
	SC	23	23	16	17	19	16	12	13	14	9	18	23	19	14	24	26
	HK	18	23	18	20	17	17	20	21	13	17	13	7	11	14	15	13
# SURVEYED		165	170	166	171	162	164	161	154	144	127	159	131	106	125	140	136
AGE	RESP	'72	'73	'74	'75	'76	'77	'78	'80	'82	'83	'84	'85	'86	'87	'88	'89
24-29	FT	57%	53%	47%	51%	57%	66%	64%	59%	59%	57%	60%	64%	65%	70%	61%	67%
	PT	8	10	9	10	12	6	7	11	11	12	12	13	7	10	15	12
	TM	3	1	2	3	2	2	3	3	4	5	1	2	2	3	1	2
	UN	7	2	7	6	5	4	2	4	8	7	4	4	4	4	3	1
	RT	0	0	0	0	0	0	0	0	0	0	0	0	0	0	0	0
	SC	4	6	4	4	3	2	5	5	5	3	3	2	5	5	7	3
	HK	23	27	30	27	21	19	19	16	13	19	19	15	15	10	11	12
# SURVEYED		230	212	211	232	226	202	241	201	244	286	230	217	216	191	214	201
AGE	RESP	'72	'73	'74	'75	'76	'77	'78	'80	'82	'83	'84	'85	'86	'87	'88	'89
30-35	FT	55%	51%	53%	54%	49%	65%	61%	65%	65%	61%	63%	67%	64%	70%	76%	66%
	PT	7	7	12	8	8	7	10	7	13	10	13	12	10	11	8	11
	TM	2	4	2	2	3	4	4	2	3	2	1	2	3	1	1	5
	UN	2	2	2	6	5	3	3	5	5	6	2	3	2	2	1	1
	RT	0	0	1	0	0	0	0	0	0	0	0	0	0	0	0	0
	SC	4	2	3	5	1	2	1	2	0	1	2	2	2	1	1	1
	HK	31	34	28	24	34	20	22	18	14	20	20	14	18	14	12	15
# SURVEYED		186	166	173	168	186	187	228	213	204	236	200	212	221	219	193	210
AGE	RESP	'72	'73	'74	'75	'76	'77	'78	'80	'82	'83	'84	'85	'86	'87	'88	'89
36-41	FT	51%	62%	46%	55%	59%	65%	56%	69%	69%	64%	66%	66%	72%	77%	70%	70%
	PT	8	8	7	16	6	6	10	9	7	8	14	10	12	8	8	11
	TM	3	1	4	3	1	3	3	3	4	4	3	3	1	2	4	2
	UN	3	1	6	5	4	2	3	1	3	7	5	2	2	2	2	4
	RT	0	0	0	1	1	0	0	0	1	0	1	1	0	1	0	0
	SC	2	1	3	1	2	2	0	2	0	2	1	2	0	2	4	1
	HK	34	27	34	21	27	23	29	17	15	15	11	16	13	9	13	12
# SURVEYED		128	172	152	154	158	168	160	149	144	171	185	182	187	183	192	196

TABLE IV: CURRENT EMPLOYMENT STATUS - BY AGE (Continued)

Question: Last week were you working full time, part-time, going to school, keeping house, or what?

Responses:

FT = Working full time
TM = With a job, but not at work because of temporary illness, vacation, strike
SC = In school
PT = Working part time
UN = Unemployed, laid off, looking for work
RT = Retired
HK = Keeping house

		YEAR															
AGE	RESP	'72	'73	'74	'75	'76	'77	'78	'80	'82	'83	'84	'85	'86	'87	'88	'89
42-47	FT	62%	54%	58%	56%	49%	58%	67%	65%	65%	59%	65%	74%	60%	65%	74%	66%
	PT	7	15	7	8	15	9	8	9	8	11	11	8	15	17	10	15
	TM	3	3	4	1	4	1	3	3	4	4	2	2	3	2	3	3
	UN	2	2	1	6	6	3	6	3	6	6	3	3	3	3	3	1
	RT	0	0	1	2	1	0	1	2	0	0	0	0	1	0	1	1
	SC	0	1	1	1	1	0	1	1	0	0	1	0	1	1	2	0
	HK	26	25	28	27	25	28	15	18	17	20	18	12	17	13	8	14
# SURVEYED		182	144	151	142	110	141	116	116	118	143	125	124	139	156	155	156
AGE	RESP	'72	'73	'74	'75	'76	'77	'78	'80	'82	'83	'84	'85	'86	'87	'88	'89
48-53	FT	64%	50%	59%	51%	56%	68%	63%	58%	56%	52%	67%	64%	57%	66%	68%	68%
	PT	5	10	5	12	5	8	6	9	11	16	5	10	7	8	10	8
	TM	3	3	2	2	2	2	6	2	1	4	3	6	4	2	4	5
	UN	1	3	2	3	3	3	2	3	3	6	3	3	5	0	3	1
	RT	2	1	3	4	2	5	2	1	5	4	2	3	2	7	3	1
	SC	1	0	1	0	0	1	1	0	1	0	0	2	1	0	1	0
	HK	25	32	29	28	32	13	20	28	23	19	20	12	25	17	10	17
# SURVEYED		187	145	146	139	132	152	126	119	110	114	99	130	105	123	91	136
AGE	RESP	'72	'73	'74	'75	'76	'77	'78	'80	'82	'83	'84	'85	'86	'87	'88	'89
54-59	FT	59%	53%	53%	51%	55%	54%	48%	50%	49%	52%	53%	48%	48%	59%	55%	61%
	PT	6	8	5	12	7	7	12	14	10	10	10	8	9	13	14	6
	TM	4	4	7	3	3	4	2	5	3	5	5	7	3	2	1	3
	UN	3	1	2	0	4	1	1	1	1	6	4	7	2	2	2	1
	RT	3	3	10	7	4	7	8	6	7	3	6	10	11	4	8	5
	SC	0	0	0	0	1	0	0	1	0	2	2	0	1	1	0	2
	HK	25	30	24	28	27	26	30	24	29	22	20	21	25	19	19	20
# SURVEYED		151	152	136	120	128	164	130	131	137	124	112	130	96	94	84	93
AGE	RESP	'72	'73	'74	'75	'76	'77	'78	'80	'82	'83	'84	'85	'86	'87	'88	'89
60-65	FT	38%	36%	36%	35%	27%	39%	30%	26%	32%	35%	32%	30%	37%	35%	28%	27%
	PT	8	11	7	6	7	6	10	8	6	8	8	13	5	9	12	5
	TM	4	2	6	5	2	1	2	5	4	1	4	2	1	1	4	0
	UN	2	1	2	0	3	1	3	0	5	2	2	2	1	0	2	1
	RT	19	28	23	20	19	21	18	27	15	23	27	34	25	28	32	37
	SC	0	0	0	0	1	1	0	0	0	1	0	0	0	0	0	0
	HK	29	23	27	34	42	31	37	34	38	30	28	20	30	26	22	29
# SURVEYED		140	120	106	108	132	114	105	115	111	130	113	127	110	95	118	110

TABLE IV: CURRENT EMPLOYMENT STATUS - BY AGE (Continued)

Question: Last week were you working full time, part-time, going to school, keeping house, or what?

Responses:
FT = Working full time
TM = With a job, but not at work because of temporary illness, vacation, strike
SC = In school
PT = Working part time
UN = Unemployed, laid off, looking for work
RT = Retired
HK = Keeping house

AGE	RESP	'72	'73	'74	'75	'76	'77	'78	'80	'82	'83	'84	'85	'86	'87	'88	'89
		YEAR															
66+	FT	5%	6%	5%	5%	3%	4%	3%	4%	5%	5%	8%	4%	3%	6%	4%	6%
	PT	7	5	5	5	4	4	6	10	7	7	6	7	4	7	7	5
	TM	1	1	1	0	0	1	2	0	0	0	1	0	1	0	1	1
	UN	0	1	0	0	0	0	1	0	0	0	0	1	0	0	0	0
	RT	50	57	54	55	56	52	54	45	54	52	49	54	58	62	60	62
	SC	0	0	0	0	0	0	0	0	0	0	0	0	0	0	0	0
	HK	36	32	34	35	35	38	35	41	33	35	35	34	33	25	27	27
# SURVEYED		215	200	227	231	250	208	228	236	252	235	231	259	260	252	275	273

****

EMPLOYMENT HISTORY

TABLE I: EMPLOYMENT HISTORY - BY TOTAL POPULATION

Question: Did you ever work for as long as one year? NOTE: Asked only of respondents who answered retired, in school or keeping house to the question "Current Employment Status."

Responses: Yes; No

RESPONSE	'72	'73	'74	'75	'76	'77	'78	'80	'82	'83	'84	'85	'86	'87	'88	'89
	YEAR															
YES	75%	77%	80%	79%	78%	80%	79%	79%	83%	82%	83%	85%	82%	86%	84%	83%
NO	25	23	20	21	22	20	21	21	17	18	17	15	18	14	16	17
# SURVEYED	658	649	641	636	658	572	598	570	551	569	509	538	562	491	523	554

TABLE II: EMPLOYMENT HISTORY - BY SEX

Question: Did you ever work for as long as one year? NOTE: Asked only of respondents who answered retired, in school, keeping house or other to the question "Current Employment Status."

Responses: Yes; No

		YEAR															
SEX	RESP	'72	'73	'74	'75	'76	'77	'78	'80	'82	'83	'84	'85	'86	'87	'88	'89
M	YES	84%	86%	92%	90%	91%	92%	94%	94%	93%	95%	93%	91%	94%	97%	90%	90%
	NO	16	14	8	10	9	8	6	6	7	5	7	9	6	3	10	10
# SURVEYED		153	174	179	169	159	150	120	138	146	127	121	148	134	133	153	141
SEX	RESP	'72	'73	'74	'75	'76	'77	'78	'80	'82	'83	'84	'85	'86	'87	'88	'89
F	YES	73%	74%	75%	75%	74%	76%	75%	74%	80%	78%	79%	83%	79%	82%	81%	81%
	NO	27	26	25	25	26	24	25	26	20	22	21	17	21	18	19	19
# SURVEYED		505	475	462	467	499	422	478	432	405	442	388	390	428	358	370	413

TABLE III: EMPLOYMENT HISTORY - BY RACE

Question: Did you ever work for as long as one year? NOTE: Asked only of respondents who answered retired, in school, keeping house or other to the question "Current Employment Status."

Responses: Yes; No

		YEAR															
RACE	RESP	'72	'73	'74	'75	'76	'77	'78	'80	'82	'83	'84	'85	'86	'87	'88	'89
WHITE	YES	76%	77%	81%	78%	78%	82%	80%	80%	84%	82%	84%	85%	83%	87%	85%	85%
	NO	24	23	19	22	23	18	20	20	16	18	16	15	17	13	15	15
# SURVEYED		561	571	560	562	600	499	534	501	484	494	425	477	481	398	443	463
RACE	RESP	'72	'73	'74	'75	'76	'77	'78	'80	'82	'83	'84	'85	'86	'87	'88	'89
BLACK	YES	74%	77%	79%	82%	84%	70%	69%	70%	81%	81%	85%	87%	75%	80%	75%	79%
	NO	26	23	21	18	16	30	31	30	19	19	15	13	25	20	25	21
# SURVEYED		96	73	76	73	55	69	58	66	59	69	66	53	69	76	61	66
RACE	RESP	'72	'73	'74	'75	'76	'77	'78	'80	'82	'83	'84	'85	'86	'87	'88	'89
OTHER	YES	00%	80%	40%	100%	67%	50%	83%	67%	75%	83%	44%	75%	75%	71%	79%	64%
	NO	0	20	60	0	33	50	17	33	25	17	56	25	25	29	21	36
# SURVEYED		1	5	5	1	3	4	6	3	8	6	18	8	12	17	19	25

TABLE IV: EMPLOYMENT HISTORY - BY AGE

Question: Did you ever work for as long as one year? NOTE: Asked only of respondents who answered retired, in school, keeping house or other to the question "Current Employment Status."

Responses: Yes; No

		YEAR															
AGE	RESP	'72	'73	'74	'75	'76	'77	'78	'80	'82	'83	'84	'85	'86	'87	'88	'89
18-23	YES	36%	41%	40%	44%	38%	44%	39%	34%	40%	49%	50%	44%	50%	39%	44%	42%
	NO	64	59	60	56	62	56	61	66	60	51	50	56	50	61	56	58
# SURVEYED		72	78	58	66	58	54	54	53	43	35	50	41	34	36	55	55
AGE	RESP	'72	'73	'74	'75	'76	'77	'78	'80	'82	'83	'84	'85	'86	'87	'88	'89
24-29	YES	67%	74%	81%	77%	65%	73%	71%	68%	73%	69%	71%	81%	69%	68%	78%	76%
	NO	33	26	19	23	35	27	29	32	27	31	29	19	31	32	22	24
# SURVEYED		63	68	73	73	55	44	59	44	45	65	51	36	45	31	41	33
AGE	RESP	'72	'73	'74	'75	'76	'77	'78	'80	'82	'83	'84	'85	'86	'87	'88	'89
30-35	YES	82%	80%	75%	71%	83%	73%	76%	74%	90%	80%	86%	85%	78%	83%	79%	67%
	NO	18	20	25	29	17	27	24	26	10	20	14	15	22	17	21	33
# SURVEYED		65	61	56	52	65	41	55	47	29	51	43	34	45	36	28	36
AGE	RESP	'72	'73	'74	'75	'76	'77	'78	'80	'82	'83	'84	'85	'86	'87	'88	'89
36-41	YES	80%	80%	84%	91%	93%	83%	80%	72%	92%	78%	82%	89%	85%	88%	85%	85%
	NO	20	20	16	9	7	17	20	28	8	22	18	11	15	12	15	15
# SURVEYED		45	51	56	34	46	41	46	29	26	32	22	36	26	25	33	27
AGE	RESP	'72	'73	'74	'75	'76	'77	'78	'80	'82	'83	'84	'85	'86	'87	'88	'89
42-47	YES	65%	85%	71%	81%	73%	80%	82%	84%	81%	83%	75%	80%	76%	83%	100%	93%
	NO	35	15	29	19	27	20	18	16	19	17	25	20	24	17	0	7
# SURVEYED		52	40	45	43	33	46	22	25	21	30	24	15	29	23	19	28
AGE	RESP	'72	'73	'74	'75	'76	'77	'78	'80	'82	'83	'84	'85	'86	'87	'88	'89
48-53	YES	87%	74%	74%	83%	71%	87%	86%	87%	76%	79%	88%	83%	72%	94%	100%	88%
	NO	13	26	26	17	29	13	14	13	24	21	12	17	28	6	0	12
# SURVEYED		53	54	47	46	45	30	35	38	33	28	25	23	32	32	14	26
AGE	RESP	'72	'73	'74	'75	'76	'77	'78	'80	'82	'83	'84	'85	'86	'87	'88	'89
54-59	YES	77%	87%	88%	90%	83%	83%	80%	87%	89%	88%	100%	95%	95%	93%	88%	91%
	NO	23	13	13	10	17	17	20	13	11	12	0	5	5	7	13	9
# SURVEYED		47	55	48	48	41	59	56	46	57	43	33	44	39	27	24	32
AGE	RESP	'72	'73	'74	'75	'76	'77	'78	'80	'82	'83	'84	'85	'86	'87	'88	'89
60-65	YES	86%	77%	85%	86%	90%	90%	95%	89%	91%	92%	92%	92%	91%	97%	92%	92%
	NO	14	23	15	14	10	10	5	11	9	8	8	8	9	3	8	8
# SURVEYED		72	62	55	64	83	63	60	74	64	72	62	72	66	58	65	73

TABLE IV: EMPLOYMENT HISTORY - BY AGE (Continued)

Question: Did you ever work for as long as one year? NOTE: Asked only of respondents who answered retired, in school, keeping house or other to the question "Current Employment Status."

Responses: Yes; No

		YEAR															
AGE	RESP	'72	'73	'74	'75	'76	'77	'78	'80	'82	'83	'84	'85	'86	'87	'88	'89
66+	YES	86%	89%	92%	85%	83%	88%	84%	88%	89%	88%	89%	88%	87%	91%	89%	91%
	NO	14	11	9	15	17	12	16	12	11	12	11	12	13	9	11	9
# SURVEYED		187	177	200	207	230	193	206	208	227	211	195	231	243	221	244	242

****

HOURS CURRENTLY EMPLOYED

TABLE I: HOURS CURRENTLY EMPLOYED - BY TOTAL POPULATION

Question: How many hours did you work last week, at all jobs? NOTE: Question not asked in 1972.

Responses: 0 - 9; 10 - 19; 20 - 29; 30 - 39; 40 - 49; 50 - 59; 60 - 69; 70 - 79; 80+

	YEAR														
RESPONSE	'73	'74	'75	'76	'77	'78	'80	'82	'83	'84	'85	'86	'87	'88	'89
0 - 9	2%	1%	2%	2%	1%	2%	2%	3%	2%	2%	3%	2%	2%	2%	2%
10-19	6	6	6	7	4	5	5	5	5	5	4	4	5	4	5
20-29	9	7	9	7	6	6	8	7	7	9	8	7	9	7	9
30-39	14	12	14	15	14	15	12	17	18	12	13	14	12	12	12
40-49	51	57	52	53	57	52	53	49	49	50	49	47	49	50	47
50-59	9	10	9	8	9	10	9	10	9	12	10	14	11	13	14
60-69	5	4	4	6	5	5	6	6	6	5	7	8	8	7	7
70-79	3	1	1	1	1	3	2	1	2	3	2	3	2	2	2
80+	1	1	1	1	1	2	3	2	2	2	3	2	2	2	2
# SURVEYED	783	741	764	747	877	855	822	847	911	876	912	835	921	890	907

TABLE II: HOURS CURRENTLY EMPLOYED - BY SEX

Question: How many hours did you work last week, at all jobs? NOTE: Question not asked in 1972.

Responses: 0 - 9; 10 - 19; 20 - 29; 30 - 39; 40 - 49; 50 - 59; 60 - 69; 70 - 79; 80+

		YEAR														
SEX	RESP	'73	'74	'75	'76	'77	'78	'80	'82	'83	'84	'85	'86	'87	'88	'89
M	0 - 9	1%	1%	1%	1%	1%	0%	2%	2%	1%	1%	1%	1%	1%	1%	1%
A	10-19	1	2	3	4	3	2	2	2	3	4	3	2	2	2	3
L	20-29	4	5	5	5	2	3	6	4	4	5	7	4	7	4	6
E	30-39	9	8	10	9	10	8	8	10	12	6	9	10	8	8	7
	40-49	57	62	58	56	59	57	55	53	51	53	50	47	51	52	48
	50-59	14	13	13	12	14	15	11	15	12	16	14	19	14	17	16
	60-69	8	5	7	9	7	6	9	10	10	8	9	9	11	9	11
	70-79	4	2	2	2	2	5	3	2	4	4	3	4	2	4	4
	80+	2	2	1	2	2	4	4	3	3	3	4	3	3	2	3
# SURVEYED		475	447	431	442	488	471	458	418	481	421	491	453	479	447	474
SEX	RESP	'73	'74	'75	'76	'77	'78	'80	'82	'83	'84	'85	'86	'87	'88	'89
F	0 - 9	3%	1%	3%	3%	2%	5%	2%	4%	3%	3%	5%	4%	3%	4%	3%
E	10-19	13	13	11	10	7	9	9	8	7	6	5	6	8	7	6
M	20-29	17	10	14	10	11	11	10	10	10	13	10	9	11	10	12
A	30-39	22	18	20	23	19	22	16	24	24	17	18	18	17	16	17
L	40-49	41	49	45	49	54	46	50	45	47	47	47	47	46	47	45
E	50-59	2	6	4	3	4	4	5	5	5	8	7	8	8	9	12
	60-69	1	2	0	1	3	3	3	3	2	3	5	6	4	6	3
	70-79	0	0	1	0	1	1	1	1	1	2	1	1	2	0	0
	80+	0	0	2	1	0	0	1	0	1	1	2	1	1	1	0
# SURVEYED		308	294	333	305	389	384	364	429	430	455	421	382	442	443	433

TABLE III: HOURS CURRENTLY EMPLOYED - BY RACE

Question: How many hours did you work last week, at all jobs? NOTE: Question not asked in 1972.

Responses: 0 - 9; 10 - 19; 20 - 29; 30 - 39; 40 - 49; 50 - 59; 60 - 69; 70 - 79; 80+

		YEAR														
RACE	RESP	'73	'74	'75	'76	'77	'78	'80	'82	'83	'84	'85	'86	'87	'88	'89
WHITE	0 - 9	2%	1%	2%	2%	1%	2%	2%	3%	2%	2%	3%	2%	2%	2%	2%
	10-19	6	6	6	6	5	5	5	5	5	5	3	4	5	5	5
	20-29	9	7	9	7	6	7	8	6	7	10	9	6	9	7	9
	30-39	14	12	14	14	14	14	12	17	17	11	13	14	12	12	11
	40-49	50	56	52	52	56	52	52	49	49	50	48	46	48	48	46
	50-59	9	11	10	9	10	10	9	10	10	12	11	15	12	14	15
	60-69	6	4	5	6	5	5	7	6	6	5	8	8	8	8	8
	70-79	3	2	1	1	1	3	3	1	2	3	3	3	2	2	2
	80+	1	1	1	1	1	2	3	2	2	2	3	2	2	1	2
# SURVEYED		687	660	684	685	770	759	749	750	820	755	795	711	782	743	793
RACE	RESP	'73	'74	'75	'76	'77	'78	'80	'82	'83	'84	'85	'86	'87	'88	'89
BLACK	0 - 9	2%	1%	1%	2%	2%	2%	5%	3%	1%	1%	5%	3%	3%	3%	4%
	10-19	6	5	10	9	1	5	6	4	6	5	9	5	7	3	6
	20-29	7	3	12	7	8	3	6	13	7	8	5	9	7	8	7
	30-39	16	13	16	21	17	17	14	20	24	22	15	11	11	12	12
	40-49	56	70	52	57	61	59	61	48	46	48	59	55	57	54	57
	50-59	9	5	6	0	6	9	6	5	1	8	2	7	8	12	8
	60-69	3	1	1	2	2	1	2	8	9	3	2	7	4	5	1
	70-79	1	0	0	0	2	3	0	0	1	4	0	2	2	1	4
	80+	0	3	1	2	0	0	2	1	4	1	3	1	3	3	1
# SURVEYED		88	79	77	56	96	87	66	80	82	92	88	100	106	111	83
RACE	RESP	'73	'74	'75	'76	'77	'78	'80	'82	'83	'84	'85	'86	'87	'88	'89
OTHER	0 - 9	0%	0%	0%	0%	0%	0%	0%	0%	0%	0%	7%	8%	3%	0%	0%
	10-19	13	50	0	0	9	22	0	0	0	3	3	0	6	3	0
	20-29	0	0	0	0	0	11	0	0	0	14	10	0	12	8	6
	30-39	0	0	33	0	9	0	29	12	0	14	17	17	15	14	32
	40-49	88	50	67	100	55	56	43	71	56	55	41	50	48	61	45
	50-59	0	0	0	0	0	0	0	12	0	3	14	13	12	6	10
	60-69	0	0	0	0	9	0	14	6	11	7	3	8	3	6	6
	70-79	0	0	0	0	9	0	0	0	22	3	3	0	0	0	0
	80+	0	0	0	0	9	11	14	0	11	0	0	4	0	3	0
# SURVEYED		8	2	3	6	11	9	7	17	9	29	29	24	33	36	31

TABLE IV: HOURS CURRENTLY EMPLOYED - BY AGE

Question: How many hours did you work last week, at all jobs? NOTE: Question not asked in 1972.

Responses: 0 - 9; 10 - 19; 20 - 29; 30 - 39; 40 - 49; 50 - 59; 60 - 69; 70 - 79; 80+

		YEAR														
AGE	RESP	'73	'74	'75	'76	'77	'78	'80	'82	'83	'84	'85	'86	'87	'88	'89
18-23	0 - 9	3%	0%	6%	3%	4%	0%	2%	7%	1%	4%	6%	4%	4%	3%	7%
	10-19	8	9	7	10	7	9	2	11	8	10	2	13	9	9	7
	20-29	8	9	11	15	6	13	12	11	10	11	20	12	21	13	13
	30-39	16	9	15	20	16	17	13	19	19	14	12	16	12	23	20
	40-49	57	67	57	47	54	48	58	41	46	45	41	46	42	35	34
	50-59	5	4	3	1	9	6	3	2	10	8	12	7	7	13	6
	60-69	0	1	0	3	2	4	8	8	4	3	5	0	5	1	8
	70-79	3	0	0	0	1	0	0	0	1	1	1	1	0	1	3
	80+	1	1	1	0	0	4	1	1	0	2	1	0	0	1	3
# SURVEYED		79	91	89	88	97	102	91	90	78	97	85	69	81	75	71
AGE	RESP	'73	'74	'75	'76	'77	'78	'80	'82	'83	'84	'85	'86	'87	'88	'89
24-29	0 - 9	3%	0%	3%	1%	1%	1%	1%	5%	3%	1%	2%	0%	1%	1%	3%
	10-19	4	8	5	7	3	2	5	2	4	2	6	2	5	5	3
	20-29	11	6	8	6	3	5	9	7	5	11	5	6	8	10	8
	30-39	11	16	13	16	14	15	11	16	18	11	11	10	12	11	15
	40-49	56	54	56	51	63	61	54	48	52	56	54	54	50	51	45
	50-59	5	9	9	8	6	6	6	13	11	13	10	15	10	13	15
	60-69	5	3	4	7	4	5	6	8	5	2	7	7	8	6	5
	70-79	3	2	1	1	2	1	3	1	2	3	2	3	4	2	4
	80+	3	1	1	3	2	2	5	1	2	1	2	4	3	1	3
# SURVEYED		133	118	142	153	145	171	141	170	199	166	167	157	153	163	156
AGE	RESP	'73	'74	'75	'76	'77	'78	'80	'82	'83	'84	'85	'86	'87	'88	'89
30-35	0 - 9	0%	2%	0%	1%	0%	3%	1%	3%	4%	3%	3%	3%	1%	2%	1%
	10-19	5	8	6	6	4	4	2	4	4	4	4	2	5	3	6
	20-29	8	5	6	4	9	3	6	7	5	9	7	7	6	4	10
	30-39	10	16	19	19	9	16	10	17	17	11	10	14	10	10	9
	40-49	52	52	47	52	56	53	60	53	54	51	55	48	48	55	44
	50-59	14	7	12	8	13	12	10	8	6	12	10	14	16	12	18
	60-69	6	6	7	9	8	5	4	5	7	7	7	7	11	11	7
	70-79	4	1	1	1	2	3	3	3	2	2	3	3	1	1	2
	80+	0	2	3	1	0	1	5	0	2	1	2	1	3	2	2
# SURVEYED		96	111	105	106	133	160	153	159	168	150	168	163	178	163	163
AGE	RESP	'73	'74	'75	'76	'77	'78	'80	'82	'83	'84	'85	'86	'87	'88	'89
36-41	0 - 9	2%	1%	0%	0%	2%	1%	3%	1%	1%	2%	1%	1%	3%	2%	1%
	10-19	5	4	7	4	5	5	3	1	5	8	2	4	3	2	3
	20-29	5	6	11	7	3	9	3	5	5	5	7	6	5	3	8
	30-39	19	11	14	12	12	10	10	15	20	13	12	17	14	8	9
	40-49	48	56	50	59	63	41	56	59	43	45	44	40	52	53	53
	50-59	9	10	7	12	10	20	12	11	11	15	15	16	13	15	11
	60-69	8	5	8	5	3	5	9	6	9	7	10	14	7	11	9
	70-79	3	5	2	1	1	5	3	1	2	2	4	1	3	3	4
	80+	1	2	0	2	3	5	0	3	3	3	6	0	3	3	3
# SURVEYED		120	81	108	104	119	105	116	109	122	146	139	154	153	150	158

TABLE IV: HOURS CURRENTLY EMPLOYED - BY AGE (Continued)

Question: How many hours did you work last week, at all jobs? NOTE: Question not asked in 1972.

Responses: 0 - 9; 10 - 19; 20 - 29; 30 - 39; 40 - 49; 50 - 59; 60 - 69; 70 - 79; 80+

		YEAR														
AGE	RESP	'73	'74	'75	'76	'77	'78	'80	'82	'83	'84	'85	'86	'87	'88	'89
42-47	0 - 9	1%	0%	1%	4%	0%	2%	1%	2%	1%	1%	2%	5%	1%	1%	3%
	10-19	8	6	3	7	3	2	4	5	5	1	2	2	4	2	6
	20-29	10	5	6	7	7	3	6	3	4	12	2	4	13	7	7
	30-39	15	11	13	17	13	14	16	10	18	14	25	12	12	13	12
	40-49	46	54	51	46	57	59	46	58	47	47	44	47	48	49	45
	50-59	10	17	22	9	11	9	7	12	12	12	11	15	10	17	17
	60-69	4	5	2	6	6	6	11	6	7	5	8	11	8	6	8
	70-79	4	1	1	3	1	3	6	0	4	6	4	3	2	2	2
	80+	1	0	0	1	2	1	4	3	2	2	3	2	2	3	0
# SURVEYED		99	98	90	70	95	87	85	86	100	95	102	102	126	128	126
AGE	RESP	'73	'74	'75	'76	'77	'78	'80	'82	'83	'84	'85	'86	'87	'88	'89
48-53	0 - 9	0%	0%	5%	1%	1%	3%	1%	0%	0%	1%	2%	2%	1%	1%	1%
	10-19	6	1	8	4	2	2	6	4	5	0	5	2	2	4	2
	20-29	10	4	6	4	5	6	6	1	10	7	8	6	8	3	8
	30-39	10	10	13	14	15	13	10	23	18	13	11	17	12	14	10
	40-49	45	70	57	56	54	55	57	51	49	59	48	40	53	51	56
	50-59	16	12	8	10	10	11	10	11	5	10	10	14	12	11	14
	60-69	7	2	3	7	9	3	6	7	6	4	10	12	5	10	9
	70-79	3	0	1	5	3	6	1	1	3	4	1	5	2	6	0
	80+	1	1	0	0	2	1	1	1	3	1	3	3	4	0	1
# SURVEYED		86	93	88	81	116	88	79	74	77	71	96	65	91	71	104
AGE	RESP	'73	'74	'75	'76	'77	'78	'80	'82	'83	'84	'85	'86	'87	'88	'89
54-59	0 - 9	2%	1%	1%	1%	1%	3%	4%	2%	0%	1%	4%	2%	5%	0%	0%
	10-19	3	1	7	3	5	6	7	6	4	3	3	5	8	9	3
	20-29	8	8	10	8	7	4	7	7	13	10	6	2	8	7	11
	30-39	16	10	12	8	20	15	10	20	17	9	14	13	6	9	16
	40-49	54	61	59	64	50	58	49	42	51	54	57	51	55	60	51
	50-59	11	11	5	10	9	6	13	11	5	10	7	20	8	7	13
	60-69	6	5	3	3	6	6	6	5	5	9	7	2	9	5	3
	70-79	0	1	1	1	0	1	1	2	1	3	1	2	2	3	2
	80+	0	1	1	3	2	0	2	4	4	1	1	4	2	0	2
# SURVEYED		93	79	73	78	100	78	83	81	78	70	72	55	66	58	63
AGE	RESP	'73	'74	'75	'76	'77	'78	'80	'82	'83	'84	'85	'86	'87	'88	'89
60-65	0 - 9	4%	4%	0%	2%	2%	7%	3%	0%	4%	2%	5%	4%	0%	7%	3%
	10-19	7	9	7	9	6	7	8	5	4	7	7	2	5	7	3
	20-29	13	9	7	5	4	5	11	7	9	4	13	6	10	4	3
	30-39	15	13	16	14	12	12	18	21	16	16	15	11	17	13	17
	40-49	51	51	50	61	65	50	45	48	48	56	49	57	57	50	60
	50-59	5	7	7	7	10	2	8	10	11	9	4	11	10	15	11
	60-69	4	0	7	2	2	5	3	7	9	0	2	2	2	4	3
	70-79	0	4	2	0	0	7	3	0	0	2	2	2	0	0	0
	80+	2	2	5	0	0	5	3	2	0	4	4	4	0	0	0
# SURVEYED		55	45	44	44	51	42	38	42	56	45	55	47	42	46	35

TABLE IV: HOURS CURRENTLY EMPLOYED - BY AGE (Continued)

Question: How many hours did you work last week, at all jobs? NOTE: Question not asked in 1972.

Responses: 0 - 9; 10 - 19; 20 - 29; 30 - 39; 40 - 49; 50 - 59; 60 - 69; 70 - 79; 80+

		YEAR														
AGE	RESP	'73	'74	'75	'76	'77	'78	'80	'82	'83	'84	'85	'86	'87	'88	'89
66+	0 - 9	14%	9%	0%	0%	7%	5%	6%	6%	14%	3%	15%	0%	10%	19%	7%
	10-19	10	17	17	32	20	30	24	19	11	18	7	16	16	9	20
	20-29	14	26	33	26	20	25	24	19	18	24	33	26	16	22	20
	30-39	5	9	8	5	13	30	18	29	21	6	15	16	26	25	10
	40-49	38	22	29	21	27	5	18	16	29	32	19	32	16	19	20
	50-59	5	13	0	11	0	5	9	3	4	6	11	5	3	3	3
	60-69	5	4	4	5	7	0	0	6	0	6	0	5	13	3	17
	70-79	5	0	4	0	7	0	0	0	4	3	0	0	0	0	0
	80+	5	0	4	0	0	0	0	0	0	3	0	0	0	0	3
# SURVEYED		21	23	24	19	15	20	33	31	28	34	27	19	31	32	30

****

INDUSTRY WORKING IN

TABLE I: INDUSTRY WORKING IN - BY TOTAL POPULATION

Question: The industry in which the respondent works. (In broad categories.)

Responses:

AG = Agriculture, mining and construction
MN = Manufacturing
TR = Transportation, communication, and other public utilities
WS = Wholesale
RT = Retail trade
FI = Finance, insurance and real estate; Business and repair service
EN = Entertainment and recreation services, professional and related services
PA = Public administration

	YEAR															
RESPONSE	'72	'73	'74	'75	'76	'77	'78	'80	'82	'83	'84	'85	'86	'87	'88	'89
AG	11%	10%	10%	10%	10%	12%	9%	10%	10%	10%	7%	11%	9%	11%	8%	9%
MN	25	25	26	25	26	26	26	25	22	22	24	19	22	20	20	19
TR	7	6	7	5	7	6	6	6	6	4	5	7	5	6	7	6
WS	4	3	2	2	2	2	3	3	3	3	3	4	3	3	2	3
RT	13	14	12	16	16	15	15	15	15	15	16	15	15	16	16	16
FI	14	15	13	14	13	13	15	12	17	14	17	16	16	16	16	16
EN	19	21	21	20	20	20	19	20	22	23	21	22	23	21	23	25
PA	7	6	9	7	7	6	7	8	5	9	7	7	7	7	7	7
# SURVEYED	1420	1338	1344	1344	1352	1416	1404	1345	1399	1486	1379	1453	1365	1392	1393	1438

TABLE II: INDUSTRY WORKING IN - BY SEX

Question: The industry in which the respondent works. (In broad categories.)

Responses:
AG = Agriculture, mining and construction
MN = Manufacturing
TR = Transportation, communication, and other public utilities
WS = Wholesale
RT = Retail trade
FI = Finance, insurance and real estate; Business and repair service
EN = Entertainment and recreation services, professional and related services
PA = Public administration

		YEAR															
SEX	RESP	'72	'73	'74	'75	'76	'77	'78	'80	'82	'83	'84	'85	'86	'87	'88	'89
M	AG	19%	19%	18%	18%	18%	22%	18%	19%	21%	19%	15%	20%	18%	20%	15%	16%
A	MN	30	28	29	29	28	28	29	30	26	26	29	23	25	25	25	21
L	TR	9	9	10	7	9	8	9	9	9	6	6	10	7	8	10	9
E	WS	5	4	2	2	3	3	4	3	3	5	4	5	4	4	3	3
	RT	10	9	8	11	12	10	9	9	11	11	11	9	11	10	13	13
	FI	8	8	9	11	10	9	11	9	12	10	12	11	13	12	12	13
	EN	10	13	13	12	11	11	12	11	12	13	12	14	14	12	13	16
	PA	10	9	11	10	10	8	10	9	6	12	10	9	8	9	10	9
# SURVEYED		767	665	669	646	654	680	636	632	623	678	587	675	611	635	621	642
SEX	RESP	'72	'73	'74	'75	'76	'77	'78	'80	'82	'83	'84	'85	'86	'87	'88	'89
F	AG	2%	1%	3%	3%	3%	2%	2%	3%	2%	3%	2%	3%	2%	3%	3%	2%
E	MN	20	22	23	21	25	24	24	21	19	19	21	15	19	16	16	18
M	TR	5	3	3	4	4	4	4	4	4	3	4	5	3	4	4	4
A	WS	3	2	2	2	2	1	2	3	3	2	2	3	2	2	2	2
L	RT	17	18	17	21	20	21	20	20	18	19	20	20	18	20	19	18
E	FI	21	21	17	17	15	16	19	15	20	17	21	21	19	20	19	19
	EN	29	29	29	28	28	28	25	28	31	32	27	29	31	29	31	31
	PA	4	3	7	4	4	5	5	7	3	6	5	5	7	6	6	5
# SURVEYED		653	673	675	698	698	736	768	713	776	808	792	778	754	757	772	796

TABLE III: INDUSTRY WORKING IN - BY RACE

Question: The industry in which the respondent works. (In broad categories.)

Responses:
AG = Agriculture, mining and construction
MN = Manufacturing
TR = Transportation, communication, and other public utilities
WS = Wholesale
RT = Retail trade
FI = Finance, insurance and real estate; Business and repair service
EN = Entertainment and recreation services, professional and related services
PA = Public administration

		YEAR															
RACE	RESP	'72	'73	'74	'75	'76	'77	'78	'80	'82	'83	'84	'85	'86	'87	'88	'89
WHITE	AG	11%	11%	10%	10%	10%	11%	9%	11%	11%	11%	7%	11%	10%	11%	9%	9%
	MN	26	25	27	25	27	27	26	26	23	21	25	19	22	21	21	20
	TR	7	6	7	6	6	6	6	6	6	4	5	7	5	6	7	6
	WS	4	3	2	2	2	2	3	3	3	3	3	4	3	3	2	2
	RT	14	15	12	16	16	16	15	16	16	15	16	15	15	16	17	17
	FI	12	14	11	13	12	12	15	12	16	14	16	16	16	15	15	15
	EN	19	21	21	20	20	20	19	19	21	23	21	21	23	21	21	24
	PA	7	6	9	7	7	6	7	8	4	8	7	6	7	7	7	7
# SURVEYED		1187	1166	1183	1192	1224	1248	1250	1217	1229	1318	1178	1266	1166	1170	1166	1245
RACE	RESP	'72	'73	'74	'75	'76	'77	'78	'80	'82	'83	'84	'85	'86	'87	'88	'89
BLACK	AG	11%	9%	11%	12%	11%	12%	5%	6%	6%	5%	4%	10%	8%	7%	5%	4%
	MN	20	24	20	21	19	19	31	22	17	27	18	13	18	17	12	16
	TR	10	8	7	4	10	8	6	8	7	5	5	8	5	8	6	6
	WS	3	1	1	2	2	1	0	2	1	4	3	3	2	3	2	4
	RT	8	9	10	14	13	12	14	8	10	11	16	14	11	11	11	9
	FI	25	19	25	21	23	20	19	18	21	13	25	14	23	24	19	22
	EN	15	22	20	20	15	20	17	27	32	21	22	29	20	21	32	32
	PA	7	8	6	6	7	8	7	10	7	15	7	10	11	9	12	7
# SURVEYED		229	160	157	148	120	155	139	119	145	151	159	145	166	174	170	141
RACE	RESP	'72	'73	'74	'75	'76	'77	'78	'80	'82	'83	'84	'85	'86	'87	'88	'89
OTHER	AG	50%	0%	0%	0%	13%	23%	7%	11%	4%	0%	14%	7%	3%	13%	16%	8%
	MN	0	33	0	25	25	15	13	22	28	24	36	19	24	19	19	23
	TR	25	0	0	0	25	0	0	11	8	0	10	5	3	4	4	4
	WS	0	8	25	0	0	0	0	0	4	0	0	2	6	0	0	6
	RT	0	0	50	0	25	23	40	11	12	24	7	14	9	19	14	17
	FI	0	8	0	25	0	8	0	11	20	12	12	21	15	27	25	13
	EN	25	25	25	50	13	23	13	33	12	35	12	29	24	17	19	23
	PA	0	25	0	0	0	8	27	0	12	6	10	2	15	2	4	6
# SURVEYED		4	12	4	4	8	13	15	9	25	17	42	42	33	48	57	52

TABLE IV: INDUSTRY WORKING IN - BY AGE

Question: The industry in which the respondent works. (In broad categories.)

Responses:
AG = Agriculture, mining and construction
MN = Manufacturing
TR = Transportation, communication, and other public utilities
WS = Wholesale
RT = Retail trade
FI = Finance, insurance and real estate; Business and repair service
EN = Entertainment and recreation services, professional and related services
PA = Public administration

		YEAR															
AGE	RESP	'72	'73	'74	'75	'76	'77	'78	'80	'82	'83	'84	'85	'86	'87	'88	'89
18-23	AG	8%	6%	8%	6%	10%	8%	11%	7%	10%	6%	11%	15%	7%	13%	11%	13%
	MN	26	25	27	23	24	25	22	30	21	12	27	11	11	14	13	13
	TR	6	2	5	4	2	3	4	4	3	1	0	4	5	5	3	8
	WS	2	2	1	2	1	1	2	2	0	7	3	2	3	0	3	3
	RT	25	29	22	24	31	26	29	26	30	38	28	29	36	33	37	29
	FI	14	12	12	18	6	13	11	9	19	16	12	17	12	17	14	20
	EN	15	19	17	17	19	17	14	16	14	16	13	18	20	15	17	13
	PA	3	5	8	6	8	7	8	7	3	4	6	4	5	3	3	2
# SURVEYED		118	121	131	135	126	134	130	120	121	108	134	110	91	104	110	104
AGE	RESP	'72	'73	'74	'75	'76	'77	'78	'80	'82	'83	'84	'85	'86	'87	'88	'89
24-29	AG	10%	10%	7%	9%	9%	11%	6%	10%	9%	12%	9%	11%	10%	9%	10%	7%
	MN	24	29	21	16	24	26	23	26	20	18	24	18	21	17	17	19
	TR	5	4	8	6	8	6	7	5	6	6	7	6	3	8	7	5
	WS	4	2	1	2	0	2	2	3	4	3	1	5	4	3	2	2
	RT	11	12	12	15	13	17	15	16	18	17	16	15	17	18	18	20
	FI	11	10	9	15	12	13	15	13	17	15	19	20	17	19	17	18
	EN	24	26	31	26	25	19	22	22	21	25	19	20	23	21	20	22
	PA	10	7	12	11	9	7	9	6	5	5	4	4	4	6	8	7
# SURVEYED		202	189	198	213	207	192	226	188	234	265	217	210	202	183	206	194
AGE	RESP	'72	'73	'74	'75	'76	'77	'78	'80	'82	'83	'84	'85	'86	'87	'88	'89
30-35	AG	10%	15%	8%	10%	9%	9%	9%	10%	7%	12%	3%	9%	11%	7%	7%	10%
	MN	23	20	27	24	32	22	26	27	20	21	19	15	20	15	21	18
	TR	10	10	4	2	5	10	5	8	10	6	5	10	4	7	7	5
	WS	6	3	3	2	3	2	4	1	2	4	4	2	2	1	2	5
	RT	13	11	11	21	13	15	13	9	13	13	11	14	13	16	14	13
	FI	14	15	16	9	11	15	15	13	16	10	19	16	18	19	16	19
	EN	20	20	23	24	23	22	21	22	27	28	31	26	25	26	25	26
	PA	5	6	8	8	4	5	7	10	7	7	8	6	6	9	7	6
# SURVEYED		173	155	160	154	174	177	217	203	200	226	194	207	211	215	188	199

TABLE IV: INDUSTRY WORKING IN - BY AGE (Continued)

Question: The industry in which the respondent works. (In broad categories.)

Responses:
AG = Agriculture, mining and construction
MN = Manufacturing
TR = Transportation, communication, and other public utilities
WS = Wholesale
RT = Retail trade
FI = Finance, insurance and real estate; Business and repair service
EN = Entertainment and recreation services, professional and related services
PA = Public administration

		YEAR															
AGE	RESP	'72	'73	'74	'75	'76	'77	'78	'80	'82	'83	'84	'85	'86	'87	'88	'89
36-41	AG	10%	9%	8%	7%	8%	11%	5%	13%	11%	9%	7%	11%	8%	13%	8%	9%
	MN	25	26	26	28	26	25	26	22	24	25	22	18	19	15	22	15
	TR	10	6	6	11	7	7	5	6	6	4	7	9	3	7	6	8
	WS	3	3	1	3	3	1	2	9	6	2	4	5	2	3	3	1
	RT	11	8	17	15	13	8	15	10	9	10	9	14	11	8	8	13
	FI	14	17	10	10	15	11	20	11	15	14	18	15	17	15	18	15
	EN	17	26	22	19	19	30	17	22	26	27	21	23	28	30	26	33
	PA	9	6	9	7	7	6	9	7	3	10	12	5	11	10	9	6
# SURVEYED		116	163	140	149	155	161	151	141	144	164	180	180	183	183	188	193
AGE	RESP	'72	'73	'74	'75	'76	'77	'78	'80	'82	'83	'84	'85	'86	'87	'88	'89
42-47	AG	12%	7%	10%	7%	11%	14%	7%	6%	7%	8%	7%	8%	12%	12%	6%	9%
	MN	26	25	28	33	30	27	22	24	21	25	18	20	20	20	19	19
	TR	7	7	7	3	3	8	10	2	8	5	6	6	5	7	12	6
	WS	3	3	2	3	1	4	3	2	4	2	3	7	5	5	3	4
	RT	13	16	7	13	12	14	15	23	13	12	17	12	11	12	13	11
	FI	14	16	14	16	12	12	16	10	15	19	18	17	19	18	19	13
	EN	18	21	22	20	22	17	22	20	30	21	26	26	21	22	21	30
	PA	7	4	10	5	8	5	5	14	2	9	7	6	7	6	8	7
# SURVEYED		164	136	137	135	105	138	115	111	112	139	120	121	133	153	156	159
AGE	RESP	'72	'73	'74	'75	'76	'77	'78	'80	'82	'83	'84	'85	'86	'87	'88	'89
48-53	AG	8%	15%	11%	10%	8%	10%	13%	11%	14%	9%	5%	12%	9%	11%	4%	11%
	MN	32	29	37	23	33	32	30	23	27	23	24	22	15	21	18	25
	TR	5	7	10	6	8	7	9	8	2	3	7	6	6	2	7	4
	WS	2	1	2	2	3	3	3	3	2	3	2	4	2	5	7	5
	RT	9	13	10	17	18	11	11	15	12	15	19	13	12	12	10	13
	FI	12	10	8	11	8	13	14	14	17	15	15	11	18	15	10	12
	EN	21	17	16	22	17	14	13	21	23	25	16	24	31	26	36	27
	PA	10	7	8	9	8	10	6	6	4	7	11	8	6	7	9	5
# SURVEYED		180	136	133	132	120	150	128	117	103	110	99	127	98	124	92	132

TABLE IV: INDUSTRY WORKING IN - BY AGE (Continued)

Question: The industry in which the respondent works. (In broad categories.)

Responses:
AG = Agriculture, mining and construction
MN = Manufacturing
TR = Transportation, communication, and other public utilities
WS = Wholesale
RT = Retail trade
FI = Finance, insurance and real estate; Business and repair service
EN = Entertainment and recreation services, professional and related services
PA = Public administration

		YEAR															
AGE	RESP	'72	'73	'74	'75	'76	'77	'78	'80	'82	'83	'84	'85	'86	'87	'88	'89
54-59	AG	16%	5%	11%	13%	10%	14%	10%	9%	12%	9%	7%	9%	8%	11%	7%	4%
	MN	22	26	24	26	23	23	29	31	25	23	30	20	28	28	22	13
	TR	8	4	7	7	9	3	6	8	2	6	3	9	6	4	4	10
	WS	5	4	3	1	3	3	2	3	4	2	3	1	3	3	1	3
	RT	17	17	5	13	18	18	11	12	12	13	18	16	16	17	15	13
	FI	16	16	12	19	11	11	11	10	12	10	14	14	16	11	18	21
	EN	12	22	28	12	20	20	23	17	25	21	22	21	13	20	21	27
	PA	5	7	8	9	7	6	8	9	7	16	4	10	8	6	12	9
# SURVEYED		144	148	131	120	122	158	126	130	138	128	114	132	97	95	82	96
AGE	RESP	'72	'73	'74	'75	'76	'77	'78	'80	'82	'83	'84	'85	'86	'87	'88	'89
60-65	AG	11%	8%	12%	10%	8%	13%	6%	10%	15%	10%	6%	14%	6%	6%	9%	1%
	MN	20	28	22	27	32	24	35	24	26	32	27	20	31	30	22	28
	TR	9	8	8	9	6	5	3	7	6	5	7	2	3	8	7	6
	WS	5	3	5	2	4	1	3	2	3	2	3	3	3	4	4	2
	RT	13	9	16	12	14	15	15	14	6	11	19	11	11	15	14	16
	FI	17	16	17	13	18	12	14	13	20	10	15	15	11	10	12	11
	EN	17	19	13	27	14	24	16	21	20	18	18	23	20	15	23	27
	PA	8	9	7	2	3	7	8	10	4	12	6	10	16	11	9	10
# SURVEYED		132	106	100	104	125	110	104	111	108	125	108	125	109	99	113	105
AGE	RESP	'72	'73	'74	'75	'76	'77	'78	'80	'82	'83	'84	'85	'86	'87	'88	'89
66+	AG	15%	16%	15%	16%	17%	14%	13%	14%	11%	12%	8%	11%	10%	13%	10%	10%
	MN	26	21	23	29	18	28	27	22	19	21	30	22	27	26	22	24
	TR	7	8	7	4	9	7	5	5	7	2	3	8	6	5	6	6
	WS	3	2	2	2	1	2	4	3	4	4	3	3	2	1	0	2
	RT	9	12	12	13	15	15	12	17	17	12	15	14	12	17	20	18
	FI	17	18	17	17	17	14	16	14	20	17	20	16	15	17	16	15
	EN	18	18	15	15	16	16	21	20	16	22	17	19	22	14	19	18
	PA	5	5	9	5	7	4	4	5	5	10	5	7	6	6	5	8
# SURVEYED		187	180	209	199	212	189	200	217	232	215	210	234	234	234	254	253

YOUR OCCUPATION

TABLE I: YOUR OCCUPATION - BY TOTAL POPULATION

Question: What kind of a job do you (did you normally) do? That is, what (is/was) your job called?

Responses:

PT = Professional, technical
MA = Managers and administrators, sales workers
CL = Clerical and kindred workers
CR = Craftsmen and kindred workers
OP = Operatives except transport
TR = Transport equipment operatives, laborers
FR = Farmers, farm laborers, etc.
SW = Service workers

	YEAR															
RESPONSE	**'72**	**'73**	**'74**	**'75**	**'76**	**'77**	**'78**	**'80**	**'82**	**'83**	**'84**	**'85**	**'86**	**'87**	**'88**	**'89**
PT	23%	24%	24%	21%	23%	22%	23%	23%	21%	22%	21%	22%	23%	22%	23%	25%
MA	13	14	13	14	14	13	14	16	12	16	16	17	18	20	17	18
CL	17	18	19	18	19	17	17	17	19	20	20	19	17	15	18	18
CR	12	11	11	12	10	12	12	11	12	11	10	11	11	12	12	11
OP	12	12	12	13	13	16	13	12	13	10	9	9	9	8	9	8
TR	7	6	6	5	6	7	6	5	6	5	7	6	5	6	6	5
FR	3	2	2	2	3	2	2	2	2	3	2	2	2	3	2	1
SW	13	14	13	14	13	12	13	14	15	13	14	14	14	14	15	13
# SURVEYED	1613	1504	1484	1490	1499	1530	1532	1468	1506	1599	1473	1534	1470	1466	1481	1537

TABLE II: YOUR OCCUPATION - BY SEX

Question: What kind of a job do you (did you normally) do? That is, what (is/was) your job called?

Responses:
PT = Professional, technical
CL = Clerical and kindred workers
OP = Operatives except transport
FR = Farmers, farm laborers, etc.
MA = Managers and administrators, sales workers
CR = Craftsmen and kindred workers
TR = Transport equipment operatives, laborers
SW = Service workers

		YEAR															
SEX	RESP	'72	'73	'74	'75	'76	'77	'78	'80	'82	'83	'84	'85	'86	'87	'88	'89
M	PT	17%	20%	17%	16%	16%	18%	17%	17%	15%	16%	16%	20%	20%	17%	20%	21%
A	MA	18	18	17	20	19	16	18	19	16	21	21	19	23	23	19	22
L	CL	7	5	6	7	5	4	4	6	7	6	7	6	6	6	7	7
E	CR	22	20	24	24	22	25	26	24	23	22	21	22	20	22	25	23
	OP	10	12	12	11	13	15	11	13	14	11	10	9	7	8	7	7
	TR	14	12	12	11	11	13	13	10	12	10	12	11	11	12	11	10
	FR	6	5	3	3	7	4	3	5	4	5	5	5	5	5	3	3
	SW	7	9	8	8	7	5	7	6	8	9	8	9	7	7	9	8
# SURVEYED		807	701	691	670	669	693	643	641	639	690	598	688	621	641	638	660
SEX	RESP	'72	'73	'74	'75	'76	'77	'78	'80	'82	'83	'84	'85	'86	'87	'88	'89
F	PT	29%	28%	30%	26%	29%	25%	27%	28%	25%	26%	24%	23%	26%	25%	25%	28%
E	MA	9	10	9	10	9	10	12	13	10	13	13	15	15	17	16	16
M	CL	28	29	30	27	29	27	26	26	29	31	28	30	25	23	26	26
A	CR	1	2	1	2	1	1	2	1	3	2	3	2	4	4	2	2
L	OP	13	12	12	14	13	16	15	11	12	9	9	8	10	9	10	9
E	TR	1	1	1	0	2	1	1	2	1	1	4	1	1	2	2	2
	FR	1	0	1	1	0	0	0	0	0	0	0	1	0	1	1	0
	SW	19	18	17	20	17	18	17	19	20	17	18	19	19	20	19	16
# SURVEYED		806	803	793	820	830	837	889	827	867	909	875	846	849	825	843	877

TABLE III: YOUR OCCUPATION - BY RACE

Question: What kind of a job do you (did you normally) do? That is, what (is/was) your job called?

Responses:

PT = Professional, technical
CL = Clerical and kindred workers
OP = Operatives except transport
FR = Farmers, farm laborers, etc.
MA = Managers and administrators, sales workers
CR = Craftsmen and kindred workers
TP = Transport equipment operatives, laborers
SW = Service workers

		YEAR															
RACE	RESP	'72	'73	'74	'75	'76	'77	'78	'80	'82	'83	'84	'85	'86	'87	'88	'89
WHITE	PT	24%	25%	25%	22%	23%	22%	24%	23%	21%	22%	21%	22%	24%	23%	23%	24%
	MA	15	15	13	15	15	14	15	17	13	17	18	19	20	22	19	20
	CL	18	19	20	19	20	17	18	18	20	21	20	20	17	15	18	19
	CR	13	11	12	12	10	13	13	12	12	11	11	11	11	11	12	12
	OP	11	11	12	12	13	16	13	11	12	9	9	8	8	8	8	8
	TR	5	6	5	4	5	6	6	5	6	5	6	5	5	6	5	5
	FR	3	2	2	2	3	2	2	2	2	3	2	2	3	3	2	2
	SW	10	11	10	13	11	10	11	12	13	12	13	12	12	12	12	11
# SURVEYED		1348	1308	1304	1323	1361	1339	1358	1318	1323	1416	1251	1338	1249	1222	1234	1319
RACE	RESP	'72	'73	'74	'75	'76	'77	'78	'80	'82	'83	'84	'85	'86	'87	'88	'89
BLACK	PT	18%	20%	15%	14%	16%	22%	18%	25%	20%	20%	16%	15%	20%	16%	19%	27%
	MA	5	3	6	6	5	1	7	2	5	8	6	3	4	10	8	7
	CL	11	7	12	11	8	15	12	11	15	15	18	14	16	20	18	16
	CR	6	7	5	10	12	6	7	6	8	8	8	9	11	14	8	5
	OP	13	17	16	20	12	15	20	13	13	19	12	9	14	8	10	10
	TR	16	10	13	10	12	11	10	9	7	7	13	11	9	8	9	10
	FR	2	3	3	4	4	4	1	1	0	2	0	3	1	1	0	1
	SW	28	32	31	25	31	26	25	31	31	21	28	35	26	24	29	24
# SURVEYED		261	183	173	163	129	176	158	140	156	165	170	152	184	191	186	157
RACE	RESP	'72	'73	'74	'75	'76	'77	'78	'80	'82	'83	'84	'85	'86	'87	'88	'89
OTHER	PT	0%	23%	43%	25%	44%	40%	25%	70%	7%	22%	37%	25%	19%	23%	25%	31%
	MA	0	0	14	0	0	13	13	0	7	22	13	9	14	11	10	11
	CL	25	31	14	25	33	7	13	10	15	17	10	16	22	8	11	11
	CR	25	15	0	25	0	13	13	10	15	11	4	7	14	13	7	10
	OP	25	8	14	0	11	7	0	0	30	17	15	14	11	11	15	16
	TR	25	8	0	0	0	13	0	0	4	0	6	7	8	4	8	5
	FR	0	8	0	0	0	0	6	0	0	0	8	2	0	6	5	0
	SW	0	8	14	25	11	7	31	10	22	11	8	20	14	25	20	15
# SURVEYED		4	13	7	4	9	15	16	10	27	18	52	44	37	53	61	61

TABLE IV: YOUR OCCUPATION - BY AGE

Question: What kind of a job do you (did you normally) do? That is, what (is/was) your job called?

Responses:

PT = Professional, technical
CL = Clerical and kindred workers
OP = Operatives except transport
FR = Farmers, farm laborers, etc.
MA = Managers and administrators, sales workers
CR = Craftsmen and kindred workers
TR = Transport equipment operatives, laborers
SW = Service workers

		YEAR															
AGE	RESP	'72	'73	'74	'75	'76	'77	'78	'80	'82	'83	'84	'85	'86	'87	'88	'89
18-23	PT	33%	35%	28%	27%	30%	21%	26%	30%	24%	19%	24%	26%	25%	23%	26%	29%
	MA	9	5	8	6	8	7	9	6	8	10	7	8	17	14	13	15
	CL	15	24	14	21	15	23	19	22	18	23	19	20	22	20	14	14
	CR	8	6	14	7	9	7	10	9	9	7	11	8	11	9	10	10
	OP	14	12	13	9	14	13	12	10	13	8	8	3	2	6	8	9
	TR	7	5	8	9	8	9	7	5	9	6	13	8	11	11	10	7
	FR	1	1	0	2	0	1	3	1	1	2	2	3	0	2	1	2
	SW	12	13	15	18	16	20	15	17	19	25	16	26	12	15	18	13
# SURVEYED		169	171	168	173	162	164	163	155	148	128	161	133	108	126	141	137
AGE	RESP	'72	'73	'74	'75	'76	'77	'78	'80	'82	'83	'84	'85	'86	'87	'88	'89
24-29	PT	27%	33%	32%	26%	27%	23%	29%	24%	20%	23%	22%	20%	25%	28%	23%	26%
	MA	10	9	8	12	10	10	13	10	12	11	12	15	22	16	17	16
	CL	22	19	26	26	23	19	15	22	21	23	27	21	12	17	18	26
	CR	16	12	11	11	12	13	13	12	14	14	13	12	10	11	14	12
	OP	8	11	8	8	9	15	12	11	13	8	9	11	9	6	7	5
	TR	6	4	6	4	8	9	7	6	6	7	5	8	6	8	5	2
	FR	1	1	0	1	3	1	0	1	1	1	1	0	4	2	2	0
	SW	10	11	8	12	8	11	11	13	15	13	11	13	12	13	14	13
# SURVEYED		231	212	212	232	226	204	244	202	246	287	232	217	218	193	215	202
AGE	RESP	'72	'73	'74	'75	'76	'77	'78	'80	'82	'83	'84	'85	'86	'87	'88	'89
30-35	PT	25%	23%	25%	23%	20%	25%	28%	30%	24%	22%	25%	23%	21%	24%	28%	28%
	MA	15	15	13	16	14	15	13	14	13	18	17	18	16	22	19	17
	CL	18	21	25	16	24	18	17	15	22	19	21	24	19	11	17	15
	CR	11	12	10	12	9	13	16	12	10	12	10	13	13	13	10	16
	OP	11	8	11	13	16	14	10	11	14	8	10	6	9	8	5	6
	TR	7	7	3	6	5	7	5	7	4	5	7	5	6	4	8	6
	FR	2	2	0	1	2	1	0	1	1	1	1	1	0	1	1	1
	SW	10	11	13	12	10	7	12	10	11	14	11	11	14	17	13	12
# SURVEYED		187	167	175	171	186	188	230	215	204	236	200	212	221	221	195	212
AGE	RESP	'72	'73	'74	'75	'76	'77	'78	'80	'82	'83	'84	'85	'86	'87	'88	'89
36-41	PT	22%	23%	20%	14%	21%	30%	16%	27%	22%	27%	21%	24%	24%	30%	23%	30%
	MA	14	13	16	14	18	11	19	22	9	17	21	23	22	23	18	22
	CL	23	21	26	18	18	18	19	15	25	19	19	18	18	11	20	14
	CR	13	7	11	16	12	11	14	12	12	14	8	11	10	15	9	10
	OP	5	14	9	16	13	14	12	10	11	10	9	6	6	6	9	7
	TR	7	9	5	5	5	5	6	4	9	3	7	5	2	5	8	8
	FR	5	2	0	0	2	2	1	3	1	1	1	3	2	2	2	1
	SW	11	10	13	17	11	10	14	7	11	8	13	9	15	10	11	9
# SURVEYED		128	175	152	154	158	168	160	150	146	173	187	184	188	186	193	198

TABLE IV: YOUR OCCUPATION - BY AGE (Continued)

Question: What kind of a job do you (did you normally) do? That is, what (is/was) your job called?

Responses:
PT = Professional, technical
MA = Managers and administrators, sales workers
CL = Clerical and kindred workers
CR = Craftsmen and kindred workers
OP = Operatives except transport
TR = Transport equipment operatives, laborers
FR = Farmers, farm laborers, etc.
SW = Service workers

		YEAR															
AGE	RESP	'72	'73	'74	'75	'76	'77	'78	'80	'82	'83	'84	'85	'86	'87	'88	'89
42-47	PT	20%	23%	28%	22%	29%	19%	22%	14%	24%	21%	21%	27%	28%	20%	19%	25%
	MA	13	16	11	17	16	14	18	21	15	19	18	23	24	20	18	23
	CL	18	20	17	14	15	18	16	23	20	26	20	16	16	17	18	17
	CR	11	12	10	13	11	14	13	15	11	8	10	10	7	11	15	14
	OP	14	10	13	17	10	16	7	8	8	12	8	9	6	8	10	5
	TR	10	4	5	1	2	10	10	5	7	4	9	4	6	7	6	7
	FR	3	1	2	2	4	2	0	2	1	3	2	1	1	3	0	1
	SW	11	15	13	13	14	8	14	14	13	6	12	10	12	13	13	9
# SURVEYED		186	146	151	143	114	147	119	117	119	145	126	124	141	157	157	161

AGE	RESP	'72	'73	'74	'75	'76	'77	'78	'80	'82	'83	'84	'85	'86	'87	'88	'89
48-53	PT	15%	21%	20%	18%	20%	16%	15%	20%	20%	22%	16%	21%	22%	15%	24%	20%
	MA	13	19	14	19	14	18	20	21	20	20	22	23	17	28	17	22
	CL	21	14	19	19	20	16	17	17	19	26	20	15	13	11	20	20
	CR	13	10	14	11	9	15	14	9	12	4	8	12	15	12	11	11
	OP	16	13	17	10	21	15	17	12	13	11	13	8	9	8	8	12
	TR	5	8	4	3	2	7	8	6	6	4	4	8	7	9	7	4
	FR	2	2	3	4	2	2	2	2	0	3	0	2	3	2	1	4
	SW	14	13	9	16	13	11	8	14	12	9	19	12	14	16	13	9
# SURVEYED		189	151	146	141	133	154	133	123	112	116	102	131	108	126	92	138

AGE	RESP	'72	'73	'74	'75	'76	'77	'78	'80	'82	'83	'84	'85	'86	'87	'88	'89
54-59	PT	16%	16%	17%	13%	15%	19%	20%	17%	18%	19%	14%	16%	10%	19%	16%	19%
	MA	17	17	14	17	19	15	18	20	14	22	19	14	19	27	19	17
	CL	17	16	18	21	19	15	20	16	19	21	19	22	24	16	24	16
	CR	10	13	12	12	8	11	9	13	13	8	11	16	12	12	14	8
	OP	12	11	12	12	14	18	15	12	14	7	11	7	11	7	8	5
	TR	6	5	8	8	9	4	4	7	6	6	10	9	5	2	2	7
	FR	9	2	1	2	3	5	1	4	1	3	3	1	4	3	1	1
	SW	13	21	17	14	13	14	11	13	15	13	13	14	14	13	15	26
# SURVEYED		156	157	139	126	129	168	137	136	144	134	114	134	99	98	85	99

AGE	RESP	'72	'73	'74	'75	'76	'77	'78	'80	'82	'83	'84	'85	'86	'87	'88	'89
60-65	PT	19%	19%	18%	16%	16%	21%	15%	20%	19%	14%	15%	20%	23%	15%	26%	21%
	MA	14	13	19	12	14	15	12	19	11	20	20	16	18	17	22	17
	CL	14	12	15	16	18	12	17	13	15	18	19	18	19	17	17	20
	CR	12	12	6	12	12	15	9	14	8	14	12	10	12	12	12	9
	OP	10	17	17	18	14	19	20	13	21	11	8	11	9	14	7	14
	TR	9	7	6	7	4	3	5	3	3	5	4	4	3	9	1	7
	FR	3	4	6	2	4	2	2	3	3	2	4	4	2	3	3	0
	SW	19	15	14	17	17	14	21	14	21	16	18	18	13	14	13	12
# SURVEYED		144	121	108	113	134	117	107	119	116	132	113	131	115	101	119	111

TABLE IV: YOUR OCCUPATION - BY AGE (Continued)

Question: What kind of a job do you (did you normally) do? That is, what (is/was) your job called?

Responses:
PT = Professional, technical
CL = Clerical and kindred workers
OP = Operatives except transport
FR = Farmers, farm laborers, etc.
MA = Managers and administrators, sales workers
CR = Craftsmen and kindred workers
TR = Transport equipment operatives, laborers
SW = Service workers

		YEAR															
AGE	RESP	'72	'73	'74	'75	'76	'77	'78	'80	'82	'83	'84	'85	'86	'87	'88	'89
66+	PT	27%	19%	20%	25%	25%	21%	26%	22%	18%	24%	24%	21%	26%	17%	19%	20%
	MA	14	18	15	14	14	10	11	15	13	14	15	16	12	15	16	18
	CL	8	12	10	10	14	15	13	11	17	11	13	17	14	19	15	19
	CR	11	11	13	14	10	11	8	9	14	11	10	7	10	11	11	9
	OP	13	13	13	16	10	19	18	15	12	14	10	13	13	13	13	12
	TR	8	7	9	3	6	6	5	4	5	4	6	3	4	3	5	3
	FR	6	7	5	4	7	5	5	5	4	6	5	5	5	6	3	3
	SW	14	14	15	13	14	14	14	19	18	17	17	16	17	15	18	15
# SURVEYED		218	200	227	232	251	213	232	242	259	241	232	261	265	253	280	275

****

PRESTIGE OF OCCUPATION

TABLE I: PRESTIGE OF OCCUPATION - BY TOTAL POPULATION

Question: Prestige of respondent's occupation.

Responses: See Appendix D for explanation and sample occupations.

	YEAR															
RESPONSE	'72	'73	'74	'75	'76	'77	'78	'80	'82	'83	'84	'85	'86	'87	'88	'89
10-19	12%	10%	10%	9%	11%	11%	10%	8%	12%	7%	11%	9%	7%	8%	7%	8%
20-29	14	17	17	17	15	16	16	17	15	17	15	13	14	13	15	12
30-39	27	25	24	26	28	29	25	24	30	23	26	25	27	26	28	29
40-49	27	27	27	26	27	22	27	27	23	28	23	25	24	23	22	21
50-59	11	11	10	11	10	10	10	15	12	14	14	15	16	19	16	16
60-69	8	7	10	8	8	10	9	7	8	9	9	9	8	8	8	10
70-79	1	2	2	1	2	2	2	2	2	2	1	3	3	2	3	4
80-89	0	0	0	0	0	0	0	0	0	0	0	0	0	0	0	0
# SURVEYED	1447	1332	1351	1349	1352	1416	1404	1349	1400	1493	1379	1453	1368	1392	1394	1440

TABLE II: PRESTIGE OF OCCUPATION - BY SEX

Question: Prestige of respondent's occupation.

Responses: See Appendix D for explanation and sample occupations.

		YEAR															
SEX	RESP	'72	'73	'74	'75	'76	'77	'78	'80	'82	'83	'84	'85	'86	'87	'88	'89
M	10-19	11%	10%	10%	8%	10%	11%	9%	9%	13%	8%	12%	10%	6%	10%	7%	7%
A	20-29	11	15	16	14	11	13	14	13	14	16	14	11	12	11	12	11
L	30-39	28	23	23	28	29	30	25	24	29	25	25	25	25	25	29	28
E	40-49	27	27	27	25	26	20	27	27	22	25	24	24	25	23	21	23
	50-59	15	14	14	15	14	14	14	19	15	16	17	16	20	23	20	19
	60-69	6	6	7	7	6	9	7	5	4	7	6	8	6	6	8	6
	70-79	2	3	3	3	3	3	3	2	3	3	2	5	4	3	3	5
	80-89	0	0	0	0	0	0	1	0	0	0	1	1	1	0	0	0
# SURVEYED		779	663	673	647	654	680	636	633	624	681	587	675	613	635	621	642
SEX	RESP	'72	'73	'74	'75	'76	'77	'78	'80	'82	'83	'84	'85	'86	'87	'88	'89
F	10-19	13%	10%	10%	11%	11%	11%	10%	8%	10%	6%	10%	9%	7%	6%	7%	9%
E	20-29	17	19	17	20	19	19	18	20	16	18	17	16	16	16	18	12
M	30-39	27	27	25	25	26	28	24	24	30	22	27	24	28	27	27	30
A	40-49	26	27	27	27	27	24	28	26	23	31	22	25	24	23	23	20
L	50-59	6	8	7	8	6	7	7	12	9	11	12	14	12	16	13	13
E	60-69	11	8	13	9	10	10	12	9	10	11	11	10	10	10	9	13
	70-79	1	1	1	0	1	1	1	1	1	1	1	1	2	2	3	3
	80-89	0	0	0	0	0	0	0	0	0	0	0	0	0	0	0	0
# SURVEYED		668	669	678	702	698	736	768	716	776	812	792	778	755	757	773	798

TABLE III: PRESTIGE OF OCCUPATION - BY RACE

Question: Prestige of respondent's occupation.

Responses: See Appendix D for explanation and sample occupations.

		YEAR															
RACE	RESP	'72	'73	'74	'75	'76	'77	'78	'80	'82	'83	'84	'85	'86	'87	'88	'89
WHITE	10-19	7%	7%	8%	8%	9%	8%	8%	7%	10%	6%	9%	7%	5%	7%	5%	7%
	20-29	13	17	16	16	15	16	16	16	14	16	14	12	14	12	14	11
	30-39	27	25	23	27	28	30	24	24	30	23	27	25	26	25	28	29
	40-49	29	29	29	27	28	23	29	27	24	29	24	26	25	24	23	22
	50-59	12	12	11	12	10	11	11	16	13	15	15	16	17	21	17	17
	60-69	9	8	11	8	8	10	10	7	8	10	9	9	9	9	9	10
	70-79	2	2	2	1	2	2	2	2	2	2	2	3	3	2	3	4
	80-89	0	0	0	0	0	0	0	0	0	0	0	0	0	0	0	0
# SURVEYED		1210	1159	1190	1195	1225	1248	1250	1220	1230	1324	1178	1266	1168	1170	1167	1246
RACE	RESP	'72	'73	'74	'75	'76	'77	'78	'80	'82	'83	'84	'85	'86	'87	'88	'89
BLACK	10-19	35%	31%	27%	23%	28%	34%	27%	21%	24%	15%	22%	28%	19%	11%	16%	16%
	20-29	15	18	20	25	23	17	19	23	18	28	25	19	17	23	22	18
	30-39	28	29	30	25	24	20	32	28	30	28	25	21	34	34	28	27
	40-49	12	14	12	19	15	17	14	18	14	19	13	21	19	19	18	19
	50-59	6	3	6	3	6	3	4	6	3	6	8	3	5	8	11	9
	60-69	3	4	4	4	4	8	3	4	11	3	8	7	4	4	5	10
	70-79	0	1	0	0	0	0	0	1	0	1	0	1	2	1	1	1
	80-89	0	0	0	0	0	0	0	0	0	0	0	1	0	0	0	0
# SURVEYED		233	162	157	150	119	155	139	120	145	152	159	145	166	174	170	142
RACE	RESP	'72	'73	'74	'75	'76	'77	'78	'80	'82	'83	'84	'85	'86	'87	'88	'89
OTHER	10-19	25%	9%	0%	25%	13%	8%	20%	11%	12%	0%	12%	10%	18%	19%	14%	12%
	20-29	0	18	50	0	13	15	20	0	24	18	21	31	18	13	26	15
	30-39	25	27	50	25	13	23	7	22	36	24	17	17	18	29	12	31
	40-49	50	36	0	25	25	15	33	22	20	29	17	17	26	19	16	13
	50-59	0	0	0	0	13	8	7	11	8	12	17	12	12	15	16	10
	60-69	0	0	0	25	25	15	7	22	0	12	12	7	6	6	11	10
	70-79	0	9	0	0	0	8	0	11	0	6	0	7	0	0	4	8
	80-89	0	0	0	0	0	8	7	0	0	0	5	0	3	0	2	2
# SURVEYED		4	11	4	4	8	13	15	9	25	17	42	42	34	48	57	52

TABLE IV: PRESTIGE OF OCCUPATION - BY AGE

Question: Prestige of respondent's occupation.

Responses: See Appendix D for explanation and sample occupations.

		YEAR															
AGE	RESP	'72	'73	'74	'75	'76	'77	'78	'80	'82	'83	'84	'85	'86	'87	'88	'89
18-23	10-19	13%	9%	15%	16%	17%	18%	15%	13%	16%	14%	22%	18%	13%	17%	13%	15%
	20-29	22	26	24	27	19	30	21	22	22	28	22	26	10	19	24	19
	30-39	33	31	31	28	40	28	33	31	40	27	29	22	37	32	35	36
	40-49	19	28	22	25	17	19	24	26	17	21	16	21	27	19	20	17
	50-59	10	4	5	2	4	4	5	8	5	8	8	8	9	11	6	10
	60-69	2	1	3	2	2	2	2	1	0	2	3	5	3	2	2	2
	70-79	2	0	1	0	0	0	1	0	0	0	0	0	0	0	0	1
	80-89	0	0	0	0	0	0	0	0	0	0	0	0	0	0	0	0
# SURVEYED		122	121	131	134	126	134	130	120	121	108	134	110	91	104	110	104
AGE	RESP	'72	'73	'74	'75	'76	'77	'78	'80	'82	'83	'84	'85	'86	'87	'88	'89
24-29	10-19	4%	5%	8%	4%	9%	9%	9%	6%	8%	7%	7%	7%	9%	5%	4%	4%
	20-29	9	17	14	13	12	15	13	16	20	18	15	12	12	13	14	14
	30-39	30	26	17	27	28	33	26	21	30	26	30	35	29	32	32	29
	40-49	36	29	33	31	30	23	28	35	23	29	26	22	22	17	22	24
	50-59	9	10	12	12	11	8	10	15	12	11	13	16	16	21	17	18
	60-69	12	8	14	13	10	9	11	4	6	8	8	6	8	10	9	9
	70-79	1	5	2	1	1	3	4	2	2	1	1	2	3	2	3	1
	80-89	0	0	0	0	0	0	0	0	0	0	0	0	0	1	0	1
# SURVEYED		210	189	197	215	207	192	226	188	234	267	217	210	204	183	206	194
AGE	RESP	'72	'73	'74	'75	'76	'77	'78	'80	'82	'83	'84	'85	'86	'87	'88	'89
30-35	10-19	5%	8%	4%	7%	8%	9%	7%	7%	10%	5%	10%	6%	6%	8%	6%	6%
	20-29	12	10	16	17	14	13	12	14	13	13	11	13	14	8	11	8
	30-39	29	24	28	32	26	31	25	21	26	23	22	20	29	27	24	29
	40-49	29	33	25	21	31	20	30	26	24	33	22	29	23	22	19	22
	50-59	14	16	13	12	10	11	12	21	14	14	19	18	17	21	26	20
	60-69	11	8	11	10	10	15	13	8	10	10	13	13	8	9	9	11
	70-79	1	2	3	2	1	2	1	2	4	2	2	2	3	3	6	5
	80-89	0	0	0	0	0	0	0	1	0	0	1	0	0	1	1	0
# SURVEYED		175	153	160	155	174	177	217	203	200	226	194	207	211	215	188	200
AGE	RESP	'72	'73	'74	'75	'76	'77	'78	'80	'82	'83	'84	'85	'86	'87	'88	'89
36-41	10-19	8%	9%	6%	9%	10%	6%	9%	4%	13%	3%	6%	5%	1%	4%	7%	7%
	20-29	11	17	14	20	12	11	14	12	10	13	14	8	11	8	12	8
	30-39	21	19	26	23	26	27	25	20	28	19	28	27	25	22	25	23
	40-49	38	31	30	27	22	26	29	29	22	31	23	21	27	24	25	19
	50-59	13	10	14	13	17	13	11	20	10	15	13	21	19	25	19	22
	60-69	8	10	8	8	8	13	10	10	12	16	12	12	12	13	7	17
	70-79	2	4	2	1	3	3	2	4	6	3	3	6	4	3	3	4
	80-89	0	0	0	0	1	1	1	0	0	0	1	1	1	0	1	1
# SURVEYED		119	162	143	151	155	161	151	142	144	166	180	180	183	183	188	193

TABLE IV: PRESTIGE OF OCCUPATION - BY AGE

Question: Prestige of respondent's occupation.

Responses: See Appendix D for explanation and sample occupations.

		YEAR															
AGE	RESP	'72	'73	'74	'75	'76	'77	'78	'80	'82	'83	'84	'85	'86	'87	'88	'89
42-47	10-19	14%	12%	8%	6%	11%	7%	11%	5%	11%	5%	10%	7%	6%	10%	8%	9%
	20-29	14	13	17	16	13	16	13	12	11	14	12	7	14	14	12	8
	30-39	30	26	25	26	23	31	23	35	29	21	31	20	23	23	28	24
	40-49	23	20	25	27	22	24	26	25	21	31	22	21	18	24	22	21
	50-59	8	13	8	13	15	13	13	12	15	18	15	21	24	20	18	22
	60-69	11	13	13	12	11	8	10	10	11	6	8	16	11	7	8	10
	70-79	0	4	3	1	4	1	3	2	2	4	2	7	2	2	3	6
	80-89	0	0	1	0	0	0	0	0	1	1	1	1	1	1	1	0
# SURVEYED		166	136	138	135	105	138	115	113	113	139	120	121	133	153	157	159
AGE	RESP	'72	'73	'74	'75	'76	'77	'78	'80	'82	'83	'84	'85	'86	'87	'88	'89
48-53	10-19	12%	10%	6%	13%	8%	12%	9%	13%	11%	3%	12%	9%	8%	10%	7%	3%
	20-29	13	22	19	14	18	14	16	14	11	15	13	12	16	16	14	13
	30-39	27	20	28	23	35	29	29	24	30	18	21	26	29	19	27	25
	40-49	29	28	27	25	23	21	25	22	24	31	26	24	16	23	21	26
	50-59	12	13	10	17	9	13	12	14	13	16	21	14	15	20	12	15
	60-69	7	6	7	7	5	8	9	12	10	13	6	10	11	10	16	13
	70-79	1	1	2	1	2	3	0	2	2	4	0	4	4	2	3	5
	80-89	0	0	0	0	0	0	0	0	0	0	0	1	0	0	0	0
# SURVEYED		182	132	134	132	120	150	128	118	103	110	99	127	99	124	92	134
AGE	RESP	'72	'73	'74	'75	'76	'77	'78	'80	'82	'83	'84	'85	'86	'87	'88	'89
54-59	10-19	12%	12%	14%	14%	11%	14%	8%	10%	11%	9%	9%	11%	5%	4%	11%	14%
	20-29	16	17	13	16	21	15	13	15	14	14	21	14	16	8	15	18
	30-39	26	28	22	26	23	21	22	28	32	26	23	27	31	34	28	31
	40-49	26	24	26	27	28	26	31	23	22	22	20	28	28	19	27	18
	50-59	12	11	11	11	11	12	15	19	12	18	13	9	14	24	10	9
	60-69	7	7	12	3	6	9	7	4	8	9	11	8	3	7	10	4
	70-79	1	1	2	2	1	3	2	1	1	3	4	2	2	3	0	6
	80-89	0	0	0	0	0	0	1	0	0	0	0	0	0	0	0	0
# SURVEYED		145	149	133	118	121	158	126	130	138	129	114	132	97	95	82	95
AGE	RESP	'72	'73	'74	'75	'76	'77	'78	'80	'82	'83	'84	'85	'86	'87	'88	'89
60-65	10-19	19%	11%	15%	13%	14%	8%	13%	5%	18%	8%	12%	8%	6%	8%	2%	10%
	20-29	13	16	13	14	18	18	26	17	17	17	14	14	14	17	13	15
	30-39	28	30	24	37	24	31	20	27	24	27	28	23	27	28	25	36
	40-49	19	24	27	21	31	19	23	27	21	26	26	26	27	24	25	14
	50-59	13	11	12	7	5	11	8	15	13	14	11	15	13	15	19	10
	60-69	4	7	9	7	7	12	6	7	7	6	8	8	10	6	12	11
	70-79	2	0	0	2	1	1	4	0	0	1	0	5	4	1	4	1
	80-89	0	1	0	0	0	0	0	1	0	0	1	1	1	0	0	1
# SURVEYED		134	107	100	104	126	110	104	111	108	126	108	125	109	99	113	105

TABLE IV: PRESTIGE OF OCCUPATION - BY AGE

Question: Prestige of respondent's occupation.

Responses: See Appendix D for explanation and sample occupations.

AGE	RESP	'72	'73	'74	'75	'76	'77	'78	'80	'82	'83	'84	'85	'86	'87	'88	'89
66+	10-19	18%	16%	14%	10%	10%	15%	10%	12%	13%	9%	13%	15%	9%	7%	8%	8%
	20-29	17	16	20	18	16	16	23	24	14	21	17	16	20	18	23	10
	30-39	22	24	19	22	25	31	20	19	30	23	24	20	21	24	27	33
	40-49	19	25	25	28	30	21	27	24	26	24	22	28	27	31	21	25
	50-59	11	12	9	14	8	7	7	11	9	11	13	11	13	14	12	12
	60-69	8	6	11	7	8	8	13	9	7	11	10	7	7	5	6	8
	70-79	4	2	2	2	2	1	1	1	0	1	1	2	2	2	2	4
	80-89	1	0	0	0	0	1	1	0	0	0	0	0	1	0	0	0
# SURVEYED		190	179	210	200	212	189	200	217	232	215	210	234	234	234	254	253

****

SELF-EMPLOYED

TABLE I: ARE YOU SELF-EMPLOYED - BY TOTAL POPULATION

Question: Respondent's self-employment status.

Responses: SL = Self-employed; SO = Someone else

RESPONSE	'72	'73	'74	'75	'76	'77	'78	'80	'82	'83	'84	'85	'86	'87	'88	'89
SL	10%	11%	9%	11%	10%	9%	10%	13%	12%	11%	12%	13%	14%	12%	12%	12%
SO	90	89	91	89	90	91	90	87	88	89	88	87	86	88	88	88
# SURVEYED	1448	1347	1354	1348	1352	1417	1404	1342	1407	1488	1380	1453	1370	1392	1390	1419

TABLE II: SELF-EMPLOYED - BY SEX

Question: Respondent's self-employment status.

Responses: SL = Self-employed; SO = Someone else

		YEAR															
SEX	RESP	'72	'73	'74	'75	'76	'77	'78	'80	'82	'83	'84	'85	'86	'87	'88	'89
M	SL	13%	15%	12%	15%	14%	14%	14%	18%	18%	17%	16%	17%	18%	17%	15%	16%
	SO	87	85	88	85	86	86	86	82	82	83	84	83	82	83	85	84
# SURVEYED		780	670	676	647	654	681	636	628	624	678	588	675	613	635	618	634
SEX	RESP	'72	'73	'74	'75	'76	'77	'78	'80	'82	'83	'84	'85	'86	'87	'88	'89
F	SL	7%	7%	5%	7%	6%	4%	7%	8%	7%	7%	10%	10%	10%	8%	9%	9%
	SO	93	93	95	93	94	96	93	92	93	93	90	90	90	92	91	91
# SURVEYED		668	677	678	701	698	736	768	714	783	810	792	778	757	757	772	785

TABLE III: SELF-EMPLOYED - BY RACE

Question: Respondent's self-employment status.

Responses: SL = Self-employed; SO = Someone else

		YEAR															
RACE	RESP	'72	'73	'74	'75	'76	'77	'78	'80	'82	'83	'84	'85	'86	'87	'88	'89
WHITE	SL	10%	12%	9%	10%	11%	10%	10%	13%	13%	12%	13%	14%	15%	14%	13%	13%
	SO	90	88	91	90	89	90	90	87	87	88	87	86	85	86	87	87
# SURVEYED		1210	1171	1193	1194	1224	1249	1250	1214	1237	1319	1179	1266	1169	1170	1165	1226
RACE	RESP	'72	'73	'74	'75	'76	'77	'78	'80	'82	'83	'84	'85	'86	'87	'88	'89
BLACK	SL	10%	5%	4%	12%	7%	3%	6%	6%	4%	3%	5%	7%	5%	5%	4%	4%
	SO	90	95	96	88	93	97	94	94	96	97	95	93	95	95	96	96
# SURVEYED		234	164	157	150	120	155	139	119	145	152	159	145	167	174	168	141
RACE	RESP	'72	'73	'74	'75	'76	'77	'78	'80	'82	'83	'84	'85	'86	'87	'88	'89
OTHER	SL	0%	0%	50%	25%	0%	23%	7%	22%	12%	12%	17%	10%	15%	10%	14%	10%
	SO	100	100	50	75	100	77	93	78	88	88	83	90	85	90	86	90
# SURVEYED		4	12	4	4	8	13	15	9	25	17	42	42	34	48	57	52

TABLE IV: SELF-EMPLOYED - BY AGE

Question: Respondent's self-employment status.

Responses: SL = Self-employed SO = Someone else

		YEAR															
AGE	RESP	'72	'73	'74	'75	'76	'77	'78	'80	'82	'83	'84	'85	'86	'87	'88	'89
18-23	SL	2%	5%	2%	4%	2%	1%	3%	4%	3%	5%	7%	2%	5%	4%	4%	6%
	SO	98	95	98	96	98	99	97	96	97	95	93	98	95	96	96	94
# SURVEYED		122	123	131	134	126	134	130	120	121	108	134	110	91	104	110	103
AGE	RESP	'72	'73	'74	'75	'76	'77	'78	'80	'82	'83	'84	'85	'86	'87	'88	'89
24-29	SL	3%	4%	3%	3%	7%	4%	7%	9%	11%	7%	8%	14%	11%	9%	8%	8%
	SO	97	96	97	97	93	96	93	91	89	93	92	86	89	91	92	92
# SURVEYED		210	192	198	215	206	192	226	188	234	266	217	210	204	183	204	192

TABLE IV: SELF-EMPLOYED - BY AGE (Continued)

Question: Respondent's self-employment status.

Responses: SL = Self-employed SO = Someone else

		YEAR															
AGE	RESP	'72	'73	'74	'75	'76	'77	'78	'80	'82	'83	'84	'85	'86	'87	'88	'89
30-35	SL	9%	12%	6%	10%	9%	8%	7%	8%	11%	10%	8%	12%	11%	7%	15%	13%
	SO	91	88	94	90	91	92	93	92	89	90	92	88	89	93	85	87
# SURVEYED		175	153	161	155	174	177	217	202	201	224	194	207	211	215	188	195
AGE	RESP	'72	'73	'74	'75	'76	'77	'78	'80	'82	'83	'84	'85	'86	'87	'88	'89
36-41	SL	8%	6%	12%	9%	8%	9%	9%	14%	9%	12%	15%	16%	17%	13%	16%	9%
	SO	92	94	88	91	92	91	91	86	91	88	85	84	83	87	84	91
# SURVEYED		119	165	143	151	155	161	151	141	144	166	181	180	184	183	188	190
AGE	RESP	'72	'73	'74	'75	'76	'77	'78	'80	'82	'83	'84	'85	'86	'87	'88	'89
42-47	SL	8%	12%	12%	11%	8%	12%	14%	18%	16%	13%	16%	15%	12%	15%	12%	13%
	SO	92	88	88	89	92	88	86	82	84	87	84	85	88	85	88	87
# SURVEYED		167	138	138	133	105	138	115	113	114	139	120	121	134	153	156	157
AGE	RESP	'72	'73	'74	'75	'76	'77	'78	'80	'82	'83	'84	'85	'86	'87	'88	'89
48-53	SL	10%	15%	10%	13%	11%	9%	16%	17%	15%	17%	9%	16%	22%	15%	11%	17%
	SO	90	85	90	87	89	91	84	83	85	83	91	84	78	85	89	83
# SURVEYED		182	137	134	133	120	150	128	118	103	109	99	127	99	124	92	131
AGE	RESP	'72	'73	'74	'75	'76	'77	'78	'80	'82	'83	'84	'85	'86	'87	'88	'89
54-59	SL	13%	12%	10%	12%	11%	15%	13%	17%	10%	14%	15%	11%	16%	19%	10%	15%
	SO	87	88	90	88	89	85	87	83	90	86	85	89	84	81	90	85
# SURVEYED		145	149	133	121	122	158	126	130	138	129	114	132	97	95	81	95
AGE	RESP	'72	'73	'74	'75	'76	'77	'78	'80	'82	'83	'84	'85	'86	'87	'88	'89
60-65	SL	15%	16%	12%	14%	12%	12%	13%	12%	15%	11%	15%	18%	14%	12%	12%	5%
	SO	85	84	88	86	88	88	87	88	85	89	85	82	86	88	88	95
# SURVEYED		133	107	100	103	126	111	104	107	110	125	108	125	109	99	114	104
AGE	RESP	'72	'73	'74	'75	'76	'77	'78	'80	'82	'83	'84	'85	'86	'87	'88	'89
66+	SL	21%	18%	12%	22%	19%	14%	12%	16%	16%	14%	17%	15%	15%	18%	13%	17%
	SO	79	82	88	78	81	86	88	84	84	86	83	85	85	82	87	83
# SURVEYED		191	179	210	199	212	189	200	216	234	215	210	234	234	234	253	249

****

TEN-YEAR EMPLOYMENT HISTORY

TABLE I: TEN-YEAR EMPLOYMENT HISTORY - BY TOTAL POPULATION

Question: At any time during the last ten years, have you been unemployed or looking for work for as long as a month? NOTE: Question not asked in 1972, 1982, 1985 and 1987.

Responses: Yes; No

	YEAR											
RESPONSE	'73	'74	'75	'76	'77	'78	'80	'83	'84	'86	'88	'89
YES	28%	26%	28%	28%	28%	29%	28%	34%	33%	30%	31%	28%
NO	72	74	72	72	72	71	72	66	67	70	69	72
# SURVEYED	1503	1482	1479	1498	1527	1530	1468	1595	1468	1466	994	1032

TABLE II: TEN-YEAR EMPLOYMENT HISTORY - BY SEX

Question: At any time during the last ten years, have you been unemployed or looking for work for as long as a month? NOTE: Question not asked in 1972, 1982, 1985 and 1987.

Responses: Yes; No

		YEAR											
SEX	RESP	'73	'74	'75	'76	'77	'78	'80	'83	'84	'86	'88	'89
M	YES	29%	28%	30%	31%	30%	33%	30%	38%	40%	34%	34%	33%
	NO	71	72	70	69	70	67	70	62	60	66	66	67
# SURVEYED		701	690	666	669	692	643	641	689	598	620	436	442
SEX	RESP	'73	'74	'75	'76	'77	'78	'80	'83	'84	'86	'88	'89
F	YES	27%	24%	25%	25%	27%	26%	26%	30%	29%	28%	29%	25%
	NO	73	76	75	75	73	74	74	70	71	72	71	75
# SURVEYED		802	792	813	829	835	887	827	906	870	846	558	590

TABLE III: TEN-YEAR EMPLOYMENT HISTORY - BY RACE

Question: At any time during the last ten years, have you been unemployed or looking for work for as long as a month? NOTE: Question not asked in 1972, 1982, 1985 and 1987.

Responses: Yes; No

		YEAR											
RACE	RESP	'73	'74	'75	'76	'77	'78	'80	'83	'84	'86	'88	'89
WHITE	YES	27%	25%	26%	26%	27%	28%	27%	33%	32%	29%	30%	27%
	NO	73	75	74	74	73	72	73	67	68	71	70	73
# SURVEYED		1307	1303	1317	1360	1336	1357	1318	1412	1246	1248	835	880
RACE	RESP	'73	'74	'75	'76	'77	'78	'80	'83	'84	'86	'88	'89
BLACK	YES	36%	37%	41%	40%	38%	41%	36%	40%	46%	40%	45%	36%
	NO	64	63	59	60	62	59	64	60	54	60	55	64
# SURVEYED		183	172	158	129	176	157	140	165	170	181	116	110
RACE	RESP	'73	'74	'75	'76	'77	'78	'80	'83	'84	'86	'88	'89
OTHER	YES	46%	14%	25%	33%	13%	31%	50%	33%	33%	32%	30%	31%
	NO	54	86	75	67	87	69	50	67	67	68	70	69
# SURVEYED		13	7	4	9	15	16	10	18	52	37	43	42

TABLE IV: TEN-YEAR EMPLOYMENT HISTORY - BY AGE

Question: At any time during the last ten years, have you been une ployed or looking for work for as long as a month? NOTE: Question not asked in 1972, 1982, 1985 and 1987.

Responses: Yes; No

		YEAR											
AGE	RESP	'73	'74	'75	'76	'77	'78	'80	'83	'84	'86	'88	'89
18-23	YES	56%	51%	51%	49%	54%	52%	47%	54%	55%	59%	52%	34%
	NO	44	49	49	51	46	48	53	46	45	41	48	66
# SURVEYED		171	168	170	162	164	163	155	128	159	108	93	93
AGE	RESP	'73	'74	'75	'76	'77	'78	'80	'83	'84	'86	'88	'89
24-29	YES	44%	45%	41%	49%	51%	56%	48%	52%	52%	51%	53%	48%
	NO	56	55	59	51	49	44	52	48	48	49	47	52
# SURVEYED		212	212	231	226	204	244	202	286	232	217	145	142

TABLE IV: TEN-YEAR EMPLOYMENT HISTORY - BY AGE (Continued)

Question: At any time during the last ten years, have you been unemployed or looking for work for as long as a month? NOTE: Question not asked in 1972, 1982, 1985 and 1987.

Responses: Yes; No

		YEAR											
AGE	RESP	'73	'74	'75	'76	'77	'78	'80	'83	'84	'86	'88	'89
30-35	YES	28%	32%	37%	36%	36%	39%	47%	50%	42%	43%	48%	41%
	NO	72	68	63	64	64	61	53	50	58	57	52	59
# SURVEYED		167	175	171	186	187	230	215	235	199	221	127	145
AGE	RESP	'73	'74	'75	'76	'77	'78	'80	'83	'84	'86	'88	'89
36-41	YES	29%	25%	29%	26%	28%	22%	27%	40%	36%	28%	37%	42%
	NO	71	75	71	74	72	78	73	60	64	72	63	58
# SURVEYED		175	152	153	157	168	160	150	173	187	188	126	132
AGE	RESP	'73	'74	'75	'76	'77	'78	'80	'83	'84	'86	'88	'89
42-47	YES	23%	19%	25%	22%	25%	25%	28%	29%	34%	39%	32%	23%
	NO	77	81	75	78	75	75	72	71	66	61	68	77
# SURVEYED		145	151	142	114	146	118	117	144	125	140	104	107
AGE	RESP	'73	'74	'75	'76	'77	'78	'80	'83	'84	'86	'88	'89
48-53	YES	26%	21%	25%	23%	18%	18%	16%	22%	30%	24%	25%	22%
	NO	74	79	75	77	82	82	84	78	70	76	75	78
# SURVEYED		151	145	140	133	153	133	123	116	102	108	57	96
AGE	RESP	'73	'74	'75	'76	'77	'78	'80	'83	'84	'86	'88	'89
54-59	YES	17%	13%	17%	18%	18%	13%	15%	22%	18%	17%	20%	22%
	NO	83	87	83	82	82	87	85	78	82	83	80	78
# SURVEYED		157	139	126	129	168	137	136	133	114	99	66	63
AGE	RESP	'73	'74	'75	'76	'77	'78	'80	'83	'84	'86	'88	'89
60-65	YES	12%	16%	11%	15%	21%	11%	13%	12%	13%	13%	15%	15%
	NO	88	84	89	85	79	89	87	88	88	87	85	85
# SURVEYED		121	107	112	134	117	107	119	132	112	115	80	75
AGE	RESP	'73	'74	'75	'76	'77	'78	'80	'83	'84	'86	'88	'89
66+	YES	11%	7%	7%	5%	4%	7%	3%	7%	10%	4%	4%	4%
	NO	90	93	93	95	96	93	97	93	90	96	96	96
# SURVEYED		200	227	229	251	213	231	242	241	232	263	192	178

****

FIVE-YEAR EMPLOYMENT HISTORY

TABLE I: FIVE-YEAR EMPLOYMENT HISTORY - BY TOTAL POPULATION

Question: Have you been unemployed during last five years? NOTE: Question not asked in 1972-1977, 1982, and 1985.

Responses:

0 = Not unemployed
1 = Unemployed during four years before last year and not main earner
2 = Unemployed during four years before last year and main earner
3 = Unemployed last year and not main earner
4 = Unemployed last year and during four previous years and not main earner
5 = Unemployed last year and not main earner and unemployed during previous four years and main earner
6 = Unemployed last year and main earner
7 = Unemployed last year and main earner and unemployed previous four years and not main earner
8 = Unemployed last year and previous four years and main earner both periods

	YEAR							
RESPONSE	'78	'80	'83	'84	'86	'87	'88	'89
0	78%	79%	75%	75%	78%	77%	76%	82%
1	5	5	5	4	6	6	7	5
2	6	6	5	7	5	6	7	5
3	2	1	2	1	1	1	2	2
4	3	3	4	4	3	3	2	2
5	0	0	1	0	0	0	0	0
6	1	2	3	2	1	2	2	2
7	1	0	0	1	1	0	0	0
8	4	3	6	5	4	4	4	3
# SURVEYED	1525	1464	1589	1457	1461	1455	992	1025

TABLE II: FIVE-YEAR EMPLOYMENT HISTORY - BY SEX

Question: Have you been unemployed during last five years? NOTE: Question not asked in 1972-1977, 1982 and 1985.

Responses:
0 = Not unemployed
1 = Unemployed during four years before last year and not main earner
2 = Unemployed during four years before last year and main earner
3 = Unemployed last year and not main earner
4 = Unemployed last year and during four previous years and not main earner
5 = Unemployed last year and not main earner and unemployed during previous four years and main earner
6 = Unemployed last year and main earner
7 = Unemployed last year and main earner and unemployed previous four years and not main earner
8 = Unemployed last year and previous four years and main earner both periods

		YEAR							
SEX	RESP	'78	'80	'83	'84	'86	'87	'88	'89
MALE	0	76%	78%	71%	70%	75%	76%	75%	79%
	1	3	5	3	4	5	4	7	4
	2	10	8	7	9	8	9	9	8
	3	0	0	2	1	1	1	1	2
	4	2	2	2	3	3	3	2	1
	5	0	0	1	1	1	0	0	1
	6	2	2	3	2	1	2	3	2
	7	1	0	1	1	1	0	0	0
	8	6	4	10	9	5	6	4	4
# SURVEYED		639	640	684	591	618	638	434	438
SEX	RESP	'78	'80	'83	'84	'86	'87	'88	'89
FEMALE	0	80%	80%	77%	79%	80%	78%	77%	84%
	1	7	6	7	5	7	7	8	5
	2	3	5	3	5	3	5	5	3
	3	2	2	2	2	1	2	2	1
	4	4	3	5	5	3	3	3	2
	5	0	0	1	0	0	0	0	0
	6	1	2	2	1	1	2	1	2
	7	1	1	0	0	0	0	1	0
	8	2	2	3	3	4	3	3	2
# SURVEYED		886	824	905	866	843	817	558	587

TABLE III: FIVE-YEAR EMPLOYMENT HISTORY - BY RACE

Question: Have you been unemployed during last five years? NOTE: Question not asked in 1972-1977, 1982 and 1985.

Responses:
0 = Not unemployed
1 = Unemployed during four years before last year and not main earner
2 = Unemployed during four years before last year and main earner
3 = Unemployed last year and not main earner
4 = Unemployed last year and during four previous years and not main earner
5 = Unemployed last year and not main earner and unemployed during previous four years and main earner
6 = Unemployed last year and main earner
7 = Unemployed last year and main earner and unemployed previous four years and not main earner
8 = Unemployed last year and previous four years and main earner both periods

		YEAR							
RACE	RESP	'78	'80	'83	'84	'86	'87	'88	'89
WHITE	0	80%	80%	75%	77%	79%	78%	78%	82%
	1	5	5	5	4	6	6	7	5
	2	6	6	5	6	5	6	6	6
	3	1	1	2	1	1	2	2	2
	4	3	3	3	4	2	2	2	1
	5	0	0	0	0	1	0	0	0
	6	1	2	3	2	1	2	1	1
	7	1	0	0	1	1	0	0	0
	8	3	3	6	4	4	4	3	2
# SURVEYED		1353	1314	1407	1238	1243	1215	832	873
RACE	RESP	'78	'80	'83	'84	'86	'87	'88	'89
BLACK	0	65%	74%	67%	63%	67%	72%	62%	77%
	1	7	7	5	6	7	6	7	3
	2	4	4	6	9	5	8	8	3
	3	3	1	4	2	2	1	3	2
	4	7	4	7	5	7	5	5	4
	5	1	0	1	0	0	0	0	1
	6	3	3	2	1	2	3	5	2
	7	1	2	1	1	1	1	1	0
	8	9	6	7	13	10	5	9	9
# SURVEYED		156	140	165	167	181	188	116	110
RACE	RESP	'78	'80	'83	'84	'86	'87	'88	'89
OTHER	0	69%	60%	76%	73%	84%	67%	73%	83%
	1	0	10	6	6	8	2	11	2
	2	6	20	6	8	5	10	9	2
	3	6	0	0	0	0	2	0	0
	4	13	0	6	2	0	8	5	2
	5	0	0	6	0	0	2	0	0
	6	6	10	0	4	3	4	0	5
	7	0	0	0	0	0	0	0	0
	8	0	0	0	8	0	6	2	5
# SURVEYED		16	10	17	52	37	52	44	42

TABLE IV: FIVE-YEAR EMPLOYMENT HISTORY - BY AGE

Question: Have you been unemployed during last five years? NOTE: Question not asked in 1972-1977, 1982 and 1985.

Responses:
0 = Not unemployed
1 = Unemployed during four years before last year and not main earner
2 = Unemployed during four years before last year and main earner
3 = Unemployed last year and not main earner
4 = Unemployed last year and during four previous years and not main earner
5 = Unemployed last year and not main earner and unemployed during previous four years and main earner
6 = Unemployed last year and main earner
7 = Unemployed last year and main earner and unemployed previous four years and not main earner
8 = Unemployed last year and previous four years and main earner both periods

		YEAR							
AGE	RESP	'78	'80	'83	'84	'86	'87	'88	'89
18-23	0	55%	55%	49%	52%	46%	52%	57%	70%
	1	17	19	15	12	20	15	14	10
	2	3	3	2	4	2	4	4	2
	3	4	5	10	6	6	9	5	7
	4	16	12	13	17	16	10	10	5
	5	1	0	2	1	1	1	1	0
	6	1	3	2	1	2	6	3	2
	7	2	1	2	2	4	1	3	0
	8	3	3	4	5	3	2	2	3
# SURVEYED		160	155	127	156	108	124	93	91
AGE	RESP	'78	'80	'83	'84	'86	'87	'88	'89
24-29	0	56%	63%	58%	58%	59%	60%	59%	65%
	1	11	13	10	10	14	11	20	11
	2	13	10	8	11	7	10	10	13
	3	3	1	2	1	3	3	1	2
	4	5	4	6	7	6	6	3	2
	5	0	0	1	0	1	0	0	1
	6	4	3	4	3	1	4	1	3
	7	2	2	0	1	1	1	0	1
	8	7	6	11	8	7	5	5	1
# SURVEYED		243	199	284	229	216	193	143	138
AGE	RESP	'78	'80	'83	'84	'86	'87	'88	'89
30-35	0	74%	69%	64%	71%	70%	69%	63%	76%
	1	5	5	8	5	7	8	10	8
	2	10	12	9	11	10	10	12	4
	3	2	2	3	1	0	0	2	2
	4	0	3	5	4	3	5	2	1
	5	1	0	1	1	0	0	0	1
	6	2	4	3	4	2	2	3	3
	7	1	1	0	2	1	0	0	0
	8	5	4	8	4	5	6	7	5
# SURVEYED		230	214	234	199	220	220	128	146

		YEAR							
AGE	RESP	'78	'80	'83	'84	'86	'87	'88	'89
36-41	0	85%	81%	71%	74%	82%	74%	74%	73%
	1	3	3	2	1	4	7	6	4
	2	5	9	6	7	6	8	10	10
	3	1	0	2	2	1	1	1	2
	4	1	2	3	1	2	2	1	1
	5	0	0	0	1	1	1	2	1
	6	1	3	5	2	1	1	2	2
	7	1	0	0	0	1	0	0	0
	8	4	3	10	13	3	6	4	7
# SURVEYED		159	150	171	186	186	184	126	132
AGE	RESP	'78	'80	'83	'84	'86	'87	'88	'89
42-47	0	81%	80%	78%	75%	74%	74%	75%	87%
	1	2	3	3	3	4	3	5	3
	2	8	5	6	7	9	9	10	6
	3	3	1	1	2	1	1	2	1
	4	1	2	1	2	1	2	2	1
	5	0	0	1	0	0	1	0	0
	6	2	3	3	2	2	2	1	0
	7	0	0	1	0	0	0	0	0
	8	3	5	5	8	9	7	6	3
# SURVEYED		118	117	144	123	139	155	104	107
AGE	RESP	'78	'80	'83	'84	'86	'87	'88	'89
48-53	0	89%	89%	82%	80%	83%	83%	82%	85%
	1	0	1	3	5	3	3	4	1
	2	5	2	3	8	3	8	5	5
	3	0	0	2	0	1	0	0	0
	4	3	2	3	1	0	1	2	1
	5	0	0	0	1	1	0	0	1
	6	0	2	2	0	3	0	4	2
	7	0	0	0	0	0	0	0	0
	8	3	3	5	5	6	5	4	4
# SURVEYED		133	123	116	100	108	124	57	95

TABLE IV: FIVE-YEAR EMPLOYMENT HISTORY - BY AGE (Continued)

Question: Have you been unemployed during last five years? NOTE: Question not asked in 1972-1977, 1982 and 1985.

Responses:
0 = Not unemployed
1 = Unemployed during four years before last year and not main earner
2 = Unemployed during four years before last year and main earner
3 = Unemployed last year and not main earner
4 = Unemployed last year and during four previous years and not main earner
5 = Unemployed last year and not main earner and unemployed during previous four years and main earner
6 = Unemployed last year and main earner
7 = Unemployed last year and main earner and unemployed previous four years and not main earner
8 = Unemployed last year and previous four years and main earner both periods

AGE	RESP	'78	'80	'83	'84	'86	'87	'88	'89
54-59	0	88%	88%	83%	85%	86%	91%	82%	87%
	1	2	3	2	1	2	3	0	3
	2	3	4	4	6	3	3	3	5
	3	0	0	1	0	0	0	3	0
	4	1	1	1	3	2	1	5	5
	5	0	0	0	0	0	0	0	0
	6	2	1	3	1	0	2	2	0
	7	0	0	0	0	0	0	2	0
	8	3	2	6	4	7	0	5	0
# SURVEYED		137	136	133	114	99	98	66	62
AGE	RESP	'78	'80	'83	'84	'86	'87	'88	'89
60-65	0	92%	92%	94%	93%	96%	91%	89%	95%
	1	1	1	0	2	2	2	3	1
	2	2	4	0	1	1	2	5	3
	3	0	1	1	0	0	0	1	0
	4	0	0	2	1	0	1	0	1
	5	0	0	0	0	0	0	0	0
	6	0	2	1	2	1	0	0	0
	7	0	0	0	0	0	0	0	0
	8	6	1	3	2	1	4	3	0
# SURVEYED		107	119	132	112	115	101	79	75
AGE	RESP	'78	'80	'83	'84	'86	'87	'88	'89
66+	0	97%	98%	99%	97%	99%	98%	98%	100%
	1	0	0	0	0	0	0	1	0
	2	2	1	0	2	0	1	1	0
	3	0	0	0	0	0	0	0	0
	4	0	0	0	0	0	0	1	0
	5	0	0	0	0	0	0	0	0
	6	0	0	0	0	0	0	0	0
	7	0	0	0	0	0	0	0	0
	8	1	0	0	0	0	0	1	0
# SURVEYED		231	242	241	232	263	253	192	178

****

UNION MEMBERSHIP

TABLE I: UNION MEMBERSHIP - BY TOTAL POPULATION

Question: Do you (or your spouse) belong to a labor union? Who? NOTE: Question not asked in 1972, 1974, 1977 and 1982.

Responses: YS = Yes, respondent belongs; SP = Yes, spouse belongs; BO = Yes, both belong; NO = No, neither belong

	YEAR											
RESPONSE	'73	'75	'76	'78	'80	'83	'84	'85	'86	'87	'88	'89
YS	15%	14%	15%	14%	13%	12%	14%	15%	9%	13%	12%	13%
SP	10	10	8	8	7	7	5	4	6	5	5	5
BO	3	2	2	2	1	2	2	1	2	2	1	1
NO	72	74	75	77	78	80	79	81	83	80	82	80
# SURVEYED	1495	1484	1482	1531	1462	1596	1458	663	1465	1456	996	1031

TABLE II: UNION MEMBERSHIP - BY SEX

Question: Do you (or your spouse) belong to a labor union? Who? NOTE: Question not asked in 1972, 1974, 1977 and 1982.

Responses: YS = Yes, respondent belongs; SP = Yes, spouse belongs; BO = Yes, both belong; NO = No, neither belong

		YEAR											
SEX	RESP	'73	'75	'76	'78	'80	'83	'84	'85	'86	'87	'88	'89
M	YS	27%	25%	24%	23%	21%	19%	21%	19%	15%	21%	18%	19%
	SP	1	2	2	2	2	3	1	4	2	2	2	2
	BO	4	2	1	2	1	2	2	1	3	2	1	1
	NO	68	71	72	73	75	76	77	77	80	75	79	77
# SURVEYED		700	668	660	643	640	690	595	387	620	639	438	442
SEX	RESP	'73	'75	'76	'78	'80	'83	'84	'85	'86	'87	'88	'89
F	YS	5%	5%	8%	7%	7%	6%	9%	9%	5%	7%	8%	8%
	SP	18	16	13	12	11	10	8	4	9	7	8	7
	BO	2	2	2	1	1	2	2	0	1	2	1	2
	NO	75	76	77	80	81	82	81	87	84	84	84	83
# SURVEYED		795	816	822	888	822	906	863	276	845	817	558	589

TABLE III: UNION MEMBERSHIP - BY RACE

Question: Do you (or your spouse) belong to a labor union? Who? NOTE: Question not asked in 1972, 1974, 1977 and 1982.

Responses: YS = Yes, respondent belongs; SP = Yes, spouse belongs; BO = Yes, both belong; NO = No, neither belong

		YEAR											
RACE	RESP	'73	'75	'76	'78	'80	'83	'84	'85	'86	'87	'88	'89
WHITE	YS	15%	14%	15%	13%	13%	11%	14%	14%	9%	12%	11%	13%
	SP	10	10	9	8	7	7	5	4	6	5	6	6
	BO	2	2	2	2	1	2	2	1	2	2	1	1
	NO	73	73	75	77	78	81	79	82	83	81	82	80
# SURVEYED		1302	1319	1351	1358	1312	1413	1237	593	1247	1215	837	879
RACE	RESP	'73	'75	'76	'78	'80	'83	'84	'85	'86	'87	'88	'89
BLACK	YS	22%	12%	20%	20%	13%	18%	14%	25%	10%	18%	17%	15%
	SP	9	7	4	4	6	7	4	2	6	5	3	3
	BO	5	1	2	2	1	4	4	0	3	2	3	2
	NO	64	80	74	73	79	72	79	74	81	75	78	80
# SURVEYED		180	161	122	157	140	165	169	57	181	188	116	110
RACE	RESP	'73	'75	'76	'78	'80	'83	'84	'85	'86	'87	'88	'89
OTHER	YS	15%	0%	33%	13%	0%	17%	10%	15%	3%	11%	14%	14%
	SP	8	25	11	0	0	6	8	8	5	4	0	5
	BO	0	0	0	0	0	0	0	0	0	2	0	0
	NO	77	75	56	88	100	78	83	77	92	83	86	81
# SURVEYED		13	4	9	16	10	18	52	13	37	53	43	42

TABLE IV: UNION MEMBERSHIP - BY AGE

Question: Do you (or your spouse) belong to a labor union? Who? NOTE: Question not asked in 1972, 1974, 1977 and 1982.

Responses: YS = Yes, respondent belongs; SP = Yes, spouse belongs; BO = Yes, both belong; NO = No, neither belong

		YEAR											
AGE	RESP	'73	'75	'76	'78	'80	'83	'84	'85	'86	'87	'88	'89
18-23	YS	12%	10%	10%	12%	7%	5%	9%	11%	5%	10%	3%	2%
	SP	8	5	3	4	9	3	1	0	2	1	2	2
	BO	2	1	1	0	1	1	1	0	0	2	0	0
	NO	77	84	87	85	83	91	89	89	94	88	95	96
# SURVEYED		169	172	158	163	155	128	161	38	108	126	92	92

TABLE IV: UNION MEMBERSHIP - BY AGE (Continued)

Question: Do you (or your spouse) belong to a labor union? Who? NOTE: Question not asked in 1972, 1974, 1977 and 1982.

Responses: YS = Yes, respondent belongs SP = Yes, spouse belongs
BO = Yes, both belong NO = No, neither belong

		YEAR											
AGE	RESP	'73	'75	'76	'78	'80	'83	'84	'85	'86	'87	'88	'89
24-29	YS	14%	17%	16%	15%	17%	11%	13%	11%	6%	7%	12%	9%
	SP	12	10	9	10	8	5	7	3	4	8	4	1
	BO	1	0	3	0	0	1	1	1	0	2	1	1
	NO	73	72	72	75	74	83	78	84	89	83	82	89
# SURVEYED		211	230	223	244	201	287	232	88	217	192	146	142
AGE	RESP	'73	'75	'76	'78	'80	'83	'84	'85	'86	'87	'88	'89
30-35	YS	11%	14%	17%	17%	18%	9%	12%	14%	8%	15%	9%	16%
	SP	11	14	12	9	6	10	7	7	10	7	7	5
	BO	4	4	0	3	1	2	4	2	3	2	1	1
	NO	74	69	71	71	75	80	77	77	79	76	84	77
# SURVEYED		167	170	185	230	215	235	195	88	221	221	128	146
AGE	RESP	'73	'75	'76	'78	'80	'83	'84	'85	'86	'87	'88	'89
36-41	YS	17%	16%	20%	16%	18%	17%	17%	17%	13%	18%	13%	16%
	SP	13	14	12	13	11	6	8	6	8	8	6	4
	BO	2	3	1	3	1	2	3	0	4	2	2	3
	NO	69	67	67	69	70	74	73	76	75	72	78	77
# SURVEYED		175	154	158	160	150	172	186	93	188	186	126	133
AGE	RESP	'73	'75	'76	'78	'80	'83	'84	'85	'86	'87	'88	'89
42-47	YS	21%	16%	13%	19%	16%	14%	13%	22%	15%	15%	14%	12%
	SP	14	13	13	7	6	12	7	5	7	4	9	7
	BO	3	1	3	3	3	3	2	0	1	6	1	2
	NO	62	69	71	72	75	71	79	72	77	76	76	79
# SURVEYED		146	143	112	118	116	145	126	58	141	156	104	107
AGE	RESP	'73	'75	'76	'78	'80	'83	'84	'85	'86	'87	'88	'89
48-53	YS	13%	14%	20%	16%	7%	14%	18%	17%	8%	19%	23%	19%
	SP	9	18	14	8	9	11	9	6	7	4	4	6
	BO	4	6	5	5	2	3	5	2	5	3	4	0
	NO	74	62	62	71	82	72	69	75	80	74	70	75
# SURVEYED		149	140	132	133	122	116	102	65	108	126	57	96
AGE	RESP	'73	'75	'76	'78	'80	'83	'84	'85	'86	'87	'88	'89
54-59	YS	21%	16%	18%	11%	16%	16%	19%	24%	12%	16%	24%	19%
	SP	16	10	11	7	7	10	9	4	7	7	8	16
	BO	6	2	3	1	0	3	2	0	1	1	2	2
	NO	57	72	68	81	77	70	70	73	80	75	67	63
# SURVEYED		155	126	129	137	135	134	114	55	99	97	66	63

TABLE IV: UNION MEMBERSHIP - BY AGE (Continued)

Question: Do you (or your spouse) belong to a labor union? Who? NOTE: Question not asked in 1972, 1974, 1977 and 1982.

Responses: YS = Yes, respondent belongs; SP = Yes, spouse belongs; BO = Yes, both belong; NO = No, neither belong

		YEAR											
AGE	RESP	'73	'75	'76	'78	'80	'83	'84	'85	'86	'87	'88	'89
60-65	YS	17%	22%	21%	14%	12%	15%	13%	16%	12%	13%	13%	15%
	SP	5	7	5	12	6	5	5	0	7	3	6	9
	BO	3	4	2	2	3	3	0	0	2	1	0	1
	NO	74	67	73	72	80	78	83	84	79	83	81	75
# SURVEYED		121	113	133	107	119	131	109	58	114	99	80	75
AGE	RESP	'73	'75	'76	'78	'80	'83	'84	'85	'86	'87	'88	'89
66+	YS	14%	7%	9%	8%	8%	7%	11%	8%	7%	7%	9%	11%
	SP	2	2	1	2	4	4	0	1	5	1	4	5
	BO	1	0	1	1	0	1	1	0	0	2	0	2
	NO	84	91	90	90	88	88	87	92	87	90	88	82
# SURVEYED		198	232	246	232	241	241	230	118	262	250	193	175

****

MILITARY SERVICE HISTORY

TABLE I: MILITARY SERVICE HISTORY - BY TOTAL POPULATION

Question: Have you ever been on active duty for military training or service for two years or more? If yes, what was your total time on active duty? NOTE: Question not asked in 1972-1973, 1976, 1980, 1986-1987.

Responses: NO = No active duty; -2 = Yes, less than two years; 24 = Yes, 2-4 years; 4+ = Yes, more than 4 years; DK = Some, don't know how long

	YEAR									
RESPONSE	'74	'75	'77	'78	'82	'83	'84	'85	'88	'89
NO	77%	78%	78%	79%	83%	82%	83%	81%	83%	83%
-2	4	6	5	4	3	4	3	4	4	4
24	12	13	13	12	11	11	9	11	9	9
4+	6	4	4	5	3	4	4	3	4	4
DK	0	0	0	0	0	0	0	0	0	0
# SURVEYED	1481	1488	1522	1527	1501	1596	1445	1531	982	986

TABLE II: MILITARY SERVICE HISTORY - BY SEX

Question: Have you ever been on active duty for military training or service for two years or more? If yes, what was your total time on active duty? NOTE: Question not asked in 1972-1973, 1976, 1980, 1986-1987.

Responses: NO = No active duty -2 = Yes, less than two years
24 = Yes, 2-4 years 4+ = Yes, more than 4 years DK = Some, don't know how long

		YEAR									
SEX	RESP	'74	'75	'77	'78	'82	'83	'84	'85	'88	'89
M	NO	53%	53%	53%	53%	62%	59%	61%	59%	63%	62%
A	-2	9	12	10	9	8	8	8	9	7	8
L	24	26	28	27	28	24	25	22	25	20	20
E	4+	12	8	9	11	7	8	9	7	9	10
	DK	0	0	0	0	0	0	0	0	0	0
# SURVEYED		691	670	688	641	637	689	585	688	435	421
SEX	RESP	'74	'75	'77	'78	'82	'83	'84	'85	'88	'89
F	NO	99%	99%	99%	98%	99%	99%	99%	99%	99%	99%
E	-2	0	1	0	1	0	0	0	1	1	1
M	24	1	0	1	1	1	1	1	1	0	1
A	4+	0	0	0	0	0	0	0	0	0	0
L	DK	0	0	0	0	0	0	0	0	0	0
E											
# SURVEYED		790	818	834	886	864	907	860	843	547	565

TABLE III: MILITARY SERVICE HISTORY - BY RACE

Question: Have you ever been on active duty for military training or service for two years or more? If yes, what was your total time on active duty? NOTE: Question not asked in 1972-1973, 1976, 1980, 1986-1987.

Responses: NO = No active duty -2 = Yes, less than two years
24 = Yes, 2-4 years 4+ = Yes, more than 4 years DK = Some, don't know how long

		YEAR									
RACE	RESP	'74	'75	'77	'78	'82	'83	'84	'85	'88	'89
WHITE	**NO**	76%	77%	77%	78%	83%	81%	83%	80%	82%	81%
	-2	5	6	5	5	4	4	4	5	4	4
	24	13	14	14	12	11	12	10	11	10	10
	4+	6	4	4	5	3	4	4	4	5	5
	DK	0	0	0	0	0	0	0	0	0	0
# SURVEYED		1301	1322	1332	1354	1319	1413	1226	1338	824	846
RACE	RESP	'74	'75	'77	'78	'82	'83	'84	'85	'88	'89
BLACK	**NO**	86%	89%	86%	85%	85%	90%	85%	83%	90%	92%
	-2	2	4	4	3	2	1	3	3	3	1
	24	10	6	7	10	8	8	8	13	6	4
	4+	2	2	3	3	5	1	4	2	2	3
	DK	0	0	0	0	0	0	0	0	0	0
# SURVEYED		173	162	175	157	155	165	168	149	124	102
RACE	RESP	'74	'75	'77	'78	'82	'83	'84	'85	'88	'89
OTHER	**NO**	100%	100%	80%	81%	89%	83%	88%	89%	94%	97%
	-2	0	0	0	0	7	0	4	2	0	3
	24	0	0	0	6	0	11	4	9	6	0
	4+	0	0	20	13	4	6	4	0	0	0
	DK	0	0	0	0	0	0	0	0	0	0
# SURVEYED		7	4	15	16	27	18	51	44	34	38

TABLE IV: MILITARY SERVICE HISTORY - BY AGE

Question: Have you ever been on active duty for military training or service for two years or more? If yes, what was your total time on active duty? NOTE: Question not asked in 1972-1973, 1976, 1980, 1986-1987.

Responses: NO = No active duty -2 = Yes, less than two years
24 = Yes, 2-4 years 4+ = Yes, more than 4 years DK = Some, don't know how long

		YEAR									
AGE	RESP	'74	'75	'77	'78	'82	'83	'84	'85	'88	'89
18-23	**NO**	94%	97%	96%	98%	96%	95%	97%	96%	98%	94%
	-2	4	3	2	1	1	2	1	1	2	5
	24	2	1	1	1	3	2	1	2	0	1
	4+	0	0	0	1	0	1	1	1	0	0
	DK	0	0	0	0	0	0	0	0	0	0
# SURVEYED		168	172	164	162	148	128	160	133	93	80

TABLE IV: MILITARY SERVICE HISTORY - BY AGE (Continued)

Question: Have you ever been on active duty for military training or service for two years or more? If yes, what was your total time on active duty? NOTE: Question not asked in 1972-1973, 1976, 1980, 1986-1987.

Responses: NO = No active duty; -2 = Yes, less than two years; 24 = Yes, 2-4 years; 4+ = Yes, more than 4 years; DK = Some, don't know how long

AGE	RESP	'74	'75	'77	'78	'82	'83	'84	'85	'88	'89
24-29	NO	76%	82%	82%	85%	91%	94%	93%	94%	93%	90%
	-2	6	6	5	4	2	1	3	1	5	3
	24	15	11	10	8	6	3	2	3	1	4
	4+	3	2	2	2	1	1	1	2	1	3
	DK	1	0	0	0	0	0	0	0	0	0
# SURVEYED		211	231	203	244	245	287	229	217	150	144
30-35	NO	82%	80%	78%	77%	83%	87%	88%	89%	95%	91%
	-2	2	6	3	3	4	3	3	3	2	2
	24	12	11	14	15	8	9	5	6	1	3
	4+	3	3	5	4	5	2	4	3	2	4
	DK	1	0	0	0	0	0	0	0	0	0
# SURVEYED		174	171	187	230	203	235	195	212	130	139
36-41	NO	76%	71%	76%	76%	84%	73%	77%	79%	85%	82%
	-2	5	7	6	5	3	5	9	8	3	6
	24	15	17	14	13	12	19	9	12	8	9
	4+	5	5	4	6	1	3	5	1	4	3
	DK	0	0	0	0	0	0	0	0	0	0
# SURVEYED		152	154	168	160	146	172	185	184	126	125
42-47	NO	66%	69%	70%	67%	79%	73%	83%	77%	66%	78%
	-2	3	6	6	3	6	6	4	7	5	3
	24	20	21	19	26	13	12	10	12	26	13
	4+	11	4	5	4	2	8	3	3	3	6
	DK	0	0	0	0	0	0	0	0	0	0
# SURVEYED		151	143	146	119	119	145	123	124	107	105
48-53	NO	62%	64%	60%	61%	74%	70%	73%	69%	85%	80%
	-2	7	8	10	11	4	6	2	6	3	4
	24	21	21	22	21	18	22	20	19	6	11
	4+	10	7	8	6	5	3	5	5	5	6
	DK	0	0	0	0	0	0	0	0	0	0
# SURVEYED		146	141	153	132	110	116	99	131	62	84

TABLE IV: MILITARY SERVICE HISTORY - BY AGE (Continued)

Question: Have you ever been on active duty for military training or service for two years or more? If yes, what was your total time on active duty? NOTE: Question not asked in 1972-1973, 1976, 1980, 1986-1987.

Responses: NO = No active duty -2 = Yes, less than two years
24 = Yes, 2-4 years 4+ = Yes, more than 4 years DK = Some, don't know how long

AGE	RESP	'74	'75	'77	'78	'82	'83	'84	'85	'88	'89
54-59	NO	63%	63%	65%	66%	76%	66%	66%	62%	73%	69%
	-2	3	6	4	4	6	7	5	11	4	6
	24	19	20	25	19	15	23	22	25	12	20
	4+	16	10	7	10	2	4	6	3	12	6
	DK	0	0	0	0	0	0	0	0	0	0
# SURVEYED		139	126	167	137	144	134	112	133	51	71
AGE	RESP	'74	'75	'77	'78	'82	'83	'84	'85	'88	'89
60-65	NO	83%	81%	78%	73%	68%	65%	65%	62%	64%	78%
	-2	3	4	3	3	3	5	4	2	3	1
	24	6	12	11	14	17	20	25	28	26	15
	4+	8	3	7	10	12	10	7	7	7	6
	DK	0	0	0	0	0	0	0	0	0	0
# SURVEYED		108	113	116	107	116	132	110	130	73	68
AGE	RESP	'74	'75	'77	'78	'82	'83	'84	'85	'88	'89
66+	NO	85%	84%	91%	89%	84%	88%	87%	82%	77%	79%
	-2	6	5	2	4	3	2	1	3	4	4
	24	5	9	5	3	11	6	8	8	11	11
	4+	3	2	2	3	2	3	4	6	8	7
	DK	1	0	0	0	0	0	0	0	0	0
# SURVEYED		226	232	211	230	258	240	228	261	189	168

****

BRANCH OF MILITARY SERVED

TABLE I: BRANCH OF MILITARY SERVED - BY TOTAL POPULATION

Question: In what branch of service was that? NOTE: Question not asked in 1972-1973, 1976, 1980, 1985-1989.

Responses:
0 = More than one
1 = Air Force Guard
2 = Air Force (Incl. reserves)
3 = Navy (Incl. reserves)
4 = Army (Incl. reserves)
5 = National Guard
6 = U.S. Marine Corps
7 = Coast Guard (Incl. reserves)
8 = Public Health

	YEAR						
RESPONSE	'74	'75	'77	'78	'82	'83	'84
0	2%	1%	1%	1%	0%	1%	2%
1	1	0	0	0	0	0	0
2	15	12	15	17	14	17	17
3	22	19	17	22	17	24	20
4	52	59	58	51	57	46	49
5	2	2	3	3	3	2	2
6	5	6	5	4	6	8	10
7	1	1	1	1	1	2	1
8	0	0	0	0	0	0	0
# SURVEYED	334	324	334	323	258	295	242

TABLE II: BRANCH OF MILITARY SERVED - BY SEX

Question: In what branch of service was that? NOTE: Question not asked in 1972-1973, 1976, 1980, 1985-1989.

Responses:
0 = More than one
1 = Air Force Guard
2 = Air Force (Incl. reserves)
3 = Navy (Incl. reserves)
4 = Army (Incl. reserves)
5 = National Guard
6 = U.S. Marine Corps
7 = Coast Guard (Incl. reserves)
8 = Public Health

SEX	RESP	'74	'75	'77	'78	'82	'83	'84
M	0	2%	1%	1%	1%	0%	1%	2%
A	1	1	0	0	0	0	0	0
L	2	15	12	14	17	13	17	17
E	3	21	19	18	22	18	24	19
	4	52	59	58	52	58	47	49
	5	2	2	3	3	3	2	2
	6	5	5	5	4	7	7	10
	7	1	1	1	1	1	1	1
	8	0	0	0	0	0	0	0
# SURVEYED		325	313	322	305	246	282	232

SEX	RESP	'74	'75	'77	'78	'82	'83	'84
F	0	0%	0%	0%	0%	0%	0%	0%
E	1	0	0	0	0	0	0	0
M	2	0	9	25	22	42	23	10
A	3	33	18	0	22	0	23	30
L	4	56	55	67	39	42	31	50
E	5	0	9	0	11	8	0	0
	6	11	9	8	6	0	15	10
	7	0	0	0	0	8	8	0
	8	0	0	0	0	0	0	0
# SURVEYED		9	11	12	18	12	13	10

TABLE III: BRANCH OF MILITARY SERVED - BY RACE

Question: In what branch of service was that? NOTE: Question not asked in 1972-1973, 1976, 1980, 1985-1989.

Responses:
0 = More than one
1 = Air Force Guard
2 = Air Force (Incl. reserves)
3 = Navy (Incl. reserves)
4 = Army (Incl. reserves)
5 = National Guard
6 = U.S. Marine Corps
7 = Coast Guard (Incl. reserves)
8 = Public Health

RACE	RESP	'74	'75	'77	'78	'82	'83	'84
WHITE	0	2%	1%	1%	1%	0%	1%	2%
	1	1	0	0	0	0	0	0
	2	16	12	15	17	14	18	18
	3	23	20	18	22	19	25	20
	4	50	58	57	51	55	45	46
	5	3	2	3	3	3	2	2
	6	5	6	5	4	6	7	10
	7	1	1	1	1	1	1	1
	8	0	0	0	0	0	0	0
# SURVEYED		309	307	306	296	231	275	210
BLACK	0	8%	0%	0%	0%	0%	0%	0%
	1	0	0	0	0	0	0	0
	2	8	6	12	13	13	12	8
	3	8	18	8	13	0	12	15
	4	76	76	72	58	79	53	69
	5	0	0	0	4	0	0	0
	6	0	0	8	13	8	18	8
	7	0	0	0	0	0	6	0
	8	0	0	0	0	0	0	0
# SURVEYED		25	17	25	24	24	17	26

RACE	RESP	'74	'75	'77	'78	'82	'83	'84
OTHER	0	0%	0%	0%	0%	0%	0%	0%
	1	0	0	0	0	0	0	0
	2	0	0	0	67	33	0	0
	3	0	0	33	33	33	0	17
	4	0	0	67	0	33	100	50
	5	0	0	0	0	0	0	0
	6	0	0	0	0	0	0	33
	7	0	0	0	0	0	0	0
	8	0	0	0	0	0	0	0
# SURVEYED		3	3	3	3	6		

TABLE IV: BRANCH OF MILITARY SERVED - BY AGE

Question: In what branch of service was that?

Responses: 0 = More than one; 1 = Air Force Guard; 2 = Air Force (Incl. reserves); 3 = Navy (Incl. reserves); 4 = Army (Incl. reserves); 5 = National Guard; 6 = U.S. Marine Corps; 7 = Coast Guard (Incl. reserves); 8 = Public Health

AGE	RESP	'74	'75	'77	'78	'82	'83	'84
18-23	0	0%	0%	0%	0%	0%	0%	0%
	1	0	0	0	0	0	0	0
	2	20	0	33	50	17	0	20
	3	10	50	17	0	33	0	20
	4	60	33	33	25	50	50	40
	5	10	0	17	25	0	17	20
	6	0	17	0	0	0	17	0
	7	0	0	0	0	0	17	0
	8	0	0	0	0	0	0	0
# SURVEYED		10	6	6	4	6	6	5

AGE	RESP	'74	'75	'77	'78	'82	'83	'84
24-29	0	0%	0%	0%	0%	0%	0%	0%
	1	0	0	0	0	0	0	0
	2	16	14	14	22	14	12	7
	3	31	21	16	17	14	29	7
	4	41	52	65	50	50	35	80
	5	4	7	3	8	0	0	0
	6	8	2	3	3	23	18	7
	7	0	2	0	0	0	6	0
	8	0	0	0	0	0	0	0
# SURVEYED		49	42	37	36	22	17	15

AGE	RESP	'74	'75	'77	'78	'82	'83	'84
30-35	0	3%	0%	0%	0%	3%	0%	0%
	1	0	0	0	0	0	3	0
	2	10	15	22	17	9	23	22
	3	19	12	17	21	26	23	13
	4	55	64	49	46	43	48	48
	5	3	0	5	4	6	3	0
	6	10	9	7	12	11	0	17
	7	0	0	0	0	0	0	0
	8	0	0	0	0	3	0	0
# SURVEYED		31	33	41	52	35	31	23

AGE	RESP	'74	'75	'77	'78	'82	'83	'84
36-41	0	0%	2%	3%	0%	0%	0%	5%
	1	0	0	3	3	0	0	0
	2	19	13	10	10	17	24	14
	3	8	22	15	28	17	15	14
	4	59	44	55	46	50	54	50
	5	3	2	5	5	4	0	7
	6	8	16	8	8	8	7	11
	7	3	0	3	0	4	0	0
	8	0	0	0	0	0	0	0
# SURVEYED		37	45	40	39	24	46	44

AGE	RESP	'74	'75	'77	'78	'82	'83	'84
42-47	0	4%	2%	2%	0%	0%	5%	0%
	1	0	0	0	0	0	0	0
	2	16	16	16	26	12	21	24
	3	22	18	20	15	8	18	14
	4	53	57	47	54	76	33	52
	5	0	0	4	3	4	5	0
	6	4	2	11	3	0	13	10
	7	2	5	0	0	0	5	0
	8	0	0	0	0	0	0	0
# SURVEYED		51	44	45	39	25	39	21

AGE	RESP	'74	'75	'77	'78	'82	'83	'84
48-53	0	5%	0%	0%	0%	0%	0%	0%
	1	0	0	0	0	0	0	0
	2	20	8	10	10	19	17	25
	3	31	35	26	33	19	40	18
	4	44	55	61	57	55	37	43
	5	0	0	0	0	0	0	0
	6	0	2	3	0	6	6	14
	7	0	0	0	0	0	0	0
	8	0	0	0	0	0	0	0
# SURVEYED		55	51	61	51	31	35	28

TABLE IV: BRANCH OF MILITARY SERVED - BY AGE (Continued)

Question: In what branch of service was that?

Responses:
0 = More than one
1 = Air Force Guard
2 = Air Force (Incl. reserves)
3 = Navy (Incl. reserves)
4 = Army (Incl. reserves)
5 = National Guard
6 = U.S. Marine Corps
7 = Coast Guard (Incl. reserves)
8 = Public Health

AGE	RESP	'74	'75	'77	'78	'82	'83	'84
54-59	0	4%	2%	0%	4%	0%	2%	5%
	1	4	0	0	0	0	0	0
	2	14	17	18	24	3	14	21
	3	12	15	7	17	21	32	32
	4	59	61	68	48	62	43	34
	5	0	0	0	0	3	0	0
	6	4	4	4	4	9	9	8
	7	4	0	4	2	3	0	0
	8	0	0	0	0	0	0	0
# SURVEYED		51	46	57	46	34	44	38
60-65	0	0%	0%	4%	3%	0%	0%	0%
	1	0	0	0	0	0	0	0
	2	11	5	8	17	30	17	13
	3	33	10	16	24	11	26	23
	4	56	71	64	55	57	46	46
	5	0	5	4	0	0	2	0
	6	0	10	0	0	0	9	13
	7	0	0	4	0	3	0	5
	8	0	0	0	0	0	0	0
# SURVEYED		18	21	25	29	37	46	39

AGE	RESP	'74	'75	'77	'78	'82	'83	'84
66+	0	0%	0%	0%	0%	0%	0%	0%
	1	0	0	0	0	0	0	0
	2	3	6	15	7	12	10	7
	3	23	6	20	15	14	14	28
	4	58	83	65	63	67	72	59
	5	10	3	0	7	7	0	3
	6	6	0	0	4	0	0	3
	7	0	3	0	4	0	3	0
	8	0	0	0	0	0	0	0
# SURVEYED		31	36	20	27	42	29	29

****

SPOUSE'S CURRENT EMPLOYMENT STATUS

TABLE I: SPOUSE'S CURRENT EMPLOYMENT STATUS - BY TOTAL POPULATION

Question: Last week was your (wife/husband) working full time, part time, going to school, keeping house, or what?

Responses:

FT = Working full time
TM = With a job, but not at work because of temporary illness, vacation, strike
SC = In school
PT = Working part time
UN = Unemployed, laid off, looking for work
RT = Retired
HK = Keeping house

	YEAR															
RESPONSE	'72	'73	'74	'75	'76	'77	'78	'80	'82	'83	'84	'85	'86	'87	'88	'89
FT	50%	55%	54%	52%	50%	52%	54%	53%	54%	53%	57%	53%	53%	59%	53%	57%
PT	8	7	7	8	8	8	9	9	9	9	7	9	11	10	9	8
TM	1	2	2	2	2	2	3	3	2	2	3	2	2	2	2	2
UN	1	1	2	3	2	2	2	2	2	4	2	2	1	2	2	2
RT	6	6	7	7	9	9	8	11	10	10	10	12	15	11	16	14
SC	1	1	1	1	1	1	1	1	1	1	1	2	1	1	1	1
HK	32	29	29	27	27	26	24	21	23	21	20	20	17	16	17	15
# SURVEYED	1137	1056	1053	987	958	964	941	876	833	949	821	858	813	788	779	830

TABLE II: SPOUSE'S CURRENT EMPLOYMENT STATUS - BY SEX

Question: Last week was your (wife/husband) working full time, part time, going to school, keeping house, or what?

Responses:

FT = Working full time
TM = With a job, but not at work because of temporary illness, vacation, strike
SC = In school
PT = Working part time
UN = Unemployed, laid off, looking for work
RT = Retired
HK = Keeping house

		YEAR															
SEX	RESP	'72	'73	'74	'75	'76	'77	'78	'80	'82	'83	'84	'85	'86	'87	'88	'89
M	FT	27%	26%	27%	26%	25%	29%	29%	34%	34%	36%	34%	35%	36%	41%	38%	44%
A	PT	11	10	10	13	11	12	15	13	13	14	13	15	18	17	12	14
L	TM	0	1	1	2	1	1	2	2	1	1	3	1	2	2	3	1
E	UN	0	0	0	1	1	1	0	1	1	2	1	1	0	1	0	0
	RT	1	2	2	3	4	2	3	5	3	3	5	6	8	5	11	8
	SC	0	1	1	0	1	1	1	1	1	2	1	2	1	1	1	1
	HK	59	60	60	55	57	54	50	44	48	43	43	40	35	33	34	31
# SURVEYED		619	506	509	478	452	463	439	419	402	463	358	430	380	374	377	402
SEX	RESP	'72	'73	'74	'75	'76	'77	'78	'80	'82	'83	'84	'85	'86	'87	'88	'89
F	FT	77%	81%	79%	77%	73%	73%	75%	71%	74%	69%	74%	71%	68%	74%	66%	70%
E	PT	4	4	4	4	5	3	4	4	4	5	3	4	4	4	6	3
M	TM	2	3	2	3	3	3	4	4	2	3	3	3	3	1	1	3
A	UN	3	1	3	4	4	3	3	3	3	7	3	3	2	2	4	3
L	RT	12	9	11	12	15	16	13	16	16	16	14	18	21	15	21	20
E	SC	1	1	1	1	1	1	1	1	1	0	1	2	0	1	0	0
	HK	0	0	0	0	0	0	1	1	0	0	2	1	2	1	2	1
# SURVEYED		518	550	544	509	506	501	502	457	431	486	463	428	433	414	402	428

TABLE III: SPOUSE'S CURRENT EMPLOYMENT STATUS - BY RACE

Question: Last week was your (wife/husband) working full time, part time, going to school, keeping house, or what?

Responses:
FT = Working full time
PT = Working part time
TM = With a job, but not at work because of temporary illness, vacation, strike
UN = Unemployed, laid off, looking for work
RT = Retired
SC = In school
HK = Keeping house

		YEAR															
RACE	RESP	'72	'73	'74	'75	'76	'77	'78	'80	'82	'83	'84	'85	'86	'87	'88	'89
WHITE	FT	50%	56%	53%	52%	50%	52%	54%	53%	54%	52%	55%	53%	52%	57%	52%	56%
	PT	8	6	7	8	8	8	9	9	9	9	8	10	10	11	10	9
	TM	2	2	2	2	2	2	3	3	2	2	3	2	2	2	2	3
	UN	2	1	2	2	2	2	2	2	2	4	2	2	2	2	2	2
	RT	5	5	7	7	9	9	8	10	10	10	11	12	15	11	17	14
	SC	1	1	1	1	1	1	1	1	1	1	1	2	1	1	1	1
	HK	33	29	29	27	27	27	24	22	23	21	20	20	18	16	17	15
# SURVEYED		980	942	956	906	898	874	861	808	763	872	719	775	724	703	683	755
RACE	RESP	'72	'73	'74	'75	'76	'77	'78	'80	'82	'83	'84	'85	'86	'87	'88	'89
BLACK	FT	52%	49%	53%	50%	46%	57%	52%	58%	58%	61%	70%	47%	59%	67%	51%	74%
	PT	6	9	4	12	6	9	10	10	7	8	4	5	11	5	7	0
	TM	0	3	1	1	2	4	1	3	2	2	4	4	6	0	3	0
	UN	1	1	3	6	2	1	1	2	4	5	3	2	0	2	3	0
	RT	12	11	8	13	17	9	8	13	15	11	4	14	14	11	15	14
	SC	1	1	0	0	4	2	3	2	0	0	0	0	1	0	1	2
	HK	28	25	30	18	23	19	24	12	15	15	14	28	8	15	19	10
# SURVEYED		155	106	92	78	52	81	71	60	55	66	69	57	71	55	67	42
RACE	RESP	'72	'73	'74	'75	'76	'77	'78	'80	'82	'83	'84	'85	'86	'87	'88	'89
OTHER	FT	50%	63%	100%	67%	75%	56%	78%	75%	53%	73%	55%	62%	67%	73%	72%	58%
	PT	0	0	0	33	13	0	11	0	0	9	6	15	11	7	0	6
	TM	0	0	0	0	0	0	11	0	0	0	0	4	0	3	0	0
	UN	0	0	0	0	0	0	0	0	7	0	3	4	0	0	0	12
	RT	0	0	0	0	0	11	0	13	0	0	6	0	6	3	3	6
	SC	0	0	0	0	0	0	0	0	7	0	3	0	0	0	0	0
	HK	50	38	0	0	13	33	0	13	33	18	27	15	17	13	24	18
# SURVEYED		2	8	5	3	8	9	9	8	15	11	33	26	18	30	29	33

TABLE IV: SPOUSE'S CURRENT EMPLOYMENT STATUS - BY AGE

Question: Last week was your (wife/husband) working full time, part time, going to school, keeping house, or what?

Responses:

FT = Working full time
TM = With a job, but not at work because of temporary illness, vacation, strike
SC = In school
PT = Working part time
UN = Unemployed, laid off, looking for work
RT = Retired
HK = Keeping house

		YEAR															
AGE	RESP	'72	'73	'74	'75	'76	'77	'78	'80	'82	'83	'84	'85	'86	'87	'88	'89
18-23	FT	64%	72%	59%	69%	65%	63%	71%	80%	65%	63%	69%	66%	74%	86%	73%	80%
	PT	5	7	9	5	4	5	11	2	7	13	8	9	11	0	8	5
	TM	4	3	1	2	2	3	4	6	2	0	0	3	0	0	0	5
	UN	4	3	7	8	4	2	2	4	13	7	0	0	5	5	3	0
	RT	0	0	0	0	0	0	0	0	0	3	0	0	0	0	0	0
	SC	2	3	1	2	11	7	2	4	2	3	5	6	0	9	5	5
	HK	22	12	22	15	15	20	11	6	11	10	18	16	11	0	11	5
# SURVEYED		55	60	68	62	54	60	56	54	46	30	39	32	19	22	37	20
AGE	RESP	'72	'73	'74	'75	'76	'77	'78	'80	'82	'83	'84	'85	'86	'87	'88	'89
24-29	FT	55%	64%	65%	65%	58%	69%	60%	66%	67%	57%	69%	73%	67%	68%	69%	77%
	PT	9	7	9	7	6	8	6	10	9	10	6	8	10	6	7	5
	TM	1	1	3	3	2	0	5	2	1	3	2	2	2	2	2	2
	UN	2	3	1	2	5	3	5	3	2	8	6	3	2	2	4	2
	RT	0	0	0	0	0	0	0	0	0	0	0	0	0	0	0	0
	SC	2	4	2	2	2	3	3	4	2	1	2	3	1	5	2	2
	HK	31	22	20	22	26	17	23	16	19	21	15	12	19	16	16	12
# SURVEYED		162	157	150	151	149	118	155	122	132	165	124	118	108	94	96	86
AGE	RESP	'72	'73	'74	'75	'76	'77	'78	'80	'82	'83	'84	'85	'86	'87	'88	'89
30-35	FT	58%	64%	66%	67%	60%	65%	64%	63%	64%	66%	73%	66%	73%	69%	74%	64%
	PT	6	6	5	6	6	6	10	7	13	6	7	11	12	12	8	11
	TM	0	4	1	0	4	4	3	3	1	4	2	1	2	2	1	2
	UN	4	0	1	4	2	1	1	3	1	4	3	3	1	5	3	4
	RT	0	0	0	0	1	1	0	0	1	0	0	1	0	0	0	0
	SC	1	1	1	1	0	1	1	1	1	2	0	1	1	2	0	1
	HK	32	26	25	22	27	23	21	23	19	18	15	17	11	10	14	18
# SURVEYED		158	141	143	132	144	140	167	137	135	163	124	140	140	132	111	124
AGE	RESP	'72	'73	'74	'75	'76	'77	'78	'80	'82	'83	'84	'85	'86	'87	'88	'89
36-41	FT	57%	60%	70%	51%	62%	60%	60%	58%	66%	64%	62%	74%	70%	76%	64%	72%
	PT	6	8	6	11	12	6	10	9	10	9	12	12	11	7	10	10
	TM	1	3	1	4	0	3	3	2	1	0	3	3	1	2	3	1
	UN	0	0	2	5	1	2	2	2	2	3	2	1	1	0	2	1
	RT	1	0	0	0	0	2	1	0	0	1	0	0	1	0	0	0
	SC	0	1	0	1	2	0	0	1	0	0	2	2	1	0	1	2
	HK	35	28	21	29	23	27	24	28	21	24	19	9	14	15	20	14
# SURVEYED		109	145	131	131	122	124	119	106	82	113	128	120	134	123	122	130

TABLE IV: SPOUSE'S CURRENT EMPLOYMENT STATUS - BY AGE (Continued)

Question: Last week was your (wife/husband) working full time, part time, going to school, keeping house, or what?

Responses:

FT = Working full time
TM = With a job, but not at work because of temporary illness, vacation, strike
SC = In school
PT = Working part time
UN = Unemployed, laid off, looking for work
RT = Retired
HK = Keeping house

		YEAR															
AGE	RESP	'72	'73	'74	'75	'76	'77	'78	'80	'82	'83	'84	'85	'86	'87	'88	'89
42-47	FT	58%	63%	62%	57%	56%	66%	59%	74%	75%	66%	71%	65%	62%	72%	69%	71%
	PT	8	7	6	16	12	6	9	6	5	6	12	12	14	11	10	9
	TM	2	3	5	0	3	2	1	5	3	2	3	1	2	2	3	3
	UN	1	1	2	2	4	1	2	2	1	7	1	3	5	2	2	4
	RT	0	2	2	3	3	2	0	0	0	2	0	0	1	2	1	2
	SC	1	0	0	1	0	0	1	0	0	1	0	1	0	0	1	0
	HK	31	24	22	21	21	24	27	13	16	16	13	18	16	11	14	13
# SURVEYED		155	112	125	107	91	116	91	84	77	100	86	78	86	107	99	112
AGE	RESP	'72	'73	'74	'75	'76	'77	'78	'80	'82	'83	'84	'85	'86	'87	'88	'89
48-53	FT	55%	61%	53%	69%	65%	47%	63%	65%	60%	69%	61%	56%	54%	66%	64%	69%
	PT	8	4	8	7	7	5	9	11	8	7	9	14	14	8	14	10
	TM	2	4	2	3	5	4	2	5	4	1	3	3	4	3	0	5
	UN	1	0	3	2	1	5	1	2	1	4	3	4	1	1	5	0
	RT	3	2	4	2	3	5	3	4	7	7	4	1	11	5	7	3
	SC	1	1	0	0	0	1	0	0	0	0	0	3	1	0	0	0
	HK	30	28	29	17	19	32	22	13	20	12	21	18	15	16	9	13
# SURVEYED		154	125	118	115	100	115	106	83	84	85	76	93	74	86	56	86
AGE	RESP	'72	'73	'74	'75	'76	'77	'78	'80	'82	'83	'84	'85	'86	'87	'88	'89
54-59	FT	50%	60%	57%	43%	45%	48%	53%	54%	51%	47%	50%	41%	51%	55%	48%	67%
	PT	10	8	4	9	5	14	6	11	10	10	7	8	3	19	10	6
	TM	2	1	0	6	1	3	4	6	1	4	8	2	3	3	4	1
	UN	2	1	0	3	1	1	1	2	2	3	0	3	0	0	0	4
	RT	5	5	8	10	15	11	13	2	12	12	10	16	21	9	15	10
	SC	0	0	0	0	0	0	0	0	0	1	0	0	0	0	0	0
	HK	30	26	32	29	33	23	23	25	24	21	25	30	22	13	23	10
# SURVEYED		129	120	104	89	95	114	83	102	103	89	72	90	63	67	52	67
AGE	RESP	'72	'73	'74	'75	'76	'77	'78	'80	'82	'83	'84	'85	'86	'87	'88	'89
60-65	FT	35%	33%	32%	29%	33%	33%	34%	27%	33%	30%	33%	24%	19%	29%	24%	27%
	PT	8	10	8	5	12	11	15	11	8	15	4	8	9	19	6	5
	TM	1	0	3	2	0	0	3	0	5	2	0	1	5	2	1	4
	UN	1	0	1	0	1	1	2	0	0	0	1	0	0	0	0	1
	RT	18	22	26	25	28	26	23	34	30	25	33	33	40	37	45	45
	SC	1	0	0	0	0	0	0	0	0	0	0	0	0	0	0	0
	HK	37	35	31	39	26	29	23	28	25	28	29	35	27	14	24	16
# SURVEYED		101	93	78	83	89	76	61	74	64	93	73	80	75	63	80	73

TABLE IV: SPOUSE'S CURRENT EMPLOYMENT STATUS - BY AGE (Continued)

Question: Last week was your (wife/husband) working full time, part time, going to school, keeping house, or what?

Responses:
- FT = Working full time
- PT = Working part time
- TM = With a job, but not at work because of temporary illness, vacation, strike
- UN = Unemployed, laid off, looking for work
- RT = Retired
- SC = In school
- HK = Keeping house

		YEAR															
AGE	RESP	'72	'73	'74	'75	'76	'77	'78	'80	'82	'83	'84	'85	'86	'87	'88	'89
66+	FT	14%	9%	12%	11%	8%	8%	7%	5%	9%	13%	17%	7%	6%	5%	5%	11%
	PT	9	4	5	8	5	8	6	8	5	11	1	5	8	4	9	8
	TM	1	0	0	1	0	0	0	1	0	0	1	3	1	0	1	2
	UN	0	0	0	1	0	0	1	0	0	1	0	0	0	0	0	0
	RT	34	29	26	33	40	45	48	54	39	44	51	53	60	53	63	55
	SC	0	0	0	0	0	0	0	0	1	0	0	0	0	0	1	0
	HK	42	58	56	46	47	38	37	31	46	30	30	33	24	37	21	24
# SURVEYED		111	102	133	115	113	99	99	112	107	106	96	106	111	91	123	131

****

CURRENT RELIGIOUS PREFERENCE

TABLE I: CURRENT RELIGIOUS PREFERENCE BY TOTAL POPULATION

Question: What is your religious preference? Is it Protestant, Catholic, Jewish, some other religion, or no religion?

Responses: PR = Protestant CT = Catholic; JW = Jewish; NO = None; OT = Other

	YEAR															
RESPONSE	'72	'73	'74	'75	'76	'77	'78	'80	'82	'83	'84	'85	'86	'87	'88	'89
PR	64%	63%	64%	66%	64%	66%	64%	64%	65%	61%	64%	62%	63%	65%	61%	63%
CT	26	26	25	24	26	24	25	25	24	28	26	27	26	24	26	25
JW	3	3	3	2	2	2	2	2	2	3	2	2	3	1	2	2
NO	5	6	7	8	8	6	8	7	7	7	7	7	7	7	8	8
OT	2	2	1	1	1	1	1	2	1	2	1	2	2	2	3	2
# SURVEYED	1608	1500	1483	1488	1497	1523	1528	1465	1498	1595	1461	1529	1467	1460	1480	1533

TABLE II: CURRENT RELIGIOUS PREFERENCE BY SEX

Question: What is your religious preference? Is it Protestant, Catholic, Jewish, some other religion, or no religion?

Responses: PR = Protestant; CT = Catholic; JW = Jewish; NO = None; OT = Other

		YEAR															
SEX	RESP	'72	'73	'74	'75	'76	'77	'78	'80	'82	'83	'84	'85	'86	'87	'88	'89
MALE	PR	61%	61%	64%	62%	62%	63%	62%	61%	61%	59%	60%	59%	57%	64%	58%	59%
	CT	27	26	24	25	25	25	23	24	24	27	26	28	27	24	25	26
	JW	3	2	2	2	2	2	3	3	2	3	2	2	3	2	2	2
	NO	7	9	10	10	10	9	11	10	12	9	10	9	10	8	12	11
	OT	1	2	1	1	2	2	2	3	2	2	1	2	3	3	4	3
# SURVEYED		804	697	690	669	668	689	642	639	632	688	594	686	620	639	638	658
SEX	RESP	'72	'73	'74	'75	'76	'77	'78	'80	'82	'83	'84	'85	'86	'87	'88	'89
FEMALE	PR	67%	64%	65%	68%	65%	69%	66%	66%	68%	63%	67%	65%	67%	66%	64%	67%
	CT	24	26	26	24	27	24	27	25	25	28	25	26	25	24	27	24
	JW	3	4	4	1	2	2	1	2	3	2	1	2	2	1	2	1
	NO	3	4	4	6	6	4	6	5	4	6	5	6	4	6	5	6
	OT	2	2	1	1	0	1	1	1	1	1	1	1	2	2	2	2
# SURVEYED		804	803	793	819	829	834	886	826	866	907	867	843	847	821	842	875

TABLE III: CURRENT RELIGIOUS PREFERENCE -- BY RACE

Question: What is your religious preference? Is it Protestant, Catholic, Jewish, some other religion, or no religion?

Responses: PR = Protestant; CT = Catholic; JW = Jewish; NO = None; OT = Other

		YEAR															
RACE	RESP	'72	'73	'74	'75	'76	'77	'78	'80	'82	'83	'84	'85	'86	'87	'88	'89
WHITE	PR	60%	60%	62%	63%	62%	63%	62%	62%	63%	58%	61%	60%	60%	62%	60%	62%
	CT	29	28	28	26	27	27	27	27	25	30	28	28	28	27	28	27
	JW	4	3	3	2	2	3	2	2	3	3	2	2	3	2	2	2
	NO	5	7	7	8	8	6	8	7	8	7	8	7	7	7	8	8
	OT	2	2	0	1	1	1	1	2	1	2	1	1	1	2	2	2
# SURVEYED		1343	1304	1304	1322	1359	1334	1354	1315	1315	1414	1239	1336	1247	1218	1233	1316
RACE	RESP	'72	'73	'74	'75	'76	'77	'78	'80	'82	'83	'84	'85	'86	'87	'88	'89
BLACK	PR	87%	83%	86%	85%	84%	89%	89%	86%	85%	88%	85%	87%	86%	86%	80%	85%
	CT	8	8	8	8	12	6	5	4	9	5	9	7	5	7	9	8
	JW	0	0	1	0	0	0	0	0	0	0	0	1	1	0	0	1
	NO	4	5	5	6	5	5	4	8	4	5	4	4	5	4	8	4
	OT	2	4	1	1	0	1	1	1	2	2	1	1	3	3	4	1
# SURVEYED		261	183	172	162	129	174	158	140	156	163	170	149	183	189	186	157
RACE	RESP	'72	'73	'74	'75	'76	'77	'78	'80	'82	'83	'84	'85	'86	'87	'88	'89
OTHER	PR	25%	46%	43%	50%	33%	20%	31%	40%	19%	39%	50%	41%	30%	53%	38%	42%
	CT	75	31	29	25	56	33	44	50	63	33	35	39	38	25	38	35
	JW	0	8	0	0	0	0	0	0	0	0	0	0	3	0	0	0
	NO	0	8	0	25	11	20	13	0	11	22	8	14	8	13	11	12
	OT	0	8	29	0	0	27	13	10	7	6	8	7	22	9	13	12
# SURVEYED		4	13	7	4	9	15	16	10	27	18	52	44	37	53	61	60

TABLE IV: CURRENT RELIGIOUS PREFERENCE -- BY AGE

Question: What is your religious preference? Is it Protestant, Catholic, Jewish, some other religion, or no religion?

Responses: PR = Protestant CT = Catholic; JW = Jewish; NO = None; OT = Other

		YEAR															
AGE	RESP	'72	'73	'74	'75	'76	'77	'78	'80	'82	'83	'84	'85	'86	'87	'88	'89
18-23	PR	55%	51%	56%	53%	51%	64%	57%	61%	56%	53%	60%	55%	56%	60%	53%	57%
	CT	25	32	27	32	30	28	27	27	26	27	28	29	30	25	28	29
	JW	3	2	2	1	0	1	1	0	1	2	1	2	0	1	2	2
	NO	12	11	13	12	18	7	13	11	15	16	9	13	14	13	16	10
	OT	4	4	2	2	1	1	2	1	3	2	2	2	0	2	1	2
# SURVEYED		166	171	168	173	162	161	163	155	148	128	159	133	108	126	141	136

TABLE IV: CURRENT RELIGIOUS PREFERENCE -- BY AGE (Continued)

Question: What is your religious preference? Is it Protestant, Catholic, Jewish, some other religion, or no religion?

Responses: PR = Protestant CT = Catholic; JW = Jewish; NO = None; OT = Other

		YEAR															
AGE	RESP	'72	'73	'74	'75	'76	'77	'78	'80	'82	'83	'84	'85	'86	'87	'88	'89
24-29	PR	57%	50%	54%	57%	55%	60%	58%	55%	51%	57%	61%	54%	63%	59%	57%	54%
	CT	30	27	32	23	28	21	26	29	33	29	25	31	25	30	28	29
	JW	3	5	4	1	2	3	1	3	0	2	2	1	2	1	1	0
	NO	9	14	9	17	13	12	12	11	14	10	12	13	7	9	11	13
	OT	1	3	1	2	2	3	3	1	2	2	0	1	3	2	3	3
# SURVEYED		231	210	212	232	225	204	244	202	246	287	231	217	217	193	215	202
AGE	RESP	'72	'73	'74	'75	'76	'77	'78	'80	'82	'83	'84	'85	'86	'87	'88	'89
30-35	PR	62%	59%	65%	63%	62%	57%	64%	58%	64%	56%	59%	67%	55%	59%	56%	53%
	CT	30	32	23	25	29	30	23	26	25	30	27	20	33	28	28	32
	JW	3	1	4	2	1	2	2	1	3	2	2	1	2	1	3	1
	NO	4	7	8	9	6	10	11	11	7	10	9	9	5	11	9	12
	OT	1	1	1	2	2	1	0	4	0	2	2	2	4	1	4	2
# SURVEYED		187	167	175	171	185	187	230	214	203	235	197	210	221	220	195	212
AGE	RESP	'72	'73	'74	'75	'76	'77	'78	'80	'82	'83	'84	'85	'86	'87	'88	'89
36-41	PR	5%	65%	62%	71%	62%	73%	54%	60%	64%	66%	59%	57%	58%	61%	58%	63%
	CT	25	26	30	24	23	19	36	23	23	25	28	28	25	24	25	22
	JW	4	2	3	1	2	2	2	1	2	3	2	2	2	1	2	1
	NO	6	4	5	5	11	7	7	11	8	5	9	8	12	11	10	10
	OT	1	3	0	0	2	0	1	5	3	1	2	4	3	4	5	4
# SURVEYED		127	175	151	153	158	168	160	150	146	173	186	183	187	185	193	198
AGE	RESP	'72	'73	'74	'75	'76	'77	'78	'80	'82	'83	'84	'85	'86	'87	'88	'89
42-47	PR	60%	62%	66%	71%	61%	62%	66%	69%	71%	63%	67%	56%	56%	61%	60%	68%
	CT	31	31	28	19	34	29	21	21	21	30	27	28	28	24	31	23
	JW	3	1	1	2	1	1	3	2	2	3	1	4	3	4	2	2
	NO	2	4	5	8	4	7	9	7	6	4	6	10	8	8	6	6
	OT	3	1	0	0	1	2	1	2	0	1	0	2	5	3	1	3
# SURVEYED		185	145	151	142	114	146	119	116	118	145	126	124	141	157	157	160
AGE	RESP	'72	'73	'74	'75	'76	'77	'78	'80	'82	'83	'84	'85	'86	'87	'88	'89
48-53	PR	1%	68%	67%	67%	67%	71%	63%	68%	66%	57%	66%	66%	74%	70%	62%	75%
	CT	28	23	23	28	26	25	31	25	26	31	27	25	16	21	25	18
	JW	5	3	3	3	2	0	2	3	2	3	3	2	3	1	4	3
	NO	4	5	6	1	5	2	2	2	5	8	3	5	7	3	4	4
	OT	2	1	1	1	1	1	2	2	1	1	1	2	0	5	4	0
# SURVEYED		189	151	146	141	133	153	132	123	111	115	102	131	108	126	92	138

TABLE IV: CURRENT RELIGIOUS PREFERENCE -- BY AGE (Continued)

Question: What is your religious preference? Is it Protestant, Catholic, Jewish, some other religion, or no religion?

Responses: PR = Protestant CT = Catholic; JW = Jewish; NO = None; OT = Other

		YEAR															
AGE	RESP	'72	'73	'74	'75	'76	'77	'78	'80	'82	'83	'84	'85	'86	'87	'88	'89
54-59	PR	67%	71%	65%	64%	74%	70%	69%	73%	71%	61%	63%	69%	65%	77%	75%	69%
	CT	24	18	27	31	23	23	24	21	23	32	27	22	25	20	15	23
	JW	3	3	2	1	2	5	1	2	1	1	3	3	7	1	1	1
	NO	4	5	6	3	2	2	5	2	3	5	4	5	3	1	6	3
	OT	1	3	0	1	0	0	1	1	1	2	3	1	0	1	2	4
# SURVEYED		156	156	139	126	129	168	136	135	143	133	114	133	99	97	84	99
AGE	RESP	'72	'73	'74	'75	'76	'77	'78	'80	'82	'83	'84	'85	'86	'87	'88	'89
60-65	PR	6%	70%	71%	70%	71%	70%	71%	67%	74%	63%	68%	65%	69%	76%	74%	65%
	CT	17	24	18	25	24	25	23	24	19	27	25	32	27	23	17	25
	JW	4	5	5	1	2	3	3	6	3	4	1	2	3	0	3	0
	NO	2	1	6	4	3	3	3	3	2	5	5	1	1	1	4	6
	OT	1	0	0	0	0	0	0	1	2	2	1	0	1	0	3	4
# SURVEYED		144	121	108	113	134	117	107	119	116	132	110	130	115	100	119	111
AGE	RESP	'72	'73	'74	'75	'76	'77	'78	'80	'82	'83	'84	'85	'86	'87	'88	'89
66+	PR	76%	72%	75%	77%	72%	70%	75%	70%	72%	69%	74%	70%	71%	73%	66%	70%
	CT	18	20	19	18	22	22	19	24	21	22	19	25	22	21	28	23
	JW	2	3	4	2	4	3	3	2	4	4	2	2	3	2	1	2
	NO	3	4	3	3	3	3	3	3	3	3	4	2	3	3	3	4
	OT	1	2	0	0	0	1	0	1	0	3	1	1	0	1	2	0
# SURVEYED		218	200	227	232	251	212	231	242	258	240	231	261	264	253	280	274

****

RELIGIOUS PREFERENCE AT AGE 16

TABLE I: RELIGIOUS PREFERENCE AT AGE 16 -- BY TOTAL POPULATION

Question: In what religion were you raised? NOTE: Question was not asked in 1972.

Responses: PR = Protestant; CT = Catholic; JW = Jewish; NO = None; OT = Other

	YEAR														
RESPONSE	'73	'74	'75	'76	'77	'78	'80	'82	'83	'84	'85	'86	'87	'88	'89
PR	65%	66%	69%	65%	68%	67%	67%	66%	63%	66%	64%	65%	67%	64%	63%
CT	28	27	25	29	26	27	27	27	30	27	29	28	27	28	29
JW	3	3	2	2	2	2	2	3	3	2	2	2	2	2	2
NO	2	3	3	3	3	3	3	3	3	3	4	3	3	4	4
OT	1	1	1	1	1	1	1	1	1	2	1	2	1	2	2
# SURVEYED	1500	1482	1490	1497	1523	1525	1466	1499	1590	1452	1529	1468	1442	1481	1533

TABLE II: RELIGIOUS PREFERENCE AT AGE 16 -- BY SEX

Question: In what religion were you raised? NOTE: Question was not asked in 1972.

Responses: PR = Protestant; CT = Catholic; JW = Jewish; NO = None; OT = Other

		YEAR														
SEX	RESP	'73	'74	'75	'76	'77	'78	'80	'82	'83	'84	'85	'86	'87	'88	'89
MALE	PR	65%	68%	67%	64%	68%	66%	65%	64%	62%	63%	62%	62%	66%	63%	60%
	CT	29	26	28	29	26	27	26	28	30	28	30	29	27	28	32
	JW	2	2	2	2	3	3	3	2	3	3	2	3	2	2	2
	NO	3	3	3	3	2	3	4	4	3	3	4	4	3	4	4
	OT	1	0	0	2	1	1	2	2	1	2	1	2	2	3	2
# SURVEYED		699	691	670	667	690	639	640	634	688	590	687	621	631	638	657
SEX	RESP	'73	'74	'75	'76	'77	'78	'80	'82	'83	'84	'85	'86	'87	'88	'89
FEMALE	PR	66%	65%	71%	65%	69%	67%	69%	67%	63%	68%	65%	67%	68%	65%	65%
	CT	27	28	24	29	26	28	27	26	30	27	28	27	27	28	27
	JW	3	4	1	2	2	1	2	3	3	2	2	2	1	2	2
	NO	2	3	3	3	3	3	3	2	3	3	4	2	3	3	4
	OT	2	1	1	1	1	0	1	1	0	1	1	2	1	2	2
# SURVEYED		801	791	820	830	833	886	826	865	902	862	842	847	811	843	876

TABLE III: RELIGIOUS PREFERENCE AT AGE 16 -- BY RACE

Question: In what religion were you raised? NOTE: Question was not asked in 1972.

Responses: PR = Protestant; CT = Catholic; JW = Jewish; NO = None; OT = Other

		YEAR														
RACE	RESP	'73	'74	'75	'76	'77	'78	'80	'82	'83	'84	'85	'86	'87	'88	'89
WHITE	PR	62%	63%	67%	63%	66%	64%	65%	64%	59%	64%	62%	62%	65%	62%	61%
	CT	31	30	28	30	28	30	29	28	33	29	31	31	29	31	31
	JW	3	4	2	2	3	2	2	3	4	2	2	3	2	3	2
	NO	2	3	3	3	3	4	3	3	3	3	4	3	3	3	4
	OT	1	0	1	1	1	1	1	1	1	1	1	1	1	2	2
# SURVEYED		1304	1302	1323	1359	1336	1352	1316	1316	1408	1232	1335	1248	1205	1234	1315
RACE	RESP	'73	'74	'75	'76	'77	'78	'80	'82	'83	'84	'85	'86	'87	'88	'89
BLACK	PR	91%	92%	93%	88%	92%	93%	92%	91%	94%	87%	91%	91%	88%	89%	87%
	CT	7	8	7	10	7	6	5	8	4	11	7	8	9	6	10
	JW	0	1	0	0	1	0	0	0	0	0	0	1	0	0	1
	NO	2	0	1	2	1	0	3	0	2	2	2	1	2	3	1
	OT	1	0	0	0	0	1	0	1	0	1	0	0	2	1	1
# SURVEYED		183	173	163	129	172	158	140	156	164	169	150	183	185	186	157
RACE	RESP	'73	'74	'75	'76	'77	'78	'80	'82	'83	'84	'85	'86	'87	'88	'89
OTHER	PR	38%	14%	0%	44%	27%	40%	30%	15%	28%	43%	27%	30%	40%	39%	34%
	CT	46	29	50	33	40	53	50	56	50	39	52	41	46	39	43
	JW	0	0	0	0	0	0	0	4	0	0	0	0	0	0	0
	NO	8	0	25	0	0	0	0	7	17	4	11	5	4	7	5
	OT	8	57	25	22	33	7	20	19	6	14	9	24	10	15	18
# SURVEYED		13	7	4	9	15	15	10	27	18	51	44	37	52	61	61

TABLE IV: RELIGIOUS PREFERENCE AT AGE 16 -- BY AGE

Question: In what religion were you raised? NOTE: Question was not asked in 1972.

Responses: PR = Protestant; CT = Catholic; JW = Jewish; NO = None; OT = Other

		YEAR														
AGE	RESP	'73	'74	'75	'76	'77	'78	'80	'82	'83	'84	'85	'86	'87	'88	'89
18-23	PR	58%	62%	55%	59%	67%	62%	61%	62%	61%	59%	58%	66%	61%	58%	57%
	CT	36	32	37	34	30	30	30	30	30	32	34	28	30	30	33
	JW	2	2	1	1	1	2	0	1	2	1	2	0	1	2	2
	NO	2	4	6	5	2	5	7	5	7	6	5	6	7	7	4
	OT	1	1	0	1	1	1	1	2	1	2	1	0	1	2	4
# SURVEYED		171	168	173	162	163	162	155	147	127	158	133	108	125	141	137

TABLE IV: RELIGIOUS PREFERENCE AT AGE 16 -- BY AGE (Continued)

Question: In what religion were you raised? NOTE: Question was not asked in 1972.

Responses: PR = Protestant; CT = Catholic; JW = Jewish; NO = None; OT = Other

		YEAR														
AGE	RESP	'73	'74	'75	'76	'77	'78	'80	'82	'83	'84	'85	'86	'87	'88	'89
24-29	PR	55%	55%	66%	59%	66%	64%	61%	54%	60%	61%	57%	60%	61%	58%	51%
	CT	36	36	27	33	27	31	32	39	33	30	36	32	34	33	37
	JW	4	5	1	2	3	1	4	0	3	3	1	1	1	1	1
	NO	3	4	5	4	3	2	2	5	3	4	6	4	4	5	7
	OT	2	0	1	2	1	2	0	2	0	2	0	2	1	4	3
# SURVEYED		211	211	232	225	203	243	202	246	287	230	215	218	190	215	202
AGE	RESP	'73	'74	'75	'76	'77	'78	'80	'82	'83	'84	'85	'86	'87	'88	'89
30-35	PR	64%	67%	69%	64%	62%	66%	66%	63%	58%	63%	69%	57%	63%	62%	55%
	CT	31	25	23	31	32	29	29	31	35	31	25	36	31	28	37
	JW	2	5	2	1	3	1	1	3	3	2	1	1	3	3	2
	NO	2	3	4	4	2	3	2	2	4	3	4	3	2	4	5
	OT	1	1	1	1	1	0	1	0	0	2	1	3	2	4	1
# SURVEYED		166	175	171	186	187	229	215	204	234	194	212	221	216	195	212
AGE	RESP	'73	'74	'75	'76	'77	'78	'80	'82	'83	'84	'85	'86	'87	'88	'89
36-41	PR	66%	64%	74%	66%	75%	60%	65%	63%	64%	62%	59%	61%	67%	64%	62%
	CT	29	32	23	28	20	35	27	27	27	32	34	31	28	28	31
	JW	1	3	1	3	2	3	1	2	5	2	1	2	1	2	1
	NO	2	2	1	3	2	2	4	5	3	2	5	3	2	4	3
	OT	3	0	1	1	1	1	3	3	1	2	1	2	2	2	3
# SURVEYED		174	152	154	157	168	160	150	146	172	185	184	187	184	193	197
AGE	RESP	'73	'74	'75	'76	'77	'78	'80	'82	'83	'84	'85	'86	'87	'88	'89
42-47	PR	66%	67%	71%	55%	64%	68%	70%	75%	63%	69%	65%	63%	61%	61%	63%
	CT	32	27	24	38	25	23	25	20	31	26	27	30	29	35	26
	JW	2	2	2	0	2	3	2	3	2	2	2	2	3	2	3
	NO	0	3	3	4	6	6	3	3	3	3	4	3	6	1	5
	OT	0	1	0	3	3	1	0	0	1	0	1	2	1	1	3
# SURVEYED		145	150	143	114	147	118	116	118	145	125	124	141	156	157	160
AGE	RESP	'73	'74	'75	'76	'77	'78	'80	'82	'83	'84	'85	'86	'87	'88	'89
48-53	PR	64%	67%	67%	65%	73%	64%	63%	70%	61%	67%	66%	76%	74%	64%	75%
	CT	26	23	26	29	24	29	29	23	31	25	24	19	22	27	20
	JW	3	3	4	2	0	2	3	4	4	4	3	3	0	4	2
	NO	5	4	1	2	2	3	3	3	4	2	6	1	1	2	4
	OT	2	3	2	2	1	2	1	0	0	2	1	1	3	2	0
# SURVEYED		151	146	141	133	153	132	123	112	114	100	130	108	126	92	138

TABLE IV: RELIGIOUS PREFERENCE AT AGE 16 -- BY AGE (Continued)

Question: In what religion were you raised? NOTE: Question was not asked in 1972.

Responses: PR = Protestant; CT = Catholic; JW = Jewish; NO = None; OT = Other

		YEAR														
AGE	RESP	'73	'74	'75	'76	'77	'78	'80	'82	'83	'84	'85	'86	'87	'88	'89
54-59	PR	72%	69%	68%	71%	73%	72%	77%	72%	63%	65%	64%	64%	77%	75%	67%
	CT	20	27	28	23	21	26	19	19	33	26	27	27	18	19	27
	JW	4	3	1	2	4	1	1	2	1	3	4	7	1	1	1
	NO	2	1	2	2	1	1	1	3	2	3	5	1	2	2	4
	OT	3	0	1	2	1	0	1	4	1	4	1	1	2	2	1
# SURVEYED		157	139	126	129	168	137	135	144	134	114	133	99	97	85	99
AGE	RESP	'73	'74	'75	'76	'77	'78	'80	'82	'83	'84	'85	'86	'87	'88	'89
60-65	PR	69%	73%	73%	70%	68%	69%	63%	71%	66%	68%	63%	68%	74%	74%	67%
	CT	22	21	26	25	26	22	27	22	28	28	34	24	22	20	29
	JW	5	5	1	2	3	3	4	4	4	1	2	3	1	3	1
	NO	4	1	1	3	3	6	3	1	2	2	0	3	2	3	1
	OT	0	0	0	0	1	0	3	2	1	1	1	3	1	1	3
# SURVEYED		121	108	113	134	117	107	119	115	132	110	130	115	99	119	111
AGE	RESP	'73	'74	'75	'76	'77	'78	'80	'82	'83	'84	'85	'86	'87	'88	'89
66+	PR	77%	75%	79%	73%	71%	75%	74%	73%	69%	78%	71%	73%	74%	69%	72%
	CT	18	20	17	21	23	19	21	21	23	16	23	21	22	26	21
	JW	3	4	2	4	3	3	2	4	4	2	3	3	2	1	3
	NO	2	1	2	2	2	3	1	1	2	2	2	3	2	3	3
	OT	1	0	0	0	0	0	1	0	2	2	1	1	1	1	1
# SURVEYED		200	227	232	251	210	231	242	258	239	231	261	264	246	280	274

****

CURRENT DEGREE OF FUNDAMENTALISM

TABLE I: CURRENT DEGREE OF FUNDAMENTALISM -- BY TOTAL POPULATION

Question: Fundamentalism/Liberalism of respondent's religion.

Responses: FN = Fundamentalist; MD = Moderate; LB = Liberal

	YEAR															
RESPONSE	'72	'73	'74	'75	'76	'77	'78	'80	'82	'83	'84	'85	'86	'87	'88	'89
FN	28%	29%	29%	29%	29%	30%	30%	31%	28%	30%	34%	34%	35%	36%	35%	33%
MD	54	53	51	52	51	52	51	49	52	51	40	40	40	38	39	41
LB	18	18	20	20	20	17	19	20	20	19	26	26	25	26	26	26
# SURVEYED	1575	1458	1462	1468	1478	1503	1508	1425	1475	1564	1433	1497	1428	1417	1426	1491

TABLE II: CURRENT DEGREE OF FUNDAMENTALISM -- BY SEX

Question: Fundamentalism/Liberalism of respondent's religion.

Responses: FN = Fundamentalist; MD = Moderate; LB = Liberal

		YEAR															
SEX	RESP	'72	'73	'74	'75	'76	'77	'78	'80	'82	'83	'84	'85	'86	'87	'88	'89
M	FN	26%	28%	27%	29%	27%	27%	27%	29%	26%	30%	31%	33%	30%	35%	32%	30%
	MD	54	53	51	51	51	53	50	49	49	48	41	40	41	39	38	41
	LB	20	20	22	21	22	19	23	22	25	22	28	26	28	26	30	29
# SURVEYED		792	675	679	660	655	677	630	617	620	672	585	668	602	615	608	637
SEX	RESP	'72	'73	'74	'75	'76	'77	'78	'80	'82	'83	'84	'85	'86	'87	'88	'89
F	FN	30%	30%	30%	28%	30%	33%	32%	33%	29%	29%	36%	34%	38%	36%	38%	35%
	MD	53	54	52	53	51	51	51	48	54	53	39	39	38	38	39	40
	LB	17	16	18	19	19	16	17	19	17	17	25	26	23	26	23	24
# SURVEYED		783	783	783	808	823	826	878	808	855	892	848	829	826	802	818	854

TABLE III: CURRENT DEGREE OF FUNDAMENTALISM -- BY RACE

Question: Fundamentalism/Liberalism of respondent's religion.

Responses: FN = Fundamentalist; MD = Moderate; LB = Liberal

		YEAR															
RACE	RESP	'72	'73	'74	'75	'76	'77	'78	'80	'82	'83	'84	'85	'86	'87	'88	'89
WHITE	FD	21%	24%	24%	24%	25%	25%	25%	27%	24%	25%	29%	30%	30%	30%	30%	29%
	MD	58	57	55	56	54	57	54	52	55	55	42	42	43	42	41	42
	LB	21	19	21	21	21	18	21	21	22	20	28	28	27	29	29	29
# SURVEYED		1314	1270	1287	1306	1340	1319	1338	1278	1298	1389	1218	1309	1223	1188	1195	1283
RACE	RESP	'72	'73	'74	'75	'76	'77	'78	'80	'82	'83	'84	'85	'86	'87	'88	'89
BLACK	FD	64%	68%	70%	71%	72%	72%	72%	75%	66%	76%	66%	65%	68%	72%	70%	65%
	MD	30	23	22	20	21	18	22	14	24	16	21	22	16	19	20	25
	LB	5	9	8	9	7	9	6	10	10	8	13	13	15	9	11	10
# SURVEYED		257	176	170	158	129	173	156	138	152	158	167	147	176	183	179	155
RACE	RESP	'72	'73	'74	'75	'76	'77	'78	'80	'82	'83	'84	'85	'86	'87	'88	'89
OTHER	FD	25%	8%	40%	25%	0%	27%	29%	33%	4%	24%	38%	39%	28%	48%	38%	38%
	MD	75	67	40	50	67	45	57	56	80	41	42	46	55	33	46	43
	LB	0	25	20	25	33	27	14	11	16	35	21	15	17	20	15	19
# SURVEYED		4	12	5	4	9	11	14	9	25	17	48	41	29	46	52	53

TABLE IV: CURRENT DEGREE OF FUNDAMENTALISM -- BY AGE

Question: Fundamentalism/Liberalism of respondent's religion.

Responses: FN = Fundamentalist; MD = Moderate; LB = Liberal

		YEAR															
AGE	RESP	'72	'73	'74	'75	'76	'77	'78	'80	'82	'83	'84	'85	'86	'87	'88	'89
18-23	FD	27%	29%	30%	24%	28%	39%	33%	34%	38%	33%	27%	37%	36%	40%	38%	34%
	MD	51	54	47	56	45	46	48	49	42	44	45	39	44	36	35	40
	LB	22	17	23	20	27	16	19	18	20	22	27	24	20	23	28	26
# SURVEYED		159	166	163	167	160	160	159	152	142	126	154	128	108	121	138	132
AGE	RESP	'72	'73	'74	'75	'76	'77	'78	'80	'82	'83	'84	'85	'86	'87	'88	'89
24-29	FD	27%	24%	26%	28%	30%	33%	32%	29%	25%	33%	32%	28%	34%	37%	32%	31%
	MD	54	51	54	45	48	45	46	50	52	49	39	41	42	45	43	45
	LB	20	26	21	27	22	22	22	22	23	18	29	31	24	18	25	24
# SURVEYED		228	203	209	228	220	196	237	199	241	282	230	214	210	189	207	196

TABLE IV: CURRENT DEGREE OF FUNDAMENTALISM -- BY AGE (Continued)

Question: Fundamentalism/Liberalism of respondent's religion.

Responses: FN = Fundamentalist; MD = Moderate; LB = Liberal

		YEAR															
AGE	RESP	'72	'73	'74	'75	'76	'77	'78	'80	'82	'83	'84	'85	'86	'87	'88	'89
30-35	FD	30%	28%	34%	31%	33%	30%	31%	33%	28%	32%	32%	37%	31%	31%	34%	26%
	MD	56	56	46	48	50	51	50	48	53	52	41	35	48	40	43	47
	LB	15	16	20	22	17	19	20	20	19	17	26	29	21	29	23	27
# SURVEYED		185	162	172	167	181	185	229	204	202	230	191	205	211	215	185	206
AGE	RESP	'72	'73	'74	'75	'76	'77	'78	'80	'82	'83	'84	'85	'86	'87	'88	'89
36-41	FD	31%	34%	29%	36%	28%	42%	30%	32%	29%	31%	31%	37%	33%	31%	31%	35%
	MD	56	53	51	48	50	41	54	45	50	51	41	40	38	40	44	38
	LB	14	13	20	16	23	17	16	22	21	18	28	22	29	29	25	28
# SURVEYED		124	166	151	152	155	168	158	143	141	169	181	174	181	176	183	189
AGE	RESP	'72	'73	'74	'75	'76	'77	'78	'80	'82	'83	'84	'85	'86	'87	'88	'89
42-47	FD	27%	27%	29%	27%	31%	28%	28%	45%	28%	33%	36%	25%	32%	35%	36%	34%
	MD	58	58	55	50	54	57	51	39	53	49	38	47	40	31	41	39
	LB	15	15	17	23	15	15	21	16	19	17	26	28	28	34	23	27
# SURVEYED		179	142	150	141	113	143	118	113	118	144	126	122	134	152	155	156
AGE	RESP	'72	'73	'74	'75	'76	'77	'78	'80	'82	'83	'84	'85	'86	'87	'88	'89
48-53	FD	26%	34%	26%	28%	27%	23%	28%	26%	30%	24%	43%	35%	37%	39%	41%	37%
	MD	52	51	51	56	52	62	54	50	47	56	36	40	29	40	36	35
	LB	22	15	23	17	21	15	18	24	23	20	22	25	34	21	23	28
# SURVEYED		184	150	143	138	130	151	129	120	110	114	101	129	108	118	88	137
AGE	RESP	'72	'73	'74	'75	'76	'77	'78	'80	'82	'83	'84	'85	'86	'87	'88	'89
54-59	FD	23%	32%	28%	29%	27%	23%	25%	40%	23%	29%	39%	36%	35%	36%	45%	33%
	MD	57	51	51	61	56	60	56	40	60	54	37	36	35	39	27	48
	LB	20	16	20	10	17	18	19	20	18	17	24	28	29	25	28	19
# SURVEYED		154	152	138	125	129	168	134	132	141	131	110	131	99	96	82	94
AGE	RESP	'72	'73	'74	'75	'76	'77	'78	'80	'82	'83	'84	'85	'86	'87	'88	'89
60-65	FD	27%	34%	30%	30%	29%	23%	30%	22%	25%	26%	34%	33%	36%	39%	40%	41%
	MD	55	51	52	53	53	62	58	60	57	54	42	43	42	45	29	39
	LB	19	15	19	17	18	15	12	18	18	20	24	24	21	16	31	21
# SURVEYED		143	121	108	113	134	117	107	118	114	128	109	130	113	100	116	106
AGE	RESP	'72	'73	'74	'75	'76	'77	'78	'80	'82	'83	'84	'85	'86	'87	'88	'89
66+	FD	34%	23%	30%	28%	27%	30%	31%	26%	27%	25%	37%	35%	39%	38%	34%	33%
	MD	49	54	55	53	54	53	48	54	54	53	36	40	36	33	38	37
	LB	17	23	16	19	20	16	21	20	19	22	27	25	25	29	28	30
# SURVEYED		214	192	222	232	250	208	231	235	257	234	226	257	258	247	268	272

****

DEGREE OF FUNDAMENTALISM AT AGE 16

TABLE I: DEGREE OF FUNDAMENTALISM AT AGE 16 -- BY TOTAL POPULATION

Question: Liberalism/Fundamentalism of religion respondent was raised in? NOTE: Question was not asked in 1972.

Responses: FN = Fundamentalist; MD = Moderate; LB = Liberal

	YEAR														
RESPONSE	'73	'74	'75	'76	'77	'78	'80	'82	'83	'84	'85	'86	'87	'88	'89
FN	30%	31%	30%	29%	32%	32%	30%	29%	30%	35%	34%	36%	38%	35%	32%
MD	55	54	56	55	54	55	54	55	54	41	41	40	39	40	44
LB	15	15	13	16	14	13	16	16	15	24	25	23	24	25	23
# SURVEYED	1466	1465	1473	1477	1504	1510	1440	1473	1578	1414	1514	1433	1408	1440	1491

TABLE II: DEGREE OF FUNDAMENTALISM AT AGE 16 -- BY SEX

Question: Liberalism/Fundamentalism of religion respondent was raised in? NOTE: Question was not asked in 1972.

Responses: FN = Fundamentalist; MD = Moderate; LB = Liberal

		YEAR														
SEX	RESP	'73	'74	'75	'76	'77	'78	'80	'82	'83	'84	'85	'86	'87	'88	'89
M	FN	29%	30%	30%	30%	30%	30%	29%	28%	32%	34%	33%	33%	38%	34%	30%
	MD	56	55	57	55	55	55	54	55	52	43	43	42	39	40	46
	LB	15	15	13	15	15	14	17	17	16	23	25	25	23	26	24
# SURVEYED		682	684	664	655	679	628	624	620	680	571	680	604	613	617	640
SEX	RESP	'73	'74	'75	'76	'77	'78	'80	'82	'83	'84	'85	'86	'87	'88	'89
F	FN	32%	32%	31%	29%	33%	33%	31%	29%	30%	36%	35%	39%	38%	36%	34%
	MD	54	53	56	54	53	54	53	55	56	40	40	38	39	39	43
	LB	14	15	13	17	14	13	15	15	14	24	25	22	24	24	23
# SURVEYED		784	781	809	822	825	882	816	853	898	843	834	829	795	823	851

TABLE III: DEGREE OF FUNDAMENTALISM AT AGE 16 -- BY RACE

Question: Liberalism/Fundamentalism of religion respondent was raised in? NOTE: Question was not asked in 1972.

Responses: FN = Fundamentalist; MD = Moderate; LB = Liberal

		YEAR														
RACE	RESP	'73	'74	'75	'76	'77	'78	'80	'82	'83	'84	'85	'86	'87	'88	'89
WHITE	FN	24%	25%	26%	25%	26%	28%	26%	24%	25%	31%	31%	32%	32%	29%	28%
	MD	60	58	60	58	58	58	57	59	58	43	42	43	41	43	46
	LB	16	17	14	17	16	15	17	17	16	26	27	25	27	28	26
# SURVEYED		1274	1291	1308	1341	1323	1339	1292	1298	1397	1205	1324	1222	1181	1207	1285
RACE	RESP	'73	'74	'75	'76	'77	'78	'80	'82	'83	'84	'85	'86	'87	'88	'89
BLACK	FN	74%	77%	70%	74%	73%	71%	76%	73%	76%	64%	64%	70%	75%	77%	66%
	MD	19	19	25	19	22	27	19	22	20	25	23	19	18	15	27
	LB	7	4	5	8	5	1	5	6	4	10	13	11	7	8	7
# SURVEYED		180	171	162	129	171	157	140	153	164	166	150	183	181	182	156
RACE	RESP	'73	'74	'75	'76	'77	'78	'80	'82	'83	'84	'85	'86	'87	'88	'89
OTHER	FN	8%	33%	0%	14%	20%	29%	13%	9%	6%	42%	23%	32%	33%	33%	34%
	MD	75	67	67	57	80	71	75	73	59	47	63	54	54	51	56
	LB	17	0	33	29	0	0	13	18	35	12	15	14	13	16	10
# SURVEYED		12	3	3	7	10	14	8	22	17	43	40	28	46	51	50

TABLE IV: DEGREE OF FUNDAMENTALISM AT AGE 16 -- BY AGE

Question: Liberalism/Fundamentalism of religion respondent was raised in? NOTE: Question was not asked in 1972.

Responses: FN = Fundamentalist; MD = Moderate; LB = Liberal

		YEAR														
AGE	RESP	'73	'74	'75	'76	'77	'78	'80	'82	'83	'84	'85	'86	'87	'88	89
18-23	FN	31%	32%	27%	28%	36%	36%	33%	41%	34%	26%	39%	43%	43%	43%	37%
	MD	57	56	58	56	51	53	51	47	51	48	42	43	38	38	43
	LB	13	12	15	17	12	12	16	12	15	25	18	15	20	20	21
# SURVEYED		167	164	173	160	162	160	151	142	126	155	132	108	122	136	131
AGE	RESP	'73	'74	'75	'76	'77	'78	'80	'82	'83	'84	'85	'86	'87	'88	'89
24-29	FN	29%	26%	30%	27%	34%	34%	32%	25%	33%	35%	27%	32%	38%	33%	28%
	MD	57	58	54	59	53	54	55	60	53	45	47	46	44	44	51
	LB	14	15	16	14	12	12	13	15	14	20	26	23	18	22	22
# SURVEYED		206	208	228	221	201	239	201	241	286	225	214	212	187	206	195

TABLE IV: DEGREE OF FUNDAMENTALISM AT AGE 16 -- BY AGE (Continued)

Question: Liberalism/Fundamentalism of religion respondent was raised in? NOTE: Question was not asked in 1972.

Responses: FN = Fundamentalist; MD = Moderate; LB = Liberal

		YEAR														
AGE	RESP	'73	'74	'75	'76	'77	'78	'80	'82	'83	'84	'85	'86	'87	'88	'89
30-35	FN	27%	35%	38%	31%	32%	30%	29%	31%	35%	32%	37%	35%	30%	35%	25%
	MD	57	46	46	51	54	56	57	57	52	44	37	47	45	42	52
	LB	15	19	16	18	15	14	14	12	13	24	27	17	25	23	23
# SURVEYED		162	174	167	184	183	228	211	203	234	188	210	213	211	186	208
AGE	RESP	'73	'74	'75	'76	'77	'78	'80	'82	'83	'84	'85	'86	'87	'88	'89
36-41	FN	35%	34%	38%	34%	42%	35%	28%	29%	30%	35%	31%	37%	39%	31%	36%
	MD	51	53	50	52	44	55	52	52	51	41	45	40	37	41	46
	LB	13	13	12	15	15	10	20	19	18	24	23	22	23	28	18
# SURVEYED		167	152	153	155	165	156	146	141	171	181	181	183	179	189	189
AGE	RESP	'73	'74	'75	'76	'77	'78	'80	'82	'83	'84	'85	'86	'87	'88	'89
42-47	FN	28%	30%	27%	30%	36%	28%	41%	25%	35%	38%	33%	31%	39%	35%	37%
	MD	57	55	58	56	49	56	49	58	51	40	40	34	36	44	36
	LB	14	15	15	14	15	15	10	17	15	23	27	34	25	21	27
# SURVEYED		145	148	142	111	143	117	116	118	144	124	122	137	154	156	154
AGE	RESP	'73	'74	'75	'76	'77	'78	'80	'82	'83	'84	'85	'86	'87	'88	'89
48-53	FN	31%	31%	28%	29%	25%	32%	29%	33%	23%	45%	38%	41%	38%	41%	34%
	MD	52	49	59	55	63	52	50	46	57	35	34	32	39	37	37
	LB	17	20	14	16	13	16	21	21	20	20	28	27	23	22	28
# SURVEYED		147	142	138	129	151	130	121	112	114	96	129	107	118	90	137
AGE	RESP	'73	'74	'75	'76	'77	'78	'80	'82	'83	'84	'85	'86	'87	'88	'89
54-59	FN	30%	32%	33%	34%	25%	28%	38%	31%	31%	38%	32%	35%	47%	46%	35%
	MD	57	52	58	50	57	59	47	53	56	39	43	36	30	30	46
	LB	13	17	9	16	17	12	15	16	13	24	25	30	23	24	19
# SURVEYED		150	139	125	127	167	137	133	138	133	106	131	98	94	83	96
AGE	RESP	'73	'74	'75	'76	'77	'78	'80	'82	'83	'84	'85	'86	'87	'88	'89
60-65	FN	33%	35%	26%	25%	22%	28%	27%	25%	24%	33%	34%	38%	39%	37%	33%
	MD	53	53	68	60	66	57	59	61	61	45	44	40	38	34	48
	LB	14	12	6	16	11	15	14	14	15	22	22	22	23	29	19
# SURVEYED		121	107	113	134	116	107	114	113	131	109	129	112	97	117	108
AGE	RESP	'73	'74	'75	'76	'77	'78	'80	'82	'83	'84	'85	'86	'87	'88	'89
66+	FN	28%	26%	28%	28%	31%	33%	24%	23%	26%	37%	35%	40%	35%	31%	32%
	MD	54	60	61	55	53	52	58	59	58	35	37	36	36	38	39
	LB	18	14	11	17	16	15	18	18	16	28	28	24	28	31	29
# SURVEYED		197	225	230	250	209	230	238	256	233	225	259	257	243	273	270

HOUSEHOLD SIZE

TABLE I: HOUSEHOLD SIZE -- BY TOTAL POPULATION

Question: Household size and number of household members.

Responses: 1 = 1; 2 = 2; 3 = 3; 4 = 4; 5 = 5; 6 = 6; 7 = 7; 8 = 8; 9 = 9; 10 = 10 or more

	YEAR															
RESPONSE	'72	'73	'74	'75	'76	'77	'78	'80	'82	'83	'84	'85	'86	'87	'88	'89
1	9%	10%	11%	13%	16%	17%	19%	20%	22%	19%	22%	22%	21%	22%	22%	21%
2	27	30	30	30	32	31	30	34	33	31	31	33	31	30	35	33
3	19	18	18	20	17	19	18	18	19	19	19	18	18	20	17	18
4	18	20	17	17	16	17	18	17	14	17	15	15	16	16	16	17
5	12	11	12	11	11	9	8	7	8	8	8	8	9	8	7	7
6	6	6	6	5	4	5	4	3	3	3	3	2	3	3	2	2
7	3	3	3	2	2	1	1	1	1	2	1	1	1	1	1	1
8	2	1	1	1	1	1	1	0	0	1	0	0	0	0	0	1
9	1	1	0	0	0	1	0	0	0	0	0	0	0	0	0	0
10	1	0	1	0	0	0	0	0	0	0	0	0	0	0	0	0
# SURVEYED	1613	1503	1482	1490	1497	1530	1532	1468	1506	1599	1473	1534	1470	1466	1481	1537

TABLE II: HOUSEHOLD SIZE -- BY SEX

Question: Household size and number of household members.

Responses: 1 = 1; 2 = 2; 3 = 3; 4 = 4; 5 = 5; 6 = 6; 7 = 7; 8 = 8; 9 = 9; 10 = 10 or more

		YEAR															
SEX	RESP	'72	'73	'74	'75	'76	'77	'78	'80	'82	'83	'84	'85	'86	'87	'88	'89
M	1	7%	10%	10%	11%	14%	17%	18%	19%	19%	18%	22%	20%	19%	22%	21%	18%
A	2	27	31	33	32	35	32	30	35	34	32	33	35	32	31	34	33
L	3	21	17	19	19	17	17	18	18	21	19	16	19	21	17	16	19
E	4	20	21	16	20	15	16	18	17	14	17	15	14	16	17	16	19
	5	12	11	12	9	11	9	9	7	8	9	9	8	10	7	8	7
	6	7	6	6	6	4	6	4	2	3	3	3	1	2	2	4	2
	7	2	2	3	2	2	1	2	1	1	1	1	1	0	1	1	1
	8	2	1	1	1	1	1	1	0	0	0	0	1	0	0	0	0
	9	1	0	0	0	0	0	0	0	0	0	0	0	0	0	0	0
	10	1	0	0	0	0	0	0	0	0	0	0	0	0	0	0	0
# SURVEYED		807	701	690	670	669	693	643	641	639	690	598	688	621	641	638	660
SEX	RESP	'72	'73	'74	'75	'76	'77	'78	'80	'82	'83	'84	'85	'86	'87	'88	'89
F	1	12%	11%	12%	16%	17%	17%	20%	20%	24%	20%	23%	24%	23%	22%	23%	23%
E	2	28	28	27	28	30	30	30	33	32	31	30	31	30	29	36	32
M	3	18	20	17	22	18	20	18	17	18	19	21	17	16	21	17	16
A	4	17	19	18	15	16	18	18	17	15	17	15	16	15	16	15	15
L	5	13	11	13	12	11	9	8	8	7	8	8	7	9	8	6	7
E	6	5	6	6	5	4	3	5	3	2	3	3	3	3	3	1	3
	7	4	3	4	2	2	1	1	2	1	2	1	1	1	1	0	2
	8	1	1	2	0	1	1	1	0	0	1	0	0	0	0	0	1
	9	1	1	0	0	0	1	0	0	0	0	0	0	0	0	0	0
	10	1	1	1	0	0	0	0	1	0	0	0	0	0	0	0	0
# SURVEYED		806	802	792	820	828	837	889	827	867	909	875	846	849	825	843	877

TABLE III: HOUSEHOLD SIZE -- BY RACE

Question: Household size and number of household members.

Responses: 1 = 1; 2 = 2; 3 = 3; 4 = 4; 5 = 5; 6 = 6; 7 = 7; 8 = 8; 9 = 9; 10 = 10 or more

		YEAR															
RACE	RESP	'72	'73	'74	'75	'76	'77	'78	'80	'82	'83	'84	'85	'86	'87	'88	'89
WHITE	**1**	10%	10%	11%	13%	15%	17%	19%	20%	22%	19%	22%	22%	21%	22%	22%	21%
	2	28	31	31	30	33	32	31	34	35	32	32	34	33	31	36	34
	3	19	18	18	20	17	18	18	17	19	19	19	18	19	19	17	18
	4	19	20	18	17	16	17	17	17	14	17	14	16	15	16	15	17
	5	13	11	13	11	11	9	8	7	7	8	8	7	8	8	6	7
	6	6	6	6	5	4	4	4	3	2	3	3	2	2	2	2	2
	7	3	3	3	2	1	1	1	1	1	1	1	1	1	1	0	1
	8	1	1	1	1	1	1	1	0	0	1	0	0	0	0	0	0
	9	1	0	0	0	0	0	0	0	0	0	0	0	0	0	0	0
	10	1	0	0	0	0	0	0	0	0	0	0	0	0	0	0	0
# SURVEYED		1348	1307	1303	1323	1359	1339	1358	1318	1323	1416	1251	1338	1249	1222	1234	1319
RACE	RESP	'72	'73	'74	'75	'76	'77	'78	'80	'82	'83	'84	'85	'86	'87	'88	'89
BLACK	**1**	8%	11%	16%	15%	24%	20%	22%	17%	25%	21%	25%	24%	22%	25%	23%	28%
	2	25	22	25	25	26	22	20	26	16	25	26	31	23	26	32	24
	3	20	21	15	19	13	22	16	21	21	19	19	17	15	21	16	15
	4	16	18	11	15	10	17	22	16	19	12	15	9	17	16	13	18
	5	11	11	11	11	13	6	9	11	12	13	7	11	13	6	11	8
	6	8	9	8	7	5	6	8	3	4	4	5	4	5	4	4	4
	7	4	3	9	3	3	2	2	4	3	4	1	1	3	2	2	1
	8	3	2	3	2	4	2	1	1	1	0	1	1	1	0	0	2
	9	2	2	1	1	2	2	1	0	0	1	0	1	1	0	0	1
	10	2	3	2	1	1	1	0	1	0	1	1	1	1	0	0	0
# SURVEYED		261	183	172	163	129	176	158	140	156	165	170	152	184	191	186	157
RACE	RESP	'72	'73	'74	'75	'76	'77	'78	'80	'82	'83	'84	'85	'86	'87	'88	'89
OTHER	**1**	0%	8%	14%	0%	0%	20%	19%	10%	15%	17%	13%	11%	19%	17%	23%	5%
	2	25	31	14	0	22	47	19	40	30	28	27	30	16	21	18	39
	3	25	23	14	75	33	7	13	20	22	22	12	18	14	21	20	15
	4	0	31	14	0	11	13	31	30	19	28	25	16	16	15	28	20
	5	25	8	0	25	11	7	19	0	7	6	15	14	22	11	3	7
	6	0	0	14	0	22	7	0	0	7	0	6	9	8	13	5	5
	7	0	0	14	0	0	0	0	0	0	0	0	2	3	0	2	7
	8	25	0	14	0	0	0	0	0	0	0	0	0	3	0	0	0
	9	0	0	0	0	0	0	0	0	0	0	0	0	0	2	2	2
	10	0	0	0	0	0	0	0	0	0	0	2	0	0	0	0	2
# SURVEYED		4	13	7	4	9	15	16	10	27	18	52	44	37	53	61	61

TABLE IV: HOUSEHOLD SIZE -- BY AGE

Question: Household size and number of household members.

Responses: 1 = 1; 2 = 2; 3 = 3; 4 = 4; 5 = 5; 6 = 6; 7 = 7; 8 = 8; 9 = 9; 10 = 10 or more

		YEAR															
AGE	RESP	'72	'73	'74	'75	'76	'77	'78	'80	'82	'83	'84	'85	'86	'87	'88	'89
18-23	1	7%	6%	5%	5%	6%	6%	11%	10%	7%	12%	14%	9%	9%	12%	8%	7%
	2	17	26	30	24	29	27	33	31	28	28	27	35	30	31	31	32
	3	20	26	26	34	23	29	23	21	31	22	25	26	22	26	25	23
	4	21	22	17	16	15	16	16	20	16	19	15	15	19	21	20	15
	5	12	12	10	9	12	9	6	5	9	9	13	7	12	4	9	11
	6	9	5	4	7	6	7	7	5	6	6	4	4	5	5	4	8
	7	4	1	5	3	4	4	3	5	2	3	1	2	3	2	2	1
	8	4	4	2	1	2	0	1	1	1	1	0	2	0	0	1	1
	9	2	0	0	1	1	2	1	0	0	0	0	0	0	0	1	2
	10	5	0	1	0	2	1	0	3	0	1	0	2	0	0	0	1
# SURVEYED		169	171	167	173	162	164	163	155	148	128	161	133	108	126	141	137
AGE	RESP	'72	'73	'74	'75	'76	'77	'78	'80	'82	'83	'84	'85	'86	'87	'88	'89
24-29	1	6%	6%	8%	10%	12%	18%	12%	13%	15%	17%	19%	18%	16%	19%	17%	16%
	2	18	24	24	28	33	25	29	28	32	25	32	33	30	31	36	31
	3	29	23	28	27	20	31	25	33	23	23	22	24	27	22	21	24
	4	24	30	25	22	22	17	20	18	19	22	19	17	16	16	19	21
	5	16	10	10	9	9	6	9	5	7	9	7	7	10	10	4	4
	6	4	4	3	3	3	2	2	1	1	2	1	2	1	2	3	3
	7	3	1	1	0	0	0	1	0	1	1	0	0	0	1	0	0
	8	1	0	0	0	1	0	1	0	0	0	0	0	0	0	0	0
	9	0	0	0	0	0	0	0	0	0	0	0	0	0	0	0	0
	10	0	0	1	0	0	0	0	0	1	0	0	0	0	0	0	0
# SURVEYED		231	211	212	232	225	204	244	202	246	287	232	217	218	193	215	202
AGE	RESP	'72	'73	'74	'75	'76	'77	'78	'80	'82	'83	'84	'85	'86	'87	'88	'89
30-35	1	3%	4%	5%	5%	4%	10%	15%	16%	13%	11%	17%	12%	13%	17%	16%	14%
	2	9	13	10	6	6	19	13	17	23	19	17	17	17	19	20	17
	3	14	12	11	24	19	19	20	19	21	24	23	25	19	21	18	25
	4	29	35	30	32	31	28	32	28	25	24	26	27	29	26	28	26
	5	26	17	25	18	22	10	14	14	14	14	10	14	14	11	12	11
	6	11	9	11	9	10	10	3	3	3	4	6	2	6	4	4	3
	7	5	7	3	4	4	2	2	1	0	3	2	1	1	1	2	2
	8	3	2	4	1	2	1	0	1	0	1	0	1	0	0	0	1
	9	0	1	1	1	1	1	0	0	0	0	0	0	0	0	1	0
	10	1	1	0	1	0	0	0	0	0	0	0	0	0	0	0	0
# SURVEYED		187	167	175	171	185	188	230	215	204	236	200	212	221	221	195	212

TABLE IV: HOUSEHOLD SIZE -- BY AGE (Continued)

Question: Household size and number of household members.

Responses: 1 = 1; 2 = 2; 3 = 3; 4 = 4; 5 = 5; 6 = 6; 7 = 7; 8 = 8; 9 = 9; 10 = 10 or more

		YEAR															
AGE	RESP	'72	'73	'74	'75	'76	'77	'78	'80	'82	'83	'84	'85	'86	'87	'88	'89
36-41	**1**	2%	7%	3%	3%	6%	12%	11%	11%	15%	13%	10%	15%	6%	13%	13%	15%
	2	14	6	5	12	14	10	9	13	16	14	18	15	19	17	18	15
	3	10	11	11	13	16	12	12	15	26	20	21	13	21	17	19	18
	4	21	22	24	25	22	27	32	35	25	30	26	28	28	30	28	33
	5	23	22	29	26	26	23	19	16	13	15	16	17	19	17	15	12
	6	9	17	15	12	9	9	12	5	3	4	9	8	3	4	5	3
	7	12	9	7	5	3	4	4	5	1	2	1	2	2	2	1	3
	8	5	3	2	3	3	2	1	1	1	1	1	1	1	0	1	2
	9	2	2	1	1	1	1	0	1	0	1	0	1	1	0	0	0
	10	2	1	2	1	1	1	1	0	1	0	0	1	0	0	0	0
# SURVEYED		128	175	151	154	158	168	160	150	146	173	187	184	188	186	193	198
AGE	RESP	'72	'73	'74	'75	'76	'77	'78	'80	'82	'83	'84	'85	'86	'87	'88	'89
42-47	**1**	4%	6%	7%	6%	6%	10%	12%	8%	13%	14%	14%	13%	18%	14%	17%	12%
	2	15	19	19	13	12	13	20	19	24	17	17	28	23	22	22	20
	3	19	14	13	20	26	23	18	22	23	19	24	24	20	22	22	23
	4	22	25	23	24	19	27	20	29	21	25	22	20	18	20	23	24
	5	15	17	17	20	24	16	14	13	11	14	14	10	13	13	11	14
	6	12	10	9	8	6	7	11	7	5	8	6	2	4	6	5	3
	7	5	3	9	5	3	1	2	2	3	3	2	1	3	0	0	3
	8	3	2	3	2	2	1	3	0	1	1	0	1	0	1	1	1
	9	2	1	0	1	0	1	0	0	0	1	0	0	1	0	0	1
	10	3	1	1	1	2	0	1	1	0	0	1	0	0	1	0	1
# SURVEYED		186	146	151	143	114	147	119	117	119	145	126	124	141	157	157	161
AGE	RESP	'72	'73	'74	'75	'76	'77	'78	'80	'82	'83	'84	'85	'86	'87	'88	'89
48-53	**1**	6%	6%	9%	10%	11%	11%	10%	14%	17%	14%	16%	17%	19%	17%	20%	22%
	2	25	25	28	26	39	34	29	37	29	40	34	38	33	30	35	34
	3	30	32	17	26	24	19	27	21	27	21	25	14	25	32	29	20
	4	19	17	15	18	18	18	17	14	13	16	13	17	9	13	10	15
	5	10	13	15	8	5	8	11	9	11	5	7	11	7	4	4	7
	6	6	3	7	6	1	6	4	4	4	3	1	2	3	2	2	1
	7	3	2	5	1	0	0	1	1	0	0	0	2	0	1	0	1
	8	1	0	3	1	2	3	2	1	0	2	1	0	3	2	0	0
	9	1	1	1	1	1	0	2	0	0	0	1	1	0	0	0	0
	10	1	1	0	1	0	1	0	0	0	0	2	0	1	0	0	0
# SURVEYED		189	151	146	141	133	154	133	123	112	116	102	131	108	126	92	138

TABLE IV: HOUSEHOLD SIZE -- BY AGE (Continued)

Question: Household size and number of household members.

Responses: 1 = 1; 2 = 2; 3 = 3; 4 = 4; 5 = 5; 6 = 6; 7 = 7; 8 = 8; 9 = 9; 10 = 10 or more

		YEAR															
AGE	RESP	'72	'73	'74	'75	'76	'77	'78	'80	'82	'83	'84	'85	'86	'87	'88	'89
54-59	1	6%	8%	12%	18%	15%	18%	26%	15%	15%	17%	22%	19%	23%	19%	24%	22%
	2	46	48	44	47	52	48	46	57	51	54	49	49	38	41	49	52
	3	21	25	27	16	16	17	15	15	20	15	19	19	21	27	16	14
	4	15	10	9	10	9	9	8	7	7	7	5	8	12	10	7	10
	5	6	6	4	5	5	7	1	4	3	5	3	2	2	3	2	2
	6	3	4	4	2	2	1	2	0	3	0	1	1	2	0	0	0
	7	1	0	1	2	1	0	1	2	1	1	1	1	0	0	1	0
	8	1	1	0	1	0	0	0	0	0	0	0	0	0	0	0	0
	9	1	0	0	0	1	0	0	0	0	0	0	0	1	0	0	0
	10	1	0	0	0	0	0	0	0	0	0	0	0	0	0	0	0
# SURVEYED		156	157	139	126	129	168	137	136	144	134	114	134	99	98	85	99
AGE	RESP	'72	'73	'74	'75	'76	'77	'78	'80	'82	'83	'84	'85	'86	'87	'88	'89
60-65	1	17%	12%	19%	19%	21%	23%	25%	28%	36%	19%	27%	30%	26%	30%	26%	27%
	2	56	63	52	62	57	59	54	61	51	52	59	53	52	50	62	59
	3	16	14	20	11	13	12	13	9	6	23	9	11	10	17	9	10
	4	4	9	3	4	5	5	7	3	2	3	3	2	3	2	2	3
	5	3	1	6	3	3	0	0	0	3	2	1	3	6	1	1	0
	6	1	0	1	2	1	0	0	0	2	0	1	0	1	0	0	1
	7	1	1	0	1	0	0	0	0	0	1	0	0	0	0	0	1
	8	0	0	0	0	0	1	0	0	0	0	0	0	0	0	0	0
	9	1	0	0	0	0	0	0	0	0	0	0	0	0	0	0	0
	10	0	0	0	0	0	0	0	0	0	0	0	0	1	0	0	0
# SURVEYED		144	121	108	113	134	117	107	119	116	132	113	131	115	101	119	111
AGE	RESP	'72	'73	'74	'75	'76	'77	'78	'80	'82	'83	'84	'85	'86	'87	'88	'89
66+	1	31%	33%	30%	38%	45%	40%	45%	46%	49%	46%	52%	51%	48%	48%	46%	44%
	2	50	50	56	50	46	48	46	46	42	45	40	41	43	42	49	49
	3	11	10	9	9	4	5	6	5	6	6	6	6	6	5	4	5
	4	7	5	3	2	2	4	3	2	2	2	0	1	2	3	0	1
	5	1	3	0	0	2	3	1	1	1	0	2	0	0	1	1	1
	6	0	1	2	0	0	0	0	0	0	1	0	1	1	0	0	0
	7	0	0	0	0	0	0	0	0	0	0	0	0	0	0	0	0
	8	0	0	0	0	0	0	0	0	0	0	0	0	0	0	0	0
	9	0	0	0	0	0	0	0	0	0	0	0	0	0	0	0	0
	10	0	0	0	0	0	0	0	0	0	0	0	0	0	0	0	0
# SURVEYED		218	200	227	232	251	213	232	242	259	241	232	261	265	253	280	275

****

HOUSEHOLD MEMBERS UNDER AGE 6

TABLE I: HOUSEHOLD MEMBERS UNDER AGE 6 -- BY TOTAL POPULATION

Question: Number of household members under age 6.

Responses: 0 = 0; 1 = 1; 2 = 2; 3 = 3; 4 = 4; 5 = 5

	YEAR															
RESPONSE	'72	'73	'74	'75	'76	'77	'78	'80	'82	'83	'84	'85	'86	'87	'88	'89
0	75%	76%	76%	78%	77%	82%	81%	81%	83%	80%	82%	81%	81%	84%	82%	81%
1	14	14	15	15	15	13	13	14	12	13	12	13	13	11	14	13
2	8	7	7	6	6	4	5	5	4	6	5	4	5	4	4	5
3	2	1	2	1	1	1	1	1	1	1	1	1	1	1	1	1
4	0	0	0	0	0	0	0	0	0	0	0	0	0	0	0	0
5	0	0	0	0	0	0	0	0	0	0	0	0	0	0	0	0
# SURVEYED	1613	1504	1482	1490	1497	1521	1518	1457	1501	1594	1468	1529	1465	1464	1470	1516

TABLE II: HOUSEHOLD MEMBERS UNDER AGE 6 -- BY SEX

Question: Number of household members under age 6.

Responses: 0 = 0; 1 = 1; 2 = 2; 3 = 3; 4 = 4; 5 = 5

		YEAR															
SEX	RESP	'72	'73	'74	'75	'76	'77	'78	'80	'82	'83	'84	'85	'86	'87	'88	'89
M	0	75%	78%	77%	80%	80%	83%	83%	82%	84%	81%	84%	85%	83%	87%	81%	84%
A	1	15	14	16	13	12	12	11	13	12	12	10	10	12	8	15	12
L	2	7	6	6	6	6	4	6	4	4	6	5	4	4	5	4	4
E	3	2	2	1	0	2	1	1	0	1	1	1	1	1	1	1	1
	4	0	0	0	0	1	0	0	0	0	0	0	0	0	0	0	0
	5	0	0	0	0	0	0	0	0	0	0	0	0	0	0	0	0
# SURVEYED		807	701	690	670	669	689	637	637	638	687	598	686	620	640	631	649
SEX	RESP	'72	'73	'74	'75	'76	'77	'78	'80	'82	'83	'84	'85	'86	'87	'88	'89
F	0	76%	75%	75%	77%	76%	81%	80%	80%	82%	79%	80%	79%	80%	83%	82%	79%
E	1	13	15	15	17	17	14	14	14	13	14	14	15	14	13	13	13
M	2	9	8	8	5	6	4	5	5	4	5	5	5	5	4	4	6
A	3	2	1	2	1	1	1	1	1	1	1	1	1	0	1	1	1
L	4	0	0	0	0	0	0	0	0	0	0	0	0	0	0	0	0
E	5	0	0	0	0	0	0	0	0	0	0	0	0	0	0	0	0
# SURVEYED		806	803	792	820	828	832	881	820	863	907	870	843	845	824	839	867

TABLE III: HOUSEHOLD MEMBERS UNDER AGE 6 -- BY RACE

Question: Number of household members under age 6.

Responses: 0 = 0; 1 = 1; 2 = 2; 3 = 3; 4 = 4; 5 = 5

		YEAR															
RACE	RESP	'72	'73	'74	'75	'76	'77	'78	'80	'82	'83	'84	'85	'86	'87	'88	'89
WHITE	0	76%	77%	77%	78%	78%	83%	82%	81%	84%	80%	84%	82%	83%	85%	83%	82%
	1	13	14	15	15	14	12	12	14	12	13	11	13	12	10	13	12
	2	8	7	6	6	6	4	5	4	4	6	5	4	5	4	3	5
	3	2	1	1	1	1	1	1	1	1	1	1	1	1	1	1	1
	4	0	0	0	0	0	0	0	0	0	0	0	0	0	0	0	0
	5	0	0	0	0	0	0	0	0	0	0	0	0	0	0	0	0
# SURVEYED		1348	1308	1303	1323	1359	1333	1347	1307	1319	1412	1247	1333	1245	1221	1225	1301
RACE	RESP	'72	'73	'74	'75	'76	'77	'78	'80	'82	'83	'84	'85	'86	'87	'88	'89
BLACK	0	70%	73%	72%	79%	74%	72%	76%	78%	75%	76%	73%	78%	72%	82%	77%	73%
	1	20	15	15	13	20	20	17	15	18	16	19	13	20	12	17	16
	2	8	8	9	6	4	6	5	4	5	4	6	5	7	6	5	8
	3	2	3	5	1	2	1	1	2	1	3	1	3	1	1	1	2
	4	1	1	1	0	0	1	1	1	0	1	0	1	1	0	0	1
	5	0	1	0	0	0	0	0	0	0	0	1	0	0	0	0	0
# SURVEYED		261	183	172	163	129	173	156	140	155	164	170	152	183	190	184	154
RACE	RESP	'72	'73	'74	'75	'76	'77	'78	'80	'82	'83	'84	'85	'86	'87	'88	'89
OTHER	0	100%	62%	43%	50%	67%	93%	73%	80%	78%	78%	73%	70%	78%	75%	70%	77%
	1	0	23	29	50	22	7	20	0	15	6	16	18	19	21	16	13
	2	0	15	29	0	11	0	7	20	4	17	10	7	3	0	11	8
	3	0	0	0	0	0	0	0	0	4	0	2	5	0	4	2	2
	4	0	0	0	0	0	0	0	0	0	0	0	0	0	0	0	0
	5	0	0	0	0	0	0	0	0	0	0	0	0	0	0	0	0
# SURVEYED		4	13	7	4	9	15	15	10	27	18	51	44	37	53	61	61

TABLE IV: HOUSEHOLD MEMBERS UNDER AGE 6 -- BY AGE

Question: Number of household members under age 6.

Responses: 0 = 0; 1 = 1; 2 = 2; 3 = 3; 4 = 4; 5 = 5

		YEAR															
AGE	RESP	'72	'73	'74	'75	'76	'77	'78	'80	'82	'83	'84	'85	'86	'87	'88	'89
18-23	0	64%	75%	67%	70%	72%	74%	78%	70%	81%	82%	78%	75%	87%	85%	73%	76%
	1	22	16	24	24	22	21	16	20	16	12	15	22	9	12	18	19
	2	9	7	7	6	4	5	4	8	3	5	6	3	3	2	7	3
	3	4	2	2	0	1	1	1	1	1	1	1	0	1	2	2	2
	4	1	1	0	0	1	0	1	1	0	1	0	0	0	0	0	1
	5	0	0	0	0	0	0	0	0	0	0	0	0	0	0	0	0
# SURVEYED		169	171	167	173	162	164	162	155	147	128	160	133	108	126	139	135

TABLE IV: HOUSEHOLD MEMBERS UNDER AGE 6 -- BY AGE (Continued)

Question: Number of household members under age 6.

Responses: 0 = 0; 1 = 1; 2 = 2; 3 = 3; 4 = 4; 5 = 5

		YEAR															
AGE	RESP	'72	'73	'74	'75	'76	'77	'78	'80	'82	'83	'84	'85	'86	'87	'88	'89
24-29	0	40%	46%	44%	50%	54%	57%	56%	57%	61%	53%	63%	61%	61%	65%	62%	61%
	1	31	25	31	31	26	30	26	30	23	29	19	23	27	24	26	26
	2	24	27	19	16	16	9	15	11	13	15	14	12	10	9	11	12
	3	4	1	6	2	4	3	3	2	3	2	3	4	1	2	1	1
	4	1	0	0	0	0	0	0	1	0	0	0	0	0	0	0	0
	5	0	0	0	0	0	0	0	0	0	0	0	0	0	0	0	0
# SURVEYED		231	212	212	232	225	201	239	196	244	286	232	216	218	192	214	201
AGE	RESP	'72	'73	'74	'75	'76	'77	'78	'80	'82	'83	'84	'85	'86	'87	'88	'89
30-35	0	39%	47%	46%	51%	37%	61%	61%	61%	58%	59%	60%	53%	53%	66%	62%	57%
	1	30	36	33	35	39	24	28	27	30	28	28	31	32	21	29	26
	2	21	11	18	12	17	13	11	11	11	11	10	12	13	12	8	15
	3	8	5	3	1	5	2	1	1	1	2	2	3	1	2	1	2
	4	1	1	1	0	2	0	0	0	0	0	0	0	0	0	0	0
	5	0	0	0	1	0	0	0	0	0	0	0	0	0	0	0	0
# SURVEYED		187	167	175	171	185	184	228	214	202	235	198	210	219	221	192	207
AGE	RESP	'72	'73	'74	'75	'76	'77	'78	'80	'82	'83	'84	'85	'86	'87	'88	'89
36-41	0	74%	66%	72%	71%	69%	74%	76%	76%	82%	76%	77%	74%	77%	77%	75%	76%
	1	17	24	21	21	23	21	18	19	16	17	19	21	17	17	22	18
	2	5	7	7	6	6	4	6	4	1	6	3	4	4	6	2	5
	3	2	2	1	2	2	1	1	1	1	1	1	1	2	0	1	1
	4	2	1	0	0	0	0	0	0	0	0	0	0	0	0	0	0
	5	0	0	0	0	0	0	0	0	0	0	0	0	0	0	0	0
# SURVEYED		128	175	151	154	158	168	157	149	146	172	186	183	186	185	188	195
AGE	RESP	'72	'73	'74	'75	'76	'77	'78	'80	'82	'83	'84	'85	'86	'87	'88	'89
42-47	0	85%	84%	87%	90%	91%	93%	94%	90%	90%	90%	93%	95%	89%	92%	87%	87%
	1	12	12	10	9	8	5	4	9	8	8	5	4	9	6	11	10
	2	3	1	3	1	1	1	2	1	1	1	2	1	2	1	3	3
	3	0	3	0	0	0	0	0	0	1	1	1	0	0	1	0	1
	4	0	0	0	0	0	0	0	0	0	0	0	0	0	0	0	0
	5	0	0	0	0	0	0	0	0	0	0	0	0	0	0	0	0
# SURVEYED		186	146	151	143	114	146	118	116	119	144	125	123	141	157	157	159
AGE	RESP	'72	'73	'74	'75	'76	'77	'78	'80	'82	'83	'84	'85	'86	'87	'88	'89
48-53	0	95%	94%	88%	94%	97%	95%	96%	93%	96%	97%	95%	92%	93%	97%	99%	96%
	1	3	5	10	5	3	4	4	7	4	3	4	6	4	3	1	2
	2	2	1	2	1	0	1	0	0	0	1	1	1	4	0	0	2
	3	1	0	0	0	0	0	0	0	0	0	0	0	0	0	0	0
	4	0	0	0	0	0	0	0	0	0	0	0	1	0	0	0	0
	5	0	1	0	0	0	0	0	0	0	0	0	0	0	0	0	0
# SURVEYED		189	151	146	141	133	154	133	122	112	116	102	131	108	126	92	136

TABLE IV: HOUSEHOLD MEMBERS UNDER AGE 6 -- BY AGE (Continued)

Question: Number of household members under age 6.

Responses: 0 = 0; 1 = 1; 2 = 2; 3 = 3; 4 = 4; 5 = 5

		YEAR															
AGE	RESP	'72	'73	'74	'75	'76	'77	'78	'80	'82	'83	'84	'85	'86	'87	'88	'89
54-59	0	94%	94%	98%	99%	98%	97%	99%	98%	96%	99%	96%	98%	97%	97%	94%	96%
	1	4	4	1	0	2	2	1	1	4	1	3	1	3	3	5	4
	2	1	2	1	1	0	1	0	1	0	0	1	1	0	0	1	0
	3	0	0	1	0	0	0	0	0	0	0	0	0	0	0	0	0
	4	0	0	0	0	0	0	0	0	0	0	0	0	0	0	0	0
	5	0	0	0	0	0	0	0	0	0	0	0	0	0	0	0	0
# SURVEYED		156	157	139	126	129	168	136	136	144	134	114	134	99	98	85	98
AGE	RESP	'72	'73	'74	'75	'76	'77	'78	'80	'82	'83	'84	'85	'86	'87	'88	'89
60-65	0	98%	98%	98%	99%	98%	99%	98%	99%	97%	98%	99%	98%	96%	99%	99%	99%
	1	1	2	1	1	1	1	2	0	3	2	1	1	3	0	1	1
	2	1	1	1	0	1	0	0	1	0	0	0	1	0	1	0	0
	3	0	0	0	0	0	0	0	0	0	0	0	0	1	0	0	0
	4	0	0	0	0	0	0	0	0	0	0	0	0	0	0	0	0
	5	0	0	0	0	0	0	0	0	0	0	0	0	0	0	0	0
# SURVEYED		144	121	108	113	134	116	107	119	116	132	113	131	114	101	119	111
AGE	RESP	'72	'73	'74	'75	'76	'77	'78	'80	'82	'83	'84	'85	'86	'87	'88	'89
66+	0	99%	99%	99%	99%	99%	98%	99%	99%	100%	100%	99%	100%	99%	99%	99%	100%
	1	1	1	1	1	1	2	1	1	0	0	0	0	1	1	0	0
	2	0	1	0	0	0	0	0	0	0	0	1	0	0	0	0	0
	3	0	0	0	0	0	0	0	0	0	0	0	0	0	0	0	0
	4	0	0	0	0	0	0	0	0	0	0	0	0	0	0	0	0
	5	0	0	0	0	0	0	0	0	0	0	0	0	0	0	0	0
# SURVEYED		218	200	227	232	251	213	232	241	259	240	232	261	265	253	280	273

****

HOUSEHOLD MEMBERS AGED 6 TO 12

TABLE I: HOUSEHOLD MEMBERS AGED 6 TO 12 -- BY TOTAL POPULATION

Question: Number of household members aged 6 to 12 years.

Responses: 0 = 0; 1 = 1; 2 = 2; 3 = 3; 4 = 4; 5 = 5; 6 = 6

	YEAR															
RESPONSE	'72	'73	'74	'75	'76	'77	'78	'80	'82	'83	'84	'85	'86	'87	'88	'89
0	72%	73%	72%	76%	76%	76%	76%	78%	81%	78%	81%	81%	80%	81%	79%	80%
1	16	14	15	14	15	14	14	14	13	14	12	12	13	12	13	13
2	8	8	9	8	7	7	7	7	5	7	6	6	5	6	5	6
3	3	3	3	2	2	2	1	1	1	1	1	1	1	1	2	1
4	1	1	0	0	0	1	0	0	0	0	0	0	1	0	0	0
5	0	0	0	0	0	0	0	0	0	0	0	0	0	0	0	0
6	0	0	0	0	0	0	0	0	0	0	0	0	0	0	0	0
# SURVEYED	1613	1504	1482	1490	1497	1521	1518	1456	1501	1593	1468	1529	1464	1464	1469	1517

TABLE II: HOUSEHOLD MEMBERS AGED 6 TO 12 -- BY SEX

Question: Number of household members aged 6 to 12 years.

Responses: 0 = 0; 1 = 1; 2 = 2; 3 = 3; 4 = 4; 5 = 5; 6 = 6

		YEAR															
SEX	RESP	'72	'73	'74	'75	'76	'77	'78	'80	'82	'83	'84	'85	'86	'87	'88	'89
M	0	75%	76%	78%	76%	78%	77%	78%	79%	83%	80%	85%	83%	83%	83%	79%	82%
A	1	15	14	13	13	15	14	12	15	10	13	10	10	11	11	13	11
L	2	8	7	7	8	5	6	8	5	5	5	5	6	4	5	5	6
E	3	2	1	2	2	2	2	1	1	2	2	1	1	2	2	3	1
	4	1	1	0	0	0	1	0	0	0	0	0	0	0	0	0	0
	5	0	0	0	0	0	0	0	0	0	0	0	0	0	0	0	0
	6	0	0	0	0	0	0	0	0	0	0	0	0	0	0	0	0
# SURVEYED		807	701	690	670	669	689	637	637	638	686	598	686	620	640	631	649
SEX	RESP	'72	'73	'74	'75	'76	'77	'78	'80	'82	'83	'84	'85	'86	'87	'88	'89
F	0	69%	71%	67%	75%	74%	75%	75%	77%	79%	75%	78%	79%	78%	79%	80%	78%
E	1	17	14	17	14	15	15	16	14	15	16	13	14	14	14	13	14
M	2	9	9	11	8	8	8	6	8	5	8	7	7	7	7	6	6
A	3	4	5	4	2	3	2	1	2	1	1	1	0	1	0	1	2
L	4	1	1	0	0	0	0	0	0	0	0	0	0	1	0	0	1
E	5	0	0	1	0	0	0	0	0	0	0	0	0	0	0	0	0
	6	0	0	0	0	0	0	0	0	0	0	0	0	0	0	0	0
# SURVEYED		806	803	792	820	828	832	881	819	863	907	870	843	844	824	838	868

TABLE III: HOUSEHOLD MEMBERS AGED 6 TO 12 -- BY RACE

Question: Number of household members aged 6 to 12 years.

Responses: 0 = 0; 1 = 1; 2 = 2; 3 = 3; 4 = 4; 5 = 5; 6 = 6

		YEAR															
RACE	RESP	'72	'73	'74	'75	'76	'77	'78	'80	'82	'83	'84	'85	'86	'87	'88	'89
WHITE	**0**	73%	73%	73%	76%	77%	77%	77%	78%	82%	79%	82%	81%	82%	82%	81%	80%
	1	16	14	16	13	15	14	14	14	12	14	11	12	12	12	13	12
	2	8	8	9	8	6	7	7	7	5	6	6	6	5	5	5	6
	3	3	3	3	2	2	2	1	1	1	1	1	1	1	1	1	1
	4	1	1	0	0	0	1	0	0	0	0	0	0	0	0	0	0
	5	0	0	0	0	0	0	0	0	0	0	0	0	0	0	0	0
	6	0	0	0	0	0	0	0	0	0	0	0	0	0	0	0	0
# SURVEYED		1348	1308	1303	1323	1359	1333	1347	1306	1319	1411	1247	1333	1244	1221	1224	1301
RACE	RESP	'72	'73	'74	'75	'76	'77	'78	'80	'82	'83	'84	'85	'86	'87	'88	'89
BLACK	**0**	68%	70%	68%	69%	72%	68%	71%	71%	70%	67%	79%	80%	70%	77%	73%	76%
	1	16	15	11	18	12	20	16	19	20	17	12	10	17	15	16	15
	2	11	8	15	7	10	8	10	7	9	13	8	9	9	7	8	6
	3	3	4	3	4	5	2	1	3	1	3	2	1	2	1	3	3
	4	2	2	1	1	1	1	1	0	1	0	0	0	2	1	0	0
	5	1	0	2	1	0	0	0	0	0	0	0	0	0	0	0	0
	6	0	0	0	0	1	1	0	0	0	0	0	1	0	0	0	0
# SURVEYED		261	183	172	163	129	173	156	140	155	164	170	152	183	190	184	155
RACE	RESP	'72	'73	'74	'75	'76	'77	'78	'80	'82	'83	'84	'85	'86	'87	'88	'89
OTHER	**0**	50%	92%	57%	75%	67%	80%	73%	90%	78%	89%	69%	75%	68%	70%	72%	72%
	1	25	8	29	25	33	20	13	10	19	11	27	18	16	13	20	18
	2	0	0	0	0	0	0	13	0	4	0	0	7	8	13	7	5
	3	25	0	14	0	0	0	0	0	0	0	4	0	8	4	2	3
	4	0	0	0	0	0	0	0	0	0	0	0	0	0	0	0	2
	5	0	0	0	0	0	0	0	0	0	0	0	0	0	0	0	0
	6	0	0	0	0	0	0	0	0	0	0	0	0	0	0	0	0
# SURVEYED		4	13	7	4	9	15	15	10	27	18	51	44	37	53	61	61

TABLE IV: HOUSEHOLD MEMBERS AGED 6 TO 12 -- BY AGE

Question: Number of household members aged 6 to 12 years.

Responses: 0 = 0; 1 = 1; 2 = 2; 3 = 3; 4 = 4; 5 = 5; 6 = 6

		YEAR															
AGE	RESP	'72	'73	'74	'75	'76	'77	'78	'80	'82	'83	'84	'85	'86	'87	'88	'89
18-23	0	80%	88%	85%	89%	83%	87%	90%	85%	86%	87%	93%	86%	88%	92%	91%	90%
	1	12	8	8	8	12	10	9	11	12	9	5	11	11	6	6	7
	2	5	3	7	3	3	4	1	3	1	4	2	2	1	2	1	1
	3	2	1	1	0	2	0	1	1	0	1	0	0	0	0	1	1
	4	1	0	0	0	1	0	0	1	0	0	0	1	0	0	0	0
	5	0	0	0	0	0	0	0	0	0	0	0	0	0	0	0	0
	6	0	0	0	0	0	0	0	0	0	0	0	0	0	0	0	0
# SURVEYED		169	171	167	173	162	164	162	155	147	128	160	133	108	126	139	135
AGE	RESP	'72	'73	'74	'75	'76	'77	'78	'80	'82	'83	'84	'85	'86	'87	'88	'89
24-29	0	79%	80%	82%	81%	83%	80%	78%	81%	82%	76%	84%	85%	81%	80%	84%	79%
	1	13	14	13	14	11	15	17	14	11	17	11	11	14	13	13	14
	2	5	3	4	5	4	5	5	4	4	6	4	5	6	7	3	7
	3	1	2	1	0	2	0	0	1	2	1	1	0	0	0	0	0
	4	1	0	0	0	0	0	0	0	0	0	0	0	0	0	0	0
	5	0	0	0	0	0	0	0	0	0	0	0	0	0	0	0	0
	6	0	0	0	0	0	0	0	0	0	0	0	0	0	0	0	0
# SURVEYED		231	212	212	232	225	201	239	196	244	286	232	216	218	192	214	201
AGE	RESP	'72	'73	'74	'75	'76	'77	'78	'80	'82	'83	'84	'85	'86	'87	'88	'89
30-35	0	39%	37%	34%	37%	38%	48%	47%	49%	55%	54%	54%	55%	57%	62%	56%	58%
	1	25	25	31	25	34	21	28	28	28	24	24	27	26	23	24	24
	2	25	23	23	29	19	23	18	20	16	17	18	17	12	14	15	12
	3	11	10	11	6	8	7	6	3	1	4	4	1	5	1	4	4
	4	1	5	0	1	0	1	1	0	0	0	0	0	1	0	1	2
	5	1	1	1	2	0	0	0	0	0	0	0	0	0	0	0	0
	6	0	0	0	0	1	0	0	0	0	0	0	0	0	0	0	0
# SURVEYED		187	167	175	171	185	184	228	214	202	235	198	210	219	221	192	208
AGE	RESP	'72	'73	'74	'75	'76	'77	'78	'80	'82	'83	'84	'85	'86	'87	'88	'89
36-41	0	30%	30%	34%	41%	44%	39%	43%	44%	55%	46%	51%	49%	55%	57%	46%	52%
	1	31	29	26	32	29	35	33	34	31	35	31	30	23	25	31	26
	2	23	27	26	16	22	17	20	17	10	15	15	17	15	15	18	18
	3	10	10	11	8	4	6	2	3	3	4	3	3	5	3	5	3
	4	4	4	1	3	1	1	1	1	1	1	1	0	2	0	0	1
	5	2	0	2	0	0	1	1	0	0	0	0	1	0	0	0	0
	6	0	0	0	0	0	1	0	0	0	0	0	1	0	0	0	0
# SURVEYED		128	175	151	154	158	168	157	149	146	171	186	183	186	185	187	195

TABLE IV: HOUSEHOLD MEMBERS AGED 6 TO 12 -- BY AGE (Continued)

Question: Number of household members aged 6 to 12 years.

Responses: 0 = 0; 1 = 1; 2 = 2; 3 = 3; 4 = 4; 5 = 5; 6 = 6

		YEAR															
AGE	RESP	'72	'73	'74	'75	'76	'77	'78	'80	'82	'83	'84	'85	'86	'87	'88	'89
42-47	0	55%	58%	54%	60%	57%	62%	68%	73%	76%	72%	76%	81%	73%	72%	68%	66%
	1	28	25	27	26	34	25	17	20	13	22	15	13	19	22	24	27
	2	12	13	13	10	7	8	14	5	9	5	8	4	5	4	4	6
	3	2	3	6	3	1	4	0	2	3	1	1	2	1	1	2	1
	4	2	1	0	1	1	2	1	0	0	0	0	0	1	0	1	1
	5	0	0	0	0	0	0	0	0	0	0	0	0	0	1	0	0
	6	1	0	0	1	0	0	0	0	0	0	0	0	0	0	0	0
# SURVEYED		186	146	151	143	114	146	118	116	119	144	125	123	141	157	157	159
AGE	RESP	'72	'73	'74	'75	'76	'77	'78	'80	'82	'83	'84	'85	'86	'87	'88	'89
48-53	0	71%	83%	68%	83%	87%	81%	78%	82%	84%	89%	88%	85%	91%	86%	88%	92%
	1	22	13	23	11	9	13	16	11	14	7	7	9	5	9	11	7
	2	6	3	9	6	3	4	3	7	1	4	4	5	5	5	1	1
	3	1	1	0	0	0	1	2	0	1	0	1	0	0	0	0	0
	4	0	1	0	0	1	1	1	0	0	0	0	0	0	1	0	0
	5	0	0	0	0	0	0	0	0	0	0	0	0	0	0	0	0
	6	0	0	0	0	0	0	0	0	0	0	0	0	0	0	0	0
# SURVEYED		189	151	146	141	133	154	133	122	112	116	102	131	107	126	92	136
AGE	RESP	'72	'73	'74	'75	'76	'77	'78	'80	'82	'83	'84	'85	'86	'87	'88	'89
54-59	0	92%	89%	91%	94%	92%	94%	96%	92%	92%	92%	97%	96%	95%	96%	92%	99%
	1	6	9	6	4	6	5	3	8	7	6	2	4	5	2	6	1
	2	1	1	1	2	1	1	1	0	1	2	1	1	0	2	1	0
	3	1	1	1	1	1	0	0	0	0	0	0	0	0	0	1	0
	4	0	0	0	0	0	0	0	0	0	0	0	0	0	0	0	0
	5	0	0	0	0	0	0	0	0	0	0	0	0	0	0	0	0
	6	0	0	0	0	0	0	0	0	0	0	0	0	0	0	0	0
# SURVEYED		156	157	139	126	129	168	136	135	144	134	114	134	99	98	85	98
AGE	RESP	'72	'73	'74	'75	'76	'77	'78	'80	'82	'83	'84	'85	'86	'87	'88	'89
60-65	0	94%	96%	97%	96%	96%	97%	97%	97%	94%	98%	99%	97%	96%	99%	99%	97%
	1	4	3	2	3	3	3	3	3	3	2	0	3	3	1	1	1
	2	0	1	1	1	0	0	0	0	3	1	1	0	0	0	0	0
	3	0	0	0	0	1	0	0	0	0	0	0	0	0	0	0	2
	4	1	0	0	0	0	0	0	0	1	0	0	0	1	0	0	0
	5	1	0	0	0	0	0	0	0	0	0	0	0	0	0	0	0
	6	0	0	0	0	0	0	0	0	0	0	0	0	0	0	0	0
# SURVEYED		144	121	108	113	134	116	107	119	116	132	113	131	114	101	119	111

TABLE IV: HOUSEHOLD MEMBERS AGED 6 TO 12 -- BY AGE (Continued)

Question: Number of household members aged 6 to 12 years.

Responses: 0 = 0; 1 = 1; 2 = 2; 3 = 3; 4 = 4; 5 = 5; 6 = 6

		YEAR															
AGE	RESP	'72	'73	'74	'75	'76	'77	'78	'80	'82	'83	'84	'85	'86	'87	'88	'89
66+	0	96%	97%	99%	97%	98%	97%	99%	99%	99%	99%	99%	100%	99%	98%	100%	99%
	1	3	2	1	2	2	3	1	1	0	1	1	0	1	1	0	0
	2	1	1	0	1	0	0	0	0	1	0	0	0	0	0	0	1
	3	0	0	0	0	0	0	0	0	0	0	0	0	0	0	0	0
	4	0	0	0	0	0	0	0	0	0	0	0	0	0	0	0	0
	5	0	0	0	0	0	0	0	0	0	0	0	0	0	0	0	0
	6	0	0	0	0	0	0	0	0	0	0	0	0	0	0	0	0
# SURVEYED		218	200	227	232	251	213	232	241	259	240	232	261	265	253	280	273

****

HOUSEHOLD MEMBERS AGED 13 TO 17

TABLE I: HOUSEHOLD MEMBERS AGED 13 TO 17 -- BY TOTAL POPULATION

Question: Number of household members aged 13 to 17 years.

Responses: 0 = 0; 1 = 1; 2 = 2; 3 = 3; 4 = 4; 5 = 5; 6 = 6; 7 = 7; 8 = 8 or more

	YEAR															
RESPONSE	'72	'73	'74	'75	'76	'77	'78	'80	'82	'83	'84	'85	'86	'87	'88	'89
0	73%	77%	75%	77%	79%	78%	79%	83%	84%	82%	83%	84%	83%	82%	85%	82%
1	16	15	15	14	12	12	13	11	11	13	11	11	13	13	11	14
2	8	6	7	7	6	7	6	5	4	5	4	4	4	4	3	3
3	2	2	3	2	2	2	2	0	1	1	1	1	1	1	1	1
4	0	0	0	0	1	0	0	0	0	0	0	0	0	0	0	0
5	0	0	0	0	0	0	0	0	0	0	0	0	0	0	0	0
6	0	0	0	0	0	0	0	0	0	0	0	0	0	0	0	0
7	0	0	0	0	0	0	0	0	0	0	0	0	0	0	0	0
8	0	0	0	0	0	0	0	0	0	0	0	0	0	0	0	0
# SURVEYED	1613	1504	1482	1490	1497	1522	1524	1458	1503	1595	1471	1531	1465	1464	1475	1522

TABLE II: HOUSEHOLD MEMBERS AGED 13 TO 17 -- BY SEX

Question: Number of household members aged 13 to 17 years.

Responses: 0 = 0; 1 = 1; 2 = 2; 3 = 3; 4 = 4; 5 = 5; 6 = 6; 7 = 7; 8 = 8 or more

		YEAR															
SEX	RESP	'72	'73	'74	'75	'76	'77	'78	'80	'82	'83	'84	'85	'86	'87	'88	'89
M	0	74%	78%	77%	77%	80%	79%	79%	84%	84%	83%	82%	84%	84%	83%	86%	82%
A	1	15	15	13	13	12	12	13	12	10	12	12	11	12	12	11	14
L	2	8	6	7	7	6	7	5	4	5	4	5	4	3	4	3	3
E	3	3	1	3	1	1	2	2	0	0	1	2	1	1	1	0	0
	4	0	0	0	1	1	0	0	0	0	0	0	0	0	0	0	0
	5	0	0	0	0	0	0	0	0	0	0	0	0	0	0	0	0
	6	0	0	0	0	0	0	0	0	0	0	0	0	0	0	0	0
	7	0	0	0	0	0	0	0	0	0	0	0	0	0	0	0	0
	8	0	0	0	0	0	0	0	0	0	0	0	0	0	0	0	0
# SURVEYED		807	701	690	670	669	689	642	637	638	688	598	686	619	640	634	650
SEX	RESP	'72	'73	'74	'75	'76	'77	'78	'80	'82	'83	'84	'85	'86	'87	'88	'89
F	0	73%	76%	73%	77%	79%	78%	79%	82%	83%	81%	84%	84%	81%	81%	84%	83%
E	1	17	14	16	14	12	13	13	11	13	14	11	11	13	13	12	13
M	2	8	7	7	6	6	7	6	6	3	5	4	4	5	4	4	3
A	3	2	2	3	2	2	2	1	1	1	1	1	1	1	1	1	1
L	4	0	0	1	0	1	1	0	0	0	0	0	0	0	0	0	0
E	5	0	0	0	0	0	0	0	0	0	0	0	0	0	0	0	0
	6	0	0	0	0	0	0	0	0	0	0	0	0	0	0	0	0
	7	0	0	0	0	0	0	0	0	0	0	0	0	0	0	0	0
	8	0	0	0	0	0	0	0	0	0	0	0	0	0	0	0	0
# SURVEYED		806	803	792	820	828	833	882	821	865	907	873	845	846	824	841	872

TABLE III: HOUSEHOLD MEMBERS AGED 13 TO 17 -- BY RACE

Question: Number of household members aged 13 to 17 years.

Responses: 0 = 0; 1 = 1; 2 = 2; 3 = 3; 4 = 4; 5 = 5; 6 = 6; 7 = 7; 8 = 8 or more

		YEAR															
RACE	RESP	'72	'73	'74	'75	'76	'77	'78	'80	'82	'83	'84	'85	'86	'87	'88	'89
WHITE	0	73%	78%	76%	77%	80%	78%	79%	84%	85%	82%	84%	84%	84%	83%	85%	83%
	1	17	15	15	14	12	13	13	11	11	13	11	11	11	12	11	13
	2	8	6	7	7	6	6	6	5	4	5	4	4	4	4	3	3
	3	2	2	3	1	1	2	2	0	1	1	1	1	1	1	1	0
	4	0	0	0	0	1	0	0	0	0	0	0	0	0	0	0	0
	5	0	0	0	0	0	0	0	0	0	0	0	0	0	0	0	0
	6	0	0	0	0	0	0	0	0	0	0	0	0	0	0	0	0
	7	0	0	0	0	0	0	0	0	0	0	0	0	0	0	0	0
	8	0	0	0	0	0	0	0	0	0	0	0	0	0	0	0	0
# SURVEYED		1348	1308	1303	1323	1359	1334	1353	1308	1321	1413	1249	1335	1245	1221	1229	1306
RACE	RESP	'72	'73	'74	'75	'76	'77	'78	'80	'82	'83	'84	'85	'86	'87	'88	'89
BLACK	0	73%	70%	70%	79%	76%	77%	77%	76%	74%	80%	82%	84%	74%	81%	83%	80%
	1	12	16	15	10	16	9	13	14	17	15	12	13	19	15	13	13
	2	10	9	9	7	5	10	8	6	8	2	5	3	7	4	4	5
	3	4	3	5	4	3	2	2	1	1	1	1	1	0	1	0	2
	4	0	1	1	1	0	1	0	1	1	1	1	0	0	0	0	0
	5	0	1	0	0	0	0	0	0	0	0	0	0	0	0	0	0
	6	0	0	0	0	0	0	0	0	0	0	0	0	0	0	0	0
	7	0	0	0	0	0	0	0	0	0	0	0	0	0	0	0	0
	8	0	0	0	0	0	0	0	0	0	0	0	0	0	0	0	0
# SURVEYED		261	183	172	163	129	173	156	140	155	164	170	152	183	190	185	155
RACE	RESP	'72	'73	'74	'75	'76	'77	'78	'80	'82	'83	'84	'85	'86	'87	'88	'89
OTHER	0	50%	100%	57%	50%	78%	80%	73%	70%	81%	89%	71%	82%	68%	74%	80%	69%
	1	25	0	14	25	11	7	27	30	7	6	15	7	24	21	16	25
	2	25	0	14	25	11	13	0	0	11	6	10	9	5	6	2	5
	3	0	0	14	0	0	0	0	0	0	0	4	2	3	0	2	2
	4	0	0	0	0	0	0	0	0	0	0	0	0	0	0	0	0
	5	0	0	0	0	0	0	0	0	0	0	0	0	0	0	0	0
	6	0	0	0	0	0	0	0	0	0	0	0	0	0	0	0	0
	7	0	0	0	0	0	0	0	0	0	0	0	0	0	0	0	0
	8	0	0	0	0	0	0	0	0	0	0	0	0	0	0	0	0
# SURVEYED		4	13	7	4	9	15	15	10	27	18	52	44	37	53	61	61

TABLE IV: HOUSEHOLD MEMBERS AGED 13 TO 17 -- BY AGE

Question: Number of household members aged 13 to 17 years.

Responses: 0 = 0; 1 = 1; 2 = 2; 3 = 3; 4 = 4; 5 = 5; 6 = 6; 7 = 7; 8 = 8 or more

		YEAR															
AGE	RESP	'72	'73	'74	'75	'76	'77	'78	'80	'82	'83	'84	'85	'86	'87	'88	'89
18-23	0	70%	75%	78%	76%	69%	71%	75%	81%	81%	78%	84%	77%	71%	82%	81%	75%
	1	15	19	14	17	18	19	15	12	13	17	11	15	22	17	16	19
	2	10	5	7	6	9	7	6	6	5	4	3	6	6	1	2	4
	3	4	1	1	1	2	3	4	1	1	1	2	2	0	0	1	1
	4	1	0	1	1	1	0	0	0	0	0	0	0	0	0	0	0
	5	0	0	0	0	0	0	0	0	0	0	0	0	0	0	0	0
	6	0	0	0	0	0	0	0	0	0	0	0	0	0	0	0	0
	7	0	0	0	0	0	0	0	0	0	0	0	0	0	0	0	0
	8	0	0	0	0	0	0	0	0	0	0	0	0	0	0	0	0
# SURVEYED		169	171	167	173	162	164	163	155	147	128	161	133	108	126	140	135
AGE	RESP	'72	'73	'74	'75	'76	'77	'78	'80	'82	'83	'84	'85	'86	'87	'88	'89
24-29	0	94%	95%	97%	97%	96%	97%	93%	97%	97%	94%	97%	97%	98%	97%	96%	94%
	1	4	3	3	3	2	2	5	2	3	5	3	2	2	3	3	5
	2	2	1	0	0	1	0	1	1	0	1	0	0	0	1	0	0
	3	0	0	0	0	0	0	0	0	0	0	0	0	0	0	0	0
	4	0	0	0	0	0	0	0	0	0	0	0	0	0	0	0	0
	5	0	0	0	0	0	0	0	0	0	0	0	0	0	0	0	0
	6	0	0	0	0	0	0	0	0	0	0	0	0	0	0	0	0
	7	0	0	0	0	0	0	0	0	0	0	0	0	0	0	0	0
	8	0	0	0	0	0	0	0	0	0	0	0	0	0	0	0	0
# SURVEYED		231	212	212	232	225	203	243	198	246	287	232	217	218	192	215	201
AGE	RESP	'72	'73	'74	'75	'76	'77	'78	'80	'82	'83	'84	'85	'86	'87	'88	'89
30-35	0	82%	83%	77%	78%	82%	86%	87%	87%	88%	84%	87%	88%	84%	83%	86%	88%
	1	14	12	16	13	14	8	8	10	9	11	9	10	12	12	10	9
	2	4	4	3	7	2	4	4	2	3	3	4	2	4	4	4	2
	3	0	1	3	1	2	1	0	0	0	1	1	0	0	0	1	0
	4	0	0	0	0	0	0	0	0	0	0	0	0	0	0	0	0
	5	0	0	0	0	0	0	0	0	0	0	0	0	0	0	0	0
	6	0	0	0	0	0	0	0	0	0	0	0	0	0	0	0	0
	7	0	0	0	0	0	0	0	0	0	0	0	0	0	0	0	0
	8	0	0	0	0	0	0	0	0	0	0	0	0	0	0	0	0
# SURVEYED		187	167	175	171	185	184	229	215	202	236	199	211	221	221	194	208
AGE	RESP	'72	'73	'74	'75	'76	'77	'78	'80	'82	'83	'84	'85	'86	'87	'88	'89
36-41	0	39%	49%	36%	48%	51%	49%	45%	56%	55%	61%	57%	58%	59%	62%	69%	64%
	1	32	22	28	31	26	27	25	23	29	26	26	25	29	25	23	27
	2	22	23	22	14	17	17	22	17	14	12	14	14	10	10	7	7
	3	7	6	12	6	4	4	6	1	1	1	2	3	2	3	1	2
	4	0	0	1	1	2	2	1	1	1	1	1	1	1	0	0	0
	5	0	0	0	0	0	0	1	1	0	0	0	0	0	0	0	0
	6	0	0	0	0	0	0	0	0	0	0	0	0	0	0	0	0
	7	0	0	0	0	0	0	0	0	0	0	0	0	0	0	0	0
	8	0	0	0	0	0	0	0	0	0	0	0	0	0	0	0	0
# SURVEYED		128	175	151	154	158	168	157	149	146	171	186	183	186	185	189	197

TABLE IV: HOUSEHOLD MEMBERS AGED 13 TO 17 -- BY AGE (Continued)

Question: Number of household members aged 13 to 17 years.

Responses: 0 = 0; 1 = 1; 2 = 2; 3 = 3; 4 = 4; 5 = 5; 6 = 6; 7 = 7; 8 = 8 or more

		YEAR															
AGE	RESP	'72	'73	'74	'75	'76	'77	'78	'80	'82	'83	'84	'85	'86	'87	'88	'89
42-47	0	39%	56%	48%	39%	40%	50%	48%	53%	57%	45%	53%	53%	59%	52%	62%	52%
	1	31	21	25	34	26	26	30	28	28	36	30	33	29	32	27	35
	2	20	18	21	22	22	16	14	18	13	16	13	11	9	13	9	11
	3	9	3	6	3	8	8	7	1	2	3	3	3	3	3	2	2
	4	2	1	0	1	4	1	1	0	0	0	0	0	0	0	0	0
	5	0	1	0	1	0	0	0	0	0	0	0	0	0	0	0	0
	6	0	0	0	0	0	0	0	0	0	0	0	0	0	0	0	0
	7	0	0	0	0	0	0	0	0	0	0	0	0	0	0	0	0
	8	0	0	0	0	0	0	0	0	0	0	0	0	0	0	0	0
# SURVEYED		186	146	151	143	114	146	119	116	119	144	126	123	141	157	157	159
AGE	RESP	'72	'73	'74	'75	'76	'77	'78	'80	'82	'83	'84	'85	'86	'87	'88	'89
48-53	0	61%	57%	57%	61%	74%	60%	58%	70%	69%	76%	74%	77%	75%	78%	71%	78%
	1	25	32	25	21	19	24	30	22	21	16	18	17	19	17	23	18
	2	10	7	10	13	8	13	10	7	9	7	7	5	5	5	7	4
	3	3	3	8	3	0	3	1	1	1	1	2	1	2	1	0	0
	4	1	1	1	1	0	0	2	0	0	0	0	1	0	0	0	0
	5	0	1	0	1	0	0	0	0	0	0	0	0	0	0	0	0
	6	1	0	0	0	0	0	0	0	0	0	0	0	0	0	0	0
	7	0	0	0	0	0	0	0	0	0	0	0	0	0	0	0	0
	8	0	0	0	0	0	0	0	0	0	0	0	0	0	0	0	0
# SURVEYED		189	151	146	141	133	153	133	122	112	116	102	131	106	126	92	137
AGE	RESP	'72	'73	'74	'75	'76	'77	'78	'80	'82	'83	'84	'85	'86	'87	'88	'89
54-59	0	74%	80%	77%	83%	83%	87%	84%	87%	85%	84%	86%	90%	85%	89%	93%	88%
	1	17	18	19	13	13	6	15	10	11	12	12	9	9	10	7	11
	2	8	1	3	3	4	6	1	2	3	4	1	1	6	1	0	1
	3	0	1	1	1	0	1	0	1	1	0	1	0	0	0	0	0
	4	0	0	0	0	0	0	0	0	0	0	0	0	0	0	0	0
	5	0	0	0	0	0	0	0	0	0	0	0	0	0	0	0	0
	6	0	0	0	0	0	0	0	0	0	0	0	0	0	0	0	0
	7	0	0	0	0	0	0	0	0	0	0	0	0	0	0	0	0
	8	1	0	0	0	0	0	0	0	0	0	0	0	0	0	0	0
# SURVEYED		156	157	139	126	129	168	136	135	144	134	114	134	99	98	85	98
AGE	RESP	'72	'73	'74	'75	'76	'77	'78	'80	'82	'83	'84	'85	'86	'87	'88	'89
60-65	0	90%	93%	93%	95%	95%	97%	95%	97%	97%	92%	97%	98%	96%	95%	95%	96%
	1	8	7	6	4	4	2	5	3	3	8	2	2	4	5	4	4
	2	2	0	1	1	1	1	0	0	1	0	1	0	0	0	1	0
	3	0	1	0	0	0	1	0	0	0	0	0	1	0	0	0	0
	4	0	0	0	0	0	0	0	0	0	0	0	0	0	0	0	0
	5	0	0	0	0	0	0	0	0	0	0	0	0	0	0	0	0
	6	0	0	0	0	0	0	0	0	0	0	0	0	0	0	0	0
	7	0	0	0	0	0	0	0	0	0	0	0	0	0	0	0	0
	8	0	0	0	0	0	0	0	0	0	0	0	0	0	0	0	0
# SURVEYED		144	121	108	113	134	116	107	119	116	132	113	131	114	101	119	111

TABLE IV: HOUSEHOLD MEMBERS AGED 13 TO 17 -- BY AGE (Continued)

Question: Number of household members aged 13 to 17 years.

Responses: 0 = 0; 1 = 1; 2 = 2; 3 = 3; 4 = 4; 5 = 5; 6 = 6; 7 = 7; 8 = 8 or more

		YEAR															
AGE	RESP	'72	'73	'74	'75	'76	'77	'78	'80	'82	'83	'84	'85	'86	'87	'88	'89
66+	0	94%	96%	97%	99%	98%	97%	98%	96%	97%	98%	97%	100%	98%	98%	99%	98%
	1	4	4	3	1	1	3	2	3	3	2	3	0	2	1	1	1
	2	1	0	0	0	1	0	0	0	0	0	0	0	0	1	0	0
	3	0	1	0	0	0	0	0	0	0	0	0	0	0	0	0	0
	4	0	0	0	0	0	0	0	0	0	0	0	0	0	0	0	0
	5	0	0	0	0	0	0	0	0	0	0	0	0	0	0	0	0
	6	0	0	0	0	0	0	0	0	0	0	0	0	0	0	0	0
	7	0	0	0	0	0	0	0	0	0	0	0	0	0	0	0	0
	8	0	0	0	0	0	0	0	0	0	0	0	0	0	0	0	0
# SURVEYED		218	200	227	232	251	213	231	240	259	240	232	261	265	253	280	274

****

HOUSEHOLD MEMBERS OVER AGE 17

TABLE I: HOUSEHOLD MEMBERS OVER AGE 17 -- BY TOTAL POPULATION

Question: Number of household members over 17 years old.

Responses: 1 = 1; 2 = 2; 3 = 3; 4 = 4; 5 = 5; 6 = 6; 7 = 7; 8 = 8 or more

	YEAR															
RESPONSE	'72	'73	'74	'75	'76	'77	'78	'80	'82	'83	'84	'85	'86	'87	'88	'89
1	12%	13%	14%	17%	20%	23%	25%	25%	28%	25%	29%	28%	26%	26%	30%	27%
2	62	64	65	60	61	59	59	60	56	59	56	56	56	55	57	56
3	17	15	14	16	13	13	12	10	11	11	10	12	13	14	10	11
4	6	6	5	4	5	4	4	3	3	4	4	3	4	3	3	4
5	1	1	2	2	1	1	1	1	1	1	1	1	1	1	0	1
6	0	0	0	0	0	0	0	0	0	0	0	0	0	0	0	0
7	0	0	0	0	0	0	0	0	0	0	0	0	0	0	0	0
8	0	0	0	0	0	0	0	0	0	0	0	0	0	0	0	0
# SURVEYED	1613	1504	1482	1490	1497	1527	1525	1461	1505	1599	1473	1534	1470	1466	1481	1537

TABLE II: HOUSEHOLD MEMBERS OVER AGE 17 -- BY SEX

Question: Number of household members over 17 years old.

Responses: 1 = 1; 2 = 2; 3 = 3; 4 = 4; 5 = 5; 6 = 6; 7 = 7; 8 = 8 or more

		YEAR															
SEX	RESP	'72	'73	'74	'75	'76	'77	'78	'80	'82	'83	'84	'85	'86	'87	'88	'89
M	1	7%	11%	11%	12%	15%	19%	20%	20%	20%	19%	24%	22%	20%	24%	23%	20%
A	2	64	65	66	64	65	60	62	65	62	64	59	59	60	56	62	61
L	3	19	15	15	17	13	15	13	10	13	10	11	15	15	15	12	13
E	4	8	7	6	6	5	4	4	4	3	6	5	3	3	4	3	4
	5	2	1	2	2	1	1	1	1	1	1	2	1	2	1	0	1
	6	0	0	0	0	0	0	0	0	0	0	0	0	0	0	0	0
	7	0	0	0	0	0	0	0	0	0	0	0	0	0	0	0	0
	8	0	0	0	0	0	0	0	0	0	0	0	0	0	0	0	0
# SURVEYED		807	701	690	670	669	692	642	639	639	690	598	688	621	641	638	660
SEX	RESP	'72	'73	'74	'75	'76	'77	'78	'80	'82	'83	'84	'85	'86	'87	'88	'89
F	1	17%	15%	18%	22%	25%	25%	28%	29%	34%	30%	32%	33%	30%	28%	35%	33%
E	2	61	64	64	56	58	58	57	57	52	54	54	53	53	55	53	53
M	3	15	15	13	16	12	12	11	10	10	12	10	9	11	13	9	10
A	4	4	5	4	3	4	4	3	3	3	3	3	4	4	3	3	3
L	5	1	1	2	2	1	1	1	1	1	1	1	0	1	0	0	1
E	6	0	0	0	0	0	0	0	0	0	0	0	0	0	0	0	0
	7	0	0	0	0	0	0	0	0	0	0	0	0	0	0	0	0
	8	0	0	0	0	0	0	0	0	0	0	0	0	0	0	0	0
# SURVEYED		806	803	792	820	828	835	883	822	866	909	875	846	849	825	843	877

TABLE III: HOUSEHOLD MEMBERS OVER AGE 17 -- BY RACE

Question: Number of household members over 17 years old.

Responses: 1 = 1; 2 = 2; 3 = 3; 4 = 4; 5 = 5; 6 = 6; 7 = 7; 8 = 8 or more

		YEAR															
RACE	RESP	'72	'73	'74	'75	'76	'77	'78	'80	'82	'83	'84	'85	'86	'87	'88	'89
WHITE	1	12%	12%	13%	17%	19%	21%	24%	25%	27%	24%	27%	28%	25%	25%	28%	26%
	2	64	66	67	61	63	61	61	61	58	60	57	57	58	57	59	59
	3	17	15	14	16	12	13	12	10	11	11	11	12	13	14	10	11
	4	5	6	5	4	4	4	3	3	3	4	4	3	4	3	3	3
	5	1	1	2	2	1	1	1	1	1	1	1	0	1	1	0	1
	6	0	0	0	0	0	0	0	0	0	0	0	0	0	0	0	0
	7	0	0	0	0	0	0	0	0	0	0	0	0	0	0	0	0
	8	0	0	0	0	0	0	0	0	0	0	0	0	0	0	0	0
# SURVEYED		1348	1308	1303	1323	1359	1337	1354	1311	1322	1416	1251	1338	1249	1222	1234	1319
RACE	RESP	'72	'73	'74	'75	'76	'77	'78	'80	'82	'83	'84	'85	'86	'87	'88	'89
BLACK	1	13%	19%	25%	25%	36%	36%	33%	31%	38%	33%	40%	36%	35%	36%	39%	45%
	2	56	54	53	49	41	45	46	50	42	48	47	45	46	44	46	36
	3	19	16	15	16	13	15	15	10	13	12	7	13	14	15	9	13
	4	9	9	5	7	5	3	5	4	4	6	4	4	4	5	5	3
	5	2	2	2	1	2	0	1	3	2	1	2	1	2	0	0	3
	6	1	1	0	2	2	1	1	0	0	0	0	2	0	1	0	1
	7	0	0	0	1	0	0	0	1	0	0	1	0	0	0	1	0
	8	0	0	0	0	0	0	0	0	0	0	0	0	0	0	0	0
# SURVEYED		261	183	172	163	129	175	156	140	156	165	170	152	184	191	186	157
RACE	RESP	'72	'73	'74	'75	'76	'77	'78	'80	'82	'83	'84	'85	'86	'87	'88	'89
OTHER	1	0%	8%	29%	0%	0%	20%	27%	10%	19%	22%	19%	16%	27%	21%	31%	15%
	2	50	54	43	100	44	60	53	90	63	56	63	61	46	57	49	62
	3	25	31	29	0	44	20	7	0	15	11	12	14	8	11	16	10
	4	25	8	0	0	11	0	13	0	0	11	4	7	8	8	2	10
	5	0	0	0	0	0	0	0	0	4	0	2	2	11	2	0	0
	6	0	0	0	0	0	0	0	0	0	0	0	0	0	2	2	3
	7	0	0	0	0	0	0	0	0	0	0	0	0	0	0	0	0
	8	0	0	0	0	0	0	0	0	0	0	0	0	0	0	0	0
# SURVEYED		4	13	7	4	9	15	15	10	27	18	52	44	37	53	61	61

TABLE IV: HOUSEHOLD MEMBERS OVER AGE 17 -- BY AGE

Question: Number of household members over 17 years old.

Responses: 1 = 1; 2 = 2; 3 = 3; 4 = 4; 5 = 5; 6 = 6; 7 = 7; 8 = 8 or more

YEAR

AGE	RESP	'72	'73	'74	'75	'76	'77	'78	'80	'82	'83	'84	'85	'86	'87	'88	'89
18-23	1	8%	10%	8%	10%	12%	9%	15%	17%	11%	15%	19%	16%	14%	17%	15%	11%
	2	41	47	53	45	44	49	53	48	44	42	40	48	35	40	47	42
	3	27	26	25	29	25	24	20	17	29	24	24	26	36	29	25	29
	4	15	11	11	10	14	12	10	13	13	14	12	8	12	11	9	9
	5	5	5	2	5	4	4	2	4	2	4	5	2	3	2	1	7
	6	2	0	0	0	0	2	0	1	1	1	0	1	0	2	2	1
	7	0	0	0	1	1	0	0	1	0	0	0	0	0	0	1	0
	8	2	0	0	0	0	0	0	0	0	0	0	0	0	0	0	0
# SURVEYED		169	171	167	173	162	164	163	155	148	128	161	133	108	126	141	137

AGE	RESP	'72	'73	'74	'75	'76	'77	'78	'80	'82	'83	'84	'85	'86	'87	'88	'89
24-29	1	11%	9%	10%	15%	17%	27%	20%	21%	21%	27%	25%	25%	22%	23%	27%	27%
	2	68	74	79	73	72	61	68	69	68	62	66	65	64	62	58	60
	3	15	12	5	9	7	9	8	9	8	5	6	8	10	10	9	9
	4	6	3	4	2	2	0	2	0	2	4	2	1	4	2	5	2
	5	0	1	1	0	1	0	1	0	1	1	1	0	1	2	0	0
	6	0	0	0	0	1	1	1	0	0	0	0	0	0	1	0	0
	7	0	0	0	0	0	0	0	0	0	0	0	0	0	0	0	0
	8	0	0	0	0	0	0	0	0	0	0	0	0	0	0	0	0
# SURVEYED		231	212	212	232	225	204	243	201	245	287	232	217	218	193	215	202

AGE	RESP	'72	'73	'74	'75	'76	'77	'78	'80	'82	'83	'84	'85	'86	'87	'88	'89
30-35	1	6%	10%	13%	12%	14%	21%	23%	27%	25%	22%	30%	22%	22%	24%	28%	26%
	2	85	83	78	80	78	74	73	69	69	72	66	73	69	67	67	66
	3	7	5	7	6	5	5	4	4	6	5	3	4	7	7	4	6
	4	1	2	1	1	2	0	0	0	0	1	2	1	1	1	1	2
	5	0	1	1	1	0	0	0	0	0	0	0	0	1	0	1	0
	6	0	0	0	0	1	0	0	0	0	0	1	0	0	0	0	0
	7	0	0	0	0	0	0	0	0	0	0	0	0	0	0	0	0
	8	0	0	0	0	0	0	0	0	0	0	0	0	0	0	0	0
# SURVEYED		187	167	175	171	185	188	229	215	204	236	200	212	221	221	195	212

AGE	RESP	'72	'73	'74	'75	'76	'77	'78	'80	'82	'83	'84	'85	'86	'87	'88	'89
36-41	1	7%	11%	8%	8%	15%	21%	21%	19%	32%	23%	24%	25%	18%	22%	30%	25%
	2	80	74	80	71	71	69	66	69	60	69	67	62	68	68	61	67
	3	9	12	11	16	11	9	11	11	9	6	6	11	12	8	7	7
	4	3	3	1	5	3	1	2	1	0	2	3	2	2	2	2	2
	5	1	0	0	0	0	0	0	0	0	0	0	0	0	1	0	0
	6	0	0	0	1	0	0	0	0	0	0	0	0	1	0	0	0
	7	0	0	0	0	0	0	0	0	0	0	0	0	0	0	0	0
	8	0	0	0	0	0	0	0	0	0	0	0	0	0	0	0	0
# SURVEYED		128	175	151	154	158	168	157	149	146	173	187	184	188	186	193	198

TABLE IV: HOUSEHOLD MEMBERS OVER AGE 17 -- BY AGE (Continued)

Question: Number of household members over 17 years old.

Responses: 1 = 1; 2 = 2; 3 = 3; 4 = 4; 5 = 5; 6 = 6; 7 = 7; 8 = 8 or more

		YEAR															
AGE	RESP	'72	'73	'74	'75	'76	'77	'78	'80	'82	'83	'84	'85	'86	'87	'88	'89
42-47	1	5%	9%	10%	16%	15%	16%	16%	12%	22%	21%	20%	23%	25%	17%	26%	19%
	2	59	61	62	47	58	57	57	50	56	48	48	56	53	59	55	55
	3	26	16	17	27	20	21	17	26	15	21	23	15	14	18	13	20
	4	6	12	9	6	5	7	8	10	5	7	7	6	6	6	4	4
	5	4	1	3	4	0	0	2	1	1	2	2	1	2	1	1	2
	6	1	1	0	0	2	0	0	0	0	1	0	0	0	0	0	1
	7	0	0	0	0	0	0	0	1	0	0	0	0	0	0	0	0
	8	0	0	0	0	0	0	0	0	1	0	0	0	0	0	0	0
# SURVEYED		186	146	151	143	114	146	119	116	119	145	126	124	141	157	157	161
AGE	RESP	'72	'73	'74	'75	'76	'77	'78	'80	'82	'83	'84	'85	'86	'87	'88	'89
48-53	1	9%	9%	13%	12%	12%	16%	16%	17%	20%	16%	17%	21%	21%	21%	26%	26%
	2	54	54	55	47	58	54	51	63	52	55	56	47	49	45	49	46
	3	24	24	22	30	21	20	25	11	21	20	18	23	19	25	23	16
	4	11	11	5	10	8	8	8	6	6	8	7	7	7	6	2	10
	5	2	2	4	1	1	1	0	3	2	0	1	2	2	1	0	1
	6	0	1	0	0	0	0	1	0	0	0	1	0	1	1	0	0
	7	0	0	0	0	0	0	0	0	0	1	1	0	0	0	0	0
	8	0	0	0	0	0	0	0	0	0	0	0	0	0	0	0	0
# SURVEYED		189	151	146	141	133	153	133	122	112	116	102	131	108	126	92	138
AGE	RESP	'72	'73	'74	'75	'76	'77	'78	'80	'82	'83	'84	'85	'86	'87	'88	'89
54-59	1	6%	10%	14%	19%	17%	20%	30%	18%	17%	19%	26%	22%	23%	20%	25%	24%
	2	61	62	59	53	60	56	51	64	60	63	55	54	49	47	58	60
	3	24	20	20	19	16	18	13	12	16	15	13	18	20	30	16	9
	4	7	8	4	6	6	5	4	4	6	1	4	5	4	3	1	6
	5	1	1	2	2	1	1	2	1	1	1	2	1	3	0	0	1
	6	1	0	1	1	1	0	0	0	1	1	0	1	0	0	0	0
	7	0	0	0	0	0	0	0	0	0	0	0	0	0	0	0	0
	8	0	0	0	0	0	0	0	0	0	0	0	0	0	0	0	0
# SURVEYED		156	157	139	126	129	168	136	135	144	134	114	134	99	98	85	99
AGE	RESP	'72	'73	'74	'75	'76	'77	'78	'80	'82	'83	'84	'85	'86	'87	'88	'89
60-65	1	17%	13%	19%	19%	21%	24%	26%	29%	38%	20%	27%	31%	26%	30%	28%	27%
	2	63	69	58	64	61	60	56	63	53	59	62	56	57	55	64	61
	3	14	14	18	11	14	13	16	7	7	16	8	11	10	14	8	11
	4	3	4	3	4	4	3	2	1	2	5	2	3	4	1	1	1
	5	1	0	3	1	0	0	0	0	0	1	1	0	3	0	0	0
	6	1	0	0	0	0	0	0	0	0	0	0	0	1	0	0	0
	7	0	0	0	1	0	0	0	0	0	0	0	0	0	0	0	0
	8	0	0	0	0	0	0	0	0	0	0	0	0	0	0	0	0
# SURVEYED		144	121	108	113	134	116	107	119	116	132	113	131	115	101	119	111

TABLE IV: HOUSEHOLD MEMBERS OVER AGE 17 -- BY AGE (Continued)

Question: Number of household members over 17 years old.

Responses: 1 = 1; 2 = 2; 3 = 3; 4 = 4; 5 = 5; 6 = 6; 7 = 7; 8 = 8 or more

		YEAR															
AGE	RESP	'72	'73	'74	'75	'76	'77	'78	'80	'82	'83	'84	'85	'86	'87	'88	'89
66+	1	33%	33%	30%	38%	45%	42%	45%	48%	50%	46%	53%	51%	48%	49%	46%	45%
	2	55	55	58	52	47	48	46	48	43	48	41	41	45	43	50	50
	3	11	9	8	8	6	7	7	4	5	4	6	7	6	6	3	5
	4	2	4	3	0	1	2	1	0	2	2	1	1	1	2	1	0
	5	0	1	1	1	1	1	0	0	0	0	0	0	0	0	0	0
	6	0	0	0	0	0	0	0	0	0	0	0	0	0	0	0	0
	7	0	0	0	0	0	0	0	0	0	0	0	0	0	0	0	0
	8	0	0	0	0	0	0	0	0	0	0	0	0	0	0	0	0
# SURVEYED		218	200	227	232	251	213	231	240	259	241	232	261	265	253	280	275

****

UNRELATED HOUSEHOLD MEMBERS

TABLE I: UNRELATED HOUSEHOLD MEMBERS -- BY TOTAL POPULATION

Question: Is everyone in the household related to you in some way? If no, how many persons in the household are not related to you in any way?

Responses: 0 = 0; 1 = 1; 2 = 2; 3 = 3; 4 = 4; 5 = 5; 6 = 6; 7 = 7; 8 = 8 or more

	YEAR															
RESPONSE	'72	'73	'74	'75	'76	'77	'78	'80	'82	'83	'84	'85	'86	'87	'88	'89
0	95%	94%	95%	95%	95%	95%	95%	93%	93%	94%	92%	91%	92%	90%	90%	90%
1	3	4	4	4	4	4	4	5	6	5	6	7	6	7	8	8
2	1	1	1	1	1	1	1	1	1	1	2	2	1	2	2	1
3	0	1	0	0	0	0	0	0	0	0	0	0	1	0	0	1
4	0	0	0	0	0	0	0	0	0	0	0	0	0	0	0	0
5	0	0	0	0	0	0	0	0	0	0	0	0	0	0	0	0
6	0	0	0	0	0	0	0	0	0	0	0	0	0	0	0	0
7	0	0	0	0	0	0	0	0	0	0	0	0	0	0	0	0
8	0	0	0	0	0	0	0	0	0	0	0	0	0	0	0	0
# SURVEYED	1457	1350	1315	1290	1263	1269	1227	1174	1173	1277	1142	1152	1142	1119	1152	1197

TABLE II: UNRELATED HOUSEHOLD MEMBERS -- BY SEX

Question: Is everyone in the household related to you in some way? If no, how many persons in the household are not related to you in any way?

Responses: 0 = 0; 1 = 1; 2 = 2; 3 = 3; 4 = 4; 5 = 5; 6 = 6; 7 = 7; 8 = 8 or more

		YEAR															
SEX	RESP	'72	'73	'74	'75	'76	'77	'78	'80	'82	'83	'84	'85	'86	'87	'88	'89
M	0	95%	93%	95%	95%	94%	94%	95%	92%	91%	94%	91%	90%	90%	89%	89%	89%
A	1	3	4	4	4	4	4	4	5	7	5	6	8	6	8	8	9
L	2	1	2	1	1	1	1	1	2	2	1	2	2	2	2	2	2
E	3	1	0	0	0	0	0	0	1	0	1	0	1	1	0	0	1
	4	0	0	0	0	0	0	0	0	0	0	0	0	0	0	0	0
	5	0	0	0	0	0	0	0	0	0	0	0	0	0	0	0	0
	6	0	0	0	0	0	0	0	0	0	0	0	0	0	0	0	0
	7	0	0	0	0	0	0	0	0	0	0	0	0	0	0	0	0
	8	0	0	0	0	0	0	0	0	0	0	0	0	0	0	0	0
# SURVEYED		750	633	621	598	574	574	521	519	517	563	466	536	498	489	504	535
SEX	RESP	'72	'73	'74	'75	'76	'77	'78	'80	'82	'83	'84	'85	'86	'87	'88	'89
F	0	96%	95%	95%	95%	95%	96%	95%	94%	94%	94%	92%	92%	93%	90%	90%	90%
E	1	3	3	4	4	4	3	4	5	5	5	6	6	5	6	9	8
M	2	1	1	1	1	1	1	1	1	0	1	2	1	1	3	1	1
A	3	0	1	0	1	0	0	0	0	0	0	0	0	1	0	0	0
L	4	0	0	0	0	0	0	0	0	0	0	0	0	0	0	0	0
E	5	0	0	0	0	0	0	0	0	0	0	0	0	0	0	0	0
	6	0	0	0	0	0	0	0	0	0	0	0	0	0	0	0	0
	7	0	0	0	0	0	0	0	0	0	0	0	0	0	0	0	0
	8	0	0	0	0	0	0	0	0	0	0	0	0	0	0	0	0
# SURVEYED		707	717	694	692	689	695	706	655	656	714	676	616	644	630	648	662

TABLE III: UNRELATED HOUSEHOLD MEMBERS -- BY RACE

Question: Is everyone in the household related to you in some way? If no, how many persons in the household are not related to you in any way?

Responses: 0 = 0; 1 = 1; 2 = 2; 3 = 3; 4 = 4; 5 = 5; 6 = 6; 7 = 7; 8 = 8 or more

		YEAR															
RACE	RESP	'72	'73	'74	'75	'76	'77	'78	'80	'82	'83	'84	'85	'86	'87	'88	'89
WHITE	0	96%	95%	95%	95%	95%	96%	95%	93%	92%	94%	91%	91%	91%	90%	90%	90%
	1	2	4	4	4	4	3	4	5	6	5	6	7	6	7	8	8
	2	1	1	1	1	1	1	1	1	1	1	2	2	2	2	2	1
	3	0	0	0	0	0	0	0	0	0	0	0	0	1	0	0	0
	4	0	0	0	0	0	0	0	0	0	0	0	0	0	0	0	0
	5	0	0	0	0	0	0	0	0	0	0	0	0	0	0	0	0
	6	0	0	0	0	0	0	0	0	0	0	0	0	0	0	0	0
	7	0	0	0	0	0	0	0	0	0	0	0	0	0	0	0	0
	8	0	0	0	0	0	0	0	0	0	0	0	0	0	0	0	0
# SURVEYED		1213	1175	1164	1148	1156	1117	1094	1049	1034	1133	970	1004	972	938	961	1027
RACE	RESP	'72	'73	'74	'75	'76	'77	'78	'80	'82	'83	'84	'85	'86	'87	'88	'89
BLACK	0	92%	93%	94%	91%	94%	94%	94%	93%	97%	94%	96%	89%	96%	90%	88%	93%
	1	6	4	5	6	3	4	6	3	3	5	2	7	4	7	11	6
	2	1	2	1	1	2	1	0	2	0	0	0	3	0	3	1	1
	3	0	2	0	1	0	0	0	0	1	1	1	1	0	1	0	0
	4	1	0	0	1	0	0	0	2	0	1	0	0	0	0	0	0
	5	0	0	0	0	1	0	0	0	0	0	1	0	0	0	0	0
	6	0	0	0	0	0	0	0	0	0	0	0	0	0	0	0	0
	7	0	0	0	0	0	1	0	0	0	0	0	0	0	0	0	0
	8	0	0	0	0	0	0	0	0	0	0	0	0	0	0	0	0
# SURVEYED		240	163	145	138	98	140	120	116	116	130	127	111	142	137	144	112
RACE	RESP	'72	'73	'74	'75	'76	'77	'78	'80	'82	'83	'84	'85	'86	'87	'88	'89
OTHER	0	100%	92%	100%	100%	89%	75%	100%	100%	91%	86%	93%	97%	89%	93%	89%	79%
	1	0	8	0	0	0	25	0	0	9	14	4	3	4	7	6	17
	2	0	0	0	0	11	0	0	0	0	0	2	0	0	0	2	2
	3	0	0	0	0	0	0	0	0	0	0	0	0	7	0	0	2
	4	0	0	0	0	0	0	0	0	0	0	0	0	0	0	0	0
	5	0	0	0	0	0	0	0	0	0	0	0	0	0	0	0	0
	6	0	0	0	0	0	0	0	0	0	0	0	0	0	0	0	0
	7	0	0	0	0	0	0	0	0	0	0	0	0	0	0	2	0
	8	0	0	0	0	0	0	0	0	0	0	0	0	0	0	0	0
# SURVEYED		4	12	6	4	9	12	13	9	23	14	45	37	28	44	47	58

TABLE IV: UNRELATED HOUSEHOLD MEMBERS -- BY AGE

Question: Is everyone in the household related to you in some way? If no, how many persons in the household are not related to you in any way?

Responses: 0 = 0; 1 = 1; 2 = 2; 3 = 3; 4 = 4; 5 = 5; 6 = 6; 7 = 7; 8 = 8 or more

		YEAR															
AGE	RESP	'72	'73	'74	'75	'76	'77	'78	'80	'82	'83	'84	'85	'86	'87	'88	'89
18-23	0	87%	86%	85%	88%	91%	93%	89%	89%	85%	81%	81%	71%	74%	74%	75%	77%
	1	8	9	11	10	6	5	11	9	10	14	13	21	16	15	17	18
	2	2	2	3	2	1	1	0	1	4	3	4	7	6	9	6	2
	3	1	1	1	0	1	1	0	0	1	2	0	2	3	2	1	1
	4	0	1	1	1	1	0	0	0	1	0	1	0	0	0	0	2
	5	0	0	0	0	0	0	0	0	0	0	0	0	0	0	1	0
	6	0	0	0	0	0	0	0	0	0	0	1	0	0	0	0	0
	7	1	0	0	0	0	1	0	0	0	0	0	0	0	0	0	0
	8	2	0	0	0	0	0	0	0	0	0	0	0	0	0	0	0
# SURVEYED		157	161	160	164	152	154	142	139	136	112	138	116	97	110	130	1
AGE	RESP	'72	'73	'74	'75	'76	'77	'78	'80	'82	'83	'84	'85	'86	'87	'88	'89
24-29	0	93%	92%	92%	91%	91%	91%	91%	88%	81%	93%	85%	82%	84%	79%	80%	75%
	1	4	7	7	7	8	6	8	9	15	4	11	15	11	15	15	19
	2	2	2	1	1	1	3	1	3	2	2	4	2	3	3	3	2
	3	0	0	1	0	1	0	0	0	0	0	1	0	2	2	1	3
	4	1	0	1	0	0	0	0	1	0	0	0	1	0	1	0	0
	5	0	0	0	0	0	0	0	0	0	0	0	1	0	0	1	0
	6	0	0	0	0	0	0	0	0	0	0	0	0	0	0	0	0
	7	0	0	0	0	0	0	0	0	0	0	0	0	0	0	1	0
	8	0	0	0	0	0	0	0	0	0	0	0	0	0	0	0	0
# SURVEYED		216	199	195	208	200	167	212	175	209	235	188	170	179	154	179	167
AGE	RESP	'72	'73	'74	'75	'76	'77	'78	'80	'82	'83	'84	'85	'86	'87	'88	'89
30-35	0	96%	98%	93%	97%	96%	98%	94%	92%	93%	95%	93%	92%	92%	92%	88%	90%
	1	3	1	5	1	3	2	3	6	6	5	5	4	7	6	10	9
	2	0	1	1	1	1	1	2	0	1	0	2	2	1	1	2	1
	3	1	0	1	0	1	0	0	2	0	0	1	2	1	0	0	0
	4	0	0	0	1	0	0	1	0	0	0	0	0	0	1	0	0
	5	0	1	1	0	0	0	0	0	0	0	0	0	0	1	0	0
	6	0	0	0	0	0	0	0	0	0	0	0	0	0	1	0	0
	7	0	0	0	0	0	0	0	0	0	0	0	0	0	0	0	0
	8	0	0	0	0	0	0	0	0	0	0	0	0	0	0	0	0
# SURVEYED		182	160	167	163	178	169	195	180	178	207	167	181	189	178	164	180
AGE	RESP	'72	'73	'74	'75	'76	'77	'78	'80	'82	'83	'84	'85	'86	'87	'88	'89
36-41	0	97%	95%	99%	97%	97%	97%	99%	93%	97%	91%	93%	95%	95%	94%	95%	93%
	1	2	1	1	2	3	2	1	6	2	8	5	5	3	5	5	5
	2	0	1	0	0	0	0	0	1	1	0	1	0	1	1	0	1
	3	1	2	0	1	0	1	0	0	0	1	0	0	1	0	0	0
	4	1	0	0	0	0	1	0	0	0	0	1	0	0	0	0	0
	5	0	0	0	0	0	0	0	0	0	0	1	0	0	0	0	0
	6	0	1	0	0	0	0	0	0	0	0	0	0	0	0	0	0
	7	0	0	0	0	0	0	0	0	0	0	0	0	0	0	0	0
	8	0	0	0	0	0	0	0	0	0	0	0	0	0	0	0	0
# SURVEYED		126	163	147	150	149	148	141	134	123	151	168	147	176	159	167	166

TABLE IV: UNRELATED HOUSEHOLD MEMBERS -- BY AGE (Continued)

Question: Is everyone in the household related to you in some way? If no, how many persons in the household are not related to you in any way?

Responses: 0 = 0; 1 = 1; 2 = 2; 3 = 3; 4 = 4; 5 = 5; 6 = 6; 7 = 7; 8 = 8 or more

		YEAR															
AGE	RESP	'72	'73	'74	'75	'76	'77	'78	'80	'82	'83	'84	'85	'86	'87	'88	'89
42-47	0	98%	96%	98%	95%	97%	95%	97%	93%	99%	98%	94%	94%	95%	93%	94%	92%
	1	2	4	1	2	2	4	3	5	1	2	4	5	4	5	6	6
	2	0	0	1	1	1	0	0	2	0	0	3	2	0	2	0	2
	3	0	0	0	1	0	0	0	0	0	0	0	0	1	0	0	0
	4	0	1	0	0	0	0	0	0	0	0	0	0	0	0	0	0
	5	0	0	0	0	0	0	0	0	0	0	0	0	1	0	0	0
	6	0	0	0	0	0	1	0	0	0	0	0	0	0	0	0	0
	7	0	0	0	0	0	0	0	0	0	0	0	0	0	0	0	0
	8	0	0	0	0	0	0	0	0	0	0	0	0	0	0	0	0
# SURVEYED		179	137	141	134	107	133	104	105	103	123	108	108	113	133	131	142
AGE	RESP	'72	'73	'74	'75	'76	'77	'78	'80	'82	'83	'84	'85	'86	'87	'88	'89
48-53	0	97%	96%	98%	99%	97%	97%	99%	95%	97%	96%	98%	98%	96%	93%	93%	94%
	1	1	4	2	1	3	2	1	3	3	3	2	1	2	3	5	6
	2	1	0	0	0	1	0	0	2	0	1	0	1	1	2	1	0
	3	0	1	0	0	0	0	0	0	0	0	0	0	0	0	0	0
	4	0	0	0	0	0	0	0	0	0	0	0	0	0	1	0	0
	5	0	0	0	0	0	0	0	0	0	0	0	0	0	1	0	0
	6	1	0	0	0	0	1	0	0	0	0	0	0	0	0	0	0
	7	0	0	0	0	0	0	0	0	0	0	0	0	0	0	0	0
	8	0	0	0	0	0	0	0	0	0	0	0	0	0	0	0	0
# SURVEYED		177	142	132	127	119	137	120	105	92	100	86	107	85	104	74	106
AGE	RESP	'72	'73	'74	'75	'76	'77	'78	'80	'82	'83	'84	'85	'86	'87	'88	'89
54-59	0	98%	97%	98%	98%	97%	96%	92%	97%	98%	97%	97%	97%	96%	96%	97%	99%
	1	1	1	2	2	3	3	7	2	2	3	3	3	3	4	3	0
	2	1	1	0	0	0	1	1	1	0	0	0	0	1	0	0	1
	3	0	1	0	0	0	0	0	0	0	0	0	0	0	0	0	0
	4	0	0	0	0	0	0	0	1	0	0	0	0	0	0	0	0
	5	0	0	1	0	0	0	0	0	0	0	0	0	0	0	0	0
	6	0	0	0	0	0	0	0	0	0	0	0	0	0	0	0	0
	7	0	0	0	0	0	0	0	0	0	0	0	0	0	0	0	0
	8	0	0	0	0	0	0	0	0	0	0	0	0	0	0	0	0
# SURVEYED		147	145	123	103	110	138	101	116	123	111	89	106	76	77	65	77
AGE	RESP	'72	'73	'74	'75	'76	'77	'78	'80	'82	'83	'84	'85	'86	'87	'88	'89
60-65	0	98%	98%	95%	96%	97%	98%	95%	95%	99%	97%	98%	97%	98%	97%	97%	96%
	1	3	2	3	2	0	2	4	2	1	2	1	3	2	3	2	4
	2	0	0	1	0	2	0	1	1	0	0	1	0	0	0	1	0
	3	0	0	0	1	0	0	0	1	0	1	0	0	0	0	0	0
	4	0	0	0	0	0	0	0	0	0	0	0	0	0	0	0	0
	5	0	0	0	1	1	0	0	0	0	0	0	0	0	0	0	0
	6	0	0	0	0	0	0	0	0	0	0	0	0	0	0	0	0
	7	0	0	0	0	0	0	0	0	0	0	0	0	0	0	0	0
	8	0	0	0	0	0	0	0	0	0	0	0	0	0	0	0	0
# SURVEYED		120	106	88	92	106	90	80	86	73	106	82	89	85	71	88	80

TABLE IV: UNRELATED HOUSEHOLD MEMBERS -- BY AGE (Continued)

Question: Is everyone in the household related to you in some way? If no, how many persons in the household are not related to you in any way?

Responses: 0 = 0: 1 = 1; 2 = 2; 3 = 3; 4 = 4; 5 = 5; 6 = 6; 7 = 7; 8 = 8 or more

		YEAR															
AGE	RESP	'72	'73	'74	'75	'76	'77	'78	'80	'82	'83	'84	'85	'86	'87	'88	'89
66+	0	95%	96%	96%	97%	93%	95%	99%	99%	98%	97%	98%	98%	99%	94%	97%	98%
	1	4	2	3	3	5	4	1	0	2	3	2	2	1	3	3	1
	2	1	1	1	0	1	2	0	0	0	0	0	0	0	2	0	1
	3	1	1	0	0	0	0	0	0	1	0	0	0	0	0	1	0
	4	0	0	0	0	0	0	0	1	0	0	0	0	0	0	0	0
	5	0	0	0	0	0	0	0	0	0	0	0	0	0	0	0	0
	6	0	0	0	0	0	0	0	0	0	0	0	0	0	1	0	0
	7	0	0	0	0	0	0	0	0	0	0	0	0	0	0	0	0
	8	0	0	0	0	0	0	0	0	0	0	0	0	0	0	0	0
# SURVEYED		149	135	159	145	138	128	128	129	131	128	112	126	137	129	150	151

****

WAGE EARNERS IN HOUSEHOLD

TABLE I: WAGE EARNERS IN HOUSEHOLD -- BY TOTAL POPULATION

Question: Just thinking about your family now, those people in the household who are related to you, how many persons in the family, including yourself, earned any money last year (71-77, 79, 81-88) from any job or employment?

Responses: 0 = 0; 1 = 1; 2 = 2; 3 = 3; 4 = 4; 5 = 5; 6 = 6; 7 = 7; 8 = 8 or more

	YEAR															
RESPONSE	'72	'73	'74	'75	'76	'77	'78	'80	'82	'83	'84	'85	'86	'87	'88	'89
0	12%	11%	13%	14%	16%	14%	15%	17%	16%	15%	16%	18%	20%	16%	19%	19%
1	43	41	41	40	42	40	41	38	42	39	42	38	35	37	38	36
2	32	34	32	33	30	32	31	33	32	34	30	33	33	34	31	31
3	9	9	9	8	8	8	7	7	7	8	8	7	7	9	9	9
4	3	4	3	4	3	4	4	4	2	3	3	4	3	3	2	3
5	1	1	1	2	1	1	1	1	1	1	1	1	1	1	1	1
6	0	0	0	0	0	0	0	0	0	0	0	0	0	0	0	0
7	0	0	0	0	0	0	0	0	0	0	0	0	0	0	0	0
8	0	0	0	0	0	0	0	0	0	0	0	0	0	0	0	0
# SURVEYED	1580	1494	1469	1482	1491	1526	1524	1449	1461	1582	1455	1523	1450	1456	1471	1525

TABLE II: WAGE EARNERS IN HOUSEHOLD -- BY SEX

Question: Just thinking about your family now, those people in the household who are related to you, how many persons in the family, including yourself, earned any money last year (71-77, 79, 81-88) from any job or employment?

Responses: 0 = 0; 1 = 1; 2 = 2; 3 = 3; 4 = 4; 5 = 5; 6 = 6; 7 = 7; 8 = 8 or more

		YEAR															
SEX	RESP	'72	'73	'74	'75	'76	'77	'78	'80	'82	'83	'84	'85	'86	'87	'88	'89
M	0	9%	9%	13%	12%	12%	12%	10%	13%	13%	11%	12%	13%	15%	11%	14%	14%
A	1	41	43	40	39	42	42	41	39	42	39	44	39	37	39	40	34
L	2	37	32	33	34	31	33	35	35	35	39	31	37	35	35	33	36
E	3	10	10	9	9	10	8	7	9	8	7	8	7	9	10	10	10
	4	3	5	3	5	3	4	4	3	2	2	4	5	3	3	2	4
	5	1	0	2	1	1	1	2	1	1	2	1	1	1	1	1	1
	6	0	0	1	0	0	0	0	0	0	0	0	0	0	0	0	0
	7	0	0	0	0	0	0	0	0	0	0	0	0	0	0	0	0
	8	0	0	0	0	0	0	0	0	0	0	0	0	0	0	0	0
# SURVEYED		789	698	680	665	667	691	639	632	621	682	592	687	616	640	634	656
SEX	RESP	'72	'73	'74	'75	'76	'77	'78	'80	'82	'83	'84	'85	'86	'87	'88	'89
F	0	15%	13%	13%	15%	18%	16%	19%	21%	18%	18%	19%	23%	25%	20%	22%	22%
E	1	46	39	41	41	42	39	41	36	42	40	41	37	33	36	37	38
M	2	27	35	32	32	29	32	29	32	31	31	30	30	32	33	29	28
A	3	7	8	9	8	7	8	7	5	7	8	8	6	6	8	9	8
L	4	4	4	4	3	3	4	3	4	2	3	2	3	3	3	2	3
E	5	1	1	1	2	1	1	1	0	0	0	1	1	1	1	1	1
	6	0	0	0	0	0	0	0	1	0	0	0	0	0	0	0	0
	7	0	0	0	0	0	0	0	0	0	0	0	0	0	0	0	0
	8	0	0	0	0	0	0	0	0	0	0	0	0	0	0	0	0
# SURVEYED		791	796	789	817	824	835	885	817	840	900	863	836	834	816	837	869

TABLE III: WAGE EARNERS IN HOUSEHOLD -- BY RACE

Question: Just thinking about your family now, those people in the household who are related to you, how many persons in the family, including yourself, earned any money last year (71-77, 79, 81-88) from any job or employment?

Responses: 0 = 0; 1 = 1; 2 = 2; 3 = 3; 4 = 4; 5 = 5; 6 = 6; 7 = 7; 8 = 8 or more

		YEAR															
RACE	RESP	'72	'73	'74	'75	'76	'77	'78	'80	'82	'83	'84	'85	'86	'87	'88	'89
WHITE	0	11%	11%	12%	13%	15%	14%	15%	17%	15%	14%	16%	18%	20%	16%	19%	18%
	1	44	41	40	40	43	39	41	38	42	38	41	38	35	36	37	35
	2	32	33	33	33	30	33	31	33	33	35	31	33	33	34	31	32
	3	8	9	9	8	8	9	7	7	7	8	8	6	7	9	10	8
	4	3	5	3	4	3	4	4	4	2	3	3	4	3	3	2	4
	5	1	1	1	2	1	1	1	1	0	1	1	1	1	1	1	1
	6	0	0	0	0	0	0	0	1	0	0	0	0	0	0	0	0
	7	0	0	0	0	0	0	0	0	0	0	0	0	0	0	0	0
	8	0	0	0	0	0	0	0	0	0	0	0	0	0	0	0	0
# SURVEYED		1321	1303	1294	1317	1356	1337	1351	1305	1286	1403	1236	1331	1234	1216	1229	1308
RACE	RESP	'72	'73	'74	'75	'76	'77	'78	'80	'82	'83	'84	'85	'86	'87	'88	'89
BLACK	0	18%	12%	19%	19%	25%	18%	13%	24%	17%	20%	20%	22%	23%	18%	21%	24%
	1	38	38	43	42	37	45	45	35	45	44	44	40	35	43	45	44
	2	30	38	27	28	29	30	34	30	26	27	31	27	32	31	26	19
	3	10	10	7	7	9	3	5	7	9	6	4	8	7	4	7	9
	4	3	1	3	2	2	3	1	2	0	1	1	2	3	3	2	3
	5	1	1	0	1	0	1	2	1	2	1	1	0	1	0	1	1
	6	0	0	1	1	0	0	0	0	0	0	0	1	0	1	0	1
	7	0	0	0	0	0	0	0	0	0	0	0	0	0	0	0	0
	8	0	0	0	0	0	0	0	0	0	0	0	0	0	0	0	0
# SURVEYED		255	178	168	161	126	174	157	134	149	162	167	148	180	187	184	157
RACE	RESP	'72	'73	'74	'75	'76	'77	'78	'80	'82	'83	'84	'85	'86	'87	'88	'89
OTHER	0	25%	0%	29%	0%	0%	7%	6%	10%	12%	12%	10%	5%	17%	9%	12%	13%
	1	0	46	29	25	44	53	44	20	35	53	60	43	31	42	36	35
	2	50	46	29	50	44	33	31	60	42	35	25	39	33	36	38	35
	3	25	8	14	25	11	7	13	10	12	0	6	2	11	11	9	13
	4	0	0	0	0	0	0	0	0	0	0	0	7	3	2	3	2
	5	0	0	0	0	0	0	6	0	0	0	0	5	3	0	2	2
	6	0	0	0	0	0	0	0	0	0	0	0	0	3	0	0	0
	7	0	0	0	0	0	0	0	0	0	0	0	0	0	0	0	0
	8	0	0	0	0	0	0	0	0	0	0	0	0	0	0	0	0
# SURVEYED		4	13	7	4	9	15	16	10	26	17	52	44	36	53	58	60

TABLE IV: WAGE EARNERS IN HOUSEHOLD -- BY AGE

Question: Just thinking about your family now, those people in the household who are related to you, how many persons in the family, including yourself, earned any money last year (71-77, 79, 81-88) from any job or employment?

Responses: 0 = 0; 1 = 1; 2 = 2; 3 = 3; 4 = 4; 5 = 5; 6 = 6; 7 = 7; 8 = 8 or more

		YEAR															
AGE	RESP	'72	'73	'74	'75	'76	'77	'78	'80	'82	'83	'84	'85	'86	'87	'88	'89
18-23	0	6%	3%	2%	3%	6%	1%	5%	4%	5%	2%	5%	5%	4%	6%	10%	8%
	1	33	35	37	28	31	29	33	34	31	35	42	36	32	45	35	30
	2	32	30	38	41	30	43	38	35	36	35	29	33	31	21	29	25
	3	16	19	13	17	19	12	13	17	17	21	14	12	16	17	15	19
	4	8	9	5	5	10	9	7	8	8	2	6	8	10	10	7	10
	5	4	2	2	5	4	5	4	1	2	6	3	4	5	2	2	6
	6	1	1	2	0	0	1	1	1	1	0	1	2	1	0	1	1
	7	0	1	0	0	0	0	0	0	0	0	0	1	0	0	0	0
	8	0	1	0	0	0	0	0	1	0	0	0	0	0	0	0	0
# SURVEYED		160	171	167	173	162	164	162	154	144	127	159	132	105	125	140	134
AGE	RESP	'72	'73	'74	'75	'76	'77	'78	'80	'82	'83	'84	'85	'86	'87	'88	'89
24-29	0	2%	3%	3%	3%	3%	3%	2%	4%	4%	5%	5%	3%	6%	5%	3%	4%
	1	47	37	49	47	46	50	51	39	48	46	50	46	45	46	50	50
	2	43	52	42	44	44	41	41	53	44	42	40	47	41	41	38	38
	3	7	5	5	3	4	3	3	3	3	3	3	3	7	6	7	6
	4	1	2	1	2	2	1	0	1	1	2	2	1	1	1	1	3
	5	0	0	0	0	0	1	2	0	1	1	0	0	0	1	0	0
	6	0	0	0	0	0	0	0	0	0	0	0	0	0	1	0	1
	7	0	0	0	0	0	0	0	0	0	0	0	0	0	0	0	0
	8	0	0	0	0	0	0	0	0	0	0	0	0	0	0	0	0
# SURVEYED		225	212	211	230	225	204	243	196	240	286	231	215	214	192	215	200
AGE	RESP	'72	'73	'74	'75	'76	'77	'78	'80	'82	'83	'84	'85	'86	'87	'88	'89
30-35	0	4%	1%	3%	4%	4%	3%	1%	6%	3%	4%	2%	3%	5%	2%	3%	6%
	1	56	54	48	46	54	44	53	48	45	41	52	44	41	43	45	43
	2	37	38	42	46	38	51	43	42	48	49	42	49	48	49	46	44
	3	1	5	5	2	2	2	2	2	5	4	4	3	5	5	5	5
	4	1	1	1	1	2	1	0	1	0	1	1	0	0	0	1	1
	5	1	0	1	1	1	0	0	0	0	0	0	0	0	0	1	1
	6	0	0	0	0	0	0	0	0	0	0	1	0	0	0	1	0
	7	0	0	1	0	0	0	0	0	0	0	0	0	0	0	0	0
	8	0	0	0	0	0	0	0	0	0	0	0	0	0	0	0	0
# SURVEYED		185	167	174	171	186	187	230	213	200	233	196	210	221	221	194	210
AGE	RESP	'72	'73	'74	'75	'76	'77	'78	'80	'82	'83	'84	'85	'86	'87	'88	'89
36-41	0	3%	4%	5%	2%	3%	3%	2%	4%	3%	3%	2%	4%	2%	1%	4%	4%
	1	47	44	40	38	41	41	47	43	46	44	42	34	32	35	45	36
	2	39	37	33	41	39	37	31	34	38	42	42	39	48	48	31	48
	3	4	7	10	11	8	12	11	8	11	9	8	11	10	9	15	9
	4	4	6	9	5	7	5	5	8	1	1	5	10	5	6	4	3
	5	2	2	3	3	1	1	3	1	1	1	1	1	2	2	1	0
	6	1	1	0	1	0	1	1	1	0	0	1	1	0	0	1	0
	7	0	0	0	0	0	0	0	0	0	0	0	1	1	0	0	0
	8	0	0	0	0	0	0	1	0	0	0	0	0	0	0	0	0
# SURVEYED		125	174	151	154	157	168	159	150	142	172	186	183	185	185	191	196

TABLE IV: WAGE EARNERS IN HOUSEHOLD -- BY AGE (Continued)

Question: Just thinking about your family now, those people in the household who are related to you, how many persons in the family, including yourself, earned any money last year (71-77, 79, 81-88) from any job or employment?

Responses: 1 = 1; 2 = 2; 3 = 3; 4 = 4; 5 = 5; 6 = 6; 7 = 7; 8 = 8 or more

		YEAR															
AGE	RESP	'72	'73	'74	'75	'76	'77	'78	'80	'82	'83	'84	'85	'86	'87	'88	'89
42-47	0	4%	1%	5%	5%	8%	3%	4%	2%	2%	6%	4%	2%	7%	3%	2%	4%
	1	35	36	30	32	35	37	33	23	40	35	37	39	35	28	32	29
	2	36	35	41	39	33	32	35	37	37	27	32	38	40	41	45	37
	3	14	14	18	15	18	18	12	19	18	21	17	16	11	18	18	16
	4	9	12	4	6	4	8	13	15	3	9	8	4	6	7	3	9
	5	2	1	2	3	2	1	2	3	1	1	2	2	1	2	1	4
	6	1	0	1	0	1	0	1	3	0	0	0	0	0	0	0	1
	7	0	1	0	0	0	0	1	0	0	0	0	0	0	0	0	1
	8	0	0	0	0	1	0	0	0	0	0	0	0	0	0	0	0
# SURVEYED		184	146	151	143	113	147	118	115	117	142	125	124	138	157	157	161
AGE	RESP	'72	'73	'74	'75	'76	'77	'78	'80	'82	'83	'84	'85	'86	'87	'88	'89
48-53	0	3%	5%	6%	9%	3%	8%	6%	9%	4%	5%	8%	7%	10%	6%	4%	4%
	1	38	34	38	30	44	39	26	38	41	36	31	33	41	39	37	38
	2	35	36	28	28	32	29	37	33	37	38	33	38	32	34	32	30
	3	19	18	19	20	17	14	18	13	13	11	20	15	10	13	21	20
	4	4	6	6	7	4	8	9	4	5	8	4	6	3	6	5	4
	5	0	0	1	4	1	2	3	2	1	1	3	1	2	2	1	2
	6	0	0	1	2	0	0	0	1	0	1	1	0	1	0	0	0
	7	0	0	0	0	0	0	1	0	0	0	0	0	1	0	0	0
	8	0	0	0	0	0	0	0	0	0	0	0	0	0	0	0	1
# SURVEYED		186	148	144	141	133	154	132	123	108	115	102	131	107	126	92	138
AGE	RESP	'72	'73	'74	'75	'76	'77	'78	'80	'82	'83	'84	'85	'86	'87	'88	'89
54-59	0	8%	4%	9%	11%	8%	8%	15%	4%	14%	8%	10%	20%	13%	11%	10%	13%
	1	39	48	47	52	50	50	50	44	45	40	50	42	40	31	49	37
	2	38	34	29	24	32	27	28	40	29	40	28	25	30	40	29	37
	3	12	12	10	7	8	10	3	8	6	10	10	6	10	16	12	8
	4	3	2	4	6	1	4	4	2	5	2	3	7	3	1	1	4
	5	1	1	0	0	2	1	1	2	0	1	0	0	4	0	0	0
	6	0	0	1	0	0	0	0	0	1	0	0	0	0	0	0	0
	7	0	0	0	0	0	0	0	1	0	0	0	0	0	0	0	0
	8	0	0	0	0	0	0	0	0	0	0	0	0	0	0	0	0
# SURVEYED		154	156	137	125	128	167	136	133	138	133	113	132	98	97	84	99
AGE	RESP	'72	'73	'74	'75	'76	'77	'78	'80	'82	'83	'84	'85	'86	'87	'88	'89
60-65	0	16%	18%	15%	21%	24%	21%	24%	36%	18%	22%	31%	25%	30%	27%	35%	34%
	1	58	49	46	54	48	50	45	40	56	45	45	48	37	42	34	49
	2	21	28	31	20	22	23	22	23	24	26	18	24	28	29	27	15
	3	4	4	7	2	6	6	7	1	2	4	4	2	4	2	3	3
	4	1	2	2	4	0	1	1	0	0	2	1	1	2	0	1	0
	5	0	0	0	0	0	0	0	0	0	0	1	0	0	0	0	0
	6	0	0	0	0	0	0	0	0	0	0	0	0	0	0	0	0
	7	0	0	0	0	0	0	0	0	0	0	0	0	0	0	0	0
	8	0	0	0	0	0	0	0	0	0	0	0	0	0	0	0	0
# SURVEYED		141	120	107	112	133	117	107	117	114	130	110	130	111	100	119	110

TABLE IV: WAGE EARNERS IN HOUSEHOLD -- BY AGE (Continued)

Question: Just thinking about your family now, those people in the household who are related to you, how many persons in the family, including yourself, earned any money last year (71-77, 79, 81-88) from any job or employment?

Responses: 0 = 0; 1 = 1; 2 = 2; 3 = 3; 4 = 4; 5 = 5; 6 = 6; 7 = 7; 8 = 8 or more

		YEAR															
AGE	RESP	'72	'73	'74	'75	'76	'77	'78	'80	'82	'83	'84	'85	'86	'87	'88	'89
66+	0	51%	53%	57%	53%	60%	66%	65%	64%	60%	62%	63%	66%	75%	63%	67%	67%
	1	38	32	31	36	32	23	26	28	32	29	28	26	17	30	24	22
	2	9	13	11	10	6	8	7	8	6	9	7	7	5	5	8	9
	3	1	2	1	1	0	1	1	0	2	0	2	0	2	2	1	1
	4	0	0	0	0	0	1	0	0	0	0	0	1	1	0	0	0
	5	0	0	0	0	0	0	0	0	0	0	0	0	0	0	0	0
	6	0	0	0	0	0	0	0	0	0	0	0	0	0	0	0	0
	7	0	0	0	0	0	0	0	0	0	0	0	0	0	0	0	0
	8	0	0	0	0	0	0	0	0	0	0	0	0	0	0	0	0
# SURVEYED		216	196	221	229	248	211	231	240	247	238	229	260	264	249	275	273

****

DWELLING TYPE

TABLE I: DWELLING TYPE -- BY TOTAL POPULATION

Question: Dwelling type. NOTE: Question not asked in 1972-1981.

Responses:
1 = Trailer
2 = Detached single family house
3 = 2-family house, 2 units side by side
4 = 2-family house, 2 units one above the other
5 = Detached 3-4 family house
6 = Row house (3 or more units in an attached row)
7 = Apartment (5 or more units, 3 stories or less)
8 = Apartment (5 or more units, 4 stories or more)
9 = Apartment in a partly commercial structure
10 = Other

	YEAR							
RESPONSE	'82	'83	'84	'85	'86	'87	'88	'89
1	7%	5%	6%	8%	7%	6%	8%	8%
2	64	67	64	62	65	66	58	67
3	5	3	5	3	3	3	4	3
4	3	3	3	3	4	3	4	3
5	2	2	2	2	2	2	3	2
6	5	5	3	5	5	4	7	4
7	9	9	11	12	11	9	12	9
8	3	3	3	3	3	3	4	3
9	1	1	1	1	1	1	1	0
10	0	1	1	1	1	2	1	3
# SURVEYED	1496	1584	1461	1515	1450	1452	1454	1510

TABLE II: DWELLING TYPE -- BY SEX

Question: Dwelling type. NOTE: Question not asked in 1972-1981.

Responses:
1 = Trailer
2 = Detached single family house
3 = 2-family house, 2 units side by side
4 = 2-family house, 2 units one above the other
5 = Detached 3-4 family house
6 = Row house (3 or more units in an attached row)
7 = Apartment (5 or more units, 3 stories or less)
8 = Apartment (5 or more units, 4 stories or more)
9 = Apartment in a partly commercial structure
10 = Other

		YEAR							
SEX	RESP	'82	'83	'84	'85	'86	'87	'88	'89
M	1	7%	5%	7%	8%	6%	7%	8%	8%
A	2	66	70	63	63	66	66	60	69
L	3	4	2	4	3	2	3	3	2
E	4	3	3	3	3	4	2	3	2
	5	2	2	3	2	2	3	2	1
	6	5	5	3	3	4	5	7	3
	7	9	8	12	13	11	10	13	9
	8	3	2	3	3	2	3	3	3
	9	1	1	1	1	1	1	1	1
	10	0	1	1	1	1	2	1	2
# SURVEYED		635	682	589	681	610	638	624	652

		YEAR							
SEX	RESP	'82	'83	'84	'85	'86	'87	'88	'89
F	1	8%	5%	5%	8%	7%	6%	8%	8%
E	2	63	65	65	61	63	66	57	65
M	3	5	3	5	3	3	4	4	3
A	4	4	4	4	3	4	4	4	3
L	5	2	2	2	2	2	1	3	2
E	6	5	6	4	6	5	3	7	5
	7	9	10	11	12	10	9	12	9
	8	3	4	4	3	4	4	5	3
	9	0	0	1	1	1	1	0	0
	10	0	1	1	1	2	1	1	3
# SURVEYED		861	902	872	834	840	814	830	858

TABLE III: DWELLING TYPE -- BY RACE

Question: Dwelling type. NOTE: Question not asked in 1972-1981.

Responses: 1 = Trailer
2 = Detached single family house
3 = 2-family house, 2 units side by side
4 = 2-family house, 2 units one above the other
5 = Detached 3-4 family house
6 = Row house (3 or more units in an attached row)
7 = Apartment (5 or more units, 3 stories or less)
8 = Apartment (5 or more units, 4 stories or more)
9 = Apartment in a partly commercial structure
10 = Other

RACE	RESP	'82	'83	'84	'85	'86	'87	'88	'89
WHITE	1	8%	6%	7%	8%	7%	6%	8%	9%
	2	67	69	67	63	67	70	61	69
	3	5	2	4	3	2	3	3	3
	4	3	3	3	3	4	2	3	3
	5	2	2	2	2	2	2	3	2
	6	4	5	2	5	4	4	6	3
	7	8	9	10	12	10	8	11	8
	8	3	3	3	3	2	2	4	2
	9	1	1	1	1	1	1	0	0
	10	0	1	1	1	1	1	1	3
# SURVEYED		1315	1403	1239	1325	1235	1213	1212	1295

RACE	RESP	'82	'83	'84	'85	'86	'87	'88	'89
BLACK	1	4%	1%	1%	4%	3%	3%	2%	1%
	2	45	53	42	49	48	46	39	53
	3	5	5	12	5	7	8	8	5
	4	6	10	2	3	2	5	10	4
	5	1	2	4	2	2	2	3	3
	6	12	9	11	7	12	7	13	15
	7	21	15	20	18	13	17	18	12
	8	6	3	8	8	9	10	7	4
	9	0	1	1	1	1	1	1	0
	10	0	1	1	2	3	2	0	3
# SURVEYED		154	163	170	147	180	186	181	155

RACE	RESP	'82	'83	'84	'85	'86	'87	'88	'89
OTHER	1	4%	6%	6%	9%	14%	17%	13%	3%
	2	56	61	56	51	60	55	54	60
	3	7	6	2	5	0	0	3	3
	4	0	0	6	7	3	6	3	2
	5	0	6	6	5	0	2	3	0
	6	7	11	2	2	0	0	0	0
	7	11	0	19	14	20	8	20	20
	8	15	6	0	5	3	8	2	10
	9	0	6	0	0	0	2	2	0
	10	0	0	4	2	0	4	0	2
# SURVEYED		27	18	52	43	35	53	61	60

TABLE IV: DWELLING TYPE -- BY AGE

Question: Dwelling type. NOTE: Question not asked in 1972-1981.

Responses:
- 1 = Trailer
- 2 = Detached single family house
- 3 = 2-family house, 2 units side by side
- 4 = 2-family house, 2 units one above the other
- 5 = Detached 3-4 family house
- 6 = Row house (3 or more units in an attached row)
- 7 = Apartment (5 or more units, 3 stories or less)
- 8 = Apartment (5 or more units, 4 stories or more)
- 9 = Apartment in a partly commercial structure
- 10 = Other

		YEAR							
AGE	RESP	'82	'83	'84	'85	'86	'87	'88	'89
18-23	1	15%	4%	5%	9%	5%	6%	9%	8%
	2	50	57	47	46	53	45	41	49
	3	6	3	6	3	2	4	6	4
	4	5	2	4	2	4	2	3	4
	5	3	4	3	3	1	5	7	0
	6	4	6	3	4	7	2	6	6
	7	14	20	26	27	19	29	24	20
	8	3	1	3	2	6	3	2	5
	9	0	2	2	2	1	0	1	2
	10	0	2	3	2	3	2	0	4
# SURVEYED		147	126	160	131	107	124	140	133

AGE	RESP	'82	'83	'84	'85	'86	'87	'88	'89
24-29	1	7%	5%	6%	9%	8%	5%	6%	10%
	2	53	56	46	47	48	45	44	45
	3	7	3	8	4	4	6	4	7
	4	5	4	6	4	7	5	5	3
	5	2	4	5	5	5	4	4	5
	6	5	7	3	4	5	6	7	5
	7	16	17	22	21	18	21	24	19
	8	5	3	1	3	3	4	5	2
	9	1	1	2	0	2	1	0	1
	10	0	1	1	3	1	3	1	4
# SURVEYED		243	286	230	215	217	191	207	197

AGE	RESP	'82	'83	'84	'85	'86	'87	'88	'89
30-35	1	6%	6%	6%	6%	7%	5%	7%	7%
	2	61	66	61	59	62	61	53	61
	3	7	1	6	3	2	5	3	3
	4	4	3	4	3	5	2	5	6
	5	5	3	2	2	1	4	3	3
	6	5	6	4	9	4	5	10	4
	7	9	12	12	14	13	9	14	9
	8	2	1	6	2	2	5	4	2
	9	0	0	0	0	1	1	2	0
	10	0	0	1	1	2	1	0	3
# SURVEYED		203	236	198	209	218	220	191	210

		YEAR							
AGE	RESP	'82	'83	'84	'85	'86	'87	'88	'89
36-41	1	5%	5%	6%	6%	5%	6%	5%	5%
	2	75	69	73	66	71	76	67	75
	3	3	3	3	4	4	3	4	2
	4	3	5	2	4	3	1	3	2
	5	3	1	2	1	2	2	2	2
	6	3	8	5	5	3	2	5	4
	7	7	5	7	12	9	4	9	5
	8	1	4	2	2	2	2	2	4
	9	0	0	0	0	0	3	0	1
	10	0	0	1	1	2	2	2	1
# SURVEYED		146	169	184	183	185	184	191	194

AGE	RESP	'82	'83	'84	'85	'86	'87	'88	'89
42-47	1	3%	5%	5%	7%	6%	5%	6%	5%
	2	74	75	74	72	69	77	67	79
	3	3	6	4	1	4	2	5	3
	4	2	3	3	2	1	2	2	2
	5	1	2	2	2	1	1	2	0
	6	5	3	2	7	4	2	6	2
	7	7	4	6	7	8	8	9	7
	8	4	2	2	2	5	3	1	3
	9	1	1	1	1	1	1	1	0
	10	0	0	1	1	1	1	0	1
# SURVEYED		118	144	125	122	137	157	155	159

AGE	RESP	'82	'83	'84	'85	'86	'87	'88	'89
48-53	1	5%	2%	4%	9%	3%	6%	3%	5%
	2	74	81	75	70	77	75	69	78
	3	3	2	3	5	1	2	6	1
	4	0	1	1	2	4	4	7	1
	5	2	1	1	1	3	0	3	0
	6	4	3	2	4	3	2	3	6
	7	8	5	8	6	7	6	6	4
	8	5	3	5	1	2	2	3	3
	9	0	0	0	2	1	1	0	0
	10	0	2	1	1	0	2	0	2
# SURVEYED		111	115	102	127	106	125	90	136

TABLE IV: DWELLING TYPE -- BY AGE (Continued)

Question: Dwelling type. NOTE: Question not asked in 1972-1981.

Responses: 1 = Trailer
2 = Detached single family house
3 = 2-family house, 2 units side by side
4 = 2-family house, 2 units one above the other
5 = Detached 3-4 family house
6 = Row house (3 or more units in an attached row)
7 = Apartment (5 or more units, 3 stories or less)
8 = Apartment (5 or more units, 4 stories or more)
9 = Apartment in a partly commercial structure
10 = Other

		YEAR							
AGE	RESP	'82	'83	'84	'85	'86	'87	'88	'89
54-59	1	6%	6%	4%	9%	8%	6%	7%	8%
	2	73	79	76	72	73	82	67	76
	3	2	2	4	2	0	2	1	1
	4	3	3	3	2	4	1	4	1
	5	1	1	3	2	0	0	0	1
	6	7	3	3	4	6	3	8	4
	7	3	2	4	6	6	4	6	4
	8	3	3	2	4	2	1	6	0
	9	2	1	0	0	0	0	0	0
	10	0	0	1	0	0	0	0	4
# SURVEYED		144	132	113	132	97	96	83	97
AGE	RESP	'82	'83	'84	'85	'86	'87	'88	'89
60-65	1	8%	6%	8%	8%	9%	10%	10%	10%
	2	66	73	76	68	71	74	65	75
	3	5	2	1	4	4	1	3	3
	4	4	5	2	0	2	2	3	3
	5	2	0	0	0	1	0	0	2
	6	3	6	5	5	5	9	3	3
	7	10	4	5	8	6	1	12	4
	8	2	3	0	3	1	2	2	1
	9	0	1	1	4	0	0	1	0
	10	0	0	2	1	1	1	1	0
# SURVEYED		116	130	113	130	114	99	116	109

		YEAR							
AGE	RESP	'82	'83	'84	'85	'86	'87	'88	'89
66+	1	8%	7%	8%	8%	6%	8%	12%	11%
	2	66	67	67	64	68	69	62	69
	3	4	4	3	3	2	3	1	2
	4	4	3	3	5	3	5	2	2
	5	2	1	2	1	1	1	2	1
	6	6	3	3	2	5	4	8	2
	7	5	8	6	8	7	3	5	7
	8	4	5	6	7	5	5	7	4
	9	0	2	1	1	1	1	0	0
	10	0	1	1	0	2	2	1	3
# SURVEYED		256	239	231	260	262	252	277	273

****

LIVE WITH PARENTS AT 16

TABLE I: LIVE WITH PARENTS AT 16 -- BY TOTAL POPULATION

Question: Were you living with both your own mother and father around the time you were 16? If not, with whom were you living around that time? NOTE: Question was not asked in 1972.

Responses:
0 = Other
1 = Both own mother and father
2 = Father and stepmother
3 = Mother and stepfather
4 = Father only
5 = Mother only
6 = Some other male relative
7 = Some other female relative
8 = Other arrangement with relatives

	YEAR															
RESPONSE	'72	'73	'74	'75	'76	'77	'78	'80	'82	'83	'84	'85	'86	'87	'88	'89
0	0%	2%	3%	2%	2%	1%	2%	3%	2%	1%	2%	2%	2%	1%	2%	3%
1	74	78	76	77	76	74	76	73	76	77	75	76	74	77	72	75
2	2	2	2	2	2	2	1	2	2	2	1	2	1	2	2	1
3	3	3	3	6	3	5	4	5	4	4	5	3	5	3	6	4
4	2	3	2	2	3	3	2	2	3	2	2	2	2	2	2	2
5	11	8	10	8	11	11	11	12	11	11	10	10	12	11	12	11
6	1	0	1	0	0	0	0	1	0	0	0	0	0	0	0	0
7	2	1	1	1	1	1	1	2	1	2	2	1	1	2	1	2
8	6	3	2	2	2	2	2	1	2	2	2	3	2	2	2	1
# SURVEYED	1613	1502	1484	1490	1496	1528	1531	1468	1504	1599	1472	1534	1470	1464	1481	1536

TABLE II: LIVE WITH PARENTS AT 16 -- BY SEX

Question: Were you living with both your own mother and father around the time you were 16? If not, with whom were you living around that time? NOTE: Question was not asked in 1972.

Responses:
0 = Other
1 = Both own mother and father
2 = Father and stepmother
3 = Mother and stepfather
4 = Father only
5 = Mother only
6 = Some other male relative
7 = Some other female relative
8 = Other arrangement with relatives

		YEAR															
SEX	RESP	'72	'73	'74	'75	'76	'77	'78	'80	'82	'83	'84	'85	'86	'87	'88	'89
M	0	0%	2%	3%	2%	2%	1%	2%	4%	2%	1%	3%	2%	3%	1%	2%	3%
A	1	77	80	76	76	78	76	79	72	78	78	74	76	76	80	73	78
L	2	1	2	1	3	1	2	1	2	2	2	2	2	1	2	2	1
E	3	2	3	3	5	3	5	4	5	2	4	6	3	6	3	6	2
	4	2	2	3	2	2	3	2	2	2	3	3	2	1	2	2	3
	5	11	7	10	8	11	10	9	12	10	10	9	10	10	10	11	10
	6	1	1	1	0	0	0	0	1	0	0	0	1	0	0	0	0
	7	1	1	1	1	1	1	1	2	1	1	1	1	2	1	1	1
	8	5	2	2	2	2	2	2	2	2	1	3	2	3	1	3	1
# SURVEYED		807	700	691	670	667	693	642	641	638	690	597	688	621	640	638	660
SEX	RESP	'72	'73	'74	'75	'76	'77	'78	'80	'82	'83	'84	'85	'86	'87	'88	'89
F	0	0%	2%	2%	1%	2%	1%	1%	2%	2%	2%	2%	2%	2%	1%	2%	3%
E	1	72	76	76	77	75	73	73	74	74	75	75	75	72	74	72	73
M	2	2	2	2	2	3	2	1	2	1	2	1	3	2	2	2	1
A	3	4	3	4	6	3	5	4	4	5	4	4	3	4	3	6	5
L	4	2	4	2	1	3	3	2	2	3	2	2	2	2	2	2	2
E	5	11	9	11	9	11	13	13	12	11	11	11	10	14	12	12	12
	6	1	0	1	0	0	0	0	0	0	0	0	0	0	0	0	0
	7	2	1	1	1	1	1	2	1	2	2	2	1	1	2	1	2
	8	7	3	2	2	3	2	3	1	2	3	2	3	2	3	2	2
# SURVEYED		806	802	793	820	829	835	889	827	866	909	875	846	849	824	843	876

TABLE III: LIVE WITH PARENTS AT 16 -- BY RACE

Question: Were you living with both your own mother and father around the time you were 16? If not, with whom were you living around that time? NOTE: Question was not asked in 1972.

Responses: 0 = Other; 1 = Both own mother and father; 2 = Father and stepmother; 3 = Mother and stepfather; 4 = Father only; 5 = Mother only; 6 = Some other male relative; 7 = Some other female relative; 8 = Other arrangement with relatives

		YEAR															
RACE	RESP	'72	'73	'74	'75	'76	'77	'78	'80	'82	'83	'84	'85	'86	'87	'88	'89
WHITE	0	0%	1%	3%	2%	2%	1%	2%	3%	2%	1%	2%	2%	2%	1%	2%	3%
	1	77	80	79	79	79	77	77	75	78	80	78	78	77	80	76	78
	2	2	2	2	2	2	2	1	2	2	2	1	2	1	2	2	1
	3	3	3	2	5	3	5	4	5	3	3	5	3	4	3	6	4
	4	2	3	3	2	3	2	2	2	3	2	2	2	2	2	2	2
	5	9	8	9	7	10	10	10	11	9	9	9	9	10	8	9	10
	6	1	0	1	0	0	0	0	1	0	0	0	1	0	0	0	0
	7	1	1	1	1	1	1	1	1	1	1	1	1	1	1	1	1
	8	5	2	2	2	2	2	2	1	2	2	2	2	2	2	2	1
# SURVEYED		1348	1307	1304	1323	1359	1337	1357	1318	1322	1416	1251	1338	1249	1221	1234	1318
RACE	RESP	'72	'73	'74	'75	'76	'77	'78	'80	'82	'83	'84	'85	'86	'87	'88	'89
BLACK	0	0%	3%	3%	3%	2%	4%	0%	3%	1%	4%	4%	2%	3%	2%	2%	4%
	1	59	68	55	55	49	55	58	56	59	52	55	58	51	57	45	52
	2	1	2	2	4	5	3	2	1	1	2	2	2	3	2	1	1
	3	4	3	9	10	6	5	4	6	5	7	7	5	8	2	10	6
	4	3	3	1	2	5	7	1	1	3	4	3	3	2	2	4	4
	5	21	13	20	15	22	21	24	23	24	22	20	19	27	27	28	23
	6	1	1	1	1	2	0	1	0	0	0	0	0	1	2	0	1
	7	4	3	3	4	6	2	3	5	3	6	5	7	3	4	5	6
	8	7	5	5	6	3	4	7	5	4	3	4	5	4	3	5	4
# SURVEYED		261	182	173	163	128	176	158	140	155	165	169	152	184	190	186	157
RACE	RESP	'72	'73	'74	'75	'76	'77	'78	'80	'82	'83	'84	'85	'86	'87	'88	'89
OTHER	0	0%	0%	0%	0%	0%	7%	0%	10%	0%	6%	6%	0%	3%	0%	2%	2%
	1	75	77	86	50	67	67	94	30	63	78	62	75	78	66	85	75
	2	0	0	0	25	0	0	0	0	4	0	2	2	5	6	3	2
	3	25	0	0	0	11	0	0	0	4	0	4	2	5	2	2	2
	4	0	15	0	0	0	7	0	0	4	6	4	0	0	4	3	2
	5	0	8	0	25	22	7	0	40	15	6	13	14	8	13	5	15
	6	0	0	0	0	0	0	0	10	0	0	0	0	0	2	0	0
	7	0	0	14	0	0	7	0	10	7	6	4	0	0	4	0	2
	8	0	0	0	0	0	7	6	0	4	0	6	7	0	4	0	2
# SURVEYED		4	13	7	4	9	15	16	10	27	18	52	44	37	53	61	61

TABLE IV: LIVE WITH PARENTS AT 16 -- BY AGE

Question: Were you living with both your own mother and father around the time you were 16? If not, with whom were you living around that time? NOTE: Question was not asked in 1972.

Responses:

0 = Other	1 = Both own mother and father	2 = Father and stepmother
3 = Mother and stepfather	4 = Father only	5 = Mother only
6 = Some other male relative	7 = Some other female relative	8 = Other arrangement with relatives

		YEAR															
AGE	RESP	'72	'73	'74	'75	'76	'77	'78	'80	'82	'83	'84	'85	'86	'87	'88	'89
18-23	0	0%	1%	2%	1%	2%	1%	2%	1%	1%	2%	4%	2%	1%	0%	1%	2%
	1	79	74	77	78	75	71	71	70	69	77	71	72	62	62	60	62
	2	0	4	1	1	2	1	1	0	2	2	2	2	1	3	2	4
	3	5	9	7	4	2	9	7	8	9	5	4	7	14	4	12	6
	4	1	2	1	2	2	2	2	1	1	2	3	1	4	4	4	3
	5	11	7	10	12	15	15	14	17	14	11	14	12	16	21	17	20
	6	0	0	1	0	0	1	0	0	0	1	0	1	0	1	0	0
	7	0	1	1	1	1	1	1	3	2	0	1	1	1	2	1	3
	8	4	3	0	2	0	1	1	0	2	1	2	2	2	3	3	0
# SURVEYED		169	171	168	173	162	164	163	155	148	128	160	133	108	126	141	137
AGE	RESP	'72	'73	'74	'75	'76	'77	'78	'80	'82	'83	'84	'85	'86	'87	'88	'89
24-29	0	0%	0%	1%	0%	0%	0%	2%	2%	2%	2%	2%	2%	2%	1%	2%	2%
	1	74	81	79	79	79	74	77	74	72	79	74	73	76	76	70	70
	2	1	1	2	1	1	1	2	0	2	2	2	2	0	3	1	1
	3	3	3	2	6	5	8	4	5	4	4	5	5	6	3	8	7
	4	3	3	1	0	2	2	2	1	3	1	2	3	1	1	1	1
	5	13	8	13	11	10	12	12	14	14	10	13	10	11	12	14	16
	6	0	0	0	0	0	0	0	1	0	0	0	1	1	0	0	0
	7	1	1	0	1	0	0	2	0	1	2	1	1	1	3	2	1
	8	4	2	1	0	2	2	1	1	2	0	1	3	1	2	2	1
# SURVEYED		231	212	212	232	223	204	243	202	246	287	232	217	218	193	215	202
AGE	RESP	'72	'73	'74	'75	'76	'77	'78	'80	'82	'83	'84	'85	'86	'87	'88	'89
30-35	0	0%	1%	3%	0%	0%	2%	0%	2%	2%	0%	2%	3%	2%	2%	3%	2%
	1	78	81	76	75	80	76	80	75	78	75	78	77	73	77	74	81
	2	2	3	1	1	2	0	2	0	0	0	1	3	1	1	1	0
	3	3	2	1	11	4	5	4	6	4	7	5	3	5	3	5	2
	4	2	1	1	0	4	4	1	2	2	2	3	2	1	2	2	1
	5	10	7	14	11	8	10	8	12	12	14	9	8	14	11	10	10
	6	1	0	1	1	0	1	1	1	0	0	0	0	0	0	0	0
	7	0	2	1	1	0	2	0	1	0	2	2	1	1	1	3	2
	8	4	2	3	2	2	1	3	0	1	1	3	2	2	2	3	1
# SURVEYED		187	167	175	171	186	188	230	215	204	236	200	212	221	221	195	212

TABLE IV: LIVE WITH PARENTS AT 16 -- BY AGE (Continued)

Question: Were you living with both your own mother and father around the time you were 16? If not, with whom were you living around that time? NOTE: Question was not asked in 1972.

Responses:
0 = Other
1 = Both own mother and father
2 = Father and stepmother
3 = Mother and stepfather
4 = Father only
5 = Mother only
6 = Some other male relative
7 = Some other female relative
8 = Other arrangement with relatives

		YEAR															
AGE	RESP	'72	'73	'74	'75	'76	'77	'78	'80	'82	'83	'84	'85	'86	'87	'88	'89
36-41	0	0%	1%	1%	4%	2%	1%	1%	2%	2%	1%	2%	1%	1%	1%	1%	4%
	1	73	80	76	73	71	78	74	79	75	79	80	80	73	81	81	79
	2	3	1	1	1	4	1	1	1	2	2	1	1	2	1	2	1
	3	2	3	7	6	3	5	6	5	3	3	5	4	5	5	4	4
	4	0	1	1	2	2	2	1	2	3	1	1	1	2	1	0	2
	5	13	11	9	8	16	9	14	9	10	12	7	8	14	11	11	8
	6	1	0	1	0	0	1	0	0	1	0	0	0	0	1	0	1
	7	2	1	2	1	1	1	1	0	1	1	1	2	1	1	1	1
	8	5	2	3	3	1	2	3	2	1	2	4	3	2	0	2	1
# SURVEYED		128	175	152	154	158	167	160	150	146	173	187	184	188	186	193	198
AGE	RESP	'72	'73	'74	'75	'76	'77	'78	'80	'82	'83	'84	'85	'86	'87	'88	'89
42-47	0	0%	4%	4%	2%	4%	2%	3%	5%	2%	1%	1%	1%	3%	1%	1%	2%
	1	77	79	72	80	72	73	73	71	77	79	74	75	78	81	76	71
	2	1	0	3	3	1	1	3	3	3	1	3	2	1	1	1	1
	3	3	1	1	2	3	6	3	6	3	4	6	3	6	4	8	6
	4	1	3	3	3	4	3	2	0	2	2	0	1	1	1	3	2
	5	9	10	11	6	10	12	15	14	12	8	13	13	9	10	8	12
	6	1	0	1	0	1	0	0	0	0	0	1	1	0	0	1	1
	7	2	0	3	1	3	1	1	0	0	1	1	0	1	1	0	1
	8	6	2	3	3	4	1	2	2	2	3	1	5	1	1	3	3
# SURVEYED		186	145	151	143	114	147	119	117	119	145	126	124	141	157	157	161
AGE	RESP	'72	'73	'74	'75	'76	'77	'78	'80	'82	'83	'84	'85	'86	'87	'88	'89
48-53	0	0%	2%	3%	3%	2%	2%	4%	2%	2%	0%	0%	4%	4%	1%	3%	3%
	1	71	75	76	81	74	75	69	68	83	76	75	82	71	83	63	82
	2	4	3	1	3	1	3	1	4	1	1	0	2	2	2	4	1
	3	4	1	3	4	4	5	2	2	3	4	5	1	1	3	8	1
	4	3	5	1	1	2	1	2	2	3	4	2	0	2	0	8	0
	5	12	9	10	4	11	10	17	14	7	10	11	11	16	8	10	12
	6	0	1	1	0	0	0	0	1	0	0	1	0	1	0	0	0
	7	2	1	2	1	2	1	2	2	0	1	5	1	2	1	2	1
	8	5	3	2	2	4	3	5	3	2	3	2	1	2	3	2	1
# SURVEYED		189	151	146	141	133	153	133	123	112	116	102	131	108	126	92	138

TABLE IV : LIVE WITH PARENTS AT 16 -- BY AGE (Continued)

Question: Were you living with both your own mother and father around the time you were 16? If not, with whom were you living around that time? NOTE: Question was not asked in 1972.

Responses: 0 = Other; 1 = Both own mother and father; 2 = Father and stepmother; 3 = Mother and stepfather; 4 = Father only; 5 = Mother only; 6 = Some other male relative; 7 = Some other female relative; 8 = Other arrangement with relatives

		YEAR															
AGE	RES	'72	'73	'74	'75	'76	'77	'78	'80	'82	'83	'84	'85	'86	'87	'88	'89
54-59	0	0%	1%	3%	2%	2%	4%	2%	3%	1%	4%	4%	2%	3%	0%	4%	7%
	1	78	76	82	77	80	73	77	72	80	76	73	77	74	74	64	70
	2	1	3	1	3	2	2	1	1	1	4	2	2	1	3	5	0
	3	3	3	1	8	2	2	1	4	3	2	5	1	4	4	7	4
	4	2	5	2	2	2	2	4	4	2	1	4	3	0	2	2	1
	5	6	8	9	3	9	13	8	10	8	10	10	9	15	10	15	14
	6	1	0	0	0	0	0	0	0	1	0	0	0	0	1	0	0
	7	3	1	1	1	2	1	1	3	2	3	1	4	1	1	0	0
	8	6	4	1	4	2	4	5	1	2	0	3	2	2	4	4	4
# SURVEYED		156	157	139	126	129	168	137	136	144	134	114	134	99	98	85	99
AGE	RESP	'72	'73	'74	'75	'76	'77	'78	'80	'82	'83	'84	'85	'86	'87	'88	'89
60-65	0	0%	2%	5%	4%	4%	0%	2%	6%	3%	2%	4%	1%	1%	1%	3%	5%
	1	65	80	69	74	73	79	77	71	72	77	76	76	83	75	76	78
	2	2	3	4	4	2	3	5	3	4	1	1	0	3	1	3	0
	3	3	2	5	4	1	3	4	3	2	1	8	1	3	3	4	2
	4	2	5	6	2	4	3	2	1	1	3	2	2	0	2	3	3
	5	15	3	10	9	11	8	6	12	8	11	7	14	6	13	10	8
	6	2	1	0	1	0	0	1	1	1	0	1	1	0	0	0	0
	7	2	1	1	1	1	0	2	2	5	2	1	2	1	1	1	4
	8	8	3	1	2	2	3	3	2	5	3	1	5	3	4	2	0
# SURVEYED		144	121	108	113	134	117	107	119	116	132	113	131	115	101	119	111
AGE	RESP	'72	'73	'74	'75	'76	'77	'78	'80	'82	'83	'84	'85	'86	'87	'88	'89
66+	0	0%	2%	3%	1%	2%	1%	2%	4%	2%	1%	2%	2%	3%	3%	2%	2%
	1	72	77	74	72	77	71	78	73	79	73	73	71	71	76	76	78
	2	1	2	2	4	2	4	0	3	2	3	2	4	1	4	1	1
	3	3	2	2	3	2	2	1	3	2	2	3	4	2	0	4	3
	4	6	3	6	3	3	5	4	3	4	5	4	7	4	4	3	6
	5	8	9	8	8	9	12	9	9	9	10	9	8	11	8	10	6
	6	0	2	1	1	1	0	0	0	0	0	1	0	0	0	0	0
	7	2	1	1	3	1	1	3	3	0	1	3	1	2	2	1	2
	8	8	3	3	4	4	4	2	2	2	5	3	2	6	2	3	1
# SURVEYED		218	199	227	232	251	213	232	242	257	241	232	261	265	253	280	275

****

FAMILY SITUATION AT 16

TABLE I: FAMILY SITUATION AT 16 -- BY TOTAL POPULATION

Question: If you were not living with both your own mother and father around the time you were 16, what happened?

Responses: 1 = One or both parents died 2 = Parents divorced or separated
3 = Father absent in armed forces 4 = One or both parents in an institution 5 = Other

	YEAR														
RESPONSE	'73	'74	'75	'76	'77	'78	'80	'82	'83	'84	'85	'86	'87	'88	'89
1	60%	59%	53%	61%	55%	55%	55%	48%	51%	49%	48%	45%	43%	41%	37%
2	32	34	40	35	37	36	33	44	43	40	40	44	40	47	47
3	0	0	0	0	0	0	0	0	0	0	0	0	1	0	0
4	1	0	1	1	1	1	0	1	0	1	0	0	0	0	1
5	6	7	7	3	6	9	12	8	7	10	13	11	16	11	15
# SURVEYED	329	355	346	350	389	370	395	360	369	344	364	367	323	386	3

TABLE II: FAMILY SITUATION AT 16 -- BY SEX

Question: If you were not living with both your own mother and father around the time you were 16, what happened?

Responses: 1 = One or both parents died 2 = Parents divorced or separated
3 = Father absent in armed forces 4 = One or both parents in an institution 5 = Other

		YEAR														
SEX	RESP	'73	'74	'75	'76	'77	'78	'80	'82	'83	'84	'85	'86	'87	'88	'89
M	1	59%	60%	55%	62%	53%	62%	55%	50%	52%	43%	47%	46%	47%	40%	36%
A	2	31	32	36	34	37	31	34	43	42	43	40	42	35	47	48
L	3	1	1	0	0	0	0	0	0	0	0	0	1	0	0	0
E	4	1	0	0	0	1	0	0	1	0	1	0	0	0	1	1
	5	8	7	9	3	9	8	11	6	5	12	13	11	19	13	14
# SURVEYED		140	164	156	143	161	131	181	140	149	145	159	138	124	164	138
SEX	RESP	'73	'74	'75	'76	'77	'78	'80	'82	'83	'84	'85	'86	'87	'88	'89
F	1	62%	57%	51%	61%	57%	51%	55%	46%	50%	53%	48%	44%	41%	41%	38%
E	2	33	36	43	35	37	38	33	45	43	37	40	45	44	48	46
M	3	0	0	0	0	0	0	0	0	0	0	0	0	1	0	0
A	4	0	0	1	1	1	1	0	0	0	1	0	0	1	0	0
L	5	5	7	5	3	4	10	12	8	7	9	12	11	14	10	16
E																
# SURVEYED		189	191	190	207	228	239	214	220	220	199	205	229	199	222	233

TABLE III: FAMILY SITUATION AT 16 -- BY RACE

Question: If you were not living with both your own mother and father around the time you were 16, what happened?

Responses: 1 = One or both parents died; 2 = Parents divorced or separated; 3 = Father absent in armed forces; 4 = One or both parents in an institution; 5 = Other

		YEAR														
RACE	RESP	'73	'74	'75	'76	'77	'78	'80	'82	'83	'84	'85	'86	'87	'88	'89
WHITE	**1**	61%	61%	55%	64%	55%	58%	55%	49%	53%	49%	49%	48%	47%	42%	39%
	2	32	32	39	34	38	34	33	42	41	41	39	42	41	46	47
	3	0	0	0	0	0	0	0	0	0	0	0	0	1	0	0
	4	1	0	0	1	1	1	0	1	0	1	0	0	0	0	1
	5	6	6	6	2	6	8	11	8	5	9	11	10	11	12	14
# SURVEYED		266	278	272	286	307	304	327	289	286	258	292	273	229	284	283
RACE	RESP	'73	'74	'75	'76	'77	'78	'80	'82	'83	'84	'85	'86	'87	'88	'89
BALCK	**1**	58%	50%	45%	51%	56%	42%	52%	46%	42%	49%	39%	35%	30%	35%	32%
	2	32	41	44	39	36	43	36	49	49	38	41	49	42	54	49
	3	0	0	0	0	0	0	0	0	0	0	0	0	0	1	0
	4	0	0	1	0	1	0	0	0	0	0	0	0	0	0	0
	5	10	9	10	10	6	15	11	5	9	13	20	16	29	11	19
# SURVEYED		60	76	73	61	77	65	61	61	79	68	61	86	77	95	74
RACE	RESP	'73	'74	'75	'76	'77	'78	'80	'82	'83	'84	'85	'86	'87	'88	'89
OTHER	**1**	67%	0%	100%	67%	60%	0%	57%	20%	50%	56%	45%	63%	53%	71%	43%
	2	33	0	0	33	0	0	14	60	0	28	36	38	29	14	36
	3	0	0	0	0	0	0	0	0	0	0	0	0	0	0	0
	4	0	0	0	0	0	0	0	0	0	0	0	0	0	0	0
	5	0	100	0	0	40	100	29	20	50	17	18	0	18	14	21
# SURVEYED		3	1	1	3	5	1	7	10	4	18	11	8	17	7	14

TABLE IV: FAMILY SITUATION AT 16 -- BY AGE

Question: If you were not living with both your own mother and father around the time you were 16, what happened?

Responses: 1 = One or both parents died 2 = Parents divorced or separated
3 = Father absent in armed forces 4 = One or both parents in an institution 5 = Other

		YEAR														
AGE	RESP	'73	'74	'75	'76	'77	'78	'80	'82	'83	'84	'85	'86	'87	'88	'89
18-23	1	34%	32%	19%	43%	40%	31%	27%	28%	24%	33%	14%	21%	16%	21%	23%
	2	59	57	76	51	53	54	64	67	66	65	78	72	64	69	69
	3	2	0	0	0	0	0	0	0	0	0	0	0	0	0	0
	4	0	0	0	0	0	0	0	0	0	0	0	0	0	0	0
	5	5	11	5	5	6	15	9	4	10	2	8	8	20	10	8
# SURVEYED		44	37	37	37	47	48	45	46	29	43	37	39	44	52	52
AGE	RESP	'73	'74	'75	'76	'77	'78	'80	'82	'83	'84	'85	'86	'87	'88	'89
24-29	1	50%	42%	38%	38%	35%	27%	36%	22%	36%	34%	34%	37%	30%	20%	17%
	2	43	53	58	53	60	65	48	65	53	55	54	53	59	66	69
	3	0	0	0	2	0	0	2	0	0	0	0	0	0	0	0
	4	3	0	2	0	0	0	0	0	0	0	0	0	0	0	0
	5	5	4	2	7	6	7	14	13	10	10	13	10	11	14	14
# SURVEYED		40	45	48	45	52	55	50	69	58	58	56	49	44	64	58
AGE	RESP	'73	'74	'75	'76	'77	'78	'80	'82	'83	'84	'85	'86	'87	'88	'89
30-35	1	48%	50%	31%	49%	40%	40%	47%	34%	36%	30%	37%	25%	25%	30%	28%
	2	39	38	62	46	53	44	45	61	58	51	52	63	48	46	55
	3	0	0	0	0	0	0	0	0	0	0	0	0	2	0	0
	4	3	0	0	5	0	0	0	0	0	0	0	0	0	0	0
	5	10	12	7	0	7	16	8	5	7	19	11	12	25	24	18
# SURVEYED		31	42	42	37	45	45	53	44	59	43	46	57	48	46	40
AGE	RESP	'73	'74	'75	'76	'77	'78	'80	'82	'83	'84	'85	'86	'87	'88	'89
36-41	1	40%	47%	51%	52%	49%	63%	44%	54%	42%	52%	29%	36%	42%	31%	27%
	2	51	47	44	41	43	29	41	40	53	36	53	53	42	57	54
	3	0	3	0	0	0	0	0	0	0	0	0	0	0	0	0
	4	0	0	0	0	3	2	0	0	0	0	0	0	0	3	2
	5	9	3	5	7	5	5	16	6	6	12	18	11	15	9	17
# SURVEYED		35	36	41	44	37	41	32	35	36	33	34	47	33	35	41
AGE	RESP	'73	'74	'75	'76	'77	'78	'80	'82	'83	'84	'85	'86	'87	'88	'89
42-47	1	61%	60%	69%	66%	53%	63%	56%	37%	40%	55%	53%	41%	43%	38%	36%
	2	26	31	28	31	37	25	35	52	53	39	43	48	43	50	45
	3	0	0	0	0	0	0	0	4	0	0	0	0	0	0	0
	4	0	0	0	0	3	0	0	0	0	0	0	0	0	0	0
	5	13	10	3	3	8	13	9	7	7	6	3	10	14	12	19
# SURVEYED		31	42	29	32	38	32	34	27	30	31	30	29	28	34	47

TABLE IV: FAMILY SITUATION AT 16 -- BY AGE (Continued)

Question: If you were not living with both your own mother and father around the time you were 16, what happened?

Responses: 1 = One or both parents died; 2 = Parents divorced or separated; 3 = Father absent in armed forces; 4 = One or both parents in an institution; 5 = Other

		YEAR														
AGE	RESP	'73	'74	'75	'76	'77	'78	'80	'82	'83	'84	'85	'86	'87	'88	'89
48-53	1	76%	66%	54%	56%	56%	63%	72%	63%	64%	42%	43%	63%	55%	44%	57%
	2	22	23	35	41	31	30	18	32	32	38	35	23	36	47	26
	3	0	0	0	0	3	0	0	0	0	0	0	0	0	0	0
	4	0	0	0	0	3	0	0	5	0	0	0	0	0	0	0
	5	3	11	12	3	8	8	10	0	4	21	22	13	9	9	17
# SURVEYED		37	35	26	34	39	40	39	19	28	24	23	30	22	32	23
AGE	RESP	'73	'74	'75	'76	'77	'78	'80	'82	'83	'84	'85	'86	'87	'88	'89
54-59	1	76%	75%	76%	81%	65%	60%	68%	59%	56%	78%	52%	65%	55%	72%	52%
	2	21	21	21	19	23	30	21	28	41	15	29	15	36	28	28
	3	0	0	0	0	0	0	0	0	0	0	0	0	5	0	0
	4	0	0	0	0	2	3	0	3	0	0	3	0	0	0	0
	5	3	4	3	0	9	7	11	10	3	7	16	19	5	0	21
# SURVEYED		38	24	29	26	43	30	38	29	32	27	31	26	22	29	29
AGE	RESP	'73	'74	'75	'76	'77	'78	'80	'82	'83	'84	'85	'86	'87	'88	'89
60-65	1	88%	74%	71%	78%	75%	84%	68%	64%	69%	59%	71%	53%	64%	38%	41%
	2	8	24	21	22	21	12	24	21	28	30	13	32	23	48	32
	3	0	0	0	0	0	0	0	0	0	0	0	0	0	0	0
	4	0	0	4	0	0	0	0	0	0	0	0	0	0	0	0
	5	4	3	4	0	4	4	9	15	3	11	16	16	14	14	27
# SURVEYED		24	34	28	36	24	25	34	33	29	27	31	19	22	29	22
AGE	RESP	'73	'74	'75	'76	'77	'78	'80	'82	'83	'84	'85	'86	'87	'88	'89
66+	1	79%	80%	72%	88%	85%	83%	74%	85%	85%	70%	77%	71%	72%	76%	71%
	2	13	15	12	11	10	10	9	11	11	18	12	20	10	16	19
	3	0	0	0	0	0	0	0	0	0	0	0	1	0	2	0
	4	0	0	0	0	0	0	0	0	2	4	0	0	2	0	2
	5	9	5	15	2	5	8	17	4	3	9	11	7	16	6	9
# SURVEYED		47	59	65	57	62	52	66	55	65	57	74	70	58	63	58

****

CITY/PLACE OF RESIDENCE AT AGE 16

TABLE I: CITY/PLACE OF RESIDENCE AT AGE 16 -- BY TOTAL POPULATION

Question: If you lived in the same state when you were 16 as you do now, were you living in this same (city/town/county)?

Responses: SC = Same state, same city; DC = Same state, different city; DS = Different state

	YEAR															
RESPONSE	'72	'73	'74	'75	'76	'77	'78	'80	'82	'83	'84	'85	'86	'87	'88	'89
SC	46%	41%	43%	43%	43%	43%	41%	43%	46%	45%	40%	40%	43%	42%	41%	41%
DC	20	24	27	25	26	25	29	26	26	24	27	28	25	25	25	26
DS	33	35	30	31	31	32	31	31	28	31	33	32	32	33	34	33
# SURVEYED	1562	1473	1438	1426	1462	1457	1521	1462	1499	1578	1464	1527	1449	1448	1465	1528

TABLE II: CITY/PLACE OF RESIDENCE AT AGE 16 -- BY SEX

Question: If you lived in the same state when you were 16 as you do now, were you living in this same (city/town/county)?

Responses: SC = Same state, same city; DC = Same state, different city; DS = Different state

		YEAR															
SEX	RESP	'72	'73	'74	'75	'76	'77	'78	'80	'82	'83	'84	'85	'86	'87	'88	'89
M	SC	47%	42%	43%	44%	45%	43%	41%	47%	48%	46%	41%	41%	43%	42%	39%	40%
	DC	19	23	27	24	24	26	26	25	24	26	24	28	25	25	25	24
	DS	33	35	30	32	31	30	32	28	28	28	35	31	31	33	36	36
# SURVEYED		782	687	675	645	653	654	639	638	636	681	595	684	615	633	630	657
SEX	RESP	'72	'73	'74	'75	'76	'77	'78	'80	'82	'83	'84	'85	'86	'87	'88	'89
F	SC	45%	40%	42%	43%	42%	43%	40%	40%	44%	45%	40%	39%	43%	43%	42%	41%
	DC	21	24	28	26	27	25	30	27	28	23	29	28	25	25	25	28
	DS	33	35	30	31	31	32	30	33	28	33	31	33	32	33	32	31
# SURVEYED		780	786	763	781	809	803	882	824	863	897	869	843	834	815	835	871

TABLE III: CITY/PLACE OF RESIDENCE AT AGE 16 -- BY RACE

Question: If you lived in the same state when you were 16 as you do now, were you living in this same (city/town/county)?

Responses: SC = Same state, same city; DC = Same state, different city; DS = Different state

		YEAR															
RACE	RESP	'72	'73	'74	'75	'76	'77	'78	'80	'82	'83	'84	'85	'86	'87	'88	'89
WHITE	SC	46%	42%	41%	44%	44%	43%	40%	43%	45%	44%	40%	40%	41%	41%	40%	40%
	DC	22	25	29	26	27	27	30	28	28	26	29	30	27	27	28	28
	DS	32	33	30	30	29	30	30	30	27	30	31	31	32	32	33	32
# SURVEYED		1314	1282	1260	1263	1332	1283	1348	1313	1318	1397	1244	1335	1232	1210	1219	1311
RACE	RESP	'72	'73	'74	'75	'76	'77	'78	'80	'82	'83	'84	'85	'86	'87	'88	'89
BLACK	SC	51%	38%	57%	43%	39%	47%	50%	50%	55%	60%	38%	44%	54%	51%	47%	54%
	DC	9	12	12	17	16	13	20	17	11	10	19	16	14	14	15	13
	DS	39	49	31	40	45	41	30	34	34	30	43	40	32	35	38	34
# SURVEYED		244	178	171	159	121	159	157	139	154	165	169	149	180	186	185	157
RACE	RESP	'72	'73	'74	'75	'76	'77	'78	'80	'82	'83	'84	'85	'86	'87	'88	'89
OTHER	SC	0%	31%	0%	25%	0%	7%	19%	10%	22%	19%	55%	42%	54%	52%	44%	33%
	DC	50	23	43	0	22	7	6	10	22	6	8	9	8	13	11	17
	DS	50	46	57	75	78	87	75	80	56	75	37	49	38	35	44	50
# SURVEYED		4	13	7	4	9	15	16	10	27	16	51	43	37	52	61	60

TABLE IV: CITY/PLACE OF RESIDENCE AT AGE 16 -- BY AGE

Question: If you lived in the same state when you were 16 as you do now, were you living in this same (city/town/county)?

Responses: SC = Same state, same city DC = Same state, different city DS = Different state

		YEAR															
AGE	RESP	'72	'73	'74	'75	'76	'77	'78	'80	'82	'83	'84	'85	'86	'87	'88	'89
18-23	SC	66%	60%	64%	65%	75%	67%	64%	69%	68%	68%	54%	53%	70%	62%	63%	67%
	DC	15	23	20	18	9	19	20	14	16	22	25	31	16	21	15	17
	DS	18	17	16	17	16	15	16	18	16	10	21	16	14	16	22	16
# SURVEYED		163	165	159	161	155	151	163	154	147	128	159	132	105	122	139	137
AGE	RESP	'72	'73	'74	'75	'76	'77	'78	'80	'82	'83	'84	'85	'86	'87	'88	'89
24-29	SC	49%	48%	46%	48%	46%	47%	45%	43%	47%	54%	53%	42%	49%	37%	46%	48%
	DC	20	21	27	26	25	25	27	33	26	22	27	32	24	33	26	26
	DS	31	30	27	26	29	27	28	24	27	24	21	26	27	30	27	27
# SURVEYED		226	211	209	221	222	194	241	201	245	280	232	216	213	193	213	200

TABLE IV: CITY/PLACE OF RESIDENCE AT AGE 16 -- BY AGE (Continued)

Question: If you lived in the same state when you were 16 as you do now, were you living in this same (city/town/county)?

Responses: SC = Same state, same city; DC = Same state, different city; DS = Different state

		YEAR															
AGE	RESP	'72	'73	'74	'75	'76	'77	'78	'80	'82	'83	'84	'85	'86	'87	'88	'89
30-35	SC	44%	35%	40%	44%	42%	44%	37%	40%	49%	46%	38%	43%	51%	47%	45%	44%
	DC	22	29	34	27	28	29	27	25	26	23	30	25	25	22	25	23
	DS	34	36	26	29	30	27	36	35	25	31	33	32	24	31	30	33
# SURVEYED		183	164	166	164	181	181	228	214	204	234	199	210	218	218	194	211
AGE	RESP	'72	'73	'74	'75	'76	'77	'78	'80	'82	'83	'84	'85	'86	'87	'88	'89
36-41	SC	49%	35%	37%	40%	41%	37%	40%	47%	42%	37%	36%	38%	40%	42%	41%	34%
	DC	19	27	24	27	27	29	32	23	31	27	32	30	28	25	29	32
	DS	32	38	39	34	32	34	28	30	28	36	32	31	31	32	30	35
# SURVEYED		122	172	147	149	153	159	160	150	144	171	186	182	186	185	192	197
AGE	RESP	'72	'73	'74	'75	'76	'77	'78	'80	'82	'83	'84	'85	'86	'87	'88	'89
42-47	SC	46%	38%	39%	28%	35%	38%	33%	40%	36%	46%	35%	30%	30%	40%	31%	35%
	DC	21	24	29	34	29	27	26	28	33	28	25	27	29	21	29	33
	DS	33	38	31	38	36	36	41	32	31	26	40	44	41	38	41	32
# SURVEYED		181	140	147	137	113	138	118	117	119	143	126	124	139	156	154	161
AGE	RESP	'72	'73	'74	'75	'76	'77	'78	'80	'82	'83	'84	'85	'86	'87	'88	'89
48-53	SC	43%	37%	41%	42%	37%	39%	35%	35%	39%	37%	30%	41%	39%	31%	32%	33%
	DC	21	22	27	18	27	26	34	29	27	26	26	27	22	32	25	25
	DS	36	41	32	40	36	35	31	36	34	37	43	32	39	37	43	42
# SURVEYED		183	150	140	137	129	148	131	122	112	114	102	131	108	125	91	136
AGE	RESP	'72	'73	'74	'75	'76	'77	'78	'80	'82	'83	'84	'85	'86	'87	'88	'89
54-59	SC	48%	37%	44%	45%	34%	45%	39%	44%	43%	43%	32%	35%	37%	40%	26%	32%
	DC	22	21	27	26	23	19	29	23	25	20	28	31	25	25	36	33
	DS	30	42	29	29	43	36	32	33	31	36	40	34	38	35	38	34
# SURVEYED		148	151	136	121	125	157	136	135	143	132	113	133	95	96	84	99
AGE	RESP	'72	'73	'74	'75	'76	'77	'78	'80	'82	'83	'84	'85	'86	'87	'88	'89
60-65	SC	39%	43%	39%	34%	41%	27%	41%	37%	36%	38%	34%	37%	34%	38%	34%	33%
	DC	22	26	28	24	30	40	27	24	29	29	23	27	29	20	23	27
	DS	40	31	33	42	29	33	32	39	34	33	44	36	37	42	43	40
# SURVEYED		139	117	106	108	131	115	107	118	116	131	110	131	115	98	118	109
AGE	RESP	'72	'73	'74	'75	'76	'77	'78	'80	'82	'83	'84	'85	'86	'87	'88	'89
66+	SC	36%	35%	36%	39%	37%	40%	31%	36%	44%	38%	37%	40%	37%	41%	38%	38%
	DC	19	21	28	25	30	20	33	34	25	22	25	23	24	23	23	24
	DS	44	44	36	35	33	41	35	31	31	40	38	37	38	36	39	37
# SURVEYED		212	199	222	224	247	207	230	242	257	238	232	261	263	252	276	275

****

COMMUNITY POPULATION

TABLE I: COMMUNITY POPULATION -- BY TOTAL POPULATION

Question: Population of respondent's place of residence.

Responses: 1 = 1,999 or less; 2 = 2000 - 20,999; 3 = 21,000 - 50,999; 4 = 51,000 - 100,999; 5 = 101,000 - 200,999; 6 = 201,000 - 400,999; 7 = 401,000 - 800,999; 8 = 801,000 - 1,000,999; 9 = 1,001,000+

	YEAR															
RESPONSE	'72	'73	'74	'75	'76	'77	'78	'80	'82	'83	'84	'85	'86	'87	'88	'89
1	7%	6%	6%	6%	10%	7%	8%	6%	6%	7%	6%	6%	4%	6%	5%	5%
2	36	42	43	47	41	45	40	45	46	44	43	43	45	45	41	43
3	12	14	14	12	14	15	14	14	15	16	13	16	12	13	19	17
4	11	10	10	7	11	9	12	9	7	11	8	12	9	8	8	8
5	6	5	5	6	5	6	7	5	5	4	9	7	10	7	10	9
6	6	6	5	6	3	5	6	6	5	6	6	4	6	6	5	6
7	12	8	8	7	6	5	6	8	7	5	7	5	7	7	5	6
8	1	1	1	1	1	1	1	1	1	0	2	1	1	1	1	1
9	10	9	9	8	8	6	5	7	7	6	7	7	6	6	6	6
# SURVEYED	1578	1469	1450	1456	1466	1511	1509	1441	1496	1583	1415	1476	1411	1408	1434	1487

TABLE II: COMMUNITY POPULATION -- BY SEX

Question: Population of respondent's place of residence.

Responses: 1 = 1,999 or less; 2 = 2000 - 20,999; 3 = 21,000 - 50,999; 4 = 51,000 - 100,999; 5 = 101,000 - 200,999; 6 = 201,000 - 400,999; 7 = 401,000 - 800,999; 8 = 801,000 - 1,000,999; 9 = 1,001,000+

		YEAR															
SEX	RESP	'72	'73	'74	'75	'76	'77	'78	'80	'82	'83	'84	'85	'86	'87	'88	'89
M	1	7%	6%	6%	6%	10%	8%	8%	6%	7%	8%	7%	7%	4%	6%	5%	5%
A	2	36	43	44	47	41	46	41	46	47	46	43	43	45	44	43	44
L	3	12	13	13	11	14	16	13	14	13	16	13	15	11	12	18	16
E	4	11	10	10	6	11	7	13	9	8	10	8	13	10	9	8	8
	5	6	5	5	6	5	5	6	4	4	4	9	5	12	7	11	9
	6	6	5	4	7	4	4	6	6	5	5	6	4	6	5	4	7
	7	12	8	8	7	6	6	6	6	7	6	9	5	6	7	4	6
	8	1	1	1	1	1	1	1	1	0	0	1	1	2	2	1	0
	9	9	9	9	8	8	7	6	8	9	6	5	6	6	7	6	5
# SURVEYED		791	685	675	652	651	681	632	631	634	681	576	663	600	612	616	637
SEX	RESP	'72	'73	'74	'75	'76	'77	'78	'80	'82	'83	'84	'85	'86	'87	'88	'89
F	1	6%	5%	6%	5%	9%	7%	8%	5%	6%	7%	5%	6%	3%	6%	6%	5%
E	2	36	41	42	46	41	45	39	44	45	43	44	43	45	45	39	42
M	3	12	15	15	13	14	14	15	14	17	15	12	16	13	14	20	17
A	4	11	10	10	8	12	9	12	9	7	12	8	11	9	8	8	8
L	5	6	5	5	5	6	6	7	5	6	5	9	8	10	7	10	9
E	6	6	6	5	6	3	5	7	6	5	7	7	4	6	6	6	6
	7	13	8	8	7	6	5	6	9	7	5	6	4	7	7	5	6
	8	1	1	1	2	1	2	1	1	1	0	2	0	1	1	1	1
	9	10	9	9	8	8	6	5	7	7	7	8	7	6	6	6	6
# SURVEYED		787	784	775	804	815	830	877	810	862	902	839	813	811	796	818	850

TABLE III: COMMUNITY POPULATION -- BY RACE

Question: Population of respondent's place of residence.

Responses: 1 = 1,999 or less; 2 = 2000 - 20,999; 3 = 21,000 - 50,999; 4 = 51,000 - 100,999; 5 = 101,000 - 200,999; 6 = 201,000 - 400,999; 7 = 401,000 - 800,999; 8 = 801,000 - 1,000,999; 9 = 1,001,000+

		YEAR															
RACE	RESP	'72	'73	'74	'75	'76	'77	'78	'80	'82	'83	'84	'85	'86	'87	'88	'89
WHITE	1	8%	7%	7%	6%	10%	7%	8%	6%	7%	8%	6%	7%	4%	7%	5%	6%
	2	39	46	46	51	43	49	43	47	49	48	45	47	47	48	43	47
	3	13	14	14	13	15	16	15	14	16	15	15	16	13	14	20	18
	4	11	10	11	6	11	9	13	9	7	12	7	12	10	8	7	8
	5	6	4	4	6	5	5	7	4	5	4	10	6	12	7	10	8
	6	5	4	4	6	3	4	6	5	5	5	6	3	5	5	5	5
	7	10	6	6	6	5	5	5	7	5	4	6	4	5	6	4	5
	8	0	1	1	1	1	1	1	1	1	0	2	1	2	2	1	0
	9	8	8	8	6	7	4	3	7	6	5	4	5	3	3	4	3
# SURVEYED		1321	1273	1270	1289	1329	1320	1335	1291	1313	1400	1195	1289	1191	1166	1190	1275
RACE	RESP	'72	'73	'74	'75	'76	'77	'78	'80	'82	'83	'84	'85	'86	'87	'88	'89
BLACK	1	1%	1%	0%	0%	5%	7%	4%	3%	0%	5%	0%	4%	1%	1%	1%	0%
	2	19	17	20	17	27	17	20	32	23	18	33	10	31	26	25	19
	3	7	15	13	9	1	9	10	9	9	19	1	15	7	4	14	9
	4	9	5	3	15	19	9	10	7	11	5	11	14	8	11	14	7
	5	6	11	13	4	5	9	8	11	7	8	5	15	5	8	11	11
	6	14	15	12	13	2	11	11	10	7	16	11	14	9	13	7	13
	7	25	17	19	18	17	11	10	14	22	11	15	10	17	13	10	16
	8	3	0	0	3	4	7	4	4	4	0	1	1	1	1	0	3
	9	15	19	19	21	21	20	22	10	17	18	22	16	20	22	18	22
# SURVEYED		254	183	173	163	128	176	158	140	156	165	168	143	183	189	183	154
RACE	RESP	'72	'73	'74	'75	'76	'77	'78	'80	'82	'83	'84	'85	'86	'87	'88	'89
OTHER	1	0%	0%	14%	0%	11%	7%	6%	0%	0%	0%	15%	2%	0%	13%	13%	0%
	2	33	15	71	25	11	47	19	10	30	11	42	30	54	40	51	19
	3	0	0	0	0	22	0	6	30	11	17	4	16	5	9	10	19
	4	0	8	14	0	11	0	13	0	7	11	6	9	11	9	3	9
	5	0	15	0	0	22	7	13	20	0	0	10	11	0	8	13	19
	6	0	31	0	0	11	7	19	10	7	0	0	2	5	0	2	14
	7	33	8	0	25	0	7	19	10	11	39	2	5	5	9	0	9
	8	0	0	0	0	0	0	0	0	7	0	2	5	3	0	0	0
	9	33	23	0	50	11	27	6	20	26	22	19	20	16	11	8	12
# SURVEYED		3	13	7	4	9	15	16	10	27	18	52	44	37	53	61	58

TABLE IV: COMMUNITY POPULATION -- BY AGE

Question: Population of respondent's place of residence.

Responses: 1 = 1,999 or less 2 = 2000 - 20,999 3 = 21,000 - 50,999
4 = 51,000 - 100,999 5 = 101,000 - 200,999 6 = 201,000 - 400,999
7 = 401,000 - 800,999 8 = 801,000 - 1,000,999 9 = 1,001,000+

		YEAR															
AGE	RESP	'72	'73	'74	'75	'76	'77	'78	'80	'82	'83	'84	'85	'86	'87	'88	'89
18-23	1	4%	4%	5%	3%	8%	10%	7%	4%	5%	9%	6%	6%	2%	4%	8%	2%
	2	33	38	34	47	44	41	41	47	42	41	37	44	37	37	40	49
	3	11	14	14	13	9	15	7	13	18	15	15	18	15	20	14	15
	4	14	11	10	6	13	9	13	5	7	11	10	11	7	10	9	6
	5	7	4	5	9	5	7	8	5	7	7	10	5	15	7	14	8
	6	8	7	8	6	4	3	6	9	6	6	7	4	7	7	4	5
	7	11	9	11	8	8	5	5	6	9	4	6	5	10	11	5	6
	8	1	2	1	3	1	2	2	1	2	0	1	4	2	2	2	0
	9	12	11	11	5	8	8	11	11	5	7	7	3	6	4	5	8
# SURVEYED		168	169	167	171	158	162	163	152	147	127	159	131	106	123	140	132
AGE	RESP	'72	'73	'74	'75	'76	'77	'78	'80	'82	'83	'84	'85	'86	'87	'88	'89
24-29	1	4%	6%	3%	5%	7%	6%	8%	5%	6%	8%	3%	8%	7%	5%	5%	4%
	2	33	36	36	46	39	44	38	44	43	44	42	37	39	38	39	39
	3	12	13	13	11	13	14	14	14	14	18	13	21	17	12	15	19
	4	13	10	14	7	12	8	13	8	6	9	9	11	10	6	6	9
	5	7	4	6	6	8	4	8	6	5	3	11	5	10	9	12	8
	6	6	8	6	8	4	6	9	9	7	6	5	5	5	7	7	9
	7	13	8	8	7	7	6	5	9	9	4	10	3	5	11	5	8
	8	1	3	1	1	0	3	1	0	0	0	2	3	3	4	1	2
	9	11	12	11	10	8	7	5	7	10	8	5	7	5	8	9	4
# SURVEYED		224	208	208	228	224	202	243	197	243	286	224	211	210	189	209	199
AGE	RESP	'72	'73	'74	'75	'76	'77	'78	'80	'82	'83	'84	'85	'86	'87	'88	'89
30-35	1	4%	4%	8%	8%	12%	4%	9%	5%	8%	9%	4%	5%	1%	5%	3%	6%
	2	39	48	44	44	44	46	39	43	40	44	39	46	48	47	45	43
	3	11	17	20	14	12	15	12	14	13	15	13	13	12	12	16	18
	4	8	9	2	5	9	11	11	9	7	13	6	15	8	7	10	10
	5	5	5	6	3	6	6	7	6	6	5	13	6	8	7	12	8
	6	4	5	3	7	2	5	9	5	7	4	10	3	6	6	3	6
	7	15	7	6	10	4	4	7	8	8	6	6	5	10	8	5	5
	8	1	0	2	1	3	1	0	2	1	0	3	0	1	1	0	0
	9	13	6	9	8	9	7	6	8	7	4	6	6	6	7	7	5
# SURVEYED		184	166	172	169	182	188	228	215	203	233	191	208	214	212	191	207

TABLE IV: COMMUNITY POPULATION -- BY AGE (Continued)

Question: Population of respondent's place of residence.

Responses:
1 = 1,999 or less | 2 = 2000 - 20,999 | 3 = 21,000 - 50,999
4 = 51,000 - 100,999 | 5 = 101,000 - 200,999 | 6 = 201,000 - 400,999
7 = 401,000 - 800,999 | 8 = 801,000 - 1,000,999 | 9 = 1,001,000+

		YEAR															
AGE	RESP	'72	'73	'74	'75	'76	'77	'78	'80	'82	'83	'84	'85	'86	'87	'88	'89
36-41	1	12%	7%	7%	3%	8%	5%	8%	4%	5%	6%	5%	8%	3%	5%	3%	3%
	2	30	44	40	52	38	48	45	47	44	40	50	39	44	51	43	42
	3	14	18	11	10	21	15	12	20	17	22	11	17	9	15	22	15
	4	13	6	13	4	9	9	13	9	8	11	8	11	15	10	7	6
	5	4	5	4	8	6	5	3	1	6	2	7	8	10	9	11	16
	6	6	5	3	5	1	5	9	5	6	6	3	2	6	4	3	6
	7	13	8	9	9	6	4	4	6	6	3	7	6	5	4	4	5
	8	0	1	3	3	1	2	2	0	0	0	1	1	2	1	1	2
	9	9	6	11	8	9	7	4	9	7	9	8	8	6	3	7	5
# SURVEYED		124	170	150	153	158	166	159	148	145	172	183	180	178	176	185	193
AGE	RESP	'72	'73	'74	'75	'76	'77	'78	'80	'82	'83	'84	'85	'86	'87	'88	'89
42-47	1	7%	6%	8%	6%	14%	5%	7%	6%	6%	8%	7%	2%	2%	4%	3%	6%
	2	39	35	44	48	38	51	39	46	50	47	48	48	55	46	44	43
	3	11	14	16	11	12	16	18	18	22	12	11	21	9	11	22	15
	4	14	11	10	8	18	8	11	8	7	15	5	13	7	10	10	5
	5	5	9	9	5	4	5	10	4	3	5	8	5	7	8	8	9
	6	6	5	2	8	2	5	7	4	2	5	7	2	4	6	3	6
	7	9	7	5	6	4	5	5	6	5	4	6	5	6	4	7	10
	8	0	0	0	0	0	0	1	1	1	0	1	0	0	1	1	0
	9	9	13	6	9	9	5	3	7	5	5	9	5	9	9	3	6
# SURVEYED		182	144	142	141	114	146	119	114	119	144	120	120	138	155	153	155
AGE	RESP	'72	'73	'74	'75	'76	'77	'78	'80	'82	'83	'84	'85	'86	'87	'88	'89
48-53	1	7%	6%	4%	2%	7%	4%	5%	2%	7%	5%	7%	12%	4%	3%	2%	5%
	2	41	48	50	47	46	53	41	48	46	48	42	35	52	47	40	42
	3	11	19	20	18	12	13	16	9	14	12	14	16	10	14	21	23
	4	5	10	11	7	16	7	16	16	8	14	8	13	9	10	9	8
	5	6	3	3	9	3	7	5	5	5	5	4	12	12	4	9	6
	6	5	2	4	6	5	5	4	5	5	4	3	3	2	4	7	8
	7	10	6	5	5	5	7	6	8	5	7	9	4	5	7	4	2
	8	1	1	0	0	1	0	1	1	0	0	3	0	1	1	2	2
	9	15	6	4	6	7	4	5	7	10	6	8	6	5	10	7	5
# SURVEYED		184	147	141	140	133	152	128	122	111	111	97	121	105	118	91	130

TABLE IV: COMMUNITY POPULATION -- BY AGE (Continued)

Question: Population of respondent's place of residence.

Responses:
1 = 1,999 or less; 2 = 2000 - 20,999; 3 = 21,000 - 50,999
4 = 51,000 - 100,999; 5 = 101,000 - 200,999; 6 = 201,000 - 400,999
7 = 401,000 - 800,999; 8 = 801,000 - 1,000,999; 9 = 1,001,000+

		YEAR															
AGE	RESP	'72	'73	'74	'75	'76	'77	'78	'80	'82	'83	'84	'85	'86	'87	'88	'89
54-59	1	14%	5%	7%	4%	8%	12%	8%	7%	5%	4%	10%	6%	5%	9%	4%	6%
	2	37	42	47	53	43	44	35	43	49	42	38	47	44	38	42	39
	3	14	13	15	12	15	15	19	14	15	19	13	13	9	14	20	19
	4	10	14	15	11	9	10	12	11	10	13	11	6	10	14	8	6
	5	5	6	1	3	3	4	8	4	5	4	7	12	14	6	8	14
	6	3	3	2	6	4	2	6	7	2	6	6	4	4	5	8	4
	7	9	7	6	7	8	2	5	7	6	6	6	2	7	8	5	4
	8	0	1	0	1	2	2	1	1	1	0	3	0	3	1	0	0
	9	9	9	8	4	9	9	5	7	6	6	6	9	3	5	4	7
# SURVEYED		154	153	137	121	127	163	134	135	144	134	108	129	96	93	83	95
AGE	RESP	'72	'73	'74	'75	'76	'77	'78	'80	'82	'83	'84	'85	'86	'87	'88	'89
60-65	1	8%	10%	7%	11%	19%	11%	9%	6%	12%	7%	5%	7%	5%	7%	6%	4%
	2	37	46	42	41	36	37	52	45	46	47	50	46	45	45	38	44
	3	14	6	10	15	10	19	15	11	12	11	12	15	13	17	29	15
	4	8	13	7	6	14	10	10	8	7	4	7	14	10	5	5	7
	5	7	3	5	1	3	5	3	8	3	6	9	6	6	8	9	11
	6	8	6	4	6	2	4	2	3	3	8	6	6	7	4	4	9
	7	15	8	13	7	8	4	8	11	8	8	7	6	6	6	6	8
	8	0	0	1	1	1	0	0	1	1	0	1	0	3	1	1	0
	9	4	8	13	11	6	8	2	7	8	8	3	2	4	6	2	3
# SURVEYED		142	115	104	109	127	115	105	116	114	131	107	123	112	98	117	110
AGE	RESP	'72	'73	'74	'75	'76	'77	'78	'80	'82	'83	'84	'85	'86	'87	'88	'89
66+	1	6%	5%	5%	9%	9%	9%	9%	10%	5%	8%	6%	5%	4%	12%	10%	8%
	2	33	45	48	44	42	45	37	47	50	46	46	46	46	50	38	45
	3	14	10	10	10	17	13	18	13	14	13	12	11	11	9	18	16
	4	11	7	9	10	7	7	12	7	7	11	5	13	9	6	6	8
	5	5	4	4	5	7	6	8	4	6	3	10	4	12	4	9	5
	6	9	7	7	5	4	6	4	4	4	8	10	7	7	6	8	5
	7	18	10	8	6	6	9	8	9	5	6	5	5	6	8	4	5
	8	1	1	1	3	1	1	1	1	2	0	0	0	0	0	0	0
	9	4	11	8	9	7	4	4	5	5	5	6	8	6	5	6	6
# SURVEYED		211	194	223	219	238	210	223	233	258	238	221	246	245	239	261	262

REGION OF COUNTRY LIVING IN

TABLE I: REGION OF COUNTRY LIVING IN -- BY TOTAL POPULATION

Question: Geographic region of interview. Note: See Appendix A for definition of regions.

Responses:
NE = New England
MA = Middle Atlantic
EN = East North Central
WN = West North Central
SA = South Atlantic
ES = East South Central
WS = West South Central
MT = Mountain
PC = Pacific

	YEAR															
RESPONSE	'72	'73	'74	'75	'76	'77	'78	'80	'82	'83	'84	'85	'86	'87	'88	'89
NE	6%	5%	5%	4%	5%	4%	5%	4%	4%	5%	5%	6%	6%	5%	5%	5%
MA	18	18	17	18	18	16	17	16	19	16	15	13	15	14	14	14
EN	19	22	23	22	21	24	21	21	22	21	19	18	18	19	18	17
WN	9	6	6	7	7	6	8	7	7	10	9	9	9	9	9	9
SA	14	19	19	20	19	20	20	18	19	16	17	17	17	18	18	19
ES	5	5	5	6	6	5	6	8	7	6	8	8	8	8	7	7
WS	12	8	8	8	8	8	7	8	7	8	9	10	8	8	9	8
MT	3	4	4	4	4	4	4	5	4	6	6	7	6	7	7	6
PC	14	13	13	12	13	13	12	13	12	13	12	12	13	12	12	14
# SURVEYED	1613	1504	1484	1490	1499	1530	1532	1468	1506	1599	1473	1534	1470	1466	1481	1537

TABLE II: REGION OF COUNTRY LIVING IN -- BY SEX

Question: Geographic region of interview. Note: See Appendix A for definition of regions.

Responses:

NE = New England	MA = Middle Atlantic	EN = East North Central
WN = West North Central	SA = South Atlantic	ES = East South Central
WS = West South Central	MT = Mountain	PC = Pacific

		YEAR															
SEX	RESP	'72	'73	'74	'75	'76	'77	'78	'80	'82	'83	'84	'85	'86	'87	'88	'89
M	NE	6%	5%	4%	4%	5%	4%	5%	3%	3%	5%	6%	7%	5%	6%	4%	5%
A	MA	19	18	17	17	17	15	18	16	21	15	13	12	15	14	13	14
L	EN	19	22	23	22	21	26	21	20	24	21	20	19	17	18	18	16
E	WN	9	6	7	8	8	6	8	8	6	10	9	9	9	9	8	8
	SA	13	19	19	20	18	20	19	18	18	17	19	16	16	19	19	20
	ES	5	5	5	5	6	4	5	7	7	6	6	7	7	5	8	7
	WS	12	7	8	8	8	8	7	9	6	9	8	10	7	9	10	9
	MT	4	4	4	3	4	3	4	5	3	5	7	8	7	7	6	6
	PC	14	13	14	13	14	13	12	13	13	13	13	12	17	13	12	15
# SURVEYED		807	701	691	670	669	693	643	641	639	690	598	688	621	641	638	660
SEX	RESP	'72	'73	'74	'75	'76	'77	'78	'80	'82	'83	'84	'85	'86	'87	'88	'89
F	NE	6%	5%	5%	4%	5%	4%	4%	4%	5%	5%	5%	6%	6%	4%	6%	6%
E	MA	18	18	18	18	19	16	17	16	17	16	16	14	15	14	15	15
M	EN	19	22	22	22	22	23	21	22	21	21	19	17	19	20	18	17
A	WN	9	6	6	6	6	5	7	6	7	10	9	9	9	8	10	10
L	SA	14	19	19	20	19	20	21	18	19	15	16	18	18	18	17	18
E	ES	5	5	5	6	5	6	6	8	6	7	9	9	8	10	6	8
	WS	13	9	9	9	7	8	8	8	9	8	9	10	9	7	8	7
	MT	3	4	4	5	5	5	4	5	4	6	5	6	5	7	8	6
	PC	14	13	13	11	12	14	12	13	12	12	12	13	10	12	12	13
# SURVEYED		806	803	793	820	830	837	889	827	867	909	875	846	849	825	843	877

TABLE III: REGION OF COUNTRY LIVING IN -- BY RACE

Question: Geographic region of interview. Note: See Appendix A for definition of regions.

Responses: NE = New England; MA = Middle Atlantic; EN = East North Central; WN = West North Central; SA = South Atlantic; ES = East South Central; WS = West South Central; MT = Mountain; PC = Pacific

		YEAR															
RACE	RESP	'72	'73	'74	'75	'76	'77	'78	'80	'82	'83	'84	'85	'86	'87	'88	'89
WHITE	NE	7%	5%	4%	5%	5%	4%	5%	4%	4%	6%	6%	7%	7%	6%	6%	5%
	MA	20	18	17	17	18	16	17	17	19	15	14	13	14	14	12	14
	EN	19	23	23	23	22	26	22	22	22	21	19	17	19	17	18	18
	WN	10	6	6	7	7	6	8	7	7	10	10	10	10	9	10	10
	SA	11	18	18	20	17	18	20	17	18	14	15	16	16	16	18	19
	ES	4	5	5	6	6	5	5	7	6	6	7	8	7	7	7	7
	WS	10	8	9	7	8	7	6	8	7	9	8	9	8	8	9	7
	MT	4	4	4	5	5	4	5	6	4	6	6	7	6	8	7	6
	PC	15	14	14	12	12	14	13	13	12	12	13	12	14	13	12	13
# SURVEYED		1348	1308	1304	1323	1361	1339	1358	1318	1323	1416	1251	1338	1249	1222	1234	1319
RACE	RESP	'72	'73	'74	'75	'76	'77	'78	'80	'82	'83	'84	'85	'86	'87	'88	'89
BLACK	NE	0%	6%	8%	0%	5%	1%	0%	3%	2%	0%	0%	2%	1%	0%	3%	6%
	MA	12	18	16	23	19	17	20	12	15	20	17	16	20	16	28	11
	EN	19	21	20	15	10	11	19	12	22	18	21	21	16	31	22	15
	WN	0	7	7	6	5	4	5	5	6	5	3	3	5	4	4	5
	SA	29	26	27	21	38	38	22	34	28	30	26	24	25	27	12	22
	ES	9	7	6	7	4	6	13	11	9	13	15	13	17	14	11	17
	WS	22	6	5	18	5	15	16	11	10	5	12	13	9	6	9	11
	MT	0	2	3	0	0	1	0	1	0	0	0	1	1	0	1	3
	PC	9	7	8	9	13	6	5	10	8	10	5	8	7	2	11	10
# SURVEYED		261	183	173	163	129	176	158	140	156	165	170	152	184	191	186	157
RACE	RESP	'72	'73	'74	'75	'76	'77	'78	'80	'82	'83	'84	'85	'86	'87	'88	'89
OTHER	NE	0%	8%	0%	0%	0%	7%	0%	10%	0%	0%	2%	2%	3%	0%	0%	5%
	MA	0	31	29	0	22	7	0	20	22	22	15	18	19	8	8	26
	EN	0	0	14	25	33	27	25	30	7	6	6	11	11	8	15	2
	WN	50	8	0	0	0	0	0	30	0	0	2	2	0	2	3	0
	SA	25	8	14	0	11	13	19	0	0	0	29	23	30	32	25	15
	ES	0	0	14	0	0	0	0	0	4	0	2	0	0	0	0	0
	WS	0	23	0	0	0	0	0	0	19	6	4	14	8	6	11	16
	MT	0	8	0	0	0	7	13	0	0	0	13	2	16	19	25	7
	PC	25	15	29	75	33	40	44	10	48	67	27	27	14	26	13	30
# SURVEYED		4	13	7	4	9	15	16	10	27	18	52	44	37	53	61	61

TABLE IV: REGION OF COUNTRY LIVING IN -- BY AGE

Question: Geographic region of interview. Note: See Appendix A for definition of regions.

Responses:
NE = New England; MA = Middle Atlantic; EN = East North Central
WN = West North Central; SA = South Atlantic; ES = East South Central
WS = West South Central; MT = Mountain; PC = Pacific

		YEAR															
AGE	RESP	'72	'73	'74	'75	'76	'77	'78	'80	'82	'83	'84	'85	'86	'87	'88	'89
18-23	NE	5%	4%	2%	6%	5%	4%	4%	1%	3%	7%	3%	7%	5%	2%	7%	5%
	MA	15	20	15	16	18	16	17	18	15	9	16	11	16	10	12	17
	EN	28	22	26	23	19	20	26	21	23	20	18	16	16	17	20	12
	WN	5	4	4	8	9	4	6	8	7	14	11	7	11	9	4	7
	SA	12	19	15	21	21	22	15	18	19	16	19	17	24	31	18	23
	ES	5	2	4	3	4	5	6	6	11	6	9	8	6	10	7	9
	WS	12	11	11	10	6	9	7	10	9	9	11	16	6	6	9	9
	MT	5	5	5	3	6	3	7	4	2	7	6	11	4	8	13	4
	PC	14	13	17	10	13	16	12	14	11	13	8	8	12	7	10	13
# SURVEYED		169	171	168	173	162	164	163	155	148	128	161	133	108	126	141	137
AGE	RESP	'72	'73	'74	'75	'76	'77	'78	'80	'82	'83	'84	'85	'86	'87	'88	'89
24-29	NE	7%	5%	6%	4%	4%	2%	3%	4%	5%	3%	6%	7%	6%	7%	4%	7%
	MA	17	17	21	21	20	13	13	16	15	16	13	12	14	13	16	13
	EN	22	24	22	18	18	25	22	20	24	22	21	18	19	19	18	19
	WN	9	5	7	6	8	6	7	8	5	8	8	7	8	8	10	8
	SA	9	18	17	19	19	22	21	18	15	14	15	13	20	16	11	20
	ES	7	4	5	6	4	4	5	10	7	5	10	7	7	5	7	5
	WS	10	8	10	8	10	9	9	9	10	11	9	13	8	10	15	8
	MT	4	4	2	4	3	3	8	2	4	7	5	8	5	7	8	4
	PC	15	15	11	15	15	15	13	13	15	14	14	14	14	16	12	15
# SURVEYED		231	212	212	232	226	204	244	202	246	287	232	217	218	193	215	202
AGE	RESP	'72	'73	'74	'75	'76	'77	'78	'80	'82	'83	'84	'85	'86	'87	'88	'89
30-35	NE	7%	5%	4%	4%	4%	6%	4%	3%	2%	6%	4%	7%	9%	5%	5%	5%
	MA	20	20	23	17	16	17	20	17	19	12	13	15	11	17	14	17
	EN	19	19	17	20	24	29	18	18	23	23	18	17	19	18	21	20
	WN	9	7	9	6	8	4	8	7	9	8	10	7	9	8	6	9
	SA	10	22	17	16	12	13	23	14	20	15	20	17	19	17	16	15
	ES	5	4	4	9	8	4	6	7	4	7	6	8	6	7	8	5
	WS	10	10	9	11	9	10	9	10	6	9	9	8	10	6	10	8
	MT	3	5	2	2	4	5	1	7	1	8	6	7	6	9	7	6
	PC	18	8	14	14	16	11	10	15	15	11	15	13	11	14	15	14
# SURVEYED		187	167	175	171	186	188	230	215	204	236	200	212	221	221	195	212

TABLE IV: REGION OF COUNTRY LIVING IN -- BY AGE (Continued)

Question: Geographic region of interview. Note: See Appendix A for definition of regions.

Responses: NE = New England; MA = Middle Atlantic; EN = East North Central; WN = West North Central; SA = South Atlantic; ES = East South Central; WS = West South Central; MT = Mountain; PC = Pacific

		YEAR															
AGE	RESP	'72	'73	'74	'75	'76	'77	'78	'80	'82	'83	'84	'85	'86	'87	'88	'89
36-41	NE	6%	5%	7%	6%	5%	5%	3%	2%	7%	6%	5%	5%	4%	6%	5%	8%
	MA	20	19	22	17	18	11	20	15	21	18	21	10	15	15	17	13
	EN	16	18	22	19	17	22	27	27	16	15	17	15	20	14	18	15
	WN	10	4	5	6	6	8	4	4	4	9	8	8	8	9	10	10
	SA	15	17	18	23	20	20	21	17	21	14	19	18	13	14	12	17
	ES	3	6	3	7	8	5	4	9	8	6	6	6	5	6	7	8
	WS	13	11	9	5	8	9	9	9	6	10	7	11	11	11	7	9
	MT	4	4	4	5	3	6	3	5	4	5	6	12	6	9	6	5
	PC	14	17	11	11	15	14	9	12	12	15	11	16	17	15	18	16
# SURVEYED		128	175	152	154	158	168	160	150	146	173	187	184	188	186	193	198
AGE	RESP	'72	'73	'74	'75	'76	'77	'78	'80	'82	'83	'84	'85	'86	'87	'88	'89
42-47	NE	9%	6%	3%	4%	4%	4%	9%	3%	3%	6%	6%	7%	5%	8%	6%	5%
	MA	20	19	15	19	24	13	18	19	22	17	17	8	19	13	13	18
	EN	18	24	30	22	19	26	21	15	23	21	21	21	21	13	21	19
	WN	6	9	6	8	5	5	8	8	5	10	8	9	6	4	8	7
	SA	16	16	19	20	22	18	14	21	25	18	11	16	11	18	18	15
	ES	2	5	3	3	3	8	5	9	6	8	6	11	4	11	7	7
	WS	13	5	6	6	11	7	7	9	6	6	13	8	9	10	12	8
	MT	3	3	3	4	3	5	3	4	3	8	8	5	9	8	6	7
	PC	12	12	15	13	9	15	14	12	8	8	10	15	17	15	9	14
# SURVEYED		186	146	151	143	114	147	119	117	119	145	126	124	141	157	157	161
AGE	RESP	'72	'73	'74	'75	'76	'77	'78	'80	'82	'83	'84	'85	'86	'87	'88	'89
48-53	NE	6%	6%	6%	4%	8%	3%	8%	4%	7%	4%	11%	5%	8%	6%	10%	4%
	MA	22	16	15	18	20	16	22	15	18	20	12	15	13	14	17	15
	EN	20	25	24	23	25	22	17	27	19	16	22	17	17	27	17	17
	WN	5	3	7	12	3	9	8	4	5	10	8	11	7	7	7	6
	SA	14	21	14	16	19	21	16	16	18	15	18	18	20	15	18	22
	ES	4	5	8	7	5	5	6	3	6	7	8	5	8	8	4	10
	WS	14	9	8	6	8	5	8	10	10	7	9	8	7	10	8	10
	MT	3	1	2	1	4	5	3	14	5	5	7	6	7	5	5	2
	PC	12	13	16	14	9	16	12	7	12	16	7	15	11	9	13	14
# SURVEYED		189	151	146	141	133	154	133	123	112	116	102	131	108	126	92	138

TABLE IV: REGION OF COUNTRY LIVING IN -- BY AGE (Continued)

Question: Geographic region of interview. Note: See Appendix A for definition of regions.

Responses: NE = New England; MA = Middle Atlantic; EN = East North Central; WN = West North Central; SA = South Atlantic; ES = East South Central; WS = West South Central; MT = Mountain; PC = Pacific

		YEAR															
AGE	RESP	'72	'73	'74	'75	'76	'77	'78	'80	'82	'83	'84	'85	'86	'87	'88	'89
54-59	NE	6%	6%	6%	5%	5%	4%	7%	3%	6%	8%	9%	2%	8%	5%	2%	1%
	MA	26	21	17	16	16	14	15	14	19	20	14	17	19	9	13	12
	EN	13	19	17	28	22	23	23	21	22	14	17	24	18	24	20	17
	WN	10	6	4	5	5	3	8	5	4	12	11	10	8	16	12	12
	SA	12	15	27	24	22	27	20	23	17	15	18	21	13	16	24	23
	ES	6	6	6	4	6	5	4	8	8	5	4	3	10	9	9	7
	WS	11	8	6	5	5	8	7	10	7	10	7	7	7	6	4	10
	MT	3	3	6	3	4	4	1	4	5	4	8	7	7	3	5	6
	PC	14	15	12	11	13	11	13	12	12	12	14	9	9	10	12	11
# SURVEYED		156	157	139	126	129	168	137	136	144	134	114	134	99	98	85	99
AGE	RESP	'72	'73	'74	'75	'76	'77	'78	'80	'82	'83	'84	'85	'86	'87	'88	'89
60-65	NE	3%	6%	6%	4%	7%	5%	1%	7%	3%	6%	4%	8%	3%	3%	8%	5%
	MA	13	12	13	18	16	22	14	17	22	21	11	16	14	15	12	12
	EN	17	21	29	26	28	29	22	17	28	27	16	18	21	19	13	11
	WN	15	10	6	5	9	5	9	8	14	8	11	10	6	10	8	15
	SA	16	24	19	16	13	16	22	18	11	17	20	20	19	21	29	15
	ES	10	8	4	5	5	3	9	8	6	5	11	8	9	9	8	10
	WS	10	4	7	13	6	9	6	3	5	4	9	9	9	4	10	7
	MT	3	3	4	5	4	2	5	6	4	2	5	2	6	6	8	9
	PC	13	12	12	8	11	9	11	17	7	11	13	9	13	14	6	15
# SURVEYED		144	121	108	113	134	117	107	119	116	132	113	131	115	101	119	111
AGE	RESP	'72	'73	'74	'75	'76	'77	'78	'80	'82	'83	'84	'85	'86	'87	'88	'89
66+	NE	2%	3%	4%	3%	3%	3%	4%	5%	3%	3%	4%	6%	5%	5%	5%	5%
	MA	13	17	13	16	16	19	17	16	17	14	13	13	15	15	12	12
	EN	17	26	21	22	22	23	19	21	22	24	22	17	16	23	16	17
	WN	12	9	9	8	8	6	10	9	8	10	9	12	14	9	16	12
	SA	19	19	24	22	20	25	22	18	20	19	15	18	17	18	22	21
	ES	5	6	7	4	7	4	5	7	5	8	12	12	13	9	7	7
	WS	15	5	6	10	6	5	4	5	6	8	6	8	5	7	6	4
	MT	4	5	6	7	6	3	5	5	5	2	3	2	5	6	5	9
	PC	13	12	11	8	12	13	13	14	14	12	15	11	9	8	11	12
# SURVEYED		218	200	227	232	251	213	232	242	259	241	232	261	265	253	280	275

****

REGION LIVED IN AT AGE 16

TABLE I: REGION LIVED IN AT AGE 16 -- BY TOTAL POPULATION

Question: In what state or foreign country were you living when you were 16 years old? NOTE: See Appendix A for regional definitions.

Responses: NE = New England; MA = Middle Atlantic; EN = East North Central; WN = West North Central; SA = South Atlantic; ES = East South Central; WS = West South Central; MT = Mountain; PC = Pacific; FR = Foreign

	YEAR															
RESPONSE	'72	'73	'74	'75	'76	'77	'78	'80	'82	'83	'84	'85	'86	'87	'88	'89
NE	4%	4%	4%	3%	4%	5%	4%	4%	4%	5%	4%	4%	5%	4%	5%	5%
MA	5	4	4	4	4	5	4	4	4	6	6	7	6	5	6	5
EN	19	17	17	17	18	16	18	16	18	17	15	14	15	15	15	15
WN	17	20	22	21	21	23	21	21	22	22	21	18	21	20	19	20
SA	11	9	10	8	10	7	9	9	8	10	10	11	10	10	10	10
ES	12	19	17	18	17	18	18	17	17	14	14	14	13	15	15	15
WS	7	7	7	8	7	7	7	9	8	8	9	10	9	10	7	8
MT	13	9	9	9	8	8	8	9	8	8	9	10	8	7	9	8
PC	3	3	3	4	3	3	3	4	4	4	4	5	5	5	5	4
FR	8	9	8	8	8	8	8	9	8	8	8	9	8	8	8	10
# SURVEYED	1613	1504	1484	1490	1499	1530	1532	1468	1506	1599	1473	1534	1470	1466	1481	1537

TABLE II: REGION LIVED IN AT AGE 16 -- BY SEX

Question: In what state or foreign country were you living when you were 16 years old? NOTE: See Appendix A for regional definitions.

Responses: NE = New England; MA = Middle Atlantic; EN = East North Central; WN = West North Central; SA = South Atlantic; ES = East South Central; WS = West South Central; MT = Mountain; PC = Pacific; FR = Foreign

		YEAR															
SEX	RESP	'72	'73	'74	'75	'76	'77	'78	'80	'82	'83	'84	'85	'86	'87	'88	'89
M	NE	4%	4%	3%	3%	5%	4%	5%	4%	5%	4%	4%	4%	5%	5%	6%	5%
A	MA	6	4	4	4	5	5	5	4	3	6	6	8	5	6	5	5
L	EN	19	17	17	18	18	15	19	16	19	16	16	14	16	15	14	16
E	WN	17	20	22	21	21	26	21	20	25	22	22	18	20	20	20	21
	SA	11	8	10	9	11	8	9	10	8	10	10	10	11	11	9	8
	ES	11	19	17	19	16	19	18	17	17	15	16	14	12	15	16	15
	WS	8	6	6	9	7	5	7	8	7	7	7	9	7	6	8	7
	MT	13	9	9	8	9	7	7	10	5	8	8	9	8	8	9	8
	PC	3	3	3	3	3	3	2	3	4	4	5	6	5	5	4	4
	FR	9	9	9	7	7	8	8	9	7	8	7	8	10	9	8	11
# SURVEYED		807	701	691	670	669	693	643	641	639	690	598	688	621	641	638	660
RESP		'72	'73	'74	'75	'76	'77	'78	'80	'82	'83	'84	'85	'86	'87	'88	'89
F	NE	5%	4%	4%	4%	4%	5%	3%	4%	3%	5%	4%	5%	5%	3%	4%	6%
E	MA	5	4	4	3	4	4	4	3	4	6	5	5	7	4	6	5
M	EN	18	17	17	17	17	16	17	16	17	17	15	14	14	15	15	15
A	WN	18	20	22	21	21	21	22	22	20	21	21	17	21	20	19	20
L	SA	11	9	10	8	9	7	9	8	9	10	9	11	9	10	11	11
E	ES	13	19	18	18	17	18	18	17	17	12	13	14	14	15	14	15
	WS	7	8	7	7	8	7	7	9	8	9	11	10	10	13	7	8
	MT	13	8	9	9	8	9	10	8	10	8	9	10	8	7	9	7
	PC	3	3	3	4	3	3	3	4	3	4	4	4	5	5	6	5
	FR	8	8	8	8	8	9	8	8	8	8	9	9	7	8	8	9
# SURVEYED		806	803	793	820	830	837	889	827	867	909	875	846	849	825	843	877

TABLE III: REGION LIVED IN AT AGE 16 -- BY RACE

Question: In what state or foreign country were you living when you were 16 years old? NOTE: See Appendix A for regional definitions.

Responses: NE = New England; MA = Middle Atlantic; EN = East North Central; WN = West North Central; SA = South Atlantic; ES = East South Central; WS = West South Central; MT = Mountain; PC = Pacific; FR = Foreign

		YEAR															
RACE	RESP	'72	'73	'74	'75	'76	'77	'78	'80	'82	'83	'84	'85	'86	'87	'88	'89
WHITE	NE	4%	4%	4%	3%	4%	4%	4%	4%	3%	4%	3%	3%	4%	3%	4%	4%
	MA	6	4	4	4	4	5	5	4	4	6	7	7	7	6	6	5
	EN	21	18	18	18	19	17	19	17	19	18	16	15	16	16	15	17
	WN	19	21	23	23	22	25	23	22	23	23	23	19	23	21	21	22
	SA	13	9	10	9	10	8	9	9	9	11	11	12	11	12	12	11
	ES	9	16	15	17	14	16	16	14	16	12	12	12	11	12	14	14
	WS	5	6	6	6	7	5	6	8	6	6	7	9	7	8	6	6
	MT	10	8	8	7	8	7	7	8	7	8	8	9	7	7	8	6
	PC	3	3	3	4	4	4	3	4	4	4	4	6	5	5	5	5
	FR	9	9	9	8	8	9	8	9	8	8	9	9	9	9	9	10
# SURVEYED		1348	1308	1304	1323	1361	1339	1358	1318	1323	1416	1251	1338	1249	1222	1234	1319
RACE	RESP	'72	'73	'74	'75	'76	'77	'78	'80	'82	'83	'84	'85	'86	'87	'88	'89
BLACK	NE	3%	2%	2%	4%	5%	3%	2%	2%	6%	5%	5%	5%	5%	4%	4%	6%
	MA	0	1	2	0	3	1	0	1	1	0	1	2	1	1	2	3
	EN	8	9	12	15	8	12	11	5	8	13	11	7	12	12	20	6
	WN	8	10	11	7	6	10	11	8	13	12	14	13	13	22	16	16
	SA	1	5	8	2	5	3	6	3	4	4	1	4	3	3	3	3
	ES	31	39	34	26	43	38	31	37	31	30	25	28	27	28	18	26
	WS	19	17	15	21	16	15	18	20	19	23	28	22	23	22	17	20
	MT	28	14	14	20	10	18	18	16	14	8	14	15	11	8	13	15
	PC	0	1	0	1	0	0	0	1	0	0	0	0	1	1	1	1
	FR	3	3	2	3	4	1	3	6	4	5	2	4	3	1	6	5
# SURVEYED		261	183	173	163	129	176	158	140	156	165	170	152	184	191	186	157
RACE	RESP	'72	'73	'74	'75	'76	'77	'78	'80	'82	'83	'84	'85	'86	'87	'88	'89
OTHER	NE	0%	31%	71%	25%	78%	60%	50%	30%	41%	61%	21%	36%	32%	21%	30%	36%
	MA	0	0	0	0	0	7	0	0	0	0	2	2	0	0	0	3
	EN	25	8	0	25	0	7	0	20	7	11	8	9	11	6	2	8
	WN	0	0	0	0	11	0	13	10	7	0	4	5	3	8	7	3
	SA	50	8	0	0	0	7	0	0	0	0	2	0	0	2	3	0
	ES	0	8	0	0	0	0	0	0	0	0	29	18	24	28	20	10
	WS	0	0	14	0	0	0	0	0	0	0	2	0	0	0	0	0
	MT	25	23	0	0	0	0	0	10	19	6	0	11	8	4	8	16
	PC	0	8	0	0	0	0	6	20	4	0	17	2	14	17	23	7
	FR	0	15	14	50	11	20	31	10	22	22	15	16	8	15	8	16
# SURVEYED		4	13	7	4	9	15	16	10	27	18	52	44	37	53	61	61

TABLE IV: REGION LIVED IN AT AGE 16 -- BY AGE

Question: In what state or foreign country were you living when you were 16 years old? NOTE: See Appendix A for regional definitions.

Responses: NE = New England; MA = Middle Atlantic; EN = East North Central; WN = West North Central; SA = South Atlantic; ES = East South Central; WS = West South Central; MT = Mountain; PC = Pacific; FR = Foreign

		YEAR															
AGE	RESP	'72	'73	'74	'75	'76	'77	'78	'80	'82	'83	'84	'85	'86	'87	'88	'89
18-23	NE	2%	1%	2%	1%	2%	2%	1%	3%	2%	1%	4%	2%	1%	1%	2%	4%
	MA	4	4	2	6	5	4	4	3	3	7	4	5	6	2	6	4
	EN	15	20	16	16	19	20	17	19	12	9	14	14	17	13	11	14
	WN	26	22	26	22	20	21	26	23	25	19	20	18	17	17	21	15
	SA	7	4	7	10	9	5	6	6	8	14	11	7	10	9	6	7
	ES	12	18	17	19	17	20	15	17	18	16	17	14	20	29	17	22
	WS	5	4	4	6	5	5	5	6	10	8	8	8	6	10	8	9
	MT	12	9	9	8	6	7	9	9	8	9	10	15	7	6	8	7
	PC	5	5	4	3	5	3	6	3	3	5	4	10	4	9	14	4
	FR	12	13	14	9	11	13	12	12	10	13	9	8	11	6	6	15
# SURVEYED		169	171	168	173	162	164	163	155	148	128	161	133	108	126	141	137
AGE	RESP	'72	'73	'74	'75	'76	'77	'78	'80	'82	'83	'84	'85	'86	'87	'88	'89
24-29	NE	3%	4%	3%	2%	7%	3%	4%	2%	5%	2%	4%	2%	4%	5%	6%	5%
	MA	7	4	5	3	3	4	2	4	4	5	5	8	6	7	3	7
	EN	21	20	21	19	20	15	14	14	15	16	15	14	13	13	15	14
	WN	18	21	18	18	17	27	21	22	21	23	23	20	20	21	19	20
	SA	8	6	10	7	9	4	8	8	7	8	9	10	9	8	10	7
	ES	9	18	15	18	17	20	19	17	15	13	13	11	17	13	10	16
	WS	9	5	8	9	4	4	7	10	9	5	11	7	9	6	5	5
	MT	10	8	10	7	10	8	10	7	9	9	6	10	5	9	12	8
	PC	4	4	1	3	2	2	3	2	5	7	4	4	4	6	7	4
	FR	12	11	9	13	11	13	12	12	11	12	10	14	12	11	13	12
# SURVEYED		231	212	212	232	226	204	244	202	246	287	232	217	218	193	215	202
AGE	RESP	'72	'73	'74	'75	'76	'77	'78	'80	'82	'83	'84	'85	'86	'87	'88	'89
30-35	NE	6%	4%	1%	4%	5%	6%	5%	5%	1%	4%	6%	4%	5%	4%	6%	6%
	MA	5	4	4	4	4	5	5	3	1	6	4	7	6	5	5	4
	EN	21	19	23	15	15	15	17	18	22	14	15	17	13	17	13	18
	WN	19	17	17	18	26	26	18	20	25	24	20	15	20	22	23	24
	SA	9	11	11	6	9	5	9	7	9	8	9	9	9	10	8	8
	ES	7	22	16	15	12	13	20	15	16	13	17	17	14	14	11	11
	WS	5	7	6	11	6	6	8	5	6	8	6	9	7	8	8	6
	MT	12	9	9	12	9	10	10	10	6	9	8	8	9	5	11	6
	PC	3	3	2	2	3	3	2	6	1	6	7	4	6	5	3	5
	FR	13	6	13	13	11	11	7	11	10	8	11	11	9	11	12	12
# SURVEYED		187	167	175	171	186	188	230	215	204	236	200	212	221	221	195	212

TABLE IV: REGION LIVED IN AT AGE 16 -- BY AGE (Continued)

Question: In what state or foreign country were you living when you were 16 years old? NOTE: See Appendix A for regional definitions.

Responses:
NE = New England
MA = Middle Atlantic
EN = East North Central
WN = West North Central
SA = South Atlantic
ES = East South Central
WS = West South Central
MT = Mountain
PC = Pacific
FR = Foreign

		YEAR															
AGE	RESP	'72	'73	'74	'75	'76	'77	'78	'80	'82	'83	'84	'85	'86	'87	'88	'89
36-41	NE	2%	5%	8%	4%	4%	8%	6%	5%	5%	5%	3%	7%	7%	7%	6%	6%
	MA	6	4	3	4	5	5	4	2	5	6	5	5	4	4	4	6
	EN	17	18	20	20	16	13	19	15	21	21	21	12	15	17	20	14
	WN	16	17	21	18	16	18	25	25	16	14	20	16	19	15	18	19
	SA	13	5	7	7	10	8	6	5	6	11	9	7	8	10	10	10
	ES	13	17	14	24	18	18	18	16	21	13	16	15	10	13	11	17
	WS	6	7	7	6	9	6	5	11	7	9	5	6	6	9	8	7
	MT	12	10	9	5	8	11	9	9	8	8	8	10	11	9	9	8
	PC	5	3	3	5	4	4	2	4	2	3	3	10	6	5	3	3
	FR	9	14	7	7	9	8	6	8	9	10	9	12	13	11	11	12
# SURVEYED		128	175	152	154	158	168	160	150	146	173	187	184	188	186	193	198
AGE	RESP	'72	'73	'74	'75	'76	'77	'78	'80	'82	'83	'84	'85	'86	'87	'88	'89
42-47	NE	2%	5%	3%	3%	10%	5%	6%	9%	5%	3%	5%	6%	7%	4%	5%	6%
	MA	8	5	1	5	4	4	7	4	3	6	6	6	4	6	8	3
	EN	20	16	18	20	22	12	19	14	19	18	15	10	21	15	17	17
	WN	16	21	28	22	20	21	18	16	20	20	20	19	19	17	19	25
	SA	9	10	9	8	6	8	10	10	8	9	8	10	6	7	8	7
	ES	16	20	17	16	15	18	13	19	24	18	11	13	10	15	16	13
	WS	5	9	6	7	5	10	9	10	7	6	9	11	6	13	5	7
	MT	15	5	8	8	11	9	8	8	9	8	13	9	11	9	12	9
	PC	2	1	3	4	2	4	1	2	2	6	7	4	4	4	2	4
	FR	8	8	6	7	4	9	8	9	3	7	7	11	12	10	8	8
# SURVEYED		186	146	151	143	114	147	119	117	119	145	126	124	141	157	157	161
AGE	RESP	'72	'73	'74	'75	'76	'77	'78	'80	'82	'83	'84	'85	'86	'87	'88	'89
48-53	NE	4%	5%	3%	6%	4%	6%	4%	2%	4%	7%	5%	5%	6%	5%	9%	5%
	MA	7	4	5	2	8	2	7	2	9	5	11	6	6	2	4	4
	EN	22	13	14	20	18	16	21	19	17	16	12	18	13	15	15	18
	WN	15	22	27	23	22	21	17	24	21	18	21	16	24	26	18	21
	SA	7	6	9	9	8	12	8	9	5	9	10	14	8	10	10	7
	ES	16	23	14	16	19	19	15	17	16	14	17	13	16	11	21	18
	WS	7	7	8	9	7	6	8	4	9	13	10	8	10	12	7	9
	MT	13	11	8	7	8	5	9	11	9	6	8	6	8	10	7	8
	PC	2	2	2	4	2	3	3	10	4	4	2	5	5	2	2	3
	FR	8	6	10	5	5	9	8	2	4	7	6	10	3	7	8	8
# SURVEYED		189	151	146	141	133	154	133	123	112	116	102	131	108	126	92	138

TABLE IV: REGION LIVED IN AT AGE 16 -- BY AGE (Continued)

Question: In what state or foreign country were you living when you were 16 years old? NOTE: See Appendix A for regional definitions.

Responses: NE = New England; MA = Middle Atlantic; EN = East North Central; WN = West North Central; SA = South Atlantic; ES = East South Central; WS = West South Central; MT = Mountain; PC = Pacific; FR = Foreign

		YEAR															
AGE	RESP	'72	'73	'74	'75	'76	'77	'78	'80	'82	'83	'84	'85	'86	'87	'88	'89
54-59	NE	1%	3%	2%	2%	2%	3%	1%	4%	6%	7%	5%	5%	1%	1%	8%	7%
	MA	7	3	7	4	4	5	6	2	4	8	10	6	7	6	6	0
	EN	23	22	18	17	17	15	19	14	19	19	11	11	16	11	11	9
	WN	12	17	19	27	22	26	22	22	24	16	18	17	22	22	18	23
	SA	18	9	6	9	10	7	11	8	5	13	12	12	10	19	12	12
	ES	10	17	24	21	22	20	18	16	14	12	13	18	12	11	21	17
	WS	9	10	7	6	10	9	7	13	9	9	7	10	12	12	9	9
	MT	13	10	9	8	7	6	8	11	7	7	11	10	10	5	5	9
	PC	2	3	4	4	2	4	1	4	6	2	7	5	6	3	2	4
	FR	5	8	4	3	5	6	7	6	7	5	7	5	3	8	8	9
# SURVEYED		156	157	139	126	129	168	137	136	144	134	114	134	99	98	85	99
AGE	RESP	'72	'73	'74	'75	'76	'77	'78	'80	'82	'83	'84	'85	'86	'87	'88	'89
60-65	NE	6%	3%	4%	2%	3%	3%	2%	6%	2%	8%	1%	3%	6%	4%	3%	4%
	MA	3	5	4	4	7	7	4	8	2	6	7	8	4	5	9	6
	EN	13	12	12	19	13	21	19	20	20	23	15	17	17	18	13	13
	WN	19	20	29	24	27	26	26	13	23	27	23	20	25	20	14	13
	SA	16	15	10	9	13	12	9	13	16	10	11	13	9	14	11	15
	ES	13	21	15	17	12	14	20	17	13	15	15	15	13	12	22	14
	WS	10	8	11	11	10	5	8	10	9	5	11	10	9	11	13	8
	MT	14	9	6	11	7	10	6	7	9	4	7	9	8	4	7	13
	PC	1	2	3	3	4	1	5	1	2	1	4	2	4	5	5	5
	FR	3	5	6	3	4	3	2	6	5	2	7	4	5	8	3	10
# SURVEYED		144	121	108	113	134	117	107	119	116	132	113	131	115	101	119	111
AGE	RESP	'72	'73	'74	'75	'76	'77	'78	'80	'82	'83	'84	'85	'86	'87	'88	'89
66+	NE	8%	6%	7%	6%	3%	7%	6%	5%	5%	7%	5%	4%	4%	3%	4%	5%
	MA	2	3	4	2	2	5	3	4	3	4	5	6	8	6	6	6
	EN	14	13	11	13	17	17	18	15	16	17	14	15	14	17	14	17
	WN	16	23	18	21	22	23	21	19	22	27	23	18	22	23	21	19
	SA	16	14	15	11	11	8	13	12	12	11	10	13	14	10	16	14
	ES	14	19	23	19	18	20	19	16	19	11	9	13	10	15	15	11
	WS	10	10	7	8	10	8	7	10	5	10	16	15	14	11	7	10
	MT	16	8	9	11	7	5	6	7	8	10	9	11	6	8	7	6
	PC	0	3	4	6	5	3	3	5	5	1	2	2	4	4	5	6
	FR	4	5	3	4	4	4	4	8	5	3	6	4	3	3	4	5
# SURVEYED		218	200	227	232	251	213	232	242	259	241	232	261	265	253	280	275

****

TYPE OF COMMUNITY LIVED IN AT AGE 16

TABLE I: TYPE OF COMMUNITY LIVED IN AT AGE 16 -- BY TOTAL POPULATION

Question: Which of the categories below comes closest to the type of place you were living in when you were 16 years old?

Responses: OC = Open country but not on a farm; FR = On a farm; TW = Small city or town (under 50,000); MC = Medium sized city (50,000 to 250,000); SB = Suburb near a large city; LC = In a large city

	YEAR															
RESPONSE	'72	'73	'74	'75	'76	'77	'78	'80	'82	'83	'84	'85	'86	'87	'88	'89
OC	9%	9%	10%	13%	11%	11%	11%	10%	10%	11%	10%	10%	10%	12%	12%	11%
FR	21	23	24	23	23	23	22	21	20	16	22	18	18	19	17	17
TW	31	32	30	29	30	34	31	32	33	34	32	34	31	28	32	32
MC	12	13	13	12	12	12	13	14	12	15	14	15	17	15	15	16
SB	6	7	8	7	8	6	8	8	9	10	9	10	9	11	10	11
LC	21	17	15	17	16	14	14	15	15	15	14	12	16	15	15	13
# SURVEYED	1610	1501	1481	1490	1497	1524	1530	1467	1499	1599	1467	1528	1470	1462	1479	1533

TABLE II: TYPE OF COMMUNITY LIVED IN AT AGE 16 -- BY SEX

Question: Which of the categories below comes closest to the type of place you were living in when you were 16 years old?

Responses:

OC = Open country but not on a farm
TW = Small city or town (under 50,000)
SB = Suburb near a large city
FR = On a farm
MC = Medium sized city (50,000 to 250,000)
LC = In a large city

		YEAR															
SEX	RESP	'72	'73	'74	'75	'76	'77	'78	'80	'82	'83	'84	'85	'86	'87	'88	'89
M	OC	9%	8%	10%	14%	11%	12%	10%	8%	12%	13%	10%	10%	12%	12%	12%	12%
A	FR	23	26	27	23	23	24	22	23	19	17	23	19	18	20	19	16
L	TW	29	31	31	29	28	35	34	33	30	32	32	34	29	27	32	31
E	MC	12	12	13	13	12	12	14	12	12	13	13	15	16	14	15	17
	SB	7	8	7	5	9	5	7	8	11	11	10	11	10	12	9	11
	LC	21	16	13	17	17	12	13	15	16	14	13	12	15	15	14	14
# SURVEYED		806	699	688	670	669	690	642	641	638	690	595	686	621	640	638	658
SEX	RESP	'72	'73	'74	'75	'76	'77	'78	'80	'82	'83	'84	'85	'86	'87	'88	'89
F	OC	9%	10%	10%	12%	10%	10%	12%	11%	9%	9%	10%	9%	8%	12%	11%	11%
E	FR	19	20	22	22	22	22	22	20	20	15	21	18	18	19	16	17
M	TW	33	33	29	29	31	34	29	31	35	34	32	35	32	28	32	33
A	MC	13	13	13	11	13	12	13	15	12	17	14	16	18	16	15	15
L	SB	5	7	9	8	7	7	9	8	9	9	9	10	9	9	10	11
E	LC	21	17	17	17	16	15	15	15	15	16	15	13	16	15	16	13
# SURVEYED		804	802	793	820	828	834	888	826	861	909	872	842	849	822	841	875

TABLE III: TYPE OF COMMUNITY LIVED IN AT AGE 16 -- BY RACE

Question: Which of the categories below comes closest to the type of place you were living in when you were 16 years old?

Responses:

OC = Open country but not on a farm
TW = Small city or town (under 50,000)
SB = Suburb near a large city
FR = On a farm
MC = Medium sized city (50,000 to 250,000)
LC = In a large city

		YEAR															
RACE	RESP	'72	'73	'74	'75	'76	'77	'78	'80	'82	'83	'84	'85	'86	'87	'88	'89
WHITE	OC	9%	9%	10%	13%	11%	12%	12%	10%	10%	11%	10%	10%	10%	12%	12%	11%
	FR	21	21	24	22	22	22	22	21	20	16	21	18	19	20	17	17
	TW	32	33	31	30	31	35	32	32	34	35	32	36	31	29	33	33
	MC	13	12	13	12	12	12	13	14	12	15	14	15	17	15	14	15
	SB	6	8	9	7	8	6	9	8	9	11	10	11	10	12	10	12
	LC	19	16	14	16	16	12	13	15	13	13	13	11	14	13	13	11
# SURVEYED		1346	1306	1304	1323	1359	1333	1356	1317	1318	1416	1247	1335	1249	1219	1233	1317
RACE	RESP	'72	'73	'74	'75	'76	'77	'78	'80	'82	'83	'84	'85	'86	'87	'88	'89
BLACK	OC	10%	9%	9%	13%	10%	7%	9%	9%	10%	10%	10%	7%	9%	12%	9%	10%
	FR	22	32	28	28	29	26	23	23	19	18	26	23	15	16	16	14
	TW	28	24	21	22	18	30	23	26	23	21	29	26	25	21	24	23
	MC	8	13	15	12	16	11	16	14	10	18	11	21	20	20	19	17
	SB	3	4	2	4	4	1	4	5	6	4	3	4	7	5	6	8
	LC	28	18	24	22	23	26	25	23	31	30	21	19	24	27	26	28
# SURVEYED		260	182	170	163	129	176	158	140	154	165	168	149	184	190	186	155
RACE	RESP	'72	'73	'74	'75	'76	'77	'78	'80	'82	'83	'84	'85	'86	'87	'88	'89
OTHER	OC	25%	0%	14%	0%	0%	7%	19%	10%	11%	11%	10%	11%	3%	17%	10%	8%
	FR	25	46	14	50	11	13	13	10	7	6	29	16	22	25	23	15
	TW	0	8	29	0	56	33	25	40	26	39	29	25	35	21	32	33
	MC	0	23	14	25	11	13	19	20	7	11	10	23	11	11	8	15
	SB	0	0	0	0	11	0	0	10	26	0	4	7	5	6	7	5
	LC	50	23	29	25	11	33	25	10	22	33	19	18	24	21	20	25
# SURVEYED		4	13	7	4	9	15	16	10	27	18	52	44	37	53	60	61

TABLE IV: TYPE OF COMMUNITY LIVED IN AT AGE 16 -- BY AGE

Question: Which of the categories below comes closest to the type of place you were living in when you were 16 years old?

Responses:

OC = Open country but not on a farm
TW = Small city or town (under 50,000)
SB = Suburb near a large city
FR = On a farm
MC = Medium sized city (50,000 to 250,000)
LC = In a large city

		YEAR															
AGE	RESP	'72	'73	'74	'75	'76	'77	'78	'80	'82	'83	'84	'85	'86	'87	'88	'89
18-23	OC	11%	12%	10%	18%	17%	13%	15%	8%	14%	13%	14%	12%	16%	15%	9%	12%
	FR	7	7	11	7	9	11	10	11	14	5	8	8	3	6	8	6
	TW	31	34	29	32	31	39	28	32	34	34	33	37	34	29	35	37
	MC	14	17	14	14	14	17	14	16	16	20	20	21	14	19	18	15
	SB	13	12	20	13	11	9	14	10	12	20	11	14	18	17	18	16
	LC	25	18	16	16	17	10	19	23	10	10	13	9	16	14	11	14
# SURVEYED		169	170	168	173	161	164	163	155	146	128	159	131	108	126	141	137
AGE	RESP	'72	'73	'74	'75	'76	'77	'78	'80	'82	'83	'84	'85	'86	'87	'88	'89
24-29	OC	11%	13%	8%	15%	12%	12%	14%	15%	9%	14%	11%	14%	15%	15%	14%	12%
	FR	9	16	12	11	14	8	11	11	12	9	8	10	12	10	6	9
	TW	32	24	32	30	31	41	28	30	34	31	38	35	27	25	35	30
	MC	16	15	18	14	16	15	18	15	16	15	15	14	19	14	17	20
	SB	13	14	12	12	14	10	14	15	15	15	13	17	13	19	12	19
	LC	19	19	18	18	13	15	14	14	13	16	15	11	15	17	15	10
# SURVEYED		231	212	211	232	226	200	244	202	245	287	232	216	218	193	214	202
AGE	RESP	'72	'73	'74	'75	'76	'77	'78	'80	'82	'83	'84	'85	'86	'87	'88	'89
30-35	OC	7%	11%	10%	14%	11%	15%	17%	9%	10%	13%	13%	9%	9%	12%	12%	11%
	FR	11	19	18	16	16	12	13	13	8	9	11	13	10	10	11	10
	TW	32	32	26	29	26	34	30	36	38	32	31	30	35	29	28	33
	MC	12	15	19	16	17	14	13	14	13	19	17	17	23	20	16	19
	SB	8	7	6	10	13	9	12	12	12	10	11	18	11	14	12	19
	LC	30	16	21	15	17	15	15	15	19	17	17	12	13	16	20	9
# SURVEYED		186	167	175	171	186	188	230	215	203	236	199	212	221	221	195	212
AGE	RESP	'72	'73	'74	'75	'76	'77	'78	'80	'82	'83	'84	'85	'86	'87	'88	'89
36-41	OC	11%	9%	11%	19%	9%	13%	11%	13%	12%	13%	12%	11%	5%	13%	15%	9%
	FR	17	18	22	21	19	23	22	16	16	17	13	13	15	14	13	11
	TW	31	36	33	26	34	35	29	30	30	27	33	39	31	28	31	35
	MC	13	10	12	14	7	10	18	13	14	14	16	16	17	16	18	18
	SB	2	9	9	5	9	8	8	13	16	16	13	10	12	13	10	13
	LC	26	18	14	15	22	12	14	15	11	13	13	10	19	16	13	15
# SURVEYED		127	175	151	154	158	168	160	149	146	173	187	183	188	186	192	197
AGE	RESP	'72	'73	'74	'75	'76	'77	'78	'80	'82	'83	'84	'85	'86	'87	'88	'89
42-47	OC	8%	6%	9%	12%	12%	12%	14%	10%	14%	10%	4%	11%	9%	15%	10%	11%
	FR	18	17	27	25	21	31	22	21	18	12	23	11	16	17	11	15
	TW	32	37	31	32	33	31	34	37	32	37	34	42	28	29	38	33
	MC	14	12	11	14	10	7	8	9	13	16	13	15	16	15	13	13
	SB	4	6	11	5	6	3	8	9	9	8	9	7	9	6	11	12
	LC	24	23	11	12	18	16	14	15	13	17	17	13	23	17	17	16
# SURVEYED		186	145	151	143	114	147	119	117	119	145	126	124	141	156	157	161

TABLE IV: TYPE OF COMMUNITY LIVED IN AT AGE 16 -- BY AGE (Continued)

Question: Which of the categories below comes closest to the type of place you were living in when you were 16 years old?

Responses:
OC = Open country but not on a farm FR = On a farm
TW = Small city or town (under 50,000) MC = Medium sized city (50,000 to 250,000)
SB = Suburb near a large city LC = In a large city

		YEAR															
AGE	RESP	'72	'73	'74	'75	'76	'77	'78	'80	'82	'83	'84	'85	'86	'87	'88	'89
48-53	OC	8%	12%	10%	9%	11%	10%	5%	10%	12%	14%	7%	8%	10%	12%	15%	22%
	FR	25	23	28	23	23	25	29	25	22	20	27	20	20	25	16	17
	TW	28	35	32	28	31	34	30	28	28	33	34	29	31	30	33	28
	MC	10	14	13	9	14	15	20	15	6	12	7	18	17	14	15	14
	SB	4	2	8	6	5	3	3	6	12	7	3	9	9	6	5	5
	LC	24	14	10	25	15	13	13	16	21	15	22	17	12	13	15	14
# SURVEYED		189	151	146	141	133	154	133	123	112	116	102	131	108	126	92	138
AGE	RESP	'72	'73	'74	'75	'76	'77	'78	'80	'82	'83	'84	'85	'86	'87	'88	'89
54-59	OC	9%	6%	12%	9%	12%	7%	7%	7%	8%	11%	10%	9%	12%	10%	7%	11%
	FR	30	32	32	31	29	27	23	35	26	21	29	23	24	24	29	22
	TW	28	29	28	27	31	31	39	29	28	32	32	33	28	27	41	30
	MC	13	11	9	14	9	11	11	15	7	14	15	14	15	9	8	10
	SB	2	6	3	3	3	3	4	2	6	7	5	5	6	11	1	5
	LC	17	16	17	16	16	22	15	12	25	15	10	17	14	18	13	21
# SURVEYED		156	157	138	126	129	168	137	136	143	134	114	133	99	98	85	98
AGE	RESP	'72	'73	'74	'75	'76	'77	'78	'80	'82	'83	'84	'85	'86	'87	'88	'89
60-65	OC	9%	6%	11%	12%	8%	11%	7%	6%	11%	5%	5%	6%	7%	10%	20%	6%
	FR	31	42	35	34	26	36	35	25	24	17	39	31	26	28	18	23
	TW	36	29	26	27	30	30	32	35	34	44	29	37	31	29	34	32
	MC	11	11	7	3	13	14	12	14	11	17	11	11	18	16	7	18
	SB	1	2	6	1	3	1	4	3	3	3	5	4	3	4	3	5
	LC	11	10	15	25	20	8	10	16	17	15	11	11	15	13	19	15
# SURVEYED		143	121	108	113	134	116	107	119	116	132	111	131	115	100	119	110
AGE	RESP	'72	'73	'74	'75	'76	'77	'78	'80	'82	'83	'84	'85	'86	'87	'88	'89
66+	OC	8%	5%	8%	8%	6%	8%	8%	9%	7%	5%	7%	5%	6%	7%	5%	7%
	FR	43	37	39	40	43	36	39	35	37	32	45	34	34	40	37	34
	TW	29	34	28	27	26	33	32	29	34	35	25	31	29	26	27	33
	MC	7	8	10	9	10	8	6	13	9	12	7	13	12	12	13	12
	SB	1	2	2	3	4	3	4	1	3	2	5	4	4	4	6	2
	LC	11	14	12	13	12	12	12	13	11	14	10	13	14	11	11	12
# SURVEYED		218	199	227	232	250	212	230	242	257	241	231	260	265	253	280	275

****

BLACKS IN NEIGHBORHOOD

TABLE I: BLACKS IN NEIGHBORHOOD -- BY TOTAL POPULATION

Question: Are there any blacks living in this neighborhood now? NOTE: Asked of non-blacks in 1972-1977. In 1978-89 it was asked of all respondents.

Responses: Yes; No

	YEAR															
RESPONSE	'72	'73	'74	'75	'76	'77	'78	'80	'82	'83	'84	'85	'86	'87	'88	'89
YES	30%	41%	44%	34%	44%	41%	50%	48%	49%	49%	53%	50%	49%	49%	56%	54%
NO	70	59	56	66	56	59	50	52	51	51	47	50	51	51	44	46
# SURVEYED	1294	1269	1265	1270	1317	1309	1476	1412	1447	1547	1406	1460	1428	1410	1409	1452

TABLE II: BLACKS IN NEIGHBORHOOD -- BY SEX

Question: Are there any blacks living in this neighborhood now? NOTE: Asked of non-blacks in 1972-1977. In 1978-89 it was asked of all respondents.

Responses: Yes; No

		YEAR															
SEX	RESP	'72	'73	'74	'75	'76	'77	'78	'80	'82	'83	'84	'85	'86	'87	'88	'89
M	YES	31%	41%	46%	35%	46%	40%	52%	48%	52%	47%	54%	51%	51%	50%	57%	55%
	NO	69	59	54	65	54	60	48	52	48	53	46	49	49	50	43	45
# SURVEYED		639	598	595	575	590	609	630	623	624	672	577	660	606	616	600	632
SEX	RESP	'72	'73	'74	'75	'76	'77	'78	'80	'82	'83	'84	'85	'86	'87	'88	'89
F	YES	29%	41%	42%	34%	42%	41%	49%	48%	46%	50%	52%	50%	48%	49%	56%	54%
	NO	71	59	58	66	58	59	51	52	54	50	48	50	52	51	44	46
# SURVEYED		655	671	670	695	727	700	846	789	823	875	829	800	822	794	809	820

TABLE III: BLACKS IN NEIGHBORHOOD -- BY RACE

Question: Are there any blacks living in this neighborhood now? NOTE: Asked of non-blacks in 1972-1977. In 1978-89 it was asked of all respondents.

Responses: Yes; No

		YEAR															
RACE	RESP	'72	'73	'74	'75	'76	'77	'78	'80	'82	'83	'84	'85	'86	'87	'88	'89
WHITE	YES	30%	41%	44%	34%	44%	40%	47%	45%	46%	45%	49%	46%	45%	45%	52%	52%
	NO	70	59	56	66	56	60	53	55	54	55	51	54	55	55	48	48
# SURVEYED		1292	1257	1259	1266	1309	1294	1304	1266	1267	1370	1191	1269	1210	1173	1171	1240
RACE	RESP	'72	'73	'74	'75	'76	'77	'78	'80	'82	'83	'84	'85	'86	'87	'88	'89
BLACK	YES	0%	0%	0%	0%	0%	0%	77%	77%	71%	81%	84%	85%	75%	82%	85%	69%
	NO	0	0	0	0	0	0	23	23	29	19	16	15	25	18	15	31
# SURVEYED		000	000	000	000	000	000	157	137	153	160	164	148	181	185	181	154
RACE	RESP	'72	'73	'74	'75	'76	'77	'78	'80	'82	'83	'84	'85	'86	'87	'88	'89
OTHER	YES	50%	92%	0%	50%	75%	67%	80%	44%	59%	71%	45%	56%	51%	38%	56%	64%
	NO	50	8	100	50	25	33	20	56	41	29	55	44	49	62	44	36
# SURVEYED		2	12	6	4	8	15	15	9	27	17	51	43	37	52	57	58

TABLE IV: BLACKS IN NEIGHBORHOOD -- BY AGE

Question: Are there any blacks living in this neighborhood now? NOTE: Asked of non-blacks in 1972-1977. In 1978-89 it was asked of all respondents.

Responses: Yes; No

		YEAR															
AGE	RESP	'72	'73	'74	'75	'76	'77	'78	'80	'82	'83	'84	'85	'86	'87	'88	'89
18-23	YES	31%	37%	54%	36%	49%	44%	55%	49%	61%	54%	64%	57%	64%	64%	57%	63%
	NO	69	63	46	64	51	56	45	51	39	46	36	43	36	36	43	37
# SURVEYED		127	140	132	145	138	135	150	148	138	124	151	126	108	122	135	131
AGE	RESP	'72	'73	'74	'75	'76	'77	'78	'80	'82	'83	'84	'85	'86	'87	'88	'89
24-29	YES	34%	42%	47%	40%	54%	49%	53%	52%	50%	53%	58%	50%	55%	58%	67%	61%
	NO	66	58	53	60	46	51	47	48	50	47	42	50	45	42	33	39
# SURVEYED		178	184	188	189	193	170	234	190	234	276	216	202	211	185	198	188

TABLE IV: BLACKS IN NEIGHBORHOOD -- BY AGE (Continued)

Question: Are there any blacks living in this neighborhood now? NOTE: Asked of non-blacks in 1972-1977. In 1978-89 it was asked of all respondents.

Responses: Yes; No

		YEAR															
AGE	RESP	'72	'73	'74	'75	'76	'77	'78	'80	'82	'83	'84	'85	'86	'87	'88	'89
30-35	YES	35%	44%	41%	38%	37%	42%	57%	56%	55%	47%	54%	49%	55%	54%	63%	56%
	NO	65	56	59	62	63	58	43	44	45	53	46	51	45	46	37	44
# SURVEYED		156	142	141	144	166	156	219	207	199	230	185	204	213	208	185	200
AGE	RESP	'72	'73	'74	'75	'76	'77	'78	'80	'82	'83	'84	'85	'86	'87	'88	'89
36-41	YES	29%	49%	52%	36%	56%	34%	56%	52%	54%	58%	53%	50%	52%	43%	61%	59%
	NO	71	51	48	64	44	66	44	48	46	42	47	50	48	57	39	41
# SURVEYED		107	147	127	129	132	140	154	145	140	171	182	176	182	176	181	184
AGE	RESP	'72	'73	'74	'75	'76	'77	'78	'80	'82	'83	'84	'85	'86	'87	'88	'89
42-47	YES	38%	49%	47%	41%	41%	31%	45%	47%	51%	54%	51%	55%	46%	52%	58%	58%
	NO	62	51	53	59	59	69	55	53	49	46	49	45	54	48	42	42
# SURVEYED		151	126	135	122	105	133	114	110	113	136	123	118	135	152	152	146
AGE	RESP	'72	'73	'74	'75	'76	'77	'78	'80	'82	'83	'84	'85	'86	'87	'88	'89
48-53	YES	23%	39%	35%	38%	50%	51%	47%	52%	50%	51%	56%	52%	49%	51%	60%	55%
	NO	77	61	65	62	50	49	53	48	50	49	44	48	51	49	40	45
# SURVEYED		154	123	127	123	118	136	128	120	109	112	99	128	106	119	87	135
AGE	RESP	'72	'73	'74	'75	'76	'77	'78	'80	'82	'83	'84	'85	'86	'87	'88	'89
54-59	YES	27%	40%	40%	25%	44%	40%	53%	55%	45%	44%	52%	50%	43%	47%	63%	53%
	NO	73	60	60	75	56	60	47	45	55	56	48	50	57	53	37	47
# SURVEYED		125	130	122	110	116	141	134	134	138	131	109	128	98	97	82	96
AGE	RESP	'72	'73	'74	'75	'76	'77	'78	'80	'82	'83	'84	'85	'86	'87	'88	'89
60-65	YES	24%	42%	38%	21%	36%	36%	42%	44%	45%	41%	42%	48%	45%	45%	48%	48%
	NO	76	58	62	79	64	64	58	56	55	59	58	52	55	55	52	52
# SURVEYED		119	106	90	102	115	106	107	114	114	128	110	121	110	98	115	106
AGE	RESP	'72	'73	'74	'75	'76	'77	'78	'80	'82	'83	'84	'85	'86	'87	'88	'89
66+	YES	24%	32%	40%	30%	33%	36%	43%	30%	35%	37%	46%	47%	37%	37%	39%	40%
	NO	76	68	60	70	67	64	57	70	65	63	54	53	63	63	61	60
# SURVEYED		174	168	198	202	229	187	231	235	252	233	225	250	259	249	271	262

****

PROXIMITY OF BLACKS

TABLE I: PROXIMITY OF BLACKS -- BY TOTAL POPULATION

Question: Are there any black families living close to you? Note: This question asked of whites only in 1972-1977; blacks and whites in terms of the opposite race in 1978, 1980, 1982-1989.

Responses: Yes; No

	YEAR															
RESPONSE	'72	'73	'74	'75	'76	'77	'78	'80	'82	'83	'84	'85	'86	'87	'88	'89
YES	74%	71%	69%	71%	73%	71%	73%	74%	74%	70%	78%	75%	73%	48%	80%	72%
NO	26	29	31	29	27	29	27	26	26	30	22	25	27	52	20	28
# SURVEYED	383	517	550	432	575	524	745	673	701	748	737	725	691	1422	776	777

TABLE II: PROXIMITY OF BLACKS -- BY SEX

Question: Are there any black families living close to you? NOTE: This question asked of whites only in 1972-1977; blacks and whites in terms of the opposite race in 1978, 1980, 1982-1989.

Responses: Yes; No

		YEAR															
SEX	RESP	'72	'73	'74	'75	'76	'77	'78	'80	'82	'83	'84	'85	'86	'87	'88	'89
M	YES	74%	70%	67%	65%	72%	69%	70%	73%	75%	68%	77%	74%	71%	47%	81%	70%
	NO	26	30	33	35	28	31	30	27	25	32	23	26	29	53	19	30
# SURVEYED		197	243	272	201	271	240	330	295	323	317	307	331	300	620	333	345
SEX	RESP	'72	'73	'74	'75	'76	'77	'78	'80	'82	'83	'84	'85	'86	'87	'88	'89
F	YES	74%	73%	70%	77%	73%	73%	75%	74%	74%	71%	78%	75%	75%	48%	79%	74%
	NO	26	27	30	23	27	27	25	26	26	29	22	25	25	52	21	26
# SURVEYED		186	274	278	231	304	284	415	378	378	431	430	394	391	802	443	432

TABLE III: PROXIMITY OF BLACKS -- BY RACE

Question: Are there any black families living close to you? NOTE: This question asked of whites only in 1972-1977; blacks and whites in terms of the opposite race in 1978, 1980, 1982-1989.

Responses: Yes; No

		YEAR															
RACE	RESP	'72	'73	'74	'75	'76	'77	'78	'80	'82	'83	'84	'85	'86	'87	'88	'89
WHITE	YES	74%	71%	69%	71%	72%	71%	70%	71%	72%	66%	75%	71%	70%	43%	77%	69%
	NO	26	29	31	29	28	29	30	29	28	34	25	29	30	57	23	31
# SURVEYED		382	506	550	430	569	514	612	564	578	607	579	575	538	1190	593	636
RACE	RESP	'72	'73	'74	'75	'76	'77	'78	'80	'82	'83	'84	'85	'86	'87	'88	'89
BLACK	YES	0%	0%	0%	0%	0%	0%	86%	85%	85%	84%	90%	91%	85%	79%	94%	90%
	NO	0	0	0	0	0	0	14	15	15	16	10	9	15	21	6	10
# SURVEYED		000	000	000	000	000	000	121	105	107	129	135	126	134	187	152	104
RACE	RESP	'72	'73	'74	'75	'76	'77	'78	'80	'82	'83	'84	'85	'86	'87	'88	'89
OTHER	YES	100%	82%	0%	50%	83%	80%	83%	75%	75%	92%	78%	79%	79%	42%	77%	68%
	NO	0	18	0	50	17	20	17	25	25	8	22	21	21	58	23	32
# SURVEYED		1	11	2	6	10	12	4	16	12	23	24	19	45	31	37	

TABLE IV: PROXIMITY OF BLACKS -- BY AGE

Question: Are there any black families living close to you? NOTE: This question asked of whites only in 1972-1977; blacks and whites in terms of the opposite race in 1978, 1980, 1982-1989.

Responses: Yes; No

		YEAR															
AGE	RESP	'72	'73	'74	'75	'76	'77	'78	'80	'82	'83	'84	'85	'86	'87	'88	'89
18-23	YES	82%	77%	63%	73%	80%	76%	80%	74%	73%	62%	82%	75%	83%	61%	87%	72%
	NO	18	23	37	27	20	24	20	26	27	38	18	25	17	39	13	28
# SURVEYED		38	52	70	52	66	58	83	72	84	66	97	72	66	124	75	83
AGE	RESP	'72	'73	'74	'75	'76	'77	'78	'80	'82	'83	'84	'85	'86	'87	'88	'89
24-29	YES	73%	74%	81%	73%	73%	67%	76%	72%	73%	74%	78%	80%	78%	57%	83%	82%
	NO	27	26	19	27	27	33	24	28	27	26	22	20	22	43	17	18
# SURVEYED		60	78	89	74	103	81	125	98	116	147	124	101	116	189	132	115
AGE	RESP	'72	'73	'74	'75	'76	'77	'78	'80	'82	'83	'84	'85	'86	'87	'88	'89
30-35	YES	64%	74%	71%	65%	71%	74%	73%	73%	71%	72%	82%	73%	74%	52%	80%	74%
	NO	36	26	29	35	29	26	27	27	29	28	18	27	26	48	20	26
# SURVEYED		55	61	58	54	62	65	124	115	110	109	98	98	117	213	113	111

TABLE IV: PROXIMITY OF BLACKS -- BY AGE (Continued)

Question: Are there any black families living close to you? NOTE: This question asked of whites only in 1972-1977; blacks and whites in terms of the opposite race in 1978, 1980, 1982-1989.

Responses: Yes; No

		YEAR															
AGE	RESP	'72	'73	'74	'75	'76	'77	'78	'80	'82	'83	'84	'85	'86	'87	'88	'89
36-41	YES	65%	71%	58%	76%	68%	67%	76%	77%	79%	73%	77%	74%	67%	46%	81%	71%
	NO	35	29	42	24	32	33	24	23	21	27	23	26	33	54	19	29
# SURVEYED		31	69	64	46	73	48	86	75	75	100	97	86	93	181	103	106
AGE	RESP	'72	'73	'74	'75	'76	'77	'78	'80	'82	'83	'84	'85	'86	'87	'88	'89
42-47	YES	76%	66%	78%	60%	70%	76%	75%	90%	76%	63%	81%	77%	75%	50%	85%	68%
	NO	24	34	22	40	30	24	25	10	24	37	19	23	25	50	15	32
# SURVEYED		58	62	63	50	43	41	51	52	58	73	63	65	59	147	88	82
AGE	RESP	'72	'73	'74	'75	'76	'77	'78	'80	'82	'83	'84	'85	'86	'87	'88	'89
48-53	YES	71%	62%	60%	74%	78%	63%	68%	69%	76%	70%	78%	75%	66%	46%	77%	68%
	NO	29	38	40	26	22	37	32	31	24	30	22	25	34	54	23	32
# SURVEYED		35	47	45	47	59	68	60	62	55	56	54	63	50	121	52	74
AGE	RESP	'72	'73	'74	'75	'76	'77	'78	'80	'82	'83	'84	'85	'86	'87	'88	'89
54-59	YES	74%	75%	57%	72%	73%	75%	69%	72%	66%	67%	79%	67%	74%	46%	79%	69%
	NO	26	25	43	28	27	25	31	28	34	33	21	33	26	54	21	31
# SURVEYED		34	52	49	25	51	55	71	74	62	58	57	64	42	98	52	51
AGE	RESP	'72	'73	'74	'75	'76	'77	'78	'80	'82	'83	'84	'85	'86	'87	'88	'89
60-65	YES	83%	70%	70%	67%	78%	76%	62%	70%	75%	60%	70%	72%	69%	43%	74%	63%
	NO	17	30	30	33	22	24	38	30	25	40	30	28	31	57	26	37
# SURVEYED		29	43	33	21	41	38	45	50	51	53	46	57	49	98	54	51
AGE	RESP	'72	'73	'74	'75	'76	'77	'78	'80	'82	'83	'84	'85	'86	'87	'88	'89
66+	YES	83%	71%	71%	75%	64%	70%	71%	67%	80%	73%	70%	75%	69%	35%	72%	73
	NO	17	29	29	25	36	30	29	33	20	27	30	25	31	65	28	27
# SURVEYED		41	52	79	61	75	66	99	70	85	85	98	116	95	247	105	102

****

DISTANCE TO BLACK HOUSEHOLD

TABLE I: DISTANCE TO BLACK HOUSEHOLD -- BY TOTAL POPULATION

Question: How many blocks (or miles) away do black families who live closest to you live? NOTE: This question asked of whites only in 1972-1977; blacks and whites in terms of the opposite race in 1978, 1980, 1982-1989.

Responses: TB = On this block, a few doors/houses away QM = 1-3 blocks away, under 1/4 mile
1M = 4-8 blocks away, 1/4 to 1 mile M+ = Over 8 blocks away, over 1 mile

	YEAR															
RESPONSE	'72	'73	'74	'75	'76	'77	'78	'80	'82	'83	'84	'85	'86	'87	'88	'89
TB	41%	38%	42%	41%	42%	39%	45%	47%	47%	47%	56%	52%	53%	28%	55%	47%
QM	39	40	35	35	32	34	36	34	34	32	31	28	31	19	32	34
1M	14	15	16	15	17	19	12	16	12	13	9	14	10	15	8	13
M+	6	6	7	9	9	8	7	4	6	8	5	6	7	38	4	6
# SURVEYED	380	518	546	430	575	525	737	663	693	740	729	723	688	1388	774	774

TABLE II: DISTANCE TO BLACK HOUSEHOLD -- BY SEX

Question: How many blocks (or miles) away do black families who live closest to you live? NOTE: This question asked of whites only in 1972-1977; blacks and whites in terms of the opposite race in 1978, 1980, 1982-1989.

Responses: TB = On this block, a few doors/houses away QM = 1-3 blocks away, under 1/4 mile
1M = 4-8 blocks away, 1/4 to 1 mile M+ = Over 8 blocks away, over 1 mile

		YEAR															
SEX	RESP	'72	'73	'74	'75	'76	'77	'78	'80	'82	'83	'84	'85	'86	'87	'88	'89
M	TB	41%	34%	39%	39%	39%	37%	42%	44%	49%	46%	53%	53%	47%	29%	54%	44%
	QM	41	45	36	33	33	35	39	35	32	29	32	25	33	18	34	35
	1M	12	16	17	18	20	18	11	18	12	15	10	13	13	15	8	14
	M+	6	5	7	10	8	10	8	2	7	9	5	9	7	38	4	7
# SURVEYED		196	244	269	198	272	240	325	289	319	310	306	329	300	602	334	343
SEX	RESP	'72	'73	'74	'75	'76	'77	'78	'80	'82	'83	'84	'85	'86	'87	'88	'89
F	TB	40%	42%	45%	44%	46%	41%	48%	49%	45%	48%	58%	51%	57%	28%	56%	48%
	QM	38	36	34	37	31	33	34	32	37	33	30	31	29	20	31	33
	1M	16	15	15	12	14	20	13	13	13	11	7	14	8	14	9	12
	M+	6	7	6	7	9	6	5	5	6	8	5	4	6	38	4	6
# SURVEYED		184	274	277	232	303	285	412	374	374	430	423	394	388	786	440	431

TABLE III: DISTANCE TO BLACK HOUSEHOLD -- BY RACE

Question: How many blocks (or miles) away do black families who live closest to you live? NOTE: This question asked of whites only in 1972-1977; blacks and whites in terms of the opposite race in 1978, 1980, 1982-1989.

Responses: TB = On this block, a few doors/houses away; QM = 1-3 blocks away, under 1/4 mile; 1M = 4-8 blocks away, 1/4 to 1 mile; M+ = Over 8 blocks away, over 1 mile

RACE	RESP	'72	'73	'74	'75	'76	'77	'78	'80	'82	'83	'84	'85	'86	'87	'88	'89
WHITE	TB	40%	38%	42%	41%	42%	39%	40%	43%	43%	41%	51%	46%	46%	23%	50%	42%
	QM	40	40	35	35	32	34	39	36	36	34	33	31	33	19	36	36
	1M	14	16	16	15	17	19	14	17	13	15	10	16	13	16	9	15
	M+	6	6	7	9	9	8	7	5	8	10	6	7	8	42	5	7
# SURVEYED		379	507	546	428	569	515	605	554	573	599	573	573	536	1150	592	633
RACE	RESP	'72	'73	'74	'75	'76	'77	'78	'80	'82	'83	'84	'85	'86	'87	'88	'89
BLACK	TB	0%	0%	0%	0%	0%	0%	73%	68%	66%	72%	77%	77%	74%	57%	77%	72%
	QM	0	0	0	0	0	0	23	23	25	22	21	17	23	24	18	20
	1M	0	0	0	0	0	0	3	9	8	5	1	4	2	11	4	5
	M+	0	0	0	0	0	0	2	1	0	1	1	2	0	8	1	3
# SURVEYED		000	000	000	000	000	000	120	105	106	129	134	126	133	187	150	104
RACE	RESP	'72	'73	'74	'75	'76	'77	'78	'80	'82	'83	'84	'85	'86	'87	'88	'89
OTHER	TB	100%	55%	0%	50%	50%	50%	75%	75%	57%	92%	68%	54%	74%	27%	50%	59%
	QM	0	27	0	50	17	30	8	25	36	8	27	25	11	10	28	32
	1M	0	9	0	0	17	20	8	0	0	0	5	13	0	4	13	3
	M+	0	9	0	0	17	0	8	0	7	0	0	8	16	59	9	5
# SURVEYED		1	11	000	2	6	10	12	4	14	12	22	24	19	51	32	37

TABLE IV: DISTANCE TO BLACK HOUSEHOLD -- BY AGE

Question: How many blocks (or miles) away do black families who live closest to you live? NOTE: This question asked of whites only in 1972-1977; blacks and whites in terms of the opposite race in 1978, 1980, 1982-1989.

Responses: TB = On this block, a few doors/houses away; QM = 1-3 blocks away, under 1/4 mile; 1M = 4-8 blocks away, 1/4 to 1 mile; M+ = Over 8 blocks away, over 1 mile

		YEAR															
AGE	RESP	'72	'73	'74	'75	'76	'77	'78	'80	'82	'83	'84	'85	'86	'87	'88	'89
18-23	TB	50%	51%	45%	55%	51%	47%	45%	56%	45%	44%	65%	56%	64%	40%	72%	43%
	QM	37	33	29	27	34	34	31	21	32	33	25	24	27	21	20	35
	1M	8	12	22	16	10	14	17	17	15	14	4	17	7	14	5	17
	M+	5	4	4	2	4	5	7	6	9	9	6	4	1	25	3	5
# SURVEYED		38	51	69	51	67	59	83	71	82	64	96	72	67	121	74	83
AGE	RESP	'72	'73	'74	'75	'76	'77	'78	'80	'82	'83	'84	'85	'86	'87	'88	'89
24-29	TB	44%	44%	51%	47%	49%	49%	58%	57%	52%	59%	67%	52%	62%	39%	62%	62%
	QM	34	35	30	31	29	29	31	26	31	23	18	32	22	18	28	30
	1M	15	16	17	14	13	18	5	14	11	10	12	11	10	11	8	5
	M+	7	5	2	8	10	4	6	3	5	8	3	5	7	32	2	3
# SURVEYED		61	77	89	74	103	82	125	97	115	146	124	101	115	180	130	115
AGE	RESP	'72	'73	'74	'75	'76	'77	'78	'80	'82	'83	'84	'85	'86	'87	'88	'89
30-35	TB	27%	44%	37%	33%	45%	27%	51%	46%	46%	44%	64%	50%	59%	32%	57%	50%
	QM	45	42	30	43	29	42	31	34	36	36	27	28	30	21	36	27
	1M	15	7	23	9	18	20	14	14	12	12	6	16	7	15	4	15
	M+	13	7	11	15	8	11	4	5	5	7	2	6	4	32	3	8
# SURVEYED		55	59	57	54	62	66	123	111	110	107	95	98	117	208	114	110
AGE	RESP	'72	'73	'74	'75	'76	'77	'78	'80	'82	'83	'84	'85	'86	'87	'88	'89
36-41	TB	23%	37%	30%	30%	41%	44%	40%	39%	44%	52%	48%	55%	50%	26%	47%	48%
	QM	48	45	36	52	22	31	43	41	43	24	41	28	28	18	39	36
	1M	19	13	24	13	27	21	12	16	11	15	8	7	12	16	7	11
	M+	10	6	9	4	11	4	6	4	3	9	3	9	10	40	8	6
# SURVEYED		31	71	66	46	74	48	86	74	75	100	96	85	92	176	105	104
AGE	RESP	'72	'73	'74	'75	'76	'77	'78	'80	'82	'83	'84	'85	'86	'87	'88	'89
42-47	TB	38%	40%	48%	29%	35%	39%	47%	67%	47%	42%	56%	54%	47%	29%	63%	41%
	QM	39	40	45	39	28	44	39	29	37	32	27	29	42	19	24	35
	1M	16	16	5	18	28	17	8	4	11	17	11	9	7	14	7	17
	M+	7	3	2	14	9	0	6	0	5	8	5	8	3	38	6	7
# SURVEYED		56	62	62	49	43	41	51	51	57	71	62	65	59	144	87	83
AGE	RESP	'72	'73	'74	'75	'76	'77	'78	'80	'82	'83	'84	'85	'86	'87	'88	'89
48-53	TB	31%	23%	36%	38%	41%	34%	36%	34%	36%	30%	57%	48%	45%	26%	52%	32%
	QM	51	44	36	40	44	31	43	47	43	46	31	37	35	21	31	44
	1M	14	23	16	17	5	16	12	19	15	11	6	11	16	15	12	14
	M+	3	10	13	4	10	18	9	0	6	13	6	5	4	37	6	10
# SURVEYED		35	48	45	47	59	67	58	62	53	56	54	63	51	121	52	72

TABLE IV: DISTANCE TO BLACK HOUSEHOLD -- BY AGE (Continued)

Question: How many blocks (or miles) away do black families who live closest to you live? NOTE: This question asked of whites only in 1972-1977; blacks and whites in terms of the opposite race in 1978, 1980, 1982-1989.

Responses: TB = On this block, a few doors/houses away; QM = 1-3 blocks away, under 1/4 mile; 1M = 4-8 blocks away, 1/4 to 1 mile; M+ = Over 8 blocks away, over 1 mile

		YEAR															
AGE	RESP	'72	'73	'74	'75	'76	'77	'78	'80	'82	'83	'84	'85	'86	'87	'88	'89
54-59	TB	36%	38%	37%	38%	36%	41%	33%	37%	40%	44%	44%	48%	43%	22%	51%	43%
	QM	45	42	46	35	40	32	46	36	32	35	42	27	36	22	31	37
	1M	15	17	9	19	18	20	12	23	19	16	11	22	14	18	18	16
	M+	3	2	9	8	6	7	9	4	8	5	4	3	7	39	0	4
# SURVEYED		33	52	46	26	50	56	69	73	62	57	55	64	42	96	51	51
AGE	RESP	'72	'73	'74	'75	'76	'77	'78	'80	'82	'83	'84	'85	'86	'87	'88	'89
60-65	TB	68%	27%	42%	29%	51%	34%	36%	42%	48%	40%	44%	46%	38%	22%	49%	43%
	QM	29	43	33	29	29	29	42	38	26	43	51	30	45	20	40	35
	1M	4	20	18	29	12	21	13	14	18	11	2	18	11	12	9	14
	M+	0	9	6	14	7	16	9	6	8	6	2	5	6	46	2	8
# SURVEYED		28	44	33	21	41	38	45	50	50	53	45	56	47	97	55	51
AGE	RESP	'72	'73	'74	'75	'76	'77	'78	'80	'82	'83	'84	'85	'86	'87	'88	'89
66+	TB	54%	36%	47%	57%	30%	37%	46%	43%	52%	53%	46%	53%	46%	18%	44%	44%
	QM	29	36	33	22	36	34	30	35	33	27	32	25	29	17	38	34
	1M	17	19	13	12	23	22	17	16	6	9	12	15	13	15	12	15
	M+	0	9	8	10	11	8	7	6	9	11	9	8	13	50	7	8
# SURVEYED		41	53	79	60	74	65	96	69	85	85	99	116	94	241	104	103

****

INTEGRATION OF NEIGHBORHOOD

TABLE I: INTEGRATION OF NEIGHBORHOOD -- BY TOTAL POPULATION

Question: Do you think the neighborhood will become all black in the next few years, or will it remain integrated? NOTE: This question asked of whites only in 1972-1977; blacks and whites in terms of blacks in 1978, 1980, 1982-1989.

Responses: AB = All black; IN = Remain integrated; MX = Mixed, but not black and white

	YEAR															
RESPONSE	'72	'73	'74	'75	'76	'77	'78	'80	'82	'83	'84	'85	'86	'87	'88	'89
AB	11%	5%	5%	7%	7%	5%	7%	7%	7%	6%	6%	5%	6%	6%	6%	5%
IN	89	95	95	93	93	95	93	93	93	94	94	95	94	94	94	95
MX	0	0	0	0	0	0	0	0	0	0	0	0	0	0	0	0
# SURVEYED	350	493	520	408	558	507	707	639	668	709	714	697	679	657	757	750

TABLE II: INTEGRATION OF NEIGHBORHOOD -- BY SEX

Question: Do you think the neighborhood will become all black in the next few years, or will it remain integrated? NOTE: This question asked of whites only in 1972-1977; blacks and whites in terms of blacks in 1978, 1980, 1982-1989.

Responses: AB = All black; IN = Remain integrated; MX = Mixed, but not black and white

		YEAR															
SEX	RESP	'72	'73	'74	'75	'76	'77	'78	'80	'82	'83	'84	'85	'86	'87	'88	'89
M	AB	12%	4%	4%	7%	6%	4%	6%	5%	9%	5%	5%	5%	4%	8%	5%	4%
	IN	88	96	96	93	94	96	94	95	91	95	95	95	96	92	95	96
	MX	0	0	0	0	0	0	0	0	0	0	0	0	0	0	0	0
# SURVEYED		181	231	260	190	266	231	316	286	308	295	298	316	296	295	327	331
SEX	RESP	'72	'73	'74	'75	'76	'77	'78	'80	'82	'83	'84	'85	'86	'87	'88	'89
F	AB	9%	6%	6%	6%	7%	5%	7%	8%	6%	7%	6%	4%	8%	5%	6%	5%
	IN	91	94	93	94	93	95	93	92	94	93	94	96	92	95	94	95
	MX	0	0	0	0	0	0	0	0	0	0	0	0	0	0	0	0
# SURVEYED		169	262	260	218	292	276	391	353	360	414	416	381	383	362	430	419

TABLE III: INTEGRATION OF NEIGHBORHOOD -- BY RACE

Question: Do you think the neighborhood will become all black in the next few years, or will it remain integrated? NOTE: This question asked of whites only in 1972-1977; blacks and whites in terms of blacks in 1978, 1980, 1982-1989.

Responses: AB = All black; IN = Remain integrated; MX = Mixed, but not black and white

		YEAR															
RACE	RESP	'72	'73	'74	'75	'76	'77	'78	'80	'82	'83	'84	'85	'86	'87	'88	'89
WHITE	AB	11%	5%	5%	6%	7%	5%	3%	5%	4%	3%	4%	3%	6%	3%	4%	3%
	IN	89	95	95	94	93	95	97	95	96	97	96	97	94	97	96	97
	MX	0	0	0	0	0	0	0	0	0	0	0	0	0	0	0	0
# SURVEYED		349	482	520	406	552	498	581	541	553	579	563	563	532	502	579	618
RACE	RESP	'72	'73	'74	'75	'76	'77	'78	'80	'82	'83	'84	'85	'86	'87	'88	'89
Black	AB	0%	0%	0%	0%	0%	0%	25%	18%	26%	22%	14%	14%	7%	18%	16%	15%
	IN	0	0	0	0	0	0	75	82	74	78	86	86	93	82	84	85
	MX	0	0	0	0	0	0	0	0	0	0	0	0	0	0	0	0
# SURVEYED		0	0	0	0	0	0	114	96	101	120	129	114	129	137	148	98
RACE	RESP	'72	'73	'74	'75	'76	'77	'78	'80	'82	'83	'84	'85	'86	'87	'88	'89
OTHER	AB	0%	0%	0%	50%	0%	0%	0%	0%	7%	10%	5%	10%	6%	6%	0%	0%
	IN	100	91	0	50	100	100	100	100	93	90	95	90	94	94	100	100
	MX	0	9	0	0	0	0	0	0	0	0	0	0	0	0	0	0
# SURVEYED		1	11	0	2	6	9	12	2	14	10	22	20	18	18	30	31

TABLE IV: INTEGRATION OF NEIGHBORHOOD -- BY AGE

Question: Do you think the neighborhood will become all black in the next few years, or will it remain integrated? NOTE: This question asked of whites only in 1972-1977; blacks and whites in terms of blacks in 1978, 1980, 1982-1989.

Responses: AB = All black; IN = Remain integrated; MX = Mixed, but not black and white

		YEAR															
AGE	RESP	'72	'73	'74	'75	'76	'77	'78	'80	'82	'83	'84	'85	'86	'87	'88	'89
18-23	AB	3%	4%	7%	13%	11%	3%	8%	15%	5%	6%	3%	6%	6%	9%	6%	9%
	IN	97	96	91	87	89	97	92	85	95	94	97	94	94	91	94	91
	MX	0	0	1	0	0	0	0	0	0	0	0	0	0	0	0	0
# SURVEYED		35	51	68	47	66	59	79	67	83	64	95	70	69	74	71	82
AGE	RESP	'72	'73	'74	'75	'76	'77	'78	'80	'82	'83	'84	'85	'86	'87	'88	'89
24-29	AB	2%	4%	7%	6%	5%	5%	7%	3%	8%	6%	6%	1%	5%	4%	2%	4%
	IN	98	95	93	94	95	95	93	97	92	94	94	99	95	96	98	96
	MX	0	1	0	0	0	0	0	0	0	0	0	0	0	0	0	0
# SURVEYED		56	74	87	70	101	78	120	93	110	143	120	94	113	103	123	110

TABLE IV: INTEGRATION OF NEIGHBORHOOD -- BY AGE (Continued)

Question: Do you think the neighborhood will become all black in the next few years, or will it remain integrated? NOTE: This question asked of whites only in 1972-1977; blacks and whites in terms of <u>blacks</u> in 1978, 1980, 1982-1989.

Responses: AB = All black; IN = Remain integrated; MX = Mixed, but not black and white

		YEAR															
AGE	RESP	'72	'73	'74	'75	'76	'77	'78	'80	'82	'83	'84	'85	'86	'87	'88	'89
30-35	AB	14%	2%	0%	4%	5%	2%	5%	11%	12%	10%	4%	2%	5%	3%	7%	1%
	IN	86	98	100	96	95	98	95	89	88	90	96	98	95	97	93	99
	MX	0	0	0	0	0	0	0	0	0	0	0	0	0	0	0	0
# SURVEYED		50	58	58	51	60	66	122	109	103	105	95	95	115	105	115	107
AGE	RESP	'72	'73	'74	'75	'76	'77	'78	'80	'82	'83	'84	'85	'86	'87	'88	'89
36-41	AB	7%	7%	2%	7%	4%	4%	6%	3%	4%	2%	7%	3%	6%	4%	6%	4%
	IN	93	93	98	93	96	96	94	97	96	98	93	97	94	96	94	96
	MX	0	0	0	0	0	0	0	0	0	0	0	0	0	0	0	0
# SURVEYED		29	69	60	46	71	46	81	74	73	94	94	86	90	73	108	102
AGE	RESP	'72	'73	'74	'75	'76	'77	'78	'80	'82	'83	'84	'85	'86	'87	'88	'89
42-47	AB	15%	9%	7%	2%	2%	5%	2%	6%	9%	4%	5%	6%	10%	8%	10%	5%
	IN	85	91	93	98	98	95	98	94	91	96	95	94	90	92	90	95
	MX	0	0	0	0	0	0	0	0	0	0	0	0	0	0	0	0
# SURVEYED		52	58	61	48	43	40	50	48	56	70	61	63	60	75	87	81
AGE	RESP	'72	'73	'74	'75	'76	'77	'78	'80	'82	'83	'84	'85	'86	'87	'88	'89
48-53	AB	8%	5%	0%	5%	5%	3%	13%	10%	6%	5%	8%	5%	4%	9%	6%	6%
	IN	92	95	100	95	95	97	88	90	94	95	92	95	96	91	94	94
	MX	0	0	0	0	0	0	0	0	0	0	0	0	0	0	0	0
# SURVEYED		36	43	41	44	56	65	56	62	53	57	49	63	51	58	51	72
AGE	RESP	'72	'73	'74	'75	'76	'77	'78	'80	'82	'83	'84	'85	'86	'87	'88	'89
54-59	AB	4%	4%	10%	8%	8%	5%	10%	1%	2%	4%	5%	7%	2%	7%	4%	4%
	IN	96	96	90	92	92	95	90	99	98	96	95	93	98	93	96	96
	MX	0	0	0	0	0	0	0	0	0	0	0	0	0	0	0	0
# SURVEYED		26	49	41	25	50	55	63	70	57	54	55	61	41	44	48	48
AGE	RESP	'72	'73	'74	'75	'76	'77	'78	'80	'82	'83	'84	'85	'86	'87	'88	'89
60-65	AB	32%	5%	0%	5%	8%	6%	5%	4%	11%	7%	12%	8%	9%	5%	4%	11%
	IN	68	95	100	95	92	94	95	96	89	93	88	92	91	95	96	89
	MX	0	0	0	0	0	0	0	0	0	0	0	0	0	0	0	0
# SURVEYED		25	43	30	20	39	36	42	47	47	46	41	51	47	39	54	47
AGE	RESP	'72	'73	'74	'75	'76	'77	'78	'80	'82	'83	'84	'85	'86	'87	'88	'89
66+	AB	15%	8%	8%	11%	11%	10%	6%	5%	7%	8%	5%	7%	10%	8%	5%	3%
	IN	85	92	92	89	89	90	94	95	93	92	95	93	90	92	95	97
	MX	0	0	0	0	0	0	0	0	0	0	0	0	0	0	0	0
# SURVEYED		39	48	74	55	70	58	93	66	82	75	101	112	90	85	98	100

****

INTEGRATION OF CHURCH

TABLE I: INTEGRATION OF CHURCH -- BY TOTAL POPULATION

Question: Do blacks/whites attend the church that you, yourself, attend most often? NOTE: Asked in terms of the opposite race. Question not asked in 1972-1977, 1982, 1985.

Responses: Yes; No

	YEAR							
RESPONSE	'78	'80	'83	'84	'86	'87	'88	'89
YES	35%	42%	36%	45%	36%	43%	48%	41%
NO	65	58	64	55	64	57	52	59
# SURVEYED	1267	1239	1344	1255	1254	1264	840	838

TABLE II: INTEGRATION OF CHURCH -- BY SEX

Question: Do blacks/whites attend the church that you, yourself, attend most often? NOTE: Asked in terms of the opposite race. Question not asked in 1972-1977, 1982, 1985.

Responses: Yes; No

		YEAR							
SEX	RESP	'78	'80	'83	'84	'86	'87	'88	'89
M	YES	34%	43%	34%	47%	37%	42%	46%	40%
	NO	66	57	66	53	63	58	54	60
# SURVEYED		513	521	557	476	509	522	349	332
SEX	RESP	'78	'80	'83	'84	'86	'87	'88	'89
F	YES	35%	42%	37%	43%	36%	44%	50%	41%
	NO	65	58	63	57	64	56	50	59
# SURVEYED		754	718	787	779	745	742	491	506

TABLE III: INTEGRATION OF CHURCH -- BY RACE

Question: Do black/whites attend the church that you, yourself, attend most often? NOTE: Asked in terms of the opposite race. Question not asked in 1972-1977, 1982, 1985.

Responses: Yes; No

		YEAR							
RACE	RESP	'78	'80	'83	'84	'86	'87	'88	'89
WHITE	YES	34%	41%	35%	43%	36%	43%	49%	40%
	NO	66	59	65	57	64	57	51	60
# SURVEYED		1107	1103	1186	1053	1050	1044	696	705
RACE	RESP	'78	'80	'83	'84	'86	'87	'88	'89
BLACK	YES	37%	50%	39%	57%	45%	46%	52%	46%
	NO	63	50	61	43	55	54	48	54
# SURVEYED		147	128	147	157	174	176	108	101
RACE	RESP	'78	'80	'83	'84	'86	'87	'88	'89
OTHER	YES	62%	50%	55%	47%	13%	36%	31%	34%
	NO	38	50	45	53	87	64	69	66
# SURVEYED		13	8	11	45	30	44	36	32

TABLE IV: INTEGRATION OF CHURCH -- BY AGE

Question: Do blacks/whites attend the church that you, yourself, attend most often? NOTE: Asked in terms of the opposite race. Question not asked in 1972-1977, 1982, 1985.

Responses: Yes; No

		YEAR							
AGE	RESP	'78	'80	'83	'84	'86	'87	'88	'89
18-23	YES	29%	44%	31%	47%	37%	43%	40%	37%
	NO	71	56	69	53	63	57	60	63
# SURVEYED		134	131	100	138	87	111	70	73
AGE	RESP	'78	'80	'83	'84	'86	'87	'88	'89
24-29	YES	34%	44%	32%	50%	32%	50%	46%	47%
	NO	66	56	68	50	68	50	54	53
# SURVEYED		183	160	228	187	182	167	119	105
AGE	RESP	'78	'80	'83	'84	'86	'87	'88	'89
30-35	YES	34%	54%	34%	42%	43%	44%	49%	44%
	NO	66	46	66	58	57	56	51	56
# SURVEYED		184	166	188	162	182	185	109	115

TABLE IV: INTEGRATION OF CHURCH -- BY AGE (Continued)

Question: Do blacks/whites attend the church that you, yourself, attend most often? NOTE: Asked in terms of the opposite race. Question not asked in 1972-1977, 1982, 1985.

Responses: Yes; No

		YEAR							
AGE	RESP	'78	'80	'83	'84	'86	'87	'88	'89
36-41	YES	40%	42%	53%	49%	37%	48%	48%	47%
	NO	60	58	47	51	63	52	52	53
# SURVEYED		136	127	144	153	159	145	104	103
AGE	RESP	'78	'80	'83	'84	'86	'87	'88	'89
42-47	YES	41%	40%	38%	43%	42%	41%	62%	37%
	NO	59	60	62	57	58	59	38	63
# SURVEYED		100	101	125	106	120	131	91	83
AGE	RESP	'78	'80	'83	'84	'86	'87	'88	'89
48-53	YES	40%	45%	40%	45%	32%	40%	51%	30%
	NO	60	55	60	55	68	60	49	70
# SURVEYED		112	107	104	93	93	110	45	80
AGE	RESP	'78	'80	'83	'84	'86	'87	'88	'89
54-59	YES	36%	36%	39%	50%	40%	37%	52%	46%
	NO	64	64	61	50	60	63	48	54
# SURVEYED		120	121	118	101	90	89	58	54
AGE	RESP	'78	'80	'83	'84	'86	'87	'88	'89
60-65	YES	25%	35%	40%	40%	31%	56%	43%	46%
	NO	75	65	60	60	69	44	57	54
# SURVEYED		92	110	122	100	102	90	72	63
AGE	RESP	'78	'80	'83	'84	'86	'87	'88	'89
66+	YES	33%	36%	25%	39%	33%	34%	47%	35%
	NO	67	64	75	61	67	66	53	65
# SURVEYED		202	210	212	209	233	232	169	160

****

SECTION 2 : OPINIONS

LIFE SATISFACTION

TABLE I: LIFE SATISFACTION -- BY TOTAL POPULATION

Question: In general, do you find life exciting, pretty routine, or dull? NOTE: Question not asked in 1972, 1975, 1978, 1983, 1986.

Responses: EX = Exciting; RT = Routine; DL = Dull

	YEAR										
RESPONSE	'73	'74	'76	'77	'80	'82	'84	'85	'87	'88	'89
EX	45%	43%	45%	44%	46%	45%	47%	48%	46%	45%	45%
RT	49	52	52	49	48	49	48	46	50	50	50
DL	5	5	4	7	6	6	5	6	4	5	5
# SURVEYED	1484	1442	1475	1496	1462	1492	1461	1517	1429	950	1017

TABLE II: LIFE SATISFACTION -- BY SEX

Question: In general, do you find life exciting, pretty routine, or dull? NOTE: Question not asked in 1972, 1975, 1978, 1983, 1986.

Responses: EX = Exciting; RT = Routine; DL = Dull

		YEAR										
SEX	RESP	'73	'74	'76	'77	'80	'82	'84	'85	'87	'88	'89
M	EX	49%	49%	47%	47%	50%	49%	50%	50%	49%	52%	47%
	RT	47	47	50	45	46	46	45	44	48	46	49
	DL	4	4	3	7	4	5	5	6	3	2	4
# SURVEYED		690	671	662	680	640	631	596	679	625	391	438
SEX	RESP	'73	'74	'76	'77	'80	'82	'84	'85	'87	'88	'89
F	EX	42%	39%	43%	42%	43%	42%	44%	46%	43%	40%	43%
	RT	52	56	53	52	50	51	51	47	52	53	51
	DL	6	5	5	6	7	7	5	7	4	7	6
# SURVEYED		794	771	813	816	822	861	865	838	804	559	579

TABLE III: LIFE SATISFACTION -- BY RACE

Question: In general, do you find life exciting, pretty routine, or dull? NOTE: Question not asked in 1972, 1975, 1978, 1983, 1986.

Responses: EX = Exciting; RT = Routine; DL = Dull

		YEAR										
RACE	RESP	'73	'74	'76	'77	'80	'82	'84	'85	'87	'88	'89
WHITE	EX	47%	45%	47%	45%	46%	46%	47%	50%	47%	45%	47%
	RT	49	51	50	49	49	48	48	45	50	51	49
	DL	4	4	3	6	4	6	5	6	3	4	5
# SURVEYED		1292	1269	1339	1311	1312	1313	1242	1326	1192	781	876
RACE	RESP	'73	'74	'76	'77	'80	'82	'84	'85	'87	'88	'89
BLACK	EX	36%	36%	28%	41%	40%	37%	46%	36%	37%	42%	29%
	RT	53	57	64	48	44	55	47	50	56	48	60
	DL	11	7	9	11	16	8	8	13	7	10	11
# SURVEYED		179	166	127	170	140	153	167	149	185	126	100
RACE	RESP	'73	'74	'76	'77	'80	'82	'84	'85	'87	'88	'89
OTHER	EX	54%	29%	22%	60%	60%	42%	46%	36%	42%	49%	39%
	RT	31	57	78	40	40	54	52	62	50	47	59
	DL	15	14	0	0	0	4	2	2	8	5	2
# SURVEYED		13	7	9	15	10	26	52	42	52	43	41

TABLE IV: LIFE SATISFACTION -- BY AGE

Question: In general, do you find life exciting, pretty routine, or dull? NOTE: Question not asked in 1972, 1975, 1978, 1983, 1986.

Responses: EX = Exciting; RT = Routine; DL = Dull

		YEAR										
AGE	RESP	'73	'74	'76	'77	'80	'82	'84	'85	'87	'88	'89
18-23	EX	55%	52%	53%	47%	46%	43%	54%	60%	46%	52%	46%
	RT	38	44	43	47	50	49	42	36	50	43	48
	DL	7	4	3	6	4	8	4	5	4	4	6
# SURVEYED		170	168	159	161	155	148	160	132	122	90	96
AGE	RESP	'73	'74	'76	'77	'80	'82	'84	'85	'87	'88	'89
24-29	EX	54%	49%	55%	52%	48%	52%	54%	57%	52%	48%	51%
	RT	43	47	44	45	47	46	44	40	45	47	47
	DL	3	4	2	4	5	2	2	3	3	5	2
# SURVEYED		209	208	222	200	201	240	230	215	191	130	115

TABLE IV: LIFE SATISFACTION -- BY AGE (Continued)

Question: In general, do you find life exciting, pretty routine, or dull? NOTE: Question not asked in 1972, 1975, 1978, 1983, 1986.

Responses: EX = Exciting; RT = Routine; DL = Dull

		YEAR										
AGE	RESP	'73	'74	'76	'77	'80	'82	'84	'85	'87	'88	'89
30-35	EX	51%	48%	51%	53%	54%	48%	42%	47%	47%	50%	48%
	RT	46	51	46	41	43	50	55	49	50	46	50
	DL	2	1	3	5	3	2	4	4	3	3	2
# SURVEYED		166	166	183	184	215	204	198	211	217	127	133
AGE	RESP	'73	'74	'76	'77	'80	'82	'84	'85	'87	'88	'89
36-41	EX	45%	43%	51%	50%	46%	52%	52%	52%	44%	56%	53%
	RT	51	53	46	48	51	41	44	45	56	43	42
	DL	4	4	3	2	3	7	5	3	0	1	5
# SURVEYED		174	148	156	165	150	146	186	183	183	129	133
AGE	RESP	'73	'74	'76	'77	'80	'82	'84	'85	'87	'88	'89
42-47	EX	45%	39%	30%	42%	44%	45%	50%	51%	50%	49%	49%
	RT	52	56	68	50	50	52	49	46	47	49	47
	DL	3	5	2	8	6	3	1	2	3	3	4
# SURVEYED		145	144	113	143	115	119	126	123	151	101	106
AGE	RESP	'73	'74	'76	'77	'80	'82	'84	'85	'87	'88	'89
48-53	EX	41%	39%	37%	47%	49%	48%	45%	40%	48%	48%	48%
	RT	54	59	60	46	49	48	47	48	46	40	47
	DL	5	1	3	7	2	5	8	12	6	12	5
# SURVEYED		149	143	130	149	123	111	102	130	124	65	94
AGE	RESP	'73	'74	'76	'77	'80	'82	'84	'85	'87	'88	'89
54-59	EX	45%	38%	40%	39%	48%	42%	50%	42%	38%	24%	42%
	RT	50	56	59	52	43	50	47	50	55	73	52
	DL	5	6	1	8	9	8	4	8	6	4	6
# SURVEYED		155	134	128	165	136	144	113	131	94	51	62
AGE	RESP	'73	'74	'76	'77	'80	'82	'84	'85	'87	'88	'89
60-65	EX	38%	42%	36%	35%	39%	31%	41%	45%	36%	43%	42%
	RT	56	50	58	59	55	60	53	47	58	54	52
	DL	6	8	5	6	5	10	6	8	6	4	6
# SURVEYED		119	104	132	116	119	114	111	130	98	80	77
AGE	RESP	'73	'74	'76	'77	'80	'82	'84	'85	'87	'88	'89
66+	EX	33%	40%	41%	31%	39%	41%	36%	40%	44%	33%	30%
	RT	58	52	51	56	51	49	53	48	51	59	61
	DL	9	9	8	13	10	9	11	13	6	9	9
# SURVEYED		193	221	246	206	239	255	230	255	245	174	198

****

HAPPINESS WITH LIFE

TABLE I: HAPPINESS WITH LIFE -- BY TOTAL POPULATION

Question: Taken all together, how would you say things are these days--would you say that you are very happy, pretty happy, or not too happy?

Responses: VH = Very happy; PH = Pretty happy; NH = Not too happy

RESPONSE	'72	'73	'74	'75	'76	'77	'78	'80	'82	'83	'84	'85	'86	'87	'88	'89
VH	30%	36%	38%	33%	34%	35%	34%	34%	33%	31%	35%	29%	32%	32%	34%	33%
PH	53	51	49	54	53	53	56	53	54	56	52	60	56	56	57	58
NH	17	13	13	13	13	12	10	13	13	13	13	11	11	12	9	10
# SURVEYED	1606	1500	1480	1485	1499	1527	1517	1462	1505	1573	1445	1530	1449	1437	1466	1526

TABLE II: HAPPINESS WITH LIFE -- BY SEX

Question: Taken all together, how would you say things are these days--would you say that you are very happy, pretty happy, or not too happy?

Responses: VH = Very happy; PH = Pretty happy; NH = Not too happy

SEX	RESP	'72	'73	'74	'75	'76	'77	'78	'80	'82	'83	'84	'85	'86	'87	'88	'89
M	VH	29%	34%	34%	32%	33%	33%	35%	31%	31%	31%	32%	29%	30%	31%	36%	32%
	PH	53	54	52	56	54	56	55	55	56	56	54	60	58	57	56	59
	NH	18	12	14	12	13	11	10	14	14	13	15	11	11	13	8	9
# SURVEYED		805	698	690	666	669	691	637	638	639	676	586	688	613	629	632	656
SEX	RESP	'72	'73	'74	'75	'76	'77	'78	'80	'82	'83	'84	'85	'86	'87	'88	'89
F	VH	32%	38%	42%	34%	35%	37%	34%	36%	35%	31%	37%	28%	34%	32%	33%	33%
	PH	53	49	46	52	53	51	57	51	53	56	51	60	55	56	57	57
	NH	15	14	12	14	12	12	9	13	12	13	12	11	11	12	10	10
# SURVEYED		801	802	790	819	830	836	880	824	866	897	859	842	836	808	834	870

TABLE III: HAPPINESS WITH LIFE -- BY RACE

Question: Taken all together, how would you say things are these days--would you say that you are very happy, pretty happy, or not too happy?

Responses: VH = Very happy; PH = Pretty happy; NH = Not too happy

		YEAR															
RACE	RESP	'72	'73	'74	'75	'76	'77	'78	'80	'82	'83	'84	'85	'86	'87	'88	'89
WHITE	VH	33%	39%	39%	35%	36%	36%	36%	35%	35%	32%	36%	30%	34%	34%	35%	34%
	PH	53	50	49	53	53	54	56	53	54	56	52	60	56	56	57	57
	NH	15	11	11	12	11	11	8	12	12	11	11	10	10	10	8	9
# SURVEYED		1342	1306	1303	1318	1361	1336	1348	1313	1323	1400	1227	1336	1233	1204	1221	1309
RACE	RESP	'72	'73	'74	'75	'76	'77	'78	'80	'82	'83	'84	'85	'86	'87	'88	'89
BLACK	VH	18%	17%	28%	20%	16%	30%	22%	20%	22%	20%	24%	19%	22%	17%	24%	19%
	PH	55	55	47	60	53	48	58	50	56	54	54	59	60	61	56	62
	NH	26	28	25	20	30	22	21	29	22	25	23	21	17	23	20	19
# SURVEYED		260	181	170	163	129	176	153	139	156	157	168	150	179	180	184	156
RACE	RESP	'72	'73	'74	'75	'76	'77	'78	'80	'82	'83	'84	'85	'86	'87	'88	'89
OTHER	VH	0%	23%	57%	25%	22%	13%	38%	20%	27%	31%	40%	30%	38%	30%	36%	28%
	PH	50	69	14	50	78	67	63	70	54	56	44	57	49	51	59	64
	NH	50	8	29	25	0	20	0	10	19	13	16	14	14	19	5	8
# SURVEYED		4	13	7	4	9	15	16	10	26	16	50	44	37	53	61	61

TABLE IV: HAPPINESS WITH LIFE -- BY AGE

Question: Taken all together, how would you say things are these days--would you say that you are very happy, pretty happy, or not too happy?

Responses: VH = Very happy; PH = Pretty happy; NH = Not too happy

		YEAR															
AGE	RESP	'72	'73	'74	'75	'76	'77	'78	'80	'82	'83	'84	'85	'86	'87	'88	'89
18-23	VH	27%	24%	23%	28%	35%	24%	31%	29%	19%	32%	26%	27%	26%	28%	35%	34%
	PH	54	60	58	58	47	64	56	57	66	51	62	64	63	54	57	58
	NH	20	16	19	14	19	12	13	14	16	17	12	9	10	18	7	7
# SURVEYED		168	171	168	173	162	164	160	155	148	121	159	133	106	126	141	137

TABLE IV: HAPPINESS WITH LIFE -- BY AGE (Continued)

Question: Taken all together, how would you say things are these days--would you say that you are very happy, pretty happy, or not too happy?

Responses: VH = Very happy; PH = Pretty happy; NH = Not too happy

		YEAR															
AGE	RESP	'72	'73	'74	'75	'76	'77	'78	'80	'82	'83	'84	'85	'86	'87	'88	'89
24-29	VH	28%	31%	34%	29%	31%	31%	34%	30%	33%	28%	31%	30%	30%	32%	30%	28%
	PH	59	57	54	58	58	55	57	56	56	59	57	61	58	58	63	61
	NH	13	12	11	13	11	13	9	14	11	13	12	9	12	10	7	11
# SURVEYED		230	211	212	231	226	204	241	202	246	283	229	217	213	185	213	202
AGE	RESP	'72	'73	'74	'75	'76	'77	'78	'80	'82	'83	'84	'85	'86	'87	'88	'89
30-35	VH	34%	39%	40%	31%	37%	35%	34%	29%	31%	28%	29%	23%	27%	30%	29%	31%
	PH	55	55	46	56	53	54	59	60	56	60	56	69	65	57	61	60
	NH	10	6	14	13	10	11	7	11	12	12	14	8	8	13	10	9
# SURVEYED		186	166	174	170	186	188	229	215	204	232	197	212	218	220	194	210
AGE	RESP	'72	'73	'74	'75	'76	'77	'78	'80	'82	'83	'84	'85	'86	'87	'88	'89
36-41	VH	28%	32%	38%	34%	35%	37%	37%	34%	28%	28%	30%	28%	36%	25%	37%	31%
	PH	57	50	50	51	58	55	56	57	59	56	55	61	60	66	55	61
	NH	15	18	12	15	7	8	7	9	13	15	15	11	4	8	8	7
# SURVEYED		128	175	151	154	158	168	160	150	146	170	183	184	186	185	190	197
AGE	RESP	'72	'73	'74	'75	'76	'77	'78	'80	'82	'83	'84	'85	'86	'87	'88	'89
42-47	VH	34%	38%	36%	36%	39%	33%	28%	35%	32%	30%	43%	28%	27%	33%	37%	31%
	PH	48	50	50	54	54	56	59	57	56	60	50	60	58	57	53	57
	NH	17	12	14	10	8	12	13	9	12	10	7	11	14	10	11	12
# SURVEYED		186	146	151	143	114	147	118	115	119	144	124	124	139	152	156	159
AGE	RESP	'72	'73	'74	'75	'76	'77	'78	'80	'82	'83	'84	'85	'86	'87	'88	'89
48-53	VH	32%	45%	41%	30%	27%	40%	36%	33%	35%	34%	31%	27%	31%	32%	30%	34%
	PH	51	42	46	55	56	47	57	55	53	51	55	53	56	54	56	57
	NH	17	13	13	14	17	13	7	11	13	15	14	20	12	14	13	9
# SURVEYED		188	151	146	141	133	153	131	123	112	115	98	131	108	125	89	136
AGE	RESP	'72	'73	'74	'75	'76	'77	'78	'80	'82	'83	'84	'85	'86	'87	'88	'89
54-59	VH	29%	41%	42%	33%	33%	37%	36%	32%	42%	28%	38%	29%	34%	28%	32%	38%
	PH	54	50	45	52	57	50	53	49	44	56	45	53	51	58	55	46
	NH	17	9	13	15	10	13	10	20	14	16	17	18	15	14	13	15
# SURVEYED		156	156	139	125	129	168	137	136	144	133	112	133	96	96	85	99
AGE	RESP	'72	'73	'74	'75	'76	'77	'78	'80	'82	'83	'84	'85	'86	'87	'88	'89
60-65	VH	28%	41%	42%	41%	33%	40%	36%	41%	29%	37%	41%	38%	39%	34%	39%	35%
	PH	52	48	49	48	51	51	52	45	57	51	45	55	46	49	52	56
	NH	20	11	9	12	16	9	11	13	14	12	14	8	15	17	9	8
# SURVEYED		143	121	107	113	134	117	105	119	115	132	109	130	114	98	117	110

TABLE IV: HAPPINESS WITH LIFE -- BY AGE (Continued)

Question: Taken all together, how would you say things are these days--would you say that you are very happy, pretty happy, or not too happy?

Responses: VH = Very happy; PH = Pretty happy; NH = Not too happy

		YEAR															
AGE	RESP	'72	'73	'74	'75	'76	'77	'78	'80	'82	'83	'84	'85	'86	'87	'88	'89
66+	VH	30%	37%	46%	38%	37%	37%	35%	42%	42%	36%	45%	29%	39%	39%	36%	35%
	PH	50	45	43	51	48	48	54	43	44	54	44	59	48	50	55	55
	NH	20	18	11	11	15	15	11	15	14	10	11	12	13	11	10	10
# SURVEYED		216	199	226	231	251	211	230	239	259	236	228	259	262	248	277	273

****

SATISFACTION WITH FAMILY LIFE

TABLE I: SATISFACTION WITH FAMILY LIFE -- BY TOTAL POPULATION

Question: How much satisfaction do you get out of your family life? NOTE: Question not asked in 1972, 1985.

Responses:

VG = A very great deal
GD = A great deal
QG = Quite a bit
FA = A fair amount
SM = Some
LT = A little
NO = None

	YEAR													
RESPONSE	'73	'74	'75	'76	'77	'78	'80	'82	'83	'84	'86	'87	'88	'89
VG	43%	43%	44%	38%	42%	39%	44%	49%	39%	45%	37%	42%	44%	42%
GD	31	34	33	38	33	36	34	27	35	31	35	32	34	33
QG	10	11	10	11	12	11	10	10	12	11	12	12	9	10
FA	9	7	7	6	7	7	6	6	7	6	9	7	6	7
SM	3	2	2	3	3	3	2	3	3	2	3	3	3	4
LT	2	2	2	2	1	2	2	2	2	2	2	2	3	2
NO	2	1	2	2	2	2	2	2	2	1	2	1	2	2
# SURVEYED	1493	1480	1482	1490	1521	1516	1459	1499	1582	1465	1448	1452	993	1028

TABLE II: SATISFACTION WITH FAMILY LIFE -- BY SEX

Question: How much satisfaction do you get out of your family life? NOTE: Question not asked in 1972, 1985.

Responses:

VG = A very great deal
GD = A great deal
QG = Quite a bit
FA = A fair amount
SM = Some
LT = A little
NO = None

		YEAR													
SEX	RESP	'73	'74	'75	'76	'77	'78	'80	'82	'83	'84	'86	'87	'88	'89
M	VG	43%	41%	41%	36%	39%	39%	44%	47%	38%	39%	35%	39%	40%	40%
A	GD	31	35	35	38	34	34	33	27	33	36	34	32	33	35
L	QG	10	11	10	12	13	11	9	9	14	11	13	12	10	10
E	FA	9	7	7	5	7	7	7	8	8	7	9	8	7	6
	SM	4	3	2	3	3	4	2	4	3	3	3	4	4	5
	LT	2	2	2	3	2	3	2	3	2	2	3	3	3	2
	NO	2	1	2	3	2	2	2	3	3	2	3	2	3	2
# SURVEYED		693	689	666	666	687	636	636	634	684	594	608	634	436	442
SEX	RESP	'73	'74	'75	'76	'77	'78	'80	'82	'83	'84	'86	'87	'88	'89
F	VG	43%	45%	46%	40%	44%	39%	45%	50%	39%	50%	38%	44%	46%	44%
E	GD	32	33	31	38	32	37	34	27	37	28	35	33	34	33
M	QG	10	10	11	10	11	11	11	12	10	11	12	12	8	10
A	FA	9	7	6	7	8	8	6	5	7	6	8	7	5	7
L	SM	3	2	3	2	3	3	2	2	3	2	3	2	3	4
E	LT	2	2	1	2	1	1	1	2	2	3	2	2	3	2
	NO	2	1	1	2	1	1	1	1	2	1	1	1	1	1
# SURVEYED		800	791	816	824	834	880	823	865	898	871	840	818	557	586

TABLE III: SATISFACTION WITH FAMILY LIFE -- BY RACE

Question: How much satisfaction do you get out of your family life? NOTE: Question not asked in 1972, 1985.

Responses:

VG = A very great deal
GD = A great deal
QG = Quite a bit
FA = A fair amount
SM = Some
LT = A little
NO = None

		YEAR													
RACE	RESP	'73	'74	'75	'76	'77	'78	'80	'82	'83	'84	'86	'87	'88	'89
WHITE	VG	46%	44%	45%	40%	42%	40%	46%	50%	39%	47%	38%	43%	44%	44%
	GD	31	33	32	37	33	35	34	27	36	31	35	32	34	33
	QG	9	11	11	11	12	11	10	10	12	11	12	12	8	10
	FA	7	7	6	6	7	7	6	6	7	6	9	7	6	6
	SM	3	2	3	3	3	3	2	3	3	2	3	3	3	4
	LT	2	2	1	2	1	2	2	2	1	2	2	2	3	2
	NO	2	1	2	2	2	2	1	2	2	1	2	1	2	1
# SURVEYED		1299	1300	1315	1353	1332	1346	1310	1316	1402	1244	1232	1212	834	877
RACE	RESP	'73	'74	'75	'76	'77	'78	'80	'82	'83	'84	'86	'87	'88	'89
BLACK	VG	24%	35%	36%	21%	41%	31%	33%	44%	36%	33%	31%	28%	43%	31%
	GD	31	38	41	45	28	40	33	24	30	34	32	39	32	36
	QG	14	10	8	14	14	11	12	16	9	13	17	12	10	8
	FA	16	7	9	12	8	13	11	6	10	11	11	12	10	11
	SM	8	5	1	4	5	2	4	4	7	4	4	4	2	8
	LT	4	1	2	1	3	2	2	5	4	4	3	4	3	3
	NO	2	4	2	3	1	1	4	1	5	2	2	2	0	3
# SURVEYED		181	173	163	128	175	154	139	156	162	169	179	187	115	109
RACE	RESP	'73	'74	'75	'76	'77	'78	'80	'82	'83	'84	'86	'87	'88	'89
OTHER	VG	31%	29%	25%	67%	14%	31%	40%	44%	44%	48%	32%	62%	48%	36%
	GD	31	43	25	22	57	44	40	22	22	29	46	17	27	45
	QG	8	14	25	0	7	13	10	4	6	8	16	4	9	10
	FA	23	14	25	0	7	13	10	26	17	8	0	8	2	2
	SM	0	0	0	0	0	0	0	0	6	4	3	8	7	5
	LT	8	0	0	11	7	0	0	0	6	4	0	0	5	2
	NO	0	0	0	0	7	0	0	4	0	0	3	2	2	0
# SURVEYED		13	7	4	9	14	16	10	27	18	52	37	53	44	42

TABLE IV: SATISFACTION WITH FAMILY LIFE -- BY AGE

Question: How much satisfaction do you get out of your family life? NOTE: Question not asked in 1972, 1985.

Responses:

VG = A very great deal
GD = A great deal
QG = Quite a bit
FA = A fair amount
SM = Some
LT = A little
NO = None

		YEAR													
AGE	RESP	'73	'74	'75	'76	'77	'78	'80	'82	'83	'84	'86	'87	'88	'89
18-23	VG	30%	39%	40%	33%	35%	33%	42%	43%	30%	36%	23%	32%	39%	41%
	GD	36	31	35	36	33	35	32	24	37	37	36	35	37	30
	QG	14	15	13	15	17	12	12	14	14	12	24	10	12	12
	FA	13	6	6	7	12	12	8	9	14	9	8	10	6	9
	SM	4	4	3	5	2	4	3	5	2	2	5	6	1	6
	LT	4	5	2	2	1	2	2	3	2	2	2	4	4	2
	NO	0	1	1	1	1	1	1	2	1	2	1	2	1	0
# SURVEYED		171	167	173	161	164	162	154	148	128	161	107	125	93	93
AGE	RESP	'73	'74	'75	'76	'77	'78	'80	'82	'83	'84	'86	'87	'88	'89
24-29	VG	46%	40%	46%	45%	40%	47%	48%	50%	37%	51%	37%	44%	40%	39%
	GD	29	33	28	35	34	31	34	28	37	26	33	29	37	30
	QG	10	12	10	9	12	9	9	10	13	10	15	15	8	12
	FA	10	8	8	5	5	9	5	6	6	5	11	7	10	7
	SM	3	3	3	3	3	2	1	3	3	3	2	2	5	7
	LT	2	3	3	2	2	1	1	2	2	3	2	2	1	3
	NO	0	0	1	1	3	2	1	1	1	2	1	2	1	2
# SURVEYED		211	212	232	225	204	242	202	244	286	231	217	191	146	142
AGE	RESP	'73	'74	'75	'76	'77	'78	'80	'82	'83	'84	'86	'87	'88	'89
30-35	VG	55%	53%	46%	44%	49%	41%	41%	54%	39%	45%	37%	39%	49%	52%
	GD	31	27	35	34	34	38	37	28	35	30	35	36	29	26
	QG	7	11	10	6	9	10	11	10	13	12	15	7	12	8
	FA	5	6	6	8	6	7	7	5	7	6	7	10	4	8
	SM	2	1	1	3	2	2	1	1	3	3	3	3	2	5
	LT	0	2	1	3	0	1	3	0	2	3	1	3	3	2
	NO	0	1	1	1	0	1	1	1	1	2	2	2	1	1
# SURVEYED		166	175	171	186	187	229	215	204	236	198	219	220	127	145
AGE	RESP	'73	'74	'75	'76	'77	'78	'80	'82	'83	'84	'86	'87	'88	'89
36-41	VG	42%	47%	52%	38%	41%	41%	46%	48%	47%	48%	42%	43%	55%	45%
	GD	30	37	34	44	36	38	36	28	33	27	38	34	27	29
	QG	13	9	6	10	11	13	12	9	9	13	8	11	7	11
	FA	7	5	5	6	6	6	4	6	7	7	6	8	4	9
	SM	5	1	1	1	3	1	1	3	2	3	3	2	6	4
	LT	1	0	1	1	2	1	1	3	2	1	1	2	1	2
	NO	2	1	0	0	1	1	0	3	1	1	2	1	1	1
# SURVEYED		175	152	154	158	168	160	147	146	172	187	186	185	126	133

TABLE IV: SATISFACTION WITH FAMILY LIFE -- BY AGE (Continued)

Question: How much satisfaction do you get out of your family life? NOTE: Question not asked in 1972, 1985.

Responses:

VG = A very great deal GD = A great deal
QG = Quite a bit FA = A fair amount
SM = Some LT = A little
NO = None

		YEAR													
AGE	RESP	'73	'74	'75	'76	'77	'78	'80	'82	'83	'84	'86	'87	'88	'89
42-47	VG	39%	40%	51%	46%	36%	37%	41%	51%	41%	42%	34%	50%	49%	36%
	GD	27	40	33	36	38	35	36	27	33	35	35	27	30	39
	QG	15	7	6	11	11	14	14	7	15	10	12	11	7	13
	FA	8	7	4	4	9	6	5	10	5	8	7	7	5	3
	SM	4	3	2	1	2	4	2	3	3	2	6	3	3	4
	LT	3	1	2	1	3	3	1	1	0	2	4	2	2	3
	NO	3	1	1	1	1	1	2	1	3	1	3	0	5	2
# SURVEYED		146	151	143	114	146	119	117	119	144	125	140	157	104	106
AGE	RESP	'73	'74	'75	'76	'77	'78	'80	'82	'83	'84	'86	'87	'88	'89
48-53	VG	50%	45%	44%	36%	49%	37%	42%	51%	45%	47%	38%	56%	36%	40%
	GD	32	29	34	40	25	41	35	30	35	33	41	23	39	40
	QG	7	14	11	11	14	11	14	8	7	11	6	9	13	11
	FA	7	7	7	8	5	8	4	4	6	4	7	6	2	5
	SM	2	2	2	2	4	2	2	1	6	2	3	2	4	2
	LT	1	1	2	2	1	1	2	4	1	3	5	2	5	0
	NO	1	1	0	1	3	1	0	3	0	0	2	2	2	2
# SURVEYED		151	145	140	132	154	131	122	112	116	102	106	126	56	95
AGE	RESP	'73	'74	'75	'76	'77	'78	'80	'82	'83	'84	'86	'87	'88	'89
54-59	VG	42%	47%	38%	32%	44%	47%	44%	51%	34%	51%	44%	39%	38%	36%
	GD	36	33	36	46	33	29	36	24	41	28	28	31	35	41
	QG	8	5	10	10	11	10	5	9	11	11	14	16	8	2
	FA	8	7	9	5	7	5	7	8	6	7	6	6	8	10
	SM	4	2	1	1	2	4	2	4	2	1	3	2	3	5
	LT	1	3	2	2	1	4	1	2	2	3	2	3	5	5
	NO	1	2	5	4	2	2	4	1	5	0	3	3	5	2
# SURVEYED		155	138	125	128	168	133	135	144	133	114	96	95	66	61
AGE	RESP	'73	'74	'75	'76	'77	'78	'80	'82	'83	'84	'86	'87	'88	'89
60-65	VG	44%	36%	42%	32%	38%	32%	53%	53%	39%	49%	38%	31%	36%	36%
	GD	36	34	30	44	39	38	27	30	34	33	39	41	41	43
	QG	7	13	13	10	10	10	8	8	11	10	11	17	9	12
	FA	7	8	7	3	9	9	8	3	10	2	6	6	8	4
	SM	1	4	4	2	2	5	3	2	2	3	3	3	0	1
	LT	2	2	2	5	1	5	0	2	1	2	2	2	1	3
	NO	2	3	3	4	2	2	1	4	3	2	2	1	5	1
# SURVEYED		121	108	112	133	116	105	118	114	131	110	112	101	80	75

TABLE IV: SATISFACTION WITH FAMILY LIFE -- BY AGE (Continued)

Question: How much satisfaction do you get out of your family life? NOTE: Question not asked in 1972, 1985.

Responses:

VG = A very great deal; GD = A great deal
QG = Quite a bit; FA = A fair amount
SM = Some; LT = A little
NO = None

		YEAR													
AGE	RESP	'73	'74	'75	'76	'77	'78	'80	'82	'83	'84	'86	'87	'88	'89
66+	VG	40%	42%	40%	35%	42%	32%	45%	44%	37%	41%	37%	40%	42%	44%
	GD	28	38	33	33	29	37	33	25	33	35	31	34	35	35
	QG	6	8	13	14	12	11	9	15	10	9	10	13	7	9
	FA	11	7	6	7	9	7	7	6	6	7	13	5	7	5
	SM	5	2	4	4	5	6	3	4	5	2	3	4	3	3
	LT	5	1	0	2	2	3	3	4	2	3	3	2	5	2
	NO	5	1	4	5	1	4	2	3	7	3	2	2	2	3
# SURVEYED		193	226	228	247	207	228	240	256	230	231	258	248	191	176

****

SATISFACTION WITH MARRIAGE

TABLE I: SATISFACTION WITH MARRIAGE -- BY TOTAL POPULATION

Question: If married, taking things all together, how would you describe your marriage? Would you say that your marriage is very happy, pretty happy, or not too happy? NOTE: Question not asked in 1972.

Responses: VH = Very happy; PH = Pretty happy; NH = Not too happy

	YEAR														
RESPONSE	'73	'74	'75	'76	'77	'78	'80	'82	'83	'84	'85	'86	'87	'88	'89
VH	68%	69%	67%	67%	65%	65%	68%	66%	62%	66%	57%	63%	65%	63%	60%
PH	30	27	30	31	31	32	29	31	34	31	40	33	32	34	37
NH	3	3	3	2	4	3	3	3	3	3	3	3	2	3	3
# SURVEYED	1072	1059	995	973	965	954	882	846	961	825	863	819	792	787	840

TABLE II: SATISFACTION WITH MARRIAGE -- BY SEX

Question: If married, taking things all together, how would you describe your marriage? Would you say that your marriage is very happy, pretty happy, or not too happy? NOTE: Question not asked in 1972.

Responses: VH = Very happy; PH = Pretty happy; NH = Not too happy

SEX	RESP	'73	'74	'75	'76	'77	'78	'80	'82	'83	'84	'85	'86	'87	'88	'89
M	VH	69%	70%	71%	69%	69%	66%	70%	65%	66%	66%	58%	61%	69%	66%	64%
	PH	29	28	28	29	29	32	27	34	32	32	38	36	30	33	35
	NH	2	2	2	1	2	2	3	1	3	3	3	3	2	1	1
# SURVEYED		507	511	478	453	459	446	420	405	463	357	430	381	372	377	405
SEX	RESP	'73	'74	'75	'76	'77	'78	'80	'82	'83	'84	'85	'86	'87	'88	'89
F	VH	67%	69%	65%	65%	62%	65%	66%	66%	59%	66%	55%	65%	62%	59%	57%
	PH	30	27	32	32	33	32	31	29	37	31	42	32	35	35	39
	NH	3	5	4	3	5	3	3	5	4	3	3	4	3	5	4
# SURVEYED		565	548	517	520	506	508	462	441	498	468	433	438	420	410	435

TABLE III: SATISFACTION WITH MARRIAGE -- BY RACE

Question: If married, taking things all together, how would you describe your marriage? Would you say that your marriage is very happy, pretty happy, or not too happy? NOTE: Question not asked in 1972.

Responses: VH = Very happy; PH = Pretty happy; NH = Not too happy

RACE	RESP	'73	'74	'75	'76	'77	'78	'80	'82	'83	'84	'85	'86	'87	'88	'89
WHITE	VH	70%	70%	69%	68%	67%	67%	69%	67%	63%	67%	58%	64%	66%	63%	62%
	PH	28	27	28	30	31	30	29	31	35	30	40	33	32	33	35
	NH	2	3	3	2	3	2	2	3	3	3	3	3	2	3	2
# SURVEYED		955	960	914	913	877	873	814	775	884	722	778	727	707	690	764
RACE	RESP	'73	'74	'75	'76	'77	'78	'80	'82	'83	'84	'85	'86	'87	'88	'89
BLACK	VH	47%	61%	49%	52%	56%	40%	57%	57%	49%	50%	45%	51%	58%	53%	44%
	PH	46	31	47	46	34	51	32	35	38	44	48	43	33	41	49
	NH	6	9	4	2	10	8	12	7	12	6	7	5	9	6	7
# SURVEYED		108	94	78	52	79	72	60	54	65	70	58	74	55	68	43
RACE	RESP	'73	'74	'75	'76	'77	'78	'80	'82	'83	'84	'85	'86	'87	'88	'89
OTHER	VH	56%	80%	67%	38%	44%	44%	50%	53%	100%	73%	52%	72%	63%	62%	39%
	PH	44	20	33	63	33	44	50	47	0	24	37	28	33	31	58
	NH	0	0	0	0	22	11	0	0	0	3	11	0	3	7	3
# SURVEYED		9	5	3	8	9	9	8	17	12	33	27	18	30	29	33

TABLE IV: SATISFACTION WITH MARRIAGE -- BY AGE

Question: If married, taking things all together, how would you describe your marriage? Would you say that your marriage is very happy, pretty happy, or not too happy? NOTE: Question not asked in 1972.

Responses: VH = Very happy; PH = Pretty happy; NH = Not too happy

		YEAR														
AGE	**RESP**	**'73**	**'74**	**'75**	**'76**	**'77**	**'78**	**'80**	**'82**	**'83**	**'84**	**'85**	**'86**	**'87**	**'88**	**'89**
18-23	**VH**	75%	70%	69%	80%	60%	74%	70%	59%	68%	80%	69%	68%	55%	75%	55%
	PH	23	25	27	16	37	26	26	36	29	20	31	32	36	19	45
	NH	2	4	3	4	3	0	4	5	3	0	0	0	9	6	0
# SURVEYED		61	67	62	55	60	57	54	44	31	40	32	19	22	36	20
AGE	**RESP**	**'73**	**'74**	**'75**	**'76**	**'77**	**'78**	**'80**	**'82**	**'83**	**'84**	**'85**	**'86**	**'87**	**'88**	**'89**
24-29	**VH**	66%	69%	69%	70%	70%	66%	68%	64%	58%	63%	63%	61%	73%	59%	59%
	PH	32	28	30	29	24	32	28	34	39	34	33	34	23	38	38
	NH	1	3	1	1	7	2	4	2	3	2	3	5	3	3	3
# SURVEYED		158	150	151	150	119	154	122	132	165	123	117	108	94	97	87
AGE	**RESP**	**'73**	**'74**	**'75**	**'76**	**'77**	**'78**	**'80**	**'82**	**'83**	**'84**	**'85**	**'86**	**'87**	**'88**	**'89**
30-35	**VH**	70%	74%	66%	66%	63%	66%	65%	64%	65%	65%	51%	55%	62%	61%	59%
	PH	28	22	30	31	35	33	32	34	32	33	46	42	37	38	39
	NH	2	4	4	3	2	2	3	2	3	2	3	4	1	2	2
# SURVEYED		141	144	132	145	137	169	137	135	163	124	140	141	132	112	125
AGE	**RESP**	**'73**	**'74**	**'75**	**'76**	**'77**	**'78**	**'80**	**'82**	**'83**	**'84**	**'85**	**'86**	**'87**	**'88**	**'89**
36-41	**VH**	62%	62%	70%	64%	58%	59%	66%	65%	58%	64%	54%	61%	62%	61%	60%
	PH	33	34	28	33	37	38	30	29	40	31	43	36	35	35	38
	NH	5	4	2	3	5	3	4	6	3	5	3	4	2	4	2
# SURVEYED		146	131	130	125	123	120	106	85	113	129	120	135	124	125	131
AGE	**RESP**	**'73**	**'74**	**'75**	**'76**	**'77**	**'78**	**'80**	**'82**	**'83**	**'84**	**'85**	**'86**	**'87**	**'88**	**'89**
42-47	**VH**	63%	66%	65%	63%	60%	58%	58%	55%	62%	65%	54%	63%	61%	70%	60%
	PH	33	29	31	37	36	35	40	41	33	31	41	31	36	25	37
	NH	4	5	4	0	3	8	1	4	5	3	5	6	3	5	4
# SURVEYED		114	125	110	93	116	92	84	80	102	86	80	89	108	99	114
AGE	**RESP**	**'73**	**'74**	**'75**	**'76**	**'77**	**'78**	**'80**	**'82**	**'83**	**'84**	**'85**	**'86**	**'87**	**'88**	**'89**
48-53	**VH**	64%	70%	63%	53%	69%	65%	69%	62%	65%	66%	48%	60%	69%	54%	60%
	PH	30	28	33	43	30	33	30	36	32	32	44	38	29	43	39
	NH	6	2	4	4	1	2	1	2	4	3	7	3	2	4	1
# SURVEYED		130	118	116	100	115	107	84	86	85	76	95	72	87	56	88
AGE	**RESP**	**'73**	**'74**	**'75**	**'76**	**'77**	**'78**	**'80**	**'82**	**'83**	**'84**	**'85**	**'86**	**'87**	**'88**	**'89**
54-59	**VH**	71%	77%	64%	67%	67%	68%	65%	75%	70%	63%	54%	66%	66%	54%	67%
	PH	28	20	33	30	27	30	30	21	26	35	43	31	33	43	27
	NH	1	3	3	3	6	2	5	4	4	3	2	3	1	4	6
# SURVEYED		123	105	89	98	119	87	104	106	94	75	92	62	67	54	70

TABLE IV: SATISFACTION WITH MARRIAGE -- BY AGE (Continued)

Question: If married, taking things all together, how would you describe your marriage? Would you say that your marriage is very happy, pretty happy, or not too happy? NOTE: Question not asked in 1972.

Responses: VH = Very happy; PH = Pretty happy; NH = Not too happy

		YEAR														
AGE	RESP	'73	'74	'75	'76	'77	'78	'80	'82	'83	'84	'85	'86	'87	'88	'89
60-65	VH	68%	64%	67%	68%	70%	68%	71%	64%	62%	66%	69%	69%	65%	68%	57%
	PH	31	31	31	32	29	31	27	34	36	29	30	27	32	30	40
	NH	1	5	2	0	1	2	1	1	2	5	1	4	3	3	3
# SURVEYED		95	80	84	91	76	65	77	67	95	73	80	77	63	80	72
AGE	RESP	'73	'74	'75	'76	'77	'78	'80	'82	'83	'84	'85	'86	'87	'88	'89
66+	VH	77%	69%	73%	74%	74%	69%	78%	76%	61%	67%	57%	75%	71%	64%	63%
	PH	22	29	27	22	22	28	21	23	36	31	41	24	28	33	35
	NH	1	2	1	4	3	3	2	1	3	2	3	1	1	3	2
# SURVEYED		103	136	120	115	98	100	112	108	108	96	106	113	95	125	133

****

SATISFACTION WITH COMMUNITY

TABLE I: SATISFACTION WITH COMMUNITY -- BY TOTAL POPULATION

Question: For each area of life I am going to name, tell me the choice that shows how much satisfaction you get from that area. The city or place you live in. NOTE: Question not asked in 1972, 1985.

Responses: VG = A very great deal; GD = A great deal; QB = Quite a bit; FA = A fair amount; SM = Some; LT = A little; NO = None

	YEAR													
RESPONSE	'73	'74	'75	'76	'77	'78	'80	'82	'83	'84	'86	'87	'88	'89
VG	23%	20%	21%	20%	19%	17%	24%	16%	16%	20%	16%	19%	18%	17%
GD	24	27	30	30	28	30	31	25	31	33	27	31	31	28
QB	17	17	15	17	17	19	15	20	18	18	19	17	19	21
FA	22	23	20	21	22	20	18	24	21	18	22	20	21	19
SM	6	7	6	7	6	7	6	8	7	6	8	7	6	7
LT	5	4	5	4	6	5	4	5	5	5	6	4	4	6
NO	3	2	3	2	2	3	2	2	2	1	2	1	2	2
# SURVEYED	1502	1483	1483	1493	1525	1525	1462	1502	1590	1461	1453	1456	993	1028

TABLE II: SATISFACTION WITH COMMUNITY -- BY SEX

Question: For each area of life I am going to name, tell me the choice that shows how much satisfaction you get from that area. The city or place you live in. NOTE: Question not asked in 1972, 1985.

Responses: VG = A very great deal; GD = A great deal; QB = Quite a bit; FA = A fair amount; SM = Some; LT = A little; NO = None

		YEAR													
SEX	RESP	'73	'74	'75	'76	'77	'78	'80	'82	'83	'84	'86	'87	'88	'89
M	VG	22%	19%	21%	19%	18%	15%	25%	14%	12%	18%	16%	18%	15%	15%
A	GD	22	26	27	30	27	29	30	23	31	34	26	32	32	28
L	QB	17	17	18	17	18	22	14	20	18	18	19	19	18	24
E	FA	24	24	21	21	22	21	18	26	22	17	22	19	21	18
	SM	6	8	6	7	7	6	6	10	9	7	9	7	6	7
	LT	6	3	5	5	6	4	5	4	6	5	6	3	5	7
	NO	3	3	3	2	2	3	2	3	2	1	2	1	3	2
# SURVEYED		700	691	667	666	689	641	639	638	688	595	610	637	435	442
SEX	RESP	'73	'74	'75	'76	'77	'78	'80	'82	'83	'84	'86	'87	'88	'89
F	VG	24%	21%	21%	20%	20%	18%	23%	17%	19%	21%	16%	20%	20%	19%
E	GD	25	27	32	30	28	31	31	27	31	32	28	30	30	27
M	QB	17	18	13	18	17	17	16	20	17	17	19	17	20	19
A	FA	21	22	19	20	21	19	18	22	20	18	21	21	21	20
L	SM	6	6	6	7	5	7	5	7	6	5	7	7	5	6
E	LT	4	4	6	3	5	5	4	5	5	5	7	4	3	6
	NO	3	1	3	2	3	3	2	2	2	2	2	2	2	3
# SURVEYED		802	792	816	827	836	884	823	864	902	866	843	819	558	586

TABLE III: SATISFACTION WITH COMMUNITY -- BY RACE

Question: For each area of life I am going to name, tell me the choice that shows how much satisfaction you get from that area. The city or place you live in. NOTE: Question not asked in 1972, 1985.

Responses: VG = A very great deal; GD = A great deal; QB = Quite a bit; FA = A fair amount; SM = Some; LT = A little; NO = None

		YEAR													
RACE	RESP	'73	'74	'75	'76	'77	'78	'80	'82	'83	'84	'86	'87	'88	'89
WHITE	VG	25%	20%	22%	20%	20%	17%	25%	16%	16%	21%	17%	20%	19%	18%
	GD	25	28	30	30	28	30	31	26	31	33	27	32	32	29
	QB	17	18	15	17	18	20	16	20	18	18	19	17	18	22
	FA	21	22	20	20	21	19	18	24	21	17	22	20	19	18
	SM	6	7	6	6	6	7	5	8	7	5	7	7	5	6
	LT	4	3	5	4	5	4	4	4	5	4	6	3	4	6
	NO	2	2	3	2	2	3	2	3	1	1	2	1	2	2
# SURVEYED		1306	1304	1316	1355	1337	1354	1314	1320	1410	1240	1235	1216	835	876
RACE	RESP	'73	'74	'75	'76	'77	'78	'80	'82	'83	'84	'86	'87	'88	'89
BLACK	VG	11%	20%	15%	12%	15%	13%	17%	14%	14%	12%	9%	10%	11%	15%
	GD	14	17	25	24	25	29	30	22	27	28	26	26	21	18
	QB	14	14	19	22	13	14	12	20	14	15	16	20	23	15
	FA	36	28	25	25	27	24	20	23	22	25	22	24	30	28
	SM	9	9	6	12	6	8	8	8	9	8	12	10	10	10
	LT	12	8	9	3	8	8	11	10	11	10	10	9	3	9
	NO	5	5	2	2	5	5	3	3	4	1	4	1	1	5
# SURVEYED		183	172	163	129	173	155	138	155	162	169	181	187	115	110
RACE	RESP	'73	'74	'75	'76	'77	'78	'80	'82	'83	'84	'86	'87	'88	'89
OTHER	VG	23%	29%	25%	11%	20%	13%	20%	7%	11%	17%	19%	23%	16%	12%
	GD	15	14	25	33	13	25	30	22	33	38	32	32	33	29
	QB	15	14	0	0	20	19	0	26	39	13	22	11	19	17
	FA	23	29	25	44	27	44	20	30	11	12	11	23	21	26
	SM	8	0	25	11	7	0	20	11	0	6	11	4	5	12
	LT	8	14	0	0	13	0	10	4	0	8	3	4	2	2
	NO	8	0	0	0	0	0	0	0	6	6	3	4	5	2
# SURVEYED		13	7	4	9	15	16	10	27	18	52	37	53	43	42

TABLE IV: SATISFACTION WITH COMMUNITY -- BY AGE

Question: For each area of life I am going to name, tell me the choice that shows how much satisfaction you get from that area. The city or place you live in. NOTE: Question not asked in 1972, 1985.

Responses: VG = A very great deal; GD = A great deal; QB = Quite a bit; FA = A fair amount; SM = Some; LT = A little; NO = None

		YEAR													
AGE	RESP	'73	'74	'75	'76	'77	'78	'80	'82	'83	'84	'86	'87	'88	'89
18-23	VG	11%	13%	14%	14%	7%	11%	12%	5%	9%	8%	7%	10%	10%	11%
	GD	18	14	17	18	21	18	25	21	31	27	23	20	24	16
	QB	20	25	17	19	21	18	21	17	13	18	17	19	20	24
	FA	28	27	28	27	27	26	23	28	23	23	27	27	23	26
	SM	12	12	10	9	11	12	6	14	13	13	10	16	9	12
	LT	8	5	8	9	9	9	8	11	6	9	13	6	11	11
	NO	3	4	5	5	4	7	5	4	4	2	3	2	4	1
# SURVEYED		171	168	173	162	164	162	154	148	128	160	107	126	93	93
AGE	RESP	'73	'74	'75	'76	'77	'78	'80	'82	'83	'84	'86	'87	'88	'89
24-29	VG	12%	10%	11%	13%	10%	7%	20%	11%	10%	14%	12%	13%	12%	8%
	GD	20	21	27	24	22	24	23	15	20	28	20	25	26	24
	QB	23	22	19	16	19	23	18	23	23	23	20	20	23	21
	FA	23	27	25	29	27	23	22	32	23	20	25	25	26	22
	SM	9	8	8	11	11	9	8	11	12	6	14	8	8	11
	LT	9	9	7	3	9	10	5	6	9	7	7	7	3	10
	NO	4	3	4	3	3	3	3	2	3	3	1	3	3	4
# SURVEYED		212	212	232	226	204	243	201	245	287	231	216	191	145	142
AGE	RESP	'73	'74	'75	'76	'77	'78	'80	'82	'83	'84	'86	'87	'88	'89
30-35	VG	17%	20%	18%	14%	21%	14%	15%	9%	11%	14%	11%	15%	14%	12%
	GD	22	21	27	34	21	29	29	24	26	23	26	29	28	26
	QB	22	14	16	18	19	22	19	24	19	23	20	22	13	29
	FA	27	29	22	18	22	23	24	25	28	24	24	20	29	24
	SM	6	8	6	5	6	5	7	10	7	7	11	10	8	4
	LT	2	6	8	7	7	4	5	6	6	8	6	3	6	3
	NO	4	2	3	3	3	3	2	4	2	2	2	2	2	3
# SURVEYED		167	175	171	185	187	230	215	204	236	198	218	221	127	144
AGE	RESP	'73	'74	'75	'76	'77	'78	'80	'82	'83	'84	'86	'87	'88	'89
36-41	VG	18%	16%	16%	19%	17%	14%	20%	13%	13%	21%	14%	15%	13%	15%
	GD	25	28	32	25	29	28	36	25	31	31	27	34	31	23
	QB	14	16	18	20	16	20	15	17	18	19	22	20	21	23
	FA	26	26	20	23	26	25	21	26	18	16	20	19	19	20
	SM	5	7	8	10	5	8	5	11	9	7	11	8	10	8
	LT	7	4	6	3	4	3	3	5	8	5	3	4	3	8
	NO	4	3	1	0	4	3	0	3	2	0	3	1	2	3
# SURVEYED		175	152	154	157	168	160	149	146	173	187	186	185	126	133

TABLE IV: SATISFACTION WITH COMMUNITY -- BY AGE (Continued)

Question: For each area of life I am going to name, tell me the choice that shows how much satisfaction you get from that area. The city or place you live in. NOTE: Question not asked in 1972, 1985.

Responses: VG = A very great deal GD = A great deal QB = Quite a bit
FA = A fair amount SM = Some LT = A little
NO = None

		YEAR													
AGE	RESP	'73	'74	'75	'76	'77	'78	'80	'82	'83	'84	'86	'87	'88	'89
42-47	VG	27%	24%	27%	23%	14%	16%	32%	14%	13%	18%	16%	23%	17%	8%
	GD	21	28	28	32	29	27	24	27	35	34	29	27	36	35
	QB	17	14	12	17	18	21	14	24	24	19	20	17	20	29
	FA	23	25	20	20	22	21	19	21	20	15	22	22	14	20
	SM	3	6	6	6	8	10	6	6	4	6	4	6	8	7
	LT	5	2	3	2	5	2	5	5	2	5	10	3	5	2
	NO	3	1	3	0	3	3	1	3	1	2	0	2	0	0
# SURVEYED		146	151	143	114	147	119	117	119	144	125	140	157	103	105
AGE	RESP	'73	'74	'75	'76	'77	'78	'80	'82	'83	'84	'86	'87	'88	'89
48-53	VG	28%	21%	21%	18%	29%	20%	26%	13%	22%	22%	25%	21%	18%	29%
	GD	25	33	39	30	23	35	29	29	34	37	22	35	35	22
	QB	16	16	14	11	18	21	20	22	15	18	23	15	18	17
	FA	19	17	19	25	19	15	18	24	18	20	19	18	21	16
	SM	7	8	4	9	3	5	3	8	6	4	6	6	2	4
	LT	5	3	3	5	7	3	4	3	4	0	5	3	2	9
	NO	1	1	0	2	1	2	0	2	1	0	0	1	5	3
# SURVEYED		151	146	140	133	154	131	123	112	116	101	107	126	57	96
AGE	RESP	'73	'74	'75	'76	'77	'78	'80	'82	'83	'84	'86	'87	'88	'89
54-59	VG	29%	26%	25%	22%	25%	21%	35%	20%	17%	21%	13%	25%	26%	18%
	GD	29	33	35	33	34	43	34	34	36	42	33	33	33	26
	QB	11	17	12	20	17	18	9	19	13	15	12	17	21	24
	FA	22	19	17	19	16	9	13	22	23	15	26	17	15	16
	SM	4	3	5	4	4	4	4	3	5	1	5	2	3	11
	LT	4	1	3	3	3	3	4	1	2	5	9	4	0	5
	NO	1	1	3	0	2	1	1	1	2	1	2	2	2	0
# SURVEYED		156	138	125	128	167	137	134	143	132	114	98	95	66	62
AGE	RESP	'73	'74	'75	'76	'77	'78	'80	'82	'83	'84	'86	'87	'88	'89
60-65	VG	34%	24%	33%	30%	22%	25%	29%	19%	17%	27%	24%	19%	15%	22%
	GD	30	29	28	35	41	30	35	28	39	41	33	44	31	35
	QB	12	19	14	17	16	20	9	23	21	12	16	15	25	11
	FA	17	22	13	13	14	18	12	22	16	15	16	19	19	22
	SM	5	2	5	3	3	5	9	3	3	3	4	3	5	3
	LT	3	2	4	2	4	2	4	3	4	2	4	1	0	5
	NO	0	2	3	0	0	1	2	1	0	1	4	0	5	3
# SURVEYED		121	108	112	133	117	106	119	116	131	110	113	101	80	74

TABLE IV: SATISFACTION WITH COMMUNITY -- BY AGE (Continued)

Question: For each area of life I am going to name, tell me the choice that shows how much satisfaction you get from that area. The city or place you live in. NOTE: Question not asked in 1972, 1985.

Responses: VG = A very great deal; GD = A great deal; QB = Quite a bit; FA = A fair amount; SM = Some; LT = A little; NO = None

		YEAR													
AGE	RESP	'73	'74	'75	'76	'77	'78	'80	'82	'83	'84	'86	'87	'88	'89
66+	VG	35%	28%	31%	26%	30%	27%	32%	30%	31%	32%	23%	30%	29%	32%
	GD	28	35	34	37	33	39	40	30	35	40	32	36	36	38
	QB	15	12	12	17	12	11	12	15	10	10	17	12	13	12
	FA	16	16	13	13	19	15	10	15	16	12	17	16	18	10
	SM	3	7	3	3	3	3	2	6	5	4	4	4	1	3
	LT	3	1	4	2	1	3	2	3	3	1	4	2	3	3
	NO	2	1	2	2	1	2	1	1	0	1	2	0	1	1
# SURVEYED		199	227	229	249	210	230	241	257	236	230	261	250	192	177

****

SATISFACTION WITH JOB

TABLE I: SATISFACTION WITH JOB -- BY TOTAL POPULATION

Question: On the whole, how satisfied are you with the work you do--would you say you are very satisfied, moderately satisfied, a little dissatisfied, or very dissatisfied?

Responses: VS = Very satisfied; MS = Moderately satisfied; LS = A little dissatisfied; VD = Very dissatisfied

	YEAR															
RESPONSE	'72	'73	'74	'75	'76	'77	'78	'80	'82	'83	'84	'85	'86	'87	'88	'89
VS	49%	49%	48%	54%	52%	48%	51%	47%	47%	49%	46%	48%	49%	44%	47%	46%
MS	37	38	37	33	34	39	36	36	38	37	35	38	39	38	39	39
LS	11	8	10	9	9	10	8	13	10	9	12	10	9	13	10	10
VD	3	4	5	4	4	3	5	5	6	5	7	4	3	5	4	4
# SURVEYED	944	1141	1223	1165	1185	1262	1280	1246	1224	1333	1208	1235	1162	1165	1153	1206

TABLE II: SATISFACTION WITH JOB -- BY SEX

Question: On the whole, how satisfied are you with the work you do--would you say you are very satisfied, moderately satisfied, a little dissatisfied, or very dissatisfied?

Responses: VS = Very satisfied MS = Moderately satisfied
LS = A little dissatisfied VD = Very dissatisfied

		YEAR															
SEX	RESP	'72	'73	'74	'75	'76	'77	'78	'80	'82	'83	'84	'85	'86	'87	'88	'89
M	VS	48%	49%	49%	55%	54%	47%	50%	46%	47%	48%	42%	45%	52%	46%	49%	47%
	MS	37	36	37	34	33	40	37	38	38	38	37	39	38	37	38	38
	LS	11	9	10	7	9	10	9	11	10	10	12	11	9	13	9	11
	VD	4	6	4	4	4	3	3	5	5	4	9	5	2	4	3	5
# SURVEYED		629	516	510	449	455	534	524	509	490	564	481	543	488	511	489	523
SEX	RESP	'72	'73	'74	'75	'76	'77	'78	'80	'82	'83	'84	'85	'86	'87	'88	'89
F	VS	50%	50%	47%	54%	51%	48%	51%	48%	47%	50%	48%	50%	47%	43%	44%	46%
	MS	37	40	38	32	35	39	36	34	38	37	34	37	40	39	41	40
	LS	11	7	10	10	9	10	8	14	9	8	12	9	9	13	11	10
	VD	2	3	5	4	5	2	5	4	6	5	6	4	3	5	4	4
# SURVEYED		315	625	713	716	730	728	756	737	734	769	727	692	674	654	664	683

TABLE III: SATISFACTION WITH JOB -- BY RACE

Question: On the whole, how satisfied are you with the work you do--would you say you are very satisfied, moderately satisfied, a little dissatisfied, or very dissatisfied?

Responses: VS = Very satisfied; MS = Moderately satisfied; LS = A little dissatisfied; VD = Very dissatisfied

		YEAR															
RACE	RESP	'72	'73	'74	'75	'76	'77	'78	'80	'82	'83	'84	'85	'86	'87	'88	'89
WHITE	VS	51%	51%	50%	55%	53%	48%	53%	48%	48%	50%	47%	49%	50%	46%	49%	48%
	MS	36	38	37	32	34	39	36	35	37	38	35	39	39	37	39	38
	LS	10	7	9	9	9	10	7	12	9	8	12	9	9	12	9	10
	VD	3	4	5	3	4	3	4	5	6	4	6	4	2	4	3	4
# SURVEYED		785	1001	1082	1040	1089	1114	1137	1123	1079	1182	1022	1076	988	980	952	1036
RACE	RESP	'72	'73	'74	'75	'76	'77	'78	'80	'82	'83	'84	'85	'86	'87	'88	'89
BLACK	VS	37%	42%	33%	44%	43%	43%	35%	38%	41%	43%	37%	42%	41%	32%	38%	31%
	MS	42	42	44	36	37	43	36	39	38	37	36	32	43	40	42	44
	LS	16	12	19	11	15	13	22	18	15	13	14	19	11	20	13	16
	VD	6	4	4	10	6	2	6	5	6	7	13	8	6	8	7	9
# SURVEYED		156	130	135	121	87	136	130	114	121	136	141	118	141	143	151	122
RACE	RESP	'72	'73	'74	'75	'76	'77	'78	'80	'82	'83	'84	'85	'86	'87	'88	'89
OTHER	VS	33%	40%	50%	50%	44%	25%	38%	22%	25%	40%	56%	49%	48%	26%	34%	38%
	MS	0	50	33	25	56	58	46	56	58	27	29	27	36	60	42	48
	LS	67	10	17	0	0	17	8	11	17	20	13	20	15	12	20	10
	VD	0	0	0	25	0	0	8	11	0	13	2	5	0	2	4	4
# SURVEYED		3	10	6	4	9	12	13	9	24	15	45	41	33	42	50	48

TABLE IV: SATISFACTION WITH JOB -- BY AGE

Question: On the whole, how satisfied are you with the work you do--would you say you are very satisfied, moderately satisfied, a little dissatisfied, or very dissatisfied?

Responses: VS = Very satisfied; MS = Moderately satisfied; LS = A little dissatisfied; VD = Very dissatisfied

		YEAR															
AGE	RESP	'72	'73	'74	'75	'76	'77	'78	'80	'82	'83	'84	'85	'86	'87	'88	'89
18-23	VS	28%	31%	31%	38%	35%	27%	44%	36%	28%	33%	30%	26%	34%	31%	33%	35%
	MS	41	47	48	43	34	50	33	39	45	44	43	47	48	45	41	51
	LS	23	15	13	14	19	18	16	17	15	12	19	21	12	14	21	11
	VD	9	7	8	6	13	5	7	8	11	11	8	5	6	10	5	4
# SURVEYED		93	113	133	122	118	131	139	134	123	111	125	99	85	104	103	95

TABLE IV: SATISFACTION WITH JOB -- BY AGE (Continued)

Question: On the whole, how satisfied are you with the work you do--would you say you are very satisfied, moderately satisfied, a little dissatisfied, or very dissatisfied?

Responses: VS = Very satisfied MS = Moderately satisfied
LS = A little dissatisfied VD = Very dissatisfied

		YEAR															
AGE	RESP	'72	'73	'74	'75	'76	'77	'78	'80	'82	'83	'84	'85	'86	'87	'88	'89
24-29	VS	38%	41%	45%	40%	43%	40%	42%	35%	41%	43%	43%	42%	40%	35%	39%	35%
	MS	38	42	33	41	41	44	41	41	43	42	33	42	47	39	47	43
	LS	18	10	15	13	11	14	13	16	11	10	16	13	12	20	11	17
	VD	7	7	7	6	5	3	4	7	5	6	8	3	2	6	3	5
# SURVEYED		159	182	197	205	204	194	229	191	231	274	218	212	202	179	197	190
AGE	RESP	'72	'73	'74	'75	'76	'77	'78	'80	'82	'83	'84	'85	'86	'87	'88	'89
30-35	VS	51%	49%	44%	55%	47%	43%	47%	42%	37%	41%	41%	46%	47%	40%	41%	44%
	MS	36	37	39	29	39	43	41	36	40	43	41	39	42	42	47	41
	LS	10	6	12	9	10	12	7	15	15	11	9	10	8	12	8	11
	VD	3	8	6	7	4	2	4	7	8	4	8	5	3	6	4	4
# SURVEYED		122	147	163	144	171	178	222	205	201	228	194	207	209	211	189	204
AGE	RESP	'72	'73	'74	'75	'76	'77	'78	'80	'82	'83	'84	'85	'86	'87	'88	'89
36-41	VS	50%	57%	43%	61%	66%	45%	49%	45%	44%	50%	42%	53%	53%	42%	53%	47%
	MS	37	30	38	27	23	42	39	42	45	33	36	33	37	40	32	40
	LS	10	11	16	6	10	11	8	10	7	11	14	10	10	16	11	9
	VD	4	2	4	5	2	3	5	3	4	6	8	5	1	3	5	4
# SURVEYED		82	155	148	142	146	159	158	145	138	161	181	175	186	177	184	191
AGE	RESP	'72	'73	'74	'75	'76	'77	'78	'80	'82	'83	'84	'85	'86	'87	'88	'89
42-47	VS	53%	47%	53%	57%	48%	49%	52%	52%	60%	55%	52%	54%	51%	46%	50%	50%
	MS	37	42	34	33	41	35	38	33	27	35	31	33	36	44	36	36
	LS	9	7	7	9	9	13	3	10	11	8	9	8	8	6	8	10
	VD	2	4	6	2	1	4	7	5	2	2	7	4	5	4	7	4
# SURVEYED		131	135	148	126	99	136	111	113	113	141	121	123	132	154	146	153
AGE	RESP	'72	'73	'74	'75	'76	'77	'78	'80	'82	'83	'84	'85	'86	'87	'88	'89
48-53	VS	52%	57%	47%	56%	46%	56%	60%	43%	54%	62%	53%	45%	54%	54%	53%	53%
	MS	41	34	46	33	44	38	28	39	34	29	30	45	34	29	30	34
	LS	6	7	7	9	4	5	9	14	6	7	11	3	9	10	12	8
	VD	1	2	1	2	6	1	3	4	6	2	5	7	3	6	5	5
# SURVEYED		135	134	138	130	126	141	120	117	101	107	92	123	100	112	86	131

TABLE IV: SATISFACTION WITH JOB -- BY AGE (Continued)

Question: On the whole, how satisfied are you with the work you do--would you say you are very satisfied, moderately satisfied, a little dissatisfied, or very dissatisfied?

Responses: VS = Very satisfied; MS = Moderately satisfied; LS = A little dissatisfied; VD = Very dissatisfied

		YEAR															
AGE	RESP	'72	'73	'74	'75	'76	'77	'78	'80	'82	'83	'84	'85	'86	'87	'88	'89
54-59	VS	50%	55%	59%	61%	64%	56%	61%	59%	58%	59%	51%	51%	52%	51%	49%	52%
	MS	36	39	32	31	25	37	28	30	34	30	30	35	41	37	42	35
	LS	11	3	4	5	9	5	5	8	5	6	11	10	5	11	7	10
	VD	3	3	5	3	2	1	5	3	4	4	8	4	2	1	3	4
# SURVEYED		109	132	120	106	114	147	116	122	125	113	98	112	81	83	74	83
AGE	RESP	'72	'73	'74	'75	'76	'77	'78	'80	'82	'83	'84	'85	'86	'87	'88	'89
60-65	VS	68%	61%	58%	63%	65%	65%	51%	64%	55%	65%	56%	63%	65%	56%	53%	54%
	MS	28	33	32	29	30	27	41	27	38	31	33	27	29	29	42	30
	LS	4	7	8	6	3	5	5	10	7	2	9	8	6	14	5	8
	VD	0	0	1	2	2	4	4	0	0	2	1	3	0	2	0	8
# SURVEYED		72	76	77	84	101	85	83	83	85	93	78	78	77	63	76	63
AGE	RESP	'72	'73	'74	'75	'76	'77	'78	'80	'82	'83	'84	'85	'86	'87	'88	'89
66+	VS	68%	52%	65%	69%	63%	64%	67%	61%	64%	55%	61%	56%	60%	61%	59%	56%
	MS	26	41	32	22	26	29	27	28	24	39	31	34	33	26	32	37
	LS	5	5	3	7	6	4	4	10	5	6	5	5	6	10	7	3
	VD	0	3	0	3	5	4	2	1	7	0	3	5	1	3	2	3
# SURVEYED		38	66	95	102	102	85	97	127	99	101	98	105	84	80	94	94

CONTINUE WORKING IF WEALTHY

TABLE I: CONTINUE WORKING IF WEALTHY -- BY TOTAL POPULATION

Question: If you are working and you were to get enough money to live as comfortably as you like for the rest of your life, would you continue to work or would you stop working? NOTE: Question not asked in 1972, 1975, 1978, 1983, 1986.

Responses: CW = Continue to work; SW = Stop working

	YEAR										
RESPONSE	'73	'74	'76	'77	'80	'82	'84	'85	'87	'88	'89
CW	69%	65%	69%	70%	77%	73%	76%	70%	75%	71%	72%
SW	31	35	31	30	23	27	24	30	25	29	28
# SURVEYED	819	821	746	940	877	933	949	978	962	620	640

TABLE II: CONTINUE WORKING IF WEALTHY -- BY SEX

Question: If you are working and you were to get enough money to live as comfortably as you like for the rest of your life, would you continue to work or would you stop working? NOTE: Question not asked in 1972, 1975, 1978, 1983, 1986.

Responses: CW = Continue to work; SW = Stop working

SEX	RESP	'73	'74	'76	'77	'80	'82	'84	'85	'87	'88	'89
M	CW	74%	69%	71%	75%	80%	75%	78%	70%	78%	74%	73%
	SW	26	31	29	25	20	25	22	30	22	26	27
# SURVEYED		505	503	444	530	495	484	467	537	503	304	344
SEX	RESP	'73	'74	'76	'77	'80	'82	'84	'85	'87	'88	'89
F	CW	61%	58%	66%	63%	73%	71%	74%	68%	71%	68%	71%
	SW	39	42	34	37	27	29	26	32	29	32	29
# SURVEYED		314	318	302	410	382	449	482	441	459	316	296

TABLE III: CONTINUE WORKING IF WEALTHY -- BY RACE

Question: If you are working and you were to get enough money to live as comfortably as you like for the rest of your life, would you continue to work or would you stop working? NOTE: Question not asked in 1972, 1975, 1978, 1983, 1986.

Responses: CW = Continue to work; SW = Stop working

RACE	RESP	'73	'74	'76	'77	'80	'82	'84	'85	'87	'88	'89
WHITE	CW	69%	66%	68%	70%	76%	72%	76%	71%	74%	71%	73%
	SW	31	34	32	30	24	28	24	29	26	29	27
# SURVEYED		710	727	684	825	798	827	812	846	816	506	557
RACE	RESP	'73	'74	'76	'77	'80	'82	'84	'85	'87	'88	'89
BLACK	CW	67%	58%	79%	69%	81%	80%	71%	58%	79%	69%	72%
	SW	33	42	21	31	19	20	29	42	21	31	28
# SURVEYED		102	92	57	104	72	88	103	96	110	85	60
RACE	RESP	'73	'74	'76	'77	'80	'82	'84	'85	'87	'88	'89
OTHER	CW	71%	50%	60%	73%	86%	72%	82%	72%	78%	79%	57%
	SW	29	50	40	27	14	28	18	28	22	21	43
# SURVEYED		7	2	5	11	7	18	34	36	36	29	23

TABLE IV: CONTINUE WORKING IF WEALTHY -- BY AGE

Question: If you are working and you were to get enough money to live as comfortably as you like for the rest of your life, would you continue to work or would you stop working? NOTE: Question not asked in 1972, 1975, 1978, 1983, 1986.

Responses: CW = Continue to work; SW = Stop working

		YEAR										
AGE	RESP	'73	'74	'76	'77	'80	'82	'84	'85	'87	'88	'89
18-23	CW	76%	70%	76%	74%	75%	77%	82%	77%	83%	81%	82%
	SW	24	30	24	26	25	23	18	23	17	19	18
# SURVEYED		87	108	87	108	96	104	109	91	88	62	60
AGE	RESP	'73	'74	'76	'77	'80	'82	'84	'85	'87	'88	'89
24-29	CW	71%	71%	78%	79%	80%	82%	82%	76%	81%	75%	83%
	SW	29	29	22	21	20	18	18	24	19	25	17
# SURVEYED		138	134	152	159	155	196	180	181	160	105	96
AGE	RESP	'73	'74	'76	'77	'80	'82	'84	'85	'87	'88	'89
30-35	CW	78%	66%	75%	75%	86%	79%	82%	81%	79%	76%	75%
	SW	22	34	25	25	14	21	18	19	21	24	25
# SURVEYED		101	116	106	146	164	170	155	174	180	104	113
AGE	RESP	'73	'74	'76	'77	'80	'82	'84	'85	'87	'88	'89
36-41	CW	80%	65%	70%	71%	75%	73%	78%	70%	72%	71%	63%
	SW	20	35	30	29	25	27	23	30	28	29	37
# SURVEYED		122	91	101	126	120	120	160	147	159	108	111
AGE	RESP	'73	'74	'76	'77	'80	'82	'84	'85	'87	'88	'89
42-47	CW	69%	67%	70%	72%	73%	76%	73%	69%	75%	74%	70%
	SW	31	33	30	28	27	24	27	31	25	26	30
# SURVEYED		103	104	73	96	89	92	101	105	134	87	90
AGE	RESP	'73	'74	'76	'77	'80	'82	'84	'85	'87	'88	'89
48-53	CW	67%	66%	57%	66%	80%	65%	73%	61%	72%	66%	71%
	SW	33	34	43	34	20	35	27	39	28	34	29
# SURVEYED		94	98	82	118	83	78	77	108	94	56	75
AGE	RESP	'73	'74	'76	'77	'80	'82	'84	'85	'87	'88	'89
54-59	CW	53%	58%	65%	51%	72%	55%	67%	51%	57%	58%	66%
	SW	47	42	35	49	28	45	33	49	43	42	34
# SURVEYED		97	89	79	108	89	87	79	85	70	38	44
AGE	RESP	'73	'74	'76	'77	'80	'82	'84	'85	'87	'88	'89
60-65	CW	55%	43%	39%	63%	56%	50%	50%	58%	56%	41%	50%
	SW	45	57	61	37	44	50	50	42	44	59	50
# SURVEYED		55	53	46	54	45	50	50	57	43	34	26

TABLE IV: CONTINUE WORKING IF WEALTHY -- BY AGE (Continued)

Question: If you are working and you were to get enough money to live as comfortably as you like for the rest of your life, would you continue to work or would you stop working? NOTE: Question not asked in 1972, 1975, 1978, 1983, 1986.

Responses: CW = Continue to work; SW = Stop working

		YEAR										
AGE	RESP	'73	'74	'76	'77	'80	'82	'84	'85	'87	'88	'89
66+	CW	52%	60%	69%	65%	76%	65%	64%	45%	81%	70%	80%
	SW	48	40	31	35	24	35	36	55	19	30	20
# SURVEYED		21	25	16	20	33	31	36	29	32	23	25

****

SATISFACTION WITH FRIENDS

TABLE I: SATISFACTION WITH FRIENDS -- BY TOTAL POPULATION

Question: How much satisfaction would you say you get from your friendships? NOTE: Question not asked in 1972, 1985.

Responses: VG = A very great deal; GD = A great deal; QB = Quite a bit; FA = A fair amount; SM = Some; LT = A little; NO = None

	YEAR													
RESPONSE	'73	'74	'75	'76	'77	'78	'80	'82	'83	'84	'86	'87	'88	'89
VG	33%	32%	29%	29%	30%	27%	34%	28%	27%	37%	24%	33%	29%	33%
GD	37	41	42	40	39	41	42	38	41	38	42	38	41	39
QB	14	14	15	16	15	17	13	18	18	12	17	15	16	15
FA	11	8	9	10	10	10	8	10	9	9	11	9	8	8
SM	3	3	3	3	3	3	2	3	3	2	4	3	3	3
LT	2	2	2	2	2	2	1	2	2	2	2	2	2	1
NO	1	1	1	1	1	0	1	1	1	0	1	1	1	1
# SURVEYED	1495	1484	1484	1492	1525	1526	1467	1502	1589	1462	1451	1456	993	1029

TABLE II: SATISFACTION WITH FRIENDS -- BY SEX

Question: How much satisfaction would you say you get from your friendships? NOTE: Question not asked in 1972, 1985.

Responses: VG = A very great deal GD = A great deal QB = Quite a bit
FA = A fair amount SM = Some LT = A little
NO = None

		YEAR													
SEX	RESP	'73	'74	'75	'76	'77	'78	'80	'82	'83	'84	'86	'87	'88	'89
M	VG	29%	30%	28%	25%	28%	25%	34%	23%	25%	32%	20%	29%	22%	30%
A	GD	38	41	40	41	40	39	41	39	39	39	40	40	43	40
L	QB	15	16	16	19	17	19	13	19	20	14	20	17	17	18
E	FA	12	7	10	10	9	12	8	11	11	11	14	9	9	8
	SM	3	3	3	3	4	4	3	4	3	2	3	3	5	3
	LT	2	2	3	1	1	1	1	2	2	1	2	1	3	2
	NO	0	0	1	1	0	1	1	1	1	0	1	1	0	1
# SURVEYED		693	691	667	667	689	642	640	637	688	595	610	637	435	443
SEX	RESP	'73	'74	'75	'76	'77	'78	'80	'82	'83	'84	'86	'87	'88	'89
F	VG	37%	33%	30%	33%	32%	29%	34%	32%	28%	40%	27%	36%	34%	36%
E	GD	35	40	43	39	38	42	42	37	42	37	43	37	39	38
M	QB	13	13	14	14	14	15	13	16	16	11	15	14	14	13
A	FA	9	9	8	9	10	9	7	10	8	8	9	8	8	8
L	SM	3	3	3	3	2	3	2	3	3	2	4	2	2	3
E	LT	3	2	2	2	3	2	2	2	2	2	2	2	2	1
	NO	1	1	0	0	1	0	1	1	1	0	1	1	1	1
# SURVEYED		802	793	817	825	836	884	827	865	901	867	841	819	558	586

TABLE III: SATISFACTION WITH FRIENDS -- BY RACE

Question: How much satisfaction would you say you get from your friendships? NOTE: Question not asked in 1972, 1985.

Responses:
VG = A very great deal | GD = A great deal | QB = Quite a bit
FA = A fair amount | SM = Some | LT = A little
NO = None

		YEAR													
RACE	RESP	'73	'74	'75	'76	'77	'78	'80	'82	'83	'84	'86	'87	'88	'89
WHITE	VG	35%	33%	30%	31%	32%	28%	35%	29%	27%	39%	26%	34%	30%	35%
	GD	38	41	42	40	40	42	41	39	41	37	43	39	42	39
	QB	13	15	15	16	15	17	13	17	18	12	16	15	14	15
	FA	10	7	8	8	9	9	7	9	9	8	10	7	8	7
	SM	2	2	3	3	3	3	2	3	3	1	3	2	3	2
	LT	2	2	2	1	2	1	1	2	2	1	2	1	2	1
	NO	0	0	0	1	0	0	1	1	0	0	1	1	0	0
# SURVEYED		1302	1304	1317	1355	1335	1355	1317	1319	1409	1244	1233	1216	834	878
RACE	RESP	'73	'74	'75	'76	'77	'78	'80	'82	'83	'84	'86	'87	'88	'89
BLACK	VG	23%	24%	16%	13%	23%	21%	24%	21%	22%	21%	11%	21%	21%	21%
	GD	28	38	45	37	33	35	44	33	33	39	34	36	36	35
	QB	17	13	12	20	20	12	11	17	15	13	22	16	20	17
	FA	16	14	15	20	12	21	13	17	15	16	17	15	12	13
	SM	9	7	5	4	5	5	6	6	7	5	9	6	3	8
	LT	6	3	6	7	6	6	2	4	4	5	6	4	7	3
	NO	2	1	1	0	1	1	1	2	4	0	2	1	1	4
# SURVEYED		180	173	163	128	176	155	140	156	162	167	181	187	115	110
RACE	RESP	'73	'74	'75	'76	'77	'78	'80	'82	'83	'84	'86	'87	'88	'89
OTHER	VG	23%	29%	25%	22%	21%	31%	20%	11%	33%	20%	27%	32%	32%	32%
	GD	46	57	50	44	43	38	70	26	50	59	46	32	30	41
	QB	8	0	0	0	7	13	0	26	11	8	22	13	25	10
	FA	23	14	0	33	7	13	10	30	6	8	5	15	5	10
	SM	0	0	0	0	7	0	0	0	0	2	0	6	7	5
	LT	0	0	25	0	0	6	0	4	0	4	0	0	0	2
	NO	0	0	0	0	14	0	0	4	0	0	0	2	2	0
# SURVEYED		13	7	4	9	14	16	10	27	18	51	37	53	44	41

TABLE IV: SATISFACTION WITH FRIENDS -- BY AGE

Question: How much satisfaction would you say you get from your friendships? NOTE: Question not asked in 1972, 1985.

Responses: VG = A very great deal GD = A great deal QB = Quite a bit
FA = A fair amount SM = Some LT = A little
NO = None

		YEAR													
AGE	RESP	'73	'74	'75	'76	'77	'78	'80	'82	'83	'84	'86	'87	'88	'89
18-23	VG	32%	35%	33%	27%	29%	33%	36%	25%	27%	36%	20%	32%	28%	45%
	GD	32	38	45	35	38	37	34	47	44	32	41	41	51	31
	QB	18	15	13	21	16	15	15	11	18	15	26	13	12	10
	FA	11	5	8	10	11	9	10	12	6	12	6	7	2	8
	SM	4	4	1	4	2	4	3	1	4	2	4	5	2	2
	LT	4	2	2	4	4	2	1	2	1	2	4	2	5	3
	NO	1	0	0	0	1	0	1	1	0	1	0	0	0	1
# SURVEYED		171	168	173	162	164	162	155	148	128	161	107	126	93	93
AGE	RESP	'73	'74	'75	'76	'77	'78	'80	'82	'83	'84	'86	'87	'88	'89
24-29	VG	30%	24%	30%	34%	25%	27%	35%	26%	28%	41%	24%	30%	23%	35%
	GD	34	42	35	39	40	42	42	36	37	34	40	32	42	30
	QB	15	21	15	12	20	16	12	21	19	10	18	21	19	18
	FA	14	10	14	8	7	10	6	12	11	10	12	10	11	11
	SM	4	2	3	3	4	3	3	4	3	2	4	3	4	5
	LT	2	1	2	3	3	1	2	1	2	4	2	2	1	2
	NO	1	0	0	1	0	0	0	0	0	0	1	1	0	0
# SURVEYED		211	212	231	225	204	243	202	245	287	231	217	191	146	142
AGE	RESP	'73	'74	'75	'76	'77	'78	'80	'82	'83	'84	'86	'87	'88	'89
30-35	VG	35%	30%	25%	30%	34%	21%	27%	24%	19%	30%	23%	24%	24%	32%
	GD	41	41	41	43	39	45	47	45	44	42	42	45	42	34
	QB	9	14	16	12	12	20	11	18	19	14	14	15	20	19
	FA	12	9	9	12	10	10	10	9	11	9	16	8	10	8
	SM	2	4	4	2	2	3	2	1	3	5	3	5	2	3
	LT	2	2	4	2	3	1	2	1	3	1	1	2	2	1
	NO	0	0	2	0	1	0	1	2	1	0	0	1	1	1
# SURVEYED		165	175	171	186	188	230	215	204	236	198	219	221	127	145
AGE	RESP	'73	'74	'75	'76	'77	'78	'80	'82	'83	'84	'86	'87	'88	'89
36-41	VG	27%	29%	26%	29%	24%	28%	34%	33%	21%	38%	20%	30%	36%	29%
	GD	36	39	44	42	40	39	41	30	43	38	43	37	43	37
	QB	18	14	18	22	19	17	15	21	21	12	19	15	11	22
	FA	14	11	8	8	9	11	7	9	9	9	13	11	6	5
	SM	1	3	3	0	5	4	2	3	2	2	5	5	2	5
	LT	3	3	1	0	2	1	1	3	2	1	1	1	2	2
	NO	1	1	0	0	0	0	1	1	1	0	0	1	0	0
# SURVEYED		174	152	154	157	168	160	150	146	173	186	186	185	126	133

TABLE IV: SATISFACTION WITH FRIENDS -- BY AGE (Continued)

Question: How much satisfaction would you say you get from your friendships? NOTE: Question not asked in 1972, 1985.

Responses: VG = A very great deal GD = A great deal QB = Quite a bit
FA = A fair amount SM = Some LT = A little
NO = None

		YEAR													
AGE	RESP	'73	'74	'75	'76	'77	'78	'80	'82	'83	'84	'86	'87	'88	'89
42-47	VG	27%	28%	33%	28%	26%	28%	37%	29%	26%	32%	21%	37%	28%	27%
	GD	38	43	38	41	46	35	35	33	42	42	36	29	35	41
	QB	21	11	15	18	12	17	15	18	17	15	22	18	20	19
	FA	9	11	6	9	12	13	9	14	8	10	12	11	12	8
	SM	2	6	5	4	2	7	2	4	5	0	5	2	4	3
	LT	3	2	3	0	3	0	2	2	1	1	3	3	2	0
	NO	1	0	0	1	0	0	1	0	1	0	1	0	0	3
# SURVEYED		146	151	143	113	145	119	117	119	143	124	140	157	104	106
AGE	RESP	'73	'74	'75	'76	'77	'78	'80	'82	'83	'84	'86	'87	'88	'89
48-53	VG	37%	34%	28%	27%	35%	23%	33%	20%	29%	37%	24%	42%	23%	35%
	GD	38	43	44	35	35	42	44	42	45	40	45	29	40	42
	QB	10	13	19	14	17	21	15	20	17	17	17	15	21	11
	FA	11	7	6	19	9	10	7	11	6	4	9	10	11	9
	SM	1	2	1	3	1	0	2	6	3	1	0	1	2	3
	LT	2	1	1	1	1	2	0	1	0	1	4	2	0	0
	NO	1	0	0	1	2	2	0	1	0	0	1	1	4	0
# SURVEYED		151	146	141	133	153	132	123	112	116	102	107	126	57	95
AGE	RESP	'73	'74	'75	'76	'77	'78	'80	'82	'83	'84	'86	'87	'88	'89
54-59	VG	37%	38%	25%	30%	38%	32%	35%	29%	27%	35%	34%	35%	30%	26%
	GD	42	36	54	41	34	42	44	43	44	47	37	43	38	53
	QB	10	12	12	16	15	14	10	17	14	12	10	13	15	5
	FA	5	8	3	8	7	7	8	6	8	4	13	5	9	6
	SM	5	1	4	2	4	3	1	2	4	1	3	2	6	6
	LT	1	1	2	2	2	1	0	3	2	0	0	1	2	3
	NO	1	3	1	0	1	1	1	0	1	0	2	1	0	0
# SURVEYED		155	139	125	128	168	137	136	144	132	114	97	95	66	62
AGE	RESP	'73	'74	'75	'76	'77	'78	'80	'82	'83	'84	'86	'87	'88	'89
60-65	VG	40%	35%	33%	25%	29%	26%	41%	28%	30%	39%	25%	31%	39%	36%
	GD	34	36	41	43	41	37	42	38	37	40	44	49	34	37
	QB	12	19	10	16	14	25	12	16	19	11	16	12	13	16
	FA	8	6	11	10	11	8	5	11	11	8	9	6	8	8
	SM	3	0	3	2	3	2	1	4	1	0	4	1	6	0
	LT	2	3	2	1	1	2	0	2	1	3	1	1	1	1
	NO	0	0	1	2	1	1	0	1	2	0	1	1	0	1
# SURVEYED		121	108	112	134	117	106	118	116	131	111	111	101	80	75

TABLE IV: SATISFACTION WITH FRIENDS -- BY AGE (Continued)

Question: How much satisfaction would you say you get from your friendships? NOTE: Question not asked in 1972, 1985.

Responses: VG = A very great deal GD = A great deal QB = Quite a bit
FA = A fair amount SM = Some LT = A little
NO = None

		YEAR													
AGE	RESP	'73	'74	'75	'76	'77	'78	'80	'82	'83	'84	'86	'87	'88	'89
66+	VG	37%	36%	26%	30%	34%	27%	36%	34%	34%	38%	26%	37%	29%	34%
	GD	37	45	42	41	40	42	42	32	36	36	45	40	42	47
	QB	11	9	13	16	12	12	12	16	14	10	13	12	12	11
	FA	9	5	10	6	10	12	6	9	8	12	8	7	7	6
	SM	4	3	5	4	2	3	2	5	3	1	3	1	4	1
	LT	3	1	3	2	0	3	2	4	4	2	3	1	4	1
	NO	1	1	1	0	1	0	1	1	1	1	2	1	1	1
# SURVEYED		197	227	230	248	211	230	242	256	236	229	260	250	190	176

****

SATISFACTION WITH HOBBY

TABLE I: SATISFACTION WITH HOBBY -- BY TOTAL POPULATION

Question: How much satisfaction would you say you get from your non-working activities --- hobbies, etc.? NOTE: Question not asked in 1972, 1985.

Responses: VG = A very great deal GD = A great deal QB = Quite a bit
FA = A fair amount SM = Some LT = A little
NO = None

	YEAR													
RESPONSE	'73	'74	'75	'76	'77	'78	'80	'82	'83	'84	'86	'87	'88	'89
VG	26%	23%	24%	22%	25%	24%	27%	22%	21%	25%	19%	25%	21%	24%
GD	29	32	33	35	29	34	34	30	32	36	34	35	36	36
QB	17	16	16	18	19	18	16	19	20	17	19	18	18	17
FA	13	13	12	11	14	13	11	15	14	12	13	12	12	11
SM	5	6	6	6	5	4	5	6	7	4	5	4	6	5
LT	6	5	5	5	4	4	4	5	3	3	5	3	4	4
NO	4	5	4	3	3	4	3	4	4	2	5	2	3	3
# SURVEYED	1487	1479	1477	1489	1519	1520	1460	1496	1583	1458	1448	1447	991	1026

TABLE II: SATISFACTION WITH HOBBY -- BY SEX

Question: How much satisfaction would you say you get from your non-working activities --- hobbies, etc.? NOTE: Question not asked in 1972, 1985.

Responses: VG = A very great deal; GD = A great deal; QB = Quite a bit; FA = A fair amount; SM = Some; LT = A little; NO = None

SEX	RESP	'73	'74	'75	'76	'77	'78	'80	'82	'83	'84	'86	'87	'88	'89
M	VG	26%	24%	24%	25%	27%	27%	29%	22%	21%	27%	18%	26%	22%	25%
A	GD	31	32	36	36	30	33	38	31	34	36	35	36	37	38
L	QB	16	17	15	16	20	18	13	19	20	18	23	18	19	18
E	FA	15	12	11	9	11	12	9	15	12	11	11	12	10	8
	SM	5	7	6	6	5	4	4	6	7	4	5	4	6	5
	LT	6	4	5	6	4	4	4	4	3	3	5	3	3	3
	NO	3	4	4	3	4	3	2	3	3	2	2	2	4	2
# SURVEYED		690	690	666	666	688	639	638	636	684	594	610	631	436	441
SEX	RESP	'73	'74	'75	'76	'77	'78	'80	'82	'83	'84	'86	'87	'88	'89
F	VG	26%	23%	25%	20%	24%	22%	26%	21%	20%	24%	19%	24%	21%	23%
E	GD	27	31	30	35	29	35	31	29	30	36	34	34	36	34
M	QB	18	15	18	20	19	19	18	19	21	17	16	18	17	17
A	FA	11	14	13	12	16	13	12	15	15	12	14	12	14	13
L	SM	6	5	6	6	5	4	5	7	6	5	5	5	6	5
E	LT	6	5	5	4	5	3	5	5	4	3	5	4	4	5
	NO	6	6	5	3	2	4	3	4	4	2	7	2	3	4
# SURVEYED		797	789	811	823	831	881	822	860	899	864	838	816	555	585

TABLE III: SATISFACTION WITH HOBBY -- BY RACE

Question: How much satisfaction would you say you get from your non-working activities --- hobbies, etc.? NOTE: Question not asked in 1972, 1985.

Responses: VG = A very great deal GD = A great deal QB = Quite a bit
FA = A fair amount SM = Some LT = A little
NO = None

		YEAR													
RACE	RESP	'73	'74	'75	'76	'77	'78	'80	'82	'83	'84	'86	'87	'88	'89
WHITE	VG	27%	24%	25%	23%	25%	25%	28%	22%	21%	27%	20%	26%	22%	25%
	GD	30	32	33	36	31	34	34	30	33	37	35	35	37	37
	QB	17	17	16	18	19	19	16	19	20	17	19	18	19	17
	FA	12	13	12	11	14	12	11	15	14	12	13	11	11	10
	SM	5	5	6	6	5	4	5	6	6	4	5	4	5	5
	LT	4	4	4	5	4	3	3	4	3	2	4	3	4	3
	NO	4	5	4	3	3	3	2	3	3	2	4	2	3	3
# SURVEYED		1293	1301	1310	1352	1330	1350	1313	1316	1403	1240	1231	1209	833	876
RACE	RESP	'73	'74	'75	'76	'77	'78	'80	'82	'83	'84	'86	'87	'88	'89
BLACK	VG	14%	19%	20%	16%	26%	15%	17%	21%	18%	16%	12%	17%	17%	15%
	GD	20	28	29	30	21	33	32	29	20	30	28	36	30	32
	QB	18	14	17	20	20	17	15	14	20	18	19	17	15	19
	FA	19	15	14	13	14	13	12	15	14	13	17	17	18	11
	SM	8	10	6	6	7	3	7	8	14	8	4	6	10	6
	LT	16	6	9	9	10	10	12	8	7	11	10	4	4	9
	NO	4	8	6	5	2	8	6	5	7	4	9	3	5	8
# SURVEYED		181	172	163	128	174	155	137	154	162	166	180	186	115	108
RACE	RESP	'73	'74	'75	'76	'77	'78	'80	'82	'83	'84	'86	'87	'88	'89
OTHER	VG	15%	33%	0%	33%	27%	20%	20%	19%	22%	21%	14%	21%	21%	12%
	GD	31	17	50	0	27	33	40	23	28	35	32	35	40	29
	QB	15	0	0	22	27	7	30	15	11	23	22	10	16	19
	FA	15	0	50	22	7	27	0	15	6	8	14	12	7	19
	SM	8	17	0	11	0	13	10	15	11	8	14	10	12	10
	LT	8	33	0	11	7	0	0	8	11	4	5	4	0	10
	NO	8	0	0	0	7	0	0	4	11	2	0	10	5	2
# SURVEYED		13	6	4	9	15	15	10	26	18	52	37	52	43	42

TABLE IV: SATISFACTION WITH HOBBY -- BY AGE

Question: How much satisfaction would you say you get from your non-working activities --- hobbies, etc.? NOTE: Question not asked in 1972, 1985.

Responses: VG = A very great deal GD = A great deal QB = Quite a bit
FA = A fair amount SM = Some LT = A little
NO = None

		YEAR													
AGE	RESP	'73	'74	'75	'76	'77	'78	'80	'82	'83	'84	'86	'87	'88	'89
18-23	VG	21%	24%	31%	22%	23%	27%	26%	18%	15%	25%	14%	20%	30%	33%
	GD	30	29	20	34	30	28	32	34	39	34	28	36	42	34
	QB	17	17	20	18	26	18	18	21	21	14	24	18	10	12
	FA	14	14	14	8	10	15	12	12	18	15	16	13	8	8
	SM	8	11	5	5	7	4	3	9	4	7	7	8	6	8
	LT	5	2	8	10	3	4	6	3	1	3	7	3	3	3
	NO	5	2	2	2	2	4	2	3	2	1	4	2	1	2
# SURVEYED		170	168	173	162	164	162	155	148	127	161	107	126	93	93
AGE	RESP	'73	'74	'75	'76	'77	'78	'80	'82	'83	'84	'86	'87	'88	'89
24-29	VG	23%	23%	24%	28%	27%	26%	28%	23%	22%	28%	16%	25%	22%	21%
	GD	34	29	32	34	28	31	38	34	26	39	35	28	37	29
	QB	15	18	16	15	20	17	15	18	23	16	23	21	15	25
	FA	13	15	15	9	14	13	11	14	16	7	11	12	12	10
	SM	6	7	6	9	4	5	4	7	7	6	7	7	7	8
	LT	6	6	4	2	6	4	3	3	4	3	5	5	5	4
	NO	3	2	3	3	1	3	0	2	2	1	3	2	2	4
# SURVEYED		211	211	231	225	204	242	201	245	286	231	217	191	145	141
AGE	RESP	'73	'74	'75	'76	'77	'78	'80	'82	'83	'84	'86	'87	'88	'89
30-35	VG	26%	23%	29%	20%	26%	23%	27%	25%	18%	20%	17%	22%	21%	28%
	GD	29	31	33	36	29	40	36	31	34	35	37	41	28	31
	QB	20	18	15	20	20	18	18	18	25	19	15	17	21	22
	FA	9	13	9	12	13	11	8	15	14	17	18	11	20	11
	SM	6	7	5	5	5	3	4	5	3	4	6	5	4	1
	LT	7	5	6	7	4	3	4	4	3	5	4	3	3	3
	NO	2	3	3	0	3	2	3	1	3	2	4	2	2	3
# SURVEYED		163	175	171	186	188	230	215	204	236	198	219	221	127	144
AGE	RESP	'73	'74	'75	'76	'77	'78	'80	'82	'83	'84	'86	'87	'88	'89
36-41	VG	21%	20%	23%	22%	21%	24%	30%	21%	16%	22%	19%	25%	27%	20%
	GD	32	32	38	35	36	37	32	25	37	34	37	38	38	35
	QB	14	14	17	15	16	15	14	21	19	22	19	15	21	21
	FA	18	16	10	15	17	14	14	14	15	14	15	15	8	14
	SM	6	5	3	6	5	3	4	8	7	4	7	2	4	5
	LT	5	7	4	3	5	3	6	9	4	2	1	2	2	2
	NO	3	7	5	2	1	3	0	4	2	2	2	2	1	2
# SURVEYED		174	152	154	156	168	160	150	146	171	185	186	182	126	132

TABLE IV: SATISFACTION WITH HOBBY -- BY AGE (Continued)

Question: How much satisfaction would you say you get from your non-working activities --- hobbies, etc.? NOTE: Question not asked in 1972, 1985.

Responses: VG = A very great deal GD = A great deal QB = Quite a bit
FA = A fair amount SM = Some LT = A little
NO = None

		YEAR													
AGE	RESP	'73	'74	'75	'76	'77	'78	'80	'82	'83	'84	'86	'87	'88	'89
42-47	VG	32%	19%	20%	19%	20%	19%	25%	27%	22%	28%	20%	29%	20%	13%
	GD	18	32	42	31	31	35	29	25	29	36	37	30	41	50
	QB	23	19	8	24	18	24	23	19	23	18	18	21	21	16
	FA	16	14	16	9	18	13	9	18	10	11	10	13	8	7
	SM	5	6	7	7	5	3	4	4	10	3	5	2	5	4
	LT	5	4	5	6	6	5	5	3	3	2	9	4	3	8
	NO	2	5	3	4	2	2	4	4	2	1	1	1	2	3
# SURVEYED		146	151	143	113	147	118	117	119	143	125	140	156	104	106
AGE	RESP	'73	'74	'75	'76	'77	'78	'80	'82	'83	'84	'86	'87	'88	'89
48-53	VG	27%	25%	24%	14%	29%	21%	24%	19%	24%	23%	21%	34%	23%	23%
	GD	31	34	35	37	28	39	40	30	32	34	36	28	27	41
	QB	12	12	19	21	18	21	18	23	17	19	18	17	21	15
	FA	13	12	11	15	10	7	8	17	10	15	8	10	9	12
	SM	5	5	4	4	6	5	7	4	9	2	3	5	5	6
	LT	7	5	4	6	3	2	2	6	3	6	7	4	7	1
	NO	5	7	4	2	5	5	1	2	3	2	7	2	7	2
# SURVEYED		149	146	140	132	153	131	121	111	115	101	107	125	56	95
AGE	RESP	'73	'74	'75	'76	'77	'78	'80	'82	'83	'84	'86	'87	'88	'89
54-59	VG	28%	25%	21%	20%	29%	27%	23%	26%	17%	21%	20%	27%	18%	29%
	GD	31	31	42	38	24	38	45	32	39	36	33	29	36	35
	QB	19	12	11	18	18	14	12	16	13	20	16	22	26	6
	FA	12	17	10	12	18	12	7	15	14	13	10	11	11	11
	SM	4	4	8	6	4	5	6	6	11	5	4	3	5	10
	LT	3	4	3	4	4	2	3	2	5	2	6	3	2	5
	NO	3	6	5	2	3	2	4	3	2	2	10	4	3	3
# SURVEYED		153	138	125	127	165	137	136	143	133	113	98	95	66	62
AGE	RESP	'73	'74	'75	'76	'77	'78	'80	'82	'83	'84	'86	'87	'88	'89
60-65	VG	26%	29%	24%	21%	21%	26%	27%	19%	28%	27%	19%	19%	18%	16%
	GD	32	34	26	43	30	29	29	26	31	39	38	39	33	36
	QB	18	16	17	14	26	22	12	23	15	18	19	17	19	19
	FA	9	5	15	8	15	19	15	17	14	5	12	12	13	15
	SM	3	4	7	4	5	3	10	3	6	3	4	6	12	5
	LT	7	8	3	4	2	1	4	9	3	5	3	6	4	5
	NO	5	5	7	6	2	1	3	3	3	5	4	1	1	3
# SURVEYED		119	107	111	133	117	105	117	115	130	111	113	100	78	74

TABLE IV: SATISFACTION WITH HOBBY -- BY AGE (Continued)

Question: How much satisfaction would you say you get from your non-working activities --- hobbies, etc.? NOTE: Question not asked in 1972, 1985.

Responses: VG = A very great deal GD = A great deal QB = Quite a bit
FA = A fair amount SM = Some LT = A little
NO = None

		YEAR													
AGE	RESP	'73	'74	'75	'76	'77	'78	'80	'82	'83	'84	'86	'87	'88	'89
66+	VG	30%	22%	21%	25%	28%	21%	31%	18%	23%	31%	21%	25%	16%	28%
	GD	23	33	31	33	30	32	29	30	27	37	29	40	38	36
	QB	15	17	20	18	15	19	14	17	18	12	19	16	16	13
	FA	11	11	10	11	10	11	13	15	11	8	13	9	14	10
	SM	4	4	5	4	4	4	5	8	5	4	4	3	5	3
	LT	8	4	5	4	5	5	3	4	4	1	6	3	4	4
	NO	10	8	8	6	8	9	5	8	11	6	9	4	7	6
# SURVEYED		198	225	225	249	206	228	239	253	235	227	254	247	192	177

****

SATISFACTION WITH HEALTH

TABLE I: SATISFACTION WITH HEALTH -- BY TOTAL POPULATION

Question: How much satisfaction would you say you get from your health and physical condition? NOTE: Question not asked in 1972, 1985.

Responses: VG = A very great deal GD = A great deal QB = Quite a bit
FA = A fair amount SM = Some LT = A little
NO = None

	YEAR													
RESPONSE	'73	'74	'75	'76	'77	'78	'80	'82	'83	'84	'86	'87	'88	'89
VG	29%	28%	25%	24%	30%	24%	29%	35%	24%	29%	23%	27%	24%	25%
GD	31	33	35	35	31	35	35	28	33	34	32	33	35	31
QB	12	13	15	15	14	15	14	14	17	14	16	16	17	17
FA	17	16	14	16	14	16	13	12	16	14	15	15	15	17
SM	5	5	5	4	4	4	4	6	5	4	5	5	4	5
LT	3	3	4	3	4	4	4	3	4	3	5	2	4	3
NO	3	2	2	2	3	2	2	2	2	2	3	2	1	2
# SURVEYED	1501	1482	1483	1494	1524	1525	1464	1500	1588	1463	1451	1455	992	1029

TABLE II: SATISFACTION WITH HEALTH -- BY SEX

Question: How much satisfaction would you say you get from your health and physical condition? NOTE: Question not asked in 1972, 1985.

Responses: VG = A very great deal; GD = A great deal; QB = Quite a bit; FA = A fair amount; SM = Some; LT = A little; NO = None

		YEAR													
SEX	RESP	'73	'74	'75	'76	'77	'78	'80	'82	'83	'84	'86	'87	'88	'89
M	VG	29%	30%	27%	25%	29%	27%	29%	36%	25%	29%	24%	27%	27%	25%
A	GD	34	34	37	38	34	36	39	28	33	35	35	35	37	31
L	QB	12	13	14	14	13	14	13	13	17	16	16	16	16	18
E	FA	16	14	11	13	14	15	11	12	15	11	13	14	12	17
	SM	5	5	4	4	4	4	4	6	6	4	5	4	3	5
	LT	3	2	4	4	3	3	3	3	3	3	4	2	3	2
	NO	2	2	2	2	3	1	2	2	1	1	3	3	1	2
# SURVEYED		700	690	666	668	688	641	637	637	686	593	608	636	434	442
SEX	RESP	'73	'74	'75	'76	'77	'78	'80	'82	'83	'84	'86	'87	'88	'89
F	VG	29%	27%	23%	24%	30%	21%	28%	35%	23%	29%	22%	28%	22%	26%
E	GD	29	32	34	33	29	35	32	28	33	33	31	31	33	32
M	QB	12	13	16	15	14	16	14	14	18	13	17	16	17	16
A	FA	18	18	16	19	15	16	14	12	16	15	17	15	17	16
L	SM	5	4	6	4	4	5	4	5	4	4	5	5	5	5
E	LT	4	4	4	3	5	4	5	4	5	4	5	3	5	3
	NO	4	2	2	2	3	2	2	2	2	2	2	2	1	3
# SURVEYED		801	792	817	826	836	884	827	863	902	870	843	819	558	587

TABLE III: SATISFACTION WITH HEALTH -- BY RACE

Question: How much satisfaction would you say you get from your health and physical condition? NOTE: Question not asked in 1972, 1985.

Responses: VG = A very great deal; GD = A great deal; QB = Quite a bit; FA = A fair amount; SM = Some; LT = A little; NO = None

		YEAR													
RACE	RESP	'73	'74	'75	'76	'77	'78	'80	'82	'83	'84	'86	'87	'88	'89
WHITE	VG	30%	29%	26%	25%	30%	23%	30%	35%	23%	29%	23%	28%	23%	26%
	GD	32	34	35	36	32	35	35	28	34	35	32	33	36	32
	QB	12	14	15	15	13	16	13	14	18	14	17	16	16	16
	FA	16	15	14	16	14	15	12	11	15	13	15	14	14	16
	SM	4	4	4	4	4	5	4	5	5	4	5	4	4	5
	LT	3	3	4	3	4	4	4	3	4	3	4	2	5	3
	NO	3	2	2	2	3	2	2	2	1	2	3	2	1	2
# SURVEYED		1305	1302	1316	1356	1334	1354	1315	1317	1408	1242	1234	1215	834	877
RACE	RESP	'73	'74	'75	'76	'77	'78	'80	'82	'83	'84	'86	'87	'88	'89
BLACK	VG	19%	24%	19%	19%	29%	26%	19%	37%	28%	26%	22%	25%	26%	26%
	GD	24	26	37	30	25	35	39	26	26	28	34	28	24	21
	QB	14	8	13	15	14	10	16	8	12	15	11	19	23	19
	FA	26	23	18	22	17	22	15	17	20	19	15	14	22	22
	SM	10	11	7	8	6	3	4	8	6	3	6	5	3	5
	LT	4	7	5	3	6	3	5	3	5	7	7	4	3	4
	NO	3	2	1	3	5	1	3	1	4	2	4	4	0	4
# SURVEYED		183	173	163	129	175	155	140	156	162	169	180	187	114	110
RACE	RESP	'73	'74	'75	'76	'77	'78	'80	'82	'83	'84	'86	'87	'88	'89
OTHER	VG	23%	29%	0%	44%	13%	31%	33%	37%	39%	27%	32%	28%	36%	19%
	GD	46	57	75	33	20	44	33	30	28	29	27	30	34	43
	QB	8	0	25	11	27	6	11	15	11	13	16	6	7	21
	FA	8	0	0	11	20	13	11	15	11	13	8	19	11	7
	SM	15	14	0	0	7	0	11	4	0	10	5	9	9	2
	LT	0	0	0	0	13	6	0	0	6	8	11	2	2	5
	NO	0	0	0	0	0	0	0	0	6	0	0	6	0	2
# SURVEYED		13	7	4	9	15	16	9	27	18	52	37	53	44	42

TABLE IV: SATISFACTION WITH HEALTH -- BY AGE

Question: How much satisfaction would you say you get from your health and physical condition? NOTE: Question not asked in 1972, 1985.

Responses: VG = A very great deal; GD = A great deal; QB = Quite a bit; FA = A fair amount; SM = Some; LT = A little; NO = None

		YEAR													
AGE	RESP	'73	'74	'75	'76	'77	'78	'80	'82	'83	'84	'86	'87	'88	'89
18-23	VG	34%	36%	34%	27%	30%	31%	30%	45%	23%	32%	22%	28%	33%	39%
	GD	32	30	36	46	35	30	44	24	39	40	36	41	42	29
	QB	16	17	15	12	18	16	14	16	20	10	21	18	16	13
	FA	12	13	10	12	12	16	6	5	12	11	14	9	4	13
	SM	2	3	3	2	4	4	3	7	2	6	1	2	3	4
	LT	2	1	2	1	1	2	3	2	5	1	3	2	1	1
	NO	3	0	0	0	1	1	0	1	0	0	3	1	0	1
# SURVEYED		171	168	173	162	164	161	155	148	128	161	107	126	93	93
AGE	RESP	'73	'74	'75	'76	'77	'78	'80	'82	'83	'84	'86	'87	'88	'89
24-29	VG	32%	33%	28%	38%	33%	32%	33%	37%	26%	35%	31%	32%	25%	28%
	GD	40	35	40	31	35	38	39	34	34	33	35	37	40	32
	QB	9	13	19	18	17	13	13	14	20	15	15	18	16	17
	FA	13	14	8	7	9	11	12	9	13	12	10	9	14	12
	SM	4	4	3	4	2	3	1	3	4	2	6	3	1	7
	LT	2	0	3	2	2	2	1	2	2	3	3	0	3	2
	NO	0	1	0	0	1	0	0	1	0	0	0	1	0	1
# SURVEYED		211	212	232	226	204	243	202	244	285	231	216	191	146	142
AGE	RESP	'73	'74	'75	'76	'77	'78	'80	'82	'83	'84	'86	'87	'88	'89
30-35	VG	39%	35%	32%	28%	42%	25%	29%	36%	20%	26%	24%	28%	28%	27%
	GD	32	38	35	42	32	40	43	31	40	35	31	29	33	33
	QB	11	10	11	12	12	16	13	16	17	21	18	19	17	23
	FA	11	10	14	11	10	11	9	10	15	13	18	16	14	15
	SM	4	2	5	2	2	5	3	4	3	2	5	5	5	1
	LT	2	2	3	3	2	3	2	2	2	2	3	2	2	1
	NO	1	1	1	2	1	0	1	1	2	1	1	0	0	0
# SURVEYED		167	175	170	186	186	230	214	204	235	198	219	221	127	145
AGE	RESP	'73	'74	'75	'76	'77	'78	'80	'82	'83	'84	'86	'87	'88	'89
36-41	VG	33%	30%	24%	25%	34%	28%	34%	40%	28%	28%	30%	26%	24%	23%
	GD	29	36	39	42	36	35	34	26	33	35	34	37	45	32
	QB	11	18	19	15	12	13	16	15	15	20	16	21	14	17
	FA	14	9	14	15	13	18	10	12	14	11	9	9	11	18
	SM	3	4	1	3	4	4	3	3	6	4	6	4	4	8
	LT	5	3	3	0	1	3	4	2	3	2	4	2	1	2
	NO	4	0	1	0	1	1	0	2	0	0	1	1	1	1
# SURVEYED		175	152	154	158	168	160	149	146	173	187	185	185	126	133

TABLE IV: SATISFACTION WITH HEALTH -- BY AGE (Continued)

Question: How much satisfaction would you say you get from your health and physical condition? NOTE: Question not asked in 1972, 1985.

Responses: VG = A very great deal GD = A great deal QB = Quite a bit FA = A fair amount SM = Some LT = A little NO = None

		YEAR													
AGE	RESP	'73	'74	'75	'76	'77	'78	'80	'82	'83	'84	'86	'87	'88	'89
42-47	VG	26%	28%	32%	29%	26%	18%	28%	29%	30%	30%	18%	32%	26%	25%
	GD	31	34	30	34	33	35	30	27	35	39	42	30	30	36
	QB	17	12	15	13	12	20	18	18	17	12	18	14	18	16
	FA	16	19	10	16	17	21	16	18	10	13	12	17	16	8
	SM	5	2	6	4	3	5	3	5	5	5	4	4	8	4
	LT	2	3	4	2	6	0	3	3	2	2	4	3	2	6
	NO	3	3	2	2	3	1	3	0	1	0	2	1	0	6
# SURVEYED		146	151	142	114	147	119	117	119	144	125	140	157	104	106
AGE	RESP	'73	'74	'75	'76	'77	'78	'80	'82	'83	'84	'86	'87	'88	'89
48-53	VG	28%	21%	24%	20%	31%	23%	26%	37%	28%	33%	21%	38%	25%	25%
	GD	25	33	45	29	32	36	32	30	31	30	37	27	32	24
	QB	9	12	11	17	13	14	17	9	16	16	13	13	19	23
	FA	23	24	12	21	12	16	12	12	12	8	12	10	12	21
	SM	8	4	4	6	6	4	6	11	5	4	5	4	4	3
	LT	3	5	4	3	3	5	2	0	4	7	4	2	7	2
	NO	5	1	0	3	3	2	5	2	3	2	7	5	2	1
# SURVEYED		151	146	140	133	154	132	121	112	116	102	107	126	57	95
AGE	RESP	'73	'74	'75	'76	'77	'78	'80	'82	'83	'84	'86	'87	'88	'89
54-59	VG	26%	26%	15%	15%	26%	22%	28%	38%	19%	26%	20%	27%	23%	18%
	GD	32	33	35	37	27	34	33	28	30	39	27	28	42	31
	QB	10	9	14	20	15	13	10	13	16	10	17	15	11	18
	FA	21	17	22	15	19	18	17	8	18	14	20	16	17	16
	SM	5	6	6	4	4	4	2	4	6	5	4	6	2	8
	LT	4	6	2	5	5	4	7	6	7	4	6	4	6	5
	NO	2	3	6	4	3	5	3	4	5	2	6	3	0	5
# SURVEYED		156	138	125	127	168	137	136	144	133	112	96	95	66	62
AGE	RESP	'73	'74	'75	'76	'77	'78	'80	'82	'83	'84	'86	'87	'88	'89
60-65	VG	20%	24%	19%	16%	23%	21%	26%	30%	23%	29%	19%	24%	23%	27%
	GD	36	32	22	35	27	31	25	30	31	33	36	30	21	27
	QB	11	13	15	11	13	14	11	8	15	9	13	9	21	7
	FA	22	12	26	24	21	20	16	17	20	17	12	24	21	26
	SM	3	4	7	6	4	5	7	9	4	4	9	6	5	7
	LT	6	9	5	6	7	8	10	5	7	4	7	5	9	5
	NO	2	6	5	3	5	2	5	2	1	5	4	3	0	1
# SURVEYED		121	108	112	133	115	106	119	115	130	111	113	101	80	74

TABLE IV: SATISFACTION WITH HEALTH -- BY AGE (Continued)

Question: How much satisfaction would you say you get from your health and physical condition? NOTE: Question not asked in 1972, 1985.

Responses: VG = A very great deal; GD = A great deal; QB = Quite a bit; FA = A fair amount; SM = Some; LT = A little; NO = None

		YEAR													
AGE	RESP	'73	'74	'75	'76	'77	'78	'80	'82	'83	'84	'86	'87	'88	'89
66+	VG	18%	18%	17%	16%	20%	12%	24%	26%	19%	22%	17%	18%	17%	19%
	GD	25	26	32	27	21	33	31	23	23	27	21	32	30	33
	QB	13	15	13	14	11	18	13	12	18	13	16	14	16	15
	FA	23	23	17	27	19	19	17	18	24	21	26	20	20	21
	SM	9	10	8	4	9	6	7	8	6	6	6	7	4	3
	LT	5	4	9	8	11	8	7	7	8	7	9	4	8	4
	NO	7	5	4	4	9	4	2	5	4	4	5	5	5	4
# SURVEYED		199	226	231	249	211	230	242	257	237	230	261	249	189	177

****

STATE OF HEALTH

TABLE I: STATE OF HEALTH -- BY TOTAL POPULATION

Question: Would you say your own health, in general, is excellent, good, fair, or poor? NOTE: Question not asked in 1978, 1983, 1986.

Responses: EX = Excellent; GD = Good; FA = Fair; PR = Poor

	YEAR												
RESPONSE	'72	'73	'74	'75	'76	'77	'80	'82	'84	'85	'87	'88	'89
EX	30%	32%	33%	32%	31%	32%	32%	32%	30%	34%	34%	31%	33%
GD	45	40	40	40	42	41	42	42	48	42	43	45	45
FA	20	21	21	21	20	20	20	19	18	18	18	18	18
PR	5	7	6	6	7	7	7	7	5	7	5	6	4
# SURVEYED	1612	1500	1480	1489	1498	1527	1466	1505	1461	1530	1464	976	1029

TABLE II: STATE OF HEALTH -- BY SEX

Question: Would you say your own health, in general, is excellent, good, fair, or poor? NOTE: Question not asked in 1978, 1983, 1986.

Responses: EX = Excellent; GD = Good; FA = Fair; PR = Poor

		YEAR												
SEX	RESP	'72	'73	'74	'75	'76	'77	'80	'82	'84	'85	'87	'88	'89
M	EX	33%	35%	36%	36%	35%	32%	34%	34%	32%	36%	36%	35%	36%
	GD	46	40	41	39	42	42	43	41	47	41	42	47	44
	FA	17	18	18	19	17	20	17	18	16	16	17	15	15
	PR	4	6	6	7	6	7	5	7	4	7	5	3	4
# SURVEYED		806	698	690	669	669	691	641	639	595	687	640	400	445
SEX	RESP	'72	'73	'74	'75	'76	'77	'80	'82	'84	'85	'87	'88	'89
F	EX	27%	29%	30%	29%	28%	32%	30%	31%	28%	32%	32%	28%	31%
	GD	44	40	39	41	42	40	41	42	48	43	43	44	45
	FA	23	23	24	24	22	21	22	20	19	19	20	20	20
	PR	6	8	7	6	8	7	8	7	5	6	5	9	4
# SURVEYED		806	802	790	820	829	836	825	866	866	843	824	576	584

TABLE III: STATE OF HEALTH -- BY RACE

Question: Would you say your own health, in general, is excellent, good, fair, or poor? NOTE: Question not asked in 1978, 1983, 1986.

Responses: EX = Excellent; GD = Good; FA = Fair; PR = Poor

RACE	RESP	'72	'73	'74	'75	'76	'77	'80	'82	'84	'85	'87	'88	'89
WHITE	EX	32%	34%	35%	34%	32%	32%	33%	32%	31%	35%	35%	32%	35%
	GD	45	40	39	40	42	42	42	42	48	42	43	45	45
	FA	18	19	20	20	19	20	19	18	17	17	17	17	17
	PR	5	7	5	7	7	6	6	7	4	6	5	6	4
# SURVEYED		1347	1305	1304	1322	1360	1336	1316	1322	1245	1337	1221	801	886
RACE	RESP	'72	'73	'74	'75	'76	'77	'80	'82	'84	'85	'87	'88	'89
BLACK	EX	17%	16%	15%	21%	19%	27%	17%	29%	24%	25%	26%	26%	25%
	GD	46	41	43	40	40	37	42	38	46	41	43	44	42
	FA	28	37	30	34	30	25	30	24	21	21	24	21	27
	PR	8	6	12	6	12	11	11	8	8	12	7	9	6
# SURVEYED		261	182	169	163	129	176	140	156	166	150	191	131	102
RACE	RESP	'72	'73	'74	'75	'76	'77	'80	'82	'84	'85	'87	'88	'89
OTHER	EX	25%	38%	43%	50%	56%	27%	60%	41%	22%	28%	35%	25%	27%
	GD	50	62	43	0	22	27	40	33	54	42	31	43	51
	FA	0	0	0	50	22	40	0	15	20	30	27	23	20
	PR	25	0	14	0	0	7	0	11	4	0	8	9	2
# SURVEYED		4	13	7	4	9	15	10	27	50	43	52	44	41

TABLE IV: STATE OF HEALTH -- BY AGE

Question: Would you say your own health, in general, is excellent, good, fair, or poor? NOTE: Question not asked in 1978, 1983, 1986.

Responses: EX = Excellent; GD = Good; FA = Fair; PR = Poor

AGE	RESP	'72	'73	'74	'75	'76	'77	'80	'82	'84	'85	'87	'88	'89
18-23	EX	40%	39%	35%	38%	47%	37%	41%	40%	33%	47%	36%	32%	39%
	GD	48	41	54	46	44	45	46	41	52	40	52	54	47
	FA	12	18	10	15	9	16	13	18	14	13	12	14	10
	PR	1	3	1	1	0	2	1	1	1	1	1	1	3
# SURVEYED		169	171	168	173	162	164	155	148	161	133	126	95	97

TABLE IV: STATE OF HEALTH -- BY AGE (Continued)

Question: Would you say your own health, in general, is excellent, good, fair, or poor? NOTE: Question not asked in 1978, 1983, 1986.

Responses: EX = Excellent; GD = Good; FA = Fair; PR = Poor

		YEAR												
AGE	RESP	'72	'73	'74	'75	'76	'77	'80	'82	'84	'85	'87	'88	'89
24-29	EX	43%	43%	51%	44%	42%	43%	37%	41%	36%	39%	44%	38%	44%
	GD	47	46	36	40	44	44	50	48	50	49	47	48	48
	FA	9	9	13	14	11	10	12	10	14	11	7	12	8
	PR	1	2	0	2	3	2	1	2	0	1	2	2	0
# SURVEYED		231	212	212	232	226	204	202	246	230	216	192	133	115
AGE	RESP	'72	'73	'74	'75	'76	'77	'80	'82	'84	'85	'87	'88	'89
30-35	EX	42%	46%	41%	45%	39%	44%	37%	39%	33%	36%	39%	36%	41%
	GD	47	36	42	37	45	41	45	49	56	49	46	54	49
	FA	9	15	14	14	13	12	17	10	10	11	13	9	10
	PR	1	4	3	4	3	3	1	2	2	4	1	1	1
# SURVEYED		186	166	175	171	186	188	215	204	198	212	221	131	136
AGE	RESP	'72	'73	'74	'75	'76	'77	'80	'82	'84	'85	'87	'88	'89
36-41	EX	35%	39%	36%	38%	39%	37%	43%	40%	33%	43%	44%	47%	40%
	GD	49	37	44	40	46	49	42	38	52	45	45	40	48
	FA	14	19	18	18	12	14	14	16	15	10	9	11	12
	PR	2	5	1	5	3	0	1	6	1	2	2	2	1
# SURVEYED		128	175	151	154	158	168	150	146	185	184	186	133	136
AGE	RESP	'72	'73	'74	'75	'76	'77	'80	'82	'84	'85	'87	'88	'89
42-47	EX	37%	36%	36%	39%	31%	29%	29%	37%	35%	41%	34%	28%	41%
	GD	40	40	37	33	44	44	44	39	45	45	48	55	41
	FA	19	18	23	25	17	16	22	21	18	13	12	13	14
	PR	3	7	3	3	9	10	5	3	2	1	5	4	4
# SURVEYED		186	146	150	143	114	147	117	119	125	124	157	102	107
AGE	RESP	'72	'73	'74	'75	'76	'77	'80	'82	'84	'85	'87	'88	'89
48-53	EX	21%	28%	32%	27%	21%	34%	29%	32%	33%	32%	37%	23%	30%
	GD	51	36	36	46	44	40	41	38	47	35	34	40	49
	FA	24	28	27	23	26	22	20	22	12	21	24	25	16
	PR	4	8	6	4	8	5	10	8	8	12	6	12	5
# SURVEYED		189	151	146	141	133	153	123	112	100	131	126	65	94

TABLE IV: STATE OF HEALTH -- BY AGE (Continued)

Question: Would you say your own health, in general, is excellent, good, fair, or poor? NOTE: Question not asked in 1978, 1983, 1986.

Responses: EX = Excellent; GD = Good; FA = Fair; PR = Poor

		YEAR												
AGE	RESP	'72	'73	'74	'75	'76	'77	'80	'82	'84	'85	'87	'88	'89
54-59	EX	19%	22%	24%	21%	24%	21%	26%	24%	30%	32%	27%	28%	22%
	GD	50	46	36	44	46	42	36	41	40	35	44	42	43
	FA	22	23	29	26	20	29	25	23	22	22	18	25	29
	PR	9	10	12	9	10	8	13	13	8	11	11	6	6
# SURVEYED		156	155	139	125	129	168	136	144	114	133	97	53	63
AGE	RESP	'72	'73	'74	'75	'76	'77	'80	'82	'84	'85	'87	'88	'89
60-65	EX	14%	20%	22%	17%	17%	23%	19%	19%	24%	25%	20%	30%	21%
	GD	41	36	45	35	35	30	31	43	41	42	35	38	38
	FA	35	32	21	34	38	32	30	27	24	24	36	23	31
	PR	10	12	12	14	11	15	19	11	11	9	10	10	10
# SURVEYED		144	121	107	113	133	117	119	116	112	130	101	84	77
AGE	RESP	'72	'73	'74	'75	'76	'77	'80	'82	'84	'85	'87	'88	'89
66+	EX	16%	12%	15%	17%	18%	14%	21%	20%	16%	16%	20%	14%	20%
	GD	32	40	32	37	35	31	40	35	41	36	33	36	40
	FA	36	33	36	30	33	36	27	29	30	32	36	32	31
	PR	16	15	17	16	15	18	12	16	13	16	11	18	9
# SURVEYED		218	199	226	232	251	211	240	259	231	260	253	177	201

****

SATISFIED WITH FINANCES

TABLE I: SATISFIED WITH FINANCES -- BY TOTAL POPULATION

Question: We are interested in how people are getting along financially these days. So far as you and your family are concerned, would you say that you are pretty well satisfied with your financial situation, more or less satisfied, or not at all satisfied?

Responses: PW = Pretty well satisfied; ML = More or less satisfied; NS = Not satisfied at all

	YEAR															
RESPONSE	'72	'73	'74	'75	'76	'77	'78	'80	'82	'83	'84	'85	'86	'87	'88	'89
PW	32%	31%	31%	31%	31%	34%	34%	29%	26%	29%	28%	30%	30%	30%	31%	31%
ML	45	46	46	42	46	44	42	45	46	41	46	44	43	48	45	44
NS	23	24	23	27	23	22	24	27	28	30	26	26	27	23	24	25
# SURVEYED	1608	1501	1478	1479	1492	1521	1529	1462	1498	1592	1464	1525	466	1461	1474	1532

TABLE II: SATISFIED WITH FINANCES -- BY SEX

Question: We are interested in how people are getting along financially these days. So far as you and your family are concerned, would you say that you are pretty well satisfied with your financial situation, more or less satisfied, or not at all satisfied?

Responses: PW = Pretty well satisfied; ML = More or less satisfied; NS = Not satisfied at all

		YEAR															
SEX	RESP	'72	'73	'74	'75	'76	'77	'78	'80	'82	'83	'84	'85	'86	'87	'88	'89
M	PW	31%	30%	32%	32%	31%	34%	35%	30%	26%	29%	29%	31%	31%	31%	31%	32%
	ML	47	46	45	42	44	44	41	44	48	41	43	44	43	47	45	42
	NS	21	24	23	27	25	22	23	27	26	30	28	25	26	22	23	26
# SURVEYED		805	701	688	665	667	690	641	639	637	689	594	685	619	640	634	658
SEX	RESP	'72	'73	'74	'75	'76	'77	'78	'80	'82	'83	'84	'85	'86	'87	'88	'89
F	PW	34%	31%	31%	30%	30%	34%	33%	28%	26%	28%	28%	28%	30%	29%	30%	30%
	ML	42	45	46	43	48	43	43	45	44	42	47	44	43	48	45	46
	NS	24	23	23	26	22	23	24	27	29	30	25	27	27	23	25	24
# SURVEYED		803	800	790	814	825	831	888	823	861	903	870	840	847	821	840	874

TABLE III: SATISFIED WITH FINANCES -- BY RACE

Question: We are interested in how people are getting along financially these days. So far as you and your family are concerned, would you say that you are pretty well satisfied with your financial situation, more or less satisfied, or not at all satisfied?

Responses: PW = Pretty well satisfied; ML = More or less satisfied; NS = Not satisfied at all

		YEAR															
RACE	RESP	'72	'73	'74	'75	'76	'77	'78	'80	'82	'83	'84	'85	'86	'87	'88	'89
WHITE	PW	34%	32%	32%	32%	32%	35%	35%	30%	28%	30%	29%	32%	32%	32%	33%	32%
	ML	46	46	46	44	46	44	44	45	45	42	47	44	43	48	45	45
	NS	20	22	22	24	22	21	21	25	27	28	24	24	25	20	22	22
# SURVEYED		1343	1305	1298	1312	1354	1331	1355	1313	1316	1411	1245	1333	1247	1219	1228	1317
RACE	RESP	'72	'73	'74	'75	'76	'77	'78	'80	'82	'83	'84	'85	'86	'87	'88	'89
BLACK	PW	25%	22%	22%	21%	11%	26%	23%	18%	14%	20%	17%	15%	20%	19%	17%	17%
	ML	41	40	46	30	47	41	32	38	45	34	38	43	40	43	41	37
	NS	34	38	32	49	42	34	45	44	41	46	45	42	40	38	42	46
# SURVEYED		261	183	173	163	129	175	158	139	155	163	167	149	182	189	185	155
RACE	RESP	'72	'73	'74	'75	'76	'77	'78	'80	'82	'83	'84	'85	'86	'87	'88	'89
OTHER	PW	25%	15%	29%	25%	67%	27%	31%	20%	15%	17%	42%	21%	38%	25%	30%	25%
	ML	25	38	29	50	22	60	25	70	67	39	40	47	38	47	48	47
	NS	50	46	43	25	11	13	44	10	19	44	17	33	24	28	23	28
# SURVEYED		4	13	7	4	9	15	16	10	27	18	52	43	37	53	61	60

TABLE IV: SATISFIED WITH FINANCES -- BY AGE

Question: We are interested in how people are getting along financially these days. So far as you and your family are concerned, would you say that you are pretty well satisfied with your financial situation, more or less satisfied, or not at all satisfied?

Responses: PW = Pretty well satisfied; ML = More or less satisfied; NS = Not satisfied at all

		YEAR															
AGE	RESP	'72	'73	'74	'75	'76	'77	'78	'80	'82	'83	'84	'85	'86	'87	'88	'89
18-23	PW	28%	30%	26%	30%	23%	29%	28%	29%	20%	21%	27%	26%	26%	23%	24%	25%
	ML	40	40	49	42	49	46	39	44	48	44	44	47	43	52	48	48
	NS	32	29	25	28	28	25	33	27	32	35	29	27	31	25	28	27
# SURVEYED		169	171	167	172	162	164	163	154	147	128	157	133	108	126	141	135
AGE	RESP	'72	'73	'74	'75	'76	'77	'78	'80	'82	'83	'84	'85	'86	'87	'88	'89
24-29	PW	25%	21%	18%	23%	27%	25%	24%	16%	19%	18%	16%	21%	22%	23%	21%	20%
	ML	50	46	53	40	39	47	48	49	43	44	55	48	45	46	47	49
	NS	25	33	28	37	34	28	29	35	38	38	28	31	33	32	31	31
# SURVEYED		231	211	211	231	225	203	242	202	246	287	231	216	218	193	213	202
AGE	RESP	'72	'73	'74	'75	'76	'77	'78	'80	'82	'83	'84	'85	'86	'87	'88	'89
30-35	PW	29%	27%	25%	24%	19%	30%	29%	19%	18%	21%	18%	24%	22%	18%	23%	25%
	ML	41	50	47	45	56	47	45	42	46	41	49	42	45	51	47	42
	NS	30	23	27	31	25	22	26	40	36	38	34	34	33	31	30	33
# SURVEYED		187	167	175	168	186	188	230	215	203	235	199	210	221	220	194	212
AGE	RESP	'72	'73	'74	'75	'76	'77	'78	'80	'82	'83	'84	'85	'86	'87	'88	'89
36-41	PW	23%	22%	30%	19%	29%	32%	21%	29%	25%	21%	24%	25%	23%	21%	21%	24%
	ML	54	49	43	45	46	43	51	43	40	41	46	41	51	58	47	47
	NS	23	29	28	35	25	26	29	28	36	38	30	34	26	21	31	29
# SURVEYED		128	175	152	154	158	167	160	150	146	173	186	183	188	185	192	198
AGE	RESP	'72	'73	'74	'75	'76	'77	'78	'80	'82	'83	'84	'85	'86	'87	'88	'89
42-47	PW	36%	31%	27%	27%	24%	32%	34%	27%	24%	31%	24%	26%	24%	30%	27%	34%
	ML	40	43	53	45	54	42	36	43	45	37	47	53	44	45	38	39
	NS	24	26	19	28	23	26	29	30	31	32	29	21	32	25	35	27
# SURVEYED		185	146	150	143	114	146	119	115	119	144	126	124	140	157	157	161
AGE	RESP	'72	'73	'74	'75	'76	'77	'78	'80	'82	'83	'84	'85	'86	'87	'88	'89
48-53	PW	34%	36%	32%	34%	33%	41%	39%	28%	28%	30%	29%	31%	34%	30%	26%	33%
	ML	49	45	42	44	45	42	44	43	54	47	50	43	36	49	52	43
	NS	16	19	26	23	22	16	17	28	19	23	21	27	30	21	22	25
# SURVEYED		189	151	145	140	132	153	133	123	112	115	101	131	105	125	92	138
AGE	RESP	'72	'73	'74	'75	'76	'77	'78	'80	'82	'83	'84	'85	'86	'87	'88	'89
54-59	PW	42%	34%	38%	33%	32%	37%	43%	28%	28%	34%	33%	34%	37%	31%	39%	43%
	ML	41	49	41	44	54	44	39	51	46	37	40	39	36	44	39	34
	NS	17	17	21	23	14	19	18	21	26	30	26	27	26	26	22	23
# SURVEYED		156	156	139	124	125	166	137	135	143	134	114	131	99	98	85	98

TABLE IV: SATISFIED WITH FINANCES -- BY AGE (Continued)

Question: We are interested in how people are getting along financially these days. So far as you and your family are concerned, would you say that you are pretty well satisfied with your financial situation, more or less satisfied, or not at all satisfied?

Responses: PW = Pretty well satisfied; ML = More or less satisfied; NS = Not satisfied at all

		YEAR															
AGE	RESP	'72	'73	'74	'75	'76	'77	'78	'80	'82	'83	'84	'85	'86	'87	'88	'89
60-65	PW	39%	40%	46%	52%	38%	42%	41%	38%	30%	41%	49%	40%	41%	47%	41%	37%
	ML	45	45	34	37	42	39	40	42	48	37	35	41	38	40	44	44
	NS	16	15	21	12	20	19	19	20	22	21	17	19	21	14	15	19
# SURVEYED		143	121	107	112	133	117	107	118	116	131	113	129	115	101	117	111
AGE	RESP	'72	'73	'74	'75	'76	'77	'78	'80	'82	'83	'84	'85	'86	'87	'88	'89
66+	PW	37%	40%	44%	43%	45%	41%	50%	42%	43%	47%	43%	40%	45%	47%	49%	40%
	ML	45	43	41	40	40	41	36	46	44	42	40	44	40	43	43	46
	NS	19	18	15	17	15	18	14	12	13	11	17	16	15	10	8	14
# SURVEYED		215	199	226	231	251	210	231	241	256	238	232	261	265	252	279	273

****

RELATIVE FINANCIAL STATUS

TABLE I: RELATIVE FINANCIAL STATUS -- BY TOTAL POPULATION

Question: Compared with American families in general, would you say your family income is far below average, below average, average, above average, or far above average?

Responses: FB = Far below average; BA = Below average; AV = Average; AA = Above average; FA = Far above average

	YEAR															
RESPONSE	'72	'73	'74	'75	'76	'77	'78	'80	'82	'83	'84	'85	'86	'87	'88	'89
FB	4%	4%	4%	4%	4%	5%	5%	5%	5%	6%	5%	6%	6%	5%	5%	4%
BA	22	19	21	24	25	24	22	24	27	23	24	23	24	24	23	23
AV	57	59	56	53	55	51	53	52	51	49	52	51	50	49	52	51
AA	16	17	18	18	15	18	18	17	16	19	18	18	19	20	18	21
FA	1	1	1	1	1	2	2	2	1	2	2	2	2	1	2	2
# SURVEYED	1599	1492	1473	1478	1484	1516	1523	1454	1487	1575	1461	1522	1459	1453	1469	1525

TABLE II: RELATIVE FINANCIAL STATUS -- BY SEX

Question: Compared with American families in general, would you say your family income is far below average, below average, average, above average, or far above average?

Responses: FB = Far below average; BA = Below average; AV = Average; AA = Above average; FA = Far above average

		YEAR															
SEX	RESP	'72	'73	'74	'75	'76	'77	'78	'80	'82	'83	'84	'85	'86	'87	'88	'89
MALE	FB	3%	4%	3%	5%	4%	4%	4%	4%	5%	5%	5%	6%	5%	6%	3%	4%
	BA	20	19	19	22	26	23	22	20	23	21	25	20	21	21	21	20
	AV	54	55	55	50	49	48	47	52	51	50	45	50	48	47	52	48
	AA	21	21	21	22	19	21	25	21	19	21	23	21	24	25	21	26
	FA	2	2	2	2	2	3	3	3	2	2	2	3	2	2	3	2
# SURVEYED		803	695	686	664	664	689	640	637	636	681	595	685	618	636	636	656
SEX	RESP	'72	'73	'74	'75	'76	'77	'78	'80	'82	'83	'84	'85	'86	'87	'88	'89
FEMALE	FB	4%	3%	5%	4%	4%	6%	5%	6%	5%	7%	5%	6%	6%	4%	6%	5%
	BA	24	19	22	25	24	24	23	26	29	25	23	26	26	27	25	25
	AV	60	62	57	55	60	54	58	53	51	49	56	53	51	52	52	52
	AA	11	14	15	15	11	15	13	14	14	17	14	15	15	17	16	17
	FA	1	1	1	1	0	1	1	1	1	2	1	1	2	1	1	1
# SURVEYED		796	797	787	814	820	827	883	817	851	894	866	837	841	817	833	869

TABLE III: RELATIVE FINANCIAL STATUS -- BY RACE

Question: Compared with American families in general, would you say your family income is far below average, below average, average, above average, or far above average?

Responses: FB = Far below average BA = Below average AV = Average
AA = Above average FA = Far above average

		YEAR															
RACE	RESP	'72	'73	'74	'75	'76	'77	'78	'80	'82	'83	'84	'85	'86	'87	'88	'89
WHITE	FB	3%	3%	3%	4%	4%	4%	4%	4%	5%	6%	4%	5%	5%	4%	4%	3%
	BA	19	18	19	21	23	22	20	21	25	22	21	21	22	23	22	21
	AV	59	59	57	54	56	52	55	54	52	50	53	52	50	49	53	52
	AA	18	19	20	20	16	19	19	18	17	20	20	19	20	22	20	22
	FA	1	2	1	1	1	2	2	2	1	3	2	2	2	1	2	2
# SURVEYED		1334	1296	1294	1311	1351	1327	1350	1307	1306	1397	1242	1330	1240	1214	1223	1308
RACE	RESP	'72	'73	'74	'75	'76	'77	'78	'80	'82	'83	'84	'85	'86	'87	'88	'89
BLACK	FB	7%	11%	8%	7%	7%	13%	10%	14%	8%	9%	12%	9%	9%	7%	10%	11%
	BA	36	26	38	45	44	33	38	43	38	36	37	40	36	33	32	39
	AV	49	56	48	45	44	48	39	38	46	49	46	46	43	51	46	41
	AA	8	6	5	2	3	7	11	3	7	5	5	5	10	9	9	7
	FA	1	1	1	1	2	0	1	2	1	0	0	1	1	1	2	1
# SURVEYED		261	183	172	163	126	174	157	137	156	160	167	149	182	187	185	157
RACE	RESP	'72	'73	'74	'75	'76	'77	'78	'80	'82	'83	'84	'85	'86	'87	'88	'89
OTHER	FB	0%	8%	0%	0%	0%	0%	0%	0%	0%	0%	4%	9%	3%	8%	8%	5%
	BA	100	38	14	25	14	27	31	40	32	50	35	37	30	27	28	27
	AV	0	46	57	50	57	47	56	40	48	22	48	40	65	50	54	53
	AA	0	8	29	25	29	27	6	10	20	17	12	14	3	13	10	13
	FA	0	0	0	0	0	0	6	10	0	11	2	0	0	2	0	2
# SURVEYED		4	13	7	4	7	15	16	10	25	18	52	43	37	52	61	60

TABLE IV: RELATIVE FINANCIAL STATUS -- BY AGE

Question: Compared with American families in general, would you say your family income is far below average, below average, average, above average, or far above average?

Responses: FB = Far below average BA = Below average AV = Average
AA = Above average FA = Far above average

		YEAR															
AGE	RESP	'72	'73	'74	'75	'76	'77	'78	'80	'82	'83	'84	'85	'86	'87	'88	'89
18-23	FB	2%	4%	7%	4%	4%	5%	5%	5%	6%	8%	4%	6%	9%	4%	6%	4%
	BA	20	20	24	19	29	22	27	22	26	20	22	24	24	24	30	18
	AV	59	60	51	61	53	61	59	57	53	54	52	53	54	53	50	61
	AA	18	16	17	15	12	10	8	16	13	17	20	14	13	18	11	15
	FA	2	0	1	1	1	2	1	1	1	1	1	3	0	1	2	1
# SURVEYED		169	169	167	173	161	164	163	153	148	127	157	133	108	126	141	137
AGE	RESP	'72	'73	'74	'75	'76	'77	'78	'80	'82	'83	'84	'85	'86	'87	'88	'89
24-29	FB	2%	5%	4%	4%	4%	5%	2%	6%	6%	6%	5%	5%	8%	4%	8%	4%
	BA	19	20	21	21	28	27	24	25	25	28	24	21	31	27	23	28
	AV	63	57	58	54	53	50	55	56	52	49	53	57	44	49	50	50
	AA	15	17	17	19	14	17	18	11	16	15	17	14	15	20	18	17
	FA	0	1	0	1	1	2	1	2	0	1	1	2	2	0	1	0
# SURVEYED		230	212	211	232	223	199	242	202	245	286	232	216	218	192	212	201
AGE	RESP	'72	'73	'74	'75	'76	'77	'78	'80	'82	'83	'84	'85	'86	'87	'88	'89
30-35	FB	4%	2%	3%	2%	4%	4%	3%	5%	4%	7%	6%	4%	4%	5%	2%	4%
	BA	15	13	21	19	25	19	17	27	29	25	24	22	22	28	20	25
	AV	60	64	55	61	54	49	52	42	49	46	51	51	56	45	60	50
	AA	20	20	21	18	16	24	25	25	18	20	18	21	18	21	18	20
	FA	1	1	1	0	1	4	2	2	0	2	1	1	1	2	1	1
# SURVEYED		186	166	175	170	186	187	229	211	202	234	199	212	221	219	193	212
AGE	RESP	'72	'73	'74	'75	'76	'77	'78	'80	'82	'83	'84	'85	'86	'87	'88	'89
36-41	FB	5%	3%	5%	6%	3%	6%	5%	4%	6%	7%	4%	7%	3%	6%	7%	5%
	BA	16	20	12	18	19	14	23	15	22	25	24	15	19	20	20	18
	AV	62	54	56	47	52	59	48	48	45	46	45	49	49	47	50	49
	AA	15	21	23	26	24	20	23	30	25	21	25	26	25	26	19	24
	FA	2	2	4	3	2	1	1	3	2	1	2	3	4	1	4	4
# SURVEYED		125	175	151	152	156	167	160	149	146	173	185	182	188	185	192	198
AGE	RESP	'72	'73	'74	'75	'76	'77	'78	'80	'82	'83	'84	'85	'86	'87	'88	'89
42-47	FB	3%	2%	4%	2%	5%	5%	7%	4%	5%	10%	6%	3%	7%	6%	3%	4%
	BA	19	13	13	23	17	19	14	19	34	21	25	22	21	21	21	19
	AV	56	57	57	49	52	52	53	58	36	39	45	42	39	47	50	43
	AA	21	25	23	22	25	22	23	16	24	26	25	32	29	24	24	33
	FA	2	3	2	4	2	1	3	3	2	4	0	1	3	2	3	2
# SURVEYED		185	144	150	141	114	147	118	116	119	145	126	124	140	155	157	161

TABLE IV: RELATIVE FINANCIAL STATUS -- BY AGE (Continued)

Question: Compared with American families in general, would you say your family income is far below average, below average, average, above average, or far above average?

Responses: FB = Far below average BA = Below average AV = Average
AA = Above average FA = Far above average

		YEAR															
AGE	RESP	'72	'73	'74	'75	'76	'77	'78	'80	'82	'83	'84	'85	'86	'87	'88	'89
48-53	FB	2%	4%	3%	6%	2%	3%	3%	3%	6%	5%	4%	5%	9%	6%	4%	6%
	BA	22	18	20	21	22	26	15	32	18	17	21	26	16	19	26	21
	AV	61	53	54	52	59	49	56	43	47	46	47	47	57	52	37	49
	AA	13	22	21	19	17	22	23	17	25	26	26	20	13	21	28	23
	FA	2	3	1	1	1	1	3	5	4	6	2	2	5	2	4	1
# SURVEYED		188	150	145	139	133	151	132	122	112	115	102	131	106	125	92	137
AGE	RESP	'72	'73	'74	'75	'76	'77	'78	'80	'82	'83	'84	'85	'86	'87	'88	'89
54-59	FB	4%	3%	1%	5%	2%	4%	6%	4%	5%	7%	5%	11%	5%	10%	8%	4%
	BA	19	18	22	22	23	26	20	21	22	19	24	27	23	13	19	15
	AV	56	63	57	56	60	44	52	52	55	48	54	46	44	48	51	53
	AA	20	15	19	16	14	23	19	21	13	22	14	13	25	28	20	26
	FA	1	1	1	1	1	2	3	3	4	4	3	3	2	1	2	2
# SURVEYED		156	156	138	125	127	167	137	135	143	131	113	131	99	98	85	98
AGE	RESP	'72	'73	'74	'75	'76	'77	'78	'80	'82	'83	'84	'85	'86	'87	'88	'89
60-65	FB	4%	7%	5%	5%	6%	9%	7%	7%	3%	4%	5%	5%	4%	1%	2%	4%
	BA	30	22	21	27	28	30	29	25	31	19	23	21	27	29	22	30
	AV	50	57	56	46	57	45	45	55	54	60	55	56	49	55	55	51
	AA	15	13	16	22	9	15	19	10	12	15	14	15	18	14	19	14
	FA	0	2	2	1	0	2	0	3	0	2	3	2	2	1	3	2
# SURVEYED		142	119	108	111	134	116	107	119	113	130	113	130	114	99	117	110
AGE	RESP	'72	'73	'74	'75	'76	'77	'78	'80	'82	'83	'84	'85	'86	'87	'88	'89
66+	FB	8%	5%	3%	5%	5%	7%	5%	5%	5%	4%	7%	7%	5%	3%	3%	3%
	BA	35	25	29	38	30	31	29	25	30	26	25	28	27	28	27	28
	AV	50	59	58	46	56	52	56	60	59	56	59	55	53	53	55	52
	AA	7	9	9	10	9	9	9	9	6	13	7	10	14	14	13	16
	FA	1	2	0	0	0	1	1	1	0	2	1	0	2	2	1	1
# SURVEYED		213	197	222	231	244	211	228	238	251	228	229	256	259	250	276	268

****

CHANGES IN FINANCES

TABLE I: CHANGES IN FINANCES -- BY TOTAL POPULATION

Question: During the last few years, has your financial situation been getting better, worse, or has it stayed the same?

Responses: GB = Getting better; GW = Getting worse; SM = Stayed the same

	YEAR															
RESPONSE	'72	'73	'74	'75	'76	'77	'78	'80	'82	'83	'84	'85	'86	'87	'88	'89
GB	43%	42%	40%	35%	36%	38%	41%	34%	31%	35%	39%	39%	40%	40%	40%	43%
GW	18	16	22	28	23	22	19	25	29	27	22	22	21	19	18	18
SM	39	41	39	37	41	40	40	40	39	38	39	40	38	41	41	39
# SURVEYED	1590	1462	1474	1479	1493	1517	1526	1462	1500	1572	1461	1527	1460	1459	1473	1530

TABLE II: CHANGES IN FINANCES -- BY SEX

Question: During the last few years, has your financial situation been getting better, worse, or has it stayed the same?

Responses: GB = Getting better; GW = Getting worse; SM = Stayed the same

		YEAR															
SEX	RESP	'72	'73	'74	'75	'76	'77	'78	'80	'82	'83	'84	'85	'86	'87	'88	'89
M	GB	48%	41%	40%	38%	39%	40%	47%	38%	36%	39%	42%	42%	46%	44%	45%	48%
	GW	17	15	21	27	22	21	18	23	27	25	21	21	19	18	15	16
	SM	34	43	39	35	40	39	36	40	37	36	37	37	35	39	40	36
# SURVEYED		799	681	686	667	667	687	642	639	636	678	592	686	617	637	637	658
SEX	RESP	'72	'73	'74	'75	'76	'77	'78	'80	'82	'83	'84	'85	'86	'87	'88	'89
F	GB	38%	43%	39%	33%	34%	37%	38%	32%	28%	32%	37%	36%	36%	37%	37%	39%
	GW	19	17	23	30	24	23	19	28	31	29	22	22	23	20	21	19
	SM	43	40	39	38	42	40	43	41	40	39	41	42	41	43	42	42
# SURVEYED		791	781	788	812	826	830	884	823	864	894	869	841	843	822	836	872

TABLE III: CHANGES IN FINANCES -- BY RACE

Question: During the last few years, has your financial situation been getting better, worse, or has it stayed the same?

Responses: GB = Getting better; GW = Getting worse; SM = Stayed the same

		YEAR															
RACE	RESP	'72	'73	'74	'75	'76	'77	'78	'80	'82	'83	'84	'85	'86	'87	'88	'89
WHITE	GB	45%	44%	40%	37%	37%	39%	43%	35%	32%	37%	40%	41%	41%	42%	41%	44%
	GW	17	16	21	28	22	21	18	25	28	26	21	21	21	19	18	18
	SM	38	41	38	36	41	40	39	39	40	37	39	38	38	39	41	39
# SURVEYED		1330	1270	1294	1312	1355	1329	1352	1312	1318	1394	1241	1334	1241	1219	1227	1314
RACE	RESP	'72	'73	'74	'75	'76	'77	'78	'80	'82	'83	'84	'85	'86	'87	'88	'89
BLACK	GB	35%	34%	35%	24%	21%	31%	31%	24%	27%	24%	27%	23%	36%	27%	37%	34%
	GW	23	20	24	33	36	32	25	24	38	35	27	28	23	20	20	21
	SM	43	46	41	43	43	37	44	52	35	41	45	49	41	53	43	46
# SURVEYED		256	179	173	163	129	174	158	140	156	160	168	149	182	187	185	156
RACE	RESP	'72	'73	'74	'75	'76	'77	'78	'80	'82	'83	'84	'85	'86	'87	'88	'89
OTHER	GB	25%	31%	14%	25%	56%	36%	44%	40%	31%	17%	48%	32%	43%	34%	39%	47%
	GW	0	31	43	25	11	14	13	40	38	33	15	23	14	23	16	13
	SM	75	38	43	50	33	50	44	20	31	50	37	45	43	43	44	40
# SURVEYED		4	13	7	4	9	14	16	10	26	18	52	44	37	53	61	60

TABLE IV: CHANGES IN FINANCES -- BY AGE

Question: During the last few years, has your financial situation been getting better, worse, or has it stayed the same?

Responses: GB = Getting better; GW = Getting worse; SM = Stayed the same

		YEAR															
AGE	RESP	'72	'73	'74	'75	'76	'77	'78	'80	'82	'83	'84	'85	'86	'87	'88	'89
18-23	GB	46%	51%	46%	38%	41%	40%	47%	45%	35%	41%	49%	47%	48%	40%	46%	50%
	GW	21	12	17	25	22	20	17	20	31	24	19	21	19	17	20	13
	SM	33	37	37	37	36	40	36	34	34	35	31	32	34	43	33	36
# SURVEYED		160	166	166	172	162	163	161	154	147	125	156	132	107	126	138	135
AGE	RESP	'72	'73	'74	'75	'76	'77	'78	'80	'82	'83	'84	'85	'86	'87	'88	'89
24-29	GB	58%	50%	47%	44%	50%	55%	57%	48%	40%	42%	54%	48%	53%	58%	55%	56%
	GW	13	16	20	31	21	18	12	21	25	22	18	19	19	17	14	17
	SM	29	33	33	25	29	27	32	32	35	35	28	32	28	25	31	27
# SURVEYED		231	207	211	232	224	201	243	202	245	285	231	217	217	192	213	202

TABLE IV: CHANGES IN FINANCES -- BY AGE (Continued)

Question: During the last few years, has your financial situation been getting better, worse, or has it stayed the same?

Responses: GB = Getting better; GW = Getting worse; SM = Stayed the same

		YEAR															
AGE	RESP	'72	'73	'74	'75	'76	'77	'78	'80	'82	'83	'84	'85	'86	'87	'88	'89
30-35	GB	51%	53%	50%	47%	46%	47%	57%	40%	43%	41%	47%	54%	49%	49%	50%	54%
	GW	17	12	23	28	22	20	14	26	30	29	24	17	20	17	16	15
	SM	32	35	26	24	32	33	28	34	27	30	29	29	31	34	34	31
# SURVEYED		187	161	175	169	186	188	229	215	204	232	199	212	221	219	194	209
AGE	RESP	'72	'73	'74	'75	'76	'77	'78	'80	'82	'83	'84	'85	'86	'87	'88	'89
36-41	GB	51%	45%	36%	37%	42%	40%	46%	33%	37%	39%	42%	42%	47%	54%	51%	47%
	GW	20	16	23	38	24	23	21	27	32	35	22	22	15	18	19	18
	SM	29	38	40	25	34	37	34	40	32	26	36	35	37	28	31	34
# SURVEYED		126	170	151	153	158	166	160	150	146	170	186	184	188	185	192	198
AGE	RESP	'72	'73	'74	'75	'76	'77	'78	'80	'82	'83	'84	'85	'86	'87	'88	'89
42-47	GB	43%	45%	40%	35%	39%	38%	45%	30%	29%	38%	36%	45%	45%	43%	45%	50%
	GW	24	21	23	31	25	21	18	29	40	34	31	18	25	20	20	24
	SM	33	35	37	34	36	42	36	41	30	28	33	37	30	37	36	26
# SURVEYED		185	141	150	143	114	146	119	116	119	144	125	124	140	157	157	161
AGE	RESP	'72	'73	'74	'75	'76	'77	'78	'80	'82	'83	'84	'85	'86	'87	'88	'89
48-53	GB	40%	42%	42%	31%	32%	35%	35%	30%	35%	37%	36%	40%	40%	34%	32%	41%
	GW	14	17	30	25	22	20	20	30	29	35	27	34	25	24	26	22
	SM	46	41	28	44	46	44	45	40	36	28	38	26	35	42	42	38
# SURVEYED		185	149	144	140	133	153	133	123	112	116	101	131	107	126	92	138
AGE	RESP	'72	'73	'74	'75	'76	'77	'78	'80	'82	'83	'84	'85	'86	'87	'88	'89
54-59	GB	42%	38%	32%	32%	32%	39%	36%	38%	26%	26%	29%	27%	23%	28%	41%	39%
	GW	15	14	22	32	25	25	24	30	38	32	25	28	31	27	20	12
	SM	43	48	46	35	43	37	39	33	36	41	46	45	46	45	39	48
# SURVEYED		155	153	139	124	126	166	137	135	143	133	114	132	98	97	85	99
AGE	RESP	'72	'73	'74	'75	'76	'77	'78	'80	'82	'83	'84	'85	'86	'87	'88	'89
60-65	GB	32%	34%	31%	30%	25%	35%	26%	25%	18%	30%	26%	29%	31%	34%	24%	27%
	GW	20	22	19	27	26	25	25	23	32	21	23	21	25	20	25	21
	SM	47	45	49	43	49	40	49	52	50	49	51	50	44	46	51	52
# SURVEYED		142	119	108	112	133	117	107	118	116	128	113	128	114	100	119	111
AGE	RESP	'72	'73	'74	'75	'76	'77	'7	'80	'82	'83	'84	'85	'86	'87	'88	'89
66+	GB	26%	22%	27%	21%	18%	17%	15	19%	17%	20%	22%	18%	23%	17%	19%	21%
	GW	21	19	20	21	21	26	24	26	21	19	15	21	22	17	16	18
	SM	54	59	53	57	61	57	61	55	62	61	63	61	56	66	65	60
# SURVEYED		214	192	225	230	251	210	231	240	258	232	231	260	261	253	279	273

****

SOCIO-ECONOMIC STATUS

TABLE I: SOCIO-ECONOMIC STATUS -- BY TOTAL POPULATION

Question: If you were asked to use one of four names for your social class, which would you say you belong in: the lower class, the working class, the middle class, or the upper class?

Responses: LC = Lower class WC = Working class MC = Middle class
UC = Upper class NO = No class (volunteered)

RESPONSE	'72	'73	'74	'75	'76	'77	'78	'80	'82	'83	'84	'85	'86	'87	'88	'89
LC	6%	4%	4%	5%	4%	4%	5%	5%	5%	6%	5%	4%	7%	5%	5%	5%
WC	47	48	47	48	46	49	47	46	48	47	46	45	43	44	45	43
MC	44	46	46	44	48	43	45	45	44	44	46	47	47	47	47	48
UC	2	3	3	3	2	4	2	3	3	4	3	4	3	4	2	4
NO	0	0	0	0	0	0	0	0	0	0	0	0	0	0	0	0
# SURVEYED	1604	748	1475	1482	1491	1518	1527	1461	1494	799	1462	1529	1457	1444	1476	1530

TABLE II: SOCIO-ECONOMIC STATUS -- BY SEX

Question: If you were asked to use one of four names for your social class, which would you say you belong in: the lower class, the working class, the middle class, or the upper class?

Responses: LC = Lower class WC = Working class MC = Middle class
UC = Upper class NO = No class (volunteered)

SEX	RESP	'72	'73	'74	'75	'76	'77	'78	'80	'82	'83	'84	'85	'86	'87	'88	'89
MALE	LC	6%	4%	4%	5%	5%	3%	5%	3%	5%	5%	4%	4%	5%	4%	4%	4%
	WC	48	52	50	47	47	52	48	48	50	48	45	48	45	45	46	43
	MC	44	42	43	46	46	41	45	45	43	42	48	44	47	47	47	48
	UC	2	2	3	3	2	3	2	4	2	5	4	4	3	3	3	5
	NO	0	0	0	0	0	0	0	0	0	0	0	0	0	0	0	0
# SURVEYED		803	345	688	666	666	686	641	639	636	485	593	687	615	630	636	657
SEX	RESP	'72	'73	'74	'75	'76	'77	'78	'80	'82	'83	'84	'85	'86	'87	'88	'89
FEMALE	LC	7%	3%	5%	5%	4%	6%	6%	7%	5%	7%	5%	4%	7%	6%	6%	6%
	WC	47	44	44	49	46	46	46	44	46	45	48	43	42	42	44	42
	MC	44	49	49	43	49	44	46	46	45	46	44	49	47	47	48	48
	UC	2	3	3	3	1	4	2	3	4	2	3	4	3	5	2	3
	NO	0	0	0	0	0	0	0	0	0	0	0	0	0	0	0	0
# SURVEYED		801	403	787	816	825	832	886	822	858	314	869	842	842	814	840	873

TABLE III: SOCIO-ECONOMIC STATUS -- BY RACE

Question: If you were asked to use one of four names for your social class, which would you say you belong in: the lower class, the working class, the middle class, or the upper class?

Responses: LC = Lower class WC = Working class MC = Middle class
UC = Upper class NO = No class (volunteered)

		YEAR															
RACE	RESP	'72	'73	'74	'75	'76	'77	'78	'80	'82	'83	'84	'85	'86	'87	'88	'89
WHITE	LC	5%	3%	4%	4%	4%	3%	5%	5%	4%	5%	3%	4%	5%	4%	4%	4%
	WC	46	47	46	47	45	47	46	45	47	44	45	43	42	42	42	41
	MC	48	48	48	47	50	46	48	47	46	47	49	50	49	50	51	51
	UC	2	2	3	3	1	4	2	3	3	4	3	4	4	4	3	4
	NO	0	0	0	0	0	0	0	0	0	0	0	0	0	0	0	0
# SURVEYED		1340	648	1299	1315	1353	1329	1353	1312	1312	708	1243	1336	1240	1208	1232	1312
RACE	RESP	'72	'73	'74	'75	'76	'77	'78	'80	'82	'83	'84	'85	'86	'87	'88	'89
BLACK	LC	17%	8%	10%	13%	12%	14%	13%	10%	10%	10%	14%	7%	15%	10%	13%	15%
	WC	56	59	55	59	58	62	58	56	56	67	57	64	51	54	59	52
	MC	25	28	30	24	28	19	27	25	27	22	25	25	31	30	27	30
	UC	2	5	5	4	2	6	3	9	6	1	4	3	2	6	2	3
	NO	0	0	0	0	0	0	0	0	0	0	0	0	0	0	0	0
# SURVEYED		260	92	169	163	129	175	158	139	155	82	167	150	181	185	184	157
RACE	RESP	'72	'73	'74	'75	'76	'77	'78	'80	'82	'83	'84	'85	'86	'87	'88	'89
OTHER	LC	0%	13%	0%	0%	0%	0%	13%	10%	4%	11%	6%	7%	11%	6%	12%	2%
	WC	100	25	14	25	44	50	44	40	59	56	52	53	44	51	53	49
	MC	0	63	86	75	56	36	38	50	37	11	40	37	44	43	35	43
	UC	0	0	0	0	0	14	6	0	0	22	2	2	0	0	0	7
	NO	0	0	0	0	0	0	0	0	0	0	0	0	0	0	0	0
# SURVEYED		4	8	7	4	9	14	16	10	27	9	52	43	36	51	60	61

TABLE IV: SOCIO-ECONOMIC STATUS -- BY AGE

Question: If you were asked to use one of four names for your social class, which would you say you belong in: the lower class, the working class, the middle class, or the upper class?

Responses: LC = Lower class WC = Working class MC = Middle class
UC = Upper class NO = No class (volunteered)

		YEAR															
AGE	RESP	'72	'73	'74	'75	'76	'77	'78	'80	'82	'83	'84	'85	'86	'87	'88	'89
18-23	LC	6%	3%	5%	4%	8%	7%	6%	5%	5%	8%	6%	3%	6%	8%	5%	5%
	WC	44	51	58	49	44	55	58	51	60	46	47	53	40	38	50	38
	MC	47	44	34	46	46	36	36	40	31	40	44	41	54	52	40	54
	UC	3	2	4	1	2	2	1	4	4	6	3	4	0	2	4	4
	NO	0	0	0	0	0	0	0	0	0	0	0	0	0	0	0	0
# SURVEYED		169	87	166	173	162	164	163	154	147	52	158	133	108	126	141	136

TABLE IV: SOCIO-ECONOMIC STATUS -- BY AGE (Continued)

Question: If you were asked to use one of four names for your social class, which would you say you belong in: the lower class, the working class, the middle class, or the upper class?

Responses: LC = Lower class WC = Working class MC = Middle class
UC = Upper class NO = No class (volunteered)

YEAR

AGE	RESP	'72	'73	'74	'75	'76	'77	'78	'80	'82	'83	'84	'85	'86	'87	'88	'89
24-29	LC	3%	4%	3%	3%	7%	2%	5%	5%	5%	6%	4%	4%	6%	6%	7%	4%
	WC	49	48	44	55	50	60	54	61	57	61	60	51	54	53	52	52
	MC	47	46	49	40	42	36	41	32	37	33	35	39	40	37	41	41
	UC	1	3	4	2	1	1	0	1	2	1	1	6	0	4	1	3
	NO	0	0	0	0	0	0	0	0	0	0	0	0	0	0	0	0
# SURVEYED		231	111	211	231	226	203	244	202	246	138	232	216	216	192	213	202

AGE	RESP	'72	'73	'74	'75	'76	'77	'78	'80	'82	'83	'84	'85	'86	'87	'88	'89
30-35	LC	6%	3%	2%	4%	3%	3%	3%	4%	5%	6%	4%	6%	6%	5%	6%	5%
	WC	49	47	47	51	49	55	44	47	53	52	48	53	47	50	45	47
	MC	43	47	47	44	46	38	51	47	41	41	46	39	44	43	49	44
	UC	1	3	3	2	1	4	1	3	1	2	2	2	3	2	0	4
	NO	0	0	0	0	0	0	0	0	0	0	0	0	0	0	0	0
# SURVEYED		186	86	175	170	185	187	230	215	203	122	199	212	220	218	195	212

AGE	RESP	'72	'73	'74	'75	'76	'77	'78	'80	'82	'83	'84	'85	'86	'87	'88	'89
36-41	LC	6%	3%	5%	7%	3%	5%	4%	5%	5%	1%	6%	1%	3%	5%	5%	9%
	WC	48	47	43	53	50	46	51	46	44	58	48	47	47	40	47	39
	MC	46	48	52	39	46	43	42	46	47	36	45	47	45	50	46	47
	UC	0	2	1	2	2	5	3	3	4	5	1	5	5	5	3	6
	NO	0	0	0	0	0	0	0	0	0	0	0	0	0	0	0	0
# SURVEYED		127	86	151	153	157	168	159	149	146	108	186	184	187	183	192	197

AGE	RESP	'72	'73	'74	'75	'76	'77	'78	'80	'82	'83	'84	'85	'86	'87	'88	'89
42-47	LC	4%	4%	4%	2%	4%	4%	3%	6%	3%	8%	6%	2%	5%	3%	3%	6%
	WC	56	46	50	50	52	47	47	50	46	41	46	41	42	52	48	38
	MC	38	49	45	47	43	47	45	40	47	44	46	54	48	42	48	51
	UC	2	1	1	1	1	2	5	4	4	8	2	2	5	3	1	5
	NO	0	0	0	0	0	0	0	0	0	0	0	0	0	0	0	0
# SURVEYED		185	74	151	141	114	146	118	116	119	66	126	123	140	155	157	160

AGE	RESP	'72	'73	'74	'75	'76	'77	'78	'80	'82	'83	'84	'85	'86	'87	'88	'89
48-53	LC	4%	0%	3%	6%	2%	7%	4%	7%	5%	5%	3%	4%	10%	6%	4%	3%
	WC	50	52	44	45	53	49	48	46	43	39	50	53	41	43	46	51
	MC	41	45	50	45	45	39	48	45	50	49	43	38	41	46	46	43
	UC	4	3	2	4	1	5	1	2	3	7	4	5	7	6	4	2
	NO	0	0	0	0	0	0	0	0	0	0	0	0	0	0	0	0
# SURVEYED		188	66	145	139	131	150	132	123	111	61	102	131	107	123	92	138

TABLE IV: SOCIO-ECONOMIC STATUS -- BY AGE (Continued)

Question: If you were asked to use one of four names for your social class, which would you say you belong in: the lower class, the working class, the middle class, or the upper class?

Responses: LC = Lower class WC = Working class MC = Middle class
UC = Upper class NO = No class (volunteered)

		YEAR															
AGE	RESP	'72	'73	'74	'75	'76	'77	'78	'80	'82	'83	'84	'85	'86	'87	'88	'89
54-59	LC	6%	3%	2%	4%	2%	5%	7%	4%	6%	3%	4%	5%	7%	4%	4%	2%
	WC	46	56	46	48	52	43	47	50	47	42	46	40	40	41	60	47
	MC	44	41	48	45	45	46	41	44	44	53	45	51	46	49	32	46
	UC	3	1	4	2	1	7	5	2	3	2	5	4	6	6	5	4
	NO	0	0	0	0	0	0	0	0	0	0	0	0	0	0	0	0
# SURVEYED		156	79	138	126	128	167	137	135	143	60	113	132	99	96	84	99
AGE	RESP	'72	'73	'74	'75	'76	'77	'78	'80	'82	'83	'84	'85	'86	'87	'88	'89
60-65	LC	7%	0%	8%	4%	2%	2%	7%	4%	3%	3%	7%	5%	9%	5%	3%	7%
	WC	48	51	56	51	49	48	40	32	42	42	36	42	35	41	41	46
	MC	44	43	33	40	47	48	48	57	53	53	53	49	55	52	52	42
	UC	1	6	3	4	2	3	6	7	3	2	4	4	2	2	4	5
	NO	0	0	0	0	0	0	0	0	0	0	0	0	0	0	0	0
# SURVEYED		142	67	108	113	134	115	107	119	116	60	111	130	113	100	119	110
AGE	RESP	'72	'73	'74	'75	'76	'77	'78	'80	'82	'83	'84	'85	'86	'87	'88	'89
66+	LC	14%	10%	6%	9%	6%	6%	10%	5%	6%	11%	2%	5%	8%	4%	8%	4%
	WC	37	37	41	36	31	36	34	34	38	29	34	30	36	33	31	33
	MC	44	50	48	50	61	53	53	56	52	54	57	62	52	55	59	60
	UC	4	3	5	5	2	5	3	4	4	6	7	3	4	7	3	3
	NO	0	0	0	0	0	0	0	0	0	0	0	0	0	0	0	0
# SURVEYED		215	90	224	231	248	211	230	239	255	127	230	261	261	247	279	272

****

IDEAL FAMILY SIZE

TABLE I: IDEAL FAMILY SIZE -- BY TOTAL POPULATION

Question: What do you think is the ideal number of children for a family to have? NOTE: Question not asked in 1973, 1980, 1984, 1987.

Responses: 0 = None 1 = 1 2 = 2 3 = 3 4 = 4
5 = 5 6 = 6 7 = 7+ 8 = As many as you want

	YEAR											
RESPONSE	'72	'74	'75	'76	'77	'78	'82	'83	'85	'86	'88	'89
0	2%	1%	1%	2%	1%	1%	1%	1%	1%	1%	2%	1%
1	1	2	2	3	2	2	3	2	3	2	2	3
2	41	45	49	52	49	51	55	52	56	52	51	55
3	24	24	24	20	23	24	20	24	22	25	26	22
4	18	16	15	13	15	13	13	13	11	13	11	9
5	3	2	1	2	2	2	2	1	2	2	2	3
6	3	1	1	1	1	1	1	1	1	1	1	1
7	1	0	0	0	1	1	1	0	1	0	0	1
8	6	8	6	6	6	6	5	6	4	5	5	5
# SURVEYED	1552	1444	1444	1461	1500	1484	1466	1556	1500	1440	968	969

TABLE II: IDEAL FAMILY SIZE -- BY SEX

Question: What do you think is the ideal number of children for a family to have? NOTE: Question not asked in 1973, 1980, 1984, 1987.

Responses: 0 = None 1 = 1 2 = 2 3 = 3 4 = 4
5 = 5 6 = 6 7 = 7+ 8 = As many as you want

		YEAR											
SEX	RESP	'72	'74	'75	'76	'77	'78	'82	'83	'85	'86	'88	'89
M	0	1%	1%	2%	2%	2%	1%	1%	1%	1%	1%	2%	2%
A	1	1	2	2	4	1	2	2	2	3	2	1	2
L	2	44	46	48	50	48	52	56	52	55	51	52	56
E	3	23	25	25	21	25	21	23	26	23	27	28	21
	4	18	13	13	11	12	12	10	10	11	10	9	9
	5	3	2	1	2	3	3	1	1	3	3	1	2
	6	1	1	1	1	1	1	0	2	1	1	1	0
	7	1	0	1	1	1	1	1	0	0	0	0	1
	8	6	9	7	7	6	7	4	5	4	5	5	6
# SURVEYED		777	671	648	647	677	620	624	665	669	610	429	416
SEX	RESP	'72	'74	'75	'76	'77	'78	'82	'83	'85	'86	'88	'89
F	0	2%	1%	1%	2%	0%	1%	1%	1%	1%	1%	2%	0%
E	1	1	2	2	3	3	1	3	2	2	2	2	3
M	2	38	45	50	53	50	50	54	52	57	52	50	55
A	3	25	23	23	20	22	26	18	22	22	24	25	23
L	4	19	19	16	15	17	14	15	14	11	15	13	9
E	5	3	2	2	2	2	2	2	2	1	1	2	3
	6	4	1	1	1	0	1	1	1	1	1	1	1
	7	1	1	0	0	1	0	1	0	1	0	0	1
	8	6	8	6	6	6	5	5	6	4	5	5	5
# SURVEYED		775	773	796	814	823	864	842	891	831	830	539	553

TABLE III: IDEAL FAMILY SIZE -- BY RACE

Question: What do you think is the ideal number of children for a family to have? NOTE: Question not asked in 1973, 1980, 1984, 1987.

Responses: 0 = None 1 = 1 2 = 2 3 = 3 4 = 4
5 = 5 6 = 6 7 = 7+ 8 = As many as you want

		YEAR											
RACE	RESP	'72	'74	'75	'76	'77	'78	'82	'83	'85	'86	'88	'89
WHITE	0	2%	1%	1%	2%	1%	1%	1%	1%	1%	1%	2%	1%
	1	1	2	2	3	2	2	2	2	3	2	2	3
	2	44	48	51	53	51	52	57	54	58	53	52	57
	3	25	24	25	21	24	25	20	24	22	26	26	22
	4	18	14	14	13	14	12	13	12	10	12	11	8
	5	2	2	1	1	2	2	1	1	1	1	1	2
	6	2	1	1	1	1	1	1	1	0	1	1	1
	7	1	0	0	0	0	1	1	0	1	0	0	1
	8	5	7	6	6	5	5	4	6	4	5	5	5
# SURVEYED		1301	1272	1283	1328	1315	1316	1291	1381	1309	1223	811	837
RACE	RESP	'72	'74	'75	'76	'77	'78	'82	'83	'85	'86	'88	'89
BLACK	0	2%	1%	2%	2%	1%	0%	1%	2%	1%	1%	2%	2%
	1	2	1	4	4	2	2	6	4	2	0	2	6
	2	27	23	35	32	32	36	41	38	43	43	44	40
	3	19	25	17	18	18	19	22	24	22	22	24	23
	4	21	28	24	19	21	24	18	18	21	19	16	18
	5	7	4	6	7	6	7	2	4	4	4	2	5
	6	5	2	3	1	2	3	1	3	2	4	2	1
	7	4	1	1	2	4	1	2	0	1	1	0	0
	8	14	14	9	16	15	9	8	8	3	7	7	4
# SURVEYED		248	165	157	124	170	152	148	157	148	181	123	95
RACE	RESP	'72	'74	'75	'76	'77	'78	'82	'83	'85	'86	'88	'89
OTHER	0	0%	0%	0%	0%	0%	0%	0%	0%	2%	0%	0%	0%
	1	0	14	0	0	0	6	0	0	5	3	0	0
	2	33	43	25	89	53	56	63	61	47	44	53	49
	3	33	14	75	11	27	6	15	33	23	19	24	22
	4	0	29	0	0	20	25	7	0	12	19	9	16
	5	0	0	0	0	0	6	4	0	5	6	6	3
	6	0	0	0	0	0	0	0	0	0	3	3	3
	7	33	0	0	0	0	0	0	0	0	0	0	0
	8	0	0	0	0	0	0	11	6	7	6	6	8
# SURVEYED		3	7	4	9	15	16	27	18	43	36	34	37

TABLE IV: IDEAL FAMILY SIZE -- BY AGE

Question: What do you think is the ideal number of children for a family to have? NOTE: Question not asked in 1973, 1980, 1984, 1987.

Responses: 0 = None 1 = 1 2 = 2 3 = 3 4 = 4
5 = 5 6 = 6 7 = 7+ 8 = As many as you want

		YEAR											
AGE	RESP	'72	'74	'75	'76	'77	'78	'82	'83	'85	'86	'88	'89
18-23	0	2%	1%	0%	3%	0%	1%	1%	1%	1%	3%	0%	0%
	1	4	5	2	6	3	1	3	2	3	2	3	4
	2	45	51	54	52	56	48	54	49	53	51	47	48
	3	23	23	28	22	21	27	21	30	27	28	34	32
	4	17	13	12	9	10	12	12	12	11	12	10	11
	5	2	2	1	2	2	5	1	3	3	2	2	2
	6	2	0	0	1	0	2	1	0	0	0	1	0
	7	1	1	0	2	1	1	1	0	0	1	0	0
	8	4	4	4	3	6	4	5	3	2	1	3	2
# SURVEYED		163	164	171	162	164	161	146	127	131	107	94	81
AGE	RESP	'72	'74	'75	'76	'77	'78	'82	'83	'85	'86	'88	'89
24-29	0	0%	0%	3%	2%	2%	2%	1%	0%	0%	0%	2%	1%
	1	0	2	4	6	5	1	5	1	3	1	2	4
	2	56	60	62	58	62	62	61	56	60	54	50	62
	3	26	23	20	22	18	21	21	24	22	30	26	22
	4	12	8	6	8	8	10	8	13	8	10	11	8
	5	0	1	0	0	1	1	2	1	2	2	1	1
	6	1	0	0	0	0	0	1	1	0	0	1	1
	7	0	0	0	0	0	0	0	0	1	0	0	0
	8	3	6	5	3	6	2	1	4	4	3	7	2
# SURVEYED		225	210	228	224	200	241	243	284	215	215	149	143
AGE	RESP	'72	'74	'75	'76	'77	'78	'82	'83	'85	'86	'88	'89
30-35	0	1%	2%	2%	2%	0%	1%	2%	0%	1%	0%	1%	1%
	1	2	2	2	7	2	3	3	3	4	2	2	4
	2	44	45	55	57	55	63	64	64	60	60	55	55
	3	24	24	19	17	24	17	18	19	24	18	28	22
	4	18	16	14	11	12	7	11	6	6	13	6	9
	5	3	2	1	2	2	2	1	2	0	1	2	1
	6	1	2	1	0	1	1	0	0	0	2	0	0
	7	1	1	0	0	0	0	1	0	0	0	1	1
	8	6	7	7	4	4	5	3	4	3	4	6	7
# SURVEYED		180	174	166	184	186	223	199	233	210	219	128	138
AGE	RESP	'72	'74	'75	'76	'77	'78	'82	'83	'85	'86	'88	'89
36-41	0	2%	0%	1%	3%	1%	3%	1%	2%	2%	2%	2%	2%
	1	1	1	1	4	2	2	3	2	3	2	0	4
	2	41	44	58	56	53	51	65	56	62	59	58	65
	3	28	21	22	21	19	23	17	21	16	22	24	14
	4	18	17	11	7	13	12	10	12	8	9	8	5
	5	4	2	1	3	1	2	1	0	3	1	2	4
	6	4	1	1	0	1	1	0	1	1	1	1	2
	7	0	1	0	0	0	1	1	0	0	0	2	0
	8	2	13	6	6	11	6	1	5	6	5	5	5
# SURVEYED		125	144	153	156	167	153	144	164	180	186	123	122

TABLE IV: IDEAL FAMILY SIZE -- BY AGE (Continued)

Question: What do you think is the ideal number of children for a family to have? NOTE: Question not asked in 1973, 1980, 1984, 1987.

Responses: 0 = None 1 = 1 2 = 2 3 = 3 4 = 4
5 = 5 6 = 6 7 = 7+ 8 = As many as you want

		YEAR											
AGE	RESP	'72	'74	'75	'76	'77	'78	'82	'83	'85	'86	'88	'89
42-47	0	1%	1%	0%	2%	1%	2%	2%	1%	1%	2%	3%	1%
	1	2	2	6	1	1	4	2	1	2	3	2	3
	2	33	44	52	53	43	60	57	56	73	51	54	57
	3	22	23	17	19	27	17	22	21	16	22	26	27
	4	23	18	14	12	14	15	9	8	4	12	8	6
	5	3	4	1	2	4	0	1	1	2	0	1	2
	6	5	1	1	0	1	1	1	1	0	1	2	1
	7	1	0	1	1	3	0	1	0	1	1	0	0
	8	10	7	8	10	6	2	5	9	1	7	4	4
# SURVEYED		183	149	139	109	145	114	112	142	123	137	106	104
AGE	RESP	'72	'74	'75	'76	'77	'78	'82	'83	'85	'86	'88	'89
48-53	0	3%	3%	2%	2%	1%	2%	0%	1%	2%	2%	2%	5%
	1	1	1	1	2	1	2	2	2	2	2	2	2
	2	40	46	39	48	47	38	56	51	59	48	54	56
	3	25	20	27	23	19	34	17	25	18	22	22	21
	4	20	17	21	14	24	15	14	11	14	18	15	7
	5	3	2	3	0	2	2	3	2	2	2	0	0
	6	2	1	1	2	0	0	3	1	0	0	0	2
	7	2	0	1	1	0	1	0	2	0	0	0	0
	8	3	10	4	8	6	6	6	6	5	7	5	6
# SURVEYED		181	143	136	128	150	129	109	114	130	106	59	82
AGE	RESP	'72	'74	'75	'76	'77	'78	'82	'83	'85	'86	'88	'89
54-59	0	3%	1%	0%	2%	1%	0%	1%	1%	1%	0%	2%	1%
	1	1	1	0	2	1	2	1	2	2	1	4	0
	2	33	40	40	48	45	41	52	48	54	50	52	55
	3	30	28	32	20	31	26	19	27	24	26	21	21
	4	17	15	16	16	12	16	15	16	13	12	8	13
	5	4	4	1	2	2	5	2	0	2	1	4	4
	6	4	1	2	1	2	2	1	2	1	3	0	0
	7	1	0	0	0	2	0	1	0	0	0	0	0
	8	7	11	9	11	4	10	8	6	3	7	8	4
# SURVEYED		150	135	122	128	163	133	141	128	127	94	48	67
AGE	RESP	'72	'74	'75	'76	'77	'78	'82	'83	'85	'86	'88	'89
60-65	0	3%	1%	1%	2%	3%	1%	1%	2%	2%	2%	1%	2%
	1	1	2	1	0	0	0	1	1	2	0	0	0
	2	40	38	37	45	46	47	56	48	48	49	58	51
	3	20	32	29	22	25	26	18	27	28	24	26	22
	4	21	16	22	19	18	16	15	15	13	15	15	14
	5	4	1	2	3	3	2	1	2	2	6	0	5
	6	3	0	1	2	0	1	0	1	0	1	0	0
	7	2	1	1	0	0	1	0	0	2	0	0	2
	8	6	9	6	7	6	6	8	4	3	5	0	6
# SURVEYED		135	102	110	129	114	104	114	130	126	109	74	65

TABLE IV: IDEAL FAMILY SIZE -- BY AGE (Continued)

Question: What do you think is the ideal number of children for a family to have? NOTE: Question not asked in 1973, 1980, 1984, 1987.

Responses: 0 = None; 1 = 1; 2 = 2; 3 = 3; 4 = 4; 5 = 5; 6 = 6; 7 = 7+; 8 = As many as you want

AGE	RESP	YEAR '72	'74	'75	'76	'77	'78	'82	'83	'85	'86	'88	'89
66+	0	2%	1%	0%	1%	2%	0%	1%	2%	1%	0%	3%	0%
	1	0	2	0	0	0	1	1	2	1	1	2	1
	2	33	33	38	44	32	37	39	40	42	42	42	47
	3	20	24	26	19	26	27	26	24	23	31	25	21
	4	20	25	23	22	25	19	23	19	20	15	18	13
	5	5	2	2	3	5	2	2	2	1	3	3	5
	6	3	3	3	2	2	1	2	2	2	2	2	1
	7	2	1	0	0	1	1	2	0	2	0	0	2
	8	13	8	7	9	5	11	6	10	8	6	5	10
# SURVEYED		205	217	216	237	204	219	248	227	251	260	186	164

****

OBEDIENCE AS A CHILDHOOD TRAIT

TABLE I: OBEDIENCE AS A CHILDHOOD TRAIT -- BY TOTAL POPULATION

Question: Considered along with the other four childhood characteristics from the list below that a child should learn to help prepare him/her for life, where would you rank "to obey?" NOTE: Question not asked in 1972-1985.

A. to obey
B. to be well liked or popular
C. to think for himself or herself
D. to work hard
E. to help others when they need help

Responses: 1 = First; 2 = Second; 3 = Third; 4 = Fourth; 5 = Fifth

RESPONSE	YEAR '86	'87	'88	'89
1	23%	21%	23%	20%
2	16	13	12	14
3	16	15	20	17
4	32	31	29	33
5	13	20	16	17
# SURVEYED	732	1452	977	1000

TABLE II: OBEDIENCE AS A CHILDHOOD TRAIT -- BY SEX

Question: Considered along with the other four childhood characteristics from the list below that a child should learn to help prepare him/her for life, where would you rank "to obey?" NOTE: Question not asked in 1972-1985.

A. to obey
B. to be well liked or popular
C. to think for himself or herself
D. to work hard
E. to help others when they need help

Responses: 1 = First; 2 = Second; 3 = Third; 4 = Fourth; 5 = Fifth

		YEAR			
SEX	RESP	'86	'87	'88	'89
MALE	1	18%	21%	22%	22%
	2	16	11	13	15
	3	16	15	20	16
	4	32	32	30	30
	5	17	21	16	18
# SURVEYED		315	636	430	432

		YEAR			
SEX	RESP	'86	'87	'88	'89
FEMALE	1	26%	20%	24%	18%
	2	16	14	12	13
	3	16	15	19	18
	4	32	30	29	35
	5	10	19	16	16
# SURVEYED		417	816	547	568

TABLE III: OBEDIENCE AS A CHILDHOOD TRAIT -- BY RACE

Question: Considered along with the other four childhood characteristics from the list below that a child should learn to help prepare him/her for life, where would you rank "to obey?" NOTE: Question not asked in 1972-1985.

A. to obey
B. to be well liked or popular
C. to think for himself or herself
D. to work hard
E. to help others when they need help

Responses: 1 = First; 2 = Second; 3 = Third; 4 = Fourth; 5 = Fifth

		YEAR			
RACE	RESP	'86	'87	'88	'89
WHITE	1	23%	18%	23%	19%
	2	14	12	12	13
	3	15	15	19	16
	4	34	32	32	35
	5	14	22	16	17
# SURVEYED		632	1212	818	858

		YEAR			
RACE	RESP	'86	'87	'88	'89
BLACK	1	23%	34%	26%	27%
	2	25	15	20	20
	3	25	16	28	24
	4	22	26	17	18
	5	5	8	9	11
# SURVEYED		79	189	116	100

		YEAR			
RACE	RESP	'86	'87	'88	'89
OTHER	1	24%	31%	23%	26%
	2	24	12	9	7
	3	19	12	16	14
	4	19	29	19	31
	5	14	16	33	21
# SURVEYED		21	51	43	42

TABLE IV: OBEDIENCE AS A CHILDHOOD TRAIT -- BY AGE

Question: Considered along with the other four childhood characteristics from the list below that a child should learn to help prepare him/her for life, where would you rank "to obey?" NOTE: Question not asked in 1972-1985.

A. to obey
B. to be well liked or popular
C. to think for himself or herself
D. to work hard
E. to help others when they need help

Responses: 1 = First; 2 = Second; 3 = Third; 4 = Fourth; 5 = Fifth

AGE	RESP	'86	'87	'88	'89
18-23	1	19%	17%	20%	18%
	2	15	19	11	12
	3	21	17	19	20
	4	29	30	40	35
	5	15	17	11	15
# SURVEYED		52	126	91	89
24-29	1	18%	14%	21%	14%
	2	17	11	9	12
	3	21	15	25	19
	4	27	35	30	36
	5	17	25	15	18
# SURVEYED		118	193	143	140
30-35	1	13%	14%	14%	14%
	2	15	11	10	17
	3	13	17	25	15
	4	47	37	32	37
	5	11	21	20	17
# SURVEYED		104	218	126	139

AGE	RESP	'86	'87	'88	'89
36-41	1	19%	9%	13%	12%
	2	15	10	13	14
	3	17	17	20	18
	4	38	37	40	37
	5	12	27	15	18
# SURVEYED		95	186	124	131
42-47	1	18%	21%	20%	16%
	2	20	10	13	15
	3	11	15	18	6
	4	37	34	29	40
	5	14	20	20	22
# SURVEYED		76	156	104	104
48-53	1	21%	23%	26%	15%
	2	16	14	18	13
	3	11	10	19	21
	4	37	32	26	36
	5	16	21	11	15
# SURVEYED		57	124	57	94

AGE	RESP	'86	'87	'88	'89
54-59	1	37%	21%	21%	16%
	2	23	18	14	10
	3	14	16	25	13
	4	23	30	25	44
	5	2	16	14	16
# SURVEYED		43	96	63	61
60-65	1	30%	30%	28%	23%
	2	14	8	12	14
	3	9	21	12	30
	4	28	29	31	23
	5	19	12	18	11
# SURVEYED		64	98	78	71
66+	1	37%	39%	39%	40%
	2	13	15	16	14
	3	21	11	14	14
	4	19	18	17	17
	5	11	17	14	15
# SURVEYED		120	250	187	169

****

INDEPENDENT THOUGHT AS A CHILDHOOD TRAIT

TABLE I: INDEPENDENT THOUGHT AS A CHILDHOOD TRAIT -- BY TOTAL POPULATION

Question: Considered along with the other four childhood characteristics from the list below that a child should learn to help prepare him/her for life, where would you rank "to think for himself or herself?" NOTE: Question not asked in 1972-1985.

A. to obey
B. to be well liked or popular
C. to think for himself or herself
D. to work hard
E. to help others when they need help

Responses: 1 = First; 2 = Second; 3 = Third; 4 = Fourth; 5 = Fifth

	YEAR			
RESPONSE	'86	'87	'88	'89
1	52%	55%	49%	53%
2	17	17	18	18
3	14	11	13	10
4	11	11	13	13
5	6	6	7	6
# SURVEYED	732	1452	977	1000

TABLE II: INDEPENDENT THOUGHT AS A CHILDHOOD TRAIT -- BY SEX

Question: Considered along with the other four childhood characteristics from the list below that a child should learn to help prepare him/her for life, where would you rank "to think for himself or herself?" NOTE: Question not asked in 1972-1985.

A. to obey
B. to be well liked or popular
C. to think for himself or herself
D. to work hard
E. to help others when they need help

Responses: 1 = First; 2 = Second; 3 = Third; 4 = Fourth; 5 = Fifth

		YEAR			
SEX	RESP	'86	'87	'88	'89
MALE	1	51%	54%	48%	48%
	2	17	16	18	20
	3	13	11	12	11
	4	13	11	14	13
	5	6	7	8	7
# SURVEYED		315	636	430	432

		YEAR			
SEX	RESP	'86	'87	'88	'89
FEMALE	1	52%	56%	50%	56%
	2	18	18	18	17
	3	14	10	14	10
	4	10	10	12	13
	5	6	6	5	5
# SURVEYED		417	816	547	568

TABLE III: INDEPENDENT THOUGHT AS A CHILDHOOD TRAIT -- BY RACE

Question: Considered along with the other four childhood characteristics from the list below that a child should learn to help prepare him/her for life, where would you rank "to think for himself or herself?" NOTE: Question not asked in 1972-1985.

A. to obey
B. to be well liked or popular.
C. to think for himself or herself
D. to work hard
E. to help others when they need help

Responses: 1 = First; 2 = Second; 3 = Third; 4 = Fourth; 5 = Fifth

RACE	RESP	'86	'87	'88	'89
		YEAR			
WHITE	1	53%	58%	51%	55%
	2	17	17	18	18
	3	14	9	12	9
	4	11	10	13	12
	5	6	6	7	6
# SURVEYED		632	1212	818	858

RACE	RESP	'86	'87	'88	'89
		YEAR			
BLACK	1	48%	42%	41%	38%
	2	22	20	24	21
	3	14	19	19	17
	4	13	14	12	20
	5	4	5	4	4
# SURVEYED		79	189	116	100

RACE	RESP	'86	'87	'88	'89
		YEAR			
OTHER	1	43%	33%	44%	38%
	2	29	20	14	21
	3	5	22	12	17
	4	19	6	19	19
	5	5	20	12	5
# SURVEYED		21	51	43	42

TABLE IV: INDEPENDENT THOUGHT AS A CHILDHOOD TRAIT -- BY AGE

Question: Considered along with the other four childhood characteristics from the list below that a child should learn to help prepare him/her for life, where would you rank "to think for himself or herself" NOTE: Question not asked in 1972-1985.

A. to obey
B. to be well liked or popular
C. to think for himself or herself
D. to work hard
E. to help others when they need help

Responses: 1 = First; 2 = Second; 3 = Third; 4 = Fourth; 5 = Fifth

AGE	RESP	'86	'87	'88	'89
		YEAR			
18-23	1	58%	44%	55%	38%
	2	13	16	13	26
	3	13	13	12	8
	4	2	18	10	20
	5	13	9	10	8
# SURVEYED		52	126	91	89

AGE	RESP	'86	'87	'88	'89
		YEAR			
24-29	1	46%	56%	48%	55%
	2	17	19	17	19
	3	14	13	15	14
	4	17	7	13	6
	5	6	5	8	7
# SURVEYED		118	193	143	140

AGE	RESP	'86	'87	'88	'89
		YEAR			
30-35	1	58%	64%	50%	58%
	2	13	14	21	19
	3	12	7	7	6
	4	15	10	17	14
	5	3	5	4	3
# SURVEYED		104	218	126	139

TABLE IV: INDEPENDENT THOUGHT AS A CHILDHOOD TRAIT -- BY AGE (Continued)

Question: Considered along with the other four childhood characteristics from the list below that a child should learn to help prepare him/her for life, where would you rank "to think for himself or herself?" NOTE: Question not asked in 1972-1985.

A. to obey
B. to be well liked or popular
C. to think for himself or herself
D. to work hard
E. to help others when they need help

Responses: 1 = First; 2 = Second; 3 = Third; 4 = Fourth; 5 = Fifth

AGE	RESP	'86	'87	'88	'89
36-41	1	66%	69%	61%	59%
	2	18	13	20	15
	3	7	6	6	10
	4	6	9	9	12
	5	2	2	3	5
# SURVEYED		95	186	124	131
42-47	1	64%	62%	59%	57%
	2	13	13	13	13
	3	12	8	14	9
	4	9	11	13	17
	5	1	6	2	4
# SURVEYED		76	156	104	104

AGE	RESP	'86	'87	'88	'89
48-53	1	51%	54%	53%	65%
	2	23	22	16	11
	3	12	7	12	10
	4	7	8	11	13
	5	7	9	9	2
# SURVEYED		57	124	57	94
54-59	1	40%	56%	49%	54%
	2	16	16	21	21
	3	21	15	11	10
	4	19	10	10	10
	5	5	3	10	5
# SURVEYED		43	96	63	6

AGE	RESP	'86	'87	'88	'89
60-65	1	47%	50%	54%	55%
	2	20	18	15	17
	3	16	14	14	7
	4	11	8	8	11
	5	6	9	9	10
# SURVEYED		64	98	78	71
66+	1	38%	40%	31%	41%
	2	23	23	22	22
	3	18	12	20	14
	4	12	14	19	14
	5	9	10	8	9
# SURVEYED		120	250	187	169

****

HELPFULNESS AS A CHILDHOOD TRAIT

TABLE I: HELPFULNESS AS A CHILDHOOD TRAIT -- BY TOTAL POPULATION

Question: Considered along with the other four childhood characteristics from the list below that a child should learn to help prepare him/her for life, where would you rank "to help others when they need help?" NOTE: Question not asked in 1972-1985.

A. to obey
B. to be well liked or popular
C. to think for himself or herself
D. to work hard
E. to help others when they need help

Responses: 1 = First; 2 = Second; 3 = Third; 4 = Fourth; 5 = Fifth

	YEAR			
RESPONSE	'86	'87	'88	'89
1	14%	12%	13%	12%
2	30	31	33	31
3	33	35	29	33
4	20	19	21	20
5	4	4	4	4
# SURVEYED	732	1452	994	1000

TABLE II: HELPFULNESS AS A CHILDHOOD TRAIT -- BY SEX

Question: Considered along with the other four childhood characteristics from the list below that a child should learn to help prepare him/her for life, where would you rank "to help others when they need help?" NOTE: Question not asked in 1972-1985.

A. to obey
B. to be well liked or popular
C. to think for himself or herself
D. to work hard
E. to help others when they need help

Responses: 1 = First; 2 = Second; 3 = Third; 4 = Fourth; 5 = Fifth

		YEAR			
SEX	RESP	'86	'87	'88	'89
MALE	1	16%	13%	14%	13%
	2	28	29	33	29
	3	34	36	29	34
	4	19	18	20	21
	5	4	5	4	3
# SURVEYED		315	636	436	432

		YEAR			
SEX	RESP	'86	'87	'88	'89
FEMALE	1	12%	11%	12%	12%
	2	31	33	34	33
	3	33	35	28	32
	4	20	19	21	19
	5	4	3	4	4
# SURVEYED		417	816	558	568

TABLE III: HELPFULNESS AS A CHILDHOOD TRAIT -- BY RACE

Question: Considered along with the other four childhood characteristics from the list below that a child should learn to help prepare him/her for life, where would you rank "to help others when they need help?" NOTE: Question not asked in 1972-1985.

A. to obey
B. to be well liked or popular
C. to think for himself or herself
D. to work hard
E. to help others when they need help

Responses: 1 = First; 2 = Second; 3 = Third; 4 = Fourth; 5 = Fifth

		YEAR			
RACE	RESP	'86	'87	'88	'89
WHITE	1	14%	11%	13%	12%
	2	31	32	35	32
	3	34	37	29	34
	4	18	16	19	18
	5	4	3	4	4
# SURVEYED		632	1212	834	858

		YEAR			
RACE	RESP	'86	'87	'88	'89
BLACK	1	14%	13%	11%	15%
	2	23	26	22	23
	3	27	24	22	23
	4	33	29	36	31
	5	4	8	9	8
# SURVEYED		79	189	116	100

		YEAR			
RACE	RESP	'86	'87	'88	'89
OTHER	1	14%	18%	14%	12%
	2	14	20	30	40
	3	48	29	32	26
	4	19	33	18	19
	5	5	0	7	2
# SURVEYED		21	51	44	42

TABLE IV: HELPFULNESS AS A CHILDHOOD TRAIT -- BY AGE

Question: Considered along with the other four childhood characteristics from the list below that a child should learn to help prepare him/her for life, where would you rank "to help others when they need help?" NOTE: Question not asked in 1972-1985.

A. to obey
B. to be well liked or popular
C. to think for himself or herself
D. to work hard
E. to help others when they need help

Responses: 1 = First; 2 = Second; 3 = Third; 4 = Fourth; 5 = Fifth

		YEAR			
AGE	RESP	'86	'87	'88	'89
18-23	1	12%	13%	11%	21%
	2	31	33	38	35
	3	29	37	30	21
	4	27	17	16	16
	5	2	1	5	7
# SURVEYED		52	126	93	89

		YEAR			
AGE	RESP	'86	'87	'88	'89
24-29	1	21%	16%	12%	12%
	2	31	32	33	29
	3	29	33	30	35
	4	17	16	21	19
	5	3	3	4	5
# SURVEYED		118	193	146	140

		YEAR			
AGE	RESP	'86	'87	'88	'89
30-35	1	13%	14%	17%	11%
	2	38	37	34	35
	3	34	32	29	29
	4	12	13	16	20
	5	4	4	4	5
# SURVEYED		104	218	128	139

TABLE IV: HELPFULNESS AS A CHILDHOOD TRAIT -- BY AGE (Continued)

Question: Considered along with the other four childhood characteristics from the list below that a child should learn to help prepare him/her for life, where would you rank "to help others when they need help?" NOTE: Question not asked in 1972-1985.

A. to obey
B. to be well liked or popular
C. to think for himself or herself
D. to work hard
E. to help others when they need help

Responses: 1 = First; 2 = Second; 3 = Third; 4 = Fourth; 5 = Fifth

AGE	RESP	'86	'87	'88	'89
36-41	1	6%	9%	13%	15%
	2	32	33	36	40
	3	34	38	32	34
	4	25	16	17	12
	5	3	4	3	0
# SURVEYED		95	186	126	131
42-47	1	8%	8%	12%	14%
	2	25	36	39	29
	3	41	37	29	41
	4	24	17	16	15
	5	3	2	4	0
# SURVEYED		76	156	104	104

AGE	RESP	'86	'87	'88	'89
48-53	1	11%	11%	12%	10%
	2	26	31	32	34
	3	40	39	28	30
	4	16	17	23	26
	5	7	2	5	1
# SURVEYED		57	124	57	94
54-59	1	16%	14%	12%	15%
	2	19	24	30	34
	3	33	32	26	34
	4	28	26	29	15
	5	5	4	3	2
# SURVEYED		43	96	66	61

AGE	RESP	'86	'87	'88	'89
60-65	1	16%	8%	11%	3%
	2	23	28	30	30
	3	41	29	30	35
	4	13	30	24	23
	5	8	6	5	10
# SURVEYED		64	98	80	71
66+	1	16%	10%	13%	11%
	2	30	23	30	21
	3	28	39	24	35
	4	22	22	27	27
	5	5	6	6	6
# SURVEYED		120	250	190	169

***

POPULARITY AS A CHILDHOOD TRAIT

TABLE I: POPULARITY AS A CHILDHOOD TRAIT -- BY TOTAL POPULATION

Question: Considered along with the other four childhood characteristics from the list below that a child should learn to help prepare him/her for life, where would you rank "to be well liked or popular?" NOTE: Question not asked in 1972-1985.

A. to obey
B. to be well liked or popular
C. to think for himself or herself
D. to work hard
E. to help others when they need help

Responses: 1 = First; 2 = Second; 3 = Third; 4 = Fourth; 5 = Fifth

	YEAR			
RESPONSE	'86	'87	'88	'89
1	1%	1%	1%	1%
2	4	4	5	3
3	5	6	6	6
4	19	23	19	19
5	72	66	70	71
# SURVEYED	732	1452	977	1000

TABLE II: POPULARITY AS A CHILDHOOD TRAIT -- BY SEX

Question: Considered along with the other four childhood characteristics from the list below that a child should learn to help prepare him/her for life, where would you rank "to be well liked or popular?" NOTE: Question not asked in 1972-1985.

A. to obey
B. to be well liked or popular
C. to think for himself or herself
D. to work hard
E. to help others when they need help

Responses: 1 = First; 2 = Second; 3 = Third; 4 = Fourth; 5 = Fifth

		YEAR			
SEX	RESP	'86	'87	'88	'89
MALE	1	1%	1%	1%	1%
	2	4	6	4	4
	3	6	7	7	7
	4	21	24	20	19
	5	68	62	68	69
# SURVEYED		315	636	430	432

		YEAR			
SEX	RESP	'86	'87	'88	'89
FEMALE	1	0%	1%	1%	1%
	2	4	3	5	3
	3	3	5	4	4
	4	18	22	19	18
	5	75	69	72	73
# SURVEYED		417	816	547	568

TABLE III: POPULARITY AS A CHILDHOOD TRAIT -- BY RACE

Question: Considered along with the other four childhood characteristics from the list below that a child should learn to help prepare him/her for life, where would you rank "to be well liked or popular?" NOTE: Question not asked in 1972-1985.

A. to obey
B. to be well liked or popular
C. to think for himself or herself
D. to work hard
E. to help others when they need help

Responses: 1 = First; 2 = Second; 3 = Third; 4 = Fourth; 5 = Fifth

RACE	RESP	'86	'87	'88	'89
		YEAR			
WHITE	1	0%	1%	0%	1%
	2	4	4	5	3
	3	4	6	6	5
	4	20	25	19	20
	5	71	65	71	71
# SURVEYED		632	1212	818	858

RACE	RESP	'86	'87	'88	'89
		YEAR			
BLACK	1	1%	1%	2%	1%
	2	4	7	4	7
	3	6	5	3	10
	4	11	11	18	11
	5	77	76	73	71
# SURVEYED		79	189	116	100

RACE	RESP	'86	'87	'88	'89
		YEAR			
OTHER	1	5%	2%	2%	5%
	2	5	8	7	5
	3	5	8	9	7
	4	19	18	33	14
	5	67	65	49	69
# SURVEYED		21	51	43	42

TABLE IV: POPULARITY AS A CHILDHOOD TRAIT -- BY AGE

Question: Considered along with the other four childhood characteristics from the list below that a child should learn to help prepare him/her for life, where would you rank "to be well liked or popular?" NOTE: Question not asked in 1972-1985.

A. to obey
B. to be well liked or popular
C. to think for himself or herself
D. to work hard
E. to help others when they need help

Responses: 1 = First; 2 = Second; 3 = Third; 4 = Fourth; 5 = Fifth

AGE	RESP	'86	'87	'88	'89
		YEAR			
18-23	1	0%	2%	0%	1%
	2	6	3	2	3
	3	2	5	3	8
	4	27	19	23	20
	5	65	71	71	67
# SURVEYED		52	126	91	89

AGE	RESP	'86	'87	'88	'89
		YEAR			
24-29	1	0%	1%	1%	1%
	2	2	4	2	5
	3	5	7	6	6
	4	23	22	20	20
	5	70	67	71	68
# SURVEYED		118	193	143	140

AGE	RESP	'86	'87	'88	'89
		YEAR			
30-35	1	0%	0%	0%	1%
	2	2	3	5	2
	3	6	3	5	8
	4	13	25	20	15
	5	79	68	71	74
# SURVEYED		104	218	126	139

****

TABLE IV: POPULARITY AS A CHILDHOOD TRAIT -- BY AGE (Continued)

Question: Considered along with the other four childhood characteristics from the list below that a child should learn to help prepare him/her for life, where would you rank "to be well liked or popular?" NOTE: Question not asked in 1972-1985.

A. to obey
B. to be well liked or popular
C. to think for himself or herself
D. to work hard
E. to help others when they need help

Responses: 1 = First; 2 = Second; 3 = Third; 4 = Fourth; 5 = Fifth

		YEAR			
AGE	RESP	'86	'87	'88	'89
36-41	1	1%	1%	0%	1%
	2	1	4	2	0
	3	4	4	5	2
	4	13	25	15	23
	5	81	66	77	74
# SURVEYED		95	186	124	131
AGE	RESP	'86	'87	'88	'89
42-47	1	0%	1%	0%	2%
	2	5	3	4	2
	3	3	4	2	5
	4	17	22	24	19
	5	75	70	70	72
# SURVEYED		76	156	104	104

		YEAR			
AGE	RESP	'86	'87	'88	'89
48-53	1	2%	2%	0%	1%
	2	2	3	4	2
	3	7	4	7	2
	4	25	26	19	15
	5	65	65	70	80
# SURVEYED		57	124	57	94
AGE	RESP	'86	'87	'88	'89
54-59	1	0%	1%	2%	0%
	2	5	4	5	0
	3	2	5	6	5
	4	12	20	17	20
	5	81	70	70	75
# SURVEYED		43	96	63	61

		YEAR			
AGE	RESP	'86	'87	'88	'89
60-65	1	2%	3%	1%	3%
	2	6	6	8	4
	3	3	7	6	6
	4	23	16	18	18
	5	66	67	67	69
# SURVEYED		64	98	78	71
AGE	RESP	'86	'87	'88	'89
66+	1	1%	0%	2%	1%
	2	8	8	9	8
	3	6	10	9	7
	4	23	24	17	18
	5	63	58	65	66
# SURVEYED		120	250	187	169

****

WORKING HARD AS A CHILDHOOD TRAIT

TABLE I: WORKING HARD AS A CHILDHOOD TRAIT -- BY TOTAL POPULATION

Question: Considered along with the other four childhood characteristics from the list below that a child should learn to help prepare him/her for life, where would you rank "to work hard?" NOTE: Question not asked in 1972-1985.

A. to obey
B. to be well liked or popular
C. to think for himself or herself
D. to work hard
E. to help others when they need help

Responses: 1 = First; 2 = Second; 3 = Third; 4 = Fourth; 5 = Fifth

	YEAR			
RESPONSE	'86	'87	'88	'89
1	11%	12%	14%	14%
2	33	35	31	34
3	33	33	33	35
4	18	17	18	16
5	5	4	4	2
# SURVEYED	732	1452	977	1000

TABLE II: WORKING HARD AS A CHILDHOOD TRAIT -- BY SEX

Question: Considered along with the other four childhood characteristics from the list below that a child should learn to help prepare him/her for life, where would you rank "to work hard?" NOTE: Question not asked in 1972-1985.

A. to obey
B. to be well liked or popular
C. to think for himself or herself
D. to work hard
E. to help others when they need help

Responses: 1 = First; 2 = Second; 3 = Third; 4 = Fourth; 5 = Fifth

		YEAR			
SEX	RESP	'86	'87	'88	'89
MALE	1	14%	11%	15%	15%
	2	35	39	32	33
	3	31	31	32	32
	4	15	15	16	17
	5	5	4	5	3
# SURVEYED		315	636	430	432

		YEAR			
SEX	RESP	'86	'87	'88	'89
FEMALE	1	9%	12%	14%	13%
	2	32	32	30	34
	3	34	35	34	36
	4	20	18	19	15
	5	6	3	3	2
# SURVEYED		417	816	547	568

TABLE III: WORKING HARD AS A CHILDHOOD TRAIT -- BY RACE

Question: Considered along with the other four childhood characteristics from the list below that a child should learn to help prepare him/her for life, where would you rank "to work hard?" NOTE: Question not asked in 1972-1985.

A. to obey
B. to be well liked or popular
C. to think for himself or herself
D. to work hard
E. to help others when they need help

Responses: 1 = First; 2 = Second; 3 = Third; 4 = Fourth; 5 = Fifth

RACE	RESP	'86	'87	'88	'89
WHITE	1	11%	12%	13%	13%
	2	34	35	31	34
	3	33	33	34	36
	4	17	17	18	15
	5	5	4	4	2
# SURVEYED		632	1212	818	858

RACE	RESP	'86	'87	'88	'89
BLACK	1	14%	10%	21%	19%
	2	27	32	30	29
	3	28	37	28	26
	4	22	19	16	20
	5	10	3	4	6
# SURVEYED		79	189	116	100

RACE	RESP	'86	'87	'88	'89
OTHER	1	14%	16%	19%	19%
	2	29	41	40	26
	3	24	29	30	36
	4	24	14	12	17
	5	10	0	0	2
# SURVEYED		21	51	43	42

TABLE IV: WORKING HARD AS A CHILDHOOD TRAIT -- BY AGE

Question: Considered along with the other four childhood characteristics from the list below that a child should learn to help prepare him/her for life, where would you rank "to work hard?" NOTE: Question not asked in 1972-1985.

A. to obey
B. to be well liked or popular
C. to think for himself or herself
D. to work hard
E. to help others when they need help

Responses: 1 = First; 2 = Second; 3 = Third; 4 = Fourth; 5 = Fifth

AGE	RESP	'86	'87	'88	'89
18-23	1	12%	25%	15%	21%
	2	35	29	36	24
	3	35	29	35	43
	4	15	15	11	9
	5	4	2	2	3
# SURVEYED		52	126	91	89
AGE	RESP	'86	'87	'88	'89
24-29	1	15%	13%	18%	18%
	2	34	34	38	36
	3	31	32	24	26
	4	16	20	17	19
	5	4	1	3	2
# SURVEYED		118	193	143	140

AGE	RESP	'86	'87	'88	'89
30-35	1	15%	7%	18%	17%
	2	33	35	31	27
	3	36	41	35	42
	4	13	15	14	14
	5	4	2	2	1
# SURVEYED		104	218	126	139
AGE	RESP	'86	'87	'88	'89
36-41	1	7%	13%	13%	14%
	2	35	40	29	32
	3	38	34	37	36
	4	18	13	19	15
	5	2	1	2	3
# SURVEYED		95	186	124	131

AGE	RESP	'86	'87	'88	'89
42-47	1	9%	8%	10%	11%
	2	37	38	32	40
	3	34	36	37	39
	4	13	15	18	8
	5	7	2	4	2
# SURVEYED		76	156	104	104
AGE	RESP	'86	'87	'88	'89
48-53	1	16%	10%	9%	10%
	2	33	31	32	40
	3	30	40	33	37
	4	16	17	21	11
	5	5	2	5	2
# SURVEYED		57	124	57	94

TABLE IV: WORKING HARD AS A CHILDHOOD TRAIT -- BY AGE (Continued)

Question: Considered along with the other four childhood characteristics from the list below that a child should learn to help prepare him/her for life, where would you rank "to work hard?" NOTE: Question not asked in 1972-1985.

A. to obey
B. to be well liked or popular
C. to think for himself or herself
D. to work hard
E. to help others when they need help

Responses: 1 = First; 2 = Second; 3 = Third; 4 = Fourth; 5 = Fifth

		YEAR			
AGE	RESP	'86	'87	'88	'89
54-59	1	7%	8%	16%	15%
	2	37	39	29	34
	3	30	32	32	38
	4	19	14	19	11
	5	7	7	5	2
# SURVEYED		43	96	63	61

		YEAR			
AGE	RESP	'86	'87	'88	'89
60-65	1	6%	9%	5%	17%
	2	36	40	35	35
	3	31	29	37	23
	4	25	17	21	25
	5	2	5	3	0
# SURVEYED		64	98	78	71

		YEAR			
AGE	RESP	'86	'87	'88	'89
66+	1	8%	10%	17%	7%
	2	28	31	22	34
	3	28	28	33	31
	4	24	21	21	24
	5	13	10	7	4
# SURVEYED		120	250	187	169

****

MULTI-GENERATION HOUSEHOLDS

TABLE I: MULTI-GENERATION HOUSEHOLDS -- BY TOTAL POPULATION

Question: As you know, many older people share a home with their grown children. Do you think this is generally a good idea or a bad idea? NOTE: Question not asked in 1972, 1974, 1977, 1982, 1985.

Responses: GI = A good idea; BI = Bad idea; DP = Depends

	YEAR										
RESPONSE	'73	'75	'76	'78	'80	'83	'84	'86	'87	'88	'89
GI	31%	31%	37%	35%	41%	43%	50%	41%	50%	45%	43%
BI	58	54	49	49	44	42	36	47	36	41	40
DP	11	15	15	17	16	15	13	12	14	14	17
# SURVEYED	1495	1480	1485	1526	1449	1593	1459	1460	1452	988	1023

TABLE II: MULTI-GENERATION HOUSEHOLDS -- BY SEX

Question: As you know, many older people share a home with their grown children. Do you think this is generally a good idea or a bad idea? NOTE: Question not asked in 1972, 1974, 1977, 1982, 1985.

Responses: GI = A good idea; BI = Bad idea; DP = Depends

		YEAR										
SEX	RESP	'73	'75	'76	'78	'80	'83	'84	'86	'87	'88	'89
M	GI	33%	32%	40%	37%	43%	46%	54%	41%	54%	46%	45%
	BI	57	53	47	47	43	43	33	47	33	40	38
	DP	10	15	13	16	14	11	12	11	13	14	17
# SURVEYED		697	665	663	641	631	688	593	615	635	436	437
SEX	RESP	'73	'75	'76	'78	'80	'83	'84	'86	'87	'88	'89
F	GI	30%	30%	34%	33%	39%	41%	47%	40%	47%	43%	41%
	BI	58	55	51	50	44	42	38	47	38	42	42
	DP	12	15	16	17	17	17	14	13	15	15	17
# SURVEYED		798	815	822	885	818	905	866	845	817	552	586

TABLE III: MULTI-GENERATION HOUSEHOLDS -- BY RACE

Question: As you know, many older people share a home with their grown children. Do you think this is generally a good idea or a bad idea? NOTE: Question not asked in 1972, 1974, 1977, 1982, 1985.

Responses: GI = A good idea; BI = Bad idea; DP = Depends

		YEAR										
RACE	RESP	'73	'75	'76	'78	'80	'83	'84	'86	'87	'88	'89
WHITE	GI	30%	29%	35%	34%	40%	41%	49%	38%	47%	41%	40%
	BI	60	56	50	50	46	45	38	49	39	44	42
	DP	10	16	14	16	15	15	14	13	14	15	18
# SURVEYED		1300	1313	1348	1352	1303	1412	1240	1241	1214	829	872
RACE	RESP	'73	'75	'76	'78	'80	'83	'84	'86	'87	'88	'89
BLACK	GI	40%	47%	48%	41%	51%	60%	53%	52%	64%	57%	58%
	BI	46	40	34	42	27	23	35	37	20	35	30
	DP	14	13	17	16	21	17	13	11	16	8	12
# SURVEYED		182	163	128	158	136	163	167	182	187	115	109
RACE	RESP	'73	'75	'76	'78	'80	'83	'84	'86	'87	'88	'89
OTHER	GI	54%	75%	44%	50%	50%	72%	85%	84%	78%	73%	57%
	BI	38	25	22	19	20	22	10	11	12	11	31
	DP	8	0	33	31	30	6	6	5	10	16	12
# SURVEYED		13	4	9	16	10	18	52	37	51	44	42

TABLE IV: MULTI-GENERATION HOUSEHOLDS -- BY AGE

Question: As you know, many older people share a home with their grown children. Do you think this is generally a good idea or a bad idea? NOTE: Question not asked in 1972, 1974, 1977, 1982, 1985.

Responses: GI = A good idea; BI = Bad idea; DP = Depends

		YEAR										
AGE	RESP	'73	'75	'76	'78	'80	'83	'84	'86	'87	'88	'89
18-23	GI	42%	49%	53%	53%	57%	55%	71%	50%	65%	54%	52%
	BI	50	38	32	35	32	32	22	38	20	35	31
	DP	8	13	15	12	12	13	7	12	15	11	18
# SURVEYED		171	172	161	162	152	128	156	107	124	92	91
AGE	RESP	'73	'75	'76	'78	'80	'83	'84	'86	'87	'88	'89
24-29	GI	39%	35%	40%	41%	52%	54%	59%	49%	60%	62%	47%
	BI	50	49	47	43	34	31	30	39	28	26	34
	DP	11	16	13	16	15	15	11	13	11	12	19
# SURVEYED		210	231	224	244	200	286	230	216	193	144	140
AGE	RESP	'73	'75	'76	'78	'80	'83	'84	'86	'87	'88	'89
30-35	GI	29%	27%	38%	37%	47%	51%	59%	47%	62%	58%	58%
	BI	60	53	49	47	37	37	27	36	28	24	27
	DP	10	19	14	16	16	12	14	17	10	17	15
# SURVEYED		167	171	184	230	213	235	198	221	218	127	144
AGE	RESP	'73	'75	'76	'78	'80	'83	'84	'86	'87	'88	'89
36-41	GI	37%	34%	43%	42%	44%	52%	55%	50%	58%	53%	48%
	BI	51	53	43	43	39	39	32	41	26	32	34
	DP	12	13	14	15	17	9	13	9	16	15	18
# SURVEYED		174	153	155	159	149	172	187	187	184	126	133
AGE	RESP	'73	'75	'76	'78	'80	'83	'84	'86	'87	'88	'89
42-47	GI	32%	30%	39%	34%	37%	40%	52%	45%	51%	49%	48%
	BI	58	57	40	42	41	39	31	40	34	37	38
	DP	10	13	21	24	22	21	17	15	15	15	14
# SURVEYED		146	142	112	119	115	145	124	139	155	103	107
AGE	RESP	'73	'75	'76	'78	'80	'83	'84	'86	'87	'88	'89
48-53	GI	28%	37%	35%	37%	50%	41%	50%	37%	52%	42%	39%
	BI	65	52	51	44	41	47	38	54	33	44	37
	DP	7	11	14	19	10	11	12	9	15	14	24
# SURVEYED		150	141	133	132	123	116	101	108	126	57	95

TABLE IV: MULTI-GENERATION HOUSEHOLDS -- BY AGE (Continued)

Question: As you know, many older people share a home with their grown children. Do you think this is generally a good idea or a bad idea? NOTE: Question not asked in 1972, 1974, 1977, 1982, 1985.

Responses: GI = A good idea; BI = Bad idea; DP = Depends

		YEAR										
AGE	RESP	'73	'75	'76	'78	'80	'83	'84	'86	'87	'88	'89
54-59	GI	27%	23%	31%	29%	35%	35%	39%	36%	46%	41%	32%
	BI	59	58	54	57	49	52	48	52	33	48	50
	DP	14	19	15	14	16	14	13	12	21	11	18
# SURVEYED		154	126	127	136	135	133	114	98	97	66	60
AGE	RESP	'73	'75	'76	'78	'80	'83	'84	'86	'87	'88	'89
60-65	GI	19%	21%	34%	17%	26%	33%	34%	28%	29%	26%	35%
	BI	69	63	56	71	58	55	48	59	58	60	55
	DP	12	17	10	12	16	13	18	13	13	14	11
# SURVEYED		120	112	134	107	117	132	112	114	99	80	75
AGE	RESP	'73	'75	'76	'78	'80	'83	'84	'86	'87	'88	'89
66+	GI	24%	21%	22%	20%	22%	22%	29%	24%	27%	19%	24%
	BI	64	64	62	60	62	56	55	65	57	64	59
	DP	12	15	16	21	16	22	16	11	16	17	17
# SURVEYED		199	228	249	230	236	239	231	263	252	189	176

****

SPANKING AS GOOD DISCIPLINE

TABLE I: SPANKING AS GOOD DISCIPLINE -- BY TOTAL POPULATION

Question: Do you strongly agree, agree, disagree, or strongly disagree that it is sometimes necessary to discipline a child with a good, hard spanking? NOTE: Question not asked in 1972-1985.

Responses: SA = Strongly agree; AG = Agree; DA = Disagree; SD = Strongly disagree

	YEAR		
RESPONSE	'86	'88	'89
SA	28%	31%	32%
AG	56	49	46
DA	13	15	17
SD	3	6	6
# SURVEYED	1460	978	994

TABLE II: SPANKING AS GOOD DISCIPLINE -- BY SEX

Question: Do you strongly agree, agree, disagree, or strongly disagree that it is sometimes necessary to discipline a child with a good, hard spanking? NOTE: Question not asked in 1972-1985.

Responses: SA = Strongly agree; AG = Agree; DA = Disagree; SD = Strongly disagree

SEX	RESP	'86	'88	'89
M	SA	26%	30%	35%
	AG	59	53	47
	DA	12	14	13
	SD	3	4	4
# SURVEYED		613	433	424

SEX	RESP	'86	'88	'89
F	SA	29%	32%	29%
	AG	54	46	45
	DA	15	16	20
	SD	3	7	6
# SURVEYED		847	545	570

TABLE III: SPANKING AS GOOD DISCIPLINE -- BY RACE

Question: Do you strongly agree, agree, disagree, or strongly disagree that it is sometimes necessary to discipline a child with a good, hard spanking? NOTE: Question not asked in 1972-1985.

Responses: SA = Strongly agree; AG = Agree; DA = Disagree; SD = Strongly disagree

RACE	RESP	'86	'88	'89
WHITE	SA	26%	28%	30%
	AG	56	50	47
	DA	14	16	18
	SD	3	6	6
# SURVEYED		1242	820	855

RACE	RESP	'86	'88	'89
BLACK	SA	36%	46%	47%
	AG	54	46	39
	DA	9	6	10
	SD	1	2	5
# SURVEYED		182	125	101

RACE	RESP	'86	'88	'89
OTHER	SA	31%	48%	34%
	AG	53	30	42
	DA	8	9	21
	SD	8	12	3
# SURVEYED		36	33	38

TABLE IV: SPANKING AS GOOD DISCIPLINE -- BY AGE

Question: Do you strongly agree, agree, disagree, or strongly disagree that it is sometimes necessary to discipline a child with a good, hard spanking? NOTE: Question not asked in 1972-1985.

Responses: SA = Strongly agree; AG = Agree; DA = Disagree; SD = Strongly disagree

AGE	RESP	'86	'88	'89
18-23	SA	21%	21%	29%
	AG	63	54	48
	DA	14	21	15
	SD	3	4	8
# SURVEYED		107	92	84
24-29	SA	30%	32%	22%
	AG	55	49	51
	DA	14	13	20
	SD	0	5	7
# SURVEYED		217	149	144
30-35	SA	29%	25%	26%
	AG	55	57	49
	DA	12	13	16
	SD	5	5	9
# SURVEYED		221	130	140

AGE	RESP	'86	'88	'89
36-41	SA	31%	30%	37%
	AG	53	46	48
	DA	14	15	12
	SD	3	9	3
# SURVEYED		188	125	127
42-47	SA	21%	36%	29%
	AG	59	43	45
	DA	14	17	19
	SD	5	5	6
# SURVEYED		138	107	108
48-53	SA	34%	37%	33%
	AG	51	47	46
	DA	11	13	15
	SD	4	3	5
# SURVEYED		106	62	84

AGE	RESP	'86	'88	'89
54-59	SA	22%	39%	42%
	AG	67	47	36
	DA	7	12	19
	SD	3	2	3
# SURVEYED		98	51	72
60-65	SA	28%	31%	37%
	AG	57	45	40
	DA	13	19	22
	SD	3	5	1
# SURVEYED		115	74	68
66+	SA	28%	33%	37%
	AG	53	48	43
	DA	16	13	16
	SD	3	7	4
# SURVEYED		263	187	164

****

MOST PEOPLE DEAL FAIRLY

TABLE I: MOST PEOPLE DEAL FAIRLY -- BY TOTAL POPULATION

Question: Do you think that most people would try to take advantage of you if they got a chance, or would they try to be fair? NOTE: Question not asked in 1974, 1977, 1982, 1985.

Responses: AD = Would take advantage of you; FR = Would try to be fair; DP = Depends (volunteered)

	YEAR											
RESPONSE	'72	'73	'75	'76	'78	'80	'83	'84	'86	'87	'88	'89
AD	34%	38%	31%	36%	30%	35%	35%	35%	34%	37%	34%	37%
FR	60	58	62	59	65	61	60	62	63	58	61	58
DP	6	5	7	4	5	4	5	3	4	4	5	5
# SURVEYED	1592	1495	1476	1491	1515	1450	1585	1467	1456	1445	984	1029

TABLE II: MOST PEOPLE DEAL FAIRLY -- BY SEX

Question: Do you think that most people would try to take advantage of you if they got a chance, or would they try to be fair? NOTE: Question not asked in 1974, 1977, 1982, 1985.

Responses: AD = Would take advantage of you; FR = Would try to be fair; DP = Depends (volunteered)

		YEAR											
SEX	RESP	'72	'73	'75	'76	'78	'80	'83	'84	'86	'87	'88	'89
M	AD	37%	41%	33%	40%	32%	38%	37%	37%	37%	38%	36%	40%
	FR	57	54	59	56	63	59	58	60	60	56	58	55
	DP	6	5	7	4	5	4	5	3	3	5	6	5
# SURVEYED		796	695	661	668	637	632	683	595	613	636	435	440
SEX	RESP	'72	'73	'75	'76	'78	'80	'83	'84	'86	'87	'88	'89
F	AD	32%	35%	29%	33%	28%	33%	33%	33%	31%	37%	32%	34%
	FR	63	61	65	63	66	62	61	64	65	60	63	61
	DP	6	5	7	4	6	5	6	3	4	3	5	6
# SURVEYED		796	800	815	823	878	818	902	872	843	809	549	589

TABLE III: MOST PEOPLE DEAL FAIRLY -- BY RACE

Question: Do you think that most people would try to take advantage of you if they got a chance, or would they try to be fair? NOTE: Question not asked in 1974, 1977, 1982, 1985.

Responses: AD = Would take advantage of you; FR = Would try to be fair; DP = Depends (volunteered)

		YEAR											
RACE	RESP	'72	'73	'75	'76	'78	'80	'83	'84	'86	'87	'88	'89
WHITE	AD	31%	34%	28%	33%	26%	32%	31%	32%	29%	33%	30%	33%
	FR	65	61	65	63	69	64	64	65	67	63	64	62
	DP	5	4	7	4	5	4	5	3	4	4	6	5
# SURVEYED		1330	1300	1310	1354	1344	1302	1406	1245	1241	1208	829	879
RACE	RESP	'72	'73	'75	'76	'78	'80	'83	'84	'86	'87	'88	'89
BLACK	AD	52%	61%	55%	70%	63%	61%	68%	51%	63%	63%	58%	62%
	FR	35	31	35	23	32	32	24	43	33	30	40	34
	DP	14	8	10	6	6	7	7	6	4	7	3	5
# SURVEYED		259	182	163	128	155	138	164	170	181	187	113	110
RACE	RESP	'72	'73	'75	'76	'78	'80	'83	'84	'86	'87	'88	'89
OTHER	AD	67%	38%	33%	22%	44%	40%	20%	42%	50%	46%	45%	45%
	FR	33	62	67	78	50	60	73	54	47	54	50	45
	DP	0	0	0	0	6	0	7	4	3	0	5	10
# SURVEYED		3	13	3	9	16	10	15	52	34	50	42	40

TABLE IV: MOST PEOPLE DEAL FAIRLY -- BY AGE

Question: Do you think that most people would try to take advantage of you if they got a chance, or would they try to be fair? NOTE: Question not asked in 1974, 1977, 1982, 1985.

Responses: AD = Would take advantage of you; FR = Would try to be fair; DP = Depends (volunteered)

		YEAR											
AGE	RESP	'72	'73	'75	'76	'78	'80	'83	'84	'86	'87	'88	'89
18-23	AD	52%	48%	43%	46%	49%	52%	50%	45%	49%	54%	38%	56%
	FR	40	47	53	48	47	44	45	53	47	44	55	37
	DP	8	5	4	6	4	4	6	2	4	2	7	8
# SURVEYED		167	171	173	162	160	155	127	161	108	126	91	93
AGE	RESP	'72	'73	'75	'76	'78	'80	'83	'84	'86	'87	'88	'89
24-29	AD	43%	42%	30%	41%	34%	46%	40%	46%	36%	52%	40%	49%
	FR	51	53	63	54	60	53	55	51	61	45	54	42
	DP	6	4	7	5	6	1	4	3	4	4	6	9
# SURVEYED		229	212	231	226	240	201	287	231	214	193	143	142

TABLE IV: MOST PEOPLE DEAL FAIRLY -- BY AGE (Continued)

Question: Do you think that most people would try to take advantage of you if they got a chance, or would they try to be fair? NOTE: Question not asked in 1974, 1977, 1982, 1985.

Responses: AD = Would take advantage of you; FR = Would try to be fair; DP = Depends (volunteered)

		YEAR											
AGE	RESP	'72	'73	'75	'76	'78	'80	'83	'84	'86	'87	'88	'89
30-35	AD	26%	40%	32%	41%	29%	45%	38%	39%	39%	41%	41%	32%
	FR	67	57	60	55	65	50	57	58	58	55	54	66
	DP	6	4	8	4	7	5	5	4	3	4	5	3
# SURVEYED		186	164	167	186	228	212	235	197	219	217	126	146
AGE	RESP	'72	'73	'75	'76	'78	'80	'83	'84	'86	'87	'88	'89
36-41	AD	28%	35%	33%	33%	30%	32%	30%	33%	34%	33%	30%	34%
	FR	66	63	59	65	67	61	63	64	63	61	63	62
	DP	6	2	8	2	3	7	7	3	4	7	7	5
# SURVEYED		126	174	152	156	160	147	169	187	188	183	126	133
AGE	RESP	'72	'73	'75	'76	'78	'80	'83	'84	'86	'87	'88	'89
42-47	AD	30%	35%	22%	32%	29%	33%	31%	29%	32%	37%	35%	34%
	FR	65	61	72	65	64	64	67	67	63	60	62	59
	DP	5	4	6	4	8	3	2	3	5	3	4	7
# SURVEYED		182	146	143	114	118	117	144	126	139	155	104	106
AGE	RESP	'72	'73	'75	'76	'78	'80	'83	'84	'86	'87	'88	'89
48-53	AD	31%	37%	28%	39%	22%	27%	32%	28%	29%	36%	37%	39%
	FR	63	59	68	58	69	69	63	71	67	61	63	57
	DP	5	4	4	3	9	3	5	1	4	3	0	4
# SURVEYED		185	150	141	132	132	121	116	102	106	126	57	96
AGE	RESP	'72	'73	'75	'76	'78	'80	'83	'84	'86	'87	'88	'89
54-59	AD	29%	32%	29%	30%	30%	26%	36%	29%	33%	35%	35%	37%
	FR	65	63	62	65	67	66	58	68	66	59	62	60
	DP	5	5	9	5	3	7	6	3	1	6	3	3
# SURVEYED		156	156	123	128	135	136	131	114	96	98	65	62
AGE	RESP	'72	'73	'75	'76	'78	'80	'83	'84	'86	'87	'88	'89
60-65	AD	24%	32%	30%	33%	27%	26%	33%	28%	23%	28%	29%	36%
	FR	69	62	58	63	68	71	61	71	75	68	65	59
	DP	7	7	13	4	5	3	6	2	3	4	5	5
# SURVEYED		142	120	111	134	106	115	132	112	115	98	78	75
AGE	RESP	'72	'73	'75	'76	'78	'80	'83	'84	'86	'87	'88	'89
66+	AD	36%	33%	30%	30%	21%	21%	26%	26%	30%	24%	26%	24%
	FR	59	59	63	65	76	74	68	69	65	70	68	72
	DP	5	8	7	4	3	5	6	6	6	5	5	4
# SURVEYED		214	198	230	247	229	237	237	231	264	245	190	174

****

MOST PEOPLE ARE HELPFUL

TABLE I: MOST PEOPLE ARE HELPFUL -- BY TOTAL POPULATION

Question: Would you say that most of the time people try to be helpful, or that mostly they are just looking out for themselves? NOTE: Question not asked in 1974, 1977, 1982, 1985.

Responses: HL = Try to be helpful; NH = Just look out for themselves; DP = Depends (volunteered)

	YEAR											
RESPONSE	'72	'73	'75	'76	'78	'80	'83	'84	'86	'87	'88	'89
HL	47%	47%	56%	43%	60%	49%	58%	52%	56%	48%	50%	50%
NH	47	49	37	51	35	47	38	44	39	48	45	45
DP	6	4	7	6	5	4	4	4	5	5	5	5
# SURVEYED	1589	1497	1480	1493	1523	1456	1588	1467	1458	1456	988	1029

TABLE II: MOST PEOPLE ARE HELPFUL -- BY SEX

Question: Would you say that most of the time people try to be helpful, or that mostly they are just looking out for themselves? NOTE: Question not asked in 1974, 1977, 1982, 1985.

Responses: HL = Try to be helpful; NH = Just look out for themselves; DP = Depends (volunteered)

		YEAR											
SEX	RESP	'72	'73	'75	'76	'78	'80	'83	'84	'86	'87	'88	'89
M	HL	40%	44%	52%	40%	52%	46%	54%	49%	52%	45%	48%	46%
	NH	52	53	42	55	43	49	41	48	43	50	48	49
	DP	8	4	6	5	5	4	5	3	5	5	5	5
# SURVEYED		796	697	665	666	640	635	686	596	616	637	434	440
SEX	RESP	'72	'73	'75	'76	'78	'80	'83	'84	'86	'87	'88	'89
F	HL	54%	50%	60%	46%	65%	51%	60%	54%	59%	50%	52%	53%
	NH	41	47	33	47	30	45	35	42	35	46	44	41
	DP	5	4	7	7	5	4	4	4	6	5	5	5
# SURVEYED		793	800	815	827	883	821	902	871	842	819	554	589

TABLE III: MOST PEOPLE ARE HELPFUL -- BY RACE

Question: Would you say that most of the time people try to be helpful, or that mostly they are just looking out for themselves? NOTE: Question not asked in 1974, 1977, 1982, 1985.

Responses: HL = Try to be helpful; NH = Just look out for themselves; DP = Depends (volunteered)

		YEAR											
RACE	RESP	'72	'73	'75	'76	'78	'80	'83	'84	'86	'87	'88	'89
WHITE	HL	50%	50%	58%	46%	63%	52%	60%	56%	59%	51%	53%	53%
	NH	44	47	36	49	32	45	35	41	36	44	42	42
	DP	6	3	6	6	5	4	4	3	5	4	5	5
# SURVEYED		1333	1305	1315	1356	1353	1306	1407	1245	1242	1217	829	878
RACE	RESP	'72	'73	'75	'76	'78	'80	'83	'84	'86	'87	'88	'89
BLACK	HL	33%	22%	41%	20%	31%	26%	36%	26%	38%	27%	34%	35%
	NH	58	68	47	73	61	65	60	66	58	66	63	60
	DP	9	10	12	7	8	9	4	8	4	8	3	5
# SURVEYED		253	179	161	128	154	140	164	170	180	186	115	110
RACE	RESP	'72	'73	'75	'76	'78	'80	'83	'84	'86	'87	'88	'89
OTHER	HL	67%	31%	25%	33%	56%	40%	59%	37%	39%	38%	41%	34%
	NH	33	62	50	44	31	50	29	62	53	58	57	63
	DP	0	8	25	22	13	10	12	2	8	4	2	2
# SURVEYED		3	13	4	9	16	10	17	52	36	53	44	41

TABLE IV: MOST PEOPLE ARE HELPFUL -- BY AGE

Question: Would you say that most of the time people try to be helpful, or that mostly they are just looking out for themselves? NOTE: Question not asked in 1974, 1977, 1982, 1985.

Responses: HL = Try to be helpful; NH = Just look out for themselves; DP = Depends (volunteered)

		YEAR											
AGE	RESP	'72	'73	'75	'76	'78	'80	'83	'84	'86	'87	'88	'89
18-23	HL	34%	34%	49%	35%	49%	32%	47%	41%	52%	37%	35%	32%
	NH	60	63	47	60	49	65	48	56	41	62	59	61
	DP	6	4	4	6	2	3	5	3	7	1	5	8
# SURVEYED		166	171	172	161	162	155	126	160	108	125	91	92
AGE	RESP	'72	'73	'75	'76	'78	'80	'83	'84	'86	'87	'88	'89
24-29	HL	38%	47%	57%	37%	52%	42%	52%	46%	47%	39%	48%	44%
	NH	58	50	37	54	44	55	45	51	45	57	49	50
	DP	5	3	7	9	4	2	2	3	8	4	3	6
# SURVEYED		226	212	229	225	243	202	286	232	218	192	144	142
AGE	RESP	'72	'73	'75	'76	'78	'80	'83	'84	'86	'87	'88	'89
30-35	HL	48%	44%	54%	47%	63%	45%	55%	50%	50%	43%	48%	49%
	NH	43	53	38	49	32	52	41	43	45	55	48	48
	DP	9	3	9	4	6	2	4	7	5	2	5	3
# SURVEYED		185	166	170	186	230	212	236	198	218	218	128	145
AGE	RESP	'72	'73	'75	'76	'78	'80	'83	'84	'86	'87	'88	'89
36-41	HL	54%	51%	58%	46%	64%	51%	63%	55%	59%	50%	52%	52%
	NH	41	45	36	48	28	46	35	42	39	46	42	44
	DP	5	4	6	6	8	3	2	3	2	4	6	5
# SURVEYED		128	175	154	157	160	149	173	187	188	186	124	133
AGE	RESP	'72	'73	'75	'76	'78	'80	'83	'84	'86	'87	'88	'89
42-47	HL	55%	53%	64%	52%	57%	56%	58%	53%	59%	58%	58%	55%
	NH	40	42	28	43	40	38	39	44	34	36	41	42
	DP	5	4	8	5	3	7	3	2	7	6	1	4
# SURVEYED		182	146	142	114	118	117	143	126	138	154	104	106
AGE	RESP	'72	'73	'75	'76	'78	'80	'83	'84	'86	'87	'88	'89
48-53	HL	53%	48%	64%	41%	65%	62%	63%	56%	56%	47%	49%	50%
	NH	39	47	33	54	29	33	32	39	41	47	46	46
	DP	8	5	3	5	6	5	5	5	4	6	5	4
# SURVEYED		184	151	140	132	132	123	116	101	106	126	57	96
AGE	RESP	'72	'73	'75	'76	'78	'80	'83	'84	'86	'87	'88	'89
54-59	HL	47%	44%	53%	45%	66%	55%	61%	55%	58%	49%	51%	62%
	NH	46	53	38	49	29	40	37	43	37	46	45	33
	DP	7	4	10	5	4	5	2	2	5	5	5	5
# SURVEYED		156	154	125	128	136	135	132	114	97	98	65	63

TABLE IV: MOST PEOPLE ARE HELPFUL -- BY AGE (Continued)

Question: Would you say that most of the time people try to be helpful, or that mostly they are just looking out for themselves? NOTE: Question not asked in 1974, 1977, 1982, 1985.

Responses: HL = Try to be helpful; NH = Just look out for themselves; DP = Depends (volunteered)

		YEAR											
AGE	RESP	'72	'73	'75	'76	'78	'80	'83	'84	'86	'87	'88	'89
60-65	HL	54%	49%	58%	41%	56%	52%	67%	56%	63%	49%	48%	56%
	NH	43	48	33	53	40	42	29	42	34	45	47	43
	DP	4	3	9	6	5	6	5	3	3	7	5	1
# SURVEYED		141	120	112	134	106	117	132	113	114	101	79	75
AGE	RESP	'72	'73	'75	'76	'78	'80	'83	'84	'86	'87	'88	'89
66+	HL	47%	54%	54%	48%	65%	54%	61%	59%	64%	55%	56%	57%
	NH	46	42	39	46	28	40	30	37	31	37	39	35
	DP	6	4	6	7	7	6	9	5	5	8	6	8
# SURVEYED		216	198	231	250	229	237	237	230	264	252	192	175

****

WORK HARD OR LUCK HELPS GET AHEAD

TABLE I: WORK HARD OR LUCK HELPS GET AHEAD -- BY TOTAL POPULATION

Question: Some people say that people get ahead by their own hard work; others say that lucky breaks or help from other people are more important. Which do you think is more important? NOTE: Question not asked in 1972, 1975, 1978, 1983, 1986.

Responses: HW = Hard work most important WL = Hard work, luck equally important
LK = Luck most important

	YEAR										
RESPONSE	'73	'74	'76	'77	'80	'82	'84	'85	'87	'88	'89
HW	66%	62%	63%	61%	64%	61%	67%	66%	66%	67%	66%
WL	24	29	24	28	28	26	18	19	19	21	20
LK	10	9	13	10	8	13	15	15	15	12	14
# SURVEYED	1478	1452	1485	1516	1454	1483	1459	1509	1451	971	1021

TABLE II: WORK HARD OR LUCK HELPS GET AHEAD -- BY SEX

Question: Some people say that people get ahead by their own hard work; others say that lucky breaks or help from other people are more important. Which do you think is more important? NOTE: Question not asked in 1972, 1975, 1978, 1983, 1986.

Responses: HW = Hard work most important WL = Hard work, luck equally important
LK = Luck most important

		YEAR										
SEX	RESP	'73	'74	'76	'77	'80	'82	'84	'85	'87	'88	'89
M	HW	65%	59%	58%	58%	61%	60%	65%	66%	65%	64%	64%
	WL	25	31	25	29	31	24	18	18	18	21	19
	LK	11	10	17	13	8	16	18	16	17	15	17
# SURVEYED		684	671	664	685	633	632	593	679	636	397	443
SEX	RESP	'73	'74	'76	'77	'80	'82	'84	'85	'87	'88	'89
F	HW	67%	65%	67%	64%	66%	62%	68%	67%	67%	69%	68%
	WL	24	27	23	28	26	26	18	20	19	21	21
	LK	10	8	10	8	8	11	13	13	13	10	12
# SURVEYED		794	781	821	831	821	851	866	830	815	574	578

TABLE III: WORK HARD OR LUCK HELPS GET AHEAD -- BY RACE

Question: Some people say that people get ahead by their own hard work; others say that lucky breaks or help from other people are more important. Which do you think is more important? NOTE: Question not asked in 1972, 1975, 1978, 1983, 1986.

Responses: HW = Hard work most important WL = Hard work, luck equally important
LK = Luck most important

		YEAR										
RACE	RESP	'73	'74	'76	'77	'80	'82	'84	'85	'87	'88	'89
WHITE	HW	67%	63%	64%	62%	64%	63%	68%	67%	67%	68%	65%
	WL	24	29	23	28	28	24	18	19	19	20	20
	LK	10	9	13	10	8	13	14	13	14	11	15
# SURVEYED		1284	1273	1348	1327	1304	1303	1242	1322	1211	800	880
RACE	RESP	'73	'74	'76	'77	'80	'82	'84	'85	'87	'88	'89
BLACK	HW	61%	58%	46%	53%	60%	52%	64%	57%	61%	60%	71%
	WL	24	33	33	32	28	32	16	19	20	27	22
	LK	14	9	21	16	12	16	20	24	19	13	8
# SURVEYED		181	172	128	174	140	153	167	144	189	128	102
RACE	RESP	'73	'74	'76	'77	'80	'82	'84	'85	'87	'88	'89
OTHER	HW	54%	71%	78%	87%	70%	44%	60%	70%	67%	65%	72%
	WL	31	29	11	0	30	41	18	7	10	16	15
	LK	15	0	11	13	0	15	22	23	24	19	13
# SURVEYED		13	7	9	15	10	27	50	43	51	43	39

TABLE IV: WORK HARD OR LUCK HELPS GET AHEAD -- BY AGE

Question: Some people say that people get ahead by their own hard work; others say that lucky breaks or help from other people are more important. Which do you think is more important? NOTE: Question not asked in 1972, 1975, 1978, 1983, 1986.

Responses: HW = Hard work most important WL = Hard work, luck equally important
LK = Luck most important

		YEAR										
AGE	RESP	'73	'74	'76	'77	'80	'82	'84	'85	'87	'88	'89
18-23	HW	70%	64%	65%	56%	63%	56%	67%	69%	73%	64%	67%
	WL	19	22	19	30	25	30	21	20	15	19	16
	LK	11	14	16	13	12	14	11	11	12	17	16
# SURVEYED		168	165	161	164	155	148	159	131	124	95	97

TABLE IV: WORK HARD OR LUCK HELPS GET AHEAD -- BY AGE (Continued)

Question: Some people say that people get ahead by their own hard work; others say that lucky breaks or help from other people are more important. Which do you think is more important? NOTE: Question not asked in 1972, 1975, 1978, 1983, 1986.

Responses: HW = Hard work most important; WL = Hard work, luck equally important; LK = Luck most important

		YEAR										
AGE	RESP	'73	'74	'76	'77	'80	'82	'84	'85	'87	'88	'89
24-29	HW	63%	61%	57%	66%	69%	60%	74%	68%	68%	67%	66%
	WL	25	28	26	25	24	23	13	20	15	19	22
	LK	12	12	17	9	6	17	14	12	17	14	12
# SURVEYED		208	207	225	204	201	244	232	215	193	133	116
AGE	RESP	'73	'74	'76	'77	'80	'82	'84	'85	'87	'88	'89
30-35	HW	69%	60%	63%	62%	64%	62%	67%	69%	69%	61%	65%
	WL	21	34	24	26	30	28	21	16	15	27	21
	LK	9	7	12	13	6	10	12	14	16	11	13
# SURVEYED		163	173	186	188	214	201	199	208	219	131	135
AGE	RESP	'73	'74	'76	'77	'80	'82	'84	'85	'87	'88	'89
36-41	HW	68%	65%	62%	63%	64%	65%	57%	67%	68%	73%	67%
	WL	26	32	26	31	29	25	18	20	21	23	21
	LK	6	3	12	6	7	10	25	13	11	5	12
# SURVEYED		175	148	155	167	148	143	187	183	184	132	133
AGE	RESP	'73	'74	'76	'77	'80	'82	'84	'85	'87	'88	'89
42-47	HW	65%	65%	69%	60%	55%	61%	68%	64%	73%	67%	64%
	WL	27	29	21	29	38	24	18	24	15	20	21
	LK	8	6	10	10	7	15	15	12	11	13	16
# SURVEYED		144	148	113	144	113	119	124	124	157	101	107
AGE	RESP	'73	'74	'76	'77	'80	'82	'84	'85	'87	'88	'89
48-53	HW	62%	56%	67%	57%	63%	59%	75%	62%	63%	69%	59%
	WL	28	32	25	33	33	26	14	16	17	18	24
	LK	10	11	8	10	5	14	11	22	20	12	17
# SURVEYED		146	142	132	151	123	111	101	129	125	65	94
AGE	RESP	'73	'74	'76	'77	'80	'82	'84	'85	'87	'88	'89
54-59	HW	67%	61%	54%	59%	63%	60%	69%	63%	53%	58%	68%
	WL	22	32	30	28	24	24	18	22	28	28	19
	LK	11	7	16	13	13	15	13	15	20	13	13
# SURVEYED		156	135	128	168	136	143	113	130	97	53	62

TABLE IV: WORK HARD OR LUCK HELPS GET AHEAD -- BY AGE (Continued)

Question: Some people say that people get ahead by their own hard work; others say that lucky breaks or help from other people are more important. Which do you think is more important? NOTE: Question not asked in 1972, 1975, 1978, 1983, 1986.

Responses: HW = Hard work most important WL = Hard work, luck equally important
LK = Luck most important

		YEAR										
AGE	RESP	'73	'74	'76	'77	'80	'82	'84	'85	'87	'88	'89
60-65	HW	70%	63%	59%	58%	65%	62%	59%	70%	63%	68%	69%
	WL	19	30	28	30	24	27	23	17	20	23	16
	LK	10	8	13	12	11	11	18	13	17	10	16
# SURVEYED		118	104	134	116	117	116	110	127	100	84	77
AGE	RESP	'73	'74	'76	'77	'80	'82	'84	'85	'87	'88	'89
66+	HW	60%	65%	69%	66%	66%	65%	66%	64%	63%	70%	70%
	WL	27	26	19	26	28	24	20	18	25	17	17
	LK	13	9	12	8	7	12	14	18	12	14	13
# SURVEYED		196	224	245	207	238	249	228	255	248	174	197

****

MOST PEOPLE ARE TRUSTWORTHY

TABLE I: MOST PEOPLE ARE TRUSTWORTHY -- BY TOTAL POPULATION

Question: Generally speaking, would you say that most people could be trusted or that you can't be too careful in dealing with people? NOTE: Question not asked in 1974, 1977, 1982, 1985.

Responses: TR = Most people can be trusted; TC = Can't be too careful; DP = Depends (volunteered)

	YEAR											
RESPONSE	'72	'73	'75	'76	'78	'80	'83	'84	'86	'87	'88	'89
TR	46%	46%	40%	44%	39%	46%	37%	48%	38%	44%	39%	41%
TC	50	51	56	52	57	51	59	50	60	52	57	55
DP	4	3	4	4	4	4	4	3	3	4	4	4
# SURVEYED	1597	1499	1478	1495	1528	1461	800	1461	1466	1459	990	1030

TABLE II: MOST PEOPLE ARE TRUSTWORTHY -- BY SEX

Question: Generally speaking, would you say that most people could be trusted or that you can't be too careful in dealing with people? NOTE: Question not asked in 1974, 1977, 1982, 1985.

Responses: TR = Most people can be trusted; TC = Can't be too careful; DP = Depends (volunteered)

		YEAR											
SEX	RESP	'72	'73	'75	'76	'78	'80	'83	'84	'86	'87	'88	'89
M	TR	48%	49%	45%	46%	44%	46%	41%	49%	41%	47%	42%	41%
	TC	48	49	51	51	52	50	54	47	57	48	53	54
	DP	4	3	4	3	4	4	5	4	2	5	5	5
# SURVEYED		804	698	665	668	642	636	487	596	620	640	433	441
SEX	RESP	'72	'73	'75	'76	'78	'80	'83	'84	'86	'87	'88	'89
F	TR	44%	44%	35%	44%	35%	45%	30%	47%	35%	42%	36%	41%
	TC	53	53	60	52	60	51	66	51	62	55	60	56
	DP	3	3	4	4	5	4	4	2	3	3	4	3
# SURVEYED		793	801	813	827	886	825	313	865	846	819	557	589

TABLE III: MOST PEOPLE ARE TRUSTWORTHY -- BY RACE

Question: Generally speaking, would you say that most people could be trusted or that you can't be too careful in dealing with people? NOTE: Question not asked in 1974, 1977, 1982, 1985.

Responses: TR = Most people can be trusted; TC = Can't be too careful; DP = Depends (volunteered)

		YEAR											
RACE	RESP	'72	'73	'75	'76	'78	'80	'83	'84	'86	'87	'88	'89
WHITE	TR	51%	50%	42%	47%	42%	48%	40%	52%	41%	49%	42%	45%
	TC	46	47	53	49	53	48	56	45	56	47	53	51
	DP	4	3	4	4	4	4	4	3	3	4	5	4
# SURVEYED		1336	1304	1312	1358	1356	1311	709	1240	1246	1218	833	878
RACE	RESP	'72	'73	'75	'76	'78	'80	'83	'84	'86	'87	'88	'89
BLACK	TR	23%	16%	17%	13%	15%	21%	10%	21%	15%	16%	17%	14%
	TC	74	82	80	83	83	74	86	78	83	82	82	82
	DP	4	2	4	4	3	6	5	2	2	2	2	5
# SURVEYED		257	182	162	128	157	140	83	169	183	188	115	110
RACE	RESP	'72	'73	'75	'76	'78	'80	'83	'84	'86	'87	'88	'89
OTHER	TR	25%	46%	75%	33%	20%	40%	25%	35%	22%	26%	36%	24%
	TC	75	54	25	67	73	60	50	63	76	70	62	71
	DP	0	0	0	0	7	0	25	2	3	4	2	5
# SURVEYED		4	13	4	9	15	10	8	52	37	53	42	42

TABLE IV: MOST PEOPLE ARE TRUSTWORTHY -- BY AGE

Question: Generally speaking, would you say that most people could be trusted or that you can't be too careful in dealing with people? NOTE: Question not asked in 1974, 1977, 1982, 1985.

Responses: TR = Most people can be trusted; TC = Can't be too careful; DP = Depends (volunteered)

		YEAR											
AGE	RESP	'72	'73	'75	'76	'78	'80	'83	'84	'86	'87	'88	'89
18-23	TR	29%	40%	37%	30%	31%	23%	37%	37%	31%	26%	30%	19%
	TC	64	57	58	67	63	74	62	61	67	73	68	75
	DP	7	4	5	2	6	3	2	3	3	2	1	5
# SURVEYED		167	171	173	161	162	155	52	160	108	125	92	93

TABLE IV: MOST PEOPLE ARE TRUSTWORTHY -- BY AGE (Continued)

Question: Generally speaking, would you say that most people could be trusted or that you can't be too careful in dealing with people? NOTE: Question not asked in 1974, 1977, 1982, 1985.

Responses: TR = Most people can be trusted; TC = Can't be too careful; DP = Depends (volunteered)

		YEAR											
AGE	RESP	'72	'73	'75	'76	'78	'80	'83	'84	'86	'87	'88	'89
24-29	TR	45%	40%	37%	37%	36%	41%	35%	39%	36%	36%	30%	32%
	TC	53	55	59	60	60	54	63	59	60	61	66	65
	DP	2	4	4	3	4	4	2	3	3	3	3	3
# SURVEYED		228	211	231	226	244	201	137	231	217	193	143	141
AGE	RESP	'72	'73	'75	'76	'78	'80	'83	'84	'86	'87	'88	'89
30-35	TR	48%	47%	38%	46%	43%	40%	33%	44%	34%	45%	35%	41%
	TC	49	50	56	50	51	55	66	53	63	51	57	57
	DP	4	4	6	4	5	4	2	3	3	4	8	2
# SURVEYED		185	167	170	186	230	215	123	198	221	221	127	146
AGE	RESP	'72	'73	'75	'76	'78	'80	'83	'84	'86	'87	'88	'89
36-41	TR	58%	49%	45%	48%	39%	56%	38%	56%	45%	49%	50%	46%
	TC	40	50	52	47	57	41	57	40	53	47	48	49
	DP	2	1	3	4	4	3	5	3	2	4	2	5
# SURVEYED		126	175	154	158	159	149	108	186	187	185	126	132
AGE	RESP	'72	'73	'75	'76	'78	'80	'83	'84	'86	'87	'88	'89
42-47	TR	60%	55%	45%	50%	42%	53%	48%	57%	40%	50%	41%	47%
	TC	38	42	48	47	52	43	42	42	57	45	53	46
	DP	2	3	7	3	6	4	10	2	2	5	6	7
# SURVEYED		186	146	141	113	119	117	67	125	141	157	104	106
AGE	RESP	'72	'73	'75	'76	'78	'80	'83	'84	'86	'87	'88	'89
48-53	TR	47%	46%	50%	45%	47%	55%	43%	62%	34%	50%	42%	44%
	TC	51	53	50	50	47	40	51	37	64	46	56	51
	DP	3	1	0	5	5	5	7	1	2	4	2	5
# SURVEYED		186	151	141	132	133	123	61	102	108	126	57	96
AGE	RESP	'72	'73	'75	'76	'78	'80	'83	'84	'86	'87	'88	'89
54-59	TR	51%	45%	43%	49%	49%	48%	39%	48%	44%	47%	45%	50%
	TC	44	52	54	47	50	48	58	50	52	49	50	48
	DP	4	4	3	5	1	4	3	3	4	4	5	2
# SURVEYED		156	155	125	129	137	136	59	113	99	98	66	62
AGE	RESP	'72	'73	'75	'76	'78	'80	'83	'84	'86	'87	'88	'89
60-65	TR	45%	1%	34%	49%	32%	46%	39%	56%	38%	47%	40%	43%
	TC	50	46	61	46	64	50	54	43	59	49	55	56
	DP	4	2	5	5	4	3	7	1	3	3	5	1
# SURVEYED		143	121	110	133	107	119	61	110	115	99	80	75

TABLE IV: MOST PEOPLE ARE TRUSTWORTHY -- BY AGE (Continued)

Question: Generally speaking, would you say that most people could be trusted or that you can't be too careful in dealing with people? NOTE: Question not asked in 1974, 1977, 1982, 1985.

Responses: TR = Most people can be trusted; TC = Can't be too careful; DP = Depends (volunteered)

		YEAR											
AGE	RESP	'72	'73	'75	'76	'78	'80	'83	'84	'86	'87	'88	'89
66+	TR	38%	46%	33%	47%	35%	51%	33%	46%	36%	45%	40%	47%
	TC	58	51	62	49	61	46	63	51	61	49	55	49
	DP	4	3	4	4	4	2	4	3	3	5	5	4
# SURVEYED		215	198	228	251	230	237	127	231	264	251	191	177

****

HUMAN CONDITION GETTING WORSE

TABLE I: HUMAN CONDITION GETTING WORSE -- BY TOTAL POPULATION

Question: Do you agree with the following statement? In spite of what some people say, the lot (situation/condition) of the average man is getting worse, not better. NOTE: Question not asked in 1972, 1975, 1978, 1983, 1986.

Responses: AG = Agree; DS = Disagree

	YEAR										
RESPONSE	'73	'74	'76	'77	'80	'82	'84	'85	'87	'88	'89
AG	56%	61%	61%	56%	69%	68%	57%	50%	64%	62%	59%
DS	44	39	39	44	31	32	43	50	36	38	41
# SURVEYED	1463	1436	1447	1463	1435	1431	1438	1467	1433	929	989

TABLE II: HUMAN CONDITION GETTING WORSE -- BY SEX

Question: Do you agree with the following statement? In spite of what some people say, the lot (situation/condition) of the average man is getting worse, not better. NOTE: Question not asked in 1972, 1975, 1978, 1983, 1986.

Responses: AG = Agree; DS = Disagree

		YEAR										
SEX	RESP	'73	'74	'76	'77	'80	'82	'84	'85	'87	'88	'89
M	AG	51%	59%	57%	54%	66%	66%	53%	47%	60%	60%	54%
	DS	49	41	43	46	34	34	47	53	40	40	46
# SURVEYED		686	674	646	670	631	610	590	668	633	388	433
SEX	RESP	'73	'74	'76	'77	'80	'82	'84	'85	'87	'88	'89
F	AG	59%	63%	63%	58%	71%	69%	60%	51%	67%	64%	64%
	DS	41	37	37	42	29	31	40	49	33	36	36
# SURVEYED		777	762	801	793	804	821	848	799	800	541	556

TABLE III: HUMAN CONDITION GETTING WORSE -- BY RACE

Question: Do you agree with the following statement? In spite of what some people say, the lot (situation/condition) of the average man is getting worse, not better. NOTE: Question not asked in 1972, 1975, 1978, 1983, 1986.

Responses: AG = Agree; DS = Disagree

		YEAR										
RACE	RESP	'73	'74	'76	'77	'80	'82	'84	'85	'87	'88	'89
WHITE	AG	52%	59%	58%	54%	68%	68%	53%	48%	60%	60%	56%
	DS	48	41	42	46	32	32	47	52	40	40	44
# SURVEYED		1271	1261	1318	1291	1289	1262	1220	1285	1195	762	850
RACE	RESP	'73	'74	'76	'77	'80	'82	'84	'85	'87	'88	'89
BLACK	AG	82%	77%	88%	73%	82%	73%	78%	65%	83%	72%	85%
	DS	18	23	12	28	18	27	22	35	17	28	15
# SURVEYED		180	168	121	160	137	148	169	139	187	127	101
RACE	RESP	'73	'74	'76	'77	'80	'82	'84	'85	'87	'88	'89
OTHER	AG	83%	86%	63%	50%	33%	62%	76%	51%	80%	75%	68%
	DS	17	14	38	50	67	38	24	49	20	25	32
# SURVEYED		12	7	8	12	9	21	49	43	51	40	38

TABLE IV: HUMAN CONDITION GETTING WORSE -- BY AGE

Question: Do you agree with the following statement? In spite of what some people say, the lot (situation/condition) of the average man is getting worse, not better. NOTE: Question not asked in 1972, 1975, 1978, 1983, 1986.

Responses: AG = Agree; DS = Disagree

		YEAR										
AGE	RESP	'73	'74	'76	'77	'80	'82	'84	'85	'87	'88	'89
18-23	AG	58%	63%	64%	65%	72%	68%	58%	46%	66%	57%	66%
	DS	42	37	36	35	28	32	42	54	34	43	34
# SURVEYED		167	163	160	158	154	140	158	128	125	90	94
AGE	RESP	'73	'74	'76	'77	'80	'82	'84	'85	'87	'88	'89
24-29	AG	59%	60%	62%	56%	74%	68%	55%	47%	63%	63%	63%
	DS	41	40	38	44	26	32	45	53	37	37	37
# SURVEYED		210	209	220	197	199	240	230	210	192	131	113
AGE	RESP	'73	'74	'76	'77	'80	'82	'84	'85	'87	'88	'89
30-35	AG	52%	68%	56%	54%	71%	71%	63%	46%	57%	57%	52%
	DS	48	32	44	46	29	30	37	54	43	43	48
# SURVEYED		164	170	183	182	214	200	193	209	218	126	134
AGE	RESP	'73	'74	'76	'77	'80	'82	'84	'85	'87	'88	'89
36-41	AG	55%	62%	62%	58%	74%	71%	51%	50%	65%	66%	65%
	DS	45	38	38	42	26	29	49	50	35	34	35
# SURVEYED		173	150	156	163	148	142	187	178	182	129	128
AGE	RESP	'73	'74	'76	'77	'80	'82	'84	'85	'87	'88	'89
42-47	AG	58%	60%	56%	54%	74%	68%	62%	44%	64%	66%	49%
	DS	42	40	44	46	26	32	38	56	36	34	51
# SURVEYED		144	150	110	144	115	113	125	121	154	100	104
AGE	RESP	'73	'74	'76	'77	'80	'82	'84	'85	'87	'88	'89
48-53	AG	48%	62%	60%	48%	65%	72%	61%	55%	68%	65%	63%
	DS	52	38	40	52	35	28	39	45	32	35	37
# SURVEYED		143	139	129	147	121	107	101	130	123	60	90
AGE	RESP	'73	'74	'76	'77	'80	'82	'84	'85	'87	'88	'89
54-59	AG	61%	50%	60%	54%	67%	72%	62%	52%	59%	57%	68%
	DS	39	50	40	46	33	28	38	48	41	43	32
# SURVEYED		153	134	124	164	132	138	111	124	97	51	60
AGE	RESP	'73	'74	'76	'77	'80	'82	'84	'85	'87	'88	'89
60-65	AG	54%	58%	60%	52%	69%	61%	50%	52%	71%	63%	56%
	DS	46	42	40	48	31	39	50	48	29	38	44
# SURVEYED		116	104	133	113	112	110	107	124	97	80	73

TABLE IV: HUMAN CONDITION GETTING WORSE -- BY AGE (Continued)

Question: Do you agree with the following statement? In spite of what some people say, the lot (situation/condition) of the average man is getting worse, not better. NOTE: Question not asked in 1972, 1975, 1978, 1983, 1986.

Responses: AG = Agree; DS = Disagree

		YEAR										
AGE	RESP	'73	'74	'76	'77	'80	'82	'84	'85	'87	'88	'89
66+	AG	53%	65%	62%	62%	57%	63%	55%	54%	65%	64%	58%
	DS	47	35	38	38	43	37	45	46	35	36	42
# SURVEYED		189	211	229	188	231	232	221	237	240	160	190

****

WORLD TOO BAD FOR NEW CHILDREN

TABLE I: WORLD TOO BAD FOR NEW CHILDREN -- BY TOTAL POPULATION

Question: Do you agree with the following statement? It's hardly fair to bring a child into the world with the way things look for the future. NOTE: Question not asked in 1972, 1975, 1978, 1983, 1986.

Responses: AG = Agree; DS = Disagree

	YEAR										
RESPONSE	'73	'74	'76	'77	'80	'82	'84	'85	'87	'88	'89
AG	37%	37%	43%	39%	48%	35%	41%	33%	40%	39%	38%
DS	63	63	57	61	52	65	59	67	60	61	62
# SURVEYED	1468	1444	1442	1481	1428	1434	1448	1486	1423	951	1005

TABLE II: WORLD TOO BAD FOR NEW CHILDREN -- BY SEX

Question: Do you agree with the following statement? It's hardly fair to bring a child into the world with the way things look for the future. NOTE: Question not asked in 1972, 1975, 1978, 1983, 1986.

Responses: AG = Agree; DS = Disagree

		YEAR										
SEX	RESP	'73	'74	'76	'77	'80	'82	'84	'85	'87	'88	'89
M	AG	34%	34%	40%	35%	47%	36%	39%	34%	35%	34%	36%
	DS	66	66	60	65	53	64	61	66	65	66	64
# SURVEYED		684	670	644	675	626	617	593	672	626	388	434
SEX	RESP	'73	'74	'76	'77	'80	'82	'84	'85	'87	'88	'89
F	AG	40%	39%	45%	42%	49%	35%	41%	33%	44%	43%	40%
	DS	60	61	55	58	51	65	59	67	56	57	60
# SURVEYED		784	774	798	806	802	817	855	814	797	563	571

TABLE III: WORLD TOO BAD FOR NEW CHILDREN -- BY RACE

Question: Do you agree with the following statement? It's hardly fair to bring a child into the world with the way things look for the future. NOTE: Question not asked in 1972, 1975, 1978, 1983, 1986.

Responses: AG = Agree; DS = Disagree

		YEAR										
RACE	RESP	'73	'74	'76	'77	'80	'82	'84	'85	'87	'88	'89
WHITE	AG	34%	35%	41%	38%	46%	34%	37%	31%	37%	36%	33%
	DS	66	65	59	62	54	66	63	69	63	64	67
# SURVEYED		1279	1270	1315	1296	1284	1258	1230	1302	1189	780	865
RACE	RESP	'73	'74	'76	'77	'80	'82	'84	'85	'87	'88	'89
BLACK	AG	55%	51%	63%	48%	64%	41%	57%	46%	54%	50%	68%
	DS	45	49	38	52	36	59	43	54	46	50	32
# SURVEYED		177	167	120	172	134	150	167	142	184	129	99
RACE	RESP	'73	'74	'76	'77	'80	'82	'84	'85	'87	'88	'89
OTHER	AG	58%	71%	29%	38%	30%	50%	69%	57%	56%	60%	71%
	DS	42	29	71	62	70	50	31	43	44	40	29
# SURVEYED		12	7	7	13	10	26	51	42	50	42	41

TABLE IV: WORLD TOO BAD FOR NEW CHILDREN -- BY AGE

Question: Do you agree with the following statement? It's hardly fair to bring a child into the world with the way things look for the future. NOTE: Question not asked in 1972, 1975, 1978, 1983, 1986.

Responses: AG = Agree; DS = Disagree

		YEAR										
AGE	RESP	'73	'74	'76	'77	'80	'82	'84	'85	'87	'88	'89
18-23	AG	42%	35%	47%	42%	45%	33%	36%	34%	47%	41%	44%
	DS	58	65	53	58	55	67	64	66	53	59	56
# SURVEYED		170	165	159	162	154	142	159	131	125	94	96
AGE	RESP	'73	'74	'76	'77	'80	'82	'84	'85	'87	'88	'89
24-29	AG	36%	31%	41%	35%	44%	30%	41%	30%	32%	32%	37%
	DS	64	69	59	65	57	70	59	70	68	68	63
# SURVEYED		208	210	219	201	200	240	227	212	190	130	115
AGE	RESP	'73	'74	'76	'77	'80	'82	'84	'85	'87	'88	'89
30-35	AG	34%	36%	36%	41%	46%	31%	40%	31%	36%	32%	31%
	DS	66	64	64	59	54	69	60	69	64	68	69
# SURVEYED		163	174	183	181	213	196	196	210	219	128	134
AGE	RESP	'73	'74	'76	'77	'80	'82	'84	'85	'87	'88	'89
36-41	AG	30%	34%	41%	31%	52%	38%	35%	25%	27%	31%	33%
	DS	70	66	59	69	48	62	65	75	73	69	67
# SURVEYED		173	148	150	167	148	142	184	178	180	132	135
AGE	RESP	'73	'74	'76	'77	'80	'82	'84	'85	'87	'88	'89
42-47	AG	36%	37%	46%	38%	50%	38%	40%	30%	38%	34%	31%
	DS	64	63	54	62	50	62	60	70	62	66	69
# SURVEYED		144	149	112	143	111	113	124	120	154	99	106
AGE	RESP	'73	'74	'76	'77	'80	'82	'84	'85	'87	'88	'89
48-53	AG	37%	36%	42%	34%	48%	34%	37%	36%	50%	37%	38%
	DS	63	64	58	66	52	66	63	64	50	63	62
# SURVEYED		148	143	130	150	122	110	102	130	121	65	90

TABLE IV: WORLD TOO BAD FOR NEW CHILDREN -- BY AGE (Continued)

Question: Do you agree with the following statement? It's hardly fair to bring a child into the world with the way things look for the future. NOTE: Question not asked in 1972, 1975, 1978, 1983, 1986.

Responses: AG = Agree; DS = Disagree

		YEAR										
AGE	RESP	'73	'74	'76	'77	'80	'82	'84	'85	'87	'88	'89
54-59	AG	36%	35%	41%	40%	46%	32%	40%	40%	40%	51%	40%
	DS	64	65	59	60	54	68	60	60	60	49	60
# SURVEYED		157	136	121	162	133	139	113	130	96	53	60
AGE	RESP	'73	'74	'76	'77	'80	'82	'84	'85	'87	'88	'89
60-65	AG	34%	34%	43%	50%	55%	42%	48%	34%	53%	46%	46%
	DS	66	66	57	50	45	58	52	66	47	54	54
# SURVEYED		116	101	128	112	114	108	110	125	97	82	74
AGE	RESP	'73	'74	'76	'77	'80	'82	'84	'85	'87	'88	'89
66+	AG	45%	50%	50%	43%	50%	42%	46%	40%	48%	52%	46%
	DS	55	50	50	57	50	58	54	60	52	48	54
# SURVEYED		185	212	234	197	224	232	228	245	236	165	192

****

ATTITUDE OF PUBLIC OFFICIALS

TABLE I: ATTITUDE OF PUBLIC OFFICIALS -- BY TOTAL POPULATION

Question: Please tell me whether you agree or disagree with this statement. Most public officials (people in public office) are not really interested in the problems of the average man. NOTE: Question not asked in 1972, 1975, 1978, 1983, 1986.

Responses: AG = Agree; DS = Disagree

	YEAR										
RESPONSE	'73	'74	'76	'77	'80	'82	'84	'85	'87	'88	'89
AG	60%	66%	67%	65%	73%	68%	70%	65%	70%	68%	66%
DS	40	34	33	35	27	32	30	35	30	32	34
# SURVEYED	1467	1444	1463	1472	1421	1440	1431	1482	1424	939	994

TABLE II: ATTITUDE OF PUBLIC OFFICIALS -- BY SEX

Question: Please tell me whether you agree or disagree with this statement. Most public officials (people in public office) are not really interested in the problems of the average man. NOTE: Question not asked in 1972, 1975, 1978, 1983, 1986.

Responses: AG = Agree; DS = Disagree

		YEAR										
SEX	RESP	'73	'74	'76	'77	'80	'82	'84	'85	'87	'88	'89
M	AG	58%	67%	66%	65%	71%	69%	70%	66%	71%	65%	65%
	DS	42	33	34	35	29	31	30	34	29	35	35
# SURVEYED		692	678	660	676	634	622	582	672	627	385	431
SEX	RESP	'73	'74	'76	'77	'80	'82	'84	'85	'87	'88	'89
F	AG	61%	64%	67%	65%	74%	68%	70%	65%	69%	70%	67%
	DS	39	36	33	35	26	32	30	35	31	30	33
# SURVEYED		775	766	803	796	787	818	849	810	797	554	563

TABLE III: ATTITUDE OF PUBLIC OFFICIALS -- BY RACE

Question: Please tell me whether you agree or disagree with this statement. Most public officials (people in public office) are not really interested in the problems of the average man. NOTE: Question not asked in 1972, 1975, 1978, 1983, 1986.

Responses: AG = Agree; DS = Disagree

		YEAR										
RACE	RESP	'73	'74	'76	'77	'80	'82	'84	'85	'87	'88	'89
WHITE	AG	57%	64%	66%	63%	72%	67%	68%	64%	68%	66%	64%
	DS	43	36	34	37	28	33	32	36	32	34	36
# SURVEYED		1274	1269	1330	1293	1275	1266	1219	1301	1194	773	859
RACE	RESP	'73	'74	'76	'77	'80	'82	'84	'85	'87	'88	'89
BLACK	AG	76%	80%	76%	76%	82%	75%	83%	76%	80%	82%	78%
	DS	24	20	24	24	18	25	17	24	20	18	22
# SURVEYED		180	169	125	167	136	150	163	141	180	125	97
RACE	RESP	'73	'74	'76	'77	'80	'82	'84	'85	'87	'88	'89
OTHER	AG	69%	50%	75%	58%	60%	83%	73%	73%	80%	71%	79%
	DS	31	50	25	42	40	17	27	28	20	29	21
# SURVEYED		13	6	8	12	10	24	49	40	50	41	38

TABLE IV: ATTITUDE OF PUBLIC OFFICIALS -- BY AGE

Question: Please tell me whether you agree or disagree with this statement. Most public officials (people in public office) are not really interested in the problems of the average man. NOTE: Question not asked in 1972, 1975, 1978, 1983, 1986.

Responses: AG = Agree; DS = Disagree

		YEAR										
AGE	RESP	'73	'74	'76	'77	'80	'82	'84	'85	'87	'88	'89
18-23	AG	63%	65%	60%	70%	67%	65%	66%	57%	62%	60%	59%
	DS	38	35	40	30	33	35	34	43	38	40	41
# SURVEYED		168	163	161	159	148	141	157	129	122	90	95
AGE	RESP	'73	'74	'76	'77	'80	'82	'84	'85	'87	'88	'89
24-29	AG	60%	61%	62%	62%	71%	69%	63%	62%	63%	67%	68%
	DS	40	39	38	38	29	31	37	38	37	33	32
# SURVEYED		211	206	220	200	198	239	223	211	183	126	113
AGE	RESP	'73	'74	'76	'77	'80	'82	'84	'85	'87	'88	'89
30-35	AG	56%	69%	68%	65%	71%	74%	68%	68%	67%	66%	65%
	DS	44	31	32	35	29	26	32	32	33	34	35
# SURVEYED		163	170	184	182	209	198	193	207	216	126	133
AGE	RESP	'73	'74	'76	'77	'80	'82	'84	'85	'87	'88	'89
36-41	AG	61%	65%	66%	69%	75%	62%	69%	64%	72%	68%	64%
	DS	39	35	34	31	25	38	31	36	28	32	36
# SURVEYED		171	150	156	163	147	141	183	179	183	130	130
AGE	RESP	'73	'74	'76	'77	'80	'82	'84	'85	'87	'88	'89
42-47	AG	59%	67%	70%	65%	70%	70%	72%	63%	70%	69%	60%
	DS	41	33	30	35	30	30	28	37	30	31	40
# SURVEYED		145	149	113	142	115	117	123	120	151	99	102
AGE	RESP	'73	'74	'76	'77	'80	'82	'84	'85	'87	'88	'89
48-53	AG	56%	63%	71%	53%	70%	65%	75%	65%	72%	66%	71%
	DS	44	37	29	47	30	35	25	35	28	34	29
# SURVEYED		142	141	130	152	122	105	100	128	123	64	91
AGE	RESP	'73	'74	'76	'77	'80	'82	'84	'85	'87	'88	'89
54-59	AG	55%	66%	67%	58%	79%	67%	72%	69%	66%	67%	77%
	DS	45	34	33	42	21	33	28	31	34	33	23
# SURVEYED		152	138	123	161	135	140	111	127	98	51	61

TABLE IV: ATTITUDE OF PUBLIC OFFICIALS -- BY AGE (Continued)

Question: Please tell me whether you agree or disagree with this statement. Most public officials (people in public office) are not really interested in the problems of the average man. NOTE: Question not asked in 1972, 1975, 1978, 1983, 1986.

Responses: AG = Agree; DS = Disagree

		YEAR										
AGE	RESP	'73	'74	'76	'77	'80	'82	'84	'85	'87	'88	'89
60-65	AG	63%	69%	68%	71%	83%	65%	76%	67%	77%	70%	68%
	DS	37	31	32	29	17	35	24	33	23	30	32
# SURVEYED		119	104	127	112	114	113	109	129	100	83	71
AGE	RESP	'73	'74	'76	'77	'80	'82	'84	'85	'87	'88	'89
66+	AG	61%	67%	70%	72%	75%	71%	75%	68%	77%	74%	69%
	DS	39	33	30	28	25	29	25	32	23	26	31
# SURVEYED		192	218	243	194	224	237	226	248	243	167	195

****

BELIEF IN AN AFTERLIFE

TABLE I: BELIEF IN AN AFTERLIFE -- BY TOTAL POPULATION

Question: Do you believe there is life after death? NOTE: Question not asked in 1972, 1974, 1977, 1982, 1985.

Responses: Yes; No

	YEAR										
RESPONSE	'73	'75	'76	'78	'80	'83	'84	'86	'87	'88	'89
YES	77%	75%	78%	77%	81%	74%	79%	82%	78%	79%	76%
NO	23	25	22	23	19	26	21	18	22	21	24
# SURVEYED	1367	1341	1372	1394	1318	1475	1352	1363	1347	1371	908

TABLE II: BELIEF IN AN AFTERLIFE -- BY SEX

Question: Do you believe there is life after death? NOTE: Question not asked in 1972, 1974, 1977, 1982, 1985.

Responses: Yes; No

		YEAR										
SEX	RESP	'73	'75	'76	'78	'80	'83	'84	'86	'87	'88	'89
M	YES	74%	72%	76%	73%	76%	72%	75%	78%	75%	77%	72%
	NO	26	28	24	27	24	28	25	22	25	23	28
# SURVEYED		630	595	623	587	573	637	548	574	586	591	391
SEX	RESP	'73	'75	'76	'78	'80	'83	'84	'86	'87	'88	'89
F	YES	79%	77%	80%	79%	85%	75%	83%	85%	81%	81%	79%
	NO	21	23	20	21	15	25	17	15	19	19	21
# SURVEYED		737	746	749	807	745	838	804	789	761	780	517

TABLE III: BELIEF IN AN AFTERLIFE -- BY RACE

Question: Do you believe there is life after death? NOTE: Question not asked in 1972, 1974, 1977, 1982, 1985.

Responses: Yes; No

		YEAR										
RACE	RESP	'73	'75	'76	'78	'80	'83	'84	'86	'87	'88	'89
WHITE	YES	77%	75%	79%	78%	81%	75%	81%	82%	78%	80%	77%
	NO	23	25	21	22	19	25	19	18	22	20	23
# SURVEYED		1193	1201	1245	1242	1183	1308	1149	1163	1127	1143	778
RACE	RESP	'73	'75	'76	'78	'80	'83	'84	'86	'87	'88	'89
BLACK	YES	78%	69%	73%	64%	84%	68%	71%	84%	77%	77%	75%
	NO	22	31	27	36	16	32	29	16	23	23	25
# SURVEYED		161	137	119	137	127	150	154	166	175	171	95
RACE	RESP	'73	'75	'76	'78	'80	'83	'84	'86	'87	'88	'89
OTHER	YES	69%	33%	75%	73%	63%	53%	57%	76%	78%	72%	66%
	NO	31	67	25	27	38	47	43	24	22	28	34
# SURVEYED		13	3	8	15	8	17	49	34	45	57	35

TABLE IV: BELIEF IN AN AFTERLIFE -- BY AGE

Question: Do you believe there is life after death? NOTE: Question not asked in 1972, 1974, 1977, 1982, 1985.

Responses: Yes; No

		YEAR										
AGE	RESP	'73	'75	'76	'78	'80	'83	'84	'86	'87	'88	'89
18-23	YES	69%	69%	70%	67%	84%	72%	76%	79%	71%	78%	78%
	NO	31	31	30	33	16	28	24	21	29	22	22
# SURVEYED		157	157	147	143	41	120	150	102	119	130	74
AGE	RESP	'73	'75	'76	'78	'80	'83	'84	'86	'87	'88	'89
24-29	YES	77%	75%	77%	75%	75%	76%	81%	87%	82%	79%	74%
	NO	23	25	23	25	25	24	19	13	18	21	26
# SURVEYED		193	209	207	226	183	266	211	205	178	198	135
AGE	RESP	'73	'75	'76	'78	'80	'83	'84	'86	'87	'88	'89
30-35	YES	75%	76%	82%	76%	83%	77%	83%	83%	80%	82%	74%
	NO	25	24	18	24	17	23	17	17	20	18	26
# SURVEYED		153	152	174	211	192	222	177	206	204	185	128

TABLE IV: BELIEF IN AN AFTERLIFE -- BY AGE (Continued)

Question: Do you believe there is life after death? NOTE: Question not asked in 1972, 1974, 1977, 1982, 1985.

Responses: Yes; No

AGE	RESP	'73	'75	'76	'78	'80	'83	'84	'86	'87	'88	'89
36-41	YES	79%	82%	82%	78%	81%	78%	79%	78%	84%	77%	76%
	NO	21	18	18	22	19	22	21	22	16	23	24
# SURVEYED		162	137	140	149	137	158	179	176	169	179	114
AGE	RESP	'73	'75	'76	'78	'80	'83	'84	'86	'87	'88	'89
42-47	YES	74%	77%	76%	73%	87%	76%	76%	85%	74%	84%	79%
	NO	26	23	24	27	13	24	24	15	26	16	21
# SURVEYED		131	129	105	107	103	135	115	131	144	149	102
AGE	RESP	'73	'75	'76	'78	'80	'83	'84	'86	'87	'88	'89
48-53	YES	77%	71%	79%	85%	79%	70%	74%	79%	80%	86%	72%
	NO	23	29	21	15	21	30	26	21	20	14	28
# SURVEYED		136	126	124	123	112	110	93	103	120	78	79
AGE	RESP	'73	'75	'76	'78	'80	'83	'84	'86	'87	'88	'89
54-59	YES	74%	75%	74%	82%	79%	73%	80%	82%	81%	78%	82%
	NO	26	25	26	18	21	27	20	18	19	23	18
# SURVEYED		144	118	115	125	129	122	109	92	91	80	68
AGE	RESP	'73	'75	'76	'78	'80	'83	'84	'86	'87	'88	'89
60-65	YES	81%	75%	79%	81%	76%	73%	83%	79%	72%	80%	75%
	NO	19	25	21	19	24	27	17	21	28	20	25
# SURVEYED		110	99	124	101	103	122	102	108	93	109	60
AGE	RESP	'73	'75	'76	'78	'80	'83	'84	'86	'87	'88	'89
66+	YES	86%	74%	81%	76%	85%	66%	81%	81%	76%	77%	75%
	NO	14	26	19	24	15	34	19	19	24	23	25
# SURVEYED		177	209	232	204	212	213	212	233	226	259	146

****

READING LORD'S PRAYER

TABLE I: READING LORD'S PRAYER -- BY TOTAL POPULATION

Question: The United States Supreme Court has ruled that no state or local government may require the reading of the Lord's Prayer or Bible verses in public schools. What are your views on this--do you approve or disapprove of the court ruling? NOTE: Question not asked in 1972, 1973, 1976, 1978, 1980, 1984, 1987.

Responses: AP = Approve; DP = Disapprove

	YEAR								
RESPONSE	'74	'75	'77	'82	'83	'85	'86	'88	'89
AP	32%	36%	34%	39%	41%	44%	38%	39%	42%
DP	68	64	66	61	59	56	62	61	58
# SURVEYED	727	1444	1492	1462	1535	1483	712	949	973

TABLE II: READING LORD'S PRAYER -- BY SEX

Question: The United States Supreme Court has ruled that no state or local government may require the reading of the Lord's Prayer or Bible verses in public schools. What are your views on this--do you approve or disapprove of the court ruling? NOTE: Question not asked in 1972, 1973, 1976, 1978, 1980, 1984, 1987.

Responses: AP = Approve; DP = Disapprove

		YEAR								
SEX	RESP	'74	'75	'77	'82	'83	'85	'86	'88	'89
M	AP	34%	38%	36%	42%	45%	47%	40%	42%	50%
	DP	66	62	64	58	55	53	60	58	50
# SURVEYED		337	645	675	616	664	663	294	420	413
SEX	RESP	'74	'75	'77	'82	'83	'85	'86	'88	'89
F	AP	30%	35%	33%	36%	38%	42%	36%	36%	36%
	DP	70	65	67	64	62	58	64	64	64
# SURVEYED		390	799	817	846	871	820	418	529	560

TABLE III: READING LORD'S PRAYER -- BY RACE

Question: The United States Supreme Court has ruled that no state or local government may require the reading of the Lord's Prayer or Bible verses in public schools. What are your views on this--do you approve or disapprove of the court ruling? NOTE: Question not asked in 1972, 1973, 1976, 1978, 1980, 1984, 1987.

Responses: AP = Approve; DP = Disapprove

		YEAR								
RACE	RESP	'74	'75	'77	'82	'83	'85	'86	'88	'89
WHITE	AP	33%	38%	36%	40%	42%	46%	40%	39%	44%
	DP	67	62	64	60	58	54	60	61	56
# SURVEYED		642	1287	1303	1287	1369	1303	596	795	840
RACE	RESP	'74	'75	'77	'82	'83	'85	'86	'88	'89
BLACK	AP	24%	27%	20%	21%	29%	33%	25%	36%	24%
	DP	76	73	80	79	71	67	75	64	76
# SURVEYED		83	154	174	151	153	141	100	121	99
RACE	RESP	'74	'75	'77	'82	'83	'85	'86	'88	'89
OTHER	AP	50%	33%	53%	46%	62%	38%	25%	39%	41%
	DP	50	67	47	54	38	62	75	61	59
# SURVEYED		2	3	15	24	13	39	16	33	34

TABLE IV: READING LORD'S PRAYER -- BY AGE

Question: The United States Supreme Court has ruled that no state or local government may require the reading of the Lord's Prayer or Bible verses in public schools. What are your views on this--do you approve or disapprove of the court ruling? NOTE: Question not asked in 1972, 1973, 1976, 1978, 1980, 1984, 1987.

Responses: AP = Approve; DP = Disapprove

		YEAR								
AGE	RESP	'74	'75	'77	'82	'83	'85	'86	'88	'89
18-23	AP	54%	52%	51%	51%	51%	56%	54%	55%	46%
	DP	46	48	49	49	49	44	46	45	54
# SURVEYED		74	162	162	138	123	132	54	91	79
AGE	RESP	'74	'75	'77	'82	'83	'85	'86	'88	'89
24-29	AP	40%	48%	52%	47%	55%	59%	44%	46%	57%
	DP	60	52	48	53	45	41	56	54	43
# SURVEYED		109	225	199	240	273	211	97	144	141

TABLE IV: READING LORD'S PRAYER -- BY AGE (Continued)

Question: The United States Supreme Court has ruled that no state or local government may require the reading of the Lord's Prayer or Bible verses in public schools. What are your views on this--do you approve or disapprove of the court ruling? NOTE: Question not asked in 1972, 1973, 1976, 1978, 1980, 1984, 1987.

Responses: AP = Approve; DP = Disapprove

		YEAR								
AGE	RESP	'74	'75	'77	'82	'83	'85	'86	'88	'89
30-35	AP	34%	41%	38%	42%	45%	54%	48%	50%	47%
	DP	66	59	62	58	55	46	52	50	53
# SURVEYED		85	164	184	200	232	198	116	127	137
AGE	RESP	'74	'75	'77	'82	'83	'85	'86	'88	'89
36-41	AP	23%	28%	31%	31%	42%	42%	41%	41%	46%
	DP	77	72	69	69	58	58	59	59	54
# SURVEYED		71	149	167	144	163	179	90	121	125
AGE	RESP	'74	'75	'77	'82	'83	'85	'86	'88	'89
42-47	AP	29%	33%	25%	38%	35%	42%	40%	36%	45%
	DP	71	67	75	62	65	58	60	64	55
# SURVEYED		68	140	144	118	141	120	65	105	105
AGE	RESP	'74	'75	'77	'82	'83	'85	'86	'88	'89
48-53	AP	22%	33%	30%	36%	37%	39%	35%	32%	31%
	DP	78	67	70	64	63	61	65	68	69
# SURVEYED		63	138	149	110	113	129	48	60	84
AGE	RESP	'74	'75	'77	'82	'83	'85	'86	'88	'89
54-59	AP	25%	33%	28%	29%	31%	35%	23%	37%	32%
	DP	75	67	72	71	69	65	77	63	68
# SURVEYED		71	125	164	141	129	128	52	49	69
AGE	RESP	'74	'75	'77	'82	'83	'85	'86	'88	'89
60-65	AP	28%	25%	26%	38%	34%	34%	22%	32%	38%
	DP	72	75	74	62	66	66	78	68	62
# SURVEYED		60	111	114	114	126	128	49	68	66
AGE	RESP	'74	'75	'77	'82	'83	'85	'86	'88	'89
66+	AP	27%	28%	21%	31%	30%	35%	26%	23%	31%
	DP	73	72	79	69	70	65	74	77	69
# SURVEYED		122	225	202	248	228	252	137	183	164

****

ALLOW ATHEIST TO SPEAK

TABLE I: ALLOW ATHEIST TO SPEAK -- BY TOTAL POPULATION

Question: If an avowed atheist wanted to make a speech in your (city/town/community) against churches and religion, should he be allowed to speak, or not? NOTE: Question not asked in 1975, 1978, 1983, 1986.

Responses: YES = Yes, allowed to speak; NO = Not allowed

	YEAR											
RESPONSE	'72	'73	'74	'76	'77	'80	'82	'84	'85	'87	'88	'89
YES	67%	66%	63%	65%	63%	67%	65%	69%	66%	70%	71%	73%
NO	33	34	37	35	37	33	35	31	34	30	29	27
# SURVEYED	1576	1493	1462	1483	1518	1456	1484	1461	1510	1456	961	1020

TABLE II: ALLOW ATHEIST TO SPEAK -- BY SEX

Question: If an avowed atheist wanted to make a speech in your (city/town/community) against churches and religion, should he be allowed to speak, or not? NOTE: Question not asked in 1975, 1978, 1983, 1986.

Responses: YES = Yes, allowed to speak; NO = Not allowed

		YEAR											
SEX	RESP	'72	'73	'74	'76	'77	'80	'82	'84	'85	'87	'88	'89
M	YES	72%	68%	63%	69%	64%	72%	70%	73%	70%	76%	74%	77%
	NO	28	32	37	31	36	28	30	27	30	24	26	23
# SURVEYED		797	698	685	666	690	639	637	595	683	638	395	444
SEX	RESP	'72	'73	'74	'76	'77	'80	'82	'84	'85	'87	'88	'89
F	YES	61%	64%	62%	61%	61%	63%	62%	66%	62%	65%	69%	69%
	NO	39	36	38	39	39	37	38	34	38	35	31	31
# SURVEYED		779	795	777	817	828	817	847	866	827	818	566	576

TABLE III: ALLOW ATHEIST TO SPEAK -- BY RACE

Question: If an avowed atheist wanted to make a speech in your (city/town/community) against churches and religion, should he be allowed to speak, or not? NOTE: Question not asked in 1975, 1978, 1983, 1986.

Responses: YES = Yes, allowed to speak; NO = Not allowed

		YEAR											
RACE	RESP	'72	'73	'74	'76	'77	'80	'82	'84	'85	'87	'88	'89
WHITE	YES	69%	68%	63%	65%	63%	68%	66%	71%	68%	71%	71%	75%
	NO	31	32	37	35	37	32	34	29	32	29	29	25
# SURVEYED		1321	1298	1291	1348	1330	1307	1304	1243	1324	1215	790	879
RACE	RESP	'72	'73	'74	'76	'77	'80	'82	'84	'85	'87	'88	'89
BLACK	YES	55%	52%	55%	55%	55%	55%	61%	60%	52%	66%	72%	61%
	NO	45	48	45	45	45	45	39	40	48	34	28	39
# SURVEYED		251	183	164	128	174	139	155	167	146	188	128	100
RACE	RESP	'72	'73	'74	'76	'77	'80	'82	'84	'85	'87	'88	'89
OTHER	YES	75%	75%	71%	100%	93%	70%	40%	47%	45%	47%	60%	59%
	NO	25	25	29	0	7	30	60	53	55	53	40	41
# SURVEYED		4	12	7	7	14	10	25	51	40	53	43	41

TABLE IV: ALLOW ATHEIST TO SPEAK -- BY AGE

Question: If an avowed atheist wanted to make a speech in your (city/town/community) against churches and religion, should he be allowed to speak, or not? NOTE: Question not asked in 1975, 1978, 1983, 1986.

Responses: YES = Yes, allowed to speak; NO = Not allowed

		YEAR											
AGE	RESP	'72	'73	'74	'76	'77	'80	'82	'84	'85	'87	'88	'89
18-23	YES	85%	84%	77%	80%	80%	76%	68%	74%	66%	71%	73%	77%
	NO	15	16	23	20	20	24	32	26	34	29	27	23
# SURVEYED		164	171	167	161	161	154	145	159	131	125	94	96
AGE	RESP	'72	'73	'74	'76	'77	'80	'82	'84	'85	'87	'88	'89
24-29	YES	85%	87%	81%	84%	81%	80%	78%	74%	78%	83%	81%	82%
	NO	15	13	19	16	19	20	22	26	22	17	19	18
# SURVEYED		227	211	211	225	201	201	244	231	214	191	130	115

TABLE IV: ALLOW ATHEIST TO SPEAK -- BY AGE (Continued)

Question: If an avowed atheist wanted to make a speech in your (city/town/community) against churches and religion, should he be allowed to speak, or not? NOTE: Question not asked in 1975, 1978, 1983, 1986.

Responses: YES = Yes, allowed to speak; NO = Not allowed

		YEAR											
AGE	RESP	'72	'73	'74	'76	'77	'80	'82	'84	'85	'87	'88	'89
30-35	YES	77%	72%	74%	75%	80%	84%	82%	78%	73%	80%	82%	79%
	NO	23	28	26	25	20	16	18	22	27	20	18	21
# SURVEYED		184	167	174	185	188	214	203	198	210	221	131	136
AGE	RESP	'72	'73	'74	'76	'77	'80	'82	'84	'85	'87	'88	'89
36-41	YES	75%	74%	69%	74%	70%	71%	75%	77%	77%	82%	82%	84%
	NO	25	26	31	26	30	29	25	23	23	18	18	16
# SURVEYED		123	175	150	157	168	150	145	185	183	186	131	134
AGE	RESP	'72	'73	'74	'76	'77	'80	'82	'84	'85	'87	'88	'89
42-47	YES	69%	74%	71%	61%	62%	74%	73%	74%	80%	69%	82%	85%
	NO	31	26	29	39	38	26	27	26	20	31	18	15
# SURVEYED		183	146	148	112	144	115	118	125	123	157	102	107
AGE	RESP	'72	'73	'74	'76	'77	'80	'82	'84	'85	'87	'88	'89
48-53	YES	62%	55%	65%	59%	53%	67%	63%	60%	67%	69%	63%	73%
	NO	38	45	35	41	47	33	38	40	33	31	37	27
# SURVEYED		186	147	143	132	154	123	112	102	131	126	63	94
AGE	RESP	'72	'73	'74	'76	'77	'80	'82	'84	'85	'87	'88	'89
54-59	YES	60%	53%	50%	54%	59%	56%	65%	62%	56%	67%	73%	71%
	NO	40	47	50	46	41	44	35	38	44	33	27	29
# SURVEYED		153	156	136	127	167	136	142	113	126	98	52	63
AGE	RESP	'72	'73	'74	'76	'77	'80	'82	'84	'85	'87	'88	'89
60-65	YES	45%	43%	49%	50%	45%	51%	45%	64%	60%	52%	61%	57%
	NO	55	58	51	50	55	49	55	36	40	48	39	43
# SURVEYED		142	120	107	134	117	119	116	112	130	101	82	74
AGE	RESP	'72	'73	'74	'76	'77	'80	'82	'84	'85	'87	'88	'89
66+	YES	38%	40%	29%	41%	31%	42%	39%	50%	42%	49%	45%	53%
	NO	62	60	71	59	69	58	61	50	58	51	55	47
# SURVEYED		210	196	221	244	211	235	249	230	255	246	173	198

****

ALLOW ATHEIST BOOKS IN PUBLIC LIBRARY

TABLE I: ALLOW ATHEIST BOOKS IN PUBLIC LIBRARY -- BY TOTAL POPULATION

Question: If some people in your community suggested that a book written by an atheist against churches and religion should be taken out of your public library, would you favor removing this book, or not? NOTE: Question not asked in 1975, 1978, 1983.

Responses: FA = Favor; NF = Not favor

	YEAR											
RESPONSE	'72	'73	'74	'76	'77	'80	'82	'84	'85	'87	'88	'89
FA	37%	38%	39%	39%	40%	36%	37%	35%	38%	33%	35%	31%
NF	63	62	61	61	60	64	63	65	62	67	65	69
# SURVEYED	1552	1471	1445	1461	1498	1430	1466	1434	1493	1427	952	998

TABLE II: ALLOW ATHEIST BOOKS INPUBLIC LIBRARY -- BY SEX

Question: If some people in your community suggested that a book written by an atheist against churches and religion should be taken out of your public library, would you favor removing this book, or not? NOTE: Question not asked in 1975, 1978, 1983.

Responses: FA = Favor; NF = Not favor

		YEAR											
SEX	RESP	'72	'73	'74	'76	'77	'80	'82	'84	'85	'87	'88	'89
M	FA	34%	36%	38%	35%	39%	34%	35%	31%	36%	27%	33%	27%
	NF	66	64	62	65	61	66	65	69	64	73	67	73
# SURVEYED		780	690	675	654	677	623	624	585	676	626	395	433
SEX	RESP	'72	'73	'74	'76	'77	'80	'82	'84	'85	'87	'88	'89
F	FA	40%	39%	39%	42%	42%	38%	39%	37%	40%	37%	36%	33%
	NF	60	61	61	58	58	62	61	63	60	63	64	67
# SURVEYED		772	781	770	807	821	807	842	849	817	801	557	565

TABLE III: ALLOW ATHEIST BOOKS IN PUBLIC LIBRARY -- BY RACE

Question: If some people in your community suggested that a book written by an atheist against churches and religion should be taken out of your public library, would you favor removing this book, or not? NOTE: Question not asked in 1975, 1978, 1983.

Responses: FA = Favor; NF = Not favor

		YEAR											
RACE	RESP	'72	'73	'74	'76	'77	'80	'82	'84	'85	'87	'88	'89
WHITE	FA	35%	36%	37%	38%	39%	36%	37%	33%	36%	31%	33%	29%
	NF	65	64	63	62	61	64	63	67	64	69	67	71
# SURVEYED		1306	1279	1274	1328	1318	1281	1291	1222	1308	1195	786	865
RACE	RESP	'72	'73	'74	'76	'77	'80	'82	'84	'85	'87	'88	'89
BLACK	FA	48%	50%	48%	46%	48%	45%	44%	47%	50%	41%	39%	43%
	NF	52	50	52	54	52	55	56	53	50	59	61	57
# SURVEYED		242	180	165	126	166	140	150	164	143	182	124	95
RACE	RESP	'72	'73	'74	'76	'77	'80	'82	'84	'85	'87	'88	'89
OTHER	FA	25%	33%	50%	29%	36%	22%	32%	42%	55%	46%	52%	42%
	NF	75	67	50	71	64	78	68	58	45	54	48	58
# SURVEYED		4	12	6	7	14	9	25	48	42	50	42	38

TABLE IV: ALLOW ATHEIST BOOKS IN PUBLIC LIBRARY -- BY AGE

Question: If some people in your community suggested that a book written by an atheist against churches and religion should be taken out of your public library, would you favor removing this book, or not? NOTE: Question not asked in 1975, 1978, 1983.

Responses: FA = Favor; NF = Not favor

		YEAR											
AGE	RESP	'72	'73	'74	'76	'77	'80	'82	'84	'85	'87	'88	'89
18-23	FA	20%	17%	22%	19%	28%	25%	35%	25%	33%	30%	34%	23%
	NF	80	83	78	81	72	75	65	75	67	70	66	77
# SURVEYED		158	169	165	160	159	152	142	154	129	123	91	90
AGE	RESP	'72	'73	'74	'76	'77	'80	'82	'84	'85	'87	'88	'89
24-29	FA	19%	18%	21%	21%	26%	17%	25%	29%	26%	22%	31%	22%
	NF	81	82	79	79	74	83	75	71	74	78	69	78
# SURVEYED		224	208	207	221	200	195	243	229	214	188	130	112

TABLE IV: ALLOW ATHEIST BOOKS IN PUBLIC LIBRARY -- BY AGE (Continued)

Question: If some people in your community suggested that a book written by an atheist against churches and religion should be taken out of your public library, would you favor removing this book, or not? NOTE: Question not asked in 1975, 1978, 1983.

Responses: FA = Favor; NF = Not favor

		YEAR											
AGE	RESP	'72	'73	'74	'76	'77	'80	'82	'84	'85	'87	'88	'89
30-35	FA	26%	34%	32%	30%	26%	23%	20%	21%	29%	21%	26%	23%
	NF	74	66	68	70	74	77	80	79	71	79	74	77
# SURVEYED		181	167	173	185	185	207	202	193	204	217	130	133
AGE	RESP	'72	'73	'74	'76	'77	'80	'82	'84	'85	'87	'88	'89
36-41	FA	34%	34%	32%	29%	34%	31%	29%	23%	27%	20%	23%	23%
	NF	66	66	68	71	66	69	71	77	73	80	77	77
# SURVEYED		120	172	148	153	165	149	145	183	182	182	131	132
AGE	RESP	'72	'73	'74	'76	'77	'80	'82	'84	'85	'87	'88	'89
42-47	FA	34%	35%	33%	50%	39%	33%	38%	27%	29%	29%	24%	23%
	NF	66	65	67	50	61	67	62	73	71	71	76	77
# SURVEYED		182	142	150	112	142	112	116	124	122	150	99	107
AGE	RESP	'72	'73	'74	'76	'77	'80	'82	'84	'85	'87	'88	'89
48-53	FA	41%	43%	37%	44%	47%	40%	42%	46%	36%	39%	44%	24%
	NF	59	57	63	56	53	60	58	54	64	61	56	76
# SURVEYED		184	145	141	128	150	121	110	101	129	124	64	94
AGE	RESP	'72	'73	'74	'76	'77	'80	'82	'84	'85	'87	'88	'89
54-59	FA	45%	52%	54%	44%	42%	50%	43%	43%	47%	35%	38%	31%
	NF	55	48	46	56	58	50	57	57	53	65	62	69
# SURVEYED		149	155	136	126	168	134	138	112	129	96	53	61
AGE	RESP	'72	'73	'74	'76	'77	'80	'82	'84	'85	'87	'88	'89
60-65	FA	57%	57%	55%	57%	52%	48%	48%	53%	43%	46%	40%	44%
	NF	43	43	45	43	48	52	52	47	57	54	60	56
# SURVEYED		141	119	104	132	116	117	113	109	127	100	83	75
AGE	RESP	'72	'73	'74	'76	'77	'80	'82	'84	'85	'87	'88	'89
66+	FA	62%	59%	64%	61%	71%	62%	61%	54%	62%	53%	53%	49%
	NF	38	41	36	39	29	38	39	46	38	47	47	51
# SURVEYED		210	191	216	239	206	234	247	223	252	242	168	191

****

ALLOW ATHEIST TO TEACH IN COLLEGE

TABLE I: ALLOW ATHEIST TO TEACH IN COLLEGE -- BY TOTAL POPULATION

Question: Should an avowed atheist be allowed to teach in a college or university, or not? NOTE: Question not asked in 1972, 1973, 1976, 1978, 1980, 1984, 1987.

Responses: YES = Yes, allowed to teach; NO = Not allowed

	YEAR											
RESPONSE	'72	'73	'74	'76	'77	'80	'82	'84	'85	'87	'88	'89
YES	42%	42%	43%	42%	40%	47%	47%	47%	47%	49%	47%	54%
NO	58	58	57	58	60	53	53	53	53	51	53	46
# SURVEYED	1538	1452	1429	1466	1497	1419	1454	1421	1485	1411	944	985

TABLE II: ALLOW ATHEIST TO TEACH IN COLLEGE -- BY SEX

Question: Should an avowed atheist be allowed to teach in a college or university, or not? NOTE: Question not asked in 1972, 1973, 1976, 1978, 1980, 1984, 1987.

Responses: YES = Yes, allowed to teach; NO = Not allowed

		YEAR											
SEX	RESP	'72	'73	'74	'76	'77	'80	'82	'84	'85	'87	'88	'89
M	YES	45	44	45	47	43	50	50	52	51	55	51	57
	NO	55	56	55	53	57	50	50	48	49	45	49	43
# SURVEYED		777	679	669	652	686	623	623	587	668	621	390	427
SEX	RESP	'72	'73	'74	'76	'77	'80	'82	'84	'85	'87	'88	'89
F	YES	38	40	42	38	37	44	45	44	44	45	44	51
	NO	62	60	58	62	63	56	55	56	56	55	56	49
# SURVEYED		761	773	760	814	811	796	831	834	817	790	554	558

TABLE III: ALLOW ATHEIST TO TEACH IN COLLEGE -- BY RACE

Question: Should an avowed atheist be allowed to teach in a college or university, or not? NOTE: Question not asked in 1972, 1973, 1976, 1978, 1980, 1984, 1987.

Responses: YES = Yes, allowed to teach; NO = Not allowed

		YEAR											
RACE	RESP	'72	'73	'74	'76	'77	'80	'82	'84	'85	'87	'88	'89
WHITE	YES	42%	43%	44%	42%	40%	47%	47%	49%	47%	50%	47%	54%
	NO	58	57	56	58	60	53	53	51	53	50	53	46
# SURVEYED		1292	1259	1260	1333	1316	1270	1278	1209	1300	1180	777	849
RACE	RESP	'72	'73	'74	'76	'77	'80	'82	'84	'85	'87	'88	'89
BLACK	YES	40%	36%	41%	44%	35%	41%	47%	41%	44%	49%	44%	46%
	NO	60	64	59	56	65	59	53	59	56	51	56	54
# SURVEYED		243	182	164	126	167	139	152	164	143	179	126	97
RACE	RESP	'72	'73	'74	'76	'77	'80	'82	'84	'85	'87	'88	'89
OTHER	YES	67%	73%	40%	71%	57%	70%	33%	35%	38%	37%	51%	54%
	NO	33	27	60	29	43	30	67	65	62	63	49	46
# SURVEYED		3	11	5	7	14	10	24	48	42	52	41	39

TABLE IV: ALLOW ATHEIST TO TEACH IN COLLEGE -- BY AGE

Question: Should an avowed atheist be allowed to teach in a college or university, or not? NOTE: Question not asked in 1972, 1973, 1976, 1978, 1980, 1984, 1987.

Responses: YES = Yes, allowed to teach; NO = Not allowed

		YEAR											
AGE	RESP	'72	'73	'74	'76	'77	'80	'82	'84	'85	'87	'88	'89
18-23	YES	70%	63%	68%	66%	66%	65%	56%	61%	60%	55%	62%	63%
	NO	30	37	33	34	34	35	44	39	40	45	38	37
# SURVEYED		155	167	160	160	157	150	144	156	130	120	92	93
AGE	RESP	'72	'73	'74	'76	'77	'80	'82	'84	'85	'87	'88	'89
24-29	YES	67%	72%	66%	69%	61%	66%	65%	59%	65%	63%	52%	63%
	NO	33	28	34	31	39	34	35	41	35	37	48	37
# SURVEYED		223	205	203	223	200	198	240	227	212	188	129	108

TABLE IV: ALLOW ATHEIST TO TEACH IN COLLEGE -- BY AGE (Continued)

Question: Should an avowed atheist be allowed to teach in a college or university, or not? NOTE: Question not asked in 1972, 1973, 1976, 1978, 1980, 1984, 1987.

Responses: YES = Yes, allowed to teach; NO = Not allowed

		YEAR											
AGE	RESP	'72	'73	'74	'76	'77	'80	'82	'84	'85	'87	'88	'89
30-35	YES	55%	49%	51%	54%	54%	63%	68%	67%	66%	64%	60%	64%
	NO	45	51	49	46	46	37	32	33	34	36	40	36
# SURVEYED		180	163	174	183	181	208	194	193	207	212	128	132
AGE	RESP	'72	'73	'74	'76	'77	'80	'82	'84	'85	'87	'88	'89
36-41	YES	41%	46%	47%	44%	41%	51%	62%	57%	63%	66%	59%	69%
	NO	59	54	53	56	59	49	38	43	37	34	41	31
# SURVEYED		121	169	146	153	165	148	141	180	179	182	128	132
AGE	RESP	'72	'73	'74	'76	'77	'80	'82	'84	'85	'87	'88	'89
42-47	YES	40%	43%	42%	41%	30%	50%	55%	46%	60%	52%	52%	65%
	NO	60	57	58	59	70	50	45	54	40	48	48	35
# SURVEYED		183	141	145	110	142	110	115	117	117	149	99	106
AGE	RESP	'72	'73	'74	'76	'77	'80	'82	'84	'85	'87	'88	'89
48-53	YES	28%	28%	39%	26%	36%	47%	44%	37%	34%	41%	46%	48%
	NO	72	72	61	74	64	53	56	63	66	59	54	52
# SURVEYED		181	143	138	130	154	119	110	100	128	124	63	89
AGE	RESP	'72	'73	'74	'76	'77	'80	'82	'84	'85	'87	'88	'89
54-59	YES	28%	28%	31%	28%	27%	26%	32%	28%	28%	37%	38%	44%
	NO	72	72	69	72	73	74	68	72	72	63	62	56
# SURVEYED		149	151	132	124	168	134	139	110	125	97	53	59
AGE	RESP	'72	'73	'74	'76	'77	'80	'82	'84	'85	'87	'88	'89
60-65	YES	25%	18%	26%	22%	23%	29%	22%	31%	28%	26%	41%	34%
	NO	75	82	74	78	77	71	78	69	72	74	59	66
# SURVEYED		138	119	106	129	115	115	112	108	129	96	82	73
AGE	RESP	'72	'73	'74	'76	'77	'80	'82	'84	'85	'87	'88	'89
66+	YES	18%	17%	15%	19%	14%	21%	18%	24%	18%	24%	19%	32%
	NO	82	83	85	81	86	79	82	76	82	76	81	68
# SURVEYED		205	190	220	248	208	228	249	224	251	238	167	190

****

FEELINGS TOWARD CATHOLICS

TABLE I: FEELINGS TOWARD CATHOLICS -- BY TOTAL POPULATION

Question: On a temperature scale from 0 to 100 how warm or cool do you feel toward Catholics? NOTE: Question not asked in 1972-1985, 1987.

Responses: 00 = 0-9 degrees 10 = 10-19 20 = 20-29 30 = 30-39 40 = 40-49 50 = 50-59 60 = 60-69 70 = 70-79 80 = 80-89 90 = 90-99

	YEAR		
RESPONSE	'86	'88	'89
00	1%	2%	2%
10	1	1	2
20	0	0	1
30	2	2	3
40	6	4	4
50	15	28	23
60	18	13	12
70	21	20	19
80	20	18	19
90	15	13	16
# SURVEYED	1410	1396	941

TABLE II: FEELINGS TOWARD CATHOLICS -- BY SEX

Question: On a temperature scale from 0 to 100 how warm or cool do you feel toward Catholics? NOTE: Question not asked in 1972-1985, 1987.

Responses: 00 = 0-9 degrees 10 = 10-19 20 = 20-29 30 = 30-39 40 = 40-49 50 = 50-59 60 = 60-69 70 = 70-79 80 = 80-89 90 = 90-99

		YEAR		
SEX	RESP	'86	'88	'89
MALE	00	1%	2%	2%
	10	1	1	2
	20	0	0	0
	30	3	2	2
	40	8	4	5
	50	17	31	26
	60	20	13	15
	70	22	19	17
	80	17	15	17
	90	10	11	13
# SURVEYED		605	604	406

		YEAR		
SEX	RESP	'86	'88	'89
FEMALE	00	1%	1%	2%
	10	1	1	2
	20	0	0	1
	30	2	2	3
	40	5	3	4
	50	13	25	21
	60	17	12	9
	70	20	20	20
	80	21	20	21
	90	19	15	18
# SURVEYED		805	792	535

TABLE III: FEELINGS TOWARD CATHOLICS -- BY RACE

Question: On a temperature scale from 0 to 100 how warm or cool do you feel toward Catholics? NOTE: Question not asked in 1972-1985, 1987.

Responses: 00 = 0-9 degrees 10 = 10-19 20 = 20-29 30 = 30-39 40 = 40-49
50 = 50-59 60 = 60-69 70 = 70-79 80 = 80-89 90 = 90-99

		YEAR		
RACE	RESP	'86	'88	'89
WHITE	00	1%	1%	2%
	10	1	1	2
	20	0	0	0
	30	2	2	3
	40	6	3	5
	50	15	28	23
	60	19	12	12
	70	21	20	19
	80	20	18	19
	90	15	14	16
# SURVEYED		1206	1171	817

		YEAR		
RACE	RESP	'86	'88	'89
BLACK	00	3%	2%	4%
	10	2	2	1
	20	1	0	1
	30	4	4	1
	40	7	7	1
	50	17	25	23
	60	20	15	11
	70	21	16	18
	80	18	18	24
	90	9	10	14
# SURVEYED		169	168	90

		YEAR		
RACE	RESP	'86	'88	'89
OTHER	00	3%	0%	3%
	10	3	2	0
	20	0	0	0
	30	0	2	0
	40	6	5	3
	50	14	32	26
	60	6	11	9
	70	14	14	21
	80	26	21	18
	90	29	14	21
# SURVEYED		35	57	34

TABLE IV: FEELINGS TOWARD CATHOLICS -- BY AGE

Question: On a temperature scale from 0 to 100 how warm or cool do you feel toward Catholics? NOTE: Question not asked in 1972-1985, 1987.

Responses: 00 = 0-9 degrees 10 = 10-19 20 = 20-29 30 = 30-39 40 = 40-49
50 = 50-59 60 = 60-69 70 = 70-79 80 = 80-89 90 = 90-99

		YEAR		
AGE	RESP	'86	'88	'89
18-23	00	2%	0%	2%
	10	2	1	5
	20	0	0	0
	30	6	1	1
	40	5	7	9
	50	15	29	22
	60	26	15	13
	70	20	20	17
	80	14	14	16
	90	10	13	15
# SURVEYED		106	135	82

		YEAR		
AGE	RESP	'86	'88	'89
24-29	00	1%	1%	2%
	10	1	0	3
	20	0	0	2
	30	1	1	6
	40	8	5	7
	50	19	33	22
	60	23	16	11
	70	17	19	18
	80	18	16	15
	90	11	9	13
# SURVEYED		212	210	142

AGE	RESP	'86	'88	'89
30-35	00	1%	2%	2%
	10	0	2	2
	20	0	1	1
	30	1	1	3
	40	6	2	5
	50	21	30	31
	60	17	14	11
	70	25	20	15
	80	13	17	19
	90	15	14	13
# SURVEYED		216	185	131

TABLE IV: FEELINGS TOWARD CATHOLICS -- BY AGE

Question: On a temperature scale from 0 to 100 how warm or cool do you feel toward Catholics? NOTE: Question not asked in 1972-1985, 1987.

Responses: 00 = 0-9 degrees 10 = 10-19 20 = 20-29 30 = 30-39 40 = 40-49
50 = 50-59 60 = 60-69 70 = 70-79 80 = 80-89 90 = 90-99

		YEAR		
AGE	RESP	'86	'88	'89
36-41	00	2%	2%	0%
	10	0	1	2
	20	0	0	0
	30	2	2	6
	40	8	4	3
	50	17	31	34
	60	18	15	13
	70	18	22	22
	80	21	15	17
	90	14	9	5
# SURVEYED		184	185	119

AGE	RESP	'86	'88	'89
42-47	00	2%	1%	2%
	10	2	1	0
	20	0	1	0
	30	3	5	1
	40	6	2	3
	50	11	26	23
	60	13	13	14
	70	24	21	19
	80	19	16	23
	90	21	15	15
# SURVEYED		139	150	103

AGE	RESP	'86	'88	'89
48-53	00	3%	1%	4%
	10	2	6	2
	20	0	0	0
	30	2	1	2
	40	5	3	2
	50	12	31	21
	60	16	14	12
	70	24	14	27
	80	23	15	13
	90	13	16	16
# SURVEYED		105	88	82

AGE	RESP	'86	'88	'89
54-59	00	2%	0%	2%
	10	2	2	2
	20	0	2	0
	30	3	2	0
	40	4	5	3
	50	5	24	20
	60	16	10	9
	70	22	18	15
	80	26	22	27
	90	18	13	23
# SURVEYED		92	82	66

AGE	RESP	'86	'88	'89
60-65	00	1%	3%	5%
	10	1	0	2
	20	0	0	0
	30	3	1	0
	40	5	3	0
	50	10	27	13
	60	15	8	6
	70	23	28	24
	80	28	24	34
	90	15	6	16
# SURVEYED		110	110	62

AGE	RESP	'86	'88	'89
66+	00	1%	2%	3%
	10	2	1	2
	20	1	0	1
	30	3	2	2
	40	6	4	6
	50	13	20	16
	60	20	9	13
	70	18	17	14
	80	21	23	18
	90	17	23	26
# SURVEYED		239	248	152

FEELINGS TOWARD JEWS

TABLE I: FEELINGS TOWARD JEWS -- BY TOTAL POPULATION

Question: On a temperature scale from 0 to 100 how warm or cool do you feel toward Jews? NOTE: Question not asked in 1972-1985, 1987.

Responses: 00 = 0-9 degrees 10 = 10-19 20 = 20-29 30 = 30-39 40 = 40-49 50 = 50-59 60 = 60-69 70 = 70-79 80 = 80-89 90 = 90-99

	YEAR		
RESPONSE	'86	'88	'89
00	3%	2%	2%
10	2	2	2
20	1	1	1
30	3	3	3
40	7	4	6
50	20	37	30
60	19	12	13
70	23	17	20
80	15	14	13
90	9	8	9
# SURVEYED	1386	1378	916

TABLE II: FEELINGS TOWARD JEWS -- BY SEX

Question: On a temperature scale from 0 to 100 how warm or cool do you feel toward Jews? NOTE: Question not asked in 1972-1985, 1987.

Responses: 00 = 0-9 degrees 10 = 10-19 20 = 20-29 30 = 30-39 40 = 40-49 50 = 50-59 60 = 60-69 70 = 70-79 80 = 80-89 90 = 90-99

		YEAR		
SEX	RESP	'86	'88	'89
MALE	00	3%	2%	3%
	10	2	2	2
	20	1	1	0
	30	4	4	3
	40	8	4	6
	50	22	37	32
	60	21	13	15
	70	21	15	21
	80	12	14	12
	90	6	6	7
# SURVEYED		598	603	397

		YEAR		
SEX	RESP	'86	'88	'89
FEMALE	00	2%	2%	2%
	10	2	1	2
	20	1	1	2
	30	2	2	3
	40	6	4	6
	50	18	37	29
	60	17	12	12
	70	25	19	19
	80	18	14	14
	90	11	8	11
# SURVEYED		788	775	519

TABLE III: FEELINGS TOWARD JEWS -- BY RACE

Question: On a temperature scale from 0 to 100 how warm or cool do you feel toward Jews. NOTE: Question not asked in 1972-1985, 1987.

Responses: 00 = 0-9 degrees; 10 = 10-19; 20 = 20-29; 30 = 30-39; 40 = 40-49; 50 = 50-59; 60 = 60-69; 70 = 70-79; 80 = 80-89; 90 = 90-99

		YEAR		
RACE	RESP	'86	'88	'89
WHITE	00	2%	1%	2%
	10	2	2	2
	20	1	1	1
	30	2	2	3
	40	7	4	6
	50	20	37	30
	60	19	13	14
	70	23	18	20
	80	16	14	13
	90	9	8	10
# SURVEYED		1190	1155	797

		YEAR		
RACE	RESP	'86	'88	'89
BLACK	00	4%	2%	5%
	10	3	2	0
	20	1	2	1
	30	6	4	5
	40	4	5	5
	50	17	36	33
	60	21	11	11
	70	23	14	17
	80	13	16	15
	90	7	7	9
# SURVEYED		162	166	88

		YEAR		
RACE	RESP	'86	'88	'89
OTHER	00	6%	11%	6%
	10	3	5	6
	20	0	2	3
	30	6	2	0
	40	12	7	10
	50	35	47	26
	60	12	5	13
	70	15	11	13
	80	3	7	13
	90	9	4	10
# SURVEYED		34	57	31

TABLE IV: FEELINGS TOWARD JEWS -- BY AGE

Question: On a temperature scale from 0 to 100 how warm or cool do you feel toward Jews? NOTE: Question not asked in 1972-1985, 1987.

Responses: 00 = 0-9 degrees; 10 = 10-19; 20 = 20-29; 30 = 30-39; 40 = 40-49; 50 = 50-59; 60 = 60-69; 70 = 70-79; 80 = 80-89; 90 = 90-99

		YEAR		
AGE	RESP	'86	'88	'89
18-23	00	3%	3%	5%
	10	4	3	5
	20	1	1	1
	30	1	5	4
	40	8	5	10
	50	29	44	37
	60	25	8	13
	70	20	16	13
	80	8	10	5
	90	2	4	8
# SURVEYED		106	134	79

		YEAR		
AGE	RESP	'86	'88	'89
24-29	00	4%	3%	2%
	10	1	3	1
	20	1	2	2
	30	2	1	3
	40	9	5	9
	50	24	43	34
	60	21	15	20
	70	24	11	15
	80	9	12	9
	90	5	4	6
# SURVEYED		211	204	138

		YEAR		
AGE	RESP	'86	'88	'89
30-35	00	3%	2%	3%
	10	1	2	5
	20	0	1	2
	30	3	2	4
	40	5	3	5
	50	25	38	38
	60	18	12	9
	70	25	19	16
	80	9	14	11
	90	11	6	8
# SURVEYED		211	185	128

TABLE IV: FEELINGS TOWARD JEWS -- BY AGE (Continued)

Question: On a temperature scale from 0 to 100 how warm or cool do you feel toward Jews? NOTE: Question not asked in 1972-1985, 1987.

Responses: 00 = 0-9 degrees; 10 = 10-19; 20 = 20-29; 30 = 30-39; 40 = 40-49; 50 = 50-59; 60 = 60-69; 70 = 70-79; 80 = 80-89; 90 = 90-99

		YEAR		
AGE	RESP	'86	'88	'89
36-41	00	1%	1%	0%
	10	1	1	3
	20	0	1	1
	30	2	1	4
	40	7	4	6
	50	23	36	32
	60	17	13	15
	70	23	19	19
	80	17	14	14
	90	8	9	5
# SURVEYED		179	181	115
AGE	RESP	'86	'88	'89
42-47	00	2%	2%	1%
	10	1	0	1
	20	0	1	0
	30	3	1	2
	40	9	4	6
	50	19	34	26
	60	16	16	10
	70	21	18	22
	80	19	13	18
	90	10	11	14
# SURVEYED		138	153	103

		YEAR		
AGE	RESP	'86	'88	'89
48-53	00	4%	1%	3%
	10	1	3	1
	20	0	0	1
	30	4	5	4
	40	4	2	4
	50	18	42	25
	60	16	11	21
	70	27	10	20
	80	15	16	13
	90	11	9	9
# SURVEYED		106	88	80
AGE	RESP	'86	'88	'89
54-59	00	0%	1%	3%
	10	5	1	0
	20	2	3	0
	30	5	4	3
	40	1	4	2
	50	7	32	25
	60	22	10	11
	70	24	22	27
	80	27	16	14
	90	8	8	16
# SURVEYED		88	79	64

		YEAR		
AGE	RESP	'86	'88	'89
60-65	00	2%	1%	2%
	10	2	1	2
	20	0	1	2
	30	2	2	0
	40	7	6	2
	50	10	30	14
	60	20	9	10
	70	23	25	36
	80	22	20	24
	90	12	6	10
# SURVEYED		109	109	59
AGE	RESP	'86	'88	'89
66+	00	3%	2%	1%
	10	2	2	1
	20	1	0	0
	30	3	4	3
	40	9	4	7
	50	15	33	28
	60	19	11	11
	70	21	17	20
	80	17	16	16
	90	10	10	14
# SURVEYED		231	242	148

****

FEELINGS TOWARD PROTESTANTS

TABLE I: FEELINGS TOWARD PROTESTANTS -- BY TOTAL POPULATION

Question: On a temperature scale from 0 to 100 how warm or cool do you feel toward Protestants? NOTE: Question not asked in 1972-1985, 1987.

Responses: 00 = 0-9 degrees 10 = 10-19 20 = 20-29 30 = 30-39 40 = 40-49
50 = 50-59 60 = 60-69 70 = 70-79 80 = 80-89 90 = 90-99

	YEAR		
RESPONSE	'86	'88	'89
00	1%	1%	1%
10	1	1	1
20	0	0	1
30	1	1	2
40	4	2	3
50	18	29	23
60	16	10	9
70	21	20	20
80	21	18	21
90	18	17	18
# SURVEYED	1397	1395	931

TABLE II: FEELINGS TOWARD PROTESTANTS -- BY SEX

Question: On a temperature scale from 0 to 100 how warm or cool do you feel toward Protestants? NOTE: Question not asked in 1972-1985, 1987.

Responses: 00 = 0-9 degrees 10 = 10-19 20 = 20-29 30 = 30-39 40 = 40-49
50 = 50-59 60 = 60-69 70 = 70-79 80 = 80-89 90 = 90-99

		YEAR		
SEX	RESP	'86	'88	'89
MALE	00	1%	0%	2%
	10	1	1	1
	20	1	0	1
	30	1	1	3
	40	4	3	4
	50	21	33	27
	60	20	11	11
	70	21	21	21
	80	20	16	18
	90	11	14	13
# SURVEYED		596	602	400

		YEAR		
SEX	RESP	'86	'88	'89
FEMALE	00	1%	1%	0%
	10	1	1	1
	20	0	1	1
	30	1	1	1
	40	3	1	3
	50	15	27	21
	60	13	9	8
	70	20	20	19
	80	21	19	24
	90	23	20	22
# SURVEYED		801	793	531

TABLE III: FEELINGS TOWARD PROTE[illegible]

Question: On a temperature scale from 0 to 100 how warm or cool do you feel t[illegible]
asked in 1972-1985, 1987.

Responses: 00 = 0-9 degrees 10 = 10-19 20 = 20-29 30 = 30-3[illegible]
50 = 50-59 60 = 60-69 70 = 70-79 80 = 80-89

		YEAR		
RACE	RESP	'86	'88	'89
WHITE	00	1%	1%	1%
	10	1	1	1
	20	0	0	1
	30	1	1	2
	40	4	2	3
	50	17	29	23
	60	16	9	9
	70	21	22	21
	80	21	18	22
	90	19	17	18
# SURVEYED		1200	1173	812

		YEAR		
RACE	RESP	'86	'88	'89
BLACK	00	3%	1%	1%
	10	2	2	1
	20	0	0	1
	30	1	0	2
	40	3	4	3
	50	16	28	23
	60	18	12	14
	70	21	15	11
	80	18	19	22
	90	18	20	22
# SURVEYED		163	170	88

		YEAR		
RACE	R[illegible]	[illegible]	[illegible]	[illegible]
OTHER	00	[illegible]	[illegible]	[illegible]
	10	[illegible]	[illegible]	[illegible]
	20	[illegible]	[illegible]	[illegible]
	30	0	[illegible]	[illegible]
	40	6	[illegible]	[illegible]
	50	41	4[illegible]	[illegible]
	60	6	12	[illegible]
	70	15	13	[illegible]
	80	15	10	1[illegible]
	90	12	4	16
# SURVEYED		34	52	31

TABLE IV: FEELINGS TOWARD PROTESTANTS -- BY AGE

Question: On a temperature scale from 0 to 100 how warm or cool do you feel toward Protestants? NOTE: Question not asked in 1972-1985, 1987.

Responses: 00 = 0-9 degrees 10 = 10-19 20 = 20-29 30 = 30-39 40 = 40-49
50 = 50-59 60 = 60-69 70 = 70-79 80 = 80-89 90 = 90-99

		YEAR		
AGE	RESP	'86	'88	'89
18-23	00	1%	0%	5%
	10	1	2	0
	20	0	2	0
	30	0	2	3
	40	3	5	4
	50	28	43	25
	60	20	4	8
	70	17	17	28
	80	22	10	14
	90	8	16	14
# SURVEYED		103	133	79

		YEAR		
AGE	RESP	'86	'88	'89
24-29	00	1%	2%	1%
	10	0	0	2
	20	0	0	1
	30	1	0	2
	40	5	2	4
	50	25	41	31
	60	20	12	13
	70	20	18	22
	80	15	15	12
	90	12	9	13
# SURVEYED		207	204	134

		YEAR		
AGE	RESP	'86	'88	'89
30-35	00	2%	1%	0%
	10	0	2	2
	20	0	1	2
	30	0	1	4
	40	6	1	4
	50	26	41	29
	60	17	11	9
	70	22	17	15
	80	12	12	22
	90	14	15	12
# SURVEYED		214	184	129

TABLE IV: FEELINGS TOWARD PROTESTANTS -- BY AGE (Continued)

On a temperature scale from 0 to 100 how warm or cool do you feel toward Protestants? NOTE: Question not 72-1985, 1987.

es: 000 = 0-9 degrees 10 = 10-19 20 = 20-29 30 = 30-39 40 = 40-49
50 = 50-59 60 = 60-69 70 = 70-79 80 = 80-89 90 = 90-99

AGE	RESP	'86	'88	'89
36-41	00	1%	1%	1%
	10	1	1	1
	20	1	0	0
	30	1	0	2
	40	3	2	5
	50	23	31	33
	60	20	14	9
	70	20	19	18
	80	16	20	21
	90	15	13	11
# SURVEYED		183	182	119

AGE	RESP	'86	'88	'89
42-47	00	1%	1%	0%
	10	1	1	0
	20	0	0	0
	30	1	1	1
	40	4	4	4
	50	18	26	24
	60	14	11	12
	70	15	22	19
	80	24	18	25
	90	21	16	17
# SURVEYED		139	151	102

AGE	RESP	'86	'88	'89
48-53	00	1%	0%	2%
	10	2	3	0
	20	1	0	1
	30	0	1	1
	40	0	1	4
	50	12	26	20
	60	10	6	11
	70	29	22	22
	80	25	24	25
	90	21	16	14
# SURVEYED		104	87	81

AGE	RESP	'86	'88	'89
54-59	00	0%	2%	0%
	10	1	0	1
	20	0	1	0
	30	2	1	1
	40	1	1	1
	50	7	22	19
	60	15	11	7
	70	21	16	18
	80	37	22	22
	90	16	24	28
# SURVEYED		92	83	67

AGE	RESP	'86	'88	'89
60-65	00	0%	0%	2%
	10	0	0	2
	20	0	1	0
	30	0	0	0
	40	2	0	0
	50	7	16	11
	60	13	7	6
	70	21	27	21
	80	31	30	32
	90	26	19	26
# SURVEYED		105	113	62

AGE	RESP	'86	'88	'89
66+	00	0%	0%	1%
	10	1	0	1
	20	0	0	1
	30	2	2	1
	40	4	2	1
	50	7	15	11
	60	14	9	6
	70	21	24	22
	80	22	20	25
	90	30	27	31
# SURVEYED		243	255	156

****

TAKE BIBLE LITERALLY

TABLE I: TAKE BIBLE LITERALLY -- BY TOTAL POPULATION

Question: Which of these statements comes closest to describing your feelings about the Bible? Chose only one code. NOTE: Question not asked 1972-1983, 1986.

Responses: AW = The Bible is the actual word of God and is to be taken literally, word for word.
IW = The Bible is the inspired word of God but not everything should be taken literally.
AB = The Bible is an ancient book of fables, legends, history, and moral precepts recorded by men.

	YEAR				
RESPONSE	'84	'85	'87	'88	'89
AW	38%	37%	37%	35%	32%
IW	47	50	47	48	51
AB	14	13	15	16	16
# SURVEYED	963	733	944	1450	970

TABLE II: TAKE BIBLE LITERALLY -- BY SEX

Question: Which of these statements comes closest to describing your feelings about the Bible? Chose only one code. NOTE: Question not asked 1972-1983, 1986.

Responses: AW = The Bible is the actual word of God and is to be taken literally, word for word.
IW = The Bible is the inspired word of God but not everything should be taken literally.
AB = The Bible is an ancient book of fables, legends, history, and moral precepts recorded by men.

		YEAR				
SEX	RESP	'84	'85	'87	'88	'89
M	AW	29%	32%	31%	29%	26%
	IW	51	53	50	50	52
	AB	19	15	19	20	22
# SURVEYED		403	418	427	622	415

		YEAR				
SEX	RESP	'84	'85	'87	'88	'89
F	AW	44%	44%	43%	39%	37%
	IW	45	45	44	46	50
	AB	10	10	13	14	12
# SURVEYED		560	315	517	828	555

TABLE III: TAKE BIBLE LITERALLY -- BY RACE

Question: Which of these statements comes closest to describing your feelings about the Bible? Chose only one code. NOTE: Question not asked 1972-1983, 1986.

Responses: AW = The Bible is the actual word of God and is to be taken literally, word for word.
IW = The Bible is the inspired word of God but not everything should be taken literally.
AB = The Bible is an ancient book of fables, legends, history, and moral precepts recorded by men.

		YEAR				
RACE	RESP	'84	'85	'87	'88	'89
WHITE	AW	35%	34%	33%	33%	29%
	IW	50	53	50	50	53
	AB	15	13	16	17	17
# SURVEYED		822	644	787	1215	836
RACE	RESP	'84	'85	'87	'88	'89
BLACK	AW	61%	64%	60%	45%	59%
	IW	33	27	26	40	30
	AB	6	9	14	14	11
# SURVEYED		112	74	124	181	99

		YEAR				
RACE	RESP	'84	'85	'87	'88	'89
OTHER	AW	48%	53%	52%	41%	29%
	IW	38	33	30	37	54
	AB	14	7	18	22	17
# SURVEYED		29	15	33	54	35

TABLE IV: TAKE BIBLE LITERALLY -- BY AGE

Question: Which of these statements comes closest to describing your feelings about the Bible? Chose only one code. NOTE: Question not asked 1972-1983, 1986.

Responses: AW = The Bible is the actual word of God and is to be taken literally, word for word.
IW = The Bible is the inspired word of God but not everything should be taken literally.
AB = The Bible is an ancient book of fables, legends, history, and moral precepts recorded by men.

		YEAR				
AGE	RESP	'84	'85	'87	'88	'89
18-23	AW	35%	35%	38%	39%	36%
	IW	49	43	53	40	49
	AB	16	23	9	21	15
# SURVEYED		82	40	87	140	81
AGE	RESP	'84	'85	'87	'88	'89
24-29	AW	37%	28%	27%	26%	30%
	IW	48	56	50	57	53
	AB	14	16	21	16	17
# SURVEYED		147	95	131	211	142

		YEAR				
AGE	RESP	'84	'85	'87	'88	'89
30-35	AW	29%	29%	28%	34%	23%
	IW	55	62	49	51	56
	AB	15	10	22	15	21
# SURVEYED		132	94	158	188	135
AGE	RESP	'84	'85	'87	'88	'89
36-41	AW	29%	30%	32%	28%	24%
	IW	52	56	50	49	57
	AB	18	13	17	22	18
# SURVEYED		126	97	117	190	119

TABLE IV: TAKE BIBLE LITERALLY -- BY AGE (Continued)

Question: Which of these statements comes closest to describing your feelings about the Bible? Chose only one code. NOTE: Question not asked 1972-1983, 1986.

Responses: AW = The Bible is the actual word of God and is to be taken literally, word for word.
IW = The Bible is the inspired word of God but not everything should be taken literally.
AB = The Bible is an ancient book of fables, legends, history, and moral precepts recorded by men.

AGE	RESP	'84	'85	'87	'88	'89
42-47	AW	39%	28%	40%	31%	27%
	IW	44	49	47	51	56
	AB	17	22	12	17	16
# SURVEYED		87	67	97	155	106
48-53	AW	37%	35%	47%	30%	27%
	IW	45	54	41	59	52
	AB	18	11	11	11	19
# SURVEYED		76	74	75	91	84
54-59	AW	38%	56%	40%	39%	36%
	IW	45	34	48	43	47
	AB	18	10	13	17	17
# SURVEYED		74	62	63	82	70

		YEAR				
AGE	RESP	'84	'85	'87	'88	'89
60-65	AW	45%	38%	44%	40%	44%
	IW	49	50	46	43	44
	AB	7	12	10	16	12
# SURVEYED		74	68	72	116	68
66+	AW	52%	50%	48%	46%	45%
	IW	41	41	36	41	43
	AB	6	8	15	12	13
# SURVEYED		160	133	143	273	164

****

LIKELIHOOD OF LOSING JOB

TABLE I: LIKELIHOOD OF LOSING JOB -- BY TOTAL POPULATION

Question: Thinking about the next twelve months, how likely do you think it is that you will lose your job or be laid off -- very likely, fairly likely, not too likely, or not at all likely? NOTE: Question not asked in 1972-1976, 1980, 1984, 1987.

Responses: VL = Very likely FL = Fairly likely NT = Not too likely
UN = Not at all likely LV = Will be leaving labor force (volunteered)

	YEAR							
RESPONSE	'77	'78	'82	'83	'85	'86	'88	'89
VL	4%	4%	7%	6%	7%	4%	4%	4%
FL	6	4	6	8	5	7	4	4
NT	24	21	26	25	23	22	25	22
UN	65	71	61	61	65	67	66	70
LV	1	0	0	0	0	0	0	0
# SURVEYED	901	880	865	925	932	850	610	608

TABLE II: LIKELIHOOD OF LOSING JOB -- BY SEX

Question: Thinking about the next twelve months, how likely do you think it is that you will lose your job or be laid off -- very likely, fairly likely, not too likely, or not at all likely? NOTE: Question not asked in 1972-1976, 1980, 1984, 1987.

Responses: VL = Very likely FL = Fairly likely NT = Not too likely
UN = Not at all likely LV = Will be leaving labor force (volunteered)

		YEAR							
SEX	RESP	'77	'78	'82	'83	'85	'86	'88	'89
MALE	VL	4%	4%	9%	8%	6%	4%	5%	4%
	FL	6	3	7	7	4	6	5	3
	NT	23	21	25	23	22	24	25	21
	UN	66	72	59	62	67	67	65	72
	LV	0	0	0	0	0	0	0	0
# SURVEYED		497	487	433	489	499	450	310	318

		YEAR							
SEX	RESP	'77	'78	'82	'83	'85	'86	'88	'89
FEMALE	VL	4%	4%	6%	4%	7%	4%	3%	4%
	FL	6	5	5	8	5	8	4	4
	NT	25	20	28	28	25	21	25	24
	UN	63	71	62	60	63	68	68	67
	LV	1	0	0	0	0	0	0	0
# SURVEYED		404	393	432	436	433	400	300	290

TABLE III: LIKELIHOOD OF LOSING JOB -- BY RACE

Question: Thinking about the next twelve months, how likely do you think it is that you will lose your job or be laid off -- very likely, fairly likely, not too likely, or not at all likely? NOTE: Question not asked in 1972-1976, 1980, 1984, 1987.

Responses: VL = Very likely FL = Fairly likely NT = Not too likely
UN = Not at all likely LV = Will be leaving labor force (volunteered)

		YEAR							
RACE	RESP	'77	'78	'82	'83	'85	'86	'88	'89
WHITE	VL	4%	4%	7%	6%	6%	3%	4%	4%
	FL	6	3	5	7	4	5	3	3
	NT	23	21	26	25	23	23	25	22
	UN	67	73	61	63	67	69	67	71
	LV	1	0	0	0	0	0	0	0
# SURVEYED		795	783	766	835	815	727	515	534
RACE	RESP	'77	'78	'82	'83	'85	'86	'88	'89
BLACK	VL	5%	8%	5%	7%	11%	7%	3%	8%
	FL	4	11	12	19	7	18	11	10
	NT	38	22	28	30	26	20	25	21
	UN	53	59	55	44	56	55	61	62
	LV	0	0	0	0	0	0	0	0
# SURVEYED		95	88	82	81	85	99	75	52

		YEAR							
RACE	RESP	'77	'78	'82	'83	'85	'86	'88	'89
OTHER	VL	0%	0%	6%	0%	6%	4%	10%	5%
	FL	18	0	12	11	6	4	5	0
	NT	18	22	29	33	31	17	25	27
	UN	64	78	53	56	56	75	60	68
	LV	0	0	0	0	0	0	0	0
# SURVEYED		11	9	17	9	32	24	20	22

TABLE IV: LIKELIHOOD OF LOSING JOB -- BY AGE

Question: Thinking about the next twelve months, how likely do you think it is that you will lose your job or be laid off -- very likely, fairly likely, not too likely, or not at all likely? NOTE: Question not asked in 1972-1976, 1980, 1984, 1987.

Responses: VL = Very likely FL = Fairly likely NT = Not too likely
UN = Not at all likely LV = Will be leaving labor force (volunteered)

		YEAR							
AGE	RESP	'77	'78	'82	'83	'85	'86	'88	'89
18-23	VL	11%	10%	7%	10%	5%	3%	2%	9%
	FL	7	3	8	4	5	12	2	0
	NT	28	27	35	23	24	29	26	21
	UN	53	60	51	63	66	57	70	70
	LV	1	0	0	0	0	0	0	0
# SURVEYED		100	101	89	78	86	69	46	43

		YEAR							
AGE	RESP	'77	'78	'82	'83	'85	'86	'88	'89
24-29	VL	6%	7%	7%	5%	11%	2%	7%	6%
	FL	4	3	6	9	3	4	5	3
	NT	27	22	31	25	28	23	22	25
	UN	60	67	57	60	59	71	66	67
	LV	3	0	0	0	0	0	0	0
# SURVEYED		146	175	177	201	170	163	116	117

TABLE IV: LIKELIHOOD OF LOSING JOB -- BY AGE

Question: Thinking about the next twelve months, how likely do you think it is that you will lose your job or be laid off -- very likely, fairly likely, not too likely, or not at all likely? NOTE: Question not asked in 1972-1976, 1980, 1984, 1987.

Responses: VL = Very likely; FL = Fairly likely; NT = Not too likely; UN = Not at all likely; LV = Will be leaving labor force (volunteered)

AGE	RESP	'77	'78	'82	'83	'85	'86	'88	'89
30-35	VL	4%	2%	9%	6%	6%	3%	4%	7%
	FL	7	5	9	8	6	8	4	4
	NT	27	23	23	27	22	19	27	32
	UN	61	70	58	59	67	69	65	56
	LV	0	0	0	0	0	0	0	0
# SURVEYED		139	167	162	170	171	170	113	112
AGE	RESP	'77	'78	'82	'83	'85	'86	'88	'89
36-41	VL	3%	2%	10%	7%	7%	3%	3%	1%
	FL	7	1	7	10	7	8	4	4
	NT	20	14	26	26	21	21	25	17
	UN	71	83	57	57	65	68	68	78
	LV	0	0	0	0	0	0	0	0
# SURVEYED		123	108	114	125	140	155	104	104
AGE	RESP	'77	'78	'82	'83	'85	'86	'88	'89
42-47	VL	2%	1%	6%	6%	8%	6%	4%	0%
	FL	11	8	3	8	6	4	5	6
	NT	21	19	25	31	19	33	25	18
	UN	66	72	66	56	68	57	66	76
	LV	0	0	0	0	0	0	0	0
# SURVEYED		97	89	89	104	105	100	93	83
AGE	RESP	'77	'78	'82	'83	'85	'86	'88	'89
48-53	VL	2%	2%	7%	4%	5%	4%	2%	4%
	FL	3	3	4	6	3	4	4	6
	NT	25	22	30	19	28	19	25	24
	UN	70	72	59	71	64	72	69	66
	LV	0	0	0	0	0	0	0	0
# SURVEYED		115	94	70	79	100	68	52	67

AGE	RESP	'77	'78	'82	'83	'85	'86	'88	'89
54-59	VL	1%	4%	2%	5%	1%	9%	0%	2%
	FL	5	1	5	7	4	7	6	2
	NT	26	20	16	27	26	15	36	16
	UN	68	75	77	61	69	69	58	80
	LV	0	0	0	0	0	0	0	0
# SURVEYED		104	79	83	83	77	54	36	45
AGE	RESP	'77	'78	'82	'83	'85	'86	'88	'89
60-65	VL	2%	2%	9%	5%	7%	4%	3%	6%
	FL	4	10	4	9	0	6	3	6
	NT	16	17	20	16	13	19	22	22
	UN	78	71	67	69	80	70	72	67
	LV	0	0	0	0	0	0	0	0
# SURVEYED		51	42	46	55	54	47	32	18
AGE	RESP	'77	'78	'82	'83	'85	'86	'88	'89
66+	VL	0%	0%	3%	4%	11%	0%	18%	0%
	FL	0	0	3	0	4	10	6	0
	NT	20	9	29	30	32	14	18	11
	UN	80	91	65	67	54	76	59	89
	LV	0	0	0	0	0	0	0	0
# SURVEYED		20	23	31	27	28	21	17	18

****

LIKELIHOOD OF FINDING A NEW JOB

TABLE I: LIKELIHOOD OF FINDING A NEW JOB -- BY TOTAL POPULATION

Question: About how easy would it be for you to find a job with another employer with approximately the same income and fringe benefits that you now have? Would you say very easy, somewhat easy, or not easy at all? NOTE: Question not asked in 1972-1976, 1980, 1984, 1987.

Responses: VE = Very easy; SE = Somewhat easy; NE = Not easy at all

	YEAR							
RESPONSE	'77	'78	'82	'83	'85	'86	'88	'89
VE	27%	28%	22%	19%	25%	28%	28%	34%
SE	30	33	26	29	32	33	37	28
NE	43	39	51	51	43	39	35	38
# SURVEYED	891	869	853	920	924	854	601	602

TABLE II: LIKELIHOOD OF FINDING A NEW JOB -- BY SEX

Question: About how easy would it be for you to find a job with another employer with approximately the same income and fringe benefits that you now have? Would you say very easy, somewhat easy, or not easy at all? NOTE: Question not asked in 1972-1976, 1980, 1984, 1987.

Responses: VE = Very easy; SE = Somewhat easy; NE = Not easy at all

		YEAR							
SEX	RESP	'77	'78	'82	'83	'85	'86	'88	'89
M	VE	28%	29%	22%	20%	25%	26%	30%	33%
	SE	29	33	26	26	30	32	33	25
	NE	43	38	52	54	44	41	36	41
# SURVEYED		490	483	426	485	493	457	305	311

		YEAR							
SEX	RESP	'77	'78	'82	'83	'85	'86	'88	'89
F	VE	26%	28%	22%	18%	26%	29%	26%	35%
	SE	32	32	27	33	33	34	40	30
	NE	42	40	51	49	41	37	34	35
# SURVEYED		401	386	427	435	431	397	296	291

TABLE III: LIKELIHOOD OF FINDING A NEW JOB -- BY RACE

Question: About how easy would it be for you to find a job with another employer with approximately the same income and fringe benefits that you now have? Would you say very easy, somewhat easy, or not easy at all? NOTE: Question not asked in 1972-1976, 1980, 1984, 1987.

Responses: VE = Very easy; SE = Somewhat easy; NE = Not easy at all

RACE	RESP	'77	'78	'82	'83	'85	'86	'88	'89
WHITE	VE	28%	29%	23%	19%	27%	29%	30%	34%
	SE	30	33	27	30	32	32	37	27
	NE	42	37	50	51	41	39	33	39
# SURVEYED		784	774	753	829	808	725	506	527
BLACK	VE	20%	17%	13%	19%	12%	20%	22%	40%
	SE	30	29	22	21	26	40	36	31
	NE	50	54	65	60	62	40	42	29
# SURVEYED		96	87	82	81	84	105	74	52

RACE	RESP	'77	'78	'82	'83	'85	'86	'88	'89
OTHER	VE	27%	38%	22%	30%	22%	29%	14%	30%
	SE	36	25	28	30	28	33	29	26
	NE	36	38	50	40	50	38	57	43
# SURVEYED		11	8	18	10	32	24	21	23

TABLE IV: LIKELIHOOD OF FINDING A NEW JOB -- BY AGE

Question: About how easy would it be for you to find a job with another employer with approximately the same income and fringe benefits that you now have? Would you say very easy, somewhat easy, or not easy at all? NOTE: Question not asked in 1972-1976, 1980, 1984, 1987.

Responses: VE = Very easy; SE = Somewhat easy; NE = Not easy at all

AGE	RESP	'77	'78	'82	'83	'85	'86	'88	'89
18-23	VE	21%	35%	22%	22%	28%	29%	28%	31%
	SE	46	33	30	37	44	43	46	31
	NE	32	31	47	41	28	29	26	38
# SURVEYED		99	102	89	76	86	70	46	42
24-29	VE	32%	27%	27%	20%	29%	29%	29%	39%
	SE	38	41	28	40	39	38	47	34
	NE	30	32	45	40	32	33	24	27
# SURVEYED		151	176	173	199	168	164	116	119

AGE	RESP	'77	'78	'82	'83	'85	'86	'88	'89
30-35	VE	31%	30%	25%	20%	29%	27%	27%	33%
	SE	30	38	28	37	37	39	49	38
	NE	39	33	47	43	34	34	25	29
# SURVEYED		137	166	164	169	169	172	113	110
36-41	VE	31%	30%	20%	18%	26%	31%	27%	36%
	SE	27	30	34	29	30	35	41	26
	NE	42	40	46	53	44	34	31	38
# SURVEYED		122	106	112	127	142	152	102	103

TABLE IV: LIKELIHOOD OF FINDING A NEW JOB -- BY AGE (Continued)

Question: About how easy would it be for you to find a job with another employer with approximately the same income and fringe benefits that you now have? Would you say very easy, somewhat easy, or not easy at all? NOTE: Question not asked in 1972-1976, 1980, 1984, 1987.

Responses: VE = Very easy; SE = Somewhat easy; NE = Not easy at all

AGE	RESP	'77	'78	'82	'83	'85	'86	'88	'89
42-47	VE	20%	29%	16%	17%	26%	30%	36%	39%
	SE	32	36	23	27	33	29	16	27
	NE	47	36	61	56	41	41	48	35
# SURVEYED		93	87	90	102	105	104	92	83
48-53	VE	27%	25%	23%	26%	24%	29%	27%	25%
	SE	21	30	18	13	25	25	25	15
	NE	52	45	59	62	51	46	47	60
# SURVEYED		117	92	71	78	100	69	51	65
54-59	VE	21%	22%	21%	15%	12%	25%	21%	32%
	SE	27	18	22	15	12	15	24	14
	NE	52	60	58	71	76	60	55	55
# SURVEYED		102	78	78	82	76	53	33	44

AGE	RESP	'77	'78	'82	'83	'85	'86	'88	'89
60-65	VE	29%	20%	14%	18%	23%	13%	18%	24%
	SE	12	16	17	11	9	22	25	18
	NE	59	64	69	71	68	65	57	59
# SURVEYED		49	44	42	55	53	46	28	17
66+	VE	20%	35%	23%	11%	21%	24%	26%	39%
	SE	13	12	23	30	29	14	26	17
	NE	67	53	55	59	50	62	47	44
# SURVEYED		15	17	31	27	24	21	19	18

****

IMPORTANCE OF LENGTH OF WORK WEEK

TABLE I: IMPORTANCE OF LENGTH OF WORK WEEK -- BY TOTAL POPULATION

Question: Consider the following job characteristics: 1) high income, 2) no danger of being fired, 3) working hours are short, lots of free time, 4) chances for advancement, 5) work important and gives a feeling of accomplishment. Among these five characteristics how would you rank "working hours are short, lots of free time?" NOTE: Question not asked in 1972, 1975, 1978, 1983, 1986.

Responses: HI = Highest; NH = Next highest; MD = Middle; NL = Next lowest; LO = Lowest

	YEAR										
RESPONSE	'73	'74	'76	'77	'80	'82	'84	'85	'87	'88	'89
HI	5%	5%	4%	4%	3%	3%	3%	3%	4%	3%	3%
NH	10	11	9	8	8	8	7	7	8	8	7
MD	13	14	12	11	11	15	10	10	10	10	9
NL	25	27	22	25	26	20	22	21	27	26	23
LO	47	43	52	52	52	54	59	59	52	52	58
# SURVEYED	1462	1454	1449	1480	1436	719	1441	1500	1430	946	980

TABLE II: IMPORTANCE OF LENGTH OF WORK WEEK -- BY SEX

Question: Consider the following job characteristics: 1) high income, 2) no danger of being fired, 3) working hours are short, lots of free time, 4) chances for advancement, 5) work important and gives a feeling of accomplishment. Among these five characteristics how would you rank "working hours are short, lots of free time?" NOTE: Question not asked in 1972, 1975, 1978, 1983, 1986.

Responses: HI = Highest; NH = Next highest; MD = Middle; NL = Next lowest; LO = Lowest

		YEAR										
SEX	RESP	'73	'74	'76	'77	'80	'82	'84	'85	'87	'88	'89
MALE	HI	6%	5%	4%	4%	4%	3%	3%	4%	5%	3%	3%
	NH	11	10	10	7	10	8	7	7	9	8	8
	MD	14	16	13	12	11	15	10	11	9	12	11
	NL	25	29	22	25	26	19	21	23	28	25	24
	LO	45	40	50	51	50	54	58	56	50	52	54
# SURVEYED		679	675	650	669	635	399	588	676	623	385	430
SEX	RESP	'73	'74	'76	'77	'80	'82	'84	'85	'87	'88	'89
FEMALE	HI	4%	5%	4%	5%	3%	3%	3%	3%	3%	2%	3%
	NH	10	12	8	8	8	9	6	7	8	8	7
	MD	13	12	12	10	11	14	9	9	11	10	7
	NL	25	25	22	25	26	20	22	20	26	27	23
	LO	48	45	54	53	53	54	59	61	53	53	61
# SURVEYED		783	779	799	811	801	320	853	824	807	561	550

TABLE III: IMPORTANCE OF LENGTH OF WORK WEEK -- BY RACE

Question: Consider the following job characteristics: 1) high income, 2) no danger of being fired, 3) working hours are short, lots of free time, 4) chances for advancement, 5) work important and gives a feeling of accomplishment. Among these five characteristics how would you rank "working hours are short, lots of free time?" NOTE: Question not asked in 1972, 1975, 1978, 1983, 1986.

Responses: HI = Highest; NH = Next highest; MD = Middle; NL = Next lowest; LO = Lowest

		YEAR										
RACE	RESP	'73	'74	'76	'77	'80	'82	'84	'85	'87	'88	'89
WHITE	HI	4%	5%	4%	4%	3%	3%	3%	3%	4%	3%	3%
	NH	10	12	9	8	9	8	6	7	8	8	7
	MD	13	14	12	10	11	15	9	10	10	11	9
	NL	26	27	23	26	27	19	23	22	27	27	23
	LO	47	43	52	52	50	55	58	59	51	51	58
# SURVEYED		1276	1277	1317	1296	1290	633	1225	1312	1193	776	844
RACE	RESP	'73	'74	'76	'77	'80	'82	'84	'85	'87	'88	'89
BLACK	HI	7%	6%	5%	4%	3%	4%	4%	5%	2%	2%	2%
	NH	12	9	13	10	8	13	9	7	8	6	8
	MD	11	15	13	18	9	15	12	10	12	8	5
	NL	23	29	18	16	18	21	15	18	26	21	24
	LO	47	42	51	52	63	47	59	59	52	64	60
# SURVEYED		173	170	123	170	136	72	165	147	187	127	96
RACE	RESP	'73	'74	'76	'77	'80	'82	'84	'85	'87	'88	'89
OTHER	HI	15%	0%	0%	7%	0%	0%	4%	7%	0%	5%	5%
	NH	8	43	0	0	0	7	12	7	10	9	10
	MD	23	0	0	7	0	7	10	15	8	14	18
	NL	15	0	22	50	50	29	8	20	20	30	25
	LO	38	57	78	36	50	57	67	51	62	42	43
# SURVEYED		13	7	9	14	10	14	51	41	50	43	40

TABLE IV: IMPORTANCE OF LENGTH OF WORK WEEK -- BY AGE

Question: Consider the following job characteristics: 1) high income, 2) no danger of being fired, 3) working hours are short, lots of free time, 4) chances for advancement, 5) work important and gives a feeling of accomplishment. Among these five characteristics how would you rank "working hours are short, lots of free time?" NOTE: Question not asked in 1972, 1975, 1978, 1983, 1986.

Responses: HI = Highest; NH = Next highest; MD = Middle; NL = Next lowest; LO = Lowest

		YEAR										
AGE	RESP	'73	'74	'76	'77	'80	'82	'84	'85	'87	'88	'89
18-23	HI	4%	4%	4%	2%	0%	4%	2%	2%	3%	3%	2%
	NH	8	10	12	7	8	16	6	5	6	9	8
	MD	12	9	8	11	9	12	11	9	9	9	11
	NL	24	22	24	22	23	16	21	22	19	28	29
	LO	53	54	53	58	60	53	60	63	63	51	50
# SURVEYED		169	166	157	161	149	57	157	132	125	92	90
AGE	RESP	'73	'74	'76	'77	'80	'82	'84	'85	'87	'88	'89
24-29	HI	5%	4%	4%	7%	4%	3%	2%	4%	3%	5%	2%
	NH	12	10	9	6	8	11	6	9	7	5	5
	MD	10	12	12	9	10	16	7	7	9	12	10
	NL	27	31	22	26	26	17	23	24	29	17	29
	LO	46	43	53	52	53	52	63	56	51	60	54
# SURVEYED		206	209	223	198	200	115	228	215	191	130	112
AGE	RESP	'73	'74	'76	'77	'80	'82	'84	'85	'87	'88	'89
30-35	HI	3%	5%	2%	5%	2%	1%	1%	1%	6%	3%	5%
	NH	14	7	9	8	9	10	7	7	9	9	9
	MD	11	18	14	9	10	16	12	9	8	8	11
	NL	27	31	28	22	30	22	18	17	29	31	22
	LO	45	38	47	57	49	51	63	66	49	50	53
# SURVEYED		165	173	183	186	214	89	198	210	218	129	132
AGE	RESP	'73	'74	'76	'77	'80	'82	'84	'85	'87	'88	'89
36-41	HI	5%	3%	6%	4%	5%	7%	6%	6%	4%	2%	3%
	NH	10	13	7	10	7	7	9	8	9	9	8
	MD	13	11	14	9	14	10	9	7	9	10	11
	NL	22	26	24	30	33	29	28	22	34	34	27
	LO	49	47	49	46	40	47	48	56	45	45	52
# SURVEYED		169	149	152	166	148	72	185	179	182	131	131
AGE	RESP	'73	'74	'76	'77	'80	'82	'84	'85	'87	'88	'89
42-47	HI	5%	3%	6%	4%	7%	5%	3%	4%	5%	5%	4%
	NH	8	13	5	4	6	2	9	7	6	9	8
	MD	16	14	7	11	12	19	11	10	12	9	8
	NL	32	27	20	25	38	19	19	33	32	27	22
	LO	39	43	63	56	38	56	58	47	45	49	59
# SURVEYED		142	150	107	144	112	64	124	123	154	99	104

TABLE IV: IMPORTANCE OF LENGTH OF WORK WEEK -- BY AGE (Continued)

Question: Consider the following job characteristics: 1) high income, 2) no danger of being fired, 3) working hours are short, lots of free time, 4) chances for advancement, 5) work important and gives a feeling of accomplishment. Among these five characteristics how would you rank "working hours are short, lots of free time?" NOTE: Question not asked in 1972, 1975, 1978, 1983, 1986.

Responses: HI = Highest; NH = Next highest; MD = Middle; NL = Next lowest; LO = Lowest

		YEAR										
AGE	RESP	'73	'74	'76	'77	'80	'82	'84	'85	'87	'88	'89
48-53	HI	5%	7%	2%	5%	3%	0%	3%	5%	2%	5%	1%
	NH	10	14	20	7	7	9	5	8	6	11	3
	MD	11	17	13	15	13	11	13	12	10	17	4
	NL	25	27	16	24	28	26	22	16	31	29	21
	LO	48	36	50	48	49	54	58	60	52	38	70
# SURVEYED		146	145	131	147	123	54	102	131	124	63	90
AGE	RESP	'73	'74	'76	'77	'80	'82	'84	'85	'87	'88	'89
54-59	HI	6%	8%	7%	6%	4%	1%	4%	3%	3%	0%	5%
	NH	9	7	4	10	10	12	7	4	13	10	10
	MD	20	12	14	10	12	22	10	10	9	12	10
	NL	23	35	25	24	16	14	23	23	25	29	23
	LO	42	37	50	49	58	51	57	60	49	50	53
# SURVEYED		154	134	123	162	135	69	113	131	97	52	62
AGE	RESP	'73	'74	'76	'77	'80	'82	'84	'85	'87	'88	'89
60-65	HI	6%	6%	5%	2%	1%	2%	0%	4%	3%	0%	3%
	NH	10	17	9	10	14	4	6	8	7	10	8
	MD	11	13	12	11	8	11	8	10	11	7	7
	NL	27	30	22	26	25	17	24	19	22	26	23
	LO	46	34	52	52	53	66	61	59	56	57	59
# SURVEYED		118	105	130	112	118	47	109	127	98	81	74
AGE	RESP	'73	'74	'76	'77	'80	'82	'84	'85	'87	'88	'89
66+	HI	5%	5%	3%	3%	3%	3%	4%	3%	3%	2%	2%
	NH	8	13	8	9	8	6	6	6	8	5	8
	MD	13	17	13	13	10	14	9	13	12	12	7
	NL	23	19	21	24	19	18	20	18	19	20	17
	LO	52	46	56	50	59	58	60	60	58	61	66
# SURVEYED		189	217	238	197	229	148	220	245	238	166	182

****

IMPORTANCE OF GOOD PAY

TABLE I: IMPORTANCE OF GOOD PAY -- BY TOTAL POPULATION

Question: Consider the following job characteristics: 1) high income, 2) no danger of being fired, 3) working hours are short, lots of free time, 4) chances for advancement, 5) work important and gives a feeling of accomplishment. Among these five characteristics how would you rank "high income?" NOTE: Question not asked in 1972, 1975, 1978, 1983, 1986.

Responses: HI = Highest; NH = Next highest; MD = Middle; NL = Next lowest; LO = Lowest

	YEAR										
RESPONSE	'73	'74	'76	'77	'80	'82	'84	'85	'87	'88	'89
HI	19%	19%	20%	21%	20%	26%	19%	19%	22%	21%	21%
NH	24	21	22	24	27	25	25	26	27	24	25
MD	31	31	32	31	32	26	33	31	31	33	32
NL	20	21	19	18	16	17	19	20	15	17	18
LO	7	9	5	6	5	5	4	4	6	5	4
# SURVEYED	1462	1454	1449	1480	1436	719	1441	1500	1430	946	980

TABLE II: IMPORTANCE OF GOOD PAY -- BY SEX

Question: Consider the following job characteristics: 1) high income, 2) no danger of being fired, 3) working hours are short, lots of free time, 4) chances for advancement, 5) work important and gives a feeling of accomplishment. Among these five characteristics how would you rank "high income?" NOTE: Question not asked in 1972, 1975, 1978, 1983, 1986.

Responses: HI = Highest; NH = Next highest; MD = Middle; NL = Next lowest; LO = Lowest

		YEAR										
SEX	RESP	'73	'74	'76	'77	'80	'82	'84	'85	'87	'88	'89
MALE	HI	19%	18%	22%	20%	20%	25%	20%	19%	25%	20%	23%
	NH	26	20	25	27	28	28	26	28	29	26	24
	MD	29	30	31	29	32	28	32	33	29	36	36
	NL	19	21	18	16	15	14	18	17	13	14	13
	LO	8	10	5	7	5	5	4	2	5	3	3
# SURVEYED		679	675	650	669	635	399	588	676	623	385	430
SEX	RESP	'73	'74	'76	'77	'80	'82	'84	'85	'87	'88	'89
FEMALE	HI	19%	19%	19%	21%	20%	28%	18%	20%	20%	22%	20%
	NH	22	21	21	22	25	22	24	24	25	23	26
	MD	33	32	34	32	33	24	33	29	32	31	29
	NL	20	20	21	19	17	20	20	22	16	19	21
	LO	7	8	5	6	5	5	4	6	6	6	4
# SURVEYED		783	779	799	811	801	320	853	824	807	561	550

TABLE III: IMPORTANCE OF GOOD PAY -- BY RACE

Question: Consider the following job characteristics: 1) high income, 2) no danger of being fired, 3) working hours are short, lots of free time, 4) chances for advancement, 5) work important and gives a feeling of accomplishment. Among these five characteristics how would you rank "high income?" NOTE: Question not asked in 1972, 1975, 1978, 1983, 1986.

Responses: HI = Highest; NH = Next highest; MD = Middle; NL = Next lowest; LO = Lowest

RACE	RESP	'73	'74	'76	'77	'80	'82	'84	'85	'87	'88	'89
WHITE	HI	16%	16%	19%	18%	19%	24%	17%	18%	19%	18%	19%
	NH	24	21	23	25	26	25	24	26	26	25	25
	MD	33	32	33	32	33	28	34	32	33	34	33
	NL	21	22	20	18	17	18	20	20	15	19	18
	LO	7	10	6	7	5	5	4	4	6	5	4
# SURVEYED		1276	1277	1317	1296	1290	633	1225	1312	1193	776	844
RACE	RESP	'73	'74	'76	'77	'80	'82	'84	'85	'87	'88	'89
BLACK	HI	40%	39%	41%	41%	30%	47%	37%	33%	37%	39%	41%
	NH	25	19	20	20	31	29	24	24	30	21	27
	MD	17	22	24	19	22	14	24	23	19	29	18
	NL	12	15	13	15	13	6	11	16	12	8	14
	LO	6	5	2	4	4	4	4	3	2	3	1
# SURVEYED		173	170	123	170	136	72	165	147	187	127	96
RACE	RESP	'73	'74	'76	'77	'80	'82	'84	'85	'87	'88	'89
OTHER	HI	8%	0%	0%	29%	0%	29%	18%	24%	36%	33%	20%
	NH	23	43	33	21	30	14	33	27	16	19	15
	MD	46	29	22	29	40	36	27	27	28	40	38
	NL	15	29	33	7	20	7	20	20	18	7	25
	LO	8	0	11	14	10	14	2	2	2	2	3
# SURVEYED		13	7	9	14	10	14	51	41	50	43	40

TABLE IV: IMPORTANCE OF GOOD PAY -- BY AGE

Question: Consider the following job characteristics: 1) high income, 2) no danger of being fired, 3) working hours are short, lots of free time, 4) chances for advancement, 5) work important and gives a feeling of accomplishment. Among these five characteristics how would you rank "high income?" NOTE: Question not asked in 1972, 1975, 1978, 1983, 1986.

Responses: HI = Highest; NH = Next highest; MD = Middle; NL = Next lowest; LO = Lowest

		YEAR										
AGE	RESP	'73	'74	'76	'77	'80	'82	'84	'85	'87	'88	'89
18-23	HI	15%	14%	25%	25%	29%	35%	24%	25%	25%	24%	39%
	NH	31	21	25	31	22	28	28	32	32	38	22
	MD	31	34	34	26	28	19	30	30	29	26	22
	NL	18	22	12	13	18	11	15	11	10	8	13
	LO	4	8	4	5	3	7	3	3	4	4	3
# SURVEYED		169	166	157	161	149	57	157	132	125	92	90
AGE	RESP	'73	'74	'76	'77	'80	'82	'84	'85	'87	'88	'89
24-29	HI	17%	13%	20%	19%	25%	37%	24%	19%	25%	28%	25%
	NH	30	26	26	28	29	24	29	27	27	27	21
	MD	29	33	28	35	34	21	29	37	32	28	36
	NL	18	18	22	15	12	16	15	15	12	15	15
	LO	7	10	4	4	2	2	4	3	5	2	3
# SURVEYED		206	209	223	198	200	115	228	215	191	130	112
AGE	RESP	'73	'74	'76	'77	'80	'82	'84	'85	'87	'88	'89
30-35	HI	26%	26%	21%	17%	19%	30%	15%	23%	22%	23%	20%
	NH	26	24	27	24	27	33	26	30	28	33	36
	MD	32	25	31	32	38	24	39	25	36	29	26
	NL	15	21	15	23	14	11	15	19	11	11	14
	LO	1	4	6	4	1	2	4	3	4	4	5
# SURVEYED		165	173	183	186	214	89	198	210	218	129	132
AGE	RESP	'73	'74	'76	'77	'80	'82	'84	'85	'87	'88	'89
36-41	HI	20%	23%	16%	24%	18%	18%	19%	18%	22%	18%	27%
	NH	24	19	19	23	33	26	32	35	27	21	27
	MD	37	32	42	31	34	35	29	28	35	36	27
	NL	14	17	13	16	11	13	17	16	11	21	16
	LO	5	8	10	5	4	8	3	3	4	4	3
# SURVEYED		169	149	152	166	148	72	185	179	182	131	131
AGE	RESP	'73	'74	'76	'77	'80	'82	'84	'85	'87	'88	'89
42-47	HI	17%	19%	17%	20%	11%	30%	23%	20%	23%	21%	16%
	NH	23	17	21	28	38	31	23	21	30	23	25
	MD	35	37	37	34	34	27	32	42	31	37	39
	NL	18	19	22	15	11	13	16	13	12	14	18
	LO	8	9	2	3	7	0	5	3	5	4	1
# SURVEYED		142	150	107	144	112	64	124	123	154	99	104

TABLE IV: IMPORTANCE OF GOOD PAY -- BY AGE (Continued)

Question: Consider the following job characteristics: 1) high income, 2) no danger of being fired, 3) working hours are short, lots of free time, 4) chances for advancement, 5) work important and gives a feeling of accomplishment. Among these five characteristics how would you rank "high income?" NOTE: Question not asked in 1972, 1975, 1978, 1983, 1986.

Responses: HI = Highest; NH = Next highest; MD = Middle; NL = Next lowest; LO = Lowest

		YEAR										
AGE	RESP	'73	'74	'76	'77	'80	'82	'84	'85	'87	'88	'89
48-53	HI	21%	17%	21%	20%	20%	28%	25%	24%	26%	30%	16%
	NH	26	21	27	26	20	22	24	21	23	21	27
	MD	31	29	31	29	36	31	37	35	29	33	37
	NL	17	21	18	19	20	11	14	19	18	10	19
	LO	5	12	4	6	5	7	1	2	5	6	2
# SURVEYED		146	145	131	147	123	54	102	131	124	63	90
AGE	RESP	'73	'74	'76	'77	'80	'82	'84	'85	'87	'88	'89
54-59	HI	19%	20%	19%	24%	20%	25%	12%	23%	29%	29%	23%
	NH	17	24	23	22	32	19	28	26	28	17	26
	MD	27	32	29	31	28	26	34	26	26	35	23
	NL	25	17	23	16	16	26	19	21	13	10	24
	LO	11	7	7	7	4	4	7	5	4	10	5
# SURVEYED		154	134	123	162	135	69	113	131	97	52	62
AGE	RESP	'73	'74	'76	'77	'80	'82	'84	'85	'87	'88	'89
60-65	HI	16%	17%	24%	19%	19%	21%	18%	9%	13%	17%	22%
	NH	21	20	19	27	22	19	13	23	21	14	23
	MD	31	30	30	27	31	34	40	34	33	48	35
	NL	23	24	24	17	19	17	27	29	21	19	18
	LO	9	10	3	11	8	9	2	5	11	2	3
# SURVEYED		118	105	130	112	118	47	109	127	98	81	74
AGE	RESP	'73	'74	'76	'77	'80	'82	'84	'85	'87	'88	'89
66+	HI	16%	18%	20%	18%	17%	18%	14%	15%	18%	12%	13%
	NH	17	15	16	13	22	22	16	18	22	18	19
	MD	27	27	32	31	28	27	32	28	26	32	38
	NL	27	27	25	23	24	24	31	29	24	31	23
	LO	13	13	8	14	9	9	7	9	9	7	7
# SURVEYED		189	217	238	197	229	148	220	245	238	166	182

****

IMPORTANCE OF ACCOMPLISHMENT

TABLE I: IMPORTANCE OF ACCOMPLISHMENT -- BY TOTAL POPULATION

Question: Consider the following job characteristics: 1) high income, 2) no danger of being fired, 3) working hours are short, lots of free time, 4) chances for advancement, 5) work important and gives feeling of accomplishment. Among these five characteristics how would you rank "work important and gives feeling of accomplishment?" NOTE: Question not asked in 1972, 1975, 1978, 1983, 1986.

Responses: HI = Highest; NH = Next highest; MD = Middle; NL = Next lowest; LO = Lowest

	YEAR										
RESPONSE	'73	'74	'76	'77	'80	'82	'84	'85	'87	'88	'89
HI	52%	51%	50%	47%	52%	43%	51%	48%	50%	49%	53%
NH	16	19	17	19	18	18	19	20	19	20	19
MD	13	13	14	13	15	15	14	16	15	13	13
NL	12	10	12	12	10	14	10	11	10	11	10
LO	8	7	7	8	5	10	6	5	6	7	4
# SURVEYED	1462	1454	1449	1480	1436	719	1441	1500	1430	946	980

TABLE II: IMPORTANCE OF ACCOMPLISHMENT -- BY SEX

Question: Consider the following job characteristics: 1) high income, 2) no danger of being fired, 3) working hours are short, lots of free time, 4) chances for advancement, 5) work important and gives feeling of accomplishment. Among these five characteristics how would you rank "work important and gives feeling of accomplishment?" NOTE: Question not asked in 1972, 1975, 1978, 1983, 1986.

Responses: HI = Highest; NH = Next highest; MD = Middle; NL = Next lowest; LO = Lowest

		YEAR										
SEX	RESP	'73	'74	'76	'77	'80	'82	'84	'85	'87	'88	'89
MALE	HI	48%	46%	48%	43%	51%	41%	48%	46%	47%	49%	52%
	NH	15	19	16	19	17	19	21	20	17	17	20
	MD	13	15	17	14	16	13	14	15	17	14	12
	NL	15	12	11	14	11	16	11	13	12	12	11
	LO	9	8	8	10	6	12	6	6	7	7	5
# SURVEYED		679	675	650	669	635	399	588	676	623	385	430
SEX	RESP	'73	'74	'76	'77	'80	'82	'84	'85	'87	'88	'89
FEMALE	HI	55%	56%	52%	50%	52%	46%	53%	49%	53%	49%	55%
	NH	17	19	18	20	19	16	19	20	20	22	18
	MD	13	10	13	13	14	18	13	16	14	12	15
	NL	9	9	12	11	10	12	9	10	8	10	9
	LO	7	6	6	7	4	8	6	5	6	6	4
# SURVEYED		783	779	799	811	801	320	853	824	807	561	550

TABLE III: IMPORTANCE OF ACCOMPLISHMENT -- BY RACE

Question: Consider the following job characteristics: 1) high income, 2) no danger of being fired, 3) working hours are short, lots of free time, 4) chances for advancement, 5) work important and gives feeling of accomplishment. Among these five characteristics how would you rank "work important and gives feeling of accomplishment?" NOTE: Question not asked in 1972, 1975, 1978, 1983, 1986.

Responses: HI = Highest; NH = Next highest; MD = Middle; NL = Next lowest; LO = Lowest

		YEAR										
RACE	RESP	'73	'74	'76	'77	'80	'82	'84	'85	'87	'88	'89
WHITE	HI	55%	54%	53%	49%	54%	46%	55%	50%	54%	54%	56%
	NH	16	20	18	20	19	18	20	20	19	19	19
	MD	12	11	14	13	13	14	12	15	14	12	12
	NL	10	9	10	11	10	13	8	10	8	9	10
	LO	6	5	6	7	4	9	6	4	5	6	4
# SURVEYED		1276	1277	1317	1296	1290	633	1225	1312	1193	776	844
RACE	RESP	'73	'74	'76	'77	'80	'82	'84	'85	'87	'88	'89
BLACK	HI	23%	27%	21%	29%	33%	17%	25%	28%	29%	24%	33%
	NH	17	12	12	18	10	19	19	21	17	26	15
	MD	19	21	23	15	29	22	24	22	19	19	28
	NL	23	18	24	21	16	24	23	19	18	20	13
	LO	18	21	20	17	12	18	10	10	17	10	11
# SURVEYED		173	170	123	170	136	72	165	147	187	127	96
RACE	RESP	'73	'74	'76	'77	'80	'82	'84	'85	'87	'88	'89
OTHER	HI	46%	57%	56%	43%	50%	36%	53%	37%	42%	33%	53%
	NH	23	0	11	21	20	14	14	15	20	26	18
	MD	15	29	11	21	30	21	14	22	22	12	15
	NL	8	14	22	14	0	21	18	15	8	16	10
	LO	8	0	0	0	0	7	2	12	8	14	5
# SURVEYED		13	7	9	14	10	14	51	41	50	43	40

TABLE IV: IMPORTANCE OF ACCOMPLISHMENT -- BY AGE

Question: Consider the following job characteristics: 1) high income, 2) no danger of being fired, 3) working hours are short, lots of free time, 4) chances for advancement, 5) work important and gives feeling of accomplishment. Among these five characteristics how would you rank "work important and gives feeling of accomplishment?" NOTE: Question not asked in 1972, 1975, 1978, 1983, 1986.

Responses: HI = Highest; NH = Next highest; MD = Middle; NL = Next lowest; LO = Lowest

		YEAR										
AGE	RESP	'73	'74	'76	'77	'80	'82	'84	'85	'87	'88	'89
18-23	HI	45%	40%	47%	38%	44%	28%	39%	39%	38%	41%	38%
	NH	16	25	17	21	21	12	23	19	18	20	18
	MD	17	13	15	18	18	26	12	23	17	15	21
	NL	15	17	11	15	13	18	15	16	20	15	18
	LO	7	5	9	8	3	16	11	4	7	9	6
# SURVEYED		169	166	157	161	149	57	157	132	125	92	90
AGE	RESP	'73	'74	'76	'77	'80	'82	'84	'85	'87	'88	'89
24-29	HI	57%	56%	49%	49%	48%	40%	48%	48%	50%	41%	51%
	NH	17	19	16	22	20	17	18	17	20	22	27
	MD	13	11	19	13	20	17	18	13	13	15	13
	NL	9	7	10	9	9	14	10	15	10	15	5
	LO	5	6	6	7	5	12	6	7	6	7	4
# SURVEYED		206	209	223	198	200	115	228	215	191	130	112
AGE	RESP	'73	'74	'76	'77	'80	'82	'84	'85	'87	'88	'89
30-35	HI	50%	53%	56%	52%	55%	46%	57%	48%	50%	51%	56%
	NH	15	17	15	23	19	18	19	19	21	16	15
	MD	13	12	13	7	13	16	12	19	13	16	14
	NL	14	10	10	10	9	12	10	11	9	9	11
	LO	8	8	5	8	4	8	3	4	7	8	4
# SURVEYED		165	173	183	186	214	89	198	210	218	129	132
AGE	RESP	'73	'74	'76	'77	'80	'82	'84	'85	'87	'88	'89
36-41	HI	54%	55%	55%	48%	57%	47%	53%	52%	55%	57%	56%
	NH	15	20	24	22	18	18	19	16	21	18	18
	MD	11	11	9	8	15	18	14	19	14	11	17
	NL	13	6	8	13	6	8	9	10	7	8	7
	LO	7	7	5	8	5	8	5	3	2	5	2
# SURVEYED		169	149	152	166	148	72	185	179	182	131	131
AGE	RESP	'73	'74	'76	'77	'80	'82	'84	'85	'87	'88	'89
42-47	HI	56%	60%	58%	50%	59%	45%	56%	53%	56%	51%	65%
	NH	20	16	13	14	18	19	14	24	14	20	14
	MD	7	11	12	13	11	9	13	12	15	11	11
	NL	8	9	13	16	8	13	11	6	6	9	6
	LO	8	4	4	7	4	14	6	5	8	9	4
# SURVEYED		142	150	107	144	112	64	124	123	154	99	104

TABLE IV: IMPORTANCE OF ACCOMPLISHMENT -- BY AGE (Continued)

Question: Consider the following job characteristics: 1) high income, 2) no danger of being fired, 3) working hours are short, lots of free time, 4) chances for advancement, 5) work important and gives feeling of accomplishment. Among these five characteristics how would you rank "work important and gives feeling of accomplishment?" NOTE: Question not asked in 1972, 1975, 1978, 1983, 1986.

Responses: HI = Highest; NH = Next highest; MD = Middle; NL = Next lowest; LO = Lowest

		YEAR										
AGE	RESP	'73	'74	'76	'77	'80	'82	'84	'85	'87	'88	'89
48-53	HI	56%	56%	52%	46%	55%	52%	54%	46%	54%	44%	59%
	NH	16	20	10	18	19	13	18	27	18	17	16
	MD	12	12	15	17	15	11	10	9	19	17	9
	NL	10	6	15	11	7	13	12	11	4	11	13
	LO	5	6	8	9	4	11	7	7	6	10	3
# SURVEYED		146	145	131	147	123	54	102	131	124	63	90
AGE	RESP	'73	'74	'76	'77	'80	'82	'84	'85	'87	'88	'89
54-59	HI	48%	47%	48%	49%	50%	54%	56%	50%	47%	46%	55%
	NH	18	19	18	12	13	12	16	20	19	21	16
	MD	14	16	18	17	18	10	16	14	18	12	13
	NL	11	9	9	12	13	16	8	10	9	21	8
	LO	10	8	7	10	7	9	4	6	7	0	8
# SURVEYED		154	134	123	162	135	69	113	131	97	52	62
AGE	RESP	'73	'74	'76	'77	'80	'82	'84	'85	'87	'88	'89
60-65	HI	51%	45%	51%	49%	47%	38%	59%	61%	51%	53%	49%
	NH	14	18	19	21	24	19	21	17	19	25	26
	MD	14	9	14	10	10	23	11	13	13	12	11
	NL	12	12	10	10	15	13	6	6	10	7	8
	LO	9	16	6	10	3	6	4	5	6	2	7
# SURVEYED		118	105	130	112	118	47	109	127	98	81	74
AGE	RESP	'73	'74	'76	'77	'80	'82	'84	'85	'87	'88	'89
66+	HI	48%	47%	42%	41%	52%	41%	46%	40%	48%	52%	50%
	NH	15	18	20	21	14	24	24	22	16	21	21
	MD	14	15	13	16	13	10	14	18	18	10	13
	NL	14	14	16	14	13	17	9	14	11	10	12
	LO	10	6	9	9	7	8	7	7	7	7	5
# SURVEYED		189	217	238	197	229	148	220	245	238	166	182

****

IMPORTANCE OF PROMOTION

TABLE I: IMPORTANCE OF PROMOTION -- BY TOTAL POPULATION

Question: Consider the following job characteristics: 1) high income, 2) no danger of being fired, 3) working hours are short, lots of free time, 4) chances for advancement, 5) work important and gives a feeling of accomplishment. Among these five characteristics how would you rank "chances for advancement?" NOTE: Question not asked in 1972, 1975, 1978, 1983, 1986.

Responses: HI = Highest; NH = Next highest; MD = Middle; NL = Next lowest; LO = Lowest

	YEAR										
RESPONSE	'73	'74	'76	'77	'80	'82	'84	'85	'87	'88	'89
HI	18%	18%	18%	20%	19%	17%	19%	22%	18%	20%	17%
NH	35	38	37	34	35	31	36	36	35	34	37
MD	23	23	21	23	25	21	24	23	24	23	25
NL	13	13	15	14	14	21	14	13	16	14	14
LO	10	8	10	9	7	10	7	6	7	8	7
# SURVEYED	1462	1454	1449	1480	1436	719	1441	1500	1430	946	980

TABLE II: IMPORTANCE OF PROMOTION -- BY SEX

Question: Consider the following job characteristics: 1) high income, 2) no danger of being fired, 3) working hours are short, lots of free time, 4) chances for advancement, 5) work important and gives a feeling of accomplishment. Among these five characteristics how would you rank "chances for advancement?" NOTE: Question not asked in 1972, 1975, 1978, 1983, 1986.

Responses: HI = Highest; NH = Next highest; MD = Middle; NL = Next lowest; LO = Lowest

		YEAR										
SEX	RESP	'73	'74	'76	'77	'80	'82	'84	'85	'87	'88	'89
M	HI	19%	21%	17%	22%	18%	20%	21%	22%	18%	19%	17%
A	NH	32	38	34	32	33	28	33	34	32	35	36
L	MD	24	20	21	22	26	22	24	22	27	22	23
E	NL	15	13	16	15	15	22	14	15	16	14	17
	LO	10	8	11	8	9	9	8	7	8	11	8
# SURVEYED		679	675	650	669	635	399	588	676	623	385	430
SEX	RESP	'73	'74	'76	'77	'80	'82	'84	'85	'87	'88	'89
F	HI	17%	16%	18%	18%	20%	14%	18%	23%	18%	21%	18%
E	NH	39	38	39	36	36	34	38	38	38	34	38
M	MD	23	25	21	24	25	20	23	23	21	24	27
A	NL	12	13	14	13	12	21	13	11	15	14	12
L	LO	10	8	8	9	6	11	7	4	7	7	6
E												
# SURVEYED		783	779	799	811	801	320	853	824	807	561	550

TABLE III: IMPORTANCE OF PROMOTION -- BY RACE

Question: Consider the following job characteristics: 1) high income, 2) no danger of being fired, 3) working hours are short, lots of free time, 4) chances for advancement, 5) work important and gives a feeling of accomplishment. Among these five characteristics how would you rank "chances for advancement?" NOTE: Question not asked in 1972, 1975, 1978, 1983, 1986.

Responses: HI = Highest; NH = Next highest; MD = Middle; NL = Next lowest; LO = Lowest

		YEAR										
RACE	RESP	'73	'74	'76	'77	'80	'82	'84	'85	'87	'88	'89
WHITE	HI	18%	18%	17%	20%	18%	17%	19%	22%	18%	19%	17%
	NH	37	39	37	35	35	32	37	37	37	35	37
	MD	23	23	21	23	25	20	24	23	24	24	25
	NL	13	13	15	13	14	21	13	12	15	13	14
	LO	9	8	9	8	7	10	7	6	7	8	7
# SURVEYED		1276	1277	1317	1296	1290	633	1225	1312	1193	776	844
RACE	RESP	'73	'74	'76	'77	'80	'82	'84	'85	'87	'88	'89
BLACK	HI	20%	18%	20%	18%	23%	18%	22%	23%	24%	27%	20%
	NH	24	33	26	28	34	15	27	31	27	30	36
	MD	26	25	23	22	24	26	21	24	24	20	24
	NL	18	15	19	18	14	26	19	16	17	16	13
	LO	12	9	13	14	5	14	10	7	9	7	7
# SURVEYED		173	170	123	170	136	72	165	147	187	127	96
RACE	RESP	'73	'74	'76	'77	'80	'82	'84	'85	'87	'88	'89
OTHER	HI	15%	29%	33%	14%	40%	7%	18%	24%	10%	21%	15%
	NH	38	14	44	57	20	36	33	37	34	28	40
	MD	8	14	22	29	20	36	29	17	20	19	23
	NL	15	29	0	0	0	21	12	12	26	19	15
	LO	23	14	0	0	20	0	8	10	10	14	8
# SURVEYED		13	7	9	14	10	14	51	41	50	43	40

TABLE IV: IMPORTANCE OF PROMOTION -- BY AGE

Question: Consider the following job characteristics: 1) high income, 2) no danger of being fired, 3) working hours are short, lots of free time, 4) chances for advancement, 5) work important and gives a feeling of accomplishment. Among these five characteristics how would you rank "chances for advancement?" NOTE: Question not asked in 1972, 1975, 1978, 1983, 1986.

Responses: HI = Highest; NH = Next highest; MD = Middle; NL = Next lowest; LO = Lowest

		YEAR										
AGE	RESP	'73	'74	'76	'77	'80	'82	'84	'85	'87	'88	'89
18-23	HI	28%	30%	18%	30%	22%	19%	29%	26%	28%	25%	18%
	NH	28	27	31	28	36	23	29	39	31	22	36
	MD	20	28	22	17	24	26	24	20	24	27	26
	NL	12	10	17	18	12	23	10	11	11	17	12
	LO	12	5	12	7	5	9	8	5	6	9	9
# SURVEYED		169	166	157	161	149	57	157	132	125	92	90
AGE	RESP	'73	'74	'76	'77	'80	'82	'84	'85	'87	'88	'89
24-29	HI	16%	17%	22%	20%	22%	16%	20%	22%	18%	18%	19%
	NH	34	38	37	34	34	29	34	37	35	32	33
	MD	28	25	22	22	26	23	27	23	26	31	28
	NL	14	14	12	17	12	24	14	11	15	16	13
	LO	8	5	7	7	8	8	5	7	6	4	8
# SURVEYED		206	209	223	198	200	115	228	215	191	130	112
AGE	RESP	'73	'74	'76	'77	'80	'82	'84	'85	'87	'88	'89
30-35	HI	16%	14%	15%	19%	19%	15%	23%	23%	18%	18%	14%
	NH	35	38	41	33	34	29	35	37	33	32	31
	MD	29	23	20	26	26	25	20	23	23	29	31
	NL	13	13	16	15	13	22	17	12	18	14	18
	LO	7	12	8	7	8	9	6	5	8	7	5
# SURVEYED		165	173	183	186	214	89	198	210	218	129	132
AGE	RESP	'73	'74	'76	'77	'80	'82	'84	'85	'87	'88	'89
36-41	HI	13%	12%	17%	18%	14%	14%	14%	17%	13%	17%	11%
	NH	38	38	35	33	33	33	30	32	33	37	43
	MD	25	27	20	25	27	24	31	32	30	26	27
	NL	14	16	18	14	17	19	16	15	17	15	11
	LO	10	7	10	10	9	10	9	4	8	6	8
# SURVEYED		169	149	152	166	148	72	185	179	182	131	131
AGE	RESP	'73	'74	'76	'77	'80	'82	'84	'85	'87	'88	'89
42-47	HI	18%	14%	12%	17%	20%	14%	14%	18%	12%	15%	12%
	NH	35	47	42	38	30	30	39	37	35	36	45
	MD	23	17	21	23	35	22	24	25	25	26	19
	NL	15	12	15	11	8	23	18	14	18	17	17
	LO	10	11	9	11	7	11	6	6	10	5	7
# SURVEYED		142	150	107	144	112	64	124	123	154	99	104

TABLE IV: IMPORTANCE OF PROMOTION -- BY AGE (Continued)

Question: Consider the following job characteristics: 1) high income, 2) no danger of being fired, 3) working hours are short, lots of free time, 4) chances for advancement, 5) work important and gives a feeling of accomplishment. Among these five characteristics how would you rank "chances for advancement?" NOTE: Question not asked in 1972, 1975, 1978, 1983, 1986.

Responses: HI = Highest; NH = Next highest; MD = Middle; NL = Next lowest; LO = Lowest

		YEAR										
AGE	RESP	'73	'74	'76	'77	'80	'82	'84	'85	'87	'88	'89
48-53	HI	11%	14%	15%	14%	13%	13%	13%	19%	12%	14%	18%
	NH	40	37	29	30	46	33	34	28	44	32	38
	MD	24	21	25	25	18	24	31	27	23	19	23
	NL	12	18	17	18	12	19	11	19	18	17	17
	LO	12	10	15	13	11	11	11	7	2	17	4
# SURVEYED		146	145	131	147	123	54	102	131	124	63	90
AGE	RESP	'73	'74	'76	'77	'80	'82	'84	'85	'87	'88	'89
54-59	HI	18%	16%	14%	14%	15%	10%	13%	14%	16%	21%	10%
	NH	37	40	38	41	33	35	40	39	33	38	32
	MD	18	23	20	25	26	17	19	24	27	19	31
	NL	15	12	16	10	19	22	17	13	14	6	21
	LO	12	9	12	10	7	16	11	10	9	15	6
# SURVEYED		154	134	123	162	135	69	113	131	97	52	62
AGE	RESP	'73	'74	'76	'77	'80	'82	'84	'85	'87	'88	'89
60-65	HI	20%	23%	14%	20%	20%	21%	14%	22%	22%	26%	23%
	NH	33	33	37	29	26	43	46	38	35	43	31
	MD	23	19	25	27	28	13	14	21	17	12	22
	NL	13	15	16	15	18	15	16	13	18	10	12
	LO	11	10	8	10	8	9	11	6	7	9	12
# SURVEYED		118	105	130	112	118	47	109	127	98	81	74
AGE	RESP	'73	'74	'76	'77	'80	'82	'84	'85	'87	'88	'89
66+	HI	23%	21%	25%	27%	22%	25%	25%	31%	24%	26%	26%
	NH	37	41	38	40	39	29	40	39	39	37	38
	MD	21	21	19	19	22	18	21	16	18	14	21
	NL	13	10	11	8	12	19	8	9	12	11	11
	LO	6	7	7	6	5	9	6	5	7	11	4
# SURVEYED		189	217	238	197	229	148	220	245	238	166	182

****

IMPORTANCE OF JOB SECURITY

TABLE I: IMPORTANCE OF JOB SECURITY -- BY TOTAL POPULATION

Question: Consider the following job characteristics: 1) high income, 2) no danger of being fired, 3) working hours are short, lots of free time, 4) chances for advancement, 5) work important and gives a feeling of accomplishment. Among these five characteristics how would you rank "no danger of being fired?" NOTE: Question not asked in 1972, 1975, 1978, 1983, 1986.

Responses: HI = Highest; NH = Next highest; MD = Middle; NL = Next lowest; LO = Lowest

	YEAR										
RESPONSE	'73	'74	'76	'77	'80	'82	'84	'85	'87	'88	'89
HI	7%	8%	8%	8%	6%	10%	8%	7%	6%	7%	5%
NH	14	11	15	14	12	18	13	11	11	14	12
MD	20	20	20	22	17	23	20	21	20	20	21
NL	30	29	32	32	34	29	36	35	33	32	35
LO	29	33	26	24	31	21	24	26	29	28	27
# SURVEYED	1462	1454	1449	1480	1436	719	1441	1500	1430	946	980

TABLE II: IMPORTANCE OF JOB SECURITY -- BY SEX

Question: Consider the following job characteristics: 1) high income, 2) no danger of being fired, 3) working hours are short, lots of free time, 4) chances for advancement, 5) work important and gives a feeling of accomplishment. Among these five characteristics how would you rank "no danger of being fired?" NOTE: Question not asked in 1972, 1975, 1978, 1983, 1986.

Responses: HI = Highest; NH = Next highest; MD = Middle; NL = Next lowest; LO = Lowest

		YEAR										
SEX	RESP	'73	'74	'76	'77	'80	'82	'84	'85	'87	'88	'89
MALE	HI	8%	10%	9%	10%	7%	11%	8%	9%	6%	8%	6%
	NH	17	12	15	14	13	17	14	11	14	15	13
	MD	21	19	19	22	16	22	19	18	18	16	18
	NL	25	25	32	30	33	30	36	33	32	34	34
	LO	29	35	25	24	31	20	23	29	30	27	29
# SURVEYED		679	675	650	669	635	399	588	676	623	385	430
SEX	RESP	'73	'74	'76	'77	'80	'82	'84	'85	'87	'88	'89
FEMALE	HI	5%	5%	7%	6%	5%	9%	7%	6%	6%	6%	5%
	NH	12	10	15	14	11	18	13	11	9	13	11
	MD	19	21	21	22	18	24	21	22	22	23	23
	NL	34	32	31	33	34	27	35	37	35	30	35
	LO	29	32	27	25	32	22	24	23	29	28	26
# SURVEYED		783	779	799	811	801	320	853	824	807	561	550

TABLE III: IMPORTANCE OF JOB SECURITY -- BY RACE

Question: Consider the following job characteristics: 1) high income, 2) no danger of being fired, 3) working hours are short, lots of free time, 4) chances for advancement, 5) work important and gives a feeling of accomplishment. Among these five characteristics how would you rank "no danger of being fired?" NOTE: Question not asked in 1972, 1975, 1978, 1983, 1986.

Responses: HI = Highest; NH = Next highest; MD = Middle; NL = Next lowest; LO = Lowest

		YEAR										
RACE	RESP	'73	'74	'76	'77	'80	'82	'84	'85	'87	'88	'89
WHITE	HI	6%	7%	7%	8%	6%	9%	7%	7%	5%	6%	5%
	NH	13	9	14	13	11	17	13	11	10	13	11
	MD	19	20	20	22	17	23	20	21	19	20	21
	NL	30	29	32	32	33	29	36	36	34	31	35
	LO	31	34	27	26	33	21	25	26	31	30	27
# SURVEYED		1276	1277	1317	1296	1290	633	1225	1312	1193	776	844
RACE	RESP	'73	'74	'76	'77	'80	'82	'84	'85	'87	'88	'89
BLACK	HI	9%	9%	13%	8%	11%	14%	12%	10%	9%	9%	4%
	NH	22	27	28	24	18	24	21	16	18	17	14
	MD	27	17	18	25	15	22	19	20	26	24	25
	NL	25	24	27	29	40	24	32	31	28	35	38
	LO	17	23	14	13	16	17	16	22	20	16	20
# SURVEYED		173	170	123	170	136	72	165	147	187	127	96
RACE	RESP	'73	'74	'76	'77	'80	'82	'84	'85	'87	'88	'89
OTHER	HI	15%	14%	11%	7%	10%	29%	8%	7%	12%	9%	8%
	NH	8	0	11	0	30	29	8	15	20	19	18
	MD	8	29	44	14	10	0	20	20	22	16	8
	NL	46	29	22	29	30	21	43	34	28	28	25
	LO	23	29	11	50	20	21	22	24	18	28	43
# SURVEYED		13	7	9	14	10	14	51	41	50	43	40

TABLE IV: IMPORTANCE OF JOB SECURITY -- BY AGE

Question: Consider the following job characteristics: 1) high income, 2) no danger of being fired, 3) working hours are short, lots of free time, 4) chances for advancement, 5) work important and gives a feeling of accomplishment. Among these five characteristics how would you rank "no danger of being fired?" NOTE: Question not asked in 1972, 1975, 1978, 1983, 1986.

Responses: HI = Highest; NH = Next highest; MD = Middle; NL = Next lowest; LO = Lowest

		YEAR										
AGE	RESP	'73	'74	'76	'77	'80	'82	'84	'85	'87	'88	'89
18-23	HI	8%	11%	6%	5%	5%	14%	6%	9%	6%	7%	3%
	NH	16	17	15	13	12	21	13	6	14	12	17
	MD	20	16	22	28	21	16	23	19	22	23	20
	NL	31	28	36	32	34	33	39	40	39	32	28
	LO	24	28	22	22	28	16	18	26	20	27	32
# SURVEYED		169	166	157	161	149	57	157	132	125	92	90
AGE	RESP	'73	'74	'76	'77	'80	'82	'84	'85	'87	'88	'89
24-29	HI	6%	10%	5%	5%	2%	3%	6%	7%	4%	8%	4%
	NH	7	7	13	10	11	19	14	10	10	14	13
	MD	20	17	18	22	11	23	20	20	20	13	14
	NL	33	30	34	33	43	29	38	34	35	38	38
	LO	34	36	30	30	34	26	22	28	31	27	31
# SURVEYED		206	209	223	198	200	115	228	215	191	130	112
AGE	RESP	'73	'74	'76	'77	'80	'82	'84	'85	'87	'88	'89
30-35	HI	5%	2%	5%	7%	5%	8%	5%	4%	5%	5%	5%
	NH	10	14	8	12	11	10	13	9	8	11	9
	MD	15	21	23	26	14	20	17	25	20	18	18
	NL	32	25	30	31	33	31	40	40	34	35	35
	LO	38	38	34	24	38	30	25	22	33	32	33
# SURVEYED		165	173	183	186	214	89	198	210	218	129	132
AGE	RESP	'73	'74	'76	'77	'80	'82	'84	'85	'87	'88	'89
36-41	HI	8%	7%	5%	5%	5%	14%	8%	7%	6%	7%	2%
	NH	12	9	15	13	9	15	9	9	9	15	5
	MD	14	18	16	26	10	14	18	13	12	18	19
	NL	36	35	38	27	33	31	29	37	31	21	39
	LO	30	30	26	30	43	26	35	34	41	40	35
# SURVEYED		169	149	152	166	148	72	185	179	182	131	131
AGE	RESP	'73	'74	'76	'77	'80	'82	'84	'85	'87	'88	'89
42-47	HI	4%	4%	7%	9%	4%	6%	4%	5%	5%	8%	3%
	NH	14	8	19	15	8	19	15	11	15	11	8
	MD	20	22	21	19	9	23	19	11	17	16	23
	NL	27	33	30	33	36	33	36	35	31	32	37
	LO	35	33	22	24	44	19	25	39	32	32	30
# SURVEYED		142	150	107	144	112	64	124	123	154	99	104

TABLE IV: IMPORTANCE OF JOB SECURITY -- BY AGE (Continued)

Question: Consider the following job characteristics: 1) high income, 2) no danger of being fired, 3) working hours are short, lots of free time, 4) chances for advancement, 5) work important and gives a feeling of accomplishment. Among these five characteristics how would you rank "no danger of being fired?" NOTE: Question not asked in 1972, 1975, 1978, 1983, 1986.

Responses: HI = Highest; NH = Next highest; MD = Middle; NL = Next lowest; LO = Lowest

		YEAR										
AGE	RESP	'73	'74	'76	'77	'80	'82	'84	'85	'87	'88	'89
48-53	HI	7%	6%	11%	15%	9%	7%	6%	7%	6%	6%	7%
	NH	8	8	15	19	8	22	20	16	9	19	17
	MD	22	21	17	14	18	22	9	17	19	13	27
	NL	35	28	34	28	33	31	42	35	30	33	30
	LO	29	37	24	24	32	17	24	25	35	29	20
# SURVEYED		146	145	131	147	123	54	102	131	124	63	90
AGE	RESP	'73	'74	'76	'77	'80	'82	'84	'85	'87	'88	'89
54-59	HI	8%	9%	12%	7%	11%	10%	15%	10%	4%	4%	8%
	NH	19	9	17	15	13	23	9	11	7	13	16
	MD	21	16	20	17	16	25	21	26	21	23	24
	NL	26	27	27	38	36	22	34	34	38	35	24
	LO	25	39	24	23	24	20	21	19	30	25	27
# SURVEYED		154	134	123	162	135	69	113	131	97	52	62
AGE	RESP	'73	'74	'76	'77	'80	'82	'84	'85	'87	'88	'89
60-65	HI	7%	10%	7%	11%	12%	17%	9%	4%	10%	4%	4%
	NH	21	11	15	13	14	15	14	15	17	9	12
	MD	22	30	20	26	23	19	27	22	26	20	26
	NL	25	19	28	32	23	38	28	34	28	38	39
	LO	25	30	30	18	28	11	22	25	19	30	19
# SURVEYED		118	105	130	112	118	47	109	127	98	81	74
AGE	RESP	'73	'74	'76	'77	'80	'82	'84	'85	'87	'88	'89
66+	HI	8%	10%	11%	11%	5%	14%	11%	11%	7%	8%	9%
	NH	23	13	19	16	17	18	15	15	14	19	14
	MD	25	20	22	20	27	31	24	26	26	32	22
	NL	23	29	29	31	32	22	32	29	34	27	37
	LO	20	28	20	22	19	16	19	19	19	14	18
# SURVEYED		189	217	238	197	229	148	220	245	238	166	182

****

BRAZIL AS A FAVORED COUNTRY

TABLE I: BRAZIL AS A FAVORED COUNTRY -- BY TOTAL POPULATION

Question: On a scale that goes from "plus 5" for a country you like very much, to the lowest position of "minus 5" for a country you dislike very much, where would you rate Brazil? NOTE: Question not asked in 1972, 1973, 1976, 1978, 1980, 1984, 1986-1989.

Responses: +5 = +5 · +4 = +4 · +3 = +3 · +2 = +2 · +1 = +1 · -1 = -1 · -2 = -2 · -3 = -3 · -4 = -4 · -5 = -5

	YEAR					
RESPONSE	'74	'75	'77	'82	'83	'85
+5	8%	6%	7%	6%	5%	5%
+4	10	8	7	9	5	7
+3	20	16	15	16	11	15
+2	15	18	15	17	18	15
+1	26	27	26	28	34	32
-1	11	11	12	12	15	12
-2	4	5	6	5	6	6
-3	3	4	5	4	4	4
-4	2	2	3	2	2	2
-5	2	2	5	2	2	3
# SURVEYED	1271	1277	1322	1280	1413	659

TABLE II: BRAZIL AS A FAVORED COUNTRY -- BY SEX

Question: On a scale that goes from "plus 5" for a country you like very much, to the lowest position of "minus 5" for a country you dislike very much, where would you rate Brazil? NOTE: Question not asked in 1972, 1973, 1976, 1978, 1980, 1984, 1986-1989.

Responses: +5 = +5 · +4 = +4 · +3 = +3 · +2 = +2 · +1 = +1 · -1 = -1 · -2 = -2 · -3 = -3 · -4 = -4 · -5 = -5

		YEAR					
SEX	RESP	'74	'75	'77	'82	'83	'85
MALE	+5	8%	6%	6%	6%	5%	5%
	+4	10	8	6	10	5	5
	+3	20	15	14	15	10	15
	+2	15	19	16	17	18	13
	+1	27	26	28	26	34	33
	-1	11	12	13	13	15	12
	-2	3	7	6	6	6	6
	-3	3	4	5	4	4	4
	-4	1	2	2	1	1	3
	-5	2	3	4	2	2	3
# SURVEYED		606	591	618	565	630	401

		YEAR					
SEX	RESP	'74	'75	'77	'82	'83	'85
FEMALE	+5	8%	6%	8%	5%	6%	4%
	+4	10	8	8	8	5	9
	+3	20	17	15	17	11	14
	+2	15	17	14	17	17	18
	+1	26	28	24	29	33	30
	-1	11	10	11	11	14	12
	-2	4	4	6	5	5	5
	-3	3	5	5	3	4	5
	-4	2	2	3	2	2	1
	-5	1	1	6	2	2	2
# SURVEYED		665	686	704	715	783	258

TABLE III: BRAZIL AS A FAVORED COUNTRY -- BY RACE

Question: On a scale that goes from "plus 5" for a country you like very much, to the lowest position of "minus 5" for a country you dislike very much, where would you rate Brazil? NOTE: Question not asked in 1972, 1973, 1976, 1978, 1980, 1984, 1986-1989.

Responses: +5 = +5 +4 = +4 +3 = +3 +2 = +2 +1 = +1 -1 = -1 -2 = -2 -3 = -3 -4 = -4 -5 = -5

		YEAR					
RACE	RESP	'74	'75	'77	'82	'83	'85
WHITE	+5	7%	6%	7%	5%	4%	4%
	+4	10	8	7	8	5	5
	+3	21	17	15	16	11	14
	+2	15	17	15	17	18	15
	+1	27	28	25	29	34	34
	-1	11	11	13	12	14	12
	-2	4	5	6	6	5	6
	-3	2	4	5	3	4	4
	-4	2	2	3	2	2	2
	-5	2	2	5	2	2	3
# SURVEYED		1131	1143	1178	1126	1262	588
RACE	RESP	'74	'75	'77	'82	'83	'85
BLACK	+5	10%	6%	11%	11%	15%	13%
	+4	12	8	13	17	5	17
	+3	14	14	11	15	11	20
	+2	16	22	9	18	16	11
	+1	24	21	25	17	27	13
	-1	10	8	8	11	14	13
	-2	2	5	8	2	7	4
	-3	5	7	6	3	2	4
	-4	2	4	2	2	1	2
	-5	5	5	6	4	1	4
# SURVEYED		133	130	131	131	135	54
RACE	RESP	'74	'75	'77	'82	'83	'85
OTHER	+5	0%	25%	8%	4%	6%	6%
	+4	14	25	0	4	0	12
	+3	43	0	0	26	25	12
	+2	0	25	31	9	19	18
	+1	14	0	38	30	25	29
	-1	0	0	15	4	25	12
	-2	0	0	0	9	0	0
	-3	29	0	0	9	0	0
	-4	0	0	0	0	0	6
	-5	0	25	8	4	0	6
# SURVEYED		7	4	13	23	16	17

TABLE IV: BRAZIL AS A FAVORED COUNTRY -- BY AGE

Question: On a scale that goes from "plus 5" for a country you like very much, to the lowest position of "minus 5" for a country you dislike very much, where would you rate Brazil? NOTE: Question not asked in 1972, 1973, 1976, 1978, 1980, 1984, 1986-1989.

Responses: +5 = +5 +4 = +4 +3 = +3 +2 = +2 +1 = +1
-1 = -1 -2 = -2 -3 = -3 -4 = -4 -5 = -5

AGE	RESP	'74	'75	'77	'82	'83	'85
18-23	+5	5%	4%	6%	4%	7%	3%
	+4	11	7	9	7	7	8
	+3	21	13	16	12	9	13
	+2	15	23	17	17	21	18
	+1	29	28	28	34	32	37
	-1	12	11	8	13	12	5
	-2	4	8	6	6	6	5
	-3	1	5	4	2	6	8
	-4	2	1	2	3	2	0
	-5	1	1	3	1	0	3
# SURVEYED		156	160	155	139	120	38
24-29	+5	5%	5%	8%	6%	3%	6%
	+4	14	7	8	8	6	8
	+3	23	16	16	12	11	10
	+2	16	16	13	20	16	24
	+1	26	33	28	31	39	27
	-1	6	9	11	12	15	12
	-2	6	7	6	6	4	6
	-3	3	2	3	3	3	4
	-4	2	3	4	2	1	2
	-5	1	1	2	2	1	0
# SURVEYED		197	214	191	225	268	97
30-35	+5	13%	7%	6%	5%	5%	2%
	+4	12	7	5	9	6	3
	+3	14	23	11	18	7	21
	+2	15	12	17	14	18	15
	+1	27	28	24	32	41	41
	-1	14	10	18	11	15	10
	-2	2	7	5	6	4	3
	-3	2	3	2	4	3	2
	-4	0	1	6	1	0	0
	-5	1	1	5	1	1	2
# SURVEYED		155	156	168	195	225	91

AGE	RESP	'74	'75	'77	'82	'83	'85
36-41	+5	10%	6%	4%	7%	7%	5%
	+4	8	8	7	9	2	8
	+3	18	18	14	21	7	16
	+2	13	21	20	19	21	11
	+1	29	24	25	24	32	31
	-1	13	13	12	8	16	16
	-2	2	2	3	4	5	5
	-3	2	5	6	4	2	4
	-4	3	1	2	1	4	1
	-5	2	1	6	4	2	2
# SURVEYED		131	139	147	136	161	93
42-47	+5	14%	6%	11%	1%	4%	5%
	+4	8	8	5	10	5	8
	+3	19	21	15	21	12	22
	+2	11	14	12	19	16	8
	+1	32	29	25	27	33	32
	-1	10	13	13	9	13	10
	-2	2	3	6	7	8	10
	-3	3	3	7	1	7	3
	-4	2	2	2	3	1	2
	-5	1	1	5	2	2	0
# SURVEYED		133	125	123	107	129	60
48-53	+5	4%	7%	8%	9%	6%	2%
	+4	7	9	6	11	5	2
	+3	20	12	14	14	13	20
	+2	17	21	13	16	15	15
	+1	29	27	24	24	32	38
	-1	11	9	14	16	12	14
	-2	6	5	9	3	10	5
	-3	3	4	6	2	3	0
	-4	1	4	3	2	1	2
	-5	2	1	4	3	3	5
# SURVEYED		127	121	140	93	100	66

TABLE IV: BRAZIL AS A FAVORED COUNTRY -- BY AGE (Continued)

Question: On a scale that goes from "plus 5" for a country you like very much, to the lowest position of "minus 5" for a country you dislike very much, where would you rate Brazil? NOTE: Question not asked in 1972, 1973, 1976, 1978, 1980, 1984, 1986-1989.

Responses: +5 = +5 +4 = +4 +3 = +3 +2 = +2 +1 = +1 -1 = -1 -2 = -2 -3 = -3 -4 = -4 -5 = -5

		YEAR					
AGE	RESP	'74	'75	'77	'82	'83	'85
54-59	+5	7%	6%	8%	8%	4%	10%
	+4	10	9	9	8	5	6
	+3	25	18	17	15	14	13
	+2	18	16	9	16	19	17
	+1	17	27	25	28	28	23
	-1	13	11	14	10	13	13
	-2	3	5	3	5	5	2
	-3	4	5	5	5	5	8
	-4	1	2	3	2	1	0
	-5	1	2	5	3	4	8
# SURVEYED		115	101	146	118	113	52
AGE	RESP	'74	'75	'77	'82	'83	'85
60-65	+5	4%	11%	7%	8%	5%	5%
	+4	8	6	7	10	5	3
	+3	20	11	15	10	14	7
	+2	15	29	10	22	17	20
	+1	26	20	29	22	30	27
	-1	12	8	9	18	18	13
	-2	2	4	8	4	3	3
	-3	3	8	8	3	4	7
	-4	3	1	2	2	3	8
	-5	6	2	7	1	2	7
# SURVEYED		89	85	92	91	109	60
AGE	RESP	'74	'75	'77	'82	'83	'85
66+	+5	7%	6%	5%	6%	7%	5%
	+4	9	10	6	10	5	11
	+3	20	14	14	18	14	12
	+2	19	14	18	12	17	9
	+1	21	20	23	23	26	30
	-1	8	14	10	14	13	12
	-2	4	6	6	6	7	9
	-3	5	6	6	6	4	4
	-4	2	3	1	1	3	5
	-5	4	6	10	3	4	3
# SURVEYED		162	175	155	171	183	100

****

CANADA AS A FAVORED COUNTRY

TABLE I: CANADA AS A FAVORED COUNTRY -- BY TOTAL POPULATION

Question: On a scale that goes from "plus 5" for a country you like very much, to the lowest position of "minus 5" for a country you dislike very much, where would you rate Canada? NOTE: Question not asked in 1972-1973, 1976, 1978, 1980, 1984, 1987.

Responses: +5 = +5 | +4 = +4 | +3 = +3 | +2 = +2 | +1 = +1 | -1 = -1 | -2 = -2 | -3 = -3 | -4 = -4 | -5 = -5

	YEAR								
RESPONSE	'74	'75	'77	'82	'83	'85	'86	'88	'89
+5	44%	38%	38%	43%	38%	41%	43%	45%	39%
+4	23	24	23	23	24	23	21	21	22
+3	15	19	19	15	19	20	17	14	17
+2	8	8	8	8	9	9	9	9	7
+1	7	7	7	6	7	5	8	8	8
-1	1	2	2	2	1	1	1	1	2
-2	1	1	1	1	1	0	0	1	2
-3	1	1	1	0	1	1	1	1	0
-4	0	0	0	0	0	0	0	0	1
-5	1	0	1	1	0	0	1	1	1
# SURVEYED	1426	1416	1436	1443	1532	1469	1436	946	957

TABLE II: CANADA AS A FAVORED COUNTRY -- BY SEX

Question: On a scale that goes from "plus 5" for a country you like very much, to the lowest position of "minus 5" for a country you dislike very much, where would you rate Canada? NOTE: Question not asked in 1972-1973, 1976, 1978, 1980, 1984, 1987.

Responses: +5 = +5 +4 = +4 +3 = +3 +2 = +2 +1 = +1
-1 = -1 -2 = -2 -3 = -3 -4 = -4 -5 = -5

SEX	RESP	'74	'75	'77	'82	'83	'85	'86	'88	'89
		YEAR								
M	+5	45%	40%	39%	45%	40%	43%	43%	44%	38%
A	+4	23	24	24	23	23	24	23	21	21
L	+3	13	17	17	16	21	17	16	15	19
E	+2	8	10	9	8	8	9	9	9	8
	+1	7	6	6	5	5	4	6	9	7
	-1	1	2	2	1	1	1	1	1	2
	-2	1	0	1	1	1	0	0	0	1
	-3	1	1	1	0	0	1	0	1	0
	-4	0	0	0	0	0	1	0	0	0
	-5	1	0	0	1	1	0	1	1	2
# SURVEYED		670	648	662	627	671	667	611	424	417
SEX	RESP	'74	'75	'77	'82	'83	'85	'86	'88	'89
F	+5	42%	36%	38%	42%	36%	39%	42%	47%	39%
E	+4	23	24	22	23	25	22	20	20	23
M	+3	16	21	20	15	17	21	17	14	16
A	+2	7	7	8	9	10	9	8	8	6
L	+1	6	7	7	7	9	6	9	7	9
E	-1	2	2	2	2	1	1	1	2	2
	-2	1	1	1	1	1	0	1	1	3
	-3	1	1	0	1	1	1	1	1	0
	-4	0	0	0	0	0	0	0	0	1
	-5	1	0	1	1	0	0	1	1	1
# SURVEYED		756	768	774	816	861	802	825	522	540

TABLE III: CANADA AS A FAVORED COUNTRY -- BY RACE

Question: On a scale that goes from "plus 5" for a country you like very much, to the lowest position of "minus 5" for a country you dislike very much, where would you rate Canada? NOTE: Question not asked in 1972-1973, 1976, 1978, 1980, 1984, 1987.

Responses: +5 = +5 +4 = +4 +3 = +3 +2 = +2 +1 = +1
-1 = -1 -2 = -2 -3 = -3 -4 = -4 -5 = -5

		YEAR								
RACE	RESP	'74	'75	'77	'82	'83	'85	'86	'88	'89
WHITE	+5	45%	39%	40%	45%	39%	42%	45%	48%	41%
	+4	24	25	24	23	25	23	21	21	22
	+3	15	19	18	15	19	19	16	14	17
	+2	7	7	8	8	8	8	8	8	7
	+1	6	6	6	5	6	5	7	6	8
	-1	1	2	2	1	1	1	0	1	2
	-2	0	1	1	1	1	0	0	0	2
	-3	1	1	1	0	0	1	0	1	0
	-4	0	0	0	0	0	0	0	0	0
	-5	1	0	1	0	0	0	0	0	1
# SURVEYED		1265	1268	1278	1272	1368	1296	1229	805	829
RACE	RESP	'74	'75	'77	'82	'83	'85	'86	'88	'89
BLACK	+5	32%	25%	31%	28%	31%	35%	25%	33%	32%
	+4	18	19	15	21	15	18	18	17	18
	+3	16	19	20	15	21	23	25	18	18
	+2	14	17	10	10	15	13	11	10	10
	+1	11	13	13	14	10	5	13	13	11
	-1	1	3	4	4	3	1	2	3	3
	-2	2	1	2	3	1	1	1	2	1
	-3	3	1	1	3	3	2	1	1	0
	-4	1	1	1	1	1	2	1	1	2
	-5	3	1	3	2	1	1	2	2	4
# SURVEYED		154	144	143	145	146	130	173	109	93
RACE	RESP	'74	'75	'77	'82	'83	'85	'86	'88	'89
OTHER	+5	43%	25%	13%	23%	17%	23%	29%	28%	20%
	+4	29	0	13	12	33	23	29	16	37
	+3	14	25	33	35	28	30	15	9	26
	+2	14	25	27	12	11	14	15	16	6
	+1	0	0	7	12	11	2	6	19	3
	-1	0	0	7	4	0	2	0	3	6
	-2	0	0	0	0	0	2	3	3	0
	-3	0	0	0	0	0	0	3	0	0
	-4	0	0	0	4	0	2	0	3	0
	-5	0	25	0	0	0	0	0	3	3
# SURVEYED		7	4	15	26	18	43	34	32	35

TABLE IV: CANADA AS A FAVORED COUNTRY -- BY AGE

Question: On a scale that goes from "plus 5" for a country you like very much, to the lowest position of "minus 5" for a country you dislike very much, where would you rate Canada? NOTE: Question not asked in 1972-1973, 1976, 1978, 1980, 1984, 1987.

Responses: +5 = +5 +4 = +4 +3 = +3 +2 = +2 +1 = +1
-1 = -1 -2 = -2 -3 = -3 -4 = -4 -5 = -5

		YEAR								
AGE	RESP	'74	'75	'77	'82	'83	'85	'86	'88	'89
18-23	+5	41%	37%	32%	35%	34%	32%	29%	32%	30%
	+4	24	30	31	20	25	24	30	25	29
	+3	16	17	19	20	16	24	17	16	16
	+2	6	5	8	12	13	11	14	14	10
	+1	10	8	6	8	8	5	10	9	10
	-1	2	2	2	2	2	3	0	1	3
	-2	0	1	1	1	1	1	0	1	3
	-3	1	1	1	1	1	0	0	0	0
	-4	0	0	1	1	1	0	0	1	0
	-5	1	0	0	0	0	0	0	1	0
# SURVEYED		165	171	159	145	127	131	107	93	80
AGE	RESP	'74	'75	'77	'82	'83	'85	'86	'88	'89
24-29	+5	45%	34%	37%	39%	37%	39%	37%	38%	36%
	+4	24	27	21	23	24	22	21	27	27
	+3	16	20	20	18	20	20	17	16	15
	+2	8	10	11	11	8	9	10	8	6
	+1	5	6	8	6	8	5	10	8	8
	-1	1	1	1	1	3	2	2	1	3
	-2	0	1	2	0	0	0	1	2	1
	-3	1	0	2	0	0	1	1	1	1
	-4	0	1	0	0	0	0	0	0	0
	-5	0	0	0	1	0	0	0	0	1
# SURVEYED		206	222	199	238	279	214	214	146	142
AGE	RESP	'74	'75	'77	'82	'83	'85	'86	'88	'89
30-35	+5	44%	39%	31%	49%	33%	35%	41%	44%	32%
	+4	22	21	23	24	27	23	23	21	27
	+3	16	23	23	11	20	27	18	18	24
	+2	8	7	7	8	11	9	8	8	4
	+1	7	5	9	4	8	4	9	7	9
	-1	1	1	2	2	1	0	0	1	2
	-2	1	1	1	0	0	0	1	0	1
	-3	1	1	1	0	0	1	0	0	1
	-4	0	1	1	0	0	0	0	0	1
	-5	1	1	2	1	0	0	0	1	1
# SURVEYED		170	163	175	204	230	209	221	125	138

TABLE IV: CANADA AS A FAVORED COUNTRY -- BY AGE (Continued)

Question: On a scale that goes from "plus 5" for a country you like very much, to the lowest position of "minus 5" for a country you dislike very much, where would you rate Canada? NOTE: Question not asked in 1972-1973, 1976, 1978, 1980, 1984, 1987.

Responses: +5 = +5 +4 = +4 +3 = +3 +2 = +2 +1 = +1
-1 = -1 -2 = -2 -3 = -3 -4 = -4 -5 = -5

		YEAR								
AGE	RESP	'74	'75	'77	'82	'83	'85	'86	'88	'89
36-41	+5	36%	34%	36%	44%	39%	39%	45%	51%	33%
	+4	28	24	24	23	27	27	20	23	27
	+3	19	19	25	15	20	17	22	11	20
	+2	8	7	6	6	6	11	8	7	8
	+1	7	11	4	6	5	4	4	6	10
	-1	2	3	3	1	1	1	0	1	0
	-2	0	1	1	1	1	0	0	0	1
	-3	0	1	1	1	1	1	1	0	0
	-4	0	0	1	1	0	0	0	1	0
	-5	0	1	0	1	1	1	0	0	2
# SURVEYED		149	149	157	144	166	178	184	124	120
AGE	RESP	'74	'75	'77	'82	'83	'85	'86	'88	'89
42-47	+5	45%	36%	43%	42%	45%	45%	38%	45%	41%
	+4	18	22	17	26	21	25	23	26	19
	+3	16	20	19	17	15	15	19	12	21
	+2	6	12	9	5	10	7	8	8	7
	+1	9	6	8	6	6	7	10	9	5
	-1	1	4	2	1	1	1	1	0	2
	-2	1	0	1	2	1	0	0	0	1
	-3	1	1	1	0	0	0	1	1	1
	-4	1	0	0	1	0	1	0	0	1
	-5	3	1	1	0	1	0	1	0	2
# SURVEYED		146	138	133	113	141	122	139	103	108
AGE	RESP	'74	'75	'77	'82	'83	'85	'86	'88	'89
48-53	+5	46%	36%	44%	50%	38%	41%	55%	39%	44%
	+4	20	26	26	21	21	19	15	25	19
	+3	16	22	12	11	20	21	14	15	14
	+2	7	9	7	7	11	11	5	7	9
	+1	7	4	6	7	7	5	8	8	9
	-1	2	2	1	2	0	0	0	2	0
	-2	0	0	2	2	0	0	1	0	4
	-3	1	1	1	1	3	1	0	2	0
	-4	0	0	0	0	0	1	1	0	1
	-5	1	0	0	0	0	1	1	2	1
# SURVEYED		140	134	148	107	112	124	104	59	81

TABLE IV: CANADA AS A FAVORED COUNTRY -- BY AGE (Continued)

Question: On a scale that goes from "plus 5" for a country you like very much, to the lowest position of "minus 5" for a country you dislike very much, where would you rate Canada? NOTE: Question not asked in 1972-1973, 1976, 1978, 1980, 1984, 1987.

Responses: +5 = +5 +4 = +4 +3 = +3 +2 = +2 +1 = +1
-1 = -1 -2 = -2 -3 = -3 -4 = -4 -5 = -5

		YEAR								
AGE	RESP	'74	'75	'77	'82	'83	'85	'86	'88	'89
54-59	+5	45%	39%	38%	54%	46%	44%	42%	53%	43%
	+4	26	21	23	22	25	25	14	10	15
	+3	10	24	19	9	13	13	22	22	18
	+2	12	8	10	7	7	9	10	6	9
	+1	5	6	6	7	7	5	7	6	9
	-1	2	0	2	1	0	2	0	2	1
	-2	2	0	1	1	0	2	1	0	1
	-3	0	3	1	0	0	0	0	0	0
	-4	0	0	0	0	0	0	2	0	0
	-5	0	0	1	1	2	1	1	0	3
# SURVEYED		132	119	157	134	127	126	97	49	67
AGE	RESP	'74	'75	'77	'82	'83	'85	'86	'88	'89
60-65	+5	46%	42%	43%	46%	34%	40%	55%	51%	41%
	+4	21	17	21	21	27	21	24	13	20
	+3	15	15	17	16	23	19	11	13	19
	+2	8	9	9	8	9	10	4	8	7
	+1	7	9	6	6	2	6	4	8	8
	-1	0	3	2	1	2	0	0	3	3
	-2	2	3	0	0	1	1	1	0	2
	-3	0	0	0	0	0	0	1	3	0
	-4	1	1	0	0	1	2	0	0	0
	-5	1	1	3	1	0	1	2	1	0
# SURVEYED		102	106	109	112	124	126	110	72	59
AGE	RESP	'74	'75	'77	'82	'83	'85	'86	'88	'89
66+	+5	45%	43%	44%	36%	39%	47%	44%	53%	51%
	+4	26	24	21	25	20	19	21	14	14
	+3	10	16	14	18	23	18	14	11	10
	+2	8	8	7	9	7	6	9	9	5
	+1	4	6	8	7	8	6	8	7	9
	-1	2	2	2	2	0	1	2	2	5
	-2	0	0	1	1	2	0	0	1	3
	-3	3	2	1	0	1	1	1	1	0
	-4	0	0	0	0	0	1	0	0	1
	-5	1	0	3	0	0	0	1	1	1
# SURVEYED		210	211	194	238	220	233	254	174	159

****

CHINA AS A FAVORED COUNTRY

TABLE I: CHINA AS A FAVORED COUNTRY -- BY TOTAL POPULATION

Question: On a scale that goes from "plus 5" for a country you like very much, to the lowest position of "minus 5" for a country you dislike very much, where would you rate China? NOTE: Question not asked in 1972-1973, 1976, 1978, 1980, 1984, 1987.

Responses: +5 = +5, +4 = +4, +3 = +3, +2 = +2, +1 = +1, -1 = -1, -2 = -2, -3 = -3, -4 = -4, -5 = -5

	YEAR								
RESPONSE	'74	'75	'77	'82	'83	'85	'86	'88	'89
+5	3%	3%	3%	4%	4%	5%	5%	7%	5%
+4	4	3	4	6	4	6	5	7	6
+3	8	8	7	12	9	16	15	15	13
+2	11	9	8	13	14	15	16	14	14
+1	18	17	18	20	22	24	25	27	31
-1	14	17	17	15	17	13	11	13	13
-2	8	9	9	9	10	7	6	5	6
-3	9	10	10	8	8	6	6	3	4
-4	7	8	7	6	4	4	4	3	2
-5	17	17	18	8	8	5	6	6	6
# SURVEYED	1389	1369	1392	1400	1496	1428	1404	911	923

TABLE II: CHINA AS A FAVORED COUNTRY -- BY SEX

Question: On a scale that goes from "plus 5" for a country you like very much, to the lowest position of "minus 5" for a country you dislike very much, where would you rate China? NOTE: Question not asked in 1972, 1973, 1976, 1978, 1980, 1984, 1987.

Responses: +5 = +5 +4 = +4 +3 = +3 +2 = +2 +1 = +1
-1 = -1 -2 = -2 -3 = -3 -4 = -4 -5 = -5

		YEAR								
SEX	RESP	'74	'75	'77	'82	'83	'85	'86	'88	'89
M	+5	4%	3%	3%	5%	4%	6%	5%	9%	4%
A	+4	3	4	4	5	5	6	5	8	5
L	+3	8	8	6	12	10	14	17	11	12
E	+2	11	8	7	14	14	16	16	14	13
	+1	21	17	19	20	23	25	26	29	36
	-1	13	16	17	13	15	13	11	13	11
	-2	8	9	8	9	10	7	7	6	7
	-3	9	10	9	9	9	6	5	2	3
	-4	6	8	7	6	3	3	3	3	2
	-5	17	17	19	7	7	4	6	6	6
# SURVEYED		653	630	646	613	659	651	608	414	409
SEX	RESP	'74	'75	'77	'82	'83	'85	'86	'88	'89
F	+5	3%	2%	3%	4%	3%	4%	5%	5%	5%
E	+4	4	3	4	7	3	6	6	7	7
M	+3	7	7	7	12	9	17	14	18	14
A	+2	11	9	8	11	14	14	16	14	14
L	+1	15	16	17	20	20	23	24	26	27
E	-1	15	17	17	16	19	13	11	12	15
	-2	9	9	9	8	9	7	6	5	5
	-3	9	10	11	7	8	7	7	3	5
	-4	8	9	6	6	5	4	4	3	2
	-5	18	18	17	8	9	6	6	7	6
# SURVEYED		736	739	746	787	837	777	796	497	514

TABLE III: CHINA AS A FAVORED COUNTRY -- BY RACE

Question: On a scale that goes from "plus 5" for a country you like very much, to the lowest position of "minus 5" for a country you dislike very much, where would you rate China? NOTE: Question not asked in 1972-1973, 1976, 1978, 1980, 1984, 1987.

Responses: +5 = +5 +4 = +4 +3 = +3 +2 = +2 +1 = +1
-1 = -1 -2 = -2 -3 = -3 -4 = -4 -5 = -5

		YEAR								
RACE	RESP	'74	'75	'77	'82	'83	'85	'86	'88	'89
WHITE	+5	3%	3%	3%	4%	3%	5%	4%	6%	4%
	+4	4	3	4	6	4	5	5	7	6
	+3	8	7	7	12	9	15	16	14	13
	+2	11	8	8	12	14	14	16	14	14
	+1	18	17	18	21	22	24	26	29	32
	-1	15	17	17	15	18	13	11	13	14
	-2	8	9	9	9	10	7	6	5	6
	-3	9	10	10	8	9	7	6	3	4
	-4	7	9	7	6	5	3	4	2	2
	-5	17	18	19	8	8	6	5	7	5
# SURVEYED		1232	1225	1242	1233	1335	1261	1200	776	796
RACE	RESP	'74	'75	'77	'82	'83	'85	'86	'88	'89
BLACK	+5	6%	5%	7%	9%	10%	7%	11%	13%	6%
	+4	5	4	7	11	7	12	10	10	11
	+3	9	10	7	13	10	18	12	18	15
	+2	14	16	7	13	13	19	12	12	11
	+1	19	16	20	11	20	16	22	18	22
	-1	9	11	13	11	16	10	10	13	8
	-2	7	8	9	9	8	6	6	7	6
	-3	8	8	9	9	5	6	5	1	5
	-4	8	6	8	8	3	3	4	5	5
	-5	17	14	13	6	8	2	8	5	13
# SURVEYED		150	140	135	140	143	124	169	104	88
RACE	RESP	'74	'75	'77	'82	'83	'85	'86	'88	'89
OTHER	+5	0%	0%	13%	4%	6%	5%	0%	13%	13%
	+4	0	25	7	0	11	12	3	3	5
	+3	0	25	7	7	11	28	20	26	10
	+2	0	0	7	33	11	19	20	16	18
	+1	0	0	20	19	11	21	9	16	26
	-1	29	25	27	0	6	2	14	6	18
	-2	0	0	13	15	17	2	9	3	0
	-3	0	0	0	4	0	5	11	6	3
	-4	29	0	0	4	11	5	0	6	3
	-5	43	25	7	15	17	2	14	3	5
# SURVEYED		7	4	15	27	18	43	35	31	39

TABLE IV: CHINA AS A FAVORED COUNTRY -- BY AGE

Question: On a scale that goes from "plus 5" for a country you like very much, to the lowest position of "minus 5" for a country you dislike very much, where would you rate China? NOTE: Question not asked in 1972-1973, 1976, 1978, 1980, 1984, 1987.

Responses: +5 = +5 +4 = +4 +3 = +3 +2 = +2 +1 = +1
-1 = -1 -2 = -2 -3 = -3 -4 = -4 -5 = -5

		YEAR								
AGE	RESP	'74	'75	'77	'82	'83	'85	'86	'88	'89
18-23	+5	3%	2%	1%	5%	4%	4%	6%	8%	6%
	+4	5	5	3	7	5	4	7	11	9
	+3	9	8	9	18	8	22	18	21	11
	+2	10	14	11	15	15	16	19	14	11
	+1	19	15	17	23	20	26	23	24	36
	-1	15	17	18	16	20	8	8	6	12
	-2	10	11	11	8	12	7	10	7	7
	-3	11	9	12	3	6	7	5	3	1
	-4	8	6	6	1	4	3	2	1	2
	-5	11	12	11	3	6	4	2	4	4
# SURVEYED		166	170	157	143	125	131	108	90	81
AGE	RESP	'74	'75	'77	'82	'83	'85	'86	'88	'89
24-29	+5	3%	2%	3%	3%	3%	5%	3%	6%	4%
	+4	3	4	5	5	5	8	3	12	9
	+3	11	7	7	13	10	17	19	17	18
	+2	15	7	9	14	13	17	17	12	14
	+1	17	18	19	20	22	24	28	29	31
	-1	13	18	21	17	19	15	12	12	12
	-2	7	12	6	6	12	6	7	7	5
	-3	10	12	9	10	8	3	6	3	4
	-4	6	5	6	7	3	1	2	1	1
	-5	15	15	15	5	5	4	3	1	2
# SURVEYED		206	222	198	238	277	213	215	142	138
AGE	RESP	'74	'75	'77	'82	'83	'85	'86	'88	'89
30-35	+5	3%	6%	2%	3%	5%	5%	6%	8%	5%
	+4	2	3	5	6	4	4	5	4	5
	+3	8	8	2	13	10	15	16	19	8
	+2	8	10	4	14	12	14	19	17	17
	+1	19	17	16	22	23	25	25	26	35
	-1	14	14	20	14	17	15	8	13	16
	-2	7	6	11	11	12	6	8	6	3
	-3	13	7	10	5	6	5	7	2	5
	-4	7	10	4	6	5	3	3	2	2
	-5	19	19	26	9	8	6	2	2	5
# SURVEYED		167	160	171	200	231	208	220	124	132

TABLE IV: CHINA AS A FAVORED COUNTRY -- BY AGE (Continued)

Question: On a scale that goes from "plus 5" for a country you like very much, to the lowest position of "minus 5" for a country you dislike very much, where would you rate China? NOTE: Question not asked in 1972-1973, 1976, 1978, 1980, 1984, 1987.

Responses: +5 = +5 +4 = +4 +3 = +3 +2 = +2 +1 = +1 -1 = -1 -2 = -2 -3 = -3 -4 = -4 -5 = -5

		YEAR								
AGE	RESP	'74	'75	'77	'82	'83	'85	'86	88	'89
36-41	+5	5%	3%	7%	7%	5%	6%	4%	7%	2%
	+4	6	3	5	6	7	7	6	6	8
	+3	7	6	10	19	12	13	12	9	11
	+2	9	8	14	19	19	18	16	11	11
	+1	28	26	20	22	28	30	25	26	26
	-1	18	21	22	9	13	9	20	20	18
	-2	6	7	5	4	7	5	6	5	11
	-3	5	9	6	8	6	6	4	7	6
	-4	10	6	4	3	1	2	3	2	0
	-5	6	11	8	3	2	4	5	7	8
# SURVEYED		143	143	147	139	162	175	179	122	114
AGE	RESP	'74	'75	'77	'82	'83	'85	'86	'88	'89
42-47	+5	3%	3%	5%	7%	6%	3%	1%	3%	1%
	+4	7	5	2	9	7	7	5	4	7
	+3	12	11	12	18	13	16	10	16	15
	+2	10	9	11	12	17	9	17	19	11
	+1	16	23	24	27	32	32	34	21	20
	-1	15	17	23	13	8	16	11	13	17
	-2	12	8	7	4	6	6	7	8	10
	-3	7	11	6	4	8	3	8	8	6
	-4	6	3	3	2	2	3	1	2	2
	-5	12	8	6	5	2	5	6	4	12
# SURVEYED		142	132	125	109	133	116	131	98	104
AGE	RESP	'74	'75	'77	'82	'83	'85	'86	'88	'89
48-53	+5	3%	2%	7%	5%	7%	7%	6%	0%	6%
	+4	7	2	6	13	5	5	7	7	8
	+3	8	5	5	13	11	9	10	5	10
	+2	11	14	13	11	8	12	15	9	15
	+1	19	22	25	30	24	30	18	31	18
	-1	15	17	19	12	17	12	15	21	19
	-2	10	10	5	3	10	13	7	3	12
	-3	4	9	8	8	7	7	8	9	3
	-4	8	9	6	3	5	2	3	3	3
	-5	15	9	7	1	7	3	11	12	6
# SURVEYED		131	127	144	98	105	121	100	58	78

TABLE IV: CHINA AS A FAVORED COUNTRY -- BY AGE (Continued)

Question: On a scale that goes from "plus 5" for a country you like very much, to the lowest position of "minus 5" for a country you dislike very much, where would you rate China? NOTE: Question not asked in 1972-1973, 1976, 1978, 1980, 1984, 1987.

Responses: +5 = +5 | +4 = +4 | +3 = +3 | +2 = +2 | +1 = +1 | -1 = -1 | -2 = -2 | -3 = -3 | -4 = -4 | -5 = -5

		YEAR								
AGE	RESP	'74	'75	'77	'82	'83	'85	'86	'88	'89
54-59	+5	3%	3%	8%	6%	6%	4%	3%	13%	5%
	+4	3	3	3	10	6	6	10	4	2
	+3	13	12	10	13	16	16	10	19	10
	+2	13	6	12	13	16	16	14	9	20
	+1	17	19	18	30	26	24	22	26	25
	-1	13	19	22	9	9	10	17	13	11
	-2	13	10	6	4	6	11	8	0	5
	-3	11	13	6	4	7	8	6	4	7
	-4	4	5	5	4	4	3	2	2	5
	-5	11	11	8	7	5	3	8	11	11
# SURVEYED		120	108	147	126	124	113	90	47	61
AGE	RESP	'74	'75	'77	'82	'83	'85	'86	'88	'89
60-65	+5	2%	3%	1%	6%	8%	3%	7%	9%	4%
	+4	5	6	3	11	10	4	10	4	5
	+3	11	11	12	13	17	11	9	21	11
	+2	17	11	11	17	18	20	11	3	11
	+1	24	15	30	25	21	23	23	21	27
	-1	10	15	21	8	11	13	12	7	20
	-2	7	9	4	7	3	5	6	7	5
	-3	12	8	7	4	5	7	10	12	5
	-4	4	9	4	2	3	3	3	3	4
	-5	8	10	6	8	3	9	8	12	7
# SURVEYED		92	97	99	103	118	115	106	67	55
AGE	RESP	'74	'75	'77	'82	'83	'85	'86	'88	'89
66+	+5	7%	4%	2%	8%	5%	6%	6%	6%	6%
	+4	7	2	8	8	9	10	5	5	4
	+3	14	10	12	22	16	16	9	8	6
	+2	11	11	16	13	15	10	13	13	15
	+1	16	17	25	20	23	22	23	27	25
	-1	12	14	9	10	10	13	13	18	16
	-2	9	12	10	6	7	9	13	8	9
	-3	10	8	6	6	6	6	6	5	6
	-4	5	9	4	2	1	5	5	3	3
	-5	10	13	8	3	6	3	8	9	11
# SURVEYED		188	186	156	202	201	206	225	142	140

****

EGYPT AS A FAVORED COUNTRY

TABLE I: EGYPT AS A FAVORED COUNTRY -- BY TOTAL POPULATION

Question: On a scale that goes from "plus 5" for a country you like very much, to the lowest position of "minus 5" for a country you dislike very much, where would you rate Egypt? NOTE: Question not asked in 1972-1973, 1976, 1978, 1980, 1984, 1987.

Responses: +5 = +5 +4 = +4 +3 = +3 +2 = +2 +1 = +1
-1 = -1 -2 = -2 -3 = -3 -4 = -4 -5 = -5

	YEAR								
RESPONSE	'74	'75	'77	'82	'83	'85	'86	'88	'89
+5	4%	3%	5%	6%	6%	5%	5%	7%	4%
+4	6	4	5	9	7	7	6	6	6
+3	10	8	11	16	14	14	10	12	10
+2	11	11	13	15	14	14	15	11	13
+1	21	23	25	25	26	28	26	26	26
-1	15	17	19	12	14	12	15	16	17
-2	9	9	7	5	7	7	7	7	9
-3	7	9	6	5	6	6	6	7	5
-4	6	6	4	3	3	3	3	2	3
-5	10	10	6	4	4	4	6	7	9
# SURVEYED	1357	1341	1344	1357	1474	1395	1376	879	890

TABLE II: EGYPT AS A FAVORED COUNTRY -- BY SEX

Question: On a scale that goes from "plus 5" for a country you like very much, to the lowest position of "minus 5" for a country you dislike very much, where would you rate Egypt? NOTE: Question not asked in 1972-1973, 1976, 1978, 1980, 1984, 1987.

Responses: +5 = +5 +4 = +4 +3 = +3 +2 = +2 +1 = +1
-1 = -1 -2 = -2 -3 = -3 -4 = -4 -5 = -5

		YEAR								
SEX	RESP	'74	'75	'77	'82	'83	'85	'86	'88	'89
M	+5	3%	3%	5%	6%	5%	5%	4%	7%	4%
A	+4	5	3	3	9	7	7	6	6	4
L	+3	10	7	11	18	15	12	9	12	11
E	+2	12	11	13	16	14	14	16	10	13
	+1	21	22	26	25	26	30	27	28	26
	-1	14	18	19	12	15	12	17	17	16
	-2	10	10	6	5	7	8	7	6	9
	-3	8	10	6	5	6	6	6	6	6
	-4	6	6	3	3	2	2	2	2	2
	-5	12	10	7	3	4	4	7	6	11
# SURVEYED		638	617	630	598	650	643	590	404	397
SEX	RESP	'74	'75	'77	'82	'83	'85	'86	'88	'89
F	+5	5%	3%	6%	5%	6%	5%	5%	7%	4%
E	+4	7	4	6	10	8	7	6	5	7
M	+3	11	10	11	15	13	16	12	13	9
A	+2	11	11	12	14	14	14	15	12	14
L	+1	21	24	24	25	27	26	25	24	25
E	-1	15	16	19	11	13	13	14	14	17
	-2	9	9	8	5	6	6	7	8	8
	-3	7	8	5	6	6	6	7	7	4
	-4	6	6	5	3	4	3	3	2	3
	-5	9	10	5	6	4	4	6	7	7
# SURVEYED		719	724	714	759	824	752	786	475	493

TABLE III: EGYPT AS A FAVORED COUNTRY -- BY RACE

Question: On a scale that goes from "plus 5" for a country you like very much, to the lowest position of "minus 5" for a country you dislike very much, where would you rate Egypt? NOTE: Question not asked in 1972-1973, 1976, 1978, 1980, 1984, 1987.

Responses: +5 = +5 | +4 = +4 | +3 = +3 | +2 = +2 | +1 = +1 | -1 = -1 | -2 = -2 | -3 = -3 | -4 = -4 | -5 = -5

		YEAR								
RACE	RESP	'74	'75	'77	'82	'83	'85	'86	'88	'89
WHITE	+5	3%	2%	4%	5%	5%	5%	3%	6%	4%
	+4	5	3	4	9	6	6	5	5	6
	+3	10	8	11	17	13	13	10	11	9
	+2	11	11	13	15	14	14	15	11	13
	+1	22	23	25	25	27	29	27	27	26
	-1	15	18	19	12	15	13	16	16	17
	-2	10	10	7	5	7	7	8	7	9
	-3	8	9	6	6	6	6	7	7	6
	-4	6	6	4	3	3	3	3	2	3
	-5	10	9	6	4	4	4	7	7	8
# SURVEYED		1207	1196	1199	1194	1312	1232	1176	749	770
RACE	RESP	'74	'75	'77	'82	'83	'85	'86	'88	'89
BLACK	+5	9%	13%	15%	15%	15%	10%	13%	11%	4%
	+4	13	6	11	14	13	17	11	9	10
	+3	15	10	10	13	19	21	16	18	20
	+2	12	14	8	14	13	10	17	11	15
	+1	17	20	22	22	19	20	21	22	14
	-1	8	10	17	7	6	8	11	14	10
	-2	4	7	8	3	6	2	3	5	5
	-3	6	6	2	4	3	6	2	3	2
	-4	5	4	2	4	3	3	1	3	5
	-5	10	11	4	4	2	2	5	4	15
# SURVEYED		143	141	132	137	144	121	167	100	84
RACE	RESP	'74	'75	'77	'82	'83	'85	'86	'88	'89
OTHER	+5	14%	0%	0%	4%	0%	2%	12%	7%	6%
	+4	0	0	0	12	17	2	6	10	0
	+3	0	25	8	19	11	21	12	17	8
	+2	29	25	15	19	17	29	18	13	6
	+1	0	0	38	12	28	24	6	20	42
	-1	14	0	15	12	11	10	18	10	22
	-2	14	0	0	4	0	5	6	7	3
	-3	14	0	8	8	11	5	6	7	0
	-4	0	25	0	4	0	2	9	0	0
	-5	14	25	15	8	6	0	6	10	14
# SURVEYED		7	4	13	26	18	42	33	30	36

TABLE IV: EGYPT AS A FAVORED COUNTRY -- BY AGE

Question: On a scale that goes from "plus 5" for a country you like very much, to the lowest position of "minus 5" for a country you dislike very much, where would you rate Egypt? NOTE: Question not asked in 1972-1973, 1976, 1978, 1980, 1984, 1987.

Responses: +5 = +5 +4 = +4 +3 = +3 +2 = +2 +1 = +1
-1 = -1 -2 = -2 -3 = -3 -4 = -4 -5 = -5

		YEAR								
AGE	RESP	'74	'75	'77	'82	'83	'85	'86	'88	'89
18-23	+5	3%	3%	8%	4%	4%	5%	4%	7%	5%
	+4	7	2	6	13	7	11	7	12	5
	+3	9	7	13	13	16	13	11	13	20
	+2	13	17	12	15	11	14	18	14	15
	+1	22	22	28	28	25	29	36	22	31
	-1	12	16	17	16	20	9	9	15	11
	-2	11	8	6	4	8	6	6	7	1
	-3	8	9	3	2	3	7	2	3	3
	-4	5	8	4	2	2	1	5	2	1
	-5	9	8	4	4	3	4	4	5	7
# SURVEYED		162	169	156	141	123	127	107	86	74
AGE	RESP	'74	'75	'77	'82	'83	'85	'86	'88	'89
24-29	+5	4%	4%	5%	5%	5%	5%	3%	9%	2%
	+4	4	5	5	7	7	6	4	6	9
	+3	9	7	14	15	12	18	11	12	9
	+2	9	13	14	14	9	18	15	10	11
	+1	22	34	26	22	28	29	28	29	27
	-1	21	11	17	12	16	12	20	14	18
	-2	9	8	8	6	8	4	4	8	9
	-3	7	4	5	7	8	4	6	7	6
	-4	5	4	4	3	5	3	2	1	3
	-5	9	10	4	8	3	2	8	4	5
# SURVEYED		204	218	195	234	274	212	213	139	133
AGE	RESP	'74	'75	'77	'82	'83	'85	'86	'88	'89
30-35	+5	5%	4%	5%	3%	7%	5%	6%	6%	6%
	+4	6	4	3	9	6	6	4	3	3
	+3	9	9	11	18	10	12	10	13	4
	+2	12	9	9	17	14	13	17	9	14
	+1	24	21	29	26	27	30	27	28	28
	-1	11	23	22	14	19	18	16	16	17
	-2	8	11	10	5	5	5	6	12	9
	-3	6	13	4	5	5	6	9	5	4
	-4	5	2	2	3	3	1	2	3	5
	-5	14	4	5	2	4	3	3	4	9
# SURVEYED		169	159	170	199	228	204	220	119	128

TABLE IV: EGYPT AS A FAVORED COUNTRY -- BY AGE (Continued)

Question: On a scale that goes from "plus 5" for a country you like very much, to the lowest position of "minus 5" for a country you dislike very much, where would you rate Egypt? NOTE: Question not asked in 1972-1973, 1976, 1978, 1980, 1984, 1987.

Responses: +5 = +5   +4 = +4   +3 = +3   +2 = +2   +1 = +1
-1 = -1   -2 = -2   -3 = -3   -4 = -4   -5 = -5

		YEAR								
AGE	RESP	'74	'75	'77	'82	'83	'85	'86	'88	'89
36-41	+5	5%	3%	7%	7%	5%	6%	4%	7%	2%
	+4	6	3	5	6	7	7	6	6	8
	+3	7	6	10	19	12	13	12	9	11
	+2	9	8	14	19	19	18	16	11	11
	+1	28	26	20	22	28	30	25	26	26
	-1	18	21	22	9	13	9	20	20	18
	-2	6	7	5	4	7	5	6	5	11
	-3	5	9	6	8	6	6	4	7	6
	-4	10	6	4	3	1	2	3	2	0
	-5	6	11	8	3	2	4	5	7	8
# SURVEYED		143	143	147	139	162	175	179	122	114
AGE	RESP	'74	'75	'77	'82	'83	'85	'86	'88	'89
42-47	+5	3%	3%	5%	7%	6%	3%	1%	3%	1%
	+4	7	5	2	9	7	7	5	4	7
	+3	12	11	12	18	13	16	10	16	15
	+2	10	9	11	12	17	9	17	19	11
	+1	16	23	24	27	32	32	34	21	20
	-1	15	17	23	13	8	16	11	13	17
	-2	12	8	7	4	6	6	7	8	10
	-3	7	11	6	4	8	3	8	8	6
	-4	6	3	3	2	2	3	1	2	2
	-5	12	8	6	5	2	5	6	4	12
# SURVEYED		142	132	125	109	133	116	131	98	104
AGE	RESP	'74	'75	'77	'82	'83	'85	'86	'88	'89
48-53	+5	3%	2%	7%	5%	7%	7%	6%	0%	6%
	+4	7	2	6	13	5	5	7	7	8
	+3	8	5	5	13	11	9	10	5	10
	+2	11	14	13	11	8	12	15	9	15
	+1	19	22	25	30	24	30	18	31	18
	-1	15	17	19	12	17	12	15	21	19
	-2	10	10	5	3	10	13	7	3	12
	-3	4	9	8	8	7	7	8	9	3
	-4	8	9	6	3	5	2	3	3	3
	-5	15	9	7	1	7	3	11	12	6
# SURVEYED		131	127	144	98	105	121	100	58	78

TABLE IV: EGYPT AS A FAVORED COUNTRY -- BY AGE (Continued)

Question: On a scale that goes from "plus 5" for a country you like very much, to the lowest position of "minus 5" for a country you dislike very much, where would you rate Egypt? NOTE: Question not asked in 1972-1973, 1976, 1978, 1980, 1984, 1987.

Responses: +5 = +5   +4 = +4   +3 = +3   +2 = +2   +1 = +1   -1 = -1   -2 = -2   -3 = -3   -4 = -4   -5 = -5

		YEAR								
AGE	RESP	'74	'75	'77	'82	'83	'85	'86	'88	'89
54-59	+5	3%	3%	8%	6%	6%	4%	3%	13%	5%
	+4	3	3	3	10	6	6	10	4	2
	+3	13	12	10	13	16	16	10	19	10
	+2	13	6	12	13	16	16	14	9	20
	+1	17	19	18	30	26	24	22	26	25
	-1	13	19	22	9	9	10	17	13	11
	-2	13	10	6	4	6	11	8	0	5
	-3	11	13	6	4	7	8	6	4	7
	-4	4	5	5	4	4	3	2	2	5
	-5	11	11	8	7	5	3	8	11	11
# SURVEYED		120	108	147	126	124	113	90	47	61
AGE	RESP	'74	'75	'77	'82	'83	'85	'86	'88	'89
60-65	+5	2%	3%	1%	6%	8%	3%	7%	9%	4%
	+4	5	6	3	11	10	4	10	4	5
	+3	11	11	12	13	17	11	9	21	11
	+2	17	11	11	17	18	20	11	3	11
	+1	24	15	30	25	21	23	23	21	27
	-1	10	15	21	8	11	13	12	7	20
	-2	7	9	4	7	3	5	6	7	5
	-3	12	8	7	4	5	7	10	12	5
	-4	4	9	4	2	3	3	3	3	4
	-5	8	10	6	8	3	9	8	12	7
# SURVEYED		92	97	99	103	118	115	106	67	55
AGE	RESP	'74	'75	'77	'82	'83	'85	'86	'88	'89
66+	+5	7%	4%	2%	8%	5%	6%	6%	6%	6%
	+4	7	2	8	8	9	10	5	5	4
	+3	14	10	12	22	16	16	9	8	6
	+2	11	11	16	13	15	10	13	13	15
	+1	16	17	25	20	23	22	23	27	25
	-1	12	14	9	10	10	13	13	18	16
	-2	9	12	10	6	7	9	13	8	9
	-3	10	8	6	6	6	6	6	5	6
	-4	5	9	4	2	1	5	5	3	3
	-5	10	13	8	3	6	3	8	9	11
# SURVEYED		188	186	156	202	201	206	225	142	140

****

ENGLAND AS A FAVORED COUNTRY

TABLE I: ENGLAND AS A FAVORED COUNTRY -- BY TOTAL POPULATION

Question: On a scale that goes from "plus 5" for a country you like very much, to the lowest position of "minus 5" for a country you dislike very much, where would you rate England? NOTE: Question not asked in 1972-1973, 1976, 1978, 1980, 1984, 1986-1989.

Responses: +5 = +5 +4 = +4 +3 = +3 +2 = +2 +1 = +1
-1 = -1 -2 = -2 -3 = -3 -4 = -4 -5 = -5

	YEAR					
RESPONSE	'74	'75	'77	'82	'83	'85
+5	18%	17%	20%	22%	22%	22%
+4	21	17	18	20	20	20
+3	25	26	23	24	23	25
+2	14	14	14	14	14	15
+1	11	14	14	12	13	12
-1	4	4	4	3	3	2
-2	2	2	2	2	2	1
-3	2	2	1	2	2	1
-4	1	1	1	1	1	1
-5	3	2	2	1	1	1
# SURVEYED	1419	1400	1406	1437	1528	712

TABLE II: ENGLAND AS A FAVORED COUNTRY -- BY SEX

Question: On a scale that goes from "plus 5" for a country you like very much, to the lowest position of "minus 5" for a country you dislike very much, where would you rate England? NOTE: Question not asked in 1972-1973, 1976, 1978, 1980, 1984, 1986-1989.

Responses: +5 = +5 +4 = +4 +3 = +3 +2 = +2 +1 = +1
-1 = -1 -2 = -2 -3 = -3 -4 = -4 -5 = -5

		YEAR					
SEX	RESP	'74	'75	'77	'82	'83	'85
MALE	+5	16%	17%	18%	21%	21%	24%
	+4	19	15	18	20	21	19
	+3	26	26	22	23	22	23
	+2	17	15	15	14	15	17
	+1	11	14	15	12	13	10
	-1	5	4	5	3	3	2
	-2	2	2	3	2	2	1
	-3	2	3	1	2	2	2
	-4	1	1	1	0	0	1
	-5	3	2	2	2	2	1
# SURVEYED		669	644	651	625	670	417

		YEAR					
SEX	RESP	'74	'75	'77	'82	'83	'85
FEMALE	+5	19%	18%	21%	22%	22%	19%
	+4	22	19	19	19	19	22
	+3	25	26	24	25	24	28
	+2	12	13	12	14	12	12
	+1	11	14	13	13	14	14
	-1	4	4	4	3	3	3
	-2	1	1	2	1	2	2
	-3	1	2	1	2	2	0
	-4	1	1	1	1	1	0
	-5	3	1	2	1	1	0
# SURVEYED		750	756	755	812	858	295

TABLE III: ENGLAND AS A FAVORED COUNTRY -- BY RACE

Question: On a scale that goes from "plus 5" for a country you like very much, to the lowest position of "minus 5" for a country you dislike very much, where would you rate England? NOTE: Question not asked in 1972-1973, 1976, 1978, 1980, 1984, 1986-1989.

Responses: +5 = +5 +4 = +4 +3 = +3 +2 = +2 +1 = +1
-1 = -1 -2 = -2 -3 = -3 -4 = -4 -5 = -5

		YEAR					
RACE	RESP	'74	'75	'77	'82	'83	'85
WHITE	+5	18%	17%	20%	22%	22%	22%
	+4	21	18	19	20	20	21
	+3	25	27	24	25	24	25
	+2	14	14	13	13	14	15
	+1	10	14	14	12	13	12
	-1	4	4	4	3	3	2
	-2	2	2	2	1	1	1
	-3	1	2	1	1	2	1
	-4	1	1	1	1	1	0
	-5	2	2	2	1	1	0
# SURVEYED		1261	1249	1257	1265	1366	636
RACE	RESP	'74	'75	'77	'82	'83	'85
BLACK	+5	13%	20%	18%	19%	17%	22%
	+4	16	11	13	14	17	14
	+3	21	22	15	18	17	27
	+2	17	13	21	14	12	14
	+1	13	20	15	17	19	8
	-1	6	5	6	2	4	7
	-2	3	3	3	6	6	3
	-3	4	2	4	5	5	0
	-4	1	2	2	1	2	3
	-5	6	3	2	5	2	2
# SURVEYED		151	147	136	145	145	59
RACE	RESP	'74	'75	'77	'82	'83	'85
OTHER	+5	14%	25%	0%	15%	18%	18%
	+4	0	0	8	15	18	29
	+3	71	25	46	30	18	24
	+2	0	0	23	22	18	6
	+1	14	50	0	7	29	12
	-1	0	0	0	0	0	0
	-2	0	0	8	4	0	0
	-3	0	0	8	0	0	6
	-4	0	0	0	4	0	6
	-5	0	0	8	4	0	0
# SURVEYED		7	4	13	27	17	17

TABLE IV: ENGLAND AS A FAVORED COUNTRY -- BY AGE

Question: On a scale that goes from "plus 5" for a country you like very much, to the lowest position of "minus 5" for a country you dislike very much, where would you rate England? NOTE: Question not asked in 1972-1973, 1976, 1978, 1980, 1984, 1986-1989.

Responses: +5 = +5 | +4 = +4 | +3 = +3 | +2 = +2 | +1 = +1 | -1 = -1 | -2 = -2 | -3 = -3 | -4 = -4 | -5 = -5

		YEAR					
AGE	RESP	'74	'75	'77	'82	'83	'85
18-23	+5	18%	15%	13%	20%	16%	18%
	+4	25	21	24	24	22	21
	+3	24	30	23	28	28	28
	+2	15	14	19	12	15	13
	+1	11	14	14	11	14	8
	-1	3	3	4	3	1	8
	-2	1	0	1	1	1	3
	-3	1	2	0	1	2	3
	-4	1	1	1	0	0	0
	-5	1	0	1	0	2	0
# SURVEYED		166	169	159	144	125	39
AGE	RESP	'74	'75	'77	'82	'83	'85
24-29	+5	13%	13%	21%	18%	17%	22%
	+4	29	19	24	16	23	20
	+3	32	35	19	26	24	32
	+2	14	12	13	18	16	13
	+1	7	14	13	11	13	9
	-1	3	2	5	5	3	1
	-2	0	2	2	2	1	1
	-3	0	1	1	2	1	0
	-4	0	0	1	0	1	0
	-5	0	1	1	2	1	1
# SURVEYED		207	222	195	238	280	99
AGE	RESP	'74	'75	'77	'82	'83	'85
30-35	+5	18%	20%	17%	20%	19%	24%
	+4	21	17	19	20	17	23
	+3	25	25	23	28	24	25
	+2	12	14	16	10	15	18
	+1	14	16	15	13	20	9
	-1	4	3	3	2	1	0
	-2	1	1	2	2	2	0
	-3	2	1	3	2	1	0
	-4	1	1	1	1	0	1
	-5	1	1	1	1	1	0
# SURVEYED		169	161	172	204	230	96

		YEAR					
AGE	RESP	'74	'75	'77	'82	'83	'85
36-41	+5	18%	21%	18%	23%	16%	18%
	+4	16	17	17	21	25	21
	+3	26	21	29	27	26	27
	+2	18	20	14	12	12	16
	+1	12	17	13	10	13	12
	-1	3	2	5	2	2	2
	-2	3	0	2	3	2	2
	-3	1	3	1	1	2	2
	-4	1	0	0	0	1	0
	-5	3	0	1	2	1	0
# SURVEYED		147	145	153	144	165	94
AGE	RESP	'74	'75	'77	'82	'83	'85
42-47	+5	14%	14%	25%	18%	26%	18%
	+4	16	15	12	25	20	29
	+3	30	26	28	21	27	26
	+2	10	16	11	11	9	12
	+1	18	16	11	17	9	12
	-1	2	6	5	3	1	2
	-2	3	1	2	2	1	0
	-3	3	3	2	1	3	0
	-4	1	0	1	2	2	2
	-5	3	2	2	1	1	0
# SURVEYED		145	136	130	114	141	66
AGE	RESP	'74	'75	'77	'82	'83	'85
48-53	+5	19%	18%	18%	25%	16%	14%
	+4	17	16	16	20	21	20
	+3	22	25	21	22	31	27
	+2	16	16	12	10	10	18
	+1	9	13	17	15	12	20
	-1	9	5	5	2	2	0
	-2	3	2	5	1	2	1
	-3	2	4	1	1	4	0
	-4	1	0	1	3	2	0
	-5	3	1	3	1	2	0
# SURVEYED		139	135	147	106	111	71

TABLE IV: ENGLAND AS A FAVORED COUNTRY -- BY AGE (Continued)

Question: On a scale that goes from "plus 5" for a country you like very much, to the lowest position of "minus 5" for a country you dislike very much, where would you rate England? NOTE: Question not asked in 1972-1973, 1976, 1978, 1980, 1984, 1986-1989.

Responses: +5 = +5 +4 = +4 +3 = +3 +2 = +2 +1 = +1
-1 = -1 -2 = -2 -3 = -3 -4 = -4 -5 = -5

		YEAR					
AGE	RESP	'74	'75	'77	'82	'83	'85
54-59	+5	18%	13%	26%	35%	31%	21%
	+4	20	16	16	18	13	18
	+3	19	30	22	19	19	25
	+2	16	16	14	12	13	13
	+1	8	15	12	9	12	15
	-1	8	2	3	2	7	2
	-2	2	1	3	1	2	3
	-3	2	3	2	0	1	2
	-4	1	2	2	1	0	0
	-5	5	3	0	1	2	2
# SURVEYED		130	117	154	137	127	61
AGE	RESP	'74	'75	'77	'82	'83	'85
60-65	+5	19%	22%	15%	19%	26%	23%
	+4	17	14	13	22	18	14
	+3	25	18	33	19	18	17
	+2	16	9	12	19	15	22
	+1	13	14	14	12	11	11
	-1	3	7	5	1	5	9
	-2	1	6	2	0	2	0
	-3	1	3	1	4	2	2
	-4	0	3	2	1	3	2
	-5	5	5	4	3	1	2
# SURVEYED		100	105	108	113	125	65
AGE	RESP	'74	'75	'77	'82	'83	'85
66+	+5	21%	21%	22%	22%	29%	29%
	+4	20	16	20	18	19	18
	+3	22	22	16	22	15	22
	+2	12	12	12	16	14	11
	+1	9	12	16	13	12	10
	-1	4	7	2	5	3	3
	-2	2	2	3	2	3	2
	-3	2	2	2	2	3	3
	-4	2	2	0	0	1	2
	-5	4	3	5	0	2	1
# SURVEYED		210	207	183	230	218	118

****

ISRAEL AS A FAVORED COUNTRY

TABLE I: ISRAEL AS A FAVORED COUNTRY -- BY TOTAL POPULATION

Question: On a scale that goes from "plus 5" for a country you like very much, to the lowest position of "minus 5" for a country you dislike very much, where would you rate Israel? NOTE: Question not asked in 1972-1973, 1976, 1978, 1980, 1984, 1987.

Responses: +5 = +5 +4 = +4 +3 = +3 +2 = +2 +1 = +1
-1 = -1 -2 = -2 -3 = -3 -4 = -4 -5 = -5

	YEAR								
RESPONSE	'74	'75	'77	'82	'83	'85	'86	'88	'89
+5	14%	11%	13%	12%	10%	12%	12%	11%	9%
+4	10	9	11	9	8	9	9	7	6
+3	17	15	15	15	11	15	13	11	12
+2	13	12	13	12	12	14	13	10	10
+1	19	20	20	17	19	18	20	17	19
-1	9	12	11	13	14	11	10	14	11
-2	4	6	5	7	7	7	6	8	8
-3	5	6	5	6	7	6	5	8	6
-4	2	4	3	4	4	3	4	3	5
-5	6	6	5	5	7	5	7	10	13
# SURVEYED	1377	1365	1372	1393	1493	1418	1391	911	916

TABLE II: ISRAEL AS A FAVORED COUNTRY -- BY SEX

Question: On a scale that goes from "plus 5" for a country you like very much, to the lowest position of "minus 5" for a country you dislike very much, where would you rate Israel? NOTE: Question not asked in 1972-1973, 1976, 1978, 1980, 1984, 1987.

Responses: +5 = +5 +4 = +4 +3 = +3 +2 = +2 +1 = +1
-1 = -1 -2 = -2 -3 = -3 -4 = -4 -5 = -5

YEAR										
SEX	RESP	'74	'75	'77	'82	'83	'85	'86	'88	'89
M	+5	13%	11%	14%	11%	9%	11%	12%	10%	9%
A	+4	11	10	11	8	7	9	8	6	6
L	+3	18	15	14	15	13	14	13	10	12
E	+2	14	12	13	12	10	14	13	11	10
	+1	18	20	20	18	19	20	21	16	19
	-1	9	12	11	13	15	11	11	15	11
	-2	3	6	4	9	7	6	6	10	9
	-3	5	7	5	6	8	5	5	8	7
	-4	2	3	3	3	4	3	3	3	4
	-5	6	5	6	5	8	6	9	10	14
# SURVEYED		647	623	639	614	660	650	597	411	410
SEX	RESP	'74	'75	'77	'82	'83	'85	'86	'88	'89
F	+5	16%	10%	12%	12%	11%	13%	12%	11%	10%
E	+4	9	8	11	9	9	9	10	7	6
M	+3	16	15	16	15	10	16	12	12	12
A	+2	12	13	12	12	12	14	13	9	11
L	+1	19	20	20	16	19	16	20	18	20
E	-1	9	12	11	13	13	11	10	13	11
	-2	5	6	7	7	7	7	6	7	7
	-3	5	5	5	5	7	6	6	9	6
	-4	3	4	3	4	5	3	5	3	5
	-5	6	6	4	6	6	5	6	11	12
# SURVEYED		730	742	733	779	833	768	794	500	506

TABLE III: ISRAEL AS A FAVORED COUNTRY -- BY RACE

Question: On a scale that goes from "plus 5" for a country you like very much, to the lowest position of "minus 5" for a country you dislike very much, where would you rate Israel? NOTE: Question not asked in 1972-1973, 1976, 1978, 1980, 1984, 1987.

Responses: +5 = +5 +4 = +4 +3 = +3 +2 = +2 +1 = +1
-1 = -1 -2 = -2 -3 = -3 -4 = -4 -5 = -5

		YEAR								
RACE	RESP	'74	'75	'77	'82	'83	'85	'86	'88	'89
WHITE	+5	14%	11%	13%	12%	10%	12%	12%	10%	10%
	+4	11	9	11	8	8	9	9	7	6
	+3	17	15	15	15	11	14	12	11	11
	+2	13	12	13	12	12	14	13	10	11
	+1	20	20	20	17	20	19	20	17	20
	-1	9	12	10	13	14	11	10	14	11
	-2	4	6	5	8	7	7	6	8	8
	-3	5	6	5	6	8	5	6	9	7
	-4	2	3	3	3	4	4	4	3	4
	-5	5	6	5	5	7	6	7	10	12
# SURVEYED		1222	1218	1226	1226	1333	1255	1191	775	794
RACE	RESP	'74	'75	'77	'82	'83	'85	'86	'88	'89
BLACK	+5	16%	8%	11%	9%	11%	14%	13%	15%	6%
	+4	7	8	9	13	11	7	8	4	7
	+3	14	16	12	12	11	20	14	10	15
	+2	14	17	10	12	11	16	11	8	9
	+1	13	20	20	16	16	11	23	15	14
	-1	11	10	15	14	14	12	10	17	11
	-2	2	6	8	6	6	5	7	9	7
	-3	5	4	5	5	6	11	4	6	5
	-4	4	4	2	6	6	2	4	5	6
	-5	14	6	7	7	8	2	7	11	20
# SURVEYED		148	143	132	140	142	122	166	106	85
RACE	RESP	'74	'75	'77	'82	'83	'85	'86	'88	'89
OTHER	+5	0%	0%	14%	15%	6%	5%	12%	7%	14%
	+4	0	0	7	4	17	12	9	13	0
	+3	0	25	7	15	22	22	12	10	11
	+2	14	25	21	19	11	24	15	20	3
	+1	0	50	21	7	0	17	15	13	24
	-1	14	0	14	11	11	2	12	7	16
	-2	14	0	7	7	11	10	0	13	0
	-3	14	0	0	11	6	2	3	3	8
	-4	29	0	0	7	6	2	9	3	8
	-5	14	0	7	4	11	2	15	10	16
# SURVEYED		7	4	14	27	18	41	34	30	37

TABLE IV: ISRAEL AS A FAVORED COUNTRY -- BY AGE

Question: On a scale that goes from "plus 5" for a country you like very much, to the lowest position of "minus 5" for a country you dislike very much, where would you rate Israel? NOTE: Question not asked in 1972-1973, 1976, 1978, 1980, 1984, 1987.

Responses: +5 = +5 · +4 = +4 · +3 = +3 · +2 = +2 · +1 = +1 · -1 = -1 · -2 = -2 · -3 = -3 · -4 = -4 · -5 = -5

		YEAR								
AGE	RESP	'74	'75	'77	'82	'83	'85	'86	'88	'89
18-23	+5	7%	8%	8%	6%	8%	7%	3%	12%	5%
	+4	10	7	9	7	7	8	7	3	4
	+3	21	12	15	13	10	13	10	9	14
	+2	13	16	15	15	11	17	12	8	6
	+1	16	15	22	21	26	23	30	15	31
	-1	11	13	11	16	14	10	13	15	16
	-2	3	7	6	7	6	10	6	13	3
	-3	6	7	4	6	7	6	9	13	5
	-4	5	8	4	4	4	3	6	3	4
	-5	8	9	6	5	8	3	5	8	12
# SURVEYED		163	169	158	141	123	128	105	86	77
AGE	RESP	'74	'75	'77	'82	'83	'85	'86	'88	'89
24-29	+5	10%	8%	14%	9%	7%	8%	9%	8%	6%
	+4	14	11	10	7	11	7	7	8	7
	+3	13	16	14	10	11	12	10	8	9
	+2	11	11	12	13	10	16	13	11	14
	+1	22	22	17	17	15	19	22	23	15
	-1	12	13	15	13	18	15	13	12	14
	-2	3	6	5	9	9	9	7	12	9
	-3	6	5	3	8	8	3	6	8	7
	-4	2	3	4	4	6	5	5	2	12
	-5	7	4	7	9	4	6	9	8	7
# SURVEYED		205	219	197	238	276	213	215	145	137
AGE	RESP	'74	'75	'77	'82	'83	'85	'86	'88	'89
30-35	+5	19%	11%	9%	10%	10%	12%	10%	10%	10%
	+4	11	10	9	9	7	7	9	9	7
	+3	17	11	14	14	7	13	13	13	6
	+2	10	14	9	14	11	12	13	8	8
	+1	18	26	28	19	19	19	19	16	17
	-1	11	11	11	18	21	13	13	18	12
	-2	4	4	8	7	7	6	10	6	9
	-3	3	7	3	5	7	7	6	6	7
	-4	2	3	2	4	5	4	1	4	7
	-5	6	3	6	3	7	5	6	10	17
# SURVEYED		169	160	173	199	230	203	219	121	129

TABLE IV: ISRAEL AS A FAVORED COUNTRY -- BY AGE (Continued)

Question: On a scale that goes from "plus 5" for a country you like very much, to the lowest position of "minus 5" for a country you dislike very much, where would you rate Israel? NOTE: Question not asked in 1972-1973, 1976, 1978, 1980, 1984, 1987.

Responses: +5 = +5 | +4 = +4 | +3 = +3 | +2 = +2 | +1 = +1 | -1 = -1 | -2 = -2 | -3 = -3 | -4 = -4 | -5 = -5

		YEAR								
AGE	RESP	'74	'75	'77	'82	'83	'85	'86	'88	'89
36-41	+5	13%	11%	13%	13%	12%	14%	14%	11%	12%
	+4	6	10	17	6	6	9	10	7	6
	+3	16	13	16	19	12	16	16	12	17
	+2	19	11	12	17	18	15	10	11	9
	+1	17	22	17	16	16	19	22	15	19
	-1	10	15	13	11	15	11	11	15	13
	-2	2	6	3	5	6	5	3	8	7
	-3	4	7	6	5	6	5	4	11	4
	-4	5	2	0	5	4	0	3	4	3
	-5	7	3	3	3	4	7	6	7	11
# SURVEYED		143	145	146	140	164	175	182	123	120
AGE	RESP	'74	'75	'77	'82	'83	'85	'86	'88	'89
42-47	+5	14%	12%	15%	14%	16%	13%	8%	10%	9%
	+4	5	7	7	11	8	6	8	9	8
	+3	17	15	16	21	16	20	14	16	16
	+2	14	12	14	9	12	11	16	15	9
	+1	19	24	23	16	19	23	27	12	20
	-1	7	16	9	11	10	12	6	12	5
	-2	14	4	4	4	3	8	8	6	10
	-3	4	5	8	6	6	4	4	8	10
	-4	2	1	1	3	4	1	2	2	2
	-5	4	4	4	4	7	3	8	9	12
# SURVEYED		140	135	127	112	135	119	131	99	105
AGE	RESP	'74	'75	'77	'82	'83	'85	'86	'88	'89
48-53	+5	15%	11%	13%	17%	10%	11%	13%	12%	10%
	+4	12	5	10	9	6	7	11	12	5
	+3	17	18	13	13	14	12	15	5	15
	+2	10	15	14	9	10	18	13	7	9
	+1	19	18	19	20	19	24	16	20	21
	-1	7	12	8	9	9	7	3	14	8
	-2	3	6	8	8	7	5	6	12	10
	-3	4	7	8	7	7	9	8	3	8
	-4	3	3	5	2	4	2	3	7	4
	-5	10	5	3	8	13	3	14	8	10
# SURVEYED		134	133	144	103	107	123	102	59	78

TABLE IV: ISRAEL AS A FAVORED COUNTRY -- BY AGE (Continued)

Question: On a scale that goes from "plus 5" for a country you like very much, to the lowest position of "minus 5" for a country you dislike very much, where would you rate Israel? NOTE: Question not asked in 1972-1973, 1976, 1978, 1980, 1984, 1987.

Responses: +5 = +5 +4 = +4 +3 = +3 +2 = +2 +1 = +1
-1 = -1 -2 = -2 -3 = -3 -4 = -4 -5 = -5

		YEAR								
AGE	RESP	'74	'75	'77	'82	'83	'85	'86	'88	'89
54-59	+5	13%	13%	17%	16%	8%	17%	14%	13%	14%
	+4	15	9	15	11	7	11	15	6	3
	+3	14	15	11	15	14	18	14	13	11
	+2	18	13	16	13	12	13	10	9	14
	+1	16	17	17	16	18	13	24	15	19
	-1	7	9	10	9	12	7	9	15	8
	-2	4	8	3	6	4	5	8	4	8
	-3	7	5	3	4	10	7	3	13	5
	-4	1	4	3	5	7	5	1	2	2
	-5	6	8	4	5	8	4	3	11	16
# SURVEYED		123	111	149	129	125	117	93	47	63
AGE	RESP	'74	'75	'77	'82	'83	'85	'86	'88	'89
60-65	+5	10%	14%	15%	10%	13%	11%	17%	14%	9%
	+4	8	11	9	10	8	10	11	4	6
	+3	20	18	18	16	13	16	8	19	15
	+2	14	9	11	8	10	17	9	7	11
	+1	33	18	18	20	27	14	20	17	22
	-1	9	10	16	11	7	13	10	7	7
	-2	1	5	4	6	7	3	2	1	6
	-3	2	7	4	6	8	7	7	13	7
	-4	0	1	4	5	3	3	8	1	2
	-5	3	7	3	7	4	7	7	16	15
# SURVEYED		91	100	102	108	120	117	107	70	54
AGE	RESP	'74	'75	'77	'82	'83	'85	'86	'88	'89
66+	+5	25%	12%	15%	12%	9%	14%	17%	11%	11%
	+4	9	9	12	11	11	14	10	3	7
	+3	19	18	19	18	10	16	13	8	7
	+2	9	10	12	10	11	10	16	11	13
	+1	13	18	16	12	20	12	13	18	16
	-1	7	9	6	14	10	10	10	16	15
	-2	3	8	5	11	11	6	5	9	6
	-3	7	3	4	5	7	6	3	6	5
	-4	1	5	4	3	3	6	6	4	3
	-5	6	8	7	5	9	6	7	16	17
# SURVEYED		203	191	171	217	207	217	231	160	150

****

JAPAN AS A FAVORED COUNTRY

TABLE I: JAPAN AS A FAVORED COUNTRY -- BY TOTAL POPULATION

Question: On a scale that goes from "plus 5" for a country you like very much, to the lowest position of "minus 5" for a country you dislike very much, where would you rate Japan? NOTE: Question not asked in 1972-1973, 1976, 1978, 1980, 1984, 1987.

Responses: +5 = +5 +4 = +4 +3 = +3 +2 = +2 +1 = +1
-1 = -1 -2 = -2 -3 = -3 -4 = -4 -5 = -5

	YEAR								
RESPONSE	'74	'75	'77	'82	'83	'85	'86	'88	'89
+5	8%	6%	7%	8%	7%	9%	8%	9%	8%
+4	11	10	7	10	8	10	11	9	10
+3	22	20	21	21	17	21	23	19	20
+2	15	15	15	14	17	17	17	15	13
+1	18	20	19	17	20	17	17	20	20
-1	7	9	9	9	10	9	8	9	9
-2	4	5	5	5	6	5	6	5	6
-3	4	6	6	5	6	6	4	5	5
-4	4	5	5	4	3	3	2	2	2
-5	6	5	7	7	5	4	5	7	8
# SURVEYED	1406	1388	1399	1423	1521	1453	1415	934	962

TABLE II: JAPAN AS A FAVORED COUNTRY -- BY SEX

Question: On a scale that goes from "plus 5" for a country you like very much, to the lowest position of "minus 5" for a country you dislike very much, where would you rate Japan? NOTE: Question not asked in 1972-1973, 1976, 1978, 1980, 1984, 1987.

Responses: +5 = +5 +4 = +4 +3 = +3 +2 = +2 +1 = +1
-1 = -1 -2 = -2 -3 = -3 -4 = -4 -5 = -5

		YEAR								
SEX	RESP	'74	'75	'77	'82	'83	'85	'86	'88	'89
M	+5	9%	8%	10%	9%	8%	9%	10%	10%	8%
A	+4	10	12	7	11	9	11	11	10	12
L	+3	26	23	21	21	18	22	25	19	19
E	+2	15	15	15	15	18	18	17	14	13
	+1	18	18	20	15	19	15	15	19	18
	-1	6	8	7	8	10	9	6	9	8
	-2	4	5	5	5	4	5	5	5	7
	-3	3	4	6	4	6	5	4	4	4
	-4	3	3	3	4	3	2	1	3	2
	-5	7	5	7	8	6	3	5	8	9
# SURVEYED		667	638	651	623	668	664	609	421	418
SEX	RESP	'74	'75	'77	'82	'83	'85	'86	'88	'89
F	+5	7%	5%	5%	7%	6%	8%	7%	8%	7%
E	+4	11	8	7	9	7	10	10	8	9
M	+3	19	17	20	21	16	19	20	20	20
A	+2	16	15	14	14	16	16	17	15	13
L	+1	18	21	19	19	21	19	19	21	22
E	-1	8	10	11	10	11	9	9	10	9
	-2	5	5	5	5	7	5	6	4	5
	-3	6	7	6	6	7	7	4	6	5
	-4	5	6	6	3	4	3	3	1	2
	-5	5	5	7	6	5	4	5	7	8
# SURVEYED		739	750	748	800	853	789	806	513	544

TABLE III: JAPAN AS A FAVORED COUNTRY -- BY RACE

Question: On a scale that goes from "plus 5" for a country you like very much, to the lowest position of "minus 5" for a country you dislike very much, where would you rate Japan? NOTE: Question not asked in 1972-1973, 1976, 1978, 1980, 1984, 1987.

Responses: +5 = +5 +4 = +4 +3 = +3 +2 = +2 +1 = +1
-1 = -1 -2 = -2 -3 = -3 -4 = -4 -5 = -5

		YEAR								
RACE	RESP	'74	'75	'77	'82	'83	'85	'86	'88	'89
WHITE	+5	7%	6%	7%	7%	6%	8%	8%	9%	6%
	+4	11	10	7	10	7	10	10	8	10
	+3	23	20	21	22	18	21	23	19	20
	+2	16	15	15	15	17	17	17	15	14
	+1	19	20	20	18	21	18	17	20	21
	-1	7	9	9	9	11	10	8	9	9
	-2	4	5	5	5	6	4	6	5	6
	-3	5	5	5	5	6	6	4	6	5
	-4	3	4	4	4	3	2	2	2	2
	-5	5	5	7	6	6	4	5	7	8
# SURVEYED		1243	1244	1249	1255	1360	1284	1211	796	831
RACE	RESP	'74	'75	'77	'82	'83	'85	'86	'88	'89
BLACK	+5	10%	9%	7%	13%	9%	13%	9%	10%	14%
	+4	10	9	9	10	13	13	14	11	11
	+3	19	15	13	15	10	15	18	18	11
	+2	13	14	13	13	15	14	17	12	12
	+1	13	16	13	12	16	12	18	17	13
	-1	6	9	8	9	10	8	9	10	8
	-2	5	6	11	3	5	10	4	4	11
	-3	4	7	10	7	8	5	4	6	4
	-4	7	7	8	4	8	6	4	1	5
	-5	12	7	9	15	5	3	5	11	12
# SURVEYED		156	140	135	141	143	126	169	107	93
RACE	RESP	'74	'75	'77	'82	'83	'85	'86	'88	'89
OTHER	+5	29%	50%	13%	26%	22%	14%	11%	10%	16%
	+4	29	0	0	4	17	9	6	13	11
	+3	14	25	27	33	17	28	20	29	37
	+2	14	25	13	4	22	14	20	13	11
	+1	0	0	20	4	6	14	11	16	13
	-1	0	0	13	4	11	7	9	3	3
	-2	0	0	0	7	0	0	3	3	0
	-3	0	0	7	7	6	7	9	3	3
	-4	0	0	7	0	0	5	3	0	0
	-5	14	0	0	11	0	2	9	10	8
# SURVEYED		7	4	15	27	18	43	35	31	38

TABLE IV: JAPAN AS A FAVORED COUNTRY -- BY AGE

Question: On a scale that goes from "plus 5" for a country you like very much, to the lowest position of "minus 5" for a country you dislike very much, where would you rate Japan? NOTE: Question not asked in 1972-1973, 1976, 1978, 1980, 1984, 1987.

Responses: +5 = +5 +4 = +4 +3 = +3 +2 = +2 +1 = +1
-1 = -1 -2 = -2 -3 = -3 -4 = -4 -5 = -5

		YEAR								
AGE	RESP	'74	'75	'77	'82	'83	'85	'86	'88	'89
18-23	+5	7%	6%	3%	8%	9%	8%	4%	6%	10%
	+4	12	9	10	14	6	11	14	12	8
	+3	24	20	19	21	14	16	22	26	25
	+2	20	21	21	17	14	19	19	16	17
	+1	15	21	20	19	24	23	19	19	16
	-1	9	10	13	10	10	8	7	6	10
	-2	4	2	4	7	6	6	6	3	5
	-3	3	4	6	1	9	4	6	2	5
	-4	1	3	2	0	2	2	1	3	2
	-5	4	4	3	3	5	2	3	5	2
# SURVEYED		162	169	160	145	125	131	108	93	83
AGE	RESP	'74	'75	'77	'82	'83	'85	'86	'88	'89
24-29	+5	9%	5%	9%	10%	6%	10%	7%	9%	4%
	+4	11	12	8	9	8	12	11	11	15
	+3	30	21	25	25	20	20	21	30	25
	+2	18	15	15	18	18	18	22	10	13
	+1	16	25	18	20	22	18	22	19	24
	-1	8	7	7	6	12	12	5	4	8
	-2	3	5	8	4	6	2	5	8	3
	-3	2	4	5	3	4	3	4	5	1
	-4	1	3	3	2	3	3	1	1	3
	-5	2	4	3	3	2	1	3	3	3
# SURVEYED		209	220	197	239	279	214	215	143	143
AGE	RESP	'74	'75	'77	'82	'83	'85	'86	'88	'89
30-35	+5	7%	9%	6%	8%	8%	7%	13%	10%	10%
	+4	13	8	8	9	7	12	11	11	10
	+3	24	19	17	28	16	21	27	23	19
	+2	13	14	21	14	18	22	17	14	11
	+1	18	25	22	20	28	21	16	19	26
	-1	8	8	10	9	8	7	6	8	4
	-2	4	4	4	4	3	3	3	5	9
	-3	6	4	4	1	3	4	5	7	4
	-4	4	3	5	1	3	2	0	1	2
	-5	4	5	4	4	6	2	1	2	4
# SURVEYED		170	160	171	204	231	208	218	124	134

TABLE IV: JAPAN AS A FAVORED COUNTRY -- BY AGE (Continued)

Question: On a scale that goes from "plus 5" for a country you like very much, to the lowest position of "minus 5" for a country you dislike very much, where would you rate Japan? NOTE: Question not asked in 1972-1973, 1976, 1978, 1980, 1984, 1987.

Responses: +5 = +5 +4 = +4 +3 = +3 +2 = +2 +1 = +1 -1 = -1 -2 = -2 -3 = -3 -4 = -4 -5 = -5

		YEAR								
AGE	RESP	'74	'75	'77	'82	'83	'85	'86	'88	'89
36-41	+5	9%	4%	7%	9%	10%	9%	10%	10%	6%
	+4	12	11	6	11	9	10	10	14	12
	+3	18	24	22	22	12	28	22	18	26
	+2	17	12	13	13	17	13	19	22	15
	+1	21	18	20	14	20	16	18	17	18
	-1	7	11	14	12	9	6	7	6	11
	-2	4	6	4	7	5	6	5	2	4
	-3	5	7	4	4	7	6	2	6	2
	-4	3	3	6	4	7	3	3	2	0
	-5	4	3	3	5	4	2	3	5	5
# SURVEYED		145	143	152	138	166	178	183	124	121
AGE	RESP	'74	'75	'77	'82	'83	'85	'86	'88	'89
42-47	+5	9%	7%	15%	11%	7%	9%	2%	9%	6%
	+4	12	12	6	11	9	11	11	9	11
	+3	22	28	24	18	22	29	28	25	25
	+2	17	14	14	16	15	21	15	18	12
	+1	20	14	19	20	17	16	23	17	18
	-1	3	7	8	8	12	6	10	9	10
	-2	3	5	2	1	6	2	5	4	2
	-3	4	7	3	8	4	2	2	4	7
	-4	3	4	5	3	2	2	2	1	1
	-5	6	1	5	4	5	2	3	4	8
# SURVEYED		143	138	130	114	138	122	133	100	108
AGE	RESP	'74	'75	'77	'82	'83	'85	'86	'88	'89
48-53	+5	7%	4%	5%	10%	9%	10%	11%	7%	13%
	+4	8	7	9	5	12	11	7	0	10
	+3	20	22	18	26	17	18	30	12	16
	+2	12	19	12	11	15	15	14	17	13
	+1	25	16	21	19	16	17	14	25	10
	-1	9	14	7	10	12	10	7	14	9
	-2	4	4	4	4	6	6	7	4	5	9
	-3	3	4	6	4	4	8	5	5	6
	-4	5	4	8	2	1	2	2	2	4
	-5	8	4	10	8	8	3	8	14	10
# SURVEYED		138	134	146	105	106	123	103	59	79

TABLE IV: JAPAN AS A FAVORED COUNTRY -- BY AGE (Continued)

Question: On a scale that goes from "plus 5" for a country you like very much, to the lowest position of "minus 5" for a country you dislike very much, where would you rate Japan? NOTE: Question not asked in 1972-1973, 1976, 1978, 1980, 1984, 1987.

Responses: +5 = +5 | +4 = +4 | +3 = +3 | +2 = +2 | +1 = +1 | -1 = -1 | -2 = -2 | -3 = -3 | -4 = -4 | -5 = -5

		YEAR								
AGE	RESP	'74	'75	'77	'82	'83	'85	'86	'88	'89
54-59	+5	7%	6%	11%	7%	7%	11%	9%	13%	13%
	+4	8	4	5	12	7	7	10	8	10
	+3	19	22	25	20	16	22	21	13	16
	+2	13	14	11	13	17	12	14	13	12
	+1	18	12	12	12	17	16	15	25	13
	-1	6	11	5	13	10	11	8	19	7
	-2	6	6	8	4	7	7	7	2	6
	-3	5	7	8	7	8	8	4	0	6
	-4	5	12	5	4	4	2	2	4	1
	-5	13	5	10	10	6	6	9	4	13
# SURVEYED		126	113	155	134	125	121	96	48	67
AGE	RESP	'74	'75	'77	'82	'83	'85	'86	'88	'89
60-65	+5	6%	6%	8%	3%	5%	6%	7%	9%	5%
	+4	9	13	4	6	6	11	12	9	10
	+3	24	12	20	14	21	16	17	7	10
	+2	11	7	10	14	18	14	13	14	18
	+1	17	21	19	20	14	15	10	23	29
	-1	6	5	10	8	10	10	11	10	6
	-2	6	7	7	5	8	6	11	1	6
	-3	9	10	11	11	7	10	3	4	5
	-4	5	8	7	11	6	4	5	1	2
	-5	7	13	6	8	6	8	11	20	10
# SURVEYED		100	103	104	112	125	124	109	69	62
AGE	RESP	'74	'75	'77	'82	'83	'85	'86	'88	'89
66+	+5	9%	5%	4%	8%	3%	9%	6%	8%	6%
	+4	10	10	6	9	7	7	9	3	4
	+3	18	12	16	15	15	15	16	12	11
	+2	14	16	12	11	16	16	16	11	12
	+1	15	19	19	13	18	14	15	20	22
	-1	8	9	8	9	10	13	11	13	11
	-2	5	6	6	8	5	6	7	7	8
	-3	5	7	6	7	11	9	7	9	7
	-4	6	5	6	7	4	4	4	3	2
	-5	10	10	17	14	10	7	9	13	17
# SURVEYED		207	204	178	224	220	226	245	173	162

****

RUSSIA AS A FAVORED COUNTRY

TABLE I: RUSSIA AS A FAVORED COUNTRY -- BY TOTAL POPULATION

Question: On a scale that goes from "plus 5" for a country you like very much, to the lowest position of "minus 5" for a country you dislike very much, where would you rate Russia? NOTE: Question not asked in 1972-1973, 1976, 1978, 1980, 1984, 1987.

Responses: +5 = +5 +4 = +4 +3 = +3 +2 = +2 +1 = +1
-1 = -1 -2 = -2 -3 = -3 -4 = -4 -5 = -5

	YEAR								
RESPONSE	'74	'75	'77	'82	'83	'85	'86	'88	'89
+5	3%	3%	2%	1%	1%	2%	1%	3%	4%
+4	3	3	1	1	1	1	1	2	4
+3	13	13	9	5	4	4	7	9	12
+2	11	11	7	5	5	5	8	11	13
+1	18	17	14	11	12	12	16	21	22
-1	11	11	13	10	13	12	14	11	11
-2	5	6	6	6	8	8	7	6	7
-3	9	9	9	9	13	12	12	9	7
-4	4	5	6	6	8	7	6	4	3
-5	23	22	32	45	36	38	28	23	17
# SURVEYED	1411	1386	1415	1445	1528	1450	1405	930	951

TABLE II: RUSSIA AS A FAVORED COUNTRY -- BY SEX

Question: On a scale that goes from "plus 5" for a country you like very much, to the lowest position of "minus 5" for a country you dislike very much, where would you rate Russia? NOTE: Question not asked in 1972-1973, 1976, 1978, 1980, 1984, 1987.

Responses: +5 = +5 +4 = +4 +3 = +3 +2 = +2 +1 = +1
-1 = -1 -2 = -2 -3 = -3 -4 = -4 -5 = -5

		YEAR								
SEX	RESP	'74	'75	'77	'82	'83	'85	'86	'88	'89
M	+5	4%	4%	2%	1%	1%	2%	1%	3%	4%
A	+4	4	3	1	1	1	2	2	3	6
L	+3	14	14	9	4	4	3	8	10	11
E	+2	11	11	7	5	5	5	9	11	14
	+1	20	16	17	11	13	12	18	24	24
	-1	9	10	12	11	15	14	14	11	11
	-2	5	6	6	7	8	10	8	5	5
	-3	8	8	9	8	13	11	13	8	6
	-4	3	4	5	6	7	7	4	5	2
	-5	22	22	31	46	34	35	24	20	16
# SURVEYED		666	637	654	626	667	657	603	415	416
SEX	RESP	'74	'75	'77	'82	'83	'85	'86	'88	'89
F	+5	2%	2%	2%	1%	0%	2%	2%	3%	4%
E	+4	3	2	2	1	1	1	1	2	3
M	+3	12	12	9	5	4	4	7	9	12
A	+2	11	11	7	4	5	4	6	11	12
L	+1	16	19	12	11	12	12	15	19	21
E	-1	13	12	14	10	12	10	13	11	10
	-2	6	5	5	5	8	6	7	6	8
	-3	10	10	9	10	14	12	11	10	7
	-4	4	6	6	6	8	7	7	4	4
	-5	24	22	33	45	37	41	30	25	18
# SURVEYED		745	749	761	819	861	793	802	515	535

TABLE III: RUSSIA AS A FAVORED COUNTRY -- BY RACE

Question: On a scale that goes from "plus 5" for a country you like very much, to the lowest position of "minus 5" for a country you dislike very much, where would you rate Russia? NOTE: Question not asked in 1972-1973, 1976, 1978, 1980, 1984, 1987.

Responses: +5 = +5 +4 = +4 +3 = +3 +2 = +2 +1 = +1
-1 = -1 -2 = -2 -3 = -3 -4 = -4 -5 = -5

		YEAR								
RACE	RESP	'74	'75	'77	'82	'83	'85	'86	'88	'89
WHITE	+5	2%	3%	2%	1%	1%	1%	1%	3%	4%
	+4	3	3	1	1	1	1	1	2	4
	+3	13	13	9	5	3	3	7	10	12
	+2	11	11	7	5	5	5	8	11	13
	+1	19	18	14	11	13	12	17	22	23
	-1	11	11	13	10	12	12	14	12	11
	-2	5	6	6	6	8	8	8	6	7
	-3	9	9	9	10	14	12	12	10	7
	-4	4	4	5	6	7	6	6	4	4
	-5	22	22	32	45	36	39	27	22	16
# SURVEYED		1248	1241	1262	1272	1366	1282	1204	793	820
RACE	RESP	'74	'75	'77	'82	'83	'85	'86	'88	'89
BLACK	+5	6%	4%	4%	5%	2%	6%	2%	5%	2%
	+4	4	3	3	3	1	2	2	3	9
	+3	10	11	6	4	10	10	7	9	12
	+2	11	10	5	4	3	2	8	12	10
	+1	11	14	14	8	9	9	13	14	17
	-1	12	14	13	11	19	8	13	7	10
	-2	5	3	6	10	6	8	7	6	9
	-3	4	7	9	6	8	11	13	7	6
	-4	3	9	9	5	9	12	8	7	1
	-5	33	25	32	45	33	33	27	31	25
# SURVEYED		156	141	139	146	144	126	166	106	93
RACE	RESP	'74	'75	'77	'82	'83	'85	'86	'88	'89
OTHER	+5	14%	0%	0%	0%	6%	2%	3%	3%	5%
	+4	0	0	0	0	0	2	0	3	0
	+3	0	0	7	0	0	5	14	3	13
	+2	14	75	7	7	11	5	6	10	11
	+1	14	0	14	4	6	19	11	29	18
	-1	0	0	7	7	0	19	11	6	11
	-2	0	0	7	11	6	5	3	3	5
	-3	0	0	14	0	0	10	6	16	5
	-4	0	0	0	4	17	7	9	3	3
	-5	57	25	43	67	56	26	37	23	29
# SURVEYED		7	4	14	27	18	42	35	31	38

TABLE IV: RUSSIA AS A FAVORED COUNTRY -- BY AGE

Question: On a scale that goes from "plus 5" for a country you like very much, to the lowest position of "minus 5" for a country you dislike very much, where would you rate Russia? NOTE: Question not asked in 1972-1973, 1976, 1978, 1980, 1984, 1987.

Responses: +5 = +5, +4 = +4, +3 = +3, +2 = +2, +1 = +1, -1 = -1, -2 = -2, -3 = -3, -4 = -4, -5 = -5

		YEAR								
AGE	RESP	'74	'75	'77	'82	'83	'85	'86	'88	'89
18-23	+5	1%	3%	2%	1%	1%	0%	1%	3%	4%
	+4	4	5	4	3	0	2	0	1	4
	+3	21	16	12	5	3	6	9	7	12
	+2	15	17	12	6	6	5	10	14	17
	+1	20	21	14	15	17	17	21	24	27
	-1	10	10	12	9	12	9	7	12	12
	-2	5	6	12	10	7	10	6	4	4
	-3	7	8	7	12	15	19	10	12	4
	-4	3	3	9	6	10	10	8	3	3
	-5	13	11	16	34	30	22	26	20	14
# SURVEYED		165	167	156	145	126	132	108	92	77
AGE	RESP	'74	'75	'77	'82	'83	'85	'86	'88	'89
24-29	+5	3%	2%	3%	1%	1%	1%	0%	4%	4%
	+4	3	3	2	3	2	0	1	4	8
	+3	15	19	15	5	3	3	8	9	15
	+2	12	15	9	3	6	6	9	14	13
	+1	20	19	16	15	15	11	19	23	24
	-1	11	9	17	13	14	11	15	6	10
	-2	4	8	8	7	9	9	10	8	4
	-3	11	7	12	10	15	13	11	10	10
	-4	6	4	5	9	8	9	5	4	1
	-5	14	14	15	34	28	37	20	17	11
# SURVEYED		207	220	197	238	279	213	213	144	142
AGE	RESP	'74	'75	'77	'82	'83	'85	'86	'88	'89
30-35	+5	4%	5%	1%	1%	1%	0%	2%	2%	3%
	+4	5	2	3	1	1	0	1	2	4
	+3	15	13	9	6	6	5	6	6	15
	+2	14	8	3	10	4	5	7	14	12
	+1	20	20	25	11	12	12	18	23	24
	-1	7	13	13	11	14	14	14	13	9
	-2	5	5	7	7	9	10	6	10	7
	-3	7	7	9	11	15	13	18	9	4
	-4	2	4	3	3	7	5	6	5	5
	-5	21	23	27	37	31	35	22	17	18
# SURVEYED		169	162	173	204	229	206	217	123	137

TABLE IV: RUSSIA AS A FAVORED COUNTRY -- BY AGE (Continued)

Question: On a scale that goes from "plus 5" for a country you like very much, to the lowest position of "minus 5" for a country you dislike very much, where would you rate Russia? NOTE: Question not asked in 1972-1973, 1976, 1978, 1980, 1984, 1987.

Responses: +5 = +5 +4 = +4 +3 = +3 +2 = +2 +1 = +1
-1 = -1 -2 = -2 -3 = -3 -4 = -4 -5 = -5

		YEAR								
AGE	RESP	'74	'75	'77	'82	'83	'85	'86	'88	'89
36-41	+5	3%	2%	1%	1%	1%	2%	1%	4%	4%
	+4	4	1	1	1	1	1	1	3	6
	+3	8	9	8	8	4	2	10	11	11
	+2	14	13	8	5	5	6	9	7	12
	+1	16	20	14	16	18	18	20	27	18
	-1	12	12	18	13	15	15	14	12	11
	-2	9	6	6	6	7	10	6	4	11
	-3	9	6	8	6	10	9	10	7	12
	-4	3	8	1	7	6	6	5	3	2
	-5	22	23	35	36	35	33	23	21	15
# SURVEYED		148	143	154	141	165	178	181	124	121
AGE	RESP	'74	'75	'77	'82	'83	'85	'86	'88	'89
42-47	+5	2%	2%	3%	2%	1%	1%	0%	1%	2%
	+4	4	2	0	2	1	2	1	3	3
	+3	6	15	9	3	3	3	9	14	16
	+2	11	13	7	7	1	5	7	16	12
	+1	27	18	10	9	12	16	19	18	18
	-1	9	10	16	14	16	14	16	16	13
	-2	5	7	4	8	9	8	7	3	6
	-3	8	10	9	9	13	13	9	6	6
	-4	2	4	7	8	9	5	8	2	8
	-5	26	18	35	38	35	34	24	20	16
# SURVEYED		142	136	134	116	140	118	134	99	105
AGE	RESP	'74	'75	'77	'82	'83	'85	'86	'88	'89
48-53	+5	3%	1%	2%	3%	0%	2%	4%	3%	8%
	+4	3	2	1	0	3	0	3	0	4
	+3	12	16	6	6	3	7	6	7	9
	+2	9	7	8	4	6	2	10	7	12
	+1	17	18	12	10	12	10	13	22	21
	-1	12	16	14	6	14	12	9	14	12
	-2	6	3	2	3	5	9	7	7	9
	-3	9	10	10	9	14	13	7	10	6
	-4	4	7	10	3	5	3	4	3	3
	-5	24	20	34	57	40	42	38	27	18
# SURVEYED		140	134	145	105	110	122	101	59	78

TABLE IV: RUSSIA AS A FAVORED COUNTRY -- BY AGE (Continued)

Question: On a scale that goes from "plus 5" for a country you like very much, to the lowest position of "minus 5" for a country you dislike very much, where would you rate Russia? NOTE: Question not asked in 1972-1973, 1976, 1978, 1980, 1984, 1987.

Responses: +5 = +5 +4 = +4 +3 = +3 +2 = +2 +1 = +1
-1 = -1 -2 = -2 -3 = -3 -4 = -4 -5 = -5

		YEAR								
AGE	RESP	'74	'75	'77	'82	'83	'85	'86	'88	'89
54-59	+5	3%	2%	4%	3%	1%	4%	0%	2%	8%
	+4	2	3	0	1	1	3	2	0	5
	+3	15	10	7	2	2	3	10	13	12
	+2	7	9	9	6	6	5	3	9	14
	+1	17	12	14	7	11	8	12	21	17
	-1	13	15	8	12	10	12	10	11	14
	-2	3	4	5	5	5	5	6	9	6
	-3	9	12	12	11	13	8	16	11	5
	-4	3	6	3	5	6	11	3	4	0
	-5	28	27	39	49	44	42	38	21	21
# SURVEYED		127	113	153	138	124	120	94	47	66
AGE	RESP	'74	'75	'77	'82	'83	'85	'86	'88	'89
50-65	+5	6%	5%	3%	0%	0%	1%	1%	0%	7%
	+4	1	2	0	1	1	2	3	3	3
	+3	13	11	4	4	1	2	6	13	12
	+2	9	9	6	1	6	2	10	13	13
	+1	13	14	11	6	10	10	9	19	22
	-1	11	11	12	8	12	10	19	7	7
	-2	2	1	4	5	8	9	12	3	7
	-3	10	11	8	6	12	8	11	9	7
	-4	2	5	7	8	10	7	6	1	0
	-5	32	30	46	61	41	48	23	32	23
# SURVEYED		99	105	112	111	126	124	108	69	60
AGE	RESP	'74	'75	'77	'82	'83	'85	'86	'88	'89
66+	+5	2%	3%	2%	1%	1%	3%	2%	4%	4%
	+4	4	3	2	0	0	1	0	2	2
	+3	8	7	6	3	5	2	5	8	6
	+2	7	6	2	2	4	5	4	5	12
	+1	11	12	10	5	6	9	13	16	24
	-1	13	9	7	7	10	11	15	10	12
	-2	6	7	3	4	9	3	7	3	7
	-3	9	11	9	8	12	11	10	11	6
	-4	6	4	8	5	7	7	6	8	5
	-5	33	36	51	64	47	48	38	33	22
# SURVEYED		208	203	186	239	222	231	246	172	162

****

COMMUNISM AS A FORM OF GOVERNMENT

TABLE I: COMMUNISM AS A FORM OF GOVERNMENT -- BY TOTAL POPULATION

Question: Thinking about all the different kinds of governments in the world today, which of these statements comes closest to how you feel about Communism as a form of government? NOTE: Question not asked in 1972, 1975, 1978, 1983, 1986.

Responses: WS = It's the worst kind of all; BD = It's bad, but no worse than some others; AR = It's all right for some countries; GD = It's a good form of government

	YEAR										
RESPONSE	'73	'74	'76	'77	'80	'82	'84	'85	'87	'88	'89
WS	44%	50%	52%	54%	59%	61%	61%	59%	56%	49%	49%
BD	28	27	26	25	27	25	26	27	29	32	35
AR	25	19	20	20	13	12	11	13	14	16	15
GD	3	3	1	1	1	2	2	1	1	2	1
# SURVEYED	1445	1438	1456	1496	1426	1464	1432	1494	1423	946	1006

TABLE II: COMMUNISM AS A FORM OF GOVERNMENT -- BY SEX

Question: Thinking about all the different kinds of governments in the world today, which of these statements comes closest to how you feel about Communism as a form of government? NOTE: Question not asked in 1972, 1975, 1978, 1983, 1986.

Responses: WS = It's the worst kind of all; BD = It's bad, but no worse than some others; AR = It's all right for some countries; GD = It's a good form of government

		YEAR										
SEX	RESP	'73	'74	'76	'77	'80	'82	'84	'85	'87	'88	'89
M	WS	39%	45%	47%	48%	52%	55%	57%	52%	49%	45%	44%
	BD	30	30	28	28	32	27	28	32	34	35	37
	AR	26	21	24	22	15	15	12	14	15	18	18
	GD	5	4	2	2	1	2	3	2	2	2	1
# SURVEYED		681	670	656	683	629	629	591	675	623	391	438
SEX	RESP	'73	'74	'76	'77	'80	'82	'84	'85	'87	'88	'89
F	WS	49%	55%	57%	58%	64%	65%	64%	64%	61%	52%	53%
	BD	26	25	25	22	23	24	25	22	25	30	33
	AR	24	18	17	19	12	10	10	12	13	15	12
	GD	2	2	1	1	1	1	1	1	1	2	1
# SURVEYED		764	768	800	813	797	835	841	819	800	555	568

TABLE III: COMMUNISM AS A FORM OF GOVERNMENT -- BY RACE

Question: Thinking about all the different kinds of governments in the world today, which of these statements comes closest to how you feel about Communism as a form of government? NOTE: Question not asked in 1972, 1975, 1978, 1983, 1986.

Responses: WS = It's the worst kind of all; BD = It's bad, but no worse than some others; AR = It's all right for some countries; GD = It's a good form of government

		YEAR										
RACE	RESP	'73	'74	'76	'77	'80	'82	'84	'85	'87	'88	'89
WHITE	WS	46%	52%	54%	55%	59%	62%	62%	61%	58%	51%	49%
	BD	28	27	26	25	28	25	26	27	29	32	37
	AR	24	19	19	19	12	11	10	11	12	15	13
	GD	3	3	1	1	1	1	2	1	1	2	1
# SURVEYED		1272	1279	1332	1321	1287	1291	1226	1313	1201	781	873
RACE	RESP	'73	'74	'76	'77	'80	'82	'84	'85	'87	'88	'89
BLACK	WS	34%	37%	36%	40%	52%	48%	53%	40%	41%	40%	51%
	BD	25	33	32	24	22	31	26	28	34	29	23
	AR	35	24	30	31	22	18	17	27	23	27	24
	GD	6	7	3	4	4	2	4	6	2	5	2
# SURVEYED		161	153	115	161	130	147	156	138	173	124	95
RACE	RESP	'73	'74	'76	'77	'80	'82	'84	'85	'87	'88	'89
OTHER	WS	42%	50%	44%	57%	44%	73%	58%	51%	55%	37%	42%
	BD	17	0	33	21	11	12	24	14	18	41	29
	AR	25	50	22	21	33	12	14	35	27	22	24
	GD	17	0	0	0	11	4	4	0	0	0	5
# SURVEYED		12	6	9	14	9	26	50	43	49	41	38

TABLE IV: COMMUNISM AS A FORM OF GOVERNMENT -- BY AGE

Question: Thinking about all the different kinds of governments in the world, which of these statements comes closest to how you feel about Communism as a form of government? NOTE: Question not asked in 1972, 1975, 1978, 1983, 1986.

Responses: WS = It's the worst kind of all; BD = It's bad, but no worse than some others; AR = It's all right for some countries; GD = It's a good form of government

AGE	RESP	'73	'74	'76	'77	'80	'82	'84	'85	'87	'88	'89
18-23	WS	31%	33%	38%	42%	46%	54%	55%	41%	45%	45%	33%
	BD	32	30	30	25	39	31	26	37	26	26	38
	AR	30	29	30	28	12	13	14	20	26	26	26
	GD	7	7	2	5	3	2	6	2	3	2	3
# SURVEYED		166	165	159	163	152	147	154	132	124	91	97
24-29	WS	29%	36%	39%	39%	54%	51%	58%	52%	42%	43%	45%
	BD	35	29	35	34	28	35	28	31	33	33	34
	AR	33	30	24	25	16	11	12	14	24	21	20
	GD	4	4	2	2	3	3	2	2	1	4	1
# SURVEYED		210	208	221	201	199	240	230	216	186	131	115
30-35	WS	47%	50%	54%	45%	45%	50%	52%	56%	50%	35%	45%
	BD	30	30	24	30	36	34	36	29	35	42	40
	AR	19	17	21	24	19	14	12	15	13	19	15
	GD	4	3	1	1	0	2	0	0	2	3	0
# SURVEYED		162	169	185	185	209	202	194	209	217	130	133
36-41	WS	47%	49%	55%	50%	58%	58%	57%	54%	53%	45%	45%
	BD	31	34	29	32	32	26	28	30	29	36	40
	AR	20	15	15	16	10	15	14	13	18	18	14
	GD	2	2	1	2	1	1	1	4	1	2	1
# SURVEYED		169	150	155	164	147	144	185	181	182	131	131
42-47	WS	38%	52%	53%	64%	61%	58%	54%	50%	66%	55%	47%
	BD	29	31	24	21	29	30	34	35	25	30	38
	AR	32	15	21	14	11	11	10	15	8	14	12
	GD	1	2	3	1	0	1	2	1	1	1	3
# SURVEYED		142	150	110	146	112	117	122	121	153	99	106
48-53	WS	52%	60%	54%	53%	63%	72%	68%	55%	66%	53%	49%
	BD	27	19	29	26	23	13	23	30	28	32	34
	AR	19	18	17	20	13	15	7	12	5	15	15
	GD	2	3	1	1	1	0	1	3	1	0	2
# SURVEYED		147	139	125	152	119	110	98	130	124	62	95

TABLE IV: COMMUNISM AS A FORM OF GOVERNMENT -- BY AGE (Continued)

Question: Thinking about all the different kinds of governments in the world today, which of these statements comes closest to how you feel about Communism as a form of government? NOTE: Question not asked in 1972, 1975, 1978, 1983, 1986.

Responses: WS = It's the worst kind of all; BD = It's bad, but no worse than some others; AR = It's all right for some countries; GD = It's a good form of government

		YEAR										
AGE	RESP	'73	'74	'76	'77	'80	'82	'84	'85	'87	'88	'89
54-59	WS	50%	59%	56%	59%	67%	69%	67%	75%	58%	60%	49%
	BD	23	24	24	21	21	20	24	15	33	27	41
	AR	26	13	18	20	11	9	8	10	8	13	8
	GD	1	3	2	0	2	2	1	0	1	0	2
# SURVEYED		151	135	126	167	133	138	111	126	95	52	61
AGE	RESP	'73	'74	'76	'77	'80	'82	'84	'85	'87	'88	'89
60-65	WS	53%	52%	60%	62%	66%	70%	75%	65%	60%	56%	63%
	BD	26	28	19	21	23	20	17	23	26	38	25
	AR	18	18	20	17	10	9	7	12	12	5	12
	GD	3	2	1	1	1	1	1	1	2	1	0
# SURVEYED		115	98	130	115	117	113	106	127	97	82	76
AGE	RESP	'73	'74	'76	'77	'80	'82	'84	'85	'87	'88	'89
66+	WS	56%	66%	63%	73%	71%	74%	71%	74%	66%	60%	60%
	BD	14	18	21	13	15	14	16	16	25	25	29
	AR	26	15	16	12	14	12	10	9	10	13	11
	GD	3	1	0	1	0	0	4	0	0	2	1
# SURVEYED		180	218	239	196	231	244	226	246	240	166	189

****

ALLOW COMMUNIST TO TEACH

TABLE I: ALLOW COMMUNIST TO TEACH IN COLLEGE -- BY TOTAL POPULATION

Question: Suppose a person who admits to being a communist is teaching in a college. Should he be allowed to teach, or not? NOTE: Question not asked in 1975, 1978, 1983, 1986.

Responses: YES = Yes, allowed to teach; NO = Not allowed

	YEAR											
RESPONSE	'72	'73	'74	'76	'77	'80	'82	'84	'85	'87	'88	'89
YES	65	58	56	56	60	57	54	52	54	51	50	46
NO	35	42	44	44	40	43	46	48	46	49	50	54
# SURVEYED	1497	1408	1389	1423	1460	1377	1405	1388	1460	1383	920	965

TABLE II: ALLOW COMMUNIST TO TEACH IN COLLEGE -- BY SEX

Question: Suppose a person who admits to being a communist is teaching in a college. Should he be allowed to teach, or not? NOTE: Question not asked in 1975, 1978, 1983, 1986.

Responses: YES = Yes, allowed to teach; NO = Not allowed

		YEAR											
SEX	RESP	'72	'73	'74	'76	'77	'80	'82	'84	'85	'87	'88	'89
M	YES	62	57	52	54	56	56	50	48	50	49	44	43
	NO	38	43	48	46	44	44	50	52	50	51	56	57
# SURVEYED		762	668	650	643	673	614	602	579	670	613	384	425
SEX	RESP	'72	'73	'74	'76	'77	'80	'82	'84	'85	'87	'88	'89
F	YES	69	60	58	59	63	58	57	54	57	53	54	49
	NO	31	40	42	41	37	42	43	46	43	47	46	51
# SURVEYED		735	740	739	780	787	763	803	809	790	770	536	540

TABLE III: ALLOW COMMUNIST TO TEACH IN COLLEGE-- BY RACE

Question: Suppose a person who admits to being a communist is teaching in a college. Should he be allowed to teach, or not? NOTE: Question not asked in 1975, 1978, 1983, 1986.

Responses: YES = Yes, allowed to teach; NO = Not allowed

		YEAR											
RACE	RESP	'72	'73	'74	'76	'77	'80	'82	'84	'85	'87	'88	'89
WHITE	YES	68	60	56	57	60	56	54	51	54	53	50	45
	NO	32	40	44	43	40	44	46	49	46	48	50	55
# SURVEYED		1278	1226	1232	1297	1280	1238	1239	1184	1286	1160	762	836
RACE	RESP	'72	'73	'74	'76	'77	'80	'82	'84	'85	'87	'88	'89
BLACK	YES	50	49	50	53	57	64	49	54	50	44	47	56
	NO	50	51	50	47	43	36	51	46	50	56	53	44
# SURVEYED		216	169	150	118	165	129	142	156	132	173	116	95
RACE	RESP	'72	'73	'74	'76	'77	'80	'82	'84	'85	'87	'88	'89
OTHER	YES	33	46	43	50	53	30	50	60	50	52	43	41
	NO	67	54	57	50	47	70	50	40	50	48	57	59
# SURVEYED		3	13	7	8	15	10	24	48	42	50	42	34

TABLE IV: ALLOW COMMUNIST TO TEACH IN COLLEGE -- BY AGE

Question: Suppose a person who admits to being a communist is teaching in a college. Should he be allowed to teach, or not? NOTE: Question not asked in 1975, 1978, 1983, 1986.

Responses: YES = Yes, allowed to teach; NO = Not allowed

		YEAR											
AGE	RESP	'72	'73	'74	'76	'77	'80	'82	'84	'85	'87	'88	'89
18-23	YES	46	35	34	38	41	47	46	39	38	41	39	34
	NO	54	65	66	63	59	53	54	61	62	59	61	66
# SURVEYED		156	164	163	152	156	148	137	152	130	118	90	93
AGE	RESP	'72	'73	'74	'76	'77	'80	'82	'84	'85	'87	'88	'89
24-29	YES	46	39	39	36	39	44	44	43	38	38	40	32
	NO	54	61	61	64	61	56	56	57	63	62	60	68
# SURVEYED		217	201	202	218	192	192	237	224	208	182	124	108
AGE	RESP	'72	'73	'74	'76	'77	'80	'82	'84	'85	'87	'88	'89
30-35	YES	69	54	47	51	48	42	37	34	43	38	34	38
	NO	31	46	53	49	52	58	63	66	57	62	66	62
# SURVEYED		171	154	165	183	185	206	196	190	204	213	127	127
AGE	RESP	'72	'73	'74	'76	'77	'80	'82	'84	'85	'87	'88	'89
36-41	YES	59	56	54	55	58	51	41	42	44	39	40	35
	NO	41	44	46	45	42	49	59	58	56	61	60	65
# SURVEYED		119	163	140	149	162	144	132	178	176	177	129	127
AGE	RESP	'72	'73	'74	'76	'77	'80	'82	'84	'85	'87	'88	'89
42-47	YES	67	55	59	64	66	55	45	54	41	49	51	43
	NO	33	45	41	36	34	45	55	46	59	51	49	57
# SURVEYED		174	137	138	108	140	111	115	116	117	147	100	100
AGE	RESP	'72	'73	'74	'76	'77	'80	'82	'84	'85	'87	'88	'89
48-53	YES	69	70	62	66	69	63	60	61	57	60	56	57
	NO	31	30	38	34	31	37	40	39	43	40	44	43
# SURVEYED		179	134	135	122	144	111	103	97	123	121	62	89
AGE	RESP	'72	'73	'74	'76	'77	'80	'82	'84	'85	'87	'88	'89
54-59	YES	78	67	69	66	66	71	62	65	70	60	63	57
	NO	22	33	31	34	34	29	38	35	30	40	37	43
# SURVEYED		143	149	129	126	164	129	134	111	126	92	49	58
AGE	RESP	'72	'73	'74	'76	'77	'80	'82	'84	'85	'87	'88	'89
60-65	YES	73	81	70	65	72	67	77	67	66	77	59	60
	NO	27	19	30	35	28	33	23	33	34	23	41	40
# SURVEYED		132	117	98	123	112	110	108	107	122	97	80	72

TABLE IV: ALLOW COMMUNIST TO TEACH IN COLLEGE -- BY AGE (Continued)

Question: Suppose a person who admits to being a communist is teaching in a college. Should he be allowed to teach, or not? NOTE: Question not asked in 1975, 1978, 1983, 1986.

Responses: YES = Yes, allowed to teach; NO = Not allowed

		YEAR											
AGE	RESP	'72	'73	'74	'76	'77	'80	'82	'84	'85	'87	'88	'89
66+	YES	83	78	75	76	82	77	75	73	81	72	72	61
	NO	17	22	25	24	18	23	25	27	19	28	28	39
# SURVEYED		202	186	215	237	199	218	236	209	248	231	156	188

****

ALLOW PRO-COMMUNIST BOOKS IN LIBRARY

TABLE I: ALLOW PRO-COMMUNIST BOOKS IN LIBRARY -- BY TOTAL POPULATION

Question: Suppose a person who admits to being a communist wrote a book that is in your public library. Somebody in your community suggests that the book should be removed from the library. Would you favor removing it or not? NOTE: Question not asked in 1975, 1978, 1983, 1986.

Responses: FA = Favor; NF = Not favor

	YEAR											
RESPONSE	'72	'73	'74	'76	'77	'80	'82	'84	'85	'87	'88	'89
FA	44%	40%	39%	42%	43%	40%	41%	38%	41%	37%	39%	36%
NF	56	60	61	58	57	60	59	62	59	63	61	64
# SURVEYED	1532	1463	1427	1439	1484	1410	1437	1418	1471	1417	944	983

TABLE II: ALLOW PRO-COMMUNIST BOOKS IN LIBRARY -- BY SEX

Question: Suppose a person who admits to being a communist wrote a book that is in your public library. Somebody in your community suggests that the book should be removed from the library. Would you favor removing it or not? NOTE: Question not asked in 1975, 1978, 1983, 1986.

Responses: FA = Favor; NF = Not favor

		YEAR											
SEX	RESP	'72	'73	'74	'76	'77	'80	'82	'84	'85	'87	'88	'89
M	FA	41%	38%	39%	37%	39%	39%	39%	33%	39%	34%	36%	32%
	NF	59	62	61	63	61	61	61	67	61	66	64	68
# SURVEYED		776	685	669	646	672	622	619	587	672	628	388	428
SEX	RESP	'72	'73	'74	'76	'77	'80	'82	'84	'85	'87	'88	'89
F	FA	48%	42%	40%	45%	47%	42%	42%	42%	42%	40%	40%	39%
	NF	52	58	60	55	53	58	58	58	58	60	60	61
# SURVEYED		756	778	758	793	812	788	818	831	799	789	556	555

TABLE III: ALLOW PRO-COMMUNIST BOOKS IN LIBRARY -- BY RACE

Question: Suppose a person who admits to being a communist wrote a book that is in your public library. Somebody in your community suggests that the book should be removed from the library. Would you favor removing it or not? NOTE: Question not asked in 1975, 1978, 1983, 1986.

Responses: FA = Favor; NF = Not favor

		YEAR											
RACE	RESP	'72	'73	'74	'76	'77	'80	'82	'84	'85	'87	'88	'89
WHITE	FA	45%	40%	39%	42%	42%	40%	39%	37%	40%	36%	38%	34%
	NF	55	60	61	58	58	60	61	63	60	64	62	66
# SURVEYED		1301	1277	1261	1312	1305	1274	1270	1214	1300	1189	781	854
RACE	RESP	'72	'73	'74	'76	'77	'80	'82	'84	'85	'87	'88	'89
BLACK	FA	44%	40%	44%	44%	51%	47%	49%	47%	47%	41%	39%	52%
	NF	56	60	56	56	49	53	51	53	53	59	61	48
# SURVEYED		227	173	159	119	166	126	143	156	131	177	120	92
RACE	RESP	'72	'73	'74	'76	'77	'80	'82	'84	'85	'87	'88	'89
OTHER	FA	0%	46%	29%	38%	46%	30%	50%	48%	53%	57%	47%	41%
	NF	100	54	71	63	54	70	50	52	48	43	53	59
# SURVEYED		4	13	7	8	13	10	24	48	40	51	43	37

TABLE IV: ALLOW PRO-COMMUNIST BOOKS IN LIBRARY -- BY AGE

Question: Suppose a person who admits to being a communist wrote a book that is in your public library. Somebody in your community suggests that the book should be removed from the library. Would you favor removing it or not? NOTE: Question not asked in 1975, 1978, 1983, 1986.

Responses: FA = Favor; NF = Not favor

		YEAR											
AGE	RESP	'72	'73	'74	'76	'77	'80	'82	'84	'85	'87	'88	'89
18-23	FA	27%	20%	27%	24%	28%	31%	37%	29%	32%	31%	29%	29%
	NF	73	80	73	76	72	69	63	71	68	69	71	71
# SURVEYED		164	168	164	154	158	150	139	153	130	124	93	92
AGE	RESP	'72	'73	'74	'76	'77	'80	'82	'84	'85	'87	'88	'89
24-29	FA	28%	24%	25%	25%	30%	28%	27%	29%	29%	22%	33%	24%
	NF	72	76	75	75	70	72	73	71	71	78	67	76
# SURVEYED		220	208	208	217	201	195	239	231	212	185	131	111
AGE	RESP	'72	'73	'74	'76	'77	'80	'82	'84	'85	'87	'88	'89
30-35	FA	37%	38%	32%	34%	30%	27%	26%	23%	30%	26%	28%	30%
	NF	63	62	68	66	70	73	74	77	70	74	72	70
# SURVEYED		177	165	170	185	184	211	202	194	206	217	128	132
AGE	RESP	'72	'73	'74	'76	'77	'80	'82	'84	'85	'87	'88	'89
36-41	FA	41%	36%	29%	36%	35%	38%	36%	28%	29%	25%	27%	24%
	NF	59	64	71	64	65	62	64	72	71	75	73	76
# SURVEYED		124	170	146	151	166	147	142	183	179	181	129	128
AGE	RESP	'72	'73	'74	'76	'77	'80	'82	'84	'85	'87	'88	'89
42-47	FA	40%	30%	36%	53%	45%	37%	34%	34%	30%	41%	31%	22%
	NF	60	70	64	47	55	63	66	66	70	59	69	78
# SURVEYED		178	142	145	109	137	112	116	123	116	153	98	104
AGE	RESP	'72	'73	'74	'76	'77	'80	'82	'84	'85	'87	'88	'89
48-53	FA	49%	42%	37%	45%	49%	41%	43%	49%	42%	43%	40%	37%
	NF	51	58	63	55	51	59	57	51	58	57	60	63
# SURVEYED		183	147	138	126	150	118	106	102	125	122	65	94
AGE	RESP	'72	'73	'74	'76	'77	'80	'82	'84	'85	'87	'88	'89
54-59	FA	52%	54%	52%	44%	43%	51%	47%	53%	52%	43%	51%	42%
	NF	48	46	48	56	57	49	53	47	48	57	49	58
# SURVEYED		147	153	134	126	165	131	140	109	126	96	53	59

TABLE IV: ALLOW PRO-COMMUNIST BOOKS IN LIBRARY -- BY AGE (Continued)

Question: Suppose a person who admits to being a communist wrote a book that is in your public library. Somebody in your community suggests that the book should be removed from the library. Would you favor removing it or not? NOTE: Question not asked in 1975, 1978, 1983, 1986.

Responses: FA = Favor; NF = Not favor

		YEAR											
AGE	RESP	'72	'73	'74	'76	'77	'80	'82	'84	'85	'87	'88	'89
60-65	FA	58%	66%	52%	53%	60%	46%	54%	53%	50%	56%	48%	47%
	NF	42	34	48	47	40	54	46	47	50	44	52	53
# SURVEYED		137	119	105	129	114	112	113	105	128	97	82	73
AGE	RESP	'72	'73	'74	'76	'77	'80	'82	'84	'85	'87	'88	'89
66+	FA	70%	60%	66%	64%	73%	65%	64%	61%	66%	57%	62%	56%
	NF	30	40	34	36	27	35	36	39	34	43	38	44
# SURVEYED		198	188	213	238	203	226	232	213	244	237	163	187

****

ALLOW A COMMUNIST TO MAKE SPEECH

TABLE I: ALLOW A COMMUNIST TO MAKE SPEECH -- BY TOTAL POPULATION

Question: Consider a person who admits to being a communist. Suppose this admitted communist wanted to make a speech in your community. Should he be allowed to speak or not? NOTE: Question not asked in 1975, 1978, 1983, 1986.

Responses: YES = Yes, allowed to speak; NO = Not allowed

	YEAR											
RESPONSE	'72	'73	'74	'76	'77	'80	'82	'84	'85	'87	'88	'89
YES	54%	61%	60%	56%	57%	57%	58%	61%	59%	61%	62%	66%
NO	46	39	40	44	43	43	42	39	41	39	38	34
# SURVEYED	1556	1468	1439	1464	1494	1430	1457	1432	1488	1440	953	1005

TABLE II: ALLOW A COMMUNIST TO MAKE SPEECH -- BY SEX

Question: Consider a person who admits to being a communist. Suppose this admitted communist wanted to make a speech in your community. Should he be allowed to speak or not? NOTE: Question not asked in 1975, 1978, 1983, 1986.

Responses: YES = Yes, allowed to speak; NO = Not allowed

		YEAR											
SEX	RESP	'72	'73	'74	'76	'77	'80	'82	'84	'85	'87	'88	'89
M	YES	59%	63%	60%	60%	61%	61%	62%	67%	63%	67%	67%	71%
	NO	41	38	40	40	39	39	38	33	37	33	33	29
# SURVEYED		789	688	673	662	686	632	626	591	676	635	392	434
SEX	RESP	'72	'73	'74	'76	'77	'80	'82	'84	'85	'87	'88	'89
F	YES	49%	60%	59%	52%	53%	53%	55%	56%	55%	56%	58%	62%
	NO	51	40	41	48	47	47	45	44	45	44	42	38
# SURVEYED		767	780	766	802	808	798	831	841	812	805	561	571

TABLE III: ALLOW A COMMUNIST TO MAKE SPEECH -- BY RACE

Question: Consider a person who admits to being a communist. Suppose this admitted communist wanted to make a speech in your community. Should he be allowed to speak or not? NOTE: Question not asked in 1975, 1978, 1983, 1986.

Responses: YES = Yes, allowed to speak; NO = Not allowed

		YEAR											
RACE	RESP	'72	'73	'74	'76	'77	'80	'82	'84	'85	'87	'88	'89
WHITE	YES	53%	61%	60%	55%	57%	57%	58%	62%	59%	60%	63%	67%
	NO	47	39	40	45	43	43	42	38	41	40	37	33
# SURVEYED		1317	1282	1272	1336	1309	1290	1286	1225	1311	1208	787	870
RACE	RESP	'72	'73	'74	'76	'77	'80	'82	'84	'85	'87	'88	'89
BLACK	YES	57%	64%	58%	61%	50%	55%	54%	51%	57%	67%	59%	55%
	NO	43	36	42	39	50	45	46	49	43	33	41	45
# SURVEYED		235	173	160	120	170	130	145	157	136	181	122	98
RACE	RESP	'72	'73	'74	'76	'77	'80	'82	'84	'85	'87	'88	'89
OTHER	YES	25%	77%	57%	50%	60%	70%	50%	50%	41%	45%	50%	59%
	NO	75	23	43	50	40	30	50	50	59	55	50	41
# SURVEYED		4	13	7	8	15	10	26	50	41	51	44	37

TABLE IV: ALLOW A COMMUNIST TO MAKE SPEECH -- BY AGE

Question: Consider a person who admits to being a communist. Suppose this admitted communist wanted to make a speech in your community. Should he be allowed to speak or not? NOTE: Question not asked in 1975, 1978, 1983, 1986.

Responses: YES = Yes, allowed to speak; NO = Not allowed

		YEAR											
AGE	RESP	'72	'73	'74	'76	'77	'80	'82	'84	'85	'87	'88	'89
18-23	YES	76%	81%	73%	73%	69%	62%	59%	66%	64%	67%	71%	69%
	NO	24	19	27	27	31	38	41	34	36	33	29	31
# SURVEYED		162	170	162	158	159	151	144	155	130	124	94	95
AGE	RESP	'72	'73	'74	'76	'77	'80	'82	'84	'85	'87	'88	'89
24-29	YES	71%	75%	78%	71%	73%	67%	67%	61%	70%	76%	66%	75%
	NO	29	25	22	29	27	34	33	39	30	24	34	25
# SURVEYED		224	210	210	223	201	200	241	231	213	187	128	113
AGE	RESP	'72	'73	'74	'76	'77	'80	'82	'84	'85	'87	'88	'89
30-35	YES	58%	66%	67%	65%	67%	72%	71%	76%	65%	70%	72%	70%
	NO	42	34	33	35	33	28	29	24	35	30	28	30
# SURVEYED		180	164	168	182	185	212	203	195	208	220	130	132
AGE	RESP	'72	'73	'74	'76	'77	'80	'82	'84	'85	'87	'88	'89
36-41	YES	62%	67%	68%	64%	60%	59%	69%	70%	70%	69%	72%	81%
	NO	38	33	32	36	40	41	31	30	30	31	28	19
# SURVEYED		125	171	150	156	167	149	143	186	182	183	130	134
AGE	RESP	'72	'73	'74	'76	'77	'80	'82	'84	'85	'87	'88	'89
42-47	YES	52%	69%	66%	49%	59%	63%	65%	66%	69%	59%	68%	80%
	NO	48	31	34	51	41	37	35	34	31	41	32	20
# SURVEYED		182	139	149	110	140	114	117	121	121	155	102	106
AGE	RESP	'72	'73	'74	'76	'77	'80	'82	'84	'85	'87	'88	'89
48-53	YES	49%	54%	56%	54%	55%	59%	58%	51%	60%	53%	58%	68%
	NO	51	46	44	46	45	41	42	49	40	47	42	32
# SURVEYED		184	143	140	128	151	119	108	100	127	124	64	95
AGE	RESP	'72	'73	'74	'76	'77	'80	'82	'84	'85	'87	'88	'89
54-59	YES	51%	50%	51%	50%	55%	45%	49%	54%	43%	64%	51%	60%
	NO	49	50	49	50	45	55	51	46	57	36	49	40
# SURVEYED		149	155	134	126	168	130	140	111	129	97	51	62
AGE	RESP	'72	'73	'74	'76	'77	'80	'82	'84	'85	'87	'88	'89
60-65	YES	38%	39%	44%	45%	40%	46%	44%	54%	53%	44%	54%	43%
	NO	62	61	56	55	60	54	56	46	47	56	46	57
# SURVEYED		138	119	104	132	113	114	113	109	125	100	84	74

TABLE IV: ALLOW A COMMUNIST TO MAKE SPEECH -- BY AGE (Continued)

Question: Consider a person who admits to being a communist. Suppose this admitted communist wanted to make a speech in your community. Should he be allowed to speak or not? NOTE: Question not asked in 1975, 1978, 1983, 1986.

Responses: YES = Yes, allowed to speak; NO = Not allowed

AGE	RESP	'72	'73	'74	'76	'77	'80	'82	'84	'85	'87	'88	'89
66+	YES	26%	40%	30%	31%	29%	37%	37%	43%	37%	41%	43%	47%
	NO	74	60	70	69	71	63	63	57	63	59	57	53
# SURVEYED		208	193	217	243	203	233	240	219	246	245	167	191

****

ALLOW FASCIST TO TEACH IN COLLEGE

TABLE I: ALLOW FASCIST TO TEACH IN COLLEGE -- BY TOTAL POPULATION

Question: Should a person who advocates doing away with elections and letting the military run the country be allowed to teach in a college or university, or not? NOTE: Question not asked in 1972-1975, 1978, 1983, 1986.

Responses: YES = Yes, allowed to teach; NO = Not allowed

	YEAR								
RESPONSE	'76	'77	'80	'82	'84	'85	'87	'88	'89
YES	38	35	41	41	42	41	41	39	42
NO	62	65	59	59	58	59	59	61	58
# SURVEYED	1439	1487	1404	1418	1423	1479	1399	937	977

TABLE II: ALLOW FASCIST TO TEACH IN COLLEGE -- BY SEX

Question: Should a person who advocates doing away with elections and letting the military run the country be allowed to teach in a college or university, or not? NOTE: Question not asked in 1972-1975, 1978, 1983, 1986.

Responses: YES = Yes, allowed to teach; NO = Not allowed

		YEAR								
SEX	RESP	'76	'77	'80	'82	'84	'85	'87	'88	'89
M	YES	40	37	41	42	44	43	43	41	45
	NO	60	63	59	58	56	57	57	59	55
# SURVEYED		650	684	630	608	590	676	624	389	428
SEX	RESP	'76	'77	'80	'82	'84	'85	'87	'88	'89
F	YES	37	33	41	40	41	40	40	37	40
	NO	63	67	59	60	59	60	60	63	60
# SURVEYED		789	803	774	810	833	803	775	548	549

TABLE III: ALLOW FASCIST TO TEACH IN COLLEGE -- BY RACE

Question: Should a person who advocates doing away with elections and letting the military run the country be allowed to teach in a college or university, or not? NOTE: Question not asked in 1972-1975, 1978, 1983, 1986.

Responses: YES = Yes, allowed to teach; NO = Not allowed

		YEAR								
RACE	RESP	'76	'77	'80	'82	'84	'85	'87	'88	'89
WHITE	YES	38	35	41	41	44	41	43	40	43
	NO	62	65	59	59	56	59	57	60	57
# SURVEYED		1309	1302	1263	1247	1215	1296	1174	770	845
RACE	RESP	'76	'77	'80	'82	'84	'85	'87	'88	'89
BLACK	YES	43	32	38	43	37	43	36	32	34
	NO	57	68	62	57	63	57	64	68	66
# SURVEYED		123	170	132	147	160	141	176	125	97
RACE	RESP	'76	'77	'80	'82	'84	'85	'87	'88	'89
OTHER	YES	57	27	67	29	33	31	29	29	43
	NO	43	73	33	71	67	69	71	71	57
# SURVEYED		7	15	9	24	48	42	49	42	35

TABLE IV: ALLOW FASCIST TO TEACH IN COLLEGE -- BY AGE

Question: Should a person who advocates doing away with elections and letting the military run the country be allowed to teach in a college or university, or not? NOTE: Question not asked in 1972-1975, 1978, 1983, 1986.

Responses: YES = Yes, allowed to teach; NO = Not allowed

		YEAR								
AGE	RESP	'76	'77	'80	'82	'84	'85	'87	'88	'89
18-23	YES	58%	60%	48%	44%	58%	52%	48%	53%	60%
	NO	42	40	52	56	42	48	52	47	40
# SURVEYED		158	162	153	138	156	130	121	92	90
AGE	RESP	'76	'77	'80	'82	'84	'85	'87	'88	'89
24-29	YES	57%	51%	56%	54%	53%	60%	50%	42%	51%
	NO	43	49	44	46	47	40	50	58	49
# SURVEYED		220	198	199	235	230	213	187	127	108
AGE	RESP	'76	'77	'80	'82	'84	'85	'87	'88	'89
30-35	YES	47%	52%	59%	61%	62%	56%	58%	49%	51%
	NO	53	48	41	39	38	44	42	51	49
# SURVEYED		180	185	207	193	193	204	215	127	129
AGE	RESP	'76	'77	'80	'82	'84	'85	'87	'88	'89
36-41	YES	44%	35%	47%	51%	50%	58%	57%	52%	61%
	NO	56	65	53	49	50	42	43	48	39
# SURVEYED		151	164	146	138	182	179	176	130	127
AGE	RESP	'76	'77	'80	'82	'84	'85	'87	'88	'89
42-47	YES	35%	25%	41%	48%	36%	51%	42%	45%	54%
	NO	65	75	59	52	64	49	58	55	46
# SURVEYED		111	140	113	113	121	119	151	98	104
AGE	RESP	'76	'77	'80	'82	'84	'85	'87	'88	'89
48-53	YES	30%	27%	36%	39%	30%	32%	34%	31%	37%
	NO	70	73	64	61	70	68	66	69	63
# SURVEYED		126	150	115	106	100	127	122	61	89
AGE	RESP	'76	'77	'80	'82	'84	'85	'87	'88	'89
54-59	YES	31%	22%	25%	26%	26%	24%	36%	25%	28%
	NO	69	78	75	74	74	76	64	75	72
# SURVEYED		121	165	130	136	110	127	95	52	61
AGE	RESP	'76	'77	'80	'82	'84	'85	'87	'88	'89
60-65	YES	23%	21%	29%	27%	27%	21%	19%	28%	24%
	NO	77	79	71	73	73	79	81	72	76
# SURVEYED		132	112	111	113	106	122	96	79	72

TABLE IV: ALLOW FASCIST TO TEACH IN COLLEGE -- BY AGE (Continued)

Question: Should a person who advocates doing away with elections and letting the military run the country be allowed to teach in a college or university, or not? NOTE: Question not asked in 1972-1975, 1978, 1983, 1986.

Responses: YES = Yes, allowed to teach; NO = Not allowed

		YEAR								
AGE	RESP	'76	'77	'80	'82	'84	'85	'87	'88	'89
66+	YES	17%	15%	21%	16%	21%	14%	18%	19%	20%
	NO	83	85	79	84	79	86	82	81	80
# SURVEYED		235	204	222	238	220	251	231	168	194

****

ALLOW PRO-FASCIST BOOKS IN LIBRARY

TABLE I: ALLOW PRO-FASCIST BOOKS IN LIBRARY -- BY TOTAL POPULATION

Question: Suppose a person wrote a book advocating doing away with elections and letting the military run the country. Somebody in your community suggests that the book be removed from the public library. Would you favor removing it, or not? NOTE: Question not asked in 1972-1975, 1978, 1983, 1986.

Responses: FA = Favor; NF = Not favor

	YEAR								
RESPONSE	'76	'77	'80	'82	'84	'85	'87	'88	'89
FA	42%	44%	40%	41%	40%	42%	40%	41%	38%
NF	58	56	60	59	60	58	60	59	62
# SURVEYED	1441	1485	1417	1440	1438	1496	1412	934	987

TABLE II: ALLOW PRO-FASCIST BOOKS IN LIBRARY -- BY SEX

Question: Suppose a person wrote a book advocating doing away with elections and letting the military run the country. Somebody in your community suggests that the book be removed from the public library. Would you favor removing it, or not? NOTE: Question not asked in 1972-1975, 1978, 1983, 1986.

Responses: FA = Favor; NF = Not favor

		YEAR								
SEX	RESP	'76	'77	'80	'82	'84	'85	'87	'88	'89
M	FA	41%	45%	40%	41%	36%	43%	39%	41%	36%
	NF	59	55	60	59	64	57	61	59	64
# SURVEYED		649	676	629	621	590	678	632	390	431
SEX	RESP	'76	'77	'80	'82	'84	'85	'87	'88	'89
F	FA	43%	43%	39%	41%	42%	42%	40%	41%	40%
	NF	57	57	61	59	58	58	60	59	60
# SURVEYED		792	809	788	819	848	818	780	544	556

TABLE III: ALLOW PRO-FASCIST BOOKS IN LIBRARY -- BY RACE

Question: Suppose a person wrote a book advocating doing away with elections and letting the military run the country. Somebody in your community suggests that the book be removed from the public library. Would you favor removing it, or not? NOTE: Question not asked in 1972-1975, 1978, 1983, 1986.

Responses: FA = Favor; NF = Not favor

		YEAR								
RACE	RESP	'76	'77	'80	'82	'84	'85	'87	'88	'89
WHITE	FA	42%	43%	39%	40%	38%	41%	38%	40%	36%
	NF	58	57	61	60	62	59	62	60	64
# SURVEYED		1313	1304	1278	1268	1228	1311	1186	768	853
RACE	RESP	'76	'77	'80	'82	'84	'85	'87	'88	'89
BLACK	FA	41%	51%	47%	52%	50%	53%	42%	44%	56%
	NF	59	49	53	48	50	47	58	56	44
# SURVEYED		121	167	130	147	162	142	177	124	98
RACE	RESP	'76	'77	'80	'82	'84	'85	'87	'88	'89
OTHER	FA	29%	43%	11%	56%	54%	49%	71%	52%	42%
	NF	71	57	89	44	46	51	29	48	58
# SURVEYED		7	14	9	25	48	43	49	42	36

TABLE IV: ALLOW PRO-FASCIST BOOKS IN LIBRARY -- BY AGE

Question: Suppose a person wrote a book advocating doing away with elections and letting the military run the country. Somebody in your community suggests that the book be removed from the public library. Would you favor removing it, or not? NOTE: Question not asked in 1972-1975, 1978, 1983, 1986.

Responses: FA = Favor; NF = Not favor

		YEAR								
AGE	RESP	'76	'77	'80	'82	'84	'85	'87	'88	'89
18-23	FA	28%	28%	35%	44%	34%	37%	34%	34%	35%
	NF	72	72	65	56	66	63	66	66	65
# SURVEYED		159	157	153	142	157	131	122	91	94
AGE	RESP	'76	'77	'80	'82	'84	'85	'87	'88	'89
24-29	FA	24%	31%	23%	26%	34%	27%	29%	40%	26%
	NF	76	69	77	74	66	73	71	60	74
# SURVEYED		220	203	198	235	230	214	188	131	109
AGE	RESP	'76	'77	'80	'82	'84	'85	'87	'88	'89
30-35	FA	35%	29%	24%	22%	22%	30%	26%	27%	32%
	NF	65	71	76	79	78	70	74	73	68
# SURVEYED		182	185	208	200	195	207	216	126	133
AGE	RESP	'76	'77	'80	'82	'84	'85	'87	'88	'89
36-41	FA	36%	37%	30%	36%	26%	28%	30%	30%	28%
	NF	64	63	70	64	74	72	70	70	72
# SURVEYED		149	164	148	142	182	179	180	128	127
AGE	RESP	'76	'77	'80	'82	'84	'85	'87	'88	'89
42-47	FA	43%	49%	35%	41%	38%	30%	40%	34%	25%
	NF	57	51	65	59	62	70	60	66	75
# SURVEYED		109	140	112	116	123	122	156	99	106
AGE	RESP	'76	'77	'80	'82	'84	'85	'87	'88	'89
48-53	FA	41%	51%	46%	46%	52%	42%	43%	46%	35%
	NF	59	49	54	54	48	58	58	54	65
# SURVEYED		128	150	118	108	102	130	120	63	94
AGE	RESP	'76	'77	'80	'82	'84	'85	'87	'88	'89
54-59	FA	48%	48%	52%	46%	50%	57%	39%	51%	42%
	NF	52	52	48	54	50	43	61	49	58
# SURVEYED		121	165	130	140	111	129	97	51	59

TABLE IV: ALLOW PRO-FASCIST BOOKS IN LIBRARY -- BY AGE (Continued)

Question: Suppose a person wrote a book advocating doing away with elections and letting the military run the country. Somebody in your community suggests that the book be removed from the public library. Would you favor removing it, or not? NOTE: Question not asked in 1972-1975, 1978, 1983, 1986.

Responses: FA = Favor; NF = Not favor

		YEAR								
AGE	RESP	'76	'77	'80	'82	'84	'85	'87	'88	'89
60-65	FA NF	56% 44	56% 44	51% 49	58% 42	56% 44	55% 45	54% 46	49% 51	57% 43
# SURVEYED		131	112	114	113	108	124	96	80	72
AGE	RESP	'76	'77	'80	'82	'84	'85	'87	'88	'89
66+	FA NF	67% 33	71% 29	64% 36	62% 38	57% 43	71% 29	63% 37	61% 39	58% 42
# SURVEYED		237	202	228	236	225	253	232	162	190

****

ALLOW A FASCIST TO MAKE SPEECH

TABLE I: ALLOW A FASCIST TO MAKE SPEECH -- BY TOTAL POPULATION

Question: Consider a person who advocates doing away with elections and letting the military run the country. If such a person wanted to make a speech in your community, should he be allowed to speak or not? NOTE: Question not asked in 1972-1975, 1978, 1983, 1986.

Responses: YES = Yes, allowed to speak; NO = Not allowed

	YEAR								
RESPONSE	'76	'77	'80	'82	'84	'85	'87	'88	'89
YES NO	55% 45	51% 49	58% 42	56% 44	58% 42	56% 44	58% 42	58% 42	60% 40
# SURVEYED	1469	1501	1436	1456	1445	1496	1420	942	1012

TABLE II: ALLOW A FASCIST TO MAKE SPEECH -- BY SEX

Question: Consider a person who advocates doing away with elections and letting the military run the country. If such a person wanted to make a speech in your community, should he be allowed to speak or not? NOTE: Question not asked in 1972-1975, 1978, 1983, 1986.

Responses: YES = Yes, allowed to speak; NO = Not allowed

		YEAR								
SEX	RESP	'76	'77	'80	'82	'84	'85	'87	'88	'89
M	YES	54%	50%	58%	57%	59%	57%	61%	58%	61%
	NO	46	50	42	43	41	43	39	42	39
# SURVEYED		664	688	637	624	592	676	631	390	439
SEX	RESP	'76	'77	'80	'82	'84	'85	'87	'88	'89
F	YES	57%	53%	58%	55%	57%	55%	56%	58%	60%
	NO	43	47	42	45	43	45	44	42	40
# SURVEYED		805	813	799	832	853	820	789	552	573

TABLE III: ALLOW A FASCIST TO MAKE SPEECH -- BY RACE

Question: Consider a person who advocates doing away with elections and letting the military run the country. If such a person wanted to make a speech in your community, should he be allowed to speak or not? NOTE: Question not asked in 1972-1975, 1978, 1983, 1986.

Responses: YES = Yes, allowed to speak; NO = Not allowed

		YEAR								
RACE	RESP	'76	'77	'80	'82	'84	'85	'87	'88	'89
WHITE	YES	56%	52%	58%	57%	60%	56%	59%	60%	62%
	NO	44	48	42	43	40	44	41	40	38
# SURVEYED		1337	1316	1295	1279	1234	1311	1190	774	875
RACE	RESP	'76	'77	'80	'82	'84	'85	'87	'88	'89
BLACK	YES	50%	46%	56%	56%	48%	55%	57%	48%	46%
	NO	50	54	44	44	52	45	43	52	54
# SURVEYED		125	171	132	151	162	143	180	125	99
RACE	RESP	'76	'77	'80	'82	'84	'85	'87	'88	'89
OTHER	YES	71%	50%	78%	35%	41%	43%	48%	37%	53%
	NO	29	50	22	65	59	57	52	63	47
# SURVEYED		7	14	9	26	49	42	50	43	38

TABLE IV: ALLOW A FASCIST TO MAKE SPEECH -- BY AGE

Question: Consider a person who advocates doing away with elections and letting the military run the country. If such a person wanted to make a speech in your community, should he be allowed to speak or not? NOTE: Question not asked in 1972-1975, 1978, 1983, 1986.

Responses: YES = Yes, allowed to speak; NO = Not allowed

		YEAR								
AGE	RESP	'76	'77	'80	'82	'84	'85	'87	'88	'89
18-23	YES	71%	69%	59%	55%	64%	65%	65%	67%	68%
	NO	29	31	41	45	36	35	35	33	32
# SURVEYED		161	160	155	146	158	129	117	93	97
AGE	RESP	'76	'77	'80	'82	'84	'85	'87	'88	'89
24-29	YES	71%	64%	77%	66%	64%	71%	69%	57%	73%
	NO	29	36	23	34	36	29	31	43	27
# SURVEYED		224	201	202	238	230	215	189	128	114
AGE	RESP	'76	'77	'80	'82	'84	'85	'87	'88	'89
30-35	YES	64%	66%	73%	76%	76%	70%	72%	67%	71%
	NO	36	34	27	24	24	30	28	33	29
# SURVEYED		183	187	213	201	196	207	219	129	135
AGE	RESP	'76	'77	'80	'82	'84	'85	'87	'88	'89
36-41	YES	60%	57%	63%	69%	64%	69%	73%	69%	73%
	NO	40	43	37	31	36	31	27	31	27
# SURVEYED		154	167	150	143	185	181	183	131	132
AGE	RESP	'76	'77	'80	'82	'84	'85	'87	'88	'89
42-47	YES	55%	46%	69%	63%	62%	64%	53%	77%	70%
	NO	45	54	31	37	38	36	47	23	30
# SURVEYED		111	140	113	118	123	122	156	98	105
AGE	RESP	'76	'77	'80	'82	'84	'85	'87	'88	'89
48-53	YES	52%	51%	56%	52%	46%	60%	55%	48%	67%
	NO	48	49	44	48	54	40	45	52	33
# SURVEYED		130	153	118	107	102	130	118	60	95
AGE	RESP	'76	'77	'80	'82	'84	'85	'87	'88	'89
54-59	YES	52%	49%	44%	51%	54%	43%	57%	48%	56%
	NO	48	51	56	49	46	57	43	52	44
# SURVEYED		126	166	132	139	112	129	97	52	62

TABLE IV: ALLOW A FASCIST TO MAKE SPEECH -- BY AGE (Continued)

Question: Consider a person who advocates doing away with elections and letting the military run the country. If such a person wanted to make a speech in your community, should he be allowed to speak or not? NOTE: Question not asked in 1972-1975, 1978, 1983, 1986.

Responses: YES = Yes, allowed to speak; NO = Not allowed

		YEAR								
AGE	RESP	'76	'77	'80	'82	'84	'85	'87	'88	'89
60-65	YES	38%	35%	41%	45%	49%	41%	42%	48%	38%
	NO	62	65	59	55	51	59	58	52	62
# SURVEYED		132	113	114	116	108	125	97	82	74
AGE	RESP	'76	'77	'80	'82	'84	'85	'87	'88	'89
66+	YES	34%	23%	37%	29%	36%	26%	33%	36%	34%
	NO	66	77	63	71	64	74	67	64	66
# SURVEYED		243	207	231	240	226	251	239	166	195

****

FEELINGS TOWARD CONSERVATIVES

TABLE I: FEELINGS TOWARD CONSERVATIVES -- BY TOTAL POPULATION

Question: On a scale of 0 to 99 degrees how warm or cold do you feel toward conservatives. NOTE: Question not asked in 1972-1985, 1987.

Responses: 0 = 0-9 degrees 1 = 10-19 2 = 20-29 3 = 30-39 4 = 40-49
5 = 50-59 6 = 60-69 7 = 70-79 8 = 80-89 9 = 90-99

	YEAR		
RESPONSE	'86	'88	'89
0	2%	2%	2%
1	2	2	2
2	1	0	1
3	5	5	5
4	11	9	9
5	18	30	27
6	27	20	20
7	19	17	18
8	11	10	13
9	4	4	4
# SURVEYED	1350	1345	905

TABLE II: FEELINGS TOWARD CONSERVATIVES -- BY SEX

Question: On a scale of 0 to 99 degrees how warm or cold do you feel toward conservatives. NOTE: Question not asked in 1972-1985, 1987.

Responses: 0 = 0-9 degrees 1 = 10-19 2 = 20-29 3 = 30-39 4 = 40-49
5 = 50-59 6 = 60-69 7 = 70-79 8 = 80-89 9 = 90-99

		YEAR		
SEX	RESP	'86	'88	'89
MALE	0	1%	3%	3%
	1	2	2	3
	2	1	0	1
	3	5	5	6
	4	12	8	10
	5	19	30	25
	6	25	19	19
	7	22	19	18
	8	10	10	12
	9	3	5	3
# SURVEYED		586	599	390

SEX	RESP	'86	'88	'89
FEMALE	0	2%	2%	2%
	1	3	3	2
	2	1	0	1
	3	4	5	4
	4	11	10	8
	5	18	30	28
	6	29	21	20
	7	16	16	17
	8	12	10	13
	9	6	3	5
# SURVEYED		764	746	515

TABLE III: FEELINGS TOWARD CONSERVATIVES -- BY RACE

Question: On a scale of 0 to 99 degrees how warm or cold do you feel toward conservatives. NOTE: Question not asked in 1972-1985, 1987.

Responses: 0 = 0-9 degrees 1 = 10-19 2 = 20-29 3 = 30-39 4 = 40-49
5 = 50-59 6 = 60-69 7 = 70-79 8 = 80-89 9 = 90-99

		YEAR		
RACE	RESP	'86	'88	'89
WHITE	0	1%	1%	2%
	1	2	2	2
	2	1	0	1
	3	4	5	4
	4	12	9	8
	5	17	29	27
	6	27	21	20
	7	19	18	18
	8	12	10	13
	9	5	4	4
# SURVEYED		1166	1128	786

		YEAR		
RACE	RESP	'86	'88	'89
BLACK	0	6%	8%	4%
	1	5	7	2
	2	1	1	2
	3	9	4	12
	4	8	10	17
	5	24	34	22
	6	26	13	16
	7	13	12	13
	8	7	6	6
	9	2	6	4
# SURVEYED		152	163	89

		YEAR		
RACE	RESP	'86	'88	'89
OTHER	0	0%	4%	3%
	1	0	6	0
	2	0	0	0
	3	3	0	7
	4	16	6	10
	5	25	35	27
	6	19	28	20
	7	25	15	20
	8	6	7	13
	9	6	0	0
# SURVEYED		32	54	30

TABLE IV: FEELINGS TOWARD CONSERVATIVES -- BY AGE

Question: On a scale of 0 to 99 degrees how warm or cold do you feel toward conservatives. NOTE: Question not asked in 1972-1985, 1987.

Responses: 0 = 0-9 degrees, 1 = 10-19, 2 = 20-29, 3 = 30-39, 4 = 40-49, 5 = 50-59, 6 = 60-69, 7 = 70-79, 8 = 80-89, 9 = 90-99

AGE	RESP	'86	'88	'89
18-23	0	1%	2%	4%
	1	2	3	1
	2	0	0	1
	3	2	6	0
	4	14	9	8
	5	25	33	24
	6	31	19	23
	7	17	21	23
	8	4	5	10
	9	4	2	6
# SURVEYED		104	126	79
24-29	0	1%	2%	1%
	1	2	2	1
	2	0	0	1
	3	2	3	7
	4	17	13	6
	5	23	32	25
	6	28	23	28
	7	15	15	20
	8	10	7	9
	9	1	3	1
# SURVEYED		208	204	138
30-35	0	1%	2%	2%
	1	3	1	1
	2	1	1	2
	3	8	8	6
	4	9	9	12
	5	20	31	38
	6	28	21	16
	7	17	17	13
	8	10	7	8
	9	3	3	2
# SURVEYED		209	181	132

AGE	RESP	'86	'88	'89
36-41	0	1%	2%	2%
	1	2	4	3
	2	1	1	1
	3	4	6	9
	4	11	10	13
	5	21	25	22
	6	33	23	20
	7	16	19	15
	8	7	6	16
	9	5	3	1
# SURVEYED		178	185	115
42-47	0	1%	3%	2%
	1	1	3	1
	2	1	0	0
	3	7	5	4
	4	13	11	9
	5	19	28	24
	6	25	18	27
	7	19	13	19
	8	9	15	12
	9	5	3	1
# SURVEYED		134	149	98
48-53	0	4%	2%	3%
	1	2	2	4
	2	0	0	1
	3	4	6	6
	4	8	6	9
	5	19	35	28
	6	21	19	20
	7	18	21	15
	8	19	7	13
	9	4	2	3
# SURVEYED		95	86	80

AGE	RESP	'86	'88	'89
54-59	0	2%	3%	2%
	1	3	4	5
	2	2	0	2
	3	4	3	2
	4	16	9	9
	5	6	25	28
	6	33	21	17
	7	17	16	17
	8	11	13	11
	9	5	8	9
# SURVEYED		94	77	65
60-65	0	0%	3%	0%
	1	3	0	5
	2	1	0	0
	3	7	3	5
	4	8	6	7
	5	12	32	20
	6	24	20	16
	7	25	16	18
	8	17	14	20
	9	4	7	9
# SURVEYED		103	101	56
66+	0	3%	1%	3%
	1	3	2	2
	2	0	0	1
	3	4	4	4
	4	7	5	9
	5	15	31	26
	6	21	17	9
	7	24	19	19
	8	16	14	17
	9	7	6	9
# SURVEYED		219	233	140

****

FEELINGS TOWARD LIBERALS

TABLE I: FEELINGS TOWARD LIBERALS -- BY TOTAL POPULATION

Question: On a scale of 0 to 99 degrees how warm or cold do you feel toward liberals. NOTE: Question not asked in 1972-1985, 1987.

Responses: 0 = 0-9 degrees 1 = 10-19 2 = 20-29 3 = 30-39 4 = 40-49
5 = 50-59 6 = 60-69 7 = 70-79 8 = 80-89 9 = 90-99

	YEAR		
RESPONSE	'86	'88	'89
0	4%	4%	4%
1	3	3	3
2	1	1	1
3	7	7	7
4	14	8	9
5	22	34	31
6	22	15	17
7	15	16	16
8	7	7	8
9	3	5	5
# SURVEYED	1351	1332	896

TABLE II: FEELINGS TOWARD LIBERALS -- BY SEX

Question: On a scale of 0 to 99 degrees how warm or cold do you feel toward liberals. NOTE: Question not asked in 1972-1985, 1987.

Responses: 0 = 0-9 degrees 1 = 10-19 2 = 20-29 3 = 30-39 4 = 40-49
5 = 50-59 6 = 60-69 7 = 70-79 8 = 80-89 9 = 90-99

		YEAR		
SEX	RESP	'86	'88	'89
MALE	0	3%	4%	4%
	1	3	3	3
	2	2	1	2
	3	9	8	9
	4	16	8	10
	5	22	32	29
	6	22	15	17
	7	15	17	16
	8	5	7	6
	9	2	5	4
# SURVEYED		585	592	389

		YEAR		
SEX	RESP	'86	'88	'89
FEMALE	0	4%	3%	4%
	1	4	3	3
	2	1	1	1
	3	5	6	5
	4	13	8	9
	5	22	36	32
	6	22	15	17
	7	16	16	16
	8	8	7	8
	9	4	4	5
# SURVEYED		766	740	507

TABLE III: FEELINGS TOWARD LIBERALS -- BY RACE

Question: On a scale of 0 to 99 degrees how warm or cold do you feel toward liberals. NOTE: Question not asked in 1972-1985, 1987.

Responses: 0 = 0-9 degrees; 1 = 10-19; 2 = 20-29; 3 = 30-39; 4 = 40-49; 5 = 50-59; 6 = 60-69; 7 = 70-79; 8 = 80-89

		YEAR		
RACE	RESP	'86	'88	'89
WHITE	0	4%	4%	4%
	1	4	3	3
	2	1	1	1
	3	7	8	7
	4	15	9	10
	5	23	34	32
	6	22	16	18
	7	15	15	15
	8	7	6	7
	9	3	4	4
# SURVEYED		1169	1118	780

		YEAR		
RACE	RESP	'86	'88	'89
BLACK	0	5%	3%	3%
	1	3	2	1
	2	1	1	1
	3	3	4	8
	4	9	2	6
	5	19	30	24
	6	23	12	9
	7	20	24	20
	8	10	12	17
	9	7	10	11
# SURVEYED		151	162	89

		YEAR		
RACE	RESP	'86	'88	'89
OTHER	0	6%	4%	4%
	1	0	2	4
	2	0	0	0
	3	3	4	11
	4	10	4	11
	5	26	44	30
	6	19	8	7
	7	23	17	26
	8	3	12	0
	9	10	6	7
# SURVEYED		31	52	27

TABLE IV: FEELINGS TOWARD LIBERALS -- BY AGE

Question: On a scale of 0 to 99 degrees how warm or cold do you feel toward liberals. NOTE: Question not asked in 1972-1985, 1987.

Responses: 0 = 0-9 degrees; 1 = 10-19; 2 = 20-29; 3 = 30-39; 4 = 40-49; 5 = 50-59; 6 = 60-69; 7 = 70-79; 8 = 80-89; 9 = 90-99

		YEAR		
AGE	RESP	'86	'88	'89
18-23	0	2%	4%	5%
	1	4	2	1
	2	1	0	1
	3	6	5	7
	4	10	5	9
	5	24	33	32
	6	32	13	12
	7	14	20	20
	8	6	10	7
	9	2	8	7
# SURVEYED		103	124	76

		YEAR		
AGE	RESP	'86	'88	'89
24-29	0	2%	1%	1%
	1	2	0	4
	2	3	1	1
	3	6	5	6
	4	15	10	8
	5	21	41	35
	6	24	12	16
	7	16	18	19
	8	6	9	4
	9	4	4	5
# SURVEYED		207	199	135

		YEAR		
AGE	RESP	'86	'88	'89
30-35	0	4%	3%	2%
	1	1	2	2
	2	2	2	0
	3	8	10	7
	4	11	8	8
	5	23	30	26
	6	24	17	19
	7	18	17	18
	8	6	7	11
	9	3	4	7
# SURVEYED		208	183	131

TABLE IV: FEELINGS TOWARD LIBERALS -- BY AGE (Continued)

Question: On a scale of 0 to 99 degrees how warm or cold do you feel toward liberals. NOTE: Question not asked in 1972-1985, 1987.

Responses: 0 = 0-9 degrees 1 = 10-19 2 = 20-29 3 = 30-39 4 = 40-49
5 = 50-59 6 = 60-69 7 = 70-79 8 = 80-89 9 = 90-99

AGE	RESP	'86	'88	'89
36-41	0	3%	4%	3%
	1	2	4	3
	2	1	1	1
	3	2	6	9
	4	18	10	14
	5	29	28	22
	6	18	19	22
	7	17	18	14
	8	9	5	8
	9	1	5	4
# SURVEYED		178	186	116
42-47	0	4%	3%	2%
	1	2	4	7
	2	1	1	0
	3	10	15	6
	4	16	7	7
	5	23	30	33
	6	22	16	20
	7	11	13	16
	8	7	7	5
	9	3	3	3
# SURVEYED		134	149	98

AGE	RESP	'86	'88	'89
48-53	0	6%	2%	5%
	1	2	8	1
	2	0	0	1
	3	9	5	6
	4	15	8	6
	5	21	41	35
	6	20	8	22
	7	18	17	14
	8	8	6	5
	9	1	5	4
# SURVEYED		96	87	79
54-59	0	5%	10%	5%
	1	3	4	0
	2	3	1	2
	3	11	3	8
	4	12	4	15
	5	19	36	33
	6	24	14	15
	7	10	16	5
	8	9	6	15
	9	4	5	2
# SURVEYED		93	77	60

AGE	RESP	'86	'88	'89
60-65	0	2%	5%	5%
	1	4	4	2
	2	0	0	2
	3	8	5	9
	4	21	13	16
	5	16	39	22
	6	23	14	14
	7	15	10	24
	8	6	6	3
	9	5	5	3
# SURVEYED		100	101	58
66+	0	6%	4%	7%
	1	8	3	4
	2	1	1	2
	3	6	7	5
	4	13	7	7
	5	20	35	36
	6	19	15	13
	7	16	16	12
	8	6	7	9
	9	6	5	5
# SURVEYED		226	223	141

****

POLITICAL LEANINGS

TABLE I: POLITICAL LEANINGS -- BY TOTAL POPULATION

Question: We hear a lot of talk these days of liberals and conservatives. I'm going to show you a seven-point scale on which the political views that people might hold are arranged from extremely liberal--point 1-- to extremely conservative--point 7. Where would you place yourself on this scale? NOTE: Question was not asked in 1972, 1973.

Responses:
XL = Extremely libral
LB = Liberal
SL = Slightly liberal
MD = Moderate, middle of the road
SC = Slightly conservative
CS = Conservative
XC = Extremely conservative

	YEAR													
RESPONSE	'74	'75	'76	'77	'78	'80	'82	'83	'84	'85	'86	'87	'88	'89
XL	2%	3%	2%	3%	2%	3%	2%	2%	2%	2%	2%	2%	2%	3%
LB	14	13	13	12	10	8	10	9	9	11	9	13	12	12
SL	15	14	13	15	17	15	15	13	13	12	13	14	13	13
MD	40	40	40	39	38	41	41	41	40	39	41	39	36	39
SC	16	17	16	17	18	18	14	18	20	19	17	17	17	17
CS	11	11	14	12	13	13	14	14	13	15	15	13	16	13
XC	2	3	2	3	2	3	4	3	3	3	3	2	2	2
# SURVEYED	1410	1397	1401	1453	1435	1429	1429	770	1410	1462	1401	1378	1416	1442

TABLE II: POLITICAL LEANINGS -- BY SEX

Question: We hear a lot of talk these days of liberals and conservatives. I'm going to show you a seven-point scale on which the political views that people might hold are arranged from extremely liberal--point 1-- to extremely conservative--point 7. Where would you place yourself on this scale? NOTE: Question was not asked in 1972, 1973.

Responses:
XL = Extremely libral
LB = Liberal
SL = Slightly liberal
MD = Moderate, middle of the road
SC = Slightly conservative
CS = Conservative
XC = Extremely conservative

		YEAR													
SEX	RESP	'74	'75	'76	'77	'78	'80	'82	'83	'84	'85	'86	'87	'88	'89
M	XL	2%	3%	3%	3%	2%	4%	3%	3%	3%	2%	1%	2%	2%	3%
A	LB	15	16	16	13	12	8	8	8	9	10	10	15	12	13
L	SL	14	14	15	15	17	16	15	13	11	14	13	13	15	14
E	MD	37	34	34	35	34	35	38	40	37	34	38	33	32	35
	SC	17	18	16	18	19	20	15	20	23	21	19	21	19	19
	CS	12	10	14	14	14	13	16	13	13	16	17	12	17	15
	XC	3	4	3	2	2	4	5	3	4	3	3	2	2	2
# SURVEYED		665	637	643	664	613	629	614	477	581	664	602	612	618	635
SEX	RESP	'74	'75	'76	'77	'78	'80	'82	'83	'84	'85	'86	'87	'88	'89
F	XL	1%	3%	2%	2%	1%	2%	2%	1%	1%	3%	2%	2%	3%	3%
E	LB	13	10	11	11	8	9	10	9	10	12	9	11	12	12
M	SL	15	14	12	15	17	14	15	13	14	10	13	14	12	13
A	MD	42	45	45	42	41	45	43	44	43	42	44	43	39	43
L	SC	14	16	16	16	18	17	14	16	17	17	16	14	16	16
E	CS	11	11	13	11	13	12	13	15	13	13	13	13	15	12
	XC	2	1	1	3	2	3	3	1	2	3	3	2	2	2
# SURVEYED		745	760	758	789	822	800	815	293	829	798	799	766	798	807

TABLE III: POLITICAL LEANINGS -- BY RACE

Question: We hear a lot of talk these days of liberals and conservatives. I'm going to show you a seven-point scale on which the political views that people might hold are arranged from extremely liberal--point 1-- to extremely conservative--point 7. Where would you place yourself on this scale? NOTE: Question was not asked in 1972, 1973.

Responses:

XL = Extremely libral
LB = Liberal
SL = Slightly liberal
MD = Moderate, middle of the road
SC = Slightly conservative
CS = Conservative
XC = Extremely conservative

		YEAR													
RACE	RESP	'74	'75	'76	'77	'78	'80	'82	'83	'84	'85	'86	'87	'88	'89
WHITE	XL	2%	3%	2%	2%	1%	2%	2%	1%	2%	2%	1%	2%	2%	2%
	LB	13	12	12	11	9	8	9	9	9	10	9	11	11	11
	SL	15	13	13	15	16	15	14	13	13	11	13	13	12	13
	MD	40	41	40	40	38	41	42	42	40	38	41	40	37	39
	SC	17	17	16	18	19	19	15	18	21	20	18	18	18	18
	CS	12	11	14	12	13	13	15	15	14	16	16	14	17	14
	XC	2	2	2	2	2	3	4	2	2	3	3	2	2	2
# SURVEYED		1252	1249	1284	1283	1284	1282	1263	686	1211	1290	1202	1166	1190	1247
RACE	RESP	'74	'75	'76	'77	'78	'80	'82	'83	'84	'85	'86	'87	'88	'89
BLACK	XL	1%	7%	1%	7%	4%	8%	5%	8%	5%	6%	4%	5%	5%	7%
	LB	27	19	30	17	12	9	17	8	14	17	15	21	23	20
	SL	14	21	17	15	21	11	24	16	12	14	13	17	20	15
	MD	36	29	38	33	41	44	33	42	43	39	39	33	29	36
	SC	8	13	8	13	9	12	11	16	10	11	16	15	13	10
	CS	10	7	6	11	11	10	6	5	10	7	10	7	8	10
	XC	3	4	1	4	2	5	4	5	7	6	2	2	3	2
# SURVEYED		154	144	109	157	138	137	140	76	152	132	166	168	173	143
RACE	RESP	'74	'75	'76	'77	'78	'80	'82	'83	'84	'85	'86	'87	'88	'89
OTHER	XL	0%	0%	0%	0%	0%	0%	4%	0%	2%	0%	3%	0%	4%	6%
	LB	50	0	25	15	31	10	12	0	9	13	12	14	13	13
	SL	0	25	25	15	31	30	12	0	13	18	9	16	13	13
	MD	25	25	25	31	23	20	35	25	36	55	48	39	38	42
	SC	25	50	13	15	8	30	4	50	26	10	12	9	21	8
	CS	0	0	13	15	8	10	27	25	9	5	15	18	8	17
	XC	0	0	0	8	0	0	8	0	6	0	0	5	4	0
# SURVEYED		4	4	8	13	13	10	26	8	47	40	33	44	53	52

TABLE IV: POLITICAL LEANINGS -- BY AGE

Question: We hear a lot of talk these days of liberals and conservatives. I'm going to show you a seven-point scale on which the political views that people might hold are arranged from extremely liberal--point 1-- to extremely conservative--point 7. Where would you place yourself on this scale? NOTE: Question was not asked in 1972, 1973.

Responses:
XL = Extremely libral
LB = Liberal
SL = Slightly liberal
MD = Moderate, middle of the road
SC = Slightly conservative
CS = Conservative
XC = Extremely conservative

		YEAR													
AGE	RESP	'74	'75	'76	'77	'78	'80	'82	'83	'84	'85	'86	'87	'88	'89
18-23	XL	1%	7%	3%	5%	2%	3%	2%	2%	0%	2%	2%	1%	2%	4%
	LB	22	20	24	18	14	10	11	13	13	15	11	14	14	19
	SL	18	17	19	18	26	26	16	27	15	13	13	14	19	11
	MD	42	36	35	38	33	39	45	38	44	47	45	42	42	38
	SC	10	13	10	11	10	14	11	13	17	17	17	14	9	13
	CS	5	7	7	8	13	8	11	6	9	6	10	13	11	13
	XC	1	1	2	1	3	1	3	0	2	1	3	2	2	3
# SURVEYED		165	165	153	158	152	152	143	52	151	130	104	118	132	133
AGE	RESP	'74	'75	'76	'77	'78	'80	'82	'83	'84	'85	'86	'87	'88	'89
24-29	XL	3%	5%	4%	3%	3%	2%	2%	2%	2%	1%	1%	3%	2%	2%
	LB	21	20	19	18	13	15	11	9	9	15	11	11	13	13
	SL	21	20	21	21	23	23	18	16	14	17	17	14	18	11
	MD	38	37	37	37	39	34	41	42	44	36	39	38	34	39
	SC	13	12	12	11	14	15	15	20	16	17	20	20	17	22
	CS	4	5	7	9	7	10	11	11	13	13	11	13	16	11
	XC	0	1	1	2	1	1	2	0	2	1	2	2	1	1
# SURVEYED		206	225	213	194	235	202	237	133	227	211	209	186	205	188
AGE	RESP	'74	'75	'76	'77	'78	'80	'82	'83	'84	'85	'86	'87	'88	'89
30-35	XL	1%	3%	2%	3%	3%	3%	6%	4%	5%	4%	2%	4%	2%	2%
	LB	16	10	12	14	9	13	9	12	10	8	12	14	16	13
	SL	12	18	13	22	19	16	23	18	15	12	18	19	19	15
	MD	37	40	42	36	38	37	39	34	41	39	37	29	31	41
	SC	17	16	19	16	23	20	11	15	18	17	20	21	20	16
	CS	13	10	10	7	7	10	12	14	8	16	10	10	12	10
	XC	4	2	1	2	1	1	2	2	4	4	1	3	1	1
# SURVEYED		164	163	177	183	222	207	200	121	195	208	215	214	189	208
AGE	RESP	'74	'75	'76	'77	'78	'80	'82	'83	'84	'85	'86	'87	'88	'89
36-41	XL	2%	3%	1%	3%	0%	1%	1%	6%	2%	6%	2%	3%	5%	4%
	LB	13	13	11	9	10	10	10	16	12	15	10	17	15	17
	SL	15	11	15	13	14	17	18	13	18	12	15	19	14	17
	MD	36	37	38	39	40	36	32	34	37	37	32	30	33	33
	SC	17	22	24	23	22	19	20	20	19	17	22	22	17	15
	CS	13	12	10	11	12	15	16	10	11	11	17	9	14	14
	XC	3	3	1	2	2	1	3	2	2	2	3	1	2	1
# SURVEYED		143	142	149	158	153	147	142	107	186	179	186	179	190	187

TABLE IV: POLITICAL LEANINGS -- BY AGE (Continued)

Question: We hear a lot of talk these days of liberals and conservatives. I'm going to show you a seven-point scale on which the political views that people might hold are arranged from extremely liberal--point 1-- to extremely conservative--point 7. Where would you place yourself on this scale? NOTE: Question was not asked in 1972, 1973.

Responses:
XL = Extremely libral
LB = Liberal
SL = Slightly liberal
MD = Moderate, middle of the road
SC = Slightly conservative
CS = Conservative
XC = Extremely conservative

		YEAR													
AGE	RESP	'74	'75	'76	'77	'78	'80	'82	'83	'84	'85	'86	'87	'88	'89
42-47	XL	1%	4%	2%	2%	0%	1%	0%	0%	1%	0%	1%	2%	3%	3%
	LB	10	8	6	9	13	5	11	9	11	14	7	14	15	10
	SL	16	9	10	12	11	11	18	9	10	8	16	12	9	17
	MD	38	35	41	34	35	40	39	41	41	33	43	40	30	36
	SC	23	24	17	23	22	20	22	23	24	23	17	13	20	22
	CS	11	16	24	18	16	21	9	14	11	19	12	18	21	11
	XC	2	3	1	2	3	4	1	5	2	2	5	1	2	2
# SURVEYED		146	139	105	133	115	111	114	66	122	121	138	146	155	152
AGE	RESP	'74	'75	'76	'77	'78	'80	'82	'83	'84	'85	'86	'87	'88	'89
48-53	XL	2%	2%	2%	1%	1%	2%	3%	0%	4%	2%	2%	1%	2%	5%
	LB	10	12	11	9	6	2	7	3	4	10	8	13	10	9
	SL	11	8	10	12	18	7	10	7	9	9	6	13	17	9
	MD	45	44	37	42	35	51	42	39	35	38	45	45	36	45
	SC	18	15	20	19	19	21	17	27	30	26	17	17	18	16
	CS	11	16	19	13	20	13	19	20	17	12	22	8	13	15
	XC	3	2	2	5	1	3	3	3	0	2	1	3	3	2
# SURVEYED		141	138	123	149	124	121	106	59	96	125	103	120	88	129
AGE	RESP	'74	'75	'76	'77	'78	'80	'82	'83	'84	'85	'86	'87	'88	'89
54-59	XL	0%	0%	1%	3%	2%	2%	1%	0%	0%	2%	3%	2%	2%	0%
	LB	11	3	9	11	9	5	7	4	7	6	11	10	16	9
	SL	11	13	9	8	14	8	9	5	6	8	8	8	12	14
	MD	40	49	46	45	31	44	47	49	40	43	40	38	30	38
	SC	13	17	18	15	22	20	9	26	24	16	17	22	16	19
	CS	21	16	15	16	19	15	17	12	17	21	16	16	19	15
	XC	5	2	2	2	3	7	9	4	6	3	5	3	5	5
# SURVEYED		131	121	118	165	129	133	137	57	108	126	93	91	83	93
AGE	RESP	'74	'75	'76	'77	'78	'80	'82	'83	'84	'85	'86	'87	'88	'89
60-65	XL	2%	3%	1%	1%	0%	6%	0%	2%	3%	2%	2%	1%	1%	1%
	LB	8	10	15	7	4	5	10	2	6	7	10	14	10	14
	SL	15	6	6	11	11	12	10	9	12	12	7	14	6	12
	MD	49	49	47	39	48	45	46	53	31	38	48	45	41	38
	SC	18	21	13	27	18	19	13	16	21	18	14	12	19	14
	CS	9	7	14	11	18	9	14	19	24	19	16	13	19	19
	XC	0	3	4	4	1	3	7	0	4	4	4	2	4	3
# SURVEYED		102	99	127	114	95	117	109	57	107	125	107	94	114	103

TABLE IV: POLITICAL LEANINGS -- BY AGE (Continued)

Question: We hear a lot of talk these days of liberals and conservatives. I'm going to show you a seven-point scale on which the political views that people might hold are arranged from extremely liberal--point 1-- to extremely conservative--point 7. Where would you place yourself on this scale? NOTE: Question was not asked in 1972, 1973.

Responses: XL = Extremely libral; LB = Liberal; SL = Slightly liberal; MD = Moderate, middle of the road; SC = Slightly conservative; CS = Conservative; XC = Extremely conservative

		YEAR													
AGE	RESP	'74	'75	'76	'77	'78	'80	'82	'83	'84	'85	'86	'87	'88	'89
66+	XL	1%	1%	3%	2%	1%	3%	2%	1%	2%	2%	2%	2%	2%	3%
	LB	12	11	10	8	7	6	9	4	8	10	7	10	7	9
	SL	12	15	10	12	9	8	11	7	9	11	9	8	8	12
	MD	39	40	40	39	44	45	41	50	43	39	48	48	44	43
	SC	16	15	13	16	19	18	15	12	18	19	12	11	18	16
	CS	16	12	20	19	16	14	19	19	14	15	21	17	19	16
	XC	4	5	3	5	3	6	5	6	5	4	3	4	3	1
# SURVEYED		207	201	231	194	203	230	234	114	214	230	239	228	257	246

****

DISCRIMINATION IS BLACKS' MAIN PROBLEM

TABLE I: DISCRIMINATION IS BLACKS' MAIN PROBLEM -- BY TOTAL POPULATION

Question: On the average, blacks have worse jobs, income, and housing than white people. Do you think these differences are mainly due to discrimination? NOTE: Question not asked in 1971-1976, 1978-1984, 1987. Asked only of non-blacks in 1977.

Responses: YES; NO

	YEAR				
RESPONSE	'77	'85	'86	'88	'89
YES	41%	45%	45%	44%	42%
NO	59	55	55	56	58
# SURVEYED	1287	1464	1422	935	943

TABLE II: DISCRIMINATION IS BLACKS' MAIN PROBLEM -- BY SEX

Question: On the average, blacks have worse jobs, income, and housing than white people. Do you think these differences are mainly due to discrimination? NOTE: Question not asked in 1971-1976, 1978-1984, 1987. Asked only of non-blacks in 1977.

Responses: YES; NO

		YEAR				
SEX	RESP	'77	'85	'86	'88	'89
M	YES	38%	44%	45%	40%	38%
	NO	62	56	55	60	62
# SURVEYED		598	663	609	421	413

		YEAR				
SEX	RESP	'77	'85	'86	'88	'89
F	YES	44%	46%	45%	48%	45%
	NO	56	54	55	52	55
# SURVEYED		689	801	813	514	530

TABLE III: DISCRIMINATION IS BLACKS' MAIN PROBLEM -- BY RACE

Question: On the average, blacks have worse jobs, income, and housing than white people. Do you think these differences are mainly due to discrimination? NOTE: Question not asked in 1971-1976, 1978-1984, 1987. Asked only of non-blacks in 1977.

Responses: YES; NO

RACE	RESP	'77	'85	'86	'88	'89
WHITE	YES	41%	41%	40%	39%	38%
	NO	59	59	60	61	62
# SURVEYED		1273	1285	1215	786	808
BLACK	YES	0%	79%	74%	80%	75%
	NO	0	21	26	20	25
# SURVEYED		000	137	172	118	100

RACE	RESP	'77	'85	'86	'88	'89
OTHER	YES	36%	48%	57%	55%	54%
	NO	64	52	43	45	46
# SURVEYED		14	42	35	31	35

TABLE IV: DISCRIMINATION IS BLACKS' MAIN PROBLEM -- BY AGE

Question: On the average, blacks have worse jobs, income, and housing than white people. Do you think these differences are mainly due to discrimination? NOTE: Question not asked in 1971-1976, 1978-1984, 1987. Asked only of non-blacks in 1977.

Responses: YES; NO

AGE	RESP	'77	'85	'86	'88	'89
18-23	YES	53%	56%	50%	47%	53%
	NO	47	44	50	53	47
# SURVEYED		135	128	104	92	81
24-29	YES	49%	44%	48%	53%	44%
	NO	51	56	52	47	56
# SURVEYED		171	210	213	141	136
30-35	YES	46%	46%	49%	45%	42%
	NO	54	54	51	55	58
# SURVEYED		164	206	218	124	132

AGE	RESP	'77	'85	'86	'88	'89
36-41	YES	36%	45%	45%	42%	45%
	NO	64	55	55	58	55
# SURVEYED		138	174	183	118	122
42-47	YES	36%	44%	39%	44%	43%
	NO	64	56	61	56	57
# SURVEYED		128	121	135	106	102
48-53	YES	32%	39%	39%	44%	38%
	NO	68	61	61	56	62
# SURVEYED		133	127	104	61	78

TABLE IV: DISCRIMINATION IS BLACKS' MAIN PROBLEM -- BY AGE (Continued)

Question: On the average, blacks have worse jobs, income, and housing than white people. Do you think these differences are mainly due to discrimination? NOTE: Question not asked in 1971-1976, 1978-1984, 1987. Asked only of non-blacks in 1977.

Responses: YES; NO

		YEAR				
AGE	RESP	'77	'85	'86	'88	'89
54-59	YES	32%	43%	41%	46%	47%
	NO	68	57	59	54	53
# SURVEYED		139	127	98	48	68
AGE	RESP	'77	'85	'86	'88	'89
60-65	YES	32%	45%	39%	35%	40%
	NO	68	55	61	65	60
# SURVEYED		103	125	111	71	65

		YEAR				
AGE	RESP	'77	'85	'86	'88	'89
66+	YES	45%	44%	45%	41%	33%
	NO	55	56	55	59	67
# SURVEYED		172	241	249	174	156

****

GENETICS IS BLACKS' MAIN PROBLEM

TABLE I: GENETICS IS BLACKS' MAIN PROBLEM -- BY TOTAL POPULATION

Question: On the average, blacks have worse jobs, income, and housing than white people. Do you think these differences are mainly because most blacks have less inborn ability to learn? NOTE: Question not asked in 1971-1976, 1978-1984, 1987. Asked only of non-blacks in 1977.

Responses: YES; NO

	YEAR				
RESPONSE	'77	'85	'86	'88	'89
YES	26%	21%	21%	19%	19%
NO	74	79	79	81	81
# SURVEYED	1281	1467	1415	941	955

TABLE II: GENETICS IS BLACKS' MAIN PROBLEM -- BY SEX

Question: On the average, blacks have worse jobs, income, and housing than white people. Do you think these differences are mainly because most blacks have less inborn ability to learn? NOTE: Question not asked in 1971-1976, 1978-1984, 1987. Asked only of non-blacks in 1977.

Responses: YES; NO

		YEAR				
SEX	RESP	'77	'85	'86	'88	'89
M	YES	29%	22%	22%	19%	19%
	NO	71	78	78	81	81
# SURVEYED		597	661	602	424	414

		YEAR				
SEX	RESP	'77	'85	'86	'88	'89
F	YES	23%	20%	20%	19%	19%
	NO	77	80	80	81	81
# SURVEYED		684	806	813	517	541

TABLE III: GENETICS IS BLACKS' MAIN PROBLEM -- BY RACE

Question: On the average, blacks have worse jobs, income, and housing than white people. Do you think these differences are mainly because most blacks have less inborn ability to learn? NOTE: Question not asked in 1971-1976, 1978-1984, 1987. Asked only of non-blacks in 1977.

Responses: YES; NO

		YEAR				
RACE	RESP	'77	'85	'86	'88	'89
WHITE	YES	26%	21%	21%	21%	19%
	NO	74	79	79	79	81
# SURVEYED		1267	1279	1203	787	819
RACE	RESP	'77	'85	'86	'88	'89
BLACK	YES	0%	18%	19%	8%	18%
	NO	0	82	81	92	82
# SURVEYED		000	146	178	122	101

		YEAR				
RACE	RESP	'77	'85	'86	'88	'89
OTHER	YES	50%	24%	26%	25%	29%
	NO	50	76	74	75	71
# SURVEYED		14	42	34	32	35

TABLE IV: GENETICS IS BLACKS' MAIN PROBLEM -- BY AGE

Question: On the average, blacks have worse jobs, income, and housing than white people. Do you think these differences are mainly because most blacks have less inborn ability to learn? NOTE: Question not asked in 1971-1976, 1978-1984, 1987. Asked only of non-blacks in 1977.

Responses: YES; NO

		YEAR				
AGE	RESP	'77	'85	'86	'88	'89
18-23	YES	16%	9%	12%	16%	14%
	NO	84	91	88	84	86
# SURVEYED		136	128	106	93	81
AGE	RESP	'77	'85	'86	'88	'89
24-29	YES	9%	14%	13%	12%	12%
	NO	91	86	87	88	88
# SURVEYED		171	214	216	143	137
AGE	RESP	'77	'85	'86	'88	'89
30-35	YES	15%	11%	10%	14%	15%
	NO	85	89	90	86	85
# SURVEYED		160	208	218	130	136
AGE	RESP	'77	'85	'86	'88	'89
36-41	YES	15%	15%	12%	14%	14%
	NO	85	85	88	86	86
# SURVEYED		137	182	182	124	122
AGE	RESP	'77	'85	'86	'88	'89
42-47	YES	27%	16%	17%	10%	23%
	NO	73	84	83	90	77
# SURVEYED		125	120	137	102	103

		YEAR				
AGE	RESP	'77	'85	'86	'88	'89
48-53	YES	31%	24%	26%	22%	21%
	NO	69	76	74	78	79
# SURVEYED		135	123	104	59	80
AGE	RESP	'77	'85	'86	'88	'89
54-59	YES	28%	31%	31%	20%	18%
	NO	72	69	69	80	82
# SURVEYED		139	121	93	50	71
AGE	RESP	'77	'85	'86	'88	'89
60-65	YES	46%	33%	23%	33%	32%
	NO	54	67	77	67	68
# SURVEYED		99	126	109	70	66
AGE	RESP	'77	'85	'86	'88	'89
66+	YES	51%	37%	43%	34%	27%
	NO	49	63	57	66	73
# SURVEYED		174	238	243	170	156

****

POOR EDUCATION AS BLACKS' MAIN PROBLEM

TABLE I: POOR EDUCATION IS BLACKS' MAIN PROBLEM -- BY TOTAL POPULATION

Question: On the average, blacks have worse jobs, income, and housing than white people. Do you think these differences are mainly because most blacks don't have the chance for education that it takes to rise out of poverty? NOTE: Question not asked in 1971-1976, 1978-1984, 1987. Asked only of non-blacks in 1977.

Responses: YES; NO

	YEAR				
RESPONSE	'77	'85	'86	'88	'89
YES	51%	54%	53%	54%	54%
NO	49	46	47	46	46
# SURVEYED	1298	1494	1432	945	963

TABLE II: POOR EDUCATION IS BLACKS' MAIN PROBLEM -- BY SEX

Question: On the average, blacks have worse jobs, income, and housing than white people. Do you think these differences are mainly because most blacks don't have the chance for education that it takes to rise out of poverty? NOTE: Question not asked in 1971-1976, 1978-1984, 1987. Asked only of non-blacks in 1977.

Responses: YES; NO

		YEAR				
SEX	RESP	'77	'85	'86	'88	'89
M	YES	48%	53%	55%	49%	47%
	NO	52	47	45	51	53
# SURVEYED		601	673	607	420	415

		YEAR				
SEX	RESP	'77	'85	'86	'88	'89
F	YES	53%	55%	52%	58%	59%
	NO	47	45	48	42	41
# SURVEYED		697	821	825	525	548

TABLE III: POOR EDUCATION IS BLACKS' MAIN PROBLEM -- BY RACE

Question: On the average, blacks have worse jobs, income, and housing than white people. Do you think these differences are mainly because most blacks don't have the chance for education that it takes to rise out of poverty? NOTE: Question not asked in 1971-1976, 1978-1984, 1987. Asked only of non-blacks in 1977.

Responses: YES; NO

		YEAR				
RACE	RESP	'77	'85	'86	'88	'89
WHITE	YES	51%	52%	51%	52%	53%
	NO	49	48	49	48	47
# SURVEYED		1284	1308	1222	790	826
RACE	RESP	'77	'85	'86	'88	'89
BLACK	YES	0%	74%	65%	68%	64%
	NO	0	26	35	32	36
# SURVEYED		000	144	175	122	102
RACE	RESP	'77	'85	'86	'88	'89
OTHER	YES	43%	50%	54%	61%	54%
	NO	57	50	46	39	46
# SURVEYED		14	42	35	33	35

TABLE IV: POOR EDUCATION IS BLACKS' MAIN PROBLEM -- BY AGE

Question: On the average, blacks have worse jobs, income, and housing than white people. Do you think these differences are mainly because most blacks don't have the chance for education that it takes to rise out of poverty? NOTE: Question not asked in 1971-1976, 1978-1984, 1987. Asked only of non-blacks in 1977.

Responses: YES; NO

		YEAR				
AGE	RESP	'77	'85	'86	'88	'89
18-23	YES	54%	58%	42%	52%	51%
	NO	46	42	58	48	49
# SURVEYED		136	132	104	90	81
AGE	RESP	'77	'85	'86	'88	'89
24-29	YES	54%	53%	63%	54%	59%
	NO	46	47	37	46	41
# SURVEYED		171	214	214	146	142
AGE	RESP	'77	'85	'86	'88	'89
30-35	YES	52%	53%	53%	56%	60%
	NO	48	47	47	44	40
# SURVEYED		165	209	218	129	134
AGE	RESP	'77	'85	'86	'88	'89
36-41	YES	50%	62%	56%	54%	48%
	NO	50	38	44	46	52
# SURVEYED		139	181	183	124	124
AGE	RESP	'77	'85	'86	'88	'89
42-47	YES	46%	52%	53%	59%	62%
	NO	54	48	47	41	38
# SURVEYED		126	122	133	104	103
AGE	RESP	'77	'85	'86	'88	'89
48-53	YES	44%	50%	45%	60%	50%
	NO	56	50	55	40	50
# SURVEYED		134	127	106	60	80

TABLE IV: POOR EDUCATION IS BLACKS' MAIN PROBLEM -- BY AGE (Continued)

Question: On the average, blacks have worse jobs, income, and housing than white people. Do you think these differences are mainly because most blacks don't have the chance for education that it takes to rise out of poverty? NOTE: Question not asked in 1971-1976, 1978-1984, 1987. Asked only of non-blacks in 1977.

Responses: YES; NO

		YEAR				
AGE	RESP	'77	'85	'86	'88	'89
54-59	YES	48%	51%	53%	52%	52%
	NO	52	49	47	48	48
# SURVEYED		141	127	96	48	69
AGE	RESP	'77	'85	'86	'88	'89
60-65	YES	54%	56%	46%	53%	57%
	NO	46	44	54	47	43
# SURVEYED		104	128	114	73	67

		YEAR				
AGE	RESP	'77	'85	'86	'88	'89
66+	YES	52%	51%	52%	50%	48%
	NO	48	49	48	50	52
# SURVEYED		177	247	257	171	160

****

POOR MOTIVATION IS BLACKS' MAIN PROBLEM

TABLE I: POOR MOTIVATION IS BLACKS' MAIN PROBLEM -- BY TOTAL POPULATION

Question: On the average, blacks have worse jobs, income, and housing than white people. Do you think these differences are mainly because most blacks just don't have the motivation or will power to pull themselves up out of their poverty? NOTE: Question not asked in 1971-1976, 1978-1984, 1987. Asked only of non-blacks in 1977.

Responses: YES; NO

	YEAR				
RESPONSE	'77	'85	'86	'88	'89
YES	66%	58%	61%	58%	60%
NO	34	42	39	42	40
# SURVEYED	1270	1455	1404	932	943

TABLE II: POOR MOTIVATION IS BLACKS' MAIN PROBLEM -- BY SEX

Question: On the average, blacks have worse jobs, income, and housing than white people. Do you think these differences are mainly because most blacks just don't have the motivation or will power to pull themselves up out of their poverty? NOTE: Question not asked in 1971-1976, 1978-1984, 1987. Asked only of non-blacks in 1977.

Responses: YES; NO

		YEAR				
SEX	RESP	'77	'85	'86	'88	'89
M	YES	68%	59%	61%	59%	63%
	NO	32	41	39	41	37
# SURVEYED		592	654	593	417	404

		YEAR				
SEX	RESP	'77	'85	'86	'88	'89
F	YES	64%	57%	61%	57%	58%
	NO	36	43	39	43	42
# SURVEYED		678	801	811	515	539

TABLE III: POOR MOTIVATION IS BLACKS' MAIN PROBLEM -- BY RACE

Question: On the average, blacks have worse jobs, income, and housing than white people. Do you think these differences are mainly because most blacks just don't have the motivation or will power to pull themselves up out of their poverty? NOTE: Question not asked in 1971-1976, 1978-1984, 1987. Asked only of non-blacks in 1977.

Responses: YES; NO

		YEAR				
RACE	RESP	'77	'85	'86	'88	'89
WHITE	YES	66%	60%	64%	61%	63%
	NO	34	40	36	39	37
# SURVEYED		1256	1275	1198	780	810
RACE	RESP	'77	'85	'86	'88	'89
BLACK	YES	0%	35%	38%	34%	35%
	NO	0	65	62	66	65
# SURVEYED		000	138	172	119	97

		YEAR				
RACE	RESP	'77	'85	'86	'88	'89
OTHER	YES	50%	69%	65%	64%	64%
	NO	50	31	35	36	36
# SURVEYED		14	42	34	33	36

TABLE IV: POOR MOTIVATION IS BLACKS' MAIN PROBLEM -- BY AGE

Question: On the average, blacks have worse jobs, income, and housing than white people. Do you think these differences are mainly because most blacks just don't have the motivation or will power to pull themselves up out of their poverty? NOTE: Question not asked in 1971-1976, 1978-1984, 1987. Asked only of non-blacks in 1977.

Responses: YES; NO

AGE	RESP	'77	'85	'86	'88	'89
18-23	YES	54%	37%	55%	55%	58%
	NO	46	63	45	45	42
# SURVEYED		137	127	100	91	79
24-29	YES	55%	51%	56%	48%	56%
	NO	45	49	44	52	44
# SURVEYED		165	211	208	143	140
30-35	YES	60%	53%	54%	54%	54%
	NO	40	47	46	46	46
# SURVEYED		161	211	216	128	130
36-41	YES	64%	54%	57%	58%	56%
	NO	36	46	43	42	44
# SURVEYED		134	178	183	123	125
42-47	YES	74%	58%	55%	51%	53%
	NO	26	42	45	49	47
# SURVEYED		121	123	135	100	104

AGE	RESP	'77	'85	'86	'88	'89
48-53	YES	70%	61%	67%	58%	57%
	NO	30	39	33	42	43
# SURVEYED		133	126	101	60	77
54-59	YES	67%	67%	66%	54%	62%
	NO	33	33	34	46	38
# SURVEYED		135	118	94	48	66
60-65	YES	75%	73%	66%	71%	70%
	NO	25	27	34	29	30
# SURVEYED		100	120	111	70	64
66+	YES	77%	71%	73%	70%	73%
	NO	23	29	27	30	27
# SURVEYED		179	235	249	169	155

****

WHITES' RIGHT TO SEGREGATION

TABLE I: WHITES' RIGHT TO SEGREGATION -- BY TOTAL POPULATION

Question: White people have a right to keep blacks out of their neighborhoods if they want to, and blacks should respect that right. NOTE: Question not asked in 1973-1975, 1978, 1983, 1986. Asked of non-blacks in 1972-1977. Since 1977 it has been asked of all respondents.

Responses: AS = Agree strongly; SL = Agree slightly; DL = Disagree slightly; DS = Disagree strongly

	YEAR									
RESPONSE	'72	'76	'77	'80	'82	'84	'85	'87	'88	'89
AS	22%	22%	22%	16%	14%	11%	10%	9%	8%	8%
SL	18	18	20	16	14	15	15	14	15	14
DL	25	26	29	28	29	26	29	26	24	23
DS	35	35	28	41	44	49	46	51	54	55
# SURVEYED	1253	1337	1309	1414	1469	1435	1487	1434	950	1001

TABLE II: WHITES' RIGHT TO SEGREGATION -- BY SEX

Question: White people have a right to keep blacks out of their neighborhoods if they want to, and blacks should respect that right. NOTE: Question not asked in 1973-1975, 1978, 1983, 1986. Asked of non-blacks in 1972-1977. Since 1977 it has been asked of all respondents.

Responses: AS = Agree strongly; SL = Agree slightly; DL = Disagree slightly; DS = Disagree strongly

		YEAR									
SEX	RESP	'72	'76	'77	'80	'82	'84	'85	'87	'88	'89
M	AS	22%	22%	22%	15%	12%	11%	10%	9%	8%	7%
	SL	17	17	19	15	14	14	14	14	14	17
	DL	26	26	29	30	31	24	30	26	25	27
	DS	35	36	29	39	44	51	45	52	54	49
# SURVEYED		637	591	607	624	628	588	668	628	396	435
SEX	RESP	'72	'76	'77	'80	'82	'84	'85	'87	'88	'89
F	AS	23%	21%	22%	16%	15%	10%	10%	9%	8%	8%
	SL	19	19	21	16	14	15	16	15	15	11
	DL	23	26	29	26	27	27	28	25	24	20
	DS	35	34	28	42	44	48	46	51	53	60
# SURVEYED		616	746	702	790	841	847	819	806	554	566

TABLE III: WHITES' RIGHT TO SEGREGATION -- BY RACE

Question: White people have a right to keep blacks out of their neighborhoods if they want to, and blacks should respect that right. NOTE: Question not asked in 1973-1975, 1978, 1983, 1986. Asked of non-blacks in 1972-1977. Since 1977 it has been asked of all respondents.

Responses: AS = Agree strongly; SL = Agree slightly; DL = Disagree slightly; DS = Disagree strongly

		YEAR									
RACE	RESP	'72	'76	'77	'80	'82	'84	'85	'87	'88	'89
WHITE	AS	22%	22%	22%	17%	15%	11%	10%	10%	9%	8%
	SL	18	18	20	16	15	15	16	16	16	14
	DL	24	26	29	29	31	27	30	28	27	25
	DS	35	35	28	38	39	47	44	46	49	53
# SURVEYED		1251	1330	1296	1271	1287	1219	1301	1199	783	861
RACE	RESP	'72	'76	'77	'80	'82	'84	'85	'87	'88	'89
BLACK	AS	0%	0%	0%	5%	5%	4%	8%	3%	3%	5%
	SL	0	0	0	9	4	10	10	8	6	5
	DL	0	0	0	19	8	16	18	8	9	9
	DS	0	0	0	67	83	70	64	82	83	81
# SURVEYED		000	000	000	134	155	166	143	185	127	101
RACE	RESP	'72	'76	'77	'80	'82	'84	'85	'87	'88	'89
OTHER	AS	0%	0%	23%	11%	4%	20%	9%	12%	3%	3%
	SL	0	14	15	11	22	16	9	8	18	18
	DL	100	29	15	0	22	24	37	30	25	36
	DS	0	57	46	78	52	40	44	50	55	44
# SURVEYED		2	7	13	9	27	50	43	50	40	39

TABLE IV: WHITES' RIGHT TO SEGREGATION -- BY AGE

Question: White people have a right to keep blacks out of their neighborhoods if they want to, and blacks should respect that right. NOTE: Question not asked in 1973-1975, 1978, 1983, 1986. Asked of non-blacks in 1972-1977. Since 1977 it has been asked of all respondents.

Responses: AS = Agree strongly; SL = Agree slightly; DL = Disagree slightly; DS = Disagree strongly

		YEAR									
AGE	RESP	'72	'76	'77	'80	'82	'84	'85	'87	'88	'89
18-23	AS	11%	14%	11%	12%	10%	4%	4%	8%	5%	9%
	SL	10	13	19	10	8	8	11	7	9	12
	DL	23	17	33	26	23	24	22	18	19	18
	DS	57	56	38	52	60	64	63	67	67	61
# SURVEYED		132	147	140	153	146	157	131	124	94	95

TABLE IV: WHITES' RIGHT TO SEGREGATION -- BY AGE (Continued)

Question: White people have a right to keep blacks out of their neighborhoods if they want to, and blacks should respect that right. NOTE: Question not asked in 1973-1975, 1978, 1983, 1986. Asked of non-blacks in 1972-1977. Since 1977 it has been asked of all respondents.

Responses: AS = Agree strongly; SL = Agree slightly; DL = Disagree slightly; DS = Disagree strongly

AGE	RESP	'72	'76	'77	'80	'82	'84	'85	'87	'88	'89
24-29	AS	17%	13%	11%	10%	10%	6%	6%	2%	5%	3%
	SL	11	12	20	16	10	12	11	8	7	9
	DL	21	27	30	22	26	23	22	22	28	18
	DS	51	49	39	51	53	59	60	68	61	71
# SURVEYED		184	197	171	201	240	231	209	192	132	116
AGE	RESP	'72	'76	'77	'80	'82	'84	'85	'87	'88	'89
30-35	AS	21%	17%	16%	8%	8%	10%	7%	7%	2%	6%
	SL	15	19	20	12	12	9	11	9	11	9
	DL	26	29	29	28	27	24	24	27	19	18
	DS	38	35	35	52	52	57	58	57	68	67
# SURVEYED		152	171	164	209	204	197	211	220	130	133
AGE	RESP	'72	'76	'77	'80	'82	'84	'85	'87	'88	'89
36-41	AS	22%	13%	17%	15%	13%	9%	6%	4%	8%	6%
	SL	18	24	23	11	14	9	11	14	8	8
	DL	23	22	28	30	27	30	28	27	20	23
	DS	37	41	33	43	46	52	55	54	64	63
# SURVEYED		104	141	138	148	145	184	181	182	132	133
AGE	RESP	'72	'76	'77	'80	'82	'84	'85	'87	'88	'89
42-47	AS	21%	24%	23%	17%	9%	9%	12%	8%	4%	6%
	SL	14	20	19	14	14	15	16	12	15	9
	DL	30	29	29	30	28	25	36	25	19	22
	DS	34	28	29	39	48	50	37	55	62	63
# SURVEYED		145	105	129	113	116	123	121	155	101	103
AGE	RESP	'72	'76	'77	'80	'82	'84	'85	'87	'88	'89
48-53	AS	27%	31%	23%	10%	11%	9%	14%	15%	10%	10%
	SL	19	20	15	20	16	21	17	15	13	17
	DL	28	24	34	39	33	36	33	30	24	22
	DS	26	24	28	31	40	34	36	41	54	51
# SURVEYED		147	119	138	119	111	100	129	124	63	94
AGE	RESP	'72	'76	'77	'80	'82	'84	'85	'87	'88	'89
54-59	AS	23%	21%	26%	17%	20%	10%	10%	14%	18%	8%
	SL	22	17	25	24	14	13	24	17	20	21
	DL	24	27	29	27	33	29	35	26	20	23
	DS	31	35	20	32	33	49	31	43	43	48
# SURVEYED		120	113	139	132	139	111	127	95	51	62

TABLE IV: WHITES' RIGHT TO SEGREGATION -- BY AGE (Continued)

Question: White people have a right to keep blacks out of their neighborhoods if they want to, and blacks should respect that right. NOTE: Question not asked in 1973-1975, 1978, 1983, 1986. Asked of non-blacks in 1972-1977. Since 1977 it has been asked of all respondents.

Responses: AS = Agree strongly; SL = Agree slightly; DL = Disagree slightly; DS = Disagree strongly

		YEAR									
AGE	RESP	'72	'76	'77	'80	'82	'84	'85	'87	'88	'89
60-65	AS	25%	23%	36%	23%	18%	21%	14%	15%	15%	14%
	SL	32	23	23	17	20	17	16	22	17	19
	DL	20	30	23	28	28	27	34	25	31	24
	DS	23	23	18	32	33	35	35	39	37	43
# SURVEYED		106	115	104	114	114	107	125	96	81	74
AGE	RESP	'72	'76	'77	'80	'82	'84	'85	'87	'88	'89
66+	AS	32%	36%	39%	28%	22%	19%	17%	14%	10%	11%
	SL	25	16	20	18	17	29	20	25	30	21
	DL	25	28	27	27	33	21	32	27	33	34
	DS	18	20	14	27	28	32	30	34	27	34
# SURVEYED		160	224	181	217	245	221	247	241	164	189

****

ALLOW RACIST TO TEACH IN COLLEGE

TABLE I: ALLOW RACIST TO TEACH IN COLLEGE -- BY TOTAL POPULATION

Question: Should a person who believes that blacks are genetically inferior be allowed to teach in a college or university, or not? NOTE: Question not asked in 1972-1975, 1978, 1983, 1986.

Responses: YES = Yes, allowed to teach; NO = No, not allowed

	YEAR								
RESPONSE	'76	'77	'80	'82	'84	'85	'87	'88	'89
YES	42%	42%	45%	44%	42%	44%	45%	43%	48%
NO	58	58	55	56	58	56	55	57	52
# SURVEYED	1442	1487	1399	1439	1418	1479	1411	940	992

TABLE II: ALLOW RACIST TO TEACH IN COLLEGE -- BY SEX

Question: Should a person who believes that blacks are genetically inferior be allowed to teach in a college or university, or not? NOTE: Question not asked in 1972-1975, 1978, 1983, 1986.

Responses: YES = Yes, allowed to teach; NO = No, not allowed

		YEAR								
SEX	RESP	'76	'77	'80	'82	'84	'85	'87	'88	'89
M	YES	46%	47%	48%	48%	46%	46%	50%	49%	54%
	NO	54	53	52	52	54	54	50	51	46
# SURVEYED		645	680	615	623	579	667	619	390	428
SEX	RESP	'76	'77	'80	'82	'84	'85	'87	'88	'89
F	YES	39%	38%	43%	42%	39%	42%	42%	39%	43%
	NO	61	62	57	58	61	58	58	61	57
# SURVEYED		797	807	784	816	839	812	792	550	564

TABLE III: ALLOW RACIST TO TEACH IN COLLEGE -- BY RACE

Question: Should a person who believes that blacks are genetically inferior be allowed to teach in a college or university, or not? NOTE: Question not asked in 1972-1975, 1978, 1983, 1986.

Responses: YES = Yes, allowed to teach; NO = No, not allowed

		YEAR								
RACE	RESP	'76	'77	'80	'82	'84	'85	'87	'88	'89
WHITE	YES	4%	4%	4%	4%	4%	4%	4%	4%	4%
	NO	57	57	54	54	56	55	53	55	51
# SURVEYED		1310	1305	1255	1262	1204	1294	1175	773	857
RACE	RESP	'76	'77	'80	'82	'84	'85	'87	'88	'89
BLACK	YES	31%	32%	31%	33%	30%	38%	37%	34%	40%
	NO	69	68	69	67	70	62	63	66	60
# SURVEYED		126	168	134	153	164	143	185	126	96
RACE	RESP	'76	'77	'80	'82	'84	'85	'87	'88	'89
OTHER	YES	67%	57%	60%	33%	40%	31%	41%	39%	46%
	NO	33	43	40	67	60	69	59	61	54
# SURVEYED		6	14	10	24	50	42	51	41	39

TABLE IV: ALLOW RACIST TO TEACH IN COLLEGE -- BY AGE

Question: Should a person who believes that blacks are genetically inferior be allowed to teach in a college or university, or not? NOTE: Question not asked in 1972-1975, 1978, 1983, 1986.

Responses: YES = Yes, allowed to teach; NO = No, not allowed

		YEAR								
AGE	RESP	'76	'77	'80	'82	'84	'85	'87	'88	'89
18-23	YES	49%	54%	41%	45%	45%	45%	36%	45%	49%
	NO	51	46	59	55	55	55	64	55	51
# SURVEYED		159	160	148	144	154	130	121	92	96
AGE	RESP	'76	'77	'80	'82	'84	'85	'87	'88	'89
24-29	YES	60%	53%	55%	52%	42%	52%	52%	40%	46%
	NO	40	47	45	48	58	48	48	60	54
# SURVEYED		220	200	197	243	227	211	187	130	111
AGE	RESP	'76	'77	'80	'82	'84	'85	'87	'88	'89
30-35	YES	51%	54%	58%	58%	56%	53%	54%	49%	50%
	NO	49	46	42	42	44	47	46	51	50
# SURVEYED		179	183	205	194	193	206	216	127	131
AGE	RESP	'76	'77	'80	'82	'84	'85	'87	'88	'89
36-41	YES	44%	39%	50%	52%	50%	53%	55%	47%	64%
	NO	56	61	50	48	50	47	45	53	36
# SURVEYED		153	162	146	140	183	180	180	129	130
AGE	RESP	'76	'77	'80	'82	'84	'85	'87	'88	'89
42-47	YES	42%	37%	45%	54%	40%	50%	51%	45%	56%
	NO	58	63	55	46	60	50	49	55	44
# SURVEYED		108	139	110	114	122	121	154	100	105
AGE	RESP	'76	'77	'80	'82	'84	'85	'87	'88	'89
48-53	YES	33%	36%	45%	43%	32%	41%	43%	40%	42%
	NO	67	64	55	57	68	59	57	60	58
# SURVEYED		129	152	117	111	99	129	121	63	91
AGE	RESP	'76	'77	'80	'82	'84	'85	'87	'88	'89
54-59	YES	30%	32%	37%	38%	31%	33%	38%	43%	33%
	NO	70	68	63	62	69	67	62	57	67
# SURVEYED		124	167	133	138	111	126	93	53	60
AGE	RESP	'76	'77	'80	'82	'84	'85	'87	'88	'89
60-65	YES	31%	29%	38%	31%	35%	30%	29%	42%	36%
	NO	69	71	62	69	65	70	71	58	64
# SURVEYED		131	112	115	108	109	125	100	81	74

TABLE IV: ALLOW RACIST TO TEACH IN COLLEGE -- BY AGE (Continued)

Question: Should a person who believes that blacks are genetically inferior be allowed to teach in a college or university, or not? NOTE: Question not asked in 1972-1975, 1978, 1983, 1986.

Responses: YES = Yes, allowed to teach; NO = No, not allowed

		YEAR								
AGE	RESP	'76	'77	'80	'82	'84	'85	'87	'88	'89
66+	YES	30%	36%	33%	27%	36%	30%	37%	38%	42%
	NO	70	64	67	73	64	70	63	62	58
# SURVEYED		233	205	219	237	214	245	234	162	191

****

ALLOW RACIST BOOK IN LIBRARY

TABLE I: ALLOW RACIST BOOK IN LIBRARY -- BY TOTAL POPULATION

Question: If some people in your community suggested that a book written by a racist which said blacks are inferior should be taken out of your public library, would you favor removing this book, or not? NOTE: Question not asked in 1972-1975, 1978, 1983, 1986.

Responses: FA = Favor; NF = Not favor

	YEAR								
RESPONSE	'76	'77	'80	'82	'84	'85	'87	'88	'89
FA	38%	37%	34%	37%	35%	38%	35%	36%	33%
NF	62	63	66	63	65	62	65	64	67
# SURVEYED	1437	1483	1411	1444	1423	1488	1422	945	995

TABLE II: ALLOW RACIST BOOK IN LIBRARY -- BY SEX

Question: If some people in your community suggested that a book written by a racist which said blacks are inferior should be taken out of your public library, would you favor removing this book, or not? NOTE: Question not asked in 1972-1975, 1978, 1983, 1986.

Responses: FA = Favor; NF = Not favor

		YEAR								
SEX	RESP	'76	'77	'80	'82	'84	'85	'87	'88	'89
M	FA	35%	36%	32%	35%	30%	36%	31%	32%	30%
	NF	65	64	68	65	70	64	69	68	70
# SURVEYED		644	671	620	620	581	673	626	389	433
SEX	RESP	'76	'77	'80	'82	'84	'85	'87	'88	'89
F	FA	40%	38%	35%	38%	38%	40%	38%	39%	35%
	NF	60	62	65	62	62	60	62	61	65
# SURVEYED		793	812	791	824	842	815	796	556	562

TABLE III: ALLOW RACIST BOOK IN LIBRARY -- BY RACE

Question: If some people in your community suggested that a book written by a racist which said blacks are inferior should be taken out of your public library, would you favor removing this book, or not? NOTE: Question not asked in 1972-1975, 1978, 1983, 1986.

Responses: FA = Favor; NF = Not favor

		YEAR								
RACE	RESP	'76	'77	'80	'82	'84	'85	'87	'88	'89
WHITE	FA	37%	36%	32%	34%	32%	36%	32%	33%	32%
	NF	63	64	68	66	68	64	68	67	68
# SURVEYED		1307	1299	1263	1264	1212	1303	1192	779	863
RACE	RESP	'76	'77	'80	'82	'84	'85	'87	'88	'89
BLACK	FA	51%	49%	49%	57%	52%	52%	48%	51%	44%
	NF	49	51	51	43	48	48	52	49	56
# SURVEYED		124	169	138	155	163	142	178	126	93
RACE	RESP	'76	'77	'80	'82	'84	'85	'87	'88	'89
OTHER	FA	17%	27%	10%	48%	46%	56%	50%	55%	33%
	NF	83	73	90	52	54	44	50	45	67
# SURVEYED		6	15	10	25	48	43	52	40	39

TABLE IV: ALLOW RACIST BOOK IN LIBRARY -- BY AGE

Question: If some people in your community suggested that a book written by a racist which said blacks are inferior should be taken out of your public library, would you favor removing this book, or not? NOTE: Question not asked in 1972-1975, 1978, 1983, 1986.

Responses: FA = Favor; NF = Not favor

		YEAR								
AGE	RESP	'76	'77	'80	'82	'84	'85	'87	'88	'89
18-23	FA	28%	33%	34%	42%	36%	42%	40%	43%	39%
	NF	72	67	66	58	64	58	60	57	61
# SURVEYED		159	161	152	143	152	130	124	92	95
AGE	RESP	'76	'77	'80	'82	'84	'85	'87	'88	'89
24-29	FA	22%	32%	20%	30%	40%	36%	29%	37%	32%
	NF	78	68	80	70	60	64	71	63	68
# SURVEYED		220	202	197	242	229	212	191	133	114
AGE	RESP	'76	'77	'80	'82	'84	'85	'87	'88	'89
30-35	FA	28%	28%	24%	24%	24%	33%	27%	32%	31%
	NF	72	72	76	76	76	67	73	68	69
# SURVEYED		179	186	212	202	192	205	219	130	132
AGE	RESP	'76	'77	'80	'82	'84	'85	'87	'88	'89
36-41	FA	33%	31%	29%	32%	25%	25%	27%	25%	24%
	NF	67	69	71	68	75	75	73	75	76
# SURVEYED		149	163	147	141	185	181	184	129	132
AGE	RESP	'76	'77	'80	'82	'84	'85	'87	'88	'89
42-47	FA	42%	35%	29%	32%	29%	28%	30%	27%	27%
	NF	58	65	71	68	71	72	70	73	73
# SURVEYED		109	136	112	115	125	121	148	99	107
AGE	RESP	'76	'77	'80	'82	'84	'85	'87	'88	'89
48-53	FA	44%	40%	39%	41%	34%	34%	38%	37%	30%
	NF	56	60	61	59	66	66	62	63	70
# SURVEYED		130	149	116	110	100	129	124	63	94
AGE	RESP	'76	'77	'80	'82	'84	'85	'87	'88	'89
54-59	FA	43%	38%	42%	32%	40%	39%	38%	38%	29%
	NF	57	62	58	68	60	61	62	62	71
# SURVEYED		125	165	130	136	110	129	95	52	58
AGE	RESP	'76	'77	'80	'82	'84	'85	'87	'88	'89
60-65	FA	52%	47%	33%	47%	43%	46%	49%	41%	42%
	NF	48	53	67	53	57	54	51	59	58
# SURVEYED		129	111	116	111	108	125	99	82	74

TABLE IV: ALLOW RACIST BOOK IN LIBRARY -- BY AGE (Continued)

Question: If some people in your community suggested that a book written by a racist which said blacks are inferior should be taken out of your public library, would you favor removing this book, or not? NOTE: Question not asked in 1972-1975, 1978, 1983, 1986.

Responses: FA = Favor; NF = Not favor

		YEAR								
AGE	RESP	'76	'77	'80	'82	'84	'85	'87	'88	'89
66+	FA	55%	54%	55%	54%	44%	55%	44%	46%	39%
	NF	45	46	45	46	56	45	56	54	61
# SURVEYED		231	203	220	235	216	251	233	162	186

****

ALLOW RACIST TO MAKE SPEECH

TABLE I: ALLOW RACIST TO MAKE SPEECH -- BY TOTAL POPULATION

Question: Consider a person who believes that all blacks are genetically inferior. If such a person wanted to make a speech in your community claiming that blacks are inferior, should he be allowed to speak, or not? NOTE: Question not asked in 1972-1975, 1978, 1983, 1986.

Responses: YES = Yes, allowed to speak; NO = No, not allowed

	YEAR								
RESPONSE	'76	'77	'80	'82	'84	'85	'87	'88	'89
YES	62%	60%	63%	61%	59%	57%	62%	63%	63%
NO	38	40	37	39	41	43	38	37	37
# SURVEYED	1467	1498	1425	1460	1438	1493	1434	952	1007

TABLE II: ALLOW RACIST TO MAKE SPEECH -- BY SEX

Question: Consider a person who believes that all blacks are genetically inferior. If such a person wanted to make a speech in your community claiming that blacks are inferior, should he be allowed to speak, or not? NOTE: Question not asked in 1972-1975, 1978, 1983, 1986.

Responses: YES = Yes, allowed to speak; NO = No, not allowed

		YEAR								
SEX	RESP	'76	'77	'80	'82	'84	'85	'87	'88	'89
M	YES	66%	62%	69%	65%	65%	63%	70%	65%	67%
	NO	34	38	31	35	35	37	30	35	33
# SURVEYED		661	681	630	624	590	675	629	394	432
SEX	RESP	'76	'77	'80	'82	'84	'85	'87	'88	'89
F	YES	58%	57%	59%	58%	54%	52%	55%	61%	60%
	NO	42	43	41	42	46	48	45	39	40
# SURVEYED		806	817	795	836	848	818	805	558	575

TABLE III: ALLOW RACIST TO MAKE SPEECH -- BY RACE

Question: Consider a person who believes that all blacks are genetically inferior. If such a person wanted to make a speech in your community claiming that blacks are inferior, should he be allowed to speak, or not? NOTE: Question not asked in 1972-1975, 1978, 1983, 1986.

Responses: YES = Yes, allowed to speak; NO = No, not allowed

		YEAR								
RACE	RESP	'76	'77	'80	'82	'84	'85	'87	'88	'89
WHITE	YES	63%	61%	64%	63%	61%	59%	63%	65%	64%
	NO	37	39	36	37	39	41	37	35	36
# SURVEYED		1331	1310	1278	1280	1223	1310	1197	783	870
RACE	RESP	'76	'77	'80	'82	'84	'85	'87	'88	'89
BLACK	YES	48%	49%	54%	47%	48%	48%	56%	57%	57%
	NO	52	51	46	53	52	52	44	43	43
# SURVEYED		128	173	137	155	165	143	185	127	98
RACE	RESP	'76	'77	'80	'82	'84	'85	'87	'88	'89
OTHER	YES	88%	80%	60%	48%	44%	33%	50%	40%	51%
	NO	13	20	40	52	56	68	50	60	49
# SURVEYED		8	15	10	25	50	40	52	42	39

TABLE IV: ALLOW RACIST TO MAKE SPEECH -- BY AGE

Question: Consider a person who believes that all blacks are genetically inferior. If such a person wanted to make a speech in your community claiming that blacks are inferior, should he be allowed to speak, or not? NOTE: Question not asked in 1972-1975, 1978, 1983, 1986.

Responses: YES = Yes, allowed to speak; NO = No, not allowed

		YEAR								
AGE	RESP	'76	'77	'80	'82	'84	'85	'87	'88	'89
18-23	YES	72%	65%	63%	55%	54%	46%	50%	49%	55%
	NO	28	35	37	45	46	54	50	51	45
# SURVEYED		161	161	153	146	155	130	122	93	97
AGE	RESP	'76	'77	'80	'82	'84	'85	'87	'88	'89
24-29	YES	77%	67%	73%	67%	58%	63%	67%	63%	73%
	NO	23	33	27	33	42	37	33	37	27
# SURVEYED		225	203	200	242	230	213	190	133	115
AGE	RESP	'76	'77	'80	'82	'84	'85	'87	'88	'89
30-35	YES	72%	71%	77%	73%	72%	65%	68%	69%	69%
	NO	28	29	23	27	28	35	32	31	31
# SURVEYED		181	188	214	202	194	206	220	127	135
AGE	RESP	'76	'77	'80	'82	'84	'85	'87	'88	'89
36-41	YES	74%	68%	64%	72%	68%	66%	73%	71%	71%
	NO	26	32	36	28	32	34	27	29	29
# SURVEYED		157	164	148	144	186	181	183	131	133
AGE	RESP	'76	'77	'80	'82	'84	'85	'87	'88	'89
42-47	YES	64%	65%	70%	74%	64%	69%	66%	74%	73%
	NO	36	35	30	26	36	31	34	26	27
# SURVEYED		109	142	111	115	125	121	152	101	107
AGE	RESP	'76	'77	'80	'82	'84	'85	'87	'88	'89
48-53	YES	53%	54%	66%	60%	52%	66%	63%	53%	64%
	NO	47	46	34	40	48	34	37	47	36
# SURVEYED		130	151	119	111	100	128	122	64	94
AGE	RESP	'76	'77	'80	'82	'84	'85	'87	'88	'89
54-59	YES	56%	56%	53%	65%	53%	54%	64%	67%	64%
	NO	44	44	47	35	47	46	36	33	36
# SURVEYED		127	165	133	139	112	128	95	52	61

TABLE IV: ALLOW RACIST TO MAKE SPEECH -- BY AGE (Continued)

Question: Consider a person who believes that all blacks are genetically inferior. If such a person wanted to make a speech in your community claiming that blacks are inferior, should he be allowed to speak, or not? NOTE: Question not asked in 1972-1975, 1978, 1983, 1986.

Responses: YES = Yes, allowed to speak; NO = No, not allowed

		YEAR								
AGE	RESP	'76	'77	'80	'82	'84	'85	'87	'88	'89
60-65	YES	44%	42%	56%	49%	51%	50%	47%	58%	51%
	NO	56	58	44	51	49	50	53	42	49
# SURVEYED		130	113	116	111	111	128	100	83	73
AGE	RESP	'76	'77	'80	'82	'84	'85	'87	'88	'89
66+	YES	43%	43%	47%	39%	48%	38%	52%	55%	51%
	NO	57	57	53	61	52	62	48	45	49
# SURVEYED		241	204	222	241	219	252	245	165	189

****

BUSING AS A SOLUTION

TABLE I: BUSING AS SOLUTION -- BY TOTAL POPULATION

Question: In general, do you favor or oppose the busing of black and white school children from one district to another? NOTE: Question not asked in 1973, 1980, 1984, 1987.

Responses: FA = Favor; OP = Oppose

	YEAR											
RESPONSE	'72	'74	'75	'76	'77	'78	'82	'83	'85	'86	'88	'89
FA	20%	21%	18%	16%	17%	21%	20%	25%	23%	30%	34%	29%
OP	80	79	82	84	83	79	80	75	77	70	66	71
# SURVEYED	1544	1427	1417	1459	1482	1459	1460	1488	1479	1424	941	944

TABLE II: BUSING AS SOLUTION -- BY SEX

Question: In general, do you favor or oppose the busing of black and white school children from one district to another? NOTE: Question not asked in 1973, 1980, 1984, 1987.

Responses: FA = Favor; OP = Oppose

		YEAR											
SEX	RESP	'72	'74	'75	'76	'77	'78	'82	'83	'85	'86	'88	'89
M	FA	20%	20%	17%	16%	16%	21%	19%	22%	23%	27%	31%	26%
	OP	80	80	83	84	84	79	81	78	77	73	69	74
# SURVEYED		779	671	643	658	674	610	626	650	666	605	420	403
SEX	RESP	'72	'74	'75	'76	'77	'78	'82	'83	'85	'86	'88	'89
F	FA	20%	22%	19%	16%	17%	21%	20%	27%	22%	33%	36%	32%
	OP	80	78	81	84	83	79	80	73	78	67	64	68
# SURVEYED		765	756	774	801	808	849	834	838	813	819	521	541

TABLE III: BUSING AS SOLUTION -- BY RACE

Question: In general, do you favor or oppose the busing of black and white school children from one district to another? NOTE: Question not asked in 1973, 1980, 1984, 1987.

Responses: FA = Favor; OP = Oppose

		YEAR											
RACE	RESP	'72	'74	'75	'76	'77	'78	'82	'83	'85	'86	'88	'89
WHITE	FA	13%	15%	14%	13%	13%	17%	16%	21%	19%	25%	29%	26%
	OP	87	85	86	87	87	83	84	79	81	75	71	74
# SURVEYED		1290	1257	1257	1324	1300	1297	1281	1328	1301	1213	789	814
RACE	RESP	'72	'74	'75	'76	'77	'78	'82	'83	'85	'86	'88	'89
BLACK	FA	55%	63%	47%	52%	48%	52%	54%	56%	57%	62%	58%	54%
	OP	45	37	53	48	52	48	46	44	43	38	43	46
# SURVEYED		250	164	156	126	168	149	153	145	137	176	120	98
RACE	RESP	'72	'74	'75	'76	'77	'78	'82	'83	'85	'86	'88	'89
OTHER	FA	25%	17%	25%	33%	29%	54%	27%	27%	24%	40%	59%	47%
	OP	75	83	75	67	71	46	73	73	76	60	41	53
# SURVEYED		4	6	4	9	14	13	26	15	41	35	32	32

TABLE IV: BUSING AS SOLUTION -- BY AGE

Question: In general, do you favor or oppose the busing of black and white school children from one district to another? NOTE: Question not asked in 1973, 1980, 1984, 1987.

Responses: FA = Favor; OP = Oppose

		YEAR											
AGE	RESP	'72	'74	'75	'76	'77	'78	'82	'83	'85	'86	'88	'89
18-23	FA	30%	34%	25%	24%	19%	31%	36%	36%	37%	44%	55%	44%
	OP	70	66	75	76	81	69	64	64	63	56	45	56
# SURVEYED		161	161	163	155	161	153	138	116	130	104	93	81
AGE	RESP	'72	'74	'75	'76	'77	'78	'82	'83	'85	'86	'88	'89
24-29	FA	23%	19%	22%	17%	22%	28%	23%	31%	28%	40%	36%	43%
	OP	77	81	78	83	78	72	77	69	72	60	64	57
# SURVEYED		222	204	221	220	193	236	242	270	207	211	137	139
AGE	RESP	'72	'74	'75	'76	'77	'78	'82	'83	'85	'86	'88	'89
30-35	FA	20%	22%	22%	14%	19%	20%	17%	28%	28%	36%	42%	35%
	OP	80	78	78	86	81	80	84	72	72	64	58	65
# SURVEYED		181	173	169	184	184	219	200	222	209	218	125	137
AGE	RESP	'72	'74	'75	'76	'77	'78	'82	'83	'85	'86	'88	'89
36-41	FA	16%	20%	16%	15%	19%	22%	21%	22%	21%	29%	32%	23%
	OP	84	80	84	85	81	78	79	78	79	71	68	77
# SURVEYED		124	147	148	156	164	153	143	162	179	183	119	120
AGE	RESP	'72	'74	'75	'76	'77	'78	'82	'83	'85	'86	'88	'89
42-47	FA	20%	19%	16%	18%	13%	16%	20%	25%	12%	25%	23%	23%
	OP	80	81	84	82	87	84	80	75	88	75	77	77
# SURVEYED		178	145	139	114	144	113	116	142	118	138	103	102
AGE	RESP	'72	'74	'75	'76	'77	'78	'82	'83	'85	'86	'88	'89
48-53	FA	17%	19%	15%	9%	16%	13%	13%	16%	20%	25%	29%	28%
	OP	83	81	85	91	84	87	87	84	80	75	71	72
# SURVEYED		180	144	135	132	149	125	107	113	128	106	62	82
AGE	RESP	'72	'74	'75	'76	'77	'78	'82	'83	'85	'86	'88	'89
54-59	FA	16%	18%	10%	20%	17%	18%	11%	16%	19%	24%	33%	30%
	OP	84	82	90	80	83	82	89	84	81	76	67	70
# SURVEYED		154	134	119	126	163	136	140	123	125	98	48	67
AGE	RESP	'72	'74	'75	'76	'77	'78	'82	'83	'85	'86	'88	'89
60-65	FA	19%	20%	11%	15%	10%	14%	13%	19%	17%	16%	25%	14%
	OP	81	80	89	85	90	86	87	81	83	84	75	86
# SURVEYED		135	103	105	129	115	98	112	121	123	110	72	65

TABLE IV: BUSING AS SOLUTION -- BY AGE (Continued)

Question: In general, do you favor or oppose the busing of black and white school children from one district to another? NOTE: Question not asked in 1973, 1980, 1984, 1987.

Responses: FA = Favor; OP = Oppose

		YEAR											
AGE	RESP	'72	'74	'75	'76	'77	'78	'82	'83	'85	'86	'88	'89
66+	FA	20%	18%	19%	16%	13%	20%	21%	21%	20%	24%	30%	21%
	OP	80	82	81	84	87	80	79	79	80	76	70	79
# SURVEYED		205	210	214	238	202	220	252	214	254	249	181	148

****

SCHOOL SEGREGATION

TABLE I: SCHOOL SEGREGATION -- BY TOTAL POPULATION

Question: Do you think white students and black students should go to the same schools or separate schools? NOTE: asked of non-blacks in 1972-1977. Since 1977 it has been asked of all respondents. Question was not asked at all in 1973-1975, 1978, 1983, 1986-1989.

Responses: SM = Same schools; SP = Separate schools

	YEAR						
RESPONSE	'72	'76	'77	'80	'82	'84	'85
SM	88%	86%	87%	89%	91%	92%	93%
SP	12	14	13	11	9	8	7
# SURVEYED	1574	1457	1495	1433	1470	1437	738

TABLE II: SCHOOL SEGREGATION -- BY SEX

Question: Do you think white students and black students should go to the same schools or separate schools? NOTE: asked of non-blacks in 1972-1977. Since 1977 it has been asked of all respondents. Question was not asked at all in 1973-1975, 1978, 1983, 1986-1989.

Responses: SM = Same schools; SP = Separate schools

		YEAR						
SEX	RESP	'72	'76	'77	'80	'82	'84	'85
M	SM	90%	87%	87%	89%	91%	92%	94%
	SP	10	13	13	11	9	8	6
# SURVEYED		785	654	676	625	622	588	421

		YEAR						
SEX	RESP	'72	'76	'77	'80	'82	'84	'85
F	SM	86%	85%	87%	88%	91%	93%	92%
	SP	14	15	13	12	9	7	8
# SURVEYED		789	803	819	808	848	849	317

TABLE III: SCHOOL SEGREGATION -- BY RACE

Question: Do you think white students and black students should go to the same schools or separate schools? NOTE: asked of non-blacks in 1972-1977. Since 1977 it has been asked of all respondents. Question was not asked at all in 1973-1975, 1978, 1983, 1986-1989.

Responses: SM = Same schools; SP = Separate schools

		YEAR						
RACE	RESP	'72	'76	'77	'80	'82	'84	'85
WHITE	SM	86%	85%	86%	88%	91%	92%	93%
	SP	14	15	14	12	9	8	7
# SURVEYED		1320	1323	1309	1287	1290	1223	648
RACE	RESP	'72	'76	'77	'80	'82	'84	'85
BLACK	SM	96%	97%	93%	97%	95%	97%	97%
	SP	4	3	7	3	5	3	3
# SURVEYED		251	126	172	136	154	165	73

		YEAR						
RACE	RESP	'72	'76	'77	'80	'82	'84	'85
OTHER	SM	100%	88%	71%	100%	96%	90%	88%
	SP	0	13	29	0	4	10	12
# SURVEYED		3	8	14	10	26	49	17

TABLE IV: SCHOOL SEGREGATION -- BY AGE

Question: Do you think white students and black students should go to the same schools or separate schools? NOTE: asked of non-blacks in 1972-1977. Since 1977 it has been asked of all respondents. Question was not asked at all in 1973-1975, 1978, 1983, 1986-1989.

Responses: SM = Same schools; SP = Separate schools

YEAR								
AGE	RESP	'72	'76	'77	'80	'82	'84	'85
18-23	SM	95%	92%	91%	94%	96%	99%	100%
	SP	5	8	9	6	4	1	0
# SURVEYED		165	158	163	155	147	158	40
AGE	RESP	'72	'76	'77	'80	'82	'84	'85
24-29	SM	94%	91%	94%	94%	95%	97%	98%
	SP	6	9	7	6	5	3	2
# SURVEYED		225	222	200	200	242	229	98
AGE	RESP	'72	'76	'77	'80	'82	'84	'85
30-35	SM	88%	90%	89%	92%	97%	94%	96%
	SP	13	10	11	8	4	6	4
# SURVEYED		184	185	186	211	200	194	95
AGE	RESP	'72	'76	'77	'80	'82	'84	'85
36-41	SM	87%	87%	91%	89%	92%	94%	98%
	SP	13	13	9	11	8	6	2
# SURVEYED		126	155	163	147	144	186	98
AGE	RESP	'72	'76	'77	'80	'82	'84	'85
42-47	SM	92%	88%	86%	88%	97%	93%	91%
	SP	8	12	14	12	3	7	9
# SURVEYED		180	113	146	114	116	123	67

YEAR								
AGE	RESP	'72	'76	'77	'80	'82	'84	'85
48-53	SM	85%	78%	89%	91%	97%	96%	99%
	SP	15	22	11	9	3	4	1
# SURVEYED		186	127	149	120	108	100	72
AGE	RESP	'72	'76	'77	'80	'82	'84	'85
54-59	SM	91%	83%	87%	84%	86%	85%	86%
	SP	9	17	13	16	14	15	14
# SURVEYED		150	126	164	132	139	110	64
AGE	RESP	'72	'76	'77	'80	'82	'84	'85
60-65	SM	85%	88%	79%	87%	85%	87%	90%
	SP	15	12	21	13	15	13	10
# SURVEYED		138	130	110	118	114	109	68
AGE	RESP	'72	'76	'77	'80	'82	'84	'85
66+	SM	75%	76%	74%	80%	80%	84%	85%
	SP	25	24	26	20	20	16	15
# SURVEYED		215	236	207	228	250	222	133

****

SCHOOL WITH FEW BLACKS

TABLE I: SCHOOL WITH FEW BLACKS -- BY TOTAL POPULATION

Question: Would you yourself have any objection to sending your children to a school where a few of the children are black? NOTE: Asked of non-blacks in 1972-1977. Since 1977 it has been asked of all respondents. Question not asked in 1973, 1976, 1980, 1984, 1987.

Responses: YES; NO

	YEAR										
RESPONSE	'72	'74	'75	'77	'78	'82	'83	'85	'86	'88	'89
YES	7%	5%	7%	7%	5%	6%	5%	4%	5%	4%	4%
NO	93	95	93	93	95	94	95	96	95	96	96
# SURVEYED	1338	1288	1304	1345	1511	1490	1581	1518	1456	973	984

TABLE II: SCHOOL WITH FEW BLACKS -- BY SEX

Question: Would you yourself have any objection to sending your children to a school where a few of the children are black? NOTE: Asked of non-blacks in 1972-1977. Since 1977 it has been asked of all respondents. Question not asked in 1973, 1976, 1980, 1984, 1987.

Responses: YES; NO

		YEAR										
SEX	RESP	'72	'74	'75	'77	'78	'82	'83	'85	'86	'88	'89
M	YES	7%	5%	8%	8%	6%	7%	5%	4%	6%	6%	5%
	NO	93	95	92	92	94	93	95	96	94	94	95
# SURVEYED		668	607	592	619	635	635	686	681	615	432	418
SEX	RESP	'72	'74	'75	'77	'78	'82	'83	'85	'86	'88	'89
F	YES	7%	5%	6%	6%	4%	5%	5%	4%	4%	3%	4%
	NO	93	95	94	94	96	95	95	96	96	97	96
# SURVEYED		670	681	712	726	876	855	895	837	841	541	566

TABLE III: SCHOOL WITH FEW BLACKS -- BY RACE

Question: Would you yourself have any objection to sending your children to a school where a few of the children are black? NOTE: Asked of non-blacks in 1972-1977. Since 1977 it has been asked of all respondents. Question not asked in 1973, 1976, 1980, 1984, 1987.

Responses: YES; NO

		YEAR										
RACE	RESP	'72	'74	'75	'77	'78	'82	'83	'85	'86	'88	'89
WHITE	YES	7%	5%	7%	7%	5%	6%	5%	4%	5%	4%	4%
	NO	93	95	93	93	95	94	95	96	95	96	96
# SURVEYED		1335	1281	1300	1330	1338	1309	1402	1327	1239	817	843
RACE	RESP	'72	'74	'75	'77	'78	'82	'83	'85	'86	'88	'89
BLACK	YES	0%	0%	0%	0%	4%	4%	3%	1%	1%	2%	4%
	NO	0	0	0	0	96	96	97	99	99	98	96
# SURVEYED		000	000	000	000	158	155	163	147	180	123	102
RACE	RESP	'72	'74	'75	'77	'78	'82	'83	'85	'86	'88	'89
OTHER	YES	0%	29%	0%	7%	0%	4%	13%	9%	11%	15%	15%
	NO	100	71	100	93	100	96	88	91	89	85	85
# SURVEYED		3	7	4	15	15	26	16	44	37	33	39

TABLE IV: SCHOOL WITH FEW BLACKS -- BY AGE

Question: Would you yourself have any objection to sending your children to a school where a few of the children are black? NOTE: Asked of non-blacks in 1972-1977. Since 1977 it has been asked of all respondents. Question not asked in 1973, 1976, 1980, 1984, 1987.

Responses: YES; NO

		YEAR										
AGE	RESP	'72	'74	'75	'77	'78	'82	'83	'85	'86	'88	'89
18-23	YES	4%	4%	2%	6%	4%	4%	2%	3%	6%	3%	6%
	NO	96	96	98	94	96	96	98	97	94	97	94
# SURVEYED		134	143	154	141	163	148	128	132	108	92	83
AGE	RESP	'72	'74	'75	'77	'78	'82	'83	'85	'86	'88	'89
24-29	YES	3%	3%	4%	5%	3%	5%	5%	3%	4%	1%	4%
	NO	97	97	96	95	97	95	95	97	96	99	96
# SURVEYED		196	195	203	175	242	243	284	215	218	149	145

TABLE IV: SCHOOL WITH FEW BLACKS -- BY AGE (Continued)

Question: Would you yourself have any objection to sending your children to a school where a few of the children are black? NOTE: Asked of non-blacks in 1972-1977. Since 1977 it has been asked of all respondents. Question not asked in 1973, 1976, 1980, 1984, 1987.

Responses: YES; NO

		YEAR										
AGE	RESP	'72	'74	'75	'77	'78	'82	'83	'85	'86	'88	'89
30-35	YES	6%	4%	4%	7%	4%	4%	3%	4%	5%	3%	4%
	NO	94	96	96	93	96	96	97	96	95	97	96
# SURVEYED		159	141	150	165	226	203	235	211	220	130	141
AGE	RESP	'72	'74	'75	'77	'78	'82	'83	'85	'86	'88	'89
36-41	YES	6%	6%	8%	4%	2%	5%	5%	1%	4%	2%	2%
	NO	94	94	92	96	98	95	95	99	96	98	98
# SURVEYED		109	126	133	142	156	145	171	184	187	126	124
AGE	RESP	'72	'74	'75	'77	'78	'82	'83	'85	'86	'88	'89
42-47	YES	4%	4%	3%	9%	8%	2%	3%	5%	1%	6%	5%
	NO	96	96	97	91	92	98	97	95	99	94	95
# SURVEYED		156	135	124	135	119	119	144	124	141	107	107
AGE	RESP	'72	'74	'75	'77	'78	'82	'83	'85	'86	'88	'89
48-53	YES	11%	5%	6%	8%	5%	2%	4%	3%	9%	5%	5%
	NO	89	95	94	92	95	98	96	97	91	95	95
# SURVEYED		159	129	125	140	130	112	114	130	107	62	84
AGE	RESP	'72	'74	'75	'77	'78	'82	'83	'85	'86	'88	'89
54-59	YES	6%	7%	8%	7%	4%	6%	2%	6%	3%	2%	4%
	NO	94	93	92	93	96	94	98	94	97	98	96
# SURVEYED		129	124	112	147	135	142	133	131	97	49	70
AGE	RESP	'72	'74	'75	'77	'78	'82	'83	'85	'86	'88	'89
60-65	YES	11%	4%	7%	7%	7%	6%	8%	3%	4%	3%	3%
	NO	89	96	93	93	93	94	92	97	96	97	97
# SURVEYED		120	92	101	106	105	114	131	126	113	74	69
AGE	RESP	'72	'74	'75	'77	'78	'82	'83	'85	'86	'88	'89
66+	YES	14%	8%	17%	12%	7%	11%	10%	8%	6%	10%	6%
	NO	86	92	83	88	93	89	90	92	94	90	94
# SURVEYED		173	198	198	189	228	255	234	258	258	183	158

****

SCHOOL WITH HALF BLACKS

TABLE I: SCHOOL WITH HALF BLACKS -- BY TOTAL POPULATION

Question: Would you yourself object to sending your children to school where half the children are black? NOTE: Asked of non-blacks in 1972-1977. Since 1977 it has been asked of all respondents. Question not asked in 1973, 1976, 1980, 1984, 1987.

Responses: YES; NO

	YEAR										
RESPONSE	'72	'74	'75	'77	'78	'82	'83	'85	'86	'88	'89
YES	18%	25%	23%	19%	18%	18%	18%	17%	18%	16%	18%
NO	82	75	77	81	82	82	82	83	82	84	82
# SURVEYED	1213	1187	1183	1222	1413	1374	1476	1432	1359	921	920

TABLE II: SCHOOL WITH HALF BLACKS -- BY SEX

Question: Would you yourself object to sending your children to school where half the children are black? NOTE: Asked of non-blacks in 1972-1977. Since 1977 it has been asked of all respondents. Question not asked in 1973, 1976, 1980, 1984, 1987.

Responses: YES; NO

		YEAR										
SEX	RESP	'72	'74	'75	'77	'78	'82	'83	'85	'86	'88	'89
M	YES	17%	25%	26%	18%	17%	17%	20%	15%	18%	15%	17%
	NO	83	75	74	82	83	83	80	85	82	85	83
# SURVEYED		612	563	527	558	590	584	638	644	568	404	386
SEX	RESP	'72	'74	'75	'77	'78	'82	'83	'85	'86	'88	'89
F	YES	18%	25%	21%	20%	19%	18%	17%	18%	18%	17%	18%
	NO	82	75	79	80	81	82	83	82	82	83	82
# SURVEYED		601	624	656	664	823	790	838	788	791	517	534

TABLE III: SCHOOL WITH HALF BLACKS -- BY RACE

Question: Would you yourself object to sending your children to school where half the children are black? NOTE: Asked of non-blacks in 1972-1977. Since 1977 it has been asked of all respondents. Question not asked in 1973, 1976, 1980, 1984, 1987.

Responses: YES; NO

		YEAR										
RACE	RESP	'72	'74	'75	'77	'78	'82	'83	'85	'86	'88	'89
WHITE	YES	18%	25%	23%	19%	20%	19%	20%	19%	21%	18%	20%
	NO	82	75	77	81	80	81	80	81	79	82	80
# SURVEYED		1210	1182	1179	1208	1246	1201	1304	1248	1150	773	792
RACE	RESP	'72	'74	'75	'77	'78	'82	'83	'85	'86	'88	'89
BLACK	YES	0%	0%	0%	0%	5%	9%	2%	1%	2%	3%	5%
	NO	0	0	0	0	95	91	98	99	98	97	95
# SURVEYED		000	000	000	000	152	148	158	144	178	121	97
RACE	RESP	'72	'74	'75	'77	'78	'82	'83	'85	'86	'88	'89
OTHER	YES	33%	20%	50%	29%	13%	20%	21%	10%	16%	22%	6%
	NO	67	80	50	71	87	80	79	90	84	78	94
# SURVEYED		3	5	4	14	15	25	14	40	31	27	31

TABLE IV: SCHOOL WITH HALF BLACKS -- BY AGE

Question: Would you yourself object to sending your children to school where half the children are black? NOTE: Asked of non-blacks in 1972-1977. Since 1977 it has been asked of all respondents. Question not asked in 1973, 1976, 1980, 1984, 1987.

Responses: YES; NO

		YEAR										
AGE	RESP	'72	'74	'75	'77	'78	'82	'83	'85	'86	'88	'89
18-23	YES	12%	16%	17%	14%	14%	17%	14%	6%	16%	10%	18%
	NO	88	84	83	86	86	83	86	94	84	90	82
# SURVEYED		130	136	145	131	157	138	124	129	100	90	77
AGE	RESP	'72	'74	'75	'77	'78	'82	'83	'85	'86	'88	'89
24-29	YES	12%	20%	19%	15%	16%	16%	17%	17%	16%	12%	15%
	NO	88	80	81	85	84	84	83	83	84	88	85
# SURVEYED		185	183	192	164	232	227	267	204	207	143	137

TABLE IV: SCHOOL WITH HALF BLACKS -- BY AGE (Continued)

Question: Would you yourself object to sending your children to school where half the children are black? NOTE: Asked of non-blacks in 1972-1977. Since 1977 it has been asked of all respondents. Question not asked in 1973, 1976, 1980, 1984, 1987.

Responses: YES; NO

		YEAR										
AGE	RESP	'72	'74	'75	'77	'78	'82	'83	'85	'86	'88	'89
30-35	YES	19%	26%	17%	13%	20%	20%	18%	13%	18%	14%	13%
	NO	81	74	83	87	80	80	82	87	82	86	87
# SURVEYED		146	133	139	149	214	194	225	203	203	125	132
AGE	RESP	'72	'74	'75	'77	'78	'82	'83	'85	'86	'88	'89
36-41	YES	18%	28%	31%	21%	22%	16%	21%	16%	13%	17%	15%
	NO	82	72	69	79	78	84	79	84	87	83	85
# SURVEYED		102	114	121	135	153	135	160	178	178	121	119
AGE	RESP	'72	'74	'75	'77	'78	'82	'83	'85	'86	'88	'89
42-47	YES	18%	23%	21%	23%	18%	14%	19%	15%	16%	18%	20%
	NO	82	77	79	78	82	86	81	85	84	82	80
# SURVEYED		146	122	117	120	107	115	134	116	135	101	101
AGE	RESP	'72	'74	'75	'77	'78	'82	'83	'85	'86	'88	'89
48-53	YES	18%	34%	25%	18%	16%	12%	22%	21%	20%	10%	14%
	NO	82	66	75	82	84	88	78	79	80	90	86
# SURVEYED		138	120	114	128	122	107	110	124	95	59	79
AGE	RESP	'72	'74	'75	'77	'78	'82	'83	'85	'86	'88	'89
54-59	YES	13%	29%	29%	20%	17%	23%	19%	24%	14%	30%	19%
	NO	87	71	71	80	83	77	81	76	86	70	81
# SURVEYED		118	110	95	133	125	128	127	122	92	47	64
AGE	RESP	'72	'74	'75	'77	'78	'82	'83	'85	'86	'88	'89
60-65	YES	24%	27%	31%	26%	25%	14%	13%	19%	21%	19%	25%
	NO	76	73	69	74	75	86	87	81	79	81	75
# SURVEYED		104	85	93	97	96	101	119	120	107	69	64
AGE	RESP	'72	'74	'75	'77	'78	'82	'83	'85	'86	'88	'89
66+	YES	30%	26%	25%	25%	18%	23%	20%	19%	25%	21%	23%
	NO	70	74	75	75	83	77	80	81	75	79	77
# SURVEYED		141	179	164	161	200	222	206	230	237	165	144

****

SCHOOLS WITH MOSTLY BLACKS

TABLE I: SCHOOL WITH MOSTLY BLACKS -- BY TOTAL POPULATION

Question: Would you yourself object to sending your children to a school where more than half the children are black? NOTE: Asked of non-blacks in 1972-1977. Since 1977 it has been asked of all respondents. Question not asked in 1973, 1976, 1980, 1984, 1987.

Responses: YES; NO

	YEAR										
RESPONSE	'72	'74	'75	'77	'78	'82	'83	'85	'86	'88	'89
YES	42%	47%	45%	47%	38%	40%	45%	42%	43%	39%	42%
NO	58	53	55	53	62	60	55	58	57	61	58
# SURVEYED	963	861	887	970	1130	1099	1175	1164	1103	750	743

TABLE II: SCHOOL WITH MOSTLY BLACKS -- BY SEX

Question: Would you yourself object to sending your children to a school where more than half the children are black? NOTE: Asked of non-blacks in 1972-1977. Since 1977 it has been asked of all respondents. Question not asked in 1973, 1976, 1980, 1984, 1987.

Responses: YES; NO

		YEAR										
SEX	RESP	'72	'74	'75	'77	'78	'82	'83	'85	'86	'88	'89
M	YES	37%	43%	41%	44%	33%	41%	44%	39%	44%	38%	41%
	NO	63	57	59	56	67	59	56	61	56	62	59
# SURVEYED		489	408	383	448	477	470	503	532	464	335	318
SEX	RESP	'72	'74	'75	'77	'78	'82	'83	'85	'86	'88	'89
F	YES	47%	51%	47%	49%	41%	39%	45%	44%	43%	39%	43%
	NO	53	49	53	51	59	61	55	56	57	61	57
# SURVEYED		474	453	504	522	653	629	672	632	639	415	425

TABLE III: SCHOOL WITH MOSTLY BLACKS -- BY RACE

Question: Would you yourself object to sending your children to a school where more than half the children are black? NOTE: Asked of non-blacks in 1972-1977. Since 1977 it has been asked of all respondents. Question not asked in 1973, 1976, 1980, 1984, 1987.

Responses: YES; NO

		YEAR										
RACE	RESP	'72	'74	'75	'77	'78	'82	'83	'85	'86	'88	'89
WHITE	YES	42%	47%	45%	47%	43%	44%	50%	48%	51%	45%	47%
	NO	58	53	55	53	57	56	50	52	49	55	53
# SURVEYED		961	857	886	960	979	946	1012	987	906	612	625
RACE	RESP	'72	'74	'75	'77	'78	'82	'83	'85	'86	'88	'89
BLACK	YES	0%	0%	0%	0%	7%	14%	11%	6%	5%	8%	13%
	NO	0	0	0	0	93	86	89	94	95	92	88
# SURVEYED		000	000	000	000	138	133	153	142	170	116	88
RACE	RESP	'72	'74	'75	'77	'78	'82	'83	'85	'86	'88	'89
OTHER	YES	0%	0%	100%	40%	8%	20%	30%	23%	41%	32%	27%
	NO	100	100	0	60	92	80	70	77	59	68	73
# SURVEYED		2	4	1	10	13	20	10	35	27	22	30

TABLE IV: SCHOOL WITH MOSTLY BLACKS -- BY AGE

Question: Would you yourself object to sending your children to a school where more than half the children are black? NOTE: Asked of non-blacks in 1972-1977. Since 1977 it has been asked of all respondents. Question not asked in 1973, 1976, 1980, 1984, 1987.

Responses: YES; NO

		YEAR										
AGE	RESP	'72	'74	'75	'77	'78	'82	'83	'85	'86	'88	'89
18-23	YES	31%	48%	45%	46%	33%	35%	46%	44%	41%	37%	34%
	NO	69	52	55	54	67	65	54	56	59	63	66
# SURVEYED		108	110	121	112	131	112	104	119	82	79	62
AGE	RESP	'72	'74	'75	'77	'78	'82	'83	'85	'86	'88	'89
24-29	YES	44%	50%	46%	36%	35%	39%	49%	44%	43%	41%	37%
	NO	56	50	54	64	65	61	51	56	57	59	63
# SURVEYED		154	142	151	133	193	186	213	166	171	121	114

TABLE IV: SCHOOL WITH MOSTLY BLACKS -- BY AGE (Continued)

Question: Would you yourself object to sending your children to a school where more than half the children are black? NOTE: Asked of non-blacks in 1972-1977. Since 1977 it has been asked of all respondents. Question not asked in 1973, 1976, 1980, 1984, 1987.

Responses: YES; NO

		YEAR										
AGE	RESP	'72	'74	'75	'77	'78	'82	'83	'85	'86	'88	'89
30-35	YES	48%	40%	55%	46%	39%	45%	43%	39%	45%	42%	46%
	NO	52	60	45	54	61	55	57	61	55	58	54
# SURVEYED		116	94	114	129	167	150	183	172	168	105	114
AGE	RESP	'72	'74	'75	'77	'78	'82	'83	'85	'86	'88	'89
36-41	YES	41%	52%	51%	52%	42%	37%	40%	39%	51%	40%	43%
	NO	59	48	49	48	58	63	60	61	49	60	57
# SURVEYED		83	79	81	104	116	113	120	147	150	100	97
AGE	RESP	'72	'74	'75	'77	'78	'82	'83	'85	'86	'88	'89
42-47	YES	38%	49%	44%	42%	40%	44%	55%	43%	44%	39%	38%
	NO	62	51	56	58	60	56	45	57	56	61	62
# SURVEYED		114	93	87	92	82	96	107	97	114	80	78
AGE	RESP	'72	'74	'75	'77	'78	'82	'83	'85	'86	'88	'89
48-53	YES	51%	54%	46%	47%	41%	40%	49%	44%	35%	35%	52%
	NO	49	46	54	53	59	60	51	56	65	65	48
# SURVEYED		110	79	87	102	98	89	85	94	75	51	67
AGE	RESP	'72	'74	'75	'77	'78	'82	'83	'85	'86	'88	'89
54-59	YES	36%	46%	36%	52%	38%	45%	43%	39%	35%	26%	39%
	NO	64	54	64	48	62	55	57	61	65	74	61
# SURVEYED		100	79	66	107	105	100	100	87	80	31	54
AGE	RESP	'72	'74	'75	'77	'78	'82	'83	'85	'86	'88	'89
60-65	YES	47%	50%	38%	63%	40%	43%	45%	41%	46%	26%	45%
	NO	53	50	62	38	60	57	55	59	54	74	55
# SURVEYED		78	60	63	72	72	84	100	96	84	54	44
AGE	RESP	'72	'74	'75	'77	'78	'82	'83	'85	'86	'88	'89
66+	YES	38%	39%	38%	44%	35%	31%	36%	44%	43%	44%	43%
	NO	62	61	62	56	65	69	64	56	57	56	57
# SURVEYED		98	122	114	114	162	162	160	183	174	128	112

****

GOVERNMENT HELP FOR BLACKS

TABLE I: GOVERNMENT HELP FOR BLACKS -- BY TOTAL POPULATION

Question: Some people think that blacks have been discriminated against for so long that the government has a special obligation to help improve their living standards. These people are at point 1 on a scale of 1 to 5. Others believe that the government should not be giving special treatment to blacks. These people are at point 5 on the scale of 1 to 5. Where would you place yourself on the scale, or haven't you made up your mind on this? NOTE: Question not asked in 1972-1974, 1976-1982, 1985.

Responses: 1 = Government help 3 = Agree with both 5 = No special treatment

	YEAR						
RESPONSE	'75	'83	'84	'86	'87	'88	'89
1	17%	8%	10%	8%	10%	8%	9%
2	9	10	10	10	11	10	10
3	21	27	31	29	29	30	28
4	12	21	18	18	18	18	19
5	41	35	31	34	32	35	34
# SURVEYED	1448	1526	1399	1427	1422	963	997

TABLE II: GOVERNMENT HELP FOR BLACKS -- BY SEX

Question: Some people think that blacks have been discriminated against for so long that the government has a special obligation to help improve their living standards. These people are at point 1 on a scale of 1 to 5. Others believe that the government should not be giving special treatment to blacks. These people are at point 5 on the scale of 1 to 5. Where would you place yourself on the scale, or haven't you made up your mind on this? NOTE: Question not asked in 1972-1974, 1976-1982, 1985.

Responses: 1 = Government help 3 = Agree with both 5 = No special treatment

		YEAR						
SEX	RESP	'75	'83	'84	'86	'87	'88	'89
MALE	1	16%	7%	11%	7%	9%	7%	8%
	2	9	8	10	13	12	9	10
	3	19	26	27	25	28	30	27
	4	13	22	18	20	18	17	22
	5	42	37	34	35	32	37	33
# SURVEYED		660	665	578	607	622	425	430

		YEAR						
SEX	RESP	'75	'83	'84	'86	'87	'88	'89
FEMALE	1	17%	8%	9%	10%	11%	8%	10%
	2	8	11	10	8	9	11	10
	3	24	27	34	33	30	29	29
	4	11	21	18	17	18	19	17
	5	40	33	29	34	32	33	35
# SURVEYED		788	861	821	820	800	538	567

TABLE III: GOVERNMENT HELP FOR BLACKS -- BY RACE

Question: Some people think that blacks have been discriminated against for so long that the government has a special obligation to help improve their living standards. These people are at point 1 on a scale of 1 to 5. Others believe that the government should not be giving special treatment to blacks. These people are at point 5 on the scale of 1 to 5. Where would you place yourself on the scale, or haven't you made up your mind on this? NOTE: Question not asked in 1972-1974, 1976-1982, 1985.

Responses: 1 = Government help   3 = Agree with both   5 = No special treatment

RACE	RESP	'75	'83	'84	'86	'87	'88	'89
WHITE	1	11%	4%	6%	4%	6%	3%	6%
	2	9	9	9	9	10	9	8
	3	22	26	31	29	29	29	27
	4	13	23	20	20	20	19	21
	5	45	38	35	38	35	39	37
# SURVEYED		1287	1358	1189	1217	1182	811	851
BLACK	1	59%	39%	34%	39%	40%	37%	33%
	2	10	18	19	17	17	22	21
	3	16	30	39	32	26	30	29
	4	6	4	4	5	5	5	7
	5	10	9	4	7	12	6	10
# SURVEYED		157	152	161	175	188	111	106

RACE	RESP	'75	'83	'84	'86	'87	'88	'89
OTHER	1	25%	19%	20%	9%	10%	12%	8%
	2	0	13	8	14	10	10	13
	3	0	38	27	43	37	41	33
	4	0	13	16	11	12	20	10
	5	75	19	29	23	33	17	38
# SURVEYED		4	16	49	35	52	41	40

TABLE IV: GOVERNMENT HELP FOR BLACKS -- BY AGE

Question: Some people think that blacks have been discriminated against for so long that the government has a special obligation to help improve their living standards. These people are at point 1 on a scale of 1 to 5. Others believe that the government should not be giving special treatment to blacks. These people are at point 5 on the scale of 1 to 5. Where would you place yourself on the scale, or haven't you made up your mind on this? NOTE: Question not asked in 1972-1974, 1976-1982, 1985.

Responses: 1 = Government help   3 = Agree with both   5 = No special treatment

AGE	RESP	'75	'83	'84	'86	'87	'88	'89
18-23	1	18%	9%	8%	9%	15%	10%	15%
	2	8	15	16	11	18	12	15
	3	29	28	33	32	21	26	27
	4	19	20	20	18	16	28	17
	5	27	28	24	29	30	25	27
# SURVEYED		171	123	153	106	122	93	89

AGE	RESP	'75	'83	'84	'86	'87	'88	'89
24-29	1	18%	6%	11%	10%	11%	6%	7%
	2	8	11	6	11	14	13	15
	3	22	24	27	26	30	37	27
	4	15	25	24	23	19	20	25
	5	38	33	32	29	25	24	26
# SURVEYED		226	282	223	214	190	142	138

TABLE IV: GOVERNMENT HELP FOR BLACKS -- BY AGE (Continued)

Question: Some people think that blacks have been discriminated against for so long that the government has a special obligation to help improve their living standards. These people are at point 1 on a scale of 1 to 5. Others believe that the government should not be giving special treatment to blacks. These people are at point 5 on the scale of 1 to 5. Where would you place yourself on the scale, or haven't you made up your mind on this? NOTE: Question not asked in 1972-1974, 1976-1982, 1985.

Responses: 1 = Government help 3 = Agree with both 5 = No special treatment

		YEAR						
AGE	RESP	'75	'83	'84	'86	'87	'88	'89
30-35	1	16%	10%	10%	6%	7%	9%	8%
	2	13	11	12	11	10	11	12
	3	18	23	24	33	29	26	28
	4	11	23	22	24	23	21	23
	5	42	34	32	27	30	33	29
# SURVEYED		166	229	187	217	214	124	139
AGE	RESP	'75	'83	'84	'86	'87	'88	'89
36-41	1	15%	6%	7%	7%	6%	9%	11%
	2	5	11	10	9	13	11	11
	3	23	28	31	30	29	28	26
	4	13	17	19	17	23	17	21
	5	42	38	33	36	28	36	31
# SURVEYED		149	167	178	184	180	120	129
AGE	RESP	'75	'83	'84	'86	'87	'88	'89
42-47	1	15%	6%	12%	6%	10%	13%	7%
	2	10	7	8	12	8	11	11
	3	15	25	34	23	28	27	28
	4	13	32	13	24	19	15	17
	5	46	29	33	35	35	35	37
# SURVEYED		142	142	120	139	154	101	103
AGE	RESP	'75	'83	'84	'86	'87	'88	'89
48-53	1	16%	4%	9%	11%	10%	2%	6%
	2	6	11	14	7	7	15	5
	3	23	25	30	32	31	27	29
	4	12	19	16	15	17	18	17
	5	42	42	32	36	35	38	42
# SURVEYED		141	112	101	104	121	55	95

		YEAR						
AGE	RESP	'75	'83	'84	'86	'87	'88	'89
54-59	1	12%	7%	7%	6%	13%	12%	11%
	2	8	7	6	14	7	8	8
	3	26	29	39	29	24	34	21
	4	10	15	19	12	20	11	16
	5	44	42	29	39	36	35	44
# SURVEYED		124	127	112	93	96	65	62
AGE	RESP	'75	'83	'84	'86	'87	'88	'89
60-65	1	14%	10%	8%	7%	12%	3%	8%
	2	8	7	8	8	8	4	3
	3	16	33	33	35	31	29	35
	4	13	20	12	18	11	13	20
	5	49	30	40	33	38	51	34
# SURVEYED		113	124	104	113	98	78	71
AGE	RESP	'75	'83	'84	'86	'87	'88	'89
66+	1	21%	12%	13%	10%	12%	5%	9%
	2	10	8	8	7	8	8	6
	3	20	28	37	28	35	31	29
	4	5	16	12	11	11	16	14
	5	43	36	30	44	34	40	41
# SURVEYED		211	214	215	250	242	182	169

****

OBJECT TO BLACK DINNER GUEST

TABLE I: OBJECT TO BLACK DINNER GUEST -- BY TOTAL POPULATION

Question: How strongly would you object if a member of your family wanted to bring a black friend home to dinner? Would you object strongly, mildly, or not at all? NOTE: Asked of non-blacks in 1972-1977. Since 1977 it has been Asked of all respondents. Question not asked in 1975, 1978, 1983, 1986-1989.

Responses: SO = Strongly; MO = Mildly; NO = Not at all

	YEAR								
RESPONSE	'72	'73	'74	'76	'77	'80	'82	'84	'85
SO	13%	16%	11%	13%	12%	10%	9%	6%	10%
MO	16	15	16	15	17	13	11	11	11
NO	71	69	73	72	72	77	80	83	80
# SURVEYED	1318	1292	1288	1332	1333	1444	1484	1450	743

TABLE II: OBJECT TO BLACK DINNER GUEST -- BY SEX

Question: How strongly would you object if a member of your family wanted to bring a black friend home to dinner? Would you object strongly, mildly, or not at all? NOTE: Asked of non-blacks in 1972-1977. Since 1977 it has been asked of all respondents. Question not asked in 1975, 1978, 1983, 1986-1989.

Responses: SO = Strongly; MO = Mildly; NO = Not at all

		YEAR								
SEX	RESP	'72	'73	'74	'76	'77	'80	'82	'84	'85
M	SO	15%	19%	10%	13%	12%	12%	10%	7%	10%
	MO	16	15	15	15	15	15	11	11	12
	NO	70	66	75	72	72	74	79	82	79
# SURVEYED		661	605	607	583	614	632	631	593	426
SEX	RESP	'72	'73	'74	'76	'77	'80	'82	'84	'85
F	SO	12%	13%	12%	13%	11%	9%	8%	6%	10%
	MO	16	15	16	14	18	12	11	11	9
	NO	73	72	72	72	71	79	81	83	81
# SURVEYED		657	687	681	749	719	812	853	857	317

TABLE III: OBJECT TO BLACK DINNER GUEST -- BY RACE

Question: How strongly would you object if a member of your family wanted to bring a black friend home to dinner? Would you object strongly, mildly, or not at all? NOTE: Asked of non-blacks in 1972-1977. Since 1977 it has been asked of all respondents. Question not asked in 1975, 1978, 1983, 1986-1989.

Responses: SO = Strongly; MO = Mildly; NO = Not at all

		YEAR								
RACE	RESP	'72	'73	'74	'76	'77	'80	'82	'84	'85
WHITE	SO	13%	16%	11%	13%	12%	11%	10%	7%	11%
	MO	16	15	16	15	17	14	12	12	12
	NO	71	69	73	72	72	74	78	81	77
# SURVEYED		1315	1279	1281	1324	1318	1295	1301	1231	653
RACE	RESP	'72	'73	'74	'76	'77	'80	'82	'84	'85
BLACK	SO	0%	0%	0%	0%	0%	3%	1%	1%	1%
	MO	0	0	0	0	0	1	6	3	1
	NO	0	0	0	0	0	96	94	96	97
# SURVEYED		000	000	000	000	000	140	156	168	73
RACE	RESP	'72	'73	'74	'76	'77	'80	'82	'84	'85
OTHER	SO	0%	8%	14%	0%	0%	0%	0%	4%	6%
	MO	33	8	14	13	7	11	11	16	0
	NO	67	85	71	88	93	89	89	80	94
# SURVEYED		3	13	7	8	15	9	27	51	17

TABLE IV: OBJECT TO BLACK DINNER GUEST -- BY AGE

Question: How strongly would you object if a member of your family wanted to bring a black friend home to dinner? Would you object strongly, mildly, or not at all? NOTE: Asked of non-blacks in 1972-1977. Since 1977 it has been asked of all respondents. Question not asked in 1975, 1978, 1983, 1986-1989.

Responses: SO = Strongly; MO = Mildly; NO = Not at all

		YEAR								
AGE	RESP	'72	'73	'74	'76	'77	'80	'82	'84	'85
18-23	SO	7%	11%	6%	8%	6%	8%	5%	4%	3%
	MO	13	18	13	12	11	8	8	5	8
	NO	80	71	81	79	84	84	87	91	90
# SURVEYED		136	151	139	146	140	155	146	158	40

TABLE IV: OBJECT TO BLACK DINNER GUEST -- BY AGE (Continued)

Question: How strongly would you object if a member of your family wanted to bring a black friend home to dinner? Would you object strongly, mildly, or not at all? NOTE: Asked of non-blacks in 1972-1977. Since 1977 it has been asked of all respondents. Question not asked in 1975, 1978, 1983, 1986-1989.

Responses: SO = Strongly; MO = Mildly; NO = Not at all

		YEAR								
AGE	RESP	'72	'73	'74	'76	'77	'80	'82	'84	'85
24-29	SO	9%	10%	5%	6%	8%	8%	6%	5%	4%
	MO	15	13	14	14	15	11	10	6	13
	NO	76	77	81	80	77	80	84	89	83
# SURVEYED		195	189	195	197	173	201	241	232	98
AGE	RESP	'72	'73	'74	'76	'77	'80	'82	'84	'85
30-35	SO	13%	16%	10%	10%	7%	6%	6%	6%	13%
	MO	19	19	13	14	13	7	5	6	5
	NO	68	65	76	77	79	88	89	88	82
# SURVEYED		154	141	144	166	165	212	203	197	96
AGE	RESP	'72	'73	'74	'76	'77	'80	'82	'84	'85
36-41	SO	13%	12%	13%	13%	11%	11%	10%	7%	7%
	MO	14	15	10	16	14	11	12	9	11
	NO	72	72	77	71	76	78	77	84	82
# SURVEYED		104	149	128	139	140	149	145	186	99
AGE	RESP	'72	'73	'74	'76	'77	'80	'82	'84	'85
42-47	SO	12%	22%	7%	13%	17%	14%	7%	6%	7%
	MO	14	10	20	14	18	12	11	14	6
	NO	74	68	72	74	65	74	82	81	87
# SURVEYED		152	130	134	103	133	114	119	125	67
AGE	RESP	'72	'73	'74	'76	'77	'80	'82	'84	'85
48-53	SO	16%	18%	13%	18%	12%	11%	5%	8%	8%
	MO	19	11	22	15	16	18	12	16	9
	NO	65	70	64	67	73	72	83	76	82
# SURVEYED		155	122	129	118	139	120	111	102	74
AGE	RESP	'72	'73	'74	'76	'77	'80	'82	'84	'85
54-59	SO	10%	11%	15%	16%	11%	13%	16%	4%	11%
	MO	19	17	15	13	17	19	10	15	17
	NO	71	73	70	71	72	68	74	81	72
# SURVEYED		130	133	125	112	147	134	142	112	64

TABLE IV: OBJECT TO BLACK DINNER GUEST -- BY AGE (Continued)

Question: How strongly would you object if a member of your family wanted to bring a black friend home to dinner? Would you object strongly, mildly, or not at all? NOTE: Asked of non-blacks in 1972-1977. Since 1977 it has been asked of all respondents. Question not asked in 1975, 1978, 1983, 1986-1989.

Responses: SO = Strongly; MO = Mildly; NO = Not at all

		YEAR								
AGE	RESP	'72	'73	'74	'76	'77	'80	'82	'84	'85
60-65	SO	15%	18%	13%	12%	18%	10%	14%	9%	15%
	MO	11	16	13	12	22	19	17	15	7
	NO	74	66	73	76	60	71	69	76	78
# SURVEYED		116	107	89	116	107	116	113	111	67
AGE	RESP	'72	'73	'74	'76	'77	'80	'82	'84	'85
66+	SO	22%	24%	16%	22%	18%	14%	13%	9%	15%
	MO	15	17	20	19	22	17	15	19	15
	NO	63	59	65	60	60	69	72	72	70
# SURVEYED		173	167	200	230	184	234	254	222	135

****

HAD BLACK GUEST

TABLE I: HAD BLACK GUEST -- BY TOTAL POPULATION

Question: During the last few years, has anyone in your family brought a friend who was a black home to dinner? NOTE: Asked of non-blacks in 1972-1977. Since 1977 it has been asked of all respondents. Question not asked in 1972, 1975, 1978, 1983, 1986.

Responses: YES; NO

	YEAR										
RESPONSE	'73	'74	'76	'77	'80	'82	'84	'85	'87	'88	'89
YES	20%	23%	23%	23%	29%	30%	31%	29%	31%	32%	30%
NO	80	77	77	77	71	70	69	71	69	68	70
# SURVEYED	1310	1300	1360	1348	1458	1496	1463	1521	1454	967	1023

TABLE II: HAD BLACK GUEST -- BY SEX

Question: During the last few years, has anyone in your family brought a friend who was a black home to dinner? NOTE: Asked of non-blacks in 1972-1977. Since 1977 it has been asked of all respondents. Question not asked in 1972, 1975, 1978, 1983, 1986.

Responses: YES; NO

		YEAR										
SEX	RESP	'73	'74	'76	'77	'80	'82	'84	'85	'87	'88	'89
M	YES	19%	23%	24%	23%	27%	30%	31%	30%	30%	30%	27%
	NO	81	77	76	77	73	70	69	70	70	70	73
# SURVEYED		614	613	600	622	635	635	595	682	637	396	442
SEX	RESP	'73	'74	'76	'77	'80	'82	'84	'85	'87	'88	'89
F	YES	21%	22%	22%	23%	30%	30%	31%	29%	31%	34%	32%
	NO	79	78	78	77	70	70	69	71	69	66	68
# SURVEYED		696	687	760	726	823	861	868	839	817	571	581

TABLE III: HAD BLACK GUEST -- BY RACE

Question: During the last few years, has anyone in your family brought a friend who was a black home to dinner? NOTE: Asked of non-blacks in 1972-1977. Since 1977 it has been asked of all respondents. Question not asked in 1972, 1975, 1978, 1983, 1986.

Responses: YES; NO

		YEAR										
RACE	RESP	'73	'74	'76	'77	'80	'82	'84	'85	'87	'88	'89
WHITE	YES	20%	23%	23%	23%	26%	27%	27%	27%	27%	28%	27%
	NO	80	77	77	77	74	73	73	73	73	72	73
# SURVEYED		1297	1293	1352	1333	1311	1314	1242	1328	1215	794	882
RACE	RESP	'73	'74	'76	'77	'80	'82	'84	'85	'87	'88	'89
BLACK	YES	0%	0%	0%	0%	52%	49%	60%	43%	55%	61%	49%
	NO	0	0	0	0	48	51	40	57	45	39	51
# SURVEYED		000	000	000	000	138	155	169	149	187	131	101
RACE	RESP	'73	'74	'76	'77	'80	'82	'84	'85	'87	'88	'89
OTHER	YES	38%	14%	63%	20%	33%	52%	31%	43%	35%	31%	38%
	NO	62	86	38	80	67	48	69	57	65	69	63
# SURVEYED		13	7	8	15	9	27	52	44	52	42	40

TABLE IV: HAD BLACK GUEST -- BY AGE

Question: During the last few years, has anyone in your family brought a friend who was a black home to dinner? NOTE: Asked of non-blacks in 1972-1977. Since 1977 it has been asked of all respondents. Question not asked in 1972, 1975, 1978, 1983, 1986.

Responses: YES; NO

		YEAR										
AGE	RESP	'73	'74	'76	'77	'80	'82	'84	'85	'87	'88	'89
18-23	YES	25%	29%	31%	28%	34%	41%	38%	39%	47%	36%	39%
	NO	75	71	69	72	66	59	62	61	53	64	61
# SURVEYED		151	143	147	140	153	147	157	133	124	95	96
AGE	RESP	'73	'74	'76	'77	'80	'82	'84	'85	'87	'88	'89
24-29	YES	26%	32%	35%	33%	37%	34%	36%	32%	41%	33%	37%
	NO	74	68	65	67	63	66	64	68	59	67	63
# SURVEYED		191	194	201	175	201	244	232	214	192	133	115
AGE	RESP	'73	'74	'76	'77	'80	'82	'84	'85	'87	'88	'89
30-35	YES	20%	26%	27%	28%	37%	41%	35%	36%	38%	46%	35%
	NO	80	74	73	72	63	59	65	64	62	54	65
# SURVEYED		143	144	171	165	213	204	198	212	219	129	135
AGE	RESP	'73	'74	'76	'77	'80	'82	'84	'85	'87	'88	'89
36-41	YES	23%	27%	31%	25%	31%	32%	33%	38%	37%	41%	40%
	NO	77	73	69	75	69	68	67	62	63	59	60
# SURVEYED		149	128	143	142	150	146	186	183	185	129	134
AGE	RESP	'73	'74	'76	'77	'80	'82	'84	'85	'87	'88	'89
42-47	YES	28%	23%	26%	22%	31%	37%	37%	33%	32%	43%	32%
	NO	72	77	74	78	69	63	63	67	68	57	68
# SURVEYED		131	136	107	136	116	119	126	124	157	101	106
AGE	RESP	'73	'74	'76	'77	'80	'82	'84	'85	'87	'88	'89
48-53	YES	17%	20%	18%	24%	33%	32%	34%	31%	33%	34%	30%
	NO	83	80	82	76	67	68	66	69	67	66	70
# SURVEYED		128	132	122	140	122	112	101	130	126	64	93
AGE	RESP	'73	'74	'76	'77	'80	'82	'84	'85	'87	'88	'89
54-59	YES	20%	17%	19%	20%	20%	24%	27%	20%	23%	34%	33%
	NO	80	83	81	80	80	76	73	80	77	66	67
# SURVEYED		136	122	116	147	136	142	113	133	98	53	63

TABLE IV: HAD BLACK GUEST -- BY AGE (Continued)

Question: During the last few years, has anyone in your family brought a friend who was a black home to dinner? NOTE: Asked of non-blacks in 1972-1977. Since 1977 it has been asked of all respondents. Question not asked in 1972, 1975, 1978, 1983, 1986.

Responses: YES; NO

		YEAR										
AGE	RESP	'73	'74	'76	'77	'80	'82	'84	'85	'87	'88	'89
60-65	YES	11%	14%	10%	20%	17%	19%	23%	21%	14%	20%	21%
	NO	89	86	90	80	83	81	77	79	86	80	79
# SURVEYED		108	92	119	107	119	116	113	127	100	84	77
AGE	RESP	'73	'74	'76	'77	'80	'82	'84	'85	'87	'88	'89
66+	YES	8%	12%	7%	9%	18%	14%	16%	16%	10%	12%	11%
	NO	92	88	93	91	82	86	84	84	90	88	89
# SURVEYED		170	204	229	191	239	256	231	258	249	176	201

****

INTERRACIAL MARRIAGES

TABLE I: INTERRACIAL MARRIAGES -- BY TOTAL POPULATION

Question: Do you think there should be laws against marriages between blacks and whites? NOTE: Asked of non-blacks in 1972-1977. Since 1977 it has been Asked of all respondents. Question not asked in 1978, 1983, 1986.

Responses: YES; NO

	YEAR												
RESPONSE	'72	'73	'74	'75	'76	'77	'80	'82	'84	'85	'87	'88	'89
YES	39%	38%	35%	39%	33%	28%	30%	30%	25%	26%	24%	23%	21%
NO	61	62	65	61	67	72	70	70	75	74	76	77	79
# SURVEYED	1309	1289	1280	1292	1330	1327	1427	1462	1383	1486	1422	945	1004

TABLE II: INTERRACIAL MARRIAGES -- BY SEX

Question: Do you think there should be laws against marriages between blacks and whites? NOTE: Asked of non-blacks in 1972-1977. Since 1977 it has been asked of all respondents. Question not asked in 1978, 1983, 1986.

Responses: YES; NO

		YEAR												
SEX	RESP	'72	'73	'74	'75	'76	'77	'80	'82	'84	'85	'87	'88	'89
M	YES	36%	38%	32%	38%	29%	27%	28%	28%	23%	26%	21%	21%	20%
	NO	64	62	68	62	71	73	72	72	77	74	79	79	80
# SURVEYED		655	606	607	588	590	614	629	622	566	671	626	387	434
SEX	RESP	'72	'73	'74	'75	'76	'77	'80	'82	'84	'85	'87	'88	'89
F	YES	42%	37%	36%	39%	36%	30%	31%	32%	27%	26%	26%	24%	22%
	NO	58	63	64	61	64	70	69	68	73	74	74	76	78
# SURVEYED		654	683	673	704	740	713	798	840	817	815	796	558	570

TABLE III: INTERRACIAL MARRIAGES -- BY RACE

Question: Do you think there should be laws against marriages between blacks and whites? NOTE: Asked of non-blacks in 1972-1977. Since 1977 it has been asked of all respondents. Question not asked in 1978, 1983, 1986.

Responses: YES; NO

		YEAR												
RACE	RESP	'72	'73	'74	'75	'76	'77	'80	'82	'84	'85	'87	'88	'89
WHITE	YES	39%	38%	35%	39%	33%	28%	31%	33%	27%	28%	27%	26%	23%
	NO	61	62	65	61	67	72	69	67	73	72	73	74	77
# SURVEYED		1306	1277	1274	1289	1322	1313	1281	1281	1192	1301	1187	775	865
RACE	RESP	'72	'73	'74	'75	'76	'77	'80	'82	'84	'85	'87	'88	'89
BLACK	YES	0%	0%	0%	0%	0%	0%	18%	6%	7%	7%	5%	5%	8%
	NO	0	0	0	0	0	0	82	94	93	93	95	95	92
# SURVEYED		136	155	142	143	182	127	102						
RACE	RESP	'72	'73	'74	'75	'76	'77	'80	'82	'84	'85	'87	'88	'89
OTHER	YES	33%	17%	17%	0%	0%	7%	10%	12%	22%	17%	21%	19%	14%
	NO	67	83	83	100	100	93	90	88	78	83	79	81	86
# SURVEYED		3	12	6	3	8	14	10	26	49	42	53	43	37

TABLE IV: INTERRACIAL MARRIAGES -- BY AGE

Question: Do you think there should be laws against marriages between blacks and whites? NOTE: Asked of non-blacks in 1972-1977. Since 1977 it has been asked of all respondents. Question not asked in 1978, 1983, 1986.

Responses: YES; NO

		YEAR												
AGE	RESP	'72	'73	'74	'75	'76	'77	'80	'82	'84	'85	'87	'88	'89
18-23	YES	20%	21%	16%	16%	16%	13%	19%	18%	10%	12%	15%	16%	14%
	NO	80	79	84	84	84	87	81	82	90	88	85	84	86
# SURVEYED		133	150	141	153	148	141	151	146	155	129	124	92	95
AGE	RESP	'72	'73	'74	'75	'76	'77	'80	'82	'84	'85	'87	'88	'89
24-29	YES	23%	23%	15%	20%	12%	11%	14%	16%	14%	15%	8%	11%	11%
	NO	77	77	85	80	88	89	86	84	86	85	92	89	89
# SURVEYED		191	190	195	199	199	173	201	240	225	211	188	130	114
AGE	RESP	'72	'73	'74	'75	'76	'77	'80	'82	'84	'85	'87	'88	'89
30-35	YES	38%	36%	21%	26%	23%	15%	17%	14%	15%	18%	15%	7%	7%
	NO	62	64	79	74	77	85	83	86	85	82	85	93	93
# SURVEYED		157	143	142	149	170	163	210	201	189	209	218	127	136
AGE	RESP	'72	'73	'74	'75	'76	'77	'80	'82	'84	'85	'87	'88	'89
36-41	YES	37%	32%	30%	43%	25%	21%	24%	21%	15%	13%	14%	13%	15%
	NO	63	68	70	57	75	79	76	79	85	87	86	87	85
# SURVEYED		108	147	128	132	144	142	148	146	173	182	182	127	133
AGE	RESP	'72	'73	'74	'75	'76	'77	'80	'82	'84	'85	'87	'88	'89
42-47	YES	34%	35%	34%	31%	32%	29%	30%	26%	26%	16%	17%	23%	15%
	NO	66	65	66	69	68	71	70	74	74	84	83	77	85
# SURVEYED		145	129	134	123	101	133	115	116	117	124	155	102	106
AGE	RESP	'72	'73	'74	'75	'76	'77	'80	'82	'84	'85	'87	'88	'89
48-53	YES	43%	46%	42%	47%	38%	23%	30%	33%	33%	32%	28%	14%	29%
	NO	57	54	58	53	62	77	70	67	67	68	72	86	71
# SURVEYED		157	125	129	125	121	137	120	110	100	127	121	63	93
AGE	RESP	'72	'73	'74	'75	'76	'77	'80	'82	'84	'85	'87	'88	'89
54-59	YES	39%	44%	43%	52%	47%	39%	42%	40%	33%	35%	28%	28%	20%
	NO	61	56	57	48	53	61	58	60	67	65	72	72	80
# SURVEYED		126	129	122	110	110	143	133	141	105	127	96	53	59
AGE	RESP	'72	'73	'74	'75	'76	'77	'80	'82	'84	'85	'87	'88	'89
60-65	YES	54%	50%	44%	61%	48%	51%	44%	45%	39%	40%	43%	42%	32%
	NO	46	50	56	39	52	49	56	55	61	60	57	58	68
# SURVEYED		117	105	91	95	116	106	114	111	102	124	98	83	77

TABLE IV: INTERRACIAL MARRIAGES -- BY AGE (Continued)

Question: Do you think there should be laws against marriages between blacks and whites? NOTE: Asked of non-blacks in 1972-1977. Since 1977 it has been asked of all respondents. Question not asked in 1978, 1983, 1986.

Responses: YES; NO

		YEAR												
AGE	RESP	'72	'73	'74	'75	'76	'77	'80	'82	'84	'85	'87	'88	'89
66+	YES	67%	61%	66%	63%	57%	55%	53%	58%	50%	49%	49%	45%	42%
	NO	33	39	34	37	43	45	47	42	50	51	51	55	58
# SURVEYED		172	168	193	202	216	184	226	241	212	246	235	165	188

****

OPEN HOUSING LAWS

TABLE I: OPEN HOUSING LAWS -- BY TOTAL POPULATION

Question: Suppose there is a community wide vote on the general housing issue. There are two possible laws to vote on. Law A says that a homeowner can decide for himself whom to sell his house to, even if he prefers not to sell to blacks Law B says that a homeowner cannot refuse to sell to someone because of their race or color. Which law would you vote for? NOTE: Asked of non-blacks in 1972-1977. Since 1977 it has been asked of all respondents. Question not asked in 1972, 1974, 1977, 1982, 1985.

Responses: A = Law A; B= Law B; N = Neither (Volunteered)

	YEAR										
RESPONSE	'73	'75	'76	'78	'80	'83	'84	'86	'87	'88	'89
A	64%	65%	63%	58%	56%	50%	46%	47%	44%	40%	38%
B	35	35	35	41	42	48	52	51	54	58	60
N	2	1	2	1	2	2	2	1	2	3	2
# SURVEYED	1296	1304	1346	1499	1441	1557	1442	1448	1430	975	1012

TABLE II: OPEN HOUSING LAWS -- BY SEX

Question: Suppose there is a community wide vote on the general housing issue. There are two possible laws to vote on. Law A says that a homeowner can decide for himself whom to sell his house to, even if he prefers not to sell to blacks Law B says that a homeowner cannot refuse to sell to someone because of their race or color. Which law would you vote for? NOTE: Asked of non-blacks in 1972-1977. Since 1977 it has been asked of all respondents. Question not asked in 1972, 1974, 1977, 1982, 1985.

Responses: A = Law A; B= Law B; N = Neither (Volunteered)

		YEAR										
SEX	RESP	'73	'75	'76	'78	'80	'83	'84	'86	'87	'88	'89
M	A	63%	69%	64%	59%	59%	53%	49%	49%	46%	40%	40%
	B	35	30	34	40	39	45	49	50	52	58	58
	N	2	1	2	1	2	2	2	1	2	2	2
# SURVEYED		604	595	596	630	634	680	594	613	626	434	439
SEX	RESP	'73	'75	'76	'78	'80	'83	'84	'86	'87	'88	'89
F	A	64%	61%	63%	57%	53%	48%	44%	46%	44%	40%	35%
	B	35	38	36	42	45	51	55	52	55	57	62
	N	1	1	2	1	1	2	2	1	1	3	2
# SURVEYED		692	709	750	869	807	877	848	835	804	541	573

TABLE III: OPEN HOUSING LAWS -- BY RACE

Question: Suppose there is a community wide vote on the general housing issue. There are two possible laws to vote on. Law A says that a homeowner can decide for himself whom to sell his house to, even if he prefers not to sell to blacks Law B says that a homeowner cannot refuse to sell to someone because of their race or color. Which law would you vote for? NOTE: Asked of non-blacks in 1972-1977. Since 1977 it has been asked of all respondents. Question not asked in 1972, 1974, 1977, 1982, 1985.

Responses: A = Law A; B= Law B; N = Neither (Volunteered)

		YEAR										
RACE	RESP	'73	'75	'76	'78	'80	'83	'84	'86	'87	'88	'89
WHITE	A	64%	65%	63%	61%	59%	53%	49%	51%	49%	45%	41%
	B	34	34	35	37	40	45	49	47	49	53	57
	N	2	1	2	1	1	2	2	1	2	2	2
# SURVEYED		1283	1300	1339	1330	1292	1382	1227	1234	1197	820	864
RACE	RESP	'73	'75	'76	'78	'80	'83	'84	'86	'87	'88	'89
BLACK	A	0%	0%	0%	27%	28%	24%	21%	20%	17%	10%	12%
	B	0	0	0	73	69	72	75	78	81	88	86
	N	0	0	0	1	4	4	3	2	3	2	2
# SURVEYED		000	000	000	154	140	160	163	179	185	116	108
RACE	RESP	'73	'75	'76	'78	'80	'83	'84	'86	'87	'88	'89
OTHER	A	31%	25%	29%	33%	44%	33%	46%	37%	33%	28%	25%
	B	69	75	71	67	56	67	50	60	63	62	70
	N	0	0	0	0	0	0	4	3	4	10	5
# SURVEYED		13	4	7	15	9	15	52	35	48	39	40

TABLE IV: OPEN HOUSING LAWS -- BY AGE

Question: Suppose there is a community wide vote on the general housing issue. There are two possible laws to vote on. Law A says that a homeowner can decide for himself whom to sell his house to, even if he prefers not to sell to blacks Law B says that a homeowner cannot refuse to sell to someone because of their race or color. Which law would you vote for? NOTE: Asked of non-blacks in 1972-1977. Since 1977 it has been asked of all respondents. Question not asked in 1972, 1974, 1977, 1982, 1985.

Responses: A = Law A; B= Law B; N = Neither (Volunteered)

		YEAR										
AGE	RESP	'73	'75	'76	'78	'80	'83	'84	'86	'87	'88	'89
18-23	A	42%	43%	52%	41%	41%	39%	31%	36%	36%	26%	26%
	B	56	56	47	58	59	61	67	63	64	71	74
	N	1	1	1	1	0	0	1	2	0	3	0
# SURVEYED		149	153	147	158	153	127	156	107	122	92	91

TABLE IV: OPEN HOUSING LAWS -- BY AGE (Continued)

Question: Suppose there is a community wide vote on the general housing issue. There are two possible laws to vote on. Law A says that a homeowner can decide for himself whom to sell his house to, even if he prefers not to sell to blacks Law B says that a homeowner cannot refuse to sell to someone because of their race or color. Which law would you vote for? NOTE: Asked of non-blacks in 1972-1977. Since 1977 it has been asked of all respondents. Question not asked in 1972, 1974, 1977, 1982, 1985.

Responses: A = Law A; B= Law B; N = Neither (Volunteered)

		YEAR										
AGE	RESP	'73	'75	'76	'78	'80	'83	'84	'86	'87	'88	'89
24-29	A	51%	49%	47%	44%	38%	35%	35%	37%	35%	28%	23%
	B	48	50	52	54	59	62	64	62	62	70	75
	N	1	0	2	2	2	2	1	1	3	2	1
# SURVEYED		190	202	199	242	202	283	232	215	191	145	138
AGE	RESP	'73	'75	'76	'78	'80	'83	'84	'86	'87	'88	'89
30-35	A	63%	61%	57%	44%	46%	39%	38%	36%	31%	31%	35%
	B	37	38	42	54	52	58	60	63	68	66	63
	N	1	1	1	2	2	3	2	1	2	3	1
# SURVEYED		144	151	170	228	212	234	198	219	219	126	142
AGE	RESP	'73	'75	'76	'78	'80	'83	'84	'86	'87	'88	'89
36-41	A	66%	67%	66%	58%	53%	49%	43%	39%	38%	33%	23%
	B	34	31	32	41	46	49	55	58	62	66	73
	N	0	2	2	1	1	2	2	3	1	1	4
# SURVEYED		149	131	143	158	150	171	184	186	180	125	132
AGE	RESP	'73	'75	'76	'78	'80	'83	'84	'86	'87	'88	'89
42-47	A	65%	62%	66%	66%	64%	52%	42%	41%	44%	36%	36%
	B	34	37	32	33	33	47	55	57	51	63	62
	N	1	1	2	1	3	1	3	1	5	1	2
# SURVEYED		128	124	106	117	115	141	126	140	153	103	105
AGE	RESP	'73	'75	'76	'78	'80	'83	'84	'86	'87	'88	'89
48-53	A	78%	74%	69%	68%	58%	63%	50%	58%	57%	38%	45%
	B	18	25	30	30	40	36	49	41	43	60	52
	N	4	1	1	2	3	2	1	1	0	2	3
# SURVEYED		127	125	119	131	120	115	101	106	123	55	92
AGE	RESP	'73	'75	'76	'78	'80	'83	'84	'86	'87	'88	'89
54-59	A	67%	72%	68%	71%	65%	57%	54%	47%	50%	45%	52%
	B	30	26	30	28	34	40	44	53	46	54	44
	N	3	2	2	1	1	2	3	0	4	2	3
# SURVEYED		132	111	115	135	135	127	114	98	96	65	63

TABLE IV: OPEN HOUSING LAWS -- BY AGE (Continued)

Question: Suppose there is a community wide vote on the general housing issue. There are two possible laws to vote on. Law A says that a homeowner can decide for himself whom to sell his house to, even if he prefers not to sell to blacks Law B says that a homeowner cannot refuse to sell to someone because of their race or color. Which law would you vote for? NOTE: Asked of non-blacks in 1972-1977. Since 1977 it has been asked of all respondents. Question not asked in 1972, 1974, 1977, 1982, 1985.

Responses: A = Law A; B= Law B; N = Neither (Volunteered)

		YEAR										
AGE	RESP	'73	'75	'76	'78	'80	'83	'84	'86	'87	'88	'89
60-65	A	75%	86%	74%	70%	72%	67%	66%	66%	62%	55%	45%
	B	22	14	24	28	25	32	34	33	38	39	53
	N	3	0	3	2	3	1	0	1	0	6	1
# SURVEYED		104	102	118	104	116	127	106	113	98	77	73
AGE	RESP	'73	'75	'76	'78	'80	'83	'84	'86	'87	'88	'89
66+	A	74%	78%	77%	72%	73%	65%	64%	67%	57%	62%	55%
	B	24	22	21	27	25	32	34	32	42	35	43
	N	3	0	3	0	1	3	2	1	1	3	2
# SURVEYED		170	200	224	219	230	225	219	257	244	183	174

****

HOUSING SEGREGATION

TABLE I: HOUSING SEGREGATION -- BY TOTAL POPULATION

Question: How strongly do you agree or disagree with the following statement? Blacks shouldn't push themselves where they are not wanted. NOTE: Asked of non-blacks in 1972-1977. Since 1977 it has been asked of all respondents. Question was not asked in 1974, 1978, 1983, 1986-1989.

Responses: AS = Agree strongly; AG = Agree slightly; DS = Disagree slightly; SD = Disagree strongly

	YEAR								
RESPONSE	'72	'73	'75	'76	'77	'80	'82	'84	'85
AS	45%	44%	46%	43%	44%	34%	27%	26%	26%
AG	31	29	28	28	29	32	30	31	33
DS	14	15	15	17	18	20	22	22	23
SD	11	11	10	12	9	14	21	21	18
# SURVEYED	1258	1299	1289	1337	1322	1428	1465	1431	729

TABLE II: HOUSING SEGREGATION -- BY SEX

Question: How strongly do you agree or disagree with the following statement? Blacks shouldn't push themselves where they are not wanted. NOTE: Asked of non-blacks in 1972-1977. Since 1977 it has been asked of all respondents. Question was not asked in 1974, 1978, 1983, 1986-1989.

Responses: AS = Agree strongly; AG = Agree slightly; DS = Disagree slightly; SD = Disagree strongly

		YEAR								
SEX	RESP	'72	'73	'75	'76	'77	'80	'82	'84	'85
M	AS	46%	47%	51%	45%	46%	36%	26%	30%	28%
	AG	31	27	27	28	29	32	35	29	33
	DS	13	16	14	16	16	19	20	21	23
	SD	10	11	9	11	9	13	19	20	16
# SURVEYED		633	606	581	592	611	626	629	589	417
SEX	RESP	'72	'73	'75	'76	'77	'80	'82	'84	'85
F	AS	43%	42%	43%	41%	43%	33%	28%	24%	24%
	AG	32	32	29	29	28	31	26	32	33
	DS	14	14	16	17	19	20	23	22	23
	SD	11	12	12	13	10	15	23	22	20
# SURVEYED		625	693	708	745	711	802	836	842	312

TABLE III: HOUSING SEGREGATION -- BY RACE

Question: How strongly do you agree or disagree with the following statement? Blacks shouldn't push themselves where they are not wanted. NOTE: Asked of non-blacks in 1972-1977. Since 1977 it has been asked of all respondents. Question was not asked in 1974, 1978, 1983, 1986-1989.

Responses: AS = Agree strongly; AG = Agree slightly; DS = Disagree slightly; SD = Disagree strongly

		YEAR								
RACE	RESP	'72	'73	'75	'76	'77	'80	'82	'84	'85
WHITE	AS	45%	44%	46%	43%	44%	36%	29%	28%	27%
	AG	31	29	28	28	29	32	32	31	34
	DS	14	15	15	17	18	20	23	22	23
	SD	11	11	10	12	9	12	16	19	16
# SURVEYED		1255	1286	1286	1330	1308	1284	1286	1217	642
RACE	RESP	'72	'73	'75	'76	'77	'80	'82	'84	'85
BLACK	AS	0%	0%	0%	0%	0%	24%	12%	12%	23%
	AG	0	0	0	0	0	22	13	26	24
	DS	0	0	0	0	0	19	13	23	24
	SD	0	0	0	0	0	35	61	39	30
# SURVEYED		000	000	000	000	000	135	153	163	71
RACE	RESP	'72	'73	'75	'76	'77	'80	'82	'84	'85
OTHER	AS	0%	38%	100%	29%	50%	11%	27%	29%	19%
	AG	100	31	0	43	29	56	23	29	25
	DS	0	15	0	29	7	22	23	18	19
	SD	0	15	0	0	14	11	27	24	38
# SURVEYED		3	13	3	7	14	9	26	51	16

TABLE IV: HOUSING SEGREGATION -- BY AGE

Question: How strongly do you agree or disagree with the following statement? Blacks shouldn't push themselves where they are not wanted. NOTE: Asked of non-blacks in 1972-1977. Since 1977 it has been asked of all respondents. Question was not asked in 1974, 1978, 1983, 1986-1989.

Responses: AS = Agree strongly; AG = Agree slightly; DS = Disagree slightly; SD = Disagree strongly

		YEAR								
AGE	RESP	'72	'73	'75	'76	'77	'80	'82	'84	'85
18-23	AS	24%	30%	26%	33%	32%	26%	17%	15%	20%
	AG	27	33	38	22	32	32	27	29	15
	DS	29	21	16	25	24	23	25	25	40
	SD	20	16	20	20	12	19	31	31	25
# SURVEYED		129	151	152	147	139	151	144	158	40

TABLE IV: HOUSING SEGREGATION -- BY AGE (Continued)

Question: How strongly do you agree or disagree with the following statement? Blacks shouldn't push themselves where they are not wanted. NOTE: Asked of non-blacks in 1972-1977. Since 1977 it has been asked of all respondents. Question was not asked in 1974, 1978, 1983, 1986-1989.

Responses: AS = Agree strongly; AG = Agree slightly; DS = Disagree slightly; SD = Disagree strongly

		YEAR								
AGE	RESP	'72	'73	'75	'76	'77	'80	'82	'84	'85
24-29	AS	38%	31%	30%	31%	25%	24%	19%	19%	14%
	AG	27	27	32	26	35	32	29	28	33
	DS	15	23	23	27	25	21	26	27	25
	SD	20	19	15	16	15	23	26	26	28
# SURVEYED		189	189	201	194	171	201	240	230	95
AGE	RESP	'72	'73	'75	'76	'77	'80	'82	'84	'85
30-35	AS	43%	40%	44%	35%	33%	20%	20%	20%	20%
	AG	30	30	23	31	25	28	26	31	32
	DS	14	15	22	21	28	30	27	22	27
	SD	14	15	10	13	13	21	26	27	21
# SURVEYED		148	144	147	171	165	206	201	193	95
AGE	RESP	'72	'73	'75	'76	'77	'80	'82	'84	'85
36-41	AS	41%	38%	51%	38%	38%	37%	25%	22%	21%
	AG	28	34	32	31	30	29	26	30	35
	DS	17	15	9	17	20	16	27	24	26
	SD	15	13	8	13	12	17	22	24	18
# SURVEYED		101	149	130	141	142	150	144	185	96
AGE	RESP	'72	'73	'75	'76	'77	'80	'82	'84	'85
42-47	AS	41%	51%	46%	37%	54%	36%	27%	23%	33%
	AG	37	26	23	30	21	37	30	28	33
	DS	15	15	19	18	16	15	20	24	16
	SD	6	8	12	15	9	12	23	25	19
# SURVEYED		140	131	124	105	130	114	115	123	64
AGE	RESP	'72	'73	'75	'76	'77	'80	'82	'84	'85
48-53	AS	59%	50%	52%	51%	50%	33%	33%	20%	30%
	AG	30	29	24	24	28	40	32	39	38
	DS	7	13	15	16	15	18	17	27	15
	SD	4	8	8	9	7	9	17	13	16
# SURVEYED		145	127	123	118	137	120	111	99	73
AGE	RESP	'72	'73	'75	'76	'77	'80	'82	'84	'85
54-59	AS	53%	54%	65%	52%	52%	46%	34%	33%	31%
	AG	30	26	26	30	30	28	35	33	40
	DS	9	11	6	7	9	21	20	20	21
	SD	8	10	4	11	8	5	12	14	8
# SURVEYED		120	132	109	115	143	130	138	111	62

TABLE IV: HOUSING SEGREGATION -- BY AGE (Continued)

Question: How strongly do you agree or disagree with the following statement? Blacks shouldn't push themselves where they are not wanted. NOTE: Asked of non-blacks in 1972-1977. Since 1977 it has been asked of all respondents. Question was not asked in 1974, 1978, 1983, 1986-1989.

Responses: AS = Agree strongly; AG = Agree slightly; DS = Disagree slightly; SD = Disagree strongly

		YEAR								
AGE	RESP	'72	'73	'75	'76	'77	'80	'82	'84	'85
60-65	AS	59%	49%	68%	51%	55%	51%	37%	42%	31%
	AG	32	32	17	32	29	28	37	30	37
	DS	5	12	9	10	10	14	12	14	18
	SD	4	7	6	7	6	7	14	14	13
# SURVEYED		114	106	99	115	103	115	115	106	67
AGE	RESP	'72	'73	'75	'76	'77	'80	'82	'84	'85
66+	AS	48%	61%	53%	57%	61%	45%	36%	44%	37%
	AG	38	29	31	29	27	32	31	32	30
	DS	11	7	10	8	9	15	18	13	22
	SD	4	4	7	6	2	9	15	12	11
# SURVEYED		170	167	199	226	187	233	249	221	134

****

BLACK PRESIDENTIAL CANDIDATE

TABLE I: BLACK PRESIDENTIAL CANDIDATE -- BY TOTAL POPULATION

Question: If your party nominated a black for President, would you vote for him if he were qualified for the job? NOTE: Question was not asked in 1973, 1976, 1980, 1984, 1987.

Responses: YES; NO

	YEAR										
RESPONSE	'72	'74	'75	'77	'78	'82	'83	'85	'86	'88	'89
YES	74%	83%	82%	78%	85%	87%	86%	85%	87%	82%	83%
NO	26	17	18	22	15	13	14	15	13	18	17
# SURVEYED	1265	1423	1247	1298	1460	1422	1526	1459	1427	937	947

TABLE II: BLACK PRESIDENTIAL CANDIDATE -- BY SEX

Question: If your party nominated a black for President, would you vote for him if he were qualified for the job? NOTE: Question was not asked in 1973, 1976, 1980, 1984, 1987.

Responses: YES; NO

YEAR												
SEX	RESP	'72	'74	'75	'77	'78	'82	'83	'85	'86	'88	'89
M	YES	75%	82%	81%	78%	85%	86%	83%	86%	87%	81%	83%
	NO	25	18	19	22	15	14	17	14	13	19	17
# SURVEYED		632	663	562	599	618	606	663	657	609	420	401
SEX	RESP	'72	'74	'75	'77	'78	'82	'83	'85	'86	'88	'89
F	YES	72%	84%	83%	77%	85%	88%	88%	84%	88%	83%	83%
	NO	28	16	17	23	15	12	12	16	12	17	17
# SURVEYED		633	760	685	699	842	816	863	802	818	517	546

TABLE III: BLACK PRESIDENTIAL CANDIDATE -- BY RACE

Question: If your party nominated a black for President, would you vote for him if he were qualified for the job? NOTE: Question was not asked in 1973, 1976, 1980, 1984, 1987.

Responses: YES; NO

YEAR												
RACE	RESP	'72	'74	'75	'77	'78	'82	'83	'85	'86	'88	'89
WHITE	YES	74%	81%	82%	78%	83%	86%	85%	83%	86%	79%	81%
	NO	26	19	18	22	17	14	15	17	14	21	19
# SURVEYED		1262	1251	1243	1284	1291	1240	1353	1270	1210	780	812
RACE	RESP	'72	'74	'75	'77	'78	'82	'83	'85	'86	'88	'89
BLACK	YES	0%	96%	0%	0%	96%	97%	95%	99%	97%	98%	96%
	NO	0	4	0	0	4	3	5	1	3	2	4
# SURVEYED		165	156	156	159	145	180	125	100			
RACE	RESP	'72	'74	'75	'77	'78	'82	'83	'85	'86	'88	'89
OTHER	YES	67%	86%	100%	57%	100%	92%	100%	82%	86%	84%	86%
	NO	33	14	0	43	0	8	0	18	14	16	14
# SURVEYED		3	7	4	14	13	26	14	44	37	32	35

TABLE IV: BLACK PRESIDENTIAL CANDIDATE -- BY AGE

Question: If your party nominated a black for President, would you vote for him if he were qualified for the job? NOTE: Question was not asked in 1973, 1976, 1980, 1984, 1987.

Responses: YES; NO

		YEAR										
AGE	RESP	'72	'74	'75	'77	'78	'82	'83	'85	'86	'88	'89
18-23	YES	88%	89%	88%	89%	92%	93%	88%	84%	90%	87%	79%
	NO	12	11	12	11	8	7	12	16	10	13	21
# SURVEYED		134	159	148	137	163	140	125	129	102	91	78
AGE	RESP	'72	'74	'75	'77	'78	'82	'83	'85	'86	'88	'89
24-29	YES	79%	87%	88%	86%	90%	89%	91%	87%	89%	92%	87%
	NO	21	13	12	14	10	11	9	13	11	8	13
# SURVEYED		187	205	198	170	237	234	277	212	214	145	140
AGE	RESP	'72	'74	'75	'77	'78	'82	'83	'85	'86	'88	'89
30-35	YES	82%	88%	88%	88%	89%	92%	88%	89%	93%	88%	88%
	NO	18	12	12	12	11	8	12	11	7	12	12
# SURVEYED		149	171	146	161	221	197	231	206	217	124	139
AGE	RESP	'72	'74	'75	'77	'78	'82	'83	'85	'86	'88	'89
36-41	YES	75%	84%	80%	81%	88%	89%	88%	90%	90%	90%	85%
	NO	25	16	20	19	12	11	12	10	10	10	15
# SURVEYED		105	147	123	138	153	142	164	177	181	125	117
AGE	RESP	'72	'74	'75	'77	'78	'82	'83	'85	'86	'88	'89
42-47	YES	83%	90%	90%	80%	83%	94%	86%	88%	91%	83%	86%
	NO	17	10	10	20	17	6	14	12	9	17	14
# SURVEYED		145	144	120	130	117	115	138	119	139	103	102
AGE	RESP	'72	'74	'75	'77	'78	'82	'83	'85	'86	'88	'89
48-53	YES	67%	82%	80%	81%	87%	91%	87%	90%	85%	83%	83%
	NO	33	18	20	19	13	9	13	10	15	17	18
# SURVEYED		145	143	121	130	128	105	111	123	104	60	80
AGE	RESP	'72	'74	'75	'77	'78	'82	'83	'85	'86	'88	'89
54-59	YES	69%	77%	78%	78%	85%	81%	82%	85%	90%	86%	80%
	NO	31	23	22	22	15	19	18	15	10	14	20
# SURVEYED		118	132	107	142	128	135	123	121	97	42	70
AGE	RESP	'72	'74	'75	'77	'78	'82	'83	'85	'86	'88	'89
60-65	YES	66%	75%	74%	57%	72%	81%	87%	81%	89%	78%	74%
	NO	34	25	26	43	28	19	13	19	11	22	26
# SURVEYED		111	104	92	103	96	113	126	125	113	72	65

TABLE IV: BLACK PRESIDENTIAL CANDIDATE -- BY AGE

Question: If your party nominated a black for President, would you vote for him if he were qualified for the job?
NOTE: Question was not asked in 1973, 1976, 1980, 1984, 1987.

Responses: YES; NO

		YEAR										
AGE	RESP	'72	'74	'75	'77	'78	'82	'83	'85	'86	'88	'89
66+	YES	55%	73%	68%	56%	71%	80%	74%	74%	75%	61%	77%
	NO	45	27	32	44	29	20	26	26	25	39	23
# SURVEYED		168	212	187	182	211	234	225	242	253	174	154

****

WORKING MOTHER RELATIONSHIP

TABLE I: WORKING MOTHER RELATIONSHIP -- BY TOTAL POPULATION

Question: Please tell me whether you strongly agree, agree, disagree, or strongly disagree with the following statement: A working mother can establish just as secure and warm a relationship with her children as a mother who does not work. NOTE: Question not asked in 1972-1976, 1978-1984, 1987.

Responses: SA = Strongly agree; AG = Agree; DS = Disagree; SD = Strongly disagree

	YEAR				
RESPONSE	'77	'85	'86	'88	'89
SA	16%	21%	22%	24%	22%
AG	33	40	40	39	42
DS	34	29	30	28	29
SD	17	10	8	9	7
# SURVEYED	1505	1518	1460	977	990

TABLE II: WORKING MOTHER RELATIONSHIP -- BY SEX

Question: Please tell me whether you strongly agree, agree, disagree, or strongly disagree with the following statement: A working mother can establish just as secure and warm a relationship with her children as a mother who does not work. NOTE: Question not asked in 1972-1976, 1978-1984, 1987.

Responses: SA = Strongly agree; AG = Agree; DS = Disagree; SD = Strongly disagree

		YEAR				
SEX	RESP	'77	'85	'86	'88	'89
M	SA	9%	13%	15%	17%	14%
	AG	33	40	41	38	45
	DS	40	34	37	35	32
	SD	18	13	7	10	9
# SURVEYED		681	682	614	433	423

		YEAR				
SEX	RESP	'77	'85	'86	'88	'89
F	SA	21%	28%	27%	29%	28%
	AG	34	39	40	40	41
	DS	28	24	24	22	26
	SD	17	8	8	8	5
# SURVEYED		824	836	846	544	567

TABLE III: WORKING MOTHER RELATIONSHIP -- BY RACE

Question: Please tell me whether you strongly agree, agree, disagree, or strongly disagree with the following statement: A working mother can establish just as secure and warm a relationship with her children as a mother who does not work. NOTE: Question not asked in 1972-1976, 1978-1984, 1987.

Responses: SA = Strongly agree; AG = Agree; DS = Disagree; SD = Strongly disagree

		YEAR				
RACE	RESP	'77	'85	'86	'88	'89
WHITE	SA	15%	21%	21%	24%	20%
	AG	33	40	40	39	43
	DS	33	29	30	29	30
	SD	18	10	8	9	7
# SURVEYED		1315	1331	1243	820	851

		YEAR				
RACE	RESP	'77	'85	'86	'88	'89
BLACK	SA	18%	26%	28%	28%	37%
	AG	38	35	42	42	35
	DA	34	28	24	18	22
	SD	10	11	6	12	7
# SURVEYED		176	144	180	123	101

		YEAR				
RACE	RESP	'77	'85	'86	'88	'89
OTHER	SA	14%	19%	27%	18%	18%
	AG	29	49	30	38	45
	DS	36	19	38	35	29
	SD	21	14	5	9	8
# SURVEYED		14	43	37	34	38

TABLE IV: WORKING MOTHER RELATIONSHIP -- BY AGE

Question: Please tell me whether you strongly agree, agree, disagree, or strongly disagree with the following statement: A working mother can establish just as secure and warm a relationship with her children as a mother who does not work. NOTE: Question not asked in 1972-1976, 1978-1984, 1987.

Responses: SA = Strongly agree; AG = Agree; DS = Disagree; SD = Strongly disagree

		YEAR				
AGE	RESP	'77	'85	'86	'88	'89
18-23	SA	21%	22%	23%	18%	20%
	AG	41	43	47	54	52
	DS	26	31	23	24	23
	SD	12	4	6	3	5
# SURVEYED		159	131	108	94	83
AGE	RESP	'77	'85	'86	'88	'89
24-29	SA	15%	22%	24%	25%	23%
	AG	45	46	46	41	53
	DS	28	28	24	29	22
	SD	11	4	6	4	2
# SURVEYED		201	216	217	150	146
AGE	RESP	'77	'85	'86	'88	'89
30-35	SA	24%	28%	30%	35%	31%
	AG	37	44	47	43	37
	DS	29	17	19	16	28
	SD	9	11	5	6	4
# SURVEYED		184	210	221	128	139

		YEAR				
AGE	RESP	'77	'85	'86	'88	'89
36-41	SA	23%	29%	32%	32%	25
	AG	36	43	42	40	47
	DS	24	20	20	18	24
	SD	18	9	6	10	4
# SURVEYED		165	183	187	126	12
AGE	RESP	'77	'85	'86	'88	'89
42-47	SA	11%	28%	29%	29%	25%
	AG	28	42	40	38	39
	DS	41	25	27	24	27
	SD	19	5	3	9	8
# SURVEYED		145	124	139	106	107
AGE	RESP	'77	'85	'86	'88	'89
48-53	SA	21%	19%	21%	32%	17%
	AG	29	39	36	24	44
	DS	32	29	35	34	32
	SD	18	13	9	10	7
# SURVEYED		153	131	107	62	84

		YEAR				
AGE	RESP	'77	'85	'86	'88	'89
54-59	SA	10%	15%	19%	20%	23%
	AG	31	33	38	29	36
	DS	37	36	38	37	26
	SD	22	15	5	14	16
# SURVEYED		167	130	98	51	70
AGE	RESP	'77	'85	'86	'88	'89
60-65	SA	9%	11%	18%	15%	15%
	AG	29	37	38	38	32
	DS	43	37	35	34	43
	SD	20	15	10	14	10
# SURVEYED		115	131	113	74	68
AGE	RESP	'77	'85	'86	'88	'89
66+	SA	6%	15%	6%	11%	13%
	AG	22	32	30	36	37
	DS	44	38	48	38	38
	SD	28	16	15	15	12
# SURVEYED		209	255	263	185	164

****

HUSBAND WORK - WIFE KEEP HOUSE

TABLE I: HUSBAND WORK - WIFE KEEP HOUSE -- BY TOTAL POPULATION

Question: Please tell me whether you strongly agree, agree, disagree, or strongly disagree with the following statement: It is much better for everyone involved if the man is the achiever outside the home and the woman takes care of the home and family. NOTE: Question not asked in 1972-1976, 1978-1984, 1987.

Responses: SA = Strongly agree; AG = Agree; DA = Disagree; SD = Strongly disagree

	YEAR				
RESPONSE	'77	'85	'86	'88	'89
SA	18%	10%	9%	9%	10%
AG	48	38	39	33	31
DA	28	38	40	41	42
SD	6	13	12	16	17
# SURVEYED	1503	1502	1444	964	977

TABLE II: HUSBAND WORK - WIFE KEEP HOUSE -- BY SEX

Question: Please tell me whether you strongly agree, agree, disagree, or strongly disagree with the following statement: It is much better for everyone involved if the man is the achiever outside the home and the woman takes care of the home and family. NOTE: Question not asked in 1972-1976, 1978-1984, 1987.

Responses: SA = Strongly agree; AG = Agree; DA = Disagree; SD = Strongly disagree

		YEAR				
SEX	RESP	'77	'85	'86	'88	'89
M	SA	19%	11%	7%	11%	11%
	AG	50	40	41	35	32
	DS	27	41	43	41	46
	SD	4	8	9	13	11
# SURVEYED		680	669	608	424	418

		YEAR				
SEX	RESP	'77	'85	'86	'88	'89
F	SA	18%	9%	11%	8%	9%
	AG	46	37	37	31	30
	DS	29	36	38	41	40
	SD	8	18	15	19	21
# SURVEYED		823	833	836	540	559

TABLE III: HUSBAND WORK - WIFE KEEP HOUSE -- BY RACE

Question: Please tell me whether you strongly agree, agree, disagree, or strongly disagree with the following statement: It is much better for everyone involved if the man is the achiever outside the home and the woman takes care of the home and family. NOTE: Question not asked in 1972-1976, 1978-1984, 1987.

Responses: SA = Strongly agree; AG = Agree; DA = Disagree; SD = Strongly disagree

RACE	RESP	'77	'85	'86	'88	'89
WHITE	SA	18%	10%	10%	10%	9%
	AG	48	38	38	32	31
	DA	27	38	39	42	42
	SD	6	14	13	17	17
# SURVEYED		1317	1314	1228	809	840

RACE	RESP	'77	'85	'86	'88	'89
BLACK	SA	17%	10%	6%	7%	11%
	AG	45	41	42	34	29
	DA	33	36	43	39	43
	SD	5	13	9	19	16
# SURVEYED		172	145	179	122	99

RACE	RESP	'77	'85	'86	'88	'89
OTHER	SA	29%	7%	3%	6%	13%
	AG	36	28	41	42	45
	DA	29	56	46	45	37
	SD	7	9	11	6	5
# SURVEYED		14	43	37	33	38

TABLE IV: HUSBAND WORK - WIFE KEEP HOUSE -- BY AGE

Question: Please tell me whether you strongly agree, agree, disagree, or strongly disagree with the following statement: It is much better for everyone involved if the man is the achiever outside the home and the woman takes care of the home and family. NOTE: Question not asked in 1972-1976, 1978-1984, 1987.

Responses: SA = Strongly agree; AG = Agree; DA = Disagree; SD = Strongly disagree

AGE	RESP	'77	'85	'86	'88	'89
18-23	SA	11%	2%	2%	2%	12%
	AG	39	24	30	16	19
	DA	40	52	45	58	49
	SD	9	21	24	24	20
# SURVEYED		161	131	105	92	81
24-29	SA	6%	6%	6%	3%	3%
	AG	36	28	26	21	23
	DA	48	44	51	52	49
	SD	10	23	17	23	25
# SURVEYED		202	215	216	147	144
30-35	SA	9%	7%	6%	3%	6%
	AG	40	27	23	23	18
	DA	42	45	52	47	52
	SD	10	21	19	27	24
# SURVEYED		184	210	221	127	136

AGE	RESP	'77	'85	'86	'88	'89
36-41	SA	18%	6%	5%	9%	4%
	AG	41	26	30	22	22
	DA	33	49	48	46	49
	SD	8	20	18	23	25
# SURVEYED		167	179	186	124	123
42-47	SA	18%	6%	4%	12%	12%
	AG	57	33	38	27	25
	DA	19	49	46	44	43
	SD	6	12	12	17	20
# SURVEYED		139	124	138	108	107
48-53	SA	19%	11%	13%	8%	7%
	AG	50	48	51	37	32
	DA	26	33	28	42	50
	SD	5	8	9	12	11
# SURVEYED		153	129	104	59	82

AGE	RESP	'77	'85	'86	'88	'89
54-59	SA	22%	15%	10%	10%	9%
	AG	62	57	48	46	37
	DA	14	21	35	30	41
	SD	2	7	6	14	13
# SURVEYED		166	124	99	50	68
60-65	SA	25%	12%	17%	11%	16%
	AG	60	54	47	56	45
	DA	12	31	32	29	30
	SD	3	2	5	4	9
# SURVEYED		115	129	109	73	67
66+	SA	37%	21%	19%	19%	18%
	AG	52	54	60	55	58
	DA	11	23	19	23	21
	SD	0	3	2	2	2
# SURVEYED		209	254	259	183	166

****

WOMEN LESS SUITABLE FOR POLITICS

TABLE I: WOMEN LESS SUITABLE FOR POLITICS -- BY TOTAL POPULATION

Question: Tell me if you agree or disagree with the following statement: Most men are better suited emotionally for politics than are most women. NOTE: Question not asked in 1972, 1973, 1976, 1980, 1984, 1987.

Responses: AG = Agree; DS = Disagree

	YEAR									
RESPONSE	'74	'75	'77	'78	'82	'83	'85	'86	'88	'89
AG	47%	50%	49%	44%	38%	36%	39%	37%	33%	30%
DS	53	50	51	56	62	64	61	63	67	70
# SURVEYED	698	1429	1454	1468	698	1526	1466	1415	950	939

TABLE II: WOMEN LESS SUITABLE FOR POLITICS -- BY SEX

Question: Tell me if you agree or disagree with the following statement: Most men are better suited emotionally for politics than are most women. NOTE: Question not asked in 1972, 1973, 1976, 1980, 1984, 1987.

Responses: AG = Agree; DS = Disagree

		YEAR									
SEX	RESP	'74	'75	'77	'78	'82	'83	'85	'86	'88	'89
M	AG	48%	47%	50%	41%	38%	38%	38%	35%	37%	34%
	DS	52	53	50	59	62	62	62	65	63	66
# SURVEYED		317	627	640	605	382	645	657	591	411	391
SEX	RESP	'74	'75	'77	'78	'82	'83	'85	'86	'88	'89
F	AG	46%	52%	49%	46%	37%	34%	39%	39%	31%	28%
	DS	54	48	51	54	63	66	61	61	69	72
# SURVEYED		381	802	814	863	316	881	809	824	539	548

TABLE III: WOMEN LESS SUITABLE FOR POLITICS -- BY RACE

Question: Tell me if you agree or disagree with the following statement: Most men are better suited emotionally for politics than are most women. NOTE: Question not asked in 1972, 1973, 1976, 1980, 1984, 1987.

Responses: AG = Agree; DS = Disagree

		YEAR									
RACE	RESP	'74	'75	'77	'78	'82	'83	'85	'86	'88	'89
WHITE	AG	47%	49%	49%	43%	36%	36%	39%	37%	32%	28%
	DS	53	51	51	57	64	64	61	63	68	72
# SURVEYED		614	1267	1274	1305	614	1354	1286	1206	798	809
RACE	RESP	'74	'75	'77	'78	'82	'83	'85	'86	'88	'89
BLACK	AG	44%	56%	48%	51%	46%	36%	39%	38%	36%	38%
	DS	56	44	52	49	54	64	61	62	64	62
# SURVEYED		82	158	165	148	70	157	139	175	121	95
RACE	RESP	'74	'75	'77	'78	'82	'83	'85	'86	'88	'89
OTHER	AG	100%	75%	60%	67%	50%	33%	29%	35%	48%	54%
	DS	0	25	40	33	50	67	71	65	52	46
# SURVEYED		2	4	15	15	14	15	41	34	31	35

TABLE IV: WOMEN LESS SUITABLE FOR POLITICS -- BY AGE

Question: Tell me if you agree or disagree with the following statement: Most men are better suited emotionally for politics than are most women. NOTE: Question not asked in 1972, 1973, 1976, 1980, 1984, 1987.

Responses: AG = Agree; DS = Disagree

		YEAR									
AGE	RESP	'74	'75	'77	'78	'82	'83	'85	'86	'88	'89
18-23	AG	34%	42%	40%	29%	43%	26%	33%	21%	33%	31%
	DS	66	58	60	71	57	74	67	79	67	69
# SURVEYED		74	165	159	160	54	122	124	105	90	77
AGE	RESP	'74	'75	'77	'78	'82	'83	'85	'86	'88	'89
24-29	AG	33%	37%	34%	34%	37%	27%	26%	34%	20%	22%
	DS	67	63	66	66	63	73	74	66	80	78
# SURVEYED		104	223	196	237	110	277	207	205	147	138

TABLE IV: WOMEN LESS SUITABLE FOR POLITICS -- BY AGE (Continued)

Question: Tell me if you agree or disagree with the following statement: Most men are better suited emotionally for politics than are most women. NOTE: Question not asked in 1972, 1973, 1976, 1980, 1984, 1987.

Responses: AG = Agree; DS = Disagree

AGE	RESP	'74	'75	'77	'78	'82	'83	'85	'86	'88	'89
30-35	AG	43%	43%	41%	33%	20%	28%	31%	27%	22%	19%
	DS	57	57	59	67	80	72	69	73	78	81
# SURVEYED		82	165	181	223	88	232	204	218	125	139
AGE	RESP	'74	'75	'77	'78	'82	'83	'85	'86	'88	'89
36-41	AG	45%	48%	45%	48%	24%	28%	39%	27%	26%	29%
	DS	55	52	55	52	76	72	61	73	74	71
# SURVEYED		71	147	161	155	70	162	176	184	122	122
AGE	RESP	'74	'75	'77	'78	'82	'83	'85	'86	'88	'89
42-47	AG	47%	41%	54%	54%	33%	41%	26%	28%	26%	24%
	DS	53	59	46	46	67	59	74	72	74	76
# SURVEYED		64	140	139	112	63	143	117	137	103	101
AGE	RESP	'74	'75	'77	'78	'82	'83	'85	'86	'88	'89
48-53	AG	50%	54%	51%	47%	44%	39%	36%	43%	34%	28%
	DS	50	46	49	53	56	61	64	57	66	72
# SURVEYED		60	135	142	129	55	112	128	102	61	81
AGE	RESP	'74	'75	'77	'78	'82	'83	'85	'86	'88	'89
54-59	AG	49%	64%	52%	47%	49%	38%	42%	43%	34%	39%
	DS	51	36	48	53	51	62	58	57	66	61
# SURVEYED		67	122	164	131	68	129	130	95	50	66
AGE	RESP	'74	'75	'77	'78	'82	'83	'85	'86	'88	'89
60-65	AG	59%	56%	64%	60%	42%	48%	54%	49%	47%	44%
	DS	41	44	36	40	58	52	46	51	53	56
# SURVEYED		58	109	111	103	45	122	127	114	72	63
AGE	RESP	'74	'75	'77	'78	'82	'83	'85	'86	'88	'89
66+	AG	63%	66%	67%	59%	46%	51%	55%	60%	55%	45%
	DS	37	34	33	41	54	49	45	40	45	55
# SURVEYED		114	219	197	211	138	222	246	248	179	150

****

PRESCHOOLER - WORKING MOTHER

TABLE I: PRESCHOOLER - WORKING MOTHER -- BY TOTAL POPULATION

Question: Please tell me whether you strongly agree, agree, disagree, or strongly disagree with the following statement: A preschool child is likely to suffer if his or her mother works. NOTE: Question not asked in 1972-1976, 1978-1984, 1987.

Responses: SA = Strongly agree; AG = Agree; DA = Disagree; SD = Strongly disagree

	YEAR				
RESPONSE	'77	'85	'86	'88	'89
SA	21%	13%	11%	11%	9%
AG	47	41	40	37	39
DA	28	36	40	41	42
SD	5	10	9	11	10
# SURVEYED	1498	1499	1442	965	974

TABLE II: PRESCHOOLER - WORKING MOTHER -- BY SEX

Question: Please tell me whether you strongly agree, agree, disagree, or strongly disagree with the following statement: A preschool child is likely to suffer if his or her mother works. NOTE: Question not asked in 1972-1976, 1978-1984, 1987.

Responses: SA = Strongly agree; AG = Agree; DA = Disagree; SD = Strongly disagree

		YEAR				
SEX	RESP	'77	'85	'86	'88	'89
M	SA	23%	15%	10%	11%	9%
	AG	51	48	48	45	46
	DA	24	33	36	37	38
	SD	3	4	6	7	7
# SURVEYED		677	671	606	424	416

		YEAR				
SEX	RESP	'77	'85	'86	'88	'89
F	SA	19%	11%	11%	11%	9%
	AG	43	36	35	32	34
	DA	32	39	42	44	45
	SD	6	14	11	14	12
# SURVEYED		821	828	836	541	558

TABLE III: PRESCHOOLER - WORKING MOTHER -- BY RACE

Question: Please tell me whether you strongly agree, agree, disagree, or strongly disagree with the following statement: A preschool child is likely to suffer if his or her mother works. NOTE: Question not asked in 1972-1976, 1978-1984, 1987.

Responses: SA = Strongly agree; AG = Agree; DA = Disagree; SD = Strongly disagree

RACE	RESP	'77	'85	'86	'88	'89
		YEAR				
WHITE	SA	22%	13%	11%	11%	9%
	AG	47	41	42	38	40
	DA	26	36	38	40	41
	SD	5	9	9	11	9
# SURVEYED		1310	1309	1223	810	835

RACE	RESP	'77	'85	'86	'88	'89
		YEAR				
BLACK	SA	10%	11%	8%	7%	9%
	AG	43	38	29	32	28
	DA	43	38	54	52	48
	SD	4	14	9	10	15
# SURVEYED		173	146	182	122	102

RACE	RESP	'77	'85	'86	'88	'89
		YEAR				
OTHER	SA	27%	14%	11%	9%	11%
	AG	33	48	46	52	38
	DA	40	32	35	30	46
	SD	0	7	8	9	5
# SURVEYED		15	44	37	33	37

TABLE IV: PRESCHOOLER - WORKING MOTHER -- BY AGE

Question: Please tell me whether you strongly agree, agree, disagree, or strongly disagree with the following statement: A preschool child is likely to suffer if his or her mother works. NOTE: Question not asked in 1972-1976, 1978-1984, 1987.

Responses: SA = Strongly agree; AG = Agree; DA = Disagree; SD = Strongly disagree

AGE	RESP	'77	'85	'86	'88	'89
		YEAR				
18-23	SA	16%	5%	8%	3%	7%
	AG	44	37	32	34	32
	DA	35	47	50	49	49
	SD	6	12	11	13	12
# SURVEYED		158	130	104	91	82
AGE	RESP	'77	'85	'86	'88	'89
24-29	SA	10%	9%	7%	6%	3%
	AG	43	31	34	33	33
	DA	41	47	49	50	54
	SD	6	13	10	12	10
# SURVEYED		204	212	215	147	144
AGE	RESP	'77	'85	'86	'88	'89
30-35	SA	16%	11%	6%	6%	4%
	AG	35	30	29	26	40
	DA	39	41	51	50	38
	SD	10	18	14	18	17
# SURVEYED		188	209	220	127	134

AGE	RESP	'77	'85	'86	'88	'89
		YEAR				
36-41	SA	20%	9%	7%	12%	6%
	AG	45	40	38	26	32
	DA	28	37	41	48	50
	SD	7	14	15	14	12
# SURVEYED		163	180	186	125	126
AGE	RESP	'77	'85	'86	'88	'89
42-47	SA	23%	10%	5%	13%	12%
	AG	50	43	37	29	36
	DA	22	40	45	42	42
	SD	5	7	12	15	9
# SURVEYED		143	121	139	106	107
AGE	RESP	'77	'85	'86	'88	'89
48-53	SA	23%	13%	11%	13%	7%
	AG	45	48	50	42	44
	DA	30	32	31	37	45
	SD	3	6	7	8	4
# SURVEYED		149	130	105	62	84

AGE	RESP	'77	'85	'86	'83	'89
		YEAR				
54-59	SA	24%	20%	12%	6%	21%
	AG	55	46	47	52	32
	DA	21	29	35	32	35
	SD	1	5	5	10	12
# SURVEYED		165	128	97	50	68
AGE	RESP	'77	'85	'86	'88	'89
60-65	SA	29%	18%	18%	15%	20%
	AG	54	51	43	42	43
	DA	16	29	33	36	28
	SD	2	2	6	7	9
# SURVEYED		115	130	114	74	65
AGE	RESP	'77	'85	'86	'88	'89
66+	SA	30%	19%	21%	19%	10%
	AG	52	49	54	56	54
	DA	18	26	22	23	32
	SD	0	6	2	3	4
# SURVEYED		207	253	256	182	161

****

LEAVE RUNNING COUNTRY TO MEN

TABLE I: LEAVE RUNNING COUNTRY TO MEN -- BY TOTAL POPULATION

Question: Do you agree or disagree with the following statement? Women should take care of running their homes and leave running the country to men. NOTE: Question not asked in 1972, 1973, 1976, 1980, 1984, 1987.

Responses: AG = Agree; DS = Disagree

	YEAR									
RESPONSE	'74	'75	'77	'78	'82	'83	'85	'86	'88	'89
AG	36%	36%	38%	32%	27%	23%	26%	24%	21%	20%
DS	64	64	62	68	73	77	74	76	79	80
# SURVEYED	1431	1446	1490	1482	1464	1539	1495	1424	950	959

TABLE II: LEAVE RUNNING COUNTRY TO MEN -- BY SEX

Question: Do you agree or disagree with the following statement? Women should take care of running their homes and leave running the country to men. NOTE: Question not asked in 1972, 1973, 1976, 1980, 1984, 1987.

Responses: AG = Agree; DS = Disagree

		YEAR									
SEX	RESP	'74	'75	'77	'78	'82	'83	'85	'86	'88	'89
M	AG	36%	35%	38%	31%	27%	23%	25%	21%	22%	23%
	DS	64	65	62	69	73	77	75	79	78	77
# SURVEYED		659	649	670	617	616	663	669	604	420	408
SEX	RESP	'74	'75	'77	'78	'82	'83	'85	'86	'88	'89
F	AG	35%	36%	39%	32%	26%	24%	27%	26%	21%	18%
	DS	65	64	61	68	74	76	73	74	79	82
# SURVEYED		772	797	820	865	848	876	826	820	530	551

TABLE III: LEAVE RUNNING COUNTRY TO MEN -- BY RACE

Question: Do you agree or disagree with the following statement? Women should take care of running their homes and leave running the country to men. NOTE: Question not asked in 1972, 1973, 1976, 1980, 1984, 1987.

Responses: AG = Agree; DS = Disagree

		YEAR									
RACE	RESP	'74	'75	'77	'78	'82	'83	'85	'86	'88	'89
WHITE	AG	34%	35%	37%	31%	26%	22%	25%	23%	20%	18%
	DS	66	65	63	69	74	78	75	77	80	82
# SURVEYED		1263	1281	1306	1315	1289	1369	1309	1216	797	823
RACE	RESP	'74	'75	'77	'78	'82	'83	'85	'86	'88	'89
BLACK	AG	44%	41%	45%	38%	30%	30%	38%	31%	25%	28%
	DS	56	59	55	62	70	70	62	69	75	72
# SURVEYED		162	161	169	152	150	155	143	174	121	100
RACE	RESP	'74	'75	'77	'78	'82	'83	'85	'86	'88	'89
OTHER	AG	67%	50%	40%	33%	36%	20%	28%	29%	38%	36%
	DS	33	50	60	67	64	80	72	71	63	64
# SURVEYED		6	4	15	15	25	15	43	34	32	36

TABLE IV: LEAVE RUNNING COUNTRY TO MEN -- BY AGE

Question: Do you agree or disagree with the following statement? Women should take care of running their homes and leave running the country to men. NOTE: Question not asked in 1972, 1973, 1976, 1980, 1984, 1987.

Responses: AG = Agree; DS = Disagree

		YEAR									
AGE	RESP	'74	'75	'77	'78	'82	'83	'85	'86	'88	'89
18-23	AG	25%	23%	22%	21%	20%	13%	12%	10%	11%	12%
	DS	75	77	78	79	80	87	88	90	89	88
# SURVEYED		163	166	161	159	143	126	130	105	92	81
AGE	RESP	'74	'75	'77	'78	'82	'83	'85	'86	'88	'89
24-29	AG	18%	19%	23%	20%	16%	15%	17%	16%	10%	11%
	DS	82	81	77	80	84	85	83	84	90	89
# SURVEYED		203	225	199	240	238	278	212	213	147	138

TABLE IV: LEAVE RUNNING COUNTRY TO MEN -- BY AGE (Continued)

Question: Do you agree or disagree with the following statement? Women should take care of running their homes and leave running the country to men. NOTE: Question not asked in 1972, 1973, 1976, 1980, 1984, 1987.

Responses: AG = Agree; DS = Disagree

		YEAR									
AGE	RESP	'74	'75	'77	'78	'82	'83	'85	'86	'88	'89
30-35	AG	29%	31%	26%	20%	13%	16%	17%	12%	8%	11%
	DS	71	69	74	80	87	84	83	88	92	89
# SURVEYED		171	166	187	225	201	231	210	217	130	139
AGE	RESP	'74	'75	'77	'78	'82	'83	'85	'86	'88	'89
36-41	AG	27%	34%	37%	28%	22%	16%	22%	15%	16%	15%
	DS	73	66	63	72	78	84	78	85	84	85
# SURVEYED		149	146	161	152	143	169	180	183	121	123
AGE	RESP	'74	'75	'77	'78	'82	'83	'85	'86	'88	'89
42-47	AG	38%	29%	44%	36%	19%	17%	17%	20%	17%	19%
	DS	62	71	56	64	81	83	83	80	83	81
# SURVEYED		143	139	142	113	116	141	122	136	102	104
AGE	RESP	'74	'75	'77	'78	'82	'83	'85	'86	'88	'89
48-53	AG	37%	40%	38%	31%	25%	23%	25%	29%	26%	20%
	DS	63	60	62	69	75	77	75	71	74	80
# SURVEYED		139	136	151	130	110	111	125	104	61	81
AGE	RESP	'74	'75	'77	'78	'82	'83	'85	'86	'88	'89
54-59	AG	46%	44%	37%	38%	32%	28%	29%	26%	18%	33%
	DS	54	56	63	62	68	72	71	74	82	67
# SURVEYED		133	126	163	129	143	131	130	98	49	67
AGE	RESP	'74	'75	'77	'78	'82	'83	'85	'86	'88	'89
60-65	AG	40%	43%	52%	44%	37%	33%	42%	35%	31%	36%
	DS	60	57	48	56	63	67	58	65	69	64
# SURVEYED		104	110	115	101	111	121	129	110	70	64
AGE	RESP	'74	'75	'77	'78	'82	'83	'85	'86	'88	'89
66+	AG	60%	59%	66%	57%	49%	47%	47%	48%	47%	33%
	DS	40	41	34	43	51	53	53	52	53	67
# SURVEYED		220	227	205	226	249	224	250	251	177	159

****

VOTE FOR FEMALE PRESIDENTIAL CANDIDATE

TABLE I: VOTE FOR FEMALE PRESIDENTIAL CANDIDATE -- BY TOTAL POPULATION

Question: If your party nominated a woman for President, would you vote for her if she were qualified for the job? NOTE: Question not asked in 1973, 1976, 1984, 1987.

Responses: YES; NO

	YEAR										
RESPONSE	'72	'74	'75	'77	'78	'82	'83	'85	'86	'88	'89
YES	74%	80%	80%	79%	82%	86%	86%	82%	86%	88%	86%
NO	26	20	20	21	18	14	13	18	14	12	14
# SURVEYED	1533	1433	1443	1484	1492	1456	1546	1481	1427	958	953

TABLE II: VOTE FOR FEMALE PRESIDENTIAL CANDIDATE -- BY SEX

Question: If your party nominated a woman for President, would you vote for her if she were qualified for the job? NOTE: Question not asked in 1973, 1976, 1984, 1987.

Responses: YES; NO

		YEAR										
SEX	RESP	'72	'74	'75	'77	'78	'82	'83	'85	'86	'88	'89
M	YES	74%	80%	82%	82%	83%	86%	86%	85%	89%	90%	84%
	NO	26	20	18	18	17	14	14	15	11	10	16
# SURVEYED		762	671	650	675	628	617	661	661	602	427	399
SEX	RESP	'72	'74	'75	'77	'78	'82	'83	'85	'86	'88	'89
F	YES	74%	80%	79%	77%	80%	86%	87%	80%	84%	86%	88%
	NO	26	20	21	23	20	14	13	20	16	14	12
# SURVEYED		771	762	793	809	864	839	885	820	825	531	554

TABLE III: VOTE FOR FEMALE PRESIDENTIAL CANDIDATE -- BY RACE

Question: If your party nominated a woman for President, would you vote for her if she were qualified for the job? NOTE: Question not asked in 1973, 1976, 1984, 1987.

Responses: YES; NO

		YEAR										
RACE	RESP	'72	'74	'75	'77	'78	'82	'83	'85	'86	'88	'89
WHITE	YES	72%	81%	81%	80%	81%	86%	86%	82%	86%	88%	87%
	NO	28	19	19	20	19	14	14	18	14	12	13
# SURVEYED		1284	1258	1278	1296	1327	1276	1373	1300	1210	805	819
RACE	RESP	'72	'74	'75	'77	'78	'82	'83	'85	'86	'88	'89
BLACK	YES	80%	78%	76%	78%	87%	91%	86%	89%	88%	88%	84%
	NO	20	22	22	22	13	9	13	11	12	12	16
# SURVEYED		245	168	161	173	150	153	157	141	180	121	98
RACE	RESP	'72	'74	'75	'77	'78	'82	'83	'85	'86	'88	'89
OTHER	YES	100%	71%	50%	60%	87%	78%	94%	75%	84%	78%	83%
	NO	0	29	50	40	13	22	6	25	16	22	17
# SURVEYED		4	7	4	15	15	27	16	40	37	32	36

TABLE IV: VOTE FOR FEMALE PRESIDENTIAL CANDIDATE -- BY AGE

Question: If your party nominated a woman for President, would you vote for her if she were qualified for the job? NOTE: Question not asked in 1973, 1976, 1984, 1987.

Responses: YES; NO

		YEAR										
AGE	RESP	'72	'74	'75	'77	'78	'82	'83	'85	'86	'88	'89
18-23	YES	79%	92%	88%	89%	94%	92%	94%	85%	95%	90%	88%
	NO	21	8	12	11	6	8	6	15	5	10	12
# SURVEYED		164	165	168	160	163	140	124	131	106	93	78
AGE	RESP	'72	'74	'75	'77	'78	'82	'83	'85	'86	'88	'89
24-29	YES	86%	89%	90%	89%	92%	90%	90%	90%	89%	94%	92%
	NO	14	11	9	11	8	10	10	10	11	6	8
# SURVEYED		224	207	225	202	237	240	276	211	211	146	142

TABLE IV: VOTE FOR FEMALE PRESIDENTIAL CANDIDATE -- BY AGE (Continued)

Question: If your party nominated a woman for President, would you vote for her if she were qualified for the job? NOTE: Question not asked in 1973, 1976, 1984, 1987.

Responses: YES; NO

		YEAR										
AGE	RESP	'72	'74	'75	'77	'78	'82	'83	'85	'86	'88	'89
30-35	YES	74%	87%	85%	91%	90%	93%	90%	90%	93%	95%	94%
	NO	26	13	15	9	10	7	10	10	7	5	6
# SURVEYED		170	165	168	184	227	201	231	207	219	129	140
AGE	RESP	'72	'74	'75	'77	'78	'82	'83	'85	'86	'88	'89
36-41	YES	76%	84%	84%	78%	84%	91%	91%	86%	92%	90%	91%
	NO	24	16	14	22	16	9	8	14	8	10	9
# SURVEYED		122	147	148	165	156	143	168	176	180	125	120
AGE	RESP	'72	'74	'75	'77	'78	'82	'83	'85	'86	'88	'89
42-47	YES	73%	84%	82%	77%	80%	94%	88%	88%	94%	88%	90%
	NO	27	16	18	23	20	6	12	12	6	12	10
# SURVEYED		176	146	141	145	115	114	143	121	138	105	96
AGE	RESP	'72	'74	'75	'77	'78	'82	'83	'85	'86	'88	'89
48-53	YES	69%	76%	78%	79%	79%	88%	89%	87%	85%	84%	84%
	NO	31	24	22	21	21	12	11	13	15	16	16
# SURVEYED		180	144	138	147	131	109	113	128	106	61	80
AGE	RESP	'72	'74	'75	'77	'78	'82	'83	'85	'86	'88	'89
54-59	YES	76%	74%	77%	88%	76%	76%	84%	81%	80%	93%	84%
	NO	24	26	23	12	24	24	16	19	20	7	16
# SURVEYED		151	133	124	158	133	140	127	126	95	45	69
AGE	RESP	'72	'74	'75	'77	'78	'82	'83	'85	'86	'88	'89
60-65	YES	62%	67%	76%	62%	71%	83%	84%	75%	83%	89%	82%
	NO	38	33	24	38	29	17	16	25	17	11	18
# SURVEYED		136	105	108	112	104	112	129	128	114	72	66
AGE	RESP	'72	'74	'75	'77	'78	'82	'83	'85	'86	'88	89%
66+	YES	66%	66%	62%	58%	61%	74%	72%	65%	71%	76%	74%
	NO	34	34	38	42	39	26	28	35	29	24	26
# SURVEYED		206	215	218	204	219	246	229	246	251	181	159

****

APPROVE OF WOMEN IN BUSINESS

TABLE I: APPROVE OF WOMEN IN BUSINESS -- BY TOTAL POPULATION

Question: Do you approve or disapprove of a married woman earning money in business or industry if she has a husband capable of supporting her? NOTE: Question was not asked in 1973, 1976, 1980, 1984, 1987.

Responses: AP = Approve; DS = Disapprove

	YEAR										
RESPONSE	'72	'74	'75	'77	'78	'82	'83	'85	'86	'88	'89
AP	65%	69%	71%	66%	73%	75%	77%	86%	78%	80%	79%
DS	35	31	29	34	27	25	23	14	22	20	21
# SURVEYED	1577	1449	1462	1506	1509	1480	1561	1488	1442	961	982

TABLE II: APPROVE OF WOMEN IN BUSINESS -- BY SEX

Question: Do you approve or disapprove of a married woman earning money in business or industry if she has a husband capable of supporting her? NOTE: Question was not asked in 1973, 1976, 1980, 1984, 1987.

Responses: AP = Approve; DS = Disapprove

		YEAR										
SEX	RESP	'72	'74	'75	'77	'78	'82	'83	'85	'86	'88	'89
M	AP	63%	66%	70%	68%	72%	74%	77%	87%	79%	82%	79%
	DS	37	34	30	32	28	26	23	13	21	18	21
# SURVEYED		793	677	658	682	632	628	671	666	610	425	419
SEX	RESP	'72	'74	'75	'77	'78	'82	'83	'85	'86	'88	'89
F	AP	68%	72%	72%	65%	74%	76%	77%	86%	77%	79%	79%
	DS	32	28	28	35	26	24	23	14	23	21	21
# SURVEYED		784	772	804	824	877	852	890	822	832	536	563

TABLE III: APPROVE OF WOMEN IN BUSINESS -- BY RACE

Question: Do you approve or disapprove of a married woman earning money in business or industry if she has a husband capable of supporting her? NOTE: Question was not asked in 1973, 1976, 1980, 1984, 1987.

Responses: AP = Approve; DS = Disapprove

		YEAR										
RACE	RESP	'72	'74	'75	'77	'78	'82	'83	'85	'86	'88	'89
WHITE	AP	64%	70%	71%	67%	74%	76%	78%	87%	78%	81%	80%
	DS	36	30	29	33	26	24	22	13	22	19	20
# SURVEYED		1319	1275	1299	1318	1338	1300	1383	1298	1226	807	845
RACE	RESP	'72	'74	'75	'77	'78	'82	'83	'85	'86	'88	'89
BLACK	AP	72%	63%	68%	64%	70%	71%	70%	83%	80%	77%	77%
	DS	28	37	32	36	30	29	30	17	20	23	23
# SURVEYED		255	167	159	173	155	153	161	147	179	121	101
RACE	RESP	'72	'74	'75	'77	'78	'82	'83	'85	'86	'88	'89
OTHER	AP	33%	86%	100%	60%	56%	70%	71%	84%	68%	73%	67%
	DS	67	14	0	40	44	30	29	16	32	27	33
# SURVEYED		3	7	4	15	16	27	17	43	37	33	36

TABLE IV: APPROVE OF WOMEN IN BUSINESS -- BY AGE

Question: Do you approve or disapprove of a married woman earning money in business or industry if she has a husband capable of supporting her? NOTE: Question was not asked in 1973, 1976, 1980, 1984, 1987.

Responses: AP = Approve; DS = Disapprove

		YEAR										
AGE	RESP	'72	'74	'75	'77	'78	'82	'83	'85	'86	'88	'89
18-23	AP	77%	85%	85%	75%	79%	83%	83%	90%	87%	82%	83%
	DS	23	15	15	25	21	17	17	10	13	18	17
# SURVEYED		166	168	172	162	157	145	126	132	108	94	83
AGE	RESP	'72	'74	'75	'77	'78	'82	'83	'85	'86	'88	'89
24-29	AP	76%	82%	86%	83%	82%	86%	84%	90%	88%	80%	86%
	DS	24	18	14	17	18	14	16	10	12	20	14
# SURVEYED		225	211	229	202	243	246	283	210	215	148	144

TABLE IV: APPROVE OF WOMEN IN BUSINESS -- BY AGE (Continued)

Question: Do you approve or disapprove of a married woman earning money in business or industry if she has a husband capable of supporting her? NOTE: Question was not asked in 1973, 1976, 1980, 1984, 1987.

Responses: AP = Approve; DS = Disapprove

		YEAR										
AGE	RESP	'72	'74	'75	'77	'78	'82	'83	'85	'86	'88	'89
30-35	AP	75%	78%	77%	77%	84%	86%	82%	88%	87%	88%	86%
	DS	25	22	23	23	16	14	18	12	13	12	14
# SURVEYED		184	171	167	185	226	201	232	211	221	129	140
AGE	RESP	'72	'74	'75	'77	'78	'82	'83	'85	'86	'88	'89
36-41	AP	70%	75%	84%	70%	81%	83%	86%	87%	85%	90%	81%
	DS	30	25	16	30	19	17	14	13	15	10	19
# SURVEYED		125	151	152	167	158	144	168	179	186	124	125
AGE	RESP	'72	'74	'75	'77	'78	'82	'83	'85	'86	'88	'89
42-47	AP	69%	70%	79%	63%	72%	83%	82%	93%	87%	91%	81%
	DS	31	30	21	37	28	17	18	7	13	9	19
# SURVEYED		185	150	140	142	118	118	141	122	137	106	108
AGE	RESP	'72	'74	'75	'77	'78	'82	'83	'85	'86	'88	'89
48-53	AP	65%	68%	64%	64%	77%	75%	80%	88%	70%	75%	84%
	DS	35	32	36	36	23	25	20	12	30	25	16
# SURVEYED		186	138	140	151	132	111	114	128	106	60	82
AGE	RESP	'72	'74	'75	'77	'78	'82	'83	'85	'86	'88	'89
54-59	YES	65%	61%	56%	68%	70%	72%	72%	83%	70%	81%	78%
	NO	35	39	44	32	30	28	28	17	30	19	22
# SURVEYED		148	133	120	163	135	138	131	127	97	48	68
AGE	RESP	'72	'74	'75	'77	'78	'82	'83	'85	'86	'88	'89
60-65	AP	57%	57%	58%	55%	59%	63%	69%	84%	71%	76%	75%
	DS	43	43	42	45	41	37	31	16	29	24	25
# SURVEYED		140	104	109	117	107	115	127	129	113	74	68
AGE	RESP	'72	'74	'75	'77	'78	'82	'83	'85	'86	'88	'89
66+	AP	37%	43%	47%	40%	52%	52%	55%	78%	56%	65%	60%
	DS	63	57	53	60	48	48	45	22	44	35	40
# SURVEYED		214	217	228	210	226	252	233	243	253	177	162

****

WOMAN SHOULD ENHANCE HUSBAND'S CAREER

TABLE I: WOMAN SHOULD ENHANCE HUSBAND'S CAREER -- BY TOTAL POPULATION

Question: Please tell me whether you strongly agree, agree, disagree, or strongly disagree with the following statement: It is more important for a wife to help her husband's career than to have one herself. NOTE: Question not asked in 1972-1976, 1978-1984, 1987.

Responses: SA = Strongly agree; AG = Agree; DA = Disagree; SD = Strongly disagree

	YEAR				
RESPONSE	'77	'85	'86	'88	'89
SA	14%	7%	6%	5%	5%
AG	43	31	30	26	22
DA	36	46	47	48	52
SD	7	16	17	21	20
# SURVEYED	1472	1472	1436	966	965

TABLE II: WOMAN SHOULD ENHANCE HUSBAND'S CAREER -- BY SEX

Question: Please tell me whether you strongly agree, agree, disagree, or strongly disagree with the following statement: It is more important for a wife to help her husband's career than to have one herself. NOTE: Question not asked in 1972-1976, 1978-1984, 1987.

Responses: SA = Strongly agree; AG = Agree; DA = Disagree; SD = Strongly disagree

		YEAR				
SEX	RESP	'77	'85	'86	'88	'89
M	SA	12%	6%	5%	6%	6%
	AG	40	31	29	28	21
	DA	42	51	52	51	60
	SD	6	12	14	15	13
# SURVEYED		660	658	600	430	406

		YEAR				
SEX	RESP	'77	'85	'86	'88	'89
F	SA	15%	7%	7%	4%	5%
	AG	45	31	30	25	24
	DA	32	42	44	46	46
	SD	7	20	18	25	25
# SURVEYED		812	814	836	536	559

TABLE III: WOMAN SHOULD ENHANCE HUSBAND'S CAREER -- BY RACE

Question: Please tell me whether you strongly agree, agree, disagree, or strongly disagree with the following statement: It is more important for a wife to help her husband's career than to have one herself. NOTE: Question not asked in 1972-1976, 1978-1984, 1987.

Responses: SA = Strongly agree; AG = Agree; DA = Disagree; SD = Strongly disagree

RACE	RESP	'77	'85	'86	'88	'89
WHITE	SA	14%	6%	6%	4%	6%
	AG	43	31	30	26	23
	DA	36	46	47	49	52
	SD	7	17	17	20	20
# SURVEYED		1288	1285	1224	809	826

RACE	RESP	'77	'85	'86	'88	'89
BLACK	SA	12%	9%	6%	6%	3%
	AG	42	26	27	23	18
	DA	38	49	54	45	55
	SD	7	16	14	27	24
# SURVEYED		169	144	177	123	101

RACE	RESP	'77	'85	'86	'88	'89
OTHER	SA	40%	9%	6%	15%	8%
	AG	47	35	34	41	32
	DA	13	47	40	32	50
	SD	0	9	20	12	11
# SURVEYED		15	43	35	34	38

TABLE IV: WOMAN SHOULD ENHANCE HUSBAND'S CAREER -- BY AGE

Question: Please tell me whether you strongly agree, agree, disagree, or strongly disagree with the following statement: It is more important for a wife to help her husband's career than to have one herself. NOTE: Question not asked in 1972-1976, 1978-1984, 1987.

Responses: SA = Strongly agree; AG = Agree; DA = Disagree; SD = Strongly disagree

AGE	RESP	'77	'85	'86	'88	'89
18-23	SA	6%	1%	5%	1%	4%
	AG	32	14	11	17	16
	DA	47	57	53	54	60
	SD	16	28	31	28	21
# SURVEYED		161	130	107	93	82
24-29	SA	6%	2%	6%	3%	3%
	AG	29	19	19	10	10
	DA	54	53	55	56	58
	SD	12	26	21	31	29
# SURVEYED		199	211	214	147	141
30-35	SA	13%	4%	4%	2%	1%
	AG	29	21	14	13	14
	DA	44	55	58	54	54
	SD	13	21	24	31	30
# SURVEYED		179	208	217	129	138

AGE	RESP	'77	'85	'86	'88	'89
36-41	SA	15%	6%	2%	2%	4%
	AG	37	17	24	16	12
	DA	42	53	48	56	59
	SD	6	24	25	27	25
# SURVEYED		162	180	185	126	123
42-47	SA	16%	3%	6%	5%	3%
	AG	43	18	23	25	20
	DA	36	61	57	49	54
	SD	4	18	14	22	22
# SURVEYED		137	115	140	105	103
48-53	SA	26%	5%	4%	7%	2%
	AG	39	39	31	28	25
	DA	34	41	53	52	53
	SD	1	15	12	13	20
# SURVEYED		146	124	106	61	81

AGE	RESP	'77	'85	'86	'88	'89
54-59	SA	8%	11%	8%	4%	7%
	AG	62	44	41	36	22
	DA	28	38	39	44	55
	SD	2	6	12	16	16
# SURVEYED		163	126	98	50	69
60-65	SA	11%	6%	6%	10%	12%
	AG	67	50	47	33	40
	DA	21	38	39	51	43
	SD	2	5	8	7	6
# SURVEYED		112	125	109	73	68
66+	SA	25%	17%	12%	11%	13%
	AG	58	54	56	55	46
	DA	16	26	29	28	35
	SD	1	4	3	6	6
# SURVEYED		206	247	253	181	157

****

ALLOW ABORTION ON DEMAND

TABLE I: ALLOW ABORTION ON DEMAND -- BY TOTAL POPULATION

Question: Please tell me whether or not you think it should be possible for a pregnant woman to obtain a legal abortion if the woman wants it for any reason? NOTE: Question not asked in 1972-1976, 1986.

Responses: YES; NO

	YEAR									
RESPONSE	'77	'78	'80	'82	'83	'84	'85	'87	'88	'89
YES	38%	33%	41%	41%	34%	39%	37%	39%	36%	40%
NO	62	67	59	59	66	61	63	61	64	60
# SURVEYED	1479	1484	1406	1436	1515	1420	1481	1394	936	989

TABLE II: ALLOW ABORTION ON DEMAND -- BY SEX

Question: Please tell me whether or not you think it should be possible for a pregnant woman to obtain a legal abortion if the woman wants it for any reason? NOTE: Question not asked in 1972-1976, 1986.

Responses: YES; NO

		YEAR									
SEX	RESP	'77	'78	'80	'82	'83	'84	'85	'87	'88	'89
M	YES	39%	35%	41%	42%	35%	40%	39%	44%	36%	43%
	NO	61	65	59	58	65	60	61	56	64	57
# SURVEYED		665	619	616	605	653	578	666	601	381	427
SEX	RESP	'77	'78	'80	'82	'83	'84	'85	'87	'88	'89
F	YES	37%	32%	41%	41%	34%	37%	35%	36%	36%	38%
	NO	63	68	59	59	66	63	65	64	64	62
# SURVEYED		814	865	790	831	862	842	815	793	555	562

TABLE III: ALLOW ABORTION ON DEMAND -- BY RACE

Question: Please tell me whether or not you think it should be possible for a pregnant woman to obtain a legal abortion if the woman wants it for any reason? NOTE: Question not asked in 1972-1976, 1986.

Responses: YES; NO

		YEAR									
RACE	RESP	'77	'78	'80	'82	'83	'84	'85	'87	'88	'89
WHITE	YES	38%	33%	42%	42%	35%	40%	38%	42%	37%	40%
	NO	62	67	58	58	65	60	63	58	63	60
# SURVEYED		1296	1315	1266	1268	1342	1209	1296	1165	767	855
RACE	RESP	'77	'78	'80	'82	'83	'84	'85	'87	'88	'89
BLACK	YES	31%	34%	34%	34%	32%	27%	34%	28%	36%	43%
	NO	69	66	66	66	68	73	66	72	64	57
# SURVEYED		169	154	131	145	158	162	142	180	126	98
RACE	RESP	'77	'78	'80	'82	'83	'84	'85	'87	'88	'89
OTHER	YES	57%	67%	33%	43%	33%	35%	30%	24%	26%	44%
	NO	43	33	67	57	67	65	70	76	74	56
# SURVEYED		14	15	9	23	15	49	43	49	43	36

TABLE IV: ALLOW ABORTION ON DEMAND -- BY AGE

Question: Please tell me whether or not you think it should be possible for a pregnant woman to obtain a legal abortion if the woman wants it for any reason? NOTE: Question not asked in 1972-1976, 1986.

Responses: YES; NO

		YEAR									
AGE	RESP	'77	'78	'80	'82	'83	'84	'85	'87	'88	'89
18-23	YES	33%	36%	43%	35%	33%	36%	35%	47%	42%	45%
	NO	67	64	57	65	67	64	65	53	58	55
# SURVEYED		159	158	150	141	124	153	130	120	91	96
AGE	RESP	'77	'78	'80	'82	'83	'84	'85	'87	'88	'89
24-29	YES	43%	40%	49%	50%	37%	44%	43%	41%	39%	40%
	NO	57	60	51	50	63	56	57	59	61	60
# SURVEYED		198	239	195	237	278	226	214	184	128	111
AGE	RESP	'77	'78	'80	'82	'83	'84	'85	'87	'88	'89

TABLE IV: ALLOW ABORTION ON DEMAND -- BY AGE (Continued)

Question: Please tell me whether or not you think it should be possible for a pregnant woman to obtain a legal abortion if the woman wants it for any reason? NOTE: Question not asked in 1972-1976, 1986.

Responses: YES; NO

		YEAR									
AGE	RESP	'77	'78	'80	'82	'83	'84	'85	'87	'88	'89
30-35	YES	42%	39%	47%	50%	37%	45%	39%	46%	43%	48%
	NO	58	61	53	50	63	55	61	54	57	52
# SURVEYED		187	226	211	197	228	196	203	213	127	128
AGE	RESP	'77	'78	'80	'82	'83	'84	'85	'87	'88	'89
36-41	YES	41%	32%	44%	50%	39%	51%	40%	51%	39%	50%
	NO	59	68	56	50	61	49	60	49	61	50
# SURVEYED		165	155	142	140	164	180	180	175	128	133
AGE	RESP	'77	'78	'80	'82	'83	'84	'85	'87	'88	'89
42-47	YES	34%	36%	43%	37%	30%	43%	53%	35%	43%	43%
	NO	66	64	57	63	70	57	47	65	57	57
# SURVEYED		143	118	112	114	139	123	121	153	98	102
AGE	RESP	'77	'78	'80	'82	'83	'84	'85	'87	'88	'89
48-53	YES	41%	30%	39%	38%	37%	30%	41%	33%	33%	41%
	NO	59	70	61	62	63	70	59	68	67	59
# SURVEYED		147	128	119	109	110	102	128	120	64	90
AGE	RESP	'77	'78	'80	'82	'83	'84	'85	'87	'88	'89
54-59	YES	32%	25%	35%	37%	38%	21%	29%	41%	32%	47%
	NO	68	75	65	63	63	79	71	59	68	53
# SURVEYED		163	134	130	140	128	111	125	94	50	58
AGE	RESP	'77	'78	'80	'82	'83	'84	'85	'87	'88	'89
60-65	YES	42%	29%	37%	40%	31%	40%	32%	24%	30%	23%
	NO	58	71	63	60	69	60	68	76	70	77
# SURVEYED		113	104	115	108	125	109	124	95	80	77
AGE	RESP	'77	'78	'80	'82	'83	'84	'85	'87	'88	'89
66+	YES	32%	27%	33%	30%	26%	28%	25%	33%	25%	30%
	NO	68	73	67	70	74	72	75	67	75	70
# SURVEYED		198	215	223	240	214	215	249	236	168	191

****

ALLOW ABORTION FOR SERIOUS DEFECT

TABLE I: ALLOW ABORTION FOR SERIOUS DEFECT -- BY TOTAL POPULATION

Question: Please tell me whether or not you think it should be possible for a pregnant woman to obtain a legal abortion if there is a strong chance of serious defect in the baby? NOTE: Question not asked in 1986.

Responses: YES; NO

	YEAR														
RESPONSE	'72	'73	'74	'75	'76	'77	'78	'80	'82	'83	'84	'85	'87	'88	'89
YES	79%	84%	85%	83%	84%	85%	82%	83%	84%	79%	80%	79%	79%	79%	81%
NO	21	16	15	17	16	15	18	17	16	21	20	21	21	21	19
# SURVEYED	1526	1464	1440	1438	1457	1487	1497	1419	1447	1514	1421	1486	1414	944	995

TABLE II: ALLOW ABORTION FOR SERIOUS DEFECT -- BY SEX

Question: Please tell me whether or not you think it should be possible for a pregnant woman to obtain a legal abortion if there is a strong chance of serious defect in the baby? NOTE: Question not asked in 1986.

Responses: YES; NO

		YEAR														
SEX	RESP	'72	'73	'74	'75	'76	'77	'78	'80	'82	'83	'84	'85	'87	'88	'89
M	YES	80%	84%	84%	81%	84%	84%	82%	85%	85%	80%	82%	80%	81%	79%	83%
	NO	20	16	16	19	16	16	18	15	15	20	18	20	19	21	17
# SURVEYED		768	681	670	644	647	670	629	618	615	649	577	668	610	394	431
SEX	RESP	'72	'73	'74	'75	'76	'77	'78	'80	'82	'83	'84	'85	'87	'88	'89
F	YES	78%	85%	86%	85%	84%	87%	82%	82%	84%	78%	79%	78%	78%	79%	80%
	NO	22	15	14	15	16	13	18	18	16	22	21	22	22	21	20
# SURVEYED		758	783	770	794	810	817	868	801	832	865	844	818	804	550	564

TABLE III: ALLOW ABORTION FOR SERIOUS DEFECT -- BY RACE

Question: Please tell me whether or not you think it should be possible for a pregnant woman to obtain a legal abortion if there is a strong chance of serious defect in the baby? NOTE: Question not asked in 1986.

Responses: YES; NO

		YEAR														
RACE	RESP	'72	'73	'74	'75	'76	'77	'78	'80	'82	'83	'84	'85	'87	'88	'89
WHITE	YES	82%	86%	87%	85%	85%	88%	84%	85%	86%	80%	82%	80%	82%	80%	81%
	NO	18	14	13	15	15	12	16	15	14	20	18	20	18	20	19
# SURVEYED		1282	1280	1263	1277	1326	1305	1328	1273	1274	1344	1214	1301	1182	776	862
RACE	RESP	'72	'73	'74	'75	'76	'77	'78	'80	'82	'83	'84	'85	'87	'88	'89
BLACK	YES	60%	71%	72%	69%	68%	70%	68%	68%	68%	69%	68%	67%	67%	71%	80%
	NO	40	29	28	31	32	30	32	32	32	31	32	33	33	29	20
# SURVEYED		240	172	170	157	122	168	154	136	148	154	157	144	182	126	93
RACE	RESP	'72	'73	'74	'75	'76	'77	'78	'80	'82	'83	'84	'85	'87	'88	'89
OTHER	YES	100%	83%	86%	100%	89%	79%	80%	90%	88%	75%	74%	83%	76%	76%	88%
	NO	0	17	14	0	11	21	20	10	12	25	26	17	24	24	13
# SURVEYED		4	12	7	4	9	14	15	10	25	16	50	41	50	42	40

TABLE IV: ALLOW ABORTION FOR SERIOUS DEFECT -- BY AGE

Question: Please tell me whether or not you think it should be possible for a pregnant woman to obtain a legal abortion if there is a strong chance of serious defect in the baby? NOTE: Question not asked in 1986.

Responses: YES; NO

		YEAR														
AGE	RESP	'72	'73	'74	'75	'76	'77	'78	'80	'82	'83	'84	'85	'87	'88	'89
18-23	YES	81%	88%	88%	84%	86%	85%	89%	84%	77%	73%	83%	80%	81%	83%	79%
	NO	19	12	12	16	14	15	11	16	23	27	17	20	19	17	21
# SURVEYED		161	170	163	166	160	160	161	152	140	123	159	128	124	95	95
AGE	RESP	'72	'73	'74	'75	'76	'77	'78	'80	'82	'83	'84	'85	'87	'88	'89
24-29	YES	87%	83%	88%	86%	89%	90%	85%	86%	88%	84%	81%	80%	76%	82%	82%
	NO	13	17	12	14	11	10	15	14	12	16	19	20	24	18	18
# SURVEYED		223	209	206	226	226	199	239	196	241	271	224	214	186	129	111

TABLE IV: ALLOW ABORTION FOR SERIOUS DEFECT -- BY AGE (Continued)

Question: Please tell me whether or not you think it should be possible for a pregnant woman to obtain a legal abortion if there is a strong chance of serious defect in the baby? NOTE: Question not asked in 1986.

Responses: YES; NO

		YEAR														
AGE	RESP	'72	'73	'74	'75	'76	'77	'78	'80	'82	'83	'84	'85	'87	'88	'89
30-35	YES	86%	88%	88%	84%	86%	87%	83%	85%	88%	84%	85%	82%	83%	83%	84%
	NO	14	12	12	16	14	13	17	15	12	16	15	18	17	17	16
# SURVEYED		181	163	170	166	183	187	226	211	199	231	196	207	216	127	132
AGE	RESP	'72	'73	'74	'75	'76	'77	'78	'80	'82	'83	'84	'85	'87	'88	'89
36-41	YES	79%	87%	86%	81%	83%	85%	78%	84%	80%	74%	81%	81%	86%	79%	83%
	NO	21	13	14	19	17	15	22	16	20	26	19	19	14	21	17
# SURVEYED		122	171	152	150	155	166	158	147	143	164	185	177	181	131	132
AGE	RESP	'72	'73	'74	'75	'76	'77	'78	'80	'82	'83	'84	'85	'87	'88	'89
42-47	YES	83%	88%	82%	86%	83%	84%	76%	85%	89%	80%	81%	84%	75%	79%	78%
	NO	17	12	18	14	17	16	24	15	11	20	19	16	25	21	22
# SURVEYED		174	141	149	137	112	141	118	112	114	139	122	121	156	98	103
AGE	RESP	'72	'73	'74	'75	'76	'77	'78	'80	'82	'83	'84	'85	'87	'88	'89
48-53	YES	77%	82%	86%	81%	83%	86%	81%	81%	91%	78%	76%	75%	82%	67%	83%
	NO	23	18	14	19	17	14	19	19	9	22	24	25	18	33	17
# SURVEYED		181	148	142	139	131	146	128	119	106	113	100	127	122	64	95
AGE	RESP	'72	'73	'74	'75	'76	'77	'78	'80	'82	'83	'84	'85	'87	'88	'89
54-59	YES	75%	78%	83%	82%	82%	90%	78%	86%	85%	74%	77%	77%	79%	80%	84%
	NO	25	22	17	18	18	10	22	14	15	26	23	23	21	20	16
# SURVEYED		147	151	136	125	122	164	135	132	140	129	111	128	95	51	57
AGE	RESP	'72	'73	'74	'75	'76	'77	'78	'80	'82	'83	'84	'85	'87	'88	'89
60-65	YES	75%	83%	86%	83%	84%	87%	86%	87%	82%	80%	77%	78%	83%	77%	82%
	NO	25	17	14	17	16	13	14	13	18	20	23	22	17	23	18
# SURVEYED		128	117	100	109	129	116	102	115	113	126	108	126	94	83	77
AGE	RESP	'72	'73	'74	'75	'76	'77	'78	'80	'82	'83	'84	'85	'87	'88	'89
66+	YES	64%	84%	80%	81%	79%	78%	80%	76%	81%	77%	77%	72%	74%	75%	79%
	NO	36	16	20	19	21	22	20	24	19	23	23	28	26	25	21
# SURVEYED		206	191	216	215	234	201	223	227	240	213	210	251	236	163	190

****0**

ALLOW ABORTION FOR HEALTH RISK

TABLE I: ALLOW ABORTION FOR HEALTH RISK -- BY TOTAL POPULATION

Question: Please tell me whether or not you think it should be possible for a pregnant woman to obtain a legal abortion if the woman's own health is seriously endangered by the pregnancy? NOTE: Question not asked in 1986.

Responses: YES; NO

	YEAR														
RESPONSE	'72	'73	'74	'75	'76	'77	'78	'80	'82	'83	'84	'85	'87	'88	'89
YES	87%	92%	92%	91%	91%	91%	91%	90%	92%	90%	90%	89%	88%	89%	90%
NO	13	8	8	9	9	9	9	10	8	10	10	11	12	11	10
# SURVEYED	1539	1476	1452	1449	1464	1488	1492	1429	1466	1520	1431	1491	1418	942	1003

TABLE II: ALLOW ABORTION FOR HEALTH RISK -- BY SEX

Question: Please tell me whether or not you think it should be possible for a pregnant woman to obtain a legal abortion if the woman's own health is seriously endangered by the pregnancy? NOTE: Question not asked in 1986.

Responses: YES; NO

		YEAR														
SEX	RESP	'72	'73	'74	'75	'76	'77	'78	'80	'82	'83	'84	'85	'87	'88	'89
M	YES	88%	93%	92%	91%	92%	91%	90%	93%	93%	90%	91%	92%	91%	90%	90%
	NO	12	7	8	9	8	9	10	7	7	10	9	8	9	10	10
# SURVEYED		772	688	679	645	656	671	631	621	626	655	584	673	619	393	437
SEX	RESP	'72	'73	'74	'75	'76	'77	'78	'80	'82	'83	'84	'85	'87	'88	'89
F	YES	86%	91%	93%	91%	90%	90%	91%	88%	91%	89%	88%	87%	86%	88%	90%
	NO	14	9	7	9	10	10	9	12	9	11	12	13	14	12	10
# SURVEYED		767	788	773	804	808	817	861	808	840	865	847	818	799	549	566

TABLE III: ALLOW ABORTION FOR HEALTH RISK -- BY RACE

Question: Please tell me whether or not you think it should be possible for a pregnant woman to obtain a legal abortion if the woman's own health is seriously endangered by the pregnancy? NOTE: Question not asked in 1986.

Responses: YES; NO

		YEAR														
RACE	RESP	'72	'73	'74	'75	'76	'77	'78	'80	'82	'83	'84	'85	'87	'88	'89
WHITE	YES	89%	94%	93%	91%	92%	92%	91%	91%	92%	91%	90%	90%	89%	89%	90%
	NO	11	6	7	9	8	8	9	9	8	9	10	10	11	11	10
# SURVEYED		1292	1286	1278	1288	1329	1301	1320	1283	1288	1346	1215	1303	1184	777	863
RACE	RESP	'72	'73	'74	'75	'76	'77	'78	'80	'82	'83	'84	'85	'87	'88	'89
BLACK	YES	74%	82%	90%	85%	83%	78%	87%	82%	88%	84%	83%	85%	85%	87%	90%
	NO	26	18	10	15	17	22	13	18	12	16	17	15	15	13	10
# SURVEYED		243	177	167	157	126	173	156	137	151	158	166	145	183	124	99
RACE	RESP	'72	'73	'74	'75	'76	'77	'78	'80	'82	'83	'84	'85	'87	'88	'89
OTHER	YES	100%	92%	100%	100%	89%	79%	81%	78%	93%	69%	90%	95%	84%	85%	93%
	NO	0	8	0	0	11	21	19	22	7	31	10	5	16	15	7
# SURVEYED		4	13	7	4	9	14	16	9	27	16	50	43	51	41	41

TABLE IV: ALLOW ABORTION FOR HEALTH RISK -- BY AGE

Question: Please tell me whether or not you think it should be possible for a pregnant woman to obtain a legal abortion if the woman's own health is seriously endangered by the pregnancy? NOTE: Question not asked in 1986.

Responses: YES; NO

		YEAR														
AGE	RESP	'72	'73	'74	'75	'76	'77	'78	'80	'82	'83	'84	'85	'87	'88	'89
18-23	YES	90%	98%	96%	96%	95%	91%	93%	91%	94%	92%	94%	89%	90%	91%	91%
	NO	10	2	4	4	5	9	7	9	6	8	6	11	10	9	9
# SURVEYED		165	169	168	168	158	160	162	155	144	123	157	131	125	93	96
AGE	RESP	'72	'73	'74	'75	'76	'77	'78	'80	'82	'83	'84	'85	'87	'88	'89
24-29	YES	94%	93%	95%	95%	96%	97%	93%	91%	95%	92%	91%	92%	89%	92%	92%
	NO	6	7	5	5	4	3	7	9	5	8	9	8	11	8	8
# SURVEYED		224	210	210	226	224	198	239	198	244	275	225	215	186	130	113

TABLE IV: ALLOW ABORTION FOR HEALTH RISK -- BY AGE (Continued)

Question: Please tell me whether or not you think it should be possible for a pregnant woman to obtain a legal abortion if the woman's own health is seriously endangered by the pregnancy? NOTE: Question not asked in 1986.

Responses: YES; NO

		YEAR														
AGE	RESP	'72	'73	'74	'75	'76	'77	'78	'80	'82	'83	'84	'85	'87	'88	'89
30-35	YES	89%	92%	93%	90%	96%	91%	92%	95%	95%	90%	90%	90%	92%	94%	94%
	NO	11	8	7	10	4	9	8	5	5	10	10	10	8	6	6
# SURVEYED		182	164	174	168	181	187	225	210	200	228	196	209	215	127	130
AGE	RESP	'72	'73	'74	'75	'76	'77	'78	'80	'82	'83	'84	'85	'87	'88	'89
36-41	YES	85%	93%	91%	91%	94%	91%	89%	93%	89%	87%	94%	92%	91%	90%	90%
	NO	15	7	9	9	6	9	11	7	11	13	6	8	9	10	10
# SURVEYED		123	173	149	150	157	163	158	149	142	167	186	179	183	130	133
AGE	RESP	'72	'73	'74	'75	'76	'77	'78	'80	'82	'83	'84	'85	'87	'88	'89
42-47	YES	90%	94%	93%	95%	86%	88%	86%	93%	92%	94%	93%	94%	85%	91%	91%
	NO	10	6	7	5	14	12	14	7	8	6	7	6	15	9	9
# SURVEYED		178	143	151	140	111	142	118	113	117	140	121	120	155	97	104
AGE	RESP	'72	'73	'74	'75	'76	'77	'78	'80	'82	'83	'84	'85	'87	'88	'89
48-53	YES	87%	89%	96%	84%	89%	92%	92%	86%	93%	83%	86%	89%	91%	78%	93%
	NO	13	11	4	16	11	8	8	14	7	17	14	11	9	22	7
# SURVEYED		180	149	141	139	131	146	128	118	110	114	100	123	120	63	94
AGE	RESP	'72	'73	'74	'75	'76	'77	'78	'80	'82	'83	'84	'85	'87	'88	'89
54-59	YES	82%	88%	89%	91%	88%	93%	89%	92%	90%	86%	84%	88%	87%	92%	91%
	NO	18	12	11	9	12	7	11	8	10	14	16	12	13	8	9
# SURVEYED		149	151	134	122	127	165	133	132	143	125	112	127	92	50	58
AGE	RESP	'72	'73	'74	'75	'76	'77	'78	'80	'82	'83	'84	'85	'87	'88	'89
60-65	YES	89%	91%	91%	89%	91%	85%	86%	90%	87%	93%	87%	89%	90%	87%	88%
	NO	11	9	9	11	9	15	14	10	13	7	13	11	10	13	12
# SURVEYED		132	116	102	110	131	115	102	117	114	125	110	126	97	83	78
AGE	RESP	'72	'73	'74	'75	'76	'77	'78	'80	'82	'83	'84	'85	'87	'88	'89
66+	YES	76%	92%	88%	84%	82%	84%	91%	83%	90%	88%	85%	84%	83%	83%	85%
	NO	24	8	12	16	18	16	9	17	10	12	15	16	17	17	15
# SURVEYED		202	197	217	222	239	206	220	228	241	219	220	255	241	167	194

****

ALLOW ABORTION FOR FAMILY SIZE

TABLE I: ALLOW ABORTION FOR FAMILY SIZE -- BY TOTAL POPULATION

Question: Please tell me whether or not you think it should be possible for a pregnant woman to obtain a legal abortion if she is married and does not want any more children? NOTE: Question not asked in 1986.

Responses: YES; NO

	YEAR														
RESPONSE	'72	'73	'74	'75	'76	'77	'78	'80	'82	'83	'84	'85	'87	'88	'89
YES	40%	48%	47%	46%	46%	47%	40%	47%	49%	39%	43%	40%	42%	40%	45%
NO	60	52	53	54	54	53	60	53	51	61	57	60	58	60	55
# SURVEYED	1528	1453	1411	1426	1447	1462	1483	1407	1436	1520	1420	1488	1411	949	991

TABLE II: ALLOW ABORTION FOR FAMILY SIZE -- BY SEX

Question: Please tell me whether or not you think it should be possible for a pregnant woman to obtain a legal abortion if she is married and does not want any more children? NOTE: Question not asked in 1986.

Responses: YES; NO

		YEAR														
SEX	RESP	'72	'73	'74	'75	'76	'77	'78	'80	'82	'83	'84	'85	'87	'88	'89
M	YES	42%	53%	48%	46%	49%	49%	42%	48%	51%	43%	45%	44%	46%	41%	49%
	NO	58	47	52	54	51	51	58	52	49	57	55	56	54	59	51
# SURVEYED		768	678	652	644	651	661	623	616	607	659	575	672	611	389	431
SEX	RESP	'72	'73	'74	'75	'76	'77	'78	'80	'82	'83	'84	'85	'87	'88	'89
F	YES	37%	43%	46%	45%	43%	45%	39%	46%	47%	36%	41%	38%	38%	39%	41%
	NO	63	57	54	55	57	55	61	54	53	64	59	62	62	61	59
# SURVEYED		760	775	759	782	796	801	860	791	829	861	845	816	800	560	560

TABLE III: ALLOW ABORTION FOR FAMILY SIZE -- BY RACE

Question: Please tell me whether or not you think it should be possible for a pregnant woman to obtain a legal abortion if she is married and does not want any more children? NOTE: Question not asked in 1986.

Responses: YES; NO

		YEAR														
RACE	RESP	'72	'73	'74	'75	'76	'77	'78	'80	'82	'83	'84	'85	'87	'88	'89
WHITE	YES	41%	49%	48%	46%	47%	47%	40%	48%	49%	39%	44%	41%	44%	40%	44%
	NO	59	51	52	54	53	53	60	52	51	61	56	59	56	60	56
# SURVEYED		1283	1266	1240	1267	1311	1276	1313	1268	1259	1349	1208	1303	1182	780	859
RACE	RESP	'72	'73	'74	'75	'76	'77	'78	'80	'82	'83	'84	'85	'87	'88	'89
BLACK	YES	32%	37%	38%	42%	39%	42%	37%	43%	40%	37%	31%	36%	28%	39%	47%
	NO	68	63	62	58	61	58	63	57	60	63	69	64	72	61	53
# SURVEYED		241	174	164	156	127	172	155	130	152	156	164	143	179	125	97
RACE	RESP	'72	'73	'74	'75	'76	'77	'78	'80	'82	'83	'84	'85	'87	'88	'89
OTHER	YES	0%	46%	29%	0%	56%	64%	67%	33%	52%	40%	38%	40%	26%	34%	37%
	NO	100	54	71	100	44	36	33	67	48	60	63	60	74	66	63
# SURVEYED		4	13	7	3	9	14	15	9	25	15	48	42	50	44	35

TABLE IV: ALLOW ABORTION FOR FAMILY SIZE -- BY AGE

Question: Please tell me whether or not you think it should be possible for a pregnant woman to obtain a legal abortion if she is married and does not want any more children? NOTE: Question not asked in 1986.

Responses: YES; NO

		YEAR														
AGE	RESP	'72	'73	'74	'75	'76	'77	'78	'80	'82	'83	'84	'85	'87	'88	'89
18-23	YES	47%	54%	54%	43%	53%	47%	42%	45%	39%	37%	39%	36%	43%	41%	45%
	NO	53	46	46	57	47	53	58	55	61	63	61	64	57	59	55
# SURVEYED		165	167	160	169	160	158	158	152	144	126	155	132	123	93	96
AGE	RESP	'72	'73	'74	'75	'76	'77	'78	'80	'82	'83	'84	'85	'87	'88	'89
24-29	YES	47%	60%	52%	54%	56%	54%	48%	53%	56%	41%	49%	44%	45%	42%	46%
	NO	53	40	48	46	44	46	52	47	44	59	51	56	55	58	54
# SURVEYED		225	209	207	227	221	199	238	197	239	278	227	213	186	129	111

TABLE IV: ALLOW ABORTION FOR FAMILY SIZE -- BY AGE (Continued)

Question: Please tell me whether or not you think it should be possible for a pregnant woman to obtain a legal abortion if she is married and does not want any more children? NOTE: Question not asked in 1986.

Responses: YES; NO

		YEAR														
AGE	RESP	'72	'73	'74	'75	'76	'77	'78	'80	'82	'83	'84	'85	'87	'88	'89
30-35	YES	39%	49%	47%	50%	50%	51%	49%	51%	59%	43%	48%	46%	42%	50%	52%
	NO	61	51	53	50	50	49	51	49	42	57	52	54	58	50	48
# SURVEYED		178	165	171	169	179	184	227	211	200	230	196	207	217	129	129
AGE	RESP	'72	'73	'74	'75	'76	'77	'78	'80	'82	'83	'84	'85	'87	'88	'89
36-41	YES	42%	44%	47%	47%	52%	48%	37%	48%	55%	45%	56%	46%	54%	43%	51%
	NO	58	56	53	53	48	52	63	52	45	55	44	54	46	57	49
# SURVEYED		120	169	151	144	154	164	158	144	139	166	184	181	177	130	129
AGE	RESP	'72	'73	'74	'75	'76	'77	'78	'80	'82	'83	'84	'85	'87	'88	'89
42-47	YES	42%	51%	47%	56%	37%	38%	39%	50%	52%	36%	45%	50%	44%	40%	48%
	NO	58	49	53	44	63	62	61	50	48	64	55	50	56	60	52
# SURVEYED		171	144	146	132	111	138	116	109	114	137	120	121	156	99	103
AGE	RESP	'72	'73	'74	'75	'76	'77	'78	'80	'82	'83	'84	'85	'87	'88	'89
48-53	YES	44%	44%	50%	43%	42%	51%	35%	50%	52%	39%	37%	45%	36%	37%	45%
	NO	56	56	50	57	58	49	65	50	48	61	63	55	64	63	55
# SURVEYED		183	147	137	139	127	145	128	116	108	109	101	128	121	65	93
AGE	RESP	'72	'73	'74	'75	'76	'77	'78	'80	'82	'83	'84	'85	'87	'88	'89
54-59	YES	32%	43%	46%	36%	44%	45%	31%	44%	43%	40%	31%	33%	43%	35%	45%
	NO	68	57	54	64	56	55	69	56	57	60	69	67	57	65	55
# SURVEYED		148	149	134	117	124	164	129	130	142	129	110	128	96	52	60
AGE	RESP	'72	'73	'74	'75	'76	'77	'78	'80	'82	'83	'84	'85	'87	'88	'89
60-65	YES	37%	45%	46%	39%	43%	49%	43%	43%	46%	35%	41%	35%	32%	33%	31%
	NO	63	55	54	61	57	51	57	57	54	65	59	65	68	67	69
# SURVEYED		135	114	98	109	132	110	105	111	111	125	107	126	96	82	77
AGE	RESP	'72	'73	'74	'75	'76	'77	'78	'80	'82	'83	'84	'85	'87	'88	'89
66+	YES	27%	37%	35%	40%	35%	35%	32%	41%	35%	31%	31%	30%	34%	34%	37%
	NO	73	63	65	60	65	65	68	59	65	69	69	70	66	66	63
# SURVEYED		199	185	203	216	234	193	217	228	228	215	215	245	235	167	190

****

ALLOW ABORTION FOR POVERTY

TABLE I: ALLOW ABORTION FOR POVERTY -- BY TOTAL POPULATION

Question: Please tell me whether or not you think it should be possible for a pregnant woman to obtain a legal abortion if the family has a very low income and cannot afford any more children? NOTE: Question not asked in 1986.

Responses: YES; NO

	YEAR														
RESPONSE	'72	'73	'74	'75	'76	'77	'78	'80	'82	'83	'84	'85	'87	'88	'89
YES	49%	53%	55%	53%	53%	53%	47%	52%	52%	44%	46%	44%	45%	42%	48%
NO	51	47	45	47	47	47	53	48	48	56	54	56	55	58	52
# SURVEYED	1507	1456	1417	1416	1434	1478	1469	1408	1441	1507	1414	1488	1405	941	992

TABLE II: ALLOW ABORTION FOR POVERTY -- BY SEX

Question: Please tell me whether or not you think it should be possible for a pregnant woman to obtain a legal abortion if the family has a very low income and cannot afford any more children? NOTE: Question not asked in 1986.

Responses: YES; NO

		YEAR														
SEX	RESP	'72	'73	'74	'75	'76	'77	'78	'80	'82	'83	'84	'85	'87	'88	'89
M	YES	50%	57%	54%	55%	56%	53%	50%	53%	52%	46%	48%	46%	49%	42%	51%
	NO	50	43	46	45	44	47	50	47	48	54	52	54	51	58	49
# SURVEYED		759	681	656	634	644	669	615	621	611	651	577	670	607	385	433
SEX	RESP	'72	'73	'74	'75	'76	'77	'78	'80	'82	'83	'84	'85	'87	'88	'89
F	YES	47%	51%	55%	52%	51%	54%	46%	50%	52%	42%	45%	42%	43%	42%	45%
	NO	53	49	45	48	49	46	54	50	48	58	55	58	57	58	55
# SURVEYED		748	775	761	782	790	809	854	787	830	856	837	818	798	556	559

TABLE III: ALLOW ABORTION FOR POVERTY -- BY RACE

Question: Please tell me whether or not you think it should be possible for a pregnant woman to obtain a legal abortion if the family has a very low income and cannot afford any more children? NOTE: Question not asked in 1986.

Responses: YES; NO

		YEAR														
RACE	RESP	'72	'73	'74	'75	'76	'77	'78	'80	'82	'83	'84	'85	'87	'88	'89
WHITE	YES	51%	55%	56%	54%	54%	54%	48%	52%	52%	44%	48%	44%	47%	43%	48%
	NO	49	45	44	46	46	46	52	48	48	56	52	56	53	57	52
# SURVEYED		1264	1269	1246	1261	1304	1296	1301	1268	1265	1336	1201	1306	1181	771	857
RACE	RESP	'72	'73	'74	'75	'76	'77	'78	'80	'82	'83	'84	'85	'87	'88	'89
BLACK	YES	39%	39%	44%	49%	43%	45%	41%	46%	52%	40%	36%	40%	33%	44%	45%
	NO	61	61	56	51	57	55	59	54	48	60	64	60	67	56	55
# SURVEYED		239	175	164	152	122	168	152	130	151	156	164	141	175	128	98
RACE	RESP	'72	'73	'74	'75	'76	'77	'78	'80	'82	'83	'84	'85	'87	'88	'89
OTHER	YES	25%	75%	57%	33%	88%	71%	63%	40%	60%	60%	43%	39%	41%	26%	46%
	NO	75	25	43	67	13	29	38	60	40	40	57	61	59	74	54
# SURVEYED		4	12	7	3	8	14	16	10	25	15	49	41	49	42	37

TABLE IV: ALLOW ABORTION FOR POVERTY -- BY AGE

Question: Please tell me whether or not you think it should be possible for a pregnant woman to obtain a legal abortion if the family has a very low income and cannot afford any more children? NOTE: Question not asked in 1986.

Responses: YES; NO

		YEAR														
AGE	RESP	'72	'73	'74	'75	'76	'77	'78	'80	'82	'83	'84	'85	'87	'88	'89
18-23	YES	53%	62%	62%	50%	59%	54%	49%	54%	45%	43%	46%	42%	49%	44%	54%
	NO	47	38	38	50	41	46	51	46	55	57	54	58	51	56	46
# SURVEYED		164	169	160	165	155	158	157	150	141	126	153	132	122	93	95
AGE	RESP	'72	'73	'74	'75	'76	'77	'78	'80	'82	'83	'84	'85	'87	'88	'89
24-29	YES	56%	59%	61%	56%	61%	58%	54%	56%	59%	45%	54%	44%	47%	44%	50%
	NO	44	41	39	44	39	42	46	44	41	55	46	56	53	56	50
# SURVEYED		222	210	203	226	221	200	237	198	234	278	226	213	183	129	112

TABLE IV: ALLOW ABORTION FOR POVERTY -- BY AGE (Continued)

Question: Please tell me whether or not you think it should be possible for a pregnant woman to obtain a legal abortion if the family has a very low income and cannot afford any more children? NOTE: Question not asked in 1986.

Responses: YES; NO

		YEAR														
AGE	RESP	'72	'73	'74	'75	'76	'77	'78	'80	'82	'83	'84	'85	'87	'88	'89
30-35	YES	48%	54%	55%	53%	55%	58%	53%	58%	58%	49%	51%	49%	48%	48%	53%
	NO	52	46	45	47	45	42	47	42	42	51	49	51	52	52	47
# SURVEYED		178	160	167	167	181	187	227	210	198	227	194	206	217	128	126
AGE	RESP	'72	'73	'74	'75	'76	'77	'78	'80	'82	'83	'84	'85	'87	'88	'89
36-41	YES	49%	50%	55%	50%	59%	51%	40%	54%	61%	48%	56%	49%	55%	44%	53%
	NO	51	50	45	50	41	49	60	46	39	52	44	51	45	56	47
# SURVEYED		119	171	151	145	152	163	156	145	142	163	183	179	179	131	134
AGE	RESP	'72	'73	'74	'75	'76	'77	'78	'80	'82	'83	'84	'85	'87	'88	'89
42-47	YES	53%	61%	45%	61%	44%	45%	48%	50%	54%	36%	51%	52%	43%	42%	48%
	NO	47	39	55	39	56	55	52	50	46	64	49	48	57	58	52
# SURVEYED		175	142	144	134	109	142	115	107	109	138	121	120	155	98	105
AGE	RESP	'72	'73	'74	'75	'76	'77	'78	'80	'82	'83	'84	'85	'87	'88	'89
48-53	YES	53%	50%	60%	49%	50%	58%	43%	49%	50%	42%	40%	47%	39%	39%	46%
	NO	47	50	40	51	50	42	57	51	50	58	60	53	61	61	54
# SURVEYED		179	147	141	139	127	147	125	119	109	107	101	128	122	64	90
AGE	RESP	'72	'73	'74	'75	'76	'77	'78	'80	'82	'83	'84	'85	'87	'88	'89
54-59	YES	42%	48%	49%	50%	50%	51%	41%	52%	46%	43%	32%	35%	46%	40%	42%
	NO	58	52	51	50	50	49	59	48	54	57	68	65	54	60	58
# SURVEYED		146	150	136	119	121	163	130	127	143	127	111	128	94	53	59
AGE	RESP	'72	'73	'74	'75	'76	'77	'78	'80	'82	'83	'84	'85	'87	'88	'89
60-65	YES	45%	51%	61%	50%	49%	57%	51%	50%	50%	40%	37%	42%	34%	37%	38%
	NO	55	49	39	50	51	43	49	50	50	60	63	58	66	63	62
# SURVEYED		127	113	100	105	130	114	102	116	111	122	108	125	92	79	77
AGE	RESP	'72	'73	'74	'75	'76	'77	'78	'80	'82	'83	'84	'85	'87	'88	'89
66+	YES	37%	46%	47%	56%	46%	48%	42%	44%	44%	43%	38%	37%	41%	37%	43%
	NO	63	54	53	44	54	52	58	56	56	57	62	63	59	63	57
# SURVEYED		193	190	209	212	233	198	213	227	243	214	212	250	237	164	192

****

ALLOW ABORTION FOR RAPE VICTIMS

TABLE I: ALLOW ABORTION FOR RAPE VICTIMS -- BY TOTAL POPULATION

Question: Please tell me whether or not you think it should be possible for a pregnant woman to obtain a legal abortion if she became pregnant as a result of a rape? NOTE: Question not asked in 1986.

Responses: YES; NO

	YEAR														
RESPONSE	'72	'73	'74	'75	'76	'77	'78	'80	'82	'83	'84	'85	'87	'88	'89
YES	79%	84%	86%	84%	84%	84%	83%	83%	87%	83%	80%	81%	81%	81%	83%
NO	21	16	14	16	16	16	17	17	13	17	20	19	19	19	17
# SURVEYED	1512	1451	1420	1422	1440	1469	1481	1411	1439	1504	1406	1474	1399	924	991

TABLE II: ALLOW ABORTION FOR RAPE VICTIMS -- BY SEX

Question: Please tell me whether or not you think it should be possible for a pregnant woman to obtain a legal abortion if she became pregnant as a result of a rape? NOTE: Question not asked in 1986.

Responses: YES; NO

		YEAR														
SEX	RESP	'72	'73	'74	'75	'76	'77	'78	'80	'82	'83	'84	'85	'87	'88	'89
M	YES	79%	84%	85%	83%	83%	84%	83%	86%	88%	84%	83%	83%	84%	83%	85%
	NO	21	16	15	17	17	16	17	14	12	16	17	17	16	17	15
# SURVEYED		751	673	668	637	645	665	620	614	609	651	579	664	606	382	433
SEX	RESP	'72	'73	'74	'75	'76	'77	'78	'80	'82	'83	'84	'85	'87	'88	'89
F	YES	79%	83%	87%	84%	84%	84%	83%	81%	86%	82%	79%	80%	78%	80%	82%
	NO	21	17	13	16	16	16	17	19	14	18	21	20	22	20	18
# SURVEYED		761	778	752	785	795	804	861	797	830	853	827	810	793	542	558

TABLE III: ALLOW ABORTION FOR RAPE VICTIMS -- BY RACE

Question: Please tell me whether or not you think it should be possible for a pregnant woman to obtain a legal abortion if she became pregnant as a result of a rape? NOTE: Question not asked in 1986.

Responses: YES; NO

		YEAR														
RACE	RESP	'72	'73	'74	'75	'76	'77	'78	'80	'82	'83	'84	'85	'87	'88	'89
WHITE	YES	82%	85%	88%	85%	85%	86%	85%	85%	88%	84%	82%	82%	82%	82%	84%
	NO	18	15	12	15	15	14	15	15	12	16	18	18	18	18	16
# SURVEYED		1274	1269	1251	1267	1306	1289	1314	1269	1268	1336	1199	1291	1174	765	854
RACE	RESP	'72	'73	'74	'75	'76	'77	'78	'80	'82	'83	'84	'85	'87	'88	'89
BLACK	YES	62%	71%	75%	73%	68%	68%	67%	73%	76%	76%	68%	78%	76%	75%	80%
	NO	38	29	25	27	32	32	33	27	24	24	32	22	24	25	20
# SURVEYED		235	170	163	151	125	166	152	133	148	154	158	143	178	125	97
RACE	RESP	'72	'73	'74	'75	'76	'77	'78	'80	'82	'83	'84	'85	'87	'88	'89
OTHER	YES	33%	67%	100%	100%	89%	79%	73%	67%	87%	86%	73%	78%	70%	76%	80%
	NO	67	33	0	0	11	21	27	33	13	14	27	23	30	24	20
# SURVEYED		3	12	6	4	9	14	15	9	23	14	49	40	47	34	40

TABLE IV: ALLOW ABORTION FOR RAPE VICTIMS -- BY AGE

Question: Please tell me whether or not you think it should be possible for a pregnant woman to obtain a legal abortion if she became pregnant as a result of a rape? NOTE: Question not asked in 1986.

Responses: YES; NO

		YEAR														
AGE	RESP	'72	'73	'74	'75	'76	'77	'78	'80	'82	'83	'84	'85	'87	'88	'89
18-23	YES	78%	84%	90%	83%	88%	80%	87%	85%	85%	83%	85%	85%	85%	86%	85%
	NO	22	16	10	17	12	20	13	15	15	17	15	15	15	14	15
# SURVEYED		158	168	164	166	161	158	159	151	138	120	151	130	123	93	93
AGE	RESP	'72	'73	'74	'75	'76	'77	'78	'80	'82	'83	'84	'85	'87	'88	'89
24-29	YES	84%	86%	91%	88%	86%	85%	88%	83%	88%	83%	84%	83%	79%	89%	88%
	NO	16	14	9	12	14	15	12	17	12	17	16	17	21	11	12
# SURVEYED		222	208	206	229	222	202	236	195	240	271	225	210	185	124	113
AGE	RESP	'72	'73	'74	'75	'76	'77	'78	'80	'82	'83	'84	'85	'87	'88	'89
30-35	YES	81%	85%	82%	81%	85%	86%	82%	81%	92%	85%	81%	82%	83%	82%	86%
	NO	19	15	18	19	15	14	18	19	8	15	19	18	17	18	14
# SURVEYED		175	160	171	167	177	184	228	208	198	230	196	207	212	128	131

TABLE IV: ALLOW ABORTION FOR RAPE VICTIMS -- BY AGE (Continued)

Question: Please tell me whether or not you think it should be possible for a pregnant woman to obtain a legal abortion if she became pregnant as a result of a rape? NOTE: Question not asked in 1986.

Responses: YES; NO

		YEAR														
AGE	RESP	'72	'73	'74	'75	'76	'77	'78	'80	'82	'83	'84	'85	'87	'88	'89
36-41	YES	78%	82%	86%	81%	82%	86%	81%	83%	84%	78%	81%	81%	85%	83%	82%
	NO	22	18	14	19	18	14	19	17	16	22	19	19	15	17	18
# SURVEYED		123	172	147	145	149	162	154	148	143	167	183	178	181	129	131
AGE	RESP	'72	'73	'74	'75	'76	'77	'78	'80	'82	'83	'84	'85	'87	'88	'89
42-47	YES	82%	90%	83%	88%	79%	78%	77%	83%	90%	81%	77%	87%	78%	77%	81%
	NO	18	10	17	12	21	22	23	17	10	19	23	13	22	23	19
# SURVEYED		173	141	146	137	109	136	117	108	115	136	122	116	148	98	102
AGE	RESP	'72	'73	'74	'75	'76	'77	'78	'80	'82	'83	'84	'85	'87	'88	'89
48-53	YES	82%	78%	89%	80%	83%	86%	85%	83%	87%	81%	69%	80%	83%	71%	86%
	NO	18	22	11	20	17	14	15	17	13	19	31	20	18	29	14
# SURVEYED		176	146	140	138	129	144	129	118	105	109	98	125	120	63	90
AGE	RESP	'72	'73	'74	'75	'76	'77	'78	'80	'82	'83	'84	'85	'87	'88	'89
54-59	YES	78%	81%	80%	84%	86%	85%	79%	85%	88%	80%	74%	75%	83%	84%	86%
	NO	22	19	20	16	14	15	21	15	12	20	26	25	17	16	14
# SURVEYED		146	149	133	119	122	163	130	130	139	126	111	127	93	50	59
AGE	RESP	'72	'73	'74	'75	'76	'77	'78	'80	'82	'83	'84	'85	'87	'88	'89
60-65	YES	80%	83%	91%	83%	84%	87%	79%	83%	86%	84%	82%	81%	78%	73%	77%
	NO	20	17	9	17	16	13	21	17	14	16	18	19	22	27	23
# SURVEYED		132	115	97	108	131	114	100	114	111	122	103	124	97	79	77
AGE	RESP	'72	'73	'74	'75	'76	'77	'78	'80	'82	'83	'84	'85	'87	'88	'89
66+	YES	69%	83%	87%	84%	80%	81%	85%	84%	85%	86%	81%	79%	76%	79%	80%
	NO	31	17	13	16	20	19	15	16	15	14	19	21	24	21	20
# SURVEYED		204	188	210	208	236	200	221	230	239	218	211	250	236	158	192

****

ALLOW ABORTION FOR SINGLE WOMEN

TABLE I: ALLOW ABORTION FOR SINGLE WOMEN -- BY TOTAL POPULATION

Question: Please tell me whether or not you think it should be possible for a pregnant woman to obtain a legal abortion if she is not married and does not want to marry the man? NOTE: Question not asked in 1986.

Responses: YES; NO

	YEAR														
RESPONSE	'72	'73	'74	'75	'76	'77	'78	'80	'82	'83	'84	'85	'87	'88	'89
YES	44%	49%	50%	48%	50%	50%	41%	48%	49%	39%	44%	41%	42%	39%	45%
NO	56	51	50	52	50	50	59	52	51	61	56	59	58	61	55
# SURVEYED	1502	1450	1420	1414	1438	1459	1473	1404	1432	1493	1420	1486	1410	932	985

TABLE II: ALLOW ABORTION FOR SINGLE WOMEN -- BY SEX

Question: Please tell me whether or not you think it should be possible for a pregnant woman to obtain a legal abortion if she is not married and does not want to marry the man? NOTE: Question not asked in 1986.

Responses: YES; NO

		YEAR														
SEX	RESP	'72	'73	'74	'75	'76	'77	'78	'80	'82	'83	'84	'85	'87	'88	'89
M	YES	46%	51%	50%	49%	54%	51%	44%	47%	49%	41%	47%	43%	46%	41%	51%
	NO	54	49	50	51	46	49	56	53	51	59	53	57	54	59	49
# SURVEYED		753	676	658	633	638	664	621	617	610	645	579	669	610	381	425
SEX	RESP	'72	'73	'74	'75	'76	'77	'78	'80	'82	'83	'84	'85	'87	'88	'89
F	YES	41%	48%	50%	47%	48%	49%	39%	49%	49%	38%	42%	40%	39%	38%	41%
	NO	59	52	50	53	52	51	61	51	51	62	58	60	61	62	59
# SURVEYED		749	774	762	781	800	795	852	787	822	848	841	817	800	551	560

TABLE III: ALLOW ABORTION FOR SINGLE WOMEN -- BY RACE

Question: Please tell me whether or not you think it should be possible for a pregnant woman to obtain a legal abortion if she is not married and does not want to marry the man? NOTE: Question not asked in 1986.

Responses: YES; NO

		YEAR														
RACE	RESP	'72	'73	'74	'75	'76	'77	'78	'80	'82	'83	'84	'85	'87	'88	'89
WHITE	YES	46%	52%	52%	49%	52%	51%	42%	50%	50%	41%	46%	42%	44%	41%	46%
	NO	54	48	48	51	48	49	58	50	50	59	54	58	56	59	54
# SURVEYED		1256	1262	1245	1258	1307	1277	1300	1261	1257	1325	1209	1299	1178	763	851
RACE	RESP	'72	'73	'74	'75	'76	'77	'78	'80	'82	'83	'84	'85	'87	'88	'89
BLACK	YES	33%	31%	34%	39%	34%	37%	33%	38%	38%	28%	31%	34%	28%	33%	44%
	NO	67	69	66	61	66	63	67	62	62	72	69	66	72	67	56
# SURVEYED		242	175	168	153	124	168	157	133	149	154	162	145	184	126	98
RACE	RESP	'72	'73	'74	'75	'76	'77	'78	'80	'82	'83	'84	'85	'87	'88	'89
OTHER	YES	0%	31%	43%	67%	86%	64%	63%	50%	46%	36%	33%	40%	31%	28%	44%
	NO	100	69	57	33	14	36	38	50	54	64	67	60	69	72	56
# SURVEYED		4	13	7	3	7	14	16	10	26	14	49	42	48	43	36

TABLE IV: ALLOW ABORTION FOR SINGLE WOMEN -- BY AGE

Question: Please tell me whether or not you think it should be possible for a pregnant woman to obtain a legal abortion if she is not married and does not want to marry the man? NOTE: Question not asked in 1986.

Responses: YES; NO

		YEAR														
AGE	RESP	'72	'73	'74	'75	'76	'77	'78	'80	'82	'83	'84	'85	'87	'88	'89
18-23	YES	49%	54%	56%	46%	52%	47%	38%	49%	41%	35%	42%	36%	43%	40%	46%
	NO	51	46	44	54	48	53	62	51	59	65	58	64	57	60	54
# SURVEYED		166	167	160	171	159	158	157	154	140	124	156	131	125	94	94
AGE	RESP	'72	'73	'74	'75	'76	'77	'78	'80	'82	'83	'84	'85	'87	'88	'89
24-29	YES	46%	55%	56%	53%	58%	52%	49%	56%	56%	40%	49%	43%	43%	39%	49%
	NO	54	45	44	47	42	49	51	44	44	60	51	57	57	61	51
# SURVEYED		221	208	200	229	219	200	239	197	238	276	228	213	184	125	110

TABLE IV: ALLOW ABORTION FOR SINGLE WOMEN -- BY AGE (Continued)

Question: Please tell me whether or not you think it should be possible for a pregnant woman to obtain a legal abortion if she is not married and does not want to marry the man? NOTE: Question not asked in 1986.

Responses: YES; NO

		YEAR														
AGE	**RESP**	**'72**	**'73**	**'74**	**'75**	**'76**	**'77**	**'78**	**'80**	**'82**	**'83**	**'84**	**'85**	**'87**	**'88**	**'89**
30-35	**YES**	45%	45%	52%	48%	56%	50%	46%	51%	56%	44%	48%	45%	45%	45%	52%
	NO	55	55	48	52	44	50	54	49	44	56	52	55	55	55	48
# SURVEYED		175	161	170	166	181	187	224	210	195	226	196	208	216	130	127
AGE	**RESP**	**'72**	**'73**	**'74**	**'75**	**'76**	**'77**	**'78**	**'80**	**'82**	**'83**	**'84**	**'85**	**'87**	**'88**	**'89**
36-41	**YES**	46%	46%	48%	50%	55%	51%	34%	44%	55%	45%	58%	46%	55%	43%	50%
	NO	54	54	52	50	45	49	66	56	45	55	42	54	45	57	50
# SURVEYED		117	171	151	145	153	164	155	146	139	165	184	181	181	129	133
AGE	**RESP**	**'72**	**'73**	**'74**	**'75**	**'76**	**'77**	**'78**	**'80**	**'82**	**'83**	**'84**	**'85**	**'87**	**'88**	**'89**
42-47	**YES**	47%	58%	45%	54%	39%	45%	48%	47%	48%	36%	50%	49%	41%	44%	51%
	NO	53	42	55	46	61	55	52	53	52	64	50	51	59	56	49
# SURVEYED		176	142	147	136	111	139	117	110	113	137	121	122	152	98	102
AGE	**RESP**	**'72**	**'73**	**'74**	**'75**	**'76**	**'77**	**'78**	**'80**	**'82**	**'83**	**'84**	**'85**	**'87**	**'88**	**'89**
48-53	**YES**	45%	46%	53%	50%	47%	53%	37%	48%	45%	42%	37%	49%	35%	36%	45%
	NO	55	54	47	50	53	47	63	52	55	58	63	51	65	64	55
# SURVEYED		178	149	139	135	128	146	129	117	109	108	101	129	122	64	92
AGE	**RESP**	**'72**	**'73**	**'74**	**'75**	**'76**	**'77**	**'78**	**'80**	**'82**	**'83**	**'84**	**'85**	**'87**	**'88**	**'89**
54-59	**YES**	41%	49%	46%	45%	52%	49%	35%	46%	45%	39%	26%	34%	45%	40%	39%
	NO	59	51	54	55	48	51	65	54	55	61	74	66	55	60	61
# SURVEYED		144	150	137	115	125	158	133	125	143	127	114	125	96	50	59
AGE	**RESP**	**'72**	**'73**	**'74**	**'75**	**'76**	**'77**	**'78**	**'80**	**'82**	**'83**	**'84**	**'85**	**'87**	**'88**	**'89**
60-65	**YES**	40%	46%	55%	43%	47%	60%	42%	50%	50%	31%	42%	40%	30%	38%	30%
	NO	60	54	45	57	53	40	58	50	50	69	58	60	70	63	70
# SURVEYED		129	110	99	106	128	109	102	113	109	117	105	124	97	80	76
AGE	**RESP**	**'72**	**'73**	**'74**	**'75**	**'76**	**'77**	**'78**	**'80**	**'82**	**'83**	**'84**	**'85**	**'87**	**'88**	**'89**
66+	**YES**	32%	42%	42%	44%	43%	45%	37%	44%	41%	37%	36%	31%	36%	31%	41%
	NO	68	58	58	56	57	55	63	56	59	63	64	69	64	69	59
# SURVEYED		192	188	213	206	229	192	210	224	236	208	210	246	233	159	189

****

GOVERNMENT ASSURE WEALTH DISTRIBUTION

TABLE I: GOVERNMENT ASSURE WEALTH DISTRIBUTION -- BY TOTAL POPULATION

Question: Some people think that the government in Washington ought to reduce the income differences between the rich and the poor, perhaps by raising the taxes of wealthy families or by giving income assistance to the poor. Others think that the government should not concern itself with reducing this income difference between the rich and the poor. Think of a scale from 1 to 7. Think of a score of 1 as meaning that the government ought to reduce the income differences between the rich and the poor, and a score of 7 meaning that the government should not concern itself with reducing income differences. What score between 1 and 7 comes closest to the way you feel? NOTE: Question not asked in 1972-1977, 1982, 1985.

Responses: 1 = Government should do something to reduce the differences between rich and poor ....2 ....3 ....4 ....5 ....6 ....7 = Government should not concern itself with income difference.

	YEAR							
RESPONSE	'78	'80	'83	'84	'86	'87	'88	'89
1	20%	17%	20%	21%	23%	19%	20%	18%
2	11	10	11	12	9	9	10	13
3	17	17	16	16	17	17	18	20
4	21	20	18	17	21	21	20	20
5	11	13	11	13	11	13	12	11
6	8	7	8	8	6	7	8	7
7	13	16	15	12	13	14	12	11
# SURVEYED	747	1423	1558	1438	1448	1444	973	1015

TABLE II: GOVERNMENT ASSURE WEALTH DISTRIBUTION -- BY SEX

Question: Some people think that the government in Washington ought to reduce the income differences between the rich and the poor, perhaps by raising the taxes of wealthy families or by giving income assistance to the poor. Others think that the government should not concern itself with reducing this income difference between the rich and the poor. Think of a scale from 1 to 7. Think of a score of 1 as meaning that the government ought to reduce the income differences between the rich and the poor, and a score of 7 meaning that the government should not concern itself with reducing income differences. What score between 1 and 7 comes closest to the way you feel? NOTE: Question not asked in 1972-1977, 1982, 1985.

Responses: 1 = Government should do something to reduce the differences between rich and poor ....2 ....3 ....4 ....5 ....6 ....7 = Government should not concern itself with income difference.

		YEAR							
SEX	RESP	'78	'80	'83	'84	'86	'87	'88	'89
M	1	18%	15%	18%	19%	22%	17%	18%	17%
A	2	10	9	11	13	10	10	8	12
L	3	17	15	16	13	16	17	16	19
E	4	19	19	17	16	20	18	20	16
	5	11	13	10	14	11	14	15	15
	6	9	10	9	10	7	8	9	9
	7	16	19	18	15	14	16	13	12
# SURVEYED		431	634	675	588	615	634	431	436

		YEAR							
SEX	RESP	'78	'80	'83	'84	'86	'87	'88	'89
F	1	22%	19%	22%	23%	25%	21%	21%	19%
E	2	13	10	11	12	8	8	11	14
M	3	18	18	17	17	18	18	20	20
A	4	24	21	18	18	21	24	20	23
L	5	10	12	12	13	11	12	11	8
E	6	6	5	8	7	5	6	7	6
	7	7	14	12	10	11	12	10	10
# SURVEYED		316	789	883	850	833	810	542	579

TABLE III: GOVERNMENT ASSURE WEALTH DISTRIBUTION -- BY RACE

Question: Some people think that the government in Washington ought to reduce the income differences between the rich and the poor, perhaps by raising the taxes of wealthy families or by giving income assistance to the poor. Others think that the government should not concern itself with reducing this income difference between the rich and the poor. Think of a scale from 1 to 7. Think of a score of 1 as meaning that the government ought to reduce the income differences between the rich and the poor, and a score of 7 meaning that the government should not concern itself with reducing income differences. What score between 1 and 7 comes closest to the way you feel? NOTE: Question not asked in 1972-1977, 1982, 1985.

Responses: 1 = Government should do something to reduce the differences between rich and poor ....2 ....3 ....4 ....5 ....6 ....7 = Government should not concern itself with income difference.

		YEAR							
RACE	RESP	'78	'80	'83	'84	'86	'87	'88	'89
WHITE	1	17%	15%	18%	19%	21%	17%	18%	17%
	2	10	9	10	12	9	9	9	12
	3	17	17	17	15	17	17	18	20
	4	21	21	18	18	21	21	21	20
	5	11	13	12	14	12	14	13	12
	6	8	8	9	9	7	7	8	8
	7	14	17	16	13	14	15	13	12
# SURVEYED		654	1279	1384	1227	1229	1206	816	870
RACE	RESP	'78	'80	'83	'84	'86	'87	'88	'89
BLACK	1	36%	40%	36%	38%	39%	35%	29%	24%
	2	16	18	15	14	8	7	18	23
	3	18	10	13	15	18	19	18	21
	4	18	16	19	18	19	20	21	19
	5	9	5	6	8	7	7	6	7
	6	1	1	4	3	2	3	4	4
	7	1	10	7	6	7	9	3	2
# SURVEYED		85	134	157	160	182	185	114	107

		YEAR							
RACE	RESP	'78	'80	'83	'84	'86	'87	'88	'89
OTHER	1	25%	0%	35%	37%	35%	26%	28%	24%
	2	13	10	12	14	11	9	9	16
	3	25	50	12	20	16	13	28	18
	4	25	0	24	12	19	23	12	26
	5	0	10	0	8	11	8	12	8
	6	13	20	6	6	5	9	5	3
	7	0	10	12	4	3	11	7	5
# SURVEYED		8	10	17	51	37	53	43	38

TABLE IV: GOVERNMENT ASSURE WEALTH DISTRIBUTION -- BY AGE

Question: Some people think that the government in Washington ought to reduce the income differences between the rich and the poor, perhaps by raising the taxes of wealthy families or by giving income assistance to the poor. Others think that the government should not concern itself with reducing this income difference between the rich and the poor. Think of a scale from 1 to 7. Think of a score of 1 as meaning that the government ought to reduce the income differences between the rich and the poor, and a score of 7 meaning that the government should not concern itself with reducing income differences. What score between 1 and 7 comes closest to the way you feel? NOTE: Question not asked in 1972-1977, 1982, 1985.

Responses: 1 = Government should do something to reduce the differences between rich and poor ....2 ....3 ....4 ....5 ....6 ....7 = Government should not concern itself with income difference.

		YEAR							
AGE	RESP	'78	'80	'83	'84	'86	'87	'88	'89
18-23	1	18%	14%	20%	18%	19%	18%	18%	16%
	2	14	14	13	18	10	7	11	14
	3	18	21	15	23	20	27	25	22
	4	24	20	17	21	22	21	16	24
	5	14	18	13	11	13	15	12	17
	6	2	8	12	5	10	6	9	3
	7	10	5	11	5	6	7	9	3
# SURVEYED		50	152	128	159	108	123	91	90
AGE	RESP	'78	'80	'83	'84	'86	'87	'88	'89
24-29	1	17%	15%	19%	20%	22%	18%	17%	15%
	2	12	9	14	16	8	13	10	16
	3	25	21	19	18	20	23	25	22
	4	19	22	15	12	16	15	13	15
	5	11	16	14	15	12	11	18	14
	6	10	7	9	11	9	7	10	10
	7	7	12	9	7	13	13	8	8
# SURVEYED		113	198	285	230	216	193	145	140
AGE	RESP	'78	'80	'83	'84	'86	'87	'88	'89
30-35	1	17%	16%	15%	16%	20%	16%	21%	13%
	2	11	6	13	13	12	10	16	17
	3	15	17	20	22	18	19	19	26
	4	21	19	17	17	23	19	16	16
	5	13	17	15	14	13	15	9	9
	6	13	8	7	6	4	9	8	11
	7	11	16	13	12	11	12	11	9
# SURVEYED		109	214	230	195	221	221	125	144
AGE	RESP	'78	'80	'83	'84	'86	'87	'88	'89
36-41	1	14%	24%	19%	19%	24%	15%	17%	16%
	2	8	11	11	8	5	9	9	11
	3	14	12	18	11	17	21	22	20
	4	24	20	18	18	18	17	19	23
	5	19	9	7	14	14	18	14	11
	6	5	8	8	12	5	8	8	9
	7	16	17	20	18	16	12	10	11
# SURVEYED		86	148	170	184	184	184	125	132

		YEAR							
AGE	RESP	'78	'80	'83	'84	'86	'87	'88	'89
42-47	1	23%	10%	24%	19%	18%	18%	19%	18%
	2	15	13	9	8	8	6	9	12
	3	11	15	14	21	17	13	21	18
	4	27	16	17	19	24	23	21	17
	5	10	10	10	8	11	14	12	15
	6	5	11	8	15	6	7	6	10
	7	10	25	17	10	15	18	13	10
# SURVEYED		62	115	144	124	140	155	101	105
AGE	RESP	'78	'80	'83	'84	'86	'87	'88	'89
48-53	1	19%	13%	14%	27%	24%	19%	21%	23%
	2	8	9	8	11	6	7	5	11
	3	13	23	14	10	15	16	9	19
	4	14	16	22	18	20	28	32	20
	5	17	11	10	17	9	8	14	8
	6	13	10	12	3	5	5	4	6
	7	17	18	19	15	22	17	16	13
# SURVEYED		64	119	113	101	105	124	57	95
AGE	RESP	'78	'80	'83	'84	'86	'87	'88	'89
54-59	1	21%	20%	30%	22%	23%	27%	26%	23%
	2	11	5	10	16	12	4	9	13
	3	21	11	14	12	18	14	12	6
	4	13	28	13	16	21	21	9	21
	5	5	7	7	10	8	12	12	13
	6	5	8	6	8	6	10	14	2
	7	25	20	19	16	12	11	17	23
# SURVEYED		63	132	125	111	97	97	65	62
AGE	RESP	'78	'80	'83	'84	'86	'87	'88	'89
60-65	1	26%	22%	23%	26%	27%	20%	30%	15%
	2	12	11	7	8	9	10	9	14
	3	14	15	19	9	15	13	10	14
	4	24	16	22	18	21	26	30	29
	5	3	11	10	17	10	9	5	10
	6	7	4	5	7	8	1	3	3
	7	14	21	15	14	10	21	13	16
# SURVEYED		58	112	129	107	113	100	77	73

TABLE IV: GOVERNMENT ASSURE WEALTH DISTRIBUTION -- BY AGE (Continued)

Question: Some people think that the government in Washington ought to reduce the income differences between the rich and the poor, perhaps by raising the taxes of wealthy families or by giving income assistance to the poor. Others think that the government should not concern itself with reducing this income difference between the rich and the poor. Think of a scale from 1 to 7. Think of a score of 1 as meaning that the government ought to reduce the income differences between the rich and the poor, and a score of 7 meaning that the government should not concern itself with reducing income differences. What score between 1 and 7 comes closest to the way you feel? NOTE: Question not asked in 1972-1977, 1982, 1985.

Responses: 1 = Government should do something to reduce the differences between rich and poor ....2 ....3 ....4 ....5 ....6 ....7 = Government should not concern itself with income difference.

		YEAR							
AGE	RESP	'78	'80	'83	'84	'86	'87	'88	'89
66+	1	24%	19%	21%	26%	29%	25%	19%	24%
	2	11	11	9	12	10	7	8	10
	3	21	16	13	11	14	10	14	20
	4	22	24	22	21	23	24	28	23
	5	7	12	12	13	8	13	13	8
	6	6	4	9	5	4	5	8	5
	7	9	16	14	13	11	16	11	11
# SURVEYED		141	225	228	222	257	242	183	172

****

ALLOW GAY TO TEACH COLLEGE

TABLE I: ALLOW GAY TO TEACH IN COLLEGE -- BY TOTAL POPULATION

Question: Should a man who admits he is a homosexual be allowed to teach in a college or university, or not? NOTE: Question not asked in 1972, 1975, 1978, 1983, 1986.

Responses: YES = Yes, allowed to teach; NO = Not allowed

	YEAR										
RESPONSE	'73	'74	'76	'77	'80	'82	'84	'85	'87	'88	'89
YES	49	53	54	51	57	57	61	60	59	60	67
NO	51	47	46	49	43	43	39	40	41	40	33
# SURVEYED	1438	1404	1448	1462	1410	1437	1409	1483	1409	927	982

TABLE II: ALLOW GAY TO TEACH IN COLLEGE -- BY SEX

Question: Should a man who admits he is a homosexual be allowed to teach in a college or university, or not? NOTE: Question not asked in 1972, 1975, 1978, 1983, 1986.

Responses: YES = Yes, allowed to teach; NO = Not allowed

		YEAR										
SEX	RESP	'73	'74	'76	'77	'80	'82	'84	'85	'87	'88	'89
M	YES	49	52	55	54	55	57	63	58	58	58	67
	NO	51	48	45	46	45	43	37	42	42	42	33
# SURVEYED		679	657	654	675	631	623	580	672	622	380	426
SEX	RESP	'73	'74	'76	'77	'80	'82	'84	'85	'87	'88	'89
F	YES	50	54	53	49	58	57	60	61	59	60	66
	NO	50	46	47	51	42	43	40	39	41	40	34
# SURVEYED		759	747	794	787	779	814	829	811	787	547	556

TABLE III: ALLOW GAY TO TEACH IN COLLEGE -- BY RACE

Question: Should a man who admits he is a homosexual be allowed to teach in a college or university, or not? NOTE: Question not asked in 1972, 1975, 1978, 1983, 1986.

Responses: YES = Yes, allowed to teach; NO = Not allowed

		YEAR										
RACE	RESP	'73	'74	'76	'77	'80	'82	'84	'85	'87	'88	'89
WHITE	YES	50	52	54	51	57	57	63	60	60	61	67
	NO	50	48	46	49	43	43	37	40	40	39	33
# SURVEYED		1244	1238	1321	1285	1267	1261	1200	1298	1172	767	849
RACE	RESP	'73	'74	'76	'77	'80	'82	'84	'85	'87	'88	'89
BLACK	YES	48	60	55	50	59	56	55	61	54	57	67
	NO	52	40	45	50	41	44	45	39	46	43	33
# SURVEYED		181	159	120	163	133	153	163	142	188	121	96
RACE	RESP	'73	'74	'76	'77	'80	'82	'84	'85	'87	'88	'89
OTHER	YES	62	57	86	64	70	70	48	53	45	41	62
	NO	38	43	14	36	30	30	52	47	55	59	38
# SURVEYED		13	7	7	14	10	23	46	43	49	39	37

TABLE IV: ALLOW GAY TO TEACH IN COLLEGE -- BY AGE

Question: Should a man who admits he is a homosexual be allowed to teach in a college or university, or not? NOTE: Question not asked in 1972, 1975, 1978, 1983, 1986.

Responses: YES = Yes, allowed to teach; NO = Not allowed

		YEAR										
AGE	RESP	'73	'74	'76	'77	'80	'82	'84	'85	'87	'88	'89
18-23	YES	65	72	67	64	65	64	67	75	62	62	72
	NO	35	28	33	36	35	36	33	25	38	38	28
# SURVEYED		169	165	161	163	154	143	155	131	125	91	95
AGE	RESP	'73	'74	'76	'77	'80	'82	'84	'85	'87	'88	'89
24-29	YES	73	80	70	71	75	71	72	73	73	66	76
	NO	27	20	30	29	25	29	28	27	27	34	24
# SURVEYED		205	205	223	199	198	242	228	211	186	128	111
AGE	RESP	'73	'74	'76	'77	'80	'82	'84	'85	'87	'88	'89
30-35	YES	51	60	64	67	73	75	78	74	72	75	73
	NO	49	40	36	33	27	25	22	26	28	25	27
# SURVEYED		160	165	181	185	212	194	191	212	217	126	132
AGE	RESP	'73	'74	'76	'77	'80	'82	'84	'85	'87	'88	'89
36-41	YES	54	60	65	53	62	66	71	71	69	70	80
	NO	46	40	35	47	38	34	29	29	31	30	20
# SURVEYED		169	143	153	165	145	143	184	179	179	130	132
AGE	RESP	'73	'74	'76	'77	'80	'82	'84	'85	'87	'88	'89
42-47	YES	55	50	55	50	59	65	67	65	66	70	81
	NO	45	50	45	50	41	35	33	35	34	30	19
# SURVEYED		139	145	110	139	111	117	119	122	151	97	99
AGE	RESP	'73	'74	'76	'77	'80	'82	'84	'85	'87	'88	'89
48-53	YES	43	51	47	48	55	51	49	55	56	53	68
	NO	57	49	53	52	45	49	51	45	44	47	32
# SURVEYED		142	138	129	146	117	109	98	130	122	60	94
AGE	RESP	'73	'74	'76	'77	'80	'82	'84	'85	'87	'88	'89
54-59	YES	42	41	44	48	45	48	55	46	54	47	58
	NO	58	59	56	52	55	52	45	54	46	53	42
# SURVEYED		148	129	123	158	129	137	109	121	93	49	59
AGE	RESP	'73	'74	'76	'77	'80	'82	'84	'85	'87	'88	'89
60-65	YES	23	37	43	36	50	38	49	45	37	49	51
	NO	77	63	57	64	50	62	51	55	63	51	49
# SURVEYED		115	103	129	110	116	112	104	125	93	80	72

TABLE IV: ALLOW GAY TO TEACH IN COLLEGE -- BY AGE (Continued)

Question: Should a man who admits he is a homosexual be allowed to teach in a college or university, or not? NOTE: Question not asked in 1972, 1975, 1978, 1983, 1986.

Responses: YES = Yes, allowed to teach; NO = Not allowed

		YEAR										
AGE	RESP	'73	'74	'76	'77	'80	'82	'84	'85	'87	'88	'89
66+	YES	28	20	29	20	27	31	34	35	34	38	45
	NO	72	80	71	80	73	69	66	65	66	62	55
# SURVEYED		188	207	234	191	219	231	216	245	238	164	185

****

ALLOW PRO-GAY BOOK IN LIBRARY

TABLE I: ALLOW PRO-GAY BOOK IN LIBRARY -- BY TOTAL POPULATION

Question: If some people suggest that a book written by a homosexual in favor of homosexuality should be taken out of the public library, would you favor removing this book, or not? NOTE: Question not asked in 1972, 1975, 1978, 1983, 1986.

Responses: FA = Favor; NF = Not favor

	YEAR										
RESPONSE	'73	'74	'76	'77	'80	'82	'84	'85	'87	'88	'89
FA	45%	43%	43%	43%	41%	42%	39%	43%	41%	37%	34%
NF	55	57	57	57	59	58	61	57	59	63	66
# SURVEYED	1463	1421	1444	1475	1434	1457	1425	1484	1426	939	996

TABLE II: ALLOW PRO-GAY BOOK IN LIBRARY -- BY SEX

Question: If some people suggest that a book written by a homosexual in favor of homosexuality should be taken out of the public library, would you favor removing this book, or not? NOTE: Question not asked in 1972, 1975, 1978, 1983, 1986.

Responses: FA = Favor; NF = Not favor

		YEAR										
SEX	RESP	'73	'74	'76	'77	'80	'82	'84	'85	'87	'88	'89
M	FA	45%	45%	39%	43%	40%	41%	37%	42%	39%	41%	33%
	NF	55	55	61	57	60	59	63	58	61	59	67
# SURVEYED		685	663	649	674	634	626	587	672	627	384	431
SEX	RESP	'73	'74	'76	'77	'80	'82	'84	'85	'87	'88	'89
F	FA	45%	41%	45%	43%	41%	43%	40%	43%	42%	35%	35%
	NF	55	59	55	57	59	57	60	57	58	65	65
# SURVEYED		778	758	795	801	800	831	838	812	799	555	565

TABLE III: ALLOW PRO-GAY BOOK IN LIBRARY -- BY RACE

Question: If some people suggest that a book written by a homosexual in favor of homosexuality should be taken out of the public library, would you favor removing this book, or not? NOTE: Question not asked in 1972, 1975, 1978, 1983, 1986.

Responses: FA = Favor; NF = Not favor

		YEAR										
RACE	RESP	'73	'74	'76	'77	'80	'82	'84	'85	'87	'88	'89
WHITE	FA	44%	42%	42%	43%	40%	42%	37%	41%	40%	37%	32%
	NF	56	58	58	57	60	58	63	59	60	63	68
# SURVEYED		1271	1253	1316	1298	1289	1281	1213	1302	1191	775	862
RACE	RESP	'73	'74	'76	'77	'80	'82	'84	'85	'87	'88	'89
BLACK	FA	50%	46%	48%	43%	45%	48%	48%	58%	40%	36%	44%
	NF	50	54	52	57	55	52	52	42	60	64	56
# SURVEYED		179	161	121	162	135	152	164	139	186	124	97
RACE	RESP	'73	'74	'76	'77	'80	'82	'84	'85	'87	'88	'89
OTHER	FA	46%	57%	14%	33%	30%	33%	42%	47%	51%	53%	41%
	NF	54	43	86	67	70	67	58	53	49	48	59
# SURVEYED		13	7	7	15	10	24	48	43	49	40	37

TABLE IV: ALLOW PRO-GAY BOOK IN LIBRARY -- BY AGE

Question: If some people suggest that a book written by a homosexual in favor of homosexuality should be taken out of the public library, would you favor removing this book, or not? NOTE: Question not asked in 1972, 1975, 1978, 1983, 1986.

Responses: FA = Favor; NF = Not favor

		YEAR										
AGE	RESP	'73	'74	'76	'77	'80	'82	'84	'85	'87	'88	'89
18-23	FA	23%	30%	32%	32%	31%	40%	37%	39%	39%	33%	34%
	NF	77	70	68	68	69	60	63	61	61	67	66
# SURVEYED		169	161	160	161	155	144	154	131	123	92	95
AGE	RESP	'73	'74	'76	'77	'80	'82	'84	'85	'87	'88	'89
24-29	FA	32%	27%	25%	28%	24%	27%	26%	31%	27%	31%	23%
	NF	68	73	75	72	76	73	74	69	73	69	77
# SURVEYED		210	207	222	202	201	240	228	212	191	129	114
AGE	RESP	'73	'74	'76	'77	'80	'82	'84	'85	'87	'88	'89
30-35	FA	37%	37%	34%	32%	24%	25%	23%	31%	26%	31%	26%
	NF	63	63	66	68	76	76	77	69	74	69	74
# SURVEYED		164	171	181	185	212	200	194	208	216	127	133
AGE	RESP	'73	'74	'76	'77	'80	'82	'84	'85	'87	'88	'89
36-41	FA	42%	33%	35%	38%	39%	35%	30%	28%	32%	24%	27%
	NF	58	67	65	62	61	65	70	72	68	76	73
# SURVEYED		170	146	153	165	147	144	185	181	180	129	130
AGE	RESP	'73	'74	'76	'77	'80	'82	'84	'85	'87	'88	'89
42-47	FA	38%	35%	43%	41%	32%	35%	37%	31%	36%	27%	25%
	NF	62	65	57	59	68	65	63	69	64	73	75
# SURVEYED		143	147	107	141	114	116	123	123	151	98	104
AGE	RESP	'73	'74	'76	'77	'80	'82	'84	'85	'87	'88	'89
48-53	FA	51%	43%	48%	45%	47%	47%	43%	44%	42%	49%	25%
	NF	49	57	52	55	53	53	57	56	58	51	75
# SURVEYED		147	138	128	148	122	110	99	129	124	63	93
AGE	RESP	'73	'74	'76	'77	'80	'82	'84	'85	'87	'88	'89
54-59	FA	48%	50%	45%	39%	50%	44%	45%	49%	41%	39%	30%
	NF	52	50	55	61	50	56	55	51	59	61	70
# SURVEYED		148	134	123	161	131	140	111	126	96	51	61
AGE	RESP	'73	'74	'76	'77	'80	'82	'84	'85	'87	'88	'89
60-65	FA	72%	58%	53%	61%	45%	54%	53%	57%	58%	43%	47%
	NF	28	42	47	39	55	46	47	43	42	57	53
# SURVEYED		118	106	129	110	118	112	107	127	99	81	73

TABLE IV: ALLOW PRO-GAY BOOK IN LIBRARY -- BY AGE (Continued)

Question: If some people suggest that a book written by a homosexual in favor of homosexuality should be taken out of the public library, would you favor removing this book, or not? NOTE: Question not asked in 1972, 1975, 1978, 1983, 1986.

Responses: FA = Favor; NF = Not favor

		YEAR										
AGE	RESP	'73	'74	'76	'77	'80	'82	'84	'85	'87	'88	'89
66+	FA	70%	73%	67%	73%	72%	71%	63%	71%	68%	58%	56%
	NF	30	27	33	27	28	29	37	29	32	42	44
# SURVEYED		191	208	236	196	225	242	218	240	241	166	190

****

ALLOW GAY TO MAKE SPEECH

TABLE I: ALLOW GAY TO MAKE MAKE SPEECH -- BY TOTAL POPULATION

Question: Consider a man who admits he is a homosexual. Suppose this admitted homosexual wanted to make a speech in your community. Should he be allowed to speak, or not? NOTE: Question not asked in 1972, 1975, 1978, 1983, 1986.

Responses: YES = Yes, allowed to speak; NO = Not allowed

	YEAR										
RESPONSE	'73	'74	'76	'77	'80	'82	'84	'85	'87	'88	'89
YES	63%	65%	64%	64%	68%	68%	71%	69%	70%	73%	78%
NO	37	35	36	36	32	32	29	31	30	27	22
# SURVEYED	1445	1416	1449	1472	1422	1441	1416	1478	1426	938	1003

TABLE II: ALLOW GAY TO MAKE SPEECH -- BY SEX

Question: Consider a man who admits he is a homosexual. Suppose this admitted homosexual wanted to make a speech in your community. Should he be allowed to speak, or not? NOTE: Question not asked in 1972, 1975, 1978, 1983, 1986.

Responses: YES = Yes, allowed to speak; NO = Not allowed

		YEAR										
SEX	RESP	'73	'74	'76	'77	'80	'82	'84	'85	'87	'88	'89
M	YES	63%	64%	66%	65%	68%	69%	72%	68%	70%	71%	78%
	NO	37	36	34	35	32	31	28	32	30	29	22
# SURVEYED		671	667	657	680	634	620	583	668	625	391	438
SEX	RESP	'73	'74	'76	'77	'80	'82	'84	'85	'87	'88	'89
F	YES	64%	66%	62%	64%	68%	67%	70%	70%	69%	74%	79%
	NO	36	34	38	36	32	33	30	30	31	26	21
# SURVEYED		774	749	792	792	788	821	833	810	801	547	565

TABLE III: ALLOW GAY TO MAKE SPEECH -- BY RACE

Question: Consider a man who admits he is a homosexual. Suppose this admitted homosexual wanted to make a speech in your community. Should he be allowed to speak, or not? NOTE: Question not asked in 1972, 1975, 1978, 1983, 1986.

Responses: YES = Yes, allowed to speak; NO = Not allowed

		YEAR										
RACE	RESP	'73	'74	'76	'77	'80	'82	'84	'85	'87	'88	'89
WHITE	YES	64%	66%	64%	65%	68%	68%	73%	70%	71%	73%	79%
	NO	36	34	36	35	32	32	27	30	29	27	21
# SURVEYED		1256	1244	1322	1291	1277	1264	1202	1296	1191	774	866
RACE	RESP	'73	'74	'76	'77	'80	'82	'84	'85	'87	'88	'89
BLACK	YES	59%	64%	61%	56%	65%	68%	59%	64%	63%	76%	78%
	NO	41	36	39	44	35	32	41	36	37	24	22
# SURVEYED		178	165	120	166	136	154	165	141	186	124	99
RACE	RESP	'73	'74	'76	'77	'80	'82	'84	'85	'87	'88	'89
OTHER	YES	64%	57%	86%	73%	67%	70%	55%	49%	55%	53%	66%
	NO	36	43	14	27	33	30	45	51	45	48	34
# SURVEYED		11	7	7	15	9	23	49	41	49	40	38

TABLE IV: ALLOW GAY TO MAKE SPEECH -- BY AGE

Question: Consider a man who admits he is a homosexual. Suppose this admitted homosexual wanted to make a speech in your community. Should he be allowed to speak, or not? NOTE: Question not asked in 1972, 1975, 1978, 1983, 1986.

Responses: YES = Yes, allowed to speak; NO = Not allowed

		YEAR										
AGE	RESP	'73	'74	'76	'77	'80	'82	'84	'85	'87	'88	'89
18-23	YES	79%	78%	75%	72%	75%	66%	69%	72%	67%	73%	77%
	NO	21	22	25	28	25	34	31	28	33	27	23
# SURVEYED		170	165	159	162	153	146	157	131	126	92	97
AGE	RESP	'73	'74	'76	'77	'80	'82	'84	'85	'87	'88	'89
24-29	YES	81%	84%	76%	78%	80%	77%	79%	79%	80%	79%	87%
	NO	19	16	24	22	21	23	21	21	20	21	13
# SURVEYED		208	209	224	201	200	243	229	214	188	127	114
AGE	RESP	'73	'74	'76	'77	'80	'82	'84	'85	'87	'88	'89
30-35	YES	71%	70%	73%	76%	80%	83%	81%	75%	81%	87%	82%
	NO	29	30	27	24	20	17	19	25	19	13	18
# SURVEYED		162	169	180	186	213	199	194	208	219	130	135
AGE	RESP	'73	'74	'76	'77	'80	'82	'84	'85	'87	'88	'89
36-41	YES	63%	74%	74%	71%	70%	75%	81%	78%	78%	82%	87%
	NO	37	26	26	29	30	25	19	22	22	18	13
# SURVEYED		171	148	156	163	148	143	182	184	181	131	134
AGE	RESP	'73	'74	'76	'77	'80	'82	'84	'85	'87	'88	'89
42-47	YES	73%	71%	64%	61%	75%	77%	76%	76%	75%	81%	90%
	NO	27	29	36	39	25	23	24	24	25	19	10
# SURVEYED		144	147	107	141	114	115	121	121	151	100	105
AGE	RESP	'73	'74	'76	'77	'80	'82	'84	'85	'87	'88	'89
48-53	YES	61%	64%	62%	63%	70%	64%	65%	71%	67%	69%	88%
	NO	39	36	38	38	30	36	35	29	33	31	12
# SURVEYED		144	138	130	152	121	108	98	129	124	62	93
AGE	RESP	'73	'74	'76	'77	'80	'82	'84	'85	'87	'88	'89
54-59	YES	55%	61%	63%	71%	58%	69%	69%	61%	78%	59%	79%
	NO	45	39	37	29	42	31	31	39	22	41	21
# SURVEYED		144	133	123	160	130	136	109	124	96	49	63

TABLE IV: ALLOW GAY TO MAKE SPEECH -- BY AGE

Question: Consider a man who admits he is a homosexual. Suppose this admitted homosexual wanted to make a speech in your community. Should he be allowed to speak, or not? NOTE: Question not asked in 1972, 1975, 1978, 1983, 1986.

Responses: YES = Yes, allowed to speak; NO = Not allowed

		YEAR										
AGE	RESP	'73	'74	'76	'77	'80	'82	'84	'85	'87	'88	'89
60-65	YES	42%	58%	55%	50%	64%	57%	63%	65%	59%	64%	66%
	NO	58	42	45	50	36	43	37	35	41	36	34
# SURVEYED		113	100	128	109	112	113	103	125	97	81	74
AGE	RESP	'73	'74	'76	'77	'80	'82	'84	'85	'87	'88	'89
66+	YES	36%	28%	38%	32%	43%	43%	49%	50%	45%	53%	58%
	NO	64	72	62	68	57	57	51	50	55	47	42
# SURVEYED		185	203	237	192	222	229	217	235	239	163	185

****

IS HOMOSEXUALITY WRONG?

TABLE I: IS HOMOSEXUALITY WRONG? -- BY TOTAL POPULATION

Question: What about sexual relations between two adults of the same sex--do you think it is always wrong, almost always wrong, wrong only sometimes, or not wrong at all? NOTE: Question not asked in 1972, 1975, 1978, 1983, 1986.

Responses: AW = Always wrong; AA = Almost always wrong; WS = Wrong sometimes; NW = Not wrong at all; OT = Other

	YEAR										
RESPONSE	'73	'74	'76	'77	'80	'82	'84	'85	'87	'88	'89
AW	73%	70%	70%	72%	73%	73%	73%	75%	77%	77%	74%
AA	7	5	6	6	6	5	5	4	4	5	4
WS	8	8	8	8	6	7	7	7	7	6	6
NW	11	13	16	15	15	15	14	14	12	13	16
OT	2	4	0	0	0	0	0	0	0	0	0
# SURVEYED	1448	1412	1426	1453	1397	1435	1412	1484	1412	937	980

TABLE II: IS HOMOSEXUALITY WRONG? -- BY SEX

Question: What about sexual relations between two adults of the same sex--do you think it is always wrong, almost always wrong, wrong only sometimes, or not wrong at all? NOTE: Question not asked in 1972, 1975, 1978, 1983, 1986.

Responses: AW = Always wrong; AA = Almost always wrong; WS = Wrong sometimes; NW = Not wrong at all; OT = Other

		YEAR										
SEX	RESP	'73	'74	'76	'77	'80	'82	'84	'85	'87	'88	'89
M	AW	72%	72%	69%	70%	73%	76%	72%	75%	77%	78%	75%
A	AA	7	5	7	6	6	6	5	4	3	4	4
L	WS	8	7	9	7	5	4	7	7	7	5	6
E	NW	12	13	15	16	16	13	16	14	12	12	14
	OT	2	3	0	0	0	0	0	0	0	0	0
# SURVEYED		681	658	645	659	615	609	582	665	616	388	428
SEX	RESP	'73	'74	'76	'77	'80	'82	'84	'85	'87	'88	'89
F	AW	74%	69%	71%	73%	74%	71%	74%	75%	77%	76%	73%
E	AA	6	5	6	5	6	4	5	4	5	5	4
M	WS	7	9	7	8	7	8	8	7	6	6	6
A	NW	10	13	17	14	14	16	13	14	12	13	17
L	OT	2	4	0	0	0	0	0	0	0	0	0
E												
# SURVEYED		767	754	781	794	782	826	830	819	796	549	552

TABLE III: IS HOMOSEXUALITY WRONG? -- BY RACE

Question: What about sexual relations between two adults of the same sex--do you think it is always wrong, almost always wrong, wrong only sometimes, or not wrong at all? NOTE: Question not asked in 1972, 1975, 1978, 1983, 1986.

Responses: AW = Always wrong, AA = Almost always wrong, WS = Wrong sometimes, NW = Not wrong at all, OT = Other

		YEAR										
RACE	RESP	'73	'74	'76	'77	'80	'82	'84	'85	'87	'88	'89
WHITE	AW	71%	70%	70%	71%	73%	72%	71%	74%	75%	75%	73%
	AA	7	6	7	6	6	5	6	4	5	5	4
	WS	7	8	8	8	6	7	8	7	8	6	7
	NW	12	13	16	15	15	15	15	14	13	14	16
	OT	2	4	0	0	0	0	0	0	0	0	0
# SURVEYED		1255	1244	1297	1271	1255	1260	1199	1299	1180	768	842
RACE	RESP	'73	'74	'76	'77	'80	'82	'84	'85	'87	'88	'89
BLACK	AW	83%	75%	75%	77%	79%	86%	88%	84%	88%	90%	80%
	AA	4	1	1	6	2	3	1	3	2	2	1
	WS	7	6	8	5	6	1	2	4	1	2	2
	NW	6	16	17	13	14	10	8	9	9	7	17
	OT	1	2	0	0	0	0	0	0	0	0	0
# SURVEYED		180	161	120	167	133	150	163	146	182	128	99
RACE	RESP	'73	'74	'76	'77	'80	'82	'84	'85	'87	'88	'89
OTHER	AW	69%	86%	67%	80%	44%	64%	80%	79%	78%	73%	82%
	AA	0	0	11	0	11	8	4	3	4	10	8
	WS	23	0	0	0	33	8	4	8	10	10	3
	NW	8	14	22	20	11	20	12	10	8	7	8
	OT	0	0	0	0	0	0	0	0	0	0	0
# SURVEYED		13	7	9	15	9	25	50	39	50	41	39

TABLE IV: IS HOMOSEXUALITY WRONG? -- BY AGE

Question: What about sexual relations between two adults of the same sex--do you think it is always wrong, almost always wrong, wrong only sometimes, or not wrong at all? NOTE: Question not asked in 1972, 1975, 1978, 1983, 1986.

Responses: AW = Always wrong; AA = Almost always wrong; WS = Wrong sometimes; NW = Not wrong at all; OT = Other

		YEAR										
AGE	RESP	'73	'74	'76	'77	'80	'82	'84	'85	'87	'88	'89
18-23	AW	55%	55%	53%	61%	66%	68%	69%	70%	73%	73%	75%
	AA	8	8	12	8	10	4	5	5	8	6	1
	WS	14	13	10	9	9	11	6	7	7	8	5
	NW	19	21	25	21	15	17	19	18	12	13	18
	OT	4	3	0	0	0	0	0	0	0	0	0
# SURVEYED		167	159	154	159	152	142	154	130	122	90	92
AGE	RESP	'73	'74	'76	'77	'80	'82	'84	'85	'87	'88	'89
24-29	AW	57%	50%	55%	57%	60%	68%	64%	67%	73%	69%	69%
	AA	6	6	7	8	9	8	5	5	4	5	7
	WS	15	15	11	10	10	11	13	10	8	9	6
	NW	21	24	27	25	21	13	18	17	15	16	17
	OT	1	4	0	0	0	0	0	0	0	0	0
# SURVEYED		204	209	220	199	191	238	229	212	187	129	109
AGE	RESP	'73	'74	'76	'77	'80	'82	'84	'85	'87	'88	'89
30-35	AW	75%	67%	66%	64%	61%	61%	61%	67%	69%	67%	71%
	AA	6	4	8	3	5	7	6	1	4	6	4
	WS	7	11	8	9	8	7	11	12	10	6	3
	NW	10	13	18	24	26	25	22	20	17	21	22
	OT	1	5	0	0	0	0	0	0	0	0	0
# SURVEYED		162	166	180	176	204	193	194	208	214	130	129
AGE	RESP	'73	'74	'76	'77	'80	'82	'84	'85	'87	'88	'89
36-41	AW	76%	72%	63%	73%	72%	62%	64%	65%	65%	76%	63%
	AA	5	5	6	6	8	8	4	6	7	3	4
	WS	6	8	12	11	5	7	8	7	9	4	11
	NW	10	10	19	10	15	23	24	22	19	17	22
	OT	2	4	0	0	0	0	0	0	0	0	0
# SURVEYED		173	145	150	162	143	140	177	178	179	124	128
AGE	RESP	'73	'74	'76	'77	'80	'82	'84	'85	'87	'88	'89
42-47	AW	64%	72%	73%	73%	72%	72%	77%	68%	75%	72%	68%
	AA	13	5	7	8	6	7	6	9	5	5	8
	WS	6	6	6	7	6	11	7	8	7	11	11
	NW	12	15	13	12	15	10	10	16	14	12	14
	OT	5	3	0	0	0	0	0	0	0	0	0
# SURVEYED		143	144	109	139	112	116	116	120	150	99	103

TABLE IV: IS HOMOSEXUALITY WRONG? -- BY AGE (Continued)

Question: What about sexual relations between two adults of the same sex--do you think it is always wrong, almost always wrong, wrong only sometimes, or not wrong at all? NOTE: Question not asked in 1972, 1975, 1978, 1983, 1986.

Responses: AW = Always wrong; AA = Almost always wrong; WS = Wrong sometimes; NW = Not wrong at all; OT = Other

		YEAR										
AGE	RESP	'73	'74	'76	'77	'80	'82	'84	'85	'87	'88	'89
48-53	AW	77%	73%	76%	71%	74%	77%	88%	76%	82%	84%	78%
	AA	7	5	6	6	8	5	0	6	6	5	2
	WS	7	4	9	8	8	5	4	9	8	3	4
	NW	7	14	10	15	10	13	8	9	4	8	15
	OT	2	4	0	0	0	0	0	0	0	0	0
# SURVEYED		144	137	127	144	119	106	99	129	120	61	92
AGE	RESP	'73	'74	'76	'77	'80	'82	'84	'85	'87	'88	'89
54-59	AW	79%	87%	77%	81%	86%	77%	79%	88%	83%	84%	75%
	AA	7	2	4	5	2	4	9	3	2	4	5
	WS	5	3	4	6	3	4	5	3	6	2	7
	NW	7	5	15	8	9	15	7	5	8	10	14
	OT	2	2	0	0	0	0	0	0	0	0	0
# SURVEYED		151	130	121	160	130	137	110	128	96	50	59
AGE	RESP	'73	'74	'76	'77	'80	'82	'84	'85	'87	'88	'89
60-65	AW	85%	79%	81%	80%	83%	82%	81%	84%	88%	84%	80%
	AA	4	5	3	6	3	3	5	1	3	3	3
	WS	3	3	6	5	4	3	7	6	2	4	4
	NW	7	9	9	9	11	11	8	9	6	10	13
	OT	1	5	0	0	0	0	0	0	0	0	0
# SURVEYED		117	103	124	110	112	115	105	128	95	79	75
AGE	RESP	'73	'74	'76	'77	'80	'82	'84	'85	'87	'88	'89
66+	AW	91%	86%	89%	89%	88%	92%	88%	92%	89%	88%	86%
	AA	3	5	3	3	4	1	5	1	1	5	3
	WS	2	4	3	2	3	1	3	1	2	2	4
	NW	3	3	5	6	5	5	5	5	8	5	7
	OT	1	2	0	0	0	0	0	0	0	0	0
# SURVEYED		183	214	236	197	226	238	222	244	245	173	190

****

ALLOW SEX EDUCATION IN SCHOOLS

TABLE I: ALLOW SEX EDUCATION IN SCHOOLS -- BY TOTAL POPULATION

Question: Would you be for or against sex education in the public schools? NOTE: Question not asked in 1972, 1973, 1976, 1978, 1980, 1984, 1987.

Responses: FO = For; AG = Against; DP = Depends on grade/age

	YEAR								
RESPONSE	'74	'75	'77	'82	'83	'85	'86	'88	'89
FO	82%	79%	79%	84%	86%	84%	84%	87%	87%
AG	18	21	21	16	14	16	16	13	13
DP	1	0	0	0	0	0	0	0	0
# SURVEYED	1431	1433	1492	1457	1551	1488	1427	957	969

TABLE II: ALLOW SEX EDUCATION IN SCHOOLS -- BY SEX

Question: Would you be for or against sex education in the public schools? NOTE: Question not asked in 1972, 1973, 1976, 1978, 1980, 1984, 1987.

Responses: FO = For; AG = Against; DP = Depends on grade/age

		YEAR								
SEX	RESP	'74	'75	'77	'82	'83	'85	'86	'88	'89
M	FO	80%	77%	78%	83%	87%	85%	86%	88%	88%
	AG	19	23	22	17	13	15	14	12	12
	DP	0	0	0	0	0	0	0	0	0
# SURVEYED		668	640	678	619	673	667	603	430	416
SEX	RESP	'74	'75	'77	'82	'83	'85	'86	'88	'89
F	FO	83%	81%	79%	85%	85%	83%	82%	86%	87%
	AG	16	19	21	15	15	17	18	14	13
	DP	1	0	0	0	0	0	0	0	0
# SURVEYED		763	793	814	838	878	821	824	527	553

TABLE III: ALLOW SEX EDUCATION IN SCHOOLS -- BY RACE

Question: Would you be for or against sex education in the public schools? NOTE: Question not asked in 1972, 1973, 1976, 1978, 1980, 1984, 1987.

Responses: FO = For; AG = Against; DP = Depends on grade/age

		YEAR								
RACE	RESP	'74	'75	'77	'82	'83	'85	'86	'88	'89
WHITE	FO	82%	80%	79%	84%	86%	84%	85%	87%	88%
	AG	18	20	21	16	14	16	15	13	12
	DP	1	0	0	0	0	0	0	0	0
# SURVEYED		1257	1274	1305	1277	1378	1303	1214	799	832
RACE	RESP	'74	'75	'77	'82	'83	'85	'86	'88	'89
BLACK	FO	81%	77%	75%	88%	87%	84%	80%	86%	86%
	AG	19	23	25	12	13	16	20	14	14
	DP	0	0	0	0	0	0	0	0	0
# SURVEYED		167	155	172	153	158	146	178	125	101
RACE	RESP	'74	'75	'77	'82	'83	'85	'86	'88	'89
OTHER	FO	71%	50%	93%	74%	73%	87%	77%	85%	83%
	AG	29	50	7	26	27	13	23	15	17
	DP	0	0	0	0	0	0	0	0	0
# SURVEYED		7	4	15	27	15	39	35	33	36

TABLE IV: ALLOW SEX EDUCATION IN SCHOOLS -- BY AGE

Question: Would you be for or against sex education in the public schools? NOTE: Question not asked in 1972, 1973, 1976, 1978, 1980, 1984, 1987.

Responses: FO = For; AG = Against; DP = Depends on grade/age

		YEAR								
AGE	RESP	'74	'75	'77	'82	'83	'85	'86	'88	'89
18-23	FO	90%	88%	87%	86%	94%	92%	97%	95%	86%
	AG	10	12	13	14	6	8	3	5	14
	DP	0	0	0	0	0	0	0	0	0
# SURVEYED		167	170	163	145	127	132	106	93	83
AGE	RESP	'74	'75	'77	'82	'83	'85	'86	'88	'89
24-29	FO	91%	93%	93%	93%	91%	92%	88%	96%	94%
	AG	8	7	7	7	9	8	12	4	6
	DP	0	0	0	0	0	0	0	0	0
# SURVEYED		207	227	202	244	281	213	217	145	143

TABLE IV: ALLOW SEX EDUCATION IN SCHOOLS -- BY AGE (Continued)

Question: Would you be for or against sex education in the public schools? NOTE: Question not asked in 1972, 1973, 1976, 1978, 1980, 1984, 1987.

Responses: FO = For; AG = Against; DP = Depends on grade/age

		YEAR								
AGE	RESP	'74	'75	'77	'82	'83	'85	'86	'88	'89
30-35	FO	90%	82%	85%	96%	90%	90%	92%	93%	96%
	AG	9	18	15	4	10	10	8	7	4
	DP	1	0	0	0	0	0	0	0	0
# SURVEYED		172	167	186	202	229	208	217	130	136
AGE	RESP	'74	'75	'77	'82	'83	'85	'86	'88	'89
36-41	FO	86%	87%	84%	93%	90%	91%	90%	90%	91%
	AG	13	13	16	7	10	9	10	10	9
	DP	1	0	0	0	0	0	0	0	0
# SURVEYED		149	148	163	142	167	181	182	127	126
AGE	RESP	'74	'75	'77	'82	'83	'85	'86	'88	'89
42-47	FO	88%	88%	77%	88%	91%	94%	91%	85%	94%
	AG	11	12	23	12	9	6	9	15	6
	DP	1	0	0	0	0	0	0	0	0
# SURVEYED		147	135	141	117	141	119	139	107	107
AGE	RESP	'74	'75	'77	'82	'83	'85	'86	'88	'89
48-53	FO	83%	79%	82%	82%	91%	84%	82%	88%	91%
	AG	16	21	18	18	9	16	18	12	9
	DP	1	0	0	0	0	0	0	0	0
# SURVEYED		139	140	152	107	116	129	105	60	81
AGE	RESP	'74	'75	'77	'82	'83	'85	'86	'88	'89
54-59	FO	78%	78%	81%	78%	85%	73%	81%	80%	91%
	AG	22	22	19	22	15	27	19	20	9
	DP	0	0	0	0	0	0	0	0	0
# SURVEYED		130	121	162	142	129	127	95	50	69
AGE	RESP	'74	'75	'77	'82	'83	'85	'86	'88	'89
60-65	FO	72%	68%	69%	75%	81%	79%	80%	88%	79%
	AG	28	32	31	25	19	21	20	12	21
	DP	0	0	0	0	0	0	0	0	0
# SURVEYED		104	110	115	113	130	125	110	68	67
AGE	RESP	'74	'75	'77	'82	'83	'85	'86	'88	'89
66+	FO	58%	51%	51%	68%	67%	67%	65%	72%	66%
	AG	40	49	49	32	33	33	35	28	34
	DP	1	0	0	0	0	0	0	0	0
# SURVEYED		210	211	201	237	225	248	249	176	155

****

SUPPLY BIRTH CONTROL INFORMATION

TABLE I: SUPPLY BIRTH CONTROL INFORMATION -- BY TOTAL POPULATION

Question: In some places in the United States, it is illegal to supply birth control information. How do you feel about this--do you think birth control information should be available to anyone who wants it, or not? NOTE: Question not asked in 1972, 1973, 1976, 1978, 1980, 1984-1989.

Responses: SB = Should be available; SN = Should not be available

	YEAR				
RESPONSE	'74	'75	'77	'82	'83
SB	92%	91%	93%	92%	92%
SN	8	9	7	8	8
# SURVEYED	1469	1457	1501	1475	1568

TABLE II: SUPPLY BIRTH CONTROL INFORMATION -- BY SEX

Question: In some places in the United States, it is illegal to supply birth control information. How do you feel about this--do you think birth control information should be available to anyone who wants it, or not? NOTE: Question not asked in 1972, 1973, 1976, 1978, 1980, 1984-1989.

Responses: SB = Should be available; SN = Should not be available

		YEAR				
SEX	RESP	'74	'75	'77	'82	'83
M	SB	90%	90%	93%	92%	92%
	SN	10	10	7	8	8
# SURVEYED		683	651	680	622	675

		YEAR				
SEX	RESP	'74	'75	'77	'82	'83
F	SB	94%	92%	92%	92%	92%
	SN	6	8	8	8	8
# SURVEYED		786	806	821	853	893

TABLE III: SUPPLY BIRTH CONTROL INFORMATION -- BY RACE

Question: In some places in the United States, it is illegal to supply birth control information. How do you feel about this--do you think birth control information should be available to anyone who wants it, or not? NOTE: Question not asked in 1972, 1973, 1976, 1978, 1980, 1984-1989.

Responses: SB = Should be available; SN = Should not be available

RACE	RESP	'74	'75	'77	'82	'83
WHITE	SB	93%	92%	93%	92%	92%
	SN	7	8	7	8	8
# SURVEYED		1292	1293	1317	1297	1392

RACE	RESP	'74	'75	'77	'82	'83
BLACK	SB	86%	83%	85%	94%	90%
	SN	14	18	15	6	10
# SURVEYED		170	160	169	153	160

RACE	RESP	'74	'75	'77	'82	'83
OTHER	SB	100%	100%	100%	84%	94%
	SN	0	0	0	16	6
# SURVEYED		7	4	15	25	16

TABLE IV: SUPPLY BIRTH CONTROL INFORMATION -- BY AGE

Question: In some places in the United States, it is illegal to supply birth control information. How do you feel about this--do you think birth control information should be available to anyone who wants it, or not? NOTE: Question not asked in 1972, 1973, 1976, 1978, 1980, 1984-1989.

Responses: SB = Should be available; SN = Should not be available

AGE	RESP	'74	'75	'77	'82	'83
18-23	SB	97%	95%	98%	95%	95%
	SN	3	5	2	5	5
# SURVEYED		167	170	163	146	128
24-29	SB	99%	98%	98%	96%	94%
	SN	1	2	2	4	6
# SURVEYED		211	232	203	245	285
30-35	SB	93%	95%	95%	97%	95%
	SN	7	5	5	3	5
# SURVEYED		175	169	186	204	234

AGE	RESP	'74	'75	'77	'82	'83
36-41	SB	95%	94%	95%	95%	91%
	SN	5	6	5	5	9
# SURVEYED		152	151	167	146	172
42-47	SB	93%	89%	90%	94%	96%
	SN	7	11	10	6	4
# SURVEYED		149	142	143	118	142
48-53	SB	94%	94%	93%	95%	91%
	SN	6	6	7	5	9
# SURVEYED		145	141	152	110	116

AGE	RESP	'74	'75	'77	'82	'83
54-59	SB	92%	87%	90%	88%	90%
	SN	8	13	10	12	10
# SURVEYED		137	119	163	142	130
60-65	SB	88%	90%	91%	88%	92%
	SN	12	10	9	12	8
# SURVEYED		105	112	116	115	131
66+	SB	81%	79%	84%	85%	84%
	SN	19	21	16	15	16
# SURVEYED		222	217	201	239	224

****

BIRTH CONTROL INFORMATION FOR TEENS

TABLE I: BIRTH CONTROL INFORMATION FOR TEENS -- BY TOTAL POPULATION

Question: Do you think that birth control information should be available to teenagers who want it, or not? NOTE: Question not asked in 1972, 1973, 1976, 1978, 1980, 1984-1989.

Responses: SB = Should be available; SN = Should not be available; DP = Depends on age/grade (volunteered)

	YEAR				
RESPONSE	'74	'75	'77	'82	'83
SB	80%	81%	84%	88%	87%
SN	20	19	16	12	13
DP	0	0	0	0	0
# SURVEYED	1434	1445	1493	1466	1553

TABLE II: BIRTH CONTROL INFORMATION FOR TEENS -- BY SEX

Question: Do you think that birth control information should be available to teenagers who want it, or not? NOTE: Question not asked in 1972, 1973, 1976, 1978, 1980, 1984-1989.

Responses: SB = Should be available; SN = Should not be available; DP = Depends on age/grade (volunteered)

		YEAR				
SEX	RESP	'74	'75	'77	'82	'83
M	SB	79%	79%	84%	90%	88%
	SN	21	21	16	10	12
	DP	0	0	0	0	0
# SURVEYED		670	652	679	620	667

		YEAR				
SEX	RESP	'74	'75	'77	'82	'83
F	SB	81%	82%	83%	86%	87%
	SN	19	18	17	14	13
	DP	0	0	0	0	0
# SURVEYED		764	793	814	846	886

TABLE III: BIRTH CONTROL INFORMATION FOR TEENS -- BY RACE

Question: Do you think that birth control information should be available to teenagers who want it, or not? NOTE: Question not asked in 1972, 1973, 1976, 1978, 1980, 1984-1989.

Responses: SB = Should be available; SN = Should not be available; DP = Depends on age/grade (volunteered)

RACE	RESP	'74	'75	'77	'82	'83
WHITE	SB	80%	81%	84%	88%	87%
	SN	19	19	16	12	13
	DP	0	0	0	0	0
# SURVEYED		1259	1286	1307	1285	1379

RACE	RESP	'74	'75	'77	'82	'83
BLACK	SB	76%	77%	81%	91%	86%
	SN	24	23	19	9	14
	DP	0	0	0	0	0
# SURVEYED		168	155	171	155	159

RACE	RESP	'74	'75	'77	'82	'83
OTHER	SB	86%	50%	67%	81%	93%
	SN	14	50	33	19	7
	DP	0	0	0	0	0
# SURVEYED		7	4	15	26	15

TABLE IV: BIRTH CONTROL INFORMATION FOR TEENS -- BY AGE

Question: Do you think that birth control information should be available to teenagers who want it, or not? NOTE: Question not asked in 1972, 1973, 1976, 1978, 1980, 1984-1989.

Responses: SB = Should be available; SN = Should not be available; DP = Depends on age/grade (volunteered)

AGE	RESP	'74	'75	'77	'82	'83
18-23	SB	93%	92%	95%	94%	94%
	SN	7	8	5	6	6
	DP	0	0	0	0	0
# SURVEYED		165	171	162	148	127
AGE	RESP	'74	'75	'77	'82	'83
24-29	SB	91%	94%	98%	94%	93%
	SN	9	6	2	6	7
	DP	0	0	0	0	0
# SURVEYED		209	231	201	244	282
AGE	RESP	'74	'75	'77	'82	'83
30-35	SB	83%	86%	90%	96%	93%
	SN	17	14	10	4	7
	DP	0	0	0	0	0
# SURVEYED		172	167	187	202	235

AGE	RESP	'74	'75	'77	'82	'83
36-41	SB	87%	88%	88%	93%	87%
	SN	13	12	12	7	13
	DP	0	0	0	0	0
# SURVEYED		151	149	164	146	169
AGE	RESP	'74	'75	'77	'82	'83
42-47	SB	84%	85%	82%	95%	93%
	SN	16	15	18	5	7
	DP	0	0	0	0	0
# SURVEYED		148	142	141	118	141
AGE	RESP	'74	'75	'77	'82	'83
48-53	SB	83%	81%	84%	88%	86%
	SN	17	19	16	12	14
	DP	0	0	0	0	0
# SURVEYED		139	139	151	110	114

AGE	RESP	'74	'75	'77	'82	'83
54-59	SB	75%	74%	84%	81%	81%
	SN	25	26	16	19	19
	DP	0	0	0	0	0
# SURVEYED		133	117	164	136	129
AGE	RESP	'74	'75	'77	'82	'83
60-65	SB	70%	72%	73%	80%	85%
	SN	29	28	27	20	15
	DP	1	0	0	0	0
# SURVEYED		101	108	116	114	130
AGE	RESP	'74	'75	'77	'82	'83
66+	SB	53%	54%	59%	74%	72%
	SN	46	46	41	26	28
	DP	1	0	0	0	0
# SURVEYED		210	217	200	238	220

****

GIVE TEENS CONTRACEPTIVES WITHOUT PARENTAL CONSENT

TABLE I: GIVE TEENS CONTRACEPTIVES WITHOUT PARENTAL CONSENT -- BY TOTAL POPULATION

Question: Do you strongly agree, agree, disagree, or strongly disagree that methods of birth control should be available to teenagers between the ages of 14 and 16 if their parents do not approve? NOTE: Question not asked in 1971-1985, 1987.

Responses: AS = Strongly agree; AG = Agree; DS = Disagree; SD = Strongly disagree

	YEAR		
RESPONSE	'86	'88	'89
AS	23%	28%	28%
AG	35	30	27
DS	25	23	25
SD	17	18	20
# SURVEYED	1427	942	976

TABLE II: GIVE TEENS CONTRACEPTIVES WITHOUT PARENTAL CONSENT -- BY SEX

Question: Do you strongly agree, agree, disagree, or strongly disagree that methods of birth control should be available to teenagers between the ages of 14 and 16 if their parents do not approve? NOTE: Question not asked in 1971-1985, 1987.

Responses: AS = Strongly agree; AG = Agree; DS = Disagree; SD = Strongly disagree

		YEAR		
SEX	RESP	'86	'88	'89
M	AS	22%	29%	25%
	AG	36	34	29
	DS	27	22	26
	SD	16	15	19
# SURVEYED		604	414	422

		YEAR		
SEX	RESP	'86	'88	'89
F	AS	24%	28%	30%
	AG	35	28	26
	DS	24	24	24
	SD	17	20	21
# SURVEYED		823	528	554

TABLE III: GIVE TEENS CONTRACEPTIVES WITHOUT PARENTAL CONSENT -- BY RACE

Question: Do you strongly agree, agree, disagree, or strongly disagree that methods of birth control should be available to teenagers between the ages of 14 and 16 if their parents do not approve? NOTE: Question not asked in 1971-1985, 1987.

Responses: AS = Strongly agree; AG = Agree; DS = Disagree; SD = Strongly disagree

		YEAR		
RACE	RESP	'86	'88	'89
WHITE	AS	23%	27%	26%
	AG	35	31	28
	DS	24	24	25
	SD	18	18	20
# SURVEYED		1215	786	836

		YEAR		
RACE	RESP	'86	'88	'89
BLACK	AS	23%	35%	41%
	AG	31	27	17
	DS	35	21	25
	SD	10	17	18
# SURVEYED		175	123	102

		YEAR		
RACE	RESP	'86	'88	'89
OTHER	AS	16%	39%	18%
	AG	43	33	29
	DS	24	9	26
	SD	16	18	26
# SURVEYED		37	33	38

TABLE IV: GIVE TEENS CONTRACEPTIVES WITHOUT PARENTAL CONSENT -- BY AGE

Question: Do you strongly agree, agree, disagree, or strongly disagree that methods of birth control should be available to teenagers between the ages of 14 and 16 if their parents do not approve? NOTE: Question not asked in 1971-1985, 1987.

Responses: AS = Strongly agree; AG = Agree; DS = Disagree; SD = Strongly disagree

		YEAR		
AGE	RESP	'86	'88	'89
18-23	AS	34%	39%	29%
	AG	41	32	34
	DS	18	20	23
	SD	7	9	14
# SURVEYED		108	93	83
AGE	RESP	'86	'88	'89
24-29	AS	30%	34%	37%
	AG	39	39	33
	DS	20	15	19
	SD	10	11	11
# SURVEYED		215	145	144
AGE	RESP	'86	'88	'89
30-35	AS	25%	35%	30%
	AG	39	28	35
	DS	25	24	23
	SD	12	13	12
# SURVEYED		216	129	140

		YEAR		
AGE	RESP	'86	'88	'89
36-41	AS	26%	31%	33%
	AG	37	30	32
	DS	25	26	15
	SD	12	14	20
# SURVEYED		187	124	127
AGE	RESP	'86	'88	'89
42-47	AS	22%	22%	30%
	AG	40	30	22
	DS	25	21	28
	SD	14	27	20
# SURVEYED		139	104	107
AGE	RESP	'86	'88	'89
48-53	AS	27%	30%	22%
	AG	30	18	28
	DS	23	32	34
	SD	20	21	17
# SURVEYED		104	57	83

		YEAR		
AGE	RESP	'86	'88	'89
54-59	AS	9%	31%	29%
	AG	32	22	19
	DS	39	27	29
	SD	20	20	24
# SURVEYED		96	49	70
AGE	RESP	'86	'88	'89
60-65	AS	17%	28%	14%
	AG	32	28	15
	DS	23	29	37
	SD	28	16	34
# SURVEYED		110	69	65
AGE	RESP	'86	'88	'89
66+	AS	15%	13%	18%
	AG	27	33	19
	DS	30	25	28
	SD	28	29	34
# SURVEYED		246	171	155

****

TEENAGE SEXUAL RELATIONS

TABLE I: TEENAGE SEXUAL RELATIONS -- BY TOTAL POPULATION

Question: For teenagers, say 14 to 16 years old, do you think sexual relations before marriage are always wrong, almost always wrong, wrong only sometimes, or not wrong at all? NOTE: Question not asked in 1972-1985, 1987.

Responses: AW = Always wrong AA = Almost always wrong
WS = Wrong only sometimes NW = Not wrong at all

	YEAR		
RESPONSE	'86	'88	'89
AW	67%	69%	71%
AA	19	16	16
WS	11	11	9
NW	3	3	4
# SURVEYED	1445	973	991

TABLE II: TEENAGE SEXUAL RELATIONS -- BY SEX

Question: For teenagers, say 14 to 16 years old, do you think sexual relations before marriage are always wrong, almost always wrong, wrong only sometimes, or not wrong at all? NOTE: Question not asked in 1972-1985, 1987.

Responses: AW = Always wrong AA = Almost always wrong
WS = Wrong only sometimes NW = Not wrong at all

		YEAR		
SEX	RESP	'86	'88	'89
M	AW	61%	64%	64%
	AA	19	19	20
	WS	14	12	12
	NW	5	5	4
# SURVEYED		607	431	420

		YEAR		
SEX	RESP	'86	'88	'89
F	AW	71%	73%	76%
	AA	19	14	13
	WS	9	10	7
	NW	2	2	4
# SURVEYED		838	542	571

TABLE III: TEENAGE SEXUAL RELATIONS -- BY RACE

Question: For teenagers, say 14 to 16 years old, do you think sexual relations before marriage are always wrong, almost always wrong, wrong only sometimes, or not wrong at all? NOTE: Question not asked in 1972-1985, 1987.

Responses: AW = Always wrong; AA = Almost always wrong; WS = Wrong only sometimes; NW = Not wrong at all

RACE	RESP	'86	'88	'89
WHITE	AW	67%	69%	70%
	AA	19	17	17
	WS	11	11	9
	NW	3	3	4
# SURVEYED		1229	819	853

RACE	RESP	'86	'88	'89
BLACK	AW	62%	70%	74%
	AA	17	9	7
	WS	13	13	9
	NW	7	8	11
# SURVEYED		181	120	102

RACE	RESP	'86	'88	'89
OTHER	AW	74%	68%	72%
	AA	11	15	17
	WS	11	12	11
	NW	3	6	0
# SURVEYED		35	34	36

TABLE IV: TEENAGE SEXUAL RELATIONS -- BY AGE

Question: For teenagers, say 14 to 16 years old, do you think sexual relations before marriage are always wrong, almost always wrong, wrong only sometimes, or not wrong at all? NOTE: Question not asked in 1972-1985, 1987.

Responses: AW = Always wrong; AA = Almost always wrong; WS = Wrong only sometimes; NW = Not wrong at all

AGE	RESP	'86	'88	'89
18-23	AW	45%	46%	48%
	AA	21	20	30
	WS	28	28	17
	NW	6	6	5
# SURVEYED		107	94	83
24-29	AW	52%	56%	58%
	AA	29	22	24
	WS	18	20	12
	NW	2	1	6
# SURVEYED		214	149	143
30-35	AW	56%	60%	63%
	AA	21	23	18
	WS	18	11	12
	NW	5	6	7
# SURVEYED		218	128	138

AGE	RESP	'86	'88	'89
36-41	AW	62%	69%	63%
	AA	24	18	23
	WS	9	8	12
	NW	5	5	2
# SURVEYED		188	125	126
42-47	AW	67%	72%	76%
	AA	26	15	10
	WS	5	10	7
	NW	1	3	6
# SURVEYED		141	107	108
48-53	AW	71%	80%	81%
	AA	17	15	7
	WS	7	3	7
	NW	5	2	5
# SURVEYED		105	60	85

AGE	RESP	'86	'88	'89
54-59	AW	80%	80%	80%
	AA	13	12	10
	WS	4	4	6
	NW	3	4	4
# SURVEYED		96	51	71
60-65	AW	88%	79%	88%
	AA	4	16	12
	WS	4	4	0
	NW	4	0	0
# SURVEYED		113	73	68
66+	AW	84%	86%	86%
	AA	10	6	8
	WS	5	5	4
	NW	1	2	2
# SURVEYED		257	185	166

****

PREMARITAL SEXUAL RELATIONS

TABLE I: PREMARITAL SEXUAL RELATIONS -- BY TOTAL POPULATION

Question: There's been a lot of discussion about the ways morals and attitudes toward sex are changing in this country. If a man and woman have sexual relations before marriage, do you think it is always wrong, almost always wrong, wrong only sometimes, or not wrong at all? NOTE: Question not asked in 1973, 1976, 1980, 1984, 1987.

Responses: AW = Always wrong AA = Almost always wrong
WS = Wrong only sometimes NW = Not wrong at all

	YEAR										
RESPONSE	'72	'74	'75	'77	'78	'82	'83	'85	'86	'88	'89
AW	37%	33%	31%	31%	29%	29%	27%	28%	28%	26%	28%
AA	12	13	12	10	12	9	10	8	9	11	9
WS	24	24	24	23	20	21	24	20	23	22	23
NW	27	31	33	37	39	41	39	43	40	41	41
# SURVEYED	1537	1429	1427	1481	1494	1455	1561	1482	1425	955	971

TABLE II: PREMARITAL SEXUAL RELATIONS -- BY SEX

Question: There's been a lot of discussion about the ways morals and attitudes toward sex are changing in this country. If a man and woman have sexual relations before marriage, do you think it is always wrong, almost always wrong, wrong only sometimes, or not wrong at all? NOTE: Question not asked in 1973, 1976, 1980, 1984, 1987.

Responses: AW = Always wrong AA = Almost always wrong
WS = Wrong only sometimes NW = Not wrong at all

		YEAR										
SEX	RESP	'72	'74	'75	'77	'78	'82	'83	'85	'86	'88	'89
M	AW	30%	30%	26%	24%	23%	23%	22%	22%	20%	23%	22%
	AA	11	12	10	8	12	8	8	8	9	8	7
	WS	24	22	24	24	20	21	25	21	23	21	24
	NW	35	37	40	44	45	47	45	49	48	48	46
# SURVEYED		778	662	641	668	625	614	672	667	609	422	416
SEX	RESP	'72	'74	'75	'77	'78	'82	'83	'85	'86	'88	'89
F	AW	44%	36%	35%	37%	34%	32%	31%	34%	33%	29%	32%
	AA	12	14	14	10	12	10	11	8	9	13	10
	WS	24	25	24	22	20	21	24	19	23	24	22
	NW	20	26	27	30	34	36	33	39	35	35	36
# SURVEYED		759	767	786	813	869	841	889	815	816	533	555

TABLE III: PREMARITAL SEXUAL RELATIONS -- BY RACE

Question: There's been a lot of discussion about the ways morals and attitudes toward sex are changing in this country. If a man and woman have sexual relations before marriage, do you think it is always wrong, almost always wrong, wrong only sometimes, or not wrong at all? NOTE: Question not asked in 1973, 1976, 1980, 1984, 1987.

Responses: AW = Always wrong; AA = Almost always wrong; WS = Wrong only sometimes; NW = Not wrong at all

		YEAR										
RACE	RESP	'72	'74	'75	'77	'78	'82	'83	'85	'86	'88	'89
WHITE	AW	39%	33%	32%	31%	30%	29%	28%	29%	28%	26%	28%
	AA	13	14	13	10	12	10	10	9	9	11	9
	WS	25	24	25	23	22	22	25	21	24	23	24
	NW	23	29	31	35	36	40	37	41	39	39	40
# SURVEYED		1288	1255	1270	1299	1324	1277	1386	1293	1217	801	833
RACE	RESP	'72	'74	'75	'77	'78	'82	'83	'85	'86	'88	'89
BLACK	AW	23%	30%	22%	28%	22%	26%	23%	20%	28%	24%	27%
	AA	9	6	10	7	9	3	6	7	8	7	10
	WS	18	17	17	20	10	18	18	12	16	18	16
	NW	50	48	52	46	59	53	53	62	49	50	46
# SURVEYED		245	168	153	167	154	152	159	146	172	121	99
RACE	RESP	'72	'74	'75	'77	'78	'82	'83	'85	'86	'88	'89
OTHER	AW	0%	33%	25%	20%	19%	23%	31%	30%	36%	30%	36%
	AA	0	17	0	7	13	12	6	7	11	9	3
	WS	50	33	50	27	19	19	50	21	22	27	23
	NW	50	17	25	47	50	46	13	42	31	33	38
# SURVEYED		4	6	4	15	16	26	16	43	36	33	39

TABLE IV: PREMARITAL SEXUAL RELATIONS -- BY AGE

Question: There's been a lot of discussion about the ways morals and attitudes toward sex are changing in this country. If a man and woman have sexual relations before marriage, do you think it is always wrong, almost always wrong, wrong only sometimes, or not wrong at all? NOTE: Question not asked in 1973, 1976, 1980, 1984, 1987.

Responses: AW = Always wrong; AA = Almost always wrong; WS = Wrong only sometimes; NW = Not wrong at all

		YEAR										
AGE	RESP	'72	'74	'75	'77	'78	'82	'83	'85	'86	'88	'89
18-23	AW	11%	11%	15%	14%	13%	14%	13%	15%	10%	13%	18%
	AA	4	8	5	7	9	7	10	5	7	3	5
	WS	34	29	32	30	28	35	30	29	35	25	27
	NW	51	52	48	50	51	44	46	52	48	59	50
# SURVEYED		164	164	170	161	160	147	127	133	107	92	82
AGE	RESP	'72	'74	'75	'77	'78	'82	'83	'85	'86	'88	'89
24-29	AW	18%	11%	12%	12%	13%	12%	15%	14%	11%	21%	10%
	AA	10	11	6	6	5	6	6	6	7	12	6
	WS	32	29	27	24	16	24	30	21	29	23	31
	NW	40	50	55	58	66	58	49	59	52	45	52
# SURVEYED		222	207	222	199	239	243	284	214	216	146	145
AGE	RESP	'72	'74	'75	'77	'78	'82	'83	'85	'86	'88	'89
30-35	AW	31%	26%	24%	20%	21%	20%	21%	17%	17%	16%	11%
	AA	12	12	11	8	5	7	7	5	9	4	6
	WS	26	24	21	22	26	20	26	20	24	25	23
	NW	31	39	43	49	48	54	46	58	50	55	60
# SURVEYED		180	172	168	184	228	203	235	210	217	130	140
AGE	RESP	'72	'74	'75	'77	'78	'82	'83	'85	'86	'88	'89
36-41	AW	43%	33%	33%	31%	28%	19%	24%	22%	23%	15%	22%
	AA	10	12	13	8	15	13	10	8	6	7	4
	WS	18	25	26	26	17	22	18	15	18	29	25
	NW	28	30	28	35	40	46	48	55	53	49	49
# SURVEYED		125	144	150	167	156	142	168	179	186	126	123
AGE	RESP	'72	'74	'75	'77	'78	'82	'83	'85	'86	'88	'89
42-47	AW	34%	33%	28%	33%	30%	25%	23%	28%	25%	23%	24%
	AA	14	13	10	12	17	7	15	7	4	14	10
	WS	28	26	27	20	22	23	25	18	24	22	21
	NW	23	27	35	35	30	44	37	48	47	40	45
# SURVEYED		175	144	136	142	115	115	142	120	138	104	104
AGE	RESP	'72	'74	'75	'77	'78	'82	'83	'85	'86	'88	'89
48-53	AW	41%	32%	38%	30%	39%	37%	31%	30%	31%	25%	34%
	AA	16	17	21	15	15	10	14	12	8	18	11
	WS	26	27	19	25	20	19	24	17	22	18	18
	NW	17	24	22	30	26	33	32	41	39	38	37
# SURVEYED		177	139	135	141	131	108	114	126	104	60	82

TABLE IV: PREMARITAL SEXUAL RELATIONS -- BY AGE (Continued)

Question: There's been a lot of discussion about the ways morals and attitudes toward sex are changing in this country. If a man and woman have sexual relations before marriage, do you think it is always wrong, almost always wrong, wrong only sometimes, or not wrong at all? NOTE: Question not asked in 1973, 1976, 1980, 1984, 1987.

Responses: AW = Always wrong AA = Almost always wrong
WS = Wrong only sometimes NW = Not wrong at all

		YEAR										
AGE	RESP	'72	'74	'75	'77	'78	'82	'83	'85	'86	'88	'89
54-59	AW	48%	52%	33%	42%	43%	42%	35%	42%	37%	35%	29%
	AA	14	13	23	11	16	12	13	14	14	8	16
	WS	16	20	27	21	18	15	22	21	17	22	18
	NW	22	14	18	26	23	31	30	23	32	35	37
# SURVEYED		148	138	120	163	136	137	127	125	92	49	68
AGE	RESP	'72	'74	'75	'77	'78	'82	'83	'85	'86	'88	'89
60-65	AW	45%	44%	41%	44%	38%	37%	38%	35%	41%	42%	54%
	AA	13	13	17	14	18	11	15	10	15	16	15
	WS	24	21	19	24	24	23	19	23	16	22	20
	NW	18	22	24	18	21	29	28	31	27	19	11
# SURVEYED		136	103	106	114	101	110	128	124	110	67	65
AGE	RESP	'72	'74	'75	'77	'78	'82	'83	'85	'86	'88	'89
66+	AW	63%	60%	58%	57%	51%	52%	48%	52%	54%	47%	57%
	AA	12	16	13	8	14	11	9	10	11	15	11
	WS	12	12	17	17	15	14	22	18	20	17	18
	NW	13	12	12	18	19	23	21	20	15	22	14
# SURVEYED		205	212	216	203	221	241	231	244	248	180	159

****

EXTRA-MARITAL SEXUAL RELATIONS

TABLE I: EXTRA-MARITAL SEXUAL RELATIONS -- BY TOTAL POPULATION

Question: What is your opinion about a married person having sexual relations with someone other than the marriage partner--is it always wrong, almost always wrong, wrong only sometimes, or not wrong at all? NOTE: Question not asked in 1972, 1975, 1978, 1983, 1986.

Responses: AW = Always wrong AA = Almost always wrong
WS = Wrong only sometimes NW = Not wrong at all

	YEAR										
RESPONSE	'73	'74	'76	'77	'80	'82	'84	'85	'87	'88	'89
AW	70%	74%	69%	73%	70%	73%	71%	75%	74%	79%	78%
AA	15	12	16	14	16	13	18	14	16	13	13
WS	12	12	11	10	10	10	9	9	8	6	7
NW	4	2	4	3	4	3	2	3	2	2	2
# SURVEYED	1491	1460	1475	1510	1444	1478	1449	1512	1444	963	1019

TABLE II: EXTRA-MARITAL SEXUAL RELATIONS -- BY SEX

Question: What is your opinion about a married person having sexual relations with someone other than the marriage partner--is it always wrong, almost always wrong, wrong only sometimes, or not wrong at all? NOTE: Question not asked in 1972, 1975, 1978, 1983, 1986.

Responses: AW = Always wrong AA = Almost always wrong
WS = Wrong only sometimes NW = Not wrong at all

		YEAR										
SEX	RESP	'73	'74	'76	'77	'80	'82	'84	'85	'87	'88	'89
M	AW	64%	69%	64%	69%	67%	70%	65%	72%	70%	74%	75%
	AA	16	14	18	15	17	15	19	14	18	15	16
	WS	14	15	13	13	12	12	13	10	9	7	7
	NW	6	3	5	4	5	3	4	4	3	4	2
# SURVEYED		690	680	662	683	633	623	588	676	628	394	440
SEX	RESP	'73	'74	'76	'77	'80	'82	'84	'85	'87	'88	'89
F	AW	74%	78%	72%	77%	73%	76%	75%	77%	77%	83%	80%
	AA	14	10	14	13	15	13	18	14	14	12	11
	WS	9	9	10	8	9	9	6	7	7	5	8
	NW	2	2	4	2	3	3	1	2	2	1	1
# SURVEYED		801	780	813	827	811	855	861	836	816	569	579

TABLE III: EXTRA-MARITAL SEXUAL RELATIONS -- BY RACE

Question: What is your opinion about a married person having sexual relations with someone other than the marriage partner--is it always wrong, almost always wrong, wrong only sometimes, or not wrong at all? NOTE: Question not asked in 1972, 1975, 1978, 1983, 1986.

Responses: AW = Always wrong AA = Almost always wrong
WS = Wrong only sometimes NW = Not wrong at all

		YEAR										
RACE	RESP	'73	'74	'76	'77	'80	'82	'84	'85	'87	'88	'89
WHITE	AW	70%	75%	70%	74%	71%	74%	70%	75%	74%	80%	78%
	AA	15	12	16	14	16	14	19	14	16	13	13
	WS	11	11	11	9	9	9	8	8	8	5	7
	NW	3	2	4	3	4	2	2	2	2	2	1
# SURVEYED		1297	1287	1343	1323	1298	1297	1232	1321	1208	791	880
RACE	RESP	'73	'74	'76	'77	'80	'82	'84	'85	'87	'88	'89
BLACK	AW	66%	63%	59%	65%	66%	71%	71%	71%	71%	75%	80%
	AA	11	12	15	10	15	9	10	12	16	15	10
	WS	13	19	20	18	15	15	16	11	9	8	6
	NW	10	6	7	7	3	5	4	5	4	2	4
# SURVEYED		181	166	123	172	136	155	166	148	184	129	100
RACE	RESP	'73	'74	'76	'77	'80	'82	'84	'85	'87	'88	'89
OTHER	AW	62%	100%	78%	67%	70%	54%	75%	70%	85%	74%	79%
	AA	23	0	11	13	20	4	20	12	10	14	8
	WS	15	0	11	13	10	35	4	14	6	9	10
	NW	0	0	0	7	0	8	2	5	0	2	3
# SURVEYED		13	7	9	15	10	26	51	43	52	43	39

TABLE IV: EXTRA-MARITAL SEXUAL RELATIONS -- BY AGE

Question: What is your opinion about a married person having sexual relations with someone other than the marriage partner--is it always wrong, almost always wrong, wrong only sometimes, or not wrong at all? NOTE: Question not asked in 1972, 1975, 1978, 1983, 1986.

Responses: AW = Always wrong AA = Almost always wrong
WS = Wrong only sometimes NW = Not wrong at all

		YEAR										
AGE	RESP	'73	'74	'76	'77	'80	'82	'84	'85	'87	'88	'89
18-23	AW	56%	61%	55%	64%	67%	72%	69%	66%	71%	78%	81%
	AA	16	20	21	17	16	16	18	20	18	12	12
	WS	23	16	17	16	14	10	12	11	9	7	5
	NW	5	4	7	3	3	2	1	3	2	3	1
# SURVEYED		171	166	161	162	153	146	157	133	126	94	97

TABLE IV: EXTRA-MARITAL SEXUAL RELATIONS -- BY AGE (Continued)

Question: What is your opinion about a married person having sexual relations with someone other than the marriage partner--is it always wrong, almost always wrong, wrong only sometimes, or not wrong at all? NOTE: Question not asked in 1972, 1975, 1978, 1983, 1986.

Responses: AW = Always wrong AA = Almost always wrong
WS = Wrong only sometimes NW = Not wrong at all

AGE	RESP	'73	'74	'76	'77	'80	'82	'84	'85	'87	'88	'89
24-29	AW	54%	60%	55%	65%	60%	62%	65%	71%	66%	82%	66%
	AA	19	16	20	21	20	22	24	17	22	13	19
	WS	19	18	18	10	14	13	8	10	11	4	14
	NW	9	5	7	5	6	3	3	2	2	2	1
# SURVEYED		209	207	225	203	199	241	232	213	190	131	114
AGE	RESP	'73	'74	'76	'77	'80	'82	'84	'85	'87	'88	'89
30-35	AW	70%	70%	65%	63%	65%	68%	64%	69%	66%	67%	76%
	AA	19	10	20	15	22	17	21	18	23	24	17
	WS	8	16	12	16	10	11	13	10	8	8	6
	NW	3	5	3	5	2	3	2	3	3	2	1
# SURVEYED		166	172	183	185	211	201	198	212	220	131	133
AGE	RESP	'73	'74	'76	'77	'80	'82	'84	'85	'87	'88	'89
36-41	AW	67%	70%	58%	70%	61%	63%	60%	66%	65%	70%	69%
	AA	17	11	21	13	21	13	21	15	22	15	16
	WS	9	17	11	12	14	21	13	15	10	11	12
	NW	7	1	9	5	4	2	7	4	3	4	3
# SURVEYED		175	149	151	166	150	142	184	180	179	130	134
AGE	RESP	'73	'74	'76	'77	'80	'82	'84	'85	'87	'88	'89
42-47	AW	67%	77%	77%	71%	64%	69%	70%	64%	73%	79%	71%
	AA	14	11	11	15	23	17	19	18	14	11	16
	WS	16	10	10	12	6	10	6	11	10	7	10
	NW	3	2	2	1	7	3	4	7	3	3	3
# SURVEYED		146	150	111	145	114	117	124	123	154	101	105
AGE	RESP	'73	'74	'76	'77	'80	'82	'84	'85	'87	'88	'89
48-53	AW	77%	77%	73%	70%	73%	76%	78%	75%	78%	86%	84%
	AA	13	15	15	16	12	9	14	14	15	11	10
	WS	9	7	11	11	11	13	7	9	6	3	4
	NW	1	1	2	3	3	2	1	2	2	0	2
# SURVEYED		149	142	131	147	122	110	100	129	124	63	94

TABLE IV: EXTRA-MARITAL SEXUAL RELATIONS -- BY AGE (Continued)

Question: What is your opinion about a married person having sexual relations with someone other than the marriage partner--is it always wrong, almost always wrong, wrong only sometimes, or not wrong at all? NOTE: Question not asked in 1972, 1975, 1978, 1983, 1986.

Responses: AW = Always wrong; AA = Almost always wrong; WS = Wrong only sometimes; NW = Not wrong at all

		YEAR										
AGE	RESP	'73	'74	'76	'77	'80	'82	'84	'85	'87	'88	'89
54-59	AW	80%	84%	73%	81%	79%	78%	77%	89%	78%	87%	81%
	AA	11	10	13	11	11	11	15	6	15	12	6
	WS	5	6	9	5	6	7	7	3	6	2	10
	NW	5	0	5	3	4	3	0	2	1	0	3
# SURVEYED		154	139	129	167	135	143	111	131	98	52	63
AGE	RESP	'73	'74	'76	'77	'80	'82	'84	'85	'87	'88	'89
60-65	AW	74%	78%	80%	82%	80%	80%	78%	79%	90%	88%	84%
	AA	16	9	8	11	9	10	15	12	3	7	12
	WS	9	11	11	6	7	9	7	8	6	4	3
	NW	2	1	1	1	4	2	0	2	1	1	1
# SURVEYED		121	106	133	117	118	113	108	129	99	83	77
AGE	RESP	'73	'74	'76	'77	'80	'82	'84	'85	'87	'88	'89
66+	AW	85%	91%	85%	91%	85%	89%	82%	89%	84%	86%	89%
	AA	9	4	9	4	8	5	13	5	8	9	7
	WS	5	4	4	4	6	3	5	4	6	3	4
	NW	2	1	2	1	1	3	1	2	2	2	1
# SURVEYED		196	223	246	211	234	254	229	255	250	175	199

****

EASIER DIVORCES

TABLE I: EASIER DIVORCES -- BY TOTAL POPULATION

Question: Should divorce in this country be easier or more difficult to obtain than it is now? NOTE: Question not asked in 1972, 1973, 1980, 1984, 1987.

Responses: ES = Easier; MD = More difficult; SM = Stay as is (volunteer)

	YEAR										
RESPONSE	'74	'75	'76	'77	'78	'82	'83	'85	'86	'88	'89
ES	34%	30%	29%	31%	28%	24%	25%	24%	28%	26%	27%
MD	44	49	52	51	43	54	55	55	54	51	54
SM	22	21	19	18	28	22	20	20	18	23	19
# SURVEYED	1404	1418	1416	1451	1446	1419	1524	1465	1408	929	943

TABLE II: EASIER DIVORCES -- BY SEX

Question: Should divorce in this country be easier or more difficult to obtain than it is now? NOTE: Question not asked in 1972, 1973, 1980, 1984, 1987.

Responses: ES = Easier; MD = More difficult; SM = Stay as is (volunteer)

		YEAR										
SEX	RESP	'74	'75	'76	'77	'78	'82	'83	'85	'86	'88	'89
M	ES	38%	34%	31%	34%	32%	28%	27%	26%	30%	28%	28%
	MD	43	44	52	50	41	51	53	52	50	45	50
	SM	19	21	17	16	26	22	20	22	20	27	22
# SURVEYED		648	636	636	656	611	601	655	662	592	409	402
SEX	RESP	'74	'75	'76	'77	'78	'82	'83	'85	'86	'88	'89
F	ES	30%	26%	27%	28%	25%	21%	23%	23%	26%	24%	26%
	MD	46	52	53	52	45	56	56	58	56	56	57
	SM	24	21	20	20	30	23	20	19	17	20	17
# SURVEYED		756	782	780	795	835	818	869	803	816	520	541

TABLE III: EASIER DIVORCES -- BY RACE

Question: Should divorce in this country be easier or more difficult to obtain than it is now? NOTE: Question not asked in 1972, 1973, 1980, 1984, 1987.

Responses: ES = Easier; MD = More difficult; SM = Stay as is (volunteer)

		YEAR										
RACE	RESP	'74	'75	'76	'77	'78	'82	'83	'85	'86	'88	'89
WHITE	ES	30%	27%	27%	27%	24%	21%	22%	21%	24%	23%	23%
	MD	47	51	54	54	46	57	57	57	56	53	57
	SM	23	22	19	19	30	23	21	22	19	24	20
# SURVEYED		1232	1260	1290	1273	1288	1247	1355	1285	1202	781	808
RACE	RESP	'74	'75	'76	'77	'78	'82	'83	'85	'86	'88	'89
BLACK	ES	59%	54%	46%	58%	60%	48%	52%	55%	49%	50%	51%
	MD	26	28	41	26	26	33	38	37	38	32	35
	SM	15	18	13	16	14	20	10	8	13	17	14
# SURVEYED		165	155	117	165	145	147	157	139	172	115	99
RACE	RESP	'74	'75	'76	'77	'78	'82	'83	'85	'86	'88	'89
OTHER	ES	57%	0%	33%	38%	31%	40%	42%	32%	35%	21%	39%
	MD	29	100	33	54	31	44	33	56	50	64	39
	SM	14	0	33	8	38	16	25	12	15	15	22
# SURVEYED		7	3	9	13	13	25	12	41	34	33	36

TABLE IV: EASIER DIVORCES -- BY AGE

Question: Should divorce in this country be easier or more difficult to obtain than it is now? NOTE: Question not asked in 1972, 1973, 1980, 1984, 1987.

Responses: ES = Easier; MD = More difficult; SM = Stay as is (volunteer)

		YEAR										
AGE	RESP	'74	'75	'76	'77	'78	'82	'83	'85	'86	'88	'89
18-23	ES	51%	36%	42%	49%	42%	30%	37%	31%	38%	38%	35%
	MD	35	44	40	34	29	48	50	52	46	40	49
	SM	14	20	18	17	30	22	13	17	17	22	16
# SURVEYED		159	168	154	159	154	141	124	127	101	90	80
AGE	RESP	'74	'75	'76	'77	'78	'82	'83	'85	'86	'88	'89
24-29	ES	49%	50%	46%	40%	38%	26%	32%	30%	28%	28%	32%
	MD	34	32	38	42	35	48	47	52	52	48	50
	SM	17	18	17	18	27	26	21	18	20	24	18
# SURVEYED		206	222	218	193	237	240	277	204	209	142	137

TABLE IV: EASIER DIVORCES -- BY AGE (Continued)

Question: Should divorce in this country be easier or more difficult to obtain than it is now? NOTE: Question not asked in 1972, 1973, 1980, 1984, 1987.

Responses: ES = Easier; MD = More difficult; SM = Stay as is (volunteer)

		YEAR										
AGE	RESP	'74	'75	'76	'77	'78	'82	'83	'85	'86	'88	'89
30-35	ES	39%	31%	38%	42%	38%	27%	27%	34%	38%	25%	30%
	MD	40	43	43	41	36	45	51	47	43	48	47
	SM	21	27	19	17	26	28	22	19	19	27	23
# SURVEYED		165	166	178	182	222	195	227	203	216	124	133
AGE	RESP	'74	'75	'76	'77	'78	'82	'83	'85	'86	'88	'89
36-41	ES	33%	34%	35%	34%	28%	30%	26%	26%	39%	27%	27%
	MD	39	45	51	50	44	49	47	47	45	45	52
	SM	27	21	14	16	28	21	27	27	17	28	21
# SURVEYED		142	141	147	161	149	138	168	180	181	122	119
AGE	RESP	'74	'75	'76	'77	'78	'82	'83	'85	'86	'88	'89
42-47	ES	24%	31%	25%	27%	21%	19%	28%	19%	22%	29%	32%
	MD	46	43	53	57	45	49	54	56	57	44	51
	SM	30	26	22	16	34	32	18	25	21	27	17
# SURVEYED		143	140	108	135	114	114	138	122	135	104	103
AGE	RESP	'74	'75	'76	'77	'78	'82	'83	'85	'86	'88	'89
48-53	ES	24%	20%	23%	18%	20%	23%	18%	20%	30%	34%	32%
	MD	49	56	60	53	49	58	55	59	46	53	51
	SM	28	24	17	30	31	20	26	21	24	12	18
# SURVEYED		136	135	126	148	127	106	114	128	103	58	79
AGE	RESP	'74	'75	'76	'77	'78	'82	'83	'85	'86	'88	'89
54-59	ES	25%	24%	16%	20%	17%	21%	23%	23%	23%	25%	31%
	MD	59	61	65	60	55	61	57	57	60	48	49
	SM	16	15	19	20	28	18	20	20	18	27	20
# SURVEYED		135	122	122	161	126	135	129	126	97	48	65
AGE	RESP	'74	'75	'76	'77	'78	'82	'83	'85	'86	'88	'89
60-65	ES	29%	15%	18%	23%	20%	23%	14%	17%	17%	19%	17%
	MD	49	58	60	61	52	63	67	72	68	59	71
	SM	22	27	22	16	29	14	20	11	15	23	12
# SURVEYED		100	106	129	112	97	108	123	123	111	70	66
AGE	RESP	'74	'75	'76	'77	'78	'82	'83	'85	'86	'88	'89
66+	ES	23%	17%	12%	18%	16%	15%	14%	15%	16%	16%	11%
	MD	55	65	67	65	56	67	70	64	68	66	66
	SM	23	17	21	17	28	18	16	21	16	18	22
# SURVEYED		212	214	229	193	213	234	217	246	249	170	158

****

FEELINGS ABOUT PORNOGRAPHY LAWS

TABLE I: FEELINGS ABOUT PORNOGRAPHY LAWS -- BY TOTAL POPULATION

Question: Which of the following statements comes closest to your feelings about pornography laws: there should be laws against the distribution of pornography whatever the age; there should be laws against the distribution of pornography to persons under 18; there should be no laws forbidding the distribution of pornography. NOTE: Question not asked in 1972, 1974, 1977, 1982, 1985.

Responses:
1 = There should be laws against the distribution of pornography whatever the age
2 = There should be laws against the distribution of pornography to persons under 18
3 = There should be no laws forbidding the distribution of pornography

	YEAR										
RESPONSE	'73	'75	'76	'78	'80	'83	'84	'86	'87	'88	'89
1	43%	41%	41%	44%	41%	42%	41%	43%	40%	44%	41%
2	48	48	51	49	53	54	55	53	56	51	54
3	9	11	8	7	6	5	4	4	4	5	5
# SURVEYED	1469	1471	1465	1515	1436	1574	1446	1455	1444	975	1018

TABLE II: FEELINGS ABOUT PORNOGRAPHY LAWS -- BY SEX

Question: Which of the following statements comes closest to your feelings about pornography laws: there should be laws against the distribution of pornography whatever the age; there should be laws against the distribution of pornography to persons under 18; there should be no laws forbidding the distribution of pornography. NOTE: Question not asked in 1972, 1974, 1977, 1982, 1985.

Responses:
1 = There should be laws against the distribution of pornography whatever the age
2 = There should be laws against the distribution of pornography to persons under 18
3 = There should be no laws forbidding the distribution of pornography

		YEAR										
SEX	RESP	'73	'75	'76	'78	'80	'83	'84	'86	'87	'88	'89
M	1	36%	34%	32%	34%	32%	31%	30%	31%	26%	34%	30%
	2	54	53	58	56	61	64	63	65	69	60	64
	3	10	13	11	10	8	5	7	4	5	6	7
# SURVEYED		683	658	657	637	631	681	593	612	629	429	437
SEX	RESP	'73	'75	'76	'78	'80	'83	'84	'86	'87	'88	'89
F	1	48%	46%	48%	51%	49%	50%	49%	52%	51%	52%	49%
	2	43	44	45	44	46	46	49	45	46	44	47
	3	9	9	6	5	5	4	3	4	3	4	3
# SURVEYED		786	813	808	878	805	893	853	843	815	546	581

TABLE III: FEELINGS ABOUT PORNOGRAPHY LAWS -- BY RACE

Question: Which of the following statements comes closest to your feelings about pornography laws: there should be laws against the distribution of pornography whatever the age; there should be laws against the distribution of pornography to persons under 18; there should be no laws forbidding the distribution of pornography. NOTE: Question not asked in 1972, 1974, 1977, 1982, 1985.

Responses:
1 = There should be laws against the distribution of pornography whatever the age
2 = There should be laws against the distribution of pornography to persons under 18
3 = There should be no laws forbidding the distribution of pornography

		YEAR										
RACE	RESP	'73	'75	'76	'78	'80	'83	'84	'86	'87	'88	'89
WHITE	1	44%	43%	42%	46%	42%	43%	42%	44%	41%	46%	41%
	2	47	47	50	47	53	53	54	53	54	50	54
	3	9	10	7	7	6	4	4	3	4	5	4
# SURVEYED		1284	1308	1333	1343	1292	1397	1234	1241	1210	817	871
RACE	RESP	'73	'75	'76	'78	'80	'83	'84	'86	'87	'88	'89
BLACK	1	28%	25%	27%	29%	36%	33%	39%	38%	31%	35%	36%
	2	56	58	55	64	53	62	55	57	65	58	56
	3	16	17	18	7	11	6	6	6	4	7	8
# SURVEYED		174	159	123	156	134	160	160	178	184	116	107
RACE	RESP	'73	'75	'76	'78	'80	'83	'84	'86	'87	'88	'89
OTHER	1	55%	50%	11%	19%	50%	29%	35%	47%	44%	36%	48%
	2	36	50	89	50	50	71	60	44	54	62	48
	3	9	0	0	31	0	0	6	8	2	2	5
# SURVEYED		11	4	9	16	10	17	52	36	50	42	40

TABLE IV: FEELINGS ABOUT PORNOGRAPHY LAWS -- BY AGE

Question: Which of the following statements comes closest to your feelings about pornography laws: there should be laws against the distribution of pornography whatever the age; there should be laws against the distribution of pornography to persons under 18; there should be no laws forbidding the distribution of pornography. NOTE: Question not asked in 1972, 1974, 1977, 1982, 1985.

Responses: 1 = There should be laws against the distribution of pornography whatever the age
2 = There should be laws against the distribution of pornography to persons under 18
3 = There should be no laws forbidding the distribution of pornography

		YEAR										
AGE	RESP	'73	'75	'76	'78	'80	'83	'84	'86	'87	'88	'89
18-23	1	16%	22%	16%	29%	20%	26%	19%	23%	24%	27%	34%
	2	68	68	68	60	73	72	74	69	72	67	62
	3	16	10	16	11	7	2	7	7	4	6	3
# SURVEYED		170	172	161	163	153	127	159	108	126	93	93
AGE	RESP	'73	'75	'76	'78	'80	'83	'84	'86	'87	'88	'89
24-29	1	21%	22%	18%	20%	22%	24%	24%	27%	26%	28%	25%
	2	65	66	72	76	70	72	72	73	70	69	71
	3	14	13	10	4	7	4	4	0	4	3	4
# SURVEYED		206	229	222	240	202	285	232	216	193	144	139
AGE	RESP	'73	'75	'76	'78	'80	'83	'84	'86	'87	'88	'89
30-35	1	31%	27%	32%	31%	22%	34%	34%	32%	28%	35%	22%
	2	56	63	63	60	70	62	63	64	67	59	76
	3	13	10	5	9	8	4	3	3	5	6	3
# SURVEYED		164	169	185	229	213	235	197	219	220	127	143
AGE	RESP	'73	'75	'76	'78	'80	'83	'84	'86	'87	'88	'89
36-41	1	42%	40%	34%	50%	34%	30%	27%	34%	29%	36%	32%
	2	53	51	56	47	59	66	68	61	67	59	66
	3	5	9	10	3	7	4	5	5	4	5	2
# SURVEYED		173	152	157	159	150	172	186	188	183	125	133
AGE	RESP	'73	'75	'76	'78	'80	'83	'84	'86	'87	'88	'89
42-47	1	48%	42%	43%	45%	43%	38%	36%	38%	39%	44%	34%
	2	45	44	50	50	52	57	61	57	59	54	59
	3	6	14	6	4	5	5	2	5	3	2	7
# SURVEYED		143	140	111	119	116	143	124	140	155	104	106
AGE	RESP	'73	'75	'76	'78	'80	'83	'84	'86	'87	'88	'89
48-53	1	48%	46%	52%	50%	57%	51%	55%	47%	50%	49%	58%
	2	48	41	45	44	40	46	42	51	46	45	35
	3	3	12	3	6	3	3	3	2	4	5	7
# SURVEYED		147	140	125	133	120	114	99	108	122	55	95

TABLE IV: FEELINGS ABOUT PORNOGRAPHY LAWS -- BY AGE (Continued)

Question: Which of the following statements comes closest to your feelings about pornography laws: there should be laws against the distribution of pornography whatever the age; there should be laws against the distribution of pornography to persons under 18; there should be no laws forbidding the distribution of pornography. NOTE: Question not asked in 1972, 1974, 1977, 1982, 1985.

Responses: 1 = There should be laws against the distribution of pornography whatever the age
2 = There should be laws against the distribution of pornography to persons under 18
3 = There should be no laws forbidding the distribution of pornography

		YEAR										
AGE	RESP	'73	'75	'76	'78	'80	'83	'84	'86	'87	'88	'89
54-59	1	57%	52%	47%	54%	53%	56%	61%	53%	48%	58%	63%
	2	34	37	46	38	43	36	31	45	49	39	29
	3	9	11	7	8	4	8	8	2	3	3	8
# SURVEYED		152	124	127	135	131	131	113	96	98	64	62
AGE	RESP	'73	'75	'76	'78	'80	'83	'84	'86	'87	'88	'89
60-65	1	64%	62%	57%	62%	58%	62%	60%	55%	65%	59%	55%
	2	30	28	29	27	35	36	35	39	32	32	38
	3	6	11	14	12	7	2	6	5	3	9	7
# SURVEYED		117	112	133	104	117	130	109	112	98	78	73
AGE	RESP	'73	'75	'76	'78	'80	'83	'84	'86	'87	'88	'89
66+	1	66%	65%	70%	70%	70%	66%	69%	71%	62%	65%	62%
	2	25	26	26	21	25	26	29	24	33	30	33
	3	9	9	4	9	5	8	2	5	5	4	5
# SURVEYED		193	228	238	226	228	232	223	261	245	181	172

****

PORNOGRAPHY PROVIDES SEX EDUCATION

TABLE I: PORNOGRAPHY PROVIDES SEX EDUCATION -- BY TOTAL POPULATION

Question: Do sexually graphic materials provide information about sex? NOTE: Question not asked in 1972, 1974, 1977, 1982, 1985.

Responses: YES; NO

	YEAR										
RESPONSE	'73	'75	'76	'78	'80	'83	'84	'86	'87	'88	'89
YES	66%	68%	61%	65%	63%	63%	61%	60%	66%	62%	60%
NO	34	32	39	35	37	37	39	40	34	38	40
# SURVEYED	1416	1359	1388	1437	1358	1512	1389	1391	1370	930	978

TABLE II: PORNOGRAPHY PROVIDES SEX EDUCATION -- BY SEX

Question: Do sexually graphic materials provide information about sex? NOTE: Question not asked in 1972, 1974, 1977, 1982, 1985.

Responses: YES; NO

		YEAR										
SEX	RESP	'73	'75	'76	'78	'80	'83	'84	'86	'87	'88	'89
M	YES	66%	68%	63%	67%	63%	66%	62%	62%	67%	64%	62%
	NO	34	32	37	33	37	34	38	38	33	36	38
# SURVEYED		663	627	640	612	608	665	581	596	610	418	426
SEX	RESP	'73	'75	'76	'78	'80	'83	'84	'86	'87	'88	'89
F	YES	65%	68%	59%	64%	63%	61%	60%	59%	65%	61%	58%
	NO	35	32	41	36	37	39	40	41	35	39	42
# SURVEYED		753	732	748	825	750	847	808	795	760	512	552

TABLE III: PORNOGRAPHY PROVIDES SEX EDUCATION -- BY RACE

Question: Do sexually graphic materials provide information about sex? NOTE: Question not asked in 1972, 1974, 1977, 1982, 1985.

Responses: YES; NO

		YEAR										
RACE	RESP	'73	'75	'76	'78	'80	'83	'84	'86	'87	'88	'89
WHITE	YES	64%	67%	60%	64%	62%	62%	60%	59%	65%	61%	58%
	NO	36	33	40	36	38	38	40	41	35	39	42
# SURVEYED		1231	1211	1265	1275	1217	1341	1187	1186	1153	783	836
RACE	RESP	'73	'75	'76	'78	'80	'83	'84	'86	'87	'88	'89
BLACK	YES	77%	81%	72%	72%	70%	69%	69%	67%	74%	75%	73%
	NO	23	19	28	28	30	31	31	33	26	25	27
# SURVEYED		176	145	116	147	132	156	154	172	168	108	106
RACE	RESP	'73	'75	'76	'78	'80	'83	'84	'86	'87	'88	'89
OTHER	YES	78%	67%	57%	80%	67%	73%	58%	76%	57%	54%	72%
	NO	22	33	43	20	33	27	42	24	43	46	28
# SURVEYED		9	3	7	15	9	15	48	33	49	39	36

TABLE IV: PORNOGRAPHY PROVIDES SEX EDUCATION -- BY AGE

Question: Do sexually graphic materials provide information about sex? NOTE: Question not asked in 1972, 1974, 1977, 1982, 1985.

Responses: YES; NO

		YEAR										
AGE	RESP	'73	'75	'76	'78	'80	'83	'84	'86	'87	'88	'89
18-23	YES	73%	72%	75%	75%	75%	69%	66%	67%	73%	73%	75%
	NO	27	28	25	25	25	31	34	33	27	27	25
# SURVEYED		169	163	159	158	151	124	155	105	121	91	92
AGE	RESP	'73	'75	'76	'78	'80	'83	'84	'86	'87	'88	'89
24-29	YES	67%	75%	67%	70%	67%	65%	68%	66%	66%	71%	66%
	NO	33	25	33	30	33	35	32	34	34	29	34
# SURVEYED		206	226	218	233	196	280	222	213	191	140	134
AGE	RESP	'73	'75	'76	'78	'80	'83	'84	'86	'87	'88	'89
30-35	YES	66%	66%	63%	66%	63%	69%	61%	56%	69%	59%	53%
	NO	34	34	37	34	37	31	39	44	31	41	47
# SURVEYED		160	164	181	226	206	232	189	216	216	123	142

TABLE IV: PORNOGRAPHY PROVIDES SEX EDUCATION -- BY AGE

Question: Do sexually graphic materials provide information about sex? NOTE: Question not asked in 1972, 1974, 1977, 1982, 1985.

Responses: YES; NO

		YEAR										
AGE	RESP	'73	'75	'76	'78	'80	'83	'84	'86	'87	'88	'89
36-41	YES	62%	73%	60%	67%	61%	61%	60%	58%	61%	61%	61%
	NO	38	27	40	33	39	39	40	42	39	39	39
# SURVEYED		167	146	149	156	143	166	183	185	179	124	131
AGE	RESP	'73	'75	'76	'78	'80	'83	'84	'86	'87	'88	'89
42-47	YES	64%	65%	45%	56%	59%	61%	49%	55%	68%	57%	58%
	NO	36	35	55	44	41	39	51	45	32	43	42
# SURVEYED		142	130	108	114	109	142	120	133	144	103	103
AGE	RESP	'73	'75	'76	'78	'80	'83	'84	'86	'87	'88	'89
48-53	YES	68%	60%	63%	68%	57%	61%	61%	62%	64%	51%	61%
	NO	32	40	37	32	43	39	39	38	36	49	39
# SURVEYED		144	131	126	124	117	111	97	101	118	53	92
AGE	RESP	'73	'75	'76	'78	'80	'83	'84	'86	'87	'88	'89
54-59	YES	70%	65%	64%	64%	61%	60%	64%	55%	58%	55%	46%
	NO	30	35	36	36	39	40	36	45	42	45	54
# SURVEYED		139	111	117	125	123	126	110	92	90	62	57
AGE	RESP	'73	'75	'76	'78	'80	'83	'84	'86	'87	'88	'89
60-65	YES	57%	64%	46%	62%	63%	58%	53%	64%	66%	61%	59%
	NO	43	36	54	38	37	42	47	36	34	39	41
# SURVEYED		111	98	122	93	108	124	104	105	93	66	68
AGE	RESP	'73	'75	'76	'78	'80	'83	'84	'86	'87	'88	'89
66+	YES	61%	65%	55%	56%	59%	59%	58%	58%	64%	63%	58%
	NO	39	35	45	44	41	41	42	42	36	37	42
# SURVEYED		175	187	203	201	197	202	207	235	215	164	158

****

PORNOGRAPHY PROVIDES OUTLET

TABLE I: PORNOGRAPHY PROVIDES OUTLET -- BY TOTAL POPULATION

Question: Do sexually graphic materials provide an outlet for bottled-up impulses? NOTE: Question not asked in 1972, 1974, 1977, 1982, 1985.

Responses: YES; NO

	YEAR										
RESPONSE	'73	'75	'76	'78	'80	'83	'84	'86	'87	'88	'89
YES	61%	67%	66%	67%	69%	65%	69%	66%	70%	65%	69%
NO	39	33	34	33	31	35	31	34	30	35	31
# SURVEYED	1348	1249	1256	1344	1258	1412	1286	1317	1269	860	888

TABLE II: PORNOGRAPHY PROVIDES OUTLET -- BY SEX

Question: Do sexually graphic materials provide an outlet for bottled-up impulses? NOTE: Question not asked in 1972, 1974, 1977, 1982, 1985.

Responses: YES; NO

		YEAR										
SEX	RESP	'73	'75	'76	'78	'80	'83	'84	'86	'87	'88	'89
M	YES	60%	65%	65%	66%	70%	63%	68%	67%	68%	64%	67%
	NO	40	35	35	34	30	37	32	33	32	36	34
# SURVEYED		631	577	582	596	580	634	540	567	571	387	400
SEX	RESP	'73	'75	'76	'78	'80	'83	'84	'86	'87	'88	'89
F	YES	61%	69%	66%	68%	68%	66%	70%	65%	71%	65%	72%
	NO	39	31	34	32	32	34	30	35	29	35	28
# SURVEYED		717	672	674	748	678	778	746	750	698	473	488

TABLE III: PORNOGRAPHY PROVIDES OUTLET -- BY RACE

Question: Do sexually graphic materials provide an outlet for bottled-up impulses? NOTE: Question not asked in 1972, 1974, 1977, 1982, 1985.

Responses: YES; NO

		YEAR										
RACE	RESP	'73	'75	'76	'78	'80	'83	'84	'86	'87	'88	'89
WHITE	YES	61%	67%	67%	67%	68%	64%	70%	66%	69%	63%	68%
	NO	39	33	33	33	32	36	30	34	31	37	32
# SURVEYED		1174	1118	1143	1201	1127	1253	1101	1131	1068	720	766
RACE	RESP	'73	'75	'76	'78	'80	'83	'84	'86	'87	'88	'89
BLACK	YES	61%	63%	56%	59%	75%	71%	65%	65%	75%	76%	76%
	NO	39	37	44	41	25	29	35	35	25	24	24
# SURVEYED		164	128	106	130	122	144	141	155	158	103	93
RACE	RESP	'73	'75	'76	'78	'80	'83	'84	'86	'87	'88	'89
OTHER	YES	80%	67%	57%	92%	78%	87%	68%	77%	72%	65%	90%
	NO	20	33	43	8	22	13	32	23	28	35	10
# SURVEYED		10	3	7	13	9	15	44	31	43	37	29

TABLE IV: PORNOGRAPHY PROVIDES OUTLET -- BY AGE

Question: Do sexually graphic materials provide an outlet for bottled-up impulses? NOTE: Question not asked in 1972, 1974, 1977, 1982, 1985.

Responses: YES; NO

		YEAR										
AGE	RESP	'73	'75	'76	'78	'80	'83	'84	'86	'87	'88	'89
18-23	YES	65%	64%	65%	68%	72%	64%	64%	64%	68%	64%	73%
	NO	35	36	35	32	28	36	36	36	32	36	27
# SURVEYED		162	159	143	148	142	118	145	101	114	86	85
AGE	RESP	'73	'75	'76	'78	'80	'83	'84	'86	'87	'88	'89
24-29	YES	59%	71%	71%	66%	73%	66%	73%	66%	72%	78%	75%
	NO	41	29	29	34	27	34	27	34	28	22	25
# SURVEYED		195	203	205	220	186	264	208	203	172	125	118

TABLE IV: PORNOGRAPHY PROVIDES OUTLET -- BY AGE

Question: Do sexually graphic materials provide an outlet for bottled-up impulses? NOTE: Question not asked in 1972, 1974, 1977, 1982, 1985.

Responses: YES; NO

		YEAR										
AGE	RESP	'73	'75	'76	'78	'80	'83	'84	'86	'87	'88	'89
30-35	YES	57%	60%	68%	62%	67%	62%	69%	65%	66%	60%	64%
	NO	43	40	32	38	33	38	31	35	34	40	36
# SURVEYED		152	151	161	205	203	221	177	211	202	120	127
AGE	RESP	'73	'75	'76	'78	'80	'83	'84	'86	'87	'88	'89
36-41	YES	60%	69%	64%	66%	65%	58%	69%	64%	68%	65%	71%
	NO	40	31	36	34	35	42	31	36	32	35	29
# SURVEYED		163	136	142	142	134	161	169	174	164	114	120
AGE	RESP	'73	'75	'76	'78	'80	'83	'84	'86	'87	'88	'89
42-47	YES	62%	61%	53%	77%	61%	64%	65%	67%	74%	63%	73%
	NO	38	39	47	23	39	36	35	33	26	37	27
# SURVEYED		133	119	99	112	100	130	110	129	136	92	95
AGE	RESP	'73	'75	'76	'78	'80	'83	'84	'86	'87	'88	'89
48-53	YES	58%	65%	66%	61%	72%	63%	72%	65%	75%	49%	63%
	NO	42	35	34	39	28	37	28	35	25	51	37
# SURVEYED		140	122	111	116	98	100	88	95	115	49	83
AGE	RESP	'73	'75	'76	'78	'80	'83	'84	'86	'87	'88	'89
54-59	YES	64%	64%	71%	67%	67%	71%	65%	67%	74%	58%	58%
	NO	36	36	29	33	33	29	35	33	26	42	42
# SURVEYED		133	100	103	121	115	120	101	84	84	55	50
AGE	RESP	'73	'75	'76	'78	'80	'83	'84	'86	'87	'88	'89
60-65	YES	63%	70%	63%	64%	70%	68%	63%	58%	66%	67%	78%
	NO	37	30	37	36	30	32	37	42	34	33	22
# SURVEYED		100	90	108	89	104	113	93	100	85	64	63
AGE	RESP	'73	'75	'76	'78	'80	'83	'84	'86	'87	'88	'89
66+	YES	62%	74%	68%	71%	69%	67%	74%	74%	65%	66%	70%
	NO	38	26	32	29	31	33	26	26	35	34	30
# SURVEYED		167	167	181	185	170	181	193	214	194	152	145

****

PORNOGRAPHY BREAKS DOWN MORALS

TABLE I: PORNOGRAPHY BREAKS DOWN MORALS -- BY TOTAL POPULATION

Question: Do sexually graphic materials lead to a breakdown in morals? NOTE: Question not asked in 1972, 1974, 1977, 1982, 1985.

Responses: YES; NO

	YEAR										
RESPONSE	'73	'75	'76	'78	'80	'83	'84	'86	'87	'88	'89
YES	56%	57%	59%	60%	65%	62%	65%	66%	66%	65%	67%
NO	44	43	41	40	35	38	35	34	34	35	33
# SURVEYED	1416	1353	1379	1451	1358	1506	1387	1385	1374	941	966

TABLE II: PORNOGRAPHY BREAKS DOWN MORALS -- BY SEX

Question: Do sexually graphic materials lead to a breakdown in morals? NOTE: Question not asked in 1972, 1974, 1977, 1982, 1985.

Responses: YES; NO

		YEAR										
SEX	RESP	'73	'75	'76	'78	'80	'83	'84	'86	'87	'88	'89
M	YES	48%	53%	54%	54%	57%	56%	54%	58%	57%	58%	56%
	NO	52	47	46	46	43	44	46	42	43	42	44
# SURVEYED		661	618	627	617	604	655	579	591	603	412	419
SEX	RESP	'73	'75	'76	'78	'80	'83	'84	'86	'87	'88	'89
F	YES	63%	60%	64%	64%	71%	66%	73%	72%	72%	71%	75%
	NO	37	40	36	36	29	34	27	28	28	29	25
# SURVEYED		755	735	752	834	754	851	808	794	771	529	547

TABLE III: PORNOGRAPHY BREAKS DOWN MORALS -- BY RACE

Question: Do sexually graphic materials lead to a breakdown in morals? NOTE: Question not asked in 1972, 1974, 1977, 1982, 1985.

Responses: YES; NO

		YEAR										
RACE	RESP	'73	'75	'76	'78	'80	'83	'84	'86	'87	'88	'89
WHITE	YES	57%	58%	60%	62%	66%	63%	65%	66%	66%	67%	66%
	NO	43	42	40	38	34	37	35	34	34	33	34
# SURVEYED		1234	1202	1261	1296	1217	1339	1187	1189	1161	793	830
RACE	RESP	'73	'75	'76	'78	'80	'83	'84	'86	'87	'88	'89
BLACK	YES	51%	46%	50%	42%	57%	56%	63%	59%	61%	52%	70%
	NO	49	54	50	58	43	44	37	41	39	48	30
# SURVEYED		173	149	110	142	132	152	151	162	165	109	100
RACE	RESP	'73	'75	'76	'78	'80	'83	'84	'86	'87	'88	'89
OTHER	YES	44%	0%	50%	62%	78%	73%	71%	76%	77%	62%	72%
	NO	56	100	50	38	22	27	29	24	23	38	28
# SURVEYED		9	2	8	13	9	15	49	34	48	39	36

TABLE IV: PORNOGRAPHY BREAKS DOWN MORALS -- BY AGE

Question: Do sexually graphic materials lead to a breakdown in morals? NOTE: Question not asked in 1972, 1974, 1977, 1982, 1985.

Responses: YES; NO

		YEAR										
AGE	RESP	'73	'75	'76	'78	'80	'83	'84	'86	'87	'88	'89
18-23	YES	38%	35%	39%	44%	58%	54%	56%	49%	59%	44%	57%
	NO	62	65	61	56	42	46	44	51	41	56	43
# SURVEYED		166	163	150	154	146	125	154	99	120	89	88
AGE	RESP	'73	'75	'76	'78	'80	'83	'84	'86	'87	'88	'89
24-29	YES	40%	33%	40%	44%	39%	50%	54%	58%	57%	53%	53%
	NO	60	67	60	56	61	50	46	42	43	47	47
# SURVEYED		207	219	214	232	191	273	220	208	187	137	131

TABLE IV: PORNOGRAPHY BREAKS DOWN MORALS -- BY AGE (Continued)

Question: Do sexually graphic materials lead to a breakdown in morals? NOTE: Question not asked in 1972, 1974, 1977, 1982, 1985.

Responses: YES; NO

		YEAR										
AGE	RESP	'73	'75	'76	'78	'80	'83	'84	'86	'87	'88	'89
30-35	YES	46%	52%	48%	47%	51%	55%	55%	57%	54%	71%	55%
	NO	54	48	52	53	49	45	45	43	46	29	45
# SURVEYED		158	159	177	221	207	228	190	209	212	123	138
AGE	RESP	'73	'75	'76	'78	'80	'83	'84	'86	'87	'88	'89
36-41	YES	55%	60%	52%	59%	58%	51%	58%	55%	58%	56%	65%
	NO	45	40	48	41	42	49	42	45	42	44	35
# SURVEYED		163	141	145	153	136	164	179	182	178	120	128
AGE	RESP	'73	'75	'76	'78	'80	'83	'84	'86	'87	'88	'89
42-47	YES	54%	51%	61%	66%	67%	64%	64%	60%	67%	72%	65%
	NO	46	49	39	34	33	36	36	40	33	28	35
# SURVEYED		142	127	110	114	107	137	121	136	144	101	100
AGE	RESP	'73	'75	'76	'78	'80	'83	'84	'86	'87	'88	'89
48-53	YES	63%	60%	76%	65%	69%	71%	75%	64%	69%	64%	74%
	NO	37	40	24	35	31	29	25	36	31	36	26
# SURVEYED		140	133	123	128	115	107	95	100	118	56	88
AGE	RESP	'73	'75	'76	'78	'80	'83	'84	'86	'87	'88	'89
54-59	YES	66%	69%	69%	71%	84%	75%	73%	83%	65%	70%	71%
	NO	34	31	31	29	16	25	27	17	35	30	29
# SURVEYED		145	112	118	127	127	127	109	92	89	61	59
AGE	RESP	'73	'75	'76	'78	'80	'83	'84	'86	'87	'88	'89
60-65	YES	73%	78%	74%	75%	81%	74%	77%	76%	84%	80%	78%
	NO	27	22	26	25	19	26	23	24	16	20	22
# SURVEYED		112	100	125	102	109	125	102	107	95	75	68
AGE	RESP	'73	'75	'76	'78	'80	'83	'84	'86	'87	'88	'89
66+	YES	78%	84%	85%	84%	87%	76%	85%	87%	83%	78%	85%
	NO	22	16	15	16	13	24	15	13	17	22	15
# SURVEYED		179	197	213	213	213	215	214	246	227	175	164

****

PORNOGRAPHY INCITES RAPE

TABLE I: PORNOGRAPHY INCITES RAPE -- BY TOTAL POPULATION

Question: Do sexually graphic materials lead people to commit rape? NOTE: Question not asked in 1972, 1974, 1977, 1982, 1985.

Responses: YES; NO

	YEAR										
RESPONSE	'73	'75	'76	'78	'80	'83	'84	'86	'87	'88	'89
YES	54%	58%	58%	61%	59%	60%	60%	61%	60%	61%	65%
NO	46	42	42	39	41	40	40	39	40	39	35
# SURVEYED	1390	1335	1356	1416	1328	1476	1348	1360	1328	909	955

TABLE II: PORNOGRAPHY INCITES RAPE -- BY SEX

Question: Do sexually graphic materials lead people to commit rape? NOTE: Question not asked in 1972, 1974, 1977, 1982, 1985.

Responses: YES; NO

		YEAR										
SEX	RESP	'73	'75	'76	'78	'80	'83	'84	'86	'87	'88	'89
M	YES	46%	50%	50%	53%	51%	51%	49%	54%	50%	51%	52%
	NO	54	50	50	47	49	49	51	46	50	49	48
# SURVEYED		653	618	613	610	591	644	560	578	580	398	413
SEX	RESP	'73	'75	'76	'78	'80	'83	'84	'86	'87	'88	'89
F	YES	61%	65%	65%	67%	66%	66%	67%	66%	67%	69%	74%
	NO	39	35	35	33	34	34	33	34	33	31	26
# SURVEYED		737	717	743	806	737	832	788	782	748	511	542

TABLE III: PORNOGRAPHY INCITES RAPE -- BY RACE

Question: Do sexually graphic materials lead people to commit rape? NOTE: Question not asked in 1972, 1974, 1977, 1982, 1985.

Responses: YES; NO

		YEAR										
RACE	RESP	'73	'75	'76	'78	'80	'83	'84	'86	'87	'88	'89
WHITE	YES	54%	58%	59%	61%	59%	60%	59%	61%	60%	62%	63%
	NO	46	42	41	39	41	40	41	39	40	38	37
# SURVEYED		1205	1188	1235	1256	1194	1316	1148	1164	1119	765	818
RACE	RESP	'73	'75	'76	'78	'80	'83	'84	'86	'87	'88	'89
BLACK	YES	54%	53%	51%	60%	66%	59%	62%	63%	53%	54%	73%
	NO	46	47	49	40	34	41	38	37	47	46	27
# SURVEYED		174	144	113	146	125	145	151	162	161	105	101
RACE	RESP	'73	'75	'76	'78	'80	'83	'84	'86	'87	'88	'89
OTHER	YES	64%	67%	38%	57%	67%	73%	63%	65%	69%	67%	72%
	NO	36	33	63	43	33	27	37	35	31	33	28
# SURVEYED		11	3	8	14	9	15	49	34	48	39	36

TABLE IV: PORNOGRAPHY INCITES RAPE -- BY AGE

Question: Do sexually graphic materials lead people to commit rape? NOTE: Question not asked in 1972, 1974, 1977, 1982, 1985.

Responses: YES; NO

		YEAR										
AGE	RESP	'73	'75	'76	'78	'80	'83	'84	'86	'87	'88	'89
18-23	YES	42%	44%	41%	53%	59%	58%	49%	50%	53%	47%	61%
	NO	58	56	59	47	41	42	51	50	47	53	39
# SURVEYED		163	160	150	155	145	118	146	101	116	90	87
AGE	RESP	'73	'75	'76	'78	'80	'83	'84	'86	'87	'88	'89
24-29	YES	35%	40%	42%	50%	40%	53%	49%	47%	52%	53%	53%
	NO	65	60	58	50	60	47	51	53	48	47	47
# SURVEYED		202	212	207	225	192	268	217	206	180	131	129
AGE	RESP	'73	'75	'76	'78	'80	'83	'84	'86	'87	'88	'89
30-35	YES	45%	53%	48%	49%	44%	50%	48%	51%	45%	56%	56%
	NO	55	47	52	51	56	50	52	49	55	44	44
# SURVEYED		158	157	172	211	200	226	185	212	202	120	135

TABLE IV: PORNOGRAPHY INCITES RAPE -- BY AGE (Continued)

Question: Do sexually graphic materials lead people to commit rape? NOTE: Question not asked in 1972, 1974, 1977, 1982, 1985.

Responses: YES; NO

AGE	RESP	'73	'75	'76	'78	'80	'83	'84	'86	'87	'88	'89
36-41	YES	48%	55%	51%	59%	55%	44%	53%	50%	47%	51%	52%
	NO	52	45	49	41	45	56	47	50	53	49	48
# SURVEYED		162	140	145	146	142	161	175	179	172	115	124
AGE	RESP	'73	'75	'76	'78	'80	'83	'84	'86	'87	'88	'89
42-47	YES	55%	49%	59%	55%	58%	62%	58%	56%	59%	61%	64%
	NO	45	51	41	45	42	38	42	44	41	39	36
# SURVEYED		135	121	106	112	102	133	117	130	139	98	100
AGE	RESP	'73	'75	'76	'78	'80	'83	'84	'86	'87	'88	'89
48-53	YES	58%	63%	69%	61%	67%	61%	73%	61%	61%	58%	69%
	NO	42	37	31	39	33	39	27	39	39	42	31
# SURVEYED		139	127	124	124	115	109	88	96	117	53	91
AGE	RESP	'73	'75	'76	'78	'80	'83	'84	'86	'87	'88	'89
54-59	YES	62%	65%	64%	73%	66%	71%	70%	79%	66%	72%	69%
	NO	38	35	36	27	34	29	30	21	34	28	31
# SURVEYED		143	113	117	126	123	123	106	90	88	54	55
AGE	RESP	'73	'75	'76	'78	'80	'83	'84	'86	'87	'88	'89
60-65	YES	73%	80%	75%	72%	75%	74%	72%	75%	78%	77%	78%
	NO	27	20	25	28	25	26	28	25	22	23	22
# SURVEYED		111	103	122	99	105	125	102	104	91	73	68
AGE	RESP	'73	'75	'76	'78	'80	'83	'84	'86	'87	'88	'89
66+	YES	76%	80%	79%	84%	83%	75%	79%	85%	83%	77%	82%
	NO	24	20	21	16	17	25	21	15	17	23	18
# SURVEYED		173	199	209	211	197	208	208	235	219	171	164

****

EUTHANASIA LAW

TABLE I: EUTHANASIA LAW -- BY TOTAL POPULATION

Question: When a person has a disease that cannot be cured, do you think doctors should be allowed by law to end the patient's life by some painless means if the patient and his family request it? NOTE: Question not asked in 1972-1976, 1980, 1984, 1987.

Responses: YES; NO

	YEAR							
RESPONSE	'77	'78	'82	'83	'85	'86	'88	'89
YES	62%	60%	64%	66%	66%	68%	69%	69%
NO	38	40	36	34	34	32	31	31
# SURVEYED	1453	1471	1430	1524	1489	1413	935	957

TABLE II: EUTHANASIA LAW -- BY SEX

Question: When a person has a disease that cannot be cured, do you think doctors should be allowed by law to end the patient's life by some painless means if the patient and his family request it? NOTE: Question not asked in 1972-1976, 1980, 1984, 1987.

Responses: YES; NO

		YEAR							
SEX	RESP	'77	'78	'82	'83	'85	'86	'88	'89
M	YES	67%	64%	68%	71%	70%	74%	74%	75%
	NO	33	36	32	29	30	26	26	25
# SURVEYED		666	620	611	664	674	594	416	414

		YEAR							
SEX	RESP	'77	'78	'82	'83	'85	'86	'88	'89
F	YES	58%	57%	61%	62%	62%	64%	66%	64%
	NO	42	43	39	38	38	36	34	36
# SURVEYED		787	851	819	860	815	819	519	543

TABLE III: EUTHANASIA LAW -- BY RACE

Question: When a person has a disease that cannot be cured, do you think doctors should be allowed by law to end the patient's life by some painless means if the patient and his family request it? NOTE: Question not asked in 1972-1976, 1980, 1984, 1987.

Responses: YES; NO

		YEAR							
RACE	RESP	'77	'78	'82	'83	'85	'86	'88	'89
WHITE	YES	65%	62%	66%	68%	67%	70%	72%	71%
	NO	35	38	34	32	33	30	28	29
# SURVEYED		1274	1302	1254	1350	1304	1205	784	824
RACE	RESP	'77	'78	'82	'83	'85	'86	'88	'89
BLACK	YES	39%	45%	47%	46%	48%	53%	50%	49%
	NO	61	55	53	54	52	47	50	51
# SURVEYED		164	155	150	157	143	173	118	98

		YEAR							
RACE	RESP	'77	'78	'82	'83	'85	'86	'88	'89
OTHER	YES	60%	50%	65%	53%	74%	74%	79%	69%
	NO	40	50	35	47	26	26	21	31
# SURVEYED		15	14	26	17	42	35	33	35

TABLE IV: EUTHANASIA LAW -- BY AGE

Question: When a person has a disease that cannot be cured, do you think doctors should be allowed by law to end the patient's life by some painless means if the patient and his family request it? NOTE: Question not asked in 1972-1976, 1980, 1984, 1987.

Responses: YES; NO

		YEAR							
AGE	RESP	'77	'78	'82	'83	'85	'86	'88	'89
18-23	YES	71%	68%	74%	74%	75%	72%	80%	81%
	NO	29	32	26	26	25	28	20	19
# SURVEYED		158	159	140	122	132	104	91	80
AGE	RESP	'77	'78	'82	'83	'85	'86	'88	'89
24-29	YES	74%	73%	74%	73%	74%	78%	73%	75%
	NO	26	27	26	27	26	22	27	25
# SURVEYED		196	236	232	277	210	208	143	142
AGE	RESP	'77	'78	'82	'83	'85	'86	'88	'89
30-35	YES	63%	67%	71%	71%	76%	73%	78%	76%
	NO	37	33	29	29	24	27	22	24
# SURVEYED		183	221	199	230	209	216	120	136

		YEAR							
AGE	RESP	'77	'78	'82	'83	'85	'86	'88	'89
36-41	YES	59%	58%	66%	64%	73%	73%	70%	70%
	NO	41	42	34	36	27	27	30	30
# SURVEYED		160	156	142	165	179	187	122	122
AGE	RESP	'77	'78	'82	'83	'85	'86	'88	'89
42-47	YES	62%	52%	64%	67%	64%	68%	70%	68%
	NO	38	48	36	33	36	32	30	32
# SURVEYED		142	118	113	141	119	137	106	103
AGE	RESP	'77	'78	'82	'83	'85	'86	'88	'89
48-53	YES	55%	50%	56%	59%	57%	65%	58%	68%
	NO	45	50	44	41	43	35	42	32
# SURVEYED		148	124	107	113	129	104	59	84

TABLE IV: EUTHANASIA LAW -- BY AGE (Continued)

Question: When a person has a disease that cannot be cured, do you think doctors should be allowed by law to end the patient's life by some painless means if the patient and his family request it? NOTE: Question not asked in 1972-1976, 1980, 1984, 1987.

Responses: YES; NO

AGE	RESP	'77	'78	'82	'83	'85	'86	'88	'89
54-59	YES	64%	49%	59%	57%	59%	60%	67%	61%
	NO	36	51	41	43	41	40	33	39
# SURVEYED		157	129	138	124	128	90	48	66
60-65	YES	60%	58%	61%	63%	58%	61%	63%	51%
	NO	40	42	39	37	42	39	37	49
# SURVEYED		112	102	109	126	127	111	68	67

AGE	RESP	'77	'78	'82	'83	'85	'86	'88	'89
66+	YES	51%	53%	50%	60%	52%	60%	61%	60%
	NO	49	47	50	40	48	40	39	40
# SURVEYED		191	219	241	220	250	249	177	154

****

SUICIDE FOR TERMINALLY ILL

TABLE I: SUICIDE FOR TERMINALLY ILL -- BY TOTAL POPULATION

Question: Do you think a person has the right to end his or her life if this person has an incurable disease? NOTE: Question not asked in 1972-1976, 1980, 1984, 1987.

Responses: YES; NO

RESPONSE	'77	'78	'82	'83	'85	'86	'88	'89
YES	39%	40%	47%	50%	46%	53%	52%	49%
NO	61	60	53	50	54	47	48	51
# SURVEYED	1475	1483	1430	1530	1480	1420	946	957

TABLE II: SUICIDE FOR TERMINALLY ILL -- BY SEX

Question: Do you think a person has the right to end his or her life if this person has an incurable disease? NOTE: Question not asked in 1972-1976, 1980, 1984, 1987.

Responses: YES; NO

SEX	RESP	'77	'78	'82	'83	'85	'86	'88	'89
		YEAR							
M	YES	43%	44%	53%	54%	50%	62%	56%	55%
	NO	57	56	47	46	50	38	44	45
# SURVEYED		672	623	615	667	664	598	423	413

SEX	RESP	'77	'78	'82	'83	'85	'86	'88	'89
		YEAR							
F	YES	36%	36%	43%	46%	42%	47%	49%	45%
	NO	64	64	57	54	58	53	51	55
# SURVEYED		803	860	815	863	816	822	523	544

TABLE III: SUICIDE FOR TERMINALLY ILL -- BY RACE

Question: Do you think a person has the right to end his or her life if this person has an incurable disease? NOTE: Question not asked in 1972-1976, 1980, 1984, 1987.

Responses: YES; NO

RACE	RESP	'77	'78	'82	'83	'85	'86	'88	'89
		YEAR							
WHITE	YES	42%	41%	49%	51%	47%	56%	55%	51%
	NO	58	59	51	49	53	44	45	49
# SURVEYED		1291	1315	1256	1358	1291	1209	794	825
RACE	RESP	'77	'78	'82	'83	'85	'86	'88	'89
BLACK	YES	21%	27%	32%	38%	30%	36%	34%	38%
	NO	79	73	68	62	70	64	66	62
# SURVEYED		170	154	149	157	147	178	121	97

RACE	RESP	'77	'78	'82	'83	'85	'86	'88	'89
		YEAR							
OTHER	YES	43%	50%	48%	47%	43%	64%	45%	40%
	NO	57	50	52	53	57	36	55	60
# SURVEYED		14	14	25	15	42	33	31	35

TABLE IV: SUICIDE FOR TERMINALLY ILL -- BY AGE

Question: Do you think a person has the right to end his or her life if this person has an incurable disease? NOTE: Question not asked in 1972-1976, 1980, 1984, 1987.

Responses: YES; NO

		YEAR							
AGE	RESP	'77	'78	'82	'83	'85	'86	'88	'89
18-23	**YES**	53%	48%	60%	65%	58%	61%	51%	49%
	NO	48	52	40	35	42	39	49	51
# SURVEYED		160	158	140	121	130	105	91	81
AGE	RESP	'77	'78	'82	'83	'85	'86	'88	'89
24-29	**YES**	55%	49%	63%	58%	58%	66%	55%	58%
	NO	45	51	37	42	42	34	45	42
# SURVEYED		201	236	237	282	212	209	146	140
AGE	RESP	'77	'78	'82	'83	'85	'86	'88	'89
30-35	**YES**	42%	52%	58%	56%	59%	64%	66%	62%
	NO	58	48	42	44	41	36	34	38
# SURVEYED		180	222	199	231	208	215	128	135
AGE	RESP	'77	'78	'82	'83	'85	'86	'88	'89
36-41	**YES**	39%	36%	52%	50%	53%	61%	61%	56%
	NO	61	64	48	50	47	39	39	44
# SURVEYED		164	155	135	163	180	181	122	123
AGE	RESP	'77	'78	'82	'83	'85	'86	'88	'89
42-47	**YES**	35%	35%	47%	52%	46%	54%	58%	48%
	NO	65	65	53	48	54	46	42	52
# SURVEYED		142	118	114	140	119	140	105	101

		YEAR							
AGE	RESP	'77	'78	'82	'83	'85	'86	'88	'89
48-53	**YES**	36%	32%	42%	44%	43%	56%	50%	52%
	NO	64	68	58	56	57	44	50	48
# SURVEYED		148	128	109	109	129	105	58	84
AGE	RESP	'77	'78	'82	'83	'85	'86	'88	'89
54-59	**YES**	31%	34%	36%	45%	37%	39%	35%	46%
	NO	69	66	64	55	63	61	65	54
# SURVEYED		164	133	140	130	127	95	48	69
AGE	RESP	'77	'78	'82	'83	'85	'86	'88	'89
60-65	**YES**	33%	23%	35%	38%	32%	39%	50%	25%
	NO	67	77	65	62	68	61	50	75
# SURVEYED		110	100	108	123	128	114	70	64
AGE	RESP	'77	'78	'82	'83	'85	'86	'88	'89
66+	**YES**	25%	32%	27%	35%	25%	35%	37%	34%
	NO	75	68	73	65	75	65	63	66
# SURVEYED		199	226	238	225	241	251	177	158

****

SUICIDE FOR BANKRUPTCY

TABLE I: SUICIDE FOR BANKRUPTCY -- BY TOTAL POPULATION

Question: Do you think a person has the right to end his or her life if this person has gone bankrupt? NOTE: Question not asked in 1972-1976, 1980, 1984, 1987.

Responses: YES; NO

	YEAR							
RESPONSE	'77	'78	'82	'83	'85	'86	'88	'89
YES	7%	6%	8%	7%	8%	7%	6%	7%
NO	93	94	92	93	92	93	94	93
# SURVEYED	1506	1521	1479	1568	1504	1458	966	987

TABLE II: SUICIDE FOR BANKRUPTCY -- BY SEX

Question: Do you think a person has the right to end his or her life if this person has gone bankrupt? NOTE: Question not asked in 1972-1976, 1980, 1984, 1987.

Responses: YES; NO

		YEAR							
SEX	RESP	'77	'78	'82	'83	'85	'86	'88	'89
M	YES	8%	7%	9%	8%	9%	7%	7%	9%
	NO	92	93	91	92	91	93	93	91
# SURVEYED		683	637	632	681	677	615	429	420

		YEAR							
SEX	RESP	'77	'78	'82	'83	'85	'86	'88	'89
F	YES	6%	4%	8%	5%	7%	6%	5%	6%
	NO	94	96	92	95	93	94	95	94
# SURVEYED		823	884	847	887	827	843	537	567

TABLE III: SUICIDE FOR BANKRUPTCY -- BY RACE

Question: Do you think a person has the right to end his or her life if this person has gone bankrupt? NOTE: Question not asked in 1972-1976, 1980, 1984, 1987.

Responses: YES; NO

		YEAR							
RACE	RESP	'77	'78	'82	'83	'85	'86	'88	'89
WHITE	YES NO	7% 93	6% 94	9% 91	7% 93	8% 92	7% 93	6% 94	7% 93
# SURVEYED		1319	1347	1297	1390	1314	1241	809	850
RACE	RESP	'77	'78	'82	'83	'85	'86	'88	'89
BLACK	YES NO	4% 96	3% 97	6% 94	6% 94	6% 94	4% 96	5% 95	6% 94
# SURVEYED		173	158	155	162	147	181	124	101

		YEAR							
RACE	RESP	'77	'78	'82	'83	'85	'86	'88	'89
OTHER	YES NO	7% 93	0% 100	4% 96	13% 88	5% 95	8% 92	3% 97	11% 89
# SURVEYED		14	16	27	16	43	36	33	36

TABLE IV: SUICIDE FOR BANKRUPTCY -- BY AGE

Question: Do you think a person has the right to end his or her life if this person has gone bankrupt? NOTE: Question not asked in 1972-1976, 1980, 1984, 1987.

Responses: YES; NO

		YEAR							
AGE	RESP	'77	'78	'82	'83	'85	'86	'88	'89
18-23	YES NO	9% 91	3% 97	7% 93	6% 94	8% 92	7% 93	10% 90	8% 93
# SURVEYED		162	162	147	127	132	105	94	80
AGE	RESP	'77	'78	'82	'83	'85	'86	'88	'89
24-29	YES NO	7% 93	9% 91	10% 90	5% 95	12% 88	6% 94	3% 97	8% 92
# SURVEYED		203	243	241	285	211	217	149	146
AGE	RESP	'77	'78	'82	'83	'85	'86	'88	'89
30-35	YES NO	7% 93	8% 92	14% 86	10% 90	9% 91	7% 93	6% 94	7% 93
# SURVEYED		185	229	200	234	207	220	126	138

		YEAR							
AGE	RESP	'77	'78	'82	'83	'85	'86	'88	'89
36-41	YES NO	8% 92	4% 96	9% 91	9% 91	9% 91	10% 90	6% 94	10% 90
# SURVEYED		166	158	145	167	183	188	127	125
AGE	RESP	'77	'78	'82	'83	'85	'86	'88	'89
42-47	YES NO	8% 92	8% 92	10% 90	6% 94	11% 89	8% 92	7% 93	5% 95
# SURVEYED		146	119	119	143	123	141	106	105
AGE	RESP	'77	'78	'82	'83	'85	'86	'88	'89
48-53	YES NO	5% 95	1% 99	8% 92	11% 89	5% 95	7% 93	10% 90	9% 91
# SURVEYED		151	131	110	114	131	107	61	82

TABLE IV: SUICIDE FOR BANKRUPTCY -- BY AGE (Continued)

Question: Do you think a person has the right to end his or her life if this person has gone bankrupt? NOTE: Question not asked in 1972-1976, 1980, 1984, 1987.

Responses: YES; NO

		YEAR							
AGE	RESP	'77	'78	'82	'83	'85	'86	'88	'89
54-59	YES	5%	8%	5%	12%	5%	6%	2%	8%
	NO	95	92	95	88	95	94	98	92
# SURVEYED		166	137	142	132	131	97	50	72
AGE	RESP	'77	'78	'82	'83	'85	'86	'88	'89
60-65	YES	6%	1%	7%	1%	7%	3%	6%	1%
	NO	94	99	93	99	93	97	94	99
# SURVEYED		112	107	114	128	129	115	71	69

		YEAR							
AGE	RESP	'77	'78	'82	'83	'85	'86	'88	'89
66+	YES	7%	3%	6%	3%	5%	5%	4%	5%
	NO	93	97	94	97	95	95	96	95
# SURVEYED		209	228	251	232	250	262	181	167

****

SUICIDE FOR DISHONOR

TABLE I: SUICIDE FOR DISHONOR -- BY TOTAL POPULATION

Question: Do you think a person has the right to end his or her life if this person has dishonored his or her family? NOTE: Question not asked in 1972-1976, 1980, 1984, 1987.

Responses: YES; NO

	YEAR							
RESPONSE	'77	'78	'82	'83	'85	'86	'88	'89
YES	8%	6%	9%	7%	8%	6%	7%	7%
NO	92	94	91	93	92	94	93	93
# SURVEYED	1505	1524	1474	1566	1494	1448	964	983

TABLE II: SUICIDE FOR DISHONOR -- BY SEX

Question: Do you think a person has the right to end his or her life if this person has dishonored his or her family? NOTE: Question not asked in 1972-1976, 1980, 1984, 1987.

Responses: YES; NO

		YEAR							
SEX	RESP	'77	'78	'82	'83	'85	'86	'88	'89
M	YES	9%	8%	9%	8%	10%	7%	8%	10%
	NO	91	92	91	92	90	93	92	90
# SURVEYED		684	636	630	676	670	609	430	419

		YEAR							
SEX	RESP	'77	'78	'82	'83	'85	'86	'88	'89
F	YES	7%	5%	8%	6%	7%	5%	6%	5%
	NO	93	95	92	94	93	95	94	95
# SURVEYED		821	888	844	890	824	839	534	564

TABLE III: SUICIDE FOR DISHONOR -- BY RACE

Question: Do you think a person has the right to end his or her life if this person has dishonored his or her family? NOTE: Question not asked in 1972-1976, 1980, 1984, 1987.

Responses: YES; NO

		YEAR							
RACE	RESP	'77	'78	'82	'83	'85	'86	'88	'89
WHITE	YES	8%	7%	9%	7%	8%	6%	7%	7%
	NO	92	93	91	93	92	94	93	93
# SURVEYED		1318	1350	1294	1389	1307	1231	807	846
RACE	RESP	'77	'78	'82	'83	'85	'86	'88	'89
BLACK	YES	4%	3%	4%	6%	6%	3%	7%	5%
	NO	96	97	96	94	94	97	93	95
# SURVEYED		173	158	153	161	145	181	125	101

		YEAR							
RACE	RESP	'77	'78	'82	'83	'85	'86	'88	'89
OTHER	YES	14%	0%	4%	19%	10%	8%	3%	8%
	NO	86	100	96	81	90	92	97	92
# SURVEYED		14	16	27	16	42	36	32	36

TABLE IV: SUICIDE FOR DISHONOR -- BY AGE

Question: Do you think a person has the right to end his or her life if this person has dishonored his or her family? NOTE: Question not asked in 1972-1976, 1980, 1984, 1987.

Responses: YES; NO

AGE	RESP	'77	'78	'82	'83	'85	'86	'88	'89
18-23	YES	9%	4%	7%	6%	10%	7%	10%	12%
	NO	91	96	93	94	90	93	90	88
# SURVEYED		163	162	147	127	132	104	94	82
24-29	YES	7%	10%	11%	6%	12%	7%	4%	7%
	NO	93	90	89	94	88	93	96	93
# SURVEYED		203	243	243	287	211	216	148	145
30-35	YES	9%	9%	15%	9%	9%	7%	6%	6%
	NO	91	91	85	91	91	93	94	94
# SURVEYED		185	228	198	233	209	221	127	138
36-41	YES	8%	4%	10%	11%	9%	9%	8%	10%
	NO	92	96	90	89	91	91	92	90
# SURVEYED		166	158	144	168	183	186	126	125
42-47	YES	8%	7%	9%	6%	10%	7%	8%	5%
	NO	92	93	91	94	90	93	92	95
# SURVEYED		146	119	117	144	120	140	106	105

AGE	RESP	'77	'78	'82	'83	'85	'86	'88	'89
48-53	YES	8%	2%	8%	11%	7%	6%	10%	9%
	NO	92	98	92	89	93	94	90	91
# SURVEYED		152	132	109	114	130	106	61	82
54-59	YES	5%	9%	4%	8%	4%	4%	2%	8%
	NO	95	91	96	92	96	96	98	92
# SURVEYED		166	137	143	130	130	97	50	72
60-65	YES	7%	2%	7%	1%	7%	3%	9%	1%
	NO	93	98	93	99	93	97	91	99
# SURVEYED		112	107	115	128	127	114	70	68
66+	YES	6%	5%	4%	6%	4%	4%	6%	6%
	NO	94	95	96	94	96	96	94	94
# SURVEYED		206	231	248	229	246	258	181	163

****

SUICIDE FOR PRIVATE REASONS

TABLE I: SUICIDE FOR PRIVATE REASONS -- BY TOTAL POPULATION

Question: Do you think a person has the right to end his or her life if this person is tired of living and ready to die? NOTE: Question not asked in 1972-1976, 1980, 1984, 1987.

Responses: YES; NO

	YEAR							
RESPONSE	'77	'78	'82	'83	'85	'86	'88	'89
YES	14%	12%	15%	15%	13%	15%	13%	14%
NO	86	88	85	85	87	85	87	86
# SURVEYED	1496	1511	1452	1549	1495	1446	954	980

TABLE II: SUICIDE FOR PRIVATE REASONS -- BY SEX

Question: Do you think a person has the right to end his or her life if this person is tired of living and ready to die? NOTE: Question not asked in 1972-1976, 1980, 1984, 1987.

Responses: YES; NO

		YEAR							
SEX	RESP	'77	'78	'82	'83	'85	'86	'88	'89
M	YES	16%	15%	17%	18%	15%	17%	13%	16%
	NO	84	85	83	82	85	83	87	84
# SURVEYED		676	636	622	677	673	607	423	419

		YEAR							
SEX	RESP	'77	'78	'82	'83	'85	'86	'88	'89
F	YES	11%	10%	13%	13%	11%	14%	12%	12%
	NO	89	90	87	87	89	86	88	88
# SURVEYED		820	875	830	872	822	839	531	561

TABLE III: SUICIDE FOR PRIVATE REASONS -- BY RACE

Question: Do you think a person has the right to end his or her life if this person is tired of living and ready to die? NOTE: Question not asked in 1972-1976, 1980, 1984, 1987.

Responses: YES; NO

RACE	RESP	'77	'78	'82	'83	'85	'86	'88	'89
WHITE	YES	14%	12%	15%	15%	13%	15%	13%	14%
	NO	86	88	85	85	87	85	87	86
# SURVEYED		1310	1340	1276	1374	1306	1231	797	842
BLACK	YES	10%	11%	13%	16%	12%	14%	14%	11%
	NO	90	89	87	84	88	86	86	89
# SURVEYED		172	156	150	160	146	179	124	101

RACE	RESP	'77	'78	'82	'83	'85	'86	'88	'89
OTHER	YES	21%	7%	4%	20%	9%	22%	9%	22%
	NO	79	93	96	80	91	78	91	78
# SURVEYED		14	15	26	15	43	36	33	37

TABLE IV: SUICIDE FOR PRIVATE REASONS -- BY AGE

Question: Do you think a person has the right to end his or her life if this person is tired of living and ready to die? NOTE: Question not asked in 1972-1976, 1980, 1984, 1987.

Responses: YES; NO

AGE	RESP	'77	'78	'82	'83	'85	'86	'88	'89
18-23	YES	18%	12%	13%	19%	17%	18%	16%	15%
	NO	82	88	87	81	83	82	84	85
# SURVEYED		161	161	146	125	132	106	90	82
24-29	YES	13%	17%	16%	14%	19%	13%	9%	15%
	NO	87	83	84	86	81	87	91	85
# SURVEYED		203	242	231	284	209	212	146	144
30-35	YES	13%	16%	21%	18%	14%	14%	14%	12%
	NO	87	84	79	82	86	86	86	88
# SURVEYED		185	226	198	233	208	221	125	137

AGE	RESP	'77	'78	'82	'83	'85	'86	'88	'89
36-41	YES	14%	6%	13%	15%	16%	21%	11%	15%
	NO	86	94	87	85	84	79	89	85
# SURVEYED		163	158	139	165	182	187	126	125
42-47	YES	14%	12%	11%	13%	15%	16%	12%	13%
	NO	86	88	89	87	85	84	88	87
# SURVEYED		147	119	115	140	123	141	105	104
48-53	YES	15%	6%	14%	19%	9%	16%	13%	13%
	NO	85	94	86	81	91	84	87	87
# SURVEYED		151	130	110	113	129	106	61	83

TABLE IV: SUICIDE FOR PRIVATE REASONS -- BY AGE (Continued)

Question: Do you think a person has the right to end his or her life if this person is tired of living and ready to die? NOTE: Question not asked in 1972-1976, 1980, 1984, 1987.

Responses: YES; NO

		YEAR							
AGE	RESP	'77	'78	'82	'83	'85	'86	'88	'89
54-59	YES	8%	14%	10%	19%	9%	9%	10%	16%
	NO	92	86	90	81	91	91	90	84
# SURVEYED		165	135	142	130	129	94	48	70
AGE	RESP	'77	'78	'82	'83	'85	'86	'88	'89
60-65	YES	16%	7%	14%	7%	10%	9%	13%	6%
	NO	84	93	86	93	90	91	87	94
# SURVEYED		112	106	114	125	128	115	70	68

		YEAR							
AGE	RESP	'77	'78	'82	'83	'85	'86	'88	'89
66+	YES	12%	11%	15%	14%	8%	18%	14%	15%
	NO	88	89	85	86	92	82	86	85
# SURVEYED		203	227	247	228	249	258	182	164

****

PRE-NUPTIAL AIDS TESTING

TABLE I: PRE-NUPTIAL AIDS TESTING -- BY TOTAL POPULATION

Question: As a measure to deal with AIDS, do you support or oppose mandatory testing for the AIDS virus before marriage? NOTE: Question was asked in 1988 only.

Responses: SP = Support; OP = Oppose

	YEAR
RESPONSE	'88
SP	89%
OP	11
# SURVEYED	727

TABLE II: PRE-NUPTIAL AIDS TESTING -- BY SEX

Question: As a measure to deal with AIDS, do you support or oppose mandatory testing for the AIDS virus before marriage? NOTE: Question was asked in 1988 only.

Responses: SP = Support; OP = Oppose

SEX	RESP	YEAR '88
M	SP	86%
	OP	14
# SURVEYED		330

SEX	RESP	YEAR '88
F	SP	92%
	OP	8
# SURVEYED		397

TABLE III: PRE-NUPTIAL AIDS TESTING -- BY RACE

Question: As a measure to deal with AIDS, do you support or oppose mandatory testing for the AIDS virus before marriage? NOTE: Question was asked in 1988 only.

Responses: SP = Support; OP = Oppose

RACE	RESP	YEAR '88
WHITE	SP	89%
	OP	11
# SURVEYED		614

RACE	RESP	YEAR '88
BLACK	SP	90%
	OP	10
# SURVEYED		84

RACE	RESP	YEAR '88
OTHER	SP	90%
	OP	10
# SURVEYED		29

TABLE IV: PRE-NUPTIAL AIDS TESTING -- BY AGE

Question: As a measure to deal with AIDS, do you support or oppose mandatory testing for the AIDS virus before marriage? NOTE: Question was asked in 1988 only.

Responses: SP = Support; OP = Oppose

AGE	RESP	YEAR '88
18-23	SP	88%
	OP	13
# SURVEYED		72

AGE	RESP	YEAR '88
24-29	SP	85%
	OP	15
# SURVEYED		99

AGE	RESP	YEAR '88
30-35	SP	87%
	OP	13
# SURVEYED		93

AGE	RESP	YEAR '88
36-41	SP	85%
	OP	15
# SURVEYED		100

AGE	RESP	YEAR '88
42-47	SP	91%
	OP	9
# SURVEYED		77

TABLE IV: PRE-NUPTIAL AIDS TESTING -- BY AGE

Question: As a measure to deal with AIDS, do you support or oppose mandatory testing for the AIDS virus before marriage? NOTE: Question was asked in 1988 only.

Responses: SP = Support; OP = Oppose

		YEAR
AGE	RESP	'88
48-53	SP	91%
	OP	9
# SURVEYED		43

		YEAR
AGE	RESP	'88
54-59	SP	88%
	OP	12
# SURVEYED		43

		YEAR
AGE	RESP	'88
60-65	SP	93%
	OP	7
# SURVEYED		58

		YEAR
AGE	RESP	'88
66+	SP	94%
	OP	6
# SURVEYED		141

****

CONFIDENCE IN THE MILITARY

TABLE I: CONFIDENCE IN THE MILITARY -- BY TOTAL POPULATION

Question: I am going to name some institutions in this country. As far as the people running these institutions are concerned, would you say you have a great deal of confidence, only some confidence, or hardly any confidence at all in them? How much confidence do you have in the people running the military in this country? NOTE: Question not asked in 1972, 1985.

Responses: GD = A great deal; SM = Only some; HA = Hardly any

	YEAR													
RESPONSE	'73	'74	'75	'76	'77	'78	'80	'82	'83	'84	'86	'87	'88	'89
GD	33%	41%	37%	42%	37%	31%	29%	31%	30%	37%	32%	36%	35%	34%
SM	51	46	48	44	52	56	54	53	56	50	54	52	51	52
HA	17	14	15	14	11	13	17	15	13	13	14	13	14	14
# SURVEYED	1457	1444	1418	1399	1478	1472	1406	1467	1548	950	1429	1415	963	990

TABLE II: CONFIDENCE IN THE MILITARY -- BY SEX

Question: I am going to name some institutions in this country. As far as the people running these institutions are concerned, would you say you have a great deal of confidence, only some confidence, or hardly any confidence at all in them? How much confidence do you have in the people running the military in this country? NOTE: Question not asked in 1972, 1985.

Responses: GD = A great deal; SM = Only some; HA = Hardly any

		YEAR													
SEX	RESP	'73	'74	'75	'76	'77	'78	'80	'82	'83	'84	'86	'87	'88	'89
M	GD	36%	41%	37%	45%	39%	32%	30%	32%	35%	38%	34%	37%	38%	36%
	SM	47	44	46	40	50	55	53	51	51	46	53	49	48	50
	HA	17	15	17	15	11	13	16	17	14	16	13	14	14	15
# SURVEYED		687	677	655	642	681	633	633	636	681	404	608	630	429	438
SEX	RESP	'73	'74	'75	'76	'77	'78	'80	'82	'83	'84	'86	'87	'88	'89
F	GD	30%	40%	37%	39%	36%	29%	28%	31%	27%	36%	31%	34%	33%	32%
	SM	55	47	50	47	54	57	55	55	61	53	54	54	53	54
	HA	16	13	13	14	10	14	17	14	13	11	15	12	14	14
# SURVEYED		770	767	763	757	797	839	773	831	867	546	821	785	534	552

TABLE III: CONFIDENCE IN THE MILITARY -- BY RACE

Question: I am going to name some institutions in this country. As far as the people running these institutions are concerned, would you say you have a great deal of confidence, only some confidence, or hardly any confidence at all in them? How much confidence do you have in the people running the military in this country? NOTE: Question not asked in 1972, 1985.

Responses: GD = A great deal; SM = Only some; HA = Hardly any

		YEAR													
RACE	RESP	'73	'74	'75	'76	'77	'78	'80	'82	'83	'84	'86	'87	'88	'89
WHITE	GD	34%	41%	38%	42%	37%	31%	28%	32%	30%	36%	31%	36%	36%	34%
	SM	51	45	48	43	53	56	54	53	57	51	55	51	50	53
	HA	15	14	15	14	10	13	17	15	13	13	14	13	15	14
# SURVEYED		1271	1266	1264	1274	1297	1305	1264	1291	1375	816	1226	1190	815	853
RACE	RESP	'73	'74	'75	'76	'77	'78	'80	'82	'83	'84	'86	'87	'88	'89
BLACK	GD	23%	36%	32%	33%	42%	28%	31%	25%	31%	40%	37%	31%	33%	32%
	SM	53	51	53	50	47	59	58	57	53	43	46	58	57	56
	HA	24	13	15	17	11	13	11	17	16	17	16	10	10	12
# SURVEYED		174	171	150	117	167	152	133	150	158	107	170	175	109	102
RACE	RESP	'73	'74	'75	'76	'77	'78	'80	'82	'83	'84	'86	'87	'88	'89
OTHER	GD	25%	71%	50%	50%	36%	33%	56%	58%	60%	59%	42%	48%	31%	43%
	SM	50	14	25	50	36	60	33	31	40	37	45	42	62	31
	HA	25	14	25	0	29	7	11	12	0	4	12	10	8	26
# SURVEYED		12	7	4	8	14	15	9	26	15	27	33	50	39	35

TABLE IV: CONFIDENCE IN THE MILITARY -- BY AGE

Question: I am going to name some institutions in this country. As far as the people running these institutions are concerned, would you say you have a great deal of confidence, only some confidence, or hardly any confidence at all in them? How much confidence do you have in the people running the military in this country? NOTE: Question not asked in 1972, 1985.

Responses: GD = A great deal; SM = Only some; HA = Hardly any

		YEAR													
AGE	RESP	'73	'74	'75	'76	'77	'78	'80	'82	'83	'84	'86	'87	'88	'89
18-23	GD	28%	40%	44%	40%	37%	33%	31%	26%	38%	49%	34%	48%	52%	41%
	SM	49	42	36	40	47	49	47	50	51	42	55	40	34	44
	HA	23	18	20	19	16	18	21	24	11	8	11	11	14	15
# SURVEYED		169	168	166	159	161	161	154	147	125	83	108	124	92	93

TABLE IV: CONFIDENCE IN THE MILITARY -- BY AGE (Continued)

Question: I am going to name some institutions in this country. As far as the people running these institutions are concerned, would you say you have a great deal of confidence, only some confidence, or hardly any confidence at all in them? How much confidence do you have in the people running the military in this country? NOTE: Question not asked in 1972, 1985.

Responses: GD = A great deal; SM = Only some; HA = Hardly any

		YEAR													
AGE	RESP	'73	'74	'75	'76	'77	'78	'80	'82	'83	'84	'86	'87	'88	'89
24-29	GD	22%	34%	28%	32%	34%	25%	23%	27%	29%	36%	35%	30%	35%	35%
	SM	48	46	48	49	51	56	55	57	56	54	49	56	54	54
	HA	30	20	24	19	14	19	22	17	15	9	16	13	11	12
# SURVEYED		209	210	225	218	202	238	195	241	282	149	215	186	141	136
AGE	RESP	'73	'74	'75	'76	'77	'78	'80	'82	'83	'84	'86	'87	'88	'89
30-35	GD	30%	38%	32%	41%	30%	23%	20%	21%	24%	33%	28%	23%	31%	27%
	SM	54	43	52	44	57	64	56	54	59	49	52	59	49	52
	HA	16	19	16	15	13	12	23	25	17	17	20	18	20	22
# SURVEYED		164	172	168	182	185	225	209	203	235	132	218	219	122	143
AGE	RESP	'73	'74	'75	'76	'77	'78	'80	'82	'83	'84	'86	'87	'88	'89
36-41	GD	33%	41%	41%	42%	31%	31%	22%	26%	24%	30%	20%	30%	24%	30%
	SM	56	44	47	46	56	54	63	62	57	47	63	53	55	54
	HA	11	15	13	12	12	15	16	13	19	23	17	17	21	16
# SURVEYED		169	150	148	146	162	157	144	144	168	124	184	184	126	126
AGE	RESP	'73	'74	'75	'76	'77	'78	'80	'82	'83	'84	'86	'87	'88	'89
42-47	GD	30%	40%	31%	44%	36%	25%	32%	28%	29%	29%	30%	33%	38%	27%
	SM	60	48	59	44	57	62	55	60	60	59	56	55	51	57
	HA	10	13	10	12	7	13	14	12	11	12	14	12	11	16
# SURVEYED		145	149	139	108	140	115	111	118	144	86	135	155	101	102
AGE	RESP	'73	'74	'75	'76	'77	'78	'80	'82	'83	'84	'86	'87	'88	'89
48-53	GD	34%	37%	40%	46%	40%	36%	32%	33%	27%	35%	35%	40%	36%	35%
	SM	49	53	54	47	54	56	55	55	63	51	57	49	52	51
	HA	18	10	6	7	6	8	14	12	10	14	8	11	13	14
# SURVEYED		148	145	132	123	151	127	117	107	114	74	106	122	56	93
AGE	RESP	'73	'74	'75	'76	'77	'78	'80	'82	'83	'84	'86	'87	'88	'89
54-59	GD	41%	51%	36%	48%	43%	34%	43%	42%	35%	35%	41%	40%	37%	37%
	SM	49	43	51	42	51	56	46	47	53	50	48	55	49	53
	HA	9	6	12	9	5	10	11	11	12	15	11	5	14	10
# SURVEYED		150	133	121	118	164	130	132	142	124	74	96	95	63	62

TABLE IV: CONFIDENCE IN THE MILITARY -- BY AGE (Continued)

Question: I am going to name some institutions in this country. As far as the people running these institutions are concerned, would you say you have a great deal of confidence, only some confidence, or hardly any confidence at all in them? How much confidence do you have in the people running the military in this country? NOTE: Question not asked in 1972, 1985.

Responses: GD = A great deal; SM = Only some; HA = Hardly any

AGE	RESP	'73	'74	'75	'76	'77	'78	'80	'82	'83	'84	'86	'87	'88	'89
60-65	GD	41%	39%	43%	46%	39%	38%	31%	38%	31%	41%	31%	41%	32%	37%
	SM	45	50	44	43	50	53	56	51	57	55	60	52	55	54
	HA	14	11	13	11	11	9	13	11	11	4	9	7	12	9
# SURVEYED		117	100	104	118	112	98	113	114	124	71	112	96	74	70
AGE	RESP	'73	'74	'75	'76	'77	'78	'80	'82	'83	'84	'86	'87	'88	'89
66+	GD	41%	48%	41%	44%	46%	37%	33%	43%	37%	44%	39%	45%	36%	39%
	SM	48	43	45	40	44	52	55	47	53	44	50	44	54	51
	HA	12	9	14	16	10	11	12	10	10	12	12	11	10	10
# SURVEYED		182	211	211	223	195	214	222	243	225	153	250	229	184	163

****

CONFIDENCE IN BUSINESS

TABLE I: CONFIDENCE IN BUSINESS -- BY TOTAL POPULATION

Question: I am going to name some institutions in this country. As far as the people running these institutions are concerned, would you say you have a great deal of confidence, only some confidence, or hardly any confidence at all in them? How much confidence do you have in the people running major companies in this country? NOTE: Question not asked in 1972, 1985.

Responses: GD = A great deal; SM = Only some; HA = Hardly any

RESPONSE	'73	'74	'75	'76	'77	'78	'80	'82	'83	'84	'86	'87	'88	'89
GD	31%	33%	20%	23%	28%	23%	29%	25%	25%	32%	25%	31%	26%	25%
SM	57	52	57	54	59	61	56	61	61	59	64	60	63	64
HA	12	15	22	23	13	17	15	15	14	9	11	9	11	11
# SURVEYED	1400	1430	1401	1416	1465	1461	1386	1423	1529	947	1411	1398	948	973

TABLE II: CONFIDENCE IN BUSINESS -- BY SEX

Question: I am going to name some institutions in this country. As far as the people running these institutions are concerned, would you say you have a great deal of confidence, only some confidence, or hardly any confidence at all in them? How much confidence do you have in the people running major companies in this country? NOTE: Question not asked in 1972, 1985.

Responses: GD = A great deal; SM = Only some; HA = Hardly any

		YEAR													
SEX	RESP	'73	'74	'75	'76	'77	'78	'80	'82	'83	'84	'86	'87	'88	'89
M	GD	35%	36%	23%	27%	32%	28%	30%	25%	29%	37%	29%	32%	30%	28%
	SM	53	48	53	50	54	56	54	59	56	53	60	58	59	61
	HA	12	16	23	23	15	16	15	16	15	10	10	9	11	11
# SURVEYED		675	679	646	647	671	623	623	626	668	408	602	617	423	429
SEX	RESP	'73	'74	'75	'76	'77	'78	'80	'82	'83	'84	'86	'87	'88	'89
F	GD	28%	29%	18%	20%	26%	19%	27%	24%	22%	28%	22%	30%	22%	22%
	SM	61	56	61	57	63	64	58	63	65	64	67	62	66	67
	HA	12	14	22	23	11	18	15	13	13	8	11	8	11	11
# SURVEYED		725	751	755	769	794	838	763	797	861	539	809	781	525	544

TABLE III: CONFIDENCE IN BUSINESS -- BY RACE

Question: I am going to name some institutions in this country. As far as the people running these institutions are concerned, would you say you have a great deal of confidence, only some confidence, or hardly any confidence at all in them? How much confidence do you have in the people running major companies in this country? NOTE: Question not asked in 1972, 1985.

Responses: GD = A great deal; SM = Only some; HA = Hardly any

		YEAR													
RACE	RESP	'73	'74	'75	'76	'77	'78	'80	'82	'83	'84	'86	'87	'88	'89
WHITE	GD	34%	35%	22%	24%	30%	24%	30%	26%	26%	35%	27%	33%	28%	26%
	SM	56	51	56	54	58	60	56	61	61	57	65	59	61	64
	HA	10	15	22	22	12	15	15	13	13	8	8	8	11	10
# SURVEYED		1226	1258	1242	1291	1287	1299	1246	1254	1356	810	1202	1168	799	835
RACE	RESP	'73	'74	'75	'76	'77	'78	'80	'82	'83	'84	'86	'87	'88	'89
BLACK	GD	13%	15%	10%	13%	18%	9%	19%	13%	15%	13%	13%	16%	13%	14%
	SM	63	67	65	58	61	64	61	58	66	73	64	72	71	66
	HA	24	18	25	29	21	27	20	28	19	14	24	12	17	20
# SURVEYED		163	166	155	116	163	147	130	142	156	109	173	180	109	101
RACE	RESP	'73	'74	'75	'76	'77	'78	'80	'82	'83	'84	'86	'87	'88	'89
OTHER	GD	18%	83%	25%	22%	13%	27%	30%	22%	18%	18%	19%	34%	20%	27%
	SM	64	0	50	67	80	40	60	63	71	75	61	50	75	65
	HA	18	17	25	11	7	33	10	15	12	7	19	16	5	8
# SURVEYED		11	6	4	9	15	15	10	27	17	28	36	50	40	37

TABLE IV: CONFIDENCE IN BUSINESS -- BY AGE

Question: I am going to name some institutions in this country. As far as the people running these institutions are concerned, would you say you have a great deal of confidence, only some confidence, or hardly any confidence at all in them? How much confidence do you have in the people running major companies in this country? NOTE: Question not asked in 1972, 1985.

Responses: GD = A great deal; SM = Only some; HA = Hardly any

		YEAR													
AGE	RESP	'73	'74	'75	'76	'77	'78	'80	'82	'83	'84	'86	'87	'88	'89
18-23	GD	21%	29%	20%	20%	16%	15%	19%	17%	24%	33%	26%	31%	29%	24%
	SM	63	52	53	52	69	65	68	67	63	59	67	65	65	70
	HA	16	19	27	28	15	20	13	15	13	9	8	4	7	6
# SURVEYED		164	167	170	159	163	161	151	144	127	82	105	124	91	90

TABLE IV: CONFIDENCE IN BUSINESS -- BY AGE (Continued)

Question: I am going to name some institutions in this country. As far as the people running these institutions are concerned, would you say you have a great deal of confidence, only some confidence, or hardly any confidence at all in them? How much confidence do you have in the people running major companies in this country? NOTE: Question not asked in 1972, 1985.

Responses: GD = A great deal; SM = Only some; HA = Hardly any

		YEAR													
AGE	RESP	'73	'74	'75	'76	'77	'78	'80	'82	'83	'84	'86	'87	'88	'89
24-29	GD	23%	23%	14%	19%	23%	15%	17%	16%	20%	28%	29%	32%	29%	27%
	SM	58	59	60	55	59	66	64	70	66	67	64	61	61	60
	HA	19	18	26	25	18	19	20	14	14	5	7	7	10	13
# SURVEYED		208	210	227	221	202	234	200	241	281	148	214	188	140	139
AGE	RESP	'73	'74	'75	'76	'77	'78	'80	'82	'83	'84	'86	'87	'88	'89
30-35	GD	27%	23%	18%	16%	19%	20%	28%	20%	23%	28%	18%	24%	21%	24%
	SM	63	56	59	64	66	61	58	60	60	65	71	66	65	64
	HA	9	21	23	20	15	20	14	20	17	7	11	10	13	12
# SURVEYED		158	169	165	178	183	224	208	202	232	132	217	217	121	140
AGE	RESP	'73	'74	'75	'76	'77	'78	'80	'82	'83	'84	'86	'87	'88	'89
36-41	GD	26%	33%	19%	24%	30%	30%	30%	23%	22%	34%	24%	28%	28%	23%
	SM	64	52	61	53	59	56	56	67	67	57	65	64	63	69
	HA	10	14	20	22	10	14	15	10	11	9	10	9	10	8
# SURVEYED		165	147	146	147	164	157	144	144	168	122	185	184	126	125
AGE	RESP	'73	'74	'75	'76	'77	'78	'80	'82	'83	'84	'86	'87	'88	'89
42-47	GD	35%	32%	27%	24%	27%	28%	33%	27%	30%	30%	25%	31%	25%	25%
	SM	56	53	63	57	62	56	47	61	56	63	61	61	60	64
	HA	9	15	11	19	12	16	20	12	13	8	14	7	15	11
# SURVEYED		140	149	139	111	138	117	110	113	142	88	138	150	100	104
AGE	RESP	'73	'74	'75	'76	'77	'78	'80	'82	'83	'84	'86	'87	'88	'89
48-53	GD	38%	40%	19%	26%	40%	27%	30%	30%	30%	31%	27%	29%	20%	24%
	SM	53	51	59	54	53	62	62	60	54	59	62	57	69	65
	HA	8	9	22	20	7	11	8	10	16	9	12	15	11	11
# SURVEYED		143	140	132	125	148	127	118	109	112	74	104	122	54	92
AGE	RESP	'73	'74	'75	'76	'77	'78	'80	'82	'83	'84	'86	'87	'88	'89
54-59	GD	49%	43%	23%	32%	41%	32%	41%	26%	30%	33%	25%	37%	28%	23%
	SM	44	51	51	48	50	58	43	57	61	55	65	56	62	67
	HA	7	6	25	20	9	10	16	16	10	12	10	7	11	11
# SURVEYED		136	131	115	124	158	134	132	136	125	73	97	95	65	57

TABLE IV: CONFIDENCE IN BUSINESS -- BY AGE (Continued)

Question: I am going to name some institutions in this country. As far as the people running these institutions are concerned, would you say you have a great deal of confidence, only some confidence, or hardly any confidence at all in them? How much confidence do you have in the people running major companies in this country? NOTE: Question not asked in 1972, 1985.

Responses: GD = A great deal; SM = Only some; HA = Hardly any

AGE	RESP	'73	'74	'75	'76	'77	'78	'80	'82	'83	'84	'86	'87	'88	'89
60-65	GD	38%	34%	28%	25%	33%	23%	32%	31%	28%	36%	31%	36%	20%	27%
	SM	52	51	52	52	54	65	52	55	57	53	58	55	61	56
	HA	11	15	20	22	13	12	16	15	15	11	11	9	19	17
# SURVEYED		112	102	101	126	111	103	109	108	126	70	109	92	74	63
AGE	RESP	'73	'74	'75	'76	'77	'78	'80	'82	'83	'84	'86	'87	'88	'89
66+	GD	35%	40%	23%	26%	29%	24%	36%	35%	24%	35%	25%	38%	28%	27%
	SM	54	46	54	48	56	56	51	50	62	52	63	53	64	62
	HA	11	14	24	26	15	20	13	15	14	13	12	10	8	11
# SURVEYED		171	209	203	221	192	198	206	218	210	153	236	221	174	161

****

CONFIDENCE IN ORGANIZED RELIGION

TABLE I: CONFIDENCE IN ORGANIZED RELIGION -- BY TOTAL POPULATION

Question: I am going to name some institutions in this country. As far as the people running these institutions are concerned, would you say you have a great deal of confidence, only some confidence, or hardly any confidence at all in them? How much confidence do you have in the people running organized religion in this country? NOTE: Question not asked in 1972, 1985.

Responses: GD = A great deal; SM = Only some; HA = Hardly any

RESPONSE	'73	'74	'75	'76	'77	'78	'80	'82	'83	'84	'86	'87	'88	'89
GD	36%	45%	26%	33%	41%	32%	37%	33%	29%	32%	26%	30%	21%	22%
SM	48	44	51	48	47	49	45	51	53	48	52	51	48	46
HA	16	11	23	20	12	19	19	16	18	19	22	19	32	31
# SURVEYED	1442	1450	1390	1397	1475	1468	1409	1453	1532	945	1417	1416	967	995

TABLE II: CONFIDENCE IN ORGANIZED RELIGION -- BY SEX

Question: I am going to name some institutions in this country. As far as the people running these institutions are concerned, would you say you have a great deal of confidence, only some confidence, or hardly any confidence at all in them? How much confidence do you have in the people running organized religion in this country? NOTE: Question not asked in 1972, 1985.

Responses: GD = A great deal; SM = Only some; HA = Hardly any

		YEAR													
SEX	RESP	'73	'74	'75	'76	'77	'78	'80	'82	'83	'84	'86	'87	'88	'89
M	GD	35%	43%	24%	33%	39%	31%	35%	31%	27%	31%	24%	27%	21%	22%
	SM	46	43	51	46	47	49	47	53	53	48	54	52	43	43
	HA	18	13	26	20	14	20	19	16	20	21	22	21	36	35
# SURVEYED		680	679	633	620	667	624	617	624	662	401	598	615	422	431
SEX	RESP	'73	'74	'75	'76	'77	'78	'80	'82	'83	'84	'86	'87	'88	'89
F	GD	37%	47%	28%	32%	43%	33%	38%	35%	31%	33%	27%	32%	20%	23%
	SM	48	44	52	49	47	49	43	50	52	48	51	50	51	49
	HA	15	9	20	19	10	18	18	15	17	18	21	18	28	28
# SURVEYED		762	771	757	777	808	844	792	829	870	544	819	801	545	564

TABLE III: CONFIDENCE IN ORGANIZED RELIGION -- BY RACE

Question: I am going to name some institutions in this country. As far as the people running these institutions are concerned, would you say you have a great deal of confidence, only some confidence, or hardly any confidence at all in them? How much confidence do you have in the people running organized religion in this country? NOTE: Question not asked in 1972, 1985.

Responses: GD = A great deal; SM = Only some; HA = Hardly any

		YEAR													
RACE	RESP	'73	'74	'75	'76	'77	'78	'80	'82	'83	'84	'86	'87	'88	'89
WHITE	GD	36%	46%	26%	33%	41%	31%	36%	34%	29%	32%	26%	29%	20%	22%
	SM	47	44	51	47	47	50	45	51	53	49	52	51	47	46
	HA	17	10	23	20	12	19	19	15	18	19	22	20	33	32
# SURVEYED		1255	1273	1236	1272	1290	1302	1268	1279	1363	806	1209	1185	816	850
RACE	RESP	'73	'74	'75	'76	'77	'78	'80	'82	'83	'84	'86	'87	'88	'89
BLACK	GD	38%	40%	29%	31%	46%	35%	45%	27%	31%	31%	30%	30%	28%	19%
	SM	47	44	53	50	43	48	39	52	49	50	51	56	50	53
	HA	15	16	19	19	11	17	16	21	20	19	18	14	23	28
# SURVEYED		176	171	150	116	171	151	132	149	153	110	174	182	111	106
RACE	RESP	'73	'74	'75	'76	'77	'78	'80	'82	'83	'84	'86	'87	'88	'89
OTHER	GD	27%	50%	0%	0%	21%	40%	44%	48%	25%	38%	12%	37%	20%	31%
	SM	64	50	100	89	57	33	56	40	69	31	59	43	53	38
	HA	9	0	0	11	21	27	0	12	6	31	29	20	28	31
# SURVEYED		11	6	4	9	14	15	9	25	16	29	34	49	40	39

TABLE IV: CONFIDENCE IN ORGANIZED RELIGION -- BY AGE

Question: I am going to name some institutions in this country. As far as the people running these institutions are concerned, would you say you have a great deal of confidence, only some confidence, or hardly any confidence at all in them? How much confidence do you have in the people running organized religion in this country? NOTE: Question not asked in 1972, 1985.

Responses: GD = A great deal; SM = Only some; HA = Hardly any

		YEAR													
AGE	RESP	'73	'74	'75	'76	'77	'78	'80	'82	'83	'84	'86	'87	'88	'89
18-23	GD	27%	43%	29%	38%	38%	30%	32%	34%	31%	23%	31%	29%	23%	20%
	SM	52	48	51	42	45	48	47	49	48	58	49	50	46	44
	HA	21	9	20	20	17	2	21	17	21	19	20	20	31	36
# SURVEYED		169	166	169	153	161	161	154	144	126	81	106	123	91	91

TABLE IV: CONFIDENCE IN ORGANIZED RELIGION -- BY AGE (Continued)

Question: I am going to name some institutions in this country. As far as the people running these institutions are concerned, would you say you have a great deal of confidence, only some confidence, or hardly any confidence at all in them? How much confidence do you have in the people running organized religion in this country? NOTE: Question not asked in 1972, 1985.

Responses: GD = A great deal; SM = Only some; HA = Hardly any

		YEAR													
AGE	RESP	'73	'74	'75	'76	'77	'78	'80	'82	'83	'84	'86	'87	'88	'89
24-29	GD	28%	38%	25%	27%	27%	22%	26%	21%	26%	38%	21%	23%	23%	19%
	SM	51	51	47	52	58	58	48	60	54	44	56	61	44	48
	HA	21	11	28	21	14	20	26	18	20	18	22	16	33	33
# SURVEYED		206	208	226	217	202	231	196	242	279	148	211	188	144	139
AGE	RESP	'73	'74	'75	'76	'77	'78	'80	'82	'83	'84	'86	'87	'88	'89
30-35	GD	32%	38%	23%	26%	40%	23%	36%	22%	24%	26%	19%	17%	18%	20%
	SM	55	49	49	50	48	56	46	58	56	61	60	57	54	46
	HA	13	13	28	24	12	22	19	20	20	13	21	25	28	34
# SURVEYED		165	172	163	174	184	225	210	201	234	129	219	216	125	142
AGE	RESP	'73	'74	'75	'76	'77	'78	'80	'82	'83	'84	'86	'87	'88	'89
36-41	GD	32%	44%	19%	30%	37%	37%	32%	30%	27%	32%	20%	29%	14%	21%
	SM	49	44	59	49	49	40	53	54	60	42	55	49	51	48
	HA	18	12	22	21	13	23	15	16	14	26	25	22	35	31
# SURVEYED		168	150	144	145	163	156	147	142	168	122	184	181	123	128
AGE	RESP	'73	'74	'75	'76	'77	'78	'80	'82	'83	'84	'86	'87	'88	'89
42-47	GD	32%	45%	21%	33%	39%	32%	36%	34%	30%	31%	22%	34%	16%	18%
	SM	52	43	57	49	50	52	44	56	55	47	53	51	51	46
	HA	16	11	21	18	11	16	20	10	14	22	26	15	33	36
# SURVEYED		141	150	136	108	141	114	109	117	141	86	137	157	104	103
AGE	RESP	'73	'74	'75	'76	'77	'78	'80	'82	'83	'84	'86	'87	'88	'89
48-53	GD	38%	43%	24%	27%	51%	30%	38%	35%	30%	28%	27%	23%	16%	18%
	SM	52	43	54	52	40	52	46	52	50	51	46	58	53	48
	HA	10	14	22	22	8	18	17	13	19	21	28	19	31	34
# SURVEYED		142	140	128	120	146	128	120	108	113	75	105	120	55	95
AGE	RESP	'73	'74	'75	'76	'77	'78	'80	'82	'83	'84	'86	'87	'88	'89
54-59	GD	48%	51%	28%	32%	45%	46%	39%	41%	34%	32%	29%	39%	20%	25%
	SM	37	44	52	45	45	43	44	45	45	52	53	47	57	38
	HA	16	5	20	23	9	11	17	14	21	16	18	14	23	37
# SURVEYED		145	136	110	128	163	134	130	141	127	73	95	95	61	60

TABLE IV: CONFIDENCE IN ORGANIZED RELIGION -- BY AGE (Continued)

Question: I am going to name some institutions in this country. As far as the people running these institutions are concerned, would you say you have a great deal of confidence, only some confidence, or hardly any confidence at all in them? How much confidence do you have in the people running organized religion in this country? NOTE: Question not asked in 1972, 1985.

Responses: GD = A great deal; SM = Only some; HA = Hardly any

		YEAR													
AGE	RESP	'73	'74	'75	'76	'77	'78	'80	'82	'83	'84	'86	'87	'88	'89
60-65	GD	48%	49%	31%	34%	49%	30%	36%	37%	33%	31%	33%	35%	22%	21%
	SM	36	37	45	41	41	52	47	47	54	53	48	47	41	54
	HA	16	14	24	25	10	17	17	16	13	16	19	18	38	25
# SURVEYED		119	104	102	119	111	103	107	112	125	70	106	97	74	71
AGE	RESP	'73	'74	'75	'76	'77	'78	'80	'82	'83	'84	'86	'87	'88	'89
66+	GD	47%	57%	32%	44%	49%	44%	51%	47%	36%	40%	35%	41%	27%	34%
	SM	39	33	48	47	39	39	34	40	46	37	46	39	41	44
	HA	14	11	20	9	12	17	15	13	18	22	19	19	32	22
# SURVEYED		184	218	208	229	198	209	228	237	213	156	248	234	186	164

****

CONFIDENCE IN THE EDUCATIONAL SYSTEM

TABLE I: CONFIDENCE IN THE EDUCATIONAL SYSTEM -- BY TOTAL POPULATION

Question: I am going to name some institutions in this country. As far as the people running these institutions are concerned, would you say you have a great deal of confidence, only some confidence, or hardly any confidence at all in them? How much confidence do you have in the people running education in this country? NOTE: Question not asked in 1972, 1985.

Responses: GD = A great deal; SM = Only some; HA = Hardly any

	YEAR													
RESPONSE	'73	'74	'75	'76	'77	'78	'80	'82	'83	'84	'86	'87	'88	'89
GD	38%	50%	31%	38%	41%	29%	31%	34%	29%	29%	28%	35%	30%	31%
SM	54	42	56	46	50	56	57	52	57	61	61	56	61	59
HA	8	8	13	16	9	15	13	14	13	11	11	9	9	11
# SURVEYED	1474	1460	1462	1459	1512	1507	1436	1476	1566	956	1444	1441	976	1015

TABLE II: CONFIDENCE IN THE EDUCATIONAL SYSTEM -- BY SEX

Question: I am going to name some institutions in this country. As far as the people running these institutions are concerned, would you say you have a great deal of confidence, only some confidence, or hardly any confidence at all in them? How much confidence do you have in the people running education in this country? NOTE: Question not asked in 1972, 1985.

Responses: GD = A great deal; SM = Only some; HA = Hardly any

		YEAR													
SEX	RESP	'73	'74	'75	'76	'77	'78	'80	'82	'83	'84	'86	'87	'88	'89
M	GD	39%	49%	32%	40%	44%	29%	27%	34%	29%	28%	29%	33%	28%	29%
	SM	53	42	53	44	47	55	59	52	56	62	60	58	63	59
	HA	8	8	15	16	9	16	14	14	15	11	11	9	9	12
# SURVEYED		686	685	664	655	685	636	633	633	680	408	609	632	431	437
SEX	RESP	'73	'74	'75	'76	'77	'78	'80	'82	'83	'84	'86	'87	'88	'89
F	GD	36%	50%	31%	37%	39%	29%	33%	34%	29%	30%	27%	37%	32%	32%
	SM	55	42	57	48	52	56	55	53	59	60	62	55	60	58
	HA	9	8	12	15	9	15	12	13	12	11	11	8	9	10
# SURVEYED		788	775	798	804	827	871	803	843	886	548	835	809	545	578

TABLE III: CONFIDENCE IN THE EDUCATIONAL SYSTEM -- BY RACE

Question: I am going to name some institutions in this country. As far as the people running these institutions are concerned, would you say you have a great deal of confidence, only some confidence, or hardly any confidence at all in them? How much confidence do you have in the people running education in this country? NOTE: Question not asked in 1972, 1985.

Responses: GD = A great deal; SM = Only some; HA = Hardly any

		YEAR													
RACE	RESP	'73	'74	'75	'76	'77	'78	'80	'82	'83	'84	'86	'87	'88	'89
WHITE	GD	37%	48%	30%	38%	40%	27%	28%	33%	28%	27%	27%	33%	30%	30%
	SM	55	44	56	46	51	57	59	53	58	61	63	58	62	59
	HA	8	9	13	16	9	16	13	14	14	11	10	9	9	11
# SURVEYED		1282	1281	1296	1324	1324	1337	1289	1299	1390	819	1229	1202	822	869
RACE	RESP	'73	'74	'75	'76	'77	'78	'80	'82	'83	'84	'86	'87	'88	'89
BLACK	GD	44%	66%	41%	41%	54%	41%	53%	39%	34%	35%	36%	48%	30%	36%
	SM	47	28	48	45	39	45	38	49	54	59	50	49	60	50
	HA	9	6	11	13	8	14	9	13	12	7	14	3	10	14
# SURVEYED		179	172	162	126	173	154	137	150	158	107	179	187	112	107
RACE	RESP	'73	'74	'75	'76	'77	'78	'80	'82	'83	'84	'86	'87	'88	'89
OTHER	GD	15%	71%	25%	44%	27%	50%	40%	52%	39%	43%	42%	46%	38%	36%
	SM	77	29	75	44	73	38	50	41	50	50	50	44	52	62
	HA	8	0	0	11	0	13	10	7	11	7	8	10	10	3
# SURVEYED		13	7	4	9	15	16	10	27	18	30	36	52	42	39

TABLE IV: CONFIDENCE IN THE EDUCATIONAL SYSTEM -- BY AGE

Question: I am going to name some institutions in this country. As far as the people running these institutions are concerned, would you say you have a great deal of confidence, only some confidence, or hardly any confidence at all in them? How much confidence do you have in the people running education in this country? NOTE: Question not asked in 1972, 1985.

Responses: GD = A great deal; SM = Only some; HA = Hardly any

		YEAR													
AGE	RESP	'73	'74	'75	'76	'77	'78	'80	'82	'83	'84	'86	'87	'88	'89
18-23	GD	34%	50%	38%	42%	40%	31%	32%	37%	41%	39%	34%	36%	30%	35%
	SM	55	43	54	42	52	54	53	49	52	55	57	58	64	58
	HA	11	7	9	16	7	15	15	14	7	6	8	6	5	6
# SURVEYED		170	168	173	159	164	163	154	147	128	83	108	125	92	93

TABLE IV: CONFIDENCE IN THE EDUCATIONAL SYSTEM -- BY AGE (Continued)

Question: I am going to name some institutions in this country. As far as the people running these institutions are concerned, would you say you have a great deal of confidence, only some confidence, or hardly any confidence at all in them? How much confidence do you have in the people running education in this country? NOTE: Question not asked in 1972, 1985.

Responses: GD = A great deal; SM = Only some; HA = Hardly any

		YEAR													
AGE	RESP	'73	'74	'75	'76	'77	'78	'80	'82	'83	'84	'86	'87	'88	'89
24-29	GD	26%	47%	30%	42%	37%	25%	28%	27%	31%	31%	28%	32%	33%	25%
	SM	62	45	59	49	53	61	56	54	52	56	60	59	60	64
	HA	12	8	11	9	10	14	15	19	17	12	12	9	6	10
# SURVEYED		209	208	231	223	204	241	202	244	284	147	214	191	144	138
AGE	RESP	'73	'74	'75	'76	'77	'78	'80	'82	'83	'84	'86	'87	'88	'89
30-35	GD	32%	47%	30%	37%	40%	22%	28%	26%	20%	21%	24%	29%	30%	34%
	SM	60	45	55	49	51	64	60	56	64	68	67	62	62	60
	HA	8	8	15	14	9	14	12	18	16	12	9	9	8	6
# SURVEYED		164	175	170	185	188	229	212	202	234	130	220	220	125	143
AGE	RESP	'73	'74	'75	'76	'77	'78	'80	'82	'83	'84	'86	'87	'88	'89
36-41	GD	32%	48%	33%	37%	36%	32%	28%	27%	27%	20%	21%	31%	26%	28%
	SM	62	40	53	49	58	53	59	55	60	69	66	58	66	62
	HA	6	11	14	14	7	15	13	18	13	11	13	10	8	10
# SURVEYED		170	149	151	155	168	158	149	145	173	124	187	185	126	130
AGE	RESP	'73	'74	'75	'76	'77	'78	'80	'82	'83	'84	'86	'87	'88	'89
42-47	GD	40%	48%	27%	40%	37%	28%	30%	34%	28%	24%	26%	34%	31%	23%
	SM	50	44	59	41	53	61	60	61	58	66	63	59	59	67
	HA	10	8	15	19	10	11	10	5	14	10	12	6	10	10
# SURVEYED		146	151	143	113	144	119	113	118	144	87	139	157	102	106
AGE	RESP	'73	'74	'75	'76	'77	'78	'80	'82	'83	'84	'86	'87	'88	'89
48-53	GD	34%	40%	29%	30%	59%	27%	31%	40%	24%	29%	25%	29%	28%	20%
	SM	61	52	61	57	39	57	57	53	61	67	64	60	58	66
	HA	5	8	10	13	3	16	12	7	15	4	10	12	14	14
# SURVEYED		150	146	138	127	152	132	121	110	115	75	107	126	57	95
AGE	RESP	'73	'74	'75	'76	'77	'78	'80	'82	'83	'84	'86	'87	'88	'89
54-59	GD	50%	51%	31%	40%	40%	35%	35%	38%	29%	29%	43%	46%	29%	39%
	SM	43	40	58	45	52	53	53	50	58	55	46	44	63	53
	HA	7	9	11	15	8	12	12	13	12	16	10	10	8	8
# SURVEYED		155	138	122	126	166	135	133	141	129	75	97	96	63	62

TABLE IV: CONFIDENCE IN THE EDUCATIONAL SYSTEM -- BY AGE (Continued)

Question: I am going to name some institutions in this country. As far as the people running these institutions are concerned, would you say you have a great deal of confidence, only some confidence, or hardly any confidence at all in them? How much confidence do you have in the people running education in this country? NOTE: Question not asked in 1972, 1985.

Responses: GD = A great deal; SM = Only some; HA = Hardly any

		YEAR													
AGE	RESP	'73	'74	'75	'76	'77	'78	'80	'82	'83	'84	'86	'87	'88	'89
60-65	GD	49%	58%	36%	36%	34%	25%	26%	33%	28%	32%	26%	37%	26%	37%
	SM	48	30	49	43	57	58	62	55	59	56	61	55	60	47
	HA	3	12	15	21	9	17	12	12	13	13	13	8	14	16
# SURVEYED		115	106	107	129	116	105	116	111	127	72	109	98	77	73
AGE	RESP	'73	'74	'75	'76	'77	'78	'80	'82	'83	'84	'86	'87	'88	'89
66+	GD	48%	59%	31%	39%	46%	36%	35%	46%	35%	35%	32%	46%	32%	38%
	SM	43	35	51	40	40	42	53	44	56	55	58	46	59	47
	HA	8	6	17	21	14	22	11	10	9	10	11	8	9	14
# SURVEYED		191	213	223	238	203	218	227	248	226	157	257	238	186	173

****

CONFIDENCE IN THE U.S. PRESIDENT

TABLE I: CONFIDENCE IN THE U.S. PRESIDENT -- BY TOTAL POPULATION

Question: I am going to name some institutions in this country. As far as the people running these institutions are concerned, would you say you have a great deal of confidence, only some confidence, or hardly any confidence at all in them? How much confidence do you have in the executive branch of the federal government in this country? NOTE: Question not asked in 1972, 1985.

Responses: GD = A great deal; SM = Only some; HA = Hardly any

	YEAR													
RESPONSE	'73	'74	'75	'76	'77	'78	'80	'82	'83	'84	'86	'87	'88	'89
GD	30%	14%	14%	14%	29%	13%	13%	20%	13%	19%	21%	19%	17%	21%
SM	51	43	56	60	56	61	52	55	56	52	55	53	55	57
HA	19	43	30	26	15	26	35	25	30	29	24	27	28	23
# SURVEYED	1469	1450	1450	1449	1477	1479	1416	1465	1545	954	1427	1416	960	984

TABLE II: CONFIDENCE IN THE U.S. PRESIDENT -- BY SEX

Question: I am going to name some institutions in this country. As far as the people running these institutions are concerned, would you say you have a great deal of confidence, only some confidence, or hardly any confidence at all in them? How much confidence do you have in the executive branch of the federal government in this country? NOTE: Question not asked in 1972, 1985.

Responses: GD = A great deal; SM = Only some; HA = Hardly any

		YEAR													
SEX	RESP	'73	'74	'75	'76	'77	'78	'80	'82	'83	'84	'86	'87	'88	'89
M	GD	32%	15%	15%	16%	30%	14%	12%	21%	16%	21%	23%	21%	20%	20%
	SM	49	40	50	57	57	59	49	54	52	50	53	50	52	57
	HA	19	45	36	26	13	27	39	25	32	29	24	29	28	24
# SURVEYED		690	678	660	651	675	632	634	634	679	407	607	625	427	431
SEX	RESP	'73	'74	'75	'76	'77	'78	'80	'82	'83	'84	'86	'87	'88	'89
F	GD	28%	13%	13%	12%	28%	12%	13%	19%	11%	18%	20%	18%	15%	21%
	SM	54	47	61	63	56	63	54	56	59	53	56	56	58	57
	HA	18	41	26	25	16	25	32	25	29	29	24	26	27	22
# SURVEYED		779	772	790	798	802	847	782	831	866	547	820	791	533	553

TABLE III: CONFIDENCE IN THE U.S. PRESIDENT -- BY RACE

Question: I am going to name some institutions in this country. As far as the people running these institutions are concerned, would you say you have a great deal of confidence, only some confidence, or hardly any confidence at all in them? How much confidence do you have in the executive branch of the federal government in this country? NOTE: Question not asked in 1972, 1985.

Responses: GD = A great deal; SM = Only some; HA = Hardly any

		YEAR													
RACE	RESP	'73	'74	'75	'76	'77	'78	'80	'82	'83	'84	'86	'87	'88	'89
WHITE	GD	32%	14%	14%	15%	28%	12%	12%	21%	14%	19%	22%	20%	18%	22%
	SM	51	43	57	61	56	61	52	56	56	52	56	54	56	56
	HA	17	43	30	24	15	26	36	23	30	29	23	26	27	22
# SURVEYED		1279	1273	1292	1316	1295	1311	1273	1290	1373	820	1216	1191	808	844
RACE	RESP	'73	'74	'75	'76	'77	'78	'80	'82	'83	'84	'86	'87	'88	'89
BLACK	GD	13%	12%	14%	3%	34%	15%	15%	8%	6%	14%	15%	12%	13%	10%
	SM	54	46	52	55	53	63	56	50	53	52	49	52	49	56
	HA	33	42	34	42	13	22	29	42	41	34	35	36	39	35
# SURVEYED		178	170	154	125	168	153	134	151	157	107	175	176	111	104
RACE	RESP	'73	'74	'75	'76	'77	'78	'80	'82	'83	'84	'86	'87	'88	'89
OTHER	GD	17%	29%	50%	0%	14%	33%	22%	33%	27%	30%	28%	20%	17%	17%
	SM	58	43	0	88	71	40	56	46	67	52	50	55	66	67
	HA	25	29	50	13	14	27	22	21	7	19	22	24	17	17
# SURVEYED		12	7	4	8	14	15	9	24	15	27	36	49	41	36

TABLE IV: CONFIDENCE IN THE U.S. PRESIDENT -- BY AGE

Question: I am going to name some institutions in this country. As far as the people running these institutions are concerned, would you say you have a great deal of confidence, only some confidence, or hardly any confidence at all in them? How much confidence do you have in the executive branch of the federal government in this country? NOTE: Question not asked in 1972, 1985.

Responses: GD = A great deal; SM = Only some; HA = Hardly any

		YEAR													
AGE	RESP	'73	'74	'75	'76	'77	'78	'80	'82	'83	'84	'86	'87	'88	'89
18-23	GD	26%	11%	15%	9%	27%	15%	13%	10%	10%	23%	28%	26%	19%	31%
	SM	48	48	55	66	55	60	55	63	65	51	56	54	60	53
	HA	26	41	30	25	18	25	32	27	25	26	16	20	20	16
# SURVEYED		170	166	171	159	162	162	152	146	124	82	107	123	88	91

TABLE IV: CONFIDENCE IN THE U.S. PRESIDENT -- BY AGE (Continued)

Question: I am going to name some institutions in this country. As far as the people running these institutions are concerned, would you say you have a great deal of confidence, only some confidence, or hardly any confidence at all in them? How much confidence do you have in the executive branch of the federal government in this country? NOTE: Question not asked in 1972, 1985.

Responses: GD = A great deal; SM = Only some; HA = Hardly any

		YEAR													
AGE	RESP	'73	'74	'75	'76	'77	'78	'80	'82	'83	'84	'86	'87	'88	'89
24-29	GD	24%	7%	9%	14%	25%	13%	12%	15%	12%	19%	22%	16%	20%	18%
	SM	50	44	56	66	62	57	55	60	59	49	55	58	54	59
	HA	26	49	35	21	13	30	33	25	29	32	22	27	26	23
# SURVEYED		208	209	227	222	200	237	199	239	280	146	210	187	139	136
AGE	RESP	'73	'74	'75	'76	'77	'78	'80	'82	'83	'84	'86	'87	'88	'89
30-35	GD	29%	8%	8%	14%	23%	11%	10%	20%	11%	15%	16%	16%	20%	19%
	SM	52	42	61	64	59	66	55	53	55	53	58	58	45	57
	HA	18	50	30	21	18	23	35	27	34	32	26	26	34	24
# SURVEYED		164	173	165	183	185	228	207	203	232	132	219	218	122	140
AGE	RESP	'73	'74	'75	'76	'77	'78	'80	'82	'83	'84	'86	'87	'88	'89
36-41	GD	29%	11%	18%	15%	25%	13%	7%	20%	14%	20%	20%	15%	20%	18%
	SM	55	50	54	60	59	64	58	54	55	45	54	52	49	59
	HA	16	39	28	25	16	23	34	27	31	35	26	33	31	23
# SURVEYED		170	150	148	156	164	157	148	143	169	123	186	185	126	128
AGE	RESP	'73	'74	'75	'76	'77	'78	'80	'82	'83	'84	'86	'87	'88	'89
42-47	GD	29%	17%	11%	11%	26%	10%	15%	19%	15%	15%	19%	26%	14%	15%
	SM	54	40	68	67	59	63	50	48	50	54	55	48	57	67
	HA	17	43	21	22	16	27	35	33	35	31	25	26	29	18
# SURVEYED		146	150	141	108	141	115	112	116	142	87	139	152	102	99
AGE	RESP	'73	'74	'75	'76	'77	'78	'80	'82	'83	'84	'86	'87	'88	'89
48-53	GD	29%	14%	15%	14%	34%	13%	10%	26%	17%	15%	22%	16%	13%	25%
	SM	56	36	58	64	57	66	55	58	47	59	59	53	53	54
	HA	16	50	27	22	9	22	35	17	36	27	19	31	35	21
# SURVEYED		147	143	137	125	152	128	119	109	114	75	105	124	55	92
AGE	RESP	'73	'74	'75	'76	'77	'78	'80	'82	'83	'84	'86	'87	'88	'89
54-59	GD	37%	22%	14%	17%	34%	14%	13%	28%	13%	15%	19%	21%	14%	16%
	SM	49	42	53	52	52	63	46	51	61	49	58	50	65	48
	HA	14	37	33	31	13	23	42	21	26	36	24	29	21	36
# SURVEYED		153	134	123	126	164	133	136	140	127	74	97	96	63	58

TABLE IV: CONFIDENCE IN THE U.S. PRESIDENT -- BY AGE (Continued)

Question: I am going to name some institutions in this country. As far as the people running these institutions are concerned, would you say you have a great deal of confidence, only some confidence, or hardly any confidence at all in them? How much confidence do you have in the executive branch of the federal government in this country? NOTE: Question not asked in 1972, 1985.

Responses: GD = A great deal; SM = Only some; HA = Hardly any

		YEAR													
AGE	RESP	'73	'74	'75	'76	'77	'78	'80	'82	'83	'84	'86	'87	'88	'89
60-65	GD	30%	20%	16%	16%	30%	12%	14%	16%	13%	29%	24%	15%	9%	14%
	SM	51	46	54	52	53	63	36	61	55	54	50	59	63	59
	HA	19	34	30	33	17	25	50	24	33	17	26	26	28	26
# SURVEYED		118	104	111	128	110	99	113	114	128	72	110	95	75	69
AGE	RESP	'73	'74	'75	'76	'77	'78	'80	'82	'83	'84	'86	'87	'88	'89
66+	GD	39%	21%	18%	16%	35%	15%	17%	25%	16%	20%	23%	23%	17%	25%
	SM	47	41	49	53	51	56	53	52	58	54	50	50	58	53
	HA	14	38	33	31	14	30	30	24	26	26	28	27	25	22
# SURVEYED		189	215	224	237	194	213	222	246	223	158	248	231	186	169

****

CONFIDENCE IN FINANCIAL INSTITUTIONS

TABLE I: CONFIDENCE IN FINANCIAL INSTITUTIONS -- BY TOTAL POPULATION

Question: I am going to name some institutions in this country. As far as the people running these institutions are concerned, would you say you have a great deal of confidence, only some confidence, or hardly any confidence at all in them? How much confidence do you have in the people running banks and financial institutions in this country? NOTE: Question not asked in 1972-1974, 1985.

Responses: GD = A great deal; SM = Only some; HA = Hardly any

	YEAR											
RESPONSE	'75	'76	'77	'78	'80	'82	'83	'84	'86	'87	'88	'89
GD	33%	41%	43%	33%	33%	27%	24%	33%	21%	28%	27%	19%
SM	56	49	48	55	52	56	60	56	61	58	59	61
HA	11	10	9	12	16	17	16	11	18	14	14	20
# SURVEYED	1444	1456	1499	1507	1423	1472	1561	953	1440	1432	971	997

TABLE II: CONFIDENCE IN FINANCIAL INSTITUTIONS -- BY SEX

Question: I am going to name some institutions in this country. As far as the people running these institutions are concerned, would you say you have a great deal of confidence, only some confidence, or hardly any confidence at all in them? How much confidence do you have in the people running banks and financial institutions in this country? NOTE: Question not asked in 1972-1974, 1985.

Responses: GD = A great deal; SM = Only some; HA = Hardly any

		YEAR											
SEX	RESP	'75	'76	'77	'78	'80	'82	'83	'84	'86	'87	'88	'89
M	GD	32%	39%	41%	36%	31%	27%	24%	30%	20%	28%	27%	17%
	SM	53	48	48	51	53	52	59	56	60	56	59	60
	HA	16	13	11	14	16	21	17	13	20	17	15	24
# SURVEYED		653	654	685	635	634	631	680	407	612	629	427	435
SEX	RESP	'75	'76	'77	'78	'80	'82	'83	'84	'86	'87	'88	'89
F	GD	34%	42%	44%	32%	33%	27%	24%	34%	22%	28%	28%	22%
	SM	58	50	49	58	51	59	60	57	61	60	59	62
	HA	8	8	7	11	15	13	15	9	17	12	13	17
# SURVEYED		791	802	814	872	789	841	881	546	828	803	544	562

TABLE III: CONFIDENCE IN FINANCIAL INSTITUTIONS -- BY RACE

Question: I am going to name some institutions in this country. As far as the people running these institutions are concerned, would you say you have a great deal of confidence, only some confidence, or hardly any confidence at all in them? How much confidence do you have in the people running banks and financial institutions in this country? NOTE: Question not asked in 1972-1974, 1985.

Responses: GD = A great deal; SM = Only some; HA = Hardly any

		YEAR											
RACE	RESP	'75	'76	'77	'78	'80	'82	'83	'84	'86	'87	'88	'89
WHITE	GD	33%	42%	44%	34%	33%	28%	24%	33%	22%	27%	27%	19%
	SM	55	49	48	55	51	57	61	56	60	58	59	61
	HA	11	9	8	11	16	16	15	10	18	15	14	20
# SURVEYED		1283	1325	1314	1337	1286	1296	1387	817	1230	1198	817	856
RACE	RESP	'75	'76	'77	'78	'80	'82	'83	'84	'86	'87	'88	'89
BLACK	GD	29%	29%	37%	31%	27%	25%	22%	28%	19%	28%	30%	17%
	SM	59	46	50	53	59	51	52	56	63	60	57	61
	HA	12	25	13	16	14	24	25	16	18	12	13	22
# SURVEYED		157	122	170	154	127	149	157	107	175	181	113	106
RACE	RESP	'75	'76	'77	'78	'80	'82	'83	'84	'86	'87	'88	'89
OTHER	GD	25%	11%	13%	19%	40%	26%	29%	24%	17%	40%	24%	29%
	SM	75	89	67	63	50	56	59	62	63	51	66	60
	HA	0	0	20	19	10	19	12	14	20	9	10	11
# SURVEYED		4	9	15	16	10	27	17	29	35	53	41	35

TABLE IV: CONFIDENCE IN FINANCIAL INSTITUTIONS -- BY AGE

Question: I am going to name some institutions in this country. As far as the people running these institutions are concerned, would you say you have a great deal of confidence, only some confidence, or hardly any confidence at all in them? How much confidence do you have in the people running banks and financial institutions in this country? NOTE: Question not asked in 1972-1974, 1985.

Responses: GD = A great deal; SM = Only some; HA = Hardly any

		YEAR											
AGE	RESP	'75	'76	'77	'78	'80	'82	'83	'84	'86	'87	'88	'89
18-23	GD	23%	35%	29%	30%	30%	27%	28%	35%	26%	26%	40%	29%
	SM	65	52	58	52	50	49	61	52	60	62	48	59
	HA	12	13	12	19	20	25	11	13	13	12	12	12
# SURVEYED		171	160	161	161	154	146	126	83	106	125	91	91

TABLE IV: CONFIDENCE IN FINANCIAL INSTITUTIONS -- BY AGE (Continued)

Question: I am going to name some institutions in this country. As far as the people running these institutions are concerned, would you say you have a great deal of confidence, only some confidence, or hardly any confidence at all in them? How much confidence do you have in the people running banks and financial institutions in this country? NOTE: Question not asked in 1972-1974, 1985.

Responses: GD = A great deal; SM = Only some; HA = Hardly any

		YEAR											
AGE	RESP	'75	'76	'77	'78	'80	'82	'83	'84	'86	'87	'88	'89
24-29	GD	22%	28%	34%	19%	23%	17%	23%	34%	19%	24%	25%	21%
	SM	62	61	53	60	54	61	57	56	61	58	57	60
	HA	17	11	13	20	23	22	20	10	20	18	18	19
# SURVEYED		229	223	204	240	198	243	282	148	218	187	142	136
AGE	RESP	'75	'76	'77	'78	'80	'82	'83	'84	'86	'87	'88	'89
30-35	GD	26%	36%	33%	26%	25%	19%	14%	31%	17%	22%	24%	13%
	SM	61	53	57	62	56	59	62	52	63	61	59	60
	HA	13	11	11	13	19	22	24	17	20	17	17	26
# SURVEYED		168	182	187	230	211	204	234	131	221	221	121	141
AGE	RESP	'75	'76	'77	'78	'80	'82	'83	'84	'86	'87	'88	'89
36-41	GD	25%	38%	36%	32%	30%	22%	23%	23%	12%	21%	25%	18%
	SM	60	49	54	59	54	61	57	63	67	62	57	60
	HA	15	13	10	9	15	17	20	15	21	17	17	22
# SURVEYED		151	152	166	159	145	144	173	124	183	186	126	127
AGE	RESP	'75	'76	'77	'78	'80	'82	'83	'84	'86	'87	'88	'89
42-47	GD	28%	36%	42%	34%	33%	25%	17%	26%	22%	24%	19%	24%
	SM	65	52	49	57	53	57	68	66	59	61	69	60
	HA	7	13	9	9	14	18	15	8	18	15	12	16
# SURVEYED		140	112	143	118	115	119	143	86	138	156	103	104
AGE	RESP	'75	'76	'77	'78	'80	'82	'83	'84	'86	'87	'88	'89
48-53	GD	32%	37%	55%	37%	31%	29%	25%	24%	23%	29%	30%	13%
	SM	58	53	39	52	58	58	59	64	59	56	57	66
	HA	10	10	6	11	11	13	16	12	18	15	13	22
# SURVEYED		133	127	152	131	119	108	113	74	105	126	56	96
AGE	RESP	'75	'76	'77	'78	'80	'82	'83	'84	'86	'87	'88	'89
54-59	GD	41%	50%	53%	41%	44%	34%	27%	25%	24%	30%	26%	11%
	SM	48	40	42	54	45	52	61	63	63	59	63	66
	HA	12	10	5	5	11	14	13	12	12	11	11	23
# SURVEYED		120	127	165	137	132	142	128	75	98	97	65	62

TABLE IV: CONFIDENCE IN FINANCIAL INSTITUTIONS -- BY AGE (Continued)

Question: I am going to name some institutions in this country. As far as the people running these institutions are concerned, would you say you have a great deal of confidence, only some confidence, or hardly any confidence at all in them? How much confidence do you have in the people running banks and financial institutions in this country? NOTE: Question not asked in 1972-1974, 1985.

Responses: GD = A great deal; SM = Only some; HA = Hardly any

		YEAR											
AGE	RESP	'75	'76	'77	'78	'80	'82	'83	'84	'86	'87	'88	'89
60-65	GD	58%	52%	51%	37%	35%	27%	20%	34%	14%	33%	31%	18%
	SM	34	41	41	58	53	64	67	61	66	51	53	61
	HA	8	7	9	5	12	9	13	6	20	16	16	21
# SURVEYED		107	132	116	102	113	113	127	71	111	94	74	72
AGE	RESP	'75	'76	'77	'78	'80	'82	'83	'84	'86	'87	'88	'89
66+	GD	50%	53%	55%	51%	44%	46%	40%	50%	32%	42%	30%	23%
	SM	42	40	39	41	46	48	52	44	53	51	62	59
	HA	8	7	6	8	10	7	9	6	15	7	8	17
# SURVEYED		220	236	199	222	227	243	229	157	254	235	189	166

****

CONFIDENCE IN THE SUPREME COURT

TABLE I: CONFIDENCE IN THE SUPREME COURT -- BY TOTAL POPULATION

Question: I am going to name some institutions in this country. As far as the people running these institutions are concerned, would you say you have a great deal of confidence, only some confidence, or hardly any confidence at all in them? How much confidence do you have in the U.S. Supreme Court? NOTE: Question not asked in 1972, 1985.

Responses: GD = A great deal; SM = Only some; HA = Hardly any

	YEAR													
RESPONSE	'73	'74	'75	'76	'77	'78	'80	'82	'83	'84	'86	'87	'88	'89
GD	33%	35%	32%	38%	37%	29%	26%	32%	28%	34%	31%	38%	36%	36%
SM	51	50	48	46	52	55	53	55	57	53	54	51	53	53
HA	16	15	19	16	11	15	21	13	15	13	15	11	11	11
# SURVEYED	1447	1415	1421	1407	1460	1458	1381	1444	1534	943	1405	1404	948	984

TABLE II: CONFIDENCE IN THE SUPREME COURT -- BY SEX

Question: I am going to name some institutions in this country. As far as the people running these institutions are concerned, would you say you have a great deal of confidence, only some confidence, or hardly any confidence at all in them? How much confidence do you have in the U.S. Supreme Court? NOTE: Question not asked in 1972, 1985.

Responses: GD = A great deal; SM = Only some; HA = Hardly any

		YEAR													
SEX	RESP	'73	'74	'75	'76	'77	'78	'80	'82	'83	'84	'86	'87	'88	'89
M	GD	33%	38%	34%	41%	40%	33%	28%	33%	32%	40%	37%	42%	41%	39%
	SM	49	44	43	42	48	51	50	54	51	45	48	47	49	49
	HA	18	18	24	17	12	16	22	13	17	15	15	11	11	12
# SURVEYED		682	678	655	645	671	628	622	624	677	404	603	627	421	430
SEX	RESP	'73	'74	'75	'76	'77	'78	'80	'82	'83	'84	'86	'87	'88	'89
F	GD	33%	31%	31%	35%	35%	27%	25%	31%	25%	30%	26%	35%	33%	34%
	SM	54	56	53	50	54	58	55	56	61	59	59	55	56	56
	HA	14	13	16	16	11	15	20	13	13	11	14	10	11	11
# SURVEYED		765	737	766	762	789	830	759	820	857	539	802	777	527	554

TABLE III: CONFIDENCE IN THE SUPREME COURT -- BY RACE

Question: I am going to name some institutions in this country. As far as the people running these institutions are concerned, would you say you have a great deal of confidence, only some confidence, or hardly any confidence at all in them? How much confidence do you have in the U.S. Supreme Court? NOTE: Question not asked in 1972, 1985.

Responses: GD = A great deal; SM = Only some; HA = Hardly any

		YEAR													
RACE	RESP	'73	'74	'75	'76	'77	'78	'80	'82	'83	'84	'86	'87	'88	'89
WHITE	GD	33%	36%	33%	38%	37%	30%	26%	32%	28%	36%	32%	40%	38%	38%
	SM	51	49	48	46	52	55	53	56	57	51	55	49	51	51
	HA	16	15	20	16	11	16	21	13	14	13	14	11	11	11
# SURVEYED		1257	1247	1265	1281	1284	1294	1243	1274	1362	812	1204	1175	803	843
RACE	RESP	'73	'74	'75	'76	'77	'78	'80	'82	'83	'84	'86	'87	'88	'89
BLACK	GD	28%	28%	28%	33%	39%	21%	30%	31%	27%	25%	25%	25%	28%	25%
	SM	54	56	55	52	50	66	52	54	56	62	54	69	63	61
	HA	17	17	18	15	11	14	18	15	17	13	21	7	10	14
# SURVEYED		179	163	152	118	164	148	128	146	157	105	166	179	105	105
RACE	RESP	'73	'74	'75	'76	'77	'78	'80	'82	'83	'84	'86	'87	'88	'89
OTHER	GD	18%	60%	50%	50%	42%	75%	50%	50%	40%	38%	34%	40%	30%	36%
	SM	73	40	0	50	50	19	40	42	53	54	46	50	58	56
	HA	9	0	50	0	8	6	10	8	7	8	20	10	13	8
# SURVEYED		11	5	4	8	12	16	10	24	15	26	35	50	40	36

TABLE IV: CONFIDENCE IN THE SUPREME COURT -- BY AGE

Question: I am going to name some institutions in this country. As far as the people running these institutions are concerned, would you say you have a great deal of confidence, only some confidence, or hardly any confidence at all in them? How much confidence do you have in the U.S. Supreme Court? NOTE: Question not asked in 1972, 1985.

Responses: GD = A great deal; SM = Only some; HA = Hardly any

		YEAR													
AGE	RESP	'73	'74	'75	'76	'77	'78	'80	'82	'83	'84	'86	'87	'88	'89
18-23	GD	31%	38%	32%	40%	33%	32%	34%	35%	43%	54%	50%	54%	51%	45%
	SM	60	49	52	49	60	55	54	55	49	35	42	38	41	51
	HA	8	13	16	11	7	13	12	9	8	11	9	8	8	4
# SURVEYED		166	164	167	156	161	163	151	148	126	83	105	123	92	91

TABLE IV: CONFIDENCE IN THE SUPREME COURT -- BY AGE (Continued)

Question: I am going to name some institutions in this country. As far as the people running these institutions are concerned, would you say you have a great deal of confidence, only some confidence, or hardly any confidence at all in them? How much confidence do you have in the U.S. Supreme Court? NOTE: Question not asked in 1972, 1985.

Responses: GD = A great deal; SM = Only some; HA = Hardly any

		YEAR													
AGE	RESP	'73	'74	'75	'76	'77	'78	'80	'82	'83	'84	'86	'87	'88	'89
24-29	GD	31%	36%	35%	39%	42%	25%	29%	34%	30%	38%	36%	39%	43%	39%
	SM	55	55	48	51	49	61	55	52	58	49	53	55	49	52
	HA	14	9	16	10	10	14	16	13	12	13	11	6	9	9
# SURVEYED		210	209	227	217	199	231	196	239	280	147	210	187	138	137
AGE	RESP	'73	'74	'75	'76	'77	'78	'80	'82	'83	'84	'86	'87	'88	'89
30-35	GD	27%	32%	29%	37%	33%	34%	29%	26%	24%	34%	31%	41%	37%	35%
	SM	52	53	56	48	57	57	53	60	64	57	57	49	51	51
	HA	21	16	16	15	10	10	18	15	12	8	12	10	12	13
# SURVEYED		164	171	167	178	182	226	207	200	232	131	219	216	121	144
AGE	RESP	'73	'74	'75	'76	'77	'78	'80	'82	'83	'84	'86	'87	'88	'89
36-41	GD	32%	39%	28%	33%	32%	27%	23%	35%	24%	29%	31%	35%	35%	37%
	SM	56	47	45	47	55	56	60	51	61	55	55	57	56	56
	HA	12	14	27	20	13	17	17	14	15	15	14	8	9	7
# SURVEYED		170	146	149	150	164	157	144	144	172	123	185	182	124	126
AGE	RESP	'73	'74	'75	'76	'77	'78	'80	'82	'83	'84	'86	'87	'88	'89
42-47	GD	37%	33%	34%	34%	32%	33%	21%	26%	23%	28%	29%	38%	30%	34%
	SM	49	52	47	50	55	53	53	63	61	57	56	53	64	57
	HA	14	15	18	16	13	15	26	11	16	15	16	9	6	9
# SURVEYED		146	147	137	112	137	116	114	116	141	86	135	150	100	105
AGE	RESP	'73	'74	'75	'76	'77	'78	'80	'82	'83	'84	'86	'87	'88	'89
48-53	GD	33%	34%	34%	39%	48%	28%	23%	33%	28%	28%	30%	34%	37%	30%
	SM	52	50	48	46	42	53	54	57	52	63	52	53	56	57
	HA	14	16	18	15	11	19	23	10	21	10	18	13	7	13
# SURVEYED		145	143	136	124	149	130	117	107	112	72	105	119	54	92
AGE	RESP	'73	'74	'75	'76	'77	'78	'80	'82	'83	'84	'86	'87	'88	'89
54-59	GD	36%	36%	33%	44%	46%	35%	26%	33%	28%	33%	27%	40%	35%	34%
	SM	42	43	45	40	43	51	50	55	51	52	55	46	52	51
	HA	22	21	22	16	11	14	23	11	21	15	18	14	13	15
# SURVEYED		149	131	121	119	162	133	129	141	127	73	95	95	63	59

TABLE IV: CONFIDENCE IN THE SUPREME COURT -- BY AGE (Continued)

Question: I am going to name some institutions in this country. As far as the people running these institutions are concerned, would you say you have a great deal of confidence, only some confidence, or hardly any confidence at all in them? How much confidence do you have in the U.S. Supreme Court? NOTE: Question not asked in 1972, 1985.

Responses: GD = A great deal; SM = Only some; HA = Hardly any

		YEAR													
AGE	RESP	'73	'74	'75	'76	'77	'78	'80	'82	'83	'84	'86	'87	'88	'89
60-65	GD	27%	34%	33%	42%	31%	27%	18%	31%	30%	31%	25%	27%	24%	24%
	SM	50	53	46	35	54	52	52	56	55	56	61	58	58	62
	HA	23	13	21	23	15	22	29	13	14	13	14	15	18	14
# SURVEYED		115	102	107	120	111	93	109	109	125	71	107	96	78	71
AGE	RESP	'73	'74	'75	'76	'77	'78	'80	'82	'83	'84	'86	'87	'88	'89
66+	GD	38%	32%	31%	33%	35%	26%	27%	32%	28%	34%	25%	34%	33%	38%
	SM	44	47	47	45	52	55	50	53	55	51	55	52	50	45
	HA	19	20	22	22	13	18	23	15	16	15	20	14	17	17
# SURVEYED		178	197	206	227	189	202	206	233	213	153	238	231	174	157

****

CONFIDENCE IN LABOR UNIONS

TABLE I: CONFIDENCE IN LABOR UNIONS -- BY TOTAL POPULATION

Question: I am going to name some institutions in this country. As far as the people running these institutions are concerned, would you say you have a great deal of confidence, only some confidence, or hardly any confidence at all in them? How much confidence do you have in organized labor in this country? NOTE: Question not asked in 1972, 1985.

Responses: GD = A great deal; SM = Only some; HA = Hardly any

	YEAR													
RESPONSE	'73	'74	'75	'76	'77	'78	'80	'82	'83	'84	'86	'87	'88	'89
GD	16%	19%	11%	13%	15%	12%	16%	13%	8%	9%	8%	11%	11%	10%
SM	57	55	58	52	52	49	53	56	51	54	50	54	53	54
HA	27	26	31	36	33	40	31	31	41	37	42	35	37	36
# SURVEYED	1433	1440	1393	1376	1465	1450	1381	1433	1531	954	1386	1383	941	966

TABLE II: CONFIDENCE IN LABOR UNIONS -- BY SEX

Question: I am going to name some institutions in this country. As far as the people running these institutions are concerned, would you say you have a great deal of confidence, only some confidence, or hardly any confidence at all in them? How much confidence do you have in organized labor in this country? NOTE: Question not asked in 1972, 1985.

Responses: GD = A great deal; SM = Only some; HA = Hardly any

		YEAR													
SEX	RESP	'73	'74	'75	'76	'77	'78	'80	'82	'83	'84	'86	'87	'88	'89
M	GD	19%	24%	12%	14%	19%	13%	17%	14%	10%	9%	8%	11%	13%	10%
	SM	55	50	52	47	46	45	47	50	44	50	45	47	47	46
	HA	26	26	36	40	35	41	36	36	45	41	47	41	40	44
# SURVEYED		679	685	645	639	675	628	630	627	677	410	597	625	419	429
SEX	RESP	'73	'74	'75	'76	'77	'78	'80	'82	'83	'84	'86	'87	'88	'89
F	GD	14%	14%	9%	12%	13%	10%	15%	12%	7%	9%	8%	10%	9%	10%
	SM	59	59	63	56	56	51	57	60	56	58	54	59	57	61
	HA	28	26	27	33	31	38	28	28	38	34	38	30	34	29
# SURVEYED		754	755	748	737	790	822	751	806	854	544	789	758	522	537

TABLE III: CONFIDENCE IN LABOR UNIONS -- BY RACE

Question: I am going to name some institutions in this country. As far as the people running these institutions are concerned, would you say you have a great deal of confidence, only some confidence, or hardly any confidence at all in them? How much confidence do you have in organized labor in this country? NOTE: Question not asked in 1972, 1985.

Responses: GD = A great deal; SM = Only some; HA = Hardly any

		YEAR													
RACE	RESP	'73	'74	'75	'76	'77	'78	'80	'82	'83	'84	'86	'87	'88	'89
WHITE	GD	15%	18%	11%	12%	14%	10%	15%	12%	7%	8%	8%	10%	10%	9%
	SM	57	55	58	51	50	48	53	55	50	53	50	52	50	53
	HA	28	27	31	36	35	42	32	33	43	39	42	38	40	37
# SURVEYED		1247	1266	1241	1252	1288	1289	1242	1259	1359	819	1189	1160	796	828
RACE	RESP	'73	'74	'75	'76	'77	'78	'80	'82	'83	'84	'86	'87	'88	'89
BLACK	GD	24%	26%	12%	16%	24%	23%	26%	15%	17%	13%	14%	16%	17%	10%
	SM	55	57	57	53	61	52	50	66	58	69	51	63	64	67
	HA	21	17	30	32	15	24	25	20	25	19	35	21	20	24
# SURVEYED		174	168	148	116	164	147	129	148	156	108	163	176	107	102
RACE	RESP	'73	'74	'75	'76	'77	'78	'80	'82	'83	'84	'86	'87	'88	'89
OTHER	GD	17%	17%	0%	13%	0%	7%	10%	27%	13%	11%	3%	19%	5%	25%
	SM	58	67	50	63	62	86	60	50	63	48	56	62	76	44
	HA	25	17	50	25	38	7	30	23	25	41	41	19	18	31
# SURVEYED		12	6	4	8	13	14	10	26	16	27	34	47	38	36

TABLE IV: CONFIDENCE IN LABOR UNIONS -- BY AGE

Question: I am going to name some institutions in this country. As far as the people running these institutions are concerned, would you say you have a great deal of confidence, only some confidence, or hardly any confidence at all in them? How much confidence do you have in organized labor in this country? NOTE: Question not asked in 1972, 1985.

Responses: GD = A great deal; SM = Only some; HA = Hardly any

		YEAR													
AGE	RESP	'73	'74	'75	'76	'77	'78	'80	'82	'83	'84	'86	'87	'88	'89
18-23	GD	17%	27%	15%	17%	16%	18%	16%	20%	15%	13%	10%	19%	15%	18%
	SM	67	58	68	59	64	54	67	58	65	64	71	63	66	66
	HA	16	14	17	24	20	27	17	21	21	23	19	19	19	16
# SURVEYED		167	166	168	153	160	158	151	142	124	83	104	118	88	88

TABLE IV: CONFIDENCE IN LABOR UNIONS -- BY AGE (Continued)

Question: I am going to name some institutions in this country. As far as the people running these institutions are concerned, would you say you have a great deal of confidence, only some confidence, or hardly any confidence at all in them? How much confidence do you have in organized labor in this country? NOTE: Question not asked in 1972, 1985.

Responses: GD = A great deal; SM = Only some; HA = Hardly any

		YEAR													
AGE	RESP	'73	'74	'75	'76	'77	'78	'80	'82	'83	'84	'86	'87	'88	'89
24-29	GD	10%	12%	7%	14%	15%	13%	18%	16%	10%	16%	13%	10%	19%	12%
	SM	58	64	66	54	54	53	53	59	56	55	55	64	60	62
	HA	32	24	27	32	32	34	30	26	35	28	33	26	22	27
# SURVEYED		209	207	225	210	200	229	193	242	281	146	208	185	139	138
AGE	RESP	'73	'74	'75	'76	'77	'78	'80	'82	'83	'84	'86	'87	'88	'89
30-35	GD	9%	16%	11%	10%	13%	8%	14%	7%	6%	8%	6%	7%	8%	11%
	SM	68	53	54	57	59	56	53	60	54	57	58	63	55	55
	HA	23	31	35	32	28	36	33	32	41	34	36	30	36	34
# SURVEYED		161	174	164	174	182	224	207	202	233	131	214	215	121	137
AGE	RESP	'73	'74	'75	'76	'77	'78	'80	'82	'83	'84	'86	'87	'88	'89
36-41	GD	10%	13%	9%	14%	12%	7%	10%	11%	5%	6%	7%	9%	9%	5%
	SM	59	55	56	52	50	50	59	49	51	50	47	58	53	54
	HA	31	32	35	34	39	43	32	41	44	45	46	33	38	41
# SURVEYED		166	149	142	142	165	155	145	142	167	123	182	182	122	126
AGE	RESP	'73	'74	'75	'76	'77	'78	'80	'82	'83	'84	'86	'87	'88	'89
42-47	GD	17%	17%	12%	5%	14%	7%	11%	12%	6%	2%	2%	12%	7%	8%
	SM	54	55	54	54	50	43	55	57	46	63	52	41	50	59
	HA	30	28	33	41	36	50	34	31	48	35	46	48	44	33
# SURVEYED		145	148	138	107	141	116	108	117	140	88	135	153	101	99
AGE	RESP	'73	'74	'75	'76	'77	'78	'80	'82	'83	'84	'86	'87	'88	'89
48-53	GD	18%	13%	10%	10%	18%	9%	17%	12%	5%	9%	10%	9%	11%	4%
	SM	53	58	57	54	51	49	53	51	46	53	42	46	53	48
	HA	29	28	33	36	31	42	29	36	49	37	48	44	36	47
# SURVEYED		143	142	128	120	149	129	116	107	112	75	105	117	55	89
AGE	RESP	'73	'74	'75	'76	'77	'78	'80	'82	'83	'84	'86	'87	'88	'89
54-59	GD	26%	22%	10%	11%	19%	14%	18%	12%	10%	4%	8%	16%	11%	3%
	SM	48	56	58	45	50	47	44	53	42	49	42	53	56	54
	HA	26	22	32	43	31	39	38	35	48	47	50	31	32	42
# SURVEYED		149	135	115	122	162	129	131	133	127	74	96	94	62	59

TABLE IV: CONFIDENCE IN LABOR UNIONS -- BY AGE (Continued)

Question: I am going to name some institutions in this country. As far as the people running these institutions are concerned, would you say you have a great deal of confidence, only some confidence, or hardly any confidence at all in them? How much confidence do you have in organized labor in this country? NOTE: Question not asked in 1972, 1985.

Responses: GD = A great deal; SM = Only some; HA = Hardly any

		YEAR													
AGE	RESP	'73	'74	'75	'76	'77	'78	'80	'82	'83	'84	'86	'87	'88	'89
60-65	GD	17%	21%	13%	12%	14%	14%	16%	11%	9%	8%	11%	11%	7%	13%
	SM	55	40	55	52	44	40	44	62	39	50	44	46	51	36
	HA	28	38	33	36	41	45	40	27	52	42	45	43	43	51
# SURVEYED		115	104	104	124	111	99	110	107	126	72	108	93	75	69
AGE	RESP	'73	'74	'75	'76	'77	'78	'80	'82	'83	'84	'86	'87	'88	'89
66+	GD	24%	28%	11%	16%	17%	14%	21%	15%	11%	8%	10%	10%	8%	13%
	SM	49	50	50	41	43	40	47	52	48	48	40	46	40	50
	HA	27	22	39	43	40	46	32	34	41	43	50	44	52	37
# SURVEYED		175	210	207	219	189	204	212	233	214	159	228	221	174	159

****

CONFIDENCE IN CONGRESS

TABLE I: CONFIDENCE IN CONGRESS -- BY TOTAL POPULATION

Question: I am going to name some institutions in this country. As far as the people running these institutions are concerned, would you say you have a great deal of confidence, only some confidence, or hardly any confidence at all in them? How much confidence do you have in the U.S. Congress? NOTE: Question not asked in 1972, 1985.

Responses: GD = A great deal; SM = Only some; HA = Hardly any

	YEAR													
RESPONSE	'73	'74	'75	'76	'77	'78	'80	'82	'83	'84	'86	'87	'88	'89
GD	24%	18%	14%	14%	20%	13%	10%	14%	10%	13%	17%	17%	16%	17%
SM	61	61	60	60	63	65	55	64	66	65	62	65	64	60
HA	15	22	26	26	18	22	35	23	24	22	21	18	20	23
# SURVEYED	1458	1436	1444	1455	1479	1479	1408	1469	1545	957	1428	1413	962	999

TABLE II: CONFIDENCE IN CONGRESS -- BY SEX

Question: I am going to name some institutions in this country. As far as the people running these institutions are concerned, would you say you have a great deal of confidence, only some confidence, or hardly any confidence at all in them? How much confidence do you have in the U.S. Congress? NOTE: Question not asked in 1972, 1985.

Responses: GD = A great deal; SM = Only some; HA = Hardly any

		YEAR													
SEX	RESP	'73	'74	'75	'76	'77	'78	'80	'82	'83	'84	'86	'87	'88	'89
M	GD	25%	20%	15%	15%	20%	14%	9%	12%	12%	14%	18%	17%	16%	18%
	SM	57	58	56	54	59	62	53	62	61	61	57	63	62	56
	HA	18	22	28	31	21	23	38	26	26	25	25	20	22	26
# SURVEYED		689	683	660	657	679	630	629	634	675	406	610	627	426	436
SEX	RESP	'73	'74	'75	'76	'77	'78	'80	'82	'83	'84	'86	'87	'88	'89
F	GD	23%	16%	12%	13%	19%	13%	10%	15%	9%	12%	16%	17%	15%	17%
	SM	64	63	64	65	66	67	57	65	69	68	66	66	66	63
	HA	13	21	24	22	15	20	33	21	22	20	18	17	19	20
# SURVEYED		769	753	784	798	800	849	779	835	870	551	818	786	536	563

TABLE III: CONFIDENCE IN CONGRESS -- BY RACE

Question: I am going to name some institutions in this country. As far as the people running these institutions are concerned, would you say you have a great deal of confidence, only some confidence, or hardly any confidence at all in them? How much confidence do you have in the U.S. Congress? NOTE: Question not asked in 1972, 1985.

Responses: GD = A great deal; SM = Only some; HA = Hardly any

		YEAR													
RACE	RESP	'73	'74	'75	'76	'77	'78	'80	'82	'83	'84	'86	'87	'88	'89
WHITE	GD	26%	18%	13%	14%	19%	13%	10%	13%	10%	13%	17%	17%	16%	18%
	SM	60	61	60	60	63	65	54	64	66	64	63	64	63	60
	HA	14	21	27	26	18	22	36	23	24	23	21	19	21	22
# SURVEYED		1272	1264	1285	1323	1299	1313	1271	1293	1372	822	1224	1183	816	858
RACE	RESP	'73	'74	'75	'76	'77	'78	'80	'82	'83	'84	'86	'87	'88	'89
BLACK	GD	14%	13%	17%	13%	26%	15%	12%	15%	11%	11%	16%	15%	15%	10%
	SM	63	63	63	58	61	66	63	60	61	70	61	73	72	66
	HA	24	24	21	29	13	19	26	26	28	19	23	12	13	25
# SURVEYED		174	165	155	124	167	150	128	151	157	107	171	179	107	105
RACE	RESP	'73	'74	'75	'76	'77	'78	'80	'82	'83	'84	'86	'87	'88	'89
OTHER	GD	8%	29%	25%	0%	8%	25%	0%	24%	25%	25%	21%	22%	21%	28%
	SM	75	71	50	75	69	69	78	56	75	71	58	69	67	50
	HA	17	0	25	25	23	6	22	20	0	4	21	10	13	22
# SURVEYED		12	7	4	8	13	16	9	25	16	28	33	51	39	36

TABLE IV: CONFIDENCE IN CONGRESS -- BY AGE

Question: I am going to name some institutions in this country. As far as the people running these institutions are concerned, would you say you have a great deal of confidence, only some confidence, or hardly any confidence at all in them? How much confidence do you have in the U.S. Congress? NOTE: Question not asked in 1972, 1985.

Responses: GD = A great deal; SM = Only some; HA = Hardly any

		YEAR													
AGE	RESP	'73	'74	'75	'76	'77	'78	'80	'82	'83	'84	'86	'87	'88	'89
18-23	GD	22%	18%	15%	10%	17%	15%	9%	11%	12%	23%	27%	21%	31%	28%
	SM	63	63	61	61	66	60	64	71	66	58	62	66	64	64
	HA	15	19	24	29	17	25	27	18	22	19	11	13	5	8
# SURVEYED		169	166	171	158	162	162	152	147	126	83	107	123	91	89

TABLE IV: CONFIDENCE IN CONGRESS -- BY AGE (Continued)

Question: I am going to name some institutions in this country. As far as the people running these institutions are concerned, would you say you have a great deal of confidence, only some confidence, or hardly any confidence at all in them? How much confidence do you have in the U.S. Congress? NOTE: Question not asked in 1972, 1985.

Responses: GD = A great deal; SM = Only some; HA = Hardly any

		YEAR													
AGE	RESP	'73	'74	'75	'76	'77	'78	'80	'82	'83	'84	'86	'87	'88	'89
24-29	GD	23%	14%	10%	12%	14%	12%	9%	12%	9%	16%	20%	20%	21%	18%
	SM	64	70	62	67	69	62	56	63	66	68	60	65	56	59
	HA	13	16	29	21	17	26	35	25	25	16	20	14	23	23
# SURVEYED		208	207	226	222	199	237	199	241	278	148	213	187	139	140
AGE	RESP	'73	'74	'75	'76	'77	'78	'80	'82	'83	'84	'86	'87	'88	'89
30-35	GD	19%	13%	10%	14%	11%	12%	10%	10%	8%	11%	13%	10%	13%	17%
	SM	65	63	65	62	74	68	55	65	65	66	66	70	70	64
	HA	16	23	25	24	16	20	36	25	27	23	21	21	17	18
# SURVEYED		164	171	165	183	185	227	208	204	232	132	219	220	121	143
AGE	RESP	'73	'74	'75	'76	'77	'78	'80	'82	'83	'84	'86	'87	'88	'89
36-41	GD	27%	24%	14%	10%	12%	14%	6%	13%	8%	11%	11%	13%	14%	17%
	SM	57	51	59	62	68	71	58	64	64	61	62	68	63	56
	HA	17	26	27	28	21	16	37	23	28	28	27	19	22	28
# SURVEYED		168	148	148	156	164	154	145	143	169	122	182	180	125	127
AGE	RESP	'73	'74	'75	'76	'77	'78	'80	'82	'83	'84	'86	'87	'88	'89
42-47	GD	26%	20%	12%	16%	24%	10%	11%	9%	8%	11%	17%	22%	16%	15%
	SM	57	60	65	66	59	71	55	67	68	64	62	64	66	66
	HA	17	21	23	18	17	19	34	24	24	25	20	14	19	19
# SURVEYED		146	146	141	111	139	117	112	119	144	88	138	152	102	105
AGE	RESP	'73	'74	'75	'76	'77	'78	'80	'82	'83	'84	'86	'87	'88	'89
48-53	GD	22%	15%	19%	14%	33%	17%	9%	19%	10%	11%	13%	15%	15%	13%
	SM	62	64	61	57	55	58	52	62	66	68	67	62	75	60
	HA	16	22	20	29	13	25	39	20	24	22	20	23	11	28
# SURVEYED		147	144	135	126	150	130	117	107	113	74	105	123	55	94
AGE	RESP	'73	'74	'75	'76	'77	'78	'80	'82	'83	'84	'86	'87	'88	'89
54-59	GD	28%	21%	17%	15%	25%	20%	7%	18%	9%	7%	16%	23%	19%	15%
	SM	59	55	59	54	56	62	59	56	72	66	63	57	56	63
	HA	13	23	24	31	20	18	34	26	19	27	21	21	25	23
# SURVEYED		152	132	123	124	163	133	134	141	126	74	97	97	64	62

TABLE IV: CONFIDENCE IN CONGRESS -- BY AGE (Continued)

Question: I am going to name some institutions in this country. As far as the people running these institutions are concerned, would you say you have a great deal of confidence, only some confidence, or hardly any confidence at all in them? How much confidence do you have in the U.S. Congress? NOTE: Question not asked in 1972, 1985.

Responses: GD = A great deal; SM = Only some; HA = Hardly any

		YEAR													
AGE	RESP	'73	'74	'75	'76	'77	'78	'80	'82	'83	'84	'86	'87	'88	'89
60-65	GD	22%	17%	17%	18%	20%	11%	9%	16%	12%	14%	15%	13%	3%	14%
	SM	58	61	54	52	60	67	50	66	69	67	65	66	71	55
	HA	20	22	28	30	20	21	41	18	19	19	21	21	26	31
# SURVEYED		116	104	109	131	114	98	112	114	126	72	110	95	76	71
AGE	RESP	'73	'74	'75	'76	'77	'78	'80	'82	'83	'84	'86	'87	'88	'89
66+	GD	28%	19%	14%	16%	25%	12%	15%	17%	16%	13%	18%	18%	12%	18%
	SM	59	58	55	55	56	67	51	61	60	65	60	64	62	57
	HA	14	23	30	29	19	21	33	22	24	22	22	18	25	25
# SURVEYED		184	213	221	239	196	214	221	245	224	160	251	231	185	166

****

CONFIDENCE IN MEDICINE

TABLE I: CONFIDENCE IN MEDICINE -- BY TOTAL POPULATION

Question: I am going to name some institutions in this country. As far as the people running these institutions are concerned, would you say you have a great deal of confidence, only some confidence, or hardly any confidence at all in them? How much confidence do you have in the people running the medical profession in this country? NOTE: Question not asked in 1972, 1985.

Responses: GD = A great deal; SM = Only some; HA = Hardly any

	YEAR													
RESPONSE	'73	'74	'75	'76	'77	'78	'80	'82	'83	'84	'86	'87	'88	'89
GD	55%	61%	51%	55%	52%	46%	53%	46%	52%	52%	47%	52%	52%	47%
SM	40	34	41	36	42	44	39	47	42	42	46	42	42	46
HA	6	5	8	9	6	9	8	8	6	6	8	5	6	7
# SURVEYED	1482	1460	1465	1472	1509	1515	1445	1485	1574	968	1447	1445	984	1015

TABLE II: CONFIDENCE IN MEDICINE -- BY SEX

Question: I am going to name some institutions in this country. As far as the people running these institutions are concerned, would you say you have a great deal of confidence, only some confidence, or hardly any confidence at all in them? How much confidence do you have in the people running the medical profession in this country? NOTE: Question not asked in 1972, 1985.

Responses: GD = A great deal; SM = Only some; HA = Hardly any

		YEAR													
SEX	RESP	'73	'74	'75	'76	'77	'78	'80	'82	'83	'84	'86	'87	'88	'89
M	GD	55%	60%	50%	56%	52%	47%	55%	47%	57%	55%	51%	54%	55%	48%
	SM	38	35	41	33	41	44	37	46	37	40	42	42	39	45
	HA	7	5	9	10	7	9	7	7	6	6	7	4	6	7
# SURVEYED		691	682	664	662	684	638	635	636	684	411	614	630	433	438
SEX	RESP	'73	'74	'75	'76	'77	'78	'80	'82	'83	'84	'86	'87	'88	'89
F	GD	55%	63%	52%	53%	52%	46%	52%	45%	49%	49%	43%	51%	49%	46%
	SM	41	33	41	38	42	45	41	47	45	44	48	43	45	47
	HA	5	4	7	9	6	10	8	8	6	7	8	6	6	7
# SURVEYED		791	778	801	810	825	877	810	849	890	557	833	815	551	577

TABLE III: CONFIDENCE IN MEDICINE -- BY RACE

Question: I am going to name some institutions in this country. As far as the people running these institutions are concerned, would you say you have a great deal of confidence, only some confidence, or hardly any confidence at all in them? How much confidence do you have in the people running the medical profession in this country? NOTE: Question not asked in 1972, 1985.

Responses: GD = A great deal; SM = Only some; HA = Hardly any

		YEAR													
RACE	RESP	'73	'74	'75	'76	'77	'78	'80	'82	'83	'84	'86	'87	'88	'89
WHITE	GD	55%	62%	51%	55%	52%	47%	53%	46%	53%	53%	47%	53%	51%	47%
	SM	39	34	41	36	42	44	40	47	41	41	46	42	42	46
	HA	6	5	8	9	7	9	8	7	6	6	7	5	6	7
# SURVEYED		1288	1282	1300	1337	1322	1344	1297	1307	1397	826	1232	1204	828	869
RACE	RESP	'73	'74	'75	'76	'77	'78	'80	'82	'83	'84	'86	'87	'88	'89
BLACK	GD	52%	58%	55%	53%	53%	45%	54%	42%	46%	44%	42%	49%	55%	43%
	SM	43	39	38	33	43	47	38	49	48	50	48	44	40	50
	HA	5	3	7	13	4	8	8	9	6	6	10	7	4	7
# SURVEYED		182	171	161	126	173	155	138	152	160	112	178	188	114	108
RACE	RESP	'73	'74	'75	'76	'77	'78	'80	'82	'83	'84	'86	'87	'88	'89
OTHER	GD	50%	86%	100%	67%	64%	50%	90%	58%	41%	50%	54%	49%	48%	50%
	SM	50	14	0	33	36	44	10	31	59	43	27	45	45	45
	HA	0	0	0	0	0	6	0	12	0	7	19	6	7	5
# SURVEYED		12	7	4	9	14	16	10	26	17	30	37	53	42	38

TABLE IV: CONFIDENCE IN MEDICINE -- BY AGE

Question: I am going to name some institutions in this country. As far as the people running these institutions are concerned, would you say you have a great deal of confidence, only some confidence, or hardly any confidence at all in them? How much confidence do you have in the people running the medical profession in this country? NOTE: Question not asked in 1972, 1985.

Responses: GD = A great deal; SM = Only some; HA = Hardly any

		YEAR													
AGE	RESP	'73	'74	'75	'76	'77	'78	'80	'82	'83	'84	'86	'87	'88	'89
18-23	GD	69%	76%	68%	64%	60%	56%	64%	54%	68%	65%	60%	64%	65%	60%
	SM	29	23	27	29	33	37	31	40	27	33	34	30	28	32
	HA	2	1	5	7	8	6	6	5	5	2	6	6	7	8
# SURVEYED		170	167	173	160	163	163	154	147	128	83	108	125	92	93

TABLE IV: CONFIDENCE IN MEDICINE -- BY AGE (Continued)

Question: I am going to name some institutions in this country. As far as the people running these institutions are concerned, would you say you have a great deal of confidence, only some confidence, or hardly any confidence at all in them? How much confidence do you have in the people running the medical profession in this country? NOTE: Question not asked in 1972, 1985.

Responses: GD = A great deal; SM = Only some; HA = Hardly any

		YEAR													
AGE	RESP	'73	'74	'75	'76	'77	'78	'80	'82	'83	'84	'86	'87	'88	'89
24-29	GD	62%	67%	53%	57%	54%	51%	53%	44%	58%	54%	54%	60%	59%	54%
	SM	32	29	41	36	42	43	39	46	35	40	40	37	39	41
	HA	6	4	6	8	4	6	7	10	7	5	7	4	1	5
# SURVEYED		209	210	230	225	203	242	202	243	283	149	215	189	143	140
AGE	RESP	'73	'74	'75	'76	'77	'78	'80	'82	'83	'84	'86	'87	'88	'89
30-35	GD	52%	62%	49%	60%	56%	49%	47%	52%	49%	50%	51%	47%	50%	47%
	SM	43	35	43	35	40	42	43	40	46	44	45	50	43	49
	HA	4	3	8	5	4	9	10	8	5	7	5	3	7	4
# SURVEYED		166	172	169	184	187	229	211	203	235	133	219	220	125	143
AGE	RESP	'73	'74	'75	'76	'77	'78	'80	'82	'83	'84	'86	'87	'88	'89
36-41	GD	54%	66%	52%	56%	47%	48%	53%	44%	50%	54%	44%	48%	48%	44%
	SM	40	29	43	36	48	47	42	50	45	42	49	46	48	52
	HA	6	5	5	7	5	5	5	6	5	4	6	6	5	4
# SURVEYED		170	149	152	154	166	159	148	144	171	125	185	186	126	127
AGE	RESP	'73	'74	'75	'76	'77	'78	'80	'82	'83	'84	'86	'87	'88	'89
42-47	GD	50%	54%	41%	53%	49%	42%	55%	47%	50%	57%	35%	54%	53%	39%
	SM	44	42	51	36	48	53	38	49	46	39	59	41	42	52
	HA	6	4	9	11	3	5	7	3	3	5	6	5	5	9
# SURVEYED		146	151	140	114	142	118	115	118	145	88	141	155	103	105
AGE	RESP	'73	'74	'75	'76	'77	'78	'80	'82	'83	'84	'86	'87	'88	'89
48-53	GD	50%	59%	49%	54%	59%	44%	48%	42%	52%	42%	46%	44%	56%	45%
	SM	46	38	43	41	39	39	43	54	41	55	45	50	37	49
	HA	5	3	7	5	2	17	9	4	7	3	9	6	7	5
# SURVEYED		151	143	138	130	153	132	120	109	115	76	107	123	57	95
AGE	RESP	'73	'74	'75	'76	'77	'78	'80	'82	'83	'84	'86	'87	'88	'89
54-59	GD	53%	57%	51%	48%	48%	39%	54%	43%	54%	45%	39%	53%	41%	38%
	SM	42	41	43	45	42	53	38	50	39	45	48	44	55	51
	HA	6	3	6	6	10	8	9	7	7	9	12	3	5	11
# SURVEYED		154	138	123	128	165	135	136	141	130	75	99	98	66	63

TABLE IV: CONFIDENCE IN MEDICINE -- BY AGE (Continued)

Question: I am going to name some institutions in this country. As far as the people running these institutions are concerned, would you say you have a great deal of confidence, only some confidence, or hardly any confidence at all in them? How much confidence do you have in the people running the medical profession in this country? NOTE: Question not asked in 1972, 1985.

Responses: GD = A great deal; SM = Only some; HA = Hardly any

		YEAR													
AGE	RESP	'73	'74	'75	'76	'77	'78	'80	'82	'83	'84	'86	'87	'88	'89
60-65	GD	52%	57%	53%	50%	50%	36%	53%	37%	45%	56%	43%	47%	42%	42%
	SM	40	34	36	39	43	51	41	54	47	36	50	46	51	53
	HA	9	9	12	11	7	12	6	9	8	8	7	6	8	5
# SURVEYED		116	106	112	132	116	105	117	115	129	72	111	97	79	74
AGE	RESP	'73	'74	'75	'76	'77	'78	'80	'82	'83	'84	'86	'87	'88	'89
66+	GD	47%	53%	46%	48%	45%	42%	54%	46%	47%	45%	43%	53%	50%	47%
	SM	44	39	41	32	43	43	40	45	45	43	45	39	40	42
	HA	9	8	13	20	11	15	6	9	8	12	12	8	10	11
# SURVEYED		196	219	224	240	207	225	233	255	231	161	255	247	189	173

****

CONFIDENCE IN THE PRESS

TABLE I: CONFIDENCE IN THE PRESS -- BY TOTAL POPULATION

Question: I am going to name some institutions in this country. As far as the people running these institutions are concerned, would you say you have a great deal of confidence, only some confidence, or hardly any confidence at all in them? How much confidence do you have in the people running the press in this country? NOTE: Question not asked in 1972, 1985.

Responses: GD = A great deal; SM = Only some; HA = Hardly any

	YEAR													
RESPONSE	'73	'74	'75	'76	'77	'78	'80	'82	'83	'84	'86	'87	'88	'89
GD	23%	26%	25%	29%	26%	20%	23%	19%	14%	17%	19%	19%	19%	17%
SM	62	56	57	53	59	59	60	60	62	60	55	57	55	55
HA	15	18	18	18	16	20	18	21	24	23	26	24	26	27
# SURVEYED	1477	1463	1442	1463	1493	1501	1424	1469	1564	959	1438	1433	961	1002

TABLE II: CONFIDENCE IN THE PRESS -- BY SEX

Question: I am going to name some institutions in this country. As far as the people running these institutions are concerned, would you say you have a great deal of confidence, only some confidence, or hardly any confidence at all in them? How much confidence do you have in the people running the press in this country? NOTE: Question not asked in 1972, 1985.

Responses: GD = A great deal; SM = Only some; HA = Hardly any

		YEAR													
SEX	RESP	'73	'74	'75	'76	'77	'78	'80	'82	'83	'84	'86	'87	'88	'89
M	GD	26%	28%	25%	30%	28%	22%	25%	20%	15%	22%	20%	19%	20%	16%
	SM	59	54	54	51	55	59	59	59	60	58	52	57	51	55
	HA	15	18	21	19	17	19	16	21	25	21	28	25	29	29
# SURVEYED		688	683	655	655	675	635	632	630	684	409	613	633	424	436
SEX	RESP	'73	'74	'75	'76	'77	'78	'80	'82	'83	'84	'86	'87	'88	'89
F	GD	21%	24%	24%	28%	24%	20%	21%	18%	13%	14%	17%	19%	18%	18%
	SM	64	58	60	55	62	60	60	61	64	61	58	57	58	56
	HA	15	17	16	17	15	21	19	21	23	25	24	24	24	26
# SURVEYED		789	780	787	808	818	866	792	839	880	550	825	800	537	566

TABLE III: CONFIDENCE IN THE PRESS -- BY RACE

Question: I am going to name some institutions in this country. As far as the people running these institutions are concerned, would you say you have a great deal of confidence, only some confidence, or hardly any confidence at all in them? How much confidence do you have in the people running the press in this country? NOTE: Question not asked in 1972, 1985.

Responses: GD = A great deal; SM = Only some; HA = Hardly any

		YEAR													
RACE	RESP	'73	'74	'75	'76	'77	'78	'80	'82	'83	'84	'86	'87	'88	'89
WHITE	GD	25%	26%	25%	29%	26%	21%	22%	18%	14%	18%	18%	18%	17%	16%
	SM	62	56	56	53	58	59	60	61	62	58	56	57	56	55
	HA	14	18	19	18	16	20	19	21	24	24	26	25	27	28
# SURVEYED		1286	1284	1281	1334	1308	1334	1282	1298	1389	822	1227	1202	810	860
RACE	RESP	'73	'74	'75	'76	'77	'78	'80	'82	'83	'84	'86	'87	'88	'89
BLACK	GD	16%	30%	23%	30%	23%	18%	30%	23%	13%	15%	21%	20%	31%	19%
	SM	61	57	62	51	62	59	60	57	65	69	51	61	48	60
	HA	23	13	15	19	15	23	10	21	21	17	28	19	21	21
# SURVEYED		179	172	157	121	172	152	132	146	159	108	175	179	110	107
RACE	RESP	'73	'74	'75	'76	'77	'78	'80	'82	'83	'84	'86	'87	'88	'89
OTHER	GD	8%	57%	25%	50%	23%	20%	40%	24%	31%	17%	19%	33%	20%	31%
	SM	83	29	75	38	46	67	50	72	56	72	58	46	63	46
	HA	8	14	0	13	31	13	10	4	13	10	22	21	17	23
# SURVEYED		12	7	4	8	13	15	10	25	16	29	36	52	41	35

TABLE IV: CONFIDENCE IN THE PRESS -- BY AGE

Question: I am going to name some institutions in this country. As far as the people running these institutions are concerned, would you say you have a great deal of confidence, only some confidence, or hardly any confidence at all in them? How much confidence do you have in the people running the press in this country? NOTE: Question not asked in 1972, 1985.

Responses: GD = A great deal; SM = Only some; HA = Hardly any

		YEAR													
AGE	RESP	'73	'74	'75	'76	'77	'78	'80	'82	'83	'84	'86	'87	'88	'89
18-23	GD	24%	36%	26%	34%	21%	22%	23%	29%	18%	30%	23%	24%	32%	22%
	SM	61	51	59	46	64	57	61	52	63	56	53	57	43	48
	HA	15	13	15	21	15	21	16	20	19	15	24	19	24	30
# SURVEYED		169	168	172	158	163	161	152	147	127	81	105	124	90	91

TABLE IV: CONFIDENCE IN THE PRESS -- BY AGE (Continued)

Question: I am going to name some institutions in this country. As far as the people running these institutions are concerned, would you say you have a great deal of confidence, only some confidence, or hardly any confidence at all in them? How much confidence do you have in the people running the press in this country? NOTE: Question not asked in 1972, 1985.

Responses: GD = A great deal; SM = Only some; HA = Hardly any

		YEAR													
AGE	RESP	'73	'74	'75	'76	'77	'78	'80	'82	'83	'84	'86	'87	'88	'89
24-29	GD	24%	27%	31%	32%	26%	22%	23%	19%	12%	18%	18%	20%	21%	18%
	SM	61	62	51	52	58	59	63	62	66	63	56	57	57	56
	HA	14	11	18	17	15	18	15	20	22	20	26	23	22	26
# SURVEYED		209	210	228	223	201	239	200	241	282	148	215	188	137	140
AGE	RESP	'73	'74	'75	'76	'77	'78	'80	'82	'83	'84	'86	'87	'88	'89
30-35	GD	20%	23%	26%	36%	23%	24%	27%	15%	14%	20%	22%	18%	14%	20%
	SM	62	62	61	49	61	56	59	68	62	59	55	58	58	52
	HA	18	15	13	15	16	20	14	16	24	21	24	23	28	28
# SURVEYED		163	172	167	183	186	227	212	203	235	133	220	219	120	143
AGE	RESP	'73	'74	'75	'76	'77	'78	'80	'82	'83	'84	'86	'87	'88	'89
36-41	GD	19%	26%	21%	25%	27%	18%	18%	23%	14%	15%	19%	19%	21%	16%
	SM	68	55	60	55	56	61	61	51	62	59	55	58	53	50
	HA	13	19	19	20	18	22	21	26	24	26	26	23	25	34
# SURVEYED		172	150	149	155	165	157	148	143	172	124	185	185	126	129
AGE	RESP	'73	'74	'75	'76	'77	'78	'80	'82	'83	'84	'86	'87	'88	'89
42-47	GD	23%	23%	17%	30%	23%	20%	23%	15%	14%	13%	14%	16%	18%	21%
	SM	63	60	66	57	63	61	60	65	67	57	63	58	52	58
	HA	14	18	17	13	13	19	17	21	19	29	22	26	30	21
# SURVEYED		145	151	138	112	142	118	109	117	145	89	139	156	102	104
AGE	RESP	'73	'74	'75	'76	'77	'78	'80	'82	'83	'84	'86	'87	'88	'89
48-53	GD	25%	17%	24%	22%	26%	20%	22%	16%	14%	17%	22%	14%	21%	13%
	SM	62	58	53	53	64	63	59	60	56	65	51	56	57	65
	HA	13	25	23	25	10	17	19	24	30	17	27	31	21	22
# SURVEYED		149	145	137	128	151	132	120	108	115	75	106	124	56	94
AGE	RESP	'73	'74	'75	'76	'77	'78	'80	'82	'83	'84	'86	'87	'88	'89
54-59	GD	30%	27%	24%	26%	28%	20%	22%	20%	13%	14%	14%	18%	14%	13%
	SM	56	55	58	57	57	60	59	55	60	57	60	57	67	54
	HA	14	18	18	17	15	19	19	25	27	30	26	26	19	33
# SURVEYED		153	137	122	126	164	134	135	142	129	74	97	97	64	61

TABLE IV: CONFIDENCE IN THE PRESS -- BY AGE (Continued)

Question: I am going to name some institutions in this country. As far as the people running these institutions are concerned, would you say you have a great deal of confidence, only some confidence, or hardly any confidence at all in them? How much confidence do you have in the people running the press in this country? NOTE: Question not asked in 1972, 1985.

Responses: GD = A great deal; SM = Only some; HA = Hardly any

		YEAR													
AGE	RESP	'73	'74	'75	'76	'77	'78	'80	'82	'83	'84	'86	'87	'88	'89
60-65	GD	24%	25%	22%	34%	31%	17%	19%	13%	12%	18%	20%	18%	13%	11%
	SM	59	49	55	55	54	62	57	72	59	56	50	59	57	60
	HA	17	26	22	11	16	21	23	15	29	26	30	23	30	29
# SURVEYED		118	104	107	129	114	103	115	115	124	73	112	96	77	72
AGE	RESP	'73	'74	'75	'76	'77	'78	'80	'82	'83	'84	'86	'87	'88	'89
66+	GD	23%	30%	25%	23%	26%	18%	23%	18%	13%	15%	16%	20%	17%	17%
	SM	62	50	53	55	52	59	58	59	63	61	56	53	54	57
	HA	15	20	22	22	22	23	19	24	24	24	28	27	29	26
# SURVEYED		195	220	217	244	200	223	225	245	228	158	252	239	186	166

****

CONFIDENCE IN SCIENCE

TABLE I: CONFIDENCE IN SCIENCE -- BY TOTAL POPULATION

Question: I am going to name some institutions in this country. As far as the people running these institutions are concerned, would you say you have a great deal of confidence, only some confidence, or hardly any confidence at all in them? How much confidence do you have in the people in the scientific community in this country? NOTE: Question not asked in 1972, 1985.

Responses: GD = A great deal; SM = Only some; HA = Hardly any

	YEAR													
RESPONSE	'73	'74	'75	'76	'77	'78	'80	'82	'83	'84	'86	'87	'88	'89
GD	41%	50%	42%	49%	44%	39%	46%	43%	44%	47%	41%	48%	42%	44%
SM	52	42	51	43	50	53	47	51	50	47	51	45	52	49
HA	7	7	7	9	6	8	7	7	6	6	8	6	6	7
# SURVEYED	1353	1324	1328	1314	1403	1401	1322	1356	1492	920	1379	1363	914	937

TABLE II: CONFIDENCE IN SCIENCE -- BY SEX

Question: I am going to name some institutions in this country. As far as the people running these institutions are concerned, would you say you have a great deal of confidence, only some confidence, or hardly any confidence at all in them? How much confidence do you have in the people in the scientific community in this country? NOTE: Question not asked in 1972, 1985.

Responses: GD = A great deal; SM = Only some; HA = Hardly any

		YEAR													
SEX	RESP	'73	'74	'75	'76	'77	'78	'80	'82	'83	'84	'86	'87	'88	'89
M	GD	44%	54%	44%	51%	49%	46%	49%	50%	50%	56%	49%	51%	49%	52%
	SM	49	38	47	41	45	48	45	44	45	40	45	42	45	43
	HA	7	8	10	8	6	7	6	6	4	4	6	7	6	6
# SURVEYED		651	627	610	598	656	601	609	600	656	395	595	605	411	413
SEX	RESP	'73	'74	'75	'76	'77	'78	'80	'82	'83	'84	'86	'87	'88	'89
F	GD	38%	47%	41%	47%	40%	35%	43%	37%	40%	41%	35%	46%	36%	38%
	SM	55	46	54	45	54	56	48	56	54	52	55	49	58	54
	HA	8	7	5	9	6	9	8	7	7	7	10	6	6	7
# SURVEYED		702	697	718	716	747	800	713	756	836	525	784	758	503	524

TABLE III: CONFIDENCE IN SCIENCE -- BY RACE

Question: I am going to name some institutions in this country. As far as the people running these institutions are concerned, would you say you have a great deal of confidence, only some confidence, or hardly any confidence at all in them? How much confidence do you have in the people in the scientific community in this country? NOTE: Question not asked in 1972, 1985.

Responses: GD = A great deal; SM = Only some; HA = Hardly any

		YEAR													
RACE	RESP	'73	'74	'75	'76	'77	'78	'80	'82	'83	'84	'86	'87	'88	'89
WHITE	GD	43%	53%	44%	50%	46%	41%	47%	44%	45%	50%	43%	50%	43%	46%
	SM	51	41	50	42	49	52	47	50	49	45	50	45	51	48
	HA	6	6	7	8	5	7	6	6	6	5	7	6	6	6
# SURVEYED		1178	1176	1181	1203	1235	1246	1190	1197	1326	788	1183	1143	773	811
RACE	RESP	'73	'74	'75	'76	'77	'78	'80	'82	'83	'84	'86	'87	'88	'89
BLACK	GD	25%	25%	28%	26%	34%	26%	35%	26%	33%	28%	25%	39%	42%	26%
	SM	58	54	59	53	55	57	50	59	59	63	57	52	52	62
	HA	17	21	13	20	11	17	15	16	7	10	18	9	6	12
# SURVEYED		165	143	143	103	155	139	122	135	150	104	163	170	103	92
RACE	RESP	'73	'74	'75	'76	'77	'78	'80	'82	'83	'84	'86	'87	'88	'89
OTHER	GD	50%	80%	50%	63%	54%	50%	70%	42%	63%	50%	52%	48%	24%	44%
	SM	40	20	50	38	38	38	20	46	38	39	42	40	68	44
	HA	10	0	0	0	8	13	10	13	0	11	6	12	8	12
# SURVEYED		10	5	4	8	13	16	10	24	16	28	33	50	38	34

TABLE IV: CONFIDENCE IN SCIENCE -- BY AGE

Question: I am going to name some institutions in this country. As far as the people running these institutions are concerned, would you say you have a great deal of confidence, only some confidence, or hardly any confidence at all in them? How much confidence do you have in the people in the scientific community in this country? NOTE: Question not asked in 1972, 1985.

Responses: GD = A great deal; SM = Only some; HA = Hardly any

		YEAR													
AGE	RESP	'73	'74	'75	'76	'77	'78	'80	'82	'83	'84	'86	'87	'88	'89
18-23	GD	42%	52%	50%	56%	44%	34%	43%	48%	54%	53%	47%	46%	50%	46%
	SM	49	40	43	37	48	53	52	45	43	38	48	49	43	49
	HA	9	7	7	7	8	13	5	7	3	9	5	5	7	5
# SURVEYED		162	164	165	147	157	158	147	143	126	81	104	122	90	85

TABLE IV: CONFIDENCE IN SCIENCE -- BY AGE (Continued)

Question: I am going to name some institutions in this country. As far as the people running these institutions are concerned, would you say you have a great deal of confidence, only some confidence, or hardly any confidence at all in them? How much confidence do you have in the people in the scientific community in this country? NOTE: Question not asked in 1972, 1985.

Responses: GD = A great deal; SM = Only some; HA = Hardly any

		YEAR													
AGE	RESP	'73	'74	'75	'76	'77	'78	'80	'82	'83	'84	'86	'87	'88	'89
24-29	GD	43%	56%	45%	44%	42%	39%	53%	46%	48%	51%	47%	54%	49%	53%
	SM	51	39	49	46	51	54	40	45	45	41	47	40	42	41
	HA	6	4	5	9	7	7	7	9	6	8	6	7	9	6
# SURVEYED		201	203	221	209	195	223	191	235	277	146	207	184	136	132
AGE	RESP	'73	'74	'75	'76	'77	'78	'80	'82	'83	'84	'86	'87	'88	'89
30-35	GD	39%	53%	37%	52%	43%	47%	49%	43%	41%	49%	45%	49%	45%	50%
	SM	54	39	55	39	55	48	45	49	53	46	49	45	50	45
	HA	6	8	7	8	2	5	7	8	6	5	6	6	5	5
# SURVEYED		147	159	155	170	176	221	200	194	230	132	218	215	117	140
AGE	RESP	'73	'74	'75	'76	'77	'78	'80	'82	'83	'84	'86	'87	'88	'89
36-41	GD	39%	47%	39%	55%	43%	37%	46%	45%	46%	54%	44%	54%	44%	46%
	SM	55	50	55	40	51	56	48	49	52	44	52	41	50	49
	HA	7	4	6	5	6	7	6	6	2	2	4	6	6	5
# SURVEYED		161	135	142	139	157	150	143	139	168	125	181	179	124	125
AGE	RESP	'73	'74	'75	'76	'77	'78	'80	'82	'83	'84	'86	'87	'88	'89
42-47	GD	40%	41%	44%	48%	44%	44%	41%	36%	42%	41%	39%	49%	33%	37%
	SM	57	49	51	45	52	50	57	59	55	55	53	49	62	55
	HA	4	10	4	8	4	6	2	6	3	4	8	3	5	8
# SURVEYED		141	142	134	101	132	112	105	109	137	80	134	148	97	99
AGE	RESP	'73	'74	'75	'76	'77	'78	'80	'82	'83	'84	'86	'87	'88	'89
48-53	GD	36%	51%	43%	44%	55%	39%	42%	29%	43%	51%	48%	43%	45%	36%
	SM	55	36	46	44	42	56	48	66	53	45	48	48	55	57
	HA	9	14	10	11	3	5	10	5	5	4	5	9	0	7
# SURVEYED		135	132	125	117	144	122	115	97	110	69	103	120	53	84
AGE	RESP	'73	'74	'75	'76	'77	'78	'80	'82	'83	'84	'86	'87	'88	'89
54-59	GD	47%	53%	43%	47%	50%	47%	49%	47%	39%	42%	27%	48%	36%	33%
	SM	44	41	47	43	43	47	40	47	55	53	58	46	59	57
	HA	9	7	10	10	7	6	11	5	6	6	15	7	5	10
# SURVEYED		139	118	108	113	157	129	124	133	119	72	95	92	58	60

TABLE IV: CONFIDENCE IN SCIENCE -- BY AGE (Continued)

Question: I am going to name some institutions in this country. As far as the people running these institutions are concerned, would you say you have a great deal of confidence, only some confidence, or hardly any confidence at all in them? How much confidence do you have in the people in the scientific community in this country? NOTE: Question not asked in 1972, 1985.

Responses: GD = A great deal; SM = Only some; HA = Hardly any

		YEAR													
AGE	RESP	'73	'74	'75	'76	'77	'78	'80	'82	'83	'84	'86	'87	'88	'89
60-65	GD	42%	51%	47%	47%	44%	32%	47%	42%	44%	50%	42%	44%	39%	35%
	SM	48	43	47	43	48	60	47	53	50	47	48	51	56	55
	HA	9	7	5	10	8	8	7	5	7	3	10	5	6	10
# SURVEYED		106	91	95	112	104	87	103	101	119	66	105	94	72	71
AGE	RESP	'73	'74	'75	'76	'77	'78	'80	'82	'83	'84	'86	'87	'88	'89
66+	GD	39%	47%	32%	44%	37%	34%	41%	39%	41%	37%	31%	44%	37%	46%
	SM	54	44	58	47	55	53	52	55	48	53	54	47	56	46
	HA	7	9	10	9	9	13	7	6	12	10	15	9	7	8
# SURVEYED		159	175	179	201	175	192	187	198	199	146	226	205	163	140

****

CONFIDENCE IN TELEVISION

TABLE I: CONFIDENCE IN TELEVISION -- BY TOTAL POPULATION

Question: I am going to name some institutions in this country. As far as the people running these institutions are concerned, would you say you have a great deal of confidence, only some confidence, or hardly any confidence at all in them? How much confidence do you have in the people running the television industry in this country? NOTE: Question not asked in 1972, 1985.

Responses: GD = A great deal; SM = Only some; HA = Hardly any

	YEAR													
RESPONSE	'73	'74	'75	'76	'77	'78	'80	'82	'83	'84	'86	'87	'88	'89
GD	19%	24%	18%	19%	18%	14%	16%	14%	13%	13%	15%	12%	14%	14%
SM	59	59	59	53	57	54	56	58	59	58	57	59	59	56
HA	22	17	23	28	25	32	28	27	29	29	28	29	27	29
# SURVEYED	1480	1464	1451	1464	1502	1498	1442	1483	1566	965	1438	1437	978	1008

TABLE II: CONFIDENCE IN TELEVISION -- BY SEX

Question: I am going to name some institutions in this country. As far as the people running these institutions are concerned, would you say you have a great deal of confidence, only some confidence, or hardly any confidence at all in them? How much confidence do you have in the people running the television industry in this country? NOTE: Question not asked in 1972, 1985.

Responses: GD = A great deal; SM = Only some; HA = Hardly any

		YEAR													
SEX	RESP	'73	'74	'75	'76	'77	'78	'80	'82	'83	'84	'86	'87	'88	'89
M	GD	19%	25%	21%	19%	20%	16%	18%	15%	14%	15%	17%	11%	14%	13%
	SM	58	55	56	49	53	52	55	57	56	58	52	59	58	54
	HA	24	20	24	31	27	32	27	28	30	27	31	29	27	33
# SURVEYED		691	685	654	657	683	631	634	633	685	408	612	630	430	436
SEX	RESP	'73	'74	'75	'76	'77	'78	'80	'82	'83	'84	'86	'87	'88	'89
F	GD	19%	22%	16%	19%	16%	12%	15%	14%	12%	12%	14%	12%	15%	15%
	SM	60	62	61	56	60	57	56	59	60	58	60	58	59	58
	HA	21	16	22	25	25	31	29	27	28	30	27	29	26	27
# SURVEYED		789	779	797	807	819	867	808	850	881	557	826	807	548	572

TABLE III: CONFIDENCE IN TELEVISION -- BY RACE

Question: I am going to name some institutions in this country. As far as the people running these institutions are concerned, would you say you have a great deal of confidence, only some confidence, or hardly any confidence at all in them? How much confidence do you have in the people running the television industry in this country? NOTE: Question not asked in 1972, 1985.

Responses: GD = A great deal; SM = Only some; HA = Hardly any

		YEAR													
RACE	RESP	'73	'74	'75	'76	'77	'78	'80	'82	'83	'84	'86	'87	'88	'89
WHITE	GD	18%	22%	17%	18%	17%	13%	16%	13%	12%	12%	15%	11%	15%	13%
	SM	59	59	59	53	56	55	56	58	59	58	57	59	58	57
	HA	23	18	24	29	27	32	29	28	30	30	29	30	27	31
# SURVEYED		1286	1287	1289	1332	1316	1326	1295	1306	1388	824	1225	1202	824	864
RACE	RESP	'73	'74	'75	'76	'77	'78	'80	'82	'83	'84	'86	'87	'88	'89
BLACK	GD	24%	32%	28%	30%	22%	21%	23%	23%	18%	19%	18%	15%	15%	24%
	SM	60	55	58	50	64	51	55	57	62	59	55	60	57	55
	HA	16	13	13	20	14	28	21	20	20	22	27	25	28	22
# SURVEYED		182	170	158	123	172	156	137	150	160	111	176	182	113	106
RACE	RESP	'73	'74	'75	'76	'77	'78	'80	'82	'83	'84	'86	'87	'88	'89
OTHER	GD	25%	57%	25%	11%	14%	25%	0%	30%	33%	30%	22%	23%	10%	26%
	SM	67	43	75	89	50	69	60	52	39	50	65	51	76	50
	HA	8	0	0	0	36	6	40	19	28	20	14	26	15	24
# SURVEYED		12	7	4	9	14	16	10	27	18	30	37	53	41	38

TABLE IV: CONFIDENCE IN TELEVISION -- BY AGE

Question: I am going to name some institutions in this country. As far as the people running these institutions are concerned, would you say you have a great deal of confidence, only some confidence, or hardly any confidence at all in them? How much confidence do you have in the people running the television industry in this country? NOTE: Question not asked in 1972, 1985.

Responses: GD = A great deal; SM = Only some; HA = Hardly any

		YEAR													
AGE	RESP	'73	'74	'75	'76	'77	'78	'80	'82	'83	'84	'86	'87	'88	'89
18-23	GD	26%	35%	27%	29%	21%	23%	21%	21%	16%	17%	21%	14%	23%	22%
	SM	53	52	55	50	53	52	53	55	63	62	61	64	59	60
	HA	21	13	18	22	26	25	27	24	20	21	19	22	18	18
# SURVEYED		170	166	173	161	163	163	154	148	128	82	107	125	92	93

TABLE IV: CONFIDENCE IN TELEVISION -- BY AGE (Continued)

Question: I am going to name some institutions in this country. As far as the people running these institutions are concerned, would you say you have a great deal of confidence, only some confidence, or hardly any confidence at all in them? How much confidence do you have in the people running the television industry in this country? NOTE: Question not asked in 1972, 1985.

Responses: GD = A great deal; SM = Only some; HA = Hardly any

		YEAR													
AGE	RESP	'73	'74	'75	'76	'77	'78	'80	'82	'83	'84	'86	'87	'88	'89
24-29	GD	15%	20%	20%	21%	17%	12%	12%	12%	14%	18%	19%	12%	15%	20%
	SM	67	64	64	52	55	58	60	56	54	58	52	58	56	51
	HA	18	15	16	27	29	30	28	31	32	24	29	30	30	29
# SURVEYED		207	211	232	223	200	238	201	245	284	149	215	189	142	138
AGE	RESP	'73	'74	'75	'76	'77	'78	'80	'82	'83	'84	'86	'87	'88	'89
30-35	GD	11%	21%	11%	14%	12%	8%	13%	11%	10%	11%	14%	10%	11%	13%
	SM	67	60	60	56	59	56	52	57	57	59	56	58	59	61
	HA	22	19	29	30	29	35	34	32	33	30	30	32	30	26
# SURVEYED		167	173	168	185	187	226	215	203	235	132	218	218	125	144
AGE	RESP	'73	'74	'75	'76	'77	'78	'80	'82	'83	'84	'86	'87	'88	'89
36-41	GD	18%	22%	17%	21%	11%	13%	9%	19%	12%	10%	12%	9%	13%	12%
	SM	61	61	60	53	62	54	65	54	53	59	61	55	53	55
	HA	21	17	23	25	27	34	25	27	35	30	27	37	34	33
# SURVEYED		172	149	148	154	166	157	150	145	170	125	185	186	124	129
AGE	RESP	'73	'74	'75	'76	'77	'78	'80	'82	'83	'84	'86	'87	'88	'89
42-47	GD	19%	17%	11%	14%	17%	13%	15%	10%	10%	11%	10%	5%	6%	13%
	SM	60	63	63	58	56	55	53	57	65	56	59	58	67	62
	HA	20	20	26	28	28	32	32	32	26	33	31	37	27	25
# SURVEYED		144	150	143	113	144	118	113	117	144	89	138	155	104	106
AGE	RESP	'73	'74	'75	'76	'77	'78	'80	'82	'83	'84	'86	'87	'88	'89
48-53	GD	15%	17%	21%	11%	21%	12%	17%	15%	15%	12%	14%	10%	25%	9%
	SM	61	67	56	53	58	56	56	64	56	59	56	61	54	62
	HA	25	16	23	36	22	32	26	22	30	29	30	29	21	29
# SURVEYED		151	145	134	129	151	130	121	110	115	75	108	126	57	93
AGE	RESP	'73	'74	'75	'76	'77	'78	'80	'82	'83	'84	'86	'87	'88	'89
54-59	GD	28%	24%	18%	15%	22%	18%	17%	12%	11%	15%	16%	9%	16%	10%
	SM	53	59	58	60	58	50	54	59	61	55	55	67	63	47
	HA	19	18	24	25	20	32	29	29	28	30	29	24	21	44
# SURVEYED		154	136	122	126	165	136	133	142	128	74	98	97	62	62

TABLE IV: CONFIDENCE IN TELEVISION -- BY AGE (Continued)

Question: I am going to name some institutions in this country. As far as the people running these institutions are concerned, would you say you have a great deal of confidence, only some confidence, or hardly any confidence at all in them? How much confidence do you have in the people running the television industry in this country? NOTE: Question not asked in 1972, 1985.

Responses: GD = A great deal; SM = Only some; HA = Hardly any

		YEAR													
AGE	RESP	'73	'74	'75	'76	'77	'78	'80	'82	'83	'84	'86	'87	'88	'89
60-65	GD	17%	23%	19%	22%	15%	15%	17%	11%	11%	14%	16%	15%	12%	7%
	SM	57	52	59	47	64	48	61	68	61	56	54	59	60	55
	HA	26	25	22	30	21	38	22	20	28	30	30	26	28	38
# SURVEYED		121	105	106	129	117	103	115	114	127	73	111	96	78	71
AGE	RESP	'73	'74	'75	'76	'77	'78	'80	'82	'83	'84	'86	'87	'88	'89
66+	GD	21%	31%	19%	21%	23%	15%	24%	18%	14%	13%	15%	20%	16%	18%
	SM	52	52	53	53	51	56	49	57	64	56	58	57	59	52
	HA	27	17	28	26	26	29	27	24	22	31	27	23	25	30
# SURVEYED		190	223	221	239	202	220	231	250	229	161	252	240	190	170

****

GOVERNMENT AID FOR POOR

TABLE I: GOVERNMENT AID FOR POOR -- BY TOTAL POPULATION

Question: Some people think the government in Washington should do everything possible to improve the standard of living of all poor Americans; they are at point 1 on a scale. Other people think that it's not the government's responsibility, and that each person should take care of himself; they are at point 5. Where would you place yourself on this scale, or haven't you made up your mind on this? NOTE: Question not asked in 1972-1974, 1976-1982, 1985.

Responses: 1) = Government ... 3) = Don't know yet ... 5) = People

	YEAR						
RESPONSE	'75	'83	'84	'86	'87	'88	'89
1	30%	18%	18%	19%	17%	18%	17%
2	10	15	11	13	12	13	15
3	36	41	47	46	46	45	45
4	11	14	15	12	14	12	14
5	13	12	9	11	11	12	9
# SURVEYED	1448	1530	1409	1430	1421	971	999

TABLE II: GOVERNMENT AID FOR POOR -- BY SEX

Question: Some people think the government in Washington should do everything possible to improve the standard of living of all poor Americans; they are at point 1 on a scale. Other people think that it's not the government's responsibility, and that each person should take care of himself; they are at point 5. Where would you place yourself on this scale, or haven't you made up your mind on this? NOTE: Question not asked in 1972-1974, 1976-1982, 1985.

Responses: 1) = Government ... 3) = Don't know yet ... 5) = People

SEX	RESP	'75	'83	'84	'86	'87	'88	'89
MALE	1	28%	15%	17%	15%	17%	14%	15%
	2	10	16	12	14	13	15	15
	3	34	39	41	45	43	41	41
	4	12	15	20	14	17	15	19
	5	16	14	10	12	10	14	10
# SURVEYED		652	665	584	609	623	425	430

SEX	RESP	'75	'83	'84	'86	'87	'88	'89
FEMALE	1	32%	19%	18%	22%	17%	20%	18%
	2	10	15	11	12	12	11	16
	3	38	43	51	46	48	49	47
	4	9	13	11	10	11	10	10
	5	11	10	8	10	12	10	8
# SURVEYED		796	865	825	821	798	546	569

TABLE III: GOVERNMENT AID FOR POOR -- BY RACE

Question: Some people think the government in Washington should do everything possible to improve the standard of living of all poor Americans; they are at point 1 on a scale. Other people think that it's not the government's responsibility, and that each person should take care of himself; they are at point 5. Where would you place yourself on this scale, or haven't you made up your mind on this? NOTE: Question not asked in 1972-1974, 1976-1982, 1985.

Responses: 1) = Government ... 3) = Don't know yet ... 5) = People

RACE	RESP	'75	'83	'84	'86	'87	'88	'89
WHITE	1	26%	14%	15%	15%	14%	13%	15%
	2	10	15	11	13	12	13	15
	3	37	42	48	47	47	47	44
	4	12	15	17	13	15	13	16
	5	14	13	9	12	12	13	10
# SURVEYED		1286	1357	1196	1218	1185	816	852
RACE	RESP	'75	'83	'84	'86	'87	'88	'89
BLACK	1	61%	43%	36%	43%	38%	42%	33%
	2	9	18	15	14	15	16	18
	3	23	31	42	36	35	33	44
	4	3	4	3	5	8	7	1
	5	4	3	4	3	5	3	5
# SURVEYED		158	157	163	176	184	113	107

RACE	RESP	'75	'83	'84	'86	'87	'88	'89
OTHER	1	25%	25%	30%	33%	19%	36%	18%
	2	0	13	14	8	13	7	18
	3	25	44	40	53	48	43	58
	4	0	6	8	0	6	12	3
	5	50	13	8	6	13	2	5
# SURVEYED		4	16	50	36	52	42	40

TABLE IV: GOVERNMENT AID FOR POOR -- BY AGE

Question: Some people think the government in Washington should do everything possible to improve the standard of living of all poor Americans; they are at point 1 on a scale. Other people think that it's not the government's responsibility, and that each person should take care of himself; they are at point 5. Where would you place yourself on this scale, or haven't you made up your mind on this? NOTE: Question not asked in 1972-1974, 1976-1982, 1985.

Responses: 1) = Government ... 3) = Don't know yet ... 5) = People

		YEAR						
AGE	RESP	'75	'83	'84	'86	'87	'88	'89
18-23	1	31%	17%	16%	15%	17%	16%	16%
	2	19	18	18	17	24	13	28
	3	37	42	48	47	38	47	44
	4	8	14	16	16	16	12	9
	5	5	9	3	6	6	12	2
# SURVEYED		165	127	154	103	122	93	88
AGE	RESP	'75	'83	'84	'86	'87	'88	'89
24-29	1	29%	17%	19%	21%	22%	16%	14%
	2	14	20	12	12	14	19	23
	3	37	44	47	45	43	46	43
	4	13	14	18	15	15	11	14
	5	8	6	4	8	6	8	5
# SURVEYED		228	280	226	217	190	143	138
AGE	RESP	'75	'83	'84	'86	'87	'88	'89
30-35	1	32%	16%	18%	17%	14%	15%	15%
	2	9	18	15	21	16	19	19
	3	35	43	45	46	49	46	42
	4	15	15	17	12	16	12	16
	5	10	8	5	4	4	8	8
# SURVEYED		165	231	189	213	215	124	142
AGE	RESP	'75	'83	'84	'86	'87	'88	'89
36-41	1	32%	14%	18%	16%	12%	20%	18%
	2	6	17	12	14	14	15	12
	3	39	37	45	48	50	38	47
	4	10	16	16	15	17	17	15
	5	13	16	9	8	7	10	8
# SURVEYED		149	163	181	183	183	122	129

		YEAR						
AGE	RESP	'75	'83	'84	'86	'87	'88	'89
42-47	1	24%	20%	13%	17%	21%	21%	14%
	2	11	9	13	9	10	9	2
	3	35	41	47	54	46	50	4
	4	15	20	14	9	12	8	2
	5	15	10	13	12	12	13	
# SURVEYED		139	138	120	138	155	102	100
AGE	RESP	'75	'83	'84	'86	'87	'88	'89
48-53	1	34%	16%	21%	21%	17%	23%	19%
	2	4	13	8	11	13	14	6
	3	37	39	45	43	43	34	43
	4	11	18	15	11	11	18	17
	5	15	14	11	13	16	11	14
# SURVEYED		139	112	100	107	123	56	93
AGE	RESP	'75	'83	'84	'86	'87	'88	'89
54-59	1	26%	16%	20%	22%	19%	22%	20%
	2	10	16	7	13	6	9	8
	3	40	37	50	41	43	42	48
	4	8	14	8	14	15	12	8
	5	17	18	15	11	16	15	16
# SURVEYED		124	125	111	96	93	65	61
AGE	RESP	'75	'83	'84	'86	'87	'88	'89
60-65	1	37%	17%	17%	18%	16%	14%	19%
	2	6	18	5	9	8	3	10
	3	29	46	48	44	51	55	52
	4	10	9	13	9	14	14	15
	5	18	10	17	20	12	14	4
# SURVEYED		112	128	105	114	93	78	73
AGE	RESP	'75	'83	'84	'86	'87	'88	'89
66+	1	28%	23%	19%	21%	19%	17%	19%
	2	9	9	9	9	6	11	8
	3	33	40	51	45	46	46	47
	4	7	10	11	8	9	10	11
	5	22	18	10	18	20	16	16
# SURVEYED		222	221	218	252	243	185	167

****

GOVERNMENT AID FOR HEALTH

TABLE I: GOVERNMENT AID FOR HEALTH -- BY TOTAL POPULATION

Question: In general, some people think that it is the responsibility of the government in Washington to see to it that people have help in paying for doctor and hospital bills. Others think these matters are not the responsibility of the federal government and that people should take care of these things themselves. Where would you place yourself on a scale of 1 to 5 where 1 indicates that the government should help much more and 5 indicates that the government should let people take care of themselves? NOTE: Question not asked in 1972-1974, 1976-1982, 1985.

Responses: 1) Government help ...3) Agree with both .. 5) People take care

	YEAR						
RESPONSE	'75	'83	'84	'86	'87	'88	'89
1	37%	27%	25%	29%	27%	27%	31%
2	13	19	19	20	21	22	23
3	29	33	36	32	36	35	31
4	8	11	12	11	9	9	8
5	13	10	8	7	8	7	8
# SURVEYED	1453	1540	1409	1427	1429	972	1010

TABLE II: GOVERNMENT AID FOR HEALTH -- BY SEX

Question: In general, some people think that it is the responsibility of the government in Washington to see to it that people have help in paying for doctor and hospital bills. Others think these matters are not the responsibility of the federal government and that people should take care of these things themselves. Where would you place yourself on a scale of 1 to 5 where 1 indicates that the government should help much more and 5 indicates that the government should let people take care of themselves? NOTE: Question not asked in 1972-1974, 1976-1982, 1985.

Responses: 1) Government help ...3) Agree with both .. 5) People take care

		YEAR						
SEX	RESP	'75	'83	'84	'86	'87	'88	'89
MALE	1	38%	27%	24%	27%	27%	28%	29%
	2	14	19	21	22	22	20	25
	3	27	31	34	30	34	34	29
	4	8	11	14	14	10	11	10
	5	13	12	8	8	8	8	7
# SURVEYED		657	669	580	602	624	427	435

		YEAR						
SEX	RESP	'75	'83	'84	'86	'87	'88	'89
FEMALE	1	35%	27%	25%	31%	27%	27%	33%
	2	12	20	18	20	20	23	21
	3	31	34	38	34	37	37	32
	4	8	10	12	10	8	7	6
	5	13	10	8	5	8	6	8
# SURVEYED		796	871	829	825	805	545	575

TABLE III: GOVERNMENT AID FOR HEALTH -- BY RACE

Question: In general, some people think that it is the responsibility of the government in Washington to see to it that people have help in paying for doctor and hospital bills. Others think these matters are not the responsibility of the federal government and that people should take care of these things themselves. Where would you place yourself on a scale of 1 to 5 where 1 indicates that the government should help much more and 5 indicates that the government should let people take care of themselves? NOTE: Question not asked in 1972-1974, 1976-1982, 1985.

Responses: 1) Government help ...3) Agree with both .. 5) People take care

RACE	RESP	'75	'83	'84	'86	'87	'88	'89
WHITE	1	34%	25%	22%	26%	24%	24%	29%
	2	13	19	20	21	21	22	24
	3	30	34	36	34	37	37	31
	4	9	11	14	13	9	10	8
	5	14	11	9	7	9	7	8
# SURVEYED		1291	1365	1194	1218	1192	816	862
BLACK	1	58%	45%	40%	49%	46%	52%	49%
	2	13	21	14	19	20	24	16
	3	22	25	36	22	25	19	30
	4	1	7	5	5	6	3	3
	5	6	3	5	5	3	2	3
# SURVEYED		158	159	165	172	186	113	108

RACE	RESP	'75	'83	'84	'86	'87	'88	'89
OTHER	1	25%	25%	26%	51%	24%	30%	35%
	2	0	19	24	3	22	21	23
	3	25	38	40	35	41	42	23
	4	25	6	8	5	6	5	5
	5	25	13	2	5	8	2	15
# SURVEYED		4	16	50	37	51	43	40

TABLE IV: GOVERNMENT AID FOR HEALTH -- BY AGE

Question: In general, some people think that it is the responsibility of the government in Washington to see to it that people have help in paying for doctor and hospital bills. Others think these matters are not the responsibility of the federal government and that people should take care of these things themselves. Where would you place yourself on a scale of 1 to 5 where 1 indicates that the government should help much more and 5 indicates that the government should let people take care of themselves? NOTE: Question not asked in 1972-1974, 1976-1982, 1985.

Responses: 1) Government help ...3) Agree with both ...5) People take care

AGE	RESP	'75	'83	'84	'86	'87	'88	'89
18-23	1	44%	26%	25%	30%	25%	23%	32%
	2	13	25	28	33	33	20	31
	3	28	28	31	19	29	39	30
	4	7	13	11	12	6	11	3
	5	8	9	6	5	7	8	4
# SURVEYED		169	125	155	105	126	92	91

AGE	RESP	'75	'83	'84	'86	'87	'88	'89
24-29	1	42%	24%	28%	28%	24%	27%	33%
	2	16	28	23	25	28	27	24
	3	24	31	33	27	32	35	22
	4	10	10	13	14	11	8	12
	5	8	6	2	5	6	2	8
# SURVEYED		226	280	223	213	189	142	138

TABLE IV: GOVERNMENT AID FOR HEALTH -- BY AGE (Continued)

Question: In general, some people think that it is the responsibility of the government in Washington to see to it that people have help in paying for doctor and hospital bills. Others think these matters are not the responsibility of the federal government and that people should take care of these things themselves. Where would you place yourself on a scale of 1 to 5 where 1 indicates that the government should help much more and 5 indicates that the government should let people take care of themselves? NOTE: Question not asked in 1972-1974, 1976-1982, 1985.

Responses: 1) Government help ...3) Agree with both ...5) People take care

AGE	RESP	'75	'83	'84	'86	'87	'88	'89
30-35	1	41%	26%	27%	30%	23%	27%	29%
	2	14	21	19	24	27	29	31
	3	24	32	32	31	36	28	27
	4	9	13	16	10	9	10	7
	5	14	8	7	4	5	6	6
# SURVEYED		170	232	186	214	216	127	143
36-41	1	36%	31%	28%	30%	25%	35%	28%
	2	12	16	22	19	22	20	25
	3	31	33	31	32	36	33	35
	4	7	8	12	14	10	7	7
	5	13	12	8	5	7	4	5
# SURVEYED		149	166	181	185	181	124	130
42-47	1	23%	28%	20%	27%	30%	22%	30%
	2	15	15	21	20	16	20	29
	3	37	34	37	31	38	39	29
	4	7	13	13	12	8	8	10
	5	17	11	8	11	8	11	4
# SURVEYED		137	141	123	138	152	103	105

AGE	RESP	'75	'83	'84	'86	'87	'88	'89
48-53	1	30%	22%	26%	33%	25%	24%	30%
	2	10	17	21	13	16	36	17
	3	31	32	27	32	40	25	35
	4	7	13	11	12	7	9	5
	5	22	16	15	9	12	5	12
# SURVEYED		138	113	100	105	124	55	93
54-59	1	30%	22%	21%	24%	30%	31%	37%
	2	10	23	12	18	16	16	13
	3	35	34	41	37	34	33	31
	4	10	9	13	11	13	14	10
	5	16	12	13	10	6	6	10
# SURVEYED		122	127	112	90	97	64	62
60-65	1	35%	31%	22%	29%	29%	26%	40%
	2	12	11	10	13	20	17	14
	3	26	37	51	41	35	43	36
	4	10	13	9	12	4	7	4
	5	17	8	8	6	12	7	7
# SURVEYED		111	126	106	112	97	76	73
66+	1	40%	31%	23%	30%	31%	26%	29%
	2	12	14	13	17	12	17	17
	3	30	34	42	37	39	39	35
	4	6	6	12	8	8	8	9
	5	12	15	10	7	10	10	11
# SURVEYED		226	224	218	258	242	186	173

****

LESS GOVERNMENT HELP

TABLE I: LESS GOVERNMENT HELP -- BY TOTAL POPULATION

Question: Some people think that the government in Washington is trying to do too many things that should be left to individuals and private businesses. They are at point 5 on a scale of 1 to 5. Others disagree and think the government should do even much more to help us solve our country's problems. They are at point 1 on the scale of 1 to 5. Still others have their opinions somewhere in-between. Where would you place yourself on this scale, or haven't you made up you mind on this? NOTE: Question not asked in 1972-1974, 1976-1982, 1985.

Responses: 1) Government do more ... 3) Agree with both ... 5) Government doing too much

	YEAR						
RESPONSE	'75	'83	'84	'86	'87	'88	'89
1	27%	13%	15%	13%	15%	15%	14%
2	12	12	13	13	15	15	15
3	31	39	39	44	40	42	41
4	13	19	18	16	16	15	17
5	18	17	15	14	15	14	14
# SURVEYED	1383	1485	1370	1386	1384	936	961

TABLE II: LESS GOVERNMENT HELP -- BY SEX

Question: Some people think that the government in Washington is trying to do too many things that should be left to individuals and private businesses. They are at point 5 on a scale of 1 to 5. Others disagree and think the government should do even much more to help us solve our country's problems. They are at point 1 on the scale of 1 to 5. Still others have their opinions somewhere in-between. Where would you place yourself on this scale, or haven't you made up you mind on this? NOTE: Question not asked in 1972-1974, 1976-1982, 1985.

Responses: 1) Government do more ... 3) Agree with both ... 5) Government doing too much

		YEAR						
SEX	RESP	'75	'83	'84	'86	'87	'88	'89
MALE	1	27%	15%	15%	11%	14%	14%	13%
	2	10	11	12	14	14	13	13
	3	26	33	35	37	39	41	39
	4	15	19	21	20	18	17	20
	5	22	22	18	18	16	15	16
# SURVEYED		631	655	578	595	612	417	427

		YEAR						
SEX	RESP	'75	'83	'84	'86	'87	'88	'89
FEMALE	1	27%	12%	15%	15%	16%	15%	15%
	2	13	12	14	13	15	16	17
	3	35	43	42	49	40	42	42
	4	10	18	15	14	14	14	14
	5	14	14	13	11	14	13	12
# SURVEYED		752	830	792	791	772	519	534

TABLE III: LESS GOVERNMENT HELP -- BY RACE

Question: Some people think that the government in Washington is trying to do too many things that should be left to individuals and private businesses. They are at point 5 on a scale of 1 to 5. Others disagree and think the government should do even much more to help us solve our country's problems. They are at point 1 on the scale of 1 to 5. Still others have their opinions somewhere in-between. Where would you place yourself on this scale, or haven't you made up you mind on this? NOTE: Question not asked in 1972-1974, 1976-1982, 1985.

Responses: 1) Government do more ... 3) Agree with both ... 5) Government doing too much

		YEAR						
RACE	RESP	'75	'83	'84	'86	'87	'88	'89
WHITE	1	24%	11%	12%	10%	12%	12%	12%
	2	11	12	13	12	14	13	14
	3	32	39	39	45	41	43	41
	4	14	20	19	19	17	17	18
	5	19	19	17	15	16	15	15
# SURVEYED		1232	1322	1167	1183	1158	786	820
RACE	RESP	'75	'83	'84	'86	'87	'88	'89
BLACK	1	52%	35%	36%	32%	34%	31%	29%
	2	16	14	15	21	16	24	24
	3	23	39	39	36	32	33	34
	4	3	6	6	4	9	4	7
	5	6	7	4	7	8	8	6
# SURVEYED		147	148	154	170	179	109	103

		YEAR						
RACE	RESP	'75	'83	'84	'86	'87	'88	'89
OTHER	1	50%	7%	14%	27%	28%	15%	21%
	2	0	13	20	21	21	24	24
	3	0	40	45	36	40	51	47
	4	25	20	14	9	4	7	3
	5	25	20	6	6	6	2	5
# SURVEYED		4	15	49	33	47	41	38

TABLE IV: LESS GOVERNMENT HELP -- BY AGE

Question: Some people think that the government in Washington is trying to do too many things that should be left to individuals and private businesses. They are at point 5 on a scale of 1 to 5. Others disagree and think the government should do even much more to help us solve our country's problems. They are at point 1 on the scale of 1 to 5. Still others have their opinions somewhere in-between. Where would you place yourself on this scale, or haven't you made up you mind on this? NOTE: Question not asked in 1972-1974, 1976-1982, 1985.

Responses: 1) Government do more ... 3) Agree with both ... 5) Government doing too much

		YEAR						
AGE	RESP	'75	'83	'84	'86	'87	'88	'89
18-23	1	36%	11%	18%	13%	16%	14%	16%
	2	19	16	27	27	24	23	24
	3	27	44	38	36	45	38	39
	4	11	23	10	17	8	13	18
	5	7	7	7	7	7	12	4
# SURVEYED		167	122	148	94	116	84	85

		YEAR						
AGE	RESP	'75	'83	'84	'86	'87	'88	'89
24-29	1	25%	17%	16%	16%	17%	16%	15%
	2	17	18	14	14	19	18	19
	3	33	36	40	45	36	41	38
	4	14	17	20	17	19	18	18
	5	10	13	10	9	10	7	9
# SURVEYED		221	272	216	211	183	138	130

TABLE IV: LESS GOVERNMENT HELP -- BY AGE (Continued)

Question: Some people think that the government in Washington is trying to do too many things that should be left to individuals and private businesses. They are at point 5 on a scale of 1 to 5. Others disagree and think the government should do even much more to help us solve our country's problems. They are at point 1 on the scale of 1 to 5. Still others have their opinions somewhere in-between. Where would you place yourself on this scale, or haven't you made up you mind on this? NOTE: Question not asked in 1972-1974, 1976-1982, 1985.

Responses: 1) Government do more ... 3) Agree with both ... 5) Government doing too much

AGE	RESP	'75	'83	'84	'86	'87	'88	'89
30-35	1	25%	12%	14%	13%	13%	19%	13%
	2	9	14	17	21	21	18	18
	3	36	41	39	42	36	31	41
	4	12	21	18	14	19	21	16
	5	19	13	12	10	12	11	12
# SURVEYED		159	224	184	212	213	124	138
36-41	1	30%	12%	13%	9%	13%	11%	12%
	2	8	8	17	13	15	17	15
	3	31	38	33	46	38	42	38
	4	10	23	23	20	19	15	22
	5	20	19	14	13	16	15	13
# SURVEYED		143	162	179	181	176	122	124
42-47	1	22%	15%	9%	13%	14%	15%	13%
	2	13	8	9	12	13	9	17
	3	32	30	40	41	38	39	40
	4	15	24	24	19	21	18	19
	5	17	24	18	15	14	19	12
# SURVEYED		134	135	118	138	151	97	101

AGE	RESP	'75	'83	'84	'86	'87	'88	'89
48-53	1	24%	15%	19%	15%	13%	16%	16%
	2	7	11	11	10	14	18	17
	3	29	33	36	45	41	42	34
	4	13	18	18	12	14	15	10
	5	26	24	17	19	18	9	23
# SURVEYED		136	114	95	102	122	55	88
54-59	1	28%	10%	14%	15%	17%	21%	12%
	2	7	7	11	10	15	10	8
	3	33	43	40	39	36	48	42
	4	12	19	17	18	17	8	15
	5	20	22	18	17	16	13	23
# SURVEYED		115	120	111	92	95	61	60
60-65	1	26%	11%	13%	6%	14%	12%	10%
	2	11	17	9	8	9	7	9
	3	30	37	42	43	47	54	55
	4	12	15	10	27	11	12	10
	5	21	21	26	16	20	16	16
# SURVEYED		107	121	104	109	92	76	69
66+	1	25%	15%	17%	15%	18%	11%	16%
	2	9	6	5	7	4	12	9
	3	30	46	44	48	46	46	43
	4	12	14	15	11	12	13	16
	5	24	20	19	19	20	19	16
# SURVEYED		197	210	210	240	232	176	164

****

SPENDING ON FOREIGN AID

TABLE I: SPENDING ON FOREIGN AID -- BY TOTAL POPULATION

Question: We are faced with many problems in this country, none of which can be solved easily and inexpensively. I'm going to name some of these problems, and for each one I'd like you to tell me whether you think we are spending too much money, or about the right amount. Foreign aid. NOTE: Question not asked in 1972.

Responses: TL = Too little; AR = About right; TM = Too much

	YEAR														
RESPONSE	'73	'74	'75	'76	'77	'78	'80	'82	'83	'84	'85	'86	'87	'88	'89
TL	4%	3%	6%	3%	4%	4%	5%	6%	4%	5%	7%	6%	8%	5%	5%
AR	21	18	17	19	25	25	21	19	18	22	25	20	21	23	23
TM	74	79	77	78	71	71	74	76	78	74	68	73	72	71	72
# SURVEYED	1421	1422	1416	1438	1421	1444	1389	1431	1509	462	718	698	462	679	715

TABLE II: SPENDING ON FOREIGN AID -- BY SEX

Question: We are faced with many problems in this country, none of which can be solved easily and inexpensively. I'm going to name some of these problems, and for each one I'd like you to tell me whether you think we are spending too much money, or about the right amount. Foreign aid. NOTE: Question not asked in 1972.

Responses: TL = Too little; AR = About right; TM = Too much

		YEAR														
SEX	RESP	'73	'74	'75	'76	'77	'78	'80	'82	'83	'84	'85	'86	'87	'88	'89
M	TL	5%	3%	6%	3%	4%	4%	3%	6%	4%	6%	6%	6%	7%	6%	4%
	AR	19	18	16	17	24	24	20	18	16	20	24	16	18	21	17
	TM	76	78	78	80	72	72	77	76	79	74	70	79	75	74	79
# SURVEYED		678	676	649	657	654	622	618	619	659	228	420	294	221	281	314
SEX	RESP	'73	'74	'75	'76	'77	'78	'80	'82	'83	'84	'85	'86	'87	'88	'89
F	TL	4%	3%	6%	3%	4%	5%	7%	5%	4%	3%	7%	7%	8%	5%	5%
	AR	23	18	19	20	26	26	21	19	19	23	27	23	23	25	28
	TM	73	79	76	77	70	69	71	76	77	74	65	70	69	70	67
# SURVEYED		743	746	767	781	767	822	771	812	850	234	298	404	241	398	401

TABLE III: SPENDING ON FOREIGN AID -- BY RACE

Question: We are faced with many problems in this country, none of which can be solved easily and inexpensively. I'm going to name some of these problems, and for each one I'd like you to tell me whether you think we are spending too much money, or about the right amount. Foreign aid. NOTE: Question not asked in 1972.

Responses: TL = Too little; AR = About right; TM = Too much

		YEAR														
RACE	RESP	'73	'74	'75	'76	'77	'78	'80	'82	'83	'84	'85	'86	'87	'88	'89
WHITE	TL	4%	2%	5%	3%	3%	3%	5%	5%	4%	4%	6%	4%	6%	5%	4%
	AR	21	19	17	19	25	25	21	19	18	21	24	19	20	23	23
	TM	75	79	78	78	72	72	74	77	78	75	70	77	74	72	73
# SURVEYED		1242	1252	1261	1309	1253	1287	1246	1259	1345	394	640	586	386	559	619
RACE	RESP	'73	'74	'75	'76	'77	'78	'80	'82	'83	'84	'85	'86	'87	'88	'89
BLACK	TL	10%	10%	12%	4%	10%	13%	13%	14%	7%	13%	16%	19%	13%	9%	6%
	AR	19	12	21	17	29	25	19	17	16	21	34	23	24	24	19
	TM	71	78	68	79	61	62	68	69	78	66	50	58	63	67	75
# SURVEYED		168	164	151	121	155	143	135	147	148	53	62	96	62	92	67
RACE	RESP	'73	'74	'75	'76	'77	'78	'80	'82	'83	'84	'85	'86	'87	'88	'89
OTHER	TL	9%	17%	0%	0%	8%	0%	0%	12%	0%	0%	6%	13%	29%	4%	14%
	AR	27	17	0	25	31	57	50	40	19	40	38	38	7	32	31
	TM	64	67	100	75	62	43	50	48	81	60	56	50	64	64	55
# SURVEYED		11	6	4	8	13	14	8	25	16	15	16	16	14	28	29

TABLE IV: SPENDING ON FOREIGN AID -- BY AGE

Question: We are faced with many problems in this country, none of which can be solved easily and inexpensively. I'm going to name some of these problems, and for each one I'd like you to tell me whether you think we are spending too much money, or about the right amount. Foreign aid. NOTE: Question not asked in 1972.

Responses: TL = Too little; AR = About right; TM = Too much

		YEAR														
AGE	RESP	'73	'74	'75	'76	'77	'78	'80	'82	'83	'84	'85	'86	'87	'88	'89
18-23	TL	9%	5%	13%	7%	7%	9%	13%	9%	8%	11%	19%	9%	18%	8%	2%
	AR	35	31	24	27	32	36	31	20	24	29	32	29	31	21	31
	TM	56	64	63	66	61	56	56	71	68	61	49	62	51	71	67
# SURVEYED		161	162	159	154	152	152	148	137	118	38	37	55	39	63	61

TABLE IV: SPENDING ON FOREIGN AID -- BY AGE (Continued)

Question: We are faced with many problems in this country, none of which can be solved easily and inexpensively. I'm going to name some of these problems, and for each one I'd like you to tell me whether you think we are spending too much money, or about the right amount. Foreign aid. NOTE: Question not asked in 1972.

Responses: TL = Too little; AR = About right; TM = Too much

		YEAR														
AGE	RESP	'73	'74	'75	'76	'77	'78	'80	'82	'83	'84	'85	'86	'87	'88	'89
24-29	TL	5%	3%	4%	4%	7%	8%	8%	9%	8%	4%	13%	8%	9%	8%	9%
	AR	21	18	19	19	31	27	24	23	21	26	29	21	28	30	20
	TM	75	79	77	77	63	65	68	68	71	70	58	71	63	63	71
# SURVEYED		204	204	224	218	193	228	194	238	273	70	97	96	68	105	79
AGE	RESP	'73	'74	'75	'76	'77	'78	'80	'82	'83	'84	'85	'86	'87	'88	'89
30-35	TL	2%	4%	4%	2%	3%	4%	7%	6%	4%	3%	11%	11%	13%	6%	6%
	AR	18	12	13	19	27	24	19	16	19	21	29	27	16	21	21
	TM	80	83	83	80	70	72	74	77	77	76	61	63	71	73	73
# SURVEYED		162	169	166	181	174	221	200	204	229	67	94	113	79	90	101
AGE	RESP	'73	'74	'75	'76	'77	'78	'80	'82	'83	'84	'85	'86	'87	'88	'89
36-41	TL	5%	5%	4%	2%	3%	4%	5%	8%	2%	4%	3%	4%	7%	7%	8%
	AR	21	16	15	16	20	28	23	26	13	16	22	18	16	26	29
	TM	74	78	81	82	77	68	72	67	85	80	75	78	77	67	63
# SURVEYED		168	146	151	151	163	149	145	141	164	55	96	89	57	89	90
AGE	RESP	'73	'74	'75	'76	'77	'78	'80	'82	'83	'84	'85	'86	'87	'88	'89
42-47	TL	2%	3%	4%	3%	2%	3%	2%	4%	1%	10%	2%	2%	6%	6%	3%
	AR	15	16	24	19	25	31	16	20	16	21	25	18	19	25	23
	TM	82	81	72	79	73	66	82	75	83	69	74	80	75	69	74
# SURVEYED		137	150	137	112	133	116	114	114	138	48	65	61	52	72	78
AGE	RESP	'73	'74	'75	'76	'77	'78	'80	'82	'83	'84	'85	'86	'87	'88	'89
48-53	TL	6%	1%	4%	4%	1%	1%	3%	5%	1%	2%	5%	9%	4%	2%	4%
	AR	24	17	10	15	27	25	20	12	16	24	22	15	25	22	21
	TM	70	83	87	81	72	74	76	83	83	73	73	77	71	76	74
# SURVEYED		143	143	135	129	146	127	118	107	112	41	73	47	28	46	70
AGE	RESP	'73	'74	'75	'76	'77	'78	'80	'82	'83	'84	'85	'86	'87	'88	'89
54-59	TL	4%	2%	3%	2%	4%	1%	1%	3%	2%	4%	5%	12%	3%	5%	6%
	AR	15	19	13	16	24	24	17	16	14	28	25	21	19	30	19
	TM	81	79	84	82	72	76	82	81	83	68	70	67	78	65	75
# SURVEYED		144	127	120	124	160	135	133	134	127	25	60	52	32	37	52
AGE	RESP	'73	'74	'75	'76	'77	'78	'80	'82	'83	'84	'85	'86	'87	'88	'89
60-65	TL	3%	1%	5%	0%	4%	2%	4%	3%	3%	6%	6%	4%	0%	2%	4%
	AR	23	17	20	16	24	19	18	13	18	18	28	24	9	18	16
	TM	75	82	76	84	72	79	78	85	79	76	66	72	91	80	80
# SURVEYED		118	104	107	129	111	100	113	112	129	33	65	46	33	56	50

TABLE IV: SPENDING ON FOREIGN AID -- BY AGE (Continued)

Question: We are faced with many problems in this country, none of which can be solved easily and inexpensively. I'm going to name some of these problems, and for each one I'd like you to tell me whether you think we are spending too much money, or about the right amount. Foreign aid. NOTE: Question not asked in 1972.

Responses: TL = Too little; AR = About right; TM = Too much

		YEAR														
AGE	RESP	'73	'74	'75	'76	'77	'78	'80	'82	'83	'84	'85	'86	'87	'88	'89
66+	TL	3%	3%	9%	3%	2%	2%	3%	3%	3%	1%	3%	2%	4%	3%	2%
	AR	19	16	19	20	17	18	19	19	19	17	22	12	22	19	23
	TM	78	81	72	77	81	80	78	78	78	82	74	86	74	78	75
# SURVEYED		180	212	214	235	182	209	216	236	213	82	129	135	73	118	132

****

SPENDING FOR DEFENSE

TABLE I: SPENDING FOR DEFENSE -- BY TOTAL POPULATION

Question: We are faced with many problems in this country, none of which can be solved easily and inexpensively. I'm going to name some of these problems, and for each one I'd like you to tell me whether you think we are spending too much money, or about the right amount. The military, armaments, and defense. NOTE: Question not asked in 1972.

Responses: TL = Too little; AR = About right; TM = Too much

	YEAR														
RESPONSE	'73	'74	'75	'76	'77	'78	'80	'82	'83	'84	'85	'86	'87	'88	'89
TL	12%	18%	18%	26%	26%	29%	60%	31%	26%	18%	15%	17%	15%	17%	15%
AR	48	49	49	45	49	47	28	38	40	43	44	40	42	42	43
TM	40	33	33	29	25	24	12	32	34	39	42	43	42	41	41
# SURVEYED	1407	1380	1387	1395	1404	1413	1370	1426	1506	469	722	691	463	672	721

TABLE II: SPENDING FOR DEFENSE -- BY SEX

Question: We are faced with many problems in this country, none of which can be solved easily and inexpensively. I'm going to name some of these problems, and for each one I'd like you to tell me whether you think we are spending too much money, or about the right amount. The military, armaments, and defense. NOTE: Question not asked in 1972.

Responses: TL = Too little; AR = About right; TM = Too much

		YEAR														
SEX	RESP	'73	'74	'75	'76	'77	'78	'80	'82	'83	'84	'85	'86	'87	'88	'89
M	TL	13%	20%	22%	31%	29%	33%	65%	33%	30%	18%	14%	18%	15%	21%	17%
	AR	44	43	44	38	44	43	23	36	34	37	44	39	42	40	38
	TM	43	37	34	31	27	24	12	31	36	45	42	43	43	39	45
# SURVEYED		677	668	648	650	664	617	624	627	674	229	425	293	221	287	325
SEX	RESP	'73	'74	'75	'76	'77	'78	'80	'82	'83	'84	'85	'86	'87	'88	'89
F	TL	11%	16%	14%	21%	23%	26%	57%	29%	22%	18%	16%	16%	15%	14%	14%
	AR	52	54	53	51	54	50	31	39	45	48	43	42	43	44	47
	TM	38	29	33	28	23	23	12	32	33	34	41	42	42	42	39
# SURVEYED		730	712	739	745	740	796	746	799	832	240	297	398	242	385	396

TABLE III: SPENDING FOR DEFENSE -- BY RACE

Question: We are faced with many problems in this country, none of which can be solved easily and inexpensively. I'm going to name some of these problems, and for each one I'd like you to tell me whether you think we are spending too much money, or about the right amount. The military, armaments, and defense. NOTE: Question not asked in 1972.

Responses: TL = Too little; AR = About right; TM = Too much

		YEAR														
RACE	RESP	'73	'74	'75	'76	'77	'78	'80	'82	'83	'84	'85	'86	'87	'88	'89
WHITE	TL	11%	18%	18%	26%	27%	30%	61%	33%	27%	18%	15%	17%	17%	18%	15%
	AR	50	49	49	44	50	46	27	37	40	43	43	39	44	44	44
	TM	39	33	33	29	23	24	12	30	34	39	42	44	39	38	40
# SURVEYED		1235	1223	1237	1273	1243	1263	1236	1250	1343	397	640	584	385	552	627
RACE	RESP	'73	'74	'75	'76	'77	'78	'80	'82	'83	'84	'85	'86	'87	'88	'89
BLACK	TL	19%	21%	19%	22%	16%	20%	54%	14%	16%	16%	17%	19%	8%	14%	15%
	AR	34	44	47	52	48	56	35	41	41	43	51	43	36	34	42
	TM	48	35	34	26	36	23	11	44	43	41	32	38	56	52	43
# SURVEYED		160	151	146	114	147	137	127	152	148	56	65	93	64	93	65
RACE	RESP	'73	'74	'75	'76	'77	'78	'80	'82	'83	'84	'85	'86	'87	'88	'89
OTHER	TL	17%	33%	25%	13%	21%	38%	43%	29%	13%	13%	12%	14%	14%	7%	14%
	AR	42	67	25	63	43	31	29	29	53	38	29	64	21	37	24
	TM	42	0	50	25	36	31	29	42	33	50	59	21	64	56	62
# SURVEYED		12	6	4	8	14	13	7	24	15	16	17	14	14	27	29

TABLE IV: SPENDING FOR DEFENSE -- BY AGE

Question: We are faced with many problems in this country, none of which can be solved easily and inexpensively. I'm going to name some of these problems, and for each one I'd like you to tell me whether you think we are spending too much money, or about the right amount. The military, armaments, and defense. NOTE: Question not asked in 1972.

Responses: TL = Too little; AR = About right; TM = Too much

		YEAR														
AGE	RESP	'73	'74	'75	'76	'77	'78	'80	'82	'83	'84	'85	'86	'87	'88	'89
18-23	TL	12%	13%	13%	18%	19%	21%	47%	24%	20%	14%	22%	9%	15%	11%	14%
	AR	48	48	42	38	48	48	35	38	41	45	30	37	44	37	41
	TM	41	39	46	44	32	31	17	39	40	40	49	54	41	52	45
# SURVEYED		164	160	168	156	154	149	150	144	123	42	37	54	41	63	66

TABLE IV: SPENDING FOR DEFENSE -- BY AGE (Continued)

Question: We are faced with many problems in this country, none of which can be solved easily and inexpensively. I'm going to name some of these problems, and for each one I'd like you to tell me whether you think we are spending too much money, or about the right amount. The military, armaments, and defense. NOTE: Question not asked in 1972.

Responses: TL = Too little; AR = About right; TM = Too much

		YEAR														
AGE	RESP	'73	'74	'75	'76	'77	'78	'80	'82	'83	'84	'85	'86	'87	'88	'89
24-29	TL	6%	12%	12%	19%	20%	22%	54%	25%	24%	23%	15%	12%	16%	16%	14%
	AR	40	42	45	44	48	48	31	39	38	45	34	43	33	39	38
	TM	54	46	43	37	32	30	15	36	38	32	51	44	51	45	49
# SURVEYED		201	204	224	215	193	227	193	236	276	71	97	97	69	106	80
AGE	RESP	'73	'74	'75	'76	'77	'78	'80	'82	'83	'84	'85	'86	'87	'88	'89
30-35	TL	12%	13%	19%	22%	19%	22%	54%	27%	25%	15%	7%	13%	13%	16%	11%
	AR	50	46	50	47	49	52	31	29	35	42	48	41	41	33	38
	TM	38	40	31	31	32	27	15	44	39	43	45	46	46	51	50
# SURVEYED		157	163	157	178	173	218	207	196	226	67	96	112	80	91	107
AGE	RESP	'73	'74	'75	'76	'77	'78	'80	'82	'83	'84	'85	'86	'87	'88	'89
36-41	TL	15%	11%	18%	25%	27%	27%	54%	32%	26%	14%	16%	18%	18%	17%	14%
	AR	45	58	46	47	47	47	28	40	36	46	44	33	30	39	43
	TM	40	31	36	28	26	26	18	28	38	41	39	48	52	44	43
# SURVEYED		168	146	144	148	154	146	142	139	163	59	97	87	56	89	91
AGE	RESP	'73	'74	'75	'76	'77	'78	'80	'82	'83	'84	'85	'86	'87	'88	'89
42-47	TL	9%	13%	20%	30%	25%	29%	62%	24%	26%	19%	14%	29%	13%	18%	17%
	AR	48	55	50	50	50	46	28	44	45	38	40	42	52	54	37
	TM	43	32	30	20	25	25	10	32	29	44	46	29	35	28	46
# SURVEYED		138	143	137	105	136	113	109	117	140	48	65	62	52	71	78
AGE	RESP	'73	'74	'75	'76	'77	'78	'80	'82	'83	'84	'85	'86	'87	'88	'89
48-53	TL	14%	33%	23%	32%	34%	35%	73%	45%	22%	20%	8%	26%	25%	17%	20%
	AR	50	42	54	44	48	49	19	30	48	32	55	45	46	41	41
	TM	36	26	23	24	18	16	8	25	31	49	37	30	29	41	39
# SURVEYED		144	132	133	124	143	129	120	106	111	41	73	47	28	46	69
AGE	RESP	'73	'74	'75	'76	'77	'78	'80	'82	'83	'84	'85	'86	'87	'88	'89
54-59	TL	17%	33%	23%	34%	26%	44%	69%	47%	27%	20%	20%	23%	13%	11%	28%
	AR	44	48	50	45	57	39	22	35	42	52	49	34	35	63	49
	TM	38	19	28	22	17	17	9	18	31	28	31	43	52	26	23
# SURVEYED		143	126	111	119	156	132	127	133	124	25	59	53	31	35	53

TABLE IV: SPENDING FOR DEFENSE -- BY AGE (Continued)

Question: We are faced with many problems in this country, none of which can be solved easily and inexpensively. I'm going to name some of these problems, and for each one I'd like you to tell me whether you think we are spending too much money, or about the right amount. The military, armaments, and defense. NOTE: Question not asked in 1972, 1979, 1981.

Responses: TL = Too little; AR = About right; TM = Too much

		YEAR														
AGE	RESP	'73	'74	'75	'76	'77	'78	'80	'82	'83	'84	'85	'86	'87	'88	'89
60-65	TL	11%	22%	19%	24%	32%	44%	70%	26%	28%	30%	21%	18%	26%	23%	16%
	AR	55	44	50	47	49	44	25	39	39	33	48	43	48	38	43
	TM	34	34	31	28	20	12	5	35	33	36	31	39	26	38	41
# SURVEYED		111	98	105	123	107	95	110	110	123	33	67	49	31	52	49
AGE	RESP	'73	'74	'75	'76	'77	'78	'80	'82	'83	'84	'85	'86	'87	'88	'89
66+	TL	12%	20%	20%	32%	33%	35%	67%	33%	31%	15%	16%	15%	11%	18%	13%
	AR	54	54	54	46	50	45	25	43	42	46	42	43	51	49	54
	TM	34	26	25	22	17	20	8	24	27	39	43	42	38	33	33
# SURVEYED		178	203	204	222	183	197	205	235	213	79	129	128	74	116	126

****

SPENDING FOR BIG CITY PROBLEMS

TABLE I: SPENDING FOR BIG CITY PROBLEMS -- BY TOTAL POPULATION

Question: We are faced with many problems in this country, none of which can be solved easily and inexpensively. I'm going to name some of these problems, and for each one I'd like you to tell me whether you think we are spending too much money, or about the right amount. Solving the problems of big cities. NOTE: Question not asked in 1972.

Responses: TL = Too little; AR = About right; TM = Too much

	YEAR														
RESPONSE	'73	'74	'75	'76	'77	'78	'80	'82	'83	'84	'85	'86	'87	'88	'89
TL	55%	59%	56%	48%	47%	44%	46%	50%	48%	51%	44%	48%	45%	54%	54%
AR	31	29	30	30	31	34	30	28	34	35	37	34	39	34	34
TM	14	13	14	22	23	22	24	23	18	14	19	18	16	12	13
# SURVEYED	1319	1258	1241	1318	1311	1334	1278	1291	1373	422	661	651	406	608	659

TABLE II: SPENDING FOR BIG CITY PROBLEMS -- BY SEX

Question: We are faced with many problems in this country, none of which can be solved easily and inexpensively. I'm going to name some of these problems, and for each one I'd like you to tell me whether you think we are spending too much money, or about the right amount. Solving the problems of big cities. NOTE: Question not asked in 1972.

Responses: TL = Too little; AR = About right; TM = Too much

		YEAR														
SEX	RESP	'73	'74	'75	'76	'77	'78	'80	'82	'83	'84	'85	'86	'87	'88	'89
M	TL	54%	57%	52%	45%	45%	40%	43%	48%	45%	51%	40%	40%	43%	50%	49%
	AR	29	28	29	28	28	31	28	25	33	31	38	38	40	37	34
	TM	17	15	19	26	27	28	30	27	22	19	23	22	18	14	16
# SURVEYED		633	609	582	610	611	573	571	572	619	213	387	277	199	251	298
SEX	RESP	'73	'74	'75	'76	'77	'78	'80	'82	'83	'84	'85	'86	'87	'88	'89
F	TL	56%	60%	60%	51%	48%	47%	48%	51%	51%	51%	51%	54%	47%	57%	57%
	AR	33	29	30	31	33	36	31	30	35	40	36	31	39	33	33
	TM	11	11	10	18	19	17	20	19	15	10	13	15	14	11	9
# SURVEYED		686	649	659	708	700	761	707	719	754	209	274	374	207	357	361

TABLE III: SPENDING FOR BIG CITY PROBLEMS -- BY RACE

Question: We are faced with many problems in this country, none of which can be solved easily and inexpensively. I'm going to name some of these problems, and for each one I'd like you to tell me whether you think we are spending too much money, or about the right amount. Solving the problems of big cities. NOTE: Question not asked in 1972.

Responses: TL = Too little; AR = About right; TM = Too much

		YEAR														
RACE	RESP	'73	'74	'75	'76	'77	'78	'80	'82	'83	'84	'85	'86	'87	'88	'89
WHITE	TL	53%	56%	55%	46%	45%	42%	43%	47%	45%	49%	42%	45%	40%	52%	50%
	AR	33	30	31	31	31	35	30	29	37	37	38	35	42	35	36
	TM	15	13	15	23	24	23	26	24	19	14	20	20	18	13	14
# SURVEYED		1137	1102	1084	1195	1156	1177	1141	1127	1209	354	583	543	334	495	563
RACE	RESP	'73	'74	'75	'76	'77	'78	'80	'82	'83	'84	'85	'86	'87	'88	'89
BLACK	TL	68%	74%	69%	68%	65%	67%	67%	68%	73%	68%	58%	67%	67%	64%	76%
	AR	23	17	24	18	23	26	23	20	14	26	31	25	26	28	20
	TM	9	9	8	14	12	7	9	12	13	6	11	9	7	8	4
# SURVEYED		171	150	153	114	143	145	129	145	147	53	62	93	61	88	70
RACE	RESP	'73	'74	'75	'76	'77	'78	'80	'82	'83	'84	'85	'86	'87	'88	'89
OTHER	TL	82%	50%	25%	56%	25%	50%	38%	63%	59%	27%	75%	53%	73%	48%	65%
	AR	18	17	25	33	33	25	38	21	24	27	19	40	18	44	27
	TM	0	33	50	11	42	25	25	16	18	47	6	7	9	8	8
# SURVEYED		11	6	4	9	12	12	8	19	17	15	16	15	11	25	26

TABLE IV: SPENDING FOR BIG CITY PROBLEMS -- BY AGE

Question: We are faced with many problems in this country, none of which can be solved easily and inexpensively. I'm going to name some of these problems, and for each one I'd like you to tell me whether you think we are spending too much money, or about the right amount. Solving the problems of big cities. NOTE: Question not asked in 1972.

Responses: TL = Too little; AR = About right; TM = Too much

		YEAR														
AGE	RESP	'73	'74	'75	'76	'77	'78	'80	'82	'83	'84	'85	'86	'87	'88	'89
18-23	TL	68%	62%	78%	61%	59%	61%	58%	59%	51%	63%	53%	57%	55%	51%	63%
	AR	27	33	18	25	30	27	25	25	38	34	32	31	39	42	30
	TM	6	5	4	14	11	12	17	16	11	3	15	11	5	7	6
# SURVEYED		157	153	161	156	152	146	143	131	114	38	34	54	38	59	63

TABLE IV: SPENDING FOR BIG CITY PROBLEMS -- BY AGE (Continued)

Question: We are faced with many problems in this country, none of which can be solved easily and inexpensively. I'm going to name some of these problems, and for each one I'd like you to tell me whether you think we are spending too much money, or about the right amount. Solving the problems of big cities. NOTE: Question not asked in 1972.

Responses: TL = Too little; AR = About right; TM = Too much

		YEAR														
AGE	RESP	'73	'74	'75	'76	'77	'78	'80	'82	'83	'84	'85	'86	'87	'88	'89
24-29	TL	62%	67%	62%	56%	56%	45%	53%	49%	57%	52%	44%	51%	54%	62%	56%
	AR	29	27	29	29	28	36	29	30	29	38	42	40	36	32	32
	TM	9	6	9	15	16	20	18	21	15	10	14	10	10	6	12
# SURVEYED		195	196	196	213	183	214	186	224	261	63	98	91	59	99	78
AGE	RESP	'73	'74	'75	'76	'77	'78	'80	'82	'83	'84	'85	'86	'87	'88	'89
30-35	TL	55%	63%	55%	47%	55%	52%	53%	56%	45%	55%	47%	53%	38%	58%	52%
	AR	33	22	30	31	29	35	27	26	37	33	41	30	45	31	39
	TM	13	15	15	22	16	13	20	18	18	13	12	17	18	12	9
# SURVEYED		152	151	152	173	171	202	193	187	211	64	91	107	74	85	97
AGE	RESP	'73	'74	'75	'76	'77	'78	'80	'82	'83	'84	'85	'86	'87	'88	'89
36-41	TL	47%	62%	52%	44%	44%	38%	43%	51%	43%	50%	47%	49%	45%	54%	52%
	AR	38	23	31	36	29	37	31	25	38	37	33	34	41	34	34
	TM	14	15	17	20	27	25	26	24	19	13	20	17	14	11	14
# SURVEYED		159	126	133	138	149	142	137	133	155	52	91	89	49	79	87
AGE	RESP	'73	'74	'75	'76	'77	'78	'80	'82	'83	'84	'85	'86	'87	'88	'89
42-47	TL	55%	57%	44%	41%	48%	43%	48%	60%	44%	54%	43%	57%	46%	59%	56%
	AR	31	34	40	34	28	39	26	19	43	27	36	25	37	30	33
	TM	13	9	16	26	24	19	26	21	13	19	21	18	17	11	11
# SURVEYED		134	124	121	98	118	108	107	107	123	48	61	60	46	63	72
AGE	RESP	'73	'74	'75	'76	'77	'78	'80	'82	'83	'84	'85	'86	'87	'88	'89
48-53	TL	54%	60%	55%	51%	42%	39%	46%	45%	47%	49%	37%	50%	35%	58%	64%
	AR	28	27	29	27	31	37	32	30	30	35	39	36	43	33	23
	TM	18	13	16	21	27	24	23	26	23	16	24	14	22	9	13
# SURVEYED		133	122	124	117	128	119	101	101	104	37	67	42	23	43	64
AGE	RESP	'73	'74	'75	'76	'77	'78	'80	'82	'83	'84	'85	'86	'87	'88	'89
54-59	TL	53%	50%	50%	43%	45%	35%	38%	43%	49%	43%	58%	49%	31%	62%	53%
	AR	30	33	37	35	31	31	30	28	31	33	23	29	42	28	28
	TM	17	17	14	22	24	34	32	29	20	24	19	22	27	10	19
# SURVEYED		131	110	101	111	143	128	112	124	113	21	57	45	26	29	43

TABLE IV: SPENDING FOR BIG CITY PROBLEMS -- BY AGE (Continued)

Question: We are faced with many problems in this country, none of which can be solved easily and inexpensively. I'm going to name some of these problems, and for each one I'd like you to tell me whether you think we are spending too much money, or about the right amount. Solving the problems of big cities. NOTE: Question not asked in 1972.

Responses: TL = Too little; AR = About right; TM = Too much

		YEAR														
AGE	RESP	'73	'74	'75	'76	'77	'78	'80	'82	'83	'84	'85	'86	'87	'88	'89
60-65	TL	50%	49%	64%	56%	33%	44%	32%	42%	49%	35%	47%	39%	41%	50%	56%
	AR	29	28	23	20	34	31	33	37	31	52	41	39	37	26	31
	TM	21	22	13	24	34	26	34	22	20	13	12	22	22	24	13
# SURVEYED		101	95	86	112	101	85	108	93	110	31	59	46	27	46	45
AGE	RESP	'73	'74	'75	'76	'77	'78	'80	'82	'83	'84	'85	'86	'87	'88	'89
66+	TL	46%	49%	44%	34%	34%	39%	35%	42%	44%	48%	35%	33%	49%	39%	43%
	AR	34	32	32	31	35	33	35	29	32	32	38	40	35	44	40
	TM	20	19	24	36	31	29	30	29	24	20	28	27	16	17	18
# SURVEYED		155	176	163	196	160	184	185	184	176	66	101	113	63	103	108

****

SPENDING FOR CRIME

TABLE I: SPENDING FOR CRIME -- BY TOTAL POPULATION

Question: We are faced with many problems in this country, none of which can be solved easily and inexpensively. I'm going to name some of these problems, and for each one I'd like you to tell me whether you think we are spending too much money, or about the right amount. Halting the rising crime rate. NOTE: Question not asked in 1972.

Responses: TL = Too little; AR = About right; TM = Too much

	YEAR														
RESPONSE	'73	'74	'75	'76	'77	'78	'80	'82	'83	'84	'85	'86	'87	'88	'89
TL	69%	70%	70%	69%	70%	67%	72%	75%	70%	70%	65%	67%	71%	72%	75%
AR	26	25	25	22	24	26	22	19	25	25	29	28	25	24	20
TM	5	5	6	8	6	6	6	5	5	5	6	5	5	4	5
# SURVEYED	1405	1405	1400	1413	1431	1460	1400	1427	1521	469	718	693	461	679	739

TABLE II: SPENDING FOR CRIME -- BY SEX

Question: We are faced with many problems in this country, none of which can be solved easily and inexpensively. I'm going to name some of these problems, and for each one I'd like you to tell me whether you think we are spending too much money, or about the right amount. Halting the rising crime rate. NOTE: Question not asked in 1972.

Responses: TL = Too little; AR = About right; TM = Too much

		YEAR														
SEX	RESP	'73	'74	'75	'76	'77	'78	'80	'82	'83	'84	'85	'86	'87	'88	'89
M	TL	68%	69%	68%	66%	67%	65%	68%	73%	66%	65%	63%	61%	69%	70%	72%
	AR	25	26	24	25	25	27	24	19	28	29	30	33	27	26	21
	TM	7	5	7	9	8	8	7	8	6	6	7	6	5	4	7
# SURVEYED		673	664	638	639	657	619	615	618	666	228	412	288	217	281	321
SEX	RESP	'73	'74	'75	'76	'77	'78	'80	'82	'83	'84	'85	'86	'87	'88	'89
F	TL	70%	72%	71%	72%	73%	69%	75%	77%	73%	75%	69%	71%	73%	73%	77%
	AR	27	23	25	20	23	26	20	19	23	22	27	25	23	23	20
	TM	3	5	4	8	5	5	6	4	4	3	4	4	5	4	3
# SURVEYED		732	741	762	774	774	841	785	809	855	241	306	405	244	398	418

TABLE III: SPENDING FOR CRIME -- BY RACE

Question: We are faced with many problems in this country, none of which can be solved easily and inexpensively. I'm going to name some of these problems, and for each one I'd like you to tell me whether you think we are spending too much money, or about the right amount. Halting the rising crime rate. NOTE: Question not asked in 1972.

Responses: TL = Too little; AR = About right; TM = Too much

		YEAR														
RACE	RESP	'73	'74	'75	'76	'77	'78	'80	'82	'83	'84	'85	'86	'87	'88	'89
WHITE	TL	68%	69%	70%	69%	70%	67%	71%	75%	69%	69%	66%	65%	71%	71%	73%
	AR	27	26	25	23	24	27	23	20	27	26	29	30	25	25	21
	TM	5	5	5	8	6	6	6	5	5	5	5	5	4	4	5
# SURVEYED		1226	1236	1242	1287	1257	1294	1254	1252	1348	397	630	585	384	558	637
RACE	RESP	'73	'74	'75	'76	'77	'78	'80	'82	'83	'84	'85	'86	'87	'88	'89
BLACK	TL	71%	78%	69%	75%	69%	72%	82%	79%	79%	77%	65%	75%	70%	77%	89%
	AR	25	18	23	13	23	22	12	15	14	18	25	21	24	17	10
	TM	4	4	8	12	8	6	6	6	6	5	10	4	6	6	1
# SURVEYED		167	162	155	119	162	153	137	149	155	56	72	92	63	94	71
RACE	RESP	'73	'74	'75	'76	'77	'78	'80	'82	'83	'84	'85	'86	'87	'88	'89
OTHER	TL	92%	43%	67%	43%	83%	69%	56%	69%	67%	75%	56%	69%	79%	67%	71%
	AR	0	14	33	43	0	31	33	19	17	25	38	25	21	30	23
	TM	8	43	0	14	17	0	11	12	17	0	6	6	0	4	6
# SURVEYED		12	7	3	7	12	13	9	26	18	16	16	16	14	27	31

TABLE IV: SPENDING FOR CRIME -- BY AGE

Question: We are faced with many problems in this country, none of which can be solved easily and inexpensively. I'm going to name some of these problems, and for each one I'd like you to tell me whether you think we are spending too much money, or about the right amount. Halting the rising crime rate. NOTE: Question not asked in 1972.

Responses: TL = Too little; AR = About right; TM = Too much

		YEAR														
AGE	RESP	'73	'74	'75	'76	'77	'78	'80	'82	'83	'84	'85	'86	'87	'88	'89
18-23	TL	66%	65%	66%	72%	68%	66%	72%	76%	69%	74%	70%	74%	74%	64%	72%
	AR	29	32	31	21	31	29	25	20	29	21	30	24	18	34	22
	TM	5	3	3	7	1	5	3	3	2	5	0	2	8	2	6
# SURVEYED		168	161	164	155	157	157	150	143	123	42	40	54	39	61	67

TABLE IV: SPENDING FOR CRIME -- BY AGE (Continued)

Question: We are faced with many problems in this country, none of which can be solved easily and inexpensively. I'm going to name some of these problems, and for each one I'd like you to tell me whether you think we are spending too much money, or about the right amount. Halting the rising crime rate. NOTE: Question not asked in 1972.

Responses: TL = Too little; AR = About right; TM = Too much

		YEAR														
AGE	RESP	'73	'74	'75	'76	'77	'78	'80	'82	'83	'84	'85	'86	'87	'88	'89
24-29	TL	64%	65%	67%	67%	72%	66%	75%	74%	70%	66%	69%	65%	64%	66%	74%
	AR	33	31	28	27	22	27	20	21	26	31	29	31	31	32	21
	TM	3	3	5	5	6	6	5	5	4	3	2	4	4	2	5
# SURVEYED		201	204	224	215	198	234	199	240	283	70	97	97	70	107	84
AGE	RESP	'73	'74	'75	'76	'77	'78	'80	'82	'83	'84	'85	'86	'87	'88	'89
30-35	TL	72%	70%	67%	69%	69%	69%	69%	74%	71%	72%	73%	63%	58%	71%	72%
	AR	25	25	23	25	27	25	27	21	24	26	23	34	35	22	23
	TM	4	5	9	6	4	6	4	5	4	1	3	4	6	6	6
# SURVEYED		159	169	166	177	181	226	210	196	224	68	94	112	79	94	106
AGE	RESP	'73	'74	'75	'76	'77	'78	'80	'82	'83	'84	'85	'86	'87	'88	'89
36-41	TL	66%	66%	71%	71%	70%	59%	74%	76%	68%	70%	57%	65%	75%	73%	73%
	AR	30	28	25	23	25	34	23	18	27	25	37	31	20	24	22
	TM	4	6	4	6	5	6	3	7	5	5	5	3	5	3	5
# SURVEYED		162	148	143	153	159	155	141	137	167	56	91	89	56	89	95
AGE	RESP	'73	'74	'75	'76	'77	'78	'80	'82	'83	'84	'85	'86	'87	'88	'89
42-47	TL	71%	76%	62%	65%	73%	70%	69%	75%	70%	69%	63%	72%	72%	85%	76%
	AR	24	22	31	23	19	24	21	20	28	24	31	24	24	14	21
	TM	5	3	7	13	8	6	10	5	2	6	6	3	4	1	4
# SURVEYED		136	143	138	111	137	116	111	116	140	49	67	58	50	72	78
AGE	RESP	'73	'74	'75	'76	'77	'78	'80	'82	'83	'84	'85	'86	'87	'88	'89
48-53	TL	68%	73%	77%	70%	69%	71%	71%	79%	67%	78%	58%	63%	77%	70%	83%
	AR	24	19	18	20	27	22	23	13	26	18	32	27	23	30	11
	TM	7	8	5	10	4	7	6	7	6	5	10	10	0	0	6
# SURVEYED		139	135	133	127	149	125	116	107	110	40	72	48	26	46	70
AGE	RESP	'73	'74	'75	'76	'77	'78	'80	'82	'83	'84	'85	'86	'87	'88	'89
54-59	TL	73%	77%	74%	73%	72%	64%	74%	76%	69%	76%	72%	81%	68%	68%	81%
	AR	26	19	21	15	19	27	20	20	25	16	22	17	26	30	17
	TM	1	4	6	11	9	9	6	4	6	8	7	2	6	3	2
# SURVEYED		145	128	117	124	152	129	129	139	124	25	60	48	31	37	53

TABLE IV: SPENDING FOR CRIME -- BY AGE (Continued)

Question: We are faced with many problems in this country, none of which can be solved easily and inexpensively. I'm going to name some of these problems, and for each one I'd like you to tell me whether you think we are spending too much money, or about the right amount. Halting the rising crime rate. NOTE: Question not asked in 1972.

Responses: TL = Too little; AR = About right; TM = Too much

		YEAR														
AGE	RESP	'73	'74	'75	'76	'77	'78	'80	'82	'83	'84	'85	'86	'87	'88	'89
60-65	TL	76%	80%	78%	77%	69%	67%	66%	74%	74%	73%	66%	79%	84%	77%	78%
	AR	17	14	15	14	22	24	21	17	18	27	27	15	13	18	18
	TM	8	6	7	8	8	9	13	9	7	0	8	6	3	5	4
# SURVEYED		115	100	104	118	107	101	110	111	125	33	64	48	32	57	51
AGE	RESP	'73	'74	'75	'76	'77	'78	'80	'82	'83	'84	'85	'86	'87	'88	'89
66+	TL	68%	69%	70%	64%	68%	71%	74%	74%	68%	63%	64%	59%	78%	70%	73%
	AR	24	23	24	25	22	24	17	21	24	28	28	33	19	20	22
	TM	8	8	6	11	11	5	9	5	8	9	8	8	3	10	5
# SURVEYED		176	211	207	228	185	210	226	228	219	82	130	135	77	114	133

****

SPENDING FOR DRUG EDUCATION

TABLE I: SPENDING FOR DRUG EDUCATION -- BY TOTAL POPULATION

Question: We are faced with many problems in this country, none of which can be solved easily and inexpensively. I'm going to name some of these problems, and for each one I'd like you to tell me whether you think we are spending too much money, or about the right amount. Dealing with drug addiction. NOTE: Question not asked in 1972.

Responses: TL = Too little; AR = About right; TM = Too much

	YEAR														
RESPONSE	'73	'74	'75	'76	'77	'78	'80	'82	'83	'84	'85	'86	'87	'88	'89
TL	70%	64%	60%	63%	60%	58%	65%	61%	63%	66%	65%	61%	66%	71%	74%
AR	23	30	31	29	31	33	27	30	31	28	30	33	29	25	20
TM	6	7	9	8	9	9	8	9	6	6	6	6	4	4	7
# SURVEYED	1399	1396	1370	1390	1410	1452	1353	1387	1507	467	715	695	471	691	736

TABLE II: SPENDING FOR DRUG EDUCATION -- BY SEX

Question: We are faced with many problems in this country, none of which can be solved easily and inexpensively. I'm going to name some of these problems, and for each one I'd like you to tell me whether you think we are spending too much money, or about the right amount. Dealing with drug addiction. NOTE: Question not asked in 1972.

Responses: TL = Too little; AR = About right; TM = Too much

		YEAR														
SEX	RESP	'73	'74	'75	'76	'77	'78	'80	'82	'83	'84	'85	'86	'87	'88	'89
M	TL	70%	65%	60%	64%	58%	56%	63%	61%	63%	64%	64%	56%	64%	73%	77%
	AR	23	28	29	26	31	33	28	28	30	28	28	36	32	22	16
	TM	8	7	12	10	11	11	9	12	7	7	8	7	5	5	8
# SURVEYED		663	659	632	634	650	624	593	599	658	227	411	294	221	286	318
SEX	RESP	'73	'74	'75	'76	'77	'78	'80	'82	'83	'84	'85	'86	'87	'88	'89
F	TL	71%	62%	60%	62%	61%	60%	66%	62%	63%	67%	65%	64%	69%	69%	71%
	AR	24	31	33	31	32	32	26	31	32	29	32	30	27	28	23
	TM	5	7	7	7	8	8	8	7	5	5	3	6	4	3	6
# SURVEYED		736	737	738	756	760	828	760	788	849	240	304	401	250	405	418

TABLE III: SPENDING FOR DRUG EDUCATION -- BY RACE

Question: We are faced with many problems in this country, none of which can be solved easily and inexpensively. I'm going to name some of these problems, and for each one I'd like you to tell me whether you think we are spending too much money, or about the right amount. Dealing with drug addiction. NOTE: Question not asked in 1972.

Responses: TL = Too little; AR = About right; TM = Too much

		YEAR														
RACE	RESP	'73	'74	'75	'76	'77	'78	'80	'82	'83	'84	'85	'86	'87	'88	'89
WHITE	TL	69%	63%	58%	62%	58%	57%	63%	60%	62%	65%	65%	59%	67%	70%	72%
	AR	24	30	32	30	32	34	29	31	32	29	30	34	29	26	21
	TM	6	6	9	8	9	10	8	9	6	5	5	7	4	4	7
# SURVEYED		1226	1224	1214	1263	1239	1286	1213	1213	1338	393	626	579	394	566	633
RACE	RESP	'73	'74	'75	'76	'77	'78	'80	'82	'83	'84	'85	'86	'87	'88	'89
BLACK	TL	77%	65%	69%	73%	67%	71%	76%	72%	68%	67%	61%	68%	67%	76%	89%
	AR	15	25	24	16	24	24	14	18	26	26	32	27	25	22	8
	TM	8	9	7	11	9	5	10	10	6	7	7	5	8	2	3
# SURVEYED		164	165	153	120	159	151	130	149	152	58	72	100	63	96	72
RACE	RESP	'73	'74	'75	'76	'77	'78	'80	'82	'83	'84	'85	'86	'87	'88	'89
OTHER	TL	89%	43%	67%	43%	75%	60%	90%	64%	53%	63%	59%	63%	50%	72%	68%
	AR	11	29	0	57	8	40	10	28	29	19	24	31	50	14	19
	TM	0	29	33	0	17	0	0	8	18	19	18	6	0	14	13
# SURVEYED		9	7	3	7	12	15	10	25	17	16	17	16	14	29	31

TABLE IV: SPENDING FOR DRUG EDUCATION -- BY AGE

Question: We are faced with many problems in this country, none of which can be solved easily and inexpensively. I'm going to name some of these problems, and for each one I'd like you to tell me whether you think we are spending too much money, or about the right amount. Dealing with drug addiction. NOTE: Question not asked in 1972.

Responses: TL = Too little; AR = About right; TM = Too much

		YEAR														
AGE	RESP	'73	'74	'75	'76	'77	'78	'80	'82	'83	'84	'85	'86	'87	'88	'89
18-23	TL	68%	53%	55%	58%	53%	59%	61%	54%	64%	61%	61%	48%	58%	55%	67%
	AR	26	42	41	30	41	33	36	40	32	34	34	46	38	38	31
	TM	6	5	4	11	6	8	3	7	4	5	5	5	5	8	1
# SURVEYED		167	163	167	158	156	160	152	138	124	41	38	56	40	64	67

TABLE IV: SPENDING FOR DRUG EDUCATION -- BY AGE (Continued)

Question: We are faced with many problems in this country, none of which can be solved easily and inexpensively. I'm going to name some of these problems, and for each one I'd like you to tell me whether you think we are spending too much money, or about the right amount. Dealing with drug addiction. NOTE: Question not asked in 1972.

Responses: TL = Too little; AR = About right; TM = Too much

		YEAR														
AGE	RESP	'73	'74	'75	'76	'77	'78	'80	'82	'83	'84	'85	'86	'87	'88	'89
24-29	TL	69%	60%	63%	61%	54%	55%	58%	55%	55%	59%	64%	56%	58%	59%	73%
	AR	25	34	27	31	38	39	34	37	39	38	30	39	39	34	18
	TM	6	6	10	8	8	7	8	8	6	3	6	5	3	6	10
# SURVEYED		202	204	224	216	196	240	196	236	276	71	98	99	72	108	84
AGE	RESP	'73	'74	'75	'76	'77	'78	'80	'82	'83	'84	'85	'86	'87	'88	'89
30-35	TL	73%	72%	62%	64%	60%	61%	63%	58%	62%	70%	71%	53%	63%	66%	68%
	AR	21	19	28	30	30	31	29	33	32	29	24	41	33	30	26
	TM	6	10	10	5	9	9	7	9	5	2	4	6	4	4	6
# SURVEYED		156	167	165	182	181	221	204	195	226	66	94	115	79	96	107
AGE	RESP	'73	'74	'75	'76	'77	'78	'80	'82	'83	'84	'85	'86	'87	'88	'89
36-41	TL	69%	58%	67%	72%	62%	61%	66%	67%	62%	64%	60%	61%	71%	72%	72%
	AR	25	36	24	23	30	32	26	28	31	29	32	31	25	25	22
	TM	6	6	9	4	9	6	8	5	7	7	9	8	4	3	7
# SURVEYED		171	146	140	149	152	157	142	141	168	58	94	89	56	89	92
AGE	RESP	'73	'74	'75	'76	'77	'78	'80	'82	'83	'84	'85	'86	'87	'88	'89
42-47	TL	71%	62%	48%	68%	62%	59%	65%	69%	68%	80%	64%	71%	65%	86%	86%
	AR	22	30	42	27	33	34	26	22	28	12	33	27	30	14	9
	TM	7	8	10	5	5	7	9	9	4	8	3	2	6	0	5
# SURVEYED		136	146	136	106	133	114	108	113	138	49	67	63	54	73	76
AGE	RESP	'73	'74	'75	'76	'77	'78	'80	'82	'83	'84	'85	'86	'87	'88	'89
48-53	TL	69%	65%	61%	60%	56%	53%	70%	68%	62%	63%	68%	72%	81%	83%	82%
	AR	27	25	33	31	36	33	21	18	32	27	31	22	19	15	13
	TM	4	9	6	9	8	14	8	15	6	10	1	7	0	2	6
SURVEYED		139	138	129	125	144	124	108	102	109	41	72	46	27	47	71
AGE	RESP	'73	'74	'75	'76	'77	'78	'80	'82	'83	'84	'85	'86	'87	'88	'89
54-59	TL	74%	69%	58%	62%	63%	58%	66%	58%	56%	60%	67%	79%	69%	78%	74%
	AR	16	26	31	30	23	29	24	32	37	28	26	21	25	22	20
	TM	10	4	10	9	14	14	10	10	7	12	7	0	6	0	6
# SURVEYED		142	121	115	115	157	125	119	132	127	25	61	48	32	37	50

TABLE IV: SPENDING FOR DRUG EDUCATION -- BY AGE (Continued)

Question: We are faced with many problems in this country, none of which can be solved easily and inexpensively. I'm going to name some of these problems, and for each one I'd like you to tell me whether you think we are spending too much money, or about the right amount. Dealing with drug addiction. NOTE: Question not asked in 1972.

Responses: TL = Too little; AR = About right; TM = Too much

		YEAR														
AGE	RESP	'73	'74	'75	'76	'77	'78	'80	'82	'83	'84	'85	'86	'87	'88	'89
60-65	TL	75%	66%	66%	64%	53%	57%	71%	66%	71%	74%	66%	60%	62%	74%	75%
	AR	19	26	23	25	34	32	19	21	23	23	27	33	32	22	19
	TM	5	8	11	11	13	11	10	13	6	3	6	6	6	4	6
# SURVEYED		113	99	94	116	103	101	109	103	124	35	62	48	34	54	53
AGE	RESP	'73	'74	'75	'76	'77	'78	'80	'82	'83	'84	'85	'86	'87	'88	'89
66+	TL	66%	68%	57%	61%	70%	60%	67%	64%	71%	61%	63%	61%	75%	73%	71%
	AR	26	25	31	29	19	29	22	26	23	30	29	28	18	21	19
	TM	8	7	12	10	12	11	11	10	6	9	8	12	7	6	10
# SURVEYED		169	206	196	219	182	204	207	219	209	77	126	127	76	120	134

****

SPENDING FOR EDUCATION

TABLE I: SPENDING FOR EDUCATION -- BY TOTAL POPULATION

Question: We are faced with many problems in this country, none of which can be solved easily and inexpensively. I'm going to name some of these problems, and for each one I'd like you to tell me whether you think we are spending too much money, or about the right amount. Improving the nation's education system. NOTE: Question not asked in 1972.

Responses: TL = Too little; AR = About right; TM = Too much

	YEAR														
RESPONSE	'73	'74	'75	'76	'77	'78	'80	'82	'83	'84	'85	'86	'87	'88	'89
TL	51%	53%	51%	52%	49%	54%	55%	58%	62%	65%	62%	62%	64%	66%	69%
AR	39	38	37	38	40	35	34	33	32	32	32	33	31	30	28
TM	9	9	12	10	10	11	11	9	6	3	5	4	6	4	3
# SURVEYED	1434	1418	1420	1449	1469	1472	1404	1445	1544	475	724	705	469	688	741

TABLE II: SPENDING FOR EDUCATION -- BY SEX

Question: We are faced with many problems in this country, none of which can be solved easily and inexpensively. I'm going to name some of these problems, and for each one I'd like you to tell me whether you think we are spending too much money, or about the right amount. Improving the nation's education system. NOTE: Question not asked in 1972.

Responses: TL = Too little; AR = About right; TM = Too much

		YEAR														
SEX	RESP	'73	'74	'75	'76	'77	'78	'80	'82	'83	'84	'85	'86	'87	'88	'89
M	TL	51%	53%	48%	49%	48%	52%	53%	54%	62%	67%	60%	60%	63%	63%	70%
	AR	38	37	36	40	40	33	34	34	31	29	33	34	31	32	26
	TM	11	10	16	11	12	14	13	11	7	5	6	6	6	5	3
# SURVEYED		676	665	647	655	675	626	620	621	675	230	417	296	220	286	322
SEX	RESP	'73	'74	'75	'76	'77	'78	'80	'82	'83	'84	'85	'86	'87	'88	'89
F	TL	51%	52%	54%	54%	51%	55%	56%	61%	62%	63%	65%	64%	64%	68%	69%
	AR	41	40	38	37	41	36	35	33	33	35	31	33	30	29	29
	TM	8	8	8	9	8	9	9	7	5	2	4	3	6	3	3
# SURVEYED		758	753	773	794	794	846	784	824	869	245	307	409	249	402	419

TABLE III: SPENDING FOR EDUCATION -- BY RACE

Question: We are faced with many problems in this country, none of which can be solved easily and inexpensively. I'm going to name some of these problems, and for each one I'd like you to tell me whether you think we are spending too much money, or about the right amount. Improving the nation's education system. NOTE: Question not asked in 1972.

Responses: TL = Too little; AR = About right; TM = Too much

		YEAR														
RACE	RESP	'73	'74	'75	'76	'77	'78	'80	'82	'83	'84	'85	'86	'87	'88	'89
WHITE	TL	48%	50%	49%	50%	47%	52%	53%	56%	61%	63%	62%	61%	62%	66%	69%
	AR	42	40	38	39	41	35	36	35	33	33	32	34	31	30	28
	TM	11	10	13	10	11	12	12	9	7	4	6	5	7	4	3
# SURVEYED		1249	1247	1260	1316	1287	1303	1259	1266	1370	404	634	590	388	563	635
RACE	RESP	'73	'74	'75	'76	'77	'78	'80	'82	'83	'84	'85	'86	'87	'88	'89
BLACK	TL	74%	71%	69%	68%	68%	65%	77%	77%	72%	75%	63%	69%	71%	69%	71%
	AR	25	25	28	28	32	32	21	21	26	25	36	30	29	29	26
	TM	1	4	3	4	1	3	2	2	1	0	1	1	0	2	3
# SURVEYED		175	165	156	125	168	154	135	154	156	55	73	100	66	96	73
RACE	RESP	'73	'74	'75	'76	'77	'78	'80	'82	'83	'84	'85	'86	'87	'88	'89
OTHER	TL	70%	67%	25%	38%	29%	53%	40%	64%	61%	63%	59%	60%	60%	66%	67%
	AR	30	33	75	63	57	40	50	28	39	38	35	33	40	34	33
	TM	0	0	0	0	14	7	10	8	0	0	6	7	0	0	0
# SURVEYED		10	6	4	8	14	15	10	25	18	16	17	15	15	29	33

TABLE IV: SPENDING FOR EDUCATION -- BY AGE

Question: We are faced with many problems in this country, none of which can be solved easily and inexpensively. I'm going to name some of these problems, and for each one I'd like you to tell me whether you think we are spending too much money, or about the right amount. Improving the nation's education system. NOTE: Question not asked in 1972.

Responses: TL = Too little; AR = About right; TM = Too much

		YEAR														
AGE	RESP	'73	'74	'75	'76	'77	'78	'80	'82	'83	'84	'85	'86	'87	'88	'89
18-23	TL	53%	55%	60%	62%	58%	54%	54%	63%	63%	72%	65%	66%	67%	46%	66%
	AR	44	42	37	36	40	40	40	33	34	26	33	32	33	48	32
	TM	4	3	4	2	3	6	6	3	3	2	3	2	0	6	2
# SURVEYED		165	163	166	159	160	160	155	147	126	43	40	56	42	65	65

TABLE IV: SPENDING FOR EDUCATION -- BY AGE (Continued)

Question: We are faced with many problems in this country, none of which can be solved easily and inexpensively. I'm going to name some of these problems, and for each one I'd like you to tell me whether you think we are spending too much money, or about the right amount. Improving the nation's education system. NOTE: Question not asked in 1972.

Responses: TL = Too little; AR = About right; TM = Too much

		YEAR														
AGE	RESP	'73	'74	'75	'76	'77	'78	'80	'82	'83	'84	'85	'86	'87	'88	'89
24-29	TL	63%	63%	61%	62%	60%	68%	64%	66%	74%	74%	68%	66%	69%	74%	76%
	AR	32	34	33	34	36	28	32	30	23	24	28	33	26	26	24
	TM	5	3	6	4	4	5	4	4	3	1	4	1	6	0	0
# SURVEYED		204	206	223	224	197	240	197	241	280	70	100	98	70	109	85
AGE	RESP	'73	'74	'75	'76	'77	'78	'80	'82	'83	'84	'85	'86	'87	'88	'89
30-35	TL	49%	62%	56%	59%	53%	60%	74%	67%	67%	76%	73%	66%	69%	71%	81%
	AR	41	31	37	36	43	35	21	27	30	22	24	31	28	25	17
	TM	9	7	7	5	4	5	5	7	3	1	3	3	2	4	2
# SURVEYED		164	165	166	182	184	222	211	200	236	68	95	116	81	93	105
AGE	RESP	'73	'74	'75	'76	'77	'78	'80	'82	'83	'84	'85	'86	'87	'88	'89
36-41	TL	57%	61%	53%	61%	53%	51%	58%	65%	68%	65%	71%	76%	75%	71%	81%
	AR	38	34	36	34	38	43	35	31	27	33	26	24	20	24	18
	TM	5	5	11	6	8	6	7	4	5	2	3	0	5	4	1
# SURVEYED		169	147	148	157	165	156	147	145	170	60	97	90	56	90	96
AGE	RESP	'73	'74	'75	'76	'77	'78	'80	'82	'83	'84	'85	'86	'87	'88	'89
42-47	TL	54%	48%	57%	50%	51%	52%	48%	65%	63%	69%	68%	70%	55%	77%	74%
	AR	37	40	31	43	42	35	37	30	31	29	26	30	42	21	25
	TM	9	12	12	7	8	13	15	5	6	2	6	0	4	3	1
# SURVEYED		142	145	140	110	142	116	115	118	141	51	66	63	53	73	80
AGE	RESP	'73	'74	'75	'76	'77	'78	'80	'82	'83	'84	'85	'86	'87	'88	'89
48-53	TL	49%	56%	47%	49%	54%	47%	53%	66%	64%	58%	54%	49%	57%	65%	72%
	AR	42	34	39	35	34	34	37	26	29	40	40	43	29	30	21
	TM	10	10	14	16	13	20	10	9	7	3	6	9	14	4	7
# SURVEYED		144	140	132	127	152	128	115	105	110	40	70	47	28	46	72
AGE	RESP	'73	'74	'75	'76	'77	'78	'80	'82	'83	'84	'85	'86	'87	'88	'89
54-59	TL	52%	42%	45%	40%	45%	44%	51%	49%	50%	73%	52%	60%	65%	62%	55%
	AR	35	51	42	42	42	36	37	35	43	23	41	38	29	32	41
	TM	13	7	13	18	13	20	13	16	8	4	7	2	6	5	4
# SURVEYED		144	130	123	123	159	135	128	137	127	26	61	50	31	37	51

TABLE IV: SPENDING FOR EDUCATION -- BY AGE (Continued)

Question: We are faced with many problems in this country, none of which can be solved easily and inexpensively. I'm going to name some of these problems, and for each one I'd like you to tell me whether you think we are spending too much money, or about the right amount. Improving the nation's education system. NOTE: Question not asked in 1972.

Responses: TL = Too little; AR = About right; TM = Too much

		YEAR														
AGE	RESP	'73	'74	'75	'76	'77	'78	'80	'82	'83	'84	'85	'86	'87	'88	'89
60-65	TL	38%	50%	47%	40%	40%	45%	45%	50%	54%	40%	64%	55%	64%	63%	57%
	AR	44	33	37	45	43	39	37	36	38	54	33	35	27	34	37
	TM	18	17	16	15	17	16	19	14	9	6	3	10	9	4	6
# SURVEYED		118	103	107	127	114	98	112	111	127	35	66	49	33	56	49
AGE	RESP	'73	'74	'75	'76	'77	'78	'80	'82	'83	'84	'85	'86	'87	'88	'89
66+	TL	41%	37%	34%	39%	29%	48%	39%	36%	46%	51%	48%	52%	50%	58%	56%
	AR	44	46	41	44	48	32	41	47	41	42	40	38	41	37	39
	TM	15	18	25	17	23	20	20	17	13	6	11	11	9	5	5
# SURVEYED		180	213	211	236	189	211	218	233	220	78	126	132	74	116	136

****

SPENDING FOR ENVIRONMENT

TABLE I: SPENDING FOR ENVIRONMENT -- BY TOTAL POPULATION

Question: We are faced with many problems in this country, none of which can be solved easily and inexpensively. I'm going to name some of these problems, and for each one I'd like you to tell me whether you think we are spending too much money, or about the right amount. Improving and protecting the environment. NOTE: Question not asked in 1972.

Responses: TL = Too little; AR = About right; TM = Too much

	YEAR														
RESPONSE	'73	'74	'75	'76	'77	'78	'80	'82	'83	'84	'85	'86	'87	'88	'89
TL	65%	63%	57%	57%	51%	55%	51%	53%	58%	61%	59%	63%	69%	68%	75%
AR	27	29	33	33	37	35	33	35	33	34	33	31	26	27	21
TM	8	8	10	10	12	10	16	12	9	5	8	6	5	5	4
# SURVEYED	1413	1378	1398	1425	1414	1448	1382	1407	1494	466	717	682	457	685	731

TABLE II: SPENDING FOR ENVIRONMENT -- BY SEX

Question: We are faced with many problems in this country, none of which can be solved easily and inexpensively. I'm going to name some of these problems, and for each one I'd like you to tell me whether you think we are spending too much money, or about the right amount. Improving and protecting the environment. NOTE: Question not asked in 1972.

Responses: TL = Too little; AR = About right; TM = Too much

		YEAR														
SEX	RESP	'73	'74	'75	'76	'77	'78	'80	'82	'83	'84	'85	'86	'87	'88	'89
M	TL	65%	65%	55%	58%	52%	51%	48%	52%	57%	61%	60%	66%	68%	66%	76%
	AR	26	25	30	30	34	34	31	32	33	33	30	28	25	29	20
	TM	10	10	15	12	14	15	21	16	10	6	10	5	7	5	5
# SURVEYED		673	646	646	643	650	618	613	609	657	230	418	283	220	283	327
SEX	RESP	'73	'74	'75	'76	'77	'78	'80	'82	'83	'84	'85	'86	'87	'88	'89
F	TL	65%	61%	58%	57%	50%	58%	53%	54%	58%	62%	57%	61%	69%	69%	75%
	AR	29	32	36	36	39	35	35	37	34	35	36	33	27	27	23
	TM	6	7	6	8	10	7	13	9	8	3	6	6	3	4	3
# SURVEYED		740	732	752	782	764	830	769	798	837	236	299	399	237	402	404

TABLE III: SPENDING FOR ENVIRONMENT -- BY RACE

Question: We are faced with many problems in this country, none of which can be solved easily and inexpensively. I'm going to name some of these problems, and for each one I'd like you to tell me whether you think we are spending too much money, or about the right amount. Improving and protecting the environment. NOTE: Question not asked in 1972.

Responses: TL = Too little; AR = About right; TM = Too much

		YEAR														
RACE	RESP	'73	'74	'75	'76	'77	'78	'80	'82	'83	'84	'85	'86	'87	'88	'89
WHITE	TL	64%	62%	56%	57%	50%	54%	49%	51%	57%	61%	58%	62%	68%	67%	75%
	AR	28	30	33	34	38	35	34	36	34	34	32	33	26	27	21
	TM	8	8	10	10	12	11	17	13	9	5	9	5	6	5	4
# SURVEYED		1236	1219	1243	1300	1242	1284	1240	1237	1325	397	633	575	381	564	636
RACE	RESP	'73	'74	'75	'76	'77	'78	'80	'82	'83	'84	'85	'86	'87	'88	'89
BLACK	TL	67%	75%	61%	65%	60%	69%	66%	65%	65%	67%	54%	71%	73%	72%	79%
	AR	25	17	30	24	30	28	26	25	26	28	43	20	26	25	18
	TM	7	8	9	11	10	3	8	10	8	6	3	9	2	3	3
# SURVEYED		165	155	152	116	161	150	133	147	153	54	68	93	62	93	67
RACE	RESP	'73	'74	'75	'76	'77	'78	'80	'82	'83	'84	'85	'86	'87	'88	'89
OTHER	TL	67%	100%	67%	44%	45%	50%	44%	87%	38%	40%	88%	64%	71%	61%	61%
	AR	25	0	33	44	36	50	33	4	56	60	13	36	29	36	36
	TM	8	0	0	11	18	0	22	9	6	0	0	0	0	4	4
# SURVEYED		12	4	3	9	11	14	9	23	16	15	16	14	14	28	28

TABLE IV: SPENDING FOR ENVIRONMENT -- BY AGE

Question: We are faced with many problems in this country, none of which can be solved easily and inexpensively. I'm going to name some of these problems, and for each one I'd like you to tell me whether you think we are spending too much money, or about the right amount. Improving and protecting the environment. NOTE: Question not asked in 1972.

Responses: TL = Too little; AR = About right; TM = Too much

		YEAR														
AGE	RESP	'73	'74	'75	'76	'77	'78	'80	'82	'83	'84	'85	'86	'87	'88	'89
18-23	TL	84%	84%	75%	79%	70%	77%	71%	75%	78%	79%	75%	89%	71%	74%	80%
	AR	14	13	22	17	28	22	23	24	20	21	18	11	27	25	17
	TM	2	3	4	4	2	1	6	1	2	0	8	0	2	2	3
# SURVEYED		168	160	171	160	159	162	147	144	123	42	40	53	41	65	66

TABLE IV: SPENDING FOR ENVIRONMENT -- BY AGE (Continued)

Question: We are faced with many problems in this country, none of which can be solved easily and inexpensively. I'm going to name some of these problems, and for each one I'd like you to tell me whether you think we are spending too much money, or about the right amount. Improving and protecting the environment. NOTE: Question not asked in 1972.

Responses: TL = Too little; AR = About right; TM = Too much

		YEAR														
AGE	RESP	'73	'74	'75	'76	'77	'78	'80	'82	'83	'84	'85	'86	'87	'88	'89
24-29	TL	78%	78%	68%	67%	66%	71%	64%	64%	67%	71%	71%	65%	74%	74%	89%
	AR	20	19	28	29	28	25	26	28	27	28	22	32	21	24	11
	TM	2	2	4	5	6	5	11	8	5	1	7	3	4	2	0
# SURVEYED		208	204	226	220	191	232	199	242	273	68	97	94	70	107	82
AGE	RESP	'73	'74	'75	'76	'77	'78	'80	'82	'83	'84	'85	'86	'87	'88	'89
30-35	TL	69%	67%	62%	60%	57%	64%	66%	67%	66%	76%	68%	76%	73%	73%	77%
	AR	26	27	26	35	38	31	23	26	27	19	27	20	25	23	18
	TM	6	5	12	4	5	5	11	7	7	4	5	4	3	4	6
# SURVEYED		163	166	165	184	181	226	207	195	229	68	96	113	80	91	108
AGE	RESP	'73	'74	'75	'76	'77	'78	'80	'82	'83	'84	'85	'86	'87	'88	'89
36-41	TL	64%	58%	52%	62%	54%	52%	52%	55%	60%	53%	67%	75%	75%	75%	83%
	AR	30	32	36	31	32	38	30	30	32	43	26	22	20	22	17
	TM	5	10	12	7	13	10	18	15	8	3	7	3	5	2	0
# SURVEYED		165	141	145	151	157	151	142	142	168	58	96	87	56	89	94
AGE	RESP	'73	'74	'75	'76	'77	'78	'80	'82	'83	'84	'85	'86	'87	'88	'89
42-47	TL	64%	68%	54%	59%	48%	47%	41%	52%	54%	58%	59%	67%	71%	73%	72%
	AR	29	27	37	28	40	39	38	37	39	31	36	31	25	23	24
	TM	7	6	10	13	12	14	21	10	7	10	5	2	4	4	4
# SURVEYED		139	145	134	108	132	114	111	115	137	48	66	61	51	74	78
AGE	RESP	'73	'74	'75	'76	'77	'78	'80	'82	'83	'84	'85	'86	'87	'88	'89
48-53	TL	62%	58%	57%	52%	43%	44%	37%	49%	53%	53%	47%	59%	59%	66%	80%
	AR	27	32	32	33	39	40	42	38	29	40	41	36	30	28	14
	TM	11	9	11	15	18	16	22	14	19	8	12	5	11	6	6
# SURVEYED		142	139	137	121	145	127	120	103	112	40	73	44	27	47	69
AGE	RESP	'73	'74	'75	'76	'77	'78	'80	'82	'83	'84	'85	'86	'87	'88	'89
54-59	TL	54%	52%	43%	46%	44%	38%	39%	38%	45%	64%	58%	54%	75%	71%	66%
	AR	30	35	46	44	41	47	37	41	39	24	30	33	21	29	25
	TM	15	13	11	10	15	16	24	21	16	12	12	13	4	0	9
# SURVEYED		145	126	113	119	158	133	129	131	120	25	60	54	28	34	53

TABLE IV: SPENDING FOR ENVIRONMENT -- BY AGE (Continued)

Question: We are faced with many problems in this country, none of which can be solved easily and inexpensively. I'm going to name some of these problems, and for each one I'd like you to tell me whether you think we are spending too much money, or about the right amount. Improving and protecting the environment. NOTE: Question not asked in 1972.

Responses: TL = Too little; AR = About right; TM = Too much

		YEAR														
AGE	RESP	'73	'74	'75	'76	'77	'78	'80	'82	'83	'84	'85	'86	'87	'88	'89
60-65	TL	47%	52%	54%	46%	38%	38%	39%	34%	44%	60%	48%	54%	58%	56%	73%
	AR	43	33	34	40	41	41	38	50	48	37	45	38	35	33	16
	TM	10	15	13	14	21	21	23	17	8	3	6	8	6	11	10
# SURVEYED		116	100	104	127	112	98	108	107	120	35	62	48	31	55	49
AGE	RESP	'73	'74	'75	'76	'77	'78	'80	'82	'83	'84	'85	'86	'87	'88	'89
66+	TL	49%	44%	38%	41%	33%	44%	35%	35%	44%	46%	44%	39%	57%	52%	60%
	AR	35	41	42	40	48	42	44	45	45	52	45	50	35	38	38
	TM	16	15	20	19	19	14	21	20	11	3	11	11	8	10	2
# SURVEYED		164	191	198	230	173	198	211	219	206	79	124	124	72	120	130

****

SPENDING FOR WELFARE

TABLE I: SPENDING FOR WELFARE -- BY TOTAL POPULATION

Question: We are faced with many problems in this country, none of which can be solved easily and inexpensively. I'm going to name some of these problems, and for each one I'd like you to tell me whether you think we are spending too much money, or about the right amount. Welfare. NOTE: Question not asked in 1972.

Responses: TL = Too little; AR = About right; TM = Too much

	YEAR														
RESPONSE	'73	'74	'75	'76	'77	'78	'80	'82	'83	'84	'85	'86	'87	'88	'89
TL	21%	23%	25%	14%	13%	14%	14%	21%	22%	25%	19%	23%	22%	24%	24%
AR	25	33	30	23	24	26	27	29	29	34	34	35	32	33	32
TM	54	44	45	63	63	61	59	51	49	41	46	42	46	43	44
# SURVEYED	1432	1422	1405	1429	1449	1473	1401	1439	1530	471	719	700	461	685	720

TABLE II: SPENDING FOR WELFARE -- BY SEX

Question: We are faced with many problems in this country, none of which can be solved easily and inexpensively. I'm going to name some of these problems, and for each one I'd like you to tell me whether you think we are spending too much money, or about the right amount. Welfare. NOTE: Question not asked in 1972.

Responses: TL = Too little; AR = About right; TM = Too much

		YEAR														
SEX	RESP	'73	'74	'75	'76	'77	'78	'80	'82	'83	'84	'85	'86	'87	'88	'89
M	TL	21%	22%	25%	13%	12%	11%	13%	19%	21%	23%	17%	19%	22%	20%	24%
	AR	24	31	29	21	23	25	25	28	29	36	34	41	36	35	31
	TM	55	46	46	66	65	64	62	53	50	41	49	41	42	45	45
# SURVEYED		679	668	652	649	657	620	616	614	665	227	416	295	215	286	311
SEX	RESP	'73	'74	'75	'76	'77	'78	'80	'82	'83	'84	'85	'86	'87	'88	'89
F	TL	20%	24%	25%	15%	14%	15%	15%	22%	23%	26%	22%	26%	22%	26%	24%
	AR	27	35	31	26	25	26	29	30	29	33	35	31	28	32	32
	TM	53	42	44	60	61	58	56	48	48	41	43	43	50	42	44
# SURVEYED		753	754	753	780	792	853	785	825	865	244	303	405	246	399	409

TABLE III: SPENDING FOR WELFARE -- BY RACE

Question: We are faced with many problems in this country, none of which can be solved easily and inexpensively. I'm going to name some of these problems, and for each one I'd like you to tell me whether you think we are spending too much money, or about the right amount. Welfare. NOTE: Question not asked in 1972.

Responses: TL = Too little; AR = About right; TM = Too much

		YEAR														
RACE	RESP	'73	'74	'75	'76	'77	'78	'80	'82	'83	'84	'85	'86	'87	'88	'89
WHITE	TL	15%	19%	21%	12%	10%	10%	11%	17%	20%	20%	16%	20%	20%	21%	21%
	AR	26	34	30	23	23	25	27	29	29	37	34	35	30	33	33
	TM	59	47	49	65	67	65	62	54	51	43	50	45	50	46	46
# SURVEYED		1249	1250	1244	1301	1275	1306	1258	1270	1357	399	635	587	386	563	621
RACE	RESP	'73	'74	'75	'76	'77	'78	'80	'82	'83	'84	'85	'86	'87	'88	'89
BLACK	TL	58%	52%	57%	37%	39%	42%	39%	52%	46%	53%	43%	43%	34%	36%	51%
	AR	25	28	30	23	32	35	30	25	28	26	33	30	39	35	15
	TM	17	20	13	41	29	23	31	23	26	21	23	27	27	29	34
# SURVEYED		172	166	157	120	161	153	135	145	156	58	69	97	62	94	71
RACE	RESP	'73	'74	'75	'76	'77	'78	'80	'82	'83	'84	'85	'86	'87	'88	'89
OTHER	TL	45%	0%	25%	13%	0%	14%	0%	25%	24%	29%	33%	19%	15%	36%	32%
	AR	27	33	0	38	38	21	25	42	12	7	53	44	54	32	39
	TM	27	67	75	50	62	64	75	33	65	64	13	38	31	32	29
# SURVEYED		11	6	4	8	13	14	8	24	17	14	15	16	13	28	28

TABLE IV: SPENDING FOR WELFARE -- BY AGE

Question: We are faced with many problems in this country, none of which can be solved easily and inexpensively. I'm going to name some of these problems, and for each one I'd like you to tell me whether you think we are spending too much money, or about the right amount. Welfare. NOTE: Question not asked in 1972.

Responses: TL = Too little; AR = About right; TM = Too much

		YEAR														
AGE	RESP	'73	'74	'75	'76	'77	'78	'80	'82	'83	'84	'85	'86	'87	'88	'89
18-23	TL	22%	27%	34%	24%	18%	28%	25%	28%	31%	21%	23%	27%	17%	31%	38%
	AR	29	41	33	26	29	22	31	37	23	36	40	36	46	41	35
	TM	49	33	33	50	53	50	43	35	46	43	38	36	37	28	26
# SURVEYED		167	162	166	151	158	158	153	142	124	42	40	55	41	64	65
AGE	RESP	'73	'74	'75	'76	'77	'78	'80	'82	'83	'84	'85	'86	'87	'88	'89
24-29	TL	25%	26%	26%	18%	13%	19%	17%	23%	25%	25%	26%	33%	24%	23%	34%
	AR	23	32	31	26	27	24	24	29	29	35	29	34	30	35	25
	TM	53	42	44	56	60	57	59	49	46	39	44	34	46	42	41
# SURVEYED		208	205	219	219	199	241	197	241	280	71	99	98	70	106	80
AGE	RESP	'73	'74	'75	'76	'77	'78	'80	'82	'83	'84	'85	'86	'87	'88	'89
30-35	TL	22%	23%	31%	12%	10%	12%	14%	20%	27%	22%	20%	22%	23%	26%	19%
	AR	26	28	24	29	23	25	26	24	27	31	33	35	29	26	30
	TM	53	48	45	60	67	63	59	57	46	46	47	42	49	48	51
# SURVEYED		160	165	166	182	183	221	209	200	230	67	94	113	80	92	104
AGE	RESP	'73	'74	'75	'76	'77	'78	'80	'82	'83	'84	'85	'86	'87	'88	'89
36-41	TL	23%	20%	23%	16%	12%	9%	10%	22%	23%	23%	14%	19%	24%	21%	21%
	AR	22	31	22	18	20	24	26	29	25	30	33	38	31	30	29
	TM	56	49	54	66	67	67	64	49	52	47	53	43	45	48	49
# SURVEYED		171	146	145	152	161	156	144	140	167	57	97	89	55	89	89
AGE	RESP	'73	'74	'75	'76	'77	'78	'80	'82	'83	'84	'85	'86	'87	'88	'89
42-47	TL	15%	24%	17%	11%	13%	11%	10%	21%	19%	32%	16%	25%	13%	23%	20%
	AR	22	30	38	21	23	23	20	27	33	32	31	28	37	27	31
	TM	63	46	44	68	64	66	70	53	49	36	53	47	50	49	49
# SURVEYED		139	149	138	112	131	114	111	116	138	50	64	64	52	73	74
AGE	RESP	'73	'74	'75	'76	'77	'78	'80	'82	'83	'84	'85	'86	'87	'88	'89
48-53	TL	19%	24%	21%	10%	11%	10%	10%	23%	18%	22%	18%	17%	12%	26%	18%
	AR	23	25	30	18	26	22	35	21	27	46	32	41	35	34	23
	TM	58	51	49	71	63	68	56	55	54	32	51	41	54	40	59
# SURVEYED		144	142	136	125	150	130	115	107	114	41	73	46	26	47	71

TABLE IV: SPENDING FOR WELFARE -- BY AGE (Continued)

Question: We are faced with many problems in this country, none of which can be solved easily and inexpensively. I'm going to name some of these problems, and for each one I'd like you to tell me whether you think we are spending too much money, or about the right amount. Welfare. NOTE: Question not asked in 1972.

Responses: TL = Too little; AR = About right; TM = Too much

		YEAR														
AGE	RESP	'73	'74	'75	'76	'77	'78	'80	'82	'83	'84	'85	'86	'87	'88	'89
54-59	TL	19%	24%	17%	13%	13%	5%	12%	13%	21%	24%	23%	35%	20%	27%	22%
	AR	26	32	32	21	18	31	23	27	26	28	35	27	33	27	36
	TM	56	44	51	66	69	64	64	60	53	48	42	37	47	46	42
# SURVEYED		144	132	117	127	159	132	132	137	128	25	60	51	30	37	50
AGE	RESP	'73	'74	'75	'76	'77	'78	'80	'82	'83	'84	'85	'86	'87	'88	'89
60-65	TL	14%	21%	25%	11%	14%	11%	14%	17%	18%	24%	25%	24%	32%	22%	29%
	AR	29	36	30	17	20	23	23	27	33	33	39	34	23	35	29
	TM	57	43	44	71	66	66	63	57	49	42	36	42	45	44	41
# SURVEYED		114	106	102	126	110	103	114	113	126	33	64	50	31	55	51
AGE	RESP	'73	'74	'75	'76	'77	'78	'80	'82	'83	'84	'85	'86	'87	'88	'89
66+	TL	23%	19%	24%	10%	13%	11%	11%	17%	15%	25%	14%	14%	24%	20%	22%
	AR	30	41	31	27	28	36	32	36	38	39	37	36	31	39	40
	TM	46	40	45	63	59	53	57	47	48	36	49	50	45	41	38
# SURVEYED		181	210	213	230	192	211	218	236	216	80	125	130	75	119	134

****

SPENDING FOR HEALTH

TABLE I: SPENDING FOR HEALTH -- BY TOTAL POPULATION

Question: We are faced with many problems in this country, none of which can be solved easily and inexpensively. I'm going to name some of these problems, and for each one I'd like you to tell me whether you think we are spending too much money, or about the right amount. Improving and protecting the nation's health. NOTE: Question not asked in 1972.

Responses: TL = Too little; AR = About right; TM = Too much

	YEAR														
RESPONSE	'73	'74	'75	'76	'77	'78	'80	'82	'83	'84	'85	'86	'87	'88	'89
TL	63%	66%	65%	63%	59%	58%	57%	59%	60%	60%	59%	61%	69%	68%	71%
AR	32	29	30	32	34	35	35	34	35	33	34	35	27	29	26
TM	5	5	5	5	7	7	8	7	5	7	6	4	4	3	3
# SURVEYED	1445	1426	1425	1441	1454	1471	1407	1424	1531	465	727	702	471	692	738

TABLE II: SPENDING FOR HEALTH -- BY SEX

Question: We are faced with many problems in this country, none of which can be solved easily and inexpensively. I'm going to name some of these problems, and for each one I'd like you to tell me whether you think we are spending too much money, or about the right amount. Improving and protecting the nation's health. NOTE: Question not asked in 1972.

Responses: TL = Too little; AR = About right; TM = Too much

		YEAR														
SEX	RESP	'73	'74	'75	'76	'77	'78	'80	'82	'83	'84	'85	'86	'87	'88	'89
M	TL	64%	68%	66%	63%	57%	57%	53%	59%	59%	57%	57%	55%	64%	66%	68%
	AR	30	27	28	30	35	34	35	34	35	33	37	39	32	32	29
	TM	6	5	7	6	9	9	12	7	6	10	7	6	4	2	4
# SURVEYED		680	673	650	649	670	627	623	612	664	228	417	292	219	283	322
SEX	RESP	'73	'74	'75	'76	'77	'78	'80	'82	'83	'84	'85	'86	'87	'88	'89
F	TL	62%	65%	65%	62%	60%	58%	60%	59%	60%	63%	63%	65%	74%	70%	73%
	AR	34	31	31	34	34	36	35	34	35	32	31	33	22	26	25
	TM	4	4	4	4	6	6	5	6	5	4	6	3	4	4	3
# SURVEYED		765	753	775	792	784	844	784	812	867	237	310	410	252	409	416

TABLE III: SPENDING FOR HEALTH -- BY RACE

Question: We are faced with many problems in this country, none of which can be solved easily and inexpensively. I'm going to name some of these problems, and for each one I'd like you to tell me whether you think we are spending too much money, or about the right amount. Improving and protecting the nation's health. NOTE: Question not asked in 1972.

Responses: TL = Too little; AR = About right; TM = Too much

		YEAR														
RACE	RESP	'73	'74	'75	'76	'77	'78	'80	'82	'83	'84	'85	'86	'87	'88	'89
WHITE	TL	62%	64%	64%	61%	57%	56%	55%	57%	58%	59%	59%	59%	68%	67%	70%
	AR	34	31	30	34	35	36	36	36	36	34	34	37	27	30	27
	TM	5	5	6	5	8	8	9	7	5	7	7	4	5	3	3
# SURVEYED		1264	1250	1264	1309	1273	1302	1259	1253	1359	395	641	589	390	567	633
RACE	RESP	'73	'74	'75	'76	'77	'78	'80	'82	'83	'84	'85	'86	'87	'88	'89
BLACK	TL	73%	80%	73%	78%	70%	69%	74%	78%	72%	71%	70%	70%	77%	73%	78%
	AR	21	16	24	18	25	31	23	18	24	24	30	28	21	25	19
	TM	6	4	3	4	5	1	3	3	5	5	0	2	2	2	3
# SURVEYED		170	169	158	123	167	154	138	146	155	55	70	98	66	96	73
RACE	RESP	'73	'74	'75	'76	'77	'78	'80	'82	'83	'84	'85	'86	'87	'88	'89
OTHER	TL	73%	57%	33%	67%	50%	80%	70%	60%	47%	53%	44%	60%	60%	76%	63%
	AR	27	29	33	33	36	13	30	32	41	47	50	27	40	17	38
	TM	0	14	33	0	14	7	0	8	12	0	6	13	0	7	0
# SURVEYED		11	7	3	9	14	15	10	25	17	15	16	15	15	29	32

TABLE IV: SPENDING FOR HEALTH -- BY AGE

Question: We are faced with many problems in this country, none of which can be solved easily and inexpensively. I'm going to name some of these problems, and for each one I'd like you to tell me whether you think we are spending too much money, or about the right amount. Improving and protecting the nation's health. NOTE: Question not asked in 1972.

Responses: TL = Too little; AR = About right; TM = Too much

		YEAR														
AGE	RESP	'73	'74	'75	'76	'77	'78	'80	'82	'83	'84	'85	'86	'87	'88	'89
18-23	TL	60%	59%	62%	67%	52%	56%	59%	57%	51%	53%	64%	55%	76%	66%	60%
	AR	39	39	35	31	42	41	37	38	46	45	33	45	21	34	34
	TM	2	1	4	2	6	3	5	5	3	3	3	0	2	0	6
# SURVEYED		166	160	167	158	160	158	153	144	124	40	39	56	42	62	68

TABLE IV: SPENDING FOR HEALTH -- BY AGE (Continued)

Question: We are faced with many problems in this country, none of which can be solved easily and inexpensively. I'm going to name some of these problems, and for each one I'd like you to tell me whether you think we are spending too much money, or about the right amount. Improving and protecting the nation's health. NOTE: Question not asked in 1972.

Responses: TL = Too little; AR = About right; TM = Too much

		YEAR														
AGE	RESP	'73	'74	'75	'76	'77	'78	'80	'82	'83	'84	'85	'86	'87	'88	'89
24-29	TL	66%	76%	71%	68%	60%	67%	58%	66%	58%	59%	68%	60%	64%	69%	68%
	AR	32	21	26	28	36	28	34	29	38	41	30	38	31	29	31
	TM	2	3	3	4	4	6	8	5	4	0	2	2	6	3	1
# SURVEYED		202	205	225	222	196	236	200	240	278	70	99	97	72	108	85
AGE	RESP	'73	'74	'75	'76	'77	'78	'80	'82	'83	'84	'85	'86	'87	'88	'89
30-35	TL	71%	72%	67%	64%	64%	66%	66%	65%	64%	63%	60%	63%	76%	68%	72%
	AR	25	23	30	34	33	30	29	28	30	27	35	35	20	29	27
	TM	4	5	3	2	3	4	6	7	6	10	5	3	4	2	1
# SURVEYED		162	166	165	182	179	225	212	196	231	67	95	115	79	95	105
AGE	RESP	'73	'74	'75	'76	'77	'78	'80	'82	'83	'84	'85	'86	'87	'88	'89
36-41	TL	70%	69%	66%	64%	58%	55%	59%	66%	72%	68%	65%	65%	77%	69%	77%
	AR	28	27	26	31	31	35	34	28	24	23	26	30	18	28	21
	TM	2	4	7	5	11	10	7	6	4	9	9	4	5	3	2
# SURVEYED		170	149	148	154	159	155	144	141	168	57	97	89	56	87	92
AGE	RESP	'73	'74	'75	'76	'77	'78	'80	'82	'83	'84	'85	'86	'87	'88	'89
42-47	TL	61%	63%	64%	64%	62%	47%	55%	64%	58%	65%	54%	61%	68%	84%	73%
	AR	34	34	27	31	31	41	37	31	35	31	35	32	28	14	28
	TM	5	3	9	5	7	12	8	4	6	4	11	6	4	3	0
# SURVEYED		142	147	139	108	136	116	113	118	141	48	65	62	53	73	80
AGE	RESP	'73	'74	'75	'76	'77	'78	'80	'82	'83	'84	'85	'86	'87	'88	'89
48-53	TL	66%	72%	67%	63%	64%	56%	54%	60%	62%	50%	61%	60%	70%	77%	73%
	AR	28	23	27	29	30	34	34	35	32	45	35	29	26	23	21
	TM	6	5	6	8	7	10	12	6	6	5	4	10	4	0	6
# SURVEYED		144	144	135	128	149	126	119	107	114	40	71	48	27	47	71
AGE	RESP	'73	'74	'75	'76	'77	'78	'80	'82	'83	'84	'85	'86	'87	'88	'89
54-59	TL	65%	60%	63%	59%	60%	54%	59%	58%	56%	62%	55%	63%	62%	71%	67%
	AR	31	35	31	33	31	39	33	33	34	31	37	33	35	21	30
	TM	5	5	6	8	9	7	8	9	9	8	8	4	3	8	4
# SURVEYED		150	133	122	123	162	135	125	134	128	26	60	52	34	38	54

TABLE IV: SPENDING FOR HEALTH -- BY AGE (Continued)

Question: We are faced with many problems in this country, none of which can be solved easily and inexpensively. I'm going to name some of these problems, and for each one I'd like you to tell me whether you think we are spending too much money, or about the right amount. Improving and protecting the nation's health. NOTE: Question not asked in 1972.

Responses: TL = Too little; AR = About right; TM = Too much

		YEAR														
AGE	RESP	'73	'74	'75	'76	'77	'78	'80	'82	'83	'84	'85	'86	'87	'88	'89
60-65	TL	61%	66%	68%	60%	54%	54%	57%	52%	64%	69%	54%	63%	75%	65%	81%
	AR	34	26	28	32	34	40	33	39	32	31	38	38	25	31	15
	TM	5	8	4	8	12	6	11	8	4	0	8	0	0	4	4
# SURVEYED		119	104	109	130	113	101	113	107	126	32	65	48	32	55	52
AGE	RESP	'73	'74	'75	'76	'77	'78	'80	'82	'83	'84	'85	'86	'87	'88	'89
66+	TL	49%	58%	60%	54%	53%	52%	47%	46%	52%	57%	55%	56%	60%	55%	67%
	AR	37	33	33	39	38	38	43	46	43	28	38	37	35	39	28
	TM	14	9	7	7	9	10	10	8	5	15	8	6	5	6	5
# SURVEYED		186	212	210	231	193	213	219	228	215	82	133	131	75	124	129

****

SPENDING FOR MASS TRANSIT

TABLE I: SPENDING FOR MASS TRANSIT -- BY TOTAL POPULATION

Question: We are faced with many problems in this country, none of which can be solved easily and inexpensively. I'm going to name some of these problems, and for each one I'd like you to tell me whether you think we are spending too much money, or about the right amount. Mass transportation. NOTE: Question not asked in 1972-1983.

Responses: TL = Too little; AR = About right; TM = Too much

	YEAR					
RESPONSE	'84	'85	'86	'87	'88	'89
TL	37%	33%	31%	33%	32%	34%
AR	51	53	55	53	56	57
TM	12	13	14	14	11	10
# SURVEYED	881	1372	1325	1295	1277	1319

TABLE II: SPENDING FOR MASS TRANSIT -- BY SEX

Question: We are faced with many problems in this country, none of which can be solved easily and inexpensively. I'm going to name some of these problems, and for each one I'd like you to tell me whether you think we are spending too much money, or about the right amount. Mass transportation. NOTE: Question not asked in 1972-1983.

Responses: TL = Too little; AR = About right; TM = Too much

		YEAR					
SEX	RESP	'84	'85	'86	'87	'88	'89
M	TL	41%	37%	31%	33%	34%	38%
	AR	43	47	53	50	53	49
	TM	16	17	17	17	14	13
# SURVEYED		395	642	574	590	575	596

		YEAR					
SEX	RESP	'84	'85	'86	'87	'88	'89
F	TL	34%	30%	32%	33%	31%	30%
	AR	57	59	57	55	60	63
	TM	9	11	11	12	10	7
# SURVEYED		486	730	751	705	702	723

TABLE III: SPENDING FOR MASS TRANSIT -- BY RACE

Question: We are faced with many problems in this country, none of which can be solved easily and inexpensively. I'm going to name some of these problems, and for each one I'd like you to tell me whether you think we are spending too much money, or about the right amount. Mass transportation. NOTE: Question not asked in 1972-1983.

Responses: TL = Too little; AR = About right; TM = Too much

		YEAR					
RACE	RESP	'84	'85	'86	'87	'88	'89
WHITE	TL	36%	34%	30%	32%	32%	33%
	AR	51	53	56	52	57	57
	TM	12	14	14	15	11	10
# SURVEYED		744	1194	1128	1083	1063	1132
RACE	RESP	'84	'85	'86	'87	'88	'89
BLACK	TL	43%	33%	37%	34%	32%	33%
	AR	43	55	48	59	56	57
	TM	14	12	15	8	12	10
# SURVEYED		109	137	162	164	165	135

		YEAR					
RACE	RESP	'84	'85	'86	'87	'88	'89
OTHER	TL	32%	29%	37%	40%	45%	37%
	AR	54	61	63	44	49	60
	TM	14	10	0	17	6	4
# SURVEYED		28	41	35	48	49	52

TABLE IV: SPENDING FOR MASS TRANSIT -- BY AGE

Question: We are faced with many problems in this country, none of which can be solved easily and inexpensively. I'm going to name some of these problems, and for each one I'd like you to tell me whether you think we are spending too much money, or about the right amount. Mass transportation. NOTE: Question not asked in 1972-1983.

Responses: TL = Too little; AR = About right; TM = Too much

AGE	RESP	'84	'85	'86	'87	'88	'89
18-23	TL	28%	22%	18%	22%	21%	18%
	AR	64	71	72	70	69	75
	TM	8	8	10	9	9	7
# SURVEYED		78	120	103	115	127	126
24-29	TL	34%	27%	30%	31%	26%	28%
	AR	58	63	58	53	65	62
	TM	8	11	11	16	9	9
# SURVEYED		134	206	201	174	188	180
30-35	TL	44%	37%	28%	33%	32%	31%
	AR	45	56	58	54	57	63
	TM	11	7	15	14	11	6
# SURVEYED		125	200	210	206	173	191
36-41	TL	39%	40%	33%	36%	32%	39%
	AR	42	47	55	51	59	51
	TM	19	13	11	12	9	10
# SURVEYED		120	171	175	169	180	175
42-47	TL	36%	35%	37%	31%	34%	38%
	AR	49	49	50	58	53	52
	TM	15	16	13	12	13	10
# SURVEYED		78	111	126	139	134	143

AGE	RESP	'84	'85	'86	'87	'88	'89
48-53	TL	44%	38%	32%	35%	42%	35%
	AR	47	44	52	50	42	47
	TM	9	18	16	16	16	19
# SURVEYED		66	117	100	113	79	118
54-59	TL	36%	37%	31%	35%	29%	37%
	AR	53	48	49	44	52	49
	TM	11	15	20	21	19	14
# SURVEYED		66	122	87	82	75	86
60-65	TL	37%	33%	35%	47%	34%	38%
	AR	54	51	47	41	52	47
	TM	10	16	18	11	14	14
# SURVEYED		63	115	102	87	104	91
66+	TL	35%	32%	35%	31%	39%	38%
	AR	48	47	52	50	51	57
	TM	17	21	13	19	10	6
# SURVEYED		146	203	216	205	213	205

****

SPENDING FOR PARKS

TABLE I: SPENDING FOR PARKS -- BY TOTAL POPULATION

Question: We are faced with many problems in this country, none of which can be solved easily and inexpensively. I'm going to name some of these problems, and for each one I'd like you to tell me whether you think we are spending too much money, or about the right amount. Parks and recreation. NOTE: Question not asked in 1972-1983.

Responses: TL = Too little; AR = About right; TM = Too much

	YEAR					
RESPONSE	'84	'85	'86	'87	'88	'89
TL	33%	32%	31%	31%	30%	35%
AR	61	61	63	63	64	60
TM	6	7	6	6	6	5
# SURVEYED	940	1465	1392	1394	1396	1434

TABLE II: SPENDING FOR PARKS -- BY SEX

Question: We are faced with many problems in this country, none of which can be solved easily and inexpensively. I'm going to name some of these problems, and for each one I'd like you to tell me whether you think we are spending too much money, or about the right amount. Parks and recreation. NOTE: Question not asked in 1972-1983.

Responses: TL = Too little; AR = About right; TM = Too much

		YEAR					
SEX	RESP	'84	'85	'86	'87	'88	'89
M	TL	36%	33%	32%	33%	33%	36%
	AR	58	59	61	60	61	57
	TM	5	8	7	7	6	7
# SURVEYED		404	670	595	617	611	633

		YEAR					
SEX	RESP	'84	'85	'86	'87	'88	'89
F	TL	31%	31%	30%	29%	28%	34%
	AR	62	62	64	65	66	62
	TM	7	7	6	6	5	4
# SURVEYED		536	795	797	777	785	801

TABLE III: SPENDING FOR PARKS -- BY RACE

Question: We are faced with many problems in this country, none of which can be solved easily and inexpensively. I'm going to name some of these problems, and for each one I'd like you to tell me whether you think we are spending too much money, or about the right amount. Parks and recreation. NOTE: Question not asked in 1972-1983.

Responses: TL = Too little; AR = About right; TM = Too much

		YEAR					
RACE	RESP	'84	'85	'86	'87	'88	'89
WHITE	TL	31%	31%	28%	28%	28%	33%
	AR	63	62	66	66	66	61
	TM	6	8	6	6	6	6
# SURVEYED		802	1281	1189	1165	1167	1237
RACE	RESP	'84	'85	'86	'87	'88	'89
BLACK	TL	46%	44%	51%	44%	47%	46%
	AR	49	53	44	51	48	50
	TM	5	4	6	4	5	4
# SURVEYED		110	140	170	178	173	145

		YEAR					
RACE	RESP	'84	'85	'86	'87	'88	'89
OTHER	TL	43%	36%	36%	43%	30%	38%
	AR	46	57	52	49	64	60
	TM	11	7	12	8	5	2
# SURVEYED		28	44	33	51	56	52

TABLE IV: SPENDING FOR PARKS -- BY AGE

Question: We are faced with many problems in this country, none of which can be solved easily and inexpensively. I'm going to name some of these problems, and for each one I'd like you to tell me whether you think we are spending too much money, or about the right amount. Parks and recreation. NOTE: Question not asked in 1972-1983.

Responses: TL = Too little; AR = About right; TM = Too much

		YEAR					
AGE	RESP	'84	'85	'86	'87	'88	'89
18-23	TL	51%	38%	44%	36%	44%	46%
	AR	47	56	54	61	53	47
	TM	2	6	2	2	3	7
# SURVEYED		83	129	104	121	135	132
AGE	RESP	'84	'85	'86	'87	'88	'89
24-29	TL	42%	34%	36%	37%	37%	35%
	AR	56	60	60	60?	61	60
	TM	2	6	4	3	2	5
# SURVEYED		144	214	212	185	208	195

		YEAR					
AGE	RESP	'84	'85	'86	'87	'88	'89
30-35	TL	36%	41%	33%	35%	33%	41%
	AR	61	54	65	60	64	55
	TM	3	6	2	5	3	4
# SURVEYED		131	211	220	217	187	201
AGE	RESP	'84	'85	'86	'87	'88	'89
36-41	TL	37%	40%	31%	34%	32%	39%
	AR	58	57	64	63	64	56
	TM	6	3	5	3	4	5
# SURVEYED		126	181	182	181	184	191

TABLE IV: SPENDING FOR PARKS -- BY AGE (Continued)

Question: We are faced with many problems in this country, none of which can be solved easily and inexpensively. I'm going to name some of these problems, and for each one I'd like you to tell me whether you think we are spending too much money, or about the right amount. Parks and recreation. NOTE: Question not asked in 1972-1983.

Responses: TL = Too little; AR = About right; TM = Too much

		YEAR					
AGE	RESP	'84	'85	'86	'87	'88	'89
42-47	TL	33%	33%	31%	28%	30%	32%
	AR	56	60	66	68	64	66
	TM	12	7	4	5	7	2
# SURVEYED		86	123	134	151	149	149
		YEAR					
AGE	RESP	'84	'85	'86	'87	'88	'89
48-53	TL	29%	21%	30%	35%	27%	32%
	AR	67	62	55	57	67	62
	TM	4	17	15	8	6	6
# SURVEYED		70	128	101	122	88	133
AGE	RESP	'84	'85	'86	'87	'88	'89
54-59	TL	27%	27%	22%	28%	25%	30%
	AR	64	65	66	62	69	65
	TM	9	8	12	10	6	4
# SURVEYED		74	124	92	92	80	89

		YEAR					
AGE	RESP	'84	'85	'86	'87	'88	'89
60-65	TL	19%	30%	34%	25%	18%	33%
	AR	78	62	61	67	76	62
	TM	3	8	5	7	6	5
# SURVEYED		68	120	103	95	114	99
AGE	RESP	'84	'85	'86	'87	'88	'89
66+	TL	24%	22%	21%	19%	21%	25%
	AR	63	69	67	69	65	66
	TM	13	8	12	12	13	9
# SURVEYED		153	228	238	225	247	241

****

SPENDING FOR CONDITION OF BLACKS

TABLE I: SPENDING FOR CONDITION OF BLACKS -- BY TOTAL POPULATION

Question: We are faced with many problems in this country, none of which can be solved easily and inexpensively. I'm going to name some of these problems, and for each one I'd like you to tell me whether you think we are spending too much money, or about the right amount. Improving the condition of blacks. NOTE: Question not asked in 1972.

Responses: TL = Too little; AR = About right; TM = Too much

	YEAR														
RESPONSE	'73	'74	'75	'76	'77	'78	'80	'82	'83	'84	'85	'86	'87	'88	'89
TL	35%	33%	29%	29%	27%	26%	26%	30%	32%	37%	33%	36%	38%	38%	36%
AR	42	45	45	43	46	47	48	48	48	46	46	46	47	45	46
TM	23	22	26	27	27	27	26	22	20	17	21	17	16	17	18
# SURVEYED	1402	1379	1372	1392	1402	1417	1347	1374	1447	455	699	666	444	655	686

TABLE II: SPENDING FOR CONDITION OF BLACKS -- BY SEX

Question: We are faced with many problems in this country, none of which can be solved easily and inexpensively. I'm going to name some of these problems, and for each one I'd like you to tell me whether you think we are spending too much money, or about the right amount. Improving the condition of blacks. NOTE: Question not asked in 1972.

Responses: TL = Too little; AR = About right; TM = Too much

		YEAR														
SEX	RESP	'73	'74	'75	'76	'77	'78	'80	'82	'83	'84	'85	'86	'87	'88	'89
M	TL	35%	31%	29%	28%	28%	27%	24%	29%	30%	39%	32%	34%	36%	33%	37%
	AR	38	45	42	40	41	43	45	46	47	42	43	44	46	47	44
	TM	27	24	29	32	32	31	31	26	23	19	25	21	17	19	20
# SURVEYED		664	650	630	640	646	613	598	595	643	219	410	281	211	272	301
SEX	RESP	'73	'74	'75	'76	'77	'78	'80	'82	'83	'84	'85	'86	'87	'88	'89
F	TL	35%	35%	29%	30%	27%	26%	28%	32%	34%	36%	35%	38%	39%	41%	36%
	AR	46	45	47	46	50	50	50	49	48	49	49	48	47	43	48
	TM	19	20	23	23	23	25	22	19	17	15	17	14	15	16	16
# SURVEYED		738	729	742	752	756	804	749	779	804	236	289	385	233	383	385

TABLE III: SPENDING FOR CONDITION OF BLACKS -- BY RACE

Question: We are faced with many problems in this country, none of which can be solved easily and inexpensively. I'm going to name some of these problems, and for each one I'd like you to tell me whether you think we are spending too much money, or about the right amount. Improving the condition of blacks. NOTE: Question not asked in 1972.

Responses: TL = Too little; AR = About right; TM = Too much

		YEAR														
RACE	RESP	'73	'74	'75	'76	'77	'78	'80	'82	'83	'84	'85	'86	'87	'88	'89
WHITE	TL	28%	26%	22%	24%	20%	19%	20%	23%	27%	32%	28%	29%	32%	31%	30%
	AR	46	48	49	46	50	50	51	52	51	49	47	51	50	48	51
	TM	26	25	29	30	30	31	29	25	23	19	24	20	18	21	20
# SURVEYED		1214	1203	1210	1259	1223	1248	1202	1199	1280	384	615	557	371	537	591
RACE	RESP	'73	'74	'75	'76	'77	'78	'80	'82	'83	'84	'85	'86	'87	'88	'89
BLACK	TL	83%	82%	84%	83%	80%	83%	80%	90%	80%	71%	70%	75%	72%	81%	83%
	AR	14	18	14	14	20	16	18	9	20	29	30	22	25	19	14
	TM	3	0	2	2	0	1	2	1	0	0	0	3	3	0	3
# SURVEYED		177	170	158	125	167	154	136	152	154	56	69	97	61	96	70
RACE	RESP	'73	'74	'75	'76	'77	'78	'80	'82	'83	'84	'85	'86	'87	'88	'89
OTHER	TL	45%	33%	25%	25%	25%	33%	22%	35%	23%	40%	53%	58%	50%	27%	52%
	AR	45	50	50	50	33	67	67	52	69	33	47	33	42	73	32
	TM	9	17	25	25	42	0	11	13	8	27	0	8	8	0	16
# SURVEYED		11	6	4	8	12	15	9	23	13	15	15	12	12	22	25

TABLE IV: SPENDING FOR CONDITION OF BLACKS -- BY AGE

Question: We are faced with many problems in this country, none of which can be solved easily and inexpensively. I'm going to name some of these problems, and for each one I'd like you to tell me whether you think we are spending too much money, or about the right amount. Improving the condition of blacks. NOTE: Question not asked in 1972.

Responses: TL = Too little; AR = About right; TM = Too much

		YEAR														
AGE	RESP	'73	'74	'75	'76	'77	'78	'80	'82	'83	'84	'85	'86	'87	'88	'89
18-23	TL	40%	37%	40%	41%	39%	39%	32%	41%	45%	47%	44%	38%	63%	32%	37%
	AR	45	47	46	39	41	46	50	44	41	50	39	53	29	55	46
	TM	15	16	14	20	20	15	18	15	14	3	17	9	8	13	16
# SURVEYED		164	155	159	153	149	151	148	136	114	38	36	55	38	60	67

TABLE IV: SPENDING FOR CONDITION OF BLACKS -- BY AGE (Continued)

Question: We are faced with many problems in this country, none of which can be solved easily and inexpensively. I'm going to name some of these problems, and for each one I'd like you to tell me whether you think we are spending too much money, or about the right amount. Improving the condition of blacks. NOTE: Question not asked in 1972.

Responses: TL = Too little; AR = About right; TM = Too much

		YEAR														
AGE	RESP	'73	'74	'75	'76	'77	'78	'80	'82	'83	'84	'85	'86	'87	'88	'89
24-29	TL	39%	37%	34%	36%	31%	32%	30%	31%	35%	49%	36%	42%	39%	48%	53%
	AR	45	45	47	43	48	44	47	48	47	36	42	42	55	36	36
	TM	16	18	19	21	21	23	23	21	18	15	22	16	6	17	12
# SURVEYED		206	203	218	214	193	222	189	229	259	67	96	93	64	101	78
AGE	RESP	'73	'74	'75	'76	'77	'78	'80	'82	'83	'84	'85	'86	'87	'88	'89
30-35	TL	33%	44%	31%	29%	29%	29%	30%	34%	34%	31%	37%	36%	41%	45%	35%
	AR	39	34	43	47	48	45	48	44	50	47	42	49	44	42	50
	TM	28	22	25	24	23	26	22	21	16	22	21	15	15	13	15
# SURVEYED		156	161	161	175	177	222	201	198	223	64	91	105	78	88	96
AGE	RESP	'73	'74	'75	'76	'77	'78	'80	'82	'83	'84	'85	'86	'87	'88	'89
36-41	TL	40%	35%	23%	33%	27%	26%	21%	29%	32%	30%	27%	32%	35%	38%	33%
	AR	39	45	49	43	42	42	49	46	49	54	46	55	51	44	51
	TM	21	20	28	24	31	32	30	25	18	16	26	13	15	18	15
# SURVEYED		165	142	144	149	156	148	138	134	157	56	91	84	55	82	84
AGE	RESP	'73	'74	'75	'76	'77	'78	'80	'82	'83	'84	'85	'86	'87	'88	'89
42-47	TL	33%	31%	26%	29%	26%	23%	20%	31%	24%	41%	40%	44%	27%	41%	41%
	AR	38	40	43	45	46	51	48	44	53	47	39	37	54	41	47
	TM	29	29	30	26	28	26	32	25	24	12	21	19	19	18	11
# SURVEYED		142	140	136	108	137	113	111	111	131	49	62	59	48	71	70
AGE	RESP	'73	'74	'75	'76	'77	'78	'80	'82	'83	'84	'85	'86	'87	'88	'89
48-53	TL	33%	29%	32%	25%	22%	25%	25%	28%	26%	37%	23%	26%	32%	37%	32%
	AR	41	48	39	38	43	44	50	51	47	39	59	51	40	46	37
	TM	26	23	29	38	35	31	25	21	27	24	17	23	28	17	31
# SURVEYED		139	138	132	125	136	124	117	104	107	41	69	47	25	46	65
AGE	RESP	'73	'74	'75	'76	'77	'78	'80	'82	'83	'84	'85	'86	'87	'88	'89
54-59	TL	33%	25%	27%	23%	27%	22%	22%	18%	28%	46%	36%	40%	31%	41%	30%
	AR	42	49	38	46	47	50	51	48	46	38	36	38	56	54	48
	TM	25	26	35	31	26	28	27	33	26	17	28	21	13	5	22
# SURVEYED		139	126	114	121	157	127	119	130	119	24	61	52	32	37	50

TABLE IV: SPENDING FOR CONDITION OF BLACKS -- BY AGE (Continued)

Question: We are faced with many problems in this country, none of which can be solved easily and inexpensively. I'm going to name some of these problems, and for each one I'd like you to tell me whether you think we are spending too much money, or about the right amount. Improving the condition of blacks. NOTE: Question not asked in 1972.

Responses: TL = Too little; AR = About right; TM = Too much

		YEAR														
AGE	RESP	'73	'74	'75	'76	'77	'78	'80	'82	'83	'84	'85	'86	'87	'88	'89
60-65	TL	21%	31%	25%	21%	23%	14%	25%	34%	33%	34%	32%	35%	39%	28%	40%
	AR	45	46	46	41	49	47	41	47	45	47	63	39	42	51	44
	TM	34	23	29	38	28	39	34	19	22	19	5	26	19	21	17
# SURVEYED		111	100	102	123	107	93	110	105	122	32	65	46	31	53	48
AGE	RESP	'73	'74	'75	'76	'77	'78	'80	'82	'83	'84	'85	'86	'87	'88	'89
66+	TL	35%	26%	22%	24%	20%	17%	23%	26%	31%	29%	29%	34%	32%	28%	28%
	AR	44	49	48	46	50	52	49	54	49	51	43	47	44	46	50
	TM	22	25	30	30	31	31	28	20	20	20	28	19	24	25	22
# SURVEYED		176	208	202	220	183	210	206	218	210	80	125	121	72	114	126

****

SPENDING FOR HIGHWAY SYSTEM

TABLE I: SPENDING FOR HIGHWAY SYSTEM -- BY TOTAL POPULATION

Question: We are faced with many problems in this country, none of which can be solved easily and inexpensively. I'm going to name some of these problems, and for each one I'd like you to tell me whether you think we are spending too much money, or about the right amount. Highways and bridges. NOTE: Question not asked in 1972-1983.

Responses: TL = Too little; AR = About right; TM = Too much

	YEAR					
RESPONSE	'84	'85	'86	'87	'88	'89
TL	48%	43%	37%	37%	38%	41%
AR	45	49	55	55	54	52
TM	7	8	9	9	8	7
# SURVEYED	936	1448	1393	1373	1396	1428

TABLE II: SPENDING FOR HIGHWAY SYSTEM -- BY SEX

Question: We are faced with many problems in this country, none of which can be solved easily and inexpensively. I'm going to name some of these problems, and for each one I'd like you to tell me whether you think we are spending too much money, or about the right amount. Highways and bridges. NOTE: Question not asked in 1972-1983.

Responses: TL = Too little; AR = About right; TM = Too much

		YEAR					
SEX	RESP	'84	'85	'86	'87	'88	'89
M	TL	53%	46%	38%	41%	41%	44%
	AR	40	45	54	52	52	48
	TM	7	9	8	7	7	7
# SURVEYED		405	666	596	614	618	638

		YEAR					
SEX	RESP	'84	'85	'86	'87	'88	'89
F	TL	45%	41%	35%	33%	35%	38%
	AR	48	52	55	57	56	54
	TM	7	7	9	10	8	7
# SURVEYED		531	782	797	759	778	790

TABLE III: SPENDING FOR HIGHWAY SYSTEM -- BY RACE

Question: We are faced with many problems in this country, none of which can be solved easily and inexpensively. I'm going to name some of these problems, and for each one I'd like you to tell me whether you think we are spending too much money, or about the right amount. Highways and bridges. NOTE: Question not asked in 1972-1983.

Responses: TL = Too little; AR = About right; TM = Too much

		YEAR					
RACE	RESP	'84	'85	'86	'87	'88	'89
WHITE	TL	49%	44%	36%	36%	38%	41%
	AR	44	49	56	55	55	52
	TM	6	8	8	9	7	7
# SURVEYED		798	1265	1190	1152	1170	1226
RACE	RESP	'84	'85	'86	'87	'88	'89
BLACK	TL	42%	41%	40%	40%	35%	42%
	AR	48	47	45	51	53	46
	TM	10	11	15	9	12	12
# SURVEYED		109	140	169	170	170	147

		YEAR					
RACE	RESP	'84	'85	'86	'87	'88	'89
OTHER	TL	41%	37%	29%	33%	39%	36%
	AR	48	58	68	63	52	60
	TM	10	5	3	4	9	4
# SURVEYED		29	43	34	51	56	55

TABLE IV: SPENDING FOR HIGHWAY SYSTEM -- BY AGE

Question: We are faced with many problems in this country, none of which can be solved easily and inexpensively. I'm going to name some of these problems, and for each one I'd like you to tell me whether you think we are spending too much money, or about the right amount. Highways and bridges. NOTE: Question not asked in 1972-1983.

Responses: TL = Too little; AR = About right; TM = Too much

AGE	RESP	'84	'85	'86	'87	'88	'89
18-23	TL	43%	37%	32%	31%	28%	27%
	AR	46	54	56	60	67	65
	TM	11	10	12	9	5	8
# SURVEYED		83	126	102	117	138	133
24-29	TL	45%	46%	31%	30%	35%	36%
	AR	49	47	59	58	54	56
	TM	6	7	10	12	10	8
# SURVEYED		140	206	213	177	206	189
30-35	TL	40%	44%	32%	39%	36%	39%
	AR	50	47	60	55	53	55
	TM	10	9	8	7	12	5
# SURVEYED		127	206	216	209	180	202
36-41	TL	52%	38%	40%	41%	35%	43%
	AR	45	55	52	53	58	48
	TM	2	7	7	6	8	9
# SURVEYED		124	180	183	180	186	188
42-47	TL	50%	39%	38%	36%	37%	41%
	AR	45	54	53	53	55	53
	TM	5	7	8	11	8	5
# SURVEYED		84	121	133	150	152	148

AGE	RESP	'84	'85	'86	'87	'88	'89
48-53	TL	49%	45%	37%	44%	44%	40%
	AR	44	46	53	47	47	49
	TM	7	9	10	9	9	11
# SURVEYED		73	127	103	123	87	131
54-59	TL	51%	45%	38%	38%	34%	42%
	AR	40	50	53	54	59	53
	TM	10	6	9	8	6	4
# SURVEYED		73	123	91	91	79	90
60-65	TL	53%	46%	50%	39%	48%	45%
	AR	43	46	45	56	45	46
	TM	4	7	6	5	7	9
# SURVEYED		70	123	109	95	113	96
66+	TL	52%	47%	38%	35%	43%	51%
	AR	40	45	52	55	51	43
	TM	8	9	10	10	6	6
# SURVEYED		157	229	237	227	251	247

****

SPENDING FOR SOCIAL SECURITY

TABLE I: SPENDING FOR SOCIAL SECURITY -- BY TOTAL POPULATION

Question: We are faced with many problems in this country, none of which can be solved easily and inexpensively. I'm going to name some of these problems, and for each one I'd like you to tell me whether you think we are spending too much money, or about the right amount. Social security. NOTE: Question not asked in 1972-1983.

Responses: TL = Too little; AR = About right; TM = Too much

	YEAR					
RESPONSE	'84	'85	'86	'87	'88	'89
TL	53%	54%	57%	57%	55%	57%
AR	37	40	37	36	39	39
TM	9	7	6	7	6	5
# SURVEYED	922	1481	1419	1393	1406	1454

TABLE II: SPENDING FOR SOCIAL SECURITY -- BY SEX

Question: We are faced with many problems in this country, none of which can be solved easily and inexpensively. I'm going to name some of these problems, and for each one I'd like you to tell me whether you think we are spending too much money, or about the right amount. Social security. NOTE: Question not asked in 1972-1983.

Responses: TL = Too little; AR = About right; TM = Too much

		YEAR					
SEX	RESP	'84	'85	'86	'87	'88	'89
M	TL	48%	50%	51%	53%	48%	51%
	AR	39	40	41	38	44	43
	TM	13	9	8	9	8	6
# SURVEYED		394	669	601	611	607	632

		YEAR					
SEX	RESP	'84	'85	'86	'87	'88	'89
F	TL	57%	56%	61%	60%	60%	61%
	AR	36	39	33	35	36	36
	TM	6	5	5	5	4	3
# SURVEYED		528	812	818	782	799	822

TABLE III: SPENDING FOR SOCIAL SECURITY -- BY RACE

Question: We are faced with many problems in this country, none of which can be solved easily and inexpensively. I'm going to name some of these problems, and for each one I'd like you to tell me whether you think we are spending too much money, or about the right amount. Social security. NOTE: Question not asked in 1972-1983.

Responses: TL = Too little; AR = About right; TM = Too much

RACE	RESP	'84	'85	'86	'87	'88	'89
WHITE	TL	51%	52%	54%	54%	52%	54%
	AR	38	41	39	39	42	41
	TM	10	8	7	7	6	5
# SURVEYED		783	1296	1208	1168	1176	1247
BLACK	TL	69%	67%	79%	77%	72%	79%
	AR	27	32	15	22	24	19
	TM	4	1	6	2	4	1
# SURVEYED		113	144	175	176	176	151

RACE	RESP	'84	'85	'86	'87	'88	'89
OTHER	TL	50%	68%	56%	67%	61%	50%
	AR	50	29	44	22	39	43
	TM	0	2	0	10	0	7
# SURVEYED		26	41	36	49	54	56

TABLE IV: SPENDING FOR SOCIAL SECURITY -- BY AGE

Question: We are faced with many problems in this country, none of which can be solved easily and inexpensively. I'm going to name some of these problems, and for each one I'd like you to tell me whether you think we are spending too much money, or about the right amount. Social security. NOTE: Question not asked in 1972-1983.

Responses: TL = Too little; AR = About right; TM = Too much

AGE	RESP	'84	'85	'86	'87	'88	'89
18-23	TL	51%	58%	65%	58%	50%	51%
	AR	43	32	28	34	39	41
	TM	6	10	7	8	10	8
# SURVEYED		82	128	102	117	135	126
24-29	TL	62%	60%	61%	62%	63%	62%
	AR	28	31	31	32	35	33
	TM	10	9	8	6	3	5
# SURVEYED		138	213	209	180	195	192

AGE	RESP	'84	'85	'86	'87	'88	'89
30-35	TL	61%	62%	68%	57%	60%	62%
	AR	26	30	25	35	34	35
	TM	13	8	7	8	5	4
# SURVEYED		125	205	215	214	187	199
36-41	TL	60%	58%	59%	64%	62%	54%
	AR	32	31	32	27	28	37
	TM	8	11	9	8	10	9
# SURVEYED		116	177	185	180	185	188

TABLE IV: SPENDING FOR SOCIAL SECURITY -- BY AGE (Continued)

Question: We are faced with many problems in this country, none of which can be solved easily and inexpensively. I'm going to name some of these problems, and for each one I'd like you to tell me whether you think we are spending too much money, or about the right amount. Social security. NOTE: Question not asked in 1972-1983.

Responses: TL = Too little; AR = About right; TM = Too much

AGE	RESP	'84	'85	'86	'87	'88	'89
42-47	TL	56%	42%	55%	55%	58%	59%
	AR	32	52	36	38	36	37
	TM	12	6	9	7	5	5
# SURVEYED		84	122	139	148	151	153
48-53	TL	42%	60%	58%	55%	52%	66%
	AR	46	35	37	36	44	30
	TM	12	5	5	8	4	4
# SURVEYED		67	129	102	119	91	134
54-59	TL	49%	55%	54%	56%	50%	53%
	AR	41	41	43	41	46	44
	TM	11	4	3	3	4	3
# SURVEYED		74	128	93	93	78	94

AGE	RESP	'84	'85	'86	'87	'88	'89
60-65	TL	49%	44%	50%	55%	52%	51%
	AR	43	52	42	40	43	47
	TM	9	4	8	5	5	2
# SURVEYED		68	124	112	99	117	105
66+	TL	44%	43%	44%	51%	44%	51%
	AR	51	53	53	45	51	47
	TM	6	4	3	5	5	2
# SURVEYED		162	250	256	238	264	259

****

SPENDING FOR SPACE RESEARCH

TABLE I: SPENDING FOR SPACE RESEARCH -- BY TOTAL POPULATION

Question: We are faced with many problems in this country, none of which can be solved easily and inexpensively. I'm going to name some of these problems, and for each one I'd like you to tell me whether you think we are spending too much money, or about the right amount. Space exploration program. NOTE: Question not asked in 1972.

Responses: TL = Too little; AR = About right; TM = Too much

RESPONSE	'73	'74	'75	'76	'77	'78	'80	'82	'83	'84	'85	'86	'87	'88	'89
TL	8%	8%	8%	9%	11%	12%	20%	13%	15%	13%	12%	12%	17%	19%	16%
AR	31	29	32	29	37	37	38	44	43	46	46	45	40	45	47
TM	61	63	61	62	53	50	43	43	42	42	42	43	43	37	37
# SURVEYED	1432	1427	1425	1459	1440	1436	1344	1411	1502	460	721	697	454	673	717

TABLE II: SPENDING FOR SPACE RESEARCH -- BY SEX

Question: We are faced with many problems in this country, none of which can be solved easily and inexpensively. I'm going to name some of these problems, and for each one I'd like you to tell me whether you think we are spending too much money, or about the right amount. Space exploration program. NOTE: Question not asked in 1972.

Responses: TL = Too little; AR = About right; TM = Too much

		YEAR														
SEX	RESP	'73	'74	'75	'76	'77	'78	'80	'82	'83	'84	'85	'86	'87	'88	'89
M	TL	12%	12%	12%	16%	16%	22%	27%	21%	23%	18%	15%	18%	24%	30%	26%
	AR	33	34	36	32	39	43	40	45	44	54	51	48	44	46	48
	TM	56	54	52	51	45	35	34	34	33	28	34	34	32	24	25
# SURVEYED		678	672	648	657	667	618	605	608	662	228	420	298	222	280	316
SEX	RESP	'73	'74	'75	'76	'77	'78	'80	'82	'83	'84	'85	'86	'87	'88	'89
F	TL	5%	5%	4%	4%	6%	5%	14%	7%	8%	7%	7%	7%	11%	11%	7%
	AR	29	24	28	26	35	33	36	43	43	37	39	43	37	44	46
	TM	66	71	68	70	59	62	50	50	49	56	54	50	53	46	46
# SURVEYED		754	755	777	802	773	818	739	803	840	232	301	399	232	393	401

TABLE III: SPENDING FOR SPACE RESEARCH -- BY RACE

Question: We are faced with many problems in this country, none of which can be solved easily and inexpensively. I'm going to name some of these problems, and for each one I'd like you to tell me whether you think we are spending too much money, or about the right amount. Space exploration program. NOTE: Question not asked in 1972.

Responses: TL = Too little; AR = About right; TM = Too much

		YEAR														
RACE	RESP	'73	'74	'75	'76	'77	'78	'80	'82	'83	'84	'85	'86	'87	'88	'89
WHITE	TL	8%	9%	8%	10%	11%	14%	21%	14%	16%	14%	13%	12%	18%	21%	17%
	AR	34	31	34	30	38	39	39	47	46	48	48	48	43	45	50
	TM	58	60	58	60	50	48	40	39	38	38	39	39	38	33	33
# SURVEYED		1251	1253	1271	1327	1261	1273	1206	1241	1336	392	637	586	382	555	623
RACE	RESP	'73	'74	'75	'76	'77	'78	'80	'82	'83	'84	'85	'86	'87	'88	'89
BLACK	TL	4%	4%	2%	2%	5%	3%	6%	3%	5%	6%	4%	8%	10%	6%	2%
	AR	9	8	13	14	24	24	26	23	20	28	30	25	22	38	27
	TM	87	87	85	84	71	73	68	73	75	67	66	67	68	57	72
# SURVEYED		169	167	150	124	165	150	130	145	148	54	67	96	59	90	64
RACE	RESP	'73	'74	'75	'76	'77	'78	'80	'82	'83	'84	'85	'86	'87	'88	'89
OTHER	TL	8%	0%	0%	0%	14%	8%	38%	16%	22%	14%	6%	7%	15%	11%	13%
	AR	17	57	50	38	36	31	25	24	28	36	29	60	23	50	37
	TM	75	43	50	63	50	62	38	60	50	50	65	33	62	39	50
# SURVEYED		12	7	4	8	14	13	8	25	18	14	17	15	13	28	30

TABLE IV: SPENDING FOR SPACE RESEARCH -- BY AGE

Question: We are faced with many problems in this country, none of which can be solved easily and inexpensively. I'm going to name some of these problems, and for each one I'd like you to tell me whether you think we are spending too much money, or about the right amount. Space exploration program. NOTE: Question not asked in 1972.

Responses: TL = Too little; AR = About right; TM = Too much

		YEAR														
AGE	RESP	'73	'74	'75	'76	'77	'78	'80	'82	'83	'84	'85	'86	'87	'88	'89
18-23	TL	10%	9%	6%	8%	12%	11%	15%	16%	17%	12%	18%	9%	11%	23%	19%
	AR	35	30	39	34	35	37	50	49	55	49	56	64	43	52	56
	TM	55	60	55	58	53	52	35	35	28	39	26	27	46	25	25
# SURVEYED		166	164	172	159	156	158	148	139	119	41	39	55	37	61	64

TABLE IV: SPENDING FOR SPACE RESEARCH -- BY AGE (Continued)

Question: We are faced with many problems in this country, none of which can be solved easily and inexpensively. I'm going to name some of these problems, and for each one I'd like you to tell me whether you think we are spending too much money, or about the right amount. Space exploration program. NOTE: Question not asked in 1972.

Responses: TL = Too little; AR = About right; TM = Too much

		YEAR														
AGE	RESP	'73	'74	'75	'76	'77	'78	'80	'82	'83	'84	'85	'86	'87	'88	'89
24-29	TL	11%	7%	10%	15%	11%	18%	23%	14%	18%	16%	11%	17%	19%	19%	22%
	AR	35	34	32	28	40	38	37	49	45	49	56	43	43	55	47
	TM	54	59	58	58	49	43	40	37	38	35	33	39	38	26	31
# SURVEYED		207	207	220	224	198	230	192	240	277	69	98	99	69	105	81
AGE	RESP	'73	'74	'75	'76	'77	'78	'80	'82	'83	'84	'85	'86	'87	'88	'89
30-35	TL	6%	8%	10%	10%	15%	15%	27%	22%	18%	20%	14%	10%	26%	15%	20%
	AR	33	25	32	31	35	38	37	47	44	46	52	57	31	44	51
	TM	61	68	57	59	50	47	37	30	38	34	35	34	43	41	29
# SURVEYED		161	170	164	183	179	222	197	198	226	65	95	115	77	91	105
AGE	RESP	'73	'74	'75	'76	'77	'78	'80	'82	'83	'84	'85	'86	'87	'88	'89
36-41	TL	10%	11%	9%	14%	17%	11%	26%	16%	19%	16%	20%	18%	16%	22%	19%
	AR	29	27	34	30	36	39	39	41	46	46	46	47	47	42	49
	TM	61	63	56	56	48	49	35	44	34	38	34	36	37	36	32
# SURVEYED		174	147	149	154	162	152	142	140	166	56	95	90	57	89	90
AGE	RESP	'73	'74	'75	'76	'77	'78	'80	'82	'83	'84	'85	'86	'87	'88	'89
42-47	TL	9%	9%	18%	11%	10%	6%	20%	11%	19%	19%	22%	20%	19%	23%	19%
	AR	37	28	36	23	41	47	34	44	40	42	40	44	44	44	38
	TM	54	63	45	66	49	46	46	44	42	40	37	36	37	33	42
# SURVEYED		142	144	137	111	137	114	109	117	139	48	67	61	52	73	78
AGE	RESP	'73	'74	'75	'76	'77	'78	'80	'82	'83	'84	'85	'86	'87	'88	'89
48-53	TL	6%	9%	6%	8%	12%	16%	19%	12%	13%	12%	7%	17%	22%	11%	22%
	AR	26	37	34	27	43	40	42	41	42	38	44	38	37	43	37
	TM	68	54	60	66	45	44	39	47	45	50	49	45	41	46	41
# SURVEYED		146	138	136	128	141	124	113	107	111	42	72	47	27	46	68
AGE	RESP	'73	'74	'75	'76	'77	'78	'80	'82	'83	'84	'85	'86	'87	'88	'89
54-59	TL	5%	8%	6%	9%	9%	14%	20%	14%	6%	12%	13%	4%	17%	14%	13%
	AR	28	30	28	33	36	35	33	42	42	50	38	49	47	42	46
	TM	68	62	66	58	55	51	48	45	52	38	48	47	37	44	40
# SURVEYED		145	135	123	124	159	131	123	132	125	26	60	53	30	36	52
AGE	RESP	'73	'74	'75	'76	'77	'78	'80	'82	'83	'84	'85	'86	'87	'88	'89
60-65	TL	4%	6%	3%	6%	6%	12%	14%	8%	13%	6%	6%	4%	17%	29%	4%
	AR	31	23	20	24	38	33	35	34	37	45	48	47	33	29	53
	TM	65	71	77	70	56	55	51	58	50	48	46	49	50	43	43
# SURVEYED		112	103	110	133	113	100	110	106	124	33	65	49	30	56	51

TABLE IV: SPENDING FOR SPACE RESEARCH -- BY AGE (Continued)

Question: We are faced with many problems in this country, none of which can be solved easily and inexpensively. I'm going to name some of these problems, and for each one I'd like you to tell me whether you think we are spending too much money, or about the right amount. Space exploration program. NOTE: Question not asked in 1972.

Responses: TL = Too little; AR = About right; TM = Too much

		YEAR														
AGE	RESP	'73	'74	'75	'76	'77	'78	'80	'82	'83	'84	'85	'86	'87	'88	'89
66+	TL	7%	5%	2%	4%	5%	5%	12%	5%	8%	1%	3%	6%	8%	14%	5%
	AR	23	23	24	28	29	31	33	42	36	44	38	29	36	44	46
	TM	70	72	74	68	67	64	55	52	56	55	59	65	55	42	49
# SURVEYED		175	214	210	238	189	198	202	224	209	77	128	125	74	113	126

****

AMOUNT OF TAXES

TABLE I: AMOUNT OF TAXES -- BY TOTAL POPULATION

Question: Do you consider the amount of federal income tax which you have to pay as too high, about right, or too low? NOTE: Question not asked in 1972-1975, 1978, 1983, 1986.

Responses: HI = Too high; RT = About right; LO = Too low; NO = Respondent pays no income tax

	YEAR								
RESPONSE	'76	'77	'80	'82	'84	'85	'87	'88	'89
HI	60%	68%	71%	72%	64%	62%	61%	57%	58%
RT	34	29	28	27	33	33	36	40	38
LO	1	1	0	0	1	0	1	1	1
NO	5	2	0	1	2	4	2	2	2
# SURVEYED	1442	1462	1383	1438	1429	1484	1398	942	993

TABLE II: AMOUNT OF TAXES -- BY SEX

Question: Do you consider the amount of federal income tax which you have to pay as too high, about right, or too low? NOTE: Question not asked in 1972-1975, 1978, 1983, 1986.

Responses: HI = Too high; RT = About right; LO = Too low; NO = Respondent pays no income tax

		YEAR								
SEX	RESP	'76	'77	'80	'82	'84	'85	'87	'88	'89
M	HI	60%	67%	69%	70%	59%	64%	58%	53%	52%
	RT	35	31	31	28	38	33	40	46	45
	LO	1	1	0	1	1	1	1	1	2
	NO	4	1	0	1	2	2	1	1	1
# SURVEYED		658	676	620	|24	589	672	623	396	440

		YEAR								
SEX	RESP	'76	'77	'80	'82	'84	'85	'87	'88	'89
F	HI	61%	69%	74%	73%	68%	61%	63%	60%	63%
	RT	33	27	26	26	30	33	34	36	33
	LO	0	1	0	0	0	0	0	1	0
	NO	6	3	0	1	2	5	3	3	4
# SURVEYED		784	786	763	814	840	812	775	546	553

TABLE III: AMOUNT OF TAXES -- BY RACE

Question: Do you consider the amount of federal income tax which you have to pay as too high, about right, or too low? NOTE: Question not asked in 1972-1975, 1978, 1983, 1986.

Responses: HI = Too high; RT = About right; LO = Too low; NO = Respondent pays no income tax

		YEAR								
RACE	RESP	'76	'77	'80	'82	'84	'85	'87	'88	'89
WHITE	HI	59%	67%	71%	71%	63%	62%	60%	55%	57%
	RT	35	30	29	27	35	34	37	43	40
	LO	1	1	0	0	1	1	1	1	1
	NO	5	2	0	1	2	4	2	1	2
# SURVEYED		1317	1292	1244	1268	1218	1302	1179	776	859
RACE	RESP	'76	'77	'80	'82	'84	'85	'87	'88	'89
BLACK	HI	72%	76%	77%	80%	74%	64%	68%	62%	61%
	RT	24	19	23	20	23	29	28	30	30
	LO	1	1	0	0	1	0	1	2	2
	NO	3	4	0	0	3	7	4	6	6
# SURVEYED		116	156	129	144	159	141	170	124	96

		YEAR								
RACE	RESP	'76	'77	'80	'82	'84	'85	'87	'88	'89
OTHER	HI	78%	64%	60%	69%	67%	71%	53%	67%	66%
	RT	22	29	40	27	29	27	45	31	24
	LO	0	0	0	4	0	0	0	0	0
	NO	0	7	0	0	4	2	2	2	11
# SURVEYED		9	14	10	26	52	41	49	42	38

TABLE IV: AMOUNT OF TAXES -- BY AGE

Question: Do you consider the amount of federal income tax which you have to pay as too high, about right, or too low? NOTE: Question not asked in 1972-1975, 1978, 1983, 1986.

Responses: HI = Too high; RT = About right; LO = Too low; NO = Respondent pays no income tax

AGE	RESP	'76	'77	'80	'82	'84	'85	'87	'88	'89
18-23	HI	54%	64%	66%	67%	60%	54%	47%	49%	52%
	RT	41	31	34	31	36	41	49	50	44
	LO	1	3	1	0	1	0	0	1	1
	NO	3	3	0	1	3	5	4	0	3
# SURVEYED		152	158	148	144	157	128	119	90	94
24-29	HI	67%	70%	76%	73%	66%	66%	67%	55%	58%
	RT	32	29	24	28	33	32	32	42	41
	LO	1	1	1	0	0	1	0	1	1
	NO	0	1	0	0	0	0	1	2	1
# SURVEYED		216	199	197	240	226	211	192	132	111
30-35	HI	64%	69%	72%	80%	69%	70%	64%	62%	64%
	RT	33	31	27	19	30	30	34	36	35
	LO	1	1	0	0	1	0	0	1	0
	NO	3	0	0	0	0	0	1	1	2
# SURVEYED		184	182	210	201	196	210	218	129	133
36-41	HI	64%	73%	76%	76%	70%	67%	71%	63%	63%
	RT	35	27	24	24	29	32	28	35	33
	LO	0	1	0	1	1	1	1	1	2
	NO	1	0	0	0	0	1	1	1	2
# SURVEYED		156	164	146	144	184	180	181	131	133
42-47	HI	65%	74%	80%	83%	66%	68%	71%	60%	67%
	RT	31	23	20	17	33	29	29	38	30
	LO	0	1	0	1	0	1	1	2	1
	NO	4	2	0	0	2	2	0	0	2
# SURVEYED		109	143	113	115	125	123	154	100	107

AGE	RESP	'76	'77	'80	'82	'84	'85	'87	'88	'89
48-53	HI	67%	72%	78%	80%	71%	72%	61%	77%	64%
	RT	30	26	22	18	28	26	37	23	34
	LO	0	1	0	2	1	0	1	0	1
	NO	3	1	0	0	0	2	1	0	1
# SURVEYED		132	147	118	111	99	130	122	65	94
54-59	HI	67%	70%	79%	71%	64%	66%	64%	68%	59%
	RT	30	29	21	28	35	29	33	28	39
	LO	2	0	0	1	0	1	1	4	0
	NO	2	1	0	0	1	4	2	0	2
# SURVEYED		129	163	131	135	114	131	95	53	61
60-65	HI	59%	76%	77%	68%	67%	56%	61%	59%	63%
	RT	34	22	23	29	31	42	37	41	36
	LO	1	2	0	0	0	0	1	0	0
	NO	6	1	0	3	2	2	1	0	1
# SURVEYED		130	115	111	109	109	125	93	81	72
66+	HI	44%	50%	51%	57%	50%	47%	43%	37%	43%
	RT	37	39	48	38	41	37	49	53	49
	LO	0	0	0	0	1	0	1	1	2
	NO	18	11	0	5	9	16	6	9	6
# SURVEYED		230	184	203	229	214	239	221	158	185

****

U.S. ACTIVE IN WORLD AFFAIRS

TABLE I: U.S. ACTIVE IN WORLD AFFAIRS -- BY TOTAL POPULATION

Question: Do you think it will be best for the future of this country if we take an active part in world affairs, or if we stay out of world affairs? NOTE: Question not asked in 1972, 1974, 1977, 1980, 1987.

Responses: AP = Active part; SO = Stay out

	YEAR										
RESPONSE	'73	'75	'76	'78	'82	'83	'84	'85	'86	'88	'89
AP	68%	63%	66%	67%	64%	68%	69%	72%	67%	67%	71%
SO	32	37	34	33	36	32	31	28	33	33	29
# SURVEYED	1443	1428	1428	1469	1432	1526	1361	727	1391	946	968

TABLE II: U.S. ACTIVE IN WORLD AFFAIRS -- BY SEX

Question: Do you think it will be best for the future of this country if we take an active part in world affairs, or if we stay out of world affairs? NOTE: Question not asked in 1972, 1974, 1977, 1980, 1987.

Responses: AP = Active part; SO = Stay out

		YEAR										
SEX	RESP	'73	'75	'76	'78	'82	'83	'84	'85	'86	'88	'89
M	AP	74%	67%	73%	73%	71%	73%	70%	78%	73%	70%	75%
	SO	26	33	27	27	29	27	30	22	27	30	25
# SURVEYED		676	649	650	626	612	670	571	421	585	428	420
SEX	RESP	'73	'75	'76	'78	'82	'83	'84	'85	'86	'88	'89
F	AP	63%	60%	61%	62%	59%	64%	69%	65%	63%	65%	68%
	SO	37	40	39	38	41	36	31	35	37	35	32
# SURVEYED		767	779	778	843	820	856	790	306	806	518	548

TABLE III: U.S. ACTIVE IN WORLD AFFAIRS -- BY RACE

Question: Do you think it will be best for the future of this country if we take an active part in world affairs, or if we stay out of world affairs? NOTE: Question not asked in 1972, 1974, 1977, 1980, 1987.

Responses: AP = Active part; SO = Stay out

		YEAR										
RACE	RESP	'73	'75	'76	'78	'82	'83	'84	'85	'86	'88	'89
WHITE	AP	72%	65%	67%	68%	66%	69%	71%	75%	70%	69%	74%
	SO	28	35	33	32	34	31	29	25	30	31	26
# SURVEYED		1257	1268	1304	1304	1260	1356	1161	639	1192	795	837
RACE	RESP	'73	'75	'76	'78	'82	'83	'84	'85	'86	'88	'89
BLACK	AP	42%	49%	53%	56%	51%	54%	58%	48%	48%	55%	52%
	SO	58	51	47	44	49	46	42	52	52	45	48
# SURVEYED		175	156	116	151	146	153	154	71	165	119	97
RACE	RESP	'73	'75	'76	'78	'82	'83	'84	'85	'86	'88	'89
OTHER	AP	55%	50%	88%	79%	54%	94%	67%	59%	53%	63%	62%
	SO	45	50	13	21	46	6	33	41	47	38	38
# SURVEYED		11	4	8	14	26	17	46	17	34	32	34

TABLE IV: U.S. ACTIVE IN WORLD AFFAIRS -- BY AGE

Question: Do you think it will be best for the future of this country if we take an active part in world affairs, or if we stay out of world affairs? NOTE: Question not asked in 1972, 1974, 1977, 1980, 1987.

Responses: AP = Active part; SO = Stay out

		YEAR										
AGE	RESP	'73	'75	'76	'78	'82	'83	'84	'85	'86	'88	'89
18-23	AP	70%	61%	65%	65%	54%	54%	62%	65%	57%	51%	65%
	SO	30	39	35	35	46	46	38	35	43	49	35
# SURVEYED		167	166	155	158	143	124	146	40	102	92	82
AGE	RESP	'73	'75	'76	'78	'82	'83	'84	'85	'86	'88	'89
24-29	AP	67%	64%	69%	71%	66%	68%	66%	72%	68%	68%	69%
	SO	33	36	31	29	34	32	34	28	32	32	31
# SURVEYED		203	225	212	235	233	276	219	99	206	144	140

TABLE IV: U.S. ACTIVE IN WORLD AFFAIRS -- BY AGE (Continued)

Question: Do you think it will be best for the future of this country if we take an active part in world affairs, or if we stay out of world affairs? NOTE: Question not asked in 1972, 1974, 1977, 1980, 1987.

Responses: AP = Active part; SO = Stay out

		YEAR										
AGE	RESP	'73	'75	'76	'78	'82	'83	'84	'85	'86	'88	'89
30-35	AP	72%	65%	72%	72%	71%	71%	72%	79%	71%	67%	73%
	SO	28	35	28	28	29	29	28	21	29	33	27
# SURVEYED		160	162	183	222	196	228	184	96	208	125	138
AGE	RESP	'73	'75	'76	'78	'82	'83	'84	'85	'86	'88	'89
36-41	AP	76%	66%	75%	67%	77%	76%	74%	81%	77%	76%	72%
	SO	24	34	25	33	23	24	26	19	23	24	28
# SURVEYED		169	145	153	153	142	167	176	96	185	123	123
AGE	RESP	'73	'75	'76	'78	'82	'83	'84	'85	'86	'88	'89
42-47	AP	72%	72%	68%	79%	68%	71%	83%	79%	73%	77%	77%
	SO	28	28	32	21	32	29	17	21	27	23	23
# SURVEYED		142	139	108	117	119	143	118	63	132	106	105
AGE	RESP	'73	'75	'76	'78	'82	'83	'84	'85	'86	'88	'89
48-53	AP	71%	70%	67%	78%	68%	77%	72%	79%	74%	69%	77%
	SO	29	30	33	22	32	23	28	21	26	31	23
# SURVEYED		143	138	131	129	103	111	95	71	102	61	84
AGE	RESP	'73	'75	'76	'78	'82	'83	'84	'85	'86	'88	'89
54-59	AP	66%	70%	64%	70%	70%	68%	71%	64%	69%	67%	74%
	SO	34	30	36	30	30	32	29	36	31	33	26
# SURVEYED		154	122	123	132	138	126	107	61	98	49	68
AGE	RESP	'73	'75	'76	'78	'82	'83	'84	'85	'86	'88	'89
60-65	AP	63%	55%	64%	61%	54%	72%	68%	68%	70%	67%	65%
	SO	37	45	36	39	46	28	32	32	30	33	35
# SURVEYED		111	108	127	101	110	124	105	66	112	67	68
AGE	RESP	'73	'75	'76	'78	'82	'83	'84	'85	'86	'88	'89
66+	AP	58%	51%	55%	45%	54%	57%	63%	61%	50%	62%	66%
	SO	42	49	45	55	46	43	38	39	50	38	34
# SURVEYED		191	219	230	215	238	220	208	132	241	178	157

****

U.S. KEEP UNITED NATIONS MEMBERSHIP

TABLE I: U.S. KEEP UNITED NATIONS MEMBERSHIP -- BY TOTAL POPULATION

Question: Do you think our government should continue to belong to the United Nations, or should it pull out of it now? NOTE: Question not asked in 1972, 1974, 1977, 1980, 1984, 1987.

Responses: BL = Continue to belong; PO = Pull out now

	YEAR									
RESPONSE	'73	'75	'76	'78	'82	'83	'85	'86	'88	'89
BL	84%	81%	79%	86%	83%	85%	82%	82%	83%	87%
PO	16	19	21	14	17	15	18	18	17	13
# SURVEYED	1412	1390	1374	1413	1409	1498	1461	1363	926	950

TABLE II: U.S. KEEP UNITED NATIONS MEMBERSHIP -- BY SEX

Question: Do you think our government should continue to belong to the United Nations, or should it pull out of it now? NOTE: Question not asked in 1972, 1974, 1977, 1980, 1984, 1987.

Responses: BL = Continue to belong; PO = Pull out now

		YEAR									
SEX	RESP	'73	'75	'76	'78	'82	'83	'85	'86	'88	'89
M	BL	83%	76%	78%	85%	83%	85%	80%	82%	82%	88%
	PO	17	24	22	15	17	15	20	18	18	12
# SURVEYED		671	642	644	623	617	663	673	579	422	416
SEX	RESP	'73	'75	'76	'78	'82	'83	'85	'86	'88	'89
F	BL	85%	85%	80%	87%	83%	86%	84%	83%	84%	87%
	PO	15	15	20	13	17	14	16	17	16	13
# SURVEYED		741	748	730	790	792	835	788	784	504	534

TABLE III: U.S. KEEP UNITED NATIONS MEMBERSHIP -- BY RACE

Question: Do you think our government should continue to belong to the United Nations, or should it pull out of it now? NOTE: Question not asked in 1972, 1974, 1977, 1980, 1984, 1987.

Responses: BL = Continue to belong; PO = Pull out now

		YEAR									
RACE	RESP	'73	'75	'76	'78	'82	'83	'85	'86	'88	'89
WHITE	BL	85%	81%	79%	86%	83%	86%	82%	83%	84%	88%
	PO	15	19	21	14	17	14	18	17	16	12
# SURVEYED		1241	1231	1253	1255	1240	1330	1284	1175	778	821
RACE	RESP	'73	'75	'76	'78	'82	'83	'85	'86	'88	'89
BLACK	BL	78%	75%	75%	84%	80%	79%	81%	82%	83%	79%
	PO	23	25	25	16	20	21	19	18	17	21
# SURVEYED		160	155	114	145	142	150	134	153	117	92
RACE	RESP	'73	'75	'76	'78	'82	'83	'85	'86	'88	'89
OTHER	BL	82%	25%	86%	92%	89%	94%	84%	77%	74%	86%
	PO	18	75	14	8	11	6	16	23	26	14
# SURVEYED		11	4	7	13	27	18	43	35	31	37

TABLE IV: U.S. KEEP UNITED NATIONS MEMBERSHIP -- BY AGE

Question: Do you think our government should continue to belong to the United Nations, or should it pull out of it now? NOTE: Question not asked in 1972, 1974, 1977, 1980, 1984, 1987.

Responses: BL = Continue to belong; PO = Pull out now

		YEAR									
AGE	RESP	'73	'75	'76	'78	'82	'83	'85	'86	'88	'89
18-23	BL	88%	89%	86%	85%	81%	91%	89%	88%	76%	77%
	PO	12	11	14	15	19	9	11	12	24	23
# SURVEYED		163	166	152	158	139	120	130	99	89	83
AGE	RESP	'73	'75	'76	'78	'82	'83	'85	'86	'88	'89
24-29	BL	89%	89%	88%	90%	86%	89%	88%	87%	92%	91%
	PO	11	11	12	10	14	11	12	13	8	9
# SURVEYED		209	219	214	224	236	272	211	205	144	137

TABLE IV: U.S. KEEP UNITED NATIONS MEMBERSHIP -- BY AGE (Continued)

Question: Do you think our government should continue to belong to the United Nations, or should it pull out of it now? NOTE: Question not asked in 1972, 1974, 1977, 1980, 1984, 1987.

Responses: BL = Continue to belong; PO = Pull out now

		YEAR									
AGE	RESP	'73	'75	'76	'78	'82	'83	'85	'86	'88	'89
30-35	BL	87%	85%	86%	91%	91%	89%	89%	87%	88%	93%
	PO	13	15	14	9	9	11	11	13	12	7
# SURVEYED		160	166	176	217	198	227	209	210	126	138
AGE	RESP	'73	'75	'76	'78	'82	'83	'85	'86	'88	'89
36-41	BL	87%	82%	80%	88%	88%	84%	86%	83%	90%	87%
	PO	13	18	20	12	12	16	14	17	10	13
# SURVEYED		166	148	148	149	145	161	177	181	124	123
AGE	RESP	'73	'75	'76	'78	'82	'83	'85	'86	'88	'89
42-47	BL	87%	86%	82%	88%	88%	86%	85%	89%	79%	89%
	PO	13	14	18	12	12	14	15	11	21	11
# SURVEYED		140	136	101	116	111	137	119	133	104	105
AGE	RESP	'73	'75	'76	'78	'82	'83	'85	'86	'88	'89
48-53	BL	79%	80%	73%	90%	83%	84%	80%	84%	88%	90%
	PO	21	20	27	10	17	16	20	16	12	10
# SURVEYED		139	133	123	125	108	111	124	98	60	80
AGE	RESP	'73	'75	'76	'78	'82	'83	'85	'86	'88	'89
54-59	BL	86%	84%	72%	83%	80%	87%	74%	76%	82%	79%
	PO	14	16	28	17	20	13	26	24	18	21
# SURVEYED		146	117	120	126	135	125	130	92	50	67
AGE	RESP	'73	'75	'76	'78	'82	'83	'85	'86	'88	'89
60-65	BL	75%	64%	77%	80%	72%	78%	75%	77%	81%	87%
	PO	25	36	23	20	28	22	25	23	19	13
# SURVEYED		111	104	122	93	106	125	122	111	63	62
AGE	RESP	'73	'75	'76	'78	'82	'83	'85	'86	'88	'89
66+	BL	76%	63%	66%	77%	75%	80%	71%	72%	73%	85%
	PO	24	37	34	23	25	20	29	28	27	15
# SURVEYED		175	197	212	198	222	214	233	229	165	152

****

U.S. IN WAR IN TEN YEARS

TABLE I: U.S. IN WAR IN TEN YEARS -- BY TOTAL POPULATION

Question: Do you expect the United States to fight in another world war in the next ten years? NOTE: Question not asked in 1972-1975, 1977-1984, 1987.

Responses: YES; NO

	YEAR				
RESPONSE	'76	'85	'86	'88	'89
YES	47%	46%	47%	42%	33%
NO	53	54	53	58	67
# SURVEYED	673	731	1396	949	952

TABLE II: U.S. IN WAR IN TEN YEARS -- BY SEX

Question: Do you expect the United States to fight in another world war in the next ten years? NOTE: Question not asked in 1972-1975, 1977-1984, 1987.

Responses: YES; NO

		YEAR				
SEX	RESP	'76	'85	'86	'88	'89
M	YES	49%	40%	39%	35%	27%
	NO	51	60	61	65	73
# SURVEYED		315	239	594	422	408

		YEAR				
SEX	RESP	'76	'85	'86	'88	'89
F	YES	45%	49%	53%	47%	37%
	NO	55	51	47	53	63
# SURVEYED		358	492	802	527	544

TABLE III: U.S. IN WAR IN TEN YEARS -- BY RACE

Question: Do you expect the United States to fight in another world war in the next ten years? NOTE: Question not asked in 1972-1975, 1977-1984, 1987.

Responses: YES; NO

		YEAR				
RACE	RESP	'76	'85	'86	'88	'89
WHITE	YES	44%	44%	45%	38%	30%
	NO	56	56	55	62	70
# SURVEYED		612	644	1195	797	820

		YEAR				
RACE	RESP	'76	'85	'86	'88	'89
BLACK	YES	72%	66%	63%	63%	63%
	NO	28	34	37	37	37
# SURVEYED		58	62	167	118	97

		YEAR				
RACE	RESP	'76	'85	'86	'88	'89
OTHER	YES	33%	48%	53%	41%	34%
	NO	67	52	47	59	66
# SURVEYED		3	25	34	34	35

TABLE IV: U.S. IN WAR IN TEN YEARS -- BY AGE

Question: Do you expect the United States to fight in another world war in the next ten years? NOTE: Question not asked in 1972-1975, 1977-1984, 1987.

Responses: YES; NO

AGE	RESP	'76	'85	'86	'88	'89
18-23	YES	53%	43%	49%	41%	40%
	NO	47	57	51	59	60
# SURVEYED		75	87	104	91	80
24-29	YES	46%	54%	43%	50%	34%
	NO	54	46	57	50	66
# SURVEYED		114	111	210	147	143
30-35	YES	42%	53%	52%	43%	36%
	NO	58	47	48	57	64
# SURVEYED		90	110	210	127	138

AGE	RESP	'76	'85	'86	'88	'89
36-41	YES	36%	45%	42%	30%	32%
	NO	64	55	58	70	68
# SURVEYED		67	83	186	125	122
42-47	YES	39%	40%	43%	42%	34%
	NO	61	60	57	58	66
# SURVEYED		49	55	133	106	104
48-53	YES	39%	33%	46%	48%	35%
	NO	61	67	54	52	65
# SURVEYED		62	51	99	61	82

AGE	RESP	'76	'85	'86	'88	'89
54-59	YES	39%	44%	48%	42%	31%
	NO	61	56	52	58	69
# SURVEYED		46	63	96	48	67
60-65	YES	57%	50%	54%	38%	22%
	NO	43	50	46	63	78
# SURVEYED		61	56	112	72	58
66+	YES	58%	42%	51%	42%	30%
	NO	42	58	49	58	70
# SURVEYED		107	111	239	171	155

FEAR IN NEIGHBORHOOD

TABLE I: FEAR IN NEIGHBORHOOD -- BY TOTAL POPULATION

Question: Is there any area right around here--that is, within a mile--where you would be afraid to walk alone at night? NOTE: Question not asked in 1972, 1975, 1978, 1983, 1986.

Responses: Yes; No

	YEAR										
RESPONSE	'73	'74	'76	'77	'80	'82	'84	'85	'87	'88	'89
YES	41%	45%	44%	45%	43%	47%	42%	41%	39%	40%	40%
NO	59	55	56	55	57	53	58	59	61	60	60
# SURVEYED	1488	1472	1492	1520	1456	1502	1451	1518	1457	966	1027

TABLE II: FEAR IN NEIGHBORHOOD -- BY SEX

Question: Is there any area right around here--that is, within a mile--where you would be afraid to walk alone at night? NOTE: Question not asked in 1972, 1975, 1978, 1983, 1986.

Responses: Yes; No

		YEAR										
SEX	RESP	'73	'74	'76	'77	'80	'82	'84	'85	'87	'88	'89
M	YES	20%	24%	23%	23%	21%	28%	19%	21%	17%	17%	19%
	NO	80	76	77	77	79	72	81	79	83	83	81
# SURVEYED		696	688	666	688	639	639	596	685	638	397	443
SEX	RESP	'73	'74	'76	'77	'80	'82	'84	'85	'87	'88	'89
F	YES	60%	63%	61%	63%	61%	61%	58%	56%	56%	57%	55%
	NO	40	37	39	37	39	39	42	44	44	43	45
# SURVEYED		792	784	826	832	817	863	855	833	819	569	584

TABLE III: FEAR IN NEIGHBORHOOD -- BY RACE

Question: Is there any area right around here--that is, within a mile--where you would be afraid to walk alone at night? NOTE: Question not asked in 1972, 1975, 1978, 1983, 1986.

Responses: Yes; No

		YEAR										
RACE	RESP	'73	'74	'76	'77	'80	'82	'84	'85	'87	'88	'89
WHITE	YES	39%	43%	44%	43%	42%	45%	40%	38%	36%	39%	38%
	NO	61	57	56	57	58	55	60	62	64	61	62
# SURVEYED		1295	1295	1355	1331	1308	1320	1235	1326	1215	795	887
RACE	RESP	'73	'74	'76	'77	'80	'82	'84	'85	'87	'88	'89
BLACK	YES	55%	61%	48%	63%	53%	63%	61%	63%	52%	52%	58%
	NO	45	39	52	37	47	37	39	37	48	48	42
# SURVEYED		181	170	128	175	138	155	165	148	190	129	100
RACE	RESP	'73	'74	'76	'77	'80	'82	'84	'85	'87	'88	'89
OTHER	YES	42%	43%	44%	21%	50%	52%	39%	52%	42%	29%	40%
	NO	58	57	56	79	50	48	61	48	58	71	60
# SURVEYED		12	7	9	14	10	27	51	44	52	42	40

TABLE IV: FEAR IN NEIGHBORHOOD -- BY AGE

Question: Is there any area right around here--that is, within a mile--where you would be afraid to walk alone at night? NOTE: Question not asked in 1972, 1975, 1978, 1983, 1986.

Responses: Yes; No

		YEAR										
AGE	RESP	'73	'74	'76	'77	'80	'82	'84	'85	'87	'88	'89
18-23	YES	38%	42%	40%	41%	44%	41%	38%	33%	43%	32%	41%
	NO	62	58	60	59	56	59	62	67	57	68	59
# SURVEYED		170	167	162	164	154	147	159	133	126	94	97
AGE	RESP	'73	'74	'76	'77	'80	'82	'84	'85	'87	'88	'89
24-29	YES	41%	45%	42%	40%	40%	47%	38%	42%	39%	39%	44%
	NO	59	55	58	60	60	53	62	58	61	61	56
# SURVEYED		209	210	225	201	202	246	226	216	192	132	116

TABLE IV: FEAR IN NEIGHBORHOOD -- BY AGE (Continued)

Question: Is there any area right around here--that is, within a mile--where you would be afraid to walk alone at night?
NOTE: Question not asked in 1972, 1975, 1978, 1983, 1986.

Responses: Yes; No

		YEAR										
AGE	RESP	'73	'74	'76	'77	'80	'82	'84	'85	'87	'88	'89
30-35	YES	41%	39%	40%	45%	41%	44%	42%	36%	35%	34%	32%
	NO	59	61	60	55	59	56	58	64	65	66	68
# SURVEYED		166	175	185	187	215	204	199	211	220	130	135
AGE	RESP	'73	'74	'76	'77	'80	'82	'84	'85	'87	'88	'89
36-41	YES	35%	44%	40%	42%	32%	47%	31%	35%	37%	30%	34%
	NO	65	56	60	58	68	53	69	65	63	70	66
# SURVEYED		174	149	158	168	149	145	186	183	186	132	136
AGE	RESP	'73	'74	'76	'77	'80	'82	'84	'85	'87	'88	'89
42-47	YES	46%	37%	44%	35%	44%	38%	38%	36%	30%	34%	33%
	NO	54	63	56	65	56	62	62	64	70	66	67
# SURVEYED		146	150	112	147	117	119	125	122	155	101	106
AGE	RESP	'73	'74	'76	'77	'80	'82	'84	'85	'87	'88	'89
48-53	YES	35%	47%	44%	43%	39%	45%	38%	38%	31%	42%	32%
	NO	65	53	56	57	61	55	62	62	69	58	68
# SURVEYED		150	145	133	154	123	112	101	131	126	64	95
AGE	RESP	'73	'74	'76	'77	'80	'82	'84	'85	'87	'88	'89
54-59	YES	47%	45%	47%	43%	42%	46%	45%	38%	36%	48%	43%
	NO	53	55	53	57	58	54	55	62	64	52	57
# SURVEYED		154	139	129	167	135	144	114	133	98	52	63
AGE	RESP	'73	'74	'76	'77	'80	'82	'84	'85	'87	'88	'89
60-65	YES	39%	52%	42%	56%	53%	47%	54%	38%	52%	43%	57%
	NO	61	48	58	44	47	53	46	62	48	57	43
# SURVEYED		119	107	133	115	116	116	110	128	101	84	77
AGE	RESP	'73	'74	'76	'77	'80	'82	'84	'85	'87	'88	'89
66+	YES	47%	54%	55%	61%	50%	56%	54%	57%	46%	58%	45%
	NO	53	46	45	39	50	44	46	43	54	42	55
# SURVEYED		196	224	250	210	236	257	225	255	249	174	199

****

HARSHNESS OF COURTS

TABLE I: HARSHNESS OF COURTS -- BY TOTAL POPULATION

Question: In general, do you think the courts in this area deal too harshly or not harshly enough with criminals?

Responses: TH = Too harshly; NH = Not harshly enough; AR = About right

	YEAR															
RESPONSE	'72	'73	'74	'75	'76	'77	'78	'80	'82	'83	'84	'85	'86	'87	'88	'89
TH	7%	5%	6%	4%	3%	4%	3%	3%	3%	4%	3%	4%	3%	3%	4%	3%
NH	74	81	84	85	86	88	90	88	90	89	85	87	89	84	86	88
AR	18	14	10	10	11	9	8	8	8	7	12	9	8	13	10	9
# SURVEYED	1436	1356	694	1379	1405	1443	1448	1378	716	1524	1397	1474	1414	1383	1406	1461

TABLE II: HARSHNESS OF COURTS -- BY SEX

Question: In general, do you think the courts in this area deal too harshly or not harshly enough with criminals?

Responses: TH = Too harshly; NH = Not harshly enough; AR = About right

		YEAR															
SEX	RESP	'72	'73	'74	'75	'76	'77	'78	'80	'82	'83	'84	'85	'86	'87	'88	'89
M	TH	7%	6%	7%	5%	4%	4%	3%	3%	2%	4%	5%	4%	4%	4%	5%	5%
	NH	74	81	84	86	86	87	90	88	89	88	82	86	88	82	82	83
	AR	19	13	10	9	11	9	7	9	9	8	12	10	8	14	13	13
# SURVEYED		736	639	328	616	638	659	622	605	392	663	576	662	596	609	612	634
SEX	RESP	'72	'73	'74	'75	'76	'77	'78	'80	'82	'83	'84	'85	'86	'87	'88	'89
F	TH	7%	4%	5%	4%	3%	3%	3%	4%	3%	3%	2%	3%	3%	3%	4%	1%
	NH	75	80	84	84	86	89	89	89	91	91	87	88	89	86	88	92
	AR	18	15	11	12	10	8	8	7	6	6	11	9	8	11	8	7
# SURVEYED		700	717	366	763	767	784	826	773	324	861	821	812	818	774	794	827

TABLE III: HARSHNESS OF COURTS -- BY RACE

Question: In general, do you think the courts in this area deal too harshly or not harshly enough with criminals?

Responses: TH = Too harshly; NH = Not harshly enough; AR = About right

		YEAR															
RACE	RESP	'72	'73	'74	'75	'76	'77	'78	'80	'82	'83	'84	'85	'86	'87	'88	'89
WHITE	TH	5%	3%	5%	3%	3%	3%	2%	3%	2%	3%	3%	3%	2%	3%	3%	3%
	NH	77	82	84	86	86	88	90	89	91	91	87	87	90	85	87	87
	AR	18	15	11	11	11	9	7	8	8	7	10	9	8	12	10	10
# SURVEYED		1205	1178	614	1226	1279	1264	1283	1236	628	1357	1192	1298	1204	1162	1180	1257
RACE	RESP	'72	'73	'74	'75	'76	'77	'78	'80	'82	'83	'84	'85	'86	'87	'88	'89
BLACK	TH	20%	18%	12%	15%	10%	8%	6%	10%	9%	12%	6%	6%	9%	7%	8%	4%
	NH	59	72	81	75	82	86	86	81	81	79	75	84	81	76	80	93
	AR	21	10	8	10	8	7	9	8	9	8	18	10	10	17	12	3
# SURVEYED		229	168	78	150	119	166	152	134	75	153	155	135	175	173	172	152
RACE	RESP	'72	'73	'74	'75	'76	'77	'78	'80	'82	'83	'84	'85	'86	'87	'88	'89
OTHER	TH	0%	30%	0%	0%	0%	8%	15%	0%	15%	0%	4%	2%	9%	8%	13%	6%
	NH	0	60	100	100	86	77	62	88	77	93	80	95	83	83	76	90
	AR	100	10	0	0	14	15	23	13	8	7	16	2	9	8	11	4
# SURVEYED		2	10	2	3	7	13	13	8	13	14	50	41	35	48	54	52

TABLE IV: HARSHNESS OF COURTS -- BY AGE

Question: In general, do you think the courts in this area deal too harshly or not harshly enough with criminals?

Responses: TH = Too harshly; NH = Not harshly enough; AR = About right

		YEAR															
AGE	RESP	'72	'73	'74	'75	'76	'77	'78	'80	'82	'83	'84	'85	'86	'87	'88	'89
18-23	TH	20%	9%	13%	13%	9%	12%	8%	11%	4%	7%	7%	7%	11%	2%	10%	7%
	NH	47	66	67	71	78	77	81	84	79	87	83	80	81	87	80	86
	AR	33	24	20	16	13	11	11	4	18	6	10	13	9	11	9	7
# SURVEYED		142	148	70	154	150	152	150	140	56	125	149	126	103	119	137	133
AGE	RESP	'72	'73	'74	'75	'76	'77	'78	'80	'82	'83	'84	'85	'86	'87	'88	'89
24-29	TH	14%	10%	7%	6%	6%	4%	4%	5%	2%	6%	6%	6%	3%	6%	6%	1%
	NH	65	73	82	82	77	86	88	85	89	87	80	84	87	83	84	89
	AR	20	17	11	12	16	10	8	10	9	7	14	11	10	11	10	10
# SURVEYED		202	183	101	207	203	190	236	191	111	277	224	207	208	174	202	195

TABLE IV: HARSHNESS OF COURTS -- BY AGE (Continued)

Question: In general, do you think the courts in this area deal too harshly or not harshly enough with criminals?

Responses: TH = Too harshly; NH = Not harshly enough; AR = About right

		YEAR															
AGE	RESP	'72	'73	'74	'75	'76	'77	'78	'80	'82	'83	'84	'85	'86	'87	'88	'89
30-35	TH	6%	6%	7%	4%	3%	1%	4%	2%	7%	2%	3%	1%	3%	4%	4%	4%
	NH	76	80	87	82	88	88	90	90	84	92	87	87	90	84	83	86
	AR	18	14	6	14	9	11	6	8	9	6	10	11	7	12	13	10
# SURVEYED		161	155	83	156	174	178	211	196	87	227	186	206	209	209	183	202
AGE	RESP	'72	'73	'74	'75	'76	'77	'78	'80	'82	'83	'84	'85	'86	'87	'88	'89
36-41	TH	4%	5%	11%	5%	3%	4%	2%	6%	1%	4%	3%	6%	5%	5%	3%	3%
	NH	83	86	82	85	88	87	92	85	87	89	85	84	88	80	85	88
	AR	13	9	8	10	9	9	6	10	12	7	12	11	7	15	12	10
# SURVEYED		114	160	65	146	148	159	154	144	69	165	178	179	182	173	185	188
AGE	RESP	'72	'73	'74	'75	'76	'77	'78	'80	'82	'83	'84	'85	'86	'87	'88	'89
42-47	TH	5%	4%	5%	3%	2%	1%	1%	1%	2%	3%	2%	3%	0%	3%	3%	1%
	NH	80	83	86	87	86	92	93	93	92	85	84	89	91	83	88	89
	AR	15	13	10	10	12	7	7	6	6	12	14	8	9	14	9	10
# SURVEYED		172	138	63	134	110	137	107	111	64	139	120	119	137	150	151	151
AGE	RESP	'72	'73	'74	'75	'76	'77	'78	'80	'82	'83	'84	'85	'86	'87	'88	'89
48-53	TH	6%	3%	0%	5%	2%	5%	2%	1%	2%	4%	2%	2%	3%	2%	1%	4%
	NH	80	82	84	88	93	84	89	89	96	91	93	94	89	85	90	90
	AR	14	15	16	8	6	11	9	11	2	4	5	3	9	13	9	6
# SURVEYED		167	137	63	133	125	151	128	114	56	113	98	127	105	123	87	133
AGE	RESP	'72	'73	'74	'75	'76	'77	'78	'80	'82	'83	'84	'85	'86	'87	'88	'89
54-59	TH	6%	2%	1%	3%	3%	2%	1%	2%	0%	3%	2%	3%	2%	5%	4%	1%
	NH	77	86	90	88	87	91	92	93	92	91	84	88	95	86	75	92
	AR	17	12	9	8	11	7	8	5	8	6	14	9	3	9	21	6
# SURVEYED		147	140	67	120	120	161	132	131	72	125	112	128	97	93	80	93
AGE	RESP	'72	'73	'74	'75	'76	'77	'78	'80	'82	'83	'84	'85	'86	'87	'88	'89
60-65	TH	2%	1%	8%	1%	1%	0%	1%	3%	4%	2%	3%	2%	3%	0%	2%	4%
	NH	77	88	82	92	93	95	91	89	93	94	90	88	88	93	89	89
	AR	21	11	10	7	6	5	8	8	2	5	7	9	9	7	9	8
# SURVEYED		131	116	60	107	126	110	102	117	46	130	108	127	112	96	116	106
AGE	RESP	'72	'73	'74	'75	'76	'77	'78	'80	'82	'83	'84	'85	'86	'87	'88	'89
66+	TH	2%	3%	3%	0%	1%	3%	0%	1%	3%	2%	0%	1%	1%	2%	3%	1%
	NH	82	83	89	92	89	92	92	89	92	90	87	90	90	83	91	86
	AR	17	14	8	8	10	5	7	10	5	7	12	8	9	15	6	13
# SURVEYED		196	175	119	217	244	198	221	226	149	216	217	249	254	241	261	256

****

DEATH PENALTY

TABLE I: DEATH PENALTY -- BY TOTAL POPULATION

Question: Do you favor or oppose the death penalty for persons convicted of murder? NOTE: Question not asked in 1972, 1973, 1980.

Responses: FA = Favor; OP = Oppose

	YEAR													
RESPONSE	'74	'75	'76	'77	'78	'80	'82	'83	'84	'85	'86	'87	'88	'89
FA	66%	64%	69%	72%	70%	72%	78%	77%	75%	80%	75%	74%	76%	78%
OP	34	36	31	28	30	28	22	23	25	20	25	26	24	22
# SURVEYED	1404	1383	1426	1423	1443	1372	1418	1523	1376	1451	1390	1366	1373	1447

TABLE II: DEATH PENALTY -- BY SEX

Question: Do you favor or oppose the death penalty for persons convicted of murder? NOTE: Question not asked in 1972, 1973, 1980.

Responses: FA = Favor; OP = Oppose

		YEAR													
SEX	RESP	'74	'75	'76	'77	'78	'80	'82	'83	'84	'85	'86	'87	'88	'89
M	FA	70%	71%	75%	77%	76%	78%	83%	84%	80%	83%	82%	77%	81%	84%
	OP	30	29	25	23	24	22	17	16	20	17	18	23	19	16
# SURVEYED		668	629	646	666	625	613	614	659	569	662	593	605	604	636
SEX	RESP	'74	'75	'76	'77	'78	'80	'82	'83	'84	'85	'86	'87	'88	'89
F	FA	63%	59%	63%	67%	66%	66%	75%	72%	71%	77%	70%	72%	72%	74%
	OP	37	41	37	33	34	34	25	28	29	23	30	28	28	26
# SURVEYED		736	754	780	757	818	759	804	864	807	789	797	761	769	811

TABLE III: DEATH PENALTY -- BY RACE

Question: Do you favor or oppose the death penalty for persons convicted of murder? NOTE: Question not asked in 1972, 1973, 1980.

Responses: FA = Favor; OP = Oppose

		YEAR													
RACE	RESP	'74	'75	'76	'77	'78	'80	'82	'83	'84	'85	'86	'87	'88	'89
WHITE	FA	70%	68%	71%	75%	73%	75%	81%	80%	79%	82%	79%	78%	81%	81%
	OP	30	32	29	25	27	25	19	20	21	18	21	22	19	19
# SURVEYED		1240	1234	1294	1249	1282	1237	1248	1355	1175	1282	1188	1150	1152	1244
RACE	RESP	'74	'75	'76	'77	'78	'80	'82	'83	'84	'85	'86	'87	'88	'89
BLACK	FA	40%	36%	43%	46%	46%	43%	50%	50%	47%	57%	48%	48%	48%	59%
	OP	60	64	57	54	54	57	50	50	53	43	52	52	52	41
# SURVEYED		158	145	123	159	148	125	147	151	154	129	167	169	168	148
RACE	RESP	'74	'75	'76	'77	'78	'80	'82	'83	'84	'85	'86	'87	'88	'89
OTHER	FA	83%	75%	89%	87%	69%	50%	83%	82%	60%	70%	77%	66%	62%	67%
	OP	17	25	11	13	31	50	17	18	40	30	23	34	38	33
# SURVEYED		6	4	9	15	13	10	23	17	47	40	35	47	53	55

TABLE IV: DEATH PENALTY -- BY AGE

Question: Do you favor or oppose the death penalty for persons convicted of murder? NOTE: Question not asked in 1972, 1973, 1980.

Responses: FA = Favor; OP = Oppose

		YEAR													
AGE	RESP	'74	'75	'76	'77	'78	'80	'82	'83	'84	'85	'86	'87	'88	'89
18-23	FA	54%	50%	57%	64%	62%	70%	72%	73%	75%	73%	72%	71%	68%	72%
	OP	46	50	43	36	38	30	28	27	25	27	28	29	32	28
# SURVEYED		164	164	155	160	156	149	136	124	154	128	100	123	136	132
AGE	RESP	'74	'75	'76	'77	'78	'80	'82	'83	'84	'85	'86	'87	'88	'89
24-29	FA	63%	62%	62%	70%	70%	68%	81%	77%	81%	80%	77%	71%	78%	76%
	OP	37	38	38	30	30	32	19	23	19	20	23	29	22	24
# SURVEYED		205	213	219	188	231	195	234	274	216	208	207	184	204	191

TABLE IV: DEATH PENALTY -- BY AGE (Continued)

Question: Do you favor or oppose the death penalty for persons convicted of murder? NOTE: Question not asked in 1972, 1973, 1980.

Responses: FA = Favor; OP = Oppose

		YEAR													
AGE	RESP	'74	'75	'76	'77	'78	'80	'82	'83	'84	'85	'86	'87	'88	'89
30-35	FA	70%	66%	70%	65%	67%	68%	78%	80%	68%	84%	70%	76%	77%	77%
	OP	30	34	30	35	33	32	22	20	32	16	30	24	23	23
# SURVEYED		161	158	182	173	217	207	192	226	186	202	215	212	181	204
AGE	RESP	'74	'75	'76	'77	'78	'80	'82	'83	'84	'85	'86	'87	'88	'89
36-41	FA	66%	64%	73%	72%	75%	71%	81%	81%	81%	79%	75%	80%	78%	80%
	OP	34	36	27	28	25	29	19	19	19	21	25	20	22	20
# SURVEYED		146	144	146	159	151	144	139	167	178	172	182	170	176	188
AGE	RESP	'74	'75	'76	'77	'78	'80	'82	'83	'84	'85	'86	'87	'88	'89
42-47	FA	68%	63%	72%	76%	71%	80%	75%	82%	70%	78%	75%	79%	77%	80%
	OP	32	38	28	24	29	20	25	18	30	22	25	21	23	20
# SURVEYED		147	136	110	133	115	108	115	132	118	117	132	141	147	154
AGE	RESP	'74	'75	'76	'77	'78	'80	'82	'83	'84	'85	'86	'87	'88	'89
48-53	FA	69%	66%	72%	76%	68%	76%	79%	71%	77%	77%	74%	74%	79%	81%
	OP	31	34	28	24	32	24	21	29	23	23	26	26	21	19
# SURVEYED		139	136	128	143	126	113	107	113	97	121	105	119	84	129
AGE	RESP	'74	'75	'76	'77	'78	'80	'82	'83	'84	'85	'86	'87	'88	'89
54-59	FA	72%	73%	74%	74%	73%	82%	80%	79%	75%	82%	80%	67%	71%	72%
	OP	28	27	26	26	27	18	20	21	25	18	20	33	29	28
# SURVEYED		123	113	121	157	131	126	141	128	110	122	96	86	79	92
AGE	RESP	'74	'75	'76	'77	'78	'80	'82	'83	'84	'85	'86	'87	'88	'89
60-65	FA	71%	70%	72%	77%	74%	71%	76%	74%	77%	83%	78%	75%	81%	81%
	OP	29	30	28	23	26	29	24	26	23	17	22	25	19	19
# SURVEYED		103	105	127	113	100	108	112	129	105	126	104	95	111	102
AGE	RESP	'74	'75	'76	'77	'78	'80	'82	'83	'84	'85	'86	'87	'88	'89
66+	FA	70%	69%	71%	75%	74%	68%	79%	73%	68%	78%	78%	72%	75%	81%
	OP	30	31	29	25	26	32	21	27	32	22	22	28	25	19
# SURVEYED		210	210	233	190	209	213	234	223	207	249	243	231	252	251

****

WIRETAPPING

TABLE I: WIRETAPPING -- BY TOTAL POPULATION

Question: Everything considered, would you say that in general, you approve or disapprove of wiretapping? NOTE: Question not asked in 1972, 1973, 1976, 1980, 1984, 1987.

Responses: AP = Approve; DS = Disapprove

	YEAR									
RESPONSE	'74	'75	'77	'78	'82	'83	'85	'86	'88	'89
AP	17%	17%	19%	20%	20%	19%	24%	23%	22%	28%
DS	83	83	81	80	80	81	76	77	78	72
# SURVEYED	1424	1428	1480	1483	1446	1535	1480	1413	927	953

TABLE II: WIRETAPPING -- BY SEX

Question: Everything considered, would you say that in general, you approve or disapprove of wiretapping? NOTE: Question not asked in 1972, 1973, 1976, 1980, 1984, 1987.

Responses: AP = Approve; DS = Disapprove

		YEAR									
SEX	RESP	'74	'75	'77	'78	'82	'83	'85	'86	'88	'89
M	AP	22%	23%	24%	27%	28%	24%	31%	27%	27%	33%
	DS	78	78	76	73	72	76	69	73	73	67
# SURVEYED		671	640	678	624	619	672	663	605	416	406
SEX	RESP	'74	'75	'77	'78	'82	'83	'85	'86	'88	'89
F	AP	13%	12%	15%	14%	15%	15%	17%	20%	17%	23%
	DS	87	88	85	86	85	85	83	80	83	77
# SURVEYED		753	788	802	859	827	863	817	808	511	547

TABLE III: WIRETAPPING -- BY RACE

Question: Everything considered, would you say that in general, you approve or disapprove of wiretapping? NOTE: Question not asked in 1972, 1973, 1976, 1980, 1984, 1987.

Responses: AP = Approve; DS = Disapprove

		YEAR									
RACE	RESP	'74	'75	'77	'78	'82	'83	'85	'86	'88	'89
WHITE	AP	19%	18%	20%	21%	22%	21%	25%	25%	22%	30%
	DS	81	82	80	79	78	79	75	75	78	70
# SURVEYED		1250	1269	1299	1315	1271	1369	1299	1204	776	818
RACE	RESP	'74	'75	'77	'78	'82	'83	'85	'86	'88	'89
BLACK	AP	7%	12%	10%	9%	5%	7%	11%	11%	15%	11%
	DS	93	88	90	91	95	93	89	89	85	89
# SURVEYED		168	155	166	154	151	151	142	174	123	98
RACE	RESP	'74	'75	'77	'78	'82	'83	'85	'86	'88	'89
OTHER	AP	17%	25%	20%	0%	21%	20%	8%	9%	25%	14%
	DS	83	75	80	100	79	80	92	91	75	86
# SURVEYED		6	4	15	14	24	15	39	35	28	37

TABLE IV: WIRETAPPING -- BY AGE

Question: Everything considered, would you say that in general, you approve or disapprove of wiretapping? NOTE: Question not asked in 1972, 1973, 1976, 1980, 1984, 1987.

Responses: AP = Approve; DS = Disapprove

		YEAR									
AGE	RESP	'74	'75	'77	'78	'82	'83	'85	'86	'88	'89
18-23	AP	11%	10%	9%	14%	11%	14%	18%	17%	22%	30%
	DS	89	90	91	86	89	86	82	83	78	70
# SURVEYED		161	168	162	161	144	125	131	106	89	82
AGE	RESP	'74	'75	'77	'78	'82	'83	'85	'86	'88	'89
24-29	AP	17%	18%	14%	15%	19%	19%	20%	19%	13%	34%
	DS	83	82	86	85	81	81	80	81	87	66
# SURVEYED		207	231	202	239	241	277	210	212	142	136
AGE	RESP	'74	'75	'77	'78	'82	'83	'85	'86	'88	'89
30-35	AP	17%	19%	19%	15%	16%	10%	18%	20%	16%	22%
	DS	83	81	81	85	84	90	82	80	84	78
# SURVEYED		169	162	181	225	202	229	204	218	127	135

TABLE IV: WIRETAPPING -- BY AGE (Continued)

Question: Everything considered, would you say that in general, you approve or disapprove of wiretapping? NOTE: Question not asked in 1972, 1973, 1976, 1980, 1984, 1987.

Responses: AP = Approve; DS = Disapprove

		YEAR									
AGE	RESP	'74	'75	'77	'78	'82	'83	'85	'86	'88	'89
36-41	AP	20%	17%	21%	21%	29%	22%	29%	26%	26%	26%
	DS	80	83	79	79	71	78	71	74	74	74
# SURVEYED		148	145	167	159	140	168	180	182	122	121
AGE	RESP	'74	'75	'77	'78	'82	'83	'85	'86	'88	'89
42-47	AP	17%	20%	15%	28%	20%	22%	31%	26%	26%	20%
	DS	83	80	85	72	80	78	69	74	74	80
# SURVEYED		149	139	142	116	115	138	118	137	102	105
AGE	RESP	'74	'75	'77	'78	'82	'83	'85	'86	'88	'89
48-53	AP	21%	15%	23%	25%	21%	23%	22%	21%	15%	37%
	DS	79	85	77	75	79	77	78	79	85	63
# SURVEYED		137	135	145	126	107	111	130	106	59	83
AGE	RESP	'74	'75	'77	'78	'82	'83	'85	'86	'88	'89
54-59	AP	20%	17%	26%	20%	25%	25%	29%	34%	21%	28%
	DS	80	83	74	80	75	75	71	66	79	72
# SURVEYED		132	126	163	129	142	128	127	91	47	69
AGE	RESP	'74	'75	'77	'78	'82	'83	'85	'86	'88	'89
60-65	AP	23%	19%	20%	23%	21%	23%	24%	28%	28%	17%
	DS	77	81	80	77	79	77	76	72	72	83
# SURVEYED		104	107	114	102	109	125	127	110	69	63
AGE	RESP	'74	'75	'77	'78	'82	'83	'85	'86	'88	'89
66+	AP	13%	19%	23%	23%	21%	22%	24%	23%	26%	31%
	DS	87	81	77	77	79	78	76	77	74	69
# SURVEYED		211	210	198	219	238	227	247	245	169	156

****

LEGALIZATION OF MARIJUANA

TABLE I: LEGALIZATION OF MARIJUANA -- BY TOTAL POPULATION

Question: Do you think the use of marijuana should be made legal or not? NOTE: Question not asked in 1972, 1974, 1977, 1982, 1985.

Responses: SD = Should; SN = Should not

	YEAR										
RESPONSE	'73	'75	'76	'78	'80	'83	'84	'86	'87	'88	'89
SD	19%	21%	29%	31%	26%	21%	24%	18%	17%	18%	17%
SN	81	79	71	69	74	79	76	82	83	82	83
# SURVEYED	1471	1414	1447	1464	1420	1546	1406	1437	1421	955	998

TABLE II: LEGALIZATION OF MARIJUANA -- BY SEX

Question: Do you think the use of marijuana should be made legal or not? NOTE: Question not asked in 1972, 1974, 1977, 1982, 1985.

Responses: SD = Should; SN = Should not

		YEAR										
SEX	RESP	'73	'75	'76	'78	'80	'83	'84	'86	'87	'88	'89
M	SD	23%	27%	34%	35%	31%	26%	29%	24%	20%	22%	21%
	SN	77	73	66	65	69	74	71	76	80	78	79
# SURVEYED		681	630	638	617	619	667	572	606	622	416	423
SEX	RESP	'73	'75	'76	'78	'80	'83	'84	'86	'87	'88	'89
F	SD	15%	17%	25%	27%	22%	17%	20%	14%	14%	15%	14%
	SN	85	83	75	73	78	83	80	86	86	85	86
# SURVEYED		790	784	809	847	801	879	834	831	799	539	575

TABLE III: LEGALIZATION OF MARIJUANA -- BY RACE

Question: Do you think the use of marijuana should be made legal or not? NOTE: Question not asked in 1972, 1974, 1977, 1982, 1985.

Responses: SD = Should; SN = Should not

		YEAR										
RACE	RESP	'73	'75	'76	'78	'80	'83	'84	'86	'87	'88	'89
WHITE	SD	19%	21%	28%	29%	25%	20%	24%	18%	18%	18%	18%
	SN	81	79	72	71	75	80	76	82	82	82	82
# SURVEYED		1282	1259	1318	1304	1273	1370	1195	1226	1188	808	855
RACE	RESP	'73	'75	'76	'78	'80	'83	'84	'86	'87	'88	'89
BLACK	SD	19%	23%	36%	39%	29%	28%	23%	22%	14%	21%	12%
	SN	81	77	64	61	71	72	77	78	86	79	88
# SURVEYED		177	151	121	146	137	160	163	175	183	107	104
RACE	RESP	'73	'75	'76	'78	'80	'83	'84	'86	'87	'88	'89
OTHER	SD	17%	25%	25%	43%	10%	31%	19%	11%	6%	15%	8%
	SN	83	75	75	57	90	69	81	89	94	85	92
# SURVEYED		12	4	8	14	10	16	48	36	50	40	39

TABLE IV: LEGALIZATION OF MARIJUANA -- BY AGE

Question: Do you think the use of marijuana should be made legal or not? NOTE: Question not asked in 1972, 1974, 1977, 1982, 1985.

Responses: SD = Should; SN = Should not

		YEAR										
AGE	RESP	'73	'75	'76	'78	'80	'83	'84	'86	'87	'88	'89
18-23	SD	43%	45%	57%	49%	43%	31%	31%	26%	20%	25%	24%
	SN	57	55	43	51	57	69	69	74	80	75	76
# SURVEYED		168	158	156	156	151	127	154	102	119	84	91
AGE	RESP	'73	'75	'76	'78	'80	'83	'84	'86	'87	'88	'89
24-29	SD	36%	39%	49%	51%	44%	30%	39%	27%	30%	24%	19%
	SN	64	61	51	49	56	70	61	73	70	76	81
# SURVEYED		206	219	216	238	196	277	222	215	184	139	136

TABLE IV: LEGALIZATION OF MARIJUANA -- BY AGE (Continued)

Question: Do you think the use of marijuana should be made legal or not? NOTE: Question not asked in 1972, 1974, 1977, 1982, 1985.

Responses: SD = Should; SN = Should not

		YEAR										
AGE	RESP	'73	'75	'76	'78	'80	'83	'84	'86	'87	'88	'89
30-35	SD	14%	24%	31%	42%	35%	23%	31%	28%	26%	22%	26%
	SN	86	76	69	58	65	77	69	72	74	78	74
# SURVEYED		164	166	183	221	208	231	192	214	212	125	140
AGE	RESP	'73	'75	'76	'78	'80	'83	'84	'86	'87	'88	'89
36-41	SD	14%	11%	27%	22%	26%	23%	28%	19%	23%	18%	17%
	SN	86	89	73	78	74	77	72	81	77	82	83
# SURVEYED		174	145	152	154	149	169	177	186	185	119	126
AGE	RESP	'73	'75	'76	'78	'80	'83	'84	'86	'87	'88	'89
42-47	SD	16%	23%	20%	21%	19%	18%	28%	11%	10%	18%	17%
	SN	84	77	80	79	81	82	72	89	90	82	83
# SURVEYED		142	138	113	117	113	138	118	139	152	102	104
AGE	RESP	'73	'75	'76	'78	'80	'83	'84	'86	'87	'88	'89
48-53	SD	16%	14%	14%	20%	12%	20%	13%	10%	11%	15%	8%
	SN	84	86	86	80	88	80	87	90	89	85	92
# SURVEYED		149	138	128	123	118	114	99	104	126	55	93
AGE	RESP	'73	'75	'76	'78	'80	'83	'84	'86	'87	'88	'89
54-59	SD	8%	8%	15%	18%	17%	18%	14%	10%	8%	17%	13%
	SN	92	92	85	82	83	82	86	90	92	83	87
# SURVEYED		151	119	126	130	131	131	110	96	97	65	62
AGE	RESP	'73	'75	'76	'78	'80	'83	'84	'86	'87	'88	'89
60-65	SD	8%	11%	24%	12%	19%	11%	14%	15%	9%	14%	16%
	SN	93	89	76	88	81	89	86	85	91	86	84
# SURVEYED		120	107	127	99	118	123	107	114	98	78	73
AGE	RESP	'73	'75	'76	'78	'80	'83	'84	'86	'87	'88	'89
66+	SD	6%	7%	13%	17%	9%	10%	5%	12%	6%	10%	11%
	SN	94	93	87	83	91	90	95	88	94	90	89
# SURVEYED		193	219	241	219	228	229	221	260	243	185	171

****

GUN LICENSING

TABLE I: GUN LICENSING -- BY TOTAL POPULATION

Question: Would you favor or oppose a law which would require a person to obtain a police permit before he or she could buy a gun? NOTE: Question not asked in 1978, 1983, 1986.

Responses: FA = Favor; OP = Oppose

	YEAR												
RESPONSE	'72	'73	'74	'75	'76	'77	'80	'82	'84	'85	'87	'88	'89
FA	72%	75%	76%	76%	73%	73%	71%	73%	72%	73%	71%	76%	79%
OP	28	25	24	24	27	27	29	27	28	27	29	24	21
# SURVEYED	1562	1470	1459	1450	1472	1499	1439	1474	1430	1511	1434	947	1015

TABLE II: GUN LICENSING -- BY SEX

Question: Would you favor or oppose a law which would require a person to obtain a police permit before he or she could buy a gun? NOTE: Question not asked in 1978, 1983, 1986.

Responses: FA = Favor; OP = Oppose

		YEAR												
SEX	RESP	'72	'73	'74	'75	'76	'77	'80	'82	'84	'85	'87	'88	'89
M	FA	63%	68%	67%	67%	64%	64%	64%	68%	63%	66%	63%	67%	70%
	OP	37	32	33	33	36	36	36	32	37	34	37	33	30
# SURVEYED		789	684	686	654	661	682	637	630	589	682	627	392	442
SEX	RESP	'72	'73	'74	'75	'76	'77	'80	'82	'84	'85	'87	'88	'89
F	FA	82%	81%	85%	82%	79%	80%	76%	77%	79%	79%	78%	82%	86%
	OP	18	19	15	18	21	20	24	23	21	21	22	18	14
# SURVEYED		773	786	773	796	811	817	802	844	841	829	807	555	573

TABLE III: GUN LICENSING -- BY RACE

Question: Would you favor or oppose a law which would require a person to obtain a police permit before he or she could buy a gun? NOTE: Question not asked in 1978, 1983, 1986.

Responses: FA = Favor; OP = Oppose

		YEAR												
RACE	RESP	'72	'73	'74	'75	'76	'77	'80	'82	'84	'85	'87	'88	'89
WHITE	FA	72%	75%	76%	74%	72%	72%	69%	72%	71%	73%	71%	76%	79%
	OP	28	25	24	26	28	28	31	28	29	28	29	24	21
# SURVEYED		1310	1281	1285	1289	1340	1312	1295	1297	1218	1320	1196	777	875
RACE	RESP	'72	'73	'74	'75	'76	'77	'80	'82	'84	'85	'87	'88	'89
BLACK	FA	73%	76%	77%	85%	76%	82%	83%	81%	80%	75%	78%	80%	80%
	OP	27	24	23	15	24	18	17	19	20	25	22	20	20
# SURVEYED		248	176	167	157	123	172	134	151	162	149	187	129	100
RACE	RESP	'72	'73	'74	'75	'76	'77	'80	'82	'84	'85	'87	'88	'89
OTHER	FA	75%	69%	100%	75%	78%	93%	100%	77%	88%	86%	71%	66%	88%
	OP	25	31	0	25	22	7	0	23	12	14	29	34	13
# SURVEYED		4	13	7	4	9	15	10	26	50	42	51	41	40

TABLE IV: GUN LICENSING -- BY AGE

Question: Would you favor or oppose a law which would require a person to obtain a police permit before he or she could buy a gun? NOTE: Question not asked in 1978, 1983, 1986.

Responses: FA = Favor; OP = Oppose

		YEAR												
AGE	RESP	'72	'73	'74	'75	'76	'77	'80	'82	'84	'85	'87	'88	'89
18-23	FA	79%	77%	77%	80%	76%	66%	74%	76%	75%	73%	73%	72%	71%
	OP	21	23	23	20	24	34	26	24	25	27	27	28	29
# SURVEYED		166	171	164	172	160	163	155	147	154	133	125	94	97
AGE	RESP	'72	'73	'74	'75	'76	'77	'80	'82	'84	'85	'87	'88	'89
24-29	FA	72%	76%	77%	79%	71%	78%	72%	77%	73%	75%	78%	75%	88%
	OP	28	24	23	21	29	22	28	23	27	25	22	25	13
# SURVEYED		226	209	211	229	220	198	200	245	226	215	190	132	112
AGE	RESP	'72	'73	'74	'75	'76	'77	'80	'82	'84	'85	'87	'88	'89
30-35	FA	73%	70%	78%	75%	77%	78%	74%	78%	75%	76%	75%	78%	75%
	OP	27	30	22	25	23	22	26	22	25	24	25	22	25
# SURVEYED		184	164	174	166	183	186	213	202	195	211	219	129	135

TABLE IV: GUN LICENSING -- BY AGE (Continued)

Question: Would you favor or oppose a law which would require a person to obtain a police permit before he or she could buy a gun? NOTE: Question not asked in 1978, 1983, 1986.

Responses: FA = Favor; OP = Oppose

		YEAR												
AGE	RESP	'72	'73	'74	'75	'76	'77	'80	'82	'84	'85	'87	'88	'89
36-41	FA	71%	74%	77%	73%	70%	65%	74%	71%	69%	70%	66%	73%	76%
	OP	29	26	23	27	30	35	26	29	31	30	34	27	24
# SURVEYED		121	170	150	149	154	165	148	142	186	184	184	131	135
AGE	RESP	'72	'73	'74	'75	'76	'77	'80	'82	'84	'85	'87	'88	'89
42-47	FA	69%	78%	73%	71%	78%	66%	66%	74%	64%	67%	70%	71%	74%
	OP	31	22	27	29	22	34	34	26	36	33	30	29	26
# SURVEYED		182	142	150	137	113	145	115	115	124	123	151	99	105
AGE	RESP	'72	'73	'74	'75	'76	'77	'80	'82	'84	'85	'87	'88	'89
48-53	FA	67%	71%	71%	75%	68%	75%	61%	64%	73%	70%	64%	78%	77%
	OP	33	29	29	25	32	25	39	36	27	30	36	22	23
# SURVEYED		186	148	144	138	132	151	118	110	101	130	124	63	95
AGE	RESP	'72	'73	'74	'75	'76	'77	'80	'82	'84	'85	'87	'88	'89
54-59	FA	70%	78%	72%	75%	68%	72%	65%	70%	66%	75%	72%	75%	83%
	OP	30	22	28	25	32	28	35	30	34	25	28	25	17
# SURVEYED		150	152	137	124	127	166	132	144	110	129	93	51	63
AGE	RESP	'72	'73	'74	'75	'76	'77	'80	'82	'84	'85	'87	'88	'89
60-65	FA	74%	68%	74%	74%	71%	74%	72%	71%	70%	73%	74%	76%	82%
	OP	26	32	26	26	29	26	28	29	30	27	26	24	18
# SURVEYED		137	117	103	112	132	114	116	114	109	128	99	82	77
AGE	RESP	'72	'73	'74	'75	'76	'77	'80	'82	'84	'85	'87	'88	'89
66+	FA	76%	80%	82%	76%	73%	80%	72%	72%	79%	74%	71%	82%	84%
	OP	24	20	18	24	27	20	28	28	21	26	29	18	16
# SURVEYED		207	194	220	218	246	204	233	246	219	251	245	163	193

****

STRIKING A STRANGER WHO IS ABUSING A FEMALE

TABLE I: STRIKING A STRANGER WHO IS ABUSING A FEMALE -- BY TOTAL POPULATION

Question: Would you approve of an adult male punching a stranger if the stranger was beating up a woman and the man saw it? NOTE: Question not asked in 1972, 1974, 1977, 1982, 1985.

Responses: Yes; No

	YEAR										
RESPONSE	'73	'75	'76	'78	'80	'83	'84	'86	'87	'88	'89
YES	87%	85%	82%	83%	84%	86%	86%	84%	86%	86%	85%
NO	13	15	18	17	16	14	14	16	14	14	15
# SURVEYED	982	1019	1434	1470	1417	1534	1404	1419	1394	947	986

TABLE II: STRIKING A STRANGER WHO IS ABUSING A FEMALE -- BY SEX

Question: Would you approve of an adult male punching a stranger if the stranger was beating up a woman and the man saw it? NOTE: Question not asked in 1972, 1974, 1977, 1982, 1985.

Responses: Yes; No

		YEAR										
SEX	RESP	'73	'75	'76	'78	'80	'83	'84	'86	'87	'88	'89
M	YES	85%	84%	80%	80%	84%	87%	86%	85%	84%	87%	86%
	NO	15	16	20	20	16	13	14	15	16	13	14
# SURVEYED		445	441	632	621	618	655	571	598	612	415	428
SEX	RESP	'73	'75	'76	'78	'80	'83	'84	'86	'87	'88	'89
F	YES	89%	85%	84%	86%	84%	85%	85%	83%	87%	86%	85%
	NO	11	15	16	14	16	15	15	17	13	14	15
# SURVEYED		537	578	802	849	799	879	833	821	782	532	558

TABLE III: STRIKING A STRANGER WHO IS ABUSING A FEMALE -- BY RACE

Question: Would you approve of an adult male punching a stranger if the stranger was beating up a woman and the man saw it? NOTE: Question not asked in 1972, 1974, 1977, 1982, 1985.

Responses: Yes; No

		YEAR										
RACE	RESP	'73	'75	'76	'78	'80	'83	'84	'86	'87	'88	'89
WHITE	YES	89%	87%	84%	85%	86%	87%	89%	86%	88%	88%	87%
	NO	11	13	16	15	14	13	11	14	12	12	13
# SURVEYED		899	936	1310	1307	1277	1367	1196	1211	1176	804	841
RACE	RESP	'73	'75	'76	'78	'80	'83	'84	'86	'87	'88	'89
BLACK	YES	61%	60%	60%	66%	66%	76%	68%	72%	75%	74%	71%
	NO	39	40	40	34	34	24	32	28	25	26	29
# SURVEYED		74	81	116	148	131	154	157	174	170	102	105
RACE	RESP	'73	'75	'76	'78	'80	'83	'84	'86	'87	'88	'89
OTHER	YES	100%	50%	63%	53%	78%	54%	63%	65%	73%	80%	83%
	NO	0	50	38	47	22	46	37	35	27	20	18
# SURVEYED		9	2	8	15	9	13	51	34	48	41	40

TABLE IV: STRIKING A STRANGER WHO IS ABUSING A FEMALE -- BY AGE

Question: Would you approve of an adult male punching a stranger if the stranger was beating up a woman and the man saw it? NOTE: Question not asked in 1972, 1974, 1977, 1982, 1985.

Responses: Yes; No

		YEAR										
AGE	RESP	'73	'75	'76	'78	'80	'83	'84	'86	'87	'88	'89
18-23	YES	88%	91%	87%	88%	91%	91%	89%	85%	90%	88%	89%
	NO	12	9	13	12	9	9	11	15	10	12	11
# SURVEYED		112	117	158	161	153	127	157	106	120	91	92
AGE	RESP	'73	'75	'76	'78	'80	'83	'84	'86	'87	'88	'89
24-29	YES	92%	90%	89%	85%	88%	90%	86%	89%	89%	89%	89%
	NO	8	10	11	15	12	10	14	11	11	11	11
# SURVEYED		157	181	218	237	198	284	223	212	186	140	136

TABLE IV: STRIKING A STRANGER WHO IS ABUSING A FEMALE -- BY AGE (Continued)

Question: Would you approve of an adult male punching a stranger if the stranger was beating up a woman and the man saw it? NOTE: Question not asked in 1972, 1974, 1977, 1982, 1985.

Responses: Yes; No

		YEAR										
AGE	RESP	**'73**	**'75**	**'76**	**'78**	**'80**	**'83**	**'84**	**'86**	**'87**	**'88**	**'89**
30-35	**YES**	91%	93%	91%	83%	86%	84%	86%	85%	88%	86%	88%
	NO	9	7	9	17	14	16	14	15	12	14	12
# SURVEYED		118	135	183	224	209	227	191	215	215	122	138
AGE	RESP	**'73**	**'75**	**'76**	**'78**	**'80**	**'83**	**'84**	**'86**	**'87**	**'88**	**'89**
36-41	**YES**	88%	82%	83%	86%	87%	85%	93%	85%	92%	85%	82%
	NO	12	18	17	14	13	15	7	15	8	15	18
# SURVEYED		126	115	152	153	147	167	177	183	178	116	128
AGE	RESP	**'73**	**'75**	**'76**	**'78**	**'80**	**'83**	**'84**	**'86**	**'87**	**'88**	**'89**
42-47	**YES**	87%	76%	85%	86%	83%	85%	87%	86%	88%	90%	85%
	NO	13	24	15	14	17	15	13	14	12	10	15
# SURVEYED		106	96	110	118	109	144	121	137	147	100	103
AGE	RESP	**'73**	**'75**	**'76**	**'78**	**'80**	**'83**	**'84**	**'86**	**'87**	**'88**	**'89**
48-53	**YES**	81%	77%	79%	81%	83%	89%	83%	84%	81%	82%	86%
	NO	19	23	21	19	17	11	17	16	19	18	14
# SURVEYED		108	104	124	128	118	111	99	105	122	55	92
AGE	RESP	**'73**	**'75**	**'76**	**'78**	**'80**	**'83**	**'84**	**'86**	**'87**	**'88**	**'89**
54-59	**YES**	87%	81%	80%	82%	78%	87%	85%	86%	84%	88%	83%
	NO	13	19	20	18	22	13	15	14	16	12	17
# SURVEYED		93	86	124	131	132	131	110	94	91	65	58
AGE	RESP	**'73**	**'75**	**'76**	**'78**	**'80**	**'83**	**'84**	**'86**	**'87**	**'88**	**'89**
60-65	**YES**	86%	87%	70%	80%	83%	82%	84%	76%	84%	81%	80%
	NO	14	13	30	20	17	18	16	24	16	19	20
# SURVEYED		66	75	129	98	115	119	102	110	97	75	71
AGE	RESP	**'73**	**'75**	**'76**	**'78**	**'80**	**'83**	**'84**	**'86**	**'87**	**'88**	**'89**
66+	**YES**	79%	78%	74%	79%	81%	80%	79%	78%	76%	84%	83%
	NO	21	22	26	21	19	20	21	22	24	16	17
# SURVEYED		94	110	231	214	227	218	219	250	234	179	166

****

FIGHT CHILD BEATER

TABLE I: FIGHT CHILD BEATER -- BY TOTAL POPULATION

Question: Would you approve of an adult male punching a stranger if the stranger had hit the man's child after the child accidently damaged the stranger's car? NOTE: Question not asked in 1972, 1974, 1977, 1982, 1985.

Responses: Yes; No

	YEAR										
RESPONSE	'73	'75	'76	'78	'80	'83	'84	'86	'87	'88	'89
YES	52%	53%	50%	54%	52%	59%	54%	58%	56%	60%	57%
NO	48	47	50	46	48	41	46	42	44	40	43
# SURVEYED	981	1041	1439	1482	1396	1534	1410	1415	1404	952	993

TABLE II: FIGHT CHILD BEATER -- BY SEX

Question: Would you approve of an adult male punching a stranger if the stranger had hit the man's child after the child accidently damaged the stranger's car? NOTE: Question not asked in 1972, 1974, 1977, 1982, 1985.

Responses: Yes; No

		YEAR										
SEX	RESP	'73	'75	'76	'78	'80	'83	'84	'86	'87	'88	'89
M	YES	57%	59%	55%	58%	52%	64%	57%	64%	63%	64%	63%
	NO	43	41	45	42	48	36	43	36	37	36	37
# SURVEYED		445	454	641	617	613	662	576	604	612	419	429
SEX	RESP	'73	'75	'76	'78	'80	'83	'84	'86	'87	'88	'89
F	YES	48%	48%	46%	51%	52%	55%	52%	54%	52%	57%	52%
	NO	52	52	54	49	48	45	48	46	48	43	48
# SURVEYED		536	587	798	865	783	872	834	811	792	533	564

TABLE III: FIGHT CHILD BEATER -- BY RACE

Question: Would you approve of an adult male punching a stranger if the stranger had hit the man's child after the child accidently damaged the stranger's car? NOTE: Question not asked in 1972, 1974, 1977, 1982, 1985.

Responses: Yes; No

		YEAR										
RACE	RESP	'73	'75	'76	'78	'80	'83	'84	'86	'87	'88	'89
WHITE	YES	53%	54%	51%	54%	54%	60%	57%	59%	57%	61%	59%
	NO	47	46	49	46	46	40	43	41	43	39	41
# SURVEYED		899	954	1309	1316	1252	1361	1198	1206	1173	799	847
RACE	RESP	'73	'75	'76	'78	'80	'83	'84	'86	'87	'88	'89
BLACK	YES	45%	38%	42%	50%	40%	47%	42%	53%	56%	60%	48%
	NO	55	62	58	50	60	53	58	47	44	40	52
# SURVEYED		73	86	122	150	134	157	160	172	180	112	107
RACE	RESP	'73	'75	'76	'78	'80	'83	'84	'86	'87	'88	'89
OTHER	YES	56%	0%	25%	19%	30%	44%	38%	46%	49%	56%	36%
	NO	44	100	75	81	70	56	62	54	51	44	64
# SURVEYED		9	1	8	16	10	16	52	37	51	41	39

TABLE IV: FIGHT CHILD BEATER -- BY AGE

Question: Would you approve of an adult male punching a stranger if the stranger had hit the man's child after the child accidently damaged the stranger's car? NOTE: Question not asked in 1972, 1974, 1977, 1982, 1985.

Responses: Yes; No

		YEAR										
AGE	RESP	'73	'75	'76	'78	'80	'83	'84	'86	'87	'88	'89
18-23	YES	66%	69%	62%	59%	66%	77%	65%	58%	61%	72%	66%
	NO	34	31	38	41	34	23	35	42	39	28	34
# SURVEYED		108	118	157	160	151	127	153	106	121	92	91
AGE	RESP	'73	'75	'76	'78	'80	'83	'84	'86	'87	'88	'89
24-29	YES	53%	65%	61%	63%	61%	69%	65%	70%	71%	70%	69%
	NO	47	35	39	38	39	31	35	30	29	30	31
# SURVEYED		155	188	217	240	198	277	227	211	188	138	137

TABLE IV: FIGHT CHILD BEATER -- BY AGE

Question: Would you approve of an adult male punching a stranger if the stranger had hit the man's child after the child accidently damaged the stranger's car? NOTE: Question not asked in 1972, 1974, 1977, 1982, 1985.

Responses: Yes; No

		YEAR										
AGE	RESP	'73	'75	'76	'78	'80	'83	'84	'86	'87	'88	'89
30-35	YES	64%	58%	60%	64%	61%	62%	60%	62%	66%	68%	64%
	NO	36	42	40	36	39	38	40	38	34	32	36
# SURVEYED		120	138	183	222	205	229	194	217	215	123	140
AGE	RESP	'73	'75	'76	'78	'80	'83	'84	'86	'87	'88	'89
36-41	YES	52%	62%	50%	60%	54%	58%	58%	69%	66%	65%	56%
	NO	48	38	50	40	46	42	42	31	34	35	44
# SURVEYED		126	111	152	157	145	166	183	180	180	121	129
AGE	RESP	'73	'75	'76	'78	'80	'83	'84	'86	'87	'88	'89
42-47	YES	50%	45%	45%	57%	50%	59%	57%	64%	56%	68%	60%
	NO	50	55	55	43	50	41	43	36	44	32	40
# SURVEYED		106	98	111	116	109	141	120	138	153	104	102
AGE	RESP	'73	'75	'76	'78	'80	'83	'84	'86	'87	'88	'89
48-53	YES	46%	37%	49%	48%	50%	54%	48%	62%	48%	61%	52%
	NO	54	63	51	52	50	46	52	38	52	39	48
# SURVEYED		108	107	130	126	118	115	97	104	124	56	93
AGE	RESP	'73	'75	'76	'78	'80	'83	'84	'86	'87	'88	'89
54-59	YES	44%	43%	48%	54%	45%	57%	55%	52%	53%	46%	59%
	NO	56	57	52	46	55	43	45	48	47	54	41
# SURVEYED		91	87	124	129	131	126	108	97	94	59	58
AGE	RESP	'73	'75	'76	'78	'80	'83	'84	'86	'87	'88	'89
60-65	YES	46%	39%	41%	31%	44%	52%	50%	47%	49%	45%	47%
	NO	54	61	59	69	56	48	50	53	51	55	53
# SURVEYED		70	76	128	106	111	122	103	108	96	77	72
AGE	RESP	'73	'75	'76	'78	'80	'83	'84	'86	'87	'88	'89
66+	YES	43%	36%	32%	37%	37%	39%	30%	40%	36%	44%	44%
	NO	57	64	68	63	63	61	70	60	64	56	56
# SURVEYED		95	116	232	219	220	224	222	247	230	178	169

****

FIGHT MISBEHAVING DRUNK

TABLE I: FIGHT MISBEHAVING DRUNK -- BY TOTAL POPULATION

Question: Would you approve of an adult male punching a stranger if the stranger was drunk and bumped into the man and his wife on the street? NOTE: Question not asked in 1972, 1974, 1977, 1982, 1985.

Responses: Yes; No

	YEAR										
RESPONSE	'73	'75	'76	'78	'80	'83	'84	'86	'87	'88	'89
YES	10%	7%	9%	9%	10%	10%	7%	8%	9%	9%	8%
NO	90	93	91	91	90	90	93	92	91	91	92
# SURVEYED	986	1054	1454	1487	1414	1547	1427	1433	1425	970	1006

TABLE II: FIGHT MISBEHAVING DRUNK -- BY SEX

Question: Would you approve of an adult male punching a stranger if the stranger was drunk and bumped into the man and his wife on the street? NOTE: Question not asked in 1972, 1974, 1977, 1982, 1985.

Responses: Yes; No

		YEAR										
SEX	RESP	'73	'75	'76	'78	'80	'83	'84	'86	'87	'88	'89
M	YES	11%	10%	10%	11%	11%	11%	9%	9%	10%	11%	8%
	NO	89	90	90	89	89	89	91	91	90	89	92
# SURVEYED		444	459	645	626	618	674	582	604	622	427	437
SEX	RESP	'73	'75	'76	'78	'80	'83	'84	'86	'87	'88	'89
F	YES	10%	5%	8%	8%	9%	8%	6%	7%	8%	9%	8%
	NO	90	95	92	92	91	92	94	93	92	91	92
# SURVEYED		542	595	809	861	796	873	845	829	803	543	569

TABLE III: FIGHT MISBEHAVING DRUNK -- BY RACE

Question: Would you approve of an adult male punching a stranger if the stranger was drunk and bumped into the man and his wife on the street? NOTE: Question not asked in 1972, 1974, 1977, 1982, 1985.

Responses: Yes; No

		YEAR										
RACE	RESP	'73	'75	'76	'78	'80	'83	'84	'86	'87	'88	'89
WHITE	YES	10%	7%	9%	9%	10%	10%	8%	8%	9%	9%	7%
	NO	90	93	91	91	90	90	92	92	91	91	93
# SURVEYED		904	964	1323	1324	1273	1373	1211	1219	1195	814	857
RACE	RESP	'73	'75	'76	'78	'80	'83	'84	'86	'87	'88	'89
BLACK	YES	12%	6%	8%	8%	10%	11%	3%	8%	6%	8%	12%
	NO	88	94	92	92	90	89	97	92	94	92	88
# SURVEYED		73	88	123	147	133	158	164	178	180	114	108
RACE	RESP	'73	'75	'76	'78	'80	'83	'84	'86	'87	'88	'89
OTHER	YES	22%	0%	13%	6%	0%	6%	6%	3%	16%	14%	15%
	NO	78	100	88	94	100	94	94	97	84	86	85
# SURVEYED		9	2	8	16	8	16	52	36	50	42	41

TABLE IV: FIGHT MISBEHAVING DRUNK -- BY AGE

Question: Would you approve of an adult male punching a stranger if the stranger was drunk and bumped into the man and his wife on the street? NOTE: Question not asked in 1972, 1974, 1977, 1982, 1985.

Responses: Yes; No

		YEAR										
AGE	RESP	'73	'75	'76	'78	'80	'83	'84	'86	'87	'88	'89
18-23	YES	7%	3%	7%	4%	7%	6%	7%	5%	8%	4%	12%
	NO	93	97	93	96	93	94	93	95	92	96	88
# SURVEYED		111	121	157	163	154	127	157	104	123	93	91
AGE	RESP	'73	'75	'76	'78	'80	'83	'84	'86	'87	'88	'89
24-29	YES	6%	4%	5%	7%	6%	8%	6%	7%	5%	13%	5%
	NO	94	96	95	93	94	92	94	93	95	87	95
# SURVEYED		159	189	222	243	196	285	230	212	190	141	137

TABLE IV: FIGHT MISBEHAVING DRUNK -- BY AGE (Continued)

Question: Would you approve of an adult male punching a stranger if the stranger was drunk and bumped into the man and his wife on the street? NOTE: Question not asked in 1972, 1974, 1977, 1982, 1985.

Responses: Yes; No

		YEAR										
AGE	RESP	'73	'75	'76	'78	'80	'83	'84	'86	'87	'88	'89
30-35	YES	8%	7%	8%	5%	6%	7%	3%	4%	3%	7%	7%
	NO	92	93	92	95	94	93	97	96	97	93	93
# SURVEYED		119	140	185	223	209	230	195	218	215	127	143
AGE	RESP	'73	'75	'76	'78	'80	'83	'84	'86	'87	'88	'89
36-41	YES	6%	9%	5%	8%	7%	7%	5%	5%	8%	4%	4%
	NO	94	91	95	92	93	93	95	95	92	96	96
# SURVEYED		126	116	154	158	148	166	181	183	182	121	132
AGE	RESP	'73	'75	'76	'78	'80	'83	'84	'86	'87	'88	'89
42-47	YES	13%	4%	8%	5%	10%	8%	7%	6%	5%	1%	10%
	NO	87	96	92	95	90	92	93	94	95	99	90
# SURVEYED		107	96	108	116	115	144	123	141	156	102	104
AGE	RESP	'73	'75	'76	'78	'80	'83	'84	'86	'87	'88	'89
48-53	YES	12%	8%	15%	6%	8%	10%	3%	7%	8%	11%	4%
	NO	88	92	85	94	92	90	97	93	92	89	96
# SURVEYED		103	107	131	126	115	115	98	104	125	56	94
AGE	RESP	'73	'75	'76	'78	'80	'83	'84	'86	'87	'88	'89
54-59	YES	11%	6%	12%	13%	11%	11%	7%	13%	10%	6%	5%
	NO	89	94	88	87	89	89	93	87	90	94	95
# SURVEYED		93	88	126	130	131	130	108	98	96	64	63
AGE	RESP	'73	'75	'76	'78	'80	'83	'84	'86	'87	'88	'89
60-65	YES	7%	15%	11%	14%	10%	14%	13%	8%	18%	14%	6%
	NO	93	85	89	86	90	86	87	92	82	86	94
# SURVEYED		70	78	129	103	115	124	108	114	94	79	70
AGE	RESP	'73	'75	'76	'78	'80	'83	'84	'86	'87	'88	'89
66+	YES	26%	12%	13%	20%	21%	17%	15%	16%	17%	17%	14%
	NO	74	88	87	80	79	83	85	84	83	83	86
# SURVEYED		96	117	236	218	222	219	222	252	240	183	170

****

FIGHT PROTESTERS

TABLE I: FIGHT PROTESTERS -- BY TOTAL POPULATION

Question: Would you approve of an adult male punching a stranger if the stranger was in a protest march showing opposition to the other man's views? NOTE: Question not asked in 1972, 1974, 1977, 1982, 1985.

Responses: Yes; No

	YEAR										
RESPONSE	'73	'75	'76	'78	'80	'83	'84	'86	'87	'88	'89
YES	6%	3%	3%	3%	4%	4%	3%	3%	3%	2%	3%
NO	94	97	97	97	96	96	97	97	97	98	97
# SURVEYED	997	1062	1467	1494	1430	1558	1439	1447	1430	976	1012

TABLE II: FIGHT PROTESTERS -- BY SEX

Question: Would you approve of an adult male punching a stranger if the stranger was in a protest march showing opposition to the other man's views? NOTE: Question not asked in 1972, 1974, 1977, 1982, 1985.

Responses: Yes; No

		YEAR										
SEX	RESP	'73	'75	'76	'78	'80	'83	'84	'86	'87	'88	'89
M	YES	7%	4%	4%	3%	5%	3%	5%	3%	5%	3%	3%
	NO	93	96	96	97	95	97	95	97	95	97	97
# SURVEYED		455	471	655	632	626	669	594	616	628	432	440
SEX	RESP	'73	'75	'76	'78	'80	'83	'84	'86	'87	'88	'89
F	YES	5%	2%	3%	4%	4%	4%	2%	4%	2%	2%	2%
	NO	95	98	97	96	96	96	98	96	98	98	98
# SURVEYED		542	591	812	862	804	889	845	831	802	544	572

TABLE III: FIGHT PROTESTERS -- BY RACE

Question: Would you approve of an adult male punching a stranger if the stranger was in a protest march showing opposition to the other man's views? NOTE: Question not asked in 1972, 1974, 1977, 1982, 1985.

Responses: Yes; No

		YEAR										
RACE	RESP	'73	'75	'76	'78	'80	'83	'84	'86	'87	'88	'89
WHITE	YES	6%	3%	3%	3%	4%	3%	3%	3%	3%	2%	2%
	NO	94	97	97	97	96	97	97	97	97	98	98
# SURVEYED		913	974	1334	1326	1284	1389	1226	1233	1196	822	865
RACE	RESP	'73	'75	'76	'78	'80	'83	'84	'86	'87	'88	'89
BLACK	YES	8%	2%	2%	4%	7%	6%	7%	4%	3%	2%	4%
	NO	92	98	98	96	93	94	93	96	97	98	96
# SURVEYED		75	86	124	153	136	154	163	178	183	111	106
RACE	RESP	'73	'75	'76	'78	'80	'83	'84	'86	'87	'88	'89
OTHER	YES	11%	0%	0%	7%	0%	7%	0%	0%	8%	9%	10%
	NO	89	100	100	93	100	93	100	100	92	91	90
# SURVEYED		9	2	9	15	10	15	50	36	51	43	41

TABLE IV: FIGHT PROTESTERS -- BY AGE

Question: Would you approve of an adult male punching a stranger if the stranger was in a protest march showing opposition to the other man's views? NOTE: Question not asked in 1972, 1974, 1977, 1982, 1985.

Responses: Yes; No

		YEAR										
AGE	RESP	'73	'75	'76	'78	'80	'83	'84	'86	'87	'88	'89
18-23	YES	5%	4%	4%	6%	6%	5%	6%	4%	4%	0%	7%
	NO	95	96	96	94	94	95	94	96	96	100	93
# SURVEYED		113	120	160	163	154	126	159	108	124	92	91
AGE	RESP	'73	'75	'76	'78	'80	'83	'84	'86	'87	'88	'89
24-29	YES	6%	2%	1%	2%	4%	2%	3%	2%	3%	6%	1%
	NO	94	98	99	98	96	98	97	98	97	94	99
# SURVEYED		159	190	223	242	199	284	231	216	191	144	142

TABLE IV: FIGHT PROTESTERS -- BY AGE (Continued)

Question: Would you approve of an adult male punching a stranger if the stranger was in a protest march showing opposition to the other man's views? NOTE: Question not asked in 1972, 1974, 1977, 1982, 1985.

Responses: Yes; No

		YEAR										
AGE	RESP	'73	'75	'76	'78	'80	'83	'84	'86	'87	'88	'89
30-35	YES	7%	3%	1%	4%	1%	3%	1%	3%	2%	2%	1%
	NO	93	97	99	96	99	97	99	97	98	98	99
# SURVEYED		119	141	186	228	214	233	196	220	218	128	142
AGE	RESP	'73	'75	'76	'78	'80	'83	'84	'86	'87	'88	'89
36-41	YES	4%	2%	5%	3%	3%	2%	3%	2%	2%	2%	1%
	NO	96	98	95	97	97	98	97	98	98	98	99
# SURVEYED		128	117	154	158	149	170	186	184	183	123	133
AGE	RESP	'73	'75	'76	'78	'80	'83	'84	'86	'87	'88	'89
42-47	YES	5%	2%	3%	3%	5%	3%	2%	3%	3%	0%	4%
	NO	95	98	97	97	95	97	98	97	97	100	96
# SURVEYED		106	97	113	117	113	143	125	141	151	101	106
AGE	RESP	'73	'75	'76	'78	'80	'83	'84	'86	'87	'88	'89
48-53	YES	8%	3%	4%	2%	5%	4%	2%	3%	2%	4%	1%
	NO	92	97	96	98	95	96	98	97	98	96	99
# SURVEYED		106	109	130	128	121	114	100	106	123	57	95
AGE	RESP	'73	'75	'76	'78	'80	'83	'84	'86	'87	'88	'89
54-59	YES	4%	3%	5%	5%	7%	5%	3%	4%	3%	2%	2%
	NO	96	97	95	95	93	95	97	96	97	98	98
# SURVEYED		97	88	125	133	130	130	112	97	96	64	63
AGE	RESP	'73	'75	'76	'78	'80	'83	'84	'86	'87	'88	'89
60-65	YES	7%	4%	2%	3%	5%	6%	7%	4%	5%	4%	6%
	NO	93	96	98	97	95	94	93	96	95	96	94
# SURVEYED		72	78	130	102	114	127	108	113	98	77	70
AGE	RESP	'73	'75	'76	'78	'80	'83	'84	'86	'87	'88	'89
66+	YES	6%	6%	4%	4%	5%	4%	3%	6%	7%	3%	4%
	NO	94	94	96	96	95	96	97	94	93	97	96
# SURVEYED		95	119	240	216	229	225	217	255	242	186	168

****

FIGHTING

TABLE I: FIGHTING -- BY TOTAL POPULATION

Question: Are there any situations you can imagine in which you would approve of a man punching an adult male stranger? NOTE: Question not asked in 1972, 1974, 1977, 1982, 1985.

Responses: Yes; No

	YEAR										
RESPONSE	'73	'75	'76	'78	'80	'83	'84	'86	'87	'88	'89
YES	67%	72%	69%	66%	65%	71%	62%	66%	66%	66%	65%
NO	33	28	31	34	35	29	38	34	34	34	35
# SURVEYED	1471	1430	1424	1453	1406	1533	1408	1387	1371	939	941

TABLE II: FIGHTING -- BY SEX

Question: Are there any situations you can imagine in which you would approve of a man punching an adult male stranger? NOTE: Question not asked in 1972, 1974, 1977, 1982, 1985.

Responses: Yes; No

		YEAR										
SEX	RESP	'73	'75	'76	'78	'80	'83	'84	'86	'87	'88	'89
M	YES	65%	70%	71%	69%	66%	75%	66%	70%	69%	68%	69%
	NO	35	30	29	31	34	25	34	30	31	32	31
# SURVEYED		688	642	642	612	624	671	573	597	610	416	411
SEX	RESP	'73	'75	'76	'78	'80	'83	'84	'86	'87	'88	'89
F	YES	68%	73%	68%	64%	64%	68%	60%	64%	65%	64%	62%
	NO	32	27	32	36	36	32	40	36	35	36	38
# SURVEYED		783	788	782	841	782	862	835	790	761	523	530

TABLE III: FIGHTING -- BY RACE

Question: Are there any situations you can imagine in which you would approve of a man punching an adult male stranger? NOTE: Question not asked in 1972, 1974, 1977, 1982, 1985.

Responses: Yes; No

		YEAR										
RACE	RESP	'73	'75	'76	'78	'80	'83	'84	'86	'87	'88	'89
WHITE	YES	70%	74%	70%	68%	66%	73%	66%	69%	68%	69%	66%
	NO	30	26	30	32	34	27	34	31	32	31	34
# SURVEYED		1278	1273	1304	1291	1265	1367	1199	1183	1155	791	808
RACE	RESP	'73	'75	'76	'78	'80	'83	'84	'86	'87	'88	'89
BLACK	YES	41%	52%	59%	54%	52%	51%	41%	51%	60%	45%	60%
	NO	59	48	41	46	48	49	59	49	40	55	40
# SURVEYED		180	154	112	146	132	152	158	170	166	108	97
RACE	RESP	'73	'75	'76	'78	'80	'83	'84	'86	'87	'88	'89
OTHER	YES	69%	33%	63%	38%	78%	71%	47%	44%	54%	48%	56%
	NO	31	67	38	63	22	29	53	56	46	53	44
# SURVEYED		13	3	8	16	9	14	51	34	50	40	36

TABLE IV: FIGHTING -- BY AGE

Question: Are there any situations you can imagine in which you would approve of a man punching an adult male stranger? NOTE: Question not asked in 1972, 1974, 1977, 1982, 1985.

Responses: Yes; No

		YEAR										
AGE	RESP	'73	'75	'76	'78	'80	'83	'84	'86	'87	'88	'89
18-23	YES	67%	69%	68%	71%	71%	70%	67%	67%	63%	64%	58%
	NO	33	31	32	29	29	30	33	33	37	36	42
# SURVEYED		169	169	155	157	150	128	154	104	123	92	89
AGE	RESP	'73	'75	'76	'78	'80	'83	'84	'86	'87	'88	'89
24-29	YES	75%	82%	77%	68%	68%	76%	64%	71%	71%	72%	77%
	NO	25	18	23	32	32	24	36	29	29	28	23
# SURVEYED		208	230	221	240	196	279	225	214	186	138	132

TABLE IV: FIGHTING -- BY AGE (Continued)

Question: Are there any situations you can imagine in which you would approve of a man punching an adult male stranger? NOTE: Question not asked in 1972, 1974, 1977, 1982, 1985.

Responses: Yes; No

		YEAR										
AGE	RESP	'73	'75	'76	'78	'80	'83	'84	'86	'87	'88	'89
30-35	YES	72%	83%	78%	75%	75%	76%	66%	71%	71%	74%	67%
	NO	28	17	22	25	25	24	34	29	29	26	33
# SURVEYED		164	161	179	225	210	233	194	216	215	118	135
AGE	RESP	'73	'75	'76	'78	'80	'83	'84	'86	'87	'88	'89
36-41	YES	74%	77%	73%	67%	74%	78%	74%	73%	77%	73%	69%
	NO	26	23	27	33	26	22	26	27	23	27	31
# SURVEYED		174	149	154	153	150	167	186	178	174	122	122
AGE	RESP	'73	'75	'76	'78	'80	'83	'84	'86	'87	'88	'89
42-47	YES	73%	69%	71%	72%	71%	76%	63%	73%	71%	74%	73%
	NO	27	31	29	28	29	24	37	27	29	26	27
# SURVEYED		142	137	105	114	112	139	120	132	147	99	100
AGE	RESP	'73	'75	'76	'78	'80	'83	'84	'86	'87	'88	'89
48-53	YES	72%	78%	70%	68%	64%	79%	55%	68%	66%	69%	71%
	NO	28	22	30	32	36	21	45	32	34	31	29
# SURVEYED		149	135	128	123	118	112	97	104	116	54	85
AGE	RESP	'73	'75	'76	'78	'80	'83	'84	'86	'87	'88	'89
54-59	YES	62%	71%	72%	69%	50%	65%	58%	67%	64%	46%	78%
	NO	38	29	28	31	50	35	42	33	36	54	22
# SURVEYED		155	120	123	127	131	126	109	93	89	61	54
AGE	RESP	'73	'75	'76	'78	'80	'83	'84	'86	'87	'88	'89
60-65	YES	58%	70%	63%	56%	54%	61%	60%	61%	62%	74%	48%
	NO	42	30	37	44	46	39	40	39	38	26	52
# SURVEYED		114	107	124	96	112	122	108	106	97	77	66
AGE	RESP	'73	'75	'76	'78	'80	'83	'84	'86	'87	'88	'89
66+	YES	47%	50%	53%	48%	54%	57%	49%	50%	50%	49%	50%
	NO	53	50	47	52	46	43	51	50	50	51	50
# SURVEYED		192	217	231	211	218	220	211	234	220	174	157

****

FIGHT ROBBER

TABLE I: FIGHT ROBBER -- BY TOTAL POPULATION

Question: Would you approve of an adult male punching a stranger if the stranger had broken into the man's house? NOTE: Question not asked in 1972, 1974, 1977, 1982, 1985.

Responses: Yes; No

RESPONSE	'73	'75	'76	'78	'80	'83	'84	'86	'87	'88	'89
YES	86%	91%	84%	84%	83%	84%	82%	86%	84%	86%	87%
NO	14	9	16	16	17	16	18	14	16	14	13
# SURVEYED	998	1060	1469	1498	1426	1559	1426	1437	1418	975	1000

TABLE II: FIGHT ROBBER -- BY SEX

Question: Would you approve of an adult male punching a stranger if the stranger had broken into the man's house? NOTE: Question not asked in 1972, 1974, 1977, 1982, 1985.

Responses: Yes; No

SEX	RESP	'73	'75	'76	'78	'80	'83	'84	'86	'87	'88	'89
M	YES	87%	92%	86%	86%	86%	88%	86%	88%	86%	90%	90%
	NO	13	8	14	14	14	12	14	12	14	10	10
# SURVEYED		456	470	658	631	629	677	577	610	627	432	436
SEX	RESP	'73	'75	'76	'78	'80	'83	'84	'86	'87	'88	'89
F	YES	86%	90%	83%	83%	81%	82%	80%	85%	83%	83%	85%
	NO	14	10	17	17	19	18	20	15	17	17	15
# SURVEYED		542	590	811	867	797	882	849	827	791	543	564

TABLE III: FIGHT ROBBER -- BY RACE

Question: Would you approve of an adult male punching a stranger if the stranger had broken into the man's house? NOTE: Question not asked in 1972, 1974, 1977, 1982, 1985.

Responses: Yes; No

		YEAR										
RACE	RESP	'73	'75	'76	'78	'80	'83	'84	'86	'87	'88	'89
WHITE	YES	87%	91%	85%	84%	84%	85%	83%	87%	84%	86%	87%
	NO	13	9	15	16	16	15	17	13	16	14	13
# SURVEYED		913	969	1335	1328	1279	1385	1212	1225	1186	820	852
RACE	RESP	'73	'75	'76	'78	'80	'83	'84	'86	'87	'88	'89
BLACK	YES	82%	87%	77%	86%	80%	82%	85%	83%	86%	85%	87%
	NO	18	13	23	14	20	18	15	17	14	15	13
# SURVEYED		76	89	125	154	137	158	163	176	181	112	108
RACE	RESP	'73	'75	'76	'78	'80	'83	'84	'86	'87	'88	'89
OTHER	YES	89%	100%	78%	69%	90%	44%	71%	78%	80%	77%	88%
	NO	11	0	22	31	10	56	29	22	20	23	13
# SURVEYED		9	2	9	16	10	16	51	36	51	43	40

TABLE IV: FIGHT ROBBER -- BY AGE

Question: Would you approve of an adult male punching a stranger if the stranger had broken into the man's house? NOTE: Question not asked in 1972, 1974, 1977, 1982, 1985.

Responses: Yes; No

		YEAR										
AGE	RESP	'73	'75	'76	'78	'80	'83	'84	'86	'87	'88	'89
18-23	YES	89%	93%	83%	85%	87%	87%	85%	88%	84%	85%	88%
	NO	11	7	17	15	13	13	15	13	16	15	12
# SURVEYED		113	120	160	162	154	126	157	104	122	91	93
AGE	RESP	'73	'75	'76	'78	'80	'83	'84	'86	'87	'88	'89
24-29	YES	93%	91%	88%	88%	83%	89%	86%	87%	85%	85%	88%
	NO	7	9	13	12	17	11	14	13	15	15	12
# SURVEYED		159	185	224	238	199	284	227	215	189	143	137

TABLE IV: FIGHT ROBBER -- BY AGE (Continued)

Question: Would you approve of an adult male punching a stranger if the stranger had broken into the man's house? NOTE: Question not asked in 1972, 1974, 1977, 1982, 1985.

Responses: Yes; No

		YEAR										
AGE	RESP	'73	'75	'76	'78	'80	'83	'84	'86	'87	'88	'89
30-35	YES	93%	94%	86%	86%	85%	82%	87%	88%	85%	88%	87%
	NO	7	6	14	14	15	18	13	12	15	12	13
# SURVEYED		121	141	181	225	213	231	196	216	215	125	142
AGE	RESP	'73	'75	'76	'78	'80	'83	'84	'86	'87	'88	'89
36-41	YES	84%	91%	85%	83%	85%	82%	84%	89%	85%	83%	89%
	NO	16	9	15	17	15	18	16	11	15	17	11
# SURVEYED		129	117	157	157	148	171	178	185	181	121	132
AGE	RESP	'73	'75	'76	'78	'80	'83	'84	'86	'87	'88	'89
42-47	YES	88%	90%	80%	85%	78%	83%	79%	89%	86%	88%	84%
	NO	12	10	20	15	22	17	21	11	14	12	16
# SURVEYED		106	100	112	118	110	142	121	140	152	102	101
AGE	RESP	'73	'75	'76	'78	'80	'83	'84	'86	'87	'88	'89
48-53	YES	76%	91%	82%	83%	85%	88%	81%	86%	81%	82%	86%
	NO	24	9	18	17	15	13	19	14	19	18	14
# SURVEYED		107	109	131	127	120	112	97	107	122	55	95
AGE	RESP	'73	'75	'76	'78	'80	'83	'84	'86	'87	'88	'89
54-59	YES	77%	93%	83%	78%	83%	82%	84%	83%	84%	82%	84%
	NO	23	7	17	22	17	18	16	17	16	18	16
# SURVEYED		96	90	127	133	133	131	110	96	93	65	62
AGE	RESP	'73	'75	'76	'78	'80	'83	'84	'86	'87	'88	'89
60-65	YES	87%	87%	80%	79%	86%	83%	78%	81%	82%	88%	83%
	NO	13	13	20	21	14	17	22	19	18	13	17
# SURVEYED		71	77	130	106	111	125	111	113	98	80	71
AGE	RESP	'73	'75	'76	'78	'80	'83	'84	'86	'87	'88	'89
66+	YES	85%	86%	83%	86%	80%	83%	76%	83%	85%	87%	90%
	NO	15	14	17	14	20	17	24	17	15	13	10
# SURVEYED		94	118	242	225	229	230	224	255	242	189	165

****

POLICE USE FORCE ON ABUSIVE PERSON

TABLE I: POLICE USE FORCE ON ABUSIVE PERSON -- BY TOTAL POPULATION

Question: Would you approve of a policeman striking a citizen who had said vulgar and obscene things to the policeman?
NOTE: Question not asked in 1972, 1974, 1977, 1982, 1985.

Responses: Yes; No

	YEAR										
RESPONSE	'73	'75	'76	'78	'80	'83	'84	'86	'87	'88	'89
YES	23%	20%	20%	18%	14%	15%	12%	14%	11%	12%	11%
NO	77	80	80	82	86	85	88	86	89	88	89
# SURVEYED	1106	1102	1453	1499	1430	1560	1434	1446	1425	975	1012

TABLE II: POLICE USE FORCE ON ABUSIVE PERSON -- BY SEX

Question: Would you approve of a policeman striking a citizen who had said vulgar and obscene things to the policeman?
NOTE: Question not asked in 1972, 1974, 1977, 1982, 1985.

Responses: Yes; No

		YEAR										
SEX	RESP	'73	'75	'76	'78	'80	'83	'84	'86	'87	'88	'89
M	YES	23%	23%	22%	20%	14%	18%	14%	14%	12%	13%	13%
	NO	77	77	78	80	86	82	86	86	88	87	87
# SURVEYED		535	513	655	630	628	673	583	612	624	429	439
SEX	RESP	'73	'75	'76	'78	'80	'83	'84	'86	'87	'88	'89
F	YES	23%	17%	19%	17%	14%	13%	11%	15%	11%	12%	10%
	NO	77	83	81	83	86	87	89	85	89	88	90
# SURVEYED		571	589	798	869	802	887	851	834	801	546	573

TABLE III: POLICE USE FORCE ON ABUSIVE PERSON -- BY RACE

Question: Would you approve of a policeman striking a citizen who had said vulgar and obscene things to the policeman? NOTE: Question not asked in 1972, 1974, 1977, 1982, 1985.

Responses: Yes; No

		YEAR										
RACE	RESP	'73	'75	'76	'78	'80	'83	'84	'86	'87	'88	'89
WHITE	YES	24%	21%	21%	19%	15%	15%	12%	14%	12%	13%	11%
	NO	76	79	79	81	85	85	88	86	88	87	89
# SURVEYED		1018	1016	1324	1327	1284	1387	1218	1231	1190	818	865
RACE	RESP	'73	'75	'76	'78	'80	'83	'84	'86	'87	'88	'89
BLACK	YES	12%	12%	10%	9%	8%	12%	7%	15%	7%	7%	9%
	NO	88	88	90	91	92	88	93	85	93	93	91
# SURVEYED		78	84	122	156	137	158	164	179	184	115	107
RACE	RESP	'73	'75	'76	'78	'80	'83	'84	'86	'87	'88	'89
OTHER	YES	20%	0%	0%	31%	0%	27%	23%	14%	14%	10%	18%
	NO	80	100	100	69	100	73	77	86	86	90	83
# SURVEYED		10	2	7	16	9	15	52	36	51	42	40

TABLE IV: POLICE USE FORCE ON ABUSIVE PERSON -- BY AGE

Question: Would you approve of a policeman striking a citizen who had said vulgar and obscene things to the policeman? NOTE: Question not asked in 1972, 1974, 1977, 1982, 1985.

Responses: Yes; No

		YEAR										
AGE	RESP	'73	'75	'76	'78	'80	'83	'84	'86	'87	'88	'89
18-23	YES	11%	12%	16%	13%	10%	13%	11%	10%	7%	14%	17%
	NO	89	88	84	87	90	87	89	90	93	86	83
# SURVEYED		112	117	161	163	154	127	157	106	123	92	93
AGE	RESP	'73	'75	'76	'78	'80	'83	'84	'86	'87	'88	'89
24-29	YES	11%	5%	9%	17%	12%	10%	12%	9%	7%	7%	8%
	NO	89	95	91	83	88	90	88	91	93	93	92
# SURVEYED		168	191	220	240	197	281	232	215	191	145	138

TABLE IV: POLICE USE FORCE ON ABUSIVE PERSON -- BY AGE (Continued)

Question: Would you approve of a policeman striking a citizen who had said vulgar and obscene things to the policeman?
NOTE: Question not asked in 1972, 1974, 1977, 1982, 1985.

Responses: Yes; No

		YEAR										
AGE	RESP	'73	'75	'76	'78	'80	'83	'84	'86	'87	'88	'89
30-35	YES	20%	16%	18%	15%	9%	10%	7%	8%	5%	5%	6%
	NO	80	84	82	85	91	90	93	92	95	95	94
# SURVEYED		130	141	182	228	211	235	194	219	217	127	143
AGE	RESP	'73	'75	'76	'78	'80	'83	'84	'86	'87	'88	'89
36-41	YES	16%	15%	20%	15%	8%	15%	11%	11%	9%	7%	6%
	NO	84	85	80	85	92	85	89	89	91	93	94
# SURVEYED		133	118	152	157	148	168	185	184	179	123	131
AGE	RESP	'73	'75	'76	'78	'80	'83	'84	'86	'87	'88	'89
42-47	YES	25%	19%	21%	17%	16%	10%	15%	11%	7%	12%	8%
	NO	75	81	79	83	84	90	85	89	93	88	92
# SURVEYED		109	108	110	116	112	143	124	141	153	101	105
AGE	RESP	'73	'75	'76	'78	'80	'83	'84	'86	'87	'88	'89
48-53	YES	25%	27%	23%	18%	9%	17%	9%	19%	15%	15%	11%
	NO	75	73	77	82	91	83	91	81	85	85	89
# SURVEYED		112	106	132	129	121	112	100	105	124	55	94
AGE	RESP	'73	'75	'76	'78	'80	'83	'84	'86	'87	'88	'89
54-59	YES	33%	27%	24%	21%	20%	19%	11%	20%	10%	13%	10%
	NO	67	73	76	79	80	81	89	80	90	88	90
# SURVEYED		112	96	127	131	133	130	113	96	97	64	62
AGE	RESP	'73	'75	'76	'78	'80	'83	'84	'86	'87	'88	'89
60-65	YES	33%	41%	22%	20%	18%	22%	22%	19%	23%	17%	21%
	NO	67	59	78	80	82	78	78	81	77	83	79
# SURVEYED		94	79	125	104	114	130	105	113	101	78	73
AGE	RESP	'73	'75	'76	'78	'80	'83	'84	'86	'87	'88	'89
66+	YES	38%	35%	31%	28%	20%	22%	15%	22%	21%	21%	18%
	NO	62	65	69	72	80	78	85	78	79	79	82
# SURVEYED		132	144	238	224	231	227	220	260	236	186	171

****

POLICE USE FORCE TO REPEL ATTACKER

TABLE I: POLICE USE FORCE TO REPEL ATTACKER -- BY TOTAL POPULATION

Question: Would you approve of a policeman striking a citizen who was attacking the policeman with his fists? NOTE: Question not asked in 1972, 1974, 1977, 1982, 1985.

Responses: Yes; No

	YEAR										
RESPONSE	'73	'75	'76	'78	'80	'83	'84	'86	'87	'88	'89
YES	97%	98%	95%	94%	95%	93%	94%	95%	93%	94%	95%
NO	3	2	5	6	5	7	6	5	7	6	5
# SURVEYED	1119	1133	1485	1515	1446	1576	1448	1450	1444	980	1018

TABLE II: POLICE USE FORCE TO REPEL ATTACKER -- BY SEX

Question: Would you approve of a policeman striking a citizen who was attacking the policeman with his fists? NOTE: Question not asked in 1972, 1974, 1977, 1982, 1985.

Responses: Yes; No

		YEAR										
SEX	RESP	'73	'75	'76	'78	'80	'83	'84	'86	'87	'88	'89
M	YES	97%	99%	95%	95%	97%	95%	95%	97%	95%	95%	96%
	NO	3	1	5	5	3	5	5	3	5	5	4
# SURVEYED		539	529	663	638	635	682	589	615	633	432	440
SEX	RESP	'73	'75	'76	'78	'80	'83	'84	'86	'87	'88	'89
F	YES	97%	98%	94%	93%	95%	91%	93%	93%	92%	92%	93%
	NO	3	2	6	7	5	9	7	7	8	8	7
# SURVEYED		580	604	822	877	811	894	859	835	811	548	578

TABLE III: POLICE USE FORCE TO REPEL ATTACKER -- BY RACE

Question: Would you approve of a policeman striking a citizen who was attacking the policeman with his fists? NOTE: Question not asked in 1972, 1974, 1977, 1982, 1985.

Responses: Yes; No

		YEAR										
RACE	RESP	'73	'75	'76	'78	'80	'83	'84	'86	'87	'88	'89
WHITE	YES	98%	99%	95%	95%	96%	94%	95%	96%	94%	94%	95%
	NO	2	1	5	5	4	6	5	4	6	6	5
# SURVEYED		1028	1044	1350	1344	1299	1405	1233	1236	1209	825	868
RACE	RESP	'73	'75	'76	'78	'80	'83	'84	'86	'87	'88	'89
BLACK	YES	93%	93%	90%	83%	86%	86%	87%	90%	89%	91%	92%
	NO	7	7	10	17	14	14	13	10	11	9	8
# SURVEYED		81	87	126	155	137	156	164	178	184	113	109
RACE	RESP	'73	'75	'76	'78	'80	'83	'84	'86	'87	'88	'89
OTHER	YES	70%	50%	67%	81%	90%	73%	82%	86%	90%	88%	93%
	NO	30	50	33	19	10	27	18	14	10	12	7
# SURVEYED		10	2	9	16	10	15	51	36	51	42	41

TABLE IV: POLICE USE FORCE TO REPEL ATTACKER -- BY AGE

Question: Would you approve of a policeman striking a citizen who was attacking the policeman with his fists? NOTE: Question not asked in 1972, 1974, 1977, 1982, 1985.

Responses: Yes; No

		YEAR										
AGE	RESP	'73	'75	'76	'78	'80	'83	'84	'86	'87	'88	'89
18-23	YES	98%	98%	96%	96%	96%	97%	93%	96%	90%	89%	92%
	NO	2	2	4	4	4	3	7	4	10	11	8
# SURVEYED		113	117	159	161	155	127	160	106	124	91	93
AGE	RESP	'73	'75	'76	'78	'80	'83	'84	'86	'87	'88	'89
24-29	YES	97%	99%	95%	92%	93%	94%	97%	95%	93%	92%	92%
	NO	3	1	5	8	7	6	3	5	7	8	8
# SURVEYED		169	191	224	243	198	285	229	214	191	144	139

TABLE IV: POLICE USE FORCE TO REPEL ATTACKER -- BY AGE (Continued)

Question: Would you approve of a policeman striking a citizen who was attacking the policeman with his fists? NOTE: Question not asked in 1972, 1974, 1977, 1982, 1985.

Responses: Yes; No

		YEAR										
AGE	RESP	'73	'75	'76	'78	'80	'83	'84	'86	'87	'88	'89
30-35	YES	98%	97%	97%	95%	95%	92%	91%	95%	95%	98%	94%
	NO	2	3	3	5	5	8	9	5	5	2	6
# SURVEYED		130	143	185	229	214	234	196	218	219	125	144
AGE	RESP	'73	'75	'76	'78	'80	'83	'84	'86	'87	'88	'89
36-41	YES	97%	100%	94%	94%	96%	96%	95%	96%	96%	94%	95%
	NO	3	0	6	6	4	4	5	4	4	6	5
# SURVEYED		135	122	157	159	149	169	185	186	183	124	133
AGE	RESP	'73	'75	'76	'78	'80	'83	'84	'86	'87	'88	'89
42-47	YES	99%	99%	96%	94%	97%	94%	91%	95%	95%	95%	94%
	NO	1	1	4	6	3	6	9	5	5	5	6
# SURVEYED		109	114	113	119	113	144	125	140	154	103	105
AGE	RESP	'73	'75	'76	'78	'80	'83	'84	'86	'87	'88	'89
48-53	YES	96%	96%	95%	95%	97%	91%	92%	95%	95%	93%	94%
	NO	4	4	5	5	3	9	8	5	5	7	6
# SURVEYED		113	109	132	131	123	115	102	107	124	57	96
AGE	RESP	'73	'75	'76	'78	'80	'83	'84	'86	'87	'88	'89
54-59	YES	97%	99%	95%	92%	99%	93%	96%	94%	95%	89%	95%
	NO	3	1	5	8	1	7	4	6	5	11	5
# SURVEYED		113	100	129	134	135	132	112	97	97	66	63
AGE	RESP	'73	'75	'76	'78	'80	'83	'84	'86	'87	'88	'89
60-65	YES	98%	99%	95%	94%	94%	88%	94%	97%	95%	91%	100%
	NO	2	1	5	6	6	12	6	3	5	9	0
# SURVEYED		95	81	132	106	117	129	110	113	101	79	71
AGE	RESP	'73	'75	'76	'78	'80	'83	'84	'86	'87	'88	'89
66+	YES	93%	98%	93%	92%	95%	90%	92%	92%	88%	96%	96%
	NO	7	2	7	8	5	10	8	8	12	4	4
# SURVEYED		138	154	248	226	234	235	225	262	247	187	172

****

POLICE USE FORCE ON ESCAPEE

TABLE I: POLICE USE FORCE ON ESCAPEE -- BY TOTAL POPULATION

Question: Would you approve of a policeman striking a citizen who was attempting to escape from custody? NOTE: Question not asked in 1972, 1974, 1977, 1982, 1985.

Responses: Yes; No

	YEAR										
RESPONSE	'73	'75	'76	'78	'80	'83	'84	'86	'87	'88	'89
YES	88%	89%	81%	78%	79%	78%	76%	75%	81%	80%	79%
NO	12	11	19	22	21	22	24	25	19	20	21
# SURVEYED	1102	1101	1434	1476	1399	1534	1406	1412	1388	946	987

TABLE II: POLICE USE FORCE ON ESCAPEE -- BY SEX

Question: Would you approve of a policeman striking a citizen who was attempting to escape from custody? NOTE: Question not asked in 1972, 1974, 1977, 1982, 1985.

Responses: Yes; No

		YEAR										
SEX	RESP	'73	'75	'76	'78	'80	'83	'84	'86	'87	'88	'89
M	YES	89%	90%	84%	82%	84%	85%	78%	80%	84%	82%	84%
	NO	11	10	16	18	16	15	22	20	16	18	16
# SURVEYED		534	516	648	618	615	671	579	606	609	420	427
SEX	RESP	'73	'75	'76	'78	'80	'83	'84	'86	'87	'88	'89
F	YES	87%	88%	78%	74%	76%	73%	74%	70%	78%	78%	76%
	NO	13	12	22	26	24	27	26	30	22	22	24
# SURVEYED		568	585	786	858	784	863	827	806	779	526	560

TABLE III: POLICE USE FORCE ON ESCAPEE -- BY RACE

Question: Would you approve of a policeman striking a citizen who was attempting to escape from custody? NOTE: Question not asked in 1972, 1974, 1977, 1982, 1985.

Responses: Yes; No

		YEAR										
RACE	RESP	'73	'75	'76	'78	'80	'83	'84	'86	'87	'88	'89
WHITE	YES	89%	90%	83%	80%	82%	81%	79%	78%	83%	83%	81%
	NO	11	10	17	20	18	19	21	22	17	17	19
# SURVEYED		1015	1017	1307	1312	1259	1365	1193	1203	1166	796	844
RACE	RESP	'73	'75	'76	'78	'80	'83	'84	'86	'87	'88	'89
BLACK	YES	75%	75%	59%	59%	53%	58%	56%	54%	68%	68%	66%
	NO	25	25	41	41	47	42	44	46	32	32	34
# SURVEYED		77	83	119	150	130	154	163	173	171	111	105
RACE	RESP	'73	'75	'76	'78	'80	'83	'84	'86	'87	'88	'89
OTHER	YES	80%	100%	75%	64%	60%	53%	64%	53%	63%	59%	68%
	NO	20	0	25	36	40	47	36	47	37	41	32
# SURVEYED		10	1	8	14	10	15	50	36	51	39	38

TABLE IV: POLICE USE FORCE ON ESCAPEE -- BY AGE

Question: Would you approve of a policeman striking a citizen who was attempting to escape from custody? NOTE: Question not asked in 1972, 1974, 1977, 1982, 1985.

Responses: Yes; No

		YEAR										
AGE	RESP	'73	'75	'76	'78	'80	'83	'84	'86	'87	'88	'89
18-23	YES	88%	89%	82%	76%	74%	84%	77%	82%	79%	78%	72%
	NO	12	11	18	24	26	16	23	18	21	22	28
# SURVEYED		110	115	158	156	148	126	156	103	121	90	88
AGE	RESP	'73	'75	'76	'78	'80	'83	'84	'86	'87	'88	'89
24-29	YES	89%	88%	78%	77%	80%	80%	76%	68%	77%	77%	78%
	NO	11	12	22	23	20	20	24	32	23	23	22
# SURVEYED		167	187	215	236	194	274	225	211	183	137	137

TABLE IV: POLICE USE FORCE ON ESCAPEE -- BY AGE (Continued)

Question: Would you approve of a policeman striking a citizen who was attempting to escape from custody? NOTE: Question not asked in 1972, 1974, 1977, 1982, 1985.

Responses: Yes; No

		YEAR										
AGE	RESP	'73	'75	'76	'78	'80	'83	'84	'86	'87	'88	'89
30-35	YES	88%	87%	84%	79%	80%	75%	79%	73%	81%	82%	74%
	NO	12	13	16	21	20	25	21	27	19	18	26
# SURVEYED		127	138	179	222	208	230	188	214	214	119	141
AGE	RESP	'73	'75	'76	'78	'80	'83	'84	'86	'87	'88	'89
36-41	YES	88%	88%	81%	78%	82%	85%	74%	75%	81%	81%	79%
	NO	12	12	19	22	18	15	26	25	19	19	21
# SURVEYED		133	116	153	157	146	167	178	182	171	121	129
AGE	RESP	'73	'75	'76	'78	'80	'83	'84	'86	'87	'88	'89
42-47	YES	92%	96%	71%	76%	80%	79%	75%	78%	85%	79%	80%
	NO	8	4	29	24	20	21	25	22	15	21	20
# SURVEYED		107	107	113	116	110	142	118	138	149	101	102
AGE	RESP	'73	'75	'76	'78	'80	'83	'84	'86	'87	'88	'89
48-53	YES	87%	88%	85%	81%	81%	80%	78%	73%	83%	76%	82%
	NO	13	12	15	19	19	20	22	27	17	24	18
# SURVEYED		111	108	130	128	119	111	101	102	124	55	90
AGE	RESP	'73	'75	'76	'78	'80	'83	'84	'86	'87	'88	'89
54-59	YES	87%	87%	84%	81%	82%	78%	75%	77%	79%	68%	79%
	NO	13	13	16	19	18	22	25	23	21	32	21
# SURVEYED		112	97	122	131	130	130	109	97	95	63	61
AGE	RESP	'73	'75	'76	'78	'80	'83	'84	'86	'87	'88	'89
60-65	YES	87%	84%	81%	78%	72%	70%	77%	79%	82%	85%	88%
	NO	13	16	19	22	28	30	23	21	18	15	12
# SURVEYED		95	80	123	104	112	125	106	111	98	79	69
AGE	RESP	'73	'75	'76	'78	'80	'83	'84	'86	'87	'88	'89
66+	YES	86%	91%	82%	74%	80%	74%	73%	74%	80%	84%	83%
	NO	14	9	18	26	20	26	27	26	20	16	17
# SURVEYED		136	151	236	219	224	222	220	248	229	178	168

****

POLICE USE FORCE ON MURDER SUSPECT

TABLE I: POLICE USE FORCE ON MURDER SUSPECT -- BY TOTAL POPULATION

Question: Would you approve of a policeman striking a citizen who was being questioned as a suspect in a murder case? NOTE: Question not asked in 1972, 1974, 1977, 1982, 1985.

Responses: Yes; No

	YEAR										
RESPONSE	'73	'75	'76	'78	'80	'83	'84	'86	'87	'88	'89
YES	8%	8%	8%	8%	9%	9%	9%	9%	10%	9%	8%
NO	92	92	92	92	91	91	91	91	90	91	92
# SURVEYED	1107	1116	1465	1480	1430	1567	1430	1446	1417	971	1005

TABLE II: POLICE USE FORCE ON MURDER SUSPECT -- BY SEX

Question: Would you approve of a policeman striking a citizen who was being questioned as a suspect in a murder case? NOTE: Question not asked in 1972, 1974, 1977, 1982, 1985.

Responses: Yes; No

		YEAR										
SEX	RESP	'73	'75	'76	'78	'80	'83	'84	'86	'87	'88	'89
M	YES	8%	10%	8%	7%	8%	9%	9%	9%	9%	8%	8%
	NO	92	90	92	93	92	91	91	91	91	92	92
# SURVEYED		536	519	658	622	626	679	585	613	623	428	438
SEX	RESP	'73	'75	'76	'78	'80	'83	'84	'86	'87	'88	'89
F	YES	9%	6%	7%	9%	9%	9%	9%	9%	11%	9%	8%
	NO	91	94	93	91	91	91	91	91	89	91	92
# SURVEYED		571	597	807	858	804	888	845	833	794	543	567

TABLE III: POLICE USE FORCE ON MURDER SUSPECT -- BY RACE

Question: Would you approve of a policeman striking a citizen who was being questioned as a suspect in a murder case? NOTE: Question not asked in 1972, 1974, 1977, 1982, 1985.

Responses: Yes; No

		YEAR										
RACE	RESP	'73	'75	'76	'78	'80	'83	'84	'86	'87	'88	'89
WHITE	YES	8%	8%	8%	8%	8%	9%	9%	9%	10%	8%	7%
	NO	92	92	92	92	92	91	91	91	90	92	93
# SURVEYED		1017	1029	1331	1309	1284	1389	1216	1231	1187	815	857
RACE	RESP	'73	'75	'76	'78	'80	'83	'84	'86	'87	'88	'89
BLACK	YES	11%	5%	9%	10%	13%	9%	8%	10%	7%	13%	13%
	NO	89	95	91	90	88	91	92	90	93	87	87
# SURVEYED		80	85	125	155	136	162	163	178	180	116	107
RACE	RESP	'73	'75	'76	'78	'80	'83	'84	'86	'87	'88	'89
OTHER	YES	10%	0%	22%	6%	10%	19%	20%	11%	16%	13%	10%
	NO	90	100	78	94	90	81	80	89	84	88	90
# SURVEYED		10	2	9	16	10	16	51	37	50	40	41

TABLE IV: POLICE USE FORCE ON MURDER SUSPECT -- BY AGE

Question: Would you approve of a policeman striking a citizen who was being questioned as a suspect in a murder case? NOTE: Question not asked in 1972, 1974, 1977, 1982, 1985.

Responses: Yes; No

		YEAR										
AGE	RESP	'73	'75	'76	'78	'80	'83	'84	'86	'87	'88	'89
18-23	YES	3%	3%	7%	5%	5%	8%	8%	7%	15%	10%	10%
	NO	97	97	93	95	95	92	92	93	85	90	90
# SURVEYED		111	116	161	158	155	128	159	107	121	92	91
AGE	RESP	'73	'75	'76	'78	'80	'83	'84	'86	'87	'88	'89
24-29	YES	4%	2%	5%	7%	7%	6%	10%	6%	8%	4%	6%
	NO	96	98	95	93	93	94	90	94	92	96	94
# SURVEYED		169	191	221	243	198	284	226	216	191	143	138

TABLE IV: POLICE USE FORCE ON MURDER SUSPECT -- BY AGE (Continued)

Question: Would you approve of a policeman striking a citizen who was being questioned as a suspect in a murder case? NOTE: Question not asked in 1972, 1974, 1977, 1982, 1985.

Responses: Yes; No

		YEAR										
AGE	RESP	'73	'75	'76	'78	'80	'83	'84	'86	'87	'88	'89
30-35	YES	4%	6%	7%	6%	8%	6%	6%	2%	6%	5%	7%
	NO	96	94	93	94	92	94	94	98	94	95	93
# SURVEYED		129	140	184	226	212	233	193	218	216	125	145
AGE	RESP	'73	'75	'76	'78	'80	'83	'84	'86	'87	'88	'89
36-41	YES	6%	7%	5%	8%	5%	9%	8%	6%	6%	7%	6%
	NO	94	93	95	92	95	91	92	94	94	93	94
# SURVEYED		134	119	156	158	147	168	186	184	181	123	133
AGE	RESP	'73	'75	'76	'78	'80	'83	'84	'86	'87	'88	'89
42-47	YES	10%	4%	8%	3%	12%	8%	6%	8%	10%	11%	5%
	NO	90	96	92	97	88	92	94	92	90	89	95
# SURVEYED		107	112	111	119	115	143	124	138	155	102	105
AGE	RESP	'73	'75	'76	'78	'80	'83	'84	'86	'87	'88	'89
48-53	YES	13%	7%	8%	8%	10%	7%	5%	7%	10%	9%	10%
	NO	87	93	92	92	90	93	95	93	90	91	90
# SURVEYED		112	108	132	127	121	114	100	107	122	56	93
AGE	RESP	'73	'75	'76	'78	'80	'83	'84	'86	'87	'88	'89
54-59	YES	7%	7%	5%	10%	10%	12%	7%	13%	6%	15%	2%
	NO	93	93	95	90	90	88	93	87	94	85	98
# SURVEYED		112	99	128	135	135	130	112	99	96	65	61
AGE	RESP	'73	'75	'76	'78	'80	'83	'84	'86	'87	'88	'89
60-65	YES	13%	19%	9%	13%	8%	16%	14%	12%	14%	8%	14%
	NO	87	81	91	87	92	84	86	88	86	92	86
# SURVEYED		94	79	129	100	113	129	109	113	99	78	73
AGE	RESP	'73	'75	'76	'78	'80	'83	'84	'86	'87	'88	'89
66+	YES	19%	17%	13%	14%	12%	14%	15%	18%	15%	13%	13%
	NO	81	83	87	86	88	86	85	82	85	87	87
# SURVEYED		135	151	238	207	226	231	216	257	232	183	164

****

SECTION 3: BEHAVIOR

ALCOHOL CONSUMPTION

TABLE I: ALCOHOL CONSUMPTION -- BY TOTAL POPULATION

Question: Do you ever have occasion to use alcoholic beverages such as liquor, wine, or beer, or are you a total abstainer? NOTE: Question not asked in 1972-1976, 1982, 1985.

Responses: UA = Use alcohol; TA = Total abstainer

	YEAR								
RESPONSE	'77	'78	'80	'83	'84	'86	'87	'88	'89
UA	72%	72%	73%	74%	73%	68%	73%	69%	67%
TA	28	28	27	26	27	32	27	31	33
# SURVEYED	1525	1529	1465	1596	1466	1468	1461	995	1033

TABLE II: ALCOHOL CONSUMPTION -- BY SEX

Question: Do you ever have occasion to use alcoholic beverages such as liquor, wine, or beer, or are you a total abstainer? NOTE: Question not asked in 1972-1976, 1982, 1985.

Responses: UA = Use alcohol; TA = Total abstainer

		YEAR								
SEX	RESP	'77	'78	'80	'83	'84	'86	'87	'88	'89
M	UA	79%	79%	82%	81%	79%	75%	80%	74%	75%
	TA	21	21	18	19	21	25	20	26	25
# SURVEYED		690	641	639	|89	596	620	641	437	444

		YEAR								
SEX	RESP	'77	'78	'80	'83	'84	'86	'87	'88	'89
F	UA	66%	68%	66%	69%	68%	62%	67%	65%	61%
	TA	34	32	34	31	32	38	33	35	39
# SURVEYED		835	888	826	907	870	848	820	558	589

TABLE III: ALCOHOL CONSUMPTION -- BY RACE

Question: Do you ever have occasion to use alcoholic beverages such as liquor, wine, or beer, or are you a total abstainer? NOTE: Question not asked in 1972-1976, 1982, 1985.

Responses: UA = Use alcohol; TA = Total abstainer

RACE	RESP	'77	'78	'80	'83	'84	'86	'87	'88	'89
WHITE	UA	75%	73%	75%	76%	74%	70%	75%	70%	70%
	TA	25	27	25	24	26	30	25	30	30
# SURVEYED		1335	1355	1315	1413	1244	1247	1219	835	881
BLACK	UA	52%	65%	59%	60%	68%	58%	62%	66%	52%
	TA	48	35	41	40	32	42	38	34	48
# SURVEYED		175	158	140	165	170	184	189	116	110

RACE	RESP	'77	'78	'80	'83	'84	'86	'87	'88	'89
OTHER	UA	73%	81%	70%	56%	58%	41%	64%	64%	38%
	TA	27	19	30	44	42	59	36	36	62
# SURVEYED		15	16	10	18	52	37	53	44	42

TABLE IV: ALCOHOL CONSUMPTION -- BY AGE

Question: Do you ever have occasion to use alcoholic beverages such as liquor, wine, or beer, or are you a total abstainer? NOTE: Question not asked in 1972-1976, 1982, 1985.

Responses: UA = Use alcohol; TA = Total abstainer

AGE	RESP	'77	'78	'80	'83	'84	'86	'87	'88	'89
18-23	UA	76%	76%	77%	74%	86%	77%	79%	72%	68%
	TA	24	24	23	26	14	23	21	28	32
# SURVEYED		164	163	155	128	160	108	126	93	93
24-29	UA	82%	84%	87%	83%	83%	79%	87%	82%	80%
	TA	18	16	13	17	17	21	13	18	20
# SURVEYED		204	244	201	287	232	218	193	146	142
30-35	UA	83%	78%	84%	82%	80%	78%	85%	79%	79%
	TA	17	22	16	18	20	22	15	21	21
# SURVEYED		187	229	215	235	199	220	221	128	145

AGE	RESP	'77	'78	'80	'83	'84	'86	'87	'88	'89
36-41	UA	77%	81%	79%	76%	78%	73%	84%	73%	77%
	TA	23	19	21	24	22	27	16	27	23
# SURVEYED		168	159	150	173	187	188	185	124	133
42-47	UA	77%	76%	75%	83%	75%	69%	68%	74%	75%
	TA	23	24	25	17	25	31	32	26	25
# SURVEYED		147	119	116	145	126	141	157	104	107
48-53	UA	71%	77%	76%	72%	70%	62%	65%	72%	58%
	TA	29	23	24	28	30	38	35	28	42
# SURVEYED		154	132	123	116	102	108	126	57	96

TABLE IV: ALCOHOL CONSUMPTION -- BY AGE (Continued)

Question: Do you ever have occasion to use alcoholic beverages such as liquor, wine, or beer, or are you a total abstainer? NOTE: Question not asked in 1972-1976, 1982, 1985.

Responses: UA = Use alcohol; TA = Total abstainer

		YEAR								
AGE	RESP	'77	'78	'80	'83	'84	'86	'87	'88	'89
54-59	UA	72%	70%	67%	70%	64%	65%	72%	76%	51%
	TA	28	30	33	30	36	35	28	24	49
# SURVEYED		168	137	135	133	114	98	98	66	63
AGE	RESP	'77	'78	'80	'83	'84	'86	'87	'88	'89
60-65	UA	65%	57%	61%	71%	65%	63%	63%	55%	52%
	TA	35	43	39	29	35	37	37	45	48
# SURVEYED		116	107	119	132	110	115	100	80	75

		YEAR								
AGE	RESP	'77	'78	'80	'83	'84	'86	'87	'88	'89
66+	UA	46%	51%	55%	53%	52%	46%	51%	49%	50%
	TA	54	49	45	47	48	54	49	51	50
# SURVEYED		210	232	242	240	232	265	251	193	178

****

ALCOHOL ABUSE

TABLE I: ALCOHOL ABUSE -- BY TOTAL POPULATION

Question: Do you sometimes drink more than you think you should? NOTE: Question not asked in 1972-1976, 1982, 1985.

Responses Yes; No

	YEAR								
RESPONSE	'77	'78	'80	'83	'84	'86	'87	'88	'89
YES	38%	35%	39%	37%	43%	34%	40%	38%	36%
NO	62	65	61	63	57	66	60	62	64
# SURVEYED	1084	1099	1057	1176	1054	984	1055	679	680

TABLE II: ALCOHOL ABUSE -- BY SEX

Question: Do you sometimes drink more than you think you should? NOTE: Question not asked in 1972-1976, 1982, 1985.

Responses Yes; No

SEX	RESP	'77	'78	'80	'83	'84	'86	'87	'88	'89
M	YES	48%	45%	46%	47%	54%	43%	49%	45%	46%
	NO	52	55	54	53	46	57	51	55	54
# SURVEYED		541	501	518	554	466	462	508	321	328

SEX	RESP	'77	'78	'80	'83	'84	'86	'87	'88	'89
F	YES	27%	27%	33%	28%	35%	26%	32%	31%	26%
	NO	73	73	67	72	65	74	68	69	74
# SURVEYED		543	598	539	622	588	522	547	358	352

TABLE III: ALCOHOL ABUSE -- BY RACE

Question: Do you sometimes drink more than you think you should? NOTE: Question not asked in 1972-1976, 1982, 1985.

Responses Yes; No

RACE	RESP	'77	'78	'80	'83	'84	'86	'87	'88	'89
WHITE	YES	38%	36%	39%	38%	45%	35%	41%	37%	36%
	NO	62	64	61	62	55	65	59	63	64
# SURVEYED		984	986	969	1068	912	862	906	577	610
RACE	RESP	'77	'78	'80	'83	'84	'86	'87	'88	'89
BLACK	YES	34%	31%	37%	22%	35%	31%	32%	39%	36%
	NO	66	69	63	78	65	69	68	61	64
# SURVEYED		89	100	81	98	112	107	116	75	55

RACE	RESP	'77	'78	'80	'83	'84	'86	'87	'88	'89
OTHER	YES	18%	15%	43%	30%	27%	40%	42%	41%	20%
	NO	82	85	57	70	73	60	58	59	80
# SURVEYED		11	13	7	10	30	15	33	27	15

TABLE IV: ALCOHOL ABUSE -- BY AGE

Question: Do you sometimes drink more than you think you should? NOTE: Question not asked in 1972-1976, 1982, 1985.

Responses Yes; No

AGE	RESP	'77	'78	'80	'83	'84	'86	'87	'88	'89
18-23	YES	48%	48%	56%	52%	60%	45%	53%	55%	50%
	NO	52	52	44	48	40	55	47	45	50
# SURVEYED		124	124	117	94	136	83	99	66	62
24-29	YES	46%	43%	51%	50%	54%	44%	53%	52%	50%
	NO	54	57	49	50	46	56	47	48	50
# SURVEYED		165	203	174	238	191	172	168	119	113
30-35	YES	38%	37%	41%	41%	47%	44%	49%	37%	42%
	NO	62	63	59	59	53	56	51	63	58
# SURVEYED		153	178	178	192	158	171	186	99	112
36-41	YES	41%	38%	41%	35%	54%	42%	44%	41%	36%
	NO	59	62	59	65	46	58	56	59	64
# SURVEYED		128	128	118	130	142	137	154	90	99
42-47	YES	42%	32%	46%	42%	44%	30%	35%	36%	34%
	NO	58	68	54	58	56	70	65	64	66
# SURVEYED		109	90	84	120	94	97	105	76	79

AGE	RESP	'77	'78	'80	'83	'84	'86	'87	'88	'89
48-53	YES	37%	40%	38%	30%	40%	29%	38%	27%	36%
	NO	63	60	62	70	60	71	62	73	64
# SURVEYED		109	99	91	83	70	66	82	41	55
54-59	YES	32%	36%	33%	30%	24%	25%	33%	38%	28%
	NO	68	64	67	70	76	75	67	62	72
# SURVEYED		120	95	88	93	71	63	69	50	32
60-65	YES	23%	22%	28%	20%	17%	14%	22%	35%	21%
	NO	77	78	72	80	83	86	78	65	79
# SURVEYED		73	60	72	93	71	70	63	43	39
66+	YES	20%	9%	13%	18%	18%	14%	15%	12%	10%
	NO	80	91	87	82	82	86	85	88	90
# SURVEYED		97	118	131	128	119	122	128	92	88

****

SMOKING HISTORY

TABLE I: SMOKING HISTORY -- BY TOTAL POPULATION

Question: If you do not smoke now, have you ever smoked regularly? NOTE: Question not asked in 1972-1977, 1982, 1985.

Responses: Yes; No

	YEAR							
RESPONSE	'78	'80	'83	'84	'86	'87	'88	'89
YES	34%	35%	33%	31%	32%	35%	33%	36%
NO	66	65	67	69	68	65	67	64
# SURVEYED	873	850	996	908	949	964	608	667

TABLE II: SMOKING HISTORY -- BY SEX

Question: If you do not smoke now, have you ever smoked regularly? NOTE: Question not asked in 1972-1977, 1982, 1985.

Responses: Yes; No

		YEAR							
SEX	RESP	'78	'80	'83	'84	'86	'87	'88	'89
M	YES	49%	51%	45%	46%	44%	43%	42%	45%
	NO	51	49	55	54	56	57	58	55
# SURVEYED		330	324	397	328	368	392	251	278

		YEAR							
SEX	RESP	'78	'80	'83	'84	'86	'87	'88	'89
F	YES	25%	25%	25%	22%	24%	29%	27%	30%
	NO	75	75	75	78	76	71	73	70
# SURVEYED		543	526	599	580	581	572	357	389

TABLE III: SMOKING HISTORY -- BY RACE

Question: If you do not smoke now, have you ever smoked regularly? NOTE: Question not asked in 1972-1977, 1982, 1985.

Responses: Yes; No

RACE	RESP	'78	'80	'83	'84	'86	'87	'88	'89
WHITE	YES	36%	37%	34%	32%	33%	36%	32%	38%
	NO	64	63	66	68	67	64	68	62
# SURVEYED		774	764	888	784	820	819	510	573
BLACK	YES	16%	22%	27%	19%	25%	30%	41%	27%
	NO	84	78	73	81	75	70	59	73
# SURVEYED		86	81	94	89	106	115	74	63
OTHER	YES	46%	40%	29%	29%	22%	20%	25%	26%
	NO	54	60	71	71	78	80	75	74
# SURVEYED		13	5	14	35	23	30	24	31

TABLE IV: SMOKING HISTORY -- BY AGE

Question: If you do not smoke now, have you ever smoked regularly? NOTE: Question not asked in 1972-1977, 1982, 1985.

Responses: Yes; No

AGE	RESP	'78	'80	'83	'84	'86	'87	'88	'89
18-23	YES	19%	29%	13%	19%	23%	15%	11%	23%
	NO	81	71	87	81	77	85	89	77
# SURVEYED		85	84	78	96	74	85	55	57
24-29	YES	30%	32%	24%	27%	20%	24%	21%	18%
	NO	70	68	76	73	80	76	79	82
# SURVEYED		135	115	167	130	138	133	77	91
30-35	YES	35%	37%	29%	20%	21%	29%	31%	27%
	NO	65	63	71	80	79	71	69	73
# SURVEYED		138	123	147	122	123	133	71	92
36-41	YES	36%	32%	31%	38%	29%	34%	33%	32%
	NO	64	68	69	62	71	66	67	68
# SURVEYED		77	75	98	101	120	116	70	81
42-47	YES	43%	43%	37%	30%	36%	46%	45%	43%
	NO	57	57	63	70	64	54	55	57
# SURVEYED		63	47	76	69	81	85	62	67
48-53	YES	52%	40%	42%	44%	50%	42%	41%	46%
	NO	48	60	58	56	50	58	59	54
# SURVEYED		62	63	65	63	60	85	32	54

TABLE IV: SMOKING HISTORY -- BY AGE (Continued)

Question: If you do not smoke now, have you ever smoked regularly? NOTE: Question not asked in 1972-1977, 1982, 1985.

Responses: Yes; No

AGE	RESP	'78	'80	'83	'84	'86	'87	'88	'89
54-59	YES	44%	41%	43%	39%	42%	49%	39%	60%
	NO	56	59	57	61	58	51	61	40
# SURVEYED		68	82	83	74	53	57	44	43
AGE	RESP	'78	'80	'83	'84	'86	'87	'88	'89
60-65	YES	33%	38%	45%	42%	43%	35%	37%	54%
	NO	67	62	55	58	57	65	63	46
# SURVEYED		69	69	87	67	83	72	46	48

AGE	RESP	'78	'80	'83	'84	'86	'87	'88	'89
66+	YES	31%	34%	39%	31%	37%	42%	39%	42%
	NO	69	66	61	69	63	58	61	58
# SURVEYED		171	183	190	181	211	194	148	134

****

CURRENT SMOKING HABIT

TABLE I: CURRENT SMOKING HABIT -- BY TOTAL POPULATION

Question: Do you smoke? NOTE: Question not asked in 1972-1976, 1982, 1985.

Responses: Yes; No

RESPONSE	'77	'78	'80	'83	'84	'86	'87	'88	'89
YES	42%	39%	41%	37%	37%	33%	31%	34%	30%
NO	58	61	59	63	63	67	69	66	70
# SURVEYED	1524	1531	1467	1597	1467	1466	1461	995	1033

TABLE II: CURRENT SMOKING HABIT -- BY SEX

Question: Do you smoke? NOTE: Question not asked in 1972-1976, 1982, 1985.

Responses: Yes; No

SEX	RESP	'77	'78	'80	'83	'84	'86	'87	'88	'89
M	YES	51%	46%	48%	42%	44%	37%	36%	39%	32%
	NO	49	54	52	58	56	63	64	61	68
# SURVEYED		690	643	640	689	596	619	641	436	444

SEX	RESP	'77	'78	'80	'83	'84	'86	'87	'88	'89
F	YES	35%	35%	35%	33%	32%	29%	27%	31%	29%
	NO	65	65	65	67	68	71	73	69	71
# SURVEYED		834	888	827	908	871	847	820	559	589

TABLE III: CURRENT SMOKING HABIT -- BY RACE

Question: Do you smoke? NOTE: Question not asked in 1972-1976, 1982, 1985.

Responses: Yes; No

RACE	RESP	'77	'78	'80	'83	'84	'86	'87	'88	'89
WHITE	YES	43%	40%	41%	36%	36%	32%	30%	34%	29%
	NO	57	60	59	64	64	68	70	66	71
# SURVEYED		1335	1357	1317	1414	1245	1246	1219	836	881
RACE	RESP	'77	'78	'80	'83	'84	'86	'87	'88	'89
BLACK	YES	39%	40%	41%	43%	45%	37%	36%	35%	40%
	NO	61	60	59	57	55	63	64	65	60
# SURVEYED		174	158	140	165	170	183	189	115	110

RACE	RESP	'77	'78	'80	'83	'84	'86	'87	'88	'89
OTHER	YES	40%	19%	50%	22%	33%	27%	38%	39%	21%
	NO	60	81	50	78	67	73	62	61	79
# SURVEYED		15	16	10	18	52	37	53	44	42

TABLE IV: CURRENT SMOKING HABIT -- BY AGE

Question: Do you smoke? NOTE: Question not asked in 1972-1976, 1982, 1985.

Responses: Yes; No

AGE	RESP	'77	'78	'80	'83	'84	'86	'87	'88	'89
18-23	YES	49%	42%	45%	38%	40%	31%	32%	38%	32%
	NO	51	58	55	62	60	69	68	62	68
# SURVEYED		164	163	155	128	161	108	126	92	93

AGE	RESP	'77	'78	'80	'83	'84	'86	'87	'88	'89
24-29	YES	45%	42%	42%	41%	43%	34%	30%	42%	33%
	NO	55	58	58	59	57	66	70	58	67
# SURVEYED		204	244	202	287	232	218	193	146	142

TABLE IV: CURRENT SMOKING HABIT -- BY AGE (Continued)

Question: Do you smoke? NOTE: Question not asked in 1972-1976, 1982, 1985.

Responses: Yes; No

		YEAR								
AGE	RESP	'77	'78	'80	'83	'84	'86	'87	'88	'89
30-35	YES	47%	39%	42%	37%	37%	42%	37%	40%	32%
	NO	53	61	58	63	63	58	63	60	68
# SURVEYED		187	230	215	235	198	221	221	128	145
AGE	RESP	'77	'78	'80	'83	'84	'86	'87	'88	'89
36-41	YES	51%	49%	49%	43%	46%	36%	35%	41%	33%
	NO	49	51	51	57	54	64	65	59	67
# SURVEYED		167	160	150	173	187	188	185	125	133
AGE	RESP	'77	'78	'80	'83	'84	'86	'87	'88	'89
42-47	YES	43%	42%	57%	47%	45%	40%	41%	35%	32%
	NO	57	58	43	53	55	60	59	65	68
# SURVEYED		147	119	117	145	126	141	157	104	107
AGE	RESP	'77	'78	'80	'83	'84	'86	'87	'88	'89
48-53	YES	46%	48%	47%	44%	34%	36%	29%	40%	40%
	NO	54	52	53	56	66	64	71	60	60
# SURVEYED		154	132	123	116	102	107	126	57	96

		YEAR								
AGE	RESP	'77	'78	'80	'83	'84	'86	'87	'88	'89
54-59	YES	42%	44%	39%	38%	33%	42%	40%	29%	27%
	NO	58	56	61	62	67	58	60	71	73
# SURVEYED		168	137	135	134	114	96	98	66	63
AGE	RESP	'77	'78	'80	'83	'84	'86	'87	'88	'89
60-65	YES	35%	33%	41%	33%	37%	26%	24%	36%	28%
	NO	65	67	59	67	63	74	76	64	72
# SURVEYED		116	107	119	132	110	115	100	80	75
AGE	RESP	'77	'78	'80	'83	'84	'86	'87	'88	'89
66+	YES	25%	23%	23%	20%	20%	17%	18%	18%	17%
	NO	75	77	77	80	80	83	82	82	83
# SURVEYED		210	232	242	240	232	265	251	193	178

****

CIGARETTE SMOKING

TABLE I: CIGARETTE SMOKING -- BY TOTAL POPULATION

Question: Do you smoke cigarettes? NOTE: Asked only of current smokers. Question not asked in 1972-1976, 1982, 1985-1989.

Responses: Yes; No

	YEAR				
RESPONSE	'77	'78	'80	'83	'84
YES	92%	91%	93%	95%	95%
NO	8	9	7	5	5
# SURVEYED	638	598	594	589	541

TABLE II: CIGARETTE SMOKING -- BY SEX

Question: Do you smoke cigarettes? NOTE: Asked only of current smokers. Question not asked in 1972-1976, 1982, 1985-1989.

Responses: Yes; No

		YEAR				
SEX	RESP	'77	'78	'80	'83	'84
M	YES	85%	83%	87%	91%	91%
	NO	15	17	13	9	9
# SURVEYED		352	293	307	286	262

		YEAR				
SEX	RESP	'77	'78	'80	'83	'84
F	YES	99%	99%	99%	100%	99%
	NO	1	1	1	0	1
# SURVEYED		286	305	287	303	279

TABLE III: CIGARETTE SMOKING -- BY RACE

Question: Do you smoke cigarettes? NOTE: Asked only of current smokers. Question not asked in 1972-1976, 1982, 1985-1989.

Responses: Yes; No

RACE	RESP	'77	'78	'80	'83	'84
WHITE	YES	92%	90%	93%	95%	95%
	NO	8	10	7	5	5
# SURVEYED		568	533	532	515	448

RACE	RESP	'77	'78	'80	'83	'84
BLACK	YES	89%	98%	93%	97%	99%
	NO	11	2	7	3	1
# SURVEYED		64	62	57	70	76

RACE	RESP	'77	'78	'80	'83	'84
OTHER	YES	100%	100%	80%	50%	82%
	NO	0	0	20	50	18
# SURVEYED		6	3	5	4	17

TABLE IV: CIGARETTE SMOKING -- BY AGE

Question: Do you smoke cigarettes? NOTE: Asked only of current smokers. Question not asked in 1972-1976, 1982, 1985-1989.

Responses: Yes; No

AGE	RESP	'77	'78	'80	'83	'84
18-23	YES	94%	96%	100%	96%	94%
	NO	6	4	0	4	6
# SURVEYED		79	68	69	49	64
24-29	YES	97%	96%	96%	96%	96%
	NO	3	4	4	4	4
# SURVEYED		89	101	83	118	100
30-35	YES	94%	96%	93%	99%	95%
	NO	6	4	7	1	5
# SURVEYED		86	89	89	86	74

AGE	RESP	'77	'78	'80	'83	'84
36-41	YES	89%	91%	97%	95%	97%
	NO	11	9	3	5	3
# SURVEYED		85	77	74	73	86
42-47	YES	95%	88%	93%	94%	95%
	NO	5	13	7	6	5
# SURVEYED		63	48	67	67	57
48-53	YES	90%	83%	95%	96%	97%
	NO	10	17	5	4	3
# SURVEYED		70	64	55	51	35

AGE	RESP	'77	'78	'80	'83	'84
54-59	YES	96%	92%	85%	98%	100%
	NO	4	8	15	2	0
# SURVEYED		70	60	53	51	38
60-65	YES	85%	89%	94%	93%	85%
	NO	15	11	6	7	15
# SURVEYED		41	35	48	44	41
66+	YES	75%	83%	77%	90%	96%
	NO	25	17	23	10	4
# SURVEYED		52	54	56	48	46

****

ATTEMPTED TO QUIT SMOKING

TABLE I: ATTEMPTED TO QUIT SMOKING -- BY TOTAL POPULATION

Question: Have you ever tried to give up smoking? NOTE: Asked only of current smokers. Question not asked in 1972-1977, 1982, 1985.

Responses: Yes; No

	YEAR							
RESPONSE	'78	'80	'83	'84	'86	'87	'88	'89
YES	69%	69%	75%	74%	73%	70%	78%	74%
NO	31	31	25	26	27	30	22	26
# SURVEYED	599	595	591	541	474	452	336	308

TABLE II: ATTEMPTED TO QUIT SMOKING -- BY SEX

Question: Have you ever tried to give up smoking? NOTE: Asked only of current smokers. Question not asked in 1972-1977, 1982, 1985.

Responses: Yes; No

		YEAR							
SEX	RESP	'78	'80	'83	'84	'86	'87	'88	'89
M	YES	70%	72%	75%	72%	74%	68%	77%	79%
	NO	30	28	25	28	26	32	23	21
# SURVEYED		294	305	288	262	232	229	166	141

		YEAR							
SEX	RESP	'78	'80	'83	'84	'86	'87	'88	'89
F	YES	68%	65%	75%	76%	71%	73%	79%	71%
	NO	32	35	25	24	29	27	21	29
# SURVEYED		305	290	303	279	242	223	170	167

TABLE III: ATTEMPTED TO QUIT SMOKING -- BY RACE

Question: Have you ever tried to give up smoking? NOTE: Asked only of current smokers. Question not asked in 1972-1977, 1982, 1985.

Responses: Yes; No

RACE	RESP	'78	'80	'83	'84	'86	'87	'88	'89
WHITE	YES	70%	70%	76%	75%	74%	72%	80%	76%
	NO	30	30	24	25	26	28	20	24
# SURVEYED		534	532	516	448	397	364	280	255
BLACK	YES	60%	55%	62%	71%	66%	57%	67%	68%
	NO	40	45	38	29	34	43	33	32
# SURVEYED		62	58	71	76	67	68	39	44
OTHER	YES	33%	60%	75%	53%	80%	80%	82%	44%
	NO	67	40	25	47	20	20	18	56
# SURVEYED		3	5	4	17	10	20	17	9

TABLE IV: ATTEMPTED TO QUIT SMOKING -- BY AGE

Question: Have you ever tried to give up smoking? NOTE: Asked only of current smokers. Question not asked in 1972-1977, 1982, 1985.

Responses: Yes; No

AGE	RESP	'78	'80	'83	'84	'86	'87	'88	'89
18-23	YES	65%	78%	82%	69%	64%	68%	69%	67%
	NO	35	22	18	31	36	33	31	33
# SURVEYED		69	69	49	64	33	40	35	30
24-29	YES	73%	66%	71%	76%	68%	68%	84%	74%
	NO	27	34	29	24	32	32	16	26
# SURVEYED		101	82	118	100	75	57	61	47
30-35	YES	73%	71%	76%	74%	75%	79%	76%	76%
	NO	27	29	24	26	25	21	24	24
# SURVEYED		88	89	86	74	92	82	50	45
36-41	YES	73%	65%	81%	74%	70%	77%	84%	73%
	NO	27	35	19	26	30	23	16	27
# SURVEYED		79	74	74	86	67	65	50	44
42-47	YES	65%	71%	78%	70%	78%	72%	67%	82%
	NO	35	29	22	30	22	28	33	18
# SURVEYED		48	66	68	57	55	64	36	34
48-53	YES	70%	65%	76%	66%	82%	62%	83%	82%
	NO	30	35	24	34	18	38	17	18
# SURVEYED		63	57	51	35	39	37	23	38
54-59	YES	72%	64%	78%	74%	77%	67%	84%	71%
	NO	28	36	22	26	23	33	16	29
# SURVEYED		60	53	51	38	39	39	19	17

TABLE IV: ATTEMPTED TO QUIT SMOKING -- BY AGE (Continued)

Question: Have you ever tried to give up smoking? NOTE: Asked only of current smokers. Question not asked in 1972-1977, 1982, 1985.

Responses: Yes; No

		YEAR							
AGE	RESP	'78	'80	'83	'84	'86	'87	'88	'89
60-65	YES	51%	71%	55%	73%	83%	58%	90%	81%
	NO	49	29	45	27	17	42	10	19
# SURVEYED		35	49	44	41	30	24	29	21
AGE	RESP	'78	'80	'83	'84	'86	'87	'88	'89
66+	YES	63%	64%	71%	85%	60%	64%	70%	61%
	NO	37	36	29	15	40	36	30	39
# SURVEYED		54	56	48	46	43	44	33	31

****

GUN IN HOUSE

TABLE I: GUN IN HOUSE -- BY TOTAL POPULATION

Question: Do you happen to have in your home or garage any guns or revolvers? NOTE: Question not asked in 1972, 1975, 1978, 1983, 1986.

Responses: YES = Yes; NO = No; RF = Refused to answer

	YEAR										
RESPONSE	'73	'74	'76	'77	'80	'82	'84	'85	'87	'88	'89
YES	47%	46%	47%	51%	48%	46%	45%	44%	46%	40%	46%
NO	52	53	52	49	52	53	54	55	53	59	54
RF	1	1	1	0	0	1	1	1	1	1	0
# SURVEYED	1495	1479	1493	1521	1457	1498	1466	1530	1464	970	1030

TABLE II: GUN IN HOUSE -- BY SEX

Question: Do you happen to have in your home or garage any guns or revolvers? NOTE: Question not asked in 1972, 1975, 1978, 1983, 1986.

Responses: YES = Yes; NO = No; RF = Refused to answer

		YEAR										
SEX	RESP	'73	'74	'76	'77	'80	'82	'84	'85	'87	'88	'89
M	YES	53%	51%	52%	55%	56%	54%	53%	54%	51%	50%	55%
	NO	46	48	47	45	44	44	46	45	48	49	45
	RF	1	1	1	0	0	2	1	1	1	1	0
# SURVEYED		696	690	666	689	637	638	596	687	640	397	446
SEX	RESP	'73	'74	'76	'77	'80	'82	'84	'85	'87	'88	'89
F	YES	43%	42%	43%	47%	41%	39%	40%	36%	43%	33%	39%
	NO	57	58	56	53	58	60	60	63	57	66	61
	RF	1	0	1	0	0	1	1	0	0	1	0
# SURVEYED		799	789	827	832	820	860	870	843	824	573	584

TABLE III: GUN IN HOUSE -- BY RACE

Question: Do you happen to have in your home or garage any guns or revolvers? NOTE: Question not asked in 1972, 1975, 1978, 1983, 1986.

Responses: YES = Yes; NO = No; RF = Refused to answer

		YEAR										
RACE	RESP	'73	'74	'76	'77	'80	'82	'84	'85	'87	'88	'89
WHITE	YES	49%	48%	48%	53%	50%	48%	48%	46%	49%	43%	50%
	NO	50	51	51	47	50	51	52	53	51	56	50
	RF	1	1	1	0	0	1	1	1	0	1	0
# SURVEYED		1303	1301	1355	1332	1308	1317	1246	1336	1221	796	887
RACE	RESP	'73	'74	'76	'77	'80	'82	'84	'85	'87	'88	'89
BLACK	YES	40%	32%	37%	34%	29%	31%	27%	29%	31%	25%	25%
	NO	60	67	62	66	71	68	72	71	68	74	75
	RF	1	1	1	0	0	1	1	0	1	2	0
# SURVEYED		179	171	129	175	139	154	169	150	190	130	102
RACE	RESP	'73	'74	'76	'77	'80	'82	'84	'85	'87	'88	'89
OTHER	YES	15%	14%	33%	36%	30%	30%	39%	30%	43%	36%	17%
	NO	85	86	67	64	70	70	61	70	57	61	83
	RF	0	0	0	0	0	0	0	0	0	2	0
# SURVEYED		13	7	9	14	10	27	51	44	53	44	41

TABLE IV: GUN IN HOUSE -- BY AGE

Question: Do you happen to have in your home or garage any guns or revolvers? NOTE: Question not asked in 1972, 1975, 1978, 1983, 1986.

Responses: YES = Yes; NO = No; RF = Refused to answer

		YEAR										
AGE	RESP	'73	'74	'76	'77	'80	'82	'84	'85	'87	'88	'89
18-23	YES	43%	39%	42%	52%	48%	44%	38%	35%	38%	36%	39%
	NO	57	60	58	48	52	56	62	65	62	64	61
	RF	0	1	0	0	0	0	0	0	0	0	0
# SURVEYED		168	167	161	164	155	147	159	133	126	94	96
AGE	RESP	'73	'74	'76	'77	'80	'82	'84	'85	'87	'88	'89
24-29	YES	45%	51%	45%	42%	47%	41%	38%	42%	35%	32%	29%
	NO	54	49	54	58	53	58	63	58	65	66	71
	RF	0	0	2	0	0	1	0	0	0	1	0
# SURVEYED		212	211	226	204	200	244	232	217	193	134	116
AGE	RESP	'73	'74	'76	'77	'80	'82	'84	'85	'87	'88	'89
30-35	YES	55%	48%	53%	49%	45%	49%	38%	41%	48%	34%	48%
	NO	44	51	47	50	55	49	62	58	52	63	52
	RF	1	1	0	1	0	1	0	1	0	3	0
# SURVEYED		167	175	186	188	213	203	198	212	221	131	136
AGE	RESP	'73	'74	'76	'77	'80	'82	'84	'85	'87	'88	'89
36-41	YES	51%	50%	52%	59%	57%	50%	50%	49%	48%	42%	45%
	NO	46	49	46	41	43	47	48	50	51	56	55
	RF	2	1	3	0	0	3	2	1	1	2	0
# SURVEYED		175	152	157	166	150	146	187	184	186	132	136
AGE	RESP	'73	'74	'76	'77	'80	'82	'84	'85	'87	'88	'89
42-47	YES	49%	51%	51%	59%	47%	55%	54%	52%	58%	50%	52%
	NO	51	48	46	41	53	45	45	48	42	50	48
	RF	0	1	3	1	0	1	1	0	0	0	0
# SURVEYED		146	151	113	147	114	119	125	124	157	101	106
AGE	RESP	'73	'74	'76	'77	'80	'82	'84	'85	'87	'88	'89
48-53	YES	46%	48%	49%	58%	54%	53%	54%	60%	54%	48%	60%
	NO	51	50	50	42	45	44	46	40	44	52	40
	RF	3	2	1	0	1	4	0	0	2	0	0
# SURVEYED		151	145	132	153	123	112	101	131	126	65	95

TABLE IV: GUN IN HOUSE -- BY AGE

Question: Do you happen to have in your home or garage any guns or revolvers? NOTE: Question not asked in 1972, 1975, 1978, 1983, 1986.

Responses: YES = Yes; YES = No; RF = Refused to answer

		YEAR										
AGE	RESP	'73	'74	'76	'77	'80	'82	'84	'85	'87	'88	'89
54-59	YES	54%	47%	53%	53%	49%	50%	59%	47%	53%	51%	47%
	NO	46	53	45	47	51	48	41	52	45	49	53
	RF	1	0	2	0	0	2	0	1	2	0	0
# SURVEYED		156	139	128	167	135	144	114	132	97	53	62
AGE	RESP	'73	'74	'76	'77	'80	'82	'84	'85	'87	'88	'89
60-65	YES	52%	44%	47%	51%	46%	50%	54%	50%	47%	51%	55%
	NO	47	55	52	49	53	50	46	50	52	49	45
	RF	1	1	1	0	1	0	0	0	1	0	0
# SURVEYED		119	107	134	116	119	116	113	130	101	81	78
AGE	RESP	'73	'74	'76	'77	'80	'82	'84	'85	'87	'88	'89
66+	YES	34%	41%	37%	41%	42%	35%	41%	35%	41%	34%	46%
	NO	65	59	62	59	58	65	57	62	58	65	54
	RF	1	0	1	0	0	0	2	2	0	1	0
# SURVEYED		197	226	250	209	239	256	232	260	253	176	202

****

GUN OWNERSHIP

TABLE I: GUN OWNERSHIP -- BY TOTAL POPULATION

Question: If you have a gun or guns in your house or garage, do any of these guns personally belong to you? NOTE: Question not asked in 1972-1978, 1983, 1986.

Responses: Yes; No

	YEAR						
RESPONSE	'80	'82	'84	'85	'87	'88	'89
YES	62%	65%	57%	66%	62%	62%	61%
NO	38	35	43	34	38	38	39
# SURVEYED	662	648	660	675	665	385	470

TABLE II: GUN OWNERSHIP -- BY SEX

Question: If you have a gun or guns in your house or garage, do any of these guns personally belong to you? NOTE: Question not asked in 1972-1978, 1983, 1986.

Responses: Yes; No

		YEAR						
SEX	RESP	'80	'82	'84	'85	'87	'88	'89
M	YES	94%	91%	87%	93%	93%	89%	91%
	NO	6	9	13	7	7	11	9
# SURVEYED		341	330	317	370	320	197	243

		YEAR						
SEX	RESP	'80	'82	'84	'85	'87	'88	'89
F	YES	28%	38%	29%	32%	32%	33%	28%
	NO	72	62	71	68	68	67	72
# SURVEYED		321	318	343	305	345	188	227

TABLE III: GUN OWNERSHIP -- BY RACE

Question: If you have a gun or guns in your house or garage, do any of these guns personally belong to you? NOTE: Question not asked in 1972-1978, 1983, 1986.

Responses: Yes; No

		YEAR						
RACE	RESP	'80	'82	'84	'85	'87	'88	'89
WHITE	YES	63%	64%	57%	65%	61%	63%	61%
	NO	37	36	43	35	39	37	39
# SURVEYED		620	595	595	618	587	338	437
RACE	RESP	'80	'82	'84	'85	'87	'88	'89
BLACK	YES	56%	73%	60%	75%	71%	58%	62%
	NO	44	27	40	25	29	42	38
# SURVEYED		39	45	45	44	55	31	26

		YEAR						
RACE	RESP	'80	'82	'84	'85	'87	'88	'89
OTHER	YES	67%	88%	55%	54%	43%	50%	43%
	NO	33	13	45	46	57	50	57
# SURVEYED		3	8	20	13	23	16	7

TABLE IV: GUN OWNERSHIP -- BY AGE

Question: If you have a gun or guns in your house or garage, do any of these guns personally belong to you? NOTE: Question not asked in 1972-1978, 1983, 1986.

Responses: Yes; No

		YEAR						
AGE	RESP	'80	'82	'84	'85	'87	'88	'89
18-23	YES	44%	39%	47%	47%	43%	26%	49%
	NO	56	61	53	53	57	74	51
# SURVEYED		72	62	60	47	47	34	37
AGE	RESP	'80	'82	'84	'85	'87	'88	'89
24-29	YES	54%	65%	55%	59%	50%	63%	47%
	NO	46	35	45	41	50	37	53
# SURVEYED		89	92	87	91	68	43	34
AGE	RESP	'80	'82	'84	'85	'87	'88	'89
30-35	YES	60%	59%	52%	55%	55%	64%	52%
	NO	40	41	48	45	45	36	48
# SURVEYED		91	97	75	87	102	44	65
AGE	RESP	'80	'82	'84	'85	'87	'88	'89
36-41	YES	67%	70%	57%	65%	72%	69%	67%
	NO	33	30	43	35	28	31	33
# SURVEYED		85	70	94	91	89	55	60
AGE	RESP	'80	'82	'84	'85	'87	'88	'89
42-47	YES	67%	67%	59%	65%	59%	61%	67%
	NO	33	33	41	35	41	39	33
# SURVEYED		52	58	68	65	91	51	55

		YEAR						
AGE	RESP	'80	'82	'84	'85	'87	'88	'89
48-53	YES	63%	63%	54%	70%	60%	73%	65%
	NO	37	38	46	30	40	27	35
# SURVEYED		63	56	54	77	68	30	55
AGE	RESP	'80	'82	'84	'85	'87	'88	'89
54-59	YES	71%	67%	54%	69%	67%	50%	54%
	NO	29	33	46	31	33	50	46
# SURVEYED		63	69	67	62	49	26	28
AGE	RESP	'80	'82	'84	'85	'87	'88	'89
60-65	YES	68%	70%	56%	80%	64%	76%	60%
	NO	32	30	44	20	36	24	40
# SURVEYED		53	57	61	65	47	41	42
AGE	RESP	'80	'82	'84	'85	'87	'88	'89
66+	YES	70%	82%	71%	77%	74%	64%	71%
	NO	30	18	29	23	26	36	29
# SURVEYED		92	87	94	90	102	59	92

****

RIFLE IN HOUSE

TABLE I: RIFLE IN HOUSE -- BY TOTAL POPULATION

Question: If you own a gun, is it a rifle? NOTE: Question not asked in 1972, 1975, 1978, 1983, 1986.

Responses: YES = Yes; NO = No; RF = Refused to answer

	YEAR										
RESPONSE	'73	'74	'76	'77	'80	'82	'84	'85	'87	'88	'89
YES	29%	27%	28%	30%	29%	28%	27%	28%	28%	24%	28%
NO	70	73	71	70	70	70	72	71	71	75	72
RF	1	1	1	0	0	2	1	1	1	1	0
# SURVEYED	1497	1479	1489	1519	1458	1501	1467	1530	1464	970	1029

TABLE II: RIFLE IN HOUSE -- BY SEX

Question: If you own a gun, is it a rifle? NOTE: Question not asked in 1972, 1975, 1978, 1983, 1986.

Responses: YES = Yes; NO = No; RF = Refused to answer

		YEAR										
SEX	RESP	'73	'74	'76	'77	'80	'82	'84	'85	'87	'88	'89
M	YES	34%	30%	33%	34%	35%	34%	34%	36%	34%	32%	34%
	NO	65	69	66	66	65	64	66	63	65	67	66
	RF	1	1	1	0	1	2	1	1	1	1	0
# SURVEYED		695	688	665	688	637	638	596	687	640	397	445
SEX	RESP	'73	'74	'76	'77	'80	'82	'84	'85	'87	'88	'89
F	YES	25%	24%	24%	27%	25%	24%	23%	22%	24%	18%	22%
	NO	74	76	75	73	75	75	76	77	76	80	78
	RF	1	0	1	0	0	1	1	0	0	1	0
# SURVEYED		802	791	824	831	821	863	871	843	824	573	584

TABLE III: RIFLE IN HOUSE -- BY RACE

Question: If you own a gun, is it a rifle? NOTE: Question not asked in 1972, 1975, 1978, 1983, 1986.

Responses: YES = Yes; NO = No; RF = Refused to answer

		YEAR										
RACE	RESP	'73	'74	'76	'77	'80	'82	'84	'85	'87	'88	'89
WHITE	YES	32%	29%	30%	33%	32%	30%	30%	31%	31%	27%	31%
	NO	67	70	69	67	68	68	70	68	69	72	69
	RF	1	1	1	0	1	2	1	1	0	1	0
# SURVEYED		1304	1299	1353	1330	1308	1319	1247	1336	1221	796	886
RACE	RESP	'73	'74	'76	'77	'80	'82	'84	'85	'87	'88	'89
BLACK	YES	11%	9%	14%	9%	7%	12%	9%	8%	13%	9%	7%
	NO	89	90	85	91	93	87	90	92	86	89	93
	RF	1	1	1	0	0	1	1	0	1	2	0
# SURVEYED		180	173	127	175	140	155	169	150	190	130	102
RACE	RESP	'73	'74	'76	'77	'80	'82	'84	'85	'87	'88	'89
OTHER	YES	15%	0%	22%	21%	10%	11%	24%	11%	26%	25%	10%
	NO	85	100	78	79	90	89	76	89	74	73	90
	RF	0	0	0	0	0	0	0	0	0	2	0
# SURVEYED		13	7	9	14	10	27	51	44	53	44	41

TABLE IV: RIFLE IN HOUSE -- BY AGE

Question: If you own a gun, is it a rifle? NOTE: Question not asked in 1972, 1975, 1978, 1983, 1986.

Responses: YES = Yes; NO = No; RF = Refused to answer

		YEAR										
AGE	RESP	'73	'74	'76	'77	'80	'82	'84	'85	'87	'88	'89
18-23	YES	29%	26%	30%	36%	30%	25%	23%	23%	24%	23%	25%
	NO	71	73	70	64	70	75	77	77	76	77	75
	RF	0	1	0	0	0	0	0	0	0	0	0
# SURVEYED		171	168	161	164	155	147	160	133	126	94	96
AGE	RESP	'73	'74	'76	'77	'80	'82	'84	'85	'87	'88	'89
24-29	YES	31%	29%	28%	23%	31%	30%	23%	28%	24%	19%	15%
	NO	68	71	70	77	70	69	77	72	76	79	85
	RF	0	0	2	0	0	1	0	0	0	1	0
# SURVEYED		212	211	226	204	200	246	232	217	193	134	116

TABLE IV: RIFLE IN HOUSE -- BY AGE

Question: If you own a gun, is it a rifle? NOTE: Question not asked in 1972, 1975, 1978, 1983, 1986.

Responses: YES = Yes; NO = No; RF = Refused to answer

		YEAR										
AGE	RESP	'73	'74	'76	'77	'80	'82	'84	'85	'87	'88	'89
30-35	**YES**	37%	31%	32%	31%	28%	31%	25%	28%	30%	21%	30%
	NO	62	69	68	68	71	67	75	71	69	76	70
	RF	1	1	0	1	0	2	0	1	0	3	0
# SURVEYED		167	175	186	188	214	203	198	212	221	131	136
AGE	RESP	'73	'74	'76	'77	'80	'82	'84	'85	'87	'88	'89
36-41	**YES**	29%	31%	29%	35%	37%	33%	29%	35%	31%	27%	29%
	NO	68	68	69	65	63	64	70	65	68	72	71
	RF	2	1	3	0	0	3	2	1	1	2	0
# SURVEYED		174	152	156	166	150	146	187	184	186	132	136
AGE	RESP	'73	'74	'76	'77	'80	'82	'84	'85	'87	'88	'89
42-47	**YES**	32%	31%	32%	42%	31%	34%	34%	35%	37%	30%	37%
	NO	68	68	65	57	68	66	65	65	63	70	63
	RF	0	1	3	1	1	1	1	0	0	0	0
# SURVEYED		145	151	112	147	114	119	125	124	157	101	106
AGE	RESP	'73	'74	'76	'77	'80	'82	'84	'85	'87	'88	'89
48-53	**YES**	23%	25%	29%	40%	36%	35%	36%	35%	36%	40%	38%
	NO	74	73	70	60	63	60	64	65	63	60	62
	RF	3	2	1	0	2	5	0	0	2	0	0
# SURVEYED		149	146	131	152	123	112	101	131	126	65	95
AGE	RESP	'73	'74	'76	'77	'80	'82	'84	'85	'87	'88	'89
54-59	**YES**	30%	27%	31%	27%	27%	27%	35%	34%	31%	30%	28%
	NO	69	73	67	73	73	71	65	65	67	70	72
	RF	1	0	2	0	0	2	0	1	2	0	0
# SURVEYED		156	137	127	166	135	144	114	132	97	53	61
AGE	RESP	'73	'74	'76	'77	'80	'82	'84	'85	'87	'88	'89
60-65	**YES**	34%	25%	32%	29%	28%	33%	32%	29%	25%	28%	28%
	NO	65	74	67	71	71	67	68	71	74	72	72
	RF	1	1	1	0	2	0	0	0	1	0	0
# SURVEYED		120	107	134	116	119	116	113	130	101	81	78
AGE	RESP	'73	'74	'76	'77	'80	'82	'84	'85	'87	'88	'89
66+	**YES**	20%	18%	19%	18%	23%	17%	22%	18%	21%	15%	23%
	NO	80	82	80	82	77	83	76	80	78	84	77
	RF	1	0	1	0	0	0	2	2	0	1	0
# SURVEYED		199	226	250	209	239	257	232	260	253	176	202

****

PISTOL IN HOUSE

TABLE I: PISTOL IN HOUSE -- BY TOTAL POPULATION

Question: If you own a gun, is it a pistol? NOTE: Question not asked in 1972, 1975, 1978, 1983, 1986.

Responses: YES = Yes; NO = No; RF = Refused to answer

	YEAR										
RESPONSE	'73	'74	'76	'77	'80	'82	'84	'85	'87	'88	'89
YES	20%	20%	22%	21%	23%	21%	21%	23%	25%	23%	25%
NO	79	80	77	79	76	77	78	76	74	76	75
RF	1	1	1	0	0	2	1	1	1	1	0
# SURVEYED	1497	1479	1489	1519	1458	1501	1467	1530	1464	970	1029

TABLE II: PISTOL IN HOUSE -- BY SEX

Question: If you own a gun, is it a pistol? NOTE: Question not asked in 1972, 1975, 1978, 1983, 1986.

Responses: YES = Yes; NO = No; RF = Refused to answer

		YEAR										
SEX	RESP	'73	'74	'76	'77	'80	'82	'84	'85	'87	'88	'89
M	YES	23%	25%	26%	23%	29%	26%	29%	29%	30%	28%	33%
	NO	76	74	73	77	70	71	71	70	69	71	67
	RF	1	1	1	0	1	2	1	1	1	1	0
# SURVEYED		695	688	665	688	637	638	596	687	640	397	445
SEX	RESP	'73	'74	'76	'77	'80	'82	'84	'85	'87	'88	'89
F	YES	17%	15%	18%	19%	19%	18%	17%	18%	22%	19%	19%
	NO	82	84	81	81	81	81	83	82	78	80	81
	RF	1	0	1	0	0	1	1	0	0	1	0
# SURVEYED		802	791	824	831	821	863	871	843	824	573	584

TABLE III: PISTOL IN HOUSE -- BY RACE

Question: If you own a gun, is it a pistol? NOTE: Question not asked in 1972, 1975, 1978, 1983, 1986.

Responses: YES = Yes; NO = No; RF = Refused to answer

		YEAR										
RACE	RESP	'73	'74	'76	'77	'80	'82	'84	'85	'87	'88	'89
WHITE	YES	20%	20%	22%	21%	24%	22%	23%	24%	26%	24%	28%
	NO	79	79	77	79	76	77	77	76	73	75	72
	RF	1	1	1	0	1	2	1	1	0	1	0
# SURVEYED		1304	1299	1353	1330	1308	1319	1247	1336	1221	796	886
RACE	RESP	'73	'74	'76	'77	'80	'82	'84	'85	'87	'88	'89
BLACK	YES	19%	16%	20%	20%	17%	19%	17%	18%	21%	17%	15%
	NO	80	83	79	80	83	80	82	82	78	82	85
	RF	1	1	1	0	0	1	1	0	1	2	0
# SURVEYED		180	173	127	175	140	155	169	150	190	130	102
RACE	RESP	'73	'74	'76	'77	'80	'82	'84	'85	'87	'88	'89
OTHER	YES	0%	0%	22%	7%	10%	11%	8%	18%	19%	18%	5%
	NO	100	100	78	93	90	89	92	82	81	80	95
	RF	0	0	0	0	0	0	0	0	0	2	0
# SURVEYED		13	7	9	14	10	27	51	44	53	44	41

TABLE IV: PISTOL IN HOUSE -- BY AGE

Question: If you own a gun, is it a pistol? NOTE: Question not asked in 1972, 1975, 1978, 1983, 1986.

Responses: YES = Yes; NO = No; RF = Refused to answer

		YEAR										
AGE	RESP	'73	'74	'76	'77	'80	'82	'84	'85	'87	'88	'89
18-23	YES	14%	13%	17%	17%	19%	16%	13%	14%	20%	17%	25%
	NO	86	86	83	83	81	84	87	86	80	83	75
	RF	0	1	0	0	0	0	0	0	0	0	0
# SURVEYED		171	168	161	164	155	147	160	133	126	94	96
AGE	RESP	'73	'74	'76	'77	'80	'82	'84	'85	'87	'88	'89
24-29	YES	16%	22%	21%	15%	20%	18%	18%	23%	20%	15%	13%
	NO	83	78	77	85	80	81	82	77	80	84	87
	RF	0	0	2	0	0	1	0	0	0	1	0
# SURVEYED		212	211	226	204	200	246	232	217	193	134	116

TABLE IV: PISTOL IN HOUSE -- BY AGE (Continued)

Question: If you own a gun, is it a pistol? NOTE: Question not asked in 1972, 1975, 1978, 1983, 1986.

Responses: YES = Yes; NO = No; RF = Refused to answer

AGE	RESP	'73	'74	'76	'77	'80	'82	'84	'85	'87	'88	'89
30-35	YES	29%	25%	21%	23%	23%	22%	19%	20%	24%	23%	29%
	NO	71	75	79	77	77	76	81	79	76	74	71
	RF	1	1	0	1	0	2	0	1	0	3	0
# SURVEYED		167	175	186	188	214	203	198	212	221	131	136
AGE	RESP	'73	'74	'76	'77	'80	'82	'84	'85	'87	'88	'89
36-41	YES	24%	21%	24%	29%	32%	31%	24%	28%	31%	24%	24%
	NO	74	78	73	71	68	66	74	72	69	74	76
	RF	2	1	3	0	0	3	2	1	1	2	0
# SURVEYED		174	152	156	166	150	146	187	184	186	132	136
AGE	RESP	'73	'74	'76	'77	'80	'82	'84	'85	'87	'88	'89
42-47	YES	22%	17%	20%	20%	28%	22%	27%	26%	31%	33%	33%
	NO	78	81	78	80	71	77	72	74	69	67	67
	RF	0	1	3	1	1	1	1	0	0	0	0
# SURVEYED		145	151	112	147	114	119	125	124	157	101	106
AGE	RESP	'73	'74	'76	'77	'80	'82	'84	'85	'87	'88	'89
48-53	YES	17%	26%	24%	24%	21%	27%	26%	34%	31%	31%	35%
	NO	81	72	75	76	77	68	74	66	67	69	65
	RF	3	2	1	0	2	5	0	0	2	0	0
# SURVEYED		149	146	131	152	123	112	101	131	126	65	95
AGE	RESP	'73	'74	'76	'77	'80	'82	'84	'85	'87	'88	'89
54-59	YES	25%	20%	31%	19%	24%	26%	27%	20%	28%	34%	23%
	NO	74	80	68	81	76	72	73	80	70	66	77
	RF	1	0	2	0	0	2	0	1	2	0	0
# SURVEYED		156	137	127	166	135	144	114	132	97	53	61
AGE	RESP	'73	'74	'76	'77	'80	'82	'84	'85	'87	'88	'89
60-65	YES	24%	16%	21%	24%	31%	24%	31%	23%	27%	27%	26%
	NO	75	83	78	76	67	76	69	77	72	73	74
	RF	1	1	1	0	2	0	0	0	1	0	0
# SURVEYED		120	107	134	116	119	116	113	130	101	81	78
AGE	RESP	'73	'74	'76	'77	'80	'82	'84	'85	'87	'88	'89
66+	YES	13%	18%	18%	18%	19%	16%	18%	22%	21%	15%	24%
	NO	87	82	81	82	81	84	80	76	78	84	76
	RF	1	0	1	0	0	0	2	2	0	1	0
# SURVEYED		199	226	250	209	239	257	232	260	253	176	202

BEHAVIORPERSONAL

SHOTGUN IN HOUSE

TABLE I: SHOTGUN IN HOUSE -- BY TOTAL POPULATION

Question: If you own a gun, is it a shotgun? NOTE: Question not asked in 1972, 1975, 1978, 1983, 1986.

Responses: Yes; No

	YEAR										
RESPONSE	'73	'74	'76	'77	'80	'82	'84	'85	'87	'88	'89
YES	28%	28%	28%	31%	30%	29%	28%	28%	29%	24%	28%
NO	72	72	72	69	70	71	72	73	71	76	72
# SURVEYED	1482	1469	1472	1517	1451	1478	1458	1520	1456	960	1029

TABLE II: SHOTGUN IN HOUSE -- BY SEX

Question: If you own a gun, is it a shotgun? NOTE: Question not asked in 1972, 1975, 1978, 1983, 1986.

Responses: Yes; No

		YEAR										
SEX	RESP	'73	'74	'76	'77	'80	'82	'84	'85	'87	'88	'89
M	YES	32%	35%	33%	38%	38%	38%	34%	35%	36%	33%	36%
	NO	68	65	67	62	62	62	66	65	64	67	64
# SURVEYED		687	679	656	688	633	624	593	680	633	394	445
SEX	RESP	'73	'74	'76	'77	'80	'82	'84	'85	'87	'88	'89
F	YES	24%	22%	25%	25%	23%	22%	23%	21%	24%	18%	21%
	NO	76	78	75	75	77	78	77	79	76	82	79
# SURVEYED		795	790	816	829	818	854	865	840	823	566	584

TABLE III: SHOTGUN IN HOUSE -- BY RACE

Question: If you own a gun, is it a shotgun? NOTE: Question not asked in 1972, 1975, 1978, 1983, 1986.

Responses: Yes; No

		YEAR										
RACE	RESP	'73	'74	'76	'77	'80	'82	'84	'85	'87	'88	'89
WHITE	YES	30%	30%	30%	33%	32%	31%	30%	30%	32%	27%	30%
	NO	70	70	70	67	68	69	70	70	68	73	70
# SURVEYED		1290	1291	1337	1328	1301	1298	1240	1326	1215	789	886
RACE	RESP	'73	'74	'76	'77	'80	'82	'84	'85	'87	'88	'89
BLACK	YES	17%	14%	13%	17%	13%	16%	15%	12%	15%	12%	14%
	NO	83	86	87	83	87	84	85	88	85	88	86
# SURVEYED		179	171	126	175	140	153	167	150	188	128	102
RACE	RESP	'73	'74	'76	'77	'80	'82	'84	'85	'87	'88	'89
OTHER	YES	0%	14%	11%	14%	10%	11%	22%	9%	23%	14%	7%
	NO	100	86	89	86	90	89	78	91	77	86	93
# SURVEYED		13	7	9	14	10	27	51	44	53	43	41

TABLE IV: SHOTGUN IN HOUSE -- BY AGE

Question: If you own a gun, is it a shotgun? NOTE: Question not asked in 1972, 1975, 1978, 1983, 1986.

Responses: Yes; No

		YEAR										
AGE	RESP	'73	'74	'76	'77	'80	'82	'84	'85	'87	'88	'89
18-23	YES	26%	20%	25%	37%	34%	30%	24%	23%	24%	21%	24%
	NO	74	80	75	63	66	70	76	77	76	79	76
# SURVEYED		171	167	161	164	155	147	160	133	126	94	96
AGE	RESP	'73	'74	'76	'77	'80	'82	'84	'85	'87	'88	'89
24-29	YES	25%	30%	26%	22%	29%	26%	23%	27%	20%	20%	23%
	NO	75	70	74	78	72	74	77	73	80	80	77
# SURVEYED		211	211	222	204	200	243	232	217	193	132	116
AGE	RESP	'73	'74	'76	'77	'80	'82	'84	'85	'87	'88	'89
30-35	YES	36%	30%	34%	28%	27%	30%	23%	28%	28%	20%	30%
	NO	64	70	66	72	73	70	77	72	72	80	70
# SURVEYED		166	174	186	187	213	199	198	210	220	127	136

TABLE IV: SHOTGUN IN HOUSE -- BY AGE (Continued)

Question: If you own a gun, is it a shotgun? NOTE: Question not asked in 1972, 1975, 1978, 1983, 1986.

Responses: Yes; No

		YEAR										
AGE	RESP	'73	'74	'76	'77	'80	'82	'84	'85	'87	'88	'89
36-41	YES	32%	32%	34%	34%	42%	32%	30%	30%	32%	27%	24%
	NO	68	68	66	66	58	68	70	70	68	73	76
# SURVEYED		170	151	152	166	150	141	184	183	185	130	136
AGE	RESP	'73	'74	'76	'77	'80	'82	'84	'85	'87	'88	'89
42-47	YES	30%	34%	34%	43%	28%	36%	40%	33%	36%	30%	34%
	NO	70	66	66	57	72	64	60	67	64	70	66
# SURVEYED		145	149	109	146	113	118	124	124	157	101	106
AGE	RESP	'73	'74	'76	'77	'80	'82	'84	'85	'87	'88	'89
48-53	YES	26%	28%	28%	38%	30%	38%	32%	34%	42%	37%	38%
	NO	74	72	72	63	70	62	68	66	58	63	62
# SURVEYED		145	143	130	152	121	106	101	131	124	65	95
AGE	RESP	'73	'74	'76	'77	'80	'82	'84	'85	'87	'88	'89
54-59	YES	30%	27%	36%	33%	34%	35%	34%	32%	34%	30%	31%
	NO	70	73	64	67	66	65	66	68	66	70	69
# SURVEYED		155	137	125	166	135	141	114	131	95	53	61
AGE	RESP	'73	'74	'76	'77	'80	'82	'84	'85	'87	'88	'89
60-65	YES	32%	30%	24%	33%	26%	31%	29%	26%	28%	25%	27%
	NO	68	70	76	67	74	69	71	74	72	75	73
# SURVEYED		119	106	133	116	117	116	113	130	100	81	78
AGE	RESP	'73	'74	'76	'77	'80	'82	'84	'85	'87	'88	'89
66+	YES	18%	24%	22%	23%	24%	19%	27%	21%	25%	20%	25%
	NO	82	76	78	77	76	81	73	79	75	80	75
# SURVEYED		198	226	248	209	238	257	228	254	252	174	202

****

HUNTING

TABLE I: HUNTING -- BY TOTAL POPULATION

Question: Do you (or does your husband/wife) go hunting? NOTE: Question not asked in 1972-1976, 1978, 1983, 1986.

Responses: 1 = Yes, respondent does 2 = Yes, spouse does
3 = Yes, both do 4 = No, neither respondent nor spouse does

	YEAR							
RESPONSE	'77	'80	'82	'84	'85	'87	'88	'89
1	17%	14%	15%	14%	15%	13%	12%	12%
2	9	9	7	9	6	7	6	6
3	3	4	3	3	3	4	2	3
4	71	74	75	75	76	76	80	79
# SURVEYED	1527	1465	1501	1467	1531	1464	976	1030

TABLE II: HUNTING -- BY SEX

Question: Do you (or does your husband/wife) go hunting? NOTE: Question not asked in 1972-1976, 1978, 1983, 1986.

Responses: 1 = Yes, respondent does 2 = Yes, spouse does
3 = Yes, both do 4 = No, neither respondent nor spouse does

		YEAR							
SEX	RESP	'77	'80	'82	'84	'85	'87	'88	'89
M	1	34%	29%	30%	31%	31%	27%	27%	25%
	2	0	0	0	0	0	0	1	0
	3	3	4	3	2	3	4	3	4
	4	63	67	68	67	66	68	70	70
# SURVEYED		692	641	638	597	688	641	399	447

		YEAR							
SEX	RESP	'77	'80	'82	'84	'85	'87	'88	'89
F	1	3%	3%	4%	3%	2%	3%	2%	2%
	2	16	15	12	14	11	13	10	10
	3	4	4	3	3	3	3	2	3
	4	77	79	81	80	83	81	86	85
# SURVEYED		835	824	863	870	843	823	577	583

TABLE III: HUNTING -- BY RACE

Question: Do you (or does your husband/wife) go hunting? NOTE: Question not asked in 1972-1976, 1978, 1983, 1986.

Responses: 1 = Yes, respondent does 2 = Yes, spouse does
3 = Yes, both do 4 = No, neither respondent nor spouse does

RACE	RESP	'77	'80	'82	'84	'85	'87	'88	'89
WHITE	1	18%	15%	16%	15%	17%	14%	13%	13%
	2	10	9	8	9	7	8	7	6
	3	4	4	3	3	3	4	2	4
	4	69	71	74	73	74	74	78	77
# SURVEYED		1336	1315	1319	1247	1337	1221	802	888
RACE	RESP	'77	'80	'82	'84	'85	'87	'88	'89
BLACK	1	13%	3%	10%	6%	6%	11%	6%	7%
	2	3	4	4	5	2	3	2	1
	3	1	0	0	0	0	0	0	0
	4	82	93	86	89	92	87	92	92
# SURVEYED		176	140	155	168	150	190	130	101

RACE	RESP	'77	'80	'82	'84	'85	'87	'88	'89
OTHER	1	13%	10%	7%	19%	11%	11%	11%	2%
	2	13	10	7	8	5	6	7	12
	3	0	0	0	0	0	2	0	0
	4	73	80	85	73	84	81	82	85
# SURVEYED		15	10	27	52	44	53	44	41

TABLE IV: HUNTING -- BY AGE

Question: Do you (or does your husband/wife) go hunting? NOTE: Question not asked in 1972-1976, 1978, 1983, 1986.

Responses: 1 = Yes, respondent does 2 = Yes, spouse does
3 = Yes, both do 4 = No, neither respondent nor spouse does

AGE	RESP	'77	'80	'82	'84	'85	'87	'88	'89
18-23	1	30%	25%	26%	27%	28%	27%	21%	19%
	2	7	10	4	9	3	5	7	3
	3	4	5	1	1	2	2	2	3
	4	59	60	69	63	68	66	69	75
# SURVEYED		163	154	147	161	133	126	95	97
AGE	RESP	'77	'80	'82	'84	'85	'87	'88	'89
24-29	1	20%	17%	20%	19%	20%	21%	13%	11%
	2	13	11	10	6	9	10	6	9
	3	3	5	4	2	4	3	3	3
	4	65	66	65	72	67	67	78	78
# SURVEYED		204	202	246	231	217	193	134	116

AGE	RESP	'77	'80	'82	'84	'85	'87	'88	'89
30-35	1	19%	13%	17%	12%	17%	11%	12%	18%
	2	13	10	11	11	9	10	7	9
	3	3	7	2	6	4	6	3	6
	4	65	71	69	72	70	73	78	67
# SURVEYED		188	215	204	199	212	221	131	135
AGE	RESP	'77	'80	'82	'84	'85	'87	'88	'89
36-41	1	19%	19%	16%	16%	15%	14%	17%	13%
	2	11	12	6	10	8	9	6	7
	3	7	6	4	3	9	5	4	4
	4	63	63	73	72	67	72	73	76
# SURVEYED		168	150	146	187	184	186	133	135

TABLE IV: HUNTING -- BY AGE (Continued)

Question: Do you (or does your husband/wife) go hunting? NOTE: Question not asked in 1972-1976, 1978, 1983, 1986.

Responses: 1 = Yes, respondent does 2 = Yes, spouse does
3 = Yes, both do 4 = No, neither respondent nor spouse does

		YEAR							
AGE	RESP	'77	'80	'82	'84	'85	'87	'88	'89
42-47	1	21%	14%	19%	15%	19%	12%	14%	12%
	2	12	8	9	12	8	10	8	4
	3	3	5	3	6	2	6	0	8
	4	63	74	69	67	70	72	78	76
# SURVEYED		147	117	118	124	124	157	101	107
AGE	RESP	'77	'80	'82	'84	'85	'87	'88	'89
48-53	1	19%	15%	14%	9%	16%	16%	8%	15%
	2	6	9	13	11	7	10	9	6
	3	3	2	3	2	5	3	3	3
	4	72	74	71	78	73	71	80	76
# SURVEYED		153	123	112	102	131	126	65	95
AGE	RESP	'77	'80	'82	'84	'85	'87	'88	'89
54-59	1	8%	13%	9%	18%	12%	10%	11%	6%
	2	9	9	7	11	8	6	11	8
	3	4	1	5	2	1	1	2	2
	4	80	77	79	69	80	83	75	84
# SURVEYED		168	136	144	114	133	98	53	63

		YEAR							
AGE	RESP	'77	'80	'82	'84	'85	'87	'88	'89
60-65	1	11%	8%	9%	9%	12%	6%	11%	8%
	2	6	4	7	11	2	4	5	5
	3	3	2	2	2	1	2	1	0
	4	80	86	83	79	85	88	83	87
# SURVEYED		117	119	115	112	130	101	84	77
AGE	RESP	'77	'80	'82	'84	'85	'87	'88	'89
66+	1	8%	7%	6%	3%	5%	7%	5%	7%
	2	3	4	1	3	1	2	2	3
	3	0	1	0	1	0	1	0	0
	4	89	88	93	93	94	90	93	89
# SURVEYED		212	240	258	231	260	252	177	202

****

NEWSPAPER READING

TABLE I: NEWSPAPER READING -- BY TOTAL POPULATION

Question: How often do you read the newspaper--every day, a few times a week, weekly, less than weekly, or never? NOTE: Question not asked in 1973, 1974, 1976, 1980, 1984.

Responses: DA = Every day; FW = A few times a week; WK = Weekly; LW = Less than weekly; NV = Never

	YEAR										
RESPONSE	'72	'75	'77	'78	'82	'83	'85	'86	'87	'88	'89
DA	69%	66%	62%	57%	54%	56%	53%	54%	55%	51%	50%
FW	15	16	17	20	22	21	21	20	21	24	25
WK	8	8	10	10	12	11	13	13	13	12	13
LW	4	5	7	7	7	8	8	8	7	9	8
NV	4	4	5	5	6	5	6	6	5	5	5
# SURVEYED	1611	1488	1527	1528	1503	1599	1530	1468	1459	988	1005

TABLE II: NEWSPAPER READING -- BY SEX

Question: How often do you read the newspaper--every day, a few times a week, weekly, less than weekly, or never? NOTE: Question not asked in 1973, 1974, 1976, 1980, 1984.

Responses: DA = Every day; FW = A few times a week; WK = Weekly; LW = Less than weekly; NV = Never

		YEAR										
SEX	RESP	'72	'75	'77	'78	'82	'83	'85	'86	'87	'88	'89
MALE	DA	72%	69%	62%	61%	56%	61%	54%	57%	58%	51%	51%
	FW	14	15	16	19	21	17	23	20	21	24	25
	WK	7	7	10	8	10	10	10	11	12	12	13
	LW	3	5	7	6	5	7	7	6	5	8	7
	NV	4	4	5	6	7	4	6	6	4	5	4
# SURVEYED		806	669	691	643	638	690	688	620	640	438	429
SEX	RESP	'72	'75	'77	'78	'82	'83	'85	'86	'87	'88	'89
FEMALE	DA	65%	63%	63%	55%	52%	52%	52%	51%	52%	51%	49%
	FW	16	16	17	21	23	23	19	20	20	23	24
	WK	9	10	10	11	13	11	15	14	13	12	13
	LW	5	6	6	8	7	8	8	9	8	9	8
	NV	4	5	4	5	5	5	6	6	6	5	5
# SURVEYED		805	819	836	885	865	909	842	848	819	550	576

TABLE III: NEWSPAPER READING -- BY RACE

Question: How often do you read the newspaper--every day, a few times a week, weekly, less than weekly, or never? NOTE: Question not asked in 1973, 1974, 1976, 1980, 1984.

Responses: DA = Every day; FW = A few times a week; WK = Weekly; LW = Less than weekly; NV = Never

		YEAR										
RACE	RESP	'72	'75	'77	'78	'82	'83	'85	'86	'87	'88	'89
WHITE	DA	71%	67%	64%	59%	55%	57%	54%	56%	56%	53%	52%
	FW	14	15	16	19	21	20	21	19	20	23	23
	WK	8	8	10	10	12	11	13	13	13	11	13
	LW	3	5	6	7	6	8	7	7	6	8	7
	NV	3	4	4	5	5	5	5	6	5	5	4
# SURVEYED		1347	1321	1337	1354	1320	1416	1336	1243	1219	829	864
RACE	RESP	'72	'75	'77	'78	'82	'83	'85	'86	'87	'88	'89
BLACK	DA	55%	54%	48%	41%	44%	48%	41%	43%	45%	38%	35%
	FW	21	21	24	28	30	25	24	24	27	31	30
	WK	7	10	10	11	10	10	10	10	10	13	12
	LW	9	6	9	13	8	8	11	14	13	11	12
	NV	9	9	9	6	8	8	15	9	5	6	11
# SURVEYED		260	163	175	158	156	165	150	183	187	125	102
RACE	RESP	'72	'75	'77	'78	'82	'83	'85	'86	'87	'88	'89
OTHER	DA	50%	75%	47%	50%	41%	50%	41%	43%	45%	32%	38%
	FW	25	0	20	6	15	28	27	30	15	21	38
	WK	0	25	13	19	19	17	20	8	17	21	13
	LW	25	0	7	6	15	0	2	5	13	24	5
	NV	0	0	13	19	11	6	9	14	9	3	5
# SURVEYED		4	4	15	16	27	18	44	37	53	34	39

TABLE IV: NEWSPAPER READING -- BY AGE

Question: How often do you read the newspaper--every day, a few times a week, weekly, less than weekly, or never? NOTE: Question not asked in 1973, 1974, 1976, 1980, 1984.

Responses: DA = Every day; FW = A few times a week; WK = Weekly; LW = Less than weekly; NV = Never

		YEAR										
AGE	RESP	'72	'75	'77	'78	'82	'83	'85	'86	'87	'88	'89
18-23	DA	45%	41%	38%	31%	26%	30%	23%	28%	33%	21%	23%
	FW	27	34	30	36	32	30	42	32	29	36	43
	WK	13	13	16	10	18	13	15	18	22	20	11
	LW	10	9	10	18	16	21	14	16	10	19	17
	NV	5	3	5	6	8	5	6	6	5	3	7
# SURVEYED		168	173	164	163	148	128	132	108	126	94	84
AGE	RESP	'72	'75	'77	'78	'82	'83	'85	'86	'87	'88	'89
24-29	DA	48%	56%	42%	41%	42%	37%	36%	35%	37%	33%	26%
	FW	29	20	25	26	29	31	33	26	35	27	29
	WK	12	10	16	14	15	17	17	19	17	23	26
	LW	7	12	11	14	9	10	10	15	7	11	14
	NV	5	3	6	5	5	5	4	6	3	5	5
# SURVEYED		231	231	204	244	245	287	216	218	192	150	146
AGE	RESP	'72	'75	'77	'78	'82	'83	'85	'86	'87	'88	'89
30-35	DA	72%	64%	56%	47%	48%	43%	41%	44%	50%	38%	40%
	FW	15	16	20	23	26	26	28	28	22	34	28
	WK	9	11	12	15	13	17	17	17	16	16	17
	LW	2	6	7	11	11	11	11	8	7	7	10
	NV	3	3	5	4	3	3	3	3	4	5	5
# SURVEYED		187	171	187	230	204	236	212	221	221	131	142
AGE	RESP	'72	'75	'77	'78	'82	'83	'85	'86	'87	'88	'89
36-41	DA	78%	70%	61%	59%	49%	58%	47%	56%	54%	50%	49%
	FW	9	14	23	23	29	18	23	23	23	31	31
	WK	5	6	7	10	9	10	17	11	11	11	11
	LW	5	5	7	2	6	11	7	4	6	4	4
	NV	3	5	2	6	8	2	6	5	5	4	5
# SURVEYED		128	154	168	160	146	173	184	188	185	127	126
AGE	RESP	'72	'75	'77	'78	'82	'83	'85	'86	'87	'88	'89
42-47	DA	79%	69%	65%	71%	61%	66%	65%	55%	56%	54%	54%
	FW	10	16	16	18	24	21	17	20	23	24	24
	WK	6	9	10	8	8	7	8	15	7	7	13
	LW	3	4	3	2	3	4	5	7	11	14	7
	NV	2	2	5	3	3	1	5	3	3	1	2
# SURVEYED		186	143	147	119	119	145	124	141	157	108	108

TABLE IV: NEWSPAPER READING -- BY AGE (Continued)

Question: How often do you read the newspaper--every day, a few times a week, weekly, less than weekly, or never? NOTE: Question not asked in 1973, 1974, 1976, 1980, 1984.

Responses: DA = Every day; FW = A few times a week; WK = Weekly; LW = Less than weekly; NV = Never

		YEAR										
AGE	RESP	'72	'75	'77	'78	'82	'83	'85	'86	'87	'88	'89
48-53	DA	76%	76%	79%	63%	59%	71%	68%	64%	63%	60%	61%
	FW	12	14	9	23	16	13	10	17	16	18	20
	WK	6	6	5	7	14	7	11	6	12	8	11
	LW	4	1	4	2	6	4	8	5	7	10	2
	NV	2	4	3	5	5	5	3	8	2	5	6
# SURVEYED		188	140	154	132	111	116	131	108	125	62	85
AGE	RESP	'72	'75	'77	'78	'82	'83	'85	'86	'87	'88	'89
54-59	DA	79%	79%	76%	69%	70%	75%	61%	69%	63%	55%	63%
	FW	9	11	8	14	15	16	15	16	15	18	21
	WK	8	6	8	9	8	4	11	6	9	8	8
	LW	3	2	5	2	1	1	6	6	4	10	3
	NV	2	3	4	6	6	4	7	2	8	10	6
# SURVEYED		156	126	168	137	144	134	133	98	98	51	72
AGE	RESP	'72	'75	'77	'78	'82	'83	'85	'86	'87	'88	'89
60-65	DA	78%	77%	83%	78%	63%	76%	72%	69%	76%	76%	67%
	FW	10	9	8	10	17	11	9	11	8	14	14
	WK	6	7	4	6	12	6	6	8	10	5	7
	LW	2	3	2	4	4	2	3	5	3	3	6
	NV	3	4	3	2	3	5	9	7	3	3	6
# SURVEYED		144	113	117	105	116	132	130	115	100	74	69
AGE	RESP	'72	'75	'77	'78	'82	'83	'85	'86	'87	'88	'89
66+	DA	72%	72%	73%	75%	69%	66%	67%	68%	66%	72%	73%
	FW	9	7	8	6	11	12	11	7	10	11	13
	WK	6	8	6	7	9	7	8	8	10	4	6
	LW	3	3	6	3	2	4	4	5	4	5	4
	NV	10	9	7	8	8	12	9	12	11	8	4
# SURVEYED		218	232	211	231	258	241	261	264	251	190	170

****

HAD VISIONS OF EVENTS FAR AWAY

TABLE I: HAD VISIONS OF EVENTS FAR AWAY -- BY TOTAL POPULATION

Question: Have you ever seen events that happened at a great distance as they were happening? NOTE: Question not asked in 1972-1983, 1985-1987.

Responses: NV = Never in my life; ON = Once in my life; SV = Several times; OF = Often

	YEAR		
RESPONSE	'84	'88	'89
NV	70%	72%	77%
ON	18	17	14
SV	9	8	7
OF	3	3	2
# SURVEYED	1434	1440	983

TABLE II: HAD VISIONS OF EVENTS FAR AWAY -- BY SEX

Question: Have you ever seen events that happened at a great distance as they were happening? NOTE: Question not asked in 1972-1983, 1985-1987.

Responses: NV = Never in my life; ON = Once in my life; SV = Several times; OF = Often

		YEAR		
SEX	RESP	'84	'88	'89
M	NV	70%	70%	75%
	ON	18	18	15
	SV	9	9	8
	OF	2	4	2
# SURVEYED		582	621	422

		YEAR		
SEX	RESP	'84	'88	'89
F	NV	70%	73%	78%
	ON	18	17	14
	SV	9	7	6
	OF	3	3	2
# SURVEYED		852	819	561

TABLE III: HAD VISIONS OF EVENTS FAR AWAY -- BY RACE

Question: Have you ever seen events that happened at a great distance as they were happening? NOTE: Question not asked in 1972-1983, 1985-1987.

Responses: NV = Never in my life; ON = Once in my life; SV = Several times; OF = Often

RACE	RESP	'84	'88	'89
WHITE	NV	73%	75%	79%
	ON	17	16	13
	SV	8	7	6
	OF	2	3	2
# SURVEYED		1223	1200	844

RACE	RESP	'84	'88	'89
BLACK	NV	55%	54%	61%
	ON	21	27	23
	SV	16	11	11
	OF	8	8	5
# SURVEYED		160	180	101

RACE	RESP	'84	'88	'89
OTHER	NV	61%	65%	68%
	ON	20	18	24
	SV	16	13	8
	OF	4	3	0
# SURVEYED		51	60	38

TABLE IV: HAD VISIONS OF EVENTS FAR AWAY -- BY AGE

Question: Have you ever seen events that happened at a great distance as they were happening? NOTE: Question not asked in 1972-1983, 1985-1987.

Responses: NV = Never in my life; ON = Once in my life; SV = Several times; OF = Often

AGE	RESP	'84	'88	'89
18-23	NV	64%	60%	63%
	ON	19	23	28
	SV	10	12	6
	OF	7	5	4
# SURVEYED		156	139	83
24-29	NV	63%	69%	74%
	ON	22	20	18
	SV	12	8	7
	OF	3	3	1
# SURVEYED		229	210	144
30-35	NV	76%	69%	77%
	ON	12	22	13
	SV	10	5	6
	OF	2	4	4
# SURVEYED		195	190	137

AGE	RESP	'84	'88	'89
36-41	NV	72%	70%	77%
	ON	19	17	11
	SV	8	10	10
	OF	1	2	2
# SURVEYED		184	189	125
42-47	NV	73%	74%	74%
	ON	18	19	19
	SV	7	6	7
	OF	2	2	1
# SURVEYED		122	151	107
48-53	NV	70%	68%	77%
	ON	18	19	11
	SV	10	9	10
	OF	2	4	2
# SURVEYED		100	91	84

AGE	RESP	'84	'88	'89
54-59	NV	69%	75%	75%
	ON	21	10	17
	SV	9	6	4
	OF	2	10	4
# SURVEYED		112	83	71
60-65	NV	77%	82%	85%
	ON	17	7	5
	SV	5	8	8
	OF	2	3	3
# SURVEYED		109	114	65
66+	NV	72%	78%	85%
	ON	16	13	9
	SV	9	6	5
	OF	3	2	1
# SURVEYED		224	269	165

****

EXPERIENCED DEJA VU

TABLE I: EXPERIENCED DEJA VU -- BY TOTAL POPULATION

Question: How often have you had the following experience? Thought you were somewhere you had been before, but knew that it was impossible. NOTE: Question not asked in 1972-1983, 1985-1987.

Responses: NV = Never in my life; ON = Once in my life; SV = Several times; OF = Often

	YEAR		
RESPONSE	'84	'88	'89
NV	33%	33%	36%
ON	26	32	30
SV	31	28	27
OF	10	7	7
# SURVEYED	1439	1456	990

TABLE II: EXPERIENCED DEJA VU -- BY SEX

Question: How often have you had the following experience? Thought you were somewhere you had been before, but knew that it was impossible. NOTE: Question not asked in 1972-1983, 1985-1987.

Responses: NV = Never in my life; ON = Once in my life; SV = Several times; OF = Often

		YEAR		
SEX	RESP	'84	'88	'89
M	NV	31%	33%	32%
	ON	30	32	30
	SV	31	30	32
	OF	8	6	7
# SURVEYED		588	629	423

		YEAR		
SEX	RESP	'84	'88	'89
F	NV	35%	33%	40%
	ON	23	33	29
	SV	31	27	24
	OF	11	7	7
# SURVEYED		851	827	567

TABLE III: EXPERIENCED DEJA VU -- BY RACE

Question: How often have you had the following experience? Thought you were somewhere you had been before, but knew that it was impossible. NOTE: Question not asked in 1972-1983, 1985-1987.

Responses: NV = Never in my life; ON = Once in my life; SV = Several times; OF = Often

RACE	RESP	'84	'88	'89
		YEAR		
WHITE	NV	33%	32%	35%
	ON	25	31	31
	SV	32	30	27
	OF	10	7	6
# SURVEYED		1225	1211	851

RACE	RESP	'84	'88	'89
		YEAR		
BLACK	NV	34%	30%	40%
	ON	33	42	22
	SV	25	20	29
	OF	9	8	10
# SURVEYED		163	184	101

RACE	RESP	'84	'88	'89
		YEAR		
OTHER	NV	35%	48%	45%
	ON	25	31	26
	SV	37	20	21
	OF	2	2	8
# SURVEYED		51	61	38

TABLE IV: EXPERIENCED DEJA VU -- BY AGE

Question: How often have you had the following experience? Thought you were somewhere you had been before, but knew that it was impossible. NOTE: Question not asked in 1972-1983, 1985-1987.

Responses: NV = Never in my life; ON = Once in my life; SV = Several times; OF = Often

AGE	RESP	'84	'88	'89
		YEAR		
18-23	NV	19%	22%	23%
	ON	27	40	37
	SV	41	28	33
	OF	14	10	7
# SURVEYED		158	141	84
24-29	NV	17%	24%	21%
	ON	27	32	32
	SV	41	35	39
	OF	15	10	8
# SURVEYED		231	212	146
30-35	NV	18%	17%	25%
	ON	29	42	34
	SV	42	32	29
	OF	11	9	11
# SURVEYED		196	193	140

AGE	RESP	'84	'88	'89
		YEAR		
36-41	NV	22%	20%	27%
	ON	28	37	32
	SV	39	36	35
	OF	12	8	6
# SURVEYED		185	193	126
42-47	NV	43%	26%	27%
	ON	25	34	27
	SV	25	34	37
	OF	7	6	8
# SURVEYED		122	152	107
48-53	NV	40%	38%	46%
	ON	34	27	28
	SV	18	32	20
	OF	7	3	6
# SURVEYED		99	92	85

AGE	RESP	'84	'88	'89
		YEAR		
54-59	NV	48%	44%	32%
	ON	20	27	31
	SV	22	25	30
	OF	10	5	7
# SURVEYED		113	85	71
60-65	NV	47%	46%	58%
	ON	25	26	30
	SV	24	26	9
	OF	4	3	3
# SURVEYED		110	116	66
66+	NV	62%	59%	67%
	ON	18	24	20
	SV	17	13	10
	OF	4	3	2
# SURVEYED		221	268	164

****

EXPERIENCED ESP

TABLE I: EXPERIENCED ESP -- BY TOTAL POPULATION

Question: Have you ever felt as though you were in touch with someone when they were far away from you? NOTE: Question not asked in 1972-1983, 1985-1987.

Responses: NV = Never in my life; ON = Once in my life; SV = Several times; OF = Often

	YEAR		
RESPONSE	'84	'88	'89
NV	33%	35%	42%
ON	29	35	30
SV	29	21	21
OF	9	8	7
# SURVEYED	1439	1456	992

TABLE II: EXPERIENCED ESP -- BY SEX

Question: Have you ever felt as though you were in touch with someone when they were far away from you? NOTE: Question not asked in 1972-1983, 1985-1987.

Responses: NV = Never in my life; ON = Once in my life; SV = Several times; OF = Often

		YEAR		
SEX	RESP	'84	'88	'89
M	NV	40%	41%	47%
	ON	32	36	30
	SV	22	19	19
	OF	6	4	5
# SURVEYED		587	627	421

		YEAR		
SEX	RESP	'84	'88	'89
F	NV	29%	31%	38%
	ON	26	35	30
	SV	33	24	23
	OF	12	11	8
# SURVEYED		852	829	571

TABLE III: EXPERIENCED ESP -- BY RACE

Question: Have you ever felt as though you were in touch with someone when they were far away from you? NOTE: Question not asked in 1972-1983, 1985-1987.

Responses: NV = Never in my life; ON = Once in my life; SV = Several times; OF = Often

RACE	RESP	'84	'88	'89
WHITE	NV	33%	35%	43%
	ON	29	35	30
	SV	28	22	21
	OF	9	8	6
# SURVEYED		1227	1211	855

RACE	RESP	'84	'88	'89
BLACK	NV	34%	38%	30%
	ON	26	34	33
	SV	29	18	27
	OF	12	10	11
# SURVEYED		161	184	101

RACE	RESP	'84	'88	'89
OTHER	NV	37%	36%	58%
	ON	27	41	19
	SV	33	16	19
	OF	2	7	3
# SURVEYED		51	61	36

TABLE IV: EXPERIENCED ESP -- BY AGE

Question: Have you ever felt as though you were in touch with someone when they were far away from you? NOTE: Question not asked in 1972-1983, 1985-1987. NOTE: Question not asked in 1972-1983, 1985-1987.

Responses: NV = Never in my life; ON = Once in my life; SV = Several times; OF = Often

AGE	RESP	'84	'88	'89
18-23	NV	32%	38%	45%
	ON	33	35	35
	SV	26	22	16
	OF	9	5	5
# SURVEYED		158	140	83
AGE	RESP	'84	'88	'89
24-29	NV	25%	39%	38%
	ON	32	38	34
	SV	31	17	21
	OF	12	6	7
# SURVEYED		232	211	145
AGE	RESP	'84	'88	'89
30-35	NV	32%	28%	37%
	ON	30	42	38
	SV	30	22	20
	OF	8	8	5
# SURVEYED		196	193	140

AGE	RESP	'84	'88	'89
36-41	NV	31%	30%	44%
	ON	32	40	25
	SV	30	20	27
	OF	6	10	4
# SURVEYED		185	192	126
AGE	RESP	'84	'88	'89
42-47	NV	39%	29%	40%
	ON	27	37	27
	SV	25	23	26
	OF	9	10	7
# SURVEYED		122	155	108
AGE	RESP	'84	'88	'89
48-53	NV	38%	36%	49%
	ON	26	33	27
	SV	27	20	18
	OF	9	12	6
# SURVEYED		100	92	85

AGE	RESP	'84	'88	'89
54-59	NV	36%	34%	27%
	ON	18	33	34
	SV	35	24	28
	OF	12	9	11
# SURVEYED		112	85	71
AGE	RESP	'84	'88	'89
60-65	NV	34%	34%	49%
	ON	27	32	25
	SV	30	26	15
	OF	9	8	12
# SURVEYED		109	116	68
AGE	RESP	'84	'88	'89
66+	NV	39%	44%	48%
	ON	26	28	26
	SV	25	22	21
	OF	11	7	6
# SURVEYED		222	268	164

****

IN TOUCH WITH THE DEAD

TABLE I: IN TOUCH WITH THE DEAD -- BY TOTAL POPULATION

Question: Have you ever felt as though you were really in touch with someone who had died? NOTE: Question not asked in 1972-1983, 1985-1987.

Responses: NV = Never in my life; ON = Once in my life; SV = Several times; OF = Often

	YEAR		
RESPONSE	'84	'88	'89
NV	58%	60%	64%
ON	23	24	23
SV	14	10	8
OF	5	6	4
# SURVEYED	1445	1459	991

TABLE II: IN TOUCH WITH THE DEAD -- BY SEX

Question: Have you ever felt as though you were really in touch with someone who had died? NOTE: Question not asked in 1972-1983, 1985-1987.

Responses: NV = Never in my life; ON = Once in my life; SV = Several times; OF = Often

		YEAR		
SEX	RESP	'84	'88	'89
M	NV	64%	66%	70%
	ON	23	25	21
	SV	10	6	6
	OF	3	4	3
# SURVEYED		588	628	422

		YEAR		
SEX	RESP	'84	'88	'89
F	NV	53%	56%	60%
	ON	24	24	24
	SV	17	13	10
	OF	6	7	6
# SURVEYED		857	831	569

TABLE III: IN TOUCH WITH THE DEAD -- BY RACE

Question: Have you ever felt as though you were really in touch with someone who had died? NOTE: Question not asked in 1972-1983, 1985-1987.

Responses: NV = Never in my life; ON = Once in my life; SV = Several times; OF = Often

RACE	RESP	'84	'88	'89
		YEAR		
WHITE	NV	59%	61%	65%
	ON	23	24	22
	SV	13	10	8
	OF	4	5	4
# SURVEYED		1229	1215	850

RACE	RESP	'84	'88	'89
		YEAR		
BLACK	NV	45%	54%	55%
	ON	25	29	28
	SV	20	10	11
	OF	9	7	6
# SURVEYED		165	183	102

RACE	RESP	'84	'88	'89
		YEAR		
OTHER	NV	63%	69%	69%
	ON	16	20	26
	SV	14	5	5
	OF	8	7	0
# SURVEYED		51	61	39

TABLE IV: IN TOUCH WITH THE DEAD -- BY AGE

Question: Have you ever felt as though you were really in touch with someone who had died? NOTE: Question not asked in 1972-1983, 1985-1987.

Responses: NV = Never in my life; ON = Once in my life; SV = Several times; OF = Often

AGE	RESP	'84	'88	'89
		YEAR		
18-23	NV	59%	66%	71%
	ON	27	28	21
	SV	9	2	4
	OF	4	4	4
# SURVEYED		158	140	84
AGE	RESP	'84	'88	'89
24-29	NV	60%	60%	69%
	ON	25	28	23
	SV	11	7	6
	OF	4	4	1
# SURVEYED		232	212	145
AGE	RESP	'84	'88	'89
30-35	NV	56%	59%	61%
	ON	28	26	29
	SV	11	12	6
	OF	5	3	4
# SURVEYED		196	193	140

AGE	RESP	'84	'88	'89
		YEAR		
36-41	NV	62%	57%	60%
	ON	24	27	25
	SV	10	11	10
	OF	5	5	4
# SURVEYED		185	192	126
AGE	RESP	'84	'88	'89
42-47	NV	60%	61%	58%
	ON	24	25	27
	SV	12	9	13
	OF	4	5	3
# SURVEYED		123	154	104
AGE	RESP	'84	'88	'89
48-53	NV	58%	58%	69%
	ON	24	27	23
	SV	15	11	7
	OF	3	4	1
SURVEYED		100	92	84

AGE	RESP	'84	'88	'89
		YEAR		
54-59	NV	58%	50%	59%
	ON	20	30	21
	SV	15	10	13
	OF	7	11	7
# SURVEYED		113	84	71
AGE	RESP	'84	'88	'89
60-65	NV	55%	66%	62%
	ON	24	18	24
	SV	15	10	7
	OF	6	6	7
# SURVEYED		109	116	68
AGE	RESP	'84	'88	'89
66+	NV	52%	61%	68%
	ON	16	15	14
	SV	25	15	10
	OF	7	8	8
# SURVEYED		225	272	167

****

OUT OF BODY EXPERIENCE

TABLE I: OUT OF BODY EXPERIENCE -- BY TOTAL POPULATION

Question: Have you ever felt as though you were very close to a powerful, spiritual force that seemed to lift you out of yourself? NOTE: Question not asked in 1972-1982, 1985-1987.

Responses: NV = Never in my life; ON = Once in my life; SV = Several times; OF = Often

	YEAR			
RESPONSE	'83	'84	'88	'89
NV	45%	59%	69%	70%
ON	28	20	18	18
SV	17	14	9	7
OF	10	7	5	5
# SURVEYED	1539	1442	1451	988

TABLE II: OUT OF BODY EXPERIENCE -- BY SEX

Question: Have you ever felt as though you were very close to a powerful, spiritual force that seemed to lift you out of yourself? NOTE: Question not asked in 1972-1982, 1985-1987.

Responses: NV = Never in my life; ON = Once in my life; SV = Several times; OF = Often

		YEAR			
SEX	RESP	'83	'84	'88	'89
M	NV	49%	62%	69%	68%
	ON	26	21	19	19
	SV	16	12	8	9
	OF	9	6	5	4
# SURVEYED		662	587	624	422

		YEAR			
SEX	RESP	'83	'84	'88	'89
F	NV	42%	58%	68%	72%
	ON	29	20	18	17
	SV	18	15	9	6
	OF	12	7	4	5
# SURVEYED		877	855	827	566

TABLE III: OUT OF BODY EXPERIENCE -- BY RACE

Question: Have you ever felt as though you were very close to a powerful, spiritual force that seemed to lift you out of yourself? NOTE: Question not asked in 1972-1982, 1985-1987.

Responses: NV = Never in my life; ON = Once in my life; SV = Several times; OF = Often

RACE	RESP	'83	'84	'88	'89
WHITE	NV	46%	61%	69%	71%
	ON	29	21	18	18
	SV	17	12	9	7
	OF	8	6	4	4
# SURVEYED		1365	1226	1210	847

RACE	RESP	'83	'84	'88	'89
BLACK	NV	33%	50%	63%	58%
	ON	21	18	20	19
	SV	20	21	9	15
	OF	27	12	7	9
# SURVEYED		158	165	182	102

RACE	RESP	'83	'84	'88	'89
OTHER	NV	50%	59%	71%	90%
	ON	31	10	20	8
	SV	13	20	3	0
	OF	6	12	5	3
# SURVEYED		16	51	59	39

TABLE IV: OUT OF BODY EXPERIENCE -- BY AGE

Question: Have you ever felt as though you were very close to a powerful, spiritual force that seemed to lift you out of yourself? NOTE: Question not asked in 1972-1982, 1985-1987.

Responses: NV = Never in my life; ON = Once in my life; SV = Several times; OF = Often

AGE	RESP	'83	'84	'88	'89
18-23	NV	51%	66%	72%	81%
	ON	29	18	19	14
	SV	12	9	4	4
	OF	8	7	5	1
# SURVEYED		125	158	140	84
24-29	NV	46%	67%	73%	72%
	ON	32	14	19	19
	SV	14	13	5	7
	OF	8	6	3	2
# SURVEYED		281	229	212	145
30-35	NV	51%	60%	70%	69%
	ON	27	24	18	21
	SV	13	12	7	5
	OF	9	4	5	5
# SURVEYED		233	196	191	139

AGE	RESP	'83	'84	'88	'89
36-41	NV	40%	60%	64%	64%
	ON	31	22	19	23
	SV	21	13	12	9
	OF	8	5	4	4
# SURVEYED		169	185	190	126
42-47	NV	44%	63%	67%	63%
	ON	28	22	21	19
	SV	18	10	9	13
	OF	10	5	3	5
# SURVEYED		142	123	153	106
48-53	NV	39%	56%	63%	81%
	ON	25	23	23	11
	SV	25	13	11	7
	OF	11	8	3	1
# SURVEYED		112	100	92	84

AGE	RESP	'83	'84	'88	'89
54-59	NV	43%	55%	61%	59%
	ON	26	18	14	18
	SV	23	19	17	14
	OF	8	8	7	8
# SURVEYED		127	113	83	71
60-65	NV	51%	54%	61%	71%
	ON	21	29	18	12
	SV	15	10	12	9
	OF	13	6	9	8
# SURVEYED		126	109	117	66
66+	NV	38%	50%	74%	73%
	ON	27	19	15	15
	SV	17	21	8	4
	OF	18	10	3	7
# SURVEYED		217	225	270	165

****

MEMBER OF FARM ORGANIZATION

TABLE I: MEMBER OF FARM ORGANIZATION -- BY TOTAL POPULATION

Question: Are you a member of any farm organizations? NOTE: Question not asked in 1972, 1973, 1976, 1982, 1985.

Responses: Yes; No

	YEAR										
RESPONSE	'74	'75	'77	'78	'80	'83	'84	'86	'87	'88	'89
YES	4%	4%	4%	4%	4%	4%	4%	4%	4%	3%	3%
NO	96	96	96	96	96	96	96	96	96	97	97
# SURVEYED	1462	1459	1515	1514	1438	1590	1449	1459	1447	984	1002

TABLE II: MEMBER OF FARM ORGANIZATION -- BY SEX

Question: Are you a member of any farm organizations? NOTE: Question not asked in 1972, 1973, 1976, 1982, 1985.

Responses: Yes; No

		YEAR										
SEX	RESP	'74	'75	'77	'78	'80	'83	'84	'86	'87	'88	'89
M	YES	6%	6%	5%	5%	6%	6%	6%	5%	5%	6%	5%
	NO	94	94	95	95	94	94	94	95	95	94	95
# SURVEYED		679	652	686	637	633	686	589	617	636	430	430
SEX	RESP	'74	'75	'77	'78	'80	'83	'84	'86	'87	'88	'89
F	YES	2%	2%	3%	2%	3%	3%	3%	3%	2%	2%	2%
	NO	98	98	97	98	97	97	97	97	98	98	98
# SURVEYED		783	807	829	877	805	904	860	842	811	554	572

TABLE III: MEMBER OF FARM ORGANIZATION -- BY RACE

Question: Are you a member of any farm organizations? NOTE: Question not asked in 1972, 1973, 1976, 1982, 1985.

Responses: Yes; No

		YEAR										
RACE	RESP	'74	'75	'77	'78	'80	'83	'84	'86	'87	'88	'89
WHITE	YES	5%	5%	4%	4%	4%	5%	5%	4%	4%	4%	4%
	NO	95	95	96	96	96	95	95	96	96	96	96
# SURVEYED		1285	1293	1327	1340	1293	1407	1230	1240	1207	825	856
RACE	RESP	'74	'75	'77	'78	'80	'83	'84	'86	'87	'88	'89
BLACK	YES	1%	1%	1%	1%	1%	1%	1%	1%	1%	1%	1%
	NO	99	99	99	99	99	99	99	99	99	99	99
# SURVEYED		170	162	173	158	136	165	167	182	188	116	106
RACE	RESP	'74	'75	'77	'78	'80	'83	'84	'86	'87	'88	'89
OTHER	YES	0%	0%	0%	0%	0%	6%	2%	0%	2%	5%	0%
	NO	100	100	100	100	100	94	98	100	98	95	100
# SURVEYED		7	4	15	16	9	18	52	37	52	43	40

TABLE IV: MEMBER OF FARM ORGANIZATION -- BY AGE

Question: Are you a member of any farm organizations? NOTE: Question not asked in 1972, 1973, 1976, 1982, 1985.

Responses: Yes; No

		YEAR										
AGE	RESP	'74	'75	'77	'78	'80	'83	'84	'86	'87	'88	'89
18-23	YES	2%	5%	1%	4%	4%	5%	6%	2%	2%	6%	4%
	NO	98	95	99	96	96	95	94	98	98	94	96
# SURVEYED		167	168	163	163	154	127	156	107	122	93	92
AGE	RESP	'74	'75	'77	'78	'80	'83	'84	'86	'87	'88	'89
24-29	YES	3%	3%	2%	1%	7%	3%	2%	5%	3%	2%	0%
	NO	97	97	98	99	93	97	98	95	97	98	100
# SURVEYED		208	229	203	243	196	285	231	218	193	144	139

TABLE IV: MEMBER OF FARM ORGANIZATION -- BY AGE (Continued)

Question: Are you a member of any farm organizations? NOTE: Question not asked in 1972, 1973, 1976, 1982, 1985.

Responses: Yes; No

		YEAR										
AGE	RESP	'74	'75	'77	'78	'80	'83	'84	'86	'87	'88	'89
30-35	YES	4%	2%	3%	2%	1%	4%	3%	1%	3%	3%	3%
	NO	96	98	97	98	99	96	97	99	97	97	97
# SURVEYED		171	170	185	228	206	233	198	220	219	128	140
AGE	RESP	'74	'75	'77	'78	'80	'83	'84	'86	'87	'88	'89
36-41	YES	5%	3%	7%	3%	3%	4%	4%	3%	3%	4%	1%
	NO	95	97	93	97	97	96	96	97	97	96	99
# SURVEYED		151	150	166	156	147	171	185	187	183	123	132
AGE	RESP	'74	'75	'77	'78	'80	'83	'84	'86	'87	'88	'89
42-47	YES	6%	4%	4%	5%	3%	3%	6%	3%	4%	1%	5%
	NO	94	96	96	95	97	97	94	97	96	99	95
# SURVEYED		148	137	147	115	115	145	125	141	154	103	101
AGE	RESP	'74	'75	'77	'78	'80	'83	'84	'86	'87	'88	'89
48-53	YES	6%	6%	5%	8%	2%	8%	1%	6%	2%	7%	5%
	NO	94	94	95	92	98	92	99	94	98	93	95
# SURVEYED		143	137	153	132	120	116	102	107	125	57	96
AGE	RESP	'74	'75	'77	'78	'80	'83	'84	'86	'87	'88	'89
54-59	YES	6%	5%	5%	4%	6%	9%	5%	7%	3%	3%	5%
	NO	94	95	95	96	94	91	95	93	97	97	95
# SURVEYED		137	122	168	134	135	134	113	97	97	64	59
AGE	RESP	'74	'75	'77	'78	'80	'83	'84	'86	'87	'88	'89
60-65	YES	7%	4%	4%	5%	3%	4%	8%	3%	4%	4%	3%
	NO	93	96	96	95	97	96	92	97	96	96	97
# SURVEYED		106	113	115	107	118	132	110	115	100	78	73
AGE	RESP	'74	'75	'77	'78	'80	'83	'84	'86	'87	'88	'89
66+	YES	3%	6%	5%	4%	6%	4%	5%	5%	6%	3%	5%
	NO	97	94	95	96	94	96	95	95	94	97	95
# SURVEYED		225	228	208	229	240	240	225	262	250	190	169

****

MEMBER OF FRATERNAL GROUP

TABLE I: MEMBER OF FRATERNAL GROUP -- BY TOTAL POPULATION

Question: Are you a member of any fraternal organizations? NOTE: Question not asked in 1972, 1973, 1976, 1982, 1985.

Responses: Yes; No

	YEAR										
RESPONSE	'74	'75	'77	'78	'80	'83	'84	'86	'87	'88	'89
YES	14%	11%	10%	10%	11%	10%	9%	9%	9%	9%	9%
NO	86	89	90	90	89	90	91	91	91	91	91
# SURVEYED	1462	1463	1518	1515	1440	1589	1450	1457	1448	987	1009

TABLE II: MEMBER OF FRATERNAL GROUP -- BY SEX

Question: Are you a member of any fraternal organizations? NOTE: Question not asked in 1972, 1973, 1976, 1982, 1985.

Responses: Yes; No

		YEAR										
SEX	RESP	'74	'75	'77	'78	'80	'83	'84	'86	'87	'88	'89
M	YES	19%	16%	15%	15%	16%	15%	14%	13%	13%	13%	13%
	NO	81	84	85	85	84	85	86	87	87	87	87
# SURVEYED		679	654	686	639	632	686	588	613	637	432	436
SEX	RESP	'74	'75	'77	'78	'80	'83	'84	'86	'87	'88	'89
F	YES	9%	7%	6%	7%	7%	6%	6%	7%	7%	5%	6%
	NO	91	93	94	93	93	94	94	93	93	95	94
# SURVEYED		783	809	832	876	808	903	862	844	811	555	573

TABLE III: MEMBER OF FRATERNAL GROUP -- BY RACE

Question: Are you a member of any fraternal organizations? NOTE: Question not asked in 1972, 1973, 1976, 1982, 1985.

Responses: Yes; No

		YEAR										
RACE	RESP	'74	'75	'77	'78	'80	'83	'84	'86	'87	'88	'89
WHITE	YES	15%	11%	10%	11%	11%	10%	10%	10%	10%	9%	10%
	NO	85	89	90	89	89	90	90	90	90	91	90
# SURVEYED		1285	1299	1330	1341	1293	1406	1231	1238	1208	829	862
RACE	RESP	'74	'75	'77	'78	'80	'83	'84	'86	'87	'88	'89
BLACK	YES	8%	10%	10%	5%	4%	6%	6%	4%	7%	5%	5%
	NO	92	90	90	95	96	94	94	96	93	95	95
# SURVEYED		170	160	174	158	137	165	167	182	188	115	107
RACE	RESP	'74	'75	'77	'78	'80	'83	'84	'86	'87	'88	'89
OTHER	YES	14%	0%	7%	6%	0%	6%	0%	0%	4%	0%	3%
	NO	86	100	93	94	100	94	100	100	96	100	98
# SURVEYED		7	4	14	16	10	18	52	37	52	43	40

TABLE IV: MEMBER OF FRATERNAL GROUP -- BY AGE

Question: Are you a member of any fraternal organizations? NOTE: Question not asked in 1972, 1973, 1976, 1982, 1985.

Responses: Yes; No

		YEAR										
AGE	RESP	'74	'75	'77	'78	'80	'83	'84	'86	'87	'88	'89
18-23	YES	4%	2%	4%	2%	1%	3%	3%	3%	3%	5%	4%
	NO	96	98	96	98	99	97	97	97	97	95	96
# SURVEYED		167	168	163	163	152	128	156	108	122	93	92
AGE	RESP	'74	'75	'77	'78	'80	'83	'84	'86	'87	'88	'89
24-29	YES	9%	7%	2%	4%	5%	5%	3%	6%	4%	6%	6%
	NO	91	93	98	96	95	95	97	94	96	94	94
# SURVEYED		208	229	204	243	197	285	230	217	193	145	139

TABLE IV: MEMBER OF FRATERNAL GROUP -- BY AGE (Continued)

Question: Are you a member of any fraternal organizations? NOTE: Question not asked in 1972, 1973, 1976, 1982, 1985.

Responses: Yes; No

		YEAR										
AGE	RESP	'74	'75	'77	'78	'80	'83	'84	'86	'87	'88	'89
30-35	YES	12%	9%	10%	7%	6%	6%	8%	5%	8%	3%	7%
	NO	88	91	90	93	94	94	92	95	92	97	93
# SURVEYED		171	170	185	229	208	234	197	220	219	128	140
AGE	RESP	'74	'75	'77	'78	'80	'83	'84	'86	'87	'88	'89
36-41	YES	11%	15%	9%	12%	11%	8%	8%	8%	9%	7%	10%
	NO	89	85	91	88	89	92	92	92	91	93	90
# SURVEYED		151	152	167	156	148	172	185	186	183	123	133
AGE	RESP	'74	'75	'77	'78	'80	'83	'84	'86	'87	'88	'89
42-47	YES	16%	19%	16%	12%	10%	8%	9%	11%	8%	7%	9%
	NO	84	81	84	88	90	92	91	89	92	93	91
# SURVEYED		149	137	146	116	115	145	125	141	155	104	104
AGE	RESP	'74	'75	'77	'78	'80	'83	'84	'86	'87	'88	'89
48-53	YES	17%	12%	20%	10%	17%	16%	14%	10%	13%	5%	5%
	NO	83	88	80	90	83	84	86	90	87	95	95
# SURVEYED		143	139	153	132	121	116	102	105	125	57	96
AGE	RESP	'74	'75	'77	'78	'80	'83	'84	'86	'87	'88	'89
54-59	YES	18%	15%	14%	13%	12%	10%	16%	15%	15%	14%	17%
	NO	82	85	86	87	88	90	84	85	85	86	83
# SURVEYED		138	124	167	135	135	134	113	98	97	63	60
AGE	RESP	'74	'75	'77	'78	'80	'83	'84	'86	'87	'88	'89
60-65	YES	18%	6%	9%	21%	20%	18%	18%	10%	11%	10%	14%
	NO	82	94	91	79	80	82	82	90	89	90	86
# SURVEYED		105	113	117	107	117	131	109	115	100	79	74
AGE	RESP	'74	'75	'77	'78	'80	'83	'84	'86	'87	'88	'89
66+	YES	22%	15%	11%	17%	17%	15%	13%	15%	14%	16%	14%
	NO	78	85	89	83	83	85	87	85	86	84	86
# SURVEYED		224	226	209	227	240	237	229	262	250	191	170

****

MEMBER OF FRATERNITY OR SORORITY

TABLE I: MEMBER OF FRATERNITY OR SORORITY -- BY TOTAL POPULATION

Question: Are you a member of any school fraternities or sororities? NOTE: Question not asked in 1972, 1973, 1976, 1982, 1985.

Responses: Yes; No

	YEAR										
RESPONSE	'74	'75	'77	'78	'80	'83	'84	'86	'87	'88	'89
YES	5%	4%	4%	4%	4%	5%	6%	5%	5%	4%	6%
NO	95	96	96	96	96	95	94	95	95	96	94
# SURVEYED	1462	1459	1518	1516	1438	1591	1450	1460	1446	986	1003

TABLE II: MEMBER OF FRATERNITY OR SORORITY -- BY SEX

Question: Are you a member of any school fraternities or sororities? NOTE: Question not asked in 1972, 1973, 1976, 1982, 1985.

Responses: Yes; No

		YEAR										
SEX	RESP	'74	'75	'77	'78	'80	'83	'84	'86	'87	'88	'89
M	YES	5%	4%	5%	4%	4%	5%	5%	6%	6%	5%	7%
	NO	95	96	95	96	96	95	95	94	94	95	93
# SURVEYED		679	652	688	638	633	685	589	616	635	431	432
SEX	RESP	'74	'75	'77	'78	'80	'83	'84	'86	'87	'88	'89
F	YES	4%	4%	4%	4%	4%	5%	6%	5%	4%	4%	5%
	NO	96	96	96	96	96	95	94	95	96	96	95
# SURVEYED		783	807	830	878	805	906	861	844	811	555	571

TABLE III: MEMBER OF FRATERNITY OR SORORITY -- BY RACE

Question: Are you a member of any school fraternities or sororities. NOTE: Question not asked in 1972, 1973, 1976, 1982, 1985.

Responses: Yes; No

		YEAR										
RACE	RESP	'74	'75	'77	'78	'80	'83	'84	'86	'87	'88	'89
WHITE	YES	5%	4%	4%	4%	4%	5%	6%	6%	5%	4%	6%
	NO	95	96	96	96	96	95	94	94	95	96	94
# SURVEYED		1285	1293	1329	1342	1293	1408	1231	1241	1206	827	855
RACE	RESP	'74	'75	'77	'78	'80	'83	'84	'86	'87	'88	'89
BLACK	YES	6%	4%	6%	3%	5%	5%	5%	4%	2%	6%	7%
	NO	94	96	94	97	95	95	95	96	98	94	93
# SURVEYED		170	162	174	158	136	165	167	182	188	116	108
RACE	RESP	'74	'75	'77	'78	'80	'83	'84	'86	'87	'88	'89
OTHER	YES	0%	0%	0%	6%	0%	0%	2%	3%	0%	0%	3%
	NO	100	100	100	94	100	100	98	97	100	100	98
# SURVEYED		7	4	15	16	9	18	52	37	52	43	40

TABLE IV: MEMBER OF FRATERNITY OR SORORITY -- BY AGE

Question: Are you a member of any school fraternities or sororities. NOTE: Question not asked in 1972, 1973, 1976, 1982, 1985.

Responses: Yes; No

		YEAR										
AGE	RESP	'74	'75	'77	'78	'80	'83	'84	'86	'87	'88	'89
18-23	YES	6%	2%	4%	2%	5%	6%	8%	6%	6%	8%	12%
	NO	94	98	96	98	95	94	92	94	94	92	88
# SURVEYED		167	169	163	163	154	128	156	107	122	93	92
AGE	RESP	'74	'75	'77	'78	'80	'83	'84	'86	'87	'88	'89
24-29	YES	6%	8%	5%	6%	6%	5%	6%	8%	5%	8%	5%
	NO	94	92	95	94	94	95	94	92	95	92	95
# SURVEYED		208	229	204	243	196	285	231	218	193	144	139

TABLE IV: MEMBER OF FRATERNITY OR SORORITY -- BY AGE (Continued)

Question: Are you a member of any school fraternities or sororities? NOTE: Question not asked in 1972, 1973, 1976, 1982, 1985.

Responses: Yes; No

		YEAR										
AGE	RESP	'74	'75	'77	'78	'80	'83	'84	'86	'87	'88	'89
30-35	YES	6%	4%	5%	4%	3%	6%	7%	5%	6%	2%	11%
	NO	94	96	95	96	97	94	93	95	94	98	89
# SURVEYED		171	170	185	229	206	233	198	220	219	128	140
AGE	RESP	'74	'75	'77	'78	'80	'83	'84	'86	'87	'88	'89
36-41	YES	7%	1%	7%	4%	5%	5%	5%	6%	4%	7%	6%
	NO	93	99	93	96	95	95	95	94	96	93	94
# SURVEYED		151	150	166	156	147	172	185	187	183	123	131
AGE	RESP	'74	'75	'77	'78	'80	'83	'84	'86	'87	'88	'89
42-47	YES	4%	6%	6%	4%	4%	3%	8%	9%	6%	4%	4%
	NO	96	94	94	96	96	97	92	91	94	96	96
# SURVEYED		148	136	147	115	115	145	125	141	154	104	103
AGE	RESP	'74	'75	'77	'78	'80	'83	'84	'86	'87	'88	'89
48-53	YES	6%	6%	4%	5%	3%	4%	3%	5%	5%	4%	4%
	NO	94	94	96	95	98	96	97	95	95	96	96
# SURVEYED		143	137	153	132	120	115	102	106	125	57	96
AGE	RESP	'74	'75	'77	'78	'80	'83	'84	'86	'87	'88	'89
54-59	YES	4%	5%	6%	3%	3%	6%	10%	5%	6%	0%	7%
	NO	96	95	94	97	97	94	90	95	94	100	93
# SURVEYED		137	122	168	134	135	134	113	98	97	64	59
AGE	RESP	'74	'75	'77	'78	'80	'83	'84	'86	'87	'88	'89
60-65	YES	1%	1%	2%	5%	5%	6%	6%	1%	1%	1%	1%
	NO	99	99	98	95	95	94	94	99	99	99	99
# SURVEYED		106	113	116	107	118	132	110	115	100	78	73
AGE	RESP	'74	'75	'77	'78	'80	'83	'84	'86	'87	'88	'89
66+	YES	3%	4%	1%	2%	3%	3%	2%	3%	3%	4%	4%
	NO	97	96	99	98	97	97	98	97	97	96	96
# SURVEYED		225	228	209	230	240	240	226	262	249	191	169

****

MEMBER OF HOBBY OR GARDEN CLUB

TABLE I: MEMBER OF HOBBY OR GARDEN CLUB -- BY TOTAL POPULATION

Question: Are you a member of any hobby or garden club? NOTE: Question not asked in 1972, 1973, 1976, 1982, 1985.

Responses: Yes; No

	YEAR										
RESPONSE	'74	'75	'77	'78	'80	'83	'84	'86	'87	'88	'89
YES	10%	9%	9%	9%	9%	10%	9%	9%	9%	10%	9%
NO	90	91	91	91	91	90	91	91	91	90	91
# SURVEYED	1462	1456	1516	1517	1443	1592	1452	1457	1446	985	1005

TABLE II: MEMBER OF HOBBY OR GARDEN CLUB -- BY SEX

Question: Are you a member of any hobby or garden club? NOTE: Question not asked in 1972, 1973, 1976, 1982, 1985.

Responses: Yes; No

		YEAR										
SEX	RESP	'74	'75	'77	'78	'80	'83	'84	'86	'87	'88	'89
M	YES	7%	8%	7%	10%	7%	9%	7%	9%	9%	12%	10%
	NO	93	92	93	90	93	91	93	91	91	88	90
# SURVEYED		679	651	687	639	635	686	589	615	635	431	432
SEX	RESP	'74	'75	'77	'78	'80	'83	'84	'86	'87	'88	'89
F	YES	12%	10%	11%	9%	9%	10%	10%	9%	10%	10%	8%
	NO	88	90	89	91	91	90	90	91	90	90	92
# SURVEYED		783	805	829	878	808	906	863	842	811	554	573

TABLE III: MEMBER OF HOBBY OR GARDEN CLUB -- BY RACE

Question: Are you a member of any hobby or garden club? NOTE: Question not asked in 1972, 1973, 1976, 1982, 1985.

Responses: Yes; No

		YEAR										
RACE	RESP	'74	'75	'77	'78	'80	'83	'84	'86	'87	'88	'89
WHITE	YES	10%	10%	10%	10%	9%	10%	9%	9%	10%	11%	10%
	NO	90	90	90	90	91	90	91	91	90	89	90
# SURVEYED		1284	1290	1328	1343	1298	1409	1233	1238	1206	826	858
RACE	RESP	'74	'75	'77	'78	'80	'83	'84	'86	'87	'88	'89
BLACK	YES	6%	4%	8%	9%	5%	7%	6%	6%	4%	9%	4%
	NO	94	96	92	91	95	93	94	94	96	91	96
# SURVEYED		171	162	173	158	136	165	167	182	188	116	107
RACE	RESP	'74	'75	'77	'78	'80	'83	'84	'86	'87	'88	'89
OTHER	YES	0%	0%	7%	6%	0%	6%	10%	8%	6%	5%	5%
	NO	100	100	93	94	100	94	90	92	94	95	95
# SURVEYED		7	4	15	16	9	18	52	37	52	43	40

TABLE IV: MEMBER OF HOBBY OR GARDEN CLUB -- BY AGE

Question: Are you a member of any hobby or garden club? NOTE: Question not asked in 1972, 1973, 1976, 1982, 1985.

Responses: Yes; No

		YEAR										
AGE	RESP	'74	'75	'77	'78	'80	'83	'84	'86	'87	'88	'89
18-23	YES	8%	10%	8%	8%	10%	9%	13%	7%	10%	9%	9%
	NO	92	90	92	92	90	91	87	93	90	91	91
# SURVEYED		167	168	163	163	154	128	156	107	122	93	92
AGE	RESP	'74	'75	'77	'78	'80	'83	'84	'86	'87	'88	'89
24-29	YES	13%	9%	12%	8%	9%	9%	10%	9%	5%	13%	5%
	NO	88	91	88	92	91	91	90	91	95	87	95
# SURVEYED		208	229	204	243	196	285	231	218	193	144	139

TABLE IV: MEMBER OF HOBBY OR GARDEN CLUB -- BY AGE (Continued)

Question: Are you a member of any hobby or garden club? NOTE: Question not asked in 1972, 1973, 1976, 1982, 1985.

Responses: Yes; No

YEAR												
AGE	RESP	'74	'75	'77	'78	'80	'83	'84	'86	'87	'88	'89
30-35	YES	11%	10%	9%	8%	11%	7%	6%	6%	10%	9%	12%
	NO	89	90	91	92	89	93	94	94	90	91	88
# SURVEYED		171	170	185	228	208	233	198	220	219	128	140
AGE	RESP	'74	'75	'77	'78	'80	'83	'84	'86	'87	'88	'89
36-41	YES	11%	9%	13%	13%	9%	8%	9%	10%	13%	11%	10%
	NO	89	91	87	87	91	92	91	90	87	89	90
# SURVEYED		151	150	167	156	149	172	185	187	183	123	132
AGE	RESP	'74	'75	'77	'78	'80	'83	'84	'86	'87	'88	'89
42-47	YES	7%	13%	9%	9%	8%	10%	11%	13%	10%	11%	6%
	NO	93	87	91	91	92	90	89	87	90	89	94
# SURVEYED		148	136	147	116	115	145	126	140	154	104	101
AGE	RESP	'74	'75	'77	'78	'80	'83	'84	'86	'87	'88	'89
48-53	YES	8%	6%	8%	10%	8%	9%	9%	15%	10%	11%	10%
	NO	92	94	92	90	92	91	91	85	90	89	90
# SURVEYED		144	136	153	132	120	116	102	106	125	57	96
AGE	RESP	'74	'75	'77	'78	'80	'83	'84	'86	'87	'88	'89
54-59	YES	9%	11%	11%	9%	6%	11%	10%	7%	9%	14%	11%
	NO	91	89	89	91	94	89	90	93	91	86	89
# SURVEYED		137	122	168	134	135	134	113	98	97	64	61
AGE	RESP	'74	'75	'77	'78	'80	'83	'84	'86	'87	'88	'89
60-65	YES	11%	4%	7%	10%	7%	13%	8%	9%	9%	5%	9%
	NO	89	96	93	90	93	87	92	91	91	95	91
# SURVEYED		106	113	116	107	118	132	110	114	100	78	74
AGE	RESP	'74	'75	'77	'78	'80	'83	'84	'86	'87	'88	'89
66+	YES	10%	8%	5%	10%	9%	11%	7%	7%	8%	9%	8%
	NO	90	92	95	90	91	89	93	93	92	91	92
SURVEYED		224	227	206	231	241	240	227	262	249	190	169

****

MEMBER OF LITERARY, ART OR STUDY GROUP

TABLE I: MEMBER OF LITERARY, ART OR STUDY GROUP -- BY TOTAL POPULATION

Question: Are you a member of any literary, art discussion or study group? NOTE: Question not asked in 1972, 1973, 1976, 1982, 1985.

Responses: Yes; No

	YEAR										
RESPONSE	'74	'75	'77	'78	'80	'83	'84	'86	'87	'88	'89
YES	9%	9%	9%	9%	9%	10%	9%	9%	7%	9%	10%
NO	91	91	91	91	91	90	91	91	93	91	90
# SURVEYED	1461	1457	1518	1513	1439	1591	1451	1460	1446	985	1006

TABLE II: MEMBER OF LITERARY, ART OR STUDY GROUP -- BY SEX

Question: Are you a member of any literary, art discussion or study groups? NOTE: Question not asked in 1972, 1973, 1976, 1982, 1985.

Responses: Yes; No

		YEAR										
SEX	RESP	'74	'75	'77	'78	'80	'83	'84	'86	'87	'88	'89
M	YES	7%	7%	6%	7%	6%	8%	6%	7%	6%	7%	10%
	NO	93	93	94	93	94	92	94	93	94	93	90
# SURVEYED		678	651	688	636	633	685	589	617	635	431	432
SEX	RESP	'74	'75	'77	'78	'80	'83	'84	'86	'87	'88	'89
F	YES	11%	11%	12%	11%	11%	12%	11%	10%	8%	10%	10%
	NO	89	89	88	89	89	88	89	90	92	90	90
# SURVEYED		783	806	830	877	806	906	862	843	811	554	574

TABLE III: MEMBER OF LITERARY, ART OR STUDY GROUP -- BY RACE

Question: Are you a member of any literary, art discussion or study groups? NOTE: Question not asked in 1972, 1973, 1976, 1982, 1985.

Responses: Yes; No

		YEAR										
RACE	RESP	'74	'75	'77	'78	'80	'83	'84	'86	'87	'88	'89
WHITE	YES	10%	10%	9%	9%	9%	10%	9%	9%	8%	9%	10%
	NO	90	90	91	91	91	90	91	91	92	91	90
# SURVEYED		1284	1290	1329	1339	1295	1408	1232	1242	1206	826	858
RACE	RESP	'74	'75	'77	'78	'80	'83	'84	'86	'87	'88	'89
BLACK	YES	5%	4%	8%	5%	6%	7%	7%	6%	4%	8%	6%
	NO	95	96	92	95	94	93	93	94	96	92	94
# SURVEYED		170	163	174	158	135	165	167	181	188	116	108
RACE	RESP	'74	'75	'77	'78	'80	'83	'84	'86	'87	'88	'89
OTHER	YES	0%	0%	7%	6%	22%	22%	6%	11%	2%	2%	8%
	NO	100	100	93	94	78	78	94	89	98	98	93
# SURVEYED		7	4	15	16	9	18	52	37	52	43	40

TABLE IV: MEMBER OF LITERARY, ART OR STUDY GROUP -- BY AGE

Question: Are you a member of any literary, art discussion or study groups? NOTE: Question not asked in 1972, 1973, 1976, 1982, 1985.

Responses: Yes; No

		YEAR										
AGE	RESP	'74	'75	'77	'78	'80	'83	'84	'86	'87	'88	'89
18-23	YES	8%	9%	6%	5%	8%	7%	9%	8%	7%	6%	9%
	NO	92	91	94	95	92	93	91	92	93	94	91
# SURVEYED		167	167	163	163	155	128	157	106	122	93	92
AGE	RESP	'74	'75	'77	'78	'80	'83	'84	'86	'87	'88	'89
24-29	YES	11%	7%	9%	6%	6%	11%	9%	10%	7%	10%	5%
	NO	89	93	91	94	94	89	91	90	93	90	95
# SURVEYED		208	229	204	243	195	285	231	218	193	144	139

TABLE IV: MEMBER OF LITERARY, ART OR STUDY GROUP -- BY AGE (Continued)

Question: Are you a member of any literary, art discussion or study groups? NOTE: Question not asked in 1972, 1973, 1976, 1982, 1985.

Responses: Yes; No

		YEAR										
AGE	RESP	'74	'75	'77	'78	'80	'83	'84	'86	'87	'88	'89
30-35	YES	13%	15%	10%	11%	11%	11%	8%	6%	9%	9%	12%
	NO	87	85	90	89	89	89	92	94	91	91	88
# SURVEYED		170	170	184	228	207	233	198	221	219	128	140
AGE	RESP	'74	'75	'77	'78	'80	'83	'84	'86	'87	'88	'89
36-41	YES	7%	9%	12%	8%	5%	8%	10%	11%	9%	9%	12%
	NO	93	91	88	92	95	92	90	89	91	91	88
# SURVEYED		151	151	167	156	147	172	185	187	183	123	132
AGE	RESP	'74	'75	'77	'78	'80	'83	'84	'86	'87	'88	'89
42-47	YES	12%	10%	10%	10%	4%	13%	11%	9%	7%	10%	14%
	NO	88	90	90	90	96	87	89	91	93	90	86
# SURVEYED		148	135	147	115	115	145	125	141	154	104	102
AGE	RESP	'74	'75	'77	'78	'80	'83	'84	'86	'87	'88	'89
48-53	YES	8%	11%	7%	13%	14%	8%	9%	7%	9%	7%	11%
	NO	92	89	93	87	86	92	91	93	91	93	89
# SURVEYED		143	138	153	132	120	116	102	107	125	57	96
AGE	RESP	'74	'75	'77	'78	'80	'83	'84	'86	'87	'88	'89
54-59	YES	8%	7%	11%	16%	7%	11%	10%	13%	11%	13%	13%
	NO	92	93	89	84	93	89	90	87	89	87	87
# SURVEYED		137	122	167	134	135	134	113	98	97	63	61
AGE	RESP	'74	'75	'77	'78	'80	'83	'84	'86	'87	'88	'89
60-65	YES	9%	7%	9%	9%	11%	11%	6%	8%	1%	9%	8%
	NO	91	93	91	91	89	89	94	92	99	91	92
# SURVEYED		106	113	116	106	118	132	110	115	100	78	74
AGE	RESP	'74	'75	'77	'78	'80	'83	'84	'86	'87	'88	'89
66+	YES	8%	8%	7%	7%	10%	10%	8%	8%	6%	7%	7%
	NO	92	92	93	93	90	90	92	92	94	93	93
# SURVEYED		225	227	210	229	240	239	226	262	249	191	169

****

MEMBER OF NATIONALITY GROUP

TABLE I: MEMBER OF NATIONALITY GROUP -- BY TOTAL POPULATION

Question: Are you a member of any nationality groups? NOTE: Question not asked in 1972, 1973, 1976, 1982, 1985.

Responses: Yes; No

	YEAR										
RESPONSE	'74	'75	'77	'78	'80	'83	'84	'86	'87	'88	'89
YES	4%	3%	3%	3%	3%	4%	3%	5%	2%	2%	3%
NO	96	97	97	97	97	96	97	95	98	98	97
# SURVEYED	1462	1454	1518	1514	1437	1592	1450	1460	1445	985	1003

TABLE II: MEMBER OF NATIONALITY GROUP -- BY SEX

Question: Are you a member of any nationality groups? NOTE: Question not asked in 1972, 1973, 1976, 1982, 1985.

Responses: Yes; No

		YEAR										
SEX	RESP	'74	'75	'77	'78	'80	'83	'84	'86	'87	'88	'89
M	YES	5%	2%	4%	4%	3%	5%	4%	6%	2%	2%	4%
	NO	95	98	96	96	97	95	96	94	98	98	96
# SURVEYED		679	650	688	637	633	686	589	617	635	431	432
SEX	RESP	'74	'75	'77	'78	'80	'83	'84	'86	'87	'88	'89
F	YES	2%	3%	3%	2%	2%	3%	3%	4%	2%	3%	3%
	NO	98	97	97	98	98	97	97	96	98	97	97
# SURVEYED		783	804	830	877	804	906	861	843	810	554	571

TABLE III: MEMBER OF NATIONALITY GROUP -- BY RACE

Question: Are you a member of any nationality groups? NOTE: Question not asked in 1972, 1973, 1976, 1982, 1985.

Responses: Yes; No

		YEAR										
RACE	RESP	'74	'75	'77	'78	'80	'83	'84	'86	'87	'88	'89
WHITE	YES	3%	2%	3%	2%	2%	3%	3%	4%	2%	2%	3%
	NO	97	98	97	98	98	97	97	96	98	98	97
# SURVEYED		1285	1288	1329	1340	1293	1409	1231	1241	1205	826	856
RACE	RESP	'74	'75	'77	'78	'80	'83	'84	'86	'87	'88	'89
BLACK	YES	5%	4%	6%	2%	6%	6%	6%	4%	5%	2%	3%
	NO	95	96	94	98	94	94	94	96	95	98	97
# SURVEYED		170	162	174	158	135	165	167	182	188	116	107
RACE	RESP	'74	'75	'77	'78	'80	'83	'84	'86	'87	'88	'89
OTHER	YES	0%	0%	0%	19%	22%	22%	10%	27%	2%	5%	8%
	NO	100	100	100	81	78	78	90	73	98	95	93
# SURVEYED		7	4	15	16	9	18	52	37	52	43	40

TABLE IV: MEMBER OF NATIONALITY GROUP -- BY AGE

Question: Are you a member of any nationality groups? NOTE: Question not asked in 1972, 1973, 1976, 1982, 1985.

Responses: Yes; No

		YEAR										
AGE	RESP	'74	'75	'77	'78	'80	'83	'84	'86	'87	'88	'89
18-23	YES	4%	3%	1%	3%	3%	1%	2%	7%	4%	1%	4%
	NO	96	97	99	97	97	99	98	93	96	99	96
# SURVEYED		167	167	163	163	154	128	156	107	122	93	92
AGE	RESP	'74	'75	'77	'78	'80	'83	'84	'86	'87	'88	'89
24-29	YES	3%	2%	1%	1%	3%	2%	2%	4%	1%	2%	2%
	NO	97	98	99	99	97	98	98	96	99	98	98
# SURVEYED		208	228	204	243	196	285	231	218	193	144	139

TABLE IV: MEMBER OF NATIONALITY GROUP -- BY AGE (Continued)

Question: Are you a member of any nationality groups? NOTE: Question not asked in 1972, 1973, 1976, 1982, 1985.

Responses: Yes; No

		YEAR										
AGE	RESP	'74	'75	'77	'78	'80	'83	'84	'86	'87	'88	'89
30-35	YES	5%	2%	3%	1%	3%	5%	5%	3%	2%	2%	3%
	NO	95	98	97	99	97	95	95	97	98	98	97
# SURVEYED		171	170	185	228	206	233	198	220	218	128	140
AGE	RESP	'74	'75	'77	'78	'80	'83	'84	'86	'87	'88	'89
36-41	YES	3%	3%	4%	4%	3%	3%	4%	5%	1%	1%	4%
	NO	97	97	96	96	97	97	96	95	99	99	96
# SURVEYED		151	150	166	156	147	172	185	188	183	123	132
AGE	RESP	'74	'75	'77	'78	'80	'83	'84	'86	'87	'88	'89
42-47	YES	4%	5%	5%	3%	2%	5%	2%	5%	3%	3%	4%
	NO	96	95	95	97	98	95	98	95	97	97	96
# SURVEYED		148	136	147	115	115	145	125	141	154	104	101
AGE	RESP	'74	'75	'77	'78	'80	'83	'84	'86	'87	'88	'89
48-53	YES	3%	4%	3%	1%	5%	3%	3%	8%	1%	5%	2%
	NO	97	96	97	99	95	97	97	92	99	95	98
# SURVEYED		143	137	153	132	119	116	102	106	125	57	96
AGE	RESP	'74	'75	'77	'78	'80	'83	'84	'86	'87	'88	'89
54-59	YES	1%	4%	8%	4%	1%	3%	6%	3%	4%	6%	3%
	NO	99	96	92	96	99	97	94	97	96	94	97
# SURVEYED		137	121	168	134	135	134	113	98	97	64	60
AGE	RESP	'74	'75	'77	'78	'80	'83	'84	'86	'87	'88	'89
60-65	YES	5%	0%	3%	5%	2%	5%	5%	7%	2%	0%	5%
	NO	95	100	97	95	98	95	95	93	98	100	95
# SURVEYED		106	113	115	107	118	132	110	115	100	78	73
AGE	RESP	'74	'75	'77	'78	'80	'83	'84	'86	'87	'88	'89
66+	YES	4%	2%	5%	3%	3%	5%	2%	4%	3%	3%	4%
	NO	96	98	95	97	97	95	98	96	97	97	96
# SURVEYED		225	227	210	229	240	240	226	262	249	190	169

****

MEMBER OF POLITICAL CLUB

TABLE I: MEMBER OF POLITICAL CLUB -- BY TOTAL POPULATION

Question: Are you a member of any political clubs? NOTE: Question not asked in 1972, 1973, 1976, 1982, 1985.

Responses: Yes; No

	YEAR										
RESPONSE	'74	'75	'77	'78	'80	'83	'84	'86	'87	'88	'89
YES	5%	4%	5%	3%	3%	5%	4%	4%	4%	4%	4%
NO	95	96	95	97	97	95	96	96	96	96	96
# SURVEYED	1464	1460	1516	1515	1444	1591	1451	1461	1446	986	1006

TABLE II: MEMBER OF POLITICAL CLUB -- BY SEX

Question: Are you a member of any political clubs? NOTE: Question not asked in 1972, 1973, 1976, 1982, 1985.

Responses: Yes; No

		YEAR										
SEX	RESP	'74	'75	'77	'78	'80	'83	'84	'86	'87	'88	'89
M	YES	5%	6%	5%	4%	3%	6%	4%	5%	4%	5%	5%
	NO	95	94	95	96	97	94	96	95	96	95	95
# SURVEYED		681	652	687	639	634	685	589	617	635	430	431
SEX	RESP	'74	'75	'77	'78	'80	'83	'84	'86	'87	'88	'89
F	YES	4%	3%	4%	3%	3%	4%	4%	4%	5%	4%	3%
	NO	96	97	96	97	97	96	96	96	95	96	97
# SURVEYED		783	808	829	876	810	906	862	844	811	556	575

TABLE III: MEMBER OF POLITICAL CLUB -- BY RACE

Question: Are you a member of any political clubs? NOTE: Question not asked in 1972, 1973, 1976, 1982, 1985.

Responses: Yes; No

		YEAR										
RACE	RESP	'74	'75	'77	'78	'80	'83	'84	'86	'87	'88	'89
WHITE	YES	4%	5%	5%	4%	3%	5%	4%	4%	5%	5%	4%
	NO	96	95	95	96	97	95	96	96	95	95	96
# SURVEYED		1286	1294	1327	1341	1297	1409	1232	1241	1206	828	859
RACE	RESP	'74	'75	'77	'78	'80	'83	'84	'86	'87	'88	'89
BLACK	YES	6%	2%	5%	2%	4%	5%	3%	5%	4%	5%	3%
	NO	94	98	95	98	96	95	97	95	96	95	97
# SURVEYED		171	162	174	158	138	164	167	183	188	115	107
RACE	RESP	'74	'75	'77	'78	'80	'83	'84	'86	'87	'88	'89
OTHER	YES	0%	0%	13%	0%	0%	0%	4%	5%	2%	0%	3%
	NO	100	100	87	100	100	100	96	95	98	100	98
# SURVEYED		7	4	15	16	9	18	52	37	52	43	40

TABLE IV: MEMBER OF POLITICAL CLUB -- BY AGE

Question: Are you a member of any political clubs? NOTE: Question not asked in 1972, 1973, 1976, 1982, 1985.

Responses: Yes; No

		YEAR										
AGE	RESP	'74	'75	'77	'78	'80	'83	'84	'86	'87	'88	'89
18-23	YES	2%	2%	2%	2%	0%	1%	3%	6%	2%	5%	2%
	NO	98	98	98	98	100	99	97	94	98	95	98
# SURVEYED		167	168	163	163	154	128	156	108	122	93	92
AGE	RESP	'74	'75	'77	'78	'80	'83	'84	'86	'87	'88	'89
24-29	YES	4%	3%	3%	3%	4%	4%	1%	3%	5%	2%	4%
	NO	96	97	97	97	96	96	99	97	95	98	96
# SURVEYED		208	229	204	243	196	285	231	218	193	144	139

TABLE IV: MEMBER OF POLITICAL CLUB -- BY AGE (Continued)

Question: Are you a member of any political clubs? NOTE: Question not asked in 1972, 1973, 1976, 1982, 1985.

Responses: Yes; No

		YEAR										
AGE	RESP	'74	'75	'77	'78	'80	'83	'84	'86	'87	'88	'89
30-35	YES	8%	5%	5%	4%	3%	4%	6%	3%	4%	5%	5%
	NO	92	95	95	96	97	96	94	97	96	95	95
# SURVEYED		172	171	185	227	209	233	198	221	219	128	140
AGE	RESP	'74	'75	'77	'78	'80	'83	'84	'86	'87	'88	'89
36-41	YES	7%	6%	4%	4%	3%	6%	3%	6%	6%	5%	6%
	NO	93	94	96	96	97	94	97	94	94	95	94
# SURVEYED		151	151	166	156	148	172	185	188	183	123	132
AGE	RESP	'74	'75	'77	'78	'80	'83	'84	'86	'87	'88	'89
42-47	YES	4%	6%	5%	3%	4%	9%	6%	4%	4%	7%	3%
	NO	96	94	95	97	96	91	94	96	96	93	97
# SURVEYED		148	137	147	115	115	145	125	141	154	103	103
AGE	RESP	'74	'75	'77	'78	'80	'83	'84	'86	'87	'88	'89
48-53	YES	3%	6%	6%	7%	5%	4%	2%	2%	6%	2%	3%
	NO	97	94	94	93	95	96	98	98	94	98	97
# SURVEYED		144	137	153	132	121	116	102	106	125	57	96
AGE	RESP	'74	'75	'77	'78	'80	'83	'84	'86	'87	'88	'89
54-59	YES	3%	5%	8%	2%	2%	9%	6%	5%	7%	2%	5%
	NO	97	95	92	98	98	91	94	95	93	98	95
# SURVEYED		137	122	168	135	135	133	113	98	97	64	60
AGE	RESP	'74	'75	'77	'78	'80	'83	'84	'86	'87	'88	'89
60-65	YES	7%	1%	6%	5%	3%	3%	4%	7%	1%	1%	4%
	NO	93	99	94	95	97	97	96	93	99	99	96
# SURVEYED		106	113	114	107	118	132	110	115	100	79	74
AGE	RESP	'74	'75	'77	'78	'80	'83	'84	'86	'87	'88	'89
66+	YES	4%	6%	4%	4%	5%	4%	5%	5%	4%	7%	2%
	NO	96	94	96	96	95	96	95	95	96	93	98
# SURVEYED		225	227	209	230	241	240	227	261	249	191	169

****

MEMBER OF PROFESSIONAL SOCIETY

TABLE I: MEMBER OF PROFESSIONAL SOCIETY -- BY TOTAL POPULATION

Question: Are you a member of any professional societies? NOTE: Question not asked in 1972, 1973, 1976, 1982, 1985.

Responses: Yes; No

	YEAR										
RESPONSE	'74	'75	'77	'78	'80	'83	'84	'86	'87	'88	'89
YES	13%	12%	13%	13%	13%	16%	16%	15%	15%	14%	18%
NO	87	88	87	87	87	84	84	85	85	86	82
# SURVEYED	1462	1461	1517	1515	1439	1592	1452	1461	1446	984	1005

TABLE II: MEMBER OF PROFESSIONAL SOCIETY -- BY SEX

Question: Are you a member of any professional societies? NOTE: Question not asked in 1972, 1973, 1976, 1982, 1985.

Responses: Yes; No

		YEAR										
SEX	RESP	'74	'75	'77	'78	'80	'83	'84	'86	'87	'88	'89
M	YES	16%	14%	16%	17%	16%	18%	19%	20%	15%	14%	21%
	NO	84	86	84	83	84	82	81	80	85	86	79
# SURVEYED		678	656	688	638	634	687	589	617	635	431	433
SEX	RESP	'74	'75	'77	'78	'80	'83	'84	'86	'87	'88	'89
F	YES	11%	10%	11%	11%	11%	14%	14%	12%	15%	14%	16%
	NO	89	90	89	89	89	86	86	88	85	86	84
# SURVEYED		784	805	829	877	805	905	863	844	811	553	572

TABLE III: MEMBER OF PROFESSIONAL SOCIETY -- BY RACE

Question: Are you a member of any professional societies? NOTE: Question not asked in 1972, 1973, 1976, 1982, 1985.

Responses: Yes; No

		YEAR										
RACE	RESP	'74	'75	'77	'78	'80	'83	'84	'86	'87	'88	'89
WHITE	YES	14%	13%	13%	14%	13%	17%	17%	17%	16%	15%	19%
	NO	86	87	87	86	87	83	83	83	84	85	81
# SURVEYED		1285	1295	1329	1341	1292	1409	1234	1242	1207	825	858
RACE	RESP	'74	'75	'77	'78	'80	'83	'84	'86	'87	'88	'89
BLACK	YES	5%	4%	9%	5%	8%	7%	7%	8%	7%	9%	9%
	NO	95	96	91	95	92	93	93	92	93	91	91
# SURVEYED		170	162	173	158	138	165	166	182	188	115	107
RACE	RESP	'74	'75	'77	'78	'80	'83	'84	'86	'87	'88	'89
OTHER	YES	0%	0%	27%	19%	33%	28%	12%	11%	4%	9%	18%
	NO	100	100	73	81	67	72	88	89	96	91	83
# SURVEYED		7	4	15	16	9	18	52	37	51	44	40

TABLE IV: MEMBER OF PROFESSIONAL SOCIETY -- BY AGE

Question: Are you a member of any professional societies? NOTE: Question not asked in 1972, 1973, 1976, 1982, 1985.

Responses: Yes; No

		YEAR										
AGE	RESP	'74	'75	'77	'78	'80	'83	'84	'86	'87	'88	'89
18-23	YES	9%	12%	3%	8%	10%	9%	14%	18%	12%	6%	13%
	NO	91	88	97	92	90	91	86	82	88	94	87
# SURVEYED		167	169	163	163	154	128	156	107	122	93	92
AGE	RESP	'74	'75	'77	'78	'80	'83	'84	'86	'87	'88	'89
24-29	YES	19%	17%	14%	18%	13%	19%	18%	20%	17%	15%	24%
	NO	81	83	86	82	87	81	82	80	83	85	76
# SURVEYED		207	228	204	243	197	286	232	218	193	145	139

TABLE IV: MEMBER OF PROFESSIONAL SOCIETY -- BY AGE (Continued)

Question: Are you a member of any professional societies? NOTE: Question not asked in 1972, 1973, 1976, 1982, 1985.

Responses: Yes; No

		YEAR										
AGE	RESP	'74	'75	'77	'78	'80	'83	'84	'86	'87	'88	'89
30-35	YES	11%	11%	17%	16%	21%	17%	18%	16%	21%	25%	23%
	NO	89	89	83	84	79	83	82	84	79	75	77
# SURVEYED		170	170	185	229	208	234	198	221	219	128	141
AGE	RESP	'74	'75	'77	'78	'80	'83	'84	'86	'87	'88	'89
36-41	YES	16%	13%	23%	15%	18%	23%	23%	24%	27%	13%	26%
	NO	84	87	77	85	82	77	77	76	73	87	74
# SURVEYED		151	150	166	155	146	172	185	187	183	122	132
AGE	RESP	'74	'75	'77	'78	'80	'83	'84	'86	'87	'88	'89
42-47	YES	19%	19%	14%	18%	13%	19%	14%	19%	13%	16%	26%
	NO	81	81	86	82	87	81	86	81	87	84	74
# SURVEYED		149	138	147	116	115	144	125	141	154	103	104
AGE	RESP	'74	'75	'77	'78	'80	'83	'84	'86	'87	'88	'89
48-53	YES	10%	14%	18%	17%	16%	16%	17%	11%	18%	19%	15%
	NO	90	86	82	83	84	84	83	89	82	81	85
# SURVEYED		144	139	152	132	120	116	102	107	125	57	96
AGE	RESP	'74	'75	'77	'78	'80	'83	'84	'86	'87	'88	'89
54-59	YES	15%	9%	15%	16%	14%	14%	15%	11%	10%	11%	15%
	NO	85	91	85	84	86	86	85	89	90	89	85
# SURVEYED		137	123	168	134	135	134	112	98	97	64	59
AGE	RESP	'74	'75	'77	'78	'80	'83	'84	'86	'87	'88	'89
AGE	RESP	'74	'75	'77	'78	'80	'83	'84	'86	'87	'88	'89
60-65	YES	10%	6%	9%	7%	11%	12%	17%	11%	5%	15%	14%
	NO	90	94	91	93	89	88	83	89	95	85	86
# SURVEYED		106	113	116	107	118	132	110	115	100	78	74
AGE	RESP	'74	'75	'77	'78	'80	'83	'84	'86	'87	'88	'89
66+	YES	9%	6%	5%	7%	5%	10%	6%	6%	6%	7%	7%
	NO	91	94	95	93	95	90	94	94	94	93	93
# SURVEYED		225	226	209	229	239	239	228	262	249	190	167

****

MEMBER OF SCHOOL SERVICE GROUP

TABLE I: MEMBER OF SCHOOL SERVICE GROUP -- BY TOTAL POPULATION

Question: Are you a member of any school service groups? NOTE: Question not asked in 1972, 1973, 1976, 1982, 1985.

Responses: Yes; No

	YEAR										
RESPONSE	'74	'75	'77	'78	'80	'83	'84	'86	'87	'88	'89
YES	18%	14%	13%	14%	10%	14%	12%	14%	12%	13%	13%
NO	82	86	87	86	90	86	88	86	88	87	87
# SURVEYED	1462	1461	1516	1515	1439	1592	1452	1459	1447	985	1006

TABLE II: MEMBER OF SCHOOL SERVICE GROUP -- BY SEX

Question: Are you a member of any school service groups? NOTE: Question not asked in 1972, 1973, 1976, 1982, 1985.

Responses: Yes; No

		YEAR										
SEX	RESP	'74	'75	'77	'78	'80	'83	'84	'86	'87	'88	'89
M	YES	12%	10%	10%	12%	7%	11%	8%	7%	8%	10%	11%
	NO	88	90	90	88	93	89	92	93	92	90	89
# SURVEYED		678	652	688	638	630	686	589	616	636	431	432
SEX	RESP	'74	'75	'77	'78	'80	'83	'84	'86	'87	'88	'89
F	YES	23%	17%	16%	16%	13%	16%	15%	19%	16%	15%	15%
	NO	77	83	84	84	87	84	85	81	84	85	85
# SURVEYED		784	809	828	877	809	906	863	843	811	554	574

TABLE III: MEMBER OF SCHOOL SERVICE GROUP -- BY RACE

Question: Are you a member of any school service groups? NOTE: Question not asked in 1972, 1973, 1976, 1982, 1985.

Responses: Yes; No

		YEAR										
RACE	RESP	'74	'75	'77	'78	'80	'83	'84	'86	'87	'88	'89
WHITE	YES	18%	14%	13%	14%	10%	14%	12%	14%	13%	13%	13%
	NO	82	86	87	86	90	86	88	86	87	87	87
# SURVEYED		1284	1295	1327	1341	1292	1409	1233	1240	1207	826	860
RACE	RESP	'74	'75	'77	'78	'80	'83	'84	'86	'87	'88	'89
BLACK	YES	18%	14%	16%	12%	10%	13%	14%	14%	7%	14%	13%
	NO	82	86	84	88	90	87	86	86	93	86	87
# SURVEYED		171	162	174	158	138	165	167	182	188	116	106
RACE	RESP	'74	'75	'77	'78	'80	'83	'84	'86	'87	'88	'89
OTHER	YES	14%	0%	7%	13%	0%	6%	13%	19%	6%	5%	13%
	NO	86	100	93	88	100	94	87	81	94	95	88
# SURVEYED		7	4	15	16	9	18	52	37	52	43	40

TABLE IV: MEMBER OF SCHOOL SERVICE GROUP -- BY AGE

Question: Are you a member of any school service groups? NOTE: Question not asked in 1972, 1973, 1976, 1982, 1985.

Responses: Yes; No

		YEAR										
AGE	RESP	'74	'75	'77	'78	'80	'83	'84	'86	'87	'88	'89
18-23	YES	7%	8%	6%	7%	10%	9%	11%	14%	10%	15%	13%
	NO	93	92	94	93	90	91	89	86	90	85	87
# SURVEYED		167	167	163	163	154	128	156	107	122	93	92
AGE	RESP	'74	'75	'77	'78	'80	'83	'84	'86	'87	'88	'89
24-29	YES	16%	14%	10%	11%	11%	12%	13%	10%	9%	10%	12%
	NO	84	86	90	89	89	88	87	90	91	90	88
# SURVEYED		207	229	204	243	197	285	231	218	193	144	139

TABLE IV: MEMBER OF SCHOOL SERVICE GROUP -- BY AGE (Continued)

Question: Are you a member of any school service groups? NOTE: Question not asked in 1972, 1973, 1976, 1982, 1985.

Responses: Yes; No

		YEAR										
AGE	RESP	'74	'75	'77	'78	'80	'83	'84	'86	'87	'88	'89
30-35	YES	30%	26%	23%	24%	16%	19%	19%	22%	15%	19%	20%
	NO	70	74	77	76	84	81	81	78	85	81	80
# SURVEYED		170	170	184	228	207	233	198	220	219	128	141
AGE	RESP	'74	'75	'77	'78	'80	'83	'84	'86	'87	'88	'89
36-41	YES	38%	25%	32%	29%	19%	24%	17%	32%	26%	24%	21%
	NO	62	75	68	71	81	76	83	68	74	76	79
# SURVEYED		151	150	167	156	148	172	186	187	183	123	131
AGE	RESP	'74	'75	'77	'78	'80	'83	'84	'86	'87	'88	'89
42-47	YES	28%	29%	22%	20%	15%	27%	17%	19%	19%	19%	22%
	NO	72	71	78	80	85	73	83	81	81	81	78
# SURVEYED		148	139	147	116	115	145	125	141	155	104	104
AGE	RESP	'74	'75	'77	'78	'80	'83	'84	'86	'87	'88	'89
48-53	YES	17%	15%	14%	17%	10%	14%	10%	12%	14%	11%	9%
	NO	83	85	86	83	90	86	90	88	86	89	91
# SURVEYED		145	137	153	132	119	116	102	106	125	57	95
AGE	RESP	'74	'75	'77	'78	'80	'83	'84	'86	'87	'88	'89
54-59	YES	14%	6%	8%	9%	4%	9%	12%	13%	13%	6%	15%
	NO	86	94	92	91	96	91	88	87	87	94	85
# SURVEYED		137	123	167	134	134	134	113	98	97	64	61
AGE	RESP	'74	'75	'77	'78	'80	'83	'84	'86	'87	'88	'89
60-65	YES	9%	4%	4%	5%	3%	10%	7%	4%	2%	6%	7%
	NO	91	96	96	95	97	90	93	96	98	94	93
# SURVEYED		106	113	115	106	117	132	110	115	100	78	74
AGE	RESP	'74	'75	'77	'78	'80	'83	'84	'86	'87	'88	'89
66+	YES	4%	3%	2%	5%	4%	3%	4%	3%	3%	3%	2%
	NO	96	97	98	95	96	98	96	97	97	97	98
# SURVEYED		225	228	209	230	241	240	227	262	249	190	168

****

MEMBER OF SERVICE CLUB

TABLE I: MEMBER OF SERVICE CLUB -- BY TOTAL POPULATION

Question: Are you a member of any service clubs? NOTE: Question not asked in 1972, 1973, 1976, 1982, 1985.

Responses: Yes; No

	YEAR										
RESPONSE	'74	'75	'77	'78	'80	'83	'84	'86	'87	'88	'89
YES	9%	8%	11%	8%	9%	10%	11%	11%	9%	11%	10%
NO	91	92	89	92	91	90	89	89	91	89	90
# SURVEYED	1461	1463	1518	1520	1441	1592	1449	1459	1447	987	1010

TABLE II: MEMBER OF SERVICE CLUB -- BY SEX

Question: Are you a member of any service clubs? NOTE: Question not asked in 1972, 1973, 1976, 1982, 1985.

Responses: Yes; No

		YEAR										
SEX	RESP	'74	'75	'77	'78	'80	'83	'84	'86	'87	'88	'89
M	YES	10%	11%	12%	8%	10%	11%	10%	12%	10%	11%	11%
	NO	90	89	88	92	90	89	90	88	90	89	89
# SURVEYED		680	654	687	641	633	686	587	616	635	431	433
SEX	RESP	'74	'75	'77	'78	'80	'83	'84	'86	'87	'88	'89
F	YES	8%	7%	10%	9%	9%	10%	11%	11%	8%	11%	9%
	NO	92	93	90	91	91	90	89	89	92	89	91
# SURVEYED		781	809	831	879	808	906	862	843	812	556	577

TABLE III: MEMBER OF SERVICE CLUB -- BY RACE

Question: Are you a member of any service clubs? NOTE: Question not asked in 1972, 1973, 1976, 1982, 1985.

Responses: Yes; No

		YEAR										
RACE	RESP	'74	'75	'77	'78	'80	'83	'84	'86	'87	'88	'89
WHITE	YES	9%	9%	11%	9%	10%	11%	11%	12%	10%	12%	11%
	NO	91	91	89	91	90	89	89	88	90	88	89
# SURVEYED		1283	1297	1330	1346	1293	1409	1230	1239	1208	827	862
RACE	RESP	'74	'75	'77	'78	'80	'83	'84	'86	'87	'88	'89
BLACK	YES	7%	6%	8%	6%	4%	4%	8%	9%	4%	12%	4%
	NO	93	94	92	94	96	96	92	91	96	88	96
# SURVEYED		171	162	173	158	138	165	167	183	187	116	108
RACE	RESP	'74	'75	'77	'78	'80	'83	'84	'86	'87	'88	'89
OTHER	YES	0%	0%	7%	19%	10%	0%	2%	14%	6%	0%	3%
	NO	100	100	93	81	90	100	98	86	94	100	98
# SURVEYED		7	4	15	16	10	18	52	37	52	44	40

TABLE IV: MEMBER OF SERVICE CLUB -- BY AGE

Question: Are you a member of any service clubs? NOTE: Question not asked in 1972, 1973, 1976, 1982, 1985.

Responses: Yes; No

		YEAR										
AGE	RESP	'74	'75	'77	'78	'80	'83	'84	'86	'87	'88	'89
18-23	YES	5%	6%	7%	6%	7%	4%	8%	15%	11%	8%	9%
	NO	95	94	93	94	93	96	92	85	89	92	91
# SURVEYED		167	168	163	163	153	128	156	108	123	93	92
AGE	RESP	'74	'75	'77	'78	'80	'83	'84	'86	'87	'88	'89
24-29	YES	5%	4%	8%	6%	8%	8%	10%	10%	9%	6%	6%
	NO	95	96	92	94	92	92	90	90	91	94	94
# SURVEYED		208	228	204	243	198	285	231	218	193	144	139

TABLE IV: MEMBER OF SERVICE CLUB -- BY AGE (Continued)

Question: Are you a member of any service clubs? NOTE: Question not asked in 1972, 1973, 1976, 1982, 1985.

Responses: Yes; No

		YEAR										
AGE	RESP	'74	'75	'77	'78	'80	'83	'84	'86	'87	'88	'89
30-35	YES	11%	9%	12%	5%	8%	10%	11%	9%	7%	9%	14%
	NO	89	91	88	95	92	90	89	91	93	91	86
# SURVEYED		171	171	185	229	207	233	198	220	219	128	140
AGE	RESP	'74	'75	'77	'78	'80	'83	'84	'86	'87	'88	'89
36-41	YES	9%	9%	13%	12%	7%	12%	14%	16%	12%	15%	14%
	NO	91	91	87	88	93	88	86	84	88	85	86
# SURVEYED		151	151	167	156	147	172	184	187	182	123	133
AGE	RESP	'74	'75	'77	'78	'80	'83	'84	'86	'87	'88	'89
42-47	YES	14%	14%	14%	11%	9%	19%	9%	10%	8%	14%	7%
	NO	86	86	86	89	91	81	91	90	92	86	93
# SURVEYED		148	138	147	117	115	145	125	141	155	104	104
AGE	RESP	'74	'75	'77	'78	'80	'83	'84	'86	'87	'88	'89
48-53	YES	11%	15%	12%	11%	15%	18%	4%	8%	10%	14%	8%
	NO	89	85	88	89	85	82	96	92	90	86	92
# SURVEYED		144	138	153	132	121	116	102	106	125	57	96
AGE	RESP	'74	'75	'77	'78	'80	'83	'84	'86	'87	'88	'89
54-59	YES	9%	7%	12%	13%	10%	11%	16%	12%	12%	9%	13%
	NO	91	93	88	87	90	89	84	88	88	91	87
# SURVEYED		137	123	167	135	135	134	112	98	97	64	61
AGE	RESP	'74	'75	'77	'78	'80	'83	'84	'86	'87	'88	'89
60-65	YES	19%	4%	9%	11%	12%	7%	10%	9%	8%	10%	8%
	NO	81	96	91	89	88	93	90	91	92	90	92
# SURVEYED		106	113	116	107	118	132	109	115	100	80	74
AGE	RESP	'74	'75	'77	'78	'80	'83	'84	'86	'87	'88	'89
66+	YES	5%	9%	10%	7%	9%	9%	11%	12%	8%	14%	10%
	NO	95	91	90	93	91	91	89	88	92	86	90
# SURVEYED		223	228	209	231	240	240	228	261	249	190	170

****

MEMBER OF SPORTS GROUP

TABLE I: MEMBER OF SPORTS GROUP -- BY TOTAL POPULATION

Question: Are you a member of any sports groups? NOTE: Question not asked in 1972, 1973, 1976, 1982, 1985.

Responses: Yes; No

	YEAR										
RESPONSE	'74	'75	'77	'78	'80	'83	'84	'86	'87	'88	'89
YES	18%	19%	19%	20%	17%	21%	21%	21%	19%	20%	22%
NO	82	81	81	80	83	79	79	79	81	80	78
# SURVEYED	1464	1464	1517	1520	1445	1593	1453	1461	1449	989	1006

TABLE II: MEMBER OF SPORTS GROUP -- BY SEX

Question: Are you a member of any sports groups? NOTE: Question not asked in 1972, 1973, 1976, 1982, 1985.

Responses: Yes; No

		YEAR										
SEX	RESP	'74	'75	'77	'78	'80	'83	'84	'86	'87	'88	'89
M	YES	23%	26%	25%	25%	23%	29%	28%	28%	25%	27%	29%
	NO	77	74	75	75	77	71	72	72	75	73	71
# SURVEYED		680	658	688	641	634	687	591	616	636	433	432
SEX	RESP	'74	'75	'77	'78	'80	'83	'84	'86	'87	'88	'89
F	YES	14%	13%	13%	15%	13%	16%	17%	16%	14%	14%	16%
	NO	86	87	87	85	87	84	83	84	86	86	84
# SURVEYED		784	806	829	879	811	906	862	845	813	556	574

TABLE III: MEMBER OF SPORTS GROUP -- BY RACE

Question: Are you a member of any sports groups? NOTE: Question not asked in 1972, 1973, 1976, 1982, 1985.

Responses: Yes; No

		YEAR										
RACE	RESP	'74	'75	'77	'78	'80	'83	'84	'86	'87	'88	'89
WHITE	YES	19%	20%	19%	20%	18%	22%	23%	22%	20%	20%	22%
	NO	81	80	81	80	82	78	77	78	80	80	78
# SURVEYED		1287	1298	1328	1346	1298	1410	1233	1241	1209	830	858
RACE	RESP	'74	'75	'77	'78	'80	'83	'84	'86	'87	'88	'89
BLACK	YES	11%	14%	17%	13%	12%	14%	11%	14%	11%	15%	15%
	NO	89	86	83	87	88	86	89	86	89	85	85
# SURVEYED		170	162	174	158	138	165	168	183	188	115	108
RACE	RESP	'74	'75	'77	'78	'80	'83	'84	'86	'87	'88	'89
OTHER	YES	14%	0%	13%	19%	11%	17%	19%	11%	17%	16%	23%
	NO	86	100	87	81	89	83	81	89	83	84	78
# SURVEYED		7	4	15	16	9	18	52	37	52	44	40

TABLE IV: MEMBER OF SPORTS GROUP -- BY AGE

Question: Are you a member of any sports groups? NOTE: Question not asked in 1972, 1973, 1976, 1982, 1985.

Responses: Yes; No

		YEAR										
AGE	RESP	'74	'75	'77	'78	'80	'83	'84	'86	'87	'88	'89
18-23	YES	25%	29%	22%	21%	28%	28%	32%	29%	27%	34%	34%
	NO	75	71	78	79	72	72	68	71	73	66	66
# SURVEYED		167	170	163	163	155	128	158	108	123	93	92
AGE	RESP	'74	'75	'77	'78	'80	'83	'84	'86	'87	'88	'89
24-29	YES	22%	20%	26%	28%	24%	29%	28%	35%	28%	23%	29%
	NO	78	80	74	72	76	71	72	65	72	77	71
# SURVEYED		208	229	204	243	197	286	232	218	193	146	139

TABLE IV: MEMBER OF SPORTS GROUP -- BY AGE (Continued)

Question: Are you a member of any sports groups? NOTE: Question not asked in 1972, 1973, 1976, 1982, 1985.

Responses: Yes; No

		YEAR										
AGE	RESP	'74	'75	'77	'78	'80	'83	'84	'86	'87	'88	'89
30-35	YES	24%	22%	22%	20%	27%	25%	23%	25%	24%	24%	29%
	NO	76	78	78	80	73	75	77	75	76	76	71
# SURVEYED		172	171	185	230	209	233	198	221	221	128	141
AGE	RESP	'74	'75	'77	'78	'80	'83	'84	'86	'87	'88	'89
36-41	YES	23%	23%	23%	23%	20%	24%	32%	27%	28%	28%	32%
	NO	77	77	77	77	80	76	68	73	72	72	68
# SURVEYED		151	151	167	156	148	172	185	187	183	124	132
AGE	RESP	'74	'75	'77	'78	'80	'83	'84	'86	'87	'88	'89
42-47	YES	23%	25%	13%	31%	18%	26%	23%	24%	18%	19%	21%
	NO	77	75	87	69	82	74	77	76	82	81	79
# SURVEYED		149	136	146	117	115	145	125	141	154	103	103
AGE	RESP	'74	'75	'77	'78	'80	'83	'84	'86	'87	'88	'89
48-53	YES	15%	24%	22%	20%	12%	17%	17%	12%	14%	25%	17%
	NO	85	76	78	80	88	83	83	88	86	75	83
# SURVEYED		143	140	153	132	121	116	102	106	125	57	96
AGE	RESP	'74	'75	'77	'78	'80	'83	'84	'86	'87	'88	'89
54-59	YES	13%	16%	16%	18%	12%	15%	13%	18%	16%	15%	12%
	NO	87	84	84	82	88	85	87	82	84	85	88
# SURVEYED		137	122	168	134	135	134	113	98	97	65	60
AGE	RESP	'74	'75	'77	'78	'80	'83	'84	'86	'87	'88	'89
60-65	YES	9%	8%	15%	13%	8%	13%	15%	9%	8%	6%	10%
	NO	91	92	85	87	92	87	85	91	92	94	90
# SURVEYED		106	113	115	107	118	132	110	115	100	79	73
AGE	RESP	'74	'75	'77	'78	'80	'83	'84	'86	'87	'88	'89
66+	YES	7%	7%	6%	6%	4%	10%	6%	7%	6%	7%	7%
	NO	93	93	94	94	96	90	94	93	94	93	93
# SURVEYED		225	227	209	231	240	240	226	262	249	190	169

****

MEMBER OF LABOR UNION

TABLE I: MEMBER OF LABOR UNION -- BY TOTAL POPULATION

Question: Are you a member of any labor unions? NOTE: Question not asked in 1972, 1973, 1976, 1982, 1985.

Responses: Yes; No

	YEAR										
RESPONSE	'74	'75	'77	'78	'80	'83	'84	'86	'87	'88	'89
YES	16%	16%	17%	15%	13%	14%	14%	11%	13%	13%	14%
NO	84	84	83	85	87	86	86	89	87	87	86
# SURVEYED	1465	1459	1519	1519	1446	1590	1450	1460	1448	984	1006

TABLE II: MEMBER OF LABOR UNION -- BY SEX

Question: Are you a member of any labor unions? NOTE: Question not asked in 1972, 1973, 1976, 1982, 1985.

Responses: Yes; No

		YEAR										
SEX	RESP	'74	'75	'77	'78	'80	'83	'84	'86	'87	'88	'89
M	YES	28%	25%	26%	25%	22%	22%	21%	17%	20%	18%	21%
	NO	72	75	74	75	78	78	79	83	80	82	79
# SURVEYED		682	653	689	640	637	686	589	617	636	432	433
SEX	RESP	'74	'75	'77	'78	'80	'83	'84	'86	'87	'88	'89
F	YES	7%	8%	10%	8%	6%	8%	10%	7%	8%	9%	9%
	NO	93	92	90	92	94	92	90	93	92	91	91
# SURVEYED		783	806	830	879	809	904	861	843	812	552	573

TABLE III: MEMBER OF LABOR UNION -- BY RACE

Question: Are you a member of any labor unions? NOTE: Question not asked in 1972, 1973, 1976, 1982, 1985.

Responses: Yes; No

		YEAR										
RACE	RESP	'74	'75	'77	'78	'80	'83	'84	'86	'87	'88	'89
WHITE	YES	17%	16%	17%	14%	14%	13%	14%	11%	13%	12%	14%
	NO	83	84	83	86	86	87	86	89	87	88	86
# SURVEYED		1288	1294	1331	1345	1300	1407	1230	1240	1208	825	858
RACE	RESP	'74	'75	'77	'78	'80	'83	'84	'86	'87	'88	'89
BLACK	YES	16%	13%	18%	23%	11%	20%	15%	14%	18%	18%	13%
	NO	84	87	82	77	89	80	85	86	82	82	87
# SURVEYED		170	161	173	158	137	165	168	183	188	116	108
RACE	RESP	'74	'75	'77	'78	'80	'83	'84	'86	'87	'88	'89
OTHER	YES	0%	0%	7%	19%	0%	17%	8%	5%	12%	12%	15%
	NO	100	100	93	81	100	83	92	95	88	88	85
# SURVEYED		7	4	15	16	9	18	52	37	52	43	40

TABLE IV: MEMBER OF LABOR UNION -- BY AGE

Question: Are you a member of any labor unions? NOTE: Question not asked in 1972, 1973, 1976, 1982, 1985.

Responses: Yes; No

		YEAR										
AGE	RESP	'74	'75	'77	'78	'80	'83	'84	'86	'87	'88	'89
18-23	YES	16%	11%	14%	12%	7%	5%	10%	5%	8%	3%	4%
	NO	84	89	86	88	93	95	90	95	92	97	96
# SURVEYED		167	167	163	163	154	128	157	108	122	93	92
AGE	RESP	'74	'75	'77	'78	'80	'83	'84	'86	'87	'88	'89
24-29	YES	14%	17%	19%	16%	16%	12%	14%	9%	9%	12%	11%
	NO	86	83	81	84	84	88	86	91	91	88	89
# SURVEYED		209	229	204	243	198	284	231	218	193	145	139

TABLE IV: MEMBER OF LABOR UNION -- BY AGE (Continued)

Question: Are you a member of any labor unions? NOTE: Question not asked in 1972, 1973, 1976, 1982, 1985.

Responses: Yes; No

		YEAR										
AGE	RESP	'74	'75	'77	'78	'80	'83	'84	'86	'87	'88	'89
30-35	YES	13%	16%	18%	19%	17%	11%	13%	10%	16%	10%	14%
	NO	87	84	82	81	83	89	87	90	84	90	86
# SURVEYED		171	171	185	227	208	232	198	220	220	128	141
AGE	RESP	'74	'75	'77	'78	'80	'83	'84	'86	'87	'88	'89
36-41	YES	14%	19%	15%	19%	18%	20%	20%	17%	18%	15%	16%
	NO	86	81	85	81	82	80	80	83	82	85	84
# SURVEYED		151	152	167	157	148	172	185	187	183	123	132
AGE	RESP	'74	'75	'77	'78	'80	'83	'84	'86	'87	'88	'89
42-47	YES	17%	18%	23%	20%	16%	17%	13%	16%	19%	17%	12%
	NO	83	82	77	80	84	83	87	84	81	83	88
# SURVEYED		149	136	147	118	115	145	125	141	154	103	103
AGE	RESP	'74	'75	'77	'78	'80	'83	'84	'86	'87	'88	'89
48-53	YES	26%	22%	24%	20%	9%	15%	17%	14%	16%	25%	19%
	NO	74	78	76	80	91	85	83	86	84	75	81
# SURVEYED		144	138	153	132	121	116	102	106	126	57	96
AGE	RESP	'74	'75	'77	'78	'80	'83	'84	'86	'87	'88	'89
54-59	YES	22%	19%	19%	13%	15%	21%	19%	10%	19%	25%	22%
	NO	78	81	81	87	85	79	81	90	81	75	78
# SURVEYED		137	123	168	135	135	134	113	98	97	64	60
AGE	RESP	'74	'75	'77	'78	'80	'83	'84	'86	'87	'88	'89
60-65	YES	18%	23%	17%	16%	14%	18%	14%	12%	10%	15%	15%
	NO	82	77	83	84	86	82	86	88	90	85	85
# SURVEYED		106	113	116	107	118	131	109	115	100	78	73
AGE	RESP	'74	'75	'77	'78	'80	'83	'84	'86	'87	'88	'89
66+	YES	13%	5%	8%	7%	10%	11%	12%	7%	7%	8%	14%
	NO	87	95	92	93	90	89	88	93	93	92	86
# SURVEYED		225	225	209	230	242	241	226	262	249	189	169

****

MEMBER OF VETERANS ORGANIZATION

TABLE I: MEMBER OF VETERANS ORGANIZATION -- BY TOTAL POPULATION

Question: Are you a member of any veterans groups? NOTE: Question not asked in 1972, 1973, 1976, 1982, 1985.

Responses: Yes; No

	YEAR										
RESPONSE	'74	'75	'77	'78	'80	'83	'84	'86	'87	'88	'89
YES	9%	8%	8%	7%	7%	7%	7%	6%	6%	9%	8%
NO	91	92	92	93	93	93	93	94	94	91	92
# SURVEYED	1464	1464	1518	1515	1441	1591	1451	1461	1447	988	1007

TABLE II: MEMBER OF VETERANS ORGANIZATION -- BY SEX

Question: Are you a member of any veterans groups? NOTE: Question not asked in 1972, 1973, 1976, 1982, 1985.

Responses: Yes; No

		YEAR										
SEX	RESP	'74	'75	'77	'78	'80	'83	'84	'86	'87	'88	'89
M	YES	14%	12%	15%	11%	13%	11%	12%	10%	10%	14%	13%
	NO	86	88	85	89	87	89	88	90	90	86	87
# SURVEYED		682	655	688	640	636	685	589	617	636	433	434
SEX	RESP	'74	'75	'77	'78	'80	'83	'84	'86	'87	'88	'89
F	YES	4%	4%	3%	3%	3%	3%	3%	4%	3%	4%	4%
	NO	96	96	97	97	97	97	97	96	97	96	96
# SURVEYED		782	809	830	875	805	906	862	844	811	555	573

TABLE III: MEMBER OF VETERANS ORGANIZATION -- BY RACE

Question: Are you a member of any veterans groups? NOTE: Question not asked in 1972, 1973, 1976, 1982, 1985.

Responses: Yes; No

		YEAR										
RACE	RESP	'74	'75	'77	'78	'80	'83	'84	'86	'87	'88	'89
WHITE	YES	10%	9%	9%	7%	8%	7%	7%	6%	7%	9%	9%
	NO	90	91	91	93	92	93	93	94	93	91	91
# SURVEYED		1287	1298	1329	1341	1295	1409	1232	1241	1207	828	860
RACE	RESP	'74	'75	'77	'78	'80	'83	'84	'86	'87	'88	'89
BLACK	YES	4%	2%	6%	3%	5%	5%	4%	5%	3%	3%	2%
	NO	96	98	94	97	95	95	96	95	97	97	98
# SURVEYED		170	162	174	158	137	164	167	183	188	116	107
RACE	RESP	'74	'75	'77	'78	'80	'83	'84	'86	'87	'88	'89
OTHER	YES	0%	0%	7%	0%	0%	11%	8%	5%	4%	7%	5%
	NO	100	100	93	100	100	89	92	95	96	93	95
# SURVEYED		7	4	15	16	9	18	52	37	52	44	40

TABLE IV: MEMBER OF VETERANS ORGANIZATION -- BY AGE

Question: Are you a member of any veterans groups? NOTE: Question not asked in 1972, 1973, 1976, 1982, 1985.

Responses: Yes; No

		YEAR										
AGE	RESP	'74	'75	'77	'78	'80	'83	'84	'86	'87	'88	'89
18-23	YES	2%	2%	0%	1%	1%	3%	2%	1%	0%	0%	3%
	NO	98	98	100	99	99	97	98	99	100	100	97
# SURVEYED		167	168	163	163	154	128	156	108	122	93	92
AGE	RESP	'74	'75	'77	'78	'80	'83	'84	'86	'87	'88	'89
24-29	YES	5%	4%	6%	5%	2%	4%	3%	3%	1%	6%	3%
	NO	95	96	94	95	98	96	97	97	99	94	97
# SURVEYED		208	229	204	243	196	285	231	218	193	145	139

TABLE IV: MEMBER OF VETERANS ORGANIZATION -- BY AGE (Continued)

Question: Are you a member of any veterans groups? NOTE: Question not asked in 1972, 1973, 1976, 1982, 1985.

Responses: Yes; No

		YEAR										
AGE	RESP	'74	'75	'77	'78	'80	'83	'84	'86	'87	'88	'89
30-35	YES	5%	3%	4%	2%	6%	3%	3%	3%	4%	2%	4%
	NO	95	97	96	98	94	97	97	97	96	98	96
# SURVEYED		171	171	185	227	208	233	198	220	219	128	140
AGE	RESP	'74	'75	'77	'78	'80	'83	'84	'86	'87	'88	'89
36-41	YES	7%	8%	5%	4%	7%	6%	6%	5%	5%	10%	2%
	NO	93	92	95	96	93	94	94	95	95	90	98
# SURVEYED		151	151	167	155	147	172	185	187	183	123	133
AGE	RESP	'74	'75	'77	'78	'80	'83	'84	'86	'87	'88	'89
42-47	YES	18%	9%	10%	5%	3%	5%	5%	1%	7%	12%	6%
	NO	82	91	90	95	97	95	95	99	93	88	94
# SURVEYED		149	136	147	115	115	145	125	141	155	104	102
AGE	RESP	'74	'75	'77	'78	'80	'83	'84	'86	'87	'88	'89
48-53	YES	14%	15%	16%	11%	14%	10%	6%	7%	7%	2%	7%
	NO	86	85	84	89	86	90	94	93	93	98	93
# SURVEYED		144	138	153	132	120	116	102	106	125	57	96
AGE	RESP	'74	'75	'77	'78	'80	'83	'84	'86	'87	'88	'89
54-59	YES	19%	17%	21%	13%	19%	13%	19%	11%	15%	15%	15%
	NO	81	83	79	87	81	87	81	89	85	85	85
# SURVEYED		137	124	168	135	135	133	113	98	97	65	61
AGE	RESP	'74	'75	'77	'78	'80	'83	'84	'86	'87	'88	'89
60-65	YES	9%	6%	10%	15%	14%	12%	19%	17%	14%	15%	23%
	NO	91	94	90	85	86	88	81	83	86	85	77
# SURVEYED		107	113	115	107	118	132	110	115	100	79	73
AGE	RESP	'74	'75	'77	'78	'80	'83	'84	'86	'87	'88	'89
66+	YES	8%	10%	7%	9%	7%	10%	9%	10%	8%	14%	15%
	NO	92	90	93	91	93	90	91	90	92	86	85
# SURVEYED		224	229	209	231	241	240	227	263	249	190	170

****

MEMBER OF YOUTH GROUP

TABLE I: MEMBER OF YOUTH GROUP -- BY TOTAL POPULATION

Question: Are you a member of any youth groups? NOTE: Question not asked in 1972, 1973, 1976, 1982, 1985.

Responses: Yes; No

	YEAR										
RESPONSE	'74	'75	'77	'78	'80	'83	'84	'86	'87	'88	'89
YES	10%	10%	10%	9%	8%	11%	10%	11%	9%	11%	10%
NO	90	90	90	91	92	89	90	89	91	89	90
# SURVEYED	1464	1462	1518	1515	1442	1591	1451	1460	1446	984	1002

TABLE II: MEMBER OF YOUTH GROUP -- BY SEX

Question: Are you a member of any youth groups? NOTE: Question not asked in 1972, 1973, 1976, 1982, 1985.

Responses: Yes; No

		YEAR										
SEX	RESP	'74	'75	'77	'78	'80	'83	'84	'86	'87	'88	'89
M	YES	11%	10%	11%	9%	8%	12%	8%	9%	8%	12%	10%
	NO	89	90	89	91	92	88	92	91	92	88	90
# SURVEYED		681	655	688	637	633	687	589	616	634	431	430
SEX	RESP	'74	'75	'77	'78	'80	'83	'84	'86	'87	'88	'89
F	YES	10%	9%	9%	9%	8%	9%	10%	12%	9%	10%	9%
	NO	90	91	91	91	92	91	90	88	91	90	91
# SURVEYED		783	807	830	878	809	904	862	844	812	553	572

TABLE III: MEMBER OF YOUTH GROUP -- BY RACE

Question: Are you a member of any youth groups? NOTE: Question not asked in 1972, 1973, 1976, 1982, 1985.

Responses: Yes; No

		YEAR										
RACE	RESP	'74	'75	'77	'78	'80	'83	'84	'86	'87	'88	'89
WHITE	YES	10%	10%	10%	9%	8%	10%	9%	10%	9%	11%	10%
	NO	90	90	90	91	92	90	91	90	91	89	90
# SURVEYED		1286	1295	1329	1341	1295	1408	1233	1240	1207	825	854
RACE	RESP	'74	'75	'77	'78	'80	'83	'84	'86	'87	'88	'89
BLACK	YES	11%	7%	16%	9%	9%	13%	11%	13%	7%	16%	9%
	NO	89	93	84	91	91	87	89	87	93	84	91
# SURVEYED		171	163	174	158	138	165	167	183	187	116	108
RACE	RESP	'74	'75	'77	'78	'80	'83	'84	'86	'87	'88	'89
OTHER	YES	14%	0%	13%	19%	22%	6%	6%	8%	6%	0%	10%
	NO	86	100	87	81	78	94	94	92	94	100	90
# SURVEYED		7	4	15	16	9	18	51	37	52	43	40

TABLE IV: MEMBER OF YOUTH GROUP -- BY AGE

Question: Are you a member of any youth groups? NOTE: Question not asked in 1972, 1973, 1976, 1982, 1985.

Responses: Yes; No

		YEAR										
AGE	RESP	'74	'75	'77	'78	'80	'83	'84	'86	'87	'88	'89
18-23	YES	14%	15%	17%	11%	14%	16%	15%	16%	17%	14%	14%
	NO	86	85	83	89	86	84	85	84	83	86	86
# SURVEYED		167	169	163	163	154	128	157	108	122	93	92
AGE	RESP	'74	'75	'77	'78	'80	'83	'84	'86	'87	'88	'89
24-29	YES	6%	7%	10%	9%	7%	12%	10%	11%	7%	10%	10%
	NO	94	93	90	91	93	88	90	89	93	90	90
# SURVEYED		208	229	204	243	197	286	230	218	193	144	139

TABLE IV: MEMBER OF YOUTH GROUP -- BY AGE (Continued)

Question: Are you a member of any youth groups? NOTE: Question not asked in 1972, 1973, 1976, 1982, 1985.

Responses: Yes; No

		YEAR										
AGE	RESP	'74	'75	'77	'78	'80	'83	'84	'86	'87	'88	'89
30-35	YES	13%	17%	14%	11%	15%	13%	11%	15%	10%	14%	19%
	NO	87	83	86	89	85	87	89	85	90	86	81
# SURVEYED		172	170	185	228	207	233	198	220	220	128	140
AGE	RESP	'74	'75	'77	'78	'80	'83	'84	'86	'87	'88	'89
36-41	YES	21%	14%	16%	17%	12%	10%	14%	17%	13%	20%	12%
	NO	79	86	84	83	88	90	86	83	87	80	88
# SURVEYED		151	152	167	156	148	172	185	187	182	123	132
AGE	RESP	'74	'75	'77	'78	'80	'83	'84	'86	'87	'88	'89
42-47	YES	18%	19%	12%	11%	8%	20%	11%	14%	12%	13%	11%
	NO	82	81	88	89	92	80	89	86	88	87	89
# SURVEYED		148	138	147	115	115	144	125	141	154	104	103
AGE	RESP	'74	'75	'77	'78	'80	'83	'84	'86	'87	'88	'89
48-53	YES	11%	8%	10%	11%	4%	12%	8%	8%	7%	14%	6%
	NO	89	92	90	89	96	88	92	92	93	86	94
# SURVEYED		144	137	153	132	121	115	102	106	125	57	96
AGE	RESP	'74	'75	'77	'78	'80	'83	'84	'86	'87	'88	'89
54-59	YES	7%	7%	8%	7%	5%	4%	9%	12%	8%	3%	8%
	NO	93	93	92	93	95	96	91	88	92	97	92
# SURVEYED		137	122	168	134	135	134	113	98	97	64	60
AGE	RESP	'74	'75	'77	'78	'80	'83	'84	'86	'87	'88	'89
60-65	YES	6%	3%	3%	6%	5%	8%	4%	2%	1%	3%	3%
	NO	94	97	97	94	95	92	96	98	99	97	97
# SURVEYED		106	113	115	107	118	132	110	115	100	78	73
AGE	RESP	'74	'75	'77	'78	'80	'83	'84	'86	'87	'88	'89
66+	YES	2%	2%	3%	1%	3%	2%	4%	2%	4%	5%	2%
	NO	98	98	97	99	97	98	96	98	96	95	98
# SURVEYED		225	227	209	230	240	240	227	262	249	189	166

****

MEMBER OF CHURCH AFFILIATED GROUP

TABLE I: MEMBER OF CHURCH AFFILIATED GROUP -- BY TOTAL POPULATION

Question: Are you a member of any church affiliated groups? NOTE: Question not asked in 1972, 1973, 1976, 1982, 1985.

Responses: Yes; No

	YEAR										
RESPONSE	'74	'75	'77	'78	'80	'83	'84	'86	'87	'88	'89
YES	42%	40%	39%	36%	30%	38%	34%	40%	30%	35%	33%
NO	58	60	61	64	70	62	66	60	70	65	67
# SURVEYED	1475	1465	1518	1524	1447	1592	1451	1462	1448	989	1001

TABLE II: MEMBER OF CHURCH AFFILIATED GROUP -- BY SEX

Question: Are you a member of any church affiliated groups? NOTE: Question not asked in 1972, 1973, 1976, 1982, 1985.

Responses: Yes; No

		YEAR										
SEX	RESP	'74	'75	'77	'78	'80	'83	'84	'86	'87	'88	'89
M	YES	37%	36%	32%	31%	24%	34%	25%	31%	24%	27%	27%
	NO	63	64	68	69	76	66	75	69	76	73	73
# SURVEYED		686	653	687	640	635	687	589	617	636	433	430
SEX	RESP	'74	'75	'77	'78	'80	'83	'84	'86	'87	'88	'89
F	YES	46%	44%	45%	40%	36%	41%	40%	46%	35%	40%	37%
	NO	54	56	55	60	64	59	60	54	65	60	63
# SURVEYED		789	812	831	884	812	905	862	845	812	556	571

TABLE III: MEMBER OF CHURCH AFFILIATED GROUP -- BY RACE

Question: Are you a member of any church affiliated groups? NOTE: Question not asked in 1972, 1973, 1976, 1982, 1985.

Responses: Yes; No

		YEAR										
RACE	RESP	'74	'75	'77	'78	'80	'83	'84	'86	'87	'88	'89
WHITE	YES	41%	39%	37%	35%	29%	37%	33%	39%	31%	35%	32%
	NO	59	61	63	65	71	63	67	61	69	65	68
# SURVEYED		1296	1300	1328	1350	1300	1410	1232	1242	1207	830	855
RACE	RESP	'74	'75	'77	'78	'80	'83	'84	'86	'87	'88	'89
BLACK	YES	50%	52%	50%	47%	41%	49%	42%	50%	32%	37%	38%
	NO	50	48	50	53	59	51	58	50	68	63	62
# SURVEYED		172	161	175	158	137	164	167	183	188	116	106
RACE	RESP	'74	'75	'77	'78	'80	'83	'84	'86	'87	'88	'89
OTHER	YES	57%	50%	27%	38%	40%	22%	27%	32%	21%	19%	30%
	NO	43	50	73	63	60	78	73	68	79	81	70
# SURVEYED		7	4	15	16	10	18	52	37	53	43	40

TABLE IV: MEMBER OF CHURCH AFFILIATED GROUP -- BY AGE

Question: Are you a member of any church affiliated groups? NOTE: Question not asked in 1972, 1973, 1976, 1982, 1985.

Responses: Yes; No

		YEAR										
AGE	RESP	'74	'75	'77	'78	'80	'83	'84	'86	'87	'88	'89
18-23	YES	29%	27%	20%	25%	13%	27%	21%	28%	24%	19%	20%
	NO	71	73	80	75	87	73	79	72	76	81	80
# SURVEYED		167	168	162	163	154	128	156	108	124	93	92
AGE	RESP	'74	'75	'77	'78	'80	'83	'84	'86	'87	'88	'89
24-29	YES	28%	27%	27%	25%	21%	28%	26%	29%	20%	30%	26%
	NO	72	73	73	75	79	72	74	71	80	70	74
# SURVEYED		209	230	204	244	198	284	231	218	192	144	139

TABLE IV: MEMBER OF CHURCH AFFILIATED GROUP -- BY AGE (Continued)

Question: Are you a member of any church affiliated groups? NOTE: Question not asked in 1972, 1973, 1976, 1982, 1985.

Responses: Yes; No

		YEAR										
AGE	RESP	'74	'75	'77	'78	'80	'83	'84	'86	'87	'88	'89
30-35	YES	38%	39%	33%	34%	32%	31%	28%	31%	25%	35%	30%
	NO	62	61	67	66	68	69	72	69	75	65	70
# SURVEYED		174	170	186	229	208	234	198	220	220	128	138
AGE	RESP	'74	'75	'77	'78	'80	'83	'84	'86	'87	'88	'89
36-41	YES	46%	47%	46%	41%	31%	38%	29%	41%	28%	34%	30%
	NO	54	53	54	59	69	62	71	59	72	66	70
# SURVEYED		152	151	167	158	148	172	185	187	183	122	132
AGE	RESP	'74	'75	'77	'78	'80	'83	'84	'86	'87	'88	'89
42-47	YES	50%	47%	41%	40%	30%	34%	35%	41%	35%	38%	28%
	NO	50	53	59	60	70	66	65	59	65	63	72
# SURVEYED		149	138	147	118	115	145	124	141	154	104	101
AGE	RESP	'74	'75	'77	'78	'80	'83	'84	'86	'87	'88	'89
48-53	YES	40%	45%	45%	44%	39%	44%	40%	43%	38%	30%	37%
	NO	60	55	55	56	61	56	60	57	62	70	63
# SURVEYED		146	139	153	133	122	116	102	107	125	57	95
AGE	RESP	'74	'75	'77	'78	'80	'83	'84	'86	'87	'88	'89
54-59	YES	49%	49%	48%	40%	33%	41%	54%	47%	37%	35%	38%
	NO	51	51	52	60	67	59	46	53	63	65	62
# SURVEYED		138	123	167	135	135	134	113	98	97	65	60
AGE	RESP	'74	'75	'77	'78	'80	'83	'84	'86	'87	'88	'89
60-65	YES	50%	40%	41%	41%	34%	52%	39%	48%	33%	41%	41%
	NO	50	60	59	59	66	48	61	52	67	59	59
# SURVEYED		107	113	116	107	118	132	110	115	100	79	73
AGE	RESP	'74	'75	'77	'78	'80	'83	'84	'86	'87	'88	'89
66+	YES	54%	48%	49%	45%	40%	51%	43%	52%	39%	43%	45%
	NO	46	52	51	55	60	49	57	48	61	57	55
# SURVEYED		227	228	209	230	242	240	228	262	249	193	170

****

BAR SOCIALIZING

TABLE I: BAR SOCIALIZING -- BY TOTAL POPULATION

Question: How often do you go to a bar or tavern? NOTE: Question not asked in 1972, 1973, 1976, 1980, 1984, 1987.

Responses: DL = Almost every day WL = Once or twice a week SM = Several times a month ML = About once a month SY = Several times a year YL = About once a year NV = Never

	YEAR									
RESPONSE	'74	'75	'77	'78	'82	'83	'85	'86	'88	'89
DL	2%	1%	3%	2%	2%	2%	2%	1%	1%	1%
WL	10	8	9	9	10	10	8	8	8	8
SM	6	7	8	9	6	9	8	6	7	6
ML	9	9	10	7	9	8	11	10	10	8
SY	12	9	11	12	12	11	11	12	11	10
YL	8	9	9	10	11	10	11	10	13	11
NV	53	56	50	51	50	50	49	53	51	56
# SURVEYED	1462	1476	1525	1528	1495	1593	1529	1463	983	1004

TABLE II: BAR SOCIALIZING -- BY SEX

Question: How often do you go to a bar or tavern? NOTE: Question not asked in 1972, 1973, 1976, 1980, 1984, 1987.

Responses: DL = Almost every day; WL = Once or twice a week; SM = Several times a month; ML = About once a month; SY = Several times a year; YL = About once a year; NV = Never

		YEAR									
SEX	RESP	'74	'75	'77	'78	'82	'83	'85	'86	'88	'89
M	DL	4%	3%	5%	4%	3%	3%	3%	2%	2%	2%
A	WL	16	12	15	12	15	15	12	12	12	12
L	SM	8	9	11	12	7	11	11	8	8	8
E	ML	11	10	11	8	10	8	11	12	11	10
	SY	12	9	11	13	14	13	11	13	11	11
	YL	7	10	9	9	11	11	10	9	14	10
	NV	43	47	39	42	40	40	42	43	43	47
# SURVEYED		682	666	690	640	632	687	687	618	435	428
SEX	RESP	'74	'75	'77	'78	'82	'83	'85	'86	'88	'89
F	DL	1%	0%	1%	1%	0%	1%	1%	0%	0%	0%
E	WL	4	4	4	6	7	6	5	5	5	5
M	SM	4	5	6	7	6	7	6	4	6	3
A	ML	8	8	9	7	8	8	11	8	9	8
L	SY	13	9	11	12	11	10	12	11	11	10
E	YL	8	9	10	11	11	10	11	11	12	12
	NV	62	64	59	57	57	58	55	61	58	62
# SURVEYED		780	810	835	888	863	906	842	845	548	576

TABLE III: BAR SOCIALIZING -- BY RACE

Question: How often do you go to a bar or tavern? NOTE: Question not asked in 1972, 1973, 1976, 1980, 1984, 1987.

Responses: DL = Almost every day; WL = Once or twice a week; SM = Several times a month; ML = About once a month; SY = Several times a year; YL = About once a year; NV = Never

		YEAR									
RACE	RESP	'74	'75	'77	'78	'82	'83	'85	'86	'88	'89
WHITE	DL	2%	1%	3%	2%	2%	2%	2%	1%	1%	1%
	WL	9	8	10	8	10	10	8	8	8	8
	SM	6	7	8	9	7	9	9	6	7	6
	ML	9	10	10	7	9	8	11	10	9	8
	SY	13	10	11	12	12	12	12	13	11	11
	YL	8	9	10	10	11	10	11	10	12	12
	NV	52	55	48	51	48	48	48	52	52	54
# SURVEYED		1287	1311	1336	1354	1313	1411	1336	1242	824	863
RACE	RESP	'74	'75	'77	'78	'82	'83	'85	'86	'88	'89
BLACK	DL	4%	2%	2%	1%	1%	1%	1%	0%	2%	2%
	WL	13	7	4	11	8	8	7	6	12	8
	SM	5	7	10	9	1	5	5	9	6	0
	ML	7	6	12	6	6	10	13	10	14	9
	SY	7	4	5	11	10	3	8	8	8	7
	YL	7	9	3	12	11	7	10	10	14	7
	NV	58	64	63	49	64	66	56	58	45	68
# SURVEYED		168	161	175	158	155	164	150	184	125	102
RACE	RESP	'74	'75	'77	'78	'82	'83	'85	'86	'88	'89
OTHER	DL	0%	0%	0%	0%	0%	0%	0%	3%	0%	0%
	WL	0	0	0	0	11	6	7	5	3	5
	SM	0	0	14	6	4	6	9	8	12	0
	ML	0	0	7	25	11	0	12	14	12	13
	SY	0	0	14	6	7	11	12	3	6	13
	YL	14	25	0	6	15	6	5	3	12	3
	NV	86	75	64	56	52	72	56	65	56	67
# SURVEYED		7	4	14	16	27	18	43	37	34	39

TABLE IV: BAR SOCIALIZING -- BY AGE

Question: How often do you go to a bar or tavern? NOTE: Question not asked in 1972, 1973, 1976, 1980, 1984, 1987.

Responses: DL = Almost every day; WL = Once or twice a week; SM = Several times a month; ML = About once a month; SY = Several times a year; YL = About once a year; NV = Never

		YEAR									
AGE	RESP	'74	'75	'77	'78	'82	'83	'85	'86	'88	'89
18-23	DL	3%	2%	5%	3%	3%	2%	2%	1%	0%	2%
	WL	18	18	15	15	18	20	17	15	18	17
	SM	12	14	16	16	12	10	17	12	10	8
	ML	14	17	13	7	13	13	17	18	14	10
	SY	14	5	5	13	14	9	10	10	6	8
	YL	7	4	9	10	9	7	9	6	5	7
	NV	32	39	38	35	31	38	29	38	47	48
# SURVEYED		167	170	164	162	147	128	133	107	94	84
AGE	RESP	'74	'75	'77	'78	'82	'83	'85	'86	'88	'89
24-29	DL	5%	2%	3%	2%	2%	2%	4%	2%	1%	0%
	WL	10	12	9	11	19	15	12	17	12	15
	SM	13	11	13	14	12	18	12	12	11	8
	ML	18	14	16	12	15	14	24	16	17	20
	SY	19	15	21	18	14	13	12	15	17	18
	YL	9	15	12	15	13	11	10	11	15	11
	NV	26	32	26	26	25	26	27	27	28	29
# SURVEYED		211	231	204	244	245	287	216	218	149	146
AGE	RESP	'74	'75	'77	'78	'82	'83	'85	'86	'88	'89
30-35	DL	5%	1%	1%	2%	1%	2%	0%	0%	1%	0%
	WL	14	6	10	9	11	12	10	11	10	11
	SM	5	5	11	11	12	12	11	7	9	11
	ML	9	14	12	10	11	9	13	15	15	11
	SY	13	13	17	21	20	17	17	18	16	16
	YL	14	14	14	12	17	12	18	17	16	13
	NV	40	47	34	35	28	36	30	32	33	37
# SURVEYED		174	171	186	229	204	234	212	218	131	141
AGE	RESP	'74	'75	'77	'78	'82	'83	'85	'86	'88	'89
36-41	DL	1%	1%	4%	3%	3%	2%	2%	1%	1%	2%
	WL	14	5	8	11	12	6	7	8	7	8
	SM	7	5	10	9	8	12	9	7	6	6
	ML	9	12	13	11	10	12	12	10	9	9
	SY	11	14	14	13	17	13	18	16	15	15
	YL	7	13	12	12	12	10	16	13	20	13
	NV	50	51	40	42	40	46	36	44	42	47
# SURVEYED		147	152	168	159	146	173	184	187	125	127

TABLE IV: BAR SOCIALIZING -- BY AGE (Continued)

Question: How often do you go to a bar or tavern? NOTE: Question not asked in 1972, 1973, 1976, 1980, 1984, 1987.

Responses: DL = Almost every day; WL = Once or twice a week; SM = Several times a month; ML = About once a month; SY = Several times a year; YL = About once a year; NV = Never

		YEAR									
AGE	RESP	'74	'75	'77	'78	'82	'83	'85	'86	'88	'89
42-47	DL	1%	2%	2%	2%	2%	3%	4%	0%	1%	1%
	WL	6	11	12	9	11	9	10	6	12	6
	SM	5	11	4	14	5	3	10	4	9	6
	ML	8	8	8	5	11	13	10	11	6	8
	SY	20	6	12	8	10	12	15	20	14	13
	YL	10	12	8	8	12	21	15	13	11	14
	NV	50	50	54	54	49	39	37	46	46	52
# SURVEYED		147	142	147	119	117	145	124	141	108	108
AGE	RESP	'74	'75	'77	'78	'82	'83	'85	'86	'88	'89
48-53	DL	3%	2%	3%	2%	2%	1%	2%	2%	2%	2%
	WL	4	6	10	8	5	7	6	6	0	4
	SM	4	3	8	6	2	9	8	5	8	6
	ML	8	7	5	9	6	3	13	6	10	4
	SY	18	14	10	12	7	14	15	10	8	9
	YL	10	7	14	11	15	11	13	10	19	13
	NV	54	61	51	53	63	55	44	62	53	62
# SURVEYED		146	140	154	133	112	116	131	108	62	85
AGE	RESP	'74	'75	'77	'78	'82	'83	'85	'86	'88	'89
54-59	DL	0%	2%	1%	1%	1%	1%	0%	1%	2%	1%
	WL	7	2	7	6	6	6	8	5	8	4
	SM	2	6	7	4	1	4	5	1	2	1
	ML	5	4	8	4	8	4	5	3	6	4
	SY	10	8	10	9	10	10	6	7	10	1
	YL	4	14	9	9	8	10	8	8	14	10
	NV	71	65	58	66	65	66	68	74	58	78
# SURVEYED		134	124	168	137	144	134	133	97	50	72
AGE	RESP	'74	'75	'77	'78	'82	'83	'85	'86	'88	'89
60-65	DL	0%	2%	1%	2%	1%	2%	2%	2%	0%	0%
	WL	8	4	8	7	3	6	2	3	7	1
	SM	5	4	1	3	3	2	3	4	4	1
	ML	7	2	9	5	3	2	4	4	8	1
	SY	5	4	3	6	12	10	7	7	4	0
	YL	7	4	4	7	10	10	8	7	11	17
	NV	68	80	73	71	69	69	74	72	66	78
# SURVEYED		107	112	116	107	115	131	130	115	73	69

TABLE IV: BAR SOCIALIZING -- BY AGE (Continued)

Question: How often do you go to a bar or tavern? NOTE: Question not asked in 1972, 1973, 1976, 1980, 1984, 1987.

Responses: DL = Almost every day; WL = Once or twice a week; SM = Several times a month; ML = About once a month; SY = Several times a year; YL = About once a year; NV = Never

		YEAR									
AGE	RESP	'74	'75	'77	'78	'82	'83	'85	'86	'88	'89
66+	DL	1%	0%	2%	0%	0%	1%	1%	1%	2%	1%
	WL	4	2	5	2	2	4	2	1	2	3
	SM	1	2	1	3	0	1	2	1	1	1
	ML	2	2	4	2	4	1	2	3	3	2
	SY	1	3	2	3	4	4	4	2	3	3
	YL	2	3	3	3	6	2	3	2	5	4
	NV	89	89	82	87	84	87	87	90	84	86
# SURVEYED		223	230	211	231	257	238	260	265	190	169

****

SOCIALIZING WITH FRIENDS

TABLE I: SOCIALIZING WITH FRIENDS -- BY TOTAL POPULATION

Question: How often do you spend a social evening with friends? NOTE: Question not asked in 1972, 1973, 1976, 1980, 1984, 1987.

Responses: DL = Almost every day; WL = Once or twice a week; SM = Several times a month; ML = About once a month; SY = Several times a year; YL = About once a year; NV = Never

	YEAR									
RESPONSE	'74	'75	'77	'78	'82	'83	'85	'86	'88	'89
DL	2%	3%	3%	2%	3%	3%	3%	2%	3%	4%
WL	20	18	19	19	18	19	19	20	18	18
SM	18	17	20	21	21	21	20	18	21	18
ML	22	23	22	17	22	22	21	23	24	23
SY	18	18	19	21	19	18	18	20	19	18
YL	8	8	7	9	7	6	9	5	6	7
NV	11	13	10	12	9	11	10	12	10	11
# SURVEYED	1478	1485	1523	1526	1497	1594	1529	1465	986	1002

TABLE II: SOCIALIZING WITH FRIENDS -- BY SEX

Question: How often do you spend a social evening with friends? NOTE: Question not asked in 1972, 1973, 1976, 1980, 1984, 1987.

Responses: DL = Almost every day; WL = Once or twice a week; SM = Several times a month; ML = About once a month; SY = Several times a year; YL = About once a year; NV = Never

		YEAR									
SEX	RESP	'74	'75	'77	'78	'82	'83	'85	'86	'88	'89
M	DL	2%	4%	3%	3%	5%	2%	4%	2%	4%	4%
A	WL	20	20	19	19	18	17	19	21	21	20
L	SM	18	18	22	19	20	22	19	18	19	17
E	ML	24	21	21	20	21	22	21	23	22	23
	SY	18	19	19	21	20	19	19	23	18	19
	YL	7	8	8	9	8	7	10	4	6	9
	NV	11	11	7	9	7	10	8	9	9	8
# SURVEYED		690	669	689	639	635	689	688	618	437	426
SEX	RESP	'74	'75	'77	'78	'82	'83	'85	'86	'88	'89
F	DL	2%	3%	2%	2%	2%	3%	2%	1%	2%	4%
E	WL	19	16	19	19	18	20	19	20	15	17
M	SM	19	17	18	22	22	21	21	18	22	19
A	ML	21	24	23	14	22	22	21	23	25	23
L	SY	18	17	19	22	18	18	18	18	19	17
E	YL	10	7	6	8	7	5	8	6	6	6
	NV	12	14	12	14	10	11	11	14	11	14
# SURVEYED		788	816	834	887	862	905	841	847	549	576

TABLE III: SOCIALIZING WITH FRIENDS -- BY RACE

Question: How often do you spend a social evening with friends? NOTE: Question not asked in 1972, 1973, 1976, 1980, 1984, 1987.

Responses: DL = Almost every day; WL = Once or twice a week; SM = Several times a month; ML = About once a month; SY = Several times a year; YL = About once a year; NV = Never

RACE	RESP	'74	'75	'77	'78	'82	'83	'85	'86	'88	'89
WHITE	DL	2%	3%	2%	2%	3%	2%	2%	2%	2%	3%
	WL	20	18	18	19	18	19	19	21	18	18
	SM	18	18	19	21	22	22	20	18	21	19
	ML	23	23	23	16	22	22	21	22	23	23
	SY	19	19	20	22	19	18	19	21	19	19
	YL	8	7	8	9	7	6	9	5	7	7
	NV	10	11	10	11	9	10	9	11	10	10
# SURVEYED		1299	1318	1334	1352	1314	1411	1335	1244	827	861
RACE	RESP	'74	'75	'77	'78	'82	'83	'85	'86	'88	'89
BLACK	DL	7%	5%	6%	4%	4%	5%	6%	1%	6%	9%
	WL	19	15	22	21	19	19	19	17	14	19
	SM	18	15	22	21	20	13	19	19	18	13
	ML	13	17	17	20	19	21	15	26	26	22
	SY	13	13	14	15	19	19	14	14	20	11
	YL	13	12	5	4	10	8	12	7	5	8
	NV	17	23	13	16	8	14	14	16	10	20
# SURVEYED		172	163	174	158	156	165	150	184	125	102
RACE	RESP	'74	'75	'77	'78	'82	'83	'85	'86	'88	'89
OTHER	DL	0%	0%	0%	0%	4%	0%	5%	0%	3%	5%
	WL	0	0	27	25	22	22	18	30	15	18
	SM	14	25	20	13	11	28	30	24	26	18
	ML	57	50	13	44	22	33	30	16	24	18
	SY	0	25	13	6	15	11	7	16	12	23
	YL	0	0	0	6	7	6	2	0	3	3
	NV	29	0	27	6	19	0	9	14	18	15
# SURVEYED		7	4	15	16	27	18	44	37	34	39

TABLE IV: SOCIALIZING WITH FRIENDS -- BY AGE

Question: How often do you spend a social evening with friends? NOTE: Question not asked in 1972, 1973, 1976, 1980, 1984, 1987.

Responses: DL = Almost every day; WL = Once or twice a week; SM = Several times a month; ML = About once a month; SY = Several times a year; YL = About once a year; NV = Never

		YEAR									
AGE	RESP	'74	'75	'77	'78	'82	'83	'85	'86	'88	'89
18-23	DL	11%	18%	13%	7%	14%	9%	9%	9%	17%	19%
	WL	40	27	31	32	29	32	38	31	26	31
	SM	19	22	25	26	24	27	32	28	22	14
	ML	14	20	14	13	15	17	10	15	17	15
	SY	7	8	9	10	8	8	7	10	10	11
	YL	4	2	5	4	3	4	2	3	1	2
	NV	5	5	2	8	6	3	2	4	7	7
# SURVEYED		167	173	164	163	147	128	133	108	94	84
AGE	RESP	'74	'75	'77	'78	'82	'83	'85	'86	'88	'89
24-29	DL	3%	4%	3%	4%	4%	3%	6%	2%	2%	5%
	WL	27	26	26	25	26	27	28	33	25	29
	SM	25	26	26	26	27	29	28	20	24	21
	ML	27	22	21	20	28	22	22	22	25	21
	SY	11	12	13	13	7	11	8	14	15	12
	YL	2	3	4	6	4	4	4	3	5	4
	NV	4	6	6	5	4	5	3	6	4	8
# SURVEYED		211	231	204	244	246	287	217	218	149	146
AGE	RESP	'74	'75	'77	'78	'82	'83	'85	'86	'88	'89
30-35	DL	1%	1%	2%	0%	3%	1%	1%	1%	2%	2%
	WL	23	16	23	21	21	19	22	21	22	23
	SM	26	22	27	29	31	27	24	23	27	17
	ML	16	26	21	21	23	24	27	26	29	24
	SY	21	20	16	20	12	18	17	20	15	16
	YL	9	7	6	6	3	5	6	4	4	8
	NV	4	9	5	3	6	6	3	4	2	10
# SURVEYED		175	171	186	228	204	234	212	220	131	141
AGE	RESP	'74	'75	'77	'78	'82	'83	'85	'86	'88	'89
36-41	DL	2%	1%	2%	3%	1%	2%	2%	0%	1%	3%
	WL	18	15	21	16	21	18	17	18	15	13
	SM	20	15	20	18	23	21	22	21	23	22
	ML	23	31	27	18	19	26	24	24	25	31
	SY	20	23	17	26	23	19	23	23	21	18
	YL	11	7	8	8	10	8	6	9	7	8
	NV	6	8	6	11	3	5	6	5	9	6
# SURVEYED		152	153	168	159	146	173	184	188	126	127

TABLE IV: SOCIALIZING WITH FRIENDS -- BY AGE (Continued)

Question: How often do you spend a social evening with friends? NOTE: Question not asked in 1972, 1973, 1976, 1980, 1984, 1987.

Responses: DL = Almost every day; WL = Once or twice a week; SM = Several times a month; ML = About once a month; SY = Several times a year; YL = About once a year; NV = Never

		YEAR									
AGE	RESP	'74	'75	'77	'78	'82	'83	'85	'86	'88	'89
42-47	DL	0%	2%	0%	1%	4%	1%	5%	2%	2%	5%
	WL	11	19	14	17	16	16	14	21	23	19
	SM	11	12	16	24	15	20	19	13	21	22
	ML	33	22	25	16	28	17	26	25	22	24
	SY	30	23	29	23	20	29	23	28	20	17
	YL	6	10	5	9	10	8	9	9	6	8
	NV	9	13	11	10	6	9	6	2	6	5
# SURVEYED		149	143	147	119	117	145	124	141	108	108
AGE	RESP	'74	'75	'77	'78	'82	'83	'85	'86	'88	'89
48-53	DL	1%	1%	1%	0%	2%	3%	2%	1%	0%	0%
	WL	14	14	16	15	14	9	17	18	11	12
	SM	21	14	16	19	13	25	10	18	26	21
	ML	26	24	19	11	25	28	22	23	27	31
	SY	21	26	26	36	31	20	25	21	21	21
	YL	8	7	10	8	8	8	12	4	6	7
	NV	9	15	11	11	6	8	12	16	8	8
# SURVEYED		146	140	154	132	112	116	131	108	62	85
AGE	RESP	'74	'75	'77	'78	'82	'83	'85	'86	'88	'89
54-59	DL	1%	1%	1%	0%	1%	2%	1%	0%	2%	0%
	WL	14	17	13	14	8	14	15	14	22	7
	SM	14	15	19	15	17	12	19	16	6	21
	ML	32	21	26	18	22	30	14	30	29	18
	SY	15	17	24	26	31	27	21	20	24	28
	YL	14	14	8	12	12	5	19	3	4	10
	NV	9	14	10	16	10	11	12	16	14	17
# SURVEYED		139	126	168	137	144	133	133	98	51	72
AGE	RESP	'74	'75	'77	'78	'82	'83	'85	'86	'88	'89
60-65	DL	0%	0%	1%	2%	0%	2%	0%	2%	0%	4%
	WL	18	18	10	13	9	14	14	13	5	4
	SM	12	9	11	12	18	14	16	14	18	13
	ML	19	19	29	22	23	22	21	23	22	18
	SY	26	27	22	23	30	21	22	27	28	26
	YL	9	12	9	12	7	6	15	7	18	7
	NV	17	15	16	15	12	20	12	14	9	26
# SURVEYED		108	113	116	107	116	132	130	115	74	68

TABLE IV: SOCIALIZING WITH FRIENDS -- BY AGE (Continued)

Question: How often do you spend a social evening with friends? NOTE: Question not asked in 1972, 1973, 1976, 1980, 1984, 1987.

Responses: DL = Almost every day WL = Once or twice a week SM = Several times a month ML = About once a month SY = Several times a year YL = About once a year NV = Never

		YEAR									
AGE	RESP	'74	'75	'77	'78	'82	'83	'85	'86	'88	'89
66+	DL	1%	2%	1%	1%	2%	2%	1%	0%	2%	1%
	WL	10	10	13	11	12	15	10	13	9	15
	SM	13	14	13	13	16	12	10	13	15	10
	ML	13	19	21	10	16	18	19	17	20	21
	SY	19	18	20	23	22	18	21	19	20	21
	YL	12	11	10	13	11	9	12	7	8	10
	NV	32	26	22	28	21	27	26	31	26	21
# SURVEYED		225	231	209	231	257	239	259	263	190	168

****

SOCIALIZING WITH NEIGHBORS

TABLE I: SOCIALIZING WITH NEIGHBORS -- BY TOTAL POPULATION

Question: How often do you spend a social evening with someone who lives in your neighborhood? NOTE: Question not asked in 1972, 1973, 1976, 1980, 1984, 1987.

Responses: DL = Almost every day WL = Once or twice a week SM = Several times a month ML = About once a month SY = Several times a year YL = About once a year NV = Never

	YEAR									
RESPONSE	'74	'75	'77	'78	'82	'83	'85	'86	'88	'89
DL	7%	6%	6%	6%	6%	6%	6%	7%	5%	5%
WL	24	22	22	24	19	20	18	21	21	17
SM	13	13	12	11	12	12	13	11	11	10
ML	17	15	16	12	17	14	14	15	15	15
SY	11	12	13	14	13	12	13	11	13	12
YL	6	8	8	9	10	9	11	9	7	11
NV	22	24	24	25	22	26	26	26	28	31
# SURVEYED	1476	1485	1524	1522	1499	1592	1527	1467	984	999

TABLE II: SOCIALIZING WITH NEIGHBORS -- BY SEX

Question: How often do you spend a social evening with someone who lives in your neighborhood? NOTE: Question not asked in 1972, 1973, 1976, 1980, 1984, 1987.

Responses: DL = Almost every day; WL = Once or twice a week; SM = Several times a month; ML = About once a month; SY = Several times a year; YL = About once a year; NV = Never

SEX	RESP	'74	'75	'77	'78	'82	'83	'85	'86	'88	'89
MALE	DL	7%	7%	6%	6%	5%	5%	6%	5%	5%	5%
	WL	22	23	22	23	20	20	18	21	20	17
	SM	12	15	10	11	12	13	14	13	12	8
	ML	18	13	16	13	17	15	14	13	16	16
	SY	12	12	13	16	16	12	14	13	12	14
	YL	7	8	10	12	9	10	11	8	9	13
	NV	21	22	24	19	20	24	22	26	26	26
# SURVEYED		689	668	688	636	635	688	687	618	435	424
SEX	RESP	'74	'75	'77	'78	'82	'83	'85	'86	'88	'89
FEMALE	DL	8%	6%	6%	6%	6%	6%	5%	8%	5%	5%
	WL	25	22	21	24	19	19	18	21	21	17
	SM	13	12	14	11	13	12	12	10	10	10
	ML	16	16	15	12	17	14	13	16	14	14
	SY	11	12	12	12	12	13	12	10	14	11
	YL	6	8	7	6	11	8	10	10	6	9
	NV	22	25	25	29	24	27	29	25	30	34
# SURVEYED		787	817	836	886	864	904	840	849	549	575

TABLE III: SOCIALIZING WITH NEIGHBORS -- BY RACE

Question: How often do you spend a social evening with someone who lives in your neighborhood? NOTE: Question not asked in 1972, 1973, 1976, 1980, 1984, 1987.

Responses: DL = Almost every day; WL = Once or twice a week; SM = Several times a month; ML = About once a month; SY = Several times a year; YL = About once a year; NV = Never

		YEAR									
RACE	RESP	'74	'75	'77	'78	'82	'83	'85	'86	'88	'89
WHITE	DL	7%	6%	5%	6%	5%	5%	5%	6%	4%	4%
	WL	23	22	21	23	20	19	18	20	20	17
	SM	12	13	12	11	12	12	14	11	11	10
	ML	18	16	16	13	17	15	14	15	16	15
	SY	12	13	13	14	14	13	14	11	14	13
	YL	7	8	9	9	11	10	11	10	8	11
	NV	21	23	24	24	21	26	25	26	28	30
# SURVEYED		1298	1318	1335	1349	1316	1409	1333	1246	825	858
RACE	RESP	'74	'75	'77	'78	'82	'83	'85	'86	'88	'89
BLACK	DL	13%	9%	13%	9%	10%	9%	11%	13%	6%	12%
	WL	26	25	25	29	19	26	21	24	28	21
	SM	15	12	14	8	15	10	11	10	11	5
	ML	12	7	11	8	12	13	11	14	13	13
	SY	6	7	10	6	10	7	8	9	6	9
	YL	3	9	4	4	8	6	9	4	2	7
	NV	26	31	24	36	26	28	29	25	33	34
# SURVEYED		171	163	174	157	156	165	150	184	125	102
RACE	RESP	'74	'75	'77	'78	'82	'83	'85	'86	'88	'89
OTHER	DL	0%	25%	7%	0%	4%	17%	9%	5%	6%	10%
	WL	14	25	20	25	7	6	18	30	18	10
	SM	29	0	20	19	11	6	9	14	15	8
	ML	14	0	7	13	33	11	9	19	15	18
	SY	0	25	13	13	11	22	14	5	18	10
	YL	0	0	0	13	0	11	9	3	0	5
	NV	43	25	33	19	33	28	32	24	29	38
# SURVEYED		7	4	15	16	27	18	44	37	34	39

TABLE IV: SOCIALIZING WITH NEIGHBORS -- BY AGE

Question: How often do you spend a social evening with someone who lives in your neighborhood? NOTE: Question not asked in 1972, 1973, 1976, 1980, 1984, 1987.

Responses: DL = Almost every day; WL = Once or twice a week; SM = Several times a month; ML = About once a month; SY = Several times a year; YL = About once a year; NV = Never

		YEAR									
AGE	RESP	'74	'75	'77	'78	'82	'83	'85	'86	'88	'89
18-23	DL	21%	17%	14%	10%	15%	16%	18%	20%	10%	18%
	WL	25	23	30	31	27	27	24	26	40	37
	SM	13	15	11	12	15	15	17	5	12	4
	ML	13	10	17	12	14	17	11	18	13	7
	SY	4	9	8	6	2	9	5	9	5	8
	YL	7	4	5	7	11	4	9	9	3	6
	NV	16	22	15	22	17	13	16	13	17	20
# SURVEYED		167	173	164	163	147	127	133	108	94	84
AGE	RESP	'74	'75	'77	'78	'82	'83	'85	'86	'88	'89
24-29	DL	9%	7%	7%	7%	4%	8%	7%	7%	3%	6%
	WL	30	29	30	25	20	28	22	25	28	21
	SM	13	12	15	14	14	11	12	13	14	10
	ML	17	13	12	14	20	16	13	15	13	12
	SY	11	13	10	7	10	8	9	9	8	10
	YL	5	7	5	9	7	6	11	9	6	8
	NV	15	18	20	26	24	24	26	22	27	34
# SURVEYED		211	230	204	244	246	287	217	218	149	146
AGE	RESP	'74	'75	'77	'78	'82	'83	'85	'86	'88	'89
30-35	DL	6%	4%	3%	7%	4%	3%	4%	5%	4%	3%
	WL	26	23	16	20	23	17	20	17	20	20
	SM	18	18	13	12	14	15	16	14	9	11
	ML	13	16	20	14	18	18	15	14	20	21
	SY	10	11	15	18	16	15	10	12	15	8
	YL	6	8	9	10	8	11	15	9	4	11
	NV	22	21	25	20	17	21	19	30	29	25
# SURVEYED		175	171	186	228	204	234	211	220	131	140
AGE	RESP	'74	'75	'77	'78	'82	'83	'85	'86	'88	'89
36-41	DL	3%	3%	5%	4%	5%	2%	3%	4%	3%	4%
	WL	22	24	17	25	14	11	17	18	11	9
	SM	13	9	13	9	12	13	13	13	14	10
	ML	22	16	20	10	20	17	17	22	18	13
	SY	16	15	11	20	12	17	16	11	17	20
	YL	5	9	12	10	18	13	13	11	8	17
	NV	20	24	22	21	20	27	22	21	29	26
# SURVEYED		152	154	167	158	146	173	184	188	125	126

TABLE IV: SOCIALIZING WITH NEIGHBORS -- BY AGE (Continued)

Question: How often do you spend a social evening with someone who lives in your neighborhood? NOTE: Question not asked in 1972, 1973, 1976, 1980, 1984, 1987.

Responses: DL = Almost every day; WL = Once or twice a week; SM = Several times a month; ML = About once a month; SY = Several times a year; YL = About once a year; NV = Never

		YEAR									
AGE	RESP	'74	'75	'77	'78	'82	'83	'85	'86	'88	'89
42-47	DL	2%	4%	1%	5%	3%	2%	4%	6%	4%	4%
	WL	18	20	13	20	15	17	14	21	16	8
	SM	14	13	13	13	12	12	11	11	9	7
	ML	18	20	18	12	22	11	18	16	16	15
	SY	16	12	15	18	17	19	23	16	19	13
	YL	8	10	11	11	9	14	10	14	9	16
	NV	24	20	30	22	21	26	21	17	27	36
# SURVEYED		148	143	147	119	118	145	124	141	108	107
AGE	RESP	'74	'75	'77	'78	'82	'83	'85	'86	'88	'89
48-53	DL	6%	5%	3%	4%	7%	4%	2%	5%	3%	4%
	WL	21	23	20	18	11	17	18	19	5	7
	SM	14	9	10	14	13	15	12	12	19	9
	ML	17	12	19	19	16	13	10	18	18	19
	SY	12	16	16	14	19	14	14	11	16	19
	YL	6	9	8	10	14	10	17	10	8	12
	NV	23	26	24	22	21	26	27	25	31	31
# SURVEYED		145	140	154	130	112	115	131	108	62	85
AGE	RESP	'74	'75	'77	'78	'82	'83	'85	'86	'88	'89
54-59	DL	4%	2%	5%	3%	3%	4%	4%	5%	2%	4%
	WL	22	19	23	22	15	17	13	13	14	8
	SM	12	20	13	8	12	8	16	9	14	8
	ML	20	20	14	13	17	13	11	13	10	18
	SY	16	9	15	18	17	12	14	13	16	18
	YL	7	10	8	7	13	11	6	10	12	8
	NV	19	20	22	29	23	35	36	36	33	35
# SURVEYED		139	126	168	136	144	133	133	98	51	72
AGE	RESP	'74	'75	'77	'78	'82	'83	'85	'86	'88	'89
60-65	DL	3%	4%	3%	7%	2%	4%	2%	3%	7%	4%
	WL	25	19	21	24	20	21	12	19	10	16
	SM	11	11	15	5	12	12	12	11	5	4
	ML	17	12	12	7	12	16	17	13	16	13
	SY	14	13	9	17	16	11	18	15	15	10
	YL	6	11	13	7	8	8	9	9	16	13
	NV	24	30	27	33	31	28	31	30	30	38
# SURVEYED		108	113	116	107	116	132	129	115	73	68

TABLE IV: SOCIALIZING WITH NEIGHBORS -- BY AGE (Continued)

Question: How often do you spend a social evening with someone who lives in your neighborhood? NOTE: Question not asked in 1972, 1973, 1976, 1980, 1984, 1987.

Responses: DL = Almost every day; WL = Once or twice a week; SM = Several times a month; ML = About once a month; SY = Several times a year; YL = About once a year; NV = Never

		YEAR									
AGE	RESP	'74	'75	'77	'78	'82	'83	'85	'86	'88	'89
66+	DL	9%	5%	9%	6%	6%	9%	6%	10%	6%	3%
	WL	20	18	23	24	21	21	19	26	25	21
	SM	9	13	8	10	10	10	10	9	8	14
	ML	16	15	10	10	14	10	12	8	13	14
	SY	8	12	12	12	15	10	13	8	11	9
	YL	6	6	5	7	9	8	7	6	5	6
	NV	31	31	33	32	25	33	33	33	33	32
# SURVEYED		225	231	211	231	258	239	259	265	190	168

****

SOCIALIZING WITH PARENTS

TABLE I: SOCIALIZING WITH PARENTS -- BY TOTAL POPULATION

Question: How often do you spend an evening with your parents? NOTE: Question not asked in 1972-1977, 1980, 1984, 1987.

Responses: NA = No such relatives; DL = Almost daily; WL = Once or twice a week; SM = Several times a month; ML = About monthly; SY = Several times a year; YL = About annually; NV = Never

	YEAR						
RESPONSE	'78	'82	'83	'85	'86	'88	'89
NA	36%	30%	31%	31%	30%	25%	24%
DL	3	7	6	6	7	7	7
WL	14	15	16	11	15	14	16
SM	11	9	10	13	8	9	9
ML	7	11	10	10	10	10	10
SY	13	11	13	12	14	14	14
YL	8	7	8	9	9	8	8
NV	7	9	7	7	7	13	12
# SURVEYED	1526	1488	1594	1527	1461	974	1002

TABLE II: SOCIALIZING WITH PARENTS -- BY SEX

Question: How often do you spend an evening with your parents? NOTE: Question not asked in 1972-1977, 1980, 1984, 1987.

Responses: NA = No such relatives; DL = Almost daily; WL = Once or twice a week; SM = Several times a month; ML = About monthly; SY = Several times a year; YL = About annually; NV = Never

SEX	RESP	'78	'82	'83	'85	'86	'88	'89
M	NA	33%	29%	29%	28%	27%	23%	19%
A	DL	3	7	5	6	6	7	6
L	WL	14	14	14	10	15	13	17
E	SM	10	9	11	12	6	10	11
	ML	9	12	10	12	13	11	10
	SY	14	13	15	14	17	15	15
	YL	9	8	9	10	11	9	10
	NV	7	8	7	7	5	12	14
# SURVEYED		639	629	688	686	616	432	427

SEX	RESP	'78	'82	'83	'85	'86	'88	'89
F	NA	39%	31%	32%	33%	33%	27%	27%
E	DL	3	8	6	6	7	7	7
M	WL	14	15	16	12	15	15	15
A	SM	11	9	9	14	9	9	8
L	ML	6	11	10	9	9	10	10
E	SY	13	10	11	11	11	13	14
	YL	7	7	8	8	7	7	7
	NV	7	9	7	7	9	13	11
# SURVEYED		887	859	906	841	845	542	575

TABLE III: SOCIALIZING WITH PARENTS -- BY RACE

Question: How often do you spend an evening with your parents? NOTE: Question not asked in 1972-1977, 1984, 1987.

Responses: NA = No such relatives; DL = Almost daily; WL = Once or twice a week; SM = Several times a month; ML = About monthly; SY = Several times a year; YL = About annually; NV = Never

RACE	RESP	'78	'82	'83	'85	'86	'88	'89
WHITE	NA	36%	32%	30%	31%	30%	26%	24%
	DL	3	6	5	5	5	6	6
	WL	14	15	16	11	14	13	15
	SM	11	9	10	13	8	10	9
	ML	8	11	11	11	12	11	11
	SY	14	12	13	13	15	14	15
	YL	8	7	8	8	9	8	8
	NV	7	8	7	7	7	13	12
# SURVEYED		1353	1306	1411	1335	1241	818	861

RACE	RESP	'78	'82	'83	'85	'86	'88	'89
BLACK	NA	36%	22%	38%	32%	30%	23%	25%
	DL	8	17	13	11	16	11	11
	WL	18	12	15	10	17	15	19
	SM	8	7	10	12	8	10	8
	ML	4	11	5	6	3	6	6
	SY	9	8	7	13	9	14	8
	YL	8	10	9	7	8	9	9
	NV	9	12	4	9	8	12	15
# SURVEYED		157	156	165	149	183	124	102

RACE	RESP	'78	'82	'83	'85	'86	'88	'89
OTHER	NA	25%	19%	33%	14%	27%	19%	10%
	DL	0	4	6	9	14	13	8
	WL	13	8	6	21	27	16	21
	SM	6	8	11	12	5	6	15
	ML	0	15	6	2	3	3	5
	SY	6	15	11	9	8	13	21
	YL	6	12	0	21	8	13	10
	NV	44	19	28	12	8	19	10
# SURVEYED		16	26	18	43	37	32	39

TABLE IV: SOCIALIZING WITH PARENTS -- BY AGE

Question: How often do you spend an evening with your parents? NOTE: Question not asked in 1972-1977, 1980, 1984, 1987.

Responses: NA = No such relatives; DL = Almost daily; WL = Once or twice a week; SM = Several times a month; ML = About monthly; SY = Several times a year; YL = About annually; NV = Never

AGE	RESP	'78	'82	'83	'85	'86	'88	'89
18-23	NA	35%	2%	13%	2%	1%	0%	1%
	DL	6	25	17	20	27	27	27
	WL	15	29	29	24	25	31	30
	SM	16	11	17	20	12	12	12
	ML	7	11	9	11	10	10	12
	SY	12	10	8	17	11	11	11
	YL	5	5	7	5	9	5	4
	NV	4	6	1	2	5	4	4
# SURVEYED		162	146	128	133	108	93	84
AGE	RESP	'78	'82	'83	'85	'86	'88	'89
24-29	NA	12%	2%	5%	2%	1%	2%	1%
	DL	5	10	10	7	12	9	8
	WL	24	23	26	18	23	24	23
	SM	17	13	18	28	11	15	9
	ML	8	23	13	17	22	15	19
	SY	20	16	16	14	20	23	22
	YL	12	9	10	9	8	7	12
	NV	2	5	2	5	2	4	7
# SURVEYED		244	244	286	215	218	148	145
AGE	RESP	'78	'82	'83	'85	'86	'88	'89
30-35	NA	5%	4%	6%	5%	4%	5%	4%
	DL	5	7	9	7	4	9	7
	WL	22	17	19	13	25	19	22
	SM	17	16	12	19	16	19	18
	ML	11	20	17	15	12	15	11
	SY	21	19	22	22	19	16	20
	YL	13	13	11	14	13	12	11
	NV	7	4	4	6	7	5	7
# SURVEYED		228	203	234	212	219	129	141
AGE	RESP	'78	'82	'83	'85	'86	'88	'89
36-41	NA	14%	12%	9%	5%	10%	11%	3%
	DL	4	4	2	5	8	4	2
	WL	16	20	13	15	16	11	13
	SM	13	12	16	17	9	11	17
	ML	17	19	18	19	17	18	19
	SY	19	14	23	19	20	20	25
	YL	11	12	13	14	12	15	13
	NV	8	5	6	5	9	9	7
# SURVEYED		159	145	173	183	188	123	127

AGE	RESP	'78	'82	'83	'85	'86	'88	'89
42-47	NA	18%	14%	12%	15%	15%	14%	10%
	DL	3	7	3	2	4	6	6
	WL	18	14	23	10	20	14	18
	SM	11	10	10	10	9	6	11
	ML	9	15	14	12	9	13	9
	SY	21	19	13	25	21	24	21
	YL	13	14	16	19	16	11	11
	NV	6	9	8	5	6	12	14
# SURVEYED		119	117	144	124	140	108	108
AGE	RESP	'78	'82	'83	'85	'86	'88	'89
48-53	NA	31%	32%	37%	29%	31%	28%	24%
	DL	3	4	4	5	6	2	7
	WL	12	13	12	8	14	8	18
	SM	9	10	3	11	6	12	5
	ML	11	7	9	15	8	13	8
	SY	15	17	9	12	18	12	15
	YL	5	8	10	11	10	12	9
	NV	13	9	14	10	7	13	14
# SURVEYED		132	112	116	131	108	60	85
AGE	RESP	'78	'82	'83	'85	'86	'88	'89
54-59	NA	58%	52%	58%	50%	49%	25%	40%
	DL	1	8	2	6	3	6	6
	WL	10	10	7	11	8	6	17
	SM	7	2	3	5	4	10	4
	ML	2	3	4	6	5	10	4
	SY	7	7	10	4	7	14	4
	YL	4	2	4	7	7	18	6
	NV	10	16	11	11	15	12	19
# SURVEYED		137	143	134	132	97	51	72
AGE	RESP	'78	'82	'83	'85	'86	'88	'89
60-65	NA	79%	69%	75%	76%	69%	57%	55%
	DL	1	3	1	2	3	1	3
	WL	6	6	6	5	4	4	4
	SM	3	3	2	4	2	1	4
	ML	1	2	2	2	3	1	3
	SY	3	1	5	2	7	1	3
	YL	2	3	1	1	4	1	1
	NV	6	12	8	10	8	32	26
# SURVEYED		107	116	132	130	114	72	69

TABLE IV: SOCIALIZING WITH PARENTS -- BY AGE (Continued)

Question: How often do you spend an evening with your parents? NOTE: Question not asked in 1972-1977, 1980, 1984, 1987.

Responses: NA = No such relatives; DL = Almost daily; WL = Once or twice a week; SM = Several times a month; ML = About monthly; SY = Several times a year; YL = About annually; NV = Never

AGE	RESP	'78	'82	'83	'85	'86	'88	'89
		YEAR						
66+	NA	87%	82%	82%	83%	87%	71%	74%
	DL	0	0	0	2	1	1	1
	WL	0	1	2	2	0	2	3
	SM	0	2	0	0	0	0	1
	ML	0	0	0	0	0	0	1
	SY	0	1	2	0	1	2	1
	YL	1	1	0	1	2	0	1
	NV	11	13	13	11	9	25	20
# SURVEYED		232	253	240	260	263	189	168

****

SOCIALIZING WITH RELATIVES

TABLE I: SOCIALIZING WITH RELATIVES -- BY TOTAL POPULATION

Question: How often do you spend a social evening with relatives? NOTE: Question not asked in 1972-1973, 1976, 1980, 1984, 1987.

Responses: DL = Almost every day; WL = Once or twice a week; SM = Several times a month; ML = About once a month; SY = Several times a year; YL = About once a year; NV = Never

RESPONSE	'74	'75	'77	'78	'82	'83	'85	'86	'88	'89
	YEAR									
DL	9%	7%	8%	7%	8%	6%	7%	10%	10%	7%
WL	29	32	29	29	27	26	28	27	27	26
SM	19	17	18	19	18	20	19	15	18	16
ML	16	16	17	14	17	16	16	17	15	16
SY	16	16	16	19	18	19	18	19	18	21
YL	8	7	6	8	8	7	7	8	8	7
NV	3	5	5	4	4	5	4	5	5	6
# SURVEYED	1482	1488	1526	1526	1497	1594	1526	1464	984	1001

TABLE II: SOCIALIZING WITH RELATIVES -- BY SEX

Question: How often do you spend a social evening with relatives? NOTE: Question not asked in 1972-1973, 1976, 1980, 1984, 1987.

Responses: DL = Almost every day WL = Once or twice a week SM = Several times a month ML = About once a month SY = Several times a year YL = About once a year NV = Never

SEX	RESP	'74	'75	'77	'78	'82	'83	'85	'86	'88	'89
M	DL	9%	5%	7%	6%	8%	6%	6%	7%	8%	8%
A	WL	26	31	27	27	24	25	26	24	26	25
L	SM	20	15	19	18	18	18	19	15	18	16
E	ML	16	19	19	16	16	17	18	19	14	15
	SY	16	17	17	21	21	21	20	21	21	23
	YL	9	9	6	9	9	8	8	9	10	8
	NV	3	4	5	4	4	6	4	5	4	4
# SURVEYED		691	669	689	639	634	689	688	617	437	426
SEX	RESP	'74	'75	'77	'78	'82	'83	'85	'86	'88	'89
F	DL	9%	9%	10%	8%	9%	7%	8%	12%	11%	7%
E	WL	31	33	30	30	30	27	30	29	28	27
M	SM	19	18	17	20	17	22	20	15	19	17
A	ML	16	14	16	13	17	15	15	15	15	17
L	SY	15	16	16	18	16	17	18	17	17	19
E	YL	7	6	6	8	7	7	6	7	5	6
	NV	4	5	5	4	4	5	4	5	5	7
# SURVEYED		791	819	837	887	863	905	838	847	547	575

TABLE III: SOCIALIZING WITH RELATIVES -- BY RACE

Question: How often do you spend a social evening with relatives? NOTE: Question not asked in 1972-1973, 1976, 1980, 1984, 1987.

Responses: DL = Almost every day; WL = Once or twice a week; SM = Several times a month; ML = About once a month; SY = Several times a year; YL = About once a year; NV = Never

		YEAR									
RACE	RESP	'74	'75	'77	'78	'82	'83	'85	'86	'88	'89
WHITE	DL	8%	7%	7%	6%	7%	6%	6%	7%	8%	7%
	WL	30	32	30	28	28	26	28	27	26	27
	SM	19	17	18	20	18	21	20	15	20	16
	ML	16	16	18	15	17	16	17	18	15	16
	SY	17	17	17	20	19	20	19	19	19	21
	YL	7	7	6	8	8	7	7	8	7	7
	NV	3	4	4	4	4	5	4	5	4	5
# SURVEYED		1302	1321	1335	1352	1314	1412	1333	1243	825	860
RACE	RESP	'74	'75	'77	'78	'82	'83	'85	'86	'88	'89
BLACK	DL	17%	12%	18%	17%	21%	11%	14%	22%	19%	12%
	WL	21	31	24	35	22	30	26	22	29	25
	SM	21	14	16	14	17	17	17	17	14	16
	ML	17	17	14	9	17	12	15	9	10	14
	SY	10	13	10	15	13	14	15	13	10	16
	YL	11	6	9	8	6	10	8	9	10	8
	NV	3	6	9	2	4	5	5	7	7	10
# SURVEYED		173	163	176	158	156	164	149	184	125	102
RACE	RESP	'74	'75	'77	'78	'82	'83	'85	'86	'88	'89
OTHER	DL	0%	0%	0%	19%	11%	11%	9%	24%	12%	5%
	WL	29	25	27	19	37	28	32	38	32	23
	SM	14	25	7	19	15	6	20	3	6	26
	ML	29	25	13	13	11	28	7	5	12	21
	SY	0	0	27	13	15	0	23	16	29	18
	YL	14	0	13	0	4	6	9	3	3	5
	NV	14	25	13	19	7	22	0	11	6	3
# SURVEYED		7	4	15	16	27	18	44	37	34	39

TABLE IV: SOCIALIZING WITH RELATIVES -- BY AGE

Question: How often do you spend a social evening with relatives? NOTE: Question not asked in 1972-1973, 1976, 1980, 1984, 1987.

Responses: DL = Almost every day WL = Once or twice a week SM = Several times a month
ML = About once a month SY = Several times a year YL = About once a year
NV = Never

		YEAR									
AGE	RESP	'74	'75	'77	'78	'82	'83	'85	'86	'88	'89
18-23	DL	20%	15%	16%	12%	14%	9%	15%	20%	21%	17%
	WL	37	35	35	31	33	31	25	23	27	26
	SM	10	16	18	19	11	18	14	17	17	12
	ML	13	9	13	12	16	14	14	16	14	15
	SY	13	17	10	18	11	17	23	14	16	18
	YL	4	4	6	7	13	9	7	6	5	10
	NV	4	4	2	1	3	2	3	4	0	2
# SURVEYED		168	173	164	163	147	128	133	108	94	84
AGE	RESP	'74	'75	'77	'78	'82	'83	'85	'86	'88	'89
24-29	DL	7%	9%	12%	9%	9%	9%	6%	10%	13%	9%
	WL	30	37	28	37	31	34	38	28	32	28
	SM	28	20	18	23	18	22	21	17	18	18
	ML	14	17	15	11	18	13	11	22	17	21
	SY	11	8	16	14	16	15	18	16	12	16
	YL	9	6	8	7	6	6	5	5	4	6
	NV	1	3	3	1	3	2	1	3	3	3
# SURVEYED		211	231	204	243	246	287	216	218	149	145
AGE	RESP	'74	'75	'77	'78	'82	'83	'85	'86	'88	'89
30-35	DL	7%	4%	7%	6%	5%	6%	9%	8%	12%	5%
	WL	25	35	28	31	22	26	23	30	28	25
	SM	21	20	20	20	28	21	22	20	23	18
	ML	20	15	23	15	16	15	18	16	12	21
	SY	18	15	13	20	19	22	17	17	15	21
	YL	7	9	6	7	7	8	7	7	5	6
	NV	2	2	2	2	3	2	2	1	4	4
# SURVEYED		175	171	188	229	203	234	212	220	131	141
AGE	RESP	'74	'75	'77	'78	'82	'83	'85	'86	'88	'89
36-41	DL	10%	8%	6%	4%	6%	3%	3%	9%	7%	2%
	WL	24	23	26	25	28	18	26	27	22	24
	SM	18	16	20	19	14	23	20	13	15	17
	ML	14	21	20	16	22	25	21	18	18	20
	SY	18	24	17	21	17	17	17	21	22	28
	YL	14	6	6	8	11	9	11	7	12	8
	NV	3	2	5	6	2	3	3	5	3	2
# SURVEYED		152	154	168	159	146	173	184	188	126	127

TABLE IV: SOCIALIZING WITH RELATIVES -- BY AGE (Continued)

Question: How often do you spend a social evening with relatives? NOTE: Question not asked in 1972-1973, 1976, 1980, 1984, 1987.

Responses: DL = Almost every day; WL = Once or twice a week; SM = Several times a month; ML = About once a month; SY = Several times a year; YL = About once a year; NV = Never

		YEAR									
AGE	RESP	'74	'75	'77	'78	'82	'83	'85	'86	'88	'89
42-47	DL	5%	4%	4%	10%	5%	6%	5%	8%	7%	7%
	WL	27	27	19	24	26	28	24	26	22	28
	SM	15	15	18	21	14	21	17	12	15	18
	ML	15	19	22	15	17	19	16	18	19	11
	SY	23	21	20	18	26	19	24	21	27	23
	YL	10	8	12	10	9	4	11	12	6	6
	NV	6	6	5	3	3	3	3	4	4	6
# SURVEYED		150	143	147	119	118	145	123	141	108	108
AGE	RESP	'74	'75	'77	'78	'82	'83	'85	'86	'88	'89
48-53	DL	9%	5%	9%	7%	10%	7%	7%	10%	5%	8%
	WL	30	29	31	27	20	19	21	21	29	25
	SM	21	21	16	16	19	25	20	13	19	19
	ML	12	18	18	20	9	14	20	15	16	12
	SY	13	16	17	21	25	22	21	21	13	23
	YL	12	8	5	6	10	9	8	13	15	6
	NV	4	4	5	3	8	3	4	6	3	7
# SURVEYED		146	140	154	132	112	116	131	108	62	84
AGE	RESP	'74	'75	'77	'78	'82	'83	'85	'86	'88	'89
54-59	DL	10%	4%	8%	4%	6%	4%	8%	9%	8%	8%
	WL	29	40	38	35	30	26	35	30	22	29
	SM	18	15	19	20	20	20	12	12	20	19
	ML	19	14	10	12	17	16	19	18	8	11
	SY	17	18	16	19	12	20	12	18	27	15
	YL	4	7	3	8	11	6	6	4	12	7
	NV	3	2	7	2	3	9	9	9	4	10
# SURVEYED		139	126	168	137	144	133	133	97	51	72
AGE	RESP	'74	'75	'77	'78	'82	'83	'85	'86	'88	'89
60-65	DL	6%	5%	7%	5%	7%	8%	4%	8%	1%	7%
	WL	31	35	30	23	28	27	27	27	24	35
	SM	17	12	19	16	18	21	25	17	22	15
	ML	21	19	16	16	22	15	12	19	11	12
	SY	17	15	20	22	16	17	22	18	32	18
	YL	6	9	4	11	3	8	8	8	5	6
	NV	2	5	4	8	6	3	3	4	4	7
# SURVEYED		108	113	116	106	116	132	130	114	74	68

TABLE IV: SOCIALIZING WITH RELATIVES -- BY AGE (Continued)

Question: How often do you spend a social evening with relatives? NOTE: Question not asked in 1972-1973, 1976, 1980, 1984, 1987.

Responses: DL = Almost every day WL = Once or twice a week SM = Several times a month ML = About once a month SY = Several times a year YL = About once a year NV = Never

AGE	RESP	'74	'75	'77	'78	'82	'83	'85	'86	'88	'89
		YEAR									
66+	DL	9%	7%	6%	6%	12%	5%	7%	10%	7%	7%
	WL	26	27	26	23	26	24	29	25	29	24
	SM	21	13	13	16	14	13	19	14	19	14
	ML	18	17	19	15	14	14	17	11	13	15
	SY	15	17	20	21	22	20	17	20	14	21
	YL	6	8	6	11	6	8	3	9	8	9
	NV	5	10	10	8	7	17	7	11	11	11
# SURVEYED		227	232	210	232	258	239	258	264	188	169

****

SOCIALIZING WITH SIBLINGS

TABLE I: SOCIALIZING WITH SIBLINGS -- BY TOTAL POPULATION

Question: How often do you spend an evening with your brother or sister? NOTE: Question not asked in 1972-1977, 1980, 1984, 1987.

Responses: NA = No such relatives DL = Almost daily WL = Once or twice a week SM = Several times a month ML = About monthly SY = Several times a year YL = About annually NV = Never

RESPONSE	'78	'82	'83	'85	'86	'88	'89
	YEAR						
NA	11%	9%	11%	9%	8%	8%	7%
DL	5	6	4	5	6	6	5
WL	14	13	14	11	13	14	13
SM	12	12	13	15	11	11	10
ML	11	14	13	13	14	13	14
SY	22	22	22	21	22	22	24
YL	16	15	13	17	16	15	16
NV	10	8	10	10	10	11	10
# SURVEYED	1523	1493	1591	1526	1458	975	1001

TABLE II: SOCIALIZING WITH SIBLINGS -- BY SEX

Question: How often do you spend an evening with your brother or sister? NOTE: Question not asked in 1972-1977, 1980, 1984, 1987.

Responses: NA = No such relatives; DL = Almost daily; WL = Once or twice a week; SM = Several times a month; ML = About monthly; SY = Several times a year; YL = About annually; NV = Never

SEX	RESP	'78	'82	'83	'85	'86	'88	'89
M	NA	11%	9%	9%	8%	7%	7%	7%
A	DL	5	6	3	4	5	5	4
L	WL	11	11	12	10	11	13	13
E	SM	10	11	12	14	9	9	10
	ML	12	15	14	14	15	13	13
	SY	23	24	24	22	25	25	23
	YL	19	17	15	19	16	17	19
	NV	10	6	11	9	11	10	10
# SURVEYED		638	634	688	686	615	432	427

SEX	RESP	'78	'82	'83	'85	'86	'88	'89
F	NA	11%	10%	12%	10%	8%	8%	7%
E	DL	5	6	5	5	7	6	6
M	WL	16	14	15	12	14	15	13
A	SM	13	12	14	15	13	13	10
L	ML	11	14	12	12	14	14	15
E	SY	20	21	21	21	19	19	25
	YL	14	14	11	15	15	14	13
	NV	10	10	10	10	10	11	10
# SURVEYED		885	859	903	840	843	543	574

TABLE III: SOCIALIZING WITH SIBLINGS -- BY RACE

Question: How often do you spend an evening with your brother or sister? NOTE: Question not asked in 1972-1977, 1980, 1984, 1987.

Responses: NA = No such relatives; DL = Almost daily; WL = Once or twice a week; SM = Several times a month; ML = About monthly; SY = Several times a year; YL = About annually; NV = Never

RACE	RESP	'78	'82	'83	'85	'86	'88	'89
WHITE	NA	11%	10%	11%	9%	8%	8%	7%
	DL	3	5	3	4	4	4	4
	WL	13	12	13	11	11	12	12
	SM	12	11	13	14	11	12	10
	ML	11	15	14	14	15	14	15
	SY	23	23	23	22	24	23	25
	YL	17	16	13	17	16	15	16
	NV	10	8	10	10	10	11	10
# SURVEYED		1349	1311	1409	1334	1239	818	860
BLACK	NA	11%	8%	10%	13%	7%	6%	7%
	DL	18	17	13	11	18	14	12
	WL	18	16	23	13	22	23	17
	SM	12	15	14	19	12	8	11
	ML	8	8	7	9	10	10	10
	SY	15	15	13	12	11	15	13
	YL	11	12	10	14	13	13	16
	NV	8	9	9	9	8	13	16
# SURVEYED		158	155	164	149	182	124	102

RACE	RESP	'78	'82	'83	'85	'86	'88	'89
OTHER	NA	13%	4%	11%	7%	0%	0%	8%
	DL	0	11	11	12	16	18	8
	WL	6	26	6	16	24	33	21
	SM	13	15	22	19	8	6	18
	ML	19	11	6	5	14	3	10
	SY	13	15	11	21	14	15	28
	YL	0	11	6	12	5	21	5
	NV	38	7	28	9	19	3	3
# SURVEYED		16	27	18	43	37	33	39

TABLE IV: SOCIALIZING WITH SIBLINGS -- BY AGE

Question: How often do you spend an evening with your brother or sister? NOTE: Question not asked in 1972-1977, 1980, 1984, 1987.

Responses: NA = No such relatives; DL = Almost daily; WL = Once or twice a week; SM = Several times a month; ML = About monthly; SY = Several times a year; YL = About annually; NV = Never

AGE	RESP	'78	'82	'83	'85	'86	'88	'89
18-23	NA	8%	6%	9%	7%	4%	4%	5%
	DL	17	16	17	16	25	17	23
	WL	22	24	21	23	21	27	19
	SM	19	12	16	14	7	16	23
	ML	10	18	13	12	13	11	11
	SY	15	14	11	18	14	16	11
	YL	6	5	6	7	10	5	4
	NV	2	4	6	2	6	4	6
# SURVEYED		162	147	128	132	108	94	84
24-29	NA	6%	4%	3%	5%	2%	5%	2%
	DL	7	7	6	6	9	7	8
	WL	19	17	21	15	19	20	17
	SM	16	14	20	26	13	12	15
	ML	14	20	18	14	20	18	15
	SY	19	18	19	19	21	22	22
	YL	14	16	8	13	10	10	14
	NV	5	4	5	4	6	6	6
# SURVEYED		244	245	287	216	218	147	144
30-35	NA	6%	6%	4%	5%	4%	2%	5%
	DL	3	5	5	5	4	10	6
	WL	13	11	13	12	20	17	15
	SM	14	16	18	17	17	14	13
	ML	13	18	11	14	14	15	17
	SY	23	25	26	26	18	27	26
	YL	19	13	17	17	17	9	14
	NV	8	6	6	5	6	6	4
# SURVEYED		229	204	234	212	220	129	141
36-41	NA	14%	8%	12%	7%	4%	6%	6%
	DL	1	4	3	3	5	2	0
	WL	10	14	12	9	9	13	10
	SM	15	12	13	13	10	12	8
	ML	12	17	15	18	19	17	19
	SY	25	24	21	22	27	20	31
	YL	12	14	13	21	19	22	20
	NV	11	6	10	7	8	8	6
# SURVEYED		159	146	173	184	188	125	127

AGE	RESP	'78	'82	'83	'85	'86	'88	'89
42-47	NA	14%	9%	13%	11%	9%	4%	6%
	DL	4	3	2	1	3	4	2
	WL	9	12	9	6	8	11	10
	SM	5	13	11	6	10	10	8
	ML	8	11	16	14	17	13	17
	SY	31	32	23	27	22	24	33
	YL	19	17	15	28	21	22	11
	NV	9	3	11	6	10	11	12
# SURVEYED		118	117	145	124	140	107	108
48-53	NA	10%	13%	9%	2%	7%	7%	5%
	DL	2	4	3	2	4	3	2
	WL	13	6	9	6	8	5	12
	SM	8	11	7	15	9	11	7
	ML	10	7	16	14	11	11	11
	SY	31	30	21	25	33	25	31
	YL	14	21	16	21	17	25	19
	NV	12	8	17	15	11	13	13
# SURVEYED		131	112	116	130	107	61	84
54-59	NA	12%	10%	14%	9%	15%	6%	8%
	DL	1	3	0	2	0	2	1
	WL	12	8	11	8	11	8	15
	SM	10	16	13	15	9	10	6
	ML	11	8	4	12	9	10	14
	SY	21	20	29	20	24	22	21
	YL	20	24	17	18	17	31	22
	NV	12	10	12	17	15	10	13
# SURVEYED		137	144	133	133	96	49	72
60-65	NA	8%	11%	11%	13%	9%	16%	16%
	DL	5	4	2	3	4	1	3
	WL	13	5	13	12	7	4	14
	SM	12	5	10	12	10	9	9
	ML	9	13	14	12	18	9	14
	SY	20	30	26	22	21	24	17
	YL	21	18	14	18	16	18	19
	NV	12	13	11	8	15	18	7
# SURVEYED		107	114	132	130	113	74	69

TABLE IV: SOCIALIZING WITH SIBLINGS -- BY AGE (Continued)

Question: How often do you spend an evening with your brother or sister? NOTE: Question not asked in 1972-1977, 1980, 1984, 1987.

Responses: NA = No such relatives; DL = Almost daily; WL = Once or twice a week; SM = Several times a month; ML = About monthly; SY = Several times a year; YL = About annually; NV = Never

AGE	RESP	'78	'82	'83	'85	'86	'88	'89
		YEAR						
66+	NA	21%	18%	22%	19%	18%	15%	11%
	DL	2	7	2	4	3	3	4
	WL	8	11	11	8	10	12	9
	SM	5	7	4	10	10	7	6
	ML	8	12	8	9	6	12	11
	SY	17	17	22	17	21	19	20
	YL	20	13	13	15	17	12	18
	NV	19	16	18	18	16	20	22
# SURVEYED		230	257	236	258	262	188	169

****

TELEVISION VIEWING

TABLE I: TELEVISION VIEWING -- BY TOTAL POPULATION

Question: On an average day, about how many hours do you personally watch television? NOTE: Question not asked in 1972-1974, 1976, 1984, 1987.

Responses: 0 = 0 hours; 1 = 1; 2 = 2; 3 = 3; 4 = 4; 5 = 5-6; 6 = 7-8; 7 = 9-10; 8 = 11-12; 9 = 13 or more hours

RESPONSE	'75	'77	'78	'80	'82	'83	'85	'86	'88	'89
	YEAR									
0	4%	4%	6%	8%	4%	6%	5%	4%	3%	3%
1	17	21	21	18	21	19	18	18	19	18
2	27	25	27	24	25	25	26	27	25	30
3	20	20	19	19	19	20	20	20	19	17
4	15	13	13	13	14	13	14	13	14	14
5	13	11	10	13	11	12	12	11	14	11
6	3	3	2	3	3	3	3	3	3	3
7	1	1	1	1	1	1	1	2	1	1
8	1	1	1	0	1	1	0	1	1	1
9	0	1	0	1	1	0	1	1	1	1
# SURVEYED	1483	1525	1528	1454	1504	1595	1523	1466	979	998

TABLE II: TELEVISION VIEWING -- BY SEX

Question: On an average day, about how many hours do you personally watch television? NOTE: Question not asked in 1972-1974, 1976, 1984, 1987.

Responses: 0 = 0 hours 1 = 1 2 = 2 3 = 3 4 = 4
5 = 5-6 6 = 7-8 7 = 9-10 8 = 11-12 9 = 13 or more hours

		YEAR									
SEX	RESP	'75	'77	'78	'80	'82	'83	'85	'86	'88	'89
M	0	3%	4%	7%	9%	4%	5%	5%	5%	3%	3%
A	1	20	24	23	20	22	20	20	19	20	19
L	2	29	28	29	26	27	26	28	28	29	33
E	3	19	20	19	19	21	21	22	21	20	20
	4	14	10	12	14	12	13	12	13	13	12
	5	11	10	8	9	10	11	8	8	11	10
	6	2	2	2	3	2	3	2	3	2	2
	7	0	1	0	0	0	1	1	1	1	1
	8	1	0	0	0	1	0	0	1	1	1
	9	0	0	0	0	0	0	1	1	1	0
# SURVEYED		668	690	643	637	638	689	685	620	435	428
SEX	RESP	'75	'77	'78	'80	'82	'83	'85	'86	'88	'89
F	0	4%	4%	5%	6%	5%	6%	5%	4%	3%	4%
E	1	15	18	19	17	20	17	16	17	18	18
M	2	25	23	26	23	23	25	24	25	22	28
A	3	20	21	19	19	18	20	19	20	19	14
L	4	15	16	13	13	15	13	15	13	15	16
E	5	14	12	12	16	11	13	16	13	16	12
	6	3	4	3	3	4	3	4	4	4	5
	7	2	1	1	2	2	1	1	2	2	1
	8	1	1	1	1	1	1	0	1	1	1
	9	0	1	1	1	1	1	1	1	1	1
# SURVEYED		815	835	885	817	866	906	838	846	544	570

TABLE III: TELEVISION VIEWING -- BY RACE

Question: On an average day, about how many hours do you personally watch television? NOTE: Question not asked in 1972-1974, 1976, 1984, 1987.

Responses: 0 = 0 hours 1 = 1 2 = 2 3 = 3 4 = 4
5 = 5-6 6 = 7-8 7 = 9-10 8 = 11-12 9 = 13 or more hours

		YEAR									
RACE	RESP	'75	'77	'78	'80	'82	'83	'85	'86	'88	'89
WHITE	0	4%	4%	6%	8%	5%	6%	5%	5%	4%	3%
	1	18	22	21	18	21	19	18	19	20	20
	2	27	26	28	25	26	26	26	28	26	31
	3	20	20	19	19	19	20	20	20	19	17
	4	14	13	13	13	13	13	14	13	14	14
	5	12	11	9	13	10	12	12	11	12	10
	6	3	3	2	3	3	2	3	3	2	3
	7	1	1	1	1	1	1	1	1	1	1
	8	0	0	0	0	1	0	0	1	1	1
	9	0	1	0	1	0	0	1	0	1	0
# SURVEYED		1318	1335	1354	1304	1321	1413	1330	1245	823	860
RACE	RESP	'75	'77	'78	'80	'82	'83	'85	'86	'88	'89
BLACK	0	5%	5%	4%	6%	2%	4%	3%	2%	1%	4%
	1	11	11	15	14	13	12	10	9	12	7
	2	20	25	20	16	17	19	27	18	14	21
	3	16	20	16	22	22	24	21	23	20	21
	4	16	15	15	17	17	13	15	17	16	15
	5	20	15	21	16	12	16	18	13	24	18
	6	5	3	3	4	8	6	3	7	8	5
	7	3	2	3	2	3	2	3	5	2	2
	8	3	2	3	2	3	2	0	2	1	4
	9	1	1	1	1	3	2	1	3	2	2
# SURVEYED		161	175	158	140	156	164	150	184	123	99
RACE	RESP	'75	'77	'78	'80	'82	'83	'85	'86	'88	'89
OTHER	0	0%	13%	0%	0%	4%	6%	5%	5%	0%	13%
	1	25	40	38	30	33	33	26	16	15	18
	2	50	7	31	30	15	17	12	30	24	33
	3	0	27	13	20	19	22	26	24	27	10
	4	25	7	0	0	11	11	16	14	12	10
	5	0	0	13	20	15	6	12	5	15	10
	6	0	7	6	0	0	6	2	5	3	3
	7	0	0	0	0	0	0	2	0	3	0
	8	0	0	0	0	4	0	0	0	0	0
	9	0	0	0	0	0	0	0	0	0	3
# SURVEYED		4	15	16	10	27	18	43	37	33	39

TABLE IV: TELEVISION VIEWING -- BY AGE

Question: On an average day, about how many hours do you personally watch television? NOTE: Question not asked in 1972-1974, 1976, 1984, 1987.

Responses: 0 = 0 hours 1 = 1 2 = 2 3 = 3 4 = 4
5 = 5-6 6 = 7-8 7 = 9-10 8 = 11-12 9 = 13 or more hours

		YEAR									
AGE	RESP	'75	'77	'78	'80	'82	'83	'85	'86	'88	'89
18-23	0	3%	1%	8%	8%	4%	6%	6%	4%	3%	4%
	1	16	18	16	16	16	13	17	15	11	13
	2	23	18	25	23	19	25	20	21	28	25
	3	17	20	17	13	18	21	22	25	16	22
	4	18	16	13	11	16	14	14	8	14	14
	5	17	16	13	18	16	13	11	19	14	11
	6	3	7	3	6	5	6	7	4	9	4
	7	1	1	2	1	2	2	2	3	2	5
	8	2	2	1	2	4	0	1	1	1	2
	9	0	1	1	3	1	0	0	0	3	0
# SURVEYED		173	164	163	154	148	127	132	108	94	83
AGE	RESP	'75	'77	'78	'80	'82	'83	'85	'86	'88	'89
24-29	0	3%	5%	7%	10%	4%	7%	7%	3%	5%	3%
	1	17	18	14	20	22	13	15	20	16	18
	2	23	24	28	21	25	30	25	28	21	37
	3	20	21	19	19	20	17	22	14	22	17
	4	15	15	12	14	11	14	13	15	17	14
	5	16	11	13	12	12	13	13	12	15	9
	6	3	3	5	4	4	3	3	4	2	2
	7	2	1	1	0	0	2	1	2	1	1
	8	0	0	1	1	1	1	0	0	1	0
	9	0	0	0	1	0	0	1	0	0	0
# SURVEYED		229	204	244	200	246	286	215	218	148	145
AGE	RESP	'75	'77	'78	'80	'82	'83	'85	'86	'88	'89
30-35	0	4%	5%	8%	11%	4%	7%	7%	4%	3%	1%
	1	19	26	25	19	23	17	21	17	26	29
	2	27	28	27	27	31	28	23	24	22	32
	3	22	18	19	17	17	20	20	27	24	16
	4	15	11	12	12	10	14	13	16	9	11
	5	9	7	8	13	9	12	12	6	12	8
	6	2	3	1	1	3	2	2	4	2	1
	7	1	2	0	0	1	0	1	0	1	1
	8	1	0	0	0	1	0	0	0	0	1
	9	1	1	0	0	0	0	0	1	0	0
# SURVEYED		171	187	230	215	204	235	210	221	130	142

TABLE IV: TELEVISION VIEWING -- BY AGE (Continued)

Question: On an average day, about how many hours do you personally watch television? NOTE: Question not asked in 1972-1974, 1976, 1984, 1987.

Responses: 0 = 0 hours 1 = 1 2 = 2 3 = 3 4 = 4
5 = 5-6 6 = 7-8 7 = 9-10 8 = 11-12 9 = 13 or more hours

AGE	RESP	'75	'77	'78	'80	'82	'83	'85	'86	'88	'89
36-41	0	4%	5%	6%	5%	8%	8%	7%	5%	6%	6%
	1	16	26	22	25	25	26	25	20	29	18
	2	25	29	30	28	23	25	29	31	26	34
	3	23	19	19	23	21	18	19	22	18	17
	4	16	13	14	13	14	11	11	9	10	12
	5	11	5	8	5	5	9	7	10	9	7
	6	3	3	0	1	2	1	1	1	1	6
	7	1	0	1	0	1	0	1	1	0	0
	8	1	1	1	0	0	1	0	1	1	0
	9	0	0	0	0	1	2	1	1	1	2
# SURVEYED		153	167	159	150	146	173	183	188	125	125
AGE	RESP	'75	'77	'78	'80	'82	'83	'85	'86	'88	'89
42-47	0	5%	4%	5%	12%	4%	5%	6%	6%	3%	5%
	1	23	26	24	22	29	22	19	24	22	28
	2	29	20	34	25	28	29	31	33	33	27
	3	18	27	17	21	19	20	26	19	17	18
	4	10	14	11	8	14	13	6	6	14	9
	5	10	6	8	12	4	8	9	6	7	8
	6	1	1	1	0	1	1	2	2	1	3
	7	2	1	0	1	1	1	1	1	3	0
	8	1	0	0	0	0	1	0	1	0	2
	9	0	1	0	0	0	0	1	1	0	1
# SURVEYED		143	147	119	116	119	145	124	140	108	108
AGE	RESP	'75	'77	'78	'80	'82	'83	'85	'86	'88	'89
48-53	0	2%	5%	5%	7%	8%	4%	5%	8%	3%	1%
	1	19	27	24	22	24	28	18	23	21	22
	2	35	33	32	26	29	25	36	27	29	36
	3	24	17	21	13	18	20	20	14	18	16
	4	10	10	8	11	12	12	11	12	8	11
	5	6	7	6	14	5	8	8	10	15	11
	6	2	0	1	3	0	1	1	3	2	2
	7	1	0	2	2	0	2	1	1	2	0
	8	0	1	1	1	2	0	1	2	2	0
	9	1	1	0	1	2	1	1	0	2	0
# SURVEYED		139	154	131	122	111	116	131	108	62	85

TABLE IV: TELEVISION VIEWING -- BY AGE (Continued)

Question: On an average day, about how many hours do you personally watch television? NOTE: Question not asked in 1972-1974, 1976, 1984, 1987.

Responses: 0 = 0 hours 1 = 1 2 = 2 3 = 3 4 = 4
5 = 5-6 6 = 7-8 7 = 9-10 8 = 11-12 9 = 13 or more hours

		YEAR									
AGE	RESP	'75	'77	'78	'80	'82	'83	'85	'86	'88	'89
54-59	0	4%	4%	4%	7%	0%	4%	2%	3%	0%	7%
	1	17	18	31	19	27	26	23	12	22	11
	2	27	25	21	27	26	25	29	30	31	34
	3	18	23	21	18	19	21	17	26	18	17
	4	18	14	12	15	13	13	17	14	10	16
	5	12	14	6	12	8	8	9	7	12	13
	6	2	2	4	0	3	1	2	3	4	1
	7	2	1	0	2	2	1	0	3	2	0
	8	0	0	0	1	0	0	0	1	0	0
	9	0	0	0	0	1	1	0	1	2	0
# SURVEYED		125	168	137	135	144	134	133	98	51	70
AGE	RESP	'75	'77	'78	'80	'82	'83	'85	'86	'88	'89
60-65	0	4%	3%	2%	4%	4%	5%	2%	1%	0%	1%
	1	15	18	21	12	12	20	13	17	18	19
	2	27	32	29	20	23	18	27	26	31	19
	3	18	25	21	25	21	23	20	17	22	15
	4	17	10	13	14	20	16	19	23	18	22
	5	14	10	9	17	14	14	15	8	11	13
	6	4	0	3	4	3	2	2	3	1	6
	7	0	1	1	5	2	0	1	2	0	3
	8	2	0	0	0	0	1	0	1	0	0
	9	1	1	0	0	1	1	2	2	0	1
# SURVEYED		113	117	107	114	116	132	129	115	74	68
AGE	RESP	'75	'77	'78	'80	'82	'83	'85	'86	'88	'89
66+	0	4%	4%	6%	5%	4%	4%	3%	5%	3%	2%
	1	15	12	16	12	13	12	12	12	10	8
	2	26	20	24	21	24	18	21	22	17	25
	3	18	17	16	22	19	25	19	19	17	17
	4	13	17	16	18	16	13	16	14	20	21
	5	17	22	15	16	16	19	20	17	22	18
	6	4	3	3	4	5	6	5	6	5	6
	7	0	1	1	1	2	2	1	3	2	1
	8	1	1	1	0	1	0	1	2	2	2
	9	0	1	1	1	1	0	2	0	2	1
# SURVEYED		232	210	231	240	258	240	259	263	186	169

****

X-RATED MOVIE VIEWING

TABLE I: X-RATED MOVIE VIEWING -- BY TOTAL POPULATION

Question: Have you seen an X-rated movie in the last year? NOTE: Question not asked in 1972, 1974, 1977, 1982, 1985.

Responses: Yes; No

	YEAR										
RESPONSE	'73	'75	'76	'78	'80	'83	'84	'86	'87	'88	'89
YES	25%	19%	18%	15%	16%	20%	24%	25%	28%	27%	23%
NO	75	81	82	85	84	80	76	75	72	73	77
# SURVEYED	1491	1482	1492	1524	1462	1588	1464	1460	1456	992	102

TABLE II: X-RATED MOVIE VIEWING -- BY SEX

Question: Have you seen an X-rated movie in the last year? NOTE: Question not asked in 1972, 1974, 1977, 1982, 1985.

Responses: Yes; No

		YEAR										
SEX	RESP	'73	'75	'76	'78	'80	'83	'84	'86	'87	'88	'89
M	YES	31%	24%	26%	20%	20%	25%	30%	31%	35%	35%	31%
	NO	69	76	74	80	80	75	70	69	65	65	69
# SURVEYED		691	667	665	640	639	683	596	617	637	436	443
SEX	RESP	'73	'75	'76	'78	'80	'83	'84	'86	'87	'88	'89
F	YES	20%	15%	12%	11%	13%	15%	19%	20%	22%	20%	17%
	NO	80	85	88	89	87	85	81	80	78	80	83
# SURVEYED		800	815	827	884	823	905	868	843	819	556	583

TABLE III: X-RATED MOVIE VIEWING -- BY RACE

Question: Have you seen an X-rated movie in the last year? NOTE: Question not asked in 1972, 1974, 1977, 1982, 1985.

Responses: Yes; No

		YEAR										
RACE	RESP	'73	'75	'76	'78	'80	'83	'84	'86	'87	'88	'89
WHITE	YES	25%	18%	18%	14%	15%	19%	23%	25%	27%	24%	23%
	NO	75	82	82	86	85	81	77	75	73	76	77
# SURVEYED		1299	1317	1357	1351	1313	1410	1243	1241	1215	833	874
RACE	RESP	'73	'75	'76	'78	'80	'83	'84	'86	'87	'88	'89
BLACK	YES	28%	23%	22%	20%	20%	27%	28%	27%	31%	44%	26%
	NO	72	77	78	80	80	73	72	73	69	56	74
# SURVEYED		180	161	126	157	139	161	169	183	189	116	110
RACE	RESP	'73	'75	'76	'78	'80	'83	'84	'86	'87	'88	'89
OTHER	YES	33%	50%	22%	25%	30%	12%	33%	22%	25%	37%	12%
	NO	67	50	78	75	70	88	67	78	75	63	88
# SURVEYED		12	4	9	16	10	17	52	36	52	43	42

TABLE IV: X-RATED MOVIE VIEWING -- BY AGE

Question: Have you seen an X-rated movie in the last year? NOTE: Question not asked in 1972, 1974, 1977, 1982, 1985.

Responses: Yes; No

		YEAR										
AGE	RESP	'73	'75	'76	'78	'80	'83	'84	'86	'87	'88	'89
18-23	YES	55%	38%	38%	23%	23%	26%	40%	42%	44%	51%	45%
	NO	45	62	62	77	77	74	60	58	56	49	55
# SURVEYED		170	173	162	162	155	128	160	108	126	93	92
AGE	RESP	'73	'75	'76	'78	'80	'83	'84	'86	'87	'88	'89
24-29	YES	42%	34%	32%	23%	24%	27%	32%	40%	38%	39%	38%
	NO	58	66	68	77	76	73	68	60	62	61	62
# SURVEYED		210	230	226	242	201	286	232	216	193	145	141

TABLE IV: X-RATED MOVIE VIEWING -- BY AGE (Continued)

Question: Have you seen an X-rated movie in the last year? NOTE: Question not asked in 1972, 1974, 1977, 1982, 1985.

Responses: Yes; No

		YEAR										
AGE	RESP	'73	'75	'76	'78	'80	'83	'84	'86	'87	'88	'89
30-35	YES	32%	26%	25%	22%	22%	28%	26%	35%	42%	33%	33%
	NO	68	74	75	78	78	72	74	65	58	67	67
# SURVEYED		164	170	185	230	215	236	198	219	218	126	146
AGE	RESP	'73	'75	'76	'78	'80	'83	'84	'86	'87	'88	'89
36-41	YES	26%	14%	20%	14%	23%	24%	29%	33%	36%	29%	31%
	NO	74	86	80	86	77	76	71	67	64	71	69
# SURVEYED		175	154	155	160	149	173	187	187	184	126	131
AGE	RESP	'73	'75	'76	'78	'80	'83	'84	'86	'87	'88	'89
42-47	YES	27%	15%	9%	18%	15%	22%	26%	26%	35%	33%	19%
	NO	73	85	91	82	85	78	74	74	65	67	81
# SURVEYED		146	142	113	118	117	145	125	141	157	104	105
AGE	RESP	'73	'75	'76	'78	'80	'83	'84	'86	'87	'88	'89
48-53	YES	13%	15%	14%	14%	14%	13%	24%	19%	18%	25%	14%
	NO	87	85	86	86	86	87	76	81	82	75	86
# SURVEYED		150	140	132	133	121	115	102	108	125	57	96
AGE	RESP	'73	'75	'76	'78	'80	'83	'84	'86	'87	'88	'89
54-59	YES	19%	8%	9%	4%	13%	8%	12%	10%	12%	17%	11%
	NO	81	92	91	96	88	92	88	90	88	83	89
# SURVEYED		155	125	128	135	136	131	114	97	97	66	63
AGE	RESP	'73	'75	'76	'78	'80	'83	'84	'86	'87	'88	'89
60-65	YES	6%	5%	5%	5%	8%	12%	13%	14%	13%	12%	5%
	NO	94	95	95	95	92	88	87	86	87	88	95
# SURVEYED		120	113	134	105	119	131	111	113	100	78	74
AGE	RESP	'73	'75	'76	'78	'80	'83	'84	'86	'87	'88	'89
66+	YES	2%	4%	4%	5%	3%	8%	7%	3%	6%	7%	3%
	NO	98	96	96	95	97	92	93	97	94	93	97
# SURVEYED		197	230	251	232	240	239	230	265	252	193	177

****

ACQUAINTANCES WITH AIDS

TABLE I: ACQUAINTANCES WITH AIDS -- BY TOTAL POPULATION

Question: How many people have you known personally, either living or dead, who came down with the disease called AIDS? NOTE: Question not asked in 1972-1987.

Responses: 0 = 0; 1 = 1; 2 = 2; etc.; 8 = 8 or more

	YEAR	
RESPONSE	'88	'89
0	91%	91%
1	6	6
2	1	2
3	1	1
4	0	0
5	0	0
6	0	0
7	0	0
8	0	0
# SURVEYED	1480	1535

TABLE II: ACQUAINTANCES WITH AIDS -- BY SEX

Question: How many people have you known personally, either living or dead, who came down with the disease called AIDS? NOTE: Question not asked in 1972-1987.

Responses: 0 = 0; 1 = 1; 2 = 2; etc.; 8 = 8 or more

		YEAR	
SEX	RESP	'88	'89
MALE	0	92%	90%
	1	5	7
	2	1	2
	3	0	1
	4	0	0
	5	0	0
	6	0	0
	7	1	0
	8	0	0
# SURVEYED		638	660

		YEAR	
SEX	RESP	'88	'89
FEMALE	0	90%	92%
	1	7	6
	2	2	2
	3	1	0
	4	0	0
	5	0	0
	6	0	0
	7	0	0
	8	0	0
# SURVEYED		842	875

TABLE III: ACQUAINTANCES WITH AIDS -- BY RACE

Question: How many people have you known personally, either living or dead, who came down with the disease called AIDS? NOTE: Question not asked in 1972-1987.

Responses: 0 = 0; 1 = 1; 2 = 2; etc.; 8 = 8 or more

		YEAR	
RACE	RESP	'88	'89
WHITE	0	91%	91%
	1	6	6
	2	1	2
	3	1	1
	4	0	0
	5	0	0
	6	0	0
	7	0	0
	8	0	0
# SURVEYED		1233	1317

		YEAR	
RACE	RESP	'88	'89
BLACK	0	86%	88%
	1	10	5
	2	3	6
	3	1	1
	4	0	0
	5	0	0
	6	0	0
	7	1	0
	8	0	0
# SURVEYED		186	157

		YEAR	
RACE	RESP	'88	'89
OTHER	0	97%	87%
	1	2	11
	2	0	0
	3	0	2
	4	0	0
	5	0	0
	6	0	0
	7	2	0
	8	0	0
# SURVEYED		61	61

TABLE IV: ACQUAINTANCES WITH AIDS -- BY AGE

Question: How many people have you known personally, either living or dead, who came down with the disease called AIDS? NOTE: Question not asked in 1972-1987.

Responses: 0 = 0; 1 = 1; 2 = 2; etc.; 8 = 8 or more

		YEAR	
AGE	RESP	'88	'89
18-23	0	94%	93%
	1	4	4
	2	1	2
	3	1	0
	4	0	1
	5	0	0
	6	0	0
	7	1	0
	8	0	0
# SURVEYED		141	137

		YEAR	
AGE	RESP	'88	'89
24-29	0	87%	90%
	1	9	6
	2	2	2
	3	0	1
	4	0	0
	5	1	0
	6	0	0
	7	1	0
	8	0	0
# SURVEYED		215	202

		YEAR	
AGE	RESP	'88	'89
30-35	0	87%	87%
	1	9	8
	2	3	3
	3	1	2
	4	0	0
	5	0	0
	6	0	0
	7	0	0
	8	0	0
# SURVEYED		195	212

TABLE IV: ACQUAINTANCES WITH AIDS -- BY AGE (Continued)

Question: How many people have you known personally, either living or dead, who came down with the disease called AIDS? NOTE: Question not asked in 1972-1987.

Responses: 0 = 0; 1 = 1; 2 = 2; etc.; 8 = 8 or more

		YEAR	
AGE	RESP	'88	'89
36-41	0	88%	83%
	1	4	12
	2	3	3
	3	3	1
	4	1	0
	5	0	1
	6	1	1
	7	1	0
	8	0	0
# SURVEYED		193	198
AGE	RESP	'88	'89
42-47	0	87%	88%
	1	9	9
	2	3	3
	3	1	1
	4	0	0
	5	1	0
	6	0	0
	7	0	0
	8	0	0
# SURVEYED		157	161

		YEAR	
AGE	RESP	'88	'89
48-53	0	90%	93%
	1	9	1
	2	0	4
	3	0	1
	4	0	1
	5	0	0
	6	0	0
	7	1	0
	8	0	1
# SURVEYED		92	138
AGE	RESP	'88	'89
54-59	0	95%	91%
	1	5	8
	2	0	1
	3	0	0
	4	0	0
	5	0	0
	6	0	0
	7	0	0
	8	0	0
# SURVEYED		85	98

		YEAR	
AGE	RESP	'88	'89
60-65	0	96%	93%
	1	3	5
	2	1	2
	3	0	0
	4	0	0
	5	0	0
	6	0	0
	7	0	0
	8	0	0
# SURVEYED		119	111
AGE	RESP	'88	'89
66+	0	96%	97%
	1	4	3
	2	0	0
	3	0	0
	4	0	0
	5	0	0
	6	0	0
	7	0	0
	8	0	0
# SURVEYED		279	275

****

RELATIONSHIP WITH AIDS VICTIMS

TABLE I: RELATIONSHIP WITH AIDS VICTIMS -- BY TOTAL POPULATION

Question: Think about the person you know best, living or dead, who came down with AIDS. Please tell me the letter which best describes your relationship with that person. NOTE: Question not asked in 1972-1987.

Responses: SP = Spouse LV = Partner or lover CH = Son or daughter RE = Other reletive FR = Friend
NB = Neighbor WK = Co-worker AQ = Acquaintance PT = Patient OT = Other

	YEAR	
RESPONSE	'88	'89
SP	1%	0%
LV	0	1
CH	0	0
RE	4	13
FR	27	28
NB	5	1
WK	15	8
AQ	38	37
PT	4	2
OT	5	8
# SURVEYED	136	142

TABLE II: RELATIONSHIP WITH AIDS VICTIMS -- BY SEX

Question: Think about the person you know best, living or dead, who came down with AIDS. Please tell me the letter which best describes your relationship with that person. NOTE: Question not asked in 1972-1987.

Responses: SP = Spouse LV = Partner or lover CH = Son or daughter RE = Other reletive FR = Friend
NB = Neighbor WK = Co-worker AQ = Acquaintance PT = Patient OT = Other

		YEAR	
SEX	RESP	'88	'89
MALE	SP	2%	0%
	LV	0	0
	CH	0	0
	RE	4	17
	FR	19	22
	NB	6	1
	WK	23	13
	AQ	38	36
	PT	2	1
	OT	6	9
# SURVEYED		52	69

		YEAR	
SEX	RESP	'88	'89
FEMALE	SP	0%	0%
	LV	0	3
	CH	0	0
	RE	4	10
	FR	32	34
	NB	5	1
	WK	11	4
	AQ	38	38
	PT	6	3
	OT	5	7
# SURVEYED		84	73

TABLE III: RELATIONSHIP WITH AIDS VICTIMS -- BY RACE

Question: Think about the person you know best, living or dead, who came down with AIDS. Please tell me the letter which best describes your relationship with that person. NOTE: Question not asked in 1972-1987.

Responses: SP = Spouse LV = Partner or lover CH = Son or daughter RE = Other reletive FR = Friend NB = Neighbor WK = Co-worker AQ = Acquaintance PT = Patient OT = Other

RACE	RESP	YEAR '88	'89
WHITE	SP	1%	0%
	LV	0	1
	CH	0	0
	RE	4	13
	FR	24	27
	NB	3	1
	WK	18	8
	AQ	41	42
	PT	5	2
	OT	6	7
# SURVEYED		108	115

RACE	RESP	YEAR '88	'89
BLACK	SP	0%	0%
	LV	0	0
	CH	0	0
	RE	4	11
	FR	42	32
	NB	12	5
	WK	8	16
	AQ	31	21
	PT	4	5
	OT	0	11
# SURVEYED		26	19

RACE	RESP	YEAR '88	'89
OTHER	SP	0%	0%
	LV	0	13
	CH	0	0
	RE	0	25
	FR	0	38
	NB	50	0
	WK	0	0
	AQ	0	13
	PT	0	0
	OT	50	13
# SURVEYED		2	8

TABLE IV: RELATIONSHIP WITH AIDS VICTIMS -- BY AGE

Question: Think about the person you know best, living or dead, who came down with AIDS. Please tell me the letter which best describes your relationship with that person. NOTE: Question not asked in 1972-1987.

Responses: SP = Spouse LV = Partner or lover CH = Son or daughter RE = Other reletive FR = Friend NB = Neighbor WK = Co-worker AQ = Acquaintance PT = Patient OT = Other

AGE	RESP	YEAR '88	'89
18-23	SP	0%	0%
	LV	0	0
	CH	0	0
	RE	22	33
	FR	33	33
	NB	0	0
	WK	11	0
	AQ	33	22
	PT	0	0
	OT	0	11
# SURVEYED		9	9

AGE	RESP	YEAR '88	'89
24-29	SP	0%	0%
	LV	0	10
	CH	0	0
	RE	3	5
	FR	45	40
	NB	3	0
	WK	10	15
	AQ	34	30
	PT	3	0
	OT	0	0
# SURVEYED		29	20

AGE	RESP	YEAR '88	'89
30-35	SP	0%	0%
	LV	0	0
	CH	0	0
	RE	8	4
	FR	23	37
	NB	0	0
	WK	19	4
	AQ	42	52
	PT	8	4
	OT	0	0
# SURVEYED		26	27

AGE	RESP	YEAR '88	'89
36-41	SP	5%	0%
	LV	0	0
	CH	0	0
	RE	0	21
	FR	23	18
	NB	5	6
	WK	23	21
	AQ	36	24
	PT	0	3
	OT	9	6
# SURVEYED		22	33

AGE	RESP	YEAR '88	'89
42-47	SP	0%	0%
	LV	0	0
	CH	0	0
	RE	0	20
	FR	25	20
	NB	5	0
	WK	30	0
	AQ	30	45
	PT	0	5
	OT	10	10
# SURVEYED		20	20

TABLE IV: RELATIONSHIP WITH AIDS VICTIMS -- BY AGE (Continued)

Question: Think about the person you know best, living or dead, who came down with AIDS. Please tell me the letter which best describes your relationship with that person. NOTE: Question not asked in 1972-1987.

Responses: SP = Spouse LV = Partner or lover CH = Son or daughter RE = Other reletive FR = Friend NB = Neighbor WK = Co-worker AQ = Acquaintance PT = Patient OT = Other

AGE	RESP	YEAR '88	YEAR '89
48-53	SP	0%	0%
	LV	0	0
	CH	0	0
	RE	0	0
	FR	11	44
	NB	22	0
	WK	0	11
	AQ	22	44
	PT	11	0
	OT	33	0
# SURVEYED		9	9

AGE	RESP	YEAR '88	YEAR '89
54-59	SP	0%	0%
	LV	0	0
	CH	0	0
	RE	0	11
	FR	0	22
	NB	0	0
	WK	0	0
	AQ	100	33
	PT	0	0
	OT	0	33
# SURVEYED		4	9

AGE	RESP	YEAR '88	YEAR '89
60-65	SP	0%	0%
	LV	0	0
	CH	0	0
	RE	0	0
	FR	40	25
	NB	0	0
	WK	0	0
	AQ	40	50
	PT	20	0
	OT	0	25
# SURVEYED		5	8

AGE	RESP	YEAR '88	YEAR '89
66+	SP	0%	0%
	LV	0	0
	CH	0	0
	RE	0	29
	FR	17	14
	NB	17	0
	WK	8	0
	AQ	50	43
	PT	8	0
	OT	0	14
# SURVEYED		12	7

****

GENDER OF AIDS VICTIM

TABLE I: GENDER OF AIDS VICTIM -- BY TOTAL POPULATION

Question: We would like to know a few more things about that person you have known who came down with AIDS. (Is/was) that person male or female? NOTE: Question not asked in 1972-1987.

Responses: MA = Male; FE = Female

RESPONSE	YEAR '88	YEAR '89
MA	96%	93%
FE	4	7
# SURVEYED	136	142

TABLE II: GENDER OF AIDS VICTIM -- BY SEX

Question: We would like to know a few more things about that person you have known who came down with AIDS. (Is/was) that person male or female? NOTE: Question not asked in 1972-1987.

Responses: MA = Male; FE = Female

SEX	RESP	YEAR '88	'89
M	MA	94%	94%
	FE	6	6
# SURVEYED		53	68

SEX	RESP	YEAR '88	'89
F	MA	98%	92%
	FE	2	8
# SURVEYED		83	74

TABLE III: GENDER OF AIDS VICTIM -- BY RACE

Question: We would like to know a few more things about that person you have known who came down with AIDS. (Is/was) that person male or female? NOTE: Question not asked in 1972-1987.

Responses: MA = Male; FE = Female

RACE	RESP	YEAR '88	'89
WHITE	MA	97%	95%
	FE	3	5
# SURVEYED		108	115

RACE	RESP	YEAR '88	'89
BLACK	MA	96%	84%
	FE	4	16
# SURVEYED		26	19

RACE	RESP	YEAR '88	'89
OTHER	MA	50%	88%
	FE	50	13
# SURVEYED		2	8

TABLE IV: GENDER OF AIDS VICTIM -- BY AGE

Question: We would like to know a few more things about that person you have known who came down with AIDS. (Is/was) that person male or female? NOTE: Question not asked in 1972-1987.

Responses: MA = Male; FE = Female

AGE	RESP	YEAR '88	'89
18-23	MA	100%	100%
	FE	0	0
# SURVEYED		9	9

AGE	RESP	YEAR '88	'89
24-29	MA	93%	100%
	FE	7	0
# SURVEYED		29	20

AGE	RESP	YEAR '88	'89
30-35	MA	100%	85%
	FE	0	15
# SURVEYED		25	27

AGE	RESP	YEAR '88	'89
36-41	MA	95%	94%
	FE	5	6
# SURVEYED		22	32

TABLE IV: GENDER OF AIDS VICTIM -- BY AGE (Continued)

Question: We would like to know a few more things about that person you have known who came down with AIDS. (Is/was) that person male or female? NOTE: Question not asked in 1972-1987.

Responses: MA = Male; FE = Female

		YEAR	
AGE	RESP	'88	'89
42-47	MA	100%	95%
	FE	0	5
# SURVEYED		21	20
AGE	RESP	'88	'89
48-53	MA	89%	100%
	FE	11	0
# SURVEYED		9	10

		YEAR	
AGE	RESP	'88	'89
54-59	MA	100%	89%
	FE	0	11
# SURVEYED		4	9

		YEAR	
AGE	RESP	'88	'89
60-65	MA	100%	88%
	FE	0	13
# SURVEYED		5	8

		YEAR	
AGE	RESP	'88	'89
66+	MA	92%	86%
	FE	8	14
# SURVEYED		12	7

****

RACE OF AIDS VICTIM

TABLE I: RACE OF AIDS VICTIM -- BY TOTAL POPULATION

Question: We would like to know a few more things about that person you have known who came down with AIDS. What (is/was) that person's race? NOTE: Question not asked in 1972-1987.

Responses: BK = Black; WT = White; HP = Hispanic; OT = Other

	YEAR	
RESPONSE	'88	'89
BK	18%	12%
WT	72	77
HP	7	11
OT	3	0
# SURVEYED	137	143

TABLE II: RACE OF AIDS VICTIM -- BY SEX

Question: We would like to know a few more things about that person you have known who came down with AIDS. What (is/was) that person's race? NOTE: Question not asked in 1972-1987.

Responses: BK = Black; WT = White; HP = Hispanic; OT = Other

SEX	RESP	YEAR '88	'89
M	BK	19%	7%
	WT	65	83
	HP	12	10
	OT	4	0
# SURVEYED		52	69

SEX	RESP	YEAR '88	'89
F	BK	18%	16%
	WT	75	72
	HP	5	12
	OT	2	0
# SURVEYED		85	74

TABLE III: RACE OF AIDS VICTIM -- BY RACE

Question: We would like to know a few more things about that person you have known who came down with AIDS. What (is/was) that person's race? NOTE: Question not asked in 1972-1987.

Responses: BK = Black; WT = White; HP = Hispanic; OT = Other

RACE	RESP	YEAR '88	'89
WHITE	BK	4%	3%
	WT	87	91
	HP	6	5
	OT	4	0
# SURVEYED		109	116

RACE	RESP	YEAR '88	'89
BLACK	BK	81%	68%
	WT	4	21
	HP	15	11
	OT	0	0
# SURVEYED		26	19

RACE	RESP	YEAR '88	'89
OTHER	BK	0%	0%
	WT	100	0
	HP	0	100
	OT	0	0
# SURVEYED		2	8

TABLE IV: RACE OF AIDS VICTIM -- BY AGE

Question: We would like to know a few more things about that person you have known who came down with AIDS. What (is/was) that person's race? NOTE: Question not asked in 1972-1987.

Responses: BK = Black; WT = White; HP = Hispanic; OT = Other

AGE	RESP	'88	'89
18-23	BK	22%	0%
	WT	67	100
	HP	11	0
	OT	0	0
# SURVEYED		9	9
24-29	BK	17%	10%
	WT	69	75
	HP	3	15
	OT	10	0
# SURVEYED		29	20
30-35	BK	23%	11%
	WT	65	81
	HP	8	7
	OT	4	0
# SURVEYED		26	27

AGE	RESP	'88	'89
36-41	BK	18%	12%
	WT	73	70
	HP	9	18
	OT	0	0
# SURVEYED		22	33
42-47	BK	24%	20%
	WT	76	70
	HP	0	10
	OT	0	0
# SURVEYED		21	20

AGE	RESP	'88	'89
48-53	BK	11%	10%
	WT	78	80
	HP	11	10
	OT	0	0
# SURVEYED		9	10
54-59	BK	25%	22%
	WT	50	67
	HP	25	11
	OT	0	0
# SURVEYED		4	9

AGE	RESP	'88	'89
60-65	BK	0%	13%
	WT	80	88
	HP	20	0
	OT	0	0
# SURVEYED		5	8
66+	BK	8%	0%
	WT	83	86
	HP	8	14
	OT	0	0
# SURVEYED		12	7

****

SEX PARTNERS IN LAST YEAR

TABLE I: SEX PARTNERS IN LAST YEAR -- BY TOTAL POPULATION

Question: How many sex partners have you had in the last 12 months? NOTE: Question not asked in 1972-1987. Question asked only of people with at least one sex partner in last year.

Responses: 1 = 1 partner 2 = 2 partners 3 = 3 partners
4 = 4 partners 5 = 5-10 partners 6 = 11-20 partners
7 = 21-100 partners 8 = More than 100 9 = More than 1 (unspecified)

	YEAR	
RESPONSE	'88	'89
1	82%	83%
2	7	8
3	5	4
4	2	2
5	2	2
6	0	0
7	0	0
8	0	0
9	1	1
# SURVEYED	1072	1088

TABLE II: SEX PARTNERS IN LAST YEAR -- BY SEX

Question: How many sex partners have you had in the last 12 months? NOTE: Question not asked in 1972-1987. Question asked only of people with at least one sex partner in last year.

Responses: 1 = 1 partner 2 = 2 partners 3 = 3 partners
4 = 4 partners 5 = 5-10 partners 6 = 11-20 partners
7 = 21-100 partners 8 = More than 100 9 = More than 1 (unspecified)

		YEAR	
SEX	RESP	'88	'89
MALE	1	77%	77%
	2	7	9
	3	6	6
	4	4	3
	5	4	4
	6	1	0
	7	1	0
	8	0	0
	9	1	1
# SURVEYED		504	512

		YEAR	
SEX	RESP	'88	'89
FEMALE	1	86%	89%
	2	8	7
	3	4	2
	4	1	1
	5	1	0
	6	0	0
	7	0	0
	8	0	0
	9	1	0
# SURVEYED		568	576

TABLE III: SEX PARTNERS IN LAST YEAR -- BY RACE

Question: How many sex partners have you had in the last 12 months? NOTE: Question not asked in 1972-1987. Question asked only of people with at least one sex partner in last year.

Responses: 1 = 1 partner 2 = 2 partners 3 = 3 partners
4 = 4 partners 5 = 5-10 partners 6 = 11-20 partners
7 = 21-100 partners 8 = More than 100 9 = More than 1 (unspecified)

RACE	RESP	'88	'89
WHITE	1	83%	84%
	2	7	8
	3	4	3
	4	2	2
	5	2	2
	6	0	0
	7	0	0
	8	0	0
	9	1	0
# SURVEYED		889	934

RACE	RESP	'88	'89
BLACK	1	69%	75%
	2	11	10
	3	8	6
	4	5	3
	5	3	4
	6	1	0
	7	2	1
	8	1	0
	9	0	2
# SURVEYED		144	109

RACE	RESP	'88	'89
OTHER	1	87%	89%
	2	8	2
	3	0	4
	4	0	2
	5	3	2
	6	3	0
	7	0	0
	8	0	0
	9	0	0
# SURVEYED		39	45

TABLE IV: SEX PARTNERS IN LAST YEAR -- BY AGE

Question: How many sex partners have you had in the last 12 months? NOTE: Question not asked in 1972-1987. Question asked only of people with at least one sex partner in last year.

Responses: 1 = 1 partner 2 = 2 partners 3 = 3 partners
4 = 4 partners 5 = 5-10 partners 6 = 11-20 partners
7 = 21-100 partners 8 = More than 100 9 = More than 1 (unspecified)

AGE	RESP	'88	'89
18-23	1	55%	55%
	2	19	24
	3	8	9
	4	6	6
	5	9	6
	6	2	1
	7	1	0
	8	0	0
	9	0	0
# SURVEYED		118	105

AGE	RESP	'88	'89
24-29	1	74%	75%
	2	10	12
	3	8	6
	4	4	3
	5	3	3
	6	0	1
	7	1	1
	8	0	0
	9	1	0
# SURVEYED		183	173

AGE	RESP	'88	'89
30-35	1	84%	83%
	2	5	8
	3	6	4
	4	3	2
	5	1	2
	6	0	0
	7	0	0
	8	0	0
	9	1	0
# SURVEYED		172	179

AGE	RESP	'88	'89
36-41	1	84%	89%
	2	6	6
	3	5	2
	4	1	1
	5	2	2
	6	1	0
	7	1	0
	8	0	0
	9	1	0
# SURVEYED		166	175

TABLE IV: SEX PARTNERS IN LAST YEAR -- BY AGE (Continued)

Question: How many sex partners have you had in the last 12 months? NOTE: Question not asked in 1972-1987.

Responses: 1 = 1 partner; 2 = 2 partners; 3 = 3 partners; 4 = 4 partners; 5 = 5-10 partners; 6 = 11-20 partners; 7 = 21-100 partners; 8 = More than 100; 9 = More than 1 (unspecified)

AGE	RESP	'88	'89
42-47	1	88%	89%
	2	6	6
	3	3	3
	4	2	0
	5	1	1
	6	1	0
	7	0	1
	8	0	0
	9	0	0
# SURVEYED		133	128
48-53	1	90%	92%
	2	3	4
	3	2	1
	4	0	1
	5	0	2
	6	2	0
	7	2	0
	8	0	0
	9	2	1
# SURVEYED		63	108

AGE	RESP	'88	'89
54-59	1	84%	90%
	2	9	2
	3	2	5
	4	0	2
	5	0	0
	6	0	0
	7	0	0
	8	2	0
	9	3	2
# SURVEYED		58	62

AGE	RESP	'88	'89
60-65	1	95%	90%
	2	4	4
	3	0	1
	4	1	0
	5	0	1
	6	0	0
	7	0	0
	8	0	0
	9	0	3
# SURVEYED		77	67

AGE	RESP	'88	'89
66+	1	93%	94%
	2	1	1
	3	3	1
	4	2	1
	5	1	0
	6	0	0
	7	0	0
	8	0	0
	9	0	2
# SURVEYED		101	90

****

SEX WITH SIGNIFICANT OTHER

TABLE I: SEX WITH SIGNIFICANT OTHER -- BY TOTAL POPULATION

Question: Was one of your sex partners in the last 12 months your husband or wife or regular sex partner? NOTE: Question not asked in 1972-1987.

Responses: Yes; No

	YEAR	
RESPONSE	'88	'89
YES	92%	92%
NO	8	8
# SURVEYED	1061	1078

TABLE II: SEX WITH SIGNIFICANT OTHER -- BY SEX

Question: Was one of your sex partners in the last 12 months your husband or wife or regular sex partner? NOTE: Question not asked in 1972-1987.

Responses: Yes; No

		YEAR	
SEX	RESP	'88	'89
M	YES	89%	90%
	NO	11	10
# SURVEYED		499	509

		YEAR	
SEX	RESP	'88	'89
F	YES	94%	93%
	NO	6	7
# SURVEYED		562	569

TABLE III: SEX WITH SIGNIFICANT OTHER -- BY RACE

Question: Was one of your sex partners in the last 12 months your husband or wife or regular sex partner? NOTE: Question not asked in 1972-1987.

Responses: Yes; No

		YEAR	
RACE	RESP	'88	'89
WHITE	YES	93%	93%
	NO	7	7
# SURVEYED		881	926

		YEAR	
RACE	RESP	'88	'89
BLACK	YES	88%	84%
	NO	12	16
# SURVEYED		141	108

RACE	RESP	'88	'89
OTHER	YES	82%	86%
	NO	18	14
# SURVEYED		39	44

TABLE IV: SEX WITH SIGNIFICANT OTHER -- BY AGE

Question: Was one of your sex partners in the last 12 months your husband or wife or regular sex partner? NOTE: Question not asked in 1972-1987.

Responses: Yes; No

AGE	RESP	'88	'89
18-23	YES	82%	81%
	NO	18	19
# SURVEYED		116	104
24-29	YES	88%	87%
	NO	12	13
# SURVEYED		180	172
30-35	YES	96%	92%
	NO	4	8
# SURVEYED		171	179
36-41	YES	94%	94%
	NO	6	6
# SURVEYED		164	175
42-47	YES	92%	94%
	NO	8	6
# SURVEYED		133	126
48-53	YES	92%	95%
	NO	8	5
# SURVEYED		62	108
54-59	YES	93%	100%
	NO	7	0
# SURVEYED		57	60
60-65	YES	93%	92%
	NO	7	8
# SURVEYED		76	65
66+	YES	94%	95%
	NO	6	5
# SURVEYED		101	88

****

SEX WITH CLOSE PERSONAL FRIEND

TABLE I: SEX WITH CLOSE PERSONAL FRIEND -- BY TOTAL POPULATION

Question: Was one of your sex partners in the last 12 months a close personal friend? NOTE: Question not asked in 1972-1987.

Responses: Yes; No

RESPONSE	'88	'89
YES	65%	69%
NO	35	31
# SURVEYED	170	160

TABLE II: SEX WITH CLOSE PERSONAL FRIEND -- BY SEX

Question: Was one of your sex partners in the last 12 months a close personal friend? NOTE: Question not asked in 1972-1987.

Responses: Yes; No

SEX	RESP	'88	'89
M	YES	65%	67%
	NO	35	33
# SURVEYED		105	100

SEX	RESP	'88	'89
F	YES	66%	73%
	NO	34	27
# SURVEYED		65	60

TABLE III: SEX WITH CLOSE PERSONAL FRIEND -- BY RACE

Question: Was one of your sex partners in the last 12 months a close personal friend? NOTE: Question not asked in 1972-1987.

Responses: Yes; No

RACE	RESP	'88	'89
WHITE	YES	65%	66%
	NO	35	34
# SURVEYED		130	129

RACE	RESP	'88	'89
BLACK	YES	64%	88%
	NO	36	13
# SURVEYED		36	24

RACE	RESP	'88	'89
OTHER	YES	100%	71%
	NO	0	29
# SURVEYED		4	7

TABLE IV: SEX WITH CLOSE PERSONAL FRIEND -- BY AGE

Question: Was one of your sex partners in the last 12 months a close personal friend? NOTE: Question not asked in 1972-1987.

Responses: Yes; No

AGE	RESP	'88	'89
18-23	YES	67%	78%
	NO	33	22
# SURVEYED		43	36

AGE	RESP	'88	'89
24-29	YES	60%	60%
	NO	40	40
# SURVEYED		45	42

AGE	RESP	'88	'89
30-35	YES	67%	63%
	NO	33	37
# SURVEYED		21	30

AGE	RESP	'88	'89
36-41	YES	71%	72%
	NO	29	28
# SURVEYED		21	18

TABLE IV: SEX WITH CLOSE PERSONAL FRIEND -- BY AGE (Continued)

Question: Was one of your sex partners in the last 12 months a close personal friend? NOTE: Question not asked in 1972-1987.

Responses: Yes; No

AGE	RESP	'88	'89
42-47	YES	68%	86%
	NO	32	14
# SURVEYED		19	14

AGE	RESP	'88	'89
48-53	YES	50%	57%
	NO	50	43
# SURVEYED		4	7

AGE	RESP	'88	'89
54-59	YES	57%	50%
	NO	43	50
# SURVEYED		7	4

AGE	RESP	'88	'89
60-65	YES	60%	83%
	NO	40	17
# SURVEYED		5	6

AGE	RESP	'88	'89
66+	YES	80%	100%
	NO	20	0
# SURVEYED		5	3

****

SEX WITH ACQUAINTANCE

TABLE I: SEX WITH ACQUAINTANCE -- BY TOTAL POPULATION

Question: Was one of your sex partners in the last 12 months a neighbor, co-worker, or a long-term acquaintance? NOTE: Question not asked in 1972-1987.

Responses: Yes; No

RESPONSE	'88	'89
YES	34%	33%
NO	66	68
# SURVEYED	170	160

TABLE II: SEX WITH ACQUAINTANCE -- BY SEX

Question: Was one of your sex partners in the last 12 months a neighbor, co-worker, or a long-term acquaintance? NOTE: Question not asked in 1972-1987.

Responses: Yes; No

SEX	RESP	'88	'89
M	YES	34%	30%
	NO	66	70
# SURVEYED		105	100

SEX	RESP	'88	'89
F	YES	32%	37%
	NO	68	63
# SURVEYED		65	60

TABLE III: SEX WITH ACQUAINTANCE -- BY RACE

Question: Was one of your sex partners in the last 12 months a neighbor, co-worker, or a long-term acquaintance? NOTE: Question not asked in 1972-1987.

Responses: Yes; No

RACE	RESP	'88	'89
WHITE	YES	36%	34%
	NO	64	66
# SURVEYED		130	129

RACE	RESP	'88	'89
BLACK	YES	28%	29%
	NO	72	71
# SURVEYED		36	24

RACE	RESP	'88	'89
OTHER	YES	0%	14%
	NO	100	86
# SURVEYED		4	7

TABLE IV: SEX WITH ACQUAINTANCE -- BY AGE

Question: Was one of your sex partners in the last 12 months a neighbor, co-worker, or a long-term acquaintance? NOTE: Question not asked in 1972-1987.

Responses: Yes; No

AGE	RESP	'88	'89
18-23	YES	33%	28%
	NO	67	72
# SURVEYED		43	36

AGE	RESP	'88	'89
24-29	YES	33%	48%
	NO	67	52
# SURVEYED		45	42

AGE	RESP	'88	'89
30-35	YES	24%	27%
	NO	76	73
# SURVEYED		21	3

AGE	RESP	'88	'89
36-41	YES	48%	28%
	NO	52	72
# SURVEYED		21	18

TABLE IV: SEX WITH ACQUAINTANCE -- BY AGE (Continued)

Question: Was one of your sex partners in the last 12 months a neighbor, co-worker, or a long-term acquaintance? NOTE: Question not asked in 1972-1987.

Responses: Yes; No

AGE	RESP	YEAR '88	YEAR '89
42-47	YES	47%	29%
	NO	53	71
# SURVEYED		19	14
48-53	YES	0%	29%
	NO	100	71
# SURVEYED		4	7
54-59	YES	29%	25%
	NO	71	75
# SURVEYED		7	4
60-65	YES	40%	33%
	NO	60	67
# SURVEYED		5	6
66+	YES	0%	0%
	NO	100	100
# SURVEYED		5	3

****

SEX WITH A CASUAL DATE

TABLE I: SEX WITH CASUAL DATE -- BY TOTAL POPULATION

Question: Was one of your sex partners in the last 12 months a casual date or pickup? NOTE: Question not asked in 1972-1987.

Responses: Yes; No

RESPONSE	YEAR '88	YEAR '89
YES	28%	26%
NO	72	74
# SURVEYED	170	160

TABLE II: SEX WITH CASUAL DATE -- BY SEX

Question: Was one of your sex partners in the last 12 months a casual date or pickup? NOTE: Question not asked in 1972-1987.

Responses: Yes; No

		YEAR	
SEX	RESP	'88	'89
M	YES	36%	36%
	NO	64	64
# SURVEYED		105	100

		YEAR	
SEX	RESP	'88	'89
F	YES	15%	10%
	NO	85	90
# SURVEYED		65	60

TABLE III: SEX WITH CASUAL DATE -- BY RACE

Question: Was one of your sex partners in the last 12 months a casual date or pickup? NOTE: Question not asked in 1972-1987.

Responses: Yes; No

		YEAR	
RACE	RESP	'88	'89
WHITE	YES	28%	28%
	NO	72	72
# SURVEYED		130	129

		YEAR	
RACE	RESP	'88	'89
BLACK	YES	33%	13%
	NO	67	88
# SURVEYED		36	24

		YEAR	
RACE	RESP	'88	'89
OTHER	YES	0%	43%
	NO	100	57
# SURVEYED		4	7

TABLE IV: SEX WITH CASUAL DATE -- BY AGE

Question: Was one of your sex partners in the last 12 months a casual date or pickup? NOTE: Question not asked in 1972-1987.

Responses: Yes; No

		YEAR	
AGE	RESP	'88	'89
18-23	YES	37%	31%
	NO	63	69
# SURVEYED		43	36

		YEAR	
AGE	RESP	'88	'89
24-29	YES	36%	38%
	NO	64	62
# SURVEYED		45	42

		YEAR	
AGE	RESP	'88	'89
30-35	YES	24%	23%
	NO	76	77
# SURVEYED		21	30

		YEAR	
AGE	RESP	'88	'89
36-41	YES	24%	11%
	NO	76	89
# SURVEYED		21	18

TABLE IV: SEX WITH CASUAL DATE -- BY AGE (Continued)

Question: Was one of your sex partners in the last 12 months a casual date or pickup? NOTE: Question not asked in 1972-1987.

Responses: Yes; No

		YEAR	
AGE	RESP	'88	'89
42-47	YES NO	11% 89	21% 79
# SURVEYED		19	14
AGE	RESP	'88	'89
48-53	YES NO	50% 50	14% 86
# SURVEYED		4	7

		YEAR	
AGE	RESP	'88	'89
54-59	YES NO	14% 86	25% 75
# SURVEYED		7	4

		YEAR	
AGE	RESP	'88	'89
60-65	YES NO	0% 100	17% 83
# SURVEYED		5	6

		YEAR	
AGE	RESP	'88	'89
66+	YES NO	20% 80	0% 100
# SURVEYED		5	3

****

SEX FOR PAY

TABLE I: SEX FOR PAY -- BY TOTAL POPULATION

Question: Was one of your sex partners in the last 12 months a person you paid or paid you for sex? NOTE: Question not asked in 1972-1987.

Responses: Yes; No

	YEAR	
RESPONSE	'88	'89
YES NO	2% 98	3% 98
# SURVEYED	170	160

TABLE II: SEX FOR PAY -- BY SEX

Question: Was one of your sex partners in the last 12 months a person you paid or paid you for sex? NOTE: Question not asked in 1972-1987.

Responses: Yes; No

SEX	RESP	'88	'89
M	YES	4%	3%
	NO	96	97
# SURVEYED		105	100

SEX	RESP	'88	'89
F	YES	0%	2%
	NO	100	98
# SURVEYED		65	60

TABLE III: SEX FOR PAY -- BY RACE

Question: Was one of your sex partners in the last 12 months a person you paid or paid you for sex? NOTE: Question not asked in 1972-1987.

Responses: Yes; No

RACE	RESP	'88	'89
WHITE	YES	2%	2%
	NO	98	98
# SURVEYED		130	129

RACE	RESP	'88	'89
BLACK	YES	6%	4%
	NO	94	96
# SURVEYED		36	24

RACE	RESP	'88	'89
OTHER	YES	0%	0%
	NO	100	100
# SURVEYED		4	7

TABLE IV: SEX FOR PAY -- BY AGE

Question: Was one of your sex partners in the last 12 months a person you paid or paid you for sex? NOTE: Question not asked in 1972-1987.

Responses: Yes; No

AGE	RESP	'88	'89
18-23	YES	0%	0%
	NO	100	100
# SURVEYED		43	36

AGE	RESP	'88	'89
24-29	YES	4%	2%
	NO	96	98
# SURVEYED		45	42

AGE	RESP	'88	'89
30-35	YES	0%	3%
	NO	100	97
# SURVEYED		21	30

AGE	RESP	'88	'89
36-41	YES	0%	0%
	NO	100	100
# SURVEYED		21	18

TABLE IV: SEX FOR PAY -- BY AGE (Continued)

Question: Was one of your sex partners in the last 12 months a person you paid or paid you for sex? NOTE: Question not asked in 1972-1987.

Responses: Yes; No

AGE	RESP	'88	'89
42-47	YES	0%	7%
	NO	100	93
# SURVEYED		19	14

AGE	RESP	'88	'89
48-53	YES	25%	14%
	NO	75	86
# SURVEYED		4	7

AGE	RESP	'88	'89
54-59	YES	0%	0%
	NO	100	100
# SURVEYED		7	4

AGE	RESP	'88	'89
60-65	YES	20%	0%
	NO	80	100
# SURVEYED		5	6

AGE	RESP	'88	'89
66+	YES	0%	0%
	NO	100	100
# SURVEYED		5	3

****

GENDER OF SEX PARTNERS

TABLE I: GENDER OF SEX PARTNERS -- BY TOTAL POPULATION

Question: Have your sex partners in the last 12 months been exclusively male, both male and female, or exclusively female? NOTE: Question not asked in 1972-1987.

Responses: MA = Exclusively male; BO = Both male and female; FE = Exclusively female

RESPONSE	'88	'89
MA	55%	53%
BO	0	0
FE	45	47
# SURVEYED	1019	1059

TABLE II: GENDER OF SEX PARTNERS -- BY SEX

Question: Have your sex partners in the last 12 months been exclusively male, both male and female, or exclusively female? NOTE: Question not asked in 1972-1987.

Responses: MA = Exclusively male; BO = Both male and female; FE = Exclusively female

SEX	RESP	YEAR '88	YEAR '89
M	MA	3%	1%
	BO	0	0
	FE	97	98
# SURVEYED		476	499

SEX	RESP	YEAR '88	YEAR '89
F	MA	100%	98%
	BO	0	0
	FE	0	1
# SURVEYED		543	560

TABLE III: GENDER OF SEX PARTNERS -- BY RACE

Question: Have your sex partners in the last 12 months been exclusively male, both male and female, or exclusively female? NOTE: Question not asked in 1972-1987.

Responses: MA = Exclusively male; BO = Both male and female; FE = Exclusively female

RACE	RESP	YEAR '88	YEAR '89
WHITE	MA	54%	50%
	BO	0	0
	FE	46	49
# SURVEYED		847	911

RACE	RESP	YEAR '88	YEAR '89
BLACK	MA	60%	70%
	BO	0	0
	FE	40	30
# SURVEYED		136	107

RACE	RESP	YEAR '88	YEAR '89
OTHER	MA	47%	56%
	BO	0	0
	FE	53	44
# SURVEYED		36	41

TABLE IV: GENDER OF SEX PARTNERS -- BY AGE

Question: Have your sex partners in the last 12 months been exclusively male, both male and female, or exclusively female? NOTE: Question not asked in 1972-1987.

Responses: MA = Exclusively male; BO = Both male and female; FE = Exclusively female

AGE	RESP	YEAR '88	YEAR '89
18-23	MA	52%	50%
	BO	0	1
	FE	48	49
# SURVEYED		113	102

AGE	RESP	YEAR '88	YEAR '89
24-29	MA	56%	58%
	BO	1	0
	FE	43	42
# SURVEYED		174	171

AGE	RESP	YEAR '88	YEAR '89
30-35	MA	65%	56%
	BO	0	1
	FE	35	43
# SURVEYED		163	176

AGE	RESP	YEAR '88	YEAR '89
36-41	MA	48%	47%
	BO	0	0
	FE	52	53
# SURVEYED		158	172

TABLE IV: GENDER OF SEX PARTNERS -- BY AGE (Continued)

Question: Have your sex partners in the last 12 months been exclusively male, both male and female, or exclusively female? NOTE: Question not asked in 1972-1987.

Responses: MA = Exclusively male; BO = Both male and female; FE = Exclusively female

		YEAR	
AGE	RESP	'88	'89
42-47	MA	52%	52%
	BO	1	0
	FE	47	48
# SURVEYED		130	121

AGE	RESP	'88	'89
48-53	MA	59%	54%
	BO	0	0
	FE	41	46
# SURVEYED		61	107

		YEAR	
AGE	RESP	'88	'89
54-59	MA	56%	57%
	BO	0	0
	FE	44	43
# SURVEYED		54	61

		YEAR	
AGE	RESP	'88	'89
60-65	MA	51%	61%
	BO	0	0
	FE	49	39
# SURVEYED		74	61

		YEAR	
AGE	RESP	'88	'89
66+	MA	48%	39%
	BO	0	0
	FE	52	61
# SURVEYED		91	87

****

FREQUENCY OF SEX

TABLE I: FREQUENCY OF SEX -- BY TOTAL POPULATION

Question: About how often did you have sex during the last six months? NOTE: Question not asked in 1972-1988.

Responses: NO = Not at all; YR = Once or twice; MN = About once a month; 3 = 2 or 3 times a month; WK = About once a week; 2W = 2 or 3 times a week; 3+ = More than 3 times a week

	YEAR
RESPONSE	'89
NO	22%
YR	7
MN	8
23	16
WK	19
2W	23
3+	5
# SURVEYED	1361

TABLE II: FREQUENCY OF SEX -- BY SEX

Question: About how often did you have sex during the last six months? NOTE: Question not asked in 1972-1988.

Responses: NO = Not at all; YR = Once or twice; MN = About once a month; 3 = 2 or 3 times a month; WK = About once a week; 2W = 2 or 3 times a week; 3+ = More than 3 times a week

SEX	RESP	YEAR '89
MALE	NO	13%
	YR	7
	MN	9
	23	17
	WK	23
	2W	26
	3+	5
# SURVEYED		584

SEX	RESP	YEAR '89
FEMALE	NO	29%
	YR	8
	MN	8
	23	16
	WK	16
	2W	20
	3+	4
# SURVEYED		777

TABLE III: FREQUENCY OF SEX -- BY RACE

Question: About how often did you have sex during the last six months? NOTE: Question not asked in 1972-1988.

Responses: NO = Not at all; YR = Once or twice; MN = About once a month; 3 = 2 or 3 times a month; WK = About once a week; 2W = 2 or 3 times a week; 3+ = More than 3 times a week

RACE	RESP	YEAR '89
WHITE	NO	22%
	YR	6
	MN	8
	23	17
	WK	20
	2W	22
	3+	5
# SURVEYED		1171

RACE	RESP	YEAR '89
BLACK	NO	20%
	YR	11
	MN	9
	23	15
	WK	12
	2W	29
	3+	4
# SURVEYED		137

RACE	RESP	YEAR '89
OTHER	NO	15%
	YR	17
	MN	15
	23	11
	WK	19
	2W	19
	3+	4
# SURVEYED		53

TABLE IV: FREQUENCY OF SEX -- BY AGE

Question: About how often did you have sex during the last six months? NOTE: Question not asked in 1972-1988.

Responses: NO = Not at all; YR = Once or twice; MN = About once a month; 3 = 2 or 3 times a month; WK = About once a week; 2W = 2 or 3 times a week; 3+ = More than 3 times a week

AGE	RESP	'89
18-23	NO	21%
	YR	7
	MN	9
	23	14
	WK	19
	2W	22
	3+	9
# SURVEYED		129
24-29	NO	7%
	YR	13
	MN	5
	23	14
	WK	14
	2W	35
	3+	11
# SURVEYED		187
30-35	NO	7%
	YR	7
	MN	6
	23	14
	WK	26
	2W	37
	3+	4
# SURVEYED		192
36-41	NO	6%
	YR	3
	MN	6
	23	18
	WK	28
	2W	33
	3+	6
# SURVEYED		180
42-47	NO	12%
	YR	6
	MN	6
	23	25
	WK	23
	2W	25
	3+	4
# SURVEYED		142
48-53	NO	13%
	YR	8
	MN	9
	23	30
	WK	17
	2W	18
	3+	4
# SURVEYED		122
54-59	NO	23%
	YR	4
	MN	18
	23	13
	WK	23
	2W	15
	3+	4
# SURVEYED		82
60-65	NO	36%
	YR	14
	MN	11
	23	17
	WK	13
	2W	9
	3+	1
# SURVEYED		94
66+	NO	64%
	YR	6
	MN	12
	23	8
	WK	10
	2W	2
	3+	0
# SURVEYED		231

****

FEMALE SEX PARTNERS SINCE AGE 18

TABLE I: FEMALE SEX PARTNERS SINCE AGE 18 -- BY TOTAL POPULATION

Question: Now thinking about the time since your 18th birthday, how many female sex partners have you had?? NOTE: Question not asked in 1972-1988.

Responses: 0 = 0; 1 = 1; 2 = 2; 3 = 3; 4 = 4 - 6; 5 = 7 - 9; 6 = 10 - 14; 7 = 15 - 24; 8 = 25 - 997

	YEAR
RESPONSE	'89
0	55%
1	11
2	3
3	4
4	10
5	2
6	4
7	5
8	6
# SURVEYED	1230

TABLE II: FEMALE SEX PARTNERS SINCE AGE 18 -- BY SEX

Question: Now thinking about the time since your 18th birthday, how many female sex partners have you had? NOTE: Question not asked in 1972-1988.

Responses: 0 = 0; 1 = 1; 2 = 2; 3 = 3; 4 = 4 - 6; 5 = 7 - 9; 6 = 10 - 14; 7 = 15 - 24; 8 = 25 - 997

		YEAR
SEX	RESP	'89
MALE	0	5%
	1	21
	2	6
	3	9
	4	21
	5	4
	6	9
	7	11
	8	13
# SURVEYED		540

		YEAR
SEX	RESP	'89
FEMALE	0	94%
	1	2
	2	1
	3	1
	4	1
	5	0
	6	0
	7	0
	8	0
# SURVEYED		690

TABLE III: FEMALE SEX PARTNERS SINCE AGE 18 -- BY RACE

Question: Now thinking about the time since your 18th birthday, how many female sex partners have you had? NOTE: Question not asked in 1972-1988.

Responses: 0 = 0; 1 = 1; 2 = 2; 3 = 3; 4 = 4 - 6; 5 = 7 - 9; 6 = 10 - 14; 7 = 15 - 24; 8 = 25 - 997

RACE	RESP	YEAR '89
WHITE	0	54%
	1	11
	2	3
	3	4
	4	10
	5	2
	6	5
	7	5
	8	6
# SURVEYED		1070

RACE	RESP	YEAR '89
BLACK	0	68%
	1	4
	2	4
	3	4
	4	6
	5	2
	6	1
	7	7
	8	5
# SURVEYED		112

RACE	RESP	YEAR '89
OTHER	0	56%
	1	13
	2	6
	3	6
	4	10
	5	0
	6	0
	7	2
	8	6
# SURVEYED		48

TABLE IV: FEMALE SEX PARTNERS SINCE AGE 18 -- BY AGE

Question: Now thinking about the time since your 18th birthday, how many female sex partners have you had? NOTE: Question not asked in 1972-1988.

Responses: 0 = 0; 1 = 1; 2 = 2; 3 = 3; 4 = 4 - 6; 5 = 7 - 9; 6 = 10 - 14; 7 = 15 - 24; 8 = 25 - 997

AGE	RESP	YEAR '89
18-23	0	52%
	1	9
	2	7
	3	7
	4	16
	5	2
	6	2
	7	2
	8	2
# SURVEYED		122

AGE	RESP	YEAR '89
24-29	0	51%
	1	9
	2	2
	3	4
	4	11
	5	3
	6	6
	7	8
	8	7
# SURVEYED		180

AGE	RESP	YEAR '89
30-35	0	51%
	1	12
	2	2
	3	3
	4	14
	5	2
	6	5
	7	4
	8	6
# SURVEYED		183

AGE	RESP	YEAR '89
36-41	0	48%
	1	10
	2	1
	3	4
	4	10
	5	1
	6	8
	7	9
	8	8
# SURVEYED		168

AGE	RESP	YEAR '89
42-47	0	56%
	1	11
	2	4
	3	2
	4	9
	5	2
	6	6
	7	4
	8	6
# SURVEYED		139

TABLE IV: FEMALE SEX PARTNERS SINCE AGE 18 -- BY AGE (Continued)

Question: Now thinking about the time since your 18th birthday, how many female sex partners have you had? NOTE: Question not asked in 1972-1988.

Responses: 0 = 0 1 = 1 2 = 2 3 = 3 4 = 4 - 6
5 = 7 - 9 6 = 10 - 14 7 = 15 - 24 8 = 25 - 997

		YEAR
AGE	RESP	'89
48-53	0	56%
	1	9
	2	5
	3	5
	4	8
	5	4
	6	4
	7	4
	8	7
# SURVEYED		104

		YEAR
AGE	RESP	'89
54-59	0	60%
	1	7
	2	0
	3	9
	4	4
	5	0
	6	1
	7	4
	8	13
# SURVEYED		67

		YEAR
AGE	RESP	'89
60-65	0	64%
	1	9
	2	3
	3	6
	4	5
	5	2
	6	2
	7	1
	8	7
# SURVEYED		86

		YEAR
AGE	RESP	'89
66+	0	65%
	1	16
	2	4
	3	2
	4	7
	5	1
	6	0
	7	2
	8	2
# SURVEYED		179

****

MALE SEX PARTNERS SINCE AGE 18

TABLE I: MALE SEX PARTNERS SINCE AGE 18 -- BY TOTAL POPULATION

Question: Now thinking about the time since your 18th birthday, how many male sex partners have you had? NOTE: Question not asked in 1972-1988.

Responses: 0 = 0 1 = 1 2 = 2 3 = 3 4 = 4 - 6
5 = 7 - 9 6 = 10 - 14 7 = 15 - 24 8 = 25 - 997

	YEAR
RESPONSE	'89
0	45%
1	25
2	8
3	6
4	9
5	2
6	2
7	2
8	2
# SURVEYED	1279

TABLE II: MALE SEX PARTNERS SINCE AGE 18 -- BY SEX

Question: Now thinking about the time since your 18th birthday, how many male sex partners have you had? NOTE: Question not asked in 1972-1988.

Responses: 0 = 0 1 = 1 2 = 2 3 = 3 4 = 4 - 6
5 = 7 - 9 6 = 10 - 14 7 = 15 - 24 8 = 25 - 997

		YEAR
SEX	RESP	'89
MALE	0	93%
	1	2
	2	1
	3	1
	4	1
	5	0
	6	0
	7	0
	8	1
# SURVEYED		563

		YEAR
SEX	RESP	'89
FEMALE	0	7%
	1	43
	2	13
	3	10
	4	15
	5	3
	6	4
	7	3
	8	2
# SURVEYED		716

TABLE III: MALE SEX PARTNERS SINCE AGE 18 -- BY RACE

Question: Now thinking about the time since your 18th birthday, how many male sex partners have you had? NOTE: Question not asked in 1972-1988.

Responses: 0 = 0 1 = 1 2 = 2 3 = 3 4 = 4 - 6
5 = 7 - 9 6 = 10 - 14 7 = 15 - 24 8 = 25 - 997

RACE	RESP	YEAR '89
WHITE	0	46%
	1	26
	2	8
	3	5
	4	7
	5	2
	6	2
	7	2
	8	2
# SURVEYED		1113

RACE	RESP	YEAR '89
BLACK	0	30%
	1	18
	2	7
	3	16
	4	20
	5	3
	6	1
	7	3
	8	3
# SURVEYED		120

RACE	RESP	YEAR '89
OTHER	0	52%
	1	26
	2	7
	3	0
	4	9
	5	2
	6	4
	7	0
	8	0
# SURVEYED		46

TABLE IV: MALE SEX PARTNERS SINCE AGE 18 -- BY AGE

Question: Now thinking about the time since your 18th birthday, how many male sex partners have you had? NOTE: Question not asked in 1972-1988.

Responses: 0 = 0 1 = 1 2 = 2 3 = 3 4 = 4 - 6
5 = 7 - 9 6 = 10 - 14 7 = 15 - 24 8 = 25 - 997

AGE	RESP	YEAR '89
18-23	0	55%
	1	23
	2	8
	3	7
	4	7
	5	0
	6	0
	7	0
	8	1
# SURVEYED		122

AGE	RESP	YEAR '89
24-29	0	45%
	1	17
	2	7
	3	9
	4	11
	5	2
	6	3
	7	2
	8	2
# SURVEYED		179

AGE	RESP	YEAR '89
30-35	0	44%
	1	19
	2	6
	3	5
	4	17
	5	1
	6	3
	7	2
	8	2
# SURVEYED		186

TABLE IV: MALE SEX PARTNERS SINCE AGE 18 -- BY AGE (Continued)

Question: Now thinking about the time since your 18th birthday, how many male sex partners have you had? NOTE: Question not asked in 1972-1988.

Responses: 0 = 0 1 = 1 2 = 2 3 = 3 4 = 4 - 6
5 = 7 - 9 6 = 10 - 14 7 = 15 - 24 8 = 25 - 997

AGE	RESP	YEAR '89
36-41	0	50%
	1	20
	2	6
	3	6
	4	7
	5	3
	6	2
	7	3
	8	2
# SURVEYED		176

AGE	RESP	'89
42-47	0	42%
	1	24
	2	8
	3	7
	4	6
	5	4
	6	6
	7	1
	8	2
# SURVEYED		139

AGE	RESP	YEAR '89
48-53	0	42%
	1	33
	2	4
	3	7
	4	6
	5	4
	6	0
	7	1
	8	3
# SURVEYED		114

AGE	RESP	'89
54-59	0	36%
	1	28
	2	11
	3	4
	4	14
	5	0
	6	1
	7	4
	8	1
# SURVEYED		72

AGE	RESP	YEAR '89
60-65	0	39%
	1	39
	2	7
	3	3
	4	6
	5	2
	6	3
	7	0
	8	0
# SURVEYED		89

AGE	RESP	'89
66+	0	45%
	1	34
	2	11
	3	2
	4	3
	5	0
	6	1
	7	1
	8	1
# SURVEYED		201

****

CURRENT RELIGIOUS AFFILIATION

TABLE I: CURRENT RELIGIOUS AFFILIATION -- BY TOTAL POPULATION

Question: If you are a protestant, what specific denomination are you, if any?

Responses: BP = Baptist MT = Methodist LT = Lutheran PB = Presbyterian
EP = Episcopal OT = Other NO = No denomination given or non-denominational

	YEAR															
RESPONSE	'72	'73	'74	'75	'76	'77	'78	'80	'82	'83	'84	'85	'86	'87	'88	'89
BP	31%	33%	34%	32%	32%	32%	33%	33%	30%	31%	32%	34%	32%	34%	35%	32%
MT	23	21	20	18	17	19	19	18	17	15	18	18	16	15	15	15
LT	14	13	12	14	11	14	12	10	13	15	10	10	13	9	8	12
PB	8	6	8	8	8	7	6	8	7	7	8	6	5	8	7	7
EP	3	4	4	5	5	4	4	4	5	4	3	4	4	3	3	4
OT	18	17	18	19	21	19	21	21	21	24	24	23	24	25	24	21
NO	3	5	4	5	6	6	5	6	7	5	6	5	6	6	7	9
# SURVEYED	1029	938	953	974	951	1004	978	936	967	968	932	954	920	949	902	968

TABLE II: CURRENT RELIGIOUS AFFILIATION -- BY SEX

Question: If you are a protestant, what specific denomination are you, if any?

Responses: BP = Baptist MT = Methodist LT = Lutheran PB = Presbyterian
EP = Episcopal OT = Other NO = No denomination given or non-denominational

		YEAR															
SEX	RESP	'72	'73	'74	'75	'76	'77	'78	'80	'82	'83	'84	'85	'86	'87	'88	'89
MALE	BP	32%	33%	32%	34%	31%	31%	31%	32%	30%	33%	30%	35%	31%	33%	35%	28%
	MT	25	21	21	18	17	21	20	19	16	13	17	15	14	14	16	17
	LT	13	14	12	14	10	14	13	11	12	13	13	10	15	9	8	10
	PB	8	7	8	8	9	6	7	8	8	7	9	7	7	9	8	6
	EP	4	4	3	4	3	4	4	3	5	5	3	5	4	3	2	4
	OT	15	18	18	18	20	19	19	22	20	25	22	24	21	24	23	22
	NO	4	4	6	5	8	6	6	7	8	5	6	4	7	9	7	12
# SURVEYED		493	427	439	416	411	431	395	389	383	403	355	403	356	405	365	385
SEX	RESP	'72	'73	'74	'75	'76	'77	'78	'80	'82	'83	'84	'85	'86	'87	'88	'89
FEMALE	BP	31%	34%	35%	30%	32%	34%	33%	34%	30%	30%	33%	33%	33%	34%	35%	34%
	MT	21	22	19	18	17	18	19	18	17	17	18	20	17	16	15	14
	LT	14	13	12	15	11	13	11	9	14	16	8	11	11	9	8	12
	PB	8	5	8	8	7	7	6	9	6	6	7	5	4	8	6	8
	EP	2	5	4	5	6	3	4	6	4	3	3	4	4	3	4	5
	OT	21	17	18	19	21	19	22	20	22	23	24	21	26	26	24	20
	NO	3	5	3	5	5	5	4	4	6	5	6	6	5	4	7	7
# SURVEYED		536	511	514	558	540	573	583	547	584	565	577	551	564	544	537	583

TABLE III: CURRENT RELIGIOUS AFFILIATION -- BY RACE

Question: If you are a protestant, what specific denomination are you, if any?

Responses: BP = Baptist MT = Methodist LT = Lutheran PB = Presbyterian
EP = Episcopal OT = Other NO = No denomination given or non-denominational

		YEAR															
RACE	RESP	'72	'73	'74	'75	'76	'77	'78	'80	'82	'83	'84	'85	'86	'87	'88	'89
WHITE	BP	22%	27%	27%	26%	26%	26%	26%	27%	25%	25%	26%	29%	25%	25%	27%	25%
	MT	22	22	21	19	18	20	20	19	18	16	19	18	16	17	18	16
	LT	17	16	14	16	12	16	14	11	15	17	12	12	15	11	10	14
	PB	10	7	9	9	9	7	7	10	8	7	9	7	6	10	8	9
	EP	4	5	4	5	6	4	4	5	5	4	3	5	5	4	4	5
	OT	21	18	20	19	22	20	23	21	22	24	24	23	26	26	24	21
	NO	4	5	5	6	7	7	5	6	8	5	7	6	7	7	8	10
# SURVEYED		801	780	802	834	840	847	832	811	830	818	761	807	752	760	730	809
RACE	RESP	'72	'73	'74	'75	'76	'77	'78	'80	'82	'83	'84	'85	'86	'87	'88	'89
BLACK	BP	64%	64%	72%	69%	76%	69%	70%	69%	64%	66%	66%	66%	64%	70%	70%	69%
	MT	25	14	13	12	9	14	16	10	11	12	14	17	15	7	4	10
	LT	0	1	0	1	0	0	0	0	2	1	1	1	2	1	1	1
	PB	1	2	1	1	1	2	0	1	1	1	1	1	1	1	0	0
	EP	1	3	1	2	1	3	1	2	4	1	2	1	1	1	1	0
	OT	8	16	10	14	12	12	11	17	17	20	15	15	15	17	20	18
	NO	1	1	2	1	1	0	2	1	2	0	1	0	1	3	4	3
# SURVEYED		227	152	148	138	108	154	141	121	132	143	145	129	157	162	149	134
RACE	RESP	'72	'73	'74	'75	'76	'77	'78	'80	'82	'83	'84	'85	'86	'87	'88	'89
OTHER	BP	0%	17%	67%	0%	0%	33%	0%	25%	0%	14%	15%	50%	45%	48%	52%	40%
	MT	0	67	0	0	0	0	20	0	20	0	4	0	9	4	4	8
	LT	0	0	0	50	0	0	0	0	20	0	4	0	9	0	0	0
	PB	0	17	33	0	33	0	0	0	0	29	12	6	0	4	4	4
	EP	0	0	0	0	0	0	0	25	20	0	8	0	0	0	0	0
	OT	100	0	0	50	33	67	80	50	40	43	58	39	27	44	39	40
	NO	0	0	0	0	33	0	0	0	0	14	0	6	9	0	0	8
# SURVEYED		1	6	3	2	3	3	5	4	5	7	26	18	11	27	23	25

TABLE IV: CURRENT RELIGIOUS AFFILIATION -- BY AGE

Question: If you are a protestant, what specific denomination are you, if any?

Responses: BP = Baptist MT = Methodist LT = Lutheran PB = Presbyterian
EP = Episcopal OT = Other NO = No denomination given or non-denominational

		YEAR															
AGE	RESP	'72	'73	'74	'75	'76	'77	'78	'80	'82	'83	'84	'85	'86	'87	'88	'89
18-23	BP	35%	41%	38%	36%	35%	43%	46%	37%	42%	43%	29%	39%	39%	47%	47%	40%
	MT	18	18	17	20	11	9	13	16	11	10	16	10	7	14	12	16
	LT	18	16	5	10	8	12	12	13	6	10	10	6	11	3	5	9
	PB	8	3	6	7	12	10	2	7	2	3	10	3	5	0	5	4
	EP	3	3	3	3	2	0	4	3	5	3	3	6	3	4	3	4
	OT	13	14	23	19	24	20	17	21	30	24	24	32	31	23	23	19
	NO	4	3	6	5	7	7	5	2	4	7	7	6	3	9	5	8
# SURVEYED		92	87	94	91	83	103	92	94	83	68	96	72	61	74	75	77
AGE	RESP	'72	'73	'74	'75	'76	'77	'78	'80	'82	'83	'84	'85	'86	'87	'88	'89
24-29	BP	31%	35%	36%	39%	34%	33%	37%	38%	34%	33%	33%	30%	29%	36%	33%	32%
	MT	23	23	16	12	11	21	18	20	14	15	20	20	15	8	18	10
	LT	9	12	15	17	11	9	8	6	10	12	9	6	15	12	8	13
	PB	6	2	10	8	6	6	6	6	8	4	6	6	9	4	3	5
	EP	3	8	3	5	1	2	4	4	4	4	0	4	4	2	3	5
	OT	23	14	15	13	28	25	23	18	23	28	24	28	24	33	22	24
	NO	5	7	6	5	8	5	4	8	7	5	9	6	6	5	12	13
# SURVEYED		131	106	115	132	123	123	142	112	125	164	140	117	136	113	121	110
AGE	RESP	'72	'73	'74	'75	'76	'77	'78	'80	'82	'83	'84	'85	'86	'87	'88	'89
30-35	BP	33%	37%	38%	31%	37%	38%	31%	31%	35%	36%	24%	33%	32%	31%	40%	29%
	MT	16	20	22	14	16	11	18	15	11	16	15	17	20	16	10	18
	LT	19	11	9	16	8	13	16	9	18	14	12	9	14	12	11	13
	PB	6	6	4	6	5	3	5	8	7	2	8	6	2	9	6	8
	EP	3	4	6	7	8	7	2	2	5	2	5	6	2	4	2	2
	OT	18	16	16	23	20	19	22	29	14	27	26	25	22	22	24	22
	NO	4	5	4	4	6	9	5	6	12	3	9	5	8	5	7	9
# SURVEYED		116	97	112	107	115	106	147	124	130	132	117	140	122	129	109	112
AGE	RESP	'72	'73	'74	'75	'76	'77	'78	'80	'82	'83	'84	'85	'86	'87	'88	'89
36-41	BP	32%	38%	34%	37%	30%	43%	38%	33%	30%	26%	33%	39%	33%	29%	27%	34%
	MT	27	16	12	12	16	13	15	14	16	14	18	10	14	18	13	10
	LT	16	13	14	18	15	11	10	13	14	13	7	11	9	10	6	10
	PB	2	4	8	7	7	7	5	8	8	8	6	7	6	9	9	7
	EP	1	4	5	4	6	3	5	4	5	4	6	4	5	3	3	6
	OT	20	20	22	19	19	19	21	21	22	27	24	25	26	22	28	19
	NO	1	4	5	3	6	3	7	6	5	8	6	4	7	9	14	13
# SURVEYED		81	112	93	108	98	122	87	90	93	113	109	105	108	112	112	125

TABLE IV: CURRENT RELIGIOUS AFFILIATION -- BY AGE (Continued)

Question: If you are a protestant, what specific denomination are you, if any?

Responses: BP = Baptist MT = Methodist LT = Lutheran PB = Presbyterian
EP = Episcopal OT = Other NO = No denomination given or non-denominational

		YEAR															
AGE	RESP	'72	'73	'74	'75	'76	'77	'78	'80	'82	'83	'84	'85	'86	'87	'88	'89
42-47	BP	32%	34%	32%	31%	30%	28%	29%	48%	29%	34%	39%	29%	41%	32%	38%	27%
	MT	23	26	20	16	14	14	23	14	26	15	20	14	13	19	15	14
	LT	11	13	13	15	12	21	15	8	12	13	11	16	6	5	10	8
	PB	10	7	9	9	7	4	8	6	5	10	11	4	4	10	3	9
	EP	3	7	1	6	4	3	4	1	6	3	1	6	9	1	1	5
	OT	18	11	21	16	28	20	15	20	19	23	14	21	20	27	26	27
	NO	4	2	3	8	4	9	6	4	4	1	4	10	8	5	7	10
# SURVEYED		111	90	99	101	69	90	79	80	84	91	84	70	79	96	94	108

AGE	RESP	'72	'73	'74	'75	'76	'77	'78	'80	'82	'83	'84	'85	'86	'87	'88	'89
48-53	BP	28%	32%	32%	30%	35%	25%	30%	26%	33%	25%	36%	34%	28%	35%	40%	30%
	MT	19	24	20	17	17	20	17	13	10	22	16	20	26	16	11	20
	LT	12	11	12	16	9	18	10	8	7	12	4	10	9	3	9	12
	PB	9	7	10	11	8	8	6	14	7	6	3	8	5	6	5	5
	EP	3	1	5	4	9	6	6	8	8	3	4	3	4	5	5	4
	OT	23	21	17	16	18	16	31	20	25	26	31	18	21	28	25	21
	NO	5	5	3	5	4	7	0	10	11	6	4	6	8	7	5	9
# SURVEYED		116	102	98	93	89	109	83	84	73	65	67	87	80	88	57	102

AGE	RESP	'72	'73	'74	'75	'76	'77	'78	'80	'82	'83	'84	'85	'86	'87	'88	'89
54-59	BP	27%	29%	36%	36%	32%	24%	28%	39%	18%	33%	43%	34%	30%	29%	46%	31%
	MT	25	21	22	22	26	34	27	14	24	10	14	16	17	11	16	12
	LT	17	19	10	12	8	14	12	6	13	19	7	9	14	11	8	15
	PB	9	7	11	4	8	7	11	7	8	7	8	9	9	13	13	6
	EP	5	3	5	2	6	7	4	7	6	6	0	4	6	4	0	3
	OT	14	17	13	16	15	13	15	22	24	21	24	23	22	27	14	24
	NO	3	5	2	7	4	3	4	4	9	4	4	5	2	5	3	9
# SURVEYED		104	111	91	81	95	118	94	98	102	81	72	92	64	75	63	67

AGE	RESP	'72	'73	'74	'75	'76	'77	'78	'80	'82	'83	'84	'85	'86	'87	'88	'89
60-65	BP	28%	36%	29%	27%	33%	26%	26%	21%	21%	31%	27%	33%	25%	36%	28%	40%
	MT	30	22	25	23	17	22	24	36	19	16	19	27	10	13	16	11
	LT	14	12	16	13	16	20	16	11	17	20	19	12	20	12	11	7
	PB	11	8	6	9	5	9	4	6	10	6	8	4	8	5	9	13
	EP	3	2	1	4	11	1	4	3	2	4	3	5	4	1	8	6
	OT	10	15	18	22	14	17	21	16	21	20	21	13	28	25	23	18
	NO	4	4	5	4	5	6	5	6	9	2	4	6	5	8	5	6
# SURVEYED		109	85	77	79	95	82	76	80	86	83	75	84	79	76	88	72

TABLE IV: CURRENT RELIGIOUS AFFILIATION -- BY AGE (Continued)

Question: If you are a protestant, what specific denomination are you, if any?

Responses: BP = Baptist MT = Methodist LT = Lutheran PB = Presbyterian
EP = Episcopal OT = Other NO = No denomination given or non-denominational

		YEAR															
AGE	RESP	'72	'73	'74	'75	'76	'77	'78	'80	'82	'83	'84	'85	'86	'87	'88	'89
66+	BP	35%	22%	29%	23%	25%	30%	29%	26%	27%	27%	28%	35%	34%	31%	29%	28%
	MT	22	22	24	25	21	25	22	22	21	17	18	21	17	20	21	21
	LT	9	12	13	12	11	9	10	12	16	19	11	14	13	9	7	15
	PB	8	9	5	9	13	7	8	11	8	11	10	7	4	11	9	8
	EP	4	6	5	5	2	4	4	5	4	5	4	3	4	4	5	5
	OT	20	24	19	22	19	20	22	19	20	17	24	19	24	22	26	18
	NO	2	5	5	4	8	4	5	5	4	4	5	2	4	3	4	5
# SURVEYED		165	144	170	179	180	148	174	169	186	166	170	182	186	183	182	193

****

IF PROTESTANT AT AGE 16, WHAT DENOMINATION

TABLE I: IF PROTESTANT AT 16, WHAT DENOMINATION -- BY TOTAL POPULATION

Question: If you were raised a protestant, what specific denomination were you, if any? NOTE: Question not asked in 1972.

Responses: BP = Baptist MT = Methodist LT = Lutheran PB = Presbyterian
EP = Episcopal OT = Other NO = No denomination given or non-denominational

	YEAR														
RESPONSE	'73	'74	'75	'76	'77	'78	'80	'82	'83	'84	'85	'86	'87	'88	'89
BP	36%	37%	33%	35%	35%	37%	34%	33%	34%	35%	36%	36%	37%	38%	33%
MT	20	22	23	20	21	22	23	23	18	21	21	19	19	19	18
LT	13	12	14	11	14	13	11	13	14	10	10	13	9	9	13
PB	7	8	7	10	7	6	9	7	6	8	7	5	8	9	8
EP	4	3	4	4	3	3	4	4	4	3	4	4	3	3	3
OT	16	15	16	17	16	17	17	17	20	20	20	20	22	18	19
NO	3	2	3	3	3	3	3	3	3	4	2	3	2	3	6
# SURVEYED	974	982	1030	970	1041	1015	980	986	995	946	978	948	963	949	964

TABLE II: IF PROTESTANT AT 16, WHAT DENOMINATION -- BY SEX

Question: If you were raised a protestant, what specific denomination were you, if any? NOTE: Question not asked in 1972.

Responses: BP = Baptist MT = Methodist LT = Lutheran PB = Presbyterian
EP = Episcopal OT = Other NO = No denomination given or non-denominational

		YEAR														
SEX	RESP	'73	'74	'75	'76	'77	'78	'80	'82	'83	'84	'85	'86	'87	'88	'89
M	BP	34%	35%	35%	36%	33%	34%	34%	32%	35%	36%	35%	35%	38%	39%	29%
A	MT	21	24	22	20	23	22	23	22	17	20	19	17	18	19	19
L	LT	14	11	14	11	13	14	10	13	12	11	10	15	9	9	13
E	PB	9	10	6	10	7	6	10	10	7	10	7	7	9	10	8
	EP	4	2	4	3	4	4	2	4	5	1	5	3	3	3	4
	OT	16	15	16	17	16	16	17	16	20	18	22	20	20	17	20
	NO	2	3	3	4	3	4	3	4	3	3	3	3	3	4	8
# SURVEYED		447	472	448	429	467	420	416	404	429	368	429	379	413	400	392
SEX	RESP	'73	'74	'75	'76	'77	'78	'80	'82	'83	'84	'85	'86	'87	'88	'89
F	BP	38%	40%	32%	35%	37%	38%	33%	34%	34%	34%	36%	37%	37%	38%	36%
E	MT	20	20	23	21	20	22	23	23	20	21	22	21	19	20	17
M	LT	13	13	15	11	14	12	11	13	16	9	10	11	8	10	12
A	PB	7	7	7	10	8	6	9	6	5	7	8	4	8	8	7
L	EP	4	4	3	5	3	2	5	4	3	4	3	4	3	3	3
E	OT	15	15	16	17	15	17	17	18	20	21	19	21	23	19	19
	NO	3	1	3	2	3	3	2	3	2	4	2	3	2	3	5
# SURVEYED		527	510	582	541	574	595	564	582	566	578	549	569	550	549	572

TABLE III: IF PROTESTANT AT 16, WHAT DENOMINATION -- BY RACE

Question: If you were raised a protestant, what specific denomination were you, if any? NOTE: Question not asked in 1972.

Responses: BP = Baptist MT = Methodist LT = Lutheran PB = Presbyterian
EP = Episcopal OT = Other NO = No denomination given or non-denominational

		YEAR														
RACE	RESP	'73	'74	'75	'76	'77	'78	'80	'82	'83	'84	'85	'86	'87	'88	'89
WHITE	BP	28%	29%	27%	29%	28%	31%	27%	26%	28%	28%	30%	28%	28%	29%	26%
	MT	22	24	24	22	22	22	24	24	19	22	21	20	21	22	19
	LT	16	14	17	13	16	15	12	15	17	12	11	15	10	11	15
	PB	9	9	8	10	9	7	11	8	7	10	9	6	10	10	9
	EP	4	4	4	4	4	3	4	4	4	3	4	4	3	4	4
	OT	18	17	18	19	18	19	18	18	22	22	22	23	25	19	20
	NO	3	3	3	3	3	3	3	4	3	4	3	3	3	4	7
# SUR EYED		804	822	879	852	879	862	848	840	836	780	830	770	781	759	806
RACE	RESP	'73	'74	'75	'76	'77	'78	'80	'82	'83	'84	'85	'86	'87	'88	'89
BLACK	BP	77%	81%	71%	81%	74%	72%	75%	71%	70%	70%	69%	72%	82%	79%	76%
	MT	12	12	17	9	15	21	15	13	15	18	21	14	9	7	10
	LT	0	0	1	0	0	0	0	1	1	0	1	1	1	1	1
	PB	2	2	0	4	1	0	1	1	0	1	0	1	1	0	0
	EP	3	1	5	1	3	1	2	4	2	2	1	2	1	1	1
	OT	6	4	6	5	6	5	8	11	12	8	7	8	7	11	11
	NO	1	0	1	0	1	1	0	0	1	1	0	2	0	1	1
# SURVEYED		165	159	151	114	158	147	129	142	154	145	136	167	162	166	137
RACE	RESP	'73	'74	'75	'76	'77	'78	'80	'82	'83	'84	'85	'86	'87	'88	'89
OTHER	BP	20%	100%	0%	25%	50%	17%	0%	25%	0%	43%	50%	55%	55%	50%	48%
	MT	60	0	0	0	25	17	0	25	0	5	8	9	10	13	5
	LT	0	0	0	0	25	0	0	0	20	0	0	0	0	0	0
	PB	20	0	0	25	0	0	0	0	40	10	8	9	5	17	5
	EP	0	0	0	0	0	0	33	25	20	5	0	0	0	0	0
	OT	0	0	0	25	0	50	67	25	20	38	33	27	30	21	33
	NO	0	0	0	25	0	17	0	0	0	0	0	0	0	0	10
# SURVEYED		5	1	4	4	6	3	4	5	21	12	11	20	24	21	

TABLE IV: IF PROTESTANT AT 16, WHAT DENOMINATION -- BY AGE

Question: If you were raised a protestant, what specific denomination were you, if any? NOTE: Question not asked in 1972.

Responses: BP = Baptist MT = Methodist LT = Lutheran PB = Presbyterian
EP = Episcopal OT = Other NO = No denomination given or non-denominational

		YEAR														
AGE	RESP	'73	'74	'75	'76	'77	'78	'80	'82	'83	'84	'85	'86	'87	'88	'89
18-23	BP	42%	38%	39%	37%	42%	48%	40%	48%	42%	30%	43%	45%	49%	51%	43%
	MT	17	21	22	16	14	18	17	13	14	20	14	6	11	11	19
	LT	14	9	7	13	13	14	9	8	9	12	4	10	4	5	9
	PB	7	6	8	13	11	3	8	5	4	9	4	4	4	4	4
	EP	3	2	4	1	1	3	3	3	5	2	4	4	4	4	3
	OT	15	20	17	17	15	13	19	19	18	23	27	30	24	22	16
	NO	1	4	3	4	5	1	3	3	8	4	4	1	4	4	6
# SURVEYED		99	104	96	95	109	100	95	91	77	94	77	71	75	82	77
AGE	RESP	'73	'74	'75	'76	'77	'78	'80	'82	'83	'84	'85	'86	'87	'88	'89
24-29	BP	42%	35%	36%	33%	37%	39%	41%	36%	33%	37%	31%	33%	45%	38%	35%
	MT	21	22	18	21	21	20	20	19	16	16	20	21	11	21	13
	LT	11	15	16	14	11	8	10	12	12	9	9	13	9	15	14
	PB	4	11	9	6	7	8	7	7	5	9	7	8	8	6	8
	EP	3	1	5	3	2	3	4	5	4	0	5	2	3	3	6
	OT	16	15	13	21	19	18	14	17	28	22	26	19	23	15	17
	NO	2	2	3	2	4	5	4	4	3	6	2	4	1	2	8
# SURVEYED		117	116	152	132	134	155	123	132	172	140	122	130	115	124	104
AGE	RESP	'73	'74	'75	'76	'77	'78	'80	'82	'83	'84	'85	'86	'87	'88	'89
30-35	BP	30%	44%	38%	41%	41%	35%	30%	42%	43%	30%	37%	40%	35%	41%	32%
	MT	25	21	17	14	13	21	24	17	13	19	19	22	16	13	21
	LT	10	6	13	10	15	15	11	15	13	12	8	17	13	9	16
	PB	10	8	6	11	5	6	11	5	7	11	8	2	10	8	9
	EP	6	6	3	7	7	5	3	4	2	5	5	2	4	3	2
	OT	17	14	23	13	16	15	18	13	22	19	20	13	20	21	16
	NO	2	2	0	4	3	3	3	5	1	4	3	3	2	5	5
# SURVEYED		105	117	118	119	115	151	141	128	136	121	146	126	135	119	117
AGE	RESP	'73	'74	'75	'76	'77	'78	'80	'82	'83	'84	'85	'86	'87	'88	'89
36-41	BP	44%	38%	39%	38%	43%	36%	31%	34%	35%	39%	36%	37%	40%	37%	37%
	MT	18	12	15	19	14	16	18	22	16	19	19	19	21	20	10
	LT	10	18	15	10	12	14	13	12	16	6	9	10	7	7	15
	PB	7	8	6	8	6	2	14	8	7	10	10	6	7	11	7
	EP	5	4	5	5	3	2	4	4	5	4	3	2	1	4	5
	OT	15	18	17	17	20	28	16	21	16	19	22	25	22	16	19
	NO	1	2	4	3	2	2	3	0	3	2	1	1	2	3	7
# SURVEYED		112	97	114	103	126	94	98	92	110	113	108	115	123	123	123

TABLE IV: IF PROTESTANT AT 16, WHAT DENOMINATION -- BY AGE (Continued)

Question: If you were raised a protestant, what specific denomination were you, if any? NOTE: Question not asked in 1972.

Responses: BP = Baptist MT = Methodist LT = Lutheran PB = Presbyterian
EP = Episcopal OT = Other NO = No denomination given or non-denominational

		YEAR														
AGE	RESP	'73	'74	'75	'76	'77	'78	'80	'82	'83	'84	'85	'86	'87	'88	'89
42-47	BP	31%	39%	31%	38%	43%	30%	47%	27%	44%	39%	30%	34%	40%	44%	36%
	MT	16	21	24	13	16	19	19	33	14	22	20	26	16	16	16
	LT	14	15	15	11	17	24	11	13	14	9	14	5	5	11	10
	PB	12	8	9	11	5	5	4	8	9	8	6	7	9	8	8
	EP	5	2	3	3	2	3	2	6	3	2	2	10	1	1	5
	OT	21	12	17	22	16	16	15	10	14	18	23	18	27	17	24
	NO	2	3	2	2	1	4	2	3	1	1	5	0	2	3	2
# SURVEYED		95	100	102	63	94	80	81	88	91	85	81	88	94	96	101
AGE	RESP	'73	'74	'75	'76	'77	'78	'80	'82	'83	'84	'85	'86	'87	'88	'89
48-53	BP	41%	38%	32%	35%	28%	39%	35%	28%	26%	42%	38%	37%	32%	44%	32%
	MT	19	20	18	20	24	20	17	21	31	17	22	17	22	14	21
	LT	11	9	20	8	20	11	10	8	9	5	12	7	7	5	12
	PB	7	11	5	8	7	6	14	8	10	5	12	7	8	10	6
	EP	5	3	5	8	5	4	4	8	6	5	3	5	2	3	3
	OT	14	17	14	20	10	20	19	26	17	24	12	21	28	20	17
	NO	3	1	6	1	5	1	1	3	1	3	1	6	2	3	9
# SURVEYED		96	98	95	86	111	85	78	78	70	66	86	82	92	59	103
AGE	RESP	'73	'74	'75	'76	'77	'78	'80	'82	'83	'84	'85	'86	'87	'88	'89
54-59	BP	33%	40%	37%	35%	27%	32%	34%	30%	38%	41%	38%	24%	41%	50%	34%
	MT	20	20	24	22	32	30	22	27	17	21	14	29	14	20	12
	LT	24	15	13	8	13	13	7	11	17	10	12	16	7	8	15
	PB	5	10	5	14	8	9	8	7	5	7	9	3	12	8	6
	EP	3	3	3	2	5	4	5	3	5	0	4	6	3	3	2
	OT	13	11	14	16	13	11	23	19	17	20	20	22	22	6	23
	NO	4	1	3	3	2	1	2	3	2	1	4	0	3	5	8
# SURVEYED		110	96	86	92	122	98	104	103	84	71	85	63	74	64	65
AGE	RESP	'73	'74	'75	'76	'77	'78	'80	'82	'83	'84	'85	'86	'87	'88	'89
60-65	BP	41%	37%	26%	31%	27%	34%	28%	24%	23%	28%	35%	33%	28%	31%	36%
	MT	24	28	35	22	29	26	38	29	24	24	27	14	22	23	14
	LT	12	10	15	15	20	14	9	15	20	12	11	19	10	13	4
	PB	5	4	2	11	8	4	5	10	3	8	5	1	7	9	12
	EP	1	3	4	3	0	3	0	1	3	1	5	4	1	6	4
	OT	11	18	15	14	13	14	19	16	23	21	16	24	31	17	20
	NO	6	1	4	4	4	7	0	5	3	5	1	4	1	1	9
# SURVEYED		83	79	82	94	79	74	74	82	87	75	82	78	72	87	74

TABLE IV: IF PROTESTANT AT 16, WHAT DENOMINATION -- BY AGE (Continued)

Question: If you were raised a protestant, what specific denomination were you, if any? NOTE: Question not asked in 1972.

Responses: BP = Baptist MT = Methodist LT = Lutheran PB = Presbyterian
EP = Episcopal OT = Other NO = No denomination given or non-denominational

		YEAR														
AGE	RESP	'73	'74	'75	'76	'77	'78	'80	'82	'83	'84	'85	'86	'87	'88	'89
66+	BP	28%	31%	26%	30%	31%	35%	26%	26%	27%	30%	34%	39%	32%	26%	26%
	MT	22	29	31	27	28	27	28	25	24	26	26	18	28	27	24
	LT	14	14	16	11	9	8	14	18	19	11	11	15	11	8	14
	PB	10	6	6	9	9	9	11	9	6	8	6	5	8	11	9
	EP	5	4	2	3	4	1	6	5	4	4	4	3	3	3	2
	OT	16	12	16	16	18	18	13	14	18	17	18	18	14	22	21
	NO	4	4	2	2	2	3	3	3	2	4	1	3	4	3	5
# SURVEYED		153	170	183	182	149	173	180	187	164	179	186	190	180	193	198

****

INTENSITY OF RELIGIOUS BELIEFS

TABLE I: INTENSITY OF RELIGIOUS BELIEFS -- BY TOTAL POPULATION

Question: Would you call yourself a strong member of your faith, or a not very strong member of your faith? NOTE: This question was asked of all who indicated any religious preference. Question not asked in 1972, 1973.

Responses: ST = Strong; NV = Not very strong; SW = Somewhat strong

	YEAR													
RESPONSE	'74	'75	'76	'77	'78	'80	'82	'83	'84	'85	'86	'87	'88	'89
ST	43%	43%	39%	41%	39%	42%	43%	44%	49%	44%	43%	43%	42%	39%
NV	49	46	46	51	53	48	48	49	42	46	46	45	46	45
SW	8	11	14	8	8	10	9	7	8	10	11	12	13	16
# SURVEYED	1364	1358	1354	1407	1397	1340	1356	1457	1334	1372	1261	1330	1198	1329

TABLE II: INTENSITY OF RELIGIOUS BELIEFS -- BY SEX

Question: Would you call yourself a strong member of your faith, or a not very strong member of your faith? NOTE: This question was asked of all who indicated any religious preference. Question not asked in 1972, 1973.

Responses: ST = Strong; NV = Not very strong; SW = Somewhat strong

		YEAR													
SEX	RESP	'74	'75	'76	'77	'78	'80	'82	'83	'84	'85	'86	'87	'88	'89
M	ST	38%	35%	32%	34%	33%	33%	39%	38%	39%	36%	37%	36%	33%	33%
	NV	54	53	54	58	59	55	53	55	51	55	52	51	53	53
	SW	8	13	14	8	8	12	9	7	10	9	11	13	14	14
# SURVEYED		615	596	585	616	566	568	544	617	520	604	521	571	483	549
SEX	RESP	'74	'75	'76	'77	'78	'80	'82	'83	'84	'85	'86	'87	'88	'89
F	ST	47%	49%	45%	47%	44%	48%	46%	49%	55%	51%	48%	48%	47%	44%
	NV	45	41	41	45	48	44	45	44	37	39	41	41	41	40
	SW	8	10	15	8	8	8	9	7	8	10	11	11	11	16
# SURVEYED		749	762	769	791	831	772	812	840	814	768	740	759	715	780

TABLE III: INTENSITY OF RELIGIOUS BELIEFS -- BY RACE

Question: Would you call yourself a strong member of your faith, or a not very strong member of your faith? NOTE: This question was asked of all who indicated any religious preference. Question not asked in 1972, 1973.

Responses: ST = Strong; NV = Not very strong; SW = Somewhat strong

		YEAR													
RACE	RESP	'74	'75	'76	'77	'78	'80	'82	'83	'84	'85	'86	'87	'88	'89
WHITE	ST	42%	41%	39%	40%	39%	40%	43%	43%	48%	43%	42%	42%	41%	39%
	NV	49	48	47	52	53	50	49	50	43	47	48	47	47	45
	SW	9	11	14	8	8	10	9	8	9	10	11	12	12	16
# SURVEYED		1196	1201	1224	1233	1235	1202	1185	1291	1126	1194	1074	1110	1007	1138
RACE	RESP	'74	'75	'76	'77	'78	'80	'82	'83	'84	'85	'86	'87	'88	'89
BLACK	ST	51%	56%	47%	53%	44%	55%	44%	55%	58%	57%	51%	48%	52%	50%
	NV	44	32	39	40	47	35	42	40	35	32	37	40	35	36
	SW	5	12	14	7	9	10	14	5	7	11	12	12	13	14
# SURVEYED		161	154	122	163	149	128	147	152	160	142	158	174	143	139
RACE	RESP	'74	'75	'76	'77	'78	'80	'82	'83	'84	'85	'86	'87	'88	'89
OTHER	ST	29%	67%	25%	64%	46%	30%	42%	57%	40%	39%	55%	50%	29%	25%
	NV	71	0	63	36	31	60	54	36	50	58	34	41	52	63
	SW	0	33	13	0	23	10	4	7	10	3	10	9	19	12
# SURVEYED		7	3	8	11	13	10	24	14	48	36	29	46	48	52

TABLE IV: INTENSITY OF RELIGIOUS BELIEFS -- BY AGE

Question: Would you call yourself a strong member of your faith, or a not very strong member of your faith? NOTE: This question was asked of all who indicated any religious preference. Question not asked in 1972, 1973.

Responses: ST = Strong; NV = Not very strong; SW = Somewhat strong

		YEAR													
AGE	RESP	'74	'75	'76	'77	'78	'80	'82	'83	'84	'85	'86	'87	'88	'89
18-23	ST	30%	42%	26%	24%	27%	38%	35%	36%	41%	25%	31%	34%	28%	32%
	NV	63	46	56	65	69	54	55	56	51	62	56	57	55	55
	SW	7	12	18	11	4	8	10	9	8	13	13	9	17	13
# SURVEYED		145	147	132	147	140	136	124	104	143	110	87	109	104	118
AGE	RESP	'74	'75	'76	'77	'78	'80	'82	'83	'84	'85	'86	'87	'88	'89
24-29	ST	31%	29%	32%	29%	26%	33%	35%	38%	43%	39%	34%	36%	29%	29%
	NV	61	59	58	63	63	61	56	55	50	54	57	49	58	54
	SW	8	11	11	8	11	6	9	7	8	7	10	15	13	17
# SURVEYED		189	192	189	178	213	174	209	256	200	183	187	173	160	167

TABLE IV: INTENSITY OF RELIGIOUS BELIEFS -- BY AGE (Continued)

Question: Would you call yourself a strong member of your faith, or a not very strong member of your faith? NOTE: This question was asked of all who indicated any religious preference. Question not asked in 1972, 1973.

Responses: ST = Strong; NV = Not very strong; SW = Somewhat strong

		YEAR													
AGE	RESP	'74	'75	'76	'77	'78	'80	'82	'83	'84	'85	'86	'87	'88	'89
30-35	ST	41%	39%	31%	35%	34%	41%	31%	48%	47%	37%	39%	32%	42%	36%
	NV	55	49	55	54	58	53	60	49	38	56	50	57	45	45
	SW	4	12	14	11	8	6	9	3	14	7	11	12	13	19
# SURVEYED		157	154	170	165	202	189	184	208	177	185	197	191	153	169
AGE	RESP	'74	'75	'76	'77	'78	'80	'82	'83	'84	'85	'86	'87	'88	'89
36-41	ST	45%	39%	37%	42%	42%	39%	43%	40%	41%	43%	39%	42%	39%	33%
	NV	46	51	47	50	52	52	49	53	54	46	52	48	49	52
	SW	9	10	15	8	7	9	8	7	5	10	9	10	12	15
# SURVEYED		142	146	139	154	149	134	133	160	167	164	151	162	152	165
AGE	RESP	'74	'75	'76	'77	'78	'80	'82	'83	'84	'85	'86	'87	'88	'89
42-47	ST	48%	38%	39%	44%	42%	41%	39%	36%	42%	42%	45%	40%	42%	38%
	NV	42	49	43	46	52	43	51	59	50	50	46	52	46	48
	SW	11	13	19	11	6	16	10	6	9	8	8	8	12	15
# SURVEYED		142	129	108	133	107	107	110	138	117	106	119	142	130	141
AGE	RESP	'74	'75	'76	'77	'78	'80	'82	'83	'84	'85	'86	'87	'88	'89
48-53	ST	34%	48%	39%	46%	38%	47%	42%	55%	49%	41%	42%	45%	37%	39%
	NV	56	43	46	50	53	46	50	42	40	47	46	43	49	47
	SW	10	9	14	3	9	8	8	4	10	12	12	12	14	14
# SURVEYED		135	138	125	145	128	118	100	106	97	123	92	120	81	120
AGE	RESP	'74	'75	'76	'77	'78	'80	'82	'83	'84	'85	'86	'87	'88	'89
54-59	ST	55%	48%	38%	43%	47%	34%	51%	46%	68%	48%	51%	53%	50%	52%
	NV	37	40	49	52	43	51	47	46	27	39	38	38	38	33
	SW	8	12	14	5	10	16	2	7	5	13	11	9	13	15
# SURVEYED		129	120	125	163	129	128	134	123	106	123	92	95	72	94
AGE	RESP	'74	'75	'76	'77	'78	'80	'82	'83	'84	'85	'86	'87	'88	'89
60-65	ST	46%	47%	44%	49%	46%	43%	49%	56%	54%	49%	52%	43%	49%	41%
	NV	44	45	38	43	43	43	41	38	39	40	38	40	39	41
	SW	11	8	18	8	11	14	10	6	7	11	10	18	12	18
# SURVEYED		101	107	126	113	104	114	107	126	104	124	103	96	104	97
AGE	RESP	'74	'75	'76	'77	'78	'80	'82	'83	'84	'85	'86	'87	'88	'89
66+	ST	55%	54%	59%	59%	55%	53%	59%	47%	60%	61%	52%	58%	52%	51%
	NV	36	34	30	33	37	35	30	39	31	29	34	30	37	34
	SW	9	11	11	7	8	11	12	14	9	10	14	12	11	15
# SURVEYED		218	221	235	203	220	232	246	233	218	247	227	240	241	255

****

TITHING AMOUNT

TABLE I: TITHING AMOUNT -- BY TOTAL POPULATION

Question: About how much do you contribute to your religion every year (not including school tuition)? NOTE: Question not asked in 1972-1986.

Responses: 1 = $1 - $50   2 = $51 = $100   3 = $101 - $250   4 = $251 - $500
5 = $501 - $1,000   6 = $1,001 - $2,500   7 = $2,501 - $5,000   8 = $5,001 - $10,000
9 = $10,000+

	YEAR		
RESPONSE	'87	'88	'89
1	42%	46%	51%
2	12	11	9
3	11	13	10
4	16	13	10
5	9	8	10
6	7	7	5
7	3	2	3
8	1	1	1
9	1	0	1
# SURVEYED	1367	1378	906

TABLE II: TITHING AMOUNT -- BY SEX

Question: About how much do you contribute to your religion every year (not including school tuition)? NOTE: Question not asked in 1972-1986.

Responses: 1 = $1 - $50   2 = $51 = $100   3 = $101 - $250   4 = $251 - $500
5 = $501 - $1,000   6 = $1,001 - $2,500   7 = $2,501 - $5,000   8 = $5,001 - $10,000
9 = $10,000+

		YEAR		
SEX	RESP	'87	'88	'89
MALE	1	44%	50%	54%
	2	10	7	8
	3	11	11	9
	4	14	10	9
	5	9	10	9
	6	6	9	5
	7	3	2	3
	8	1	1	1
	9	1	0	1
# SURVEYED		602	596	390

		YEAR		
SEX	RESP	'87	'88	'89
FEMALE	1	40%	42%	49%
	2	13	13	9
	3	11	14	10
	4	18	15	11
	5	8	8	10
	6	7	5	5
	7	2	2	3
	8	0	1	2
	9	1	0	1
# SURVEYED		765	782	516

TABLE III: TITHING AMOUNT -- BY RACE

Question: About how much do you contribute to your religion every year (not including school tuition)? NOTE: Question not asked in 1972-1986.

Responses: 1 = $1 - $50 2 = $51 = $100 3 = $101 - $250 4 = $251 - $500 5 = $501 - $1,000 6 = $1,001 - $2,500 7 = $2,501 - $5,000 8 = $5,001 - $10,000 9 = $10,000+

RACE	RESP	'87	'88	'89
WHITE	1	41%	45%	51%
	2	11	10	8
	3	10	12	10
	4	16	14	10
	5	9	9	9
	6	7	7	6
	7	3	2	3
	8	1	1	2
	9	1	0	1
# SURVEYED		1144	1154	781

RACE	RESP	'87	'88	'89
BLACK	1	42%	43%	43%
	2	13	17	14
	3	15	14	10
	4	16	11	10
	5	7	8	14
	6	5	5	5
	7	2	1	2
	8	1	1	1
	9	1	0	1
# SURVEYED		176	168	88

RACE	RESP	'87	'88	'89
OTHER	1	55%	61%	59%
	2	13	13	14
	3	13	14	8
	4	13	5	8
	5	2	7	11
	6	2	0	0
	7	2	0	0
	8	0	0	0
	9	0	0	0
# SURVEYED		47	56	37

TABLE IV: TITHING AMOUNT -- BY AGE

Question: About how much do you contribute to your religion every year (not including school tuition)? NOTE: Question not asked in 1972-1986.

Responses: 1 = $1 - $50 2 = $51 = $100 3 = $101 - $250 4 = $251 - $500 5 = $501 - $1,000 6 = $1,001 - $2,500 7 = $2,501 - $5,000 8 = $5,001 - $10,000 9 = $10,000+

AGE	RESP	'87	'88	'89
18-23	1	73%	75%	76%
	2	10	9	11
	3	8	6	8
	4	5	3	4
	5	2	4	1
	6	2	3	0
	7	0	1	0
	8	0	0	0
	9	0	0	0
# SURVEYED		119	134	79

AGE	RESP	'87	'88	'89
24-29	1	58%	57%	71%
	2	14	13	10
	3	10	11	7
	4	10	11	7
	5	3	5	2
	6	3	1	2
	7	2	2	0
	8	1	0	0
	9	0	0	0
# SURVEYED		184	207	136

AGE	RESP	'87	'88	'89
30-35	1	46%	47%	54%
	2	17	9	11
	3	8	11	9
	4	14	14	10
	5	7	6	7
	6	6	8	5
	7	0	3	2
	8	0	1	0
	9	0	0	2
# SURVEYED		213	179	131

TABLE IV: TITHING AMOUNT -- BY AGE

Question: About how much do you contribute to your religion every year (not including school tuition)? NOTE: Question not asked in 1972-1986.

Responses: 1 = $1 - $50 2 = $51 = $100 3 = $101 - $250 4 = $251 - $500 5 = $501 - $1,000 6 = $1,001 - $2,500 7 = $2,501 - $5,000 8 = $5,001 - $10,000 9 = $10,000+

AGE	RESP	'87	'88	'89
		YEAR		
36-41	1	40%	46%	49%
	2	7	10	9
	3	14	12	11
	4	18	12	8
	5	8	12	10
	6	9	7	4
	7	3	2	7
	8	1	1	3
	9	0	0	0
# SURVEYED		174	182	119

AGE	RESP	'87	'88	'89
42-47	1	32%	38%	43%
	2	13	9	9
	3	8	15	9
	4	20	17	13
	5	13	8	10
	6	9	12	4
	7	4	1	6
	8	1	1	3
	9	0	0	2
# SURVEYED		142	151	98

AGE	RESP	'87	'88	'89
		YEAR		
48-53	1	32%	40%	47%
	2	12	12	11
	3	15	16	5
	4	12	11	13
	5	12	12	13
	6	6	4	7
	7	6	4	4
	8	1	1	0
	9	3	0	0
# SURVEYED		114	82	75

AGE	RESP	'87	'88	'89
54-59	1	22%	36%	42%
	2	9	13	3
	3	12	14	10
	4	29	17	11
	5	12	13	18
	6	9	8	6
	7	5	0	5
	8	0	0	2
	9	2	0	3
# SURVEYED		91	78	62

AGE	RESP	'87	'88	'89
		YEAR		
60-65	1	32%	42%	36%
	2	5	7	5
	3	14	12	10
	4	23	14	19
	5	3	6	14
	6	13	11	15
	7	6	6	0
	8	1	1	2
	9	2	1	0
# SURVEYED		94	108	59

AGE	RESP	'87	'88	'89
66+	1	31%	31%	35%
	2	11	12	7
	3	12	18	16
	4	20	18	12
	5	15	12	18
	6	6	7	8
	7	2	1	1
	8	1	1	3
	9	3	0	1
# SURVEYED		234	254	146

****

SUNDAY SCHOOL ATTENDANCE IN YOUTH

TABLE I: SUNDAY SCHOOL ATTENDANCE IN YOUTH -- BY TOTAL POPULATION

Question: When you were growing up, did you attend Sunday school or religious instruction classes regularly, most of the time, some of the time, or never? NOTE: Question not asked in 1972-1987, 1989.

Responses: RG = Regularly MT = Most of the time ST = Some of the time
NV = Never PR = Went to parochial school

	YEAR
RESPONSE	'88
RG	52%
MT	17
ST	21
NV	8
PR	3
# SURVEYED	1475

TABLE II: SUNDAY SCHOOL ATTENDANCE IN YOUTH -- BY SEX

Question: When you were growing up, did you attend Sunday school or religious instruction classes regularly, most of the time, some of the time, or never? NOTE: Question not asked in 1972-1987, 1989.

Responses: RG = Regularly MT = Most of the time ST = Some of the time
NV = Never PR = Went to parochial school

		YEAR
SEX	RESP	'88
MALE	RG	46%
	MT	16
	ST	25
	NV	11
	PR	3
# SURVEYED		636

		YEAR
SEX	RESP	'88
FEMALE	RG	56%
	MT	17
	ST	17
	NV	5
	PR	4
# SURVEYED		839

TABLE III: SUNDAY SCHOOL ATTENDANCE IN YOUTH -- BY RACE

Question: When you were growing up, did you attend Sunday school or religious instruction classes regularly, most of the time, some of the time, or never? NOTE: Question not asked in 1972-1987, 1989.

Responses: RG = Regularly MT = Most of the time ST = Some of the time
NV = Never PR = Went to parochial school

RACE	RESP	'88
WHITE	RG	51%
	MT	17
	ST	21
	NV	8
	PR	4
# SURVEYED		1230

RACE	RESP	'88
BLACK	RG	59%
	MT	18
	ST	17
	NV	5
	PR	0
# SURVEYED		185

RACE	RESP	'88
OTHER	RG	47%
	MT	15
	ST	20
	NV	18
	PR	0
# SURVEYED		60

TABLE IV: SUNDAY SCHOOL ATTENDANCE IN YOUTH -- BY AGE

Question: When you were growing up, did you attend Sunday school or religious instruction classes regularly, most of the time, some of the time, or never? NOTE: Question not asked in 1972-1987, 1989.

Responses: RG = Regularly; MT = Most of the time; ST = Some of the time;
NV = Never; PR = Went to parochial school

AGE	RESP	'88
18-23	RG	40%
	MT	18
	ST	28
	NV	12
	PR	2
# SURVEYED		141
24-29	RG	43%
	MT	21
	ST	25
	NV	8
	PR	3
# SURVEYED		214

AGE	RESP	'88
30-35	RG	55%
	MT	13
	ST	18
	NV	9
	PR	5
# SURVEYED		195
36-41	RG	54%
	MT	17
	ST	19
	NV	6
	PR	3
# SURVEYED		191

AGE	RESP	'88
42-47	RG	57%
	MT	15
	ST	20
	NV	5
	PR	3
# SURVEYED		157
48-53	RG	50%
	MT	12
	ST	29
	NV	6
	PR	3
# SURVEYED		90

AGE	RESP	'88
54-59	RG	65%
	MT	14
	ST	14
	NV	6
	PR	1
# SURVEYED		85
60-65	RG	54%
	MT	16
	ST	23
	NV	8
	PR	0
# SURVEYED		119

AGE	RESP	'88
66+	RG	52%
	MT	19
	ST	16
	NV	8
	PR	5
# SURVEYED		279

****

RELIGIOUS SCHOOL ATTENDANCE

TABLE I: RELIGIOUS SCHOOL ATTENDANCE -- BY TOTAL POPULATION

Question: If you received part of your grade school or high school education in parochial schools or other schools run by religious groups, how many years did you attend these schools? NOTE: Question not asked in 1972-1987.

Responses: 1 = 1 year 2 = 2 3 = 3 4 = 4 5 = 5
6 = 6 7 = 7 8 = 8 9 = 9 10 = 10 or more

	YEAR	
RESPONSE	'88	'89
1	8%	7%
2	10	7
3	6	11
4	7	6
5	5	7
6	9	10
7	5	4
8	22	17
9	5	3
10	24	28
# SURVEYED	288	188

TABLE II: RELIGIOUS SCHOOL ATTENDANCE -- BY SEX

Question: If you received part of your grade school or high school education in parochial schools or other schools run by religious groups, how many years did you attend these schools? NOTE: Question not asked in 1972-1987.

Responses: 1 = 1 year 2 = 2 3 = 3 4 = 4 5 = 5
6 = 6 7 = 7 8 = 8 9 = 9 10 = 10 or more

		YEAR	
SEX	RESP	'88	'89
MALE	1	9%	10%
	2	10	5
	3	7	12
	4	9	6
	5	3	6
	6	11	8
	7	3	1
	8	21	15
	9	5	4
	10	22	33
# SURVEYED		115	100

		YEAR	
SEX	RESP	'88	'89
FEMALE	1	8%	5%
	2	10	9
	3	5	9
	4	6	7
	5	6	8
	6	7	13
	7	6	7
	8	22	19
	9	5	2
	10	25	22
# SURVEYED		173	88

TABLE III: RELIGIOUS SCHOOL ATTENDANCE -- BY RACE

Question: If you received part of your grade school or high school education in parochial schools or other schools run by religious groups, how many years did you attend these schools? NOTE: Question not asked in 1972-1987.

Responses: 1 = 1 year 2 = 2 3 = 3 4 = 4 5 = 5
6 = 6 7 = 7 8 = 8 9 = 9 10 = 10 or more

RACE	RESP	YEAR '88	'89
WHITE	1	8%	8%
	2	10	6
	3	6	10
	4	6	7
	5	4	6
	6	10	10
	7	5	4
	8	20	17
	9	6	3
	10	24	28
# SURVEYED		250	174

RACE	RESP	YEAR '88	'89
BLACK	1	12%	0%
	2	12	22
	3	4	11
	4	8	0
	5	8	11
	6	0	11
	7	0	0
	8	28	22
	9	4	0
	10	24	22
# SURVEYED		25	9

RACE	RESP	YEAR '88	'89
OTHER	1	8%	0%
	2	8	20
	3	8	20
	4	15	0
	5	15	20
	6	0	0
	7	0	0
	8	31	0
	9	0	20
	10	15	20
# SURVEYED		13	5

TABLE IV: RELIGIOUS SCHOOL ATTENDANCE -- BY AGE

Question: If you received part of your grade school or high school education in parochial schools or other schools run by religious groups, how many years did you attend these schools? NOTE: Question not asked in 1972-1987.

Responses: 1 = 1 year 2 = 2 3 = 3 4 = 4 5 = 5
6 = 6 7 = 7 8 = 8 9 = 9 10 = 10 or more

AGE	RESP	YEAR '88	'89
18-23	1	12%	21%
	2	8	14
	3	4	0
	4	12	0
	5	8	14
	6	16	7
	7	4	14
	8	8	14
	9	8	7
	10	20	7
# SURVEYED		25	14

AGE	RESP	YEAR '88	'89
24-29	1	12%	7%
	2	6	4
	3	10	7
	4	6	11
	5	4	11
	6	10	15
	7	6	0
	8	19	15
	9	6	4
	10	23	26
# SURVEYED		52	27

AGE	RESP	YEAR '88	'89
30-35	1	2%	8%
	2	10	8
	3	13	3
	4	13	3
	5	10	3
	6	8	3
	7	6	0
	8	13	22
	9	4	0
	10	21	50
# SURVEYED		48	36

TABLE IV: RELIGIOUS SCHOOL ATTENDANCE -- BY AGE (Continued)

Question: If you received part of your grade school or high school education in parochial schools or other schools run by religious groups, how many years did you attend these schools? NOTE: Question not asked in 1972-1987.

Responses: 1 = 1 year 2 = 2 3 = 3 4 = 4 5 = 5
6 = 6 7 = 7 8 = 8 9 = 9 10 = 10 or more

AGE	RESP	'88	'89
36-41	1	14%	6%
	2	14	12
	3	3	18
	4	6	3
	5	0	6
	6	6	12
	7	3	6
	8	17	9
	9	3	6
	10	34	24
# SURVEYED		35	34
42-47	1	12%	8%
	2	12	0
	3	6	12
	4	3	12
	5	6	4
	6	6	15
	7	3	4
	8	21	15
	9	12	4
	10	21	27
# SURVEYED		34	26

AGE	RESP	'88	'89
48-53	1	5%	0%
	2	15	18
	3	0	18
	4	5	9
	5	5	0
	6	10	0
	7	5	9
	8	15	18
	9	0	0
	10	40	27
# SURVEYED		20	11
54-59	1	0%	7%
	2	14	0
	3	14	13
	4	0	0
	5	0	7
	6	0	0
	7	0	7
	8	57	33
	9	0	7
	10	14	27
# SURVEYED		7	15

AGE	RESP	'88	'89
60-65	1	7%	11%
	2	13	0
	3	0	22
	4	7	22
	5	0	22
	6	13	11
	7	13	0
	8	13	11
	9	7	0
	10	27	0
# SURVEYED		15	9
66+	1	6%	0%
	2	8	6
	3	2	13
	4	6	6
	5	6	6
	6	8	25
	7	2	0
	8	42	19
	9	4	0
	10	17	25
# SURVEYED		52	16

****

VOTED IN 1968

TABLE I: VOTED IN 1968 -- BY TOTAL POPULATION

Question: In 1968, you remember that Hubert Humphrey ran for President on the Democratic ticket against Richard Nixon for the Republicans, and George Wallace as an Independent. Do you remember whether you voted in that election? NOTE: Question not asked in 1974-1989.

Responses: VT = Voted; NV = Did not vote; IN = Ineligible; RF = Refused to answer

	YEAR	
RESPONSE	'72	'73
VT	67%	63%
NV	25	29
IN	8	8
RF	0	0
# SURVEYED	1588	1476

TABLE II: VOTED IN 1968 -- BY SEX

Question: In 1968, you remember that Hubert Humphrey ran for President on the Democratic ticket against Richard Nixon for the Republicans, and George Wallace as an Independent. Do you remember whether you voted in that election? NOTE: Question not asked in 1974-1989.

Responses: VT = Voted; NV = Did not vote; IN = Ineligible; RF = Refused to answer

		YEAR	
SEX	RESP	'72	'73
M	VT	68%	64%
	NV	22	27
	IN	10	9
	RF	0	0
# SURVEYED		795	695

		YEAR	
SEX	RESP	'72	'73
F	VT	66%	62%
	NV	27	30
	IN	6	7
	RF	0	0
# SURVEYED		793	781

TABLE III: VOTED IN 1968 -- BY RACE

Question: In 1968, you remember that Hubert Humphrey ran for President on the Democratic ticket against Richard Nixon for the Republicans, and George Wallace as an Independent. Do you remember whether you voted in that election? NOTE: Question not asked in 1974-1989.

Responses: VT = Voted; NV = Did not vote; IN = Ineligible; RF = Refused to answer

RACE	RESP	'72	'73
WHITE	VT	69%	64%
	NV	22	27
	IN	9	8
	RF	0	0
# SURVEYED		1333	1287
BLACK	VT	57%	56%
	NV	38	38
	IN	4	6
	RF	0	0
# SURVEYED		251	177
OTHER	VT	50%	25%
	NV	50	50
	IN	0	25
	RF	0	0
# SURVEYED		4	12

TABLE IV: VOTED IN 1968 -- BY AGE

Question: In 1968, you remember that Hubert Humphrey ran for President on the Democratic ticket against Richard Nixon for the Republicans, and George Wallace as an Independent. Do you remember whether you voted in that election? NOTE: Question not asked in 1974-1989.

Responses: VT = Voted; NV = Did not vote; IN = Ineligible; RF = Refused to answer

AGE	RESP	'72	'73
18-23	VT	1%	2%
	NV	41	55
	IN	58	44
	RF	0	0
# SURVEYED		167	170
24-29	VT	52%	37%
	NV	37	49
	IN	10	14
	RF	0	0
# SURVEYED		230	210
30-35	VT	70%	69%
	NV	28	29
	IN	3	2
	RF	0	0
# SURVEYED		185	164
36-41	VT	74%	75%
	NV	25	21
	IN	1	3
	RF	0	0
# SURVEYED		126	173
42-47	VT	80%	81%
	NV	20	17
	IN	0	2
	RF	0	0
# SURVEYED		179	145
48-53	VT	81%	78%
	NV	17	20
	IN	2	1
	RF	0	1
# SURVEYED		185	148
54-59	VT	87%	80%
	NV	12	18
	IN	1	1
	RF	0	1
# SURVEYED		156	151
60-65	VT	87%	80%
	NV	12	19
	IN	1	1
	RF	0	1
# SURVEYED		142	118
66+	VT	77%	80%
	NV	23	20
	IN	0	0
	RF	0	0
# SURVEYED		213	194

****

VOTED IN 1972

TABLE I: VOTED IN 1972 -- BY TOTAL POPULATION

Question: In 1972, you remember that George McGovern ran for President on the Democratic ticket against incumbent Richard Nixon for the Republicans. Do you remember whether you voted in that election? NOTE: Question not asked in 1972, 1978-1989.

Responses: VT = Voted NV = Did not vote IN = Ineligible RF = Refused to answer

	YEAR				
RESPONSE	'73	'74	'75	'76	'77
VT	70%	69%	66%	64%	61%
NV	28	28	28	27	26
IN	2	2	6	8	13
RF	0	0	0	0	0
# SURVEYED	1499	1470	1460	1477	1496

TABLE II: VOTED IN 1972 -- BY SEX

Question: In 1972, you remember that George McGovern ran for President on the Democratic ticket against incumbent Richard Nixon for the Republicans. Do you remember whether you voted in that election? NOTE: Question not asked in 1972, 1978-1989.

Responses: VT = Voted NV = Did not vote IN = Ineligible RF = Refused to answer

		YEAR				
SEX	RESP	'73	'74	'75	'76	'77
M	VT	70%	72%	68%	65%	64%
	NV	27	25	26	26	24
	IN	2	2	5	9	12
	RF	0	0	0	0	0
# SURVEYED		699	686	660	664	680

		YEAR				
SEX	RESP	'73	'74	'75	'76	'77
F	VT	69%	66%	64%	64%	59%
	NV	29	31	30	28	28
	IN	2	2	6	8	13
	RF	0	1	0	0	0
# SURVEYED		800	784	800	813	816

TABLE III: VOTED IN 1972 -- BY RACE

Question: In 1972, you remember that George McGovern ran for President on the Democratic ticket against incumbent Richard Nixon for the Republicans. Do you remember whether you voted in that election? NOTE: Question not asked in 1972, 1978-1989.

Responses: VT = Voted NV = Did not vote IN = Ineligible RF = Refused to answer

RACE	RESP	'73	'74	'75	'76	'77
WHITE	VT	71%	71%	67%	65%	63%
	NV	27	27	27	26	24
	IN	2	2	5	8	12
	RF	0	0	0	0	0
# SURVEYED		1305	1292	1300	1344	1313
BLACK	VT	65%	57%	53%	56%	47%
	NV	34	39	38	37	39
	IN	1	2	8	6	14
	RF	0	2	1	0	0
# SURVEYED		181	171	156	124	168
OTHER	VT	31%	29%	50%	11%	33%
	NV	54	71	25	78	27
	IN	15	0	25	11	40
	RF	0	0	0	0	0
# SURVEYED		13	7	4	9	15

TABLE IV: VOTED IN 1972 -- BY AGE

Question: In 1972, you remember that George McGovern ran for President on the Democratic ticket against incumbent Richard Nixon for the Republicans. Do you remember whether you voted in that election? NOTE: Question not asked in 1972, 1978-1989.

Responses: VT = Voted NV = Did not vote IN = Ineligible RF = Refused to answer

AGE	RESP	'73	'74	'75	'76	'77
18-23	VT	55%	35%	24%	16%	0%
	NV	41	52	43	16	1
	IN	4	13	33	68	99
	RF	0	1	0	0	0
# SURVEYED		171	168	172	161	164
24-29	VT	63%	65%	59%	52%	46%
	NV	34	33	38	46	50
	IN	3	2	3	2	4
	RF	0	0	0	0	0
# SURVEYED		212	210	229	222	204
30-35	VT	71%	70%	64%	61%	56%
	NV	28	30	30	39	42
	IN	1	0	5	1	2
	RF	0	1	0	0	0
# SURVEYED		167	175	169	184	183
36-41	VT	71%	79%	67%	67%	70%
	NV	26	17	29	32	27
	IN	2	4	3	1	2
	RF	0	0	1	0	1
# SURVEYED		174	150	153	157	162
42-47	VT	72%	70%	71%	67%	67%
	NV	26	29	27	31	33
	IN	2	1	1	2	1
	RF	1	0	1	0	0
# SURVEYED		145	149	140	112	141
48-53	VT	71%	75%	79%	80%	77%
	NV	27	25	20	19	20
	IN	1	0	1	1	3
	RF	1	0	1	0	0
# SURVEYED		149	146	136	130	154
54-59	VT	78%	81%	80%	80%	83%
	NV	20	18	20	18	16
	IN	2	0	0	1	1
	RF	0	1	0	1	1
# SURVEYED		157	137	125	128	166
60-65	VT	79%	79%	81%	83%	78%
	NV	20	21	18	17	20
	IN	1	1	1	1	2
	RF	1	0	0	0	0
# SURVEYED		121	107	107	133	111
66+	VT	72%	74%	78%	80%	80%
	NV	28	24	21	19	19
	IN	0	0	1	0	0
	RF	0	1	0	1	0
# SURVEYED		199	222	224	245	204

****

VOTED IN 1976

TABLE I: VOTED IN 1976 -- BY TOTAL POPULATION

Question: In 1976, you remember that Jimmy Carter ran for President on the Democratic ticket against incumbent Gerald Ford for the Republicans. Do you remember whether you voted in that election? NOTE: Question not asked in 1972-1976, 1983-1989.

Responses: VT = Voted NV = Did not vote IN = Ineligible RF = Refused to answer

	YEAR			
RESPONSE	'77	'78	'80	'82
VT	65%	64%	62%	61%
NV	31	30	30	26
IN	4	5	7	12
RF	0	0	0	0
# SURVEYED	1521	1514	1443	1457

TABLE II: VOTED IN 1976 -- BY SEX

Question: In 1976, you remember that Jimmy Carter ran for President on the Democratic ticket against incumbent Gerald Ford for the Republicans. Do you remember whether you voted in that election? NOTE: Question not asked in 1972-1976, 1983-1989.

Responses: VT = Voted NV = Did not vote IN = Ineligible RF = Refused to answer

		YEAR			
SEX	RESP	'77	'78	'80	'82
M	VT	64%	68%	67%	60%
	NV	33	27	27	26
	IN	3	4	6	13
	RF	0	0	0	0
# SURVEYED		687	633	628	622

		YEAR			
SEX	RESP	'77	'78	'80	'82
F	VT	65%	61%	58%	62%
	NV	31	32	33	26
	IN	4	6	8	11
	RF	0	0	0	0
# SURVEYED		834	881	815	835

TABLE III: VOTED IN 1976 -- BY RACE

Question: In 1976, you remember that Jimmy Carter ran for President on the Democratic ticket against incumbent Gerald Ford for the Republicans. Do you remember whether you voted in that election? NOTE: Question not asked in 1972-1976, 1983-1989.

Responses: VT = Voted NV = Did not vote IN = Ineligible RF = Refused to answer

RACE	RESP	'77	'78	'80	'82
WHITE	VT	66%	65%	63%	63%
	NV	31	30	29	26
	IN	3	5	7	11
	RF	0	0	0	0
# SURVEYED		1332	1340	1295	1284

RACE	RESP	'77	'78	'80	'82
BLACK	VT	59%	57%	52%	56%
	NV	37	33	39	28
	IN	3	9	9	16
	RF	0	1	0	0
# SURVEYED		174	158	138	147

RACE	RESP	'77	'78	'80	'82
OTHER	VT	40%	44%	20%	31%
	NV	20	13	80	38
	IN	40	44	0	31
	RF	0	0	0	0
# SURVEYED		15	16	10	26

TABLE IV: VOTED IN 1976 -- BY AGE

Question: In 1976, you remember that Jimmy Carter ran for President on the Democratic ticket against incumbent Gerald Ford for the Republicans. Do you remember whether you voted in that election? NOTE: Question not asked in 1972-1976, 1983-1989.

Responses: VT = Voted NV = Did not vote IN = Ineligible RF = Refused to answer

AGE	RESP	'77	'78	'80	'82
18-23	VT	30%	24%	12%	0%
	NV	49	37	25	0
	IN	21	39	63	100
	RF	0	0	0	0
# SURVEYED		164	161	155	148
24-29	VT	50%	53%	47%	42%
	NV	48	44	52	52
	IN	1	3	1	7
	RF	0	0	0	0
# SURVEYED		203	242	199	238
30-35	VT	60%	63%	57%	62%
	NV	38	35	43	36
	IN	2	1	0	2
	RF	0	0	0	0
# SURVEYED		186	224	214	198

AGE	RESP	'77	'78	'80	'82
36-41	VT	69%	64%	68%	69%
	NV	28	33	32	28
	IN	2	3	0	3
	RF	1	0	0	0
# SURVEYED		167	159	147	141
42-47	VT	67%	77%	73%	75%
	NV	32	22	24	24
	IN	1	1	3	1
	RF	0	0	0	1
# SURVEYED		146	119	113	114
48-53	VT	78%	76%	78%	79%
	NV	19	24	22	21
	IN	3	0	0	0
	RF	0	0	0	0
# SURVEYED		154	130	121	109

AGE	RESP	'77	'78	'80	'82
54-59	VT	81%	82%	80%	80%
	NV	18	18	18	18
	IN	1	1	2	1
	RF	1	0	0	0
# SURVEYED		168	136	131	141
60-65	VT	80%	75%	78%	81%
	NV	18	24	22	18
	IN	2	1	0	1
	RF	0	1	0	0
# SURVEYED		116	106	118	114
66+	VT	73%	77%	78%	80%
	NV	26	22	22	19
	IN	1	0	0	0
	RF	0	0	0	0
# SURVEYED		210	231	236	243

****

VOTED IN 1980

TABLE I: VOTED IN 1980 -- BY TOTAL POPULATION

Question: In 1980, you remember that incumbent Jimmy Carter ran for President on the Democratic ticket against Ronald Reagan for the Republicans, and John Anderson as an Independent. Do you remember whether you voted in that election? NOTE: Question not asked in 1972-1981, 1986, 1988-1989.

Responses: VT = Voted NV = Did not vote IN = Ineligible RF = Refused to answer

	YEAR				
RESPONSE	'82	'83	'84	'85	'87
VT	66%	67%	65%	68%	66%
NV	30	28	27	24	21
IN	4	5	7	9	13
RF	0	0	0	0	0
# SURVEYED	1487	1582	1445	1508	1413

TABLE II: VOTED IN 1980 -- BY SEX

Question: In 1980, you remember that incumbent Jimmy Carter ran for President on the Democratic ticket against Ronald Reagan for the Republicans, and John Anderson as an Independent. Do you remember whether you voted in that election? NOTE: Question not asked in 1972-1981, 1986, 1988-1989.

Responses: VT = Voted NV = Did not vote IN = Ineligible RF = Refused to answer

		YEAR				
SEX	RESP	'82	'83	'84	'85	'87
M	VT	66%	68%	67%	68%	66%
	NV	29	26	24	24	21
	IN	4	5	9	8	13
	RF	0	0	0	0	0
# SURVEYED		632	680	589	680	629

		YEAR				
SEX	RESP	'82	'83	'84	'85	'87
F	VT	65%	67%	65%	67%	66%
	NV	31	29	29	24	21
	IN	3	4	6	9	13
	RF	0	0	0	0	0
# SURVEYED		855	902	856	828	784

TABLE III: VOTED IN 1980 -- BY RACE

Question: In 1980, you remember that incumbent Jimmy Carter ran for President on the Democratic ticket against Ronald Reagan for the Republicans, and John Anderson as an Independent. Do you remember whether you voted in that election? NOTE: Question not asked in 1972-1981, 1986, 1988-1989.

Responses: VT = Voted NV = Did not vote IN = Ineligible RF = Refused to answer

		YEAR				
RACE	RESP	'82	'83	'84	'85	'87
WHITE	VT	66%	69%	68%	69%	68%
	NV	30	27	25	23	20
	IN	3	4	7	8	12
	RF	0	0	0	0	0
# SURVEYED		1305	1404	1228	1318	1182

		YEAR				
RACE	RESP	'82	'83	'84	'85	'87
BLACK	VT	63%	56%	57%	63%	59%
	NV	32	37	34	28	22
	IN	4	6	7	9	19
	RF	1	1	2	0	0
# SURVEYED		155	161	166	147	181

		YEAR				
RACE	RESP	'82	'83	'84	'85	'87
OTHER	VT	44%	59%	37%	53%	44%
	NV	44	12	43	30	32
	IN	11	24	20	16	20
	RF	0	6	0	0	4
# SURVEYED		27	17	51	43	50

TABLE IV: VOTED IN 1980 -- BY AGE

Question: In 1980, you remember that incumbent Jimmy Carter ran for President on the Democratic ticket against Ronald Reagan for the Republicans, and John Anderson as an Independent. Do you remember whether you voted in that election? NOTE: Question not asked in 1972-1981, 1986, 1988-1989.

Responses: VT = Voted NV = Did not vote IN = Ineligible RF = Refused to answer

		YEAR				
AGE	RESP	'82	'83	'84	'85	'87
18 23	VT	29%	27%	22%	5%	0%
	NV	41	29	22	13	0
	IN	29	44	57	83	100
	RF	1	0	0	0	0
# SURVEYED		145	126	161	132	126
AGE	RESP	'82	'83	'84	'85	'87
24-29	VT	55%	51%	53%	52%	38%
	NV	44	47	45	47	41
	IN	1	1	2	1	21
	RF	0	0	0	0	0
# SURVEYED		244	285	228	211	185
AGE	RESP	'82	'83	'84	'85	'87
30-35	VT	67%	65%	66%	69%	67%
	NV	32	33	32	29	29
	IN	1	2	2	2	3
	RF	0	0	0	0	0
# SURVEYED		202	235	196	209	214

		YEAR				
AGE	RESP	'82	'83	'84	'85	'87
36-41	VT	68%	72%	72%	71%	75%
	NV	30	25	28	26	21
	IN	2	2	1	3	3
	RF	0	1	0	0	1
# SURVEYED		143	169	183	182	177
AGE	RESP	'82	'83	'84	'85	'87
42-47	VT	73%	74%	75%	81%	73%
	NV	26	24	25	17	25
	IN	1	1	0	2	2
	RF	1	0	0	0	0
# SURVEYED		117	145	122	123	154
AGE	RESP	'82	'83	'84	'85	'87
48-53	VT	75%	79%	72%	77%	86%
	NV	25	20	26	22	13
	IN	0	0	2	1	1
	RF	0	1	0	0	0
# SURVEYED		112	114	101	129	122

		YEAR				
AGE	RESP	'82	'83	'84	'85	'87
54-59	VT	77%	77%	83%	82%	86%
	NV	22	21	16	18	14
	IN	1	2	1	0	0
	RF	0	1	0	0	0
# SURVEYED		144	132	114	129	92
AGE	RESP	'82	'83	'84	'85	'87
60-65	VT	74%	86%	74%	84%	85%
	NV	25	13	26	14	13
	IN	1	1	0	2	2
	RF	0	0	0	0	0
# SURVEYED		116	131	109	129	99
AGE	RESP	'82	'83	'84	'85	'87
66+	VT	77%	82%	82%	83%	84%
	NV	22	17	17	16	15
	IN	0	1	1	1	0
	RF	0	0	0	0	0
# SURVEYED		253	238	225	258	241

****

VOTED IN 1984

TABLE I: VOTED IN 1984 -- BY TOTAL POPULATION

Question: In 1984, you remember that Walter Mondale ran for President on the Democratic ticket against incumbent Ronald Reagan for the Republicans. Do you remember whether you voted in that election? NOTE: Question not asked in 1972-1984.

Responses: VT = Voted NV = Did not vote IN = Ineligible RF = Refused to answer

	YEAR				
RESPONSE	'85	'86	'87	'88	'89
VT	69%	68%	68%	63%	65%
NV	28	28	27	29	24
IN	2	3	5	8	9
RF	0	0	0	0	1
# SURVEYED	1523	1447	1425	1443	1501

TABLE II: VOTED IN 1984 -- BY SEX

Question: In 1984, you remember that Walter Mondale ran for President on the Democratic ticket against incumbent Ronald Reagan for the Republicans. Do you remember whether you voted in that election? NOTE: Question not asked in 1972-1984.

Responses: VT = Voted NV = Did not vote IN = Ineligible RF = Refused to answer

		YEAR				
SEX	RESP	'85	'86	'87	'88	'89
M	VT	68%	68%	66%	60%	65%
	NV	30	27	29	30	24
	IN	2	4	5	10	10
	RF	0	0	0	0	1
# SURVEYED		685	615	626	620	652

		YEAR				
SEX	RESP	'85	'86	'87	'88	'89
F	VT	71%	68%	69%	65%	65%
	NV	27	30	26	28	24
	IN	2	3	6	7	9
	RF	0	0	0	0	1
# SURVEYED		838	832	799	823	849

TABLE III: VOTED IN 1984 -- BY RACE

Question: In 1984, you remember that Walter Mondale ran for President on the Democratic ticket against incumbent Ronald Reagan for the Republicans. Do you remember whether you voted in that election? NOTE: Question not asked in 1972-1984.

Responses: VT = Voted NV = Did not vote IN = Ineligible RF = Refused to answer

RACE	RESP	'85	'86	'87	'88	'89
WHITE	VT	70%	70%	70%	65%	68%
	NV	28	27	25	28	23
	IN	2	3	4	7	8
	RF	0	0	0	0	1
# SURVEYED		1330	1233	1192	1209	1292

RACE	RESP	'85	'86	'87	'88	'89
BLACK	VT	65%	61%	60%	57%	56%
	NV	32	33	32	33	30
	IN	3	6	9	10	12
	RF	0	0	0	1	2
# SURVEYED		149	180	183	175	151

RACE	RESP	'85	'86	'87	'88	'89
OTHER	VT	55%	35%	30%	42%	31%
	NV	36	53	50	34	40
	IN	9	12	20	22	28
	RF	0	0	0	2	2
# SURVEYED		44	34	50	59	58

TABLE IV: VOTED IN 1984 -- BY AGE

Question: In 1984, you remember that Walter Mondale ran for President on the Democratic ticket against incumbent Ronald Reagan for the Republicans. Do you remember whether you voted in that election? NOTE: Question not asked in 1972-1984.

Responses: VT = Voted NV = Did not vote IN = Ineligible RF = Refused to answer

AGE	RESP	'85	'86	'87	'88	'89
18-23	VT	41%	38%	22%	12%	7%
	NV	48	36	34	22	8
	IN	11	25	43	66	85
	RF	1	0	0	0	0
# SURVEYED		132	107	125	139	135
24-29	VT	57%	53%	56%	49%	51%
	NV	42	45	42	47	46
	IN	1	3	2	4	3
	RF	0	0	0	0	1
# SURVEYED		215	215	189	212	199
30-35	VT	71%	62%	71%	57%	60%
	NV	27	34	27	40	35
	IN	1	3	2	2	2
	RF	0	1	0	1	2
# SURVEYED		211	218	217	188	209

AGE	RESP	'85	'86	'87	'88	'89
36-41	VT	68%	75%	68%	71%	75%
	NV	29	22	29	26	22
	IN	3	3	3	2	2
	RF	0	0	0	2	1
# SURVEYED		183	187	177	187	191
42-47	VT	80%	72%	68%	72%	70%
	NV	17	28	29	26	26
	IN	3	1	3	1	3
	RF	0	0	1	0	1
# SURVEYED		123	137	153	155	156
48-53	VT	74%	78%	81%	69%	76%
	NV	25	21	17	30	22
	IN	1	1	2	0	2
	RF	0	0	0	1	0
# SURVEYED		130	107	122	91	137

AGE	RESP	'85	'86	'87	'88	'89
54-59	VT	75%	77%	78%	82%	80%
	NV	24	22	22	16	19
	IN	1	1	0	2	0
	RF	0	0	0	0	1
# SURVEYED		133	97	93	83	94
60-65	VT	82%	81%	84%	81%	77%
	NV	16	18	14	19	19
	IN	2	1	2	0	3
	RF	0	0	0	0	1
# SURVEYED		129	113	98	116	109
66+	VT	77%	78%	80%	78%	84%
	NV	22	21	20	22	13
	IN	1	0	0	0	1
	RF	0	1	0	0	1
# SURVEYED		261	260	247	268	268

****

VOTED IN 1988

TABLE I: VOTED IN 1988 -- BY TOTAL POPULATION

Question: In 1988, you remember that Michael Dukakis ran for President on the Democratic ticket against George Bush for the Republicans. Do you remember whether you voted in that election? NOTE: Question not asked in 1972-1988.

Responses: VT = Voted NV = Did not vote IN = Ineligible RF = Refused to answer

RESPONSE	YEAR '89
VT	64%
NV	32
IN	2
RF	1
# SURVEYED	1529

TABLE II: VOTED IN 1988 -- BY SEX

Question: In 1988, you remember that Michael Dukakis ran for President on the Democratic ticket against George Bush for the Republicans. Do you remember whether you voted in that election? NOTE: Question not asked in 1972-1988.

Responses: VT = Voted NV = Did not vote IN = Ineligible RF = Refused to answer

SEX	RESP	YEAR '89
M	VT	65%
	NV	33
	IN	2
	RF	1
# SURVEYED		658

SEX	RESP	YEAR '89
F	VT	64%
	NV	31
	IN	3
	RF	1
# SURVEYED		871

TABLE III: VOTED IN 1988 -- BY RACE

Question: In 1988, you remember that Michael Dukakis ran for President on the Democratic ticket against George Bush for the Republicans. Do you remember whether you voted in that election? NOTE: Question not asked in 1972-1988.

Responses: VT = Voted NV = Did not vote IN = Ineligible RF = Refused to answer

RACE	RESP	'89
WHITE	VT	67%
	NV	31
	IN	2
	RF	1
# SURVEYED		1312

RACE	RESP	'89
BLACK	VT	60%
	NV	35
	IN	4
	RF	2
# SURVEYED		156

RACE	RESP	'89
OTHER	VT	33%
	NV	54
	IN	11
	RF	2
# SURVEYED		61

TABLE IV: VOTED IN 1988 -- BY AGE

Question: In 1988, you remember that Michael Dukakis ran for President on the Democratic ticket against George Bush for the Republicans. Do you remember whether you voted in that election? NOTE: Question not asked in 1972-1988.

Responses: VT = Voted NV = Did not vote IN = Ineligible RF = Refused to answer

AGE	RESP	'89
18-23	VT	40%
	NV	49
	IN	10
	RF	1
# SURVEYED		136
24-29	VT	52%
	NV	45
	IN	2
	RF	0
# SURVEYED		201

AGE	RESP	'89
30-35	VT	61%
	NV	35
	IN	2
	RF	2
# SURVEYED		212
36-41	VT	64%
	NV	32
	IN	2
	RF	2
# SURVEYED		196

AGE	RESP	'89
42-47	VT	65%
	NV	31
	IN	2
	RF	1
# SURVEYED		159
48-53	VT	74%
	NV	26
	IN	0
	RF	0
# SURVEYED		138

AGE	RESP	'89
54-59	VT	73%
	NV	26
	IN	0
	RF	1
# SURVEYED		99
60-65	VT	74%
	NV	23
	IN	2
	RF	1
# SURVEYED		111

AGE	RESP	'89
66+	VT	77%
	NV	21
	IN	1
	RF	1
# SURVEYED		273

PRESIDENTIAL CHOICE IN 1968

TABLE I: PRESIDENTIAL CHOICE IN 1968 -- BY TOTAL POPULATION

Question: If you voted in 1968, did you vote for Hubert Humphry, Richard Nixon, or George Wallace? If not, who would you have voted for, for President, if you had voted? NOTE: Question not asked in 1974-1989.

Responses: HM = Humphry; NX = Nixon; WL = Wallace; OT = Other; RF = Refused to answer

	YEAR	
RESPONSE	'72	'73
HM	42%	39%
NX	46	45
WL	9	14
OT	1	1
RF	2	1
# SURVEYED	1030	910

TABLE II: PRESIDENTIAL CHOICE IN 1968 -- BY SEX

Question: If you voted in 1968, did you vote for Hubert Humphry, Richard Nixon, or George Wallace? If not, who would you have voted for, for President, if you had voted? NOTE: Question not asked in 1974-1989.

Responses: HM = Humphry; NX = Nixon; WL = Wallace; OT = Other; RF = Refused to answer

		YEAR	
SEX	RESP	'72	'73
MALE	HM	40%	38%
	NX	44	42
	WL	13	18
	OT	1	1
	RF	2	2
# SURVEYED		528	437

		YEAR	
SEX	RESP	'72	'73
FEMALE	HM	43%	40%
	NX	49	48
	WL	5	11
	OT	1	1
	RF	2	1
# SURVEYED		502	473

TABLE III: PRESIDENTIAL CHOICE IN 1968 -- BY RACE

Question: If you voted in 1968, did you vote for Hubert Humphry, Richard Nixon, or George Wallace? If not, who would you have voted for, for President, if you had voted? NOTE: Question not asked in 1974-1989.

Responses: HM = Humphry; NX = Nixon; WL = Wallace; OT = Other; RF = Refused to answer

RACE	RESP	'72	'73
		YEAR	
WHITE	HM	35%	33%
	NX	52	49
	WL	10	16
	OT	1	1
	RF	2	1
# SURVEYED		886	812

RACE	RESP	'72	'73
		YEAR	
BLACK	HM	84%	95%
	NX	14	5
	WL	1	0
	OT	1	0
	RF	0	0
# SURVEYED		142	95

RACE	RESP	'72	'73
		YEAR	
OTHER	HM	100%	33%
	NX	0	67
	WL	0	0
	OT	0	0
	RF	0	0
# SURVEYED		2	3

TABLE IV: PRESIDENTIAL CHOICE IN 1968 -- BY AGE

Question: If you voted in 1968, did you vote for Hubert Humphry, Richard Nixon, or George Wallace? If not, who would you have voted for, for President, if you had voted? NOTE: Question not asked in 1974-1989.

Responses: HM = Humphry; NX = Nixon; WL = Wallace; OT = Other; RF = Refused to answer

AGE	RESP	'72	'73
		YEAR	
18-23	HM	50%	100%
	NX	50	0
	WL	0	0
	OT	0	0
	RF	0	0
# SURVEYED		2	3
AGE	RESP	'72	'73
24-29	HM	44%	43%
	NX	43	35
	WL	10	19
	OT	2	3
	RF	1	0
# SURVEYED		118	74
AGE	RESP	'72	'73
30-35	HM	36%	34%
	NX	42	52
	WL	19	13
	OT	0	0
	RF	2	1
# SURVEYED		125	112

AGE	RESP	'72	'73
		YEAR	
36-41	HM	39%	41%
	NX	49	41
	WL	11	17
	OT	0	1
	RF	1	1
# SURVEYED		90	128
AGE	RESP	'72	'73
42-47	HM	48%	41%
	NX	40	39
	WL	10	18
	OT	0	2
	RF	2	0
# SURVEYED		140	116
AGE	RESP	'72	'73
48-53	HM	46%	34%
	NX	45	50
	WL	5	14
	OT	2	0
	RF	2	2
# SURVEYED		143	111

AGE	RESP	'72	'73
		YEAR	
54-59	HM	38%	40%
	NX	55	43
	WL	4	12
	OT	2	1
	RF	2	4
# SURVEYED		133	119
AGE	RESP	'72	'73
60-65	HM	46%	43%
	NX	43	42
	WL	7	13
	OT	1	0
	RF	3	1
# SURVEYED		119	92
AGE	RESP	'72	'73
66+	HM	36%	38%
	NX	53	52
	WL	8	9
	OT	1	1
	RF	3	1
# SURVEYED		158	152

****

PRESIDENTIAL CHOICE IN 1972

TABLE I: PRESIDENTIAL CHOICE IN 1972 -- BY TOTAL POPULATION

Question: If you voted in 1972, did you vote for George McGovern or Richard Nixon? NOTE: Question not asked in 1972, 1978-1989.

Responses: MG = McGovern; NX = Nixon;
OT = Other; RF = Refused to answer; NV = Voted, but not for president

	YEAR				
RESPONSE	'73	'74	'75	'76	'77
MG	39%	38%	35%	37%	37%
NX	57	56	61	59	61
OT	2	4	3	3	2
RG	2	2	0	0	0
NV	0	0	1	0	1
# SURVEYED	1035	993	936	923	889

TABLE II: PRESIDENTIAL CHOICE IN 1972 -- BY SEX

Question: If you voted in 1972, did you vote for George McGovern or Richard Nixon? NOTE: Question not asked in 1972, 1978-1989.

Responses: MG = McGovern; NX = Nixon;
OT = Other; RF = Refused to answer; NV = Voted, but not for president

		YEAR				
SEX	RESP	'73	'74	'75	'76	'77
M	**MG**	37%	40%	33%	37%	37%
A	**NX**	57	53	61	59	60
L	**OT**	2	5	5	4	2
E	**RF**	3	2	0	0	0
	NV	0	0	2	0	1
# SURVEYED		485	488	444	422	423

		YEAR				
SEX	RESP	'73	'74	'75	'76	'77
F	**MG**	41%	37%	37%	38%	37%
E	**NX**	57	59	60	59	61
M	**OT**	1	3	2	3	2
A	**RF**	1	1	0	0	0
L	**NV**	0	0	1	0	0
E						
# SURVEYED		550	505	492	501	466

TABLE III: PRESIDENTIAL CHOICE IN 1972 -- BY RACE

Question: If you voted in 1972, did you vote for George McGovern or Richard Nixon? NOTE: Question not asked in 1972, 1978-1989.

Responses: MG = McGovern; NX = Nixon; OT = Other; RF = Refused to answer; NV = Voted, but not for president

RACE	RESP	'73	'74	'75	'76	'77
WHITE	MG	33%	33%	30%	34%	33%
	NX	63	61	65	62	65
	OT	2	4	3	3	2
	RF	2	2	0	0	0
	NV	0	0	2	0	1
# SURVEYED		916	895	853	856	807

RACE	RESP	'73	'74	'75	'76	'77
BLACK	MG	87%	84%	84%	80%	83%
	NX	10	11	14	15	17
	OT	1	2	2	5	0
	RF	2	2	0	0	0
	NV	0	0	0	0	0
# SURVEYED		115	96	81	66	77

RACE	RESP	'73	'74	'75	'76	'77
OTHER	MG	25%	100%	0%	0%	20%
	NX	75	0	100	100	80
	OT	0	0	0	0	0
	RF	0	0	0	0	0
	NV	0	0	0	0	0
# SURVEYED		4	2	2	1	5

TABLE IV: PRESIDENTIAL CHOICE IN 1972 -- BY AGE

Question: If you voted in 1972, did you vote for George McGovern or Richard Nixon? NOTE: Question not asked in 1972, 1978-1989.

Responses: MG = McGovern; NX = Nixon; OT = Other; RF = Refused to answer; NV = Voted, but not for president

AGE	RESP	'73	'74	'75	'76	'77
18-23	MG	58	50	45	46	0
	NX	39	43	52	54	0
	OT	3	7	0	0	0
	RF	0	0	0	0	0
	NV	0	0	2	0	0
# SURVEYED		93	58	42	24	0
24-29	MG	56%	55%	54%	48%	46%
	NX	41	40	42	48	53
	OT	2	4	4	4	0
	RF	2	0	0	0	0
	NV	0	0	0	0	1
# SURVEYED		133	136	132	113	92

AGE	RESP	'73	'74	'75	'76	'77
30-35	MG	32%	41%	36%	45%	53%
	NX	64	57	59	50	44
	OT	3	1	4	5	3
	RF	2	2	0	0	0
	NV	0	0	1	0	0
# SURVEYED		118	120	106	111	100
36-41	MG	36%	38%	33%	31%	34%
	NX	62	59	65	66	62
	OT	2	3	2	3	3
	RF	1	1	0	0	0
	NV	0	0	0	0	1
# SURVEYED		123	116	101	101	111

AGE	RESP	'73	'74	'75	'76	'77
42-47	MG	33%	34%	32%	36%	26%
	NX	63	60	65	63	68
	OT	2	5	2	0	3
	RF	2	1	0	0	0
	NV	0	0	1	1	3
# SURVEYED		102	101	98	73	90
48-53	MG	33%	35%	36%	28%	26%
	NX	64	55	57	69	73
	OT	2	7	4	3	1
	RF	1	3	0	0	0
	NV	0	0	4	0	0
# SURVEYED		105	108	106	101	118

TABLE IV: PRESIDENTIAL CHOICE IN 1972 -- BY AGE (Continued)

Question: If you voted in 1972, did you vote for George McGovern or Richard Nixon? NOTE: Question not asked in 1972, 1978-1989.

Responses: MG = McGovern; NX = Nixon; OT = Other; RF = Refused to answer; NV = Voted, but not for president

AGE	RESP	'73	'74	'75	'76	'77
54-59	MG	30%	30%	28%	43%	39%
	NX	63	66	69	53	59
	OT	1	3	1	4	2
	RF	7	2	0	0	0
	NV	0	0	2	0	0
# SURVEYED		120	108	98	102	130

AGE	RESP	'73	'74	'75	'76	'77
60-65	MG	38%	27%	23%	33%	39%
	NX	57	68	73	61	60
	OT	3	2	4	4	0
	RF	2	2	0	0	0
	NV	0	0	0	2	1
# SURVEYED		95	82	82	106	85

AGE	RESP	'73	'74	'75	'76	'77
66+	MG	36%	34%	31%	34%	35%
	NX	63	59	63	62	63
	OT	0	4	4	4	1
	RF	1	3	0	0	0
	NV	0	0	2	0	0
# SURVEYED		142	160	168	188	158

****

PRESIDENTIAL CHOICE IN 1976

TABLE I: PRESIDENTIAL CHOICE IN 1976 -- BY TOTAL POPULATION

Question: If you voted in the 1976 presidential election, did you vote for Jimmy Carter or Gerald Ford? NOTE: Question not asked in 1972-1976, 1983-1989.

Responses: CR = Carter; FD = Ford; OT = Other; RF = Refused to answer; NV = Voted, but not for President

RESPONSE	'77	'78	'80	'82
CR	55%	53%	56%	59%
FD	44	45	41	40
OT	1	2	1	1
RF	0	0	1	1
NV	0	0	1	0
# SURVEYED	965	944	879	869

TABLE II: PRESIDENTIAL CHOICE IN 1976 -- BY SEX

Question: If you voted in the 1976 presidential election, did you vote for Jimmy Carter or Gerald Ford? NOTE: Question not asked in 1972-1976, 1983-1989.

Responses: CR = Carter; FD = Ford; OT = Other; RF = Refused to answer; NV = Voted, but not for Preident

SEX	RESP	'77	'78	'80	'82
M	CR	56%	53%	56%	57%
A	FD	43	44	42	41
L	OT	1	3	0	1
E	RF	0	1	0	1
	NV	0	0	1	0
# SURVEYED		430	421	413	367

SEX	RESP	'77	'78	'80	'82
F	CR	53%	53%	56%	60%
E	FD	45	46	40	39
M	OT	1	1	2	0
A	RF	0	0	2	1
L	NV	1	0	0	0
E					
# SURVEYED		535	523	466	502

TABLE III: PRESIDENTIAL CHOICE IN 1976 -- BY RACE

Question: If you voted in the 1976 presidential election, did you vote for Jimmy Carter or Gerald Ford? NOTE: Question not asked in 1972-1976, 1983-1989.

Responses: CR = Carter; FD = Ford; OT = Other; RF = Refused to answer; NV = Voted, but not for president

RACE	RESP	'77	'78	'80	'82
WHITE	CR	51%	48%	53%	55%
	FR	48	50	44	43
	OT	1	2	1	1
	RF	0	0	1	1
	NF	0	0	1	0
# SURVEYED		859	851	806	780

RACE	RESP	'77	'78	'80	'8
BLACK	CR	93%	97%	89%	95
	FR	7	3	10	5
	OT	0	0	1	0
	RF	0	0	0	0
	NF	0	0	0	0
# SURVEYED		100	86	71	82

RACE	RESP	'77	'78	'80	'89
OTHER	CR	17%	71%	100%	71
	FR	83	29	0	29
	OT	0	0	0	0
	RF	0	0	0	0
	NF	0	0	0	0
# SURVEYED		6	7	2	7

TABLE IV: PRESIDENTIAL CHOICE IN 1976 -- BY AGE

Question: If you voted in the 1976 presidential election, did you vote for Jimmy Carter or Gerald Ford? NOTE: Question not asked in 1972-1976, 1983-1989.

Responses: CR = Carter; FD = Ford; OT = Other; RF = Refused to answer; NV = Voted, but not for president

AGE	RESP	'77	'78	'80	'82
18-23	CR	52%	57%	32%	0%
	FR	44	38	68	0
	OT	2	5	0	0
	RF	0	0	0	0
	NF	2	0	0	0
# SURVEYED		48	37	19	
24-29	CR	58%	54%	65%	51%
	FR	39	43	34	48
	OT	3	3	1	0
	RF	0	0	0	1
	NF	0	0	0	0
# SURVEYED		101	123	92	96
30-35	CR	56%	59%	61%	66%
	FR	42	39	34	31
	OT	1	2	3	2
	RF	0	0	2	1
	NF	1	0	1	0
# SURVEYED		111	134	119	118

AGE	RESP	'77	'78	'80	'82
36-41	CR	57%	58%	51%	68%
	FR	43	40	47	32
	OT	0	1	0	0
	RF	0	1	1	0
	NF	0	0	1	0
# SURVEYED		115	97	97	94
42-47	CR	52%	50%	64%	63%
	FR	48	48	31	36
	OT	0	2	1	0
	RF	0	0	4	1
	NF	0	0	0	0
# SURVEYED		97	90	81	83
48-53	CR	46%	50%	54%	52%
	FR	54	50	45	44
	OT	0	0	0	2
	RF	0	0	1	1
	NF	0	0	0	0
# SURVEYED		118	96	92	84

AGE	RESP	'77	'78	'80	'82
54-59	CR	56%	50%	52%	58%
	FR	43	47	44	40
	OT	1	2	1	1
	RF	0	1	1	1
	NF	0	0	2	0
# SURVEYED		133	109	102	110
60-65	CR	63%	49%	60%	60%
	FR	34	49	39	37
	OT	1	0	1	0
	RF	0	3	0	2
	NF	1	0	0	0
# SURVEYED		90	78	89	91
66+	CR	53%	49%	53%	55%
	FR	45	51	44	45
	OT	1	1	1	0
	RF	0	0	2	1
	NF	0	0	1	0
# SURVEYED		148	175	183	190

****

PRESIDENTIAL CHOICE IN 1980

TABLE I: PRESIDENTIAL CHOICE IN 1980 -- BY TOTAL POPULATION

Question: If you voted in the 1980 presidential election, did you vote for Jimmy Carter, Ronald Reagan, or John Anderson? NOTE: Question not asked in 1972-1981, 1988-1989.

Responses: CR = Carter; RG = Reagan; AN = Anderson; OT =Other; RF = Refused to answer

	YEAR				
RESPONSE	'82	'83	'84	'85	'87
CR	46%	46%	45%	47%	50%
RG	45	45	45	47	45
AN	7	7	7	5	6
OT	0	0	1	1	0
RF	1	1	1	1	0
# SURVEYED	964	1042	925	1007	905

TABLE II: PRESIDENTIAL CHOICE IN 1980 -- BY SEX

Question: If you voted in the 1980 presidential election, did you vote for Jimmy Carter, Ronald Reagan, or John Anderson? NOTE: Question not asked in 1972-1981, 1988-1989.

Responses: CR = Carter; RG = Reagan; AN = Anderson; OT =Other; RF = Refused to answer

		YEAR				
SEX	RESP	'82	'83	'84	'85	'87
MALE	CR	43%	43%	40%	44%	46%
	RG	48	47	51	50	48
	AN	7	7	6	4	6
	OT	0	1	1	1	1
	RF	1	2	1	2	0
# SURVEYED		413	455	387	457	400

		YEAR				
SEX	RESP	'82	'83	'84	'85	'87
FEMALE	CR	48%	49%	49%	49%	52%
	RG	44	44	41	44	42
	AN	7	6	8	5	5
	OT	0	0	1	0	0
	RF	1	1	1	1	0
# SURVEYED		551	587	538	550	505

TABLE III: PRESIDENTIAL CHOICE IN 1980 -- BY RACE

Question: If you voted in the 1980 presidential election, did you vote for Jimmy Carter, Ronald Reagan, or John Anderson? NOTE: Question not asked in 1972-1981, 1988-1989.

Responses: CR = Carter; RG = Reagan; AN = Anderson; OT =Other; RF = Refused to answer

		YEAR				
RACE	RESP	'82	'83	'84	'85	'87
WHITE	CR	40%	42%	39%	41%	43%
	RG	51	49	51	52	51
	AN	7	7	8	5	6
	OT	0	0	1	1	1
	RF	1	1	1	1	0
# SURVEYED		855	942	813	894	779

		YEAR				
RACE	RESP	'82	'83	'84	'85	'87
BLACK	CR	96%	92%	95%	96%	96%
	RG	0	4	3	2	4
	AN	2	3	2	0	0
	OT	0	0	0	1	0
	RF	2	0	0	1	0
# SURVEYED		98	90	93	90	105

		YEAR				
RACE	RESP	'82	'83	'84	'85	'87
OTHER	CR	55%	30%	68%	61%	71%
	RG	45	60	26	35	24
	AN	0	10	0	0	5
	OT	0	0	0	0	0
	RF	0	0	5	4	0
# SURVEYED		11	10	19	23	21

TABLE IV: PRESIDENTIAL CHOICE IN 1980 -- BY AGE

Question: If you voted in the 1980 presidential election, did you vote for Jimmy Carter, Ronald Reagan, or John Anderson? NOTE: Question not asked in 1972-1981, 1988-1989.

Responses: CR = Carter; RG = Reagan; AN = Anderson; OT =Other; RF = Refused to answer

		YEAR				
AGE	RESP	'82	'83	'84	'85	'87
18-23	CR	54%	48%	37%	0%	0%
	RG	29	36	40	100	0
	AN	15	12	23	0	0
	OT	2	0	0	0	0
	RF	0	0	0	0	0
# SURVEYED		41	33	35	6	0
AGE	RESP	'82	'83	'84	'85	'87
24-29	CR	47%	44%	34%	31%	32RG
	RG	45	46	53	57	54
	AN	7	9	11	9	14
	OT	0	0	1	2	0
	RF	1	1	1	1	0
# SURVEYED		134	142	117	109	69
AGE	RESP	'82	'83	'84	'85	'87
30-35	CR	50%	46%	44%	44%	44%
	RG	36	46	42	47	43
	AN	11	7	11	7	13
	OT	1	1	2	1	0
	RF	1	0	1	1	0
# SURVEYED		135	148	128	143	141

		YEAR				
AGE	RESP	'82	'83	'84	'85	'87
36-41	CR	48%	43%	44%	40%	45
	RG	41	44	43	49	44
	AN	8	10	10	9	9
	OT	1	1	2	1	2
	RF	1	2	1	1	0
# SURVEYED		95	120	127	126	132
AGE	RESP	'82	'83	'84	'85	'87
42-47	CR	44%	43%	55%	48%	48%
	RG	46	48	40	46	47
	AN	7	6	2	2	6
	OT	0	1	0	1	0
	RF	1	1	2	2	0
# SURVEYED		84	106	89	99	107
AGE	RESP	'82	'83	'84	'85	'87
48-53	CR	42%	38%	53%	53%	60%
	RG	52	50	43	42	40
	AN	5	10	3	3	0
	OT	0	0	1	0	0
	RF	1	2	0	1	0
# SURVEYED		84	90	72	96	99

		YEAR				
AGE	RESP	'82	'83	'84	'85	'87
54-59	CR	38%	49%	51%	51%	48%
	RG	52	46	42	44	49
	AN	7	5	6	2	0
	OT	0	0	0	1	3
	RF	1	0	1	1	0
# SURVEYED		107	98	95	105	77
AGE	RESP	'82	'83	'84	'85	'87
60-65	CR	49%	51%	39%	53%	55%
	RG	45	44	53	43	44
	AN	4	4	4	4	1
	OT	0	0	0	0	0
	RF	2	2	4	1	0
# SURVEYED		85	110	80	108	82
AGE	RESP	'82	'83	'84	'85	'87
66+	CR	44%	52%	48%	52%	56%
	RG	51	42	48	45	43
	AN	3	4	3	2	1
	OT	0	0	0	0	0
	RF	1	2	1	1	0
# SURVEYED		195	190	178	211	197

****

PRESIDENTIAL CHOICE IN 1984

TABLE I: PRESIDENTIAL CHOICE IN 1984 -- BY TOTAL POPULATION

Question: If you voted in the 1984 presidential election, did you vote for Walter Mondale or Ronald Reagan? NOTE: Question not asked in 1972-1984.

Responses: MD = Mondale; RG = Reagan; OT = Other; RF = Refused to answer; NV = Voted, but not for president

	YEAR				
RESPONSE	'85	'86	'87	'88	'89
MD	38%	38%	40%	35%	35%
RG	59	60	58	62	64
OT	0	1	1	1	1
RF	2	1	1	1	0
NV	1	0	0	1	0
# SURVEYED	1050	975	930	879	936

TABLE II: PRESIDENTIAL CHOICE IN 1984 -- BY SEX

Question: If you voted in the 1984 presidential election, did you vote for Walter Mondale or Ronald Reagan? NOTE: Question not asked in 1972-1984.

Responses: MD = Mondale; RG = Reagan; OT = Other; RF = Refused to answer; NV = Voted, but not for president

		YEAR				
SEX	RESP	'85	'86	'87	'88	'89
MALE	MD	36%	33%	42%	32%	34%
	RG	60	65	57	66	65
	OT	0	1	1	2	1
	RF	2	1	1	0	0
	NV	1	0	0	0	0
# SURVEYED		459	417	394	364	404

		YEAR				
SEX	RESP	'85	'86	'87	'88	'89
FEMALE	MD	40%	42%	39%	38%	36%
	RG	58	56	60	59	63
	OT	0	1	1	1	1
	RF	1	1	0	1	0
	NV	1	1	0	1	0
# SURVEYED		591	558	536	515	532

TABLE III: PRESIDENTIAL CHOICE IN 1984 -- BY RACE

Question: If you voted in the 1984 presidential election, did you vote for Walter Mondale or Ronald Reagan? NOTE: Question not asked in 1972-1984.

Responses: MD = Mondale; RG = Reagan; OT = Other; RF = Refused to answer; NV = Voted, but not for president for president

RACE	RESP	'85	'86	'87	'88	'89
WHITE	MD	33%	32%	34%	29%	30%
	RG	64	66	65	69	69
	OT	0	1	1	1	1
	RF	1	1	0	1	0
	NV	1	0	0	0	0
# SURVEYED		930	853	809	763	838

RACE	RESP	'85	'86	'87	'88	'89
BLACK	MD	84%	86%	84%	88%	86%
	RG	8	13	13	11	14
	OT	0	1	1	0	0
	RF	5	0	2	1	0
	NV	2	0	0	0	0
# SURVEYED		96	110	106	94	81

RACE	RESP	'85	'86	'87	'88	'89
OTHER	MD	46%	50%	53%	41%	47%
	RG	50	50	47	50	47
	OT	0	0	0	0	6
	RF	4	0	0	0	0
	NV	0	0	0	9	0
# SURVEYED		24	12	15	22	17

TABLE IV: PRESIDENTIAL CHOICE IN 1984 -- BY AGE

Question: If you voted in the 1984 presidential election, did you vote for Walter Mondale or Ronald Reagan? NOTE: Question not asked in 1972-1984.

Responses: MD = Mondale; RG = Reagan; OT = Other; RF = Refused to answer; NV = Voted, but not for president for president

AGE	RESP	'85	'86	'87	'88	'89
18-23	MD	32%	34%	33%	25%	33%
	RG	66	66	67	75	67
	OT	2	0	0	0	0
	RF	0	0	0	0	0
	NV	0	0	0	0	0
# SURVEYED		53	41	27	16	9
AGE	RESP	'85	'86	'87	'88	'89
24-29	MD	34%	33%	31%	34%	23%
	RG	59	63	67	62	77
	OT	1	3	1	2	0
	RF	6	0	1	1	0
	NV	1	1	0	1	0
# SURVEYED		123	112	104	101	100

AGE	RESP	'85	'86	'87	'88	'89
30-35	MD	37%	45%	42%	43%	34%
	RG	60	54	56	54	64
	OT	0	1	1	2	2
	RF	2	0	1	1	0
	NV	1	0	0	0	0
# SURVEYED		149	134	144	107	120
AGE	RESP	'85	'86	'87	'88	'89
36-41	MD	32%	35%	37%	31%	43%
	RG	66	63	61	66	55
	OT	0	0	2	2	1
	RF	2	2	1	1	0
	NV	0	0	0	1	1
# SURVEYED		124	139	119	127	136

AGE	RESP	'85	'86	'87	'88	'89
42-47	MD	41%	41%	40%	29%	35%
	RG	55	58	60	65	65
	OT	1	0	0	2	0
	RF	1	1	0	3	0
	NV	2	0	0	1	0
# SURVEYED		96	98	99	107	101
AGE	RESP	'85	'86	'87	'88	'89
48-53	MD	40%	36%	43%	33%	36%
	RG	56	61	57	63	61
	OT	0	1	0	2	2
	RF	1	1	0	2	0
	NV	2	0	0	0	1
# SURVEYED		94	83	97	60	102

TABLE IV: PRESIDENTIAL CHOICE IN 1984 -- BY AGE (Continued)

Question: If you voted in the 1984 presidential election, did you vote for Walter Mondale or Ronald Reagan? NOTE: Question not asked in 1972-1984.

Responses: MD = Mondale; RG = Reagan; OT = Other; RF = Refused to answer; NV = Voted, but not for president

AGE	RESP	'85	'86	'87	'88	'89
54-59	MD	36%	39%	46%	49%	37%
	RG	60	61	49	51	63
	OT	1	0	3	0	0
	RF	1	0	3	0	0
	NV	2	0	0	0	0
# SURVEYED		100	75	70	67	68

AGE	RESP	'85	'86	'87	'88	'89
60-65	MD	39%	32%	40%	35%	36%
	RG	60	64	60	61	62
	OT	0	2	0	2	1
	RF	1	1	0	0	0
	NV	0	0	0	1	0
# SURVEYED		106	90	80	93	77

AGE	RESP	'85	'86	'87	'88	'89
66+	MD	45%	42%	44%	35%	36%
	RG	54	56	56	65	63
	OT	0	1	0	0	0
	RF	1	1	0	0	0
	NV	1	1	0	0	0
# SURVEYED		200	199	190	201	221

****

PRESIDENTIAL CHOICE IN 1988

TABLE I: PRESIDENTIAL CHOICE IN 1988 -- BY TOTAL POPULATION

Question: If you voted in the 1988 election, did you vote for Michael Dukakis or George Bush? NOTE: Question not asked in 1972-1988.

Responses: DK = Dukakis; BS = Bush; OT = Other; RF = Refused to answer; NV = Voted, but not for President

RESPONSE	'89
DK	45%
BS	53
OT	1
RF	0
NV	0
# SURVEYED	948

TABLE II: PRESIDENTIAL CHOICE IN 1988 -- BY SEX

Question: If you voted in the 1988 election, did you vote for Michael Dukakis or George Bush? NOTE: Question not asked in 1972-1988.

Responses: DK = Dukakis; BS = Bush; OT = Other; RF = Refused to answer; NV = Voted, but not for President

SEX	RESP	YEAR '89
MALE	MD	44%
	RG	54
	OT	1
	RF	0
	NV	0
# SURVEYED		409

SEX	RESP	YEAR '89
FEMALE	MD	46%
	RG	53
	OT	0
	RF	0
	NV	1
# SURVEYED		539

TABLE III: PRESIDENTIAL CHOICE IN 1988 -- BY RACE

Question: If you voted in the 1988 election, did you vote for Michael Dukakis or George Bush? NOTE: Question not asked in 1972-1988.

Responses: DK = Dukakis; BS = Bush; OT = Other; RF = Refused to answer; NV = Voted, but not for President

RACE	RESP	YEAR '89
WHITE	DK	41%
	BS	58
	OT	1
	RF	0
	NV	0
# SURVEYED		840

RACE	RESP	YEAR '89
BLACK	DK	88%
	BS	9
	OT	1
	RF	1
	NV	1
# SURVEYED		89

RACE	RESP	YEAR '89
OTHER	DK	63%
	BS	37
	OT	0
	RF	0
	NV	0
# SURVEYED		19

TABLE IV: PRESIDENTIAL CHOICE IN 1988 -- BY AGE

Question: If you voted in the 1988 election, did you vote for Michael Dukakis or George Bush? NOTE: Question not asked in 1972-1988.

Responses: DK = Dukakis; BS = Bush; OT = Other; RF = Refused to answer; NV = Voted, but not for President

AGE	RESP	'89
18-23	DK	56%
	BS	44
	OT	0
	RF	0
	NV	0
# SURVEYED		52

AGE	RESP	'89
24-29	DK	40%
	BS	60
	OT	0
	RF	0
	NV	0
# SURVEYED		102

AGE	RESP	'89
30-35	DK	46%
	BS	53
	OT	2
	RF	0
	NV	0
# SURVEYED		125

AGE	RESP	'89
36-41	DK	47%
	BS	50
	OT	2
	RF	0
	NV	1
# SURVEYED		119

AGE	RESP	'89
42-47	DK	49%
	BS	49
	OT	0
	RF	0
	NV	1
# SURVEYED		99

AGE	RESP	'89
48-53	DK	43%
	BS	54
	OT	3
	RF	0
	NV	0
# SURVEYED		100

AGE	RESP	'89
54-59	DK	54%
	BS	45
	OT	2
	RF	0
	NV	0
# SURVEYED		65

AGE	RESP	'89
60-65	DK	38%
	BS	59
	OT	0
	RF	1
	NV	1
# SURVEYED		76

AGE	RESP	'89
66+	DK	44%
	BS	56
	OT	0
	RF	0
	NV	0
# SURVEYED		208

****

VICTIM OF VIOLENCE

TABLE I: VICTIM OF VIOLENCE -- BY TOTAL POPULATION

Question: Have you ever been punched or beaten by another person? NOTE: Question not asked in 1972, 1974, 1977, 1982, 1985.

Responses: Yes; No

	YEAR										
RESPONSE	'73	'75	'76	'78	'80	'83	'84	'86	'87	'88	'89
YES	27%	32%	28%	35%	33%	46%	40%	36%	36%	35%	37%
NO	73	68	72	65	67	54	60	64	64	65	63
# SURVEYED	1503	1489	1499	1530	1467	1597	1470	1470	1464	995	1035

TABLE II: VICTIM OF VIOLENCE -- BY SEX

Question: Have you ever been punched or beaten by another person? NOTE: Question not asked in 1972, 1974, 1977, 1982, 1985.

Responses: Yes; No

		YEAR										
SEX	RESP	'73	'75	'76	'78	'80	'83	'84	'86	'87	'88	'89
M	YES	44%	51%	46%	55%	51%	68%	60%	55%	54%	52%	54%
	NO	56	49	54	45	49	32	40	45	46	48	46
# SURVEYED		700	669	669	643	641	690	598	621	641	437	444
SEX	RESP	'73	'75	'76	'78	'80	'83	'84	'86	'87	'88	'89
F	YES	13%	16%	14%	21%	20%	29%	26%	23%	21%	23%	23%
	NO	87	84	86	79	80	71	74	77	79	77	77
# SURVEYED		803	820	830	887	826	907	872	849	823	558	591

TABLE III: VICTIM OF VIOLENCE -- BY RACE

Question: Have you ever been punched or beaten by another person? NOTE: Question not asked in 1972, 1974, 1977, 1982, 1985.

Responses: Yes; No

		YEAR										
RACE	RESP	'73	'75	'76	'78	'80	'83	'84	'86	'87	'88	'89
WHITE	YES	28%	32%	28%	34%	33%	45%	40%	37%	36%	35%	38%
	NO	72	68	72	66	67	55	60	63	64	65	62
# SURVEYED		1307	1322	1361	1356	1317	1415	1249	1249	1222	835	883
RACE	RESP	'73	'75	'76	'78	'80	'83	'84	'86	'87	'88	'89
BLACK	YES	22%	31%	32%	39%	34%	50%	40%	29%	38%	35%	30%
	NO	78	69	68	61	66	50	60	71	62	65	70
# SURVEYED		183	163	129	158	140	164	169	184	189	116	110
RACE	RESP	'73	'75	'76	'78	'80	'83	'84	'86	'87	'88	'89
OTHER	YES	8%	50%	22%	50%	50%	28%	33%	46%	32%	36%	31%
	NO	92	50	78	50	50	72	67	54	68	64	69
# SURVEYED		13	4	9	16	10	18	52	37	53	44	42

TABLE IV: VICTIM OF VIOLENCE -- BY AGE

Question: Have you ever been punched or beaten by another person? NOTE: Question not asked in 1972, 1974, 1977, 1982, 1985.

Responses: Yes; No

		YEAR										
AGE	RESP	'73	'75	'76	'78	'80	'83	'84	'86	'87	'88	'89
18-23	YES	44%	38%	47%	50%	43%	54%	55%	45%	44%	54%	49%
	NO	56	62	53	50	57	46	45	55	56	46	51
# SURVEYED		171	173	162	163	155	128	161	108	126	93	93
AGE	RESP	'73	'75	'76	'78	'80	'83	'84	'86	'87	'88	'89
24-29	YES	40%	40%	40%	47%	46%	54%	48%	45%	49%	44%	51%
	NO	60	60	60	53	54	46	52	55	51	56	49
# SURVEYED		212	232	226	244	202	287	232	218	193	146	142

TABLE IV: VICTIM OF VIOLENCE -- BY AGE (Continued)

Question: Have you ever been punched or beaten by another person? NOTE: Question not asked in 1972, 1974, 1977, 1982, 1985.

Responses: Yes; No

		YEAR										
AGE	RESP	'73	'75	'76	'78	'80	'83	'84	'86	'87	'88	'89
30-35	YES	35%	38%	30%	39%	46%	57%	45%	43%	42%	43%	42%
	NO	65	62	70	61	54	43	55	57	58	57	58
# SURVEYED		167	171	186	230	215	235	198	221	221	128	146
AGE	RESP	'73	'75	'76	'78	'80	'83	'84	'86	'87	'88	'89
36-41	YES	26%	40%	33%	38%	41%	52%	51%	45%	42%	49%	43%
	NO	74	60	67	62	59	48	49	55	58	51	57
# SURVEYED		175	154	158	159	150	173	186	188	186	126	133
AGE	RESP	'73	'75	'76	'78	'80	'83	'84	'86	'87	'88	'89
42-47	YES	27%	40%	23%	39%	37%	46%	41%	42%	44%	35%	44%
	NO	73	60	77	61	63	54	59	58	56	65	56
# SURVEYED		146	142	114	119	117	145	126	141	156	104	107
AGE	RESP	'73	'75	'76	'78	'80	'83	'84	'86	'87	'88	'89
48-53	YES	22%	29%	25%	34%	26%	41%	32%	40%	38%	39%	30%
	NO	78	71	75	66	74	59	68	60	62	61	70
# SURVEYED		151	141	133	133	123	116	102	108	126	56	96
AGE	RESP	'73	'75	'76	'78	'80	'83	'84	'86	'87	'88	'89
54-59	YES	24%	20%	25%	28%	24%	40%	31%	29%	23%	32%	29%
	NO	76	80	75	72	76	60	69	71	77	68	71
# SURVEYED		157	126	129	137	136	134	114	99	98	66	63
AGE	RESP	'73	'75	'76	'78	'80	'83	'84	'86	'87	'88	'89
60-65	YES	18%	24%	18%	15%	24%	36%	27%	27%	18%	25%	20%
	NO	82	76	82	85	76	64	73	73	82	75	80
# SURVEYED		121	113	134	106	119	132	113	115	101	80	75
AGE	RESP	'73	'75	'76	'78	'80	'83	'84	'86	'87	'88	'89
66+	YES	9%	16%	13%	19%	15%	25%	21%	17%	18%	11%	17%
	NO	91	84	87	81	85	75	79	83	82	89	83
# SURVEYED		199	232	251	232	241	240	232	265	253	192	178

****

STRUCK AS A CHILD OR ADULT

TABLE I: STRUCK AS A CHILD OR ADULT -- BY TOTAL POPULATION

Question: If you have ever been hit or beaten, did this happen to you as a child or as an adult? NOTE: Question not asked in 1972, 1974, 1977, 1982, 1985.

Responses: CH = Child; AD = Adult; BT = Both

	YEAR										
RESPONSE	'73	'75	'76	'78	'80	'83	'84	'86	'87	'88	'89
CH	43%	46%	42%	44%	43%	43%	44%	40%	41%	41%	43%
AD	30	33	36	33	37	33	33	37	37	40	36
BT	26	21	23	23	20	25	22	23	22	19	21
# SURVEYED	412	468	423	537	489	727	584	532	521	349	377

TABLE II: STRUCK AS A CHILD OR ADULT -- BY SEX

Question: If you have ever been hit or beaten, did this happen to you as a child or as an adult? NOTE: Question not asked in 1972, 1974, 1977, 1982, 1985.

Responses: CH = Child; AD = Adult; BT = Both

		YEAR										
SEX	RESP	'73	'75	'76	'78	'80	'83	'84	'86	'87	'88	'89
M	CH	45%	50%	46%	50%	50%	48%	51%	45%	48%	51%	51%
	AD	24	26	26	24	29	25	22	28	26	29	25
	BT	31	24	27	26	21	27	28	27	26	20	25
# SURVEYED		306	340	306	352	325	469	358	343	348	223	240
SEX	RESP	'73	'75	'76	'78	'80	'83	'84	'86	'87	'88	'89
F	CH	40%	34%	29%	34%	28%	33%	35%	31%	28%	24%	28%
	AD	47	52	60	50	54	47	51	53	58	59	55
	BT	13	14	11	16	18	20	14	16	14	17	16
# SURVEYED		106	128	117	185	164	258	226	189	173	126	137

TABLE III: STRUCK AS A CHILD OR ADULT -- BY RACE

Question: If you have ever been hit or beaten, did this happen to you as a child or as an adult? NOTE: Question not asked in 1972, 1974, 1977, 1982, 1985.

Responses: CH = Child; AD = Adult; BT = Both

		YEAR										
RACE	RESP	'73	'75	'76	'78	'80	'83	'84	'86	'87	'88	'89
WHITE	CH	43%	45%	42%	43%	44%	43%	45%	40%	42%	41%	43%
	AD	30	32	35	34	36	33	32	36	36	41	36
	BT	27	22	23	23	20	24	23	24	22	18	22
# SURVEYED		371	416	380	467	437	640	501	461	432	292	331
RACE	RESP	'73	'75	'76	'78	'80	'83	'84	'86	'87	'88	'89
BLACK	CH	53%	48%	41%	52%	30%	38%	36%	46%	38%	41%	33%
	AD	28	38	39	24	51	33	44	35	39	39	45
	BT	20	14	20	24	19	29	20	19	24	20	21
# SURVEYED		40	50	41	62	47	82	66	54	72	41	33
RACE	RESP	'73	'75	'76	'78	'80	'83	'84	'86	'87	'88	'89
OTHER	CH	0%	50%	50%	38%	60%	40%	47%	18%	41%	44%	69%
	AD	100	50	50	63	40	40	41	59	35	19	15
	BT	0	0	0	0	0	20	12	24	24	38	15
# SURVEYED		1	2	2	8	5	5	17	17	17	16	13

TABLE IV: STRUCK AS A CHILD OR ADULT -- BY AGE

Question: If you have ever been hit or beaten, did this happen to you as a child or as an adult? NOTE: Question not asked in 1972, 1974, 1977, 1982, 1985.

Responses: CH = Child; AD = Adult; BT = Both

		YEAR										
AGE	RESP	'73	'75	'76	'78	'80	'83	'84	'86	'87	'88	'89
18-23	CH	53%	49%	57%	53%	55%	48%	56%	43%	46%	48%	61%
	AD	23	28	24	21	23	28	22	33	31	36	24
	BT	24	23	20	26	23	25	23	24	22	16	15
# SURVEYED		75	65	76	81	66	69	88	49	54	50	46
AGE	RESP	'73	'75	'76	'78	'80	'83	'84	'86	'87	'88	'89
24-29	CH	37%	48%	42%	43%	43%	44%	50%	50%	42%	41%	35%
	AD	24	31	38	33	39	31	29	29	39	41	42
	BT	39	21	20	24	17	25	21	21	19	17	23
# SURVEYED		84	91	91	114	92	155	112	98	95	63	71

TABLE IV: STRUCK AS A CHILD OR ADULT -- BY AGE (Continued)

Question: If you have ever been hit or beaten, did this happen to you as a child or as an adult? NOTE: Question not asked in 1972, 1974, 1977, 1982, 1985.

Responses: CH = Child; AD = Adult; BT = Both

		YEAR										
AGE	RESP	'73	'75	'76	'78	'80	'83	'84	'86	'87	'88	'89
30-35	CH	40%	40%	36%	48%	37%	41%	42%	40%	39%	38%	42%
	AD	33	38	36	23	43	31	31	37	46	40	39
	BT	28	22	29	29	20	27	27	24	15	22	19
# SURVEYED		58	65	56	90	97	135	90	93	92	55	62
AGE	RESP	'73	'75	'76	'78	'80	'83	'84	'86	'87	'88	'89
36-41	CH	39%	57%	46%	32%	49%	43%	32%	40%	42%	47%	40%
	AD	37	27	29	48	36	26	46	40	29	37	33
	BT	24	17	25	20	15	31	22	20	30	17	26
# SURVEYED		46	60	52	60	61	90	94	85	77	60	57
AGE	RESP	'73	'75	'76	'78	'80	'83	'84	'86	'87	'88	'89
42-47	CH	41%	35%	42%	43%	33%	44%	48%	32%	37%	36%	38%
	AD	31	35	38	37	44	33	25	46	31	36	45
	BT	28	30	19	20	23	23	27	22	31	28	17
# SURVEYED		39	57	26	46	43	66	52	59	67	36	47
AGE	RESP	'73	'75	'76	'78	'80	'83	'84	'86	'87	'88	'89
48-53	CH	33%	41%	30%	42%	34%	44%	45%	30%	46%	45%	41%
	AD	39	32	39	36	47	35	27	23	33	27	34
	BT	27	27	30	22	19	21	27	47	21	27	24
# SURVEYED		33	41	33	45	32	48	33	43	48	22	29
AGE	RESP	'73	'75	'76	'78	'80	'83	'84	'86	'87	'88	'89
54-59	CH	54%	52%	42%	37%	38%	40%	43%	29%	35%	52%	28%
	AD	27	28	39	39	31	34	31	54	43	33	28
	BT	19	20	19	24	31	26	26	18	22	14	44
# SURVEYED		37	25	31	38	32	53	35	28	23	21	18
AGE	RESP	'73	'75	'76	'78	'80	'83	'84	'86	'87	'88	'89
60-65	CH	50%	44%	33%	56%	31%	33%	27%	33%	28%	15%	47%
	AD	45	44	46	31	41	44	53	37	44	55	20
	BT	5	11	21	13	28	23	20	30	28	30	33
# SURVEYED		22	27	24	16	29	48	30	30	18	20	15
AGE	RESP	'73	'75	'76	'78	'80	'83	'84	'86	'87	'88	'89
66+	CH	50%	43%	24%	45%	54%	45%	46%	47%	49%	32%	52%
	AD	33	43	52	41	32	42	46	44	40	64	39
	BT	17	14	24	14	14	13	8	9	11	5	10
# SURVEYED		18	37	33	44	37	60	48	45	45	22	31

****

THREATENED WITH A GUN

TABLE I: THREATENED WITH A GUN -- BY TOTAL POPULATION

Question: Have you ever been threatened with a gun, or shot at? NOTE: Question not asked in 1972, 1974, 1977, 1982, 1985.

Responses: Yes; No

	YEAR										
RESPONSE	'73	'75	'76	'78	'80	'83	'84	'86	'87	'88	'89
YES	16%	17%	17%	20%	21%	20%	20%	20%	20%	22%	19%
NO	84	83	83	80	79	80	80	80	80	78	81
# SURVEYED	1502	1486	1497	1531	1464	1596	1470	1467	1465	996	1032

TABLE II: THREATENED WITH A GUN -- BY SEX

Question: Have you ever been threatened with a gun, or shot at? NOTE: Question not asked in 1972, 1974, 1977, 1982, 1985.

Responses: Yes; No

		YEAR										
SEX	RESP	'73	'75	'76	'78	'80	'83	'84	'86	'87	'88	'89
M	YES	28%	31%	29%	33%	34%	35%	32%	34%	32%	33%	32%
	NO	72	69	71	67	66	65	68	66	68	67	68
# SURVEYED		699	666	667	643	639	688	597	621	641	437	444
SEX	RESP	'73	'75	'76	'78	'80	'83	'84	'86	'87	'88	'89
F	YES	6%	6%	7%	11%	11%	9%	11%	10%	11%	13%	10%
	NO	94	94	93	89	89	91	89	90	89	87	90
# SURVEYED		803	820	830	888	825	908	873	846	824	559	588

TABLE III: THREATENED WITH A GUN -- BY RACE

Question: Have you ever been threatened with a gun, or shot at? NOTE: Question not asked in 1972, 1974, 1977, 1982, 1985.

Responses: Yes; No

		YEAR										
RACE	RESP	'73	'75	'76	'78	'80	'83	'84	'86	'87	'88	'89
WHITE	YES	16%	17%	16%	20%	21%	20%	19%	20%	19%	21%	19%
	NO	84	83	84	80	79	80	81	80	81	79	81
# SURVEYED		1307	1319	1359	1357	1314	1414	1249	1247	1222	836	880
RACE	RESP	'73	'75	'76	'78	'80	'83	'84	'86	'87	'88	'89
BLACK	YES	20%	23%	25%	27%	24%	22%	29%	23%	26%	28%	25%
	NO	80	77	75	73	76	78	71	77	74	72	75
# SURVEYED		182	163	129	158	140	164	169	183	190	116	110
RACE	RESP	'73	'75	'76	'78	'80	'83	'84	'86	'87	'88	'89
OTHER	YES	8%	25%	0%	13%	20%	17%	17%	22%	19%	27%	10%
	NO	92	75	100	88	80	83	83	78	81	73	90
# SURVEYED		13	4	9	16	10	18	52	37	53	44	42

TABLE IV: THREATENED WITH A GUN -- BY AGE

Question: Have you ever been threatened with a gun, or shot at? NOTE: Question not asked in 1972, 1974, 1977, 1982, 1985.

Responses: Yes; No

		YEAR										
AGE	RESP	'73	'75	'76	'78	'80	'83	'84	'86	'87	'88	'89
18-23	YES	18%	17%	19%	20%	19%	20%	17%	20%	16%	17%	15%
	NO	82	83	81	80	81	80	83	80	84	83	85
# SURVEYED		171	173	162	163	155	128	161	108	126	93	93
AGE	RESP	'73	'75	'76	'78	'80	'83	'84	'86	'87	'88	'89
24-29	YES	21%	18%	19%	23%	23%	24%	19%	22%	22%	27%	22%
	NO	79	82	81	77	77	76	81	78	78	73	78
# SURVEYED		212	231	226	244	201	287	232	217	193	146	141

TABLE IV: THREATENED WITH A GUN -- BY AGE (Continued)

Question: Have you ever been threatened with a gun, or shot at? NOTE: Question not asked in 1972, 1974, 1977, 1982, 1985.

Responses: Yes; No

		YEAR										
AGE	RESP	'73	'75	'76	'78	'80	'83	'84	'86	'87	'88	'89
30-35	YES	18%	25%	17%	25%	31%	25%	22%	24%	20%	20%	21%
	NO	82	75	83	75	69	75	78	76	80	80	79
# SURVEYED		167	170	186	230	215	236	198	221	221	128	146
AGE	RESP	'73	'75	'76	'78	'80	'83	'84	'86	'87	'88	'89
36-41	YES	16%	19%	19%	28%	26%	25%	29%	21%	25%	34%	25%
	NO	84	81	81	72	74	75	71	79	75	66	75
# SURVEYED		175	153	158	160	150	173	187	188	186	125	133
AGE	RESP	'73	'75	'76	'78	'80	'83	'84	'86	'87	'88	'89
42-47	YES	21%	26%	21%	18%	28%	17%	23%	26%	24%	24%	29%
	NO	79	74	79	82	72	83	77	74	76	76	71
# SURVEYED		145	143	114	119	117	145	126	141	157	104	106
AGE	RESP	'73	'75	'76	'78	'80	'83	'84	'86	'87	'88	'89
48-53	YES	18%	17%	17%	18%	19%	19%	20%	25%	25%	26%	21%
	NO	82	83	83	82	81	81	80	75	75	74	79
# SURVEYED		150	141	133	133	123	116	101	108	126	57	96
AGE	RESP	'73	'75	'76	'78	'80	'83	'84	'86	'87	'88	'89
54-59	YES	14%	14%	20%	19%	18%	22%	18%	24%	21%	20%	24%
	NO	86	86	80	81	82	78	82	76	79	80	76
# SURVEYED		157	126	129	137	135	134	114	99	98	66	63
AGE	RESP	'73	'75	'76	'78	'80	'83	'84	'86	'87	'88	'89
60-65	YES	14%	12%	14%	17%	20%	20%	21%	19%	14%	18%	15%
	NO	86	88	86	83	80	80	79	81	86	83	85
# SURVEYED		121	113	134	106	119	132	113	114	101	80	75
AGE	RESP	'73	'75	'76	'78	'80	'83	'84	'86	'87	'88	'89
66+	YES	9%	10%	12%	13%	9%	11%	12%	8%	13%	12%	7%
	NO	92	90	88	87	91	89	88	92	87	88	93
# SURVEYED		200	231	249	232	240	239	232	264	253	193	177

****

THREATENED WITH A GUN AS A CHILD OR ADULT

TABLE I: THREATENED WITH A GUN AS A CHILD OR ADULT -- BY TOTAL POPULATION

Question: If you have ever been threatened by a gun or shot at, did this happen to you as a child or as an adult? NOTE: Question not asked in 1972, 1974, 1977, 1982, 1985.

Responses: CH = Child; AD = Adult; BT = Both

	YEAR										
RESPONSE	'73	'75	'76	'78	'80	'83	'84	'86	'87	'88	'89
CH	12%	13%	15%	14%	12%	13%	16%	12%	13%	15%	11%
AD	86	85	81	80	83	83	80	84	83	81	82
BT	2	3	5	5	4	5	3	4	3	4	7
# SURVEYED	242	253	255	310	308	323	290	292	293	214	199

TABLE II: THREATENED WITH A GUN AS A CHILD OR ADULT -- BY SEX

Question: If you have ever been threatened by a gun or shot at, did this happen to you as a child or as an adult? NOTE: Question not asked in 1972, 1974, 1977, 1982, 1985.

Responses: CH = Child; AD = Adult; BT = Both

		YEAR										
SEX	RESP	'73	'75	'76	'78	'80	'83	'84	'86	'87	'88	'89
M	CH	12%	12%	12%	16%	15%	14%	15%	11%	11%	15%	12%
	AD	85	85	82	76	80	80	80	85	84	80	80
	BT	3	3	6	8	5	6	5	4	5	6	8
# SURVEYED		195	202	195	211	219	240	191	213	206	143	142
SEX	RESP	'73	'75	'76	'78	'80	'83	'84	'86	'87	'88	'89
F	CH	11%	16%	22%	10%	7%	10%	19%	15%	18%	15%	9%
	AD	87	84	77	90	91	89	81	82	82	85	88
	BT	2	0	2	0	2	1	0	3	0	0	4
# SURVEYED		47	51	60	99	89	83	99	79	87	71	57

TABLE III: THREATENED WITH A GUN AS A CHILD OR ADULT -- BY RACE

Question: If you have ever been threatened by a gun or shot at, did this happen to you as a child or as an adult? NOTE: Question not asked in 1972, 1974, 1977, 1982, 1985.

Responses: CH = Child; AD = Adult; BT = Both

		YEAR										
RACE	RESP	'73	'75	'76	'78	'80	'83	'84	'86	'87	'88	'89
WHITE	CH	11%	11%	15%	12%	12%	13%	18%	12%	12%	15%	10%
	AD	87	87	80	83	84	83	78	85	85	80	83
	BT	2	2	5	5	4	4	4	4	3	4	7
# SURVEYED		206	215	224	265	272	284	232	243	234	169	167
RACE	RESP	'73	'75	'76	'78	'80	'83	'84	'86	'87	'88	'89
BLACK	CH	14%	24%	13%	26%	12%	8%	6%	20%	16%	15%	18%
	AD	80	70	84	65	82	78	92	76	78	82	75
	BT	6	5	3	9	6	14	2	5	6	3	7
# SURVEYED		35	37	31	43	34	36	49	41	49	33	28
RACE	RESP	'73	'75	'76	'78	'80	'83	'84	'86	'87	'88	'89
OTHER	CH	100%	0%	0%	0%	50%	33%	22%	0%	20%	8%	0%
	AD	0	100	0	100	50	67	78	100	80	92	75
	BT	0	0	0	0	0	0	0	0	0	0	25
# SURVEYED		1	1	2	2	3	9	8	10	12	4	

TABLE IV: THREATENED WITH A GUN AS A CHILD OR ADULT -- BY AGE

Question: If you have ever been threatened by a gun or shot at, did this happen to you as a child or as an adult? NOTE: Question not asked in 1972, 1974, 1977, 1982, 1985.

Responses: CH = Child; AD = Adult; BT = Both

		YEAR										
AGE	RESP	'73	'75	'76	'78	'80	'83	'84	'86	'87	'88	'89
18-23	CH	19%	24%	37%	15%	30%	31%	46%	36%	42%	6%	21%
	AD	74	69	57	76	63	58	50	64	53	94	64
	BT	6	7	7	9	7	12	4	0	5	0	14
# SURVEYED		31	29	30	33	30	26	28	22	19	16	14
AGE	RESP	'73	'75	'76	'78	'80	'83	'84	'86	'87	'88	'89
24-29	CH	11%	15%	26%	20%	20%	18%	23%	24%	21%	23%	13%
	AD	82	79	67	71	78	81	70	70	79	72	77
	BT	7	5	7	9	2	1	7	7	0	5	10
# SURVEYED		44	39	43	56	46	68	43	46	42	39	31

TABLE IV: THREATENED WITH A GUN AS A CHILD OR ADULT -- BY AGE (Continued)

Question: If you have ever been threatened by a gun or shot at, did this happen to you as a child or as an adult? NOTE: Question not asked in 1972, 1974, 1977, 1982, 1985.

Responses: CH = Child; AD = Adult; BT = Both

		YEAR										
AGE	RESP	'73	'75	'76	'78	'80	'83	'84	'86	'87	'88	'89
30-35	CH	20%	16%	10%	16%	7%	14%	14%	11%	14%	32%	23%
	AD	80	84	87	74	90	83	84	81	86	60	77
	BT	0	0	3	11	3	3	2	8	0	8	0
# SURVEYED		30	43	31	57	67	59	43	53	44	25	30
AGE	RESP	'73	'75	'76	'78	'80	'83	'84	'86	'87	'88	'89
36-41	CH	7%	14%	10%	16%	10%	2%	9%	8%	11%	14%	6%
	AD	93	79	80	80	90	86	89	88	87	81	91
	BT	0	7	10	4	0	12	2	5	2	5	3
# SURVEYED		28	29	30	45	39	43	54	40	47	42	33
AGE	RESP	'73	'75	'76	'78	'80	'83	'84	'86	'87	'88	'89
42-47	CH	0%	8%	8%	19%	12%	13%	10%	8%	5%	12%	6%
	AD	100	92	88	76	82	87	86	89	87	80	84
	BT	0	0	4	5	6	0	3	3	8	8	10
# SURVEYED		30	37	24	21	33	23	29	36	38	25	31
AGE	RESP	'73	'75	'76	'78	'80	'83	'84	'86	'87	'88	'89
48-53	CH	0%	0%	4%	8%	13%	18%	20%	4%	13%	20%	5%
	AD	100	96	91	92	83	68	80	93	84	80	90
	BT	0	4	4	0	4	14	0	4	3	0	5
# SURVEYED		25	23	23	24	23	22	20	27	32	15	20
AGE	RESP	'73	'75	'76	'78	'80	'83	'84	'86	'87	'88	'89
54-59	CH	14%	11%	4%	0%	8%	3%	5%	5%	5%	0%	20%
	AD	82	89	96	100	79	93	90	95	90	100	73
	BT	5	0	0	0	13	3	5	0	5	0	7
# SURVEYED		22	18	26	26	24	30	21	22	21	13	15
AGE	RESP	'73	'75	'76	'78	'80	'83	'84	'86	'87	'88	'89
60-65	CH	25%	8%	21%	6%	4%	12%	8%	0%	0%	0%	0%
	AD	75	92	74	94	92	88	88	100	100	100	91
	BT	0	0	5	0	4	0	4	0	0	0	9
# SURVEYED		16	13	19	17	24	26	24	22	14	14	11
AGE	RESP	'73	'75	'76	'78	'80	'83	'84	'86	'87	'88	'89
66+	CH	19%	9%	3%	17%	5%	4%	11%	14%	12%	8%	0%
	AD	81	91	97	83	91	96	85	86	79	92	85
	BT	0	0	0	0	5	0	4	0	9	0	15
# SURVEYED		16	22	29	30	22	25	27	21	33	24	13

****

VICTIMIZED BY BURGLARS

TABLE I: VICTIMIZED BY BURGLARS -- BY TOTAL POPULATION

Question: During the last year did anyone break into or somehow illegally get into your home or apartment? NOTE: Question not asked in 1972, 1975, 1978, 1983, 1986.

Responses: Yes; No

	YEAR										
RESPONSE	'73	'74	'76	'77	'80	'82	'84	'85	'87	'88	'89
YES	8%	8%	7%	7%	8%	8%	7%	7%	7%	7%	6%
NO	92	92	93	93	92	92	93	93	93	93	94
# SURVEYED	1504	1481	1496	1527	1465	1504	1471	1531	1462	977	1033

TABLE II: VICTIMIZED BY BURGLARS -- BY SEX

Question: During the last year did anyone break into or somehow illegally get into your home or apartment? NOTE: Question not asked in 1972, 1975, 1978, 1983, 1986.

Responses: Yes; No

		YEAR										
SEX	RESP	'73	'74	'76	'77	'80	'82	'84	'85	'87	'88	'89
M	YES	7%	7%	7%	7%	8%	8%	5%	7%	5%	7%	7%
	NO	93	93	93	93	92	92	95	93	95	93	93
# SURVEYED		701	690	667	692	641	639	597	688	638	400	447
SEX	RESP	'73	'74	'76	'77	'80	'82	'84	'85	'87	'88	'89
F	YES	8%	8%	7%	6%	9%	8%	7%	7%	8%	7%	5%
	NO	92	92	93	94	91	92	93	93	92	93	95
# SURVEYED		803	791	829	835	824	865	874	843	824	577	586

TABLE III: VICTIMIZED BY BURGLARS -- BY RACE

Question: During the last year did anyone break into or somehow illegally get into your home or apartment? NOTE: Question not asked in 1972, 1975, 1978, 1983, 1986.

Responses: Yes; No

		YEAR										
RACE	RESP	'73	'74	'76	'77	'80	'82	'84	'85	'87	'88	'89
WHITE	YES	7%	7%	7%	6%	8%	7%	6%	6%	6%	6%	5%
	NO	93	93	93	94	92	93	94	94	94	94	95
# SURVEYED		1308	1302	1358	1336	1315	1322	1250	1337	1219	802	890
RACE	RESP	'73	'74	'76	'77	'80	'82	'84	'85	'87	'88	'89
BLACK	YES	11%	16%	10%	9%	14%	13%	13%	10%	9%	11%	10%
	NO	89	84	90	91	86	87	87	90	91	89	90
# SURVEYED		183	172	129	176	140	155	169	150	190	131	102
RACE	RESP	'73	'74	'76	'77	'80	'82	'84	'85	'87	'88	'89
OTHER	YES	0%	0%	0%	7%	20%	19%	10%	7%	4%	5%	10%
	NO	100	100	100	93	80	81	90	93	96	95	90
# SURVEYED		13	7	9	15	10	27	52	44	53	44	41

TABLE IV: VICTIMIZED BY BURGLARS -- BY AGE

Question: During the last year did anyone break into or somehow illegally get into your home or apartment? NOTE: Question not asked in 1972, 1975, 1978, 1983, 1986.

Responses: Yes; No

		YEAR										
AGE	RESP	'73	'74	'76	'77	'80	'82	'84	'85	'87	'88	'89
18-23	YES	11%	8%	9%	8%	15%	9%	12%	8%	11%	6%	11%
	NO	89	92	91	92	85	91	88	92	89	94	89
# SURVEYED		171	168	162	164	155	148	161	133	126	95	97
AGE	RESP	'73	'74	'76	'77	'80	'82	'84	'85	'87	'88	'89
24-29	YES	8%	9%	11%	8%	11%	11%	8%	13%	10%	6%	7%
	NO	92	91	89	92	89	89	92	87	90	94	93
# SURVEYED		212	210	225	203	202	245	232	217	193	134	116

TABLE IV: VICTIMIZED BY BURGLARS -- BY AGE (Continued)

Question: During the last year did anyone break into or somehow illegally get into your home or apartment? NOTE: Question not asked in 1972, 1975, 1978, 1983, 1986.

Responses: Yes; No

		YEAR										
AGE	RESP	'73	'74	'76	'77	'80	'82	'84	'85	'87	'88	'89
30-35	YES	10%	9%	6%	6%	13%	7%	8%	7%	5%	11%	4%
	NO	90	91	94	94	87	93	92	93	95	89	96
# SURVEYED		167	175	186	188	215	204	199	212	220	131	136
AGE	RESP	'73	'74	'76	'77	'80	'82	'84	'85	'87	'88	'89
36-41	YES	6%	10%	6%	7%	10%	11%	8%	9%	5%	11%	4%
	NO	94	90	94	93	90	89	92	91	95	89	96
# SURVEYED		175	152	158	168	150	146	187	184	186	133	136
AGE	RESP	'73	'74	'76	'77	'80	'82	'84	'85	'87	'88	'89
42-47	YES	8%	5%	5%	7%	4%	8%	6%	5%	7%	9%	8%
	NO	92	95	95	93	96	92	94	95	93	91	92
# SURVEYED		146	151	114	147	117	119	125	124	156	102	107
AGE	RESP	'73	'74	'76	'77	'80	'82	'84	'85	'87	'88	'89
48-53	YES	7%	8%	9%	8%	7%	5%	4%	4%	4%	6%	5%
	NO	93	92	91	92	93	95	96	96	96	94	95
# SURVEYED		151	145	132	153	122	112	102	131	125	65	95
AGE	RESP	'73	'74	'76	'77	'80	'82	'84	'85	'87	'88	'89
54-59	YES	5%	7%	5%	7%	5%	6%	6%	5%	5%	4%	10%
	NO	95	93	95	93	95	94	94	95	95	96	90
# SURVEYED		157	139	129	168	135	144	114	133	98	53	63
AGE	RESP	'73	'74	'76	'77	'80	'82	'84	'85	'87	'88	'89
60-65	YES	6%	8%	8%	4%	3%	3%	3%	6%	6%	2%	4%
	NO	94	92	92	96	97	97	97	94	94	98	96
# SURVEYED		121	108	133	117	119	116	113	130	101	84	78
AGE	RESP	'73	'74	'76	'77	'80	'82	'84	'85	'87	'88	'89
66+	YES	7%	5%	4%	5%	4%	7%	3%	3%	5%	4%	5%
	NO	93	95	96	95	96	93	97	97	95	96	95
# SURVEYED		200	227	251	212	241	258	232	260	253	177	202

****

VICTIMIZED BY ROBBERS

TABLE I: VICTIMIZED BY ROBBERS -- BY TOTAL POPULATION

Question: During the last year, did anyone take something directly from you by using force--such as a stickup, mugging, or threat? NOTE: Question not asked in 1972, 1975, 1978, 1983, 1986.

Responses: Yes; No

	YEAR										
RESPONSE	'73	'74	'76	'77	'80	'82	'84	'85	'87	'88	'89
YES	2%	4%	2%	2%	2%	2%	2%	2%	2%	2%	1%
NO	98	96	98	98	98	98	98	98	98	98	99
# SURVEYED	1500	1473	1491	1525	1466	1504	1471	1531	1462	976	1026

TABLE II: VICTIMIZED BY ROBBERS -- BY SEX

Question: During the last year, did anyone take something directly from you by using force--such as a stickup, mugging, or threat? NOTE: Question not asked in 1972, 1975, 1978, 1983, 1986.

Responses: Yes; No

		YEAR										
SEX	RESP	'73	'74	'76	'77	'80	'82	'84	'85	'87	'88	'89
M	YES	2%	3%	1%	2%	2%	3%	2%	2%	2%	2%	1%
	NO	98	97	99	98	98	97	98	98	98	98	99
# SURVEYED		697	687	664	691	640	638	597	688	640	399	446
SEX	RESP	'73	'74	'76	'77	'80	'82	'84	'85	'87	'88	'89
F	YES	1%	4%	2%	2%	2%	2%	2%	2%	2%	1%	1%
	NO	99	96	98	98	98	98	98	98	98	99	99
# SURVEYED		803	786	827	834	826	866	874	843	822	577	580

TABLE III: VICTIMIZED BY ROBBERS -- BY RACE

Question: During the last year, did anyone take something directly from you by using force--such as a stickup, mugging, or threat? NOTE: Question not asked in 1972, 1975, 1978, 1983, 1986.

Responses: Yes; No

		YEAR										
RACE	RESP	'73	'74	'76	'77	'80	'82	'84	'85	'87	'88	'89
WHITE	YES	1%	3%	2%	2%	2%	2%	2%	2%	2%	2%	1%
	NO	99	97	98	98	98	98	98	98	98	98	99
# SURVEYED		1305	1299	1354	1334	1316	1321	1250	1337	1220	802	883
RACE	RESP	'73	'74	'76	'77	'80	'82	'84	'85	'87	'88	'89
BLACK	YES	4%	10%	1%	3%	4%	3%	2%	6%	5%	1%	3%
	NO	96	90	99	97	96	97	98	94	95	99	97
# SURVEYED		182	167	128	176	140	156	169	150	189	130	102
RACE	RESP	'73	'74	'76	'77	'80	'82	'84	'85	'87	'88	'89
OTHER	YES	0%	0%	0%	0%	0%	7%	2%	2%	0%	2%	0%
	NO	100	100	100	100	100	93	98	98	100	98	100
# SURVEYED		13	7	9	15	10	27	52	44	53	44	41

TABLE IV: VICTIMIZED BY ROBBERS -- BY AGE

Question: During the last year, did anyone take something directly from you by using force--such as a stickup, mugging, or threat? NOTE: Question not asked in 1972, 1975, 1978, 1983, 1986.

Responses: Yes; No

		YEAR										
AGE	RESP	'73	'74	'76	'77	'80	'82	'84	'85	'87	'88	'89
18-23	YES	1%	3%	4%	7%	3%	5%	4%	3%	3%	1%	1%
	NO	99	97	96	93	97	95	96	97	97	99	99
# SURVEYED		171	167	162	164	155	148	161	133	126	95	97
AGE	RESP	'73	'74	'76	'77	'80	'82	'84	'85	'87	'88	'89
24-29	YES	2%	5%	2%	2%	3%	3%	1%	4%	4%	0%	3%
	NO	98	95	98	98	97	97	99	96	96	100	97
# SURVEYED		211	211	226	203	202	246	232	217	192	134	115

APPENDIX B: Questions and Corresponding Variable Names

names are found on the SPSS statistical package systems file that accompanies the General Social Survey tapes
ey are acquired through Roper or the Inter-University Consortium for Political and Social Research.

Question	Variable Name
Acquaintances with AIDS	AIDSKNOW
Age When First Married	AGEWED
Alcohol Abuse	DRUNK
Alcohol Consumption	DRINK
Allow a Communist to Make Speech	SPKCOM
Allow a Fascist to Make Speech	SPKMIL
Allow a Fascist to Teach in College	COLMIL
Allow Abortion for Family Size	ABNOMORE
Allow Abortion for Health Risk	ABHLTH
Allow Abortion for Poverty	ABPOOR
Allow Abortion for Rape Victims	ABRAPE
Allow Abortion for Serious Defect	ABDEFECT
Allow Abortion for Single Women	ABSINGLE
Allow Abortion on Demand	ABANY
Allow Atheist Books in Public Library	LIBATH
Allow Atheist to Speak	SPKATH
Allow Atheist to Teach in College	COLATH
Allow Communist to Make Speech	SPKCOM
Allow Communist to Teach in a College	COLCOM
Allow Gay to Make Speech	SPKHOMO
Allow Gay to Teach in College	COLHOMO
Allow Pro-Communist Books in Library	LIBCOM
Allow Pro-Fascist Books in Library	LIBMIL
Allow Pro-Gay Book in Library	LIBHOMO
Allow Racist Book in Library	LIBRAC
Allow Racist to Make Speech	SPKRAC
Allow Racist to Teach in College	COLRAC
Allow Sex Education in Schools	SEXEDUC
Amount of Taxes	TAX
Approve of Women in Business	FEWORK
Are You Self-Employed	WRKSLF
Attempted to Quit Smoking	QUITSMK
Attitude of Public Officials	ANOMIA7
Bar Socializing	SOCBAR
Belief in an Afterlife	POSTLIFE
Birth Control Information for Teens	TEENPILL
Black Presidential Candidate	RACPRES
Blacks in Neighborhood	RACLIVE
Branch of Military Served	VETKIND
Brazil as a Favored Country	BRAZIL
Busing as a Solution	BUSING
Canada as a Favored Country	CANADA
Changes in Finances	FINALTER
China as a Favored Country	CHINA
Cigarette Smoking	SMOKECIG
City/Place of Residence at Age 16	MOBILE16
Communism as a Form of Government	COMMUN
Community Population	SIZE
Confidence in Business	CONBUS
Confidence in Congress	CONLEGIS
Confidence in Financial Institutions	CONFINAN
Confidence in Labor Unions	CONLABOR
Confidence in Medicine	CONMEDIC

TABLE IV: VICTIMIZED BY ROBBERS -- BY AGE (Continued)

Question: During the last year, did anyone take something directly from you by using force--such as a stickup, mugging, or threat? NOTE: Question not asked in 1972, 1975, 1978, 1983, 1986.

Responses: Yes; No

		YEAR										
AGE	RESP	'73	'74	'76	'77	'80	'82	'84	'85	'87	'88	'89
30-35	YES	2%	5%	2%	0%	2%	2%	3%	2%	0%	1%	2%
	NO	98	95	98	100	98	98	97	98	100	99	98
# SURVEYED		166	171	184	187	215	204	199	212	220	131	134
AGE	RESP	'73	'74	'76	'77	'80	'82	'84	'85	'87	'88	'89
36-41	YES	2%	4%	1%	0%	1%	1%	2%	1%	3%	4%	1%
	NO	98	96	99	100	99	99	98	99	97	96	99
# SURVEYED		175	151	158	168	150	146	187	184	186	132	135
AGE	RESP	'73	'74	'76	'77	'80	'82	'84	'85	'87	'88	'89
42-47	YES	4%	3%	0%	1%	4%	2%	2%	2%	1%	5%	0%
	NO	96	97	100	99	96	98	98	98	99	95	100
# SURVEYED		146	151	112	147	117	119	125	124	157	102	107
AGE	RESP	'73	'74	'76	'77	'80	'82	'84	'85	'87	'88	'89
48-53	YES	1%	1%	2%	1%	2%	2%	1%	3%	0%	3%	0%
	NO	99	99	98	99	98	98	99	97	100	97	100
# SURVEYED		151	145	133	153	122	112	102	131	125	65	95
AGE	RESP	'73	'74	'76	'77	'80	'82	'84	'85	'87	'88	'89
54-59	YES	0%	4%	0%	1%	1%	3%	0%	1%	2%	0%	2%
	NO	100	96	100	99	99	97	100	99	98	100	98
# SURVEYED		157	138	128	167	136	144	114	133	98	53	61
AGE	RESP	'73	'74	'76	'77	'80	'82	'84	'85	'87	'88	'89
60-65	YES	1%	4%	2%	3%	1%	2%	0%	2%	1%	0%	1%
	NO	99	96	98	97	99	98	100	98	99	100	99
# SURVEYED		120	107	133	117	119	116	113	130	101	84	78
AGE	RESP	'73	'74	'76	'77	'80	'82	'84	'85	'87	'88	'89
66+	YES	2%	4%	1%	2%	1%	2%	0%	1%	2%	1%	1%
	NO	98	96	99	98	99	98	100	99	98	99	99
# SURVEYED		199	226	250	212	241	258	232	260	253	177	201

***

APPENDIX A: Geographic Designations

The responses to questions concerning the region of the country in which the respondent live are divided into several ambiguous regions. Appendix A fully defines the regions.

NEW ENGLAND

Maine
Vermont
New Hampshire
Connecticut
Rhode Island

MIDDLE ATLANTIC

New York
New Jersey
Pennsylvania

EAST NORTH CENTRAL

Wisconsin
Illinois
Indiana
Michigan
Ohio

WEST NORTH CENTRAL

Minnesota
Iowa
Missouri
North dakota
South Dakota
Nebraska
Kansas

SOUTH ATLANTIC

Delaware
Maryland
West Virginia
Virginia
North Carolina
South Carolina
Georgia
Florida
District of Columbia

EAST SOUTH CENTRAL

Kentucky
Tennessee
Alabama
Mississippi

WEST SOUT

Arkansas
Oklahoma
Louisiana
Texas

MOUNTAIN

Montana
Idaho
Nevada
Utah
Colorado
Arizona
New Mexico

PACIFIC

Washington
Oregon
California
Alaska
Hawaii

APPENDIX B: Questions and Corresponding Variable Names (Continued)

Question	Variable
Confidence in Organized Religion	CONCLERG
Confidence in Science	CONSCI
Confidence in Television	CONTV
Confidence in the Educational System	CONEDUC
Confidence in the Military	CONARMY
Confidence in the Press	CONPRESS
Confidence in the Supreme Court	CONJUDGE
Confidence in the U.S. President	CONFED
Continue Working If Wealthy	RICHWORK
Current Degree of Fundamentalism	FUND
Current Employment Status	WRKSTAT
Current Marital Status	MARITAL
Current Religious Affiliation	DENOM
Current Religious Preference	RELIG
Current Smoking Habit	SMOKE
Death Penalty	CAPPUN
Degree of Fundamentalism at Age 16	FUND16
Discrimination is Blacks' Main Problem	RACDIF1
Distance to Black Household	RACDIS
Dwelling Type	DWELLING
Easier Divorces	DIVLAW
Egypt as a Favored Country	EGYPT
Employment History	EVWORK
England as a Favored Country	ENGLAND
Euthanasia Law	LETDIE1
Ever Divorced	DIVORCED
Ever Widowed	WIDOWED
Experienced Deja Vu	DEJAVU
Experienced ESP	ESP
Extra-Marital Sexual Relations	XMARSEX
Family Situation at Age 16	FAMDIF16
Fear in Neighborhood	FEAR
Feelings about Pornography Laws	PORNLAW
Feelings toward Catholics	CATHTEMP
Feelings toward Conservatives	CONTEMP
Feelings toward Jews	JEWTEMP
Feelings toward Liberals	LIBTEMP
Feelings toward Protestants	PROTTEMP
Female Sex Partners since Age 18	NUMWOMEN
Fight Child Beater	HITCHILD
Fight Misbehaving Drunk	HITDRUNK
Fight Protesters	HITMARCH
Fight Robber	HITROBBR
Fighting	HITBEATR
Five-Year Employment History	UNEMP5
Frequency of Sex	SEXFREQ
Gender of AIDS Victim	AIDSSEX
Gender of Sex Partners	SEXSEX
Genetics is Blacks' Main Problem	RACDIF2
Give Teens Contraceptives without Parental Consent	PILLOK
Government Aid for Health	HELPSICK
Government Aid for Poor	HELPPOOR
Government Assure Wealth Distribution	EQWLTH
Government Help for Blacks	HELPBLK
Gun in House	OWNGUN
Gun Licensing	GUNLAW
Gun Ownership	ROWNGUN
Had Black Guest	RACHOME
Had Visions of Events Far Away	VISIONS
Happiness with Life	HAPPY
Harshness of Courts	COURTS

APPENDIX B: Questions and Corresponding Variable Names (Continued)

Helpfulness as a Childhood Trait .... HELPOTH
Highest Degree Earned .... DEGREE
Hours Currently Employed HRS1
Household Members Aged 13 to 17 .... TEENS
Household Members Aged 6 to 12 .... PRETEEN
Household Members Over Age 17 .... ADULTS
Household Members Under Age 6 .... BABIES
Household Size .... HOMPOP
Housing Segregation .... RACPUSH
Human Condition Getting Worse ANOMIA5
Hunting .... HUNT
Husband Work - Wife Keep House .... FEFAM
Ideal Family Size .... CHLDIDEL
If Protestant at 16, What Denomination DENOM16
Importance of Accomplishment .... JOBMEANS
Importance of Good Pay .... JOBINC
Importance of Job Security .... JOBSEC
Importance of Length of Work Week .... JOBHOUR
Importance of Promotion .... JOBPROMO
In Touch with the Dead .... SPIRITS
Independent Thought as a Childhood Trait .... THNKSELF
Industry Working In .... INDUSTRY
Integration of Church .... RACCHURH
Integration of Neighborhood .... RACINTEG
Intensity of Religious Beliefs .... RELITEN
Interracial Marriages .... RACMAR
Is Homosexuality Wrong? .... HOMOSEX
Israel as a Favored Country .... ISRAEL
Japan as a Favored Country .... JAPAN
Leave Running Country to Men .... FEHOME
Legalization of Marijuana .... GRASS
Less Government Help .... HELPNOT
Life Satisfaction .... LIFE
Likelihood of Finding a New Job .... JOBFIND
Likelihood of Losing Job .... JOBLOSE
Live with Parents at Age 16 .... FAMILY16
Male Sex Partners since Age 18 .... NUMMEN
Member of Church Affiliated Group .... MEMCHURH
Member of Farm Organization .... MEMFARM
Member of Fraternal Group .... MEMFRAT
Member of Fraternity or Sorority .... MEMGREEK
Member of Hobby or Garden Club .... MEMHOBBY
Member of Labor Union .... MEMUNION
Member of Literary, Art, or Study Group .... MEMLIT
Member of Nationality Group .... MEMNAT
Member of Political Club .... MEMPOLIT
Member of Professional Society .... MEMPRO
Member of School Service Group .... MEMSCHL
Member of Service Club .... MEMSERV
Member of Sports Group .... MEMSPORT
Member of Veterans Organization .... MEMVET
Member of Youth Group .... MEMYOUTH
Military Service History .... VETYEARS
Most People are Helpful .... HELPFUL
Most People are Trustworthy .... TRUST
Most People Deal Fairly .... FAIR
Mother Employed Pre-School Age .... MAWKBORN
Multi-Generation Households .... AGED
Newspaper Reading .... NEWS
Number of Children You Have Had .... CHILDS
Obedience as a Childhood Trait .... OBEY
Object to Black Dinner Guest .... RACDIN

APPENDIX B: Questions and Corresponding Variable Names (Continued)

Question	Variable
Open Housing Laws	RACOPEN
Out of Body Experience	GRACE
Parent's Birthplace	PARBORN
Pistol in House	PISTOL
Police Use Force on Abusive Person	POLABUSE
Police Use Force on Escapee	POLESCAP
Police Use Force on Murder Suspect	POLMURDR
Police Use Force to Repel Attacker	POLATTAK
Political Leanings	POLVIEWS
Poor Education is Blacks' Main Problem	RACDIF3
Poor Motivation is Blacks' Main Problem	RACDIF4
Popularity as a Childhood Trait	POPULAR
Pornography Breaks Down Morals	PORNMORL
Pornography Incites Rape	PORNRAPE
Pornography Provides Outlet	PORNOUT
Pornography Provides Sex Education	PORNINFO
Pre-Nuptial AIDS Testing	AIDSMAR
Premarital Sexual Relations	PREMARSX
Preschooler - Working Mother	FEPRESCH
Presidential Choice in 1968	PRES68
Presidential Choice in 1972	PRES72
Presidential Choice in 1976	PRES76
Presidential Choice in 1980	PRES80
Presidential Choice in 1984	PRES84
Presidential Choice in 1988	PRES88
Prestige of Occupation	PRESTIGE
Proximity of Blacks	RACCLOS
Race of AIDS Victim	AIDSRACE
Reading Lord's Prayer	PRAYER
Region Lived In at Age 16	REG16
Region of Country Living In	REGION
Relationship with AIDS Victims	AIDSWHO
Relative Financial Status	FINRELA
Religious Preference at Age 16	RELIG16
Religious School Attendance	CHURHSCH
Respondent's Age	AGE
Respondent's Birthplace	BORN
Respondent's Month of Birth	BIRTHMO
Respondent's Race	RACE
Respondent's Sex	SEX
Rifle in House	RIFLE
Russia as a Favored Country	RUSSIA
Satisfaction with Community	SATCITY
Satisfaction with Family Life	SATFAM
Satisfaction with Friends	SATFRND
Satisfaction with Health	SATHEALT
Satisfaction with Hobby	SATHOBBY
Satisfaction with Job	SATJOB
Satisfaction with Marriage	HAPMAR
Satisfied with Finances	SATFIN
School Segregation	RACSCHOL
School with Few Blacks	RACFEW
School with Half Blacks	RACHAF
School with Mostly Blacks	RACMOST
Sex for Pay	PAIDSEX
Sex Partners in Last Year	PARTNERS
Sex with Acquaintance	ACQNTSEX
Sex with Casual Date	PIKUPSEX
Sex with Close Personal Friend	FRNDSEX
Sex with Significant Other	MATESEX
Shotgun in House	SHOTGUN
Siblings	SIBS

APPENDIX B: Questions and Corresponding Variable Names (Continued)

Smoking History .... EVSMOKE
Socializing with Friends .... SOCFREND
Socializing with Neighbors .... SOCUMMUN
Socializing with Parents .... SOCPARS
Socializing with Relatives .... SOCREL
Socializing with Siblings .... SOCSIBS
Socio-Economic Status .... CLASS
Spanking as Good Discipline .... SPANKING
Spending for Big City Problems .... NATCITY
Spending for Condition of Blacks .... NATRACE
Spending for Crime .... NATCRIME
Spending for Defense .... NATARMS
Spending for Drug Education .... NATDRUG
Spending for Education .... NATEDUC
Spending for Environment .... NATENVIR
Spending for Health .... NATHEAL
Spending for Highway System .... NATROAD
Spending for Mass Transit .... NATMASS
Spending for Parks .... NATPARK
Spending for Social Security .... NATSOC
Spending for Space Research .... NATSPAC
Spending for Welfare .... NATFARE
Spending on Foreign Aid .... NATAID
Spouse's Current Employment Status .... SPWRKSTA
State of Health .... HEALTH
Striking a Stranger Who is Abusing a Female .... HITBEATR
Struck as a Child or Adult .... HITAGE
Suicide for Bankruptcy SUICIDE2
Suicide for Dishonor SUICIDE3
Suicide for Private Reasons SUICIDE4
Suicide for Terminally Ill SUICIDE1
Sunday School Attendance in Youth SUNSCH16
Supply Birth Control Information .... PILL
Take Bible Literally .... BIBLE
Teenage Sexual Relations .... TEENSEX
Television Viewing .... TVHOURS
Ten-Year Employment History .... UNEMP
Threatened with a Gun .... GUN
Threatened with a Gun as a Child or Adult .... GUNAGE
Tithing Amount .... TITHING
Type of Community Lived In at Age 16 .... RES16
U.S. Active in World Affairs .... USINTL
U.S. in War in Ten Years .... USWARY
U.S. Keep United Nations Membership .... USUN
Union Membership .... UNION
Unrelated Household Members .... UNRELAT
Victim of Violence .... HIT
Victimized by Burglars .... BURGLR
Victimized by Robbers .... ROBBRY
Vote for Female Presidential Candidate .... FEPRES
Voted in 1968 .... VOTE68
Voted in 1972 .... VOTE72
Voted in 1976 .... VOTE76
Voted in 1980 .... VOTE80
Voted in 1984 .... VOTE84
Voted in 1988 .... VOTE88
Wage Earners in Household .... EARNRS
Whites' Right to Segregation .... RACSEG
Wiretapping .... WIRTAP
Woman Should Enhance Husband's Career .... FEHELP
Women Less Suitable for Politics .... FEPOL

APPENDIX B: Questions and Corresponding Variable Names (Continued)

Work Hard or Luck Helps Get Ahead .... GETAHEAD
Working Hard as a Childhood Trait .... WORKHARD
Working Mother Relationship .... FECHLD
World Too Bad for New Children ANOMIA6
X-rated Movie Viewing .... XMOVIE
Years of Education .... EDUC
Your Occupation .... OCC

APPENDIX C: What Race Do You Consider Yourself?

General Social Survey interviewers are instructed to identify the race of a respondent, if the race is obvious. If the respondent's race is not obvious the interviewer is to ask the respondent "What race do you consider yourself?" Appenxic C lists the responses given in the 366 cases where the above question was asked, along with the number of times that particular response was given. These cases were all recorded in the "Other" response catagory.

American Indian	85
Asian	30
Chinese	13
Creole	1
Cuban	2
Philipino	20
Guayanese	1
Hawaiian	4
Hindu	5
Hispanic	69
Human	1
Indian (Asian)	11
Indonesian	1
Iranian	1
Japanese	19
Korean	2
Latin	1
Latino	1
Mexican	24
Mulatto	3
Oriental	33
Polynesian	3
Puerto Rican	13
Spanish	12
Thai	2
Vietnamese	2
"Mixed"	1
"Brown"	3
"1/2 Am. Ind., 1/2 Hisp."	1
"Yellow"	1
"halfbreed"	1

APPENDIX D: Prestige Of Occupation

The prestige of occupations was determined by a survey conducted in 1963-1965. Given a list of occupations, respondents were asked to rate them for prestige on a nine point score. Appendix D lists a sample of occupations and their prestige score. This list in not complete but is meant to show the relative differences in prestige between occupations. The complete list appears in the General Social Survey codebook.

Occupation	Score
Accountants	57
Actors	55
Actuaries	55
Air Traffic Controllers	43
Airline Stewardesses	36
Airplane Pilots	70
Architects	71
Auctioneers	32
Automobile Mechanics	37
Bank Tellers	50
Biological Scientist	68
Bootblacks	9
Bulldozer Operators	33
Bus Drivers	32
Carpenters	40
Cashiers	31
Chemical Engineers	67
Child Care Workers, Private Household	23
Cleaners and Charwomen	12
Clergymen	69
Clinical Laboratory Technicians	61
College Professors	78
Computer Systems Analyst	51
Cooks, Except Private Households	26
Dental Assistants	48
Dental Hygienists	61
Dentists	74
Dieticians	52
Draftsmen	56
Dry Wall Installers and Lathers	27
Economists	57
Editors and Reporters	51
Elementary School Teachers	60
Farm Laborers	18
Farmers (owners and tenants)	41
Foresters and Conservationists	54
Funeral Directors	52
Garage workers and Gas Station Attendants	22
Garbage Collectors	17

APPENDIX D: Prestige Of Occupation (Continued)

Occupation	Score
Judges	76
Lawyers	76
Librarians	55
Lumbermen, Raftsmen and Woodchoppers	26
Maids and Servants, Private Household	18
Mathematicians	65
Mechanical Engineers	62
Physicians	82
Physicist and Astronomers	74
Plumbers and Pipe fitters	41
Policemen and Detectives	48
Postal Clerks	43
Practical Nurses	42
Psychologists	71
Real Estate Agents	44
Receptionists	39
Registered Nurses	62
Riveter and Fasteners	29
Sailors and Deck hands	34
Sales Clerks, Retail Trade	29
Sales Representative, Wholesale Trade	40
School Administrators, Elementary and Secondary.	60
Secondary School Teachers	63
Secretaries	46
Sheriffs an Bailiffs	55
Social Workers	52
Surveyors	53
Taxicab Drivers and Chauffeurs	22
Typists	41
Waiters	20
Welders and Flame-cutters	40

APPENDIX E: Crime

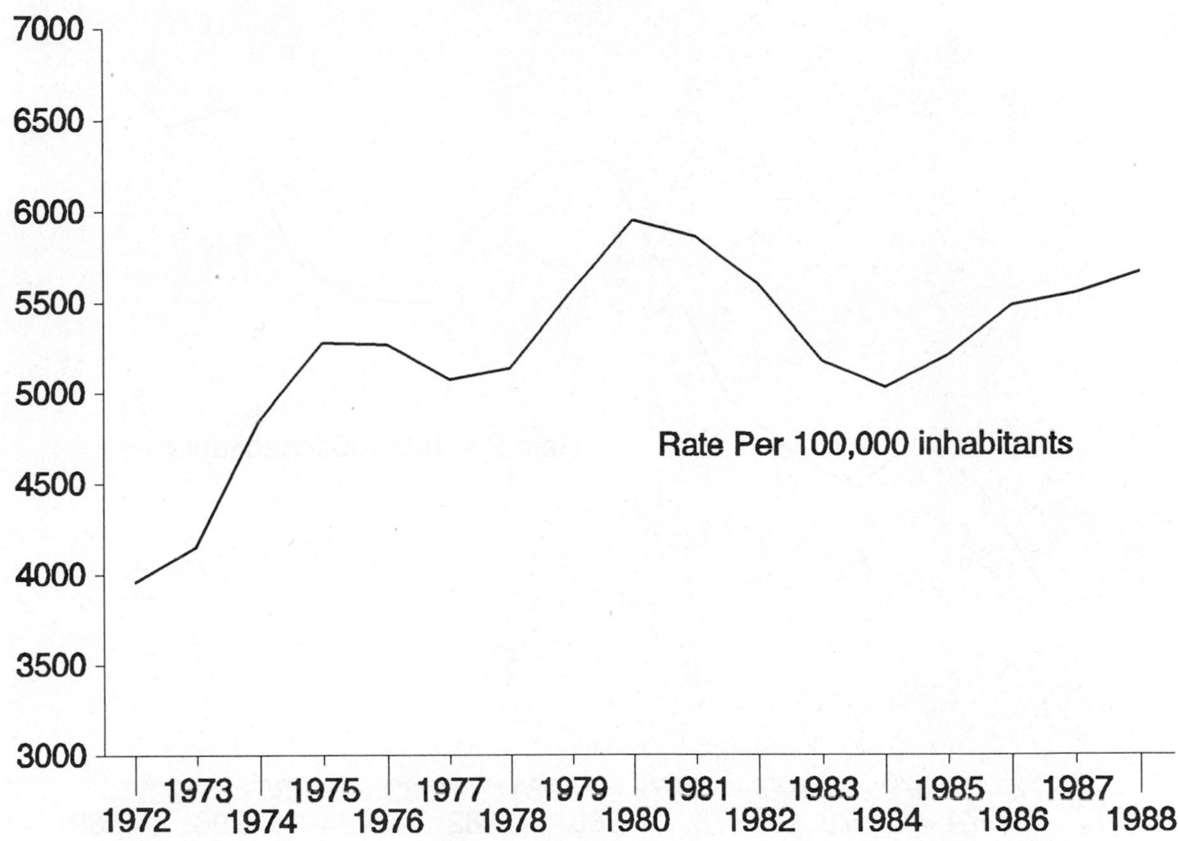

Note: 1972-1973 data taken from the 1978 edition, 1974-1976 data taken from the 1983 edition, 1977-1978 data taken from the 1986 edition, and 1979-1988 data taken from the 1988 edition of Crime in the United States.
Source: Crime in the United States. (Uniform Crime Reports) U.S. Department of Justice, Federal Bureau of Investigation. Washington, DC: USGPO.

APPENDIX E: Crime (Continued)

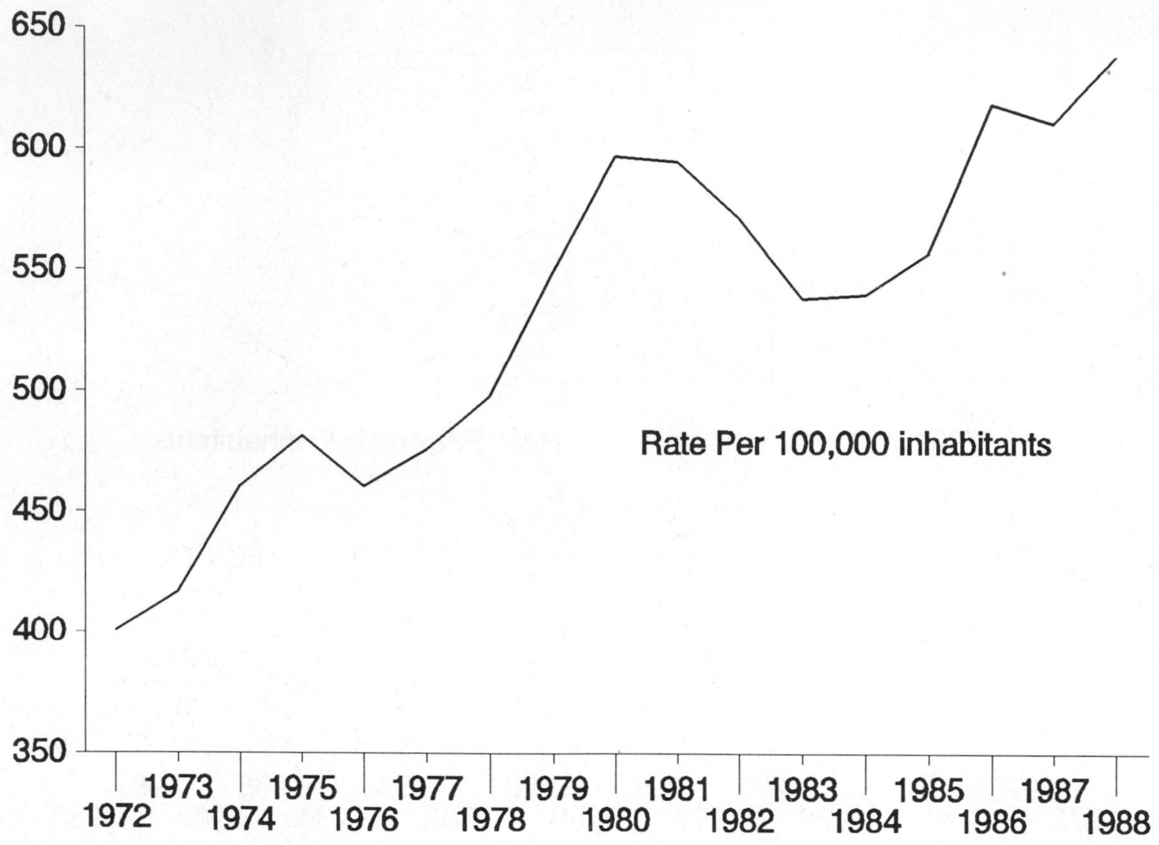

Note: 1972-1973 data taken from the 1978 edition, 1974-1976 data taken from the 1983 edition, 1977-1978 data taken from the 1986 edition, and 1979-1988 data taken from the 1988 edition of Crime in the United States.
Source: Crime in the United States. (Uniform Crime Reports) U.S. Department of Justice, Federal Bureau of Investigation. Washington, DC: USGPO.

APPENDIX E: Crime (Continued)

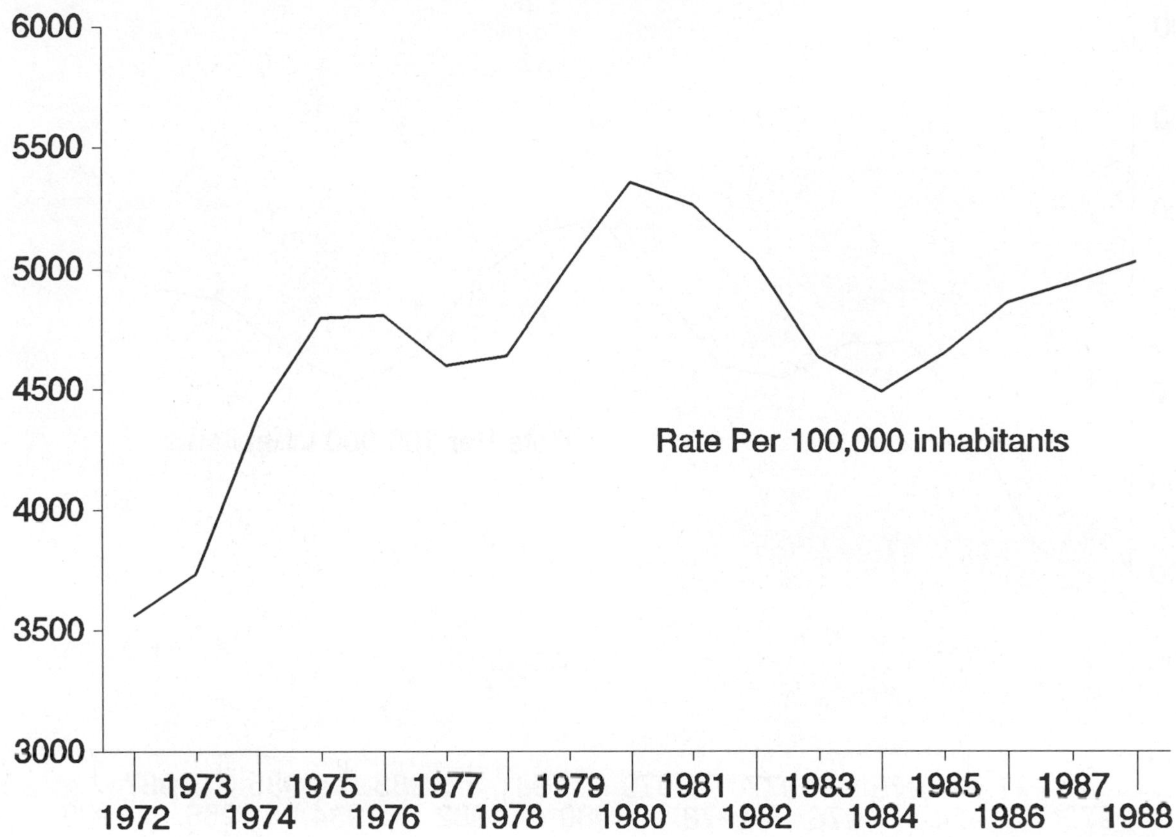

Note: 1972-1973 data taken from the 1978 edition, 1974-1976 data taken from the 1983 edition, 1977-1978 data taken from the 1986 edition, and 1979-1988 data taken from the 1988 edition of Crime in the United States.
Source: Crime in the United States. (Uniform Crime Reports) U.S. Department of Justice, Federal Bureau of Investigation. Washington, DC: USGPO.

APPENDIX F: Unemployment

The Index of Crime, United States, 1972-1988.

The Crime Index Total.

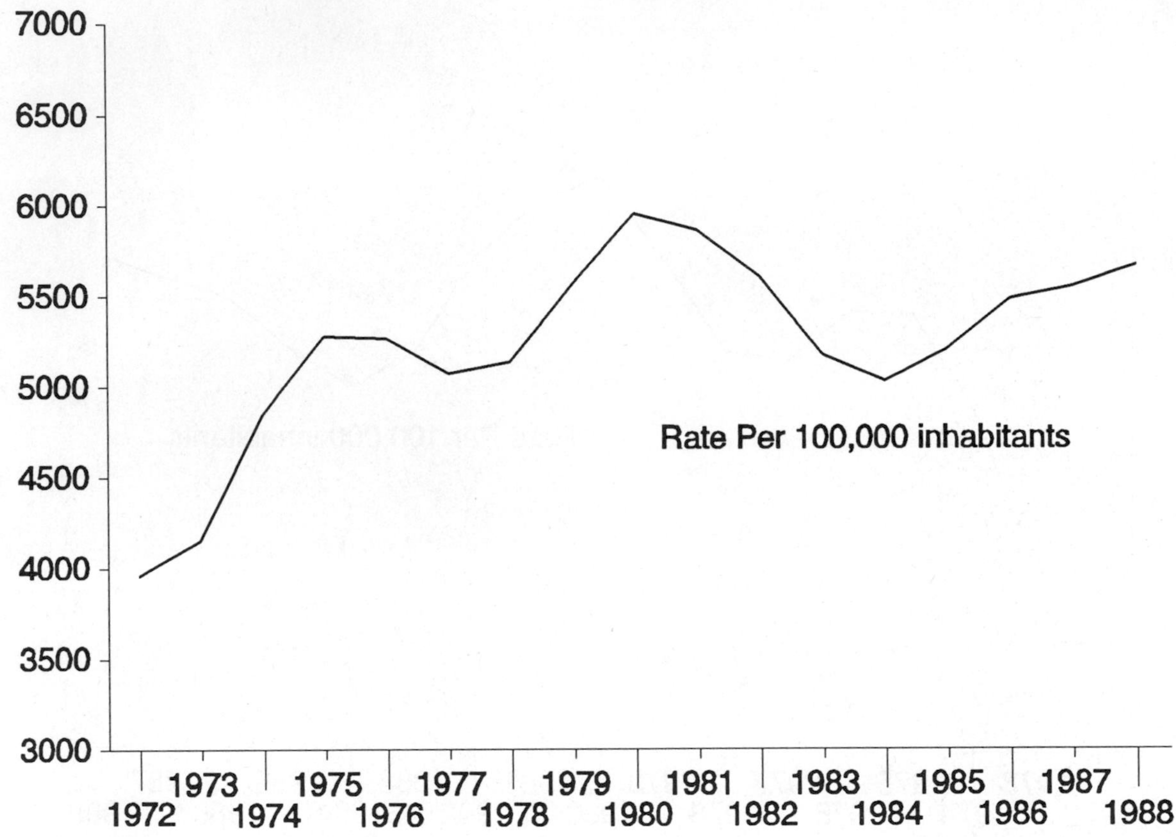

Source: Economic Report of the President - 1990. Washington, DC: USGPO, 1990.

APPENDIX F: Unemployment (Continued)

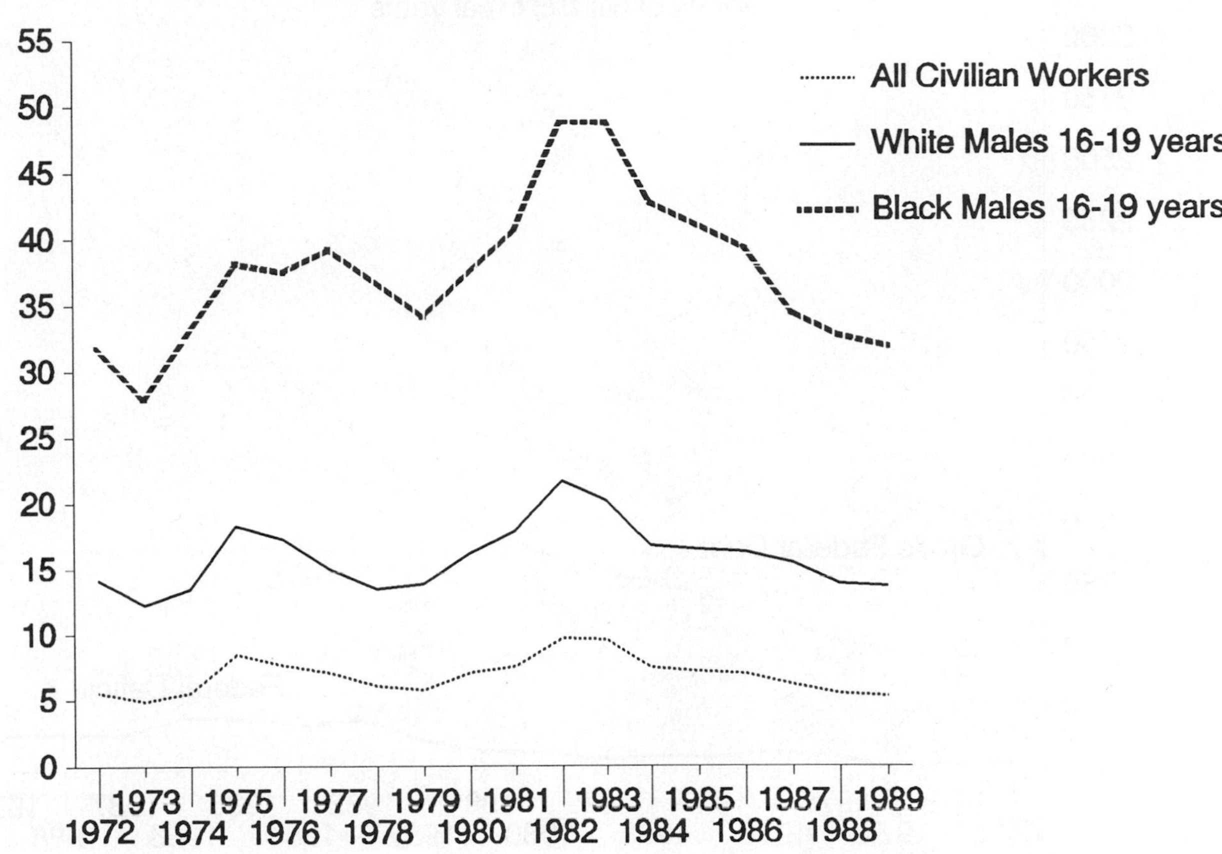

Source: Economic Report of the President - 1990. Washington, DC: USGPO, 1990.

APPENDIX G: Economy

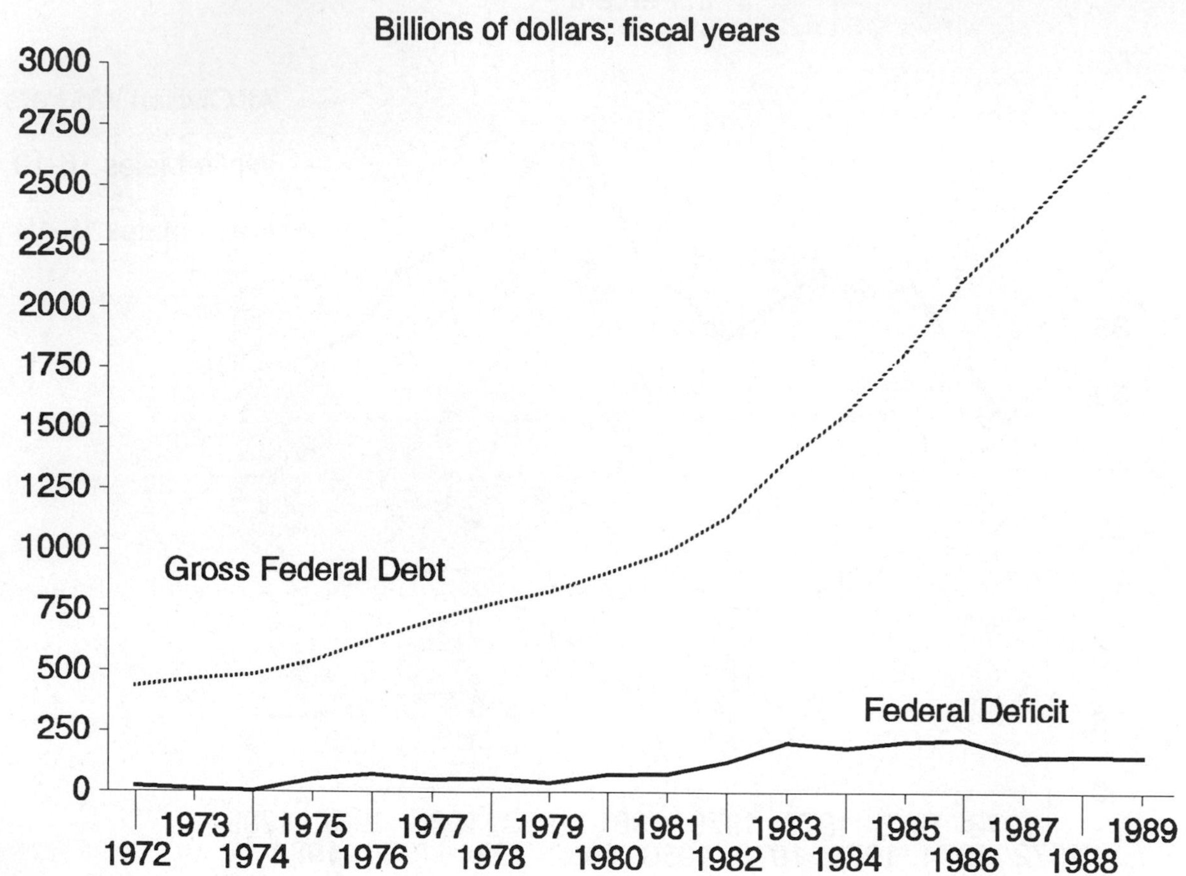

Source: Economic Report of the President - 1990. Washington, DC: USGPO, 1990.

APPENDIX G: Economy (Continued)

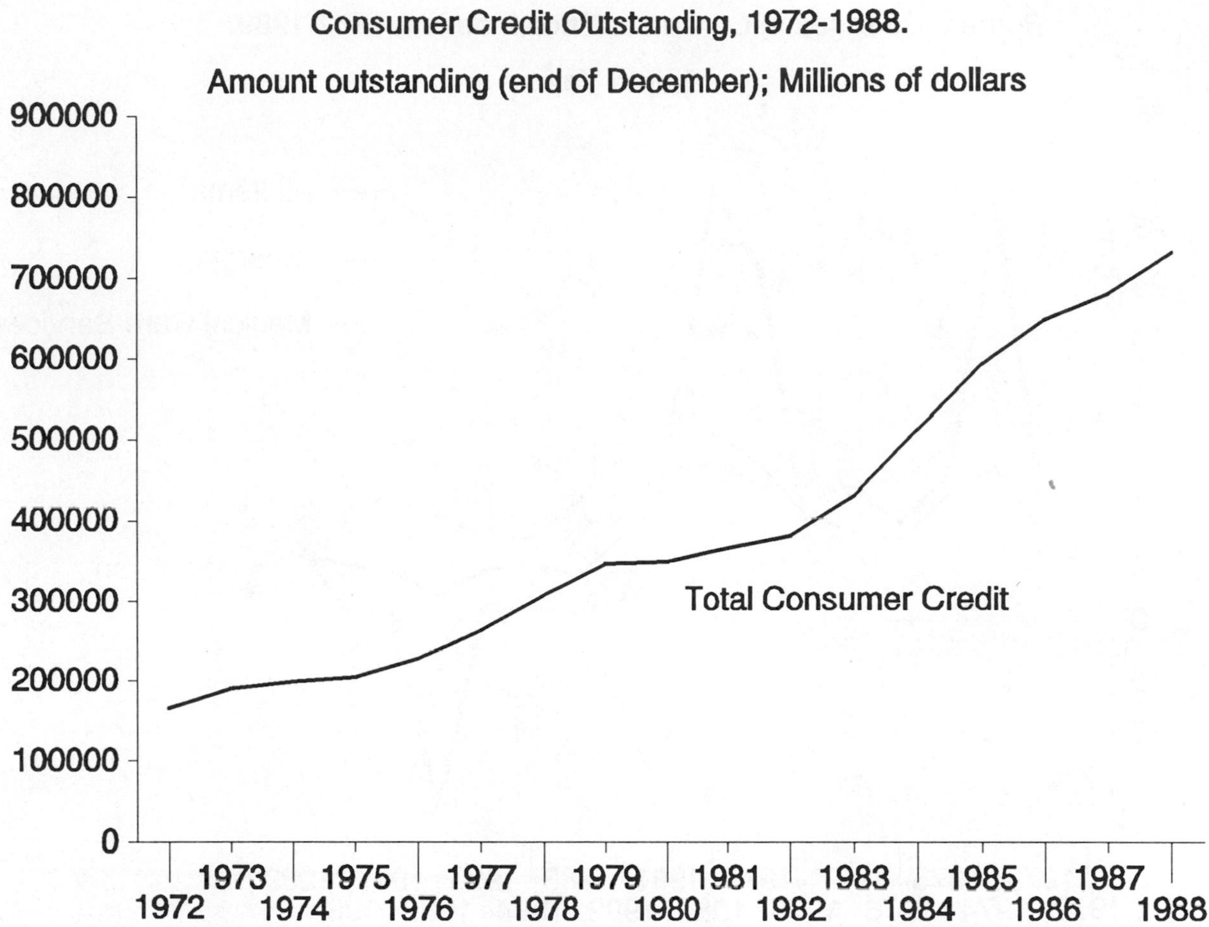

Source: Economic Report of the President - 1990. Washington, DC: USGPO, 1990.

APPENDIX G: Economy (Continued)

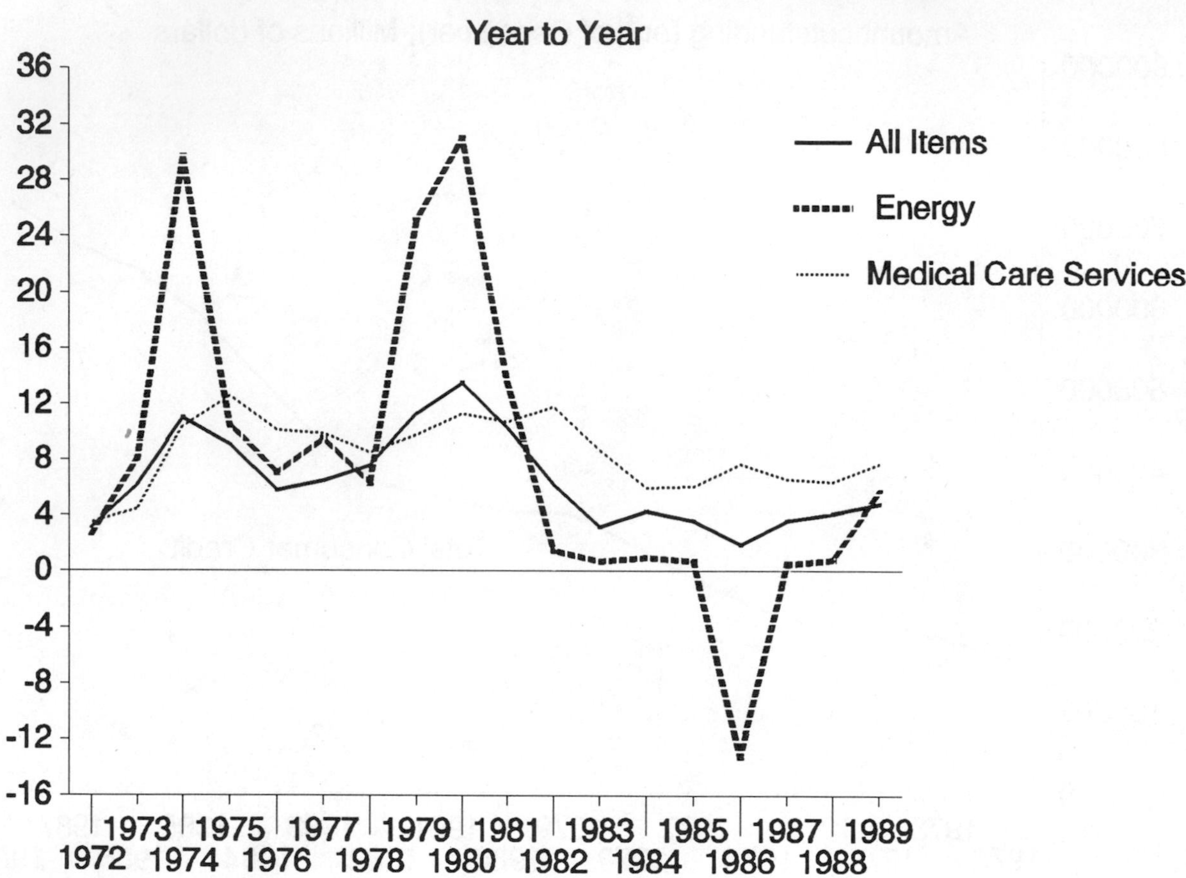

Note: "Through fiscal year 1976, the fiscal year was on a July 1-June 30 basis; beginning October 1976 (fiscal year 1977), the fiscal year is on an October 1-September 30 basis. The 3-month period from July 1, 1976 through September 30, 1976 is a separate fiscal period known as the transition quarter." The graph above does not include the transition quarter.

Source: Economic Report of the President - 1990. Washington, DC: USGPO, 1990.

APPENDIX G: Economy (Continued)

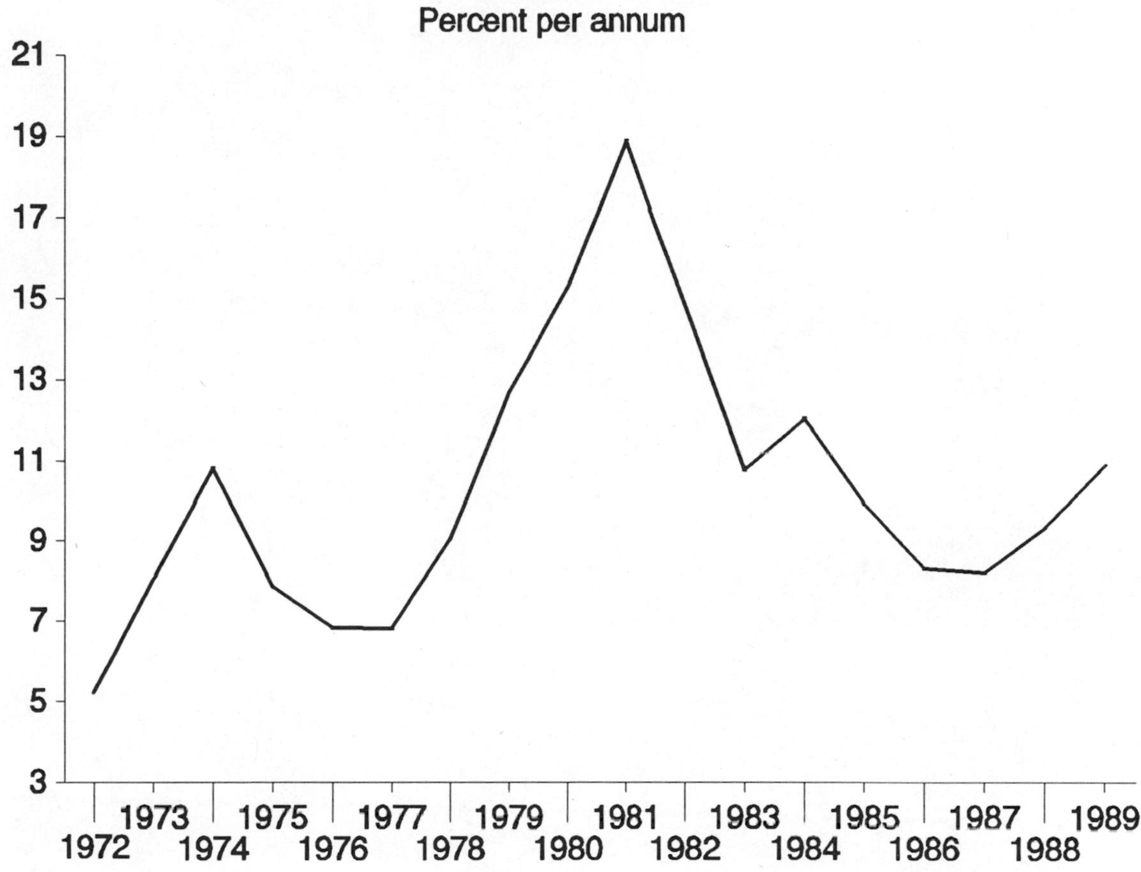

Source: Economic Report of the President - 1990. Washington, DC: USGPO, 1990.

INDEX

This index includes all titles of the questions found in the Outline of Contents. Each title is listed alphabetically by name as well as by principal keyword, by other important words in the title, and by any added keywords which have been assigned by the editors to facilitate access. Any added key words precede the title of the question in parenthesis.